Chapters 1–18

Accounting

Charles T. Horngren Series in Accounting

Auditing and Assurance Services: An Integrated Approach, 10th ed.
Arens/Elder/Beasley

Essentials of Auditing and Assurance Services, 1st ed.
Arens/Elder/Beasley

Governmental and Nonprofit Accounting: Theory and Practice, 7th ed.
Freeman/Shoulders

Financial Accounting, 5th ed.
Harrison/Horngren

Cases in Financial Reporting, 4th ed.
Hirst/McAnally

Cost Accounting: A Managerial Emphasis, 11th ed.
Horngren/Datar/Foster

Accounting, 6th ed.
Horngren/Harrison/Bamber

Introduction to Financial Accounting, 8th ed.
Horngren/Sundem/Elliott

Introduction to Management Accounting, 13th ed.
Horngren/Sundem/Stratton

Budgeting, 7th ed.
Welsch/Hilton/Gordon

Chapters 1–18

Accounting

Sixth Edition

Charles T. Horngren

Stanford University

Walter T. Harrison Jr.

Baylor University

Linda Smith Bamber

University of Georgia

PEARSON
Prentice Hall

Upper Saddle River, New Jersey 07458

Library of Congress Cataloging-in-Publication Data

Horngren, Charles T.
Accounting / Charles T. Horngren, Walter T. Harrison, Jr., Linda Smith Bamber.—6th ed.
1216 p. cm.
Includes indexes.
ISBN 0-13-143596-5
1. Accounting. I. Harrison, Walter T. II. Bamber, Linda S. (Linda Smith), III.
Title.

HF5635.H8 2003
657—dc22 2003065606

Editor-in-Chief: P.J. Boardman
Assistant Editor: Sam Goffinet
Editorial Assistant: Jane Avery
Director of Development: Stephen Deitmer
Senior Development Editor: Jeannine Ciliotta
Senior Media Project Manager: Nancy Welcher
Executive Marketing Manager: Beth Toland
Managing Editor (Production): Cynthia Regan
Senior Production Editor: Anne Graydon
Production Assistant: Joe DeProspero
Permissions Supervisor: Suzanne Grappi
Associate Director, Manufacturing: Vincent Scelta
Production Manager, Manufacturing: Arnold Vila
Design Manager: Maria Lange
Designer: Steve Frim
Interior Design: Jill Little; Atelier de ZIN
Cover Design: Steve Frim
Cover Photo: David Mager/Pearson Learning Group Photo Studio
Illustrator (Interior): Precision Graphics
Photo Researcher: Julie Tesser; Elaine Soares
Image Permission Coordinator: Michelina Viscusi
Manager, Print Production: Christy Mahon
Composition/Full-Service: UG / GGS Information Services, Inc.
Project Management: UG / GGS Information Services, Inc.
Printer/Binder: R.R. Donnelley, Willard

Credits and acknowledgments borrowed from other sources and reproduced, with permission, in this textbook: **Page 3** AP/Wide World Photos; **7** AP/Wide World Photos; **43** PhotoEdit; **65** Hisham F. Ibrahim/Getty Images, Inc.-Photodisc; **91** It's Just Lunch! Inc.; **95** Laurence Manning/CORBIS BETTMANN; **139** AP/Wide World Photos; **156** Dell Computer Corporation; **139** AP/Wide World Photos; **194** Amazon.com; **247** Raymond Watt/Albuquerque International Balloon Fiesta ®; **261** Athlete's Foot; **281** PriceKubecha, PLLC; **286** TADOnline; **323** James Leynse/Corbis/SABA Press Photos, Inc.; **327** Getty Images, Inc.-Hilton Archive Photos; **361** Marvin Jones/Getty Images, Inc.-Hilton Archive Photos; **371** Index Stock Imagery, Inc.; **399** Lawrence Manning/CORBIS-NY; **418** AP/Wide World Photos; **435** Michael Newman/PhotoEdit; **438** Don Farrall/Getty Images, Inc.-Photodisc; **469** Taxi/Getty Images, Inc.-Taxi; **474** James Nielsen/CORBIS-NY; **505** The Image Works; **514** Alex Farnsworth/The Image Works; **543** John Van Hasselt/CORBIS/Sygma; **551** Deluxe Corporation; **579** Mario Tama/Getty Images Inc.-Hilton Archive Photos; **598** AP/Wide World Photos; **625** Steven Harris/Getty Images Inc.-Hilton Archive Photos; **640** Marty Lederhandler/AP/Wide World Photos; **657** David McNew/Getty Images Inc.-Hilton Archive Photos; **660** Taxi/Getty Images Inc.-Taxi; **705** Robin Laurance/Photo Researchers, Inc.; **724** Expedia.com; **751** Regal Marine Industries, Inc.; **770** The Image Works; **797** Courtesy of Dell Computer Corp.; **806** Intermec Technologies Corporation; **845** Used with permission from Jelly Belly Candy Company; **869** Levi Strauss & Co.; **897** Al Richmond/Grand Canyon Railway; **906** Neeme Frederic/CORBIS BETTMANN; **939** Courtesy of Amazon.com; **956** Fossil, Inc.; **985** Roberto Brosan/Getty Images Time Life Pictures; **998** AP/Wide World Photos; **1033** Dell Computer Corporation; **1054** Texas Instruments Incorporated; **1078** Eric Schramm/Eric Schramm Photography; **1089** Courtesy of International Business Machines Corporation. Unauthorized use not permitted.

Pearson Education LTD.
Pearson Education Singapore, Pte. Ltd
Pearson Education, Canada, Ltd
Pearson Education–Japan
Pearson Education Australia PTY, Limited
Pearson Education North Asia Ltd
Pearson Educación de Mexico, S.A. de C.V.
Pearson Education Malaysia, Pte. Ltd

PEARSON
Prentice Hall

10 9 8 7 6 5 4 3
ISBN: 0-13-143631-7

To Betsy Willis and Becky Jones for their wisdom on learning and teaching over a 15-year period and to Michael Bamber for his insight on business practices and ethical issues in management accounting.

Brief Contents

Contents

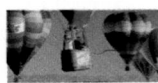

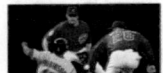

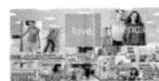

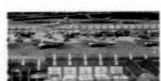

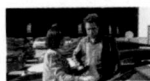

About the Authors

Charles T. Horngren is the Edmund W. Littlefield Professor of Accounting, Emeritus, at Stanford University. A graduate of Marquette University, he received his MBA from Harvard University and his Ph.D. from the University of Chicago. He is also the recipient of honorary doctorates from Marquette University and DePaul University.

A Certified Public Accountant, Horngren served on the Accounting Principles Board for six years, the Financial Accounting Standards Board Advisory Council for five years, and the Council of the American Institute of Certified Public Accountants for three years. For six years, he served as a trustee of the Financial Accounting Foundation, which oversees the Financial Accounting Standards Board and the Government Accounting Standards Board.

Horngren is a member of the Accounting Hall of Fame.

A member of the American Accounting Association, Horngren has been its President and its Director of Research. He received its first annual Outstanding Accounting Educator Award.

The California Certified Public Accountants Foundation gave Horngren its Faculty Excellence Award and its Distinguished Professor Award. He is the first person to have received both awards.

The American Institute of Certified Public Accountants presented its first Outstanding Educator Award to Horngren.

Horngren was named Accountant of the Year, Education, by the national professional accounting fraternity, Beta Alpha Psi.

Professor Horngren is also a member of the Institute of Management Accountants, from whom he has received its Distinguished Service Award. He was a member of the Institute's Board of Regents, which administers the Certified Management Accountant examinations.

Horngren is the author of other accounting books published by Prentice-Hall: *Cost Accounting: A Managerial Emphasis*, Eleventh Edition, 2003 (with Srikant Datar and George Foster); *Introduction to Financial Accounting*, Eighth Edition, 2002 (with Gary L. Sundem and John A. Elliott); *Introduction to Management Accounting*, Thirteenth Edition, 2005 (with Gary L. Sundem and William Stratton); *Financial Accounting*, Fifth Edition, 2004 (with Walter T. Harrison, Jr.).

Horngren is the Consulting Editor for Prentice-Hall's Charles T. Horngren Series in Accounting.

Walter T. Harrison, Jr. is Professor of Accounting at the Hankamer School of Business, Baylor University. He received his B.B.A. degree from Baylor University, his M.S. from Oklahoma State University, and his Ph.D. from Michigan State University.

Professor Harrison, recipient of numerous teaching awards from student groups as well as from university administrators, has also taught at Cleveland State Community College, Michigan State University, the University of Texas, and Stanford University.

A member of the American Accounting Association and the American Institute of Certified Public Accountants, Professor Harrison has served as Chairman of the Financial Accounting Standards Committee of the American Accounting Association, on the Teaching/Curriculum Development Award Committee, on the Program Advisory Committee for Accounting Education and Teaching, and on the Notable Contributions to Accounting Literature Committee.

Professor Harrison has lectured in several foreign countries and published articles in numerous journals, including *The Accounting Review, Journal of Accounting Research, Journal of Accountancy, Journal of Accounting and Public Policy, Economic Consequences of Financial Accounting Standards, Accounting Horizons, Issues in Accounting Education*, and *Journal of Law and Commerce*.

He is co-author of *Financial Accounting*, Fifth Edition, 2004 (with Charles T. Horngren), published by Prentice Hall. Professor Harrison has received scholarships, fellowships, and research grants or awards from PriceWaterhouse Coopers, Deloitte & Touche, the Ernst & Young Foundation, and the KPMG Foundation.

Linda Smith Bamber holds the J.M. Tull Chair of Accounting at the J.M. Tull School of Accounting at the University of Georgia. She graduated summa cum laude from Wake Forest University, where she was a member of Phi Beta Kappa. She is a Certified Public Accountant, and received an Elijah Watt Sells Award as well as the North Carolina Bronze Medal for her performance on the CPA examination. Before returning to graduate school, Professor Bamber gained professional experience working in management accounting at R.J. Reynolds, Inc. She then earned an MBA from Arizona State University, and a Ph.D. from The Ohio State University.

Professor Bamber has received numerous teaching awards from The Ohio State University, the University of Florida, and the University of Georgia.

She has lectured in Canada and Australia, in addition to the U.S., and her research has appeared in numerous journals, including *The Accounting Review, Journal of Accounting Research, Journal of Accounting and Economics, Journal of Finance, Contemporary Accounting Research, Accounting Horizons, Issues in Accounting Education*, and *The CPA Journal*. She also developed the annotations for the *Annotated Instructor's Edition* of Horngren, Foster, and Datar's *Cost Accounting: A Managerial Emphasis*, Seventh, Eighth, and Ninth Editions.

A member of the Institute of Management Accounting, the American Accounting Association (AAA) and the AAA's Management Accounting Section and Financial Accounting and Reporting Section, Professor Bamber has chaired the AAA New Faculty Consortium and the AAA Competitive Manuscript Award Committees, served on the AAA Council, the AAA Research Advisory Committee, the AAA Nominations Committee, and numerous other AAA and section committees. She served as Associate Editor of *Accounting Horizons*, and as editor of *The Accounting Review*.

Preface

From The Authors

This new sixth edition of *Accounting* has been tailored to meet instructors' needs and to help students master accounting. We think our efforts have made this revision much easier for instructors to teach and students to learn from. Throughout the text, we have streamlined the presentation and focused the content on the core topics of first-year accounting. To better prepare students for the business world, wherever possible we have used actual documents and real situations.

The text revisions and the new design, combined with an outstanding resource package, provide excellent tools for success in accounting. We hope you agree.

Charles Horngren ☆ **Tom Harrison** ☆ **Linda Bamber**

For The Student

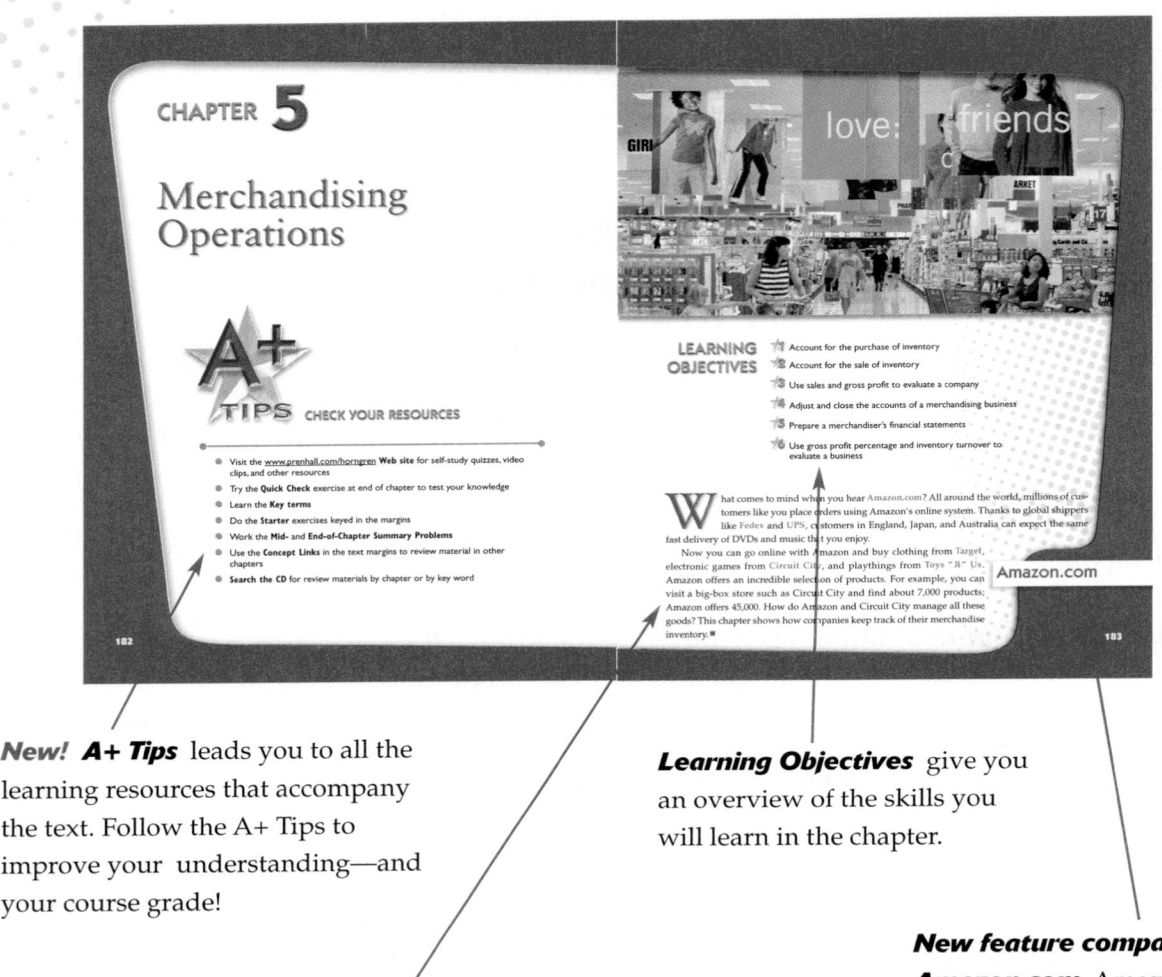

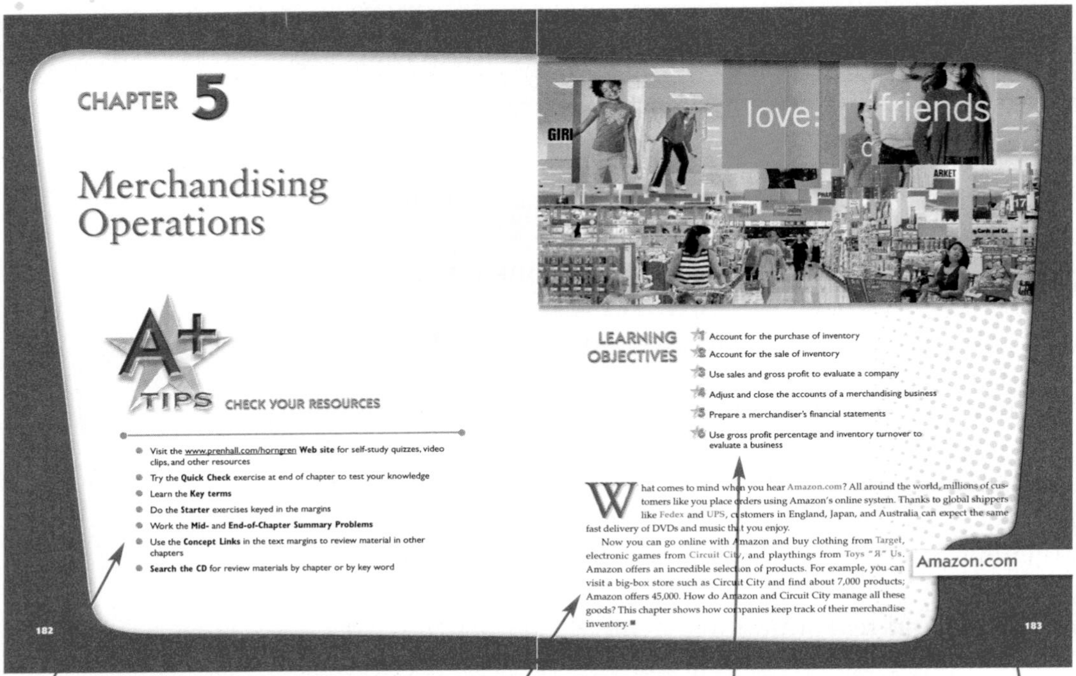

CHAPTER 5

Merchandising Operations

A+ TIPS CHECK YOUR RESOURCES

- Visit the www.prenhall.com/horngren **Web site** for self-study quizzes, video clips, and other resources
- Try the **Quick Check** exercise at end of chapter to test your knowledge
- Learn the **Key terms**
- Do the **Starter** exercises keyed in the margins
- Work the **Mid-** and **End-of-Chapter Summary Problems**
- Use the **Concept Links** in the text margins to review material in other chapters
- **Search the CD** for review materials by chapter or by key word

182

LEARNING OBJECTIVES

1. Account for the purchase of inventory
2. Account for the sale of inventory
3. Use sales and gross profit to evaluate a company
4. Adjust and close the accounts of a merchandising business
5. Prepare a merchandiser's financial statements
6. Use gross profit percentage and inventory turnover to evaluate a business

What comes to mind when you hear Amazon.com? All around the world, millions of customers like you place orders using Amazon's online system. Thanks to global shippers like Fedex and UPS, customers in England, Japan, and Australia can expect the same fast delivery of DVDs and music that you enjoy.

Now you can go online with Amazon and buy clothing from Target, electronic games from Circuit City, and playthings from Toys "Я" Us. Amazon offers an incredible selection of products. For example, you can visit a big-box store such as Circuit City and find about 7,000 products; Amazon offers 45,000. How do Amazon and Circuit City manage all these goods? This chapter shows how companies keep track of their merchandise inventory. ■

Amazon.com

183

New! A+ Tips leads you to all the learning resources that accompany the text. Follow the A+ Tips to improve your understanding—and your course grade!

Learning Objectives give you an overview of the skills you will learn in the chapter.

Chapter-opening vignettes take you into the real world of accounting—where business decisions affect the future of actual organizations. Each vignette introduces you to the central issues covered in the chapter. Many of the vignettes—on Jelly Belly, Oracle, Dell—are linked to unique, custom-created ***On Location!*** **Videos** available on the **Student and Instructor Resource CD-ROMs**.

New feature company: Amazon.com Amazon.com's annual report is bound into the book; Amazon is also the feature company in several chapter-opening vignettes, and in end-of-chapter financial statement cases.

Features

New! Sitemaps appear at the beginning of each chapter and at main headings throughout the chapter as a roadmap to show you where you are and what is coming next.

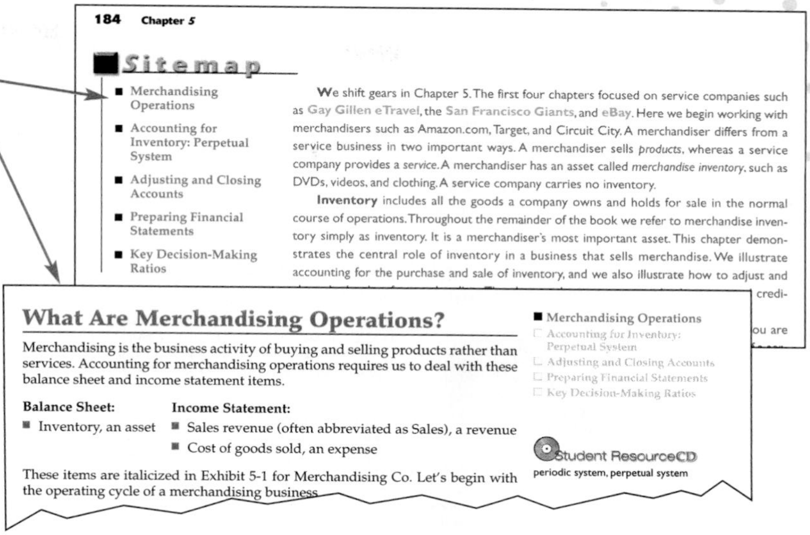
184 Chapter 5

Sitemap

- Merchandising Operations
- Accounting for Inventory: Perpetual System
- Adjusting and Closing Accounts
- Preparing Financial Statements
- Key Decision-Making Ratios

We shift gears in Chapter 5. The first four chapters focused on service companies such as Gay Gillen eTravel, the San Francisco Giants, and eBay. Here we begin working with merchandisers such as Amazon.com, Target, and Circuit City. A merchandiser differs from a service business in two important ways. A merchandiser sells *products*, whereas a service company provides a *service*. A merchandiser has an asset called *merchandise inventory*, such as DVDs, videos, and clothing. A service company carries no inventory.

Inventory includes all the goods a company owns and holds for sale in the normal course of operations. Throughout the remainder of the book we refer to merchandise inventory simply as inventory. It is a merchandiser's most important asset. This chapter demonstrates the central role of inventory in a business that sells merchandise. We illustrate accounting for the purchase and sale of inventory, and we also illustrate how to adjust and ... credi- ... ou are

What Are Merchandising Operations?

Merchandising is the business activity of buying and selling products rather than services. Accounting for merchandising operations requires us to deal with these balance sheet and income statement items.

Balance Sheet:
- Inventory, an asset

Income Statement:
- Sales revenue (often abbreviated as Sales), a revenue
- Cost of goods sold, an expense

These items are italicized in Exhibit 5-1 for Merchandising Co. Let's begin with the operating cycle of a merchandising business.

- Merchandising Operations
- Accounting for Inventory: Perpetual System
- Adjusting and Closing Accounts
- Preparing Financial Statements
- Key Decision-Making Ratios

Student ResourceCD
periodic system, perpetual system

New! An open and reader-friendly **text design** includes many new exhibits and infographics.

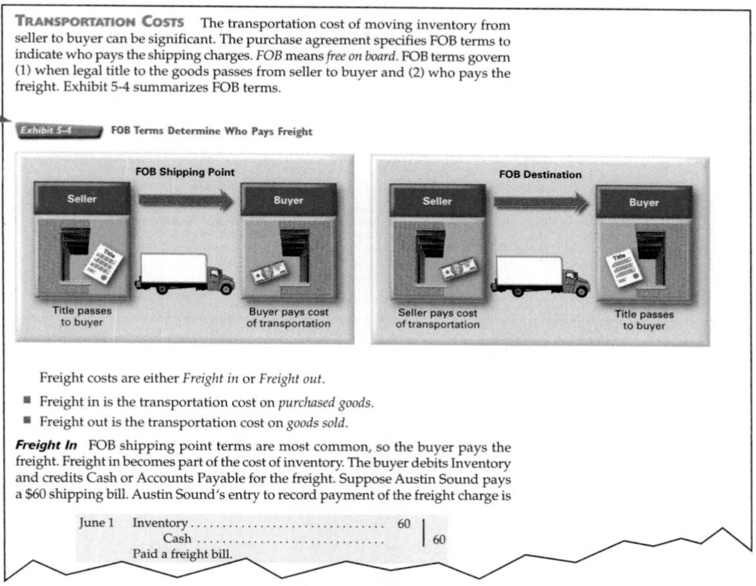
Transportation Costs The transportation cost of moving inventory from seller to buyer can be significant. The purchase agreement specifies FOB terms to indicate who pays the shipping charges. *FOB* means *free on board*. FOB terms govern (1) when legal title to the goods passes from seller to buyer and (2) who pays the freight. Exhibit 5-4 summarizes FOB terms.

Exhibit 5-4 FOB Terms Determine Who Pays Freight

Freight costs are either *Freight in* or *Freight out*.
- Freight in is the transportation cost on *purchased goods*.
- Freight out is the transportation cost on *goods sold*.

Freight In FOB shipping point terms are most common, so the buyer pays the freight. Freight in becomes part of the cost of inventory. The buyer debits Inventory and credits Cash or Accounts Payable for the freight. Suppose Austin Sound pays a $60 shipping bill. Austin Sound's entry to record payment of the freight charge is

June 1	Inventory	60	
	Cash		60
	Paid a freight bill.		

A Running Glossary provides a full definition when a term is introduced. A list of terms appears at the end of each chapter, and there is a complete Glossary at the end of the book.

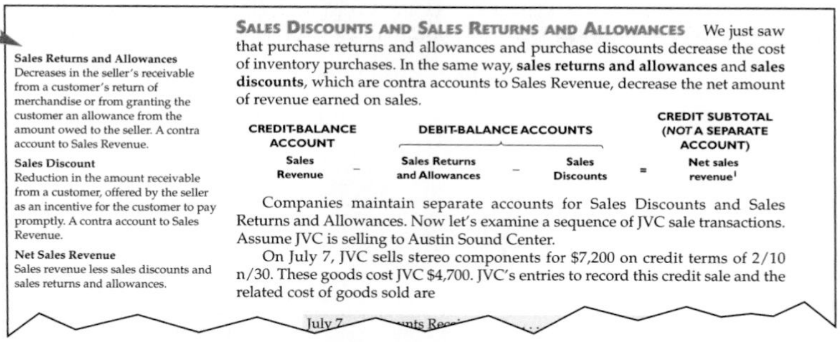
Sales Returns and Allowances
Decreases in the seller's receivable from a customer's return of merchandise or from granting the customer an allowance from the amount owed to the seller. A contra account to Sales Revenue.

Sales Discount
Reduction in the amount receivable from a customer, offered by the seller as an incentive for the customer to pay promptly. A contra account to Sales Revenue.

Net Sales Revenue
Sales revenue less sales discounts and sales returns and allowances.

Sales Discounts and Sales Returns and Allowances We just saw that purchase returns and allowances and purchase discounts decrease the cost of inventory purchases. In the same way, **sales returns and allowances** and **sales discounts**, which are contra accounts to Sales Revenue, decrease the net amount of revenue earned on sales.

CREDIT-BALANCE ACCOUNT		DEBIT-BALANCE ACCOUNTS				CREDIT SUBTOTAL (*NOT* A SEPARATE ACCOUNT)
Sales Revenue	−	Sales Returns and Allowances	−	Sales Discounts	=	Net sales revenue[1]

Companies maintain separate accounts for Sales Discounts and Sales Returns and Allowances. Now let's examine a sequence of JVC sale transactions. Assume JVC is selling to Austin Sound Center.

On July 7, JVC sells stereo components for $7,200 on credit terms of 2/10 n/30. These goods cost JVC $4,700. JVC's entries to record this credit sale and the related cost of goods sold are

Unique! Concept Links help you remember material learned earlier. Concept links in the side margins point you to relevant topics covered earlier: they provide both a rationale for the material and a chapter and text page cross reference.

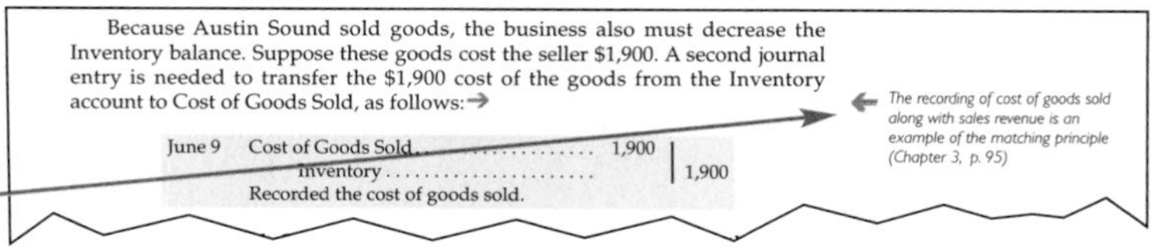
Because Austin Sound sold goods, the business also must decrease the Inventory balance. Suppose these goods cost the seller $1,900. A second journal entry is needed to transfer the $1,900 cost of the goods from the Inventory account to Cost of Goods Sold, as follows:

June 9	Cost of Goods Sold	1,900	
	Inventory		1,900
	Recorded the cost of goods sold.		

The recording of cost of goods sold along with sales revenue is an example of the matching principle (Chapter 3, p. 95)

Stop & Think

This Stop & Think example is exactly like the preceding one, but with freight in. On September 15, Austin Sound purchased $1,000 of merchandise, with *$80 freight added*, for an invoice total of $1,080. Austin returns $100 of the goods for credit on September 20 and pays the account payable in full on September 25. Journalize these transactions.

Answer

Purchase:	Sept. 15	Inventory ($1,000 + $80)	1,080	
		Accounts Payable		1,080
Return:	Sept. 20	Accounts Payable	100	
		Inventory		100
Payment:	Sept. 25	Accounts Payable ($1,080 − $100)	980	
		Inventory [($1,000 − $100) × 0.02]		18
		Cash ($1,000 + $80 − $100 − $18)		962

There is no discount on freight.

Stop & Think exercise boxes appear within the text in every chapter. The exercises encourage you to assess your understanding of concepts by providing immediate practice of what you have just learned.

Accounting.com

Amazon.com: For E-Tailers Free Shipping Isn't Free, But It's Not a Cost, Either

Like most accounting students, Jennifer didn't have time to go Christmas shopping. She cruised the online mall and ended up buying all her presents from Amazon.com, the largest player in online retailing. Jennifer was lured by Amazon.com's huge selection and an offer of free shipping for all orders over $25.

Amazon.com views free shipping as a key factor in boosting its growth—revenue jumped 233% to $851 million in one year. Yet, the company doesn't send packages via eight trusty reindeer. Amazon has to pay freight companies to deliver DVD players, books, and blenders to customers around the world. How does an e-tailer—one that is just barely making a profit—account for these shipping and handling costs?

Fortunately for Amazon and other e-tailers, in the process of revolutionizing business, e-commerce has also bent certain accounting rules. One such rule is that the cost of products sold to customers is usually recorded as Cost of Goods Sold, a merchandiser's major expense. But online powerhouses like Amazon.com and Buy.com count some of this cost as "sales and marketing expenses." By listing these "fulfillment costs" as marketing expenses, both e-tailers and catalog houses such as L. L. Bean don't have to subtract the expense in arriving at gross profit.

Small wonder that this controversial approach came under investigation by the Financial Accounting Standards Board (FASB). The dot-com bubble had burst, and e-tailers were poised to reclassify shipping and handling costs as costs of goods sold. That would restate gross profit downward. However, the Emerging Issues Task Force of the FASB recommended that shipping and handling *revenue* should be included in sales, without giving any guidance about how to account for shipping and handling *costs*. So Amazon and other e-tailers are free to continue including shipping and handling costs under marketing expense. The result: Gross profits are still high.

Based on: Nick Winfield, "Survival Strategy: Amazon Takes Page from Wal-Mart to Prosper on Web—Internet Retailer Cuts Prices and Keeps Eye on Costs in Bid for High Volumes—Betting Big on Free Shipping," *The Wall Street Journal*, November 22, 2002, p. A1. Saul Hansell, "Amazon's Loss in Quarter Shows a Sharp Decrease," *The New York Times*, October 25, 2002, p. 8. Katherine Hobson, "Silver Lining: FASB Spares E-Tailers in Cost Ruling," *The Street.com*, August 8, 2000.

Accounting.com boxes Nothing has changed business more in recent years than the Internet. Horngren/Harrison/Bamber's Accounting.com boxes identify accounting issues affecting companies doing business on the Web.

MID-CHAPTER *Summary Problem*

Suppose Amazon.com engaged in the following transactions during June of the current year:

June 3 Purchased inventory on credit terms of 1/10 net eom (end of month), $1,600.
9 Returned 40% of the inventory purchased on June 3. It was defective.
12 Sold goods for cash, $920 (cost, $550).
15 Purchased goods for $5,000. Credit terms were 3/15 net 30.
16 Paid a $260 freight bill on goods purchased.
18 Sold inventory on credit terms of 2/10 n/30, $2,000 (cost, $1,180).
22 Received returned goods from the customer of the June 18 sale, $800 (cost, $480).
24 Borrowed money from the bank to take advantage of the discount

A+ TIPS
CHECK YOUR RESOURCES

Summary Problems This unique Horngren/Harrison/Bamber feature enables you to pause and assess your progress at two locations within each chapter—midway and again at the end of the chapter text. Solutions appear with the problems for immediate feedback.

END-OF-CHAPTER *Summary Problem*

A+ TIPS
CHECK YOUR RESOURCES

The adjustment data and trial balance of Jan King Distributing Company follow. (*The solution to Requirement 1 is on page 208.*)

Adjustment data at December 31, 20X6:

a. Supplies used during the year, $2,580.
b. Prepaid rent in force, $1,000.
c. Unearned sales revenue still not earned, $2,400.
d. Depreciation. The furniture and fixtures' estimated useful life is 10 years, and they are expected to be worthless when they are retired from service.
e. Accrued salaries, $1,300.
f. Accrued interest expense, $600.
g. Inventory on hand, $65,800.

Required

1. Enter the trial balance on a work sheet and complete the work sheet.
2. Journalize the adjusting and closing entries at December 31. Post to the Income Summary account as an accuracy check on the entries affecting that account. The credit balance closed out of Income Summary should equal net income computed on the work sheet.
3. Prepare the company's multi-step income statement, statement of owner's equity, and balance sheet in account format. Draw arrows linking the statements.
4. Compute the inventory turnover for 20X6. Inventory at December 31, 20X5, was $61,000. Turnover for 20X5 was 2.1 times. Would you expect Jan King Distributing Company to be more profitable or less profitable in 20X6 than in 20X5? Give your reason.

A+ Tips reminders appear with both Mid-Chapter and End-of-Chapter review problems.

Unique! Decision Guidelines show when, why, and how managers—not just accountants—use accounting information to make good business decisions.

Decision Guidelines

MERCHANDISING OPERATIONS AND THE ACCOUNTING CYCLE

Amazon.com and Kinko's Copy Centers are two very different companies. How do Amazon and Kinko's differ? How are they similar? The Decision Guidelines answer these questions.

Decision	Guidelines
How do merchandisers differ from service entities?	• Merchandisers, such as Amazon.com, buy and sell *merchandise inventory*. • Service entities, such as Kinko's, perform a *service*.
How do a merchandiser's financial statements differ from the statements of a service business?	
Income Statement: ***Merchandiser*** Sales revenue .... $XXX −Cost of goods sold .... (X) = Gross profit .... XX −Operating expenses .... (X) = Net income .... $ X	**Balance sheet:** • Merchandiser has *inventory*, an asset. • Service business has no inventory. ***Service Business*** Service revenue .... $ XX −Operating expenses .... (X) = Net income .... $ X
Statements of Owner's Equity:	No difference
Which type of inventory system to use?	• *Perpetual system* shows the amount of *inventory* on hand (the asset) and the cost of goods sold (the expense) at all times. • *Periodic system* shows the correct balances of inventory and cost of goods sold only after a physical count of the inventory, which occurs at least once each year.

Excel Application Exercises Every business professional must know how to use Excel, and Horngren/Harrison/Bamber provides the tools you need to master it. Excel Application Exercises appear in each chapter, with instructions for creating your own spreadsheets. Spreadsheet templates appear on the CD.

Excel Application Exercise

Goal: Create a spreadsheet to compute Amazon.com's gross profit percentage and inventory turnover for the past three years.

Scenario: You are intrigued by Amazon's ability to sell merchandise via the Internet and would like to invest in such a venture. Before doing so, however, you remember from your accounting course that ratio analysis is an important part of making an investment decision. You decide to calculate two key ratios: gross profit percentage and inventory turnover. (You may need to visit Amazon.com on the Web to find inventory data from past years. Look under Investor Relations at the bottom of the Home page.) When you have completed your worksheet, answer the following questions:

1. What has happened to Amazon's gross profit percentage over the past three years?
2. What can you tell about Amazon's inventory operations from its inventory turnover ratio for the past two years?

Step-by-Step:

1. Open a new Excel spreadsheet.
2. In column 1, create a bold-faced heading as follows:
   a. Chapter 5 Excel Application Exercise
   b. Evaluating Amazon Inventory Operations
   c. Today's Date
3. Two rows down and two columns over, create bold and underlined headings for the most recent three years (e.g., 2002, 2001, and 2000).
4. In column A, enter the following (one per row):
   a. Net Sales (in thousands)
   b. Cost of Goods Sold (Cost of Sales)
   c. Gross Profit
   d. Inventory
   e. Gross Profit Percentage
   f. Inventory Turnover
5. Locate the data for items **a-d** in the Amazon.com annual report (or on the Web) and enter it in the appropriate columns.
6. Calculate gross profit percentage and inventory turnover. To help visualize the data trends, use the Chart Wizard to create a bar graph of performance.
7. Format all columns, rows, and data as needed. Save your work and print a copy for your files.

Assignment Materials

New! Starters Starters serve as warm-ups and confidence builders at the beginning of the assignment material. Try to solve these easy, single-concept exercises. Each Starter is referenced within the chapter so that if you need more guidance, you know exactly what material to review to complete the exercise.

ASSESS *Your Progress*

A+ online homework

See *www.prenhall.com/horngren* for selected Starters, Exercises, and Problems.

Starters

Recording purchase and cash payment transactions
(Obj. 1)

S5-1 You may have shopped at a **Gap** store. Suppose Gap purchases 2,000 pairs of slacks on account for $50,000. Credit terms are 2/10 n/30. Gap paid within the discount period. Journalize the following transactions for Gap:

a. Purchase of inventory. **b.** Payment on account.

Accounting for the purchase of inventory—purchase discount
(Obj. 1)

S5-2 Toys "Я" Us purchases inventory from a variety of suppliers, including **Mattel**, **Hasbro**, and **Tonka**. Suppose Toys "Я" Us buys $150,000 worth of **Lego** toys on credit terms of 3/15 n/45. Some of the goods are damaged in shipment, so Toys "Я" Us returns $50,000 (original amount, before any discounts) of the merchandise to Lego.

How much must Toys "Я" Us pay Lego

a. After the discount period? **b.** Within the discount period?

Recording purchase, purchase return, and cash payment transactions.
(Obj. 1)

S5-3 Refer to the **Toys "Я" Us** situation in Starter 5-2 and journalize the following transactions on the books of Toys "Я" Us. Explanations are not required.

a. Purchase of the goods on May 6, 20X5.

... the first

✔ Starter 5-2
✔ Starter 5-3
✔ Starter 5-4

Assets	=	Liabilities	+	Owner's Equity
Inventory		Accounts Payable		
−$100	=	−$100	+	$0

Stop & Think

On September 15, Austin Sound purchases $1,000 of merchandise on account, with terms 2/10, n/30. Austin returns $100 of merchandise for credit on September 20, then makes payment in full on September 25. Journalize these transactions.

Answer: Three separate journal entries are needed. The purchase entry is

1. **Purchase:** Sep. 15	Inventory	1,000	
	Accounts Payable		1,000

The second entry records the return of inventory, as follows:

2. **Return:** Sep. 20	Accounts Payable	100	
	Inventory		100

Accounts Payable

Return	100	Purchase	1,000
		Bal.	900

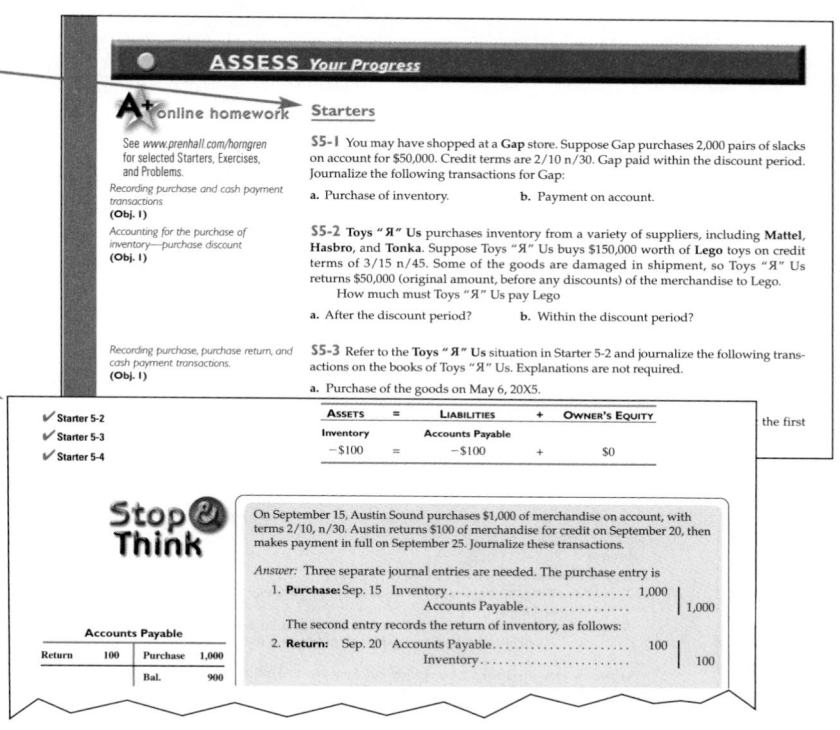

REVIEW ***Merchandising Operations***

Quick Check

1. Which account does a merchandiser, but not a service company, use?
   a. Inventory
   b. Sales revenue
   c. Cost of goods sold
   d. All of the above
2. The two main inventory accounting systems are the
   a. Purchase and sale
   b. Perpetual and periodic
   c. Cash and accrual
   d. Returns and allowances
3. The journal entry for the purchase of inventory on account is

a.	Inventory	XXX	
	Accounts Receivable		XXX
b.	Accounts Payable	XXX	
	Inventory		XXX
c.	Inventory	XXX	
	Accounts Payable		XXX

New! Quick Check These new multiple-choice questions appear at the ends of chapters so you can test your understanding of material before taking multiple-choice exams. Answers to Quick Checks appear in Appendix D at the end of the book.

E5-14 Marcia Walker's consulting practice performs systems consulting. Walker has also begun selling accounting software. During January, the business completed these transactions:

Accounting for both merchandising and service operations
(Obj. 1, 2, 4, 5)

Student ResourceCD
General Ledger, Peachtree, QuickBooks

Jan.	2	Completed a consulting engagement and received cash of $7,200.
	2	Prepaid three months' office rent, $1,500.
	7	Purchased accounting software inventory on account, $4,000.
	16	Paid employee salary, $1,400.

A+ Online homework

Problems

(Group A)

Explaining the perpetual inventory system
(Obj. 1, 2)

P5-1A Lens Masters is a regional chain of optical shops. The company offers a large selection of eyeglass frames, and Lens Masters stores provide while-you-wait service. The company has launched a vigorous advertising campaign to promote two-for-the-price-of-one frame sales.

Required

Lens Masters expects to grow rapidly and to increase its level of inventory. As the chief accountant of this company, you wish to install a perpetual inventory system. Write a one-paragraph business memo to the company president to explain how that system would work for the purchase and sale of eyeglasses. Use the following heading for your memo:

Exercises and Problems Exercises and Problems give you plenty of practice in solving accounting dilemmas and checking your understanding of major concepts in the chapter.

APPLY ***Your Knowledge***

Decision Cases

Expanding a business
(Obj. 5)

Case 1. Lauren Sever and Trey Hagins opened Party-Time T-Shirts to sell T-shirts for parties at their college. The company completed the first year of operations, and Sever and Hagins are generally pleased with operating results, as shown by the following income statement:

Party-Time T-Shirts
Income Statement
Year Ended December 31, 20X6

Net sales revenue	$350,000
Cost of goods sold	210,000
Gross margin	140,000
Operating expenses:	
Selling expense	40,000

Ethical Issue

Hunter Glass Company makes all sales under terms of FOB shipping point. The company usually receives orders for sales approximately one week before shipping inventory to customers. For orders received late in December, Donny Hunter, the owner, decides when

Financial Statement Case

Closing entries and the gross profit percentage
(Obj. 4, 6)

This case uses both the income statement (statement of operations) and the balance sheet of Amazon.com in Appendix A. It will help you understand the closing process of a business.

Required

1. Journalize Amazon.com's closing entries for the revenues and expenses of 2002. Show all amounts in thousands as in the Amazon financial statements. You may be unfamiliar with certain revenues and expenses, but treat each item on the income statement as either a revenue or an expense. For example, Net Sales is the first revenue, and Interest Income is also a revenue. The last revenue is Cumulative Effect of Change in Accounting Principle. A loss is like an expense. In your closing entries

Team Project

With a small team of classmates, visit one or more merchandising businesses in your area. Interview a responsible official of the company to learn about its inventory policies and accounting system. Obtain answers to the following questions, write a report, and be prepared to make a presentation to the class if your instructor so directs:

Required

1. What merchandise inventory does the business sell?
2. From whom does the business buy its inventory? Is the relationship with the supplier new or longstanding?
3. What are the FOB terms on inventory purchases? Who pays the freight, the buyer or the seller? Is freight a significant amount? What percentage of total inventory cost is the freight?
4. What are the credit terms on inventory purchases—2/10 n/30, or other? Does the business pay early to get purchase discounts? If so, why? If not, why not?
5. How does the business actually pay its suppliers? Does it mail a check or pay elec-

Comprehensive Problem for Chapters 1–7

COMPLETING THE ACCOUNTING CYCLE FOR A MERCHANDISING ENTITY—USING SPECIAL JOURNALS

Digital Meter Company closes its books and prepares financial statements at the end of each month. Digital uses the perpetual inventory system. The company completed the following transactions during August:

Aug.	1	Issued check no. 682 for August office rent of $1,000. (Debit Rent Expense.)
	2	Issued check no. 683 to pay the salary payable of $1,250 from July 31.
	2	Issued invoice no. 503 for sale on account to R. T. Loeb, $600. Digital's cost of this merchandise was $190.
	3	Purchased inventory on credit terms of 1/15 n/60 from Grant, Inc., $1,400.

Cases A variety of cases, plus ***Team Projects***—and ***Comprehensive Problems*** at the ends of groups of chapters—give you opportunities to practice decision-making in real business situations. Cases include ***Decision Cases***, ***Ethical Issues***, and ***Financial Statement Cases*** that use the ***Amazon.com*** annual report at the end of the book.

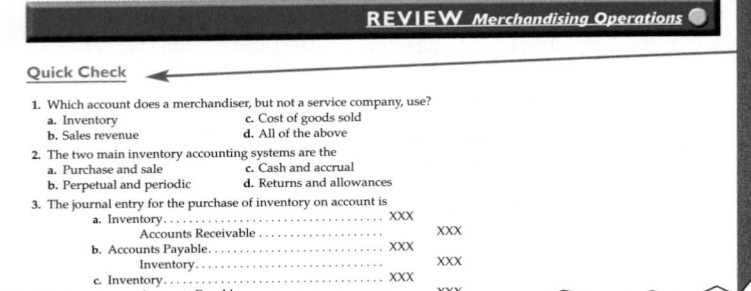

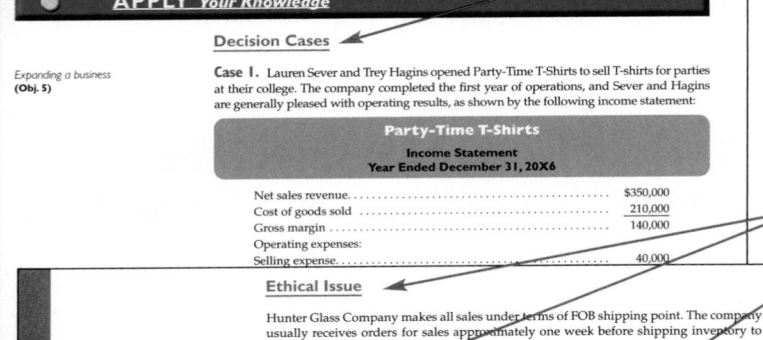

Study Aids And Resources

Throughout the book, margin icons indicate resources available on the **Student Resource CD**. Selected end-of-chapter problems appear in **spreadsheet templates** on the CD, and also in **General Ledger (GL)**, **QuickBooks (QB)**, and **Peachtree (PT)** formats. Other assignments are linked to Prentice Hall's new online homework program that includes a variety of assignments whose results feed directly into the grading program. The program includes algorithm-based problems, to give you extensive practice on a single concept.

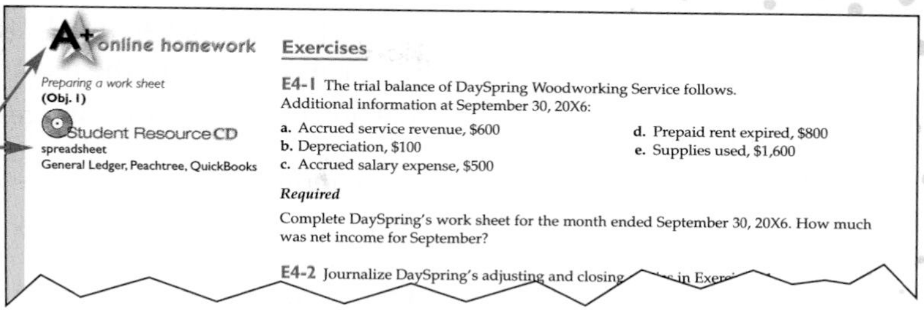
A+ online homework

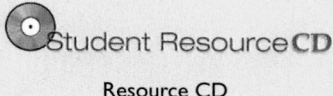

Preparing a work sheet
(Obj. 1)

Student Resource CD
spreadsheet
General Ledger, Peachtree, QuickBooks

Exercises

E4-1 The trial balance of DaySpring Woodworking Service follows. Additional information at September 30, 20X6:

a. Accrued service revenue, $600
b. Depreciation, $100
c. Accrued salary expense, $500
d. Prepaid rent expired, $800
e. Supplies used, $1,600

Required

Complete DaySpring's work sheet for the month ended September 30, 20X6. How much was net income for September?

E4-2 Journalize DaySpring's adjusting and closing

New Student and Instructor Resource CD-ROMs This innovative product includes all resources for the text—Powerpoint files, video clips, spreadsheet templates, tutorial software, General Ledger software, and Peachtree and QuickBooks software. You can access resources by chapter or by keyword (like "LIFO"). The student version of the CD allows you to create your own individualized review program. Free with new texts.

Student Resource CD

Text Icons

A+ TIPS CHECK YOUR RESOURCES

Resources

Student Resource CD

Resource CD

Writing Assignment

A+ online homework

Online homework program

Study Guide This chapter-by-chapter learning aid systematically and effectively helps you study accounting and get the maximum benefit from study time. Each chapter provides a Chapter Overview and Review, a Featured Exercise that covers in a single exercise all of the most important topics in the chapter, and Review Questions and Exercises that test your understanding of the material.

Powerpoint slides help you review concepts by providing a summary of important points. *Remember!* You can choose to review **Powerpoints** by chapter or by keyword.

Video Clips include a series of **tutorial videos** designed to help you review concepts, plus **On Location! Videos** that take you inside companies such as **Jelly Belly** and **It's Just Lunch** to show you how managers use accounting information to make everyday business decisions. *Remember!* You can choose to review **videos** by chapter or by keyword.

Spreadsheet templates Selected end-of-chapter exercises and problems appear on pre-created templates for you to use in solving these assignments. If you need additional help in using Excel, you may opt to review the tutorial segment.

More Study Aids

General Ledger Software enables you to complete homework assignments using a general ledger software package. You may also enter and solve your own problems. E-Working Papers are available for each chapter.

New! Getting Started If your professor has chosen to package one of the Getting Started series manuals with your text, you may access the data files to use with the manuals.

Companion Web site www.prenhall.com/horngren Prentice Hall's Learning on the Internet Partnership offers extensive Internet-based support. Our Web sites provide a wealth of free resources for you, including Student Study Hall, Online Tutorial Assistance, Study Guide with Quizzes, Internet Exercises, and much more.

For The Instructor

WHAT'S NEW FOR THE SIXTH EDITION? HORNGREN MAKES IT EASIER TO MOTIVATE STUDENTS TO SUCCEED!

(A complete list of chapter-by-chapter highlights follows this overview)

Text & Assignment Material

- ***New Amazon.com Annual Report & Financial Statement Analysis Cases!*** New copies of the text now include the Amazon.com annual report. This is linked to many of the chapter-opening vignettes, and end-of-chapter financial statement analysis cases.
- ***New Theme: Show More. Say Less.*** Throughout the text, the authors have worked hard to tighten and focus the content on core topics in first year accounting.
- ***New, more open and student-friendly design*** includes many new exhibits to aid in student understanding.
- ***New Chapter Organization.*** The chapters on merchandising and inventory (previously Chapters 5 & 9) are now Chapters 5-6 to enable students to link these topics more easily.
- ***New A+Tips*** at each chapter opening list resources to help students learn key concepts; reminders appear within the chapter.
- ***New Quick Check Questions.*** New multiple-choice exercises at the ends of chapters enable students to test their understanding before taking multiple-choice examinations. Answers appear in Appendix D.
- ***New Starters*** (previously called "Daily Exercises") serve as warm-ups/confidence builders at the beginning of the assignment material. Students solve these easy, single-concept exercises (many using real companies). Each problem is referenced to material within the chapter so that if students need more guidance, they know exactly what to review to complete the exercise.
- ***New Excel Application Exercises***, now for each chapter in the book, with spreadsheet solutions.

Grading & Practice

- ***New Peachtree, QuickBooks, and General Ledger Assignments.*** Selected end-of-chapter problems are available on templates for Peachtree, QuickBooks, and General Ledger software. In addition, instructors may opt to package a brief introductory manual on the latest release of Peachtree or QuickBooks at no charge with new texts.
- ***New Manual and Computerized Practice Sets*** include optional exercises using Peachtree and QuickBooks. Package any Practice Set at 50% off with new texts.
- ***New Automatic Homework Grading!*** Prentice Hall's online homework program includes a variety of in-text assignments for students to complete online—and results feed directly into the grading program. The program includes

A+ online homework

algorithm-based problems that enable students to have extensive practice on a single concept. They *reduce cheating* because two students sitting next to one another could see different versions of the problem (the instructor determines whether the problem is viewed in static or algorithm-based format). Students get extensive feedback to help them understand where they went wrong.

The New CD

Student Resource CD

- *New Instructor and Student Resource CD-ROMs:* This innovative CD-ROM includes all resources for the text and allows instructors to create custom multi-media lectures in less than 5 minutes! Access the resources by chapter or keyword (e.g., "LIFO"). A student version of the CD enables students to create individualized review programs. Free with new texts.

Chapter-by-Chapter Highlights

CHAPTER 1 Accounting and the Business Environment

- New chapter opener focuses on **Amazon.com**, the feature company for this edition.
- Discussion of ethics in accounting features **Enron**, **WorldCom**, and **Xerox**.
- New illustration of the effects of transactions on balance sheet and income statement.

CHAPTER 2 Recording Business Transactions

- New chapter opener features **Frito-Lay**.
- New notations for journal entries clarify the rules of debit and credit.
- New roadmap shows how accounts, ledgers, journals, and the trial balance fit together.

CHAPTER 3 The Adjusting Process

- New notations for adjusting entries clarify the rules of debit and credit.
- New graphic shows the difference between the accrual basis and the cash basis.

CHAPTER 4 Completing the Accounting Cycle

- New chapter opener features the **Chicago Cubs** baseball team.
- New exhibit illustrates the closing process.
- Dell Computer's balance sheet illustrates the accounts covered to date.

CHAPTER 5 Merchandising Operations

- New chapter opener features **Amazon.com**.
- This completely revised chapter begins with purchase of merchandise, then moves to sales, all based on the perpetual system.
- Appendix on the periodic system.

CHAPTER 6 Merchandise Inventory

- New chapter opener features **Columbia Sportswear** and the **International Balloon Festival**.
- New exhibits! One shows the effect of merchandising on the financial statements; another shows FIFO, LIFO, and average costing; and others show the relationship between transactions in a perpetual system and related journal entries.
- New, streamlined coverage of accounting for inventory in a periodic system.

CHAPTER 7 Accounting Information Systems

- New discussion of Enterprise Resource Planning (ERP) systems.
- New explanation of the relationship between manual and computerized systems.

CHAPTER 8 Internal Control and Cash

- Discussion of the Sarbanes-Oxley Act and internal controls.
- Streamlined discussion of the bank reconciliation.
- New graphics: internal controls for cash receipts and cash payments.
- New: Enron examples to illustrate ethics in accounting.

CHAPTER 9 Receivables

- Simplified examples to illustrate accounting for uncollectibles.
- New graphics: integration of order entry, shipping, and billing of receivables.

CHAPTER 10 Plant Assets and Intangible Assets

- New chapter opener features airlines and their assets.
- New exhibit: relationship between plant assets and related expenses.
- New graphic: relative-sales-value method.
- Streamlined coverage of Depreciation and Income Taxes.
- Simplified coverage of Partial-Year Depreciation.
- Updated accounting for goodwill.

CHAPTER 11 Current Liabilities and Payroll

- New chapter opener features General Motors, Sony, and Goodyear.
- New graphic: how to allocate interest expense to the appropriate period.
- Streamlined accounting for sales tax payable.
- Beefed up—and streamlined—coverage of accounting for contingencies.
- Simplified payroll illustrations.
- Added Form 941, Employer's Quarterly Federal Tax Return.

CHAPTER 12 Partnerships

- New chapter opener on the fragility of partnerships, featuring the Arthur Andersen debacle.
- New graphics illustrate the various ways to start a partnership.

CHAPTER 13 Corporations: Paid-in Capital and the Balance Sheet

- New discussion of closing net income for a corporation.
- Streamlined accounting for income tax by a corporation.

CHAPTER 14 Retained Earnings, Treasury Stock, and the Income Statement

- New chapter opener features Coca-Cola, Dell Computer, and Pier 1 Imports.
- New graphic: retained earnings are not cash.
- New coverage of stock dividends.
- Scaled-down treatment of the corporate income statement.
- Simplified treatment of earnings per share.

CHAPTER 15 Long-term Liabilities

- Revised chapter opener features Amazon.com.
- New roadmap guides students through issuing bonds payable to borrow money.
- Deleted sections on Leases and Pensions.

CHAPTER 16 Investments and International Operations

- New chapter opener features McDonald's, Panasonic, and Nokia.
- Scaled-down coverage of accounting for international operations.

CHAPTER 17 The Statement of Cash Flows

- New chapter opener features eBay.
- Completely revised chapter: Two distinct sections for the indirect method and the direct method. Each section features step-by-step preparation of the statement.
- Scaled-down level of complexity for both methods—fewer accounts to analyze.
- New graphics: how cash is affected by changes in the other current accounts.

CHAPTER 18 Financial Statement Analysis

- New chapter opener features Bristol-Myers Squibb.
- Revised chapter organized around decisions and the need for financial statement analysis.
- New graphics illustrate horizontal analysis and vertical analysis.
- Scaled-down financial statements—fewer accounts to analyze.
- Revised discussions of the ratios—shorter paragraphs, fewer words.
- New section on Red Flags in Financial Statement Analysis.
- New section on Analyzing Nonfinancial Data.

CHAPTER 19 Introduction to Management Accounting

- New chapter opener and **On Location!** video on Regal Marine.
- New infographics.
- New exhibit simplifies and clarifies the distinction between merchandisers' and manufacturers' income statements.
- Simplified discussion of cost of goods manufactured, linking the flow of activities.
- Brief new discussion of ERP systems.

CHAPTER 20 Job Costing

- Updated chapter opener: why and how Dell figures the cost of a built-to-order computer.
- Emphasis on why all managers need to know how much it costs to produce a product or to serve a customer.
- Reorganized and simplified discussion of accounting for materials and labor.
- Exciting new team project asks students to compare the cost (and profits) of regular airlines' versus budget airlines' flights, using real-world data.

CHAPTER 21 Process Costing

- New chapter opener and **On Location!** video feature Jelly Belly.
- Text discussion uses Jelly Belly to illustrate key process costing principles.
- *First half* of chapter enables students to grasp the basics of process costing without complications caused by the presence of beginning work in process inventory. Instructors who prefer to introduce the basics of process costing can assign just the first half of the chapter. There is plenty of relevant assignment material.
- The *second half* of the chapter allows for beginning inventories. Scaled-back coverage focuses on the process costing method students find easiest to grasp—weighted average.
- Full and self-contained coverage of the more complex FIFO method appears in a new appendix. Instructors can add—or substitute—the FIFO-based appendix for the second half of the chapter.
- Several new Decision Guidelines emphasize the big picture—job versus process costing, the checks and balances in the 5-step process costing approach illustrated in the chapter, the goal of process costing, and how managers use the production cost report.

CHAPTER 22 Cost-Volume-Profit Analysis

- Streamlined presentation of variable, fixed, and mixed costs.
- Significantly reorganized chapter: Illustrations proceed from cost behavior, to basic CVP analysis, to using CVP analysis for profit planning, to conducting sensitivity analyses with CVP.
- Chapter midpoint now follows basic CVP analysis. This speed bump prompts students to reinforce their understanding of the basics.
- Significantly revised discussion of sensitivity analyses includes realistic business decision contexts for changing various components of the CVP analysis, covers the margin of safety, and explains how managers use information technology.

CHAPTER 23 The Master Budget and Responsibility Accounting

- New chapter opener features Amazon.com CEO Jeff Bezos' use of budgets to control costs.
- Focus on Amazon.com throughout chapter, including new Decision Guidelines contexts, new end-of-chapter multiple-choice questions, and several new infographics.
- New pedagogy moves from students' personal budgets, to a simple budget for a small company, to the main example featuring a retail store's budget, to how large companies use software to roll up individual unit budgets into the companywide budget.
- Emphasizes how managers *use* the budget to plan and control, and also considers behavioral issues such as tips for increasing employees' acceptance of the budget.
- New infographic organization chart coupled with a new exhibit showing a responsibility performance report illustrate how responsibility accounting works in a real-world context.

CHAPTER 24 The Flexible Budget and Standard Costs

- New introductory example based on students' daily life shows why variances are important guides to future action.
- Mid-chapter Decision Guidelines and new Excel exercise show how students can use flexible budgets and variances to plan and control costs in start-up businesses.
- New discussion of how managers set price and quantity standards.
- Significantly streamlined discussion of allocating manufacturing overhead in a standard costing system
- Streamlined explanation of overhead variances: more visuals, fewer words.

CHAPTER 25 Activity Based Costing and Other Cost Management Tools

- Streamlined and updated discussion of how managers use activity-based management in pricing, product mix, and cost-cutting decisions.

(*continued*)

(*Chapter 25 continued*)

- Streamlined discussion of when ABC passes the cost-benefit test.
- Simplified discussion of the just-in-time philosophy and total quality management.
- New Financial Statement Case highlights Amazon.com's unique activities as an e-tailer.

CHAPTER 26 Special Business Decisions and Capital Budgeting

- New graphics: decision rules for special short-term decisions such as special orders, product mix, and sell or process further.
- Simplified coverage of special sales orders.
- Discussion and new examples of the trend toward outsourcing all kinds of business functions.
- Simplified illustration of opportunity costs in the context of decisions on best use of facilities and outsourcing.
- New graphics: decision rules for long-term capital budgeting decisions.
- Simplified coverage of net present value.
- New Financial Statement Case asks students to apply payback, accounting rate of return, and discounted cash flow techniques to Amazon.com's investments.

Instructor Resources

Everything you need where you need it. The Prentice Hall Instructor Resource Center/CD-ROM increases your effectiveness and saves you time and effort. Harness the power of having all of your resources in one well-organized place. Because resources should simplify, not overwhelm.

Technology Resources: How Horngren Makes It Easier for You to Test and Grade

NEW! Instructor and Student Resource CD-ROMs

These CD's are powerful teaching and learning tools. They first serve as a roadmap through the chapters to identify key concepts and then guide students to other resources on the CD-ROM, where they can further develop their skills.

- Available in separate versions for faculty and students, this unique tool enables faculty to **save time** and **quickly prepare highly effective and interactive multimedia classroom presentations**.
- Using a **highly accessible menu**, students and faculty can easily customize study programs or presentations. By simply clicking on a chapter or keyword, they can access an interactive library of resources.
- Instructor's CD-ROM contains all ancillaries. Student CD-ROM contains tutorial software, On Location! video clips, PowerPoints, General Ledger software, Excel tutorial, spreadsheet templates, and much more.

These CD-ROMs also contain a special option for instructors who wish to build their own online courses! Faculty can pick and choose from the various supplements (organized by chapter and topic), and export them to their hard drive in HTML. From hard drive to online course is an easy step!

The IRCD contains all print and technology (e.g., spreadsheets, videos) supplements on a single CD-ROM. Enjoy the freedom to transport the entire package from office, to home, to classroom. This enables you to customize any of the ancillaries, print only the chapters or materials you wish to use, or access any item from the package within the classroom!

NEW! Computerized Accounting Practice Sets

Containing lots of simulated real-world examples, the **A-1 Photography** and **Runners Corporation** practice sets are available complete with data files for Peachtree, QuickBooks, and PH General Ledger. Each practice set also includes business stationery for manual entry work.

NEW! Prentice Hall Automatic Homework Grading!

An outstanding Web-based homework solution. Students can work end-of-chapter problems at their own pace online. In addition, the algorithmically generated numbers ensure that problems are never repetitive.

NEW! Getting Started Series

Upon request, faculty may package their choice of one of these approximately 70-page manuals on the latest professional accounting software packages with **Accounting, 6th ed.**, at no charge. Each manual introduces students to the concepts of Excel, Peachtree, QuickBooks, or PH General Ledger.

NEW! Special Offers - Professional Accounting Software Packages

Package your choice of the latest software releases of Peachtree or QuickBooks, for less than $15, with new text purchases.

- ***General Ledger Software*** General Ledger software enables students to complete homework assignments using a general ledger software package. Students may also enter and solve their own problems. Available on the Student CD-ROM, Instructor CD-ROM, and downloadable from Companion Web site.
- ***Working Papers and e-Working Papers*** Working Papers contain tailormade spreadsheets for all end-of-chapter Excel problems. A sample set of working papers is packaged free with every Student Resource CD-ROM.
- ***INNOVATION! Standard Online Courses in WebCT, CourseCompass, and BlackBoard*** Teach a complete online course or a Web-enhanced course. Add your own course materials, take advantage of online testing and Gradebook opportunities, and utilize the bulletin board and discussion board functions. Free upon request. This is an excellent time to build your own course using our CD-ROMs with your choice of platform.
- ***Companion Web site www.prenhall.com/horngren*** Prentice Hall's Learning on the Internet Partnership offers extensive Internet-based support. Our Web site provides a wealth of resources for students and faculty including: Student Study Hall, Online Tutorial Assistance, Study Guide with Quizzes, Internet Exercises, and much more.

More Instructor Resources: Horngren makes it easier for you to prepare your classes!

- ***Annotated Instructor's Edition*** Replete with teaching tips, real-world examples, short exercises, ethical insights, and discussion, this annotated edition is ideal for instructors wishing to augment their classroom discussions.
- ***Instructor's Resource Manual*** Each chapter of this comprehensive resource consists of a list of the student learning objectives, a narrative overview of main topics, and an outline with teaching tips interspersed.
- ***Test Item File*** The printed Test Item File consists of over 2,900 questions, including true/false questions, conceptual and quantitative multiple-choice questions, critical thinking problems, and exercises. Each question identifies the difficulty level and the corresponding learning objective. Prentice Hall TestGenEQ can create exams, and evaluate and track student results. New to this edition are algorithmically generated conceptual questions integrated throughout the TestGen.
- ***Solutions Manual*** In addition to fully worked-out and accuracy-checked solutions for every question, exercise, problem, and case in the text, this manual provides a categorization of assignment material. In addition, every page of the Solutions Manual has been reproduced in acetate form for use on the overhead projector.
- ***On Location! Videos*** These brief videos take students "on location" to real companies where real accounting situations are discussed and explained.

Acknowledgments

Special Thanks to:

Professor Michael Bamber of the University of Georgia for his substantive contributions to the ethics cases and team projects in Chapters 19–26.

Professor Lynn Mazzola of Nassau Community College for her help in checking assignment material and reading the text of Chapters 19–26.

Professors Becky Jones and Betsy Willis for writing the Instructor's Manual and Professor Jones for coordinating the accuracy checking of the Solutions Manual.

Professor Robert Bauman of Allan Hancock College for providing the annotations for the Instructor's Edition.

Pradeep Nagar at the University of Georgia for helping ensure the clarity and accuracy of all the assignments in Chapters 19–26.

Writer Nancy Brandwein for the Accounting.com boxes.

We also want to thank the reviewers of the Sixth Edition and the Focus Group participants, who gave of their time and talents to help us streamline the new edition and focus on the essentials. We especially want to thank the reviewers of Chapters 5 and 6, who provided so many useful comments and suggestions.

Finally, we want to thank the hard-working members of our Prentice Hall team, all of whom contributed so much to this edition: P. J. Boardman, editor-in-chief; Jeannine Ciliotta, senior development editor; Beth Toland, executive marketing manager; Sam Goffinet, assistant editor; Jane Avery, senior editorial assistant; Melene Kubat, administrative assistant; Steve Frim, designer; Anne Graydon, production editor; Arnold Vila, production manager; Christy Mahon, manager, multimedia production; and Nancy Welcher, media project manager.

Reviewers of Accounting, 6th ed.

[alphabetized by school]

Jenny Davis *Angelo State University*
Paulette Ratliff *Arkansas State University*
Frank Marino *Assumption College*
Terry Willyard *Baker College*
Charles Birnberg *Bergen Community College*
Robert D. Collmier *Bloomfield College*
Bonnie Giraldi *Cecil Community College*
Jeffrey Jones *Community College of Southern Nevada*
Kimberly Smith *County College of Morris*
Patty Holmes
Tom Turner *DesMoines Area Community College*
Rachel Ezelle *East Mississippi Community College*
John L. Stancil *Florida Southern College*
Rebecca Floor *Greenville Tech*
Linda Tarrago *Hillsborough Community College*
Judy Isonhood *Hinds Community College*
Cynthia Beier-Greeson
Warren Smock
Cynthia Vanoosterum *Ivy Tech State College*
Suzie Cordes *Johnson County Community College*
Tara Laken *Joliet Junior College*
Ron Carlin *Lamar University-Pt. Arthur*
Susan Logorda *Lehigh Carbon Community College*
Fred R. Jex *Macomb Community College*
David Grooms *Maui Community College*
Bruce Swindle *McNeese State University*
Josie Mathias *Mercer County Community College*
Judith Garcia *Miami Dade Community College—ESL*
Pamela Bogart *University of Michigan—ESL*
Joe Flynn *Moraine Valley Community College*
Cheryl McKay *Monroe County Community College*
Laura Prosser *National American University*
Laura Ilcisin *University of Nebraska*
Toni Clegg *Palm Beach Community College*
Randy Kidd *Penn Valley*
Shifei Chung
Stephanie Weidman *Rowan Community College*
Merrily Hoffman
Jeff Jackson
Randall Whitmore *San Jacinto College Central*
Patricia Halliday *Santa Monica College*
Ann Gregory *South Plains College*
Patricia Novak *Southeast Community College*
Gloria Worthy *Southwest Tennessee Community College*
Jack Fatica *Terra Community College*
Tracy Burdis *Sylvan Learning Center*
Julie Dailey *Tidewater Community College*
Michael Stemkoski *Utah Valley State College*
Chuck Bunn *Wake Tech*
Clyde Galbraith *West Chester University*
Jerry Kreuze *Western Michigan University*
Jim Murray *Western Wisconsin Technical College*
Rajeev Parikh *Wilmington College*

Focus Group Participants

Sheila Arnouts
Thomas Badley *Baker College*
Janet Grange *Chicago State University*
William Harvey *Henry Ford Community College*
Linda Tarrago *Hillsborough Community College*
Dennis Valenti *Hudson County Community College*
Shirley Glass
Fred R. Jex *Macomb Community College*
Cheryl McKay *Monroe County Community College*
Nashwa George *Montclair State University*
Zach Holmes
Meg Costello Lambert *Oakland Community College*
Daniel Clark *Owens Community College*
Patricia Halliday *Santa Monica College*
Ruth Henderson *Union County College*
Michael Stemkoski *Utah Valley State College*

Resource Authors and Technical Reviewers

Instructor's Manual

Becky Jones, *Baylor University*

Betsy Willis, *Baylor University*

Alice Sineath, *Forsyth Technical Community College*

Solutions Manual & Solutions Transparencies

Charles T. Horngren, *Stanford University*

Walter T. Harrison, *Baylor University*

Linda Smith Bamber, *University of Georgia*

Working Papers

Ellen Sweatt, *Georgia Perimeter College*

Test Item File

Alice Sineath, *Forsyth Technical Community College*

Study Guide

Ann B. DeCapite

A1 Photography & Runner's Corporation Practice Sets

Jean Insinga, *Middlesex Community College*

On Location! Videos

Beverly Amer, *Northern Arizona University*

Companion Web site Online Student Self-Tests

Timothy Carse

Online Courses (WebCT, Blackboard, CourseCompass)

PowerPoints by Timothy Carse, with audio developed and created by Beverly Amer, *Northern Arizona University*. Original course content by Tony Fortini, *Camden Community College*, revised by Beverly Amer

Prentice Hall's Online Homework Program

Larry Kallio of the *Universtiy of Minnesota at Mankato*, with many thanks to Nancy Welcher of PH Business Publishing for extensive project coordination and support.

TestGenEQ Software

Alice B. Sineath, with algorithms selected and created by Alfonse Oddo of *Niagara University*. Software by Tamarack Software, Inc.

Student Resource CD-ROM

Instructor's Resource CD-ROM

PowerPoint Presentations by Olga Quintana of the *University of Miami*.

PH General Ledger by Jean Insinga and Carol Goetters. Spreadsheet Templates by Al Fisher of the *Community College of Southern Nevada*. Instructions to the templates provided by Diane Fisher & Associates.

Technical Reviewers

Lynn Mazzola, *Nassau Community College*; Robert Bauman, *Allan Hancock College*; Carolyn Stroebel; Becky Jones, *Baylor University*; Timothy Carse; Tom How; Pradeep Nagar, *University of Georgia*

CHAPTER 1

Accounting and the Business Environment

A+ TIPS CHECK YOUR RESOURCES

- Visit the www.prenhall.com/horngren **Web site** for self-study quizzes, video clips, and other resources
- Try the **Quick Check** exercise at the end of the chapter to test your knowledge
- Learn the **key terms**
- Do the **Starter** exercises keyed in the margins
- Work the **end-of-chapter summary problems**
- Use the **Concept Links** to review material in other chapters
- Search the **CD** for review materials by chapter or by key word
- Watch the **tutorial videos** to review key concepts
- Watch the **On Location Accounting and Business** video for an overview of the accounting function.

LEARNING OBJECTIVES

1. Use accounting vocabulary
2. Apply accounting concepts and principles
3. Use the accounting equation
4. Analyze business transactions
5. Prepare the financial statements
6. Evaluate business performance

Like most other people, you've probably bought **Amazon.com** products by shopping online. And like most other people, you've probably been amazed at how easy it is. Amazon.com is one of the most interesting organizations on earth. Consider these facts about the company:

- Amazon.com opened its virtual doors in 1995.
- In only a few years, millions of people in 220 countries have made it the world's leading online shopping site.
- It offers the world's largest selection of products.
- On Amazon.com's busiest shopping day of 2002, customers ordered 1.7 million units. That's 20 items per second, around the clock.
- There is still no Amazon.com store anywhere except online.

Amazon.com

Amazon.com continues to add partners and merchandise at breakneck speed. But it took from 1995 to 2002 for the company to post a profit. And it reported the figures using standard accounting methods.

What does all this mean? What does "profitable" mean? What are standard accounting methods? How can a company keep growing if it isn't making money? Lots of questions: And here's where accounting comes in. "Profitable" means that the company earns more revenue than its expenses. Accounting methods govern how companies keep track of their activities. This book will help you understand revenues, expenses, profit and loss, and other business concepts. After completing this first accounting course, you will be able to decide whether a company is a good (or bad) investment. You will be able to evaluate an auto loan and manage your own money. You will also be able to use accounting in your business career. ■

Sitemap

- The Language of Business
- Regulating Accounting
- Business Organizations
- Concepts and Principles
- The Accounting Equation
- Business Transactions
- Evaluating Transactions

We'll start our study with a small, single-person business known as a proprietorship. We need to begin by asking exactly what accounting is.

■ The Language of Business
□ Regulating Accounting
□ Business Organizations
□ Concepts and Principles
□ The Accounting Equation
□ Business Transactions
□ Evaluating Transactions

Student Resource CD
financial statements

Use accounting vocabulary

Accounting
The information system that measures business activities, processes that information into reports, and communicates the results to decision makers.

Financial Statements
Documents that report on a business in monetary amounts, providing information to help people make informed business decisions.

Accounting: The Language of Business

Accounting is the information system that measures business activity, processes the information into reports, and communicates the results to decision makers. Accounting is "the language of business." The better you understand the language, the better your decisions will be, and the better you can manage your finances. For example, how will you decide whether to borrow money? You had better consider your income: The concept of income comes straight from accounting.

A key product of accounting is a set of documents called financial statements. **Financial statements** report on a business in monetary terms. Is Amazon.com making a profit? Should Amazon expand? Answering these questions calls for Amazon's financial statements.

Exhibit 1-1 illustrates the role of accounting in business. The process starts and ends with people making decisions.

Exhibit 1-1 **The Accounting System: The Flow of Information**

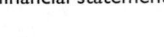

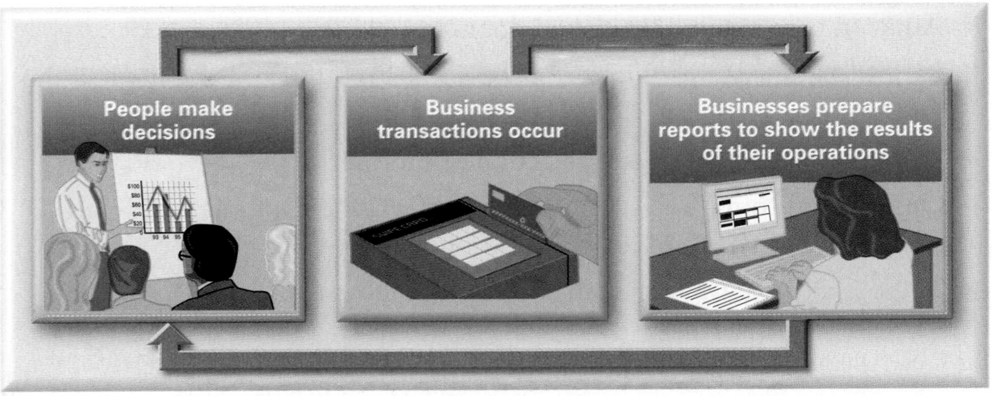

Decision Makers: The Users of Accounting Information

Decision makers need information. The bigger the decision, the greater the need. Here are some decision makers who use accounting information.

INDIVIDUALS You use accounting information to manage your bank account, evaluate a new job prospect, and decide whether to rent or buy a house. Amazon.com employees in Seattle, Washington, make the same decisions that you do.

BUSINESSES Managers use accounting information to set goals for their organizations. They also evaluate progress toward those goals, and they take corrective action when it's needed. For example, Amazon must decide which software to purchase, how many DVDs and books to keep on hand, and how much money to borrow. Accounting provides the information for making these decisions.

INVESTORS Investors provide the money to get a business going. To decide whether to invest, a person predicts the amount of income on the investment. This means analyzing the financial statements and keeping up with company developments—using, for example, www.yahoo.com (click on Finance), www.hoovers.com (click on Companies), the SEC's EDGAR database, and *The Wall Street Journal*.

CREDITORS Before lending money, a bank evaluates the borrower's ability to make the payments. This evaluation includes a report on the borrower's financial position and predicted income. To borrow money before striking it rich, Jeff Bezos, the president of Amazon.com, probably had to document his income and financial position.

GOVERNMENT REGULATORY AGENCIES Most organizations face government regulation. For example, the Securities and Exchange Commission (SEC), a federal agency, requires businesses to report their financial information to the public.

TAXING AUTHORITIES Local, state, and federal governments levy taxes. Income tax is figured using accounting information. Sales tax depends upon a company's sales.

NONPROFIT ORGANIZATIONS Nonprofit organizations—churches, hospitals, and colleges—use accounting information the same way as Amazon.com and The Coca-Cola Company.

Financial Accounting and Management Accounting

Accounting can be divided into two fields—financial accounting and management accounting.

Financial accounting provides information for people outside the company. Lenders and outside investors are not part of day-to-day management. These people use the company's financial statements. Chapters 2–18 of this book deal primarily with financial accounting.

Financial Accounting
The branch of accounting that focuses on information for people outside the firm.

Management accounting focuses on information for internal decision makers, such as the company's executives and the administrators of a hospital. Chapters 19 through 26 cover management accounting. Exhibit 1-2 illustrates the difference between financial accounting and management accounting.

Management Accounting
The branch of accounting that focuses on information for internal decision makers of a business.

Exhibit 1-2 Financial Accounting and Management Accounting

Investors:
Should we invest in Amazon.com?
Is the company profitable?
Investors use financial accounting information to measure profitability.
Amazon.com
Jeff Bezos, president, and other managers use management accounting information to operate the company.
Creditors:
Should we lend money to Amazon.com?
Can the company pay us back?
Creditors use financial accounting information to decide whether to make a loan.

The Language of Business
Regulating Accounting
Business Organizations
Concepts and Principles
The Accounting Equation
Business Transactions
Evaluating Transactions

Student Resource CD
ethics

Regulating Accounting

All professions have regulations. Let's see the organizations that most influence the accounting profession.

Governing Organizations

Financial Accounting Standards Board (FASB)
The private organization that determines how accounting is practiced in the United States.

Certified Public Accountant (CPA)
A licensed accountant who serves the general public rather than one particular company.

In the United States, a private organization called the **Financial Accounting Standards Board (FASB)** formulates accounting standards. The FASB works with a governmental agency, the SEC, and two private groups, the American Institute of Certified Public Accountants (AICPA) and the Institute of Management Accountants (IMA). **Certified public accountants**, or **CPAs**, are professional accountants who are licensed to serve the general public. **Certified management accountants**, or **CMAs**, are professional accountants who work for a single company. Both groups of accountants have passed qualifying exams.

The rules that govern public accounting information are called *generally accepted accounting principles (GAAP)*. Exhibit 1-3 diagrams the relationships among the various accounting organizations.

Exhibit 1-3

Key Accounting Organizations

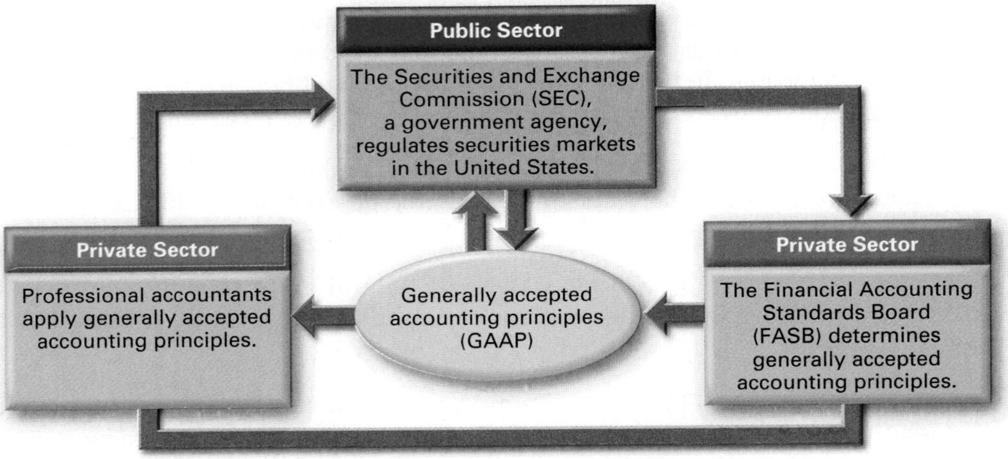

Ethics in Accounting and Business

Certified Management Accountant (CMA)
A licensed accountant who works for a single company.

Audit
An examination of a company's financial situation.

Ethical considerations affect everything accountants do. Investors and creditors need relevant and reliable information about a company such as Amazon.com or General Motors. The companies naturally want to make themselves look as good as possible in order to attract investors. There is potential for conflict here. To provide reliable information for the public, the SEC requires companies to have their financial statements audited by independent accountants. An **audit** is a financial examination. The accountants then certify that the financial statements give a true picture of the company's situation.

The vast majority of accountants do their jobs quietly, professionally, and ethically. We never hear about them. Unfortunately, only those who bend the rules make the headlines. In recent years we've seen more accounting scandals than at any time since the 1920s.

Enron Corp., for example, was the seventh-largest company in the United States before the company admitted reporting fewer debts than it really owed. WorldCom, a major long-distance telephone provider, admitted accounting for expenses as though they were assets (resources). Xerox Corp. was accused of manipulating reported profits. These and other scandals rocked the business community and hurt investor confidence. Innocent people lost their jobs, and the stock market suffered. The courts are still sorting out who was responsible for the flawed information and its consequences.

Accounting.com

The New Economy: Pumping Up Revenue via Round-Trip Trades

The stock market can get obsessed with revenue, and that can put intense pressure on companies to boost their revenue figures. "Round-trip trades" are one technique for reporting high revenues. These deals typically involve a swap of assets or services without any real gains. Two companies get together and set a price for advertising on each other's Web sites at, say, $1 million. They then swap banners and each declares $1 million as revenue and $1 million for expenses—but not a single penny changes hands. Here are some examples:

- In 1999, the women's Web site **iVillage** revealed that 20% of its revenue came from round-trip trades of online advertising.
- In 2001, **CMS Energy** and **Dynegy** completed two electricity trades worth $1.7 billion on Dynegy's online trading platform. The trades cancelled each other out, but the companies cited the artificially boosted revenues in their press releases.
- With revenues lagging, telecom companies **Global Crossing** and **Qwest** began booking revenue from capacity swaps in 1999.

The SEC began investigating round-trip trades when it learned that many of the transactions served only to inflate revenue, and in 2002 it barred telecom trades that inflate revenue. Earlier, in 1999, the FASB forced companies to disclose online advertising swaps as "barter revenue." Yet, scrutiny from shareholders and accounting regulatory agencies hasn't stopped everyone.

Homestore, Inc., an online real estate company, and **America Online** are now under investigation for complex multiparty deals in which Homestore allegedly bought products from a third company, which then bought ads on America Online. The days of round-trip trades may be over.

Based on: Dennis K. Berman, Julia Angwin, and Chip Cummins, "What's Wrong?—Tricks of the Trade: As Market Bubble Neared End, Bogus Swaps Provided a Lift," *The Wall Street Journal*, December 23, 2002, p. A1. David Wessel, "What's Wrong?—Venal Sins: Why the Bad Guys of the Boardroom Emerged en Masse," *The Wall Street Journal*, June 20, 2002, p. A1. Susan Pulliam and Rebecca Blumenstein, "SEC Broadens Investigation into Revenue-Boosting Tricks," *The Wall Street Journal*, May 16, 2002, p. A1.

Standards of Professional Conduct

The AICPA's Code of Professional Conduct for Accountants provides guidance to CPAs in their work. Ethical standards are designed to produce relevant and reliable information for decision making. The preamble to the Code states: "[A] certified public accountant assumes an obligation of self-discipline above and beyond the requirements of laws and regulations . . . [and] an unswerving commitment to honorable behavior. . . ."

The opening paragraph of the Standards of Ethical Conduct of the Institute of Management Accountants (IMA) states: "Management accountants have an obligation to the organizations they serve, their profession, the public, and themselves to maintain the highest standards of ethical conduct." The requirements are similar to those in the AICPA code.

Most corporations also set standards of ethical conduct for employees. For example, **The Boeing Company**, a leading manufacturer of aircraft, has a highly developed set of business conduct guidelines. The chairperson of the board states: "We owe our success as much to our reputation for integrity as we do to the quality and dependability of our products and services. This reputation is fragile and can easily be lost." As one chief executive has stated, "Ethical practice is simply good business."

Truth is always better than dishonesty—in accounting, in business, and in life.

☐ The Language of Business
☐ Regulating Accounting
■ Business Organizations
☐ Concepts and Principles
☐ The Accounting Equation
☐ Business Transactions
☐ Evaluating Transactions

Student ResourceCD
corporation, partnership, proprietorship

Types of Business Organizations

A business can have one of three forms of organization: proprietorship, partnership, or corporation. You should understand the differences among the three.

Proprietorship
A business with a single owner.

PROPRIETORSHIPS A **proprietorship** has a single owner, called the proprietor, who is often the manager. Proprietorships tend to be small retail stores or professional businesses, such as physicians, attorneys, and accountants. From the accounting viewpoint, each proprietorship is distinct from its proprietor: The accounting records of the proprietorship do *not* include the proprietor's personal financial records. However, from a legal perspective, the business *is* the proprietor. In this book, we begin the accounting process with a proprietorship.

Partnership
A business with two or more owners.

PARTNERSHIPS A **partnership** joins two or more individuals as co-owners. Each owner is a partner. Many retail establishments and professional organizations of physicians, attorneys, and accountants are partnerships. Most partnerships are small or medium-sized, but some are gigantic, exceeding 2,000 partners. Accounting treats the partnership as a separate organization, distinct from the personal affairs of each partner. But again, from a legal perspective, a partnership *is* the partners.

Corporation
A business owned by stockholders; it begins when the state approves its articles of incorporation. A corporation is a legal entity, an "artificial person," in the eyes of the law.

Stockholder
A person who owns stock in a corporation. Also called a **shareholder**.

CORPORATIONS A **corporation** is a business owned by **stockholders**, or **shareholders**. These are the people who own shares of ownership in the business. A business becomes a corporation when the state approves its articles of incorporation. A corporation is a legal entity that conducts business in its own name. Unlike the proprietorship and the partnership, the corporation is not defined by its owners.

Corporations differ significantly from proprietorships and partnerships in another way. If a proprietorship or a partnership cannot pay its debts, lenders can take the owners' personal assets—their cash—to satisfy the business's obligations. But if a corporation goes bankrupt, lenders cannot take the personal assets of the stockholders. This *limited liability* of stockholders for corporate debts explains why corporations are so popular: People can invest in corporations with limited personal risk.

Another factor in corporate growth is the division of ownership into individual shares. The Coca-Cola Company, for example, has billions of shares of stock owned by many stockholders. An investor with no personal relationship to Coca-Cola can become a stockholder by buying 50, 100, 5,000, or any number of shares of its stock.

Exhibit 1-4 summarizes the differences among the three types of business organization.

Exhibit 1-4 **Comparison of the Three Forms of Business Organization**

	Proprietorship	Partnership	Corporation
1. Owner(s)	Proprietor—there is only one owner	Partners—there are two or more owners	Stockholders—there are generally many owners
2. Life of the organization	Limited by the owner's choice, or death	Limited by the owners' choices, or death	Indefinite
3. Personal liability of the owner(s) for the business's debts	Proprietor is personally liable	Partners are personally liable	Stockholders are not personally liable
4. Legal status of the organization	The proprietorship is the proprietor	The partnership is the partners	The corporation is separate from the stockholders

Accounting Concepts and Principles

- □ The Language of Business
- □ Regulating Accounting
- □ Business Organizations
- ■ Concepts and Principles
- □ The Accounting Equation
- □ Business Transactions
- □ Evaluating Transactions

The rules that govern accounting fall under the heading **GAAP**, which stands for **generally accepted accounting principles**. GAAP is the "law" of accounting—rules for providing the information that is acceptable to the majority of Americans.

GAAP rests on a conceptual framework written by the FASB: *The primary objective of financial reporting is to provide information useful for making investment and lending decisions*. To be useful, information must be relevant, reliable, and comparable. We begin the discussion of GAAP by introducing basic accounting concepts and principles.

Student ResourceCD
accounting principles

2 *Apply accounting concepts and principles*

Generally Accepted Accounting Principles (GAAP)
Accounting guidelines, formulated by the Financial Accounting Standards Board, that govern how accountants measure, process, and communicate financial information.

Entity
An organization or a section of an organization that, for accounting purposes, stands apart from other organizations and individuals as a separate economic unit.

The Entity Concept

The most basic concept in accounting is that of the **entity**. An accounting entity is an organization or a section of an organization that stands apart as a separate economic unit. In accounting, boundaries are drawn around each entity so as not to confuse its affairs with those of other entities.

Consider Amazon.com. Assume Jeff Bezos started Amazon.com on his own. Suppose he began with $5,000 obtained from a bank loan. Following the entity concept, Bezos would account for the $5,000 separately from his personal assets, such as his clothing, house, and automobile. To mix the $5,000 of business cash with his personal assets would make it difficult to measure the financial position of Amazon.com.

Consider Toyota, a huge organization with several divisions. Toyota management evaluates each division as a separate accounting entity. If sales in the Lexus division are dropping, Toyota can find out why. But if sales figures from all divisions of the company are combined, management will not know that Lexus sales are going down. Thus, the entity concept applies *to any economic unit that needs to be evaluated separately*.

The Reliability (Objectivity) Principle

Accounting information is based on the most reliable data available. This guideline is the *reliability principle*, also called the *objectivity principle*. Reliable data are verifiable. They may be confirmed by any independent observer. For example, an Amazon.com bank loan is supported by a promissory note. This is objective evidence of the loan. Without the reliability principle, accounting data might be based on whims and opinions.

Suppose you want to open an electronics store. For a store location, you transfer a small building to the business. You believe the building is worth $150,000. To confirm its cost to the business, you hire two real estate appraisers, who value the building at $140,000. Which is the more reliable estimate of the building's value, your estimate of $150,000 or the $140,000 professional appraisal? The appraisal of $140,000 is more reliable because it is supported by an independent observation. The business should record the building cost as $140,000.

The Cost Principle

The *cost principle* states that acquired assets and services should be recorded at their actual cost (also called *historical cost*). Even though the purchaser may believe the price is a bargain, the item is recorded at the price actually paid and not at the "expected" cost. Suppose your electronics store purchases TV equipment from a supplier who is going out of business. Assume that you get a good deal and pay only $2,000 for equipment that would have cost you $3,000 elsewhere. The cost principle requires you to record the equipment at its actual cost of $2,000, not the $3,000 that you believe the equipment is worth.

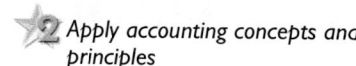

The cost principle also holds that the accounting records should maintain the historical cost of an asset over its useful life. Why? Because cost is a reliable measure. Suppose your store holds the TV equipment for six months. During that time TV prices rise, and the equipment can be sold for $3,500. Should its accounting value—the figure "on the books"—be the actual cost of $2,000 or the current market value of $3,500? By the cost principle, the accounting value of the equipment remains at actual cost: $2,000.

Stop & Think

You are considering the purchase of land for future expansion. The seller is asking $50,000 for land that cost her $35,000. An appraisal shows a value of $47,000. You first offer $44,000. The seller counteroffers with $48,000, and you agree on a price of $46,000. What dollar value for this land is reported on your financial statement? Which accounting concept or principle guides your answers?

Answer: According to the cost principle, assets and services should be recorded at their actual cost. You paid $46,000 for the land, so report the land at $46,000.

The Going-Concern Concept

Another reason for measuring assets at historical cost is the *going-concern concept*. This concept assumes that the entity will remain in operation for the foreseeable future. Under the going-concern concept, accountants assume that the business will remain in operation long enough to use existing resources for their intended purpose.

To understand the going-concern concept better, consider the alternative—which is to go out of business. A store holding a going-out-of-business sale is trying to sell everything. In that case, instead of historical cost, the relevant measure is current market value. But going out of business is the exception rather than the rule.

The Stable-Monetary-Unit Concept

In the United States, we record transactions in dollars because the dollar is the medium of exchange. British accountants record transactions in pounds sterling. French and German transactions are measured in euros. The Japanese record transactions in yen. The value of a dollar or a Mexican peso changes over time. A rise in the price level is called *inflation*. During inflation, a dollar will purchase less milk, less gas for your car, and less of other goods. When prices are stable—when there is little inflation—the purchasing power of money is also stable.

Accountants assume that the dollar's purchasing power is stable. It allows us to add and subtract dollar amounts as though each dollar has the same purchasing power as any other dollar at any other time.

- ☐ The Language of Business
- ☐ Regulating Accounting
- ☐ Business Organizations
- ☐ Concepts and Principles
- ■ The Accounting Equation
- ☐ Business Transactions
- ☐ Evaluating Transactions

The Accounting Equation

Student ResourceCD
accounting equation, asset, liability, owner's equity

3 *Use the accounting equation*

Accounting Equation
The basic tool of accounting, measuring the resources of the business and the claims to those resources: Assets = Liabilities + Owner's Equity.

Asset
An economic resource that is expected to be of benefit in the future.

The basic tool of accounting is the **accounting equation**. It measures the resources of a business and the claims to those resources.

Assets and Liabilities

Assets are economic resources that are expected to be of benefit in the future. Cash, merchandise inventory, furniture, and land are assets.

Claims to those assets come from two sources. **Liabilities** are *outsider* claims—debts that are payable to outsiders. These outside parties are called *creditors*. For example, a creditor who has loaned money to Amazon.com has a claim to some of Amazon's assets until Amazon pays the debt.

Insider claims to Amazon.com's assets are called **owner's equity**, or **capital**. These insider claims are held by the owners of the business. Owners have a claim to some of the assets because they have invested in the business.

The accounting equation shows how assets, liabilities, and owner's equity are related. Assets appear on the left side of the equation, and the liabilities and owner's equity appear on the right side. Exhibit 1-5 shows that the two sides must always be equal:

(Economic Resources)		(Claims to Economic Resources)
ASSETS	=	LIABILITIES + OWNER'S EQUITY

Exhibit 1-5

The Accounting Equation

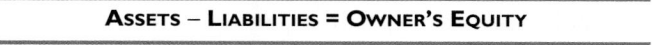

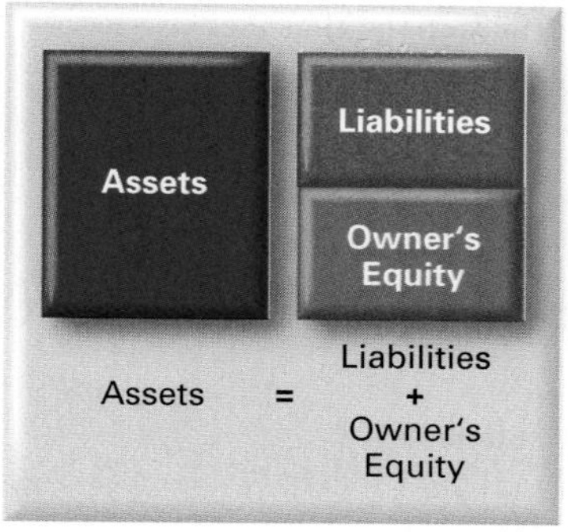

Stop & Think

1. If the assets of a business are $170,000 and the liabilities total $80,000, how much is the owner's equity?
2. If the owner's equity in a business is $22,000 and the liabilities are $36,000, how much are the assets?

Answers: To answer both questions, use the accounting equation:

1.

ASSETS	–	LIABILITIES	=	OWNER'S EQUITY
$170,000	–	$80,000	=	$90,000

2.

ASSETS	=	LIABILITIES	+	OWNER'S EQUITY
$58,000	=	$36,000	+	$22,000

Liability
An economic obligation (a debt) payable to an individual or an organization outside the business.

Owner's Equity
The claim of a business owner to the assets of the business. Also called **capital**.

Here is an example that illustrates the elements of the accounting equation. Sony supplies cell phones to Amazon.com. Amazon may buy the cell phones on credit and promise to pay Sony later. Sony's claim against Amazon.com is an **account receivable**, an asset that will benefit Sony. A *written* promise for future collection is called a **note receivable**.

Amazon.com has a debt to pay Sony. This liability is an **account payable**. It is backed only by the reputation and the credit standing of Amazon. A written promise of future payment is called a **note payable**.

All receivables are assets. All payables are liabilities. Most businesses have both receivables and payables.

Owner's Equity

Owner's equity is the amount of an entity's assets that remain after its liabilities are subtracted.

$$\text{ASSETS} - \text{LIABILITIES} = \text{OWNER'S EQUITY}$$

The purpose of business is to increase owner's equity through revenues. **Revenues** are increases in owner's equity earned by delivering goods or services to customers. Revenues also increase assets, or they decrease liabilities. As a result, the owner's share of the business's assets increases. Exhibit 1-6 shows that owner investments and revenues increase the owner's equity of the business.

Account Receivable
A promise to receive cash from customers to whom the business has sold goods or for whom the business has performed services.

Note Receivable
A written promise for future collection of cash.

Account Payable
A liability backed by the general reputation and credit standing of the debtor.

Note Payable
A written promise of future payment.

Revenue
Amounts earned by delivering goods or services to customers. Revenues increase owner's equity.

Exhibit 1-6

Transactions That Increase or Decrease Owner's Equity

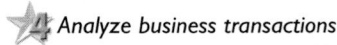

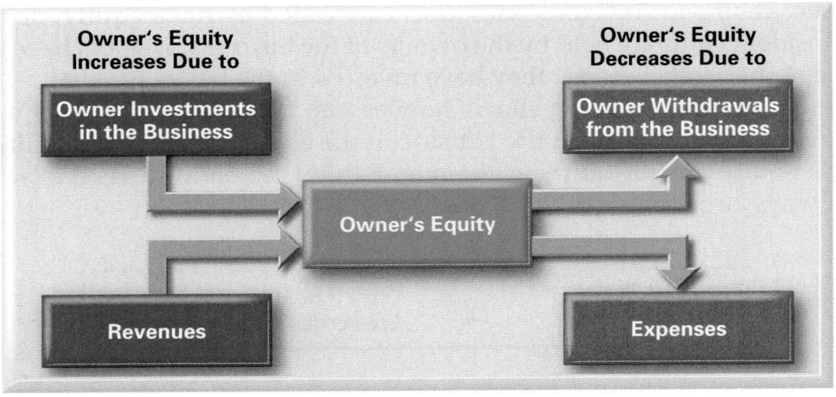

✔ Starter 1-1

✔ Starter 1-2

Exhibit 1-6 also shows that owner withdrawals and expenses decrease owner's equity. **Owner withdrawals** are amounts removed from the business by the owner. Withdrawals are the opposite of owner investments. **Expenses** are decreases in owner's equity that occur from using assets or increasing liabilities to deliver goods and services to customers. Expenses are the cost of doing business; they are the opposite of revenues. Expenses include the cost of:

Owner Withdrawals
Amounts removed from the business by an owner.

Expense
Decrease in owner's equity that occurs from using assets or increasing liabilities in the course of delivering goods or services to customers.

- Office rent
- Salaries of employees
- Advertisements
- Utility payments
- Interest on loans
- Insurance
- Property taxes
- Supplies used up

✔ Starter 1-3

✔ Starter 1-4

□ The Language of Business
□ Regulating Accounting
□ Business Organizations
□ Concepts and Principles
□ The Accounting Equation
■ Business Transactions
□ Evaluating Transactions

Accounting for Business Transactions

Accounting records are based on actual transactions. A **transaction** is any event that affects the financial position of the business *and* can be recorded reliably. Many events affect a company, including elections and economic booms. Accountants do not record the effects of those events because they can't be measured reliably. An accountant records only those events with effects that can be measured reliably, such as the purchase of a building, a sale of merchandise to a customer, and the payment of rent. The dollar amounts of these events can be measured reliably, so accountants record these transactions.

Student ResourceCD
transaction analysis

Transaction
An event that affects the financial position of a particular entity and can be recorded reliably.

What are some of your personal transactions? You may have bought a DVD player. Your purchase was a transaction. If you are making payments on an auto loan, your payments are also transactions. You need to record all your business transactions just as Amazon.com does in order to manage your personal affairs.

To illustrate accounting for a business, let's use Gay Gillen eTravel. Gillen operates a travel agency. Online customers plan and pay for their trips through the Gillen Web site. The Web site is linked to airlines, hotels, and cruise lines, so clients can obtain the latest information 24 hours a day, 7 days a week. Gillen's Web site allows the agency to transact more business than it could through the phone, fax, or e-mail. As a result, Gillen can operate with few employees, and this saves on expenses. She can pass along the cost savings to clients by charging them lower commissions. That builds up her business.

Now let's analyze some of Gillen eTravel's transactions.

4 *Analyze business transactions*

Transaction 1: Starting the Business Gay Gillen invests $30,000 of her own money to start the business. She deposits $30,000 in a bank account titled Gay Gillen eTravel. The effect of this transaction on the accounting equation of the Gay Gillen eTravel business entity is

Assets		Liabilities	+	Owner's Equity	Type of Owner's Equity Transaction
Cash	=			Gay Gillen, Capital	
(1) +30,000				+30,000	*Owner investment*

For every transaction, the amount on the left side of the equation must equal the amount on the right side. The first transaction increases both the assets (in this case, Cash) and the owner's equity (Gay Gillen, Capital) of the business. To the right of the transaction, we write "Owner investment" to keep track of the source of the owner's equity.

Immediately after this first transaction, Gay Gillen eTravel can prepare a balance sheet. A **balance sheet** reports the assets, liabilities, and owner's equity of the business. Gillen's initial balance sheet would appear as follows on April 1, 20X5:

Balance Sheet
An entity's assets, liabilities, and owner's equity as of a specific date. Also called the **statement of financial position**.

Gay Gillen eTravel
Balance Sheet
April 1, 20X5

Assets		=	Liabilities	
Cash	$30,000		None	$0
			+	
			Owner's Equity	
			Gay Gillen, capital	30,000
Total assets	$30,000		Total liabilities and owner's equity	$30,000

A balance sheet reports the financial position of the entity at a moment in time—in this case at the stroke of midnight on April 1. Gay Gillen eTravel has $30,000 of cash, owes no liabilities, and has owner's equity of $30,000.

TRANSACTION 2: PURCHASE OF LAND Gillen purchases land for an office location, paying cash of $20,000. The effect of this transaction on the accounting equation is

	Assets				Liabilities	+	Owner's Equity	Type of Owner's Equity Transaction
	Cash	+	Land				Gay Gillen, Capital	
(1)	30,000			=			30,000	*Owner investment*
(2)	−20,000	+	20,000					
Bal.	10,000		20,000				30,000	
	30,000						30,000	

✔ Starter 1-5

✔ Starter 1-6

✔ Starter 1-7

The cash purchase of land increases one asset, Land, and decreases another asset, Cash, by the same amount. After the transaction is completed, Gillen's business has cash of $10,000, land of $20,000, no liabilities, and owner's equity of $30,000. Note that the sums of the balances (abbreviated Bal.) on both sides of the equation must always be equal.

With software, such as QuickBooks and Peachtree, a business can print a balance sheet at any time to see where it stands financially. Gillen can use QuickBooks to prepare a balance sheet—this time after two transactions. The business's balance sheet on April 2 follows:

Gay Gillen eTravel
Balance Sheet
April 2, 20X5

Assets		Liabilities	
Cash..................	$10,000	None..................	$0
Land..................	20,000		
		Owner's Equity	
		Gay Gillen, capital	30,000
		Total liabilities and	
Total assets	$30,000	owner's equity	$30,000

Now the business holds two assets, with the liabilities and owner's equity unchanged. After we move through a sequence of transactions, we will return to Gillen's balance sheet. It's most common to prepare a balance sheet at the end of the accounting period. Now let's account for additional transactions of Gay Gillen eTravel.

Transaction 3: Purchase of Office Supplies Gillen buys stationery and other office supplies, agreeing to pay $500 within 30 days. This transaction increases both the assets and the liabilities of the business. Its effect on the accounting equation is

	Assets					=	Liabilities	+	Owner's Equity
	Cash	+	Office Supplies	+	Land		Accounts Payable	+	Gay Gillen, Capital
Bal.	10,000				20,000	=			30,000
(3)			+500				+500		
Bal.	10,000		500		20,000		500		30,000
			30,500					30,500	

Office Supplies is an asset, not an expense, because the supplies can be used in the future. The liability created by this transaction is an account payable. Recall that a *payable* is a liability.

Stop & Think

Prepare the balance sheet of Gay Gillen eTravel on April 9, after transaction 3.

Answer:

Gay Gillen eTravel
Balance Sheet
April 9, 20X5

Assets		Liabilities	
Cash	$10,000	Accounts payable	$500
Office supplies	500	**Owner's Equity**	
Land	20,000	Gay Gillen, capital	30,000
		Total liabilities and	
Total assets	$30,500	owner's equity	$30,500

Transaction 4: Earning of Service Revenue Gay Gillen eTravel earns service revenue by providing travel services for clients. She earns $5,500 revenue and collects this amount in cash. The effect on the accounting equation is an increase in the asset Cash and an increase in Gay Gillen, Capital, as follows:

	Assets					=	Liabilities	+	Owner's Equity	Type of Owner's Equity Transaction
	Cash	+	Office Supplies	+	Land	=	Accounts Payable	+	Gay Gillen, Capital	
Bal.	10,000		500		20,000		500		30,000	
(4)	+5,500								+5,500	*Service revenue*
Bal.	15,500		500		20,000		500		35,500	
			36,000					36,000		

A revenue transaction grows the business, as shown by the increases in assets and owner's equity. A company like Amazon.com or Wal-Mart that sells goods to customers is a merchandising business. Its revenue is called *sales revenue*. By contrast, Gay Gillen eTravel performs services for clients; Gillen's revenue is called *service revenue*.

✔ Starter 1-8

Transaction 5: Earning of Service Revenue on Account Gillen performs services for clients who do not pay immediately. In return for her travel services, Gillen receives clients' promises to pay $3,000 within one month. This promise is an asset to Gillen, an account receivable because she expects to collect the cash in the future. In accounting, we say that Gillen performed this service *on account*. When the business performs service for a client, the business earns the revenue.

The act of performing the service, not collecting the cash, earns the revenue. This $3,000 of service revenue increases the wealth of Gillen's business just like the $5,500 of revenue that she collected immediately in transaction 4. Gillen records $3,000 of revenue on account as follows:

	Assets							=	Liabilities	+	Owner's Equity	Type of Owner's Equity Transaction
	Cash	+	Accounts Receivable	+	Office Supplies	+	Land	=	Accounts Payable	+	Gay Gillen, Capital	
Bal.	15,500				500		20,000		500		35,500	
(5)			+3,000								+3,000	*Service revenue*
Bal.	15,500		3,000		500		20,000		500		38,500	
				39,000						39,000		

Transaction 6: Payment of Expenses During the month, Gillen pays $3,300 in cash expenses: lease expense on a computer, $600; office rent, $1,100; employee salary, $1,200 (part-time assistant); and utilities, $400. The effects on the accounting equation are

	Assets							=	Liabilities	+	Owner's Equity	Type of Owner's Equity Transaction
	Cash	+	Accounts Receivable	+	Office Supplies	+	Land	=	Accounts Payable	+	Gay Gillen, Capital	
Bal.	15,500		3,000		500		20,000		500		38,500	
(6)	− 600										− 600	*Lease expense, computer*
(6)	− 1,100										− 1,100	*Rent expense, office*
(6)	− 1,200										− 1,200	*Salary expense*
(6)	− 400										− 400	*Utilities expense*
Bal.	12,200		3,000		500		20,000		500		35,200	
				35,700						35,700		

Expenses have the opposite effect of revenues. Expenses cause the business to shrink, as shown by the decreased balances of assets and owner's equity.

Each expense is recorded separately. The expenses are listed together here for simplicity. We could record the cash payment in a single amount for the sum of the four expenses: $3,300 ($600 + $1,100 + $1,200 + $400). In all cases, the "balance" of the equation holds, as we know it must.

After any transaction, the business can prepare a balance sheet, as we illustrated earlier. Click on "Print Balance Sheet" and the software will produce the document.

After Gillen's revenue and expense transactions, Gay Gillen will want to know how well the travel agency is performing. Is the business profitable, or is it losing money? To answer this important question, Gillen can use QuickBooks to print an income statement. An income statement reports revenues and expenses to measure profits (called **net income**, **net earnings**, or **net profit**) and losses (called **net loss**). Gillen's income statement for the month ended April 30 would appear as follows:

Net Income
Excess of total revenues over total expenses. Also called **net earnings** or **net profit**.

Net Loss
Excess of total expenses over total revenues.

Gay Gillen eTravel
Income Statement
Month Ended April 30, 20X5

Revenue:		
Service revenue ($5,500 + $3,000)		$8,500
Expenses:		
Salary expense	$1,200	
Rent expense, office	1,100	
Lease expense, computer	600	
Utilities expense	400	
Total expenses		3,300
Net income		$5,200

The business had more revenues than expenses, so it was profitable during April. It earned net income of $5,200—not bad for a start-up company. We will revisit the income statement later.

TRANSACTION 7: PAYMENT ON ACCOUNT Gillen pays $300 to the store where she purchased $500 worth of office supplies in transaction 3. In accounting, we say that she pays $300 *on account*. The effect on the accounting equation is a decrease in the asset Cash and a decrease in the liability Accounts Payable, as shown next.

	ASSETS								=	LIABILITIES	+	OWNER'S EQUITY
	Cash	+	Accounts Receivable	+	Office Supplies	+	Land			Accounts Payable	+	Gay Gillen, Capital
Bal.	12,200		3,000		500		20,000		=	500		35,200
(7)	– 300									–300		
Bal.	11,900		3,000		500		20,000			200		35,200
			35,400								35,400	

The payment of cash on account has no effect on Office Supplies because the payment does not affect the supplies available to the business. Likewise, the payment on account does not affect expenses. Gillen was paying off a liability, not an expense.

TRANSACTION 8: PERSONAL TRANSACTION Gillen remodels her home at a cost of $40,000, paying cash from personal funds. This event is *not* a transaction of Gay Gillen eTravel. It has no effect on the travel agency and therefore is not recorded by the business. It is a transaction of the Gay Gillen *personal* entity, not Gay Gillen eTravel. This transaction illustrates the *entity concept*.

TRANSACTION 9: COLLECTION ON ACCOUNT In transaction 5, Gillen performed services for a client on account. The business now collects $1,000 from the client. We say that Gillen collects the cash *on account*. Gillen will record an increase in the asset Cash. Should she also record an increase in service revenue? No, because she already recorded the revenue when she earned it in transaction 5. The phrase "collect cash on account" means to record an increase in Cash and a decrease in Accounts Receivable. The effect on the accounting equation of Gay Gillen eTravel is

	ASSETS					LIABILITIES +	OWNER'S EQUITY
	Cash +	Accounts Receivable +	Office Supplies +	Land		Accounts Payable +	Gay Gillen, Capital
Bal.	11,900	3,000	500	20,000	=	200	35,200
(9)	+ 1,000	−1,000					
Bal.	12,900	2,000	500	20,000		200	35,200
	35,400					35,400	

Total assets are unchanged from the preceding total. Why? Because Gillen merely exchanged one asset for another. Also, total liabilities and owner's equity are unchanged.

✔ Starter 1-9

TRANSACTION 10: SALE OF LAND Gillen sells some land owned by the travel agency. The sale price of $9,000 is equal to Gillen's cost of the land. Gillen's business receives $9,000 cash. The effect on the accounting equation of the travel agency follows:

	ASSETS					LIABILITIES +	OWNER'S EQUITY
	Cash +	Accounts Receivable +	Office Supplies +	Land		Accounts Payable +	Gay Gillen, Capital
Bal.	12,900	2,000	500	20,000	=	200	35,200
(10)	+ 9,000			− 9,000			
Bal.	21,900	2,000	500	11,000		200	35,200
	35,400					35,400	

TRANSACTION 11: WITHDRAWAL OF CASH Gillen withdraws $2,000 cash from the business for personal use. The effect on the accounting equation is

	ASSETS					LIABILITIES +	OWNER'S EQUITY	TYPE OF OWNER'S EQUITY TRANSACTION
	Cash +	Accounts Receivable +	Office Supplies +	Land		Accounts Payable +	Gay Gillen, Capital	
Bal.	21,900	2,000	500	11,000	=	200	35,200	
(11)	− 2,000						− 2,000	*Owner withdrawal*
Bal.	19,900	2,000	500	11,000		200	33,200	
	33,400					33,400		

Gillen's withdrawal of $2,000 cash decreases the asset Cash and also the owner's equity of the business. *The withdrawal does not represent an expense because the cash is used for the owner's personal affairs.* We record this decrease in owner's equity as Withdrawals or as Drawings. The double underlines below each column indicate a final total.

✔ Starter 1-10

- ☐ The Language of Business
- ☐ Regulating Accounting
- ☐ Business Organizations
- ☐ Concepts and Principles
- ☐ The Accounting Equation
- ☐ Business Transactions
- ■ Evaluating Transactions

Evaluating Business Transactions

Exhibit 1-7 summarizes Gay Gillen eTravel's transactions. Panel A lists the details of the transactions, and Panel B shows the analysis. As you study the exhibit, note that every transaction maintains the equality

ASSETS = LIABILITIES + OWNER'S EQUITY

5 Prepare the financial statements

Student ResourceCD
balance sheet, financial statements, income statement, statement of cash flows, statement of owner's equity

The Financial Statements

After analyzing transactions, we need a way to present the results. We look now at the *financial statements*, which report the entity's financial information to interested parties such as Gay Gillen. If Gillen ever needs a loan, her banker will also want to see her financial statements. Earlier we prepared Gillen's income statement and balance sheet after a few transactions. Now we are ready to examine all the business's financial statements at the end of the period.

The financial statements are the

- Income statement
- Balance sheet
- Statement of owner's equity
- Statement of cash flows

Income Statement
Summary of an entity's revenues, expenses, and net income or net loss for a specific period. Also called the **statement of earnings** or the **statement of operations**.

INCOME STATEMENT The **income statement** presents a summary of an entity's revenues and expenses for specific period of time, such as a month or a year. The income statement, also called the **statement of earnings** or **statement of operations**, is like a video—it presents a moving picture of operations during the period. The income statement holds one of the most important pieces of information about a business—whether it earned:

- ***Net income*** (total revenues greater than total expenses) or
- ***Net loss*** (total expenses greater than total revenues)

Net income is good news about operations. A net loss is bad news. What was the result of Gay Gillen eTravel's operations during April? Good news—the business earned net income (see the top part of Exhibit 1-8, page 21).

Statement of Owner's Equity
Summary of the changes in an entity's owner's equity during a specific period.

STATEMENT OF OWNER'S EQUITY The **statement of owner's equity** shows the changes in *owner's equity* during a specific time period, such as a month or a year, as follows:

Increases in owner's equity come from:

- Owner investments
- Net income

Decreases in owner's equity result from:

- Owner withdrawals
- Net loss

BALANCE SHEET The *balance sheet* lists all the entity's assets, liabilities, and owner's equity as of a specific date, usually the end of a month or a year. The balance sheet is like a snapshot of the entity. For this reason, it is also called the *statement of financial position* (see the middle of Exhibit 1-8, page 21).

Statement of Cash Flows
Reports cash receipts and cash payments during a period.

STATEMENT OF CASH FLOWS The **statement of cash flows** reports the cash coming in (cash receipts) and the amount of cash going out (*cash payments*) during a period. Business activities result in a net cash inflow (receipts greater than payments) or a net cash outflow (payments greater than receipts). The statement of cash flows shows the net increase or decrease in cash during the period and the ending cash balance. (We focus on the statement of cash flows in Chapter 17.)

Exhibit 1-7 Analysis of Transactions, Gay Gillen eTravel

PANEL A—Details of Transactions

(1) Gillen invested $30,000 cash in the business.
(2) Paid $20,000 cash for land.
(3) Bought $500 of office supplies on account.
(4) Received $5,500 cash from clients for service revenue earned.
(5) Performed travel service for clients on account, $3,000.
(6) Paid cash expenses: computer lease, $600; office rent, $1,100; employee salary, $1,200; utilities, $400.
(7) Paid $300 on the account payable created in transaction 3.
(8) Remodeled Gillen's personal residence. This is *not* a transaction of the business.
(9) Collected $1,000 on the account receivable created in transaction 5.
(10) Sold land for cash at its cost of $9,000.
(11) Withdrew $2,000 cash for personal expenses.

PANEL B—Analysis of Transactions

	ASSETS				=	LIABILITIES +	OWNER'S EQUITY	TYPE OF OWNER'S EQUITY TRANSACTION
	Cash +	Accounts Receivable +	Office Supplies +	Land		Accounts Payable +	Gay Gillen, Capital	
(1)	+30,000						+30,000	*Owner investment*
Bal.	30,000						30,000	
(2)	−20,000			+20,000				
Bal.	10,000			20,000			30,000	
(3)			+500			+500		
Bal.	10,000		500	20,000		500	30,000	
(4)	+ 5,500						+ 5,500	*Service revenue*
Bal.	15,500		500	20,000		500	35,500	
(5)		+3,000					+ 3,000	*Service revenue*
Bal.	15,500	3,000	500	20,000		500	38,500	
(6)	− 600						− 600	*Lease expense, computer*
(6)	− 1,100						− 1,100	*Rent expense, office*
(6)	− 1,200						− 1,200	*Salary expense*
(6)	− 400						− 400	*Utilities expense*
Bal.	12,200	3,000	500	20,000		500	35,200	
(7)	− 300					−300		
Bal.	11,900	3,000	500	20,000		200	35,200	
(8)	Not a transaction of the business							
(9)	+ 1,000	−1,000						
Bal.	12,900	2,000	500	20,000		200	35,200	
(10)	+ 9,000			− 9,000				
Bal.	21,900	2,000	500	11,000		200	35,200	
(11)	− 2,000						− 2,000	*Owner withdrawal*
Bal.	19,900	2,000	500	11,000		200	33,200	
	33,400					33,400		

✔ Starter 1-11

Financial Statement Headings

Each financial statement has a heading giving three pieces of data:

- Name of the business (such as Gay Gillen eTravel)
- Name of the financial statement (income statement, balance sheet, and so on)
- Date or time period covered by the statement (April 30, 20X5, for the balance sheet; month ended April 30, 20X5, for the income statement)

An income statement (or a statement of owner's equity) that covers a year ended in December 20X5 is dated "Year Ended December 31, 20X5." A monthly income statement (or statement of owner's equity) for September 20X4 shows "Month Ended September 30, 20X4," or "For the Month of September 20X4." Income must be identified with a particular time period.

6 *Evaluate business performance*

Relationships Among the Financial Statements

Exhibit 1-8 illustrates all four financial statements. Their data come from the transaction analysis in Exhibit 1-7 which covers the month of April 20X5. Study the exhibit carefully. Specifically, observe the following in Exhibit 1-8:

1. The *income statement* for the month ended April 30, 20X5:
   a. Reports April's revenues and expenses. Expenses are listed in decreasing order of their amount, with the largest expense first.
   b. Reports *net income* of the period if total revenues exceed total expenses. If total expenses exceed total revenues, a *net loss* is reported instead.
2. The *statement of owner's equity* for the month ended April 30, 20X5:
   a. Opens with the owner's capital balance at the beginning of the period.
   b. Adds *investments by the owner* and also adds net income (or subtracts net loss, as the case may be). Net income or net loss come directly from the income statement (see arrow ① in Exhibit 1-8).
   c. Subtracts withdrawals by the owner. Parentheses indicate a subtraction.
   d. Ends with the owner's capital balance at the end of the period.
3. The *balance sheet* at April 30, 20X5:
   a. Reports all assets, all liabilities, and owner's equity at the end of the period.
   b. Reports that total assets equal total liabilities plus total owner's equity.
   c. Reports the owner's ending capital balance, taken directly from the statement of owner's equity (see arrow ②).
4. The *statement of cash flows* for the month ended April 30, 20X5:
   a. Reports cash flows from three types of business activities (*operating, investing,* and *financing activities*) during the month. Each category of cash-flow activities includes both cash receipts (positive amounts), and cash payments (negative amounts denoted by parentheses).
   b. Reports a net increase in cash during the month and ends with the cash balance at April 30, 20X5. This is the amount of cash to report on the balance sheet (see arrow ③).

Have you ever thought of having your own business? The Decision Guidelines feature shows how to make some of the decisions that you will face if you start a business. Decision Guidelines appear in each chapter.

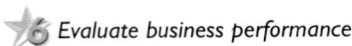

Exhibit 1-8

Financial Statements of Gay Gillen eTravel

Gay Gillen eTravel

Income Statement
Month Ended April 30, 20X5

Revenue		
Service revenue		$8,500
Expenses:		
Salary expense	$1,200	
Rent expense, office	1,100	
Lease expense, computer	600	
Utilities expense	400	
Total expenses		3,300
Net income		$5,200

Gay Gillen eTravel

Statement of Owner's Equity
Month Ended April 30, 20X5

Gay Gillen, capital, April 1, 20X5	$ 0
Add: Investments by owner	30,000
Net income for the month	5,200
	35,200
Less: Withdrawals by owner	(2,000)
Gay Gillen, capital, April 30, 20X5	$33,200

①

Gay Gillen eTravel

Balance Sheet
April 30, 20X5

②

Assets		Liabilities	
Cash	$19,900	Accounts payable	$ 200
Accounts receivable	2,000		
Office supplies	500	**Owner's Equity**	
Land	11,000	Gay Gillen, capital	33,200
		Total liabilities and	
Total assets	$33,400	owner's equity	$33,400

✔ Starter 1-12

✔ Starter 1-13

✔ Starter 1-14

✔ Starter 1-15

Gay Gillen eTravel

Statement of Cash Flows*
Month Ended April 30, 20X5

③

Cash flows from **operating** activities:		
Receipts:		
Collections from customers ($5,500 + $1,000)		$ 6,500
Payments:		
To suppliers ($600 + $1,100 + $400 + $300)	$ (2,400)	
To employees	(1,200)	(3,600)
Net cash inflow from operating activities		2,900
Cash flows from **investing** activities:		
Acquisition of land	$(20,000)	
Sale of land	9,000	
Net cash outflow from investing activities		(11,000)
Cash flows from **financing** activities:		
Investment by owner	$30,000	
Withdrawal by owner	(2,000)	
Net cash inflow from financing activities		28,000
Net increase in cash		19,900
Cash balance, April 1, 20X5		0
Cash balance, April 30, 20X5		$19,900

*Chapter 17 shows how to prepare this statement.

Decision Guidelines

MAJOR BUSINESS DECISIONS

Suppose you open a business to take photos at parties at your college. You hire a professional photographer and line up suppliers for party favors and photo albums. Here are some factors you must consider if you expect to be profitable.

Decision	Guidelines
How to organize the business?	If a single owner—a *proprietorship*. If two or more owners, but not incorporated—a *partnership*. If the business issues stock to stockholders—a *corporation*.
What to account for?	Account for the business, a separate entity apart from its owner *(entity concept)*. Account for transactions and events that affect the business and can be measured reliably.
How much to record for assets and liabilities?	Actual historical amount (*cost principle*).
How to analyze a transaction?	The accounting equation: Assets = Liabilities + Owner's Equity
How to measure profits and losses?	Income statement: Revenues − Expenses = Net Income (or Net Loss)
Did owner's equity increase or decrease?	Statement of owner's equity: Beginning capital + Owner investments + Net income (or − Net loss) − Owner withdrawals = Ending capital
Where does the business stand financially?	Balance sheet (accounting equation): Assets = Liabilities + Owner's Equity

Excel Application Exercise

Goal: Create a simple spreadsheet that a stockholder or creditor could use to quickly analyze the financial performance of a company.

Scenario: After buying some books and DVDs from **Amazon.com**, you are thinking about investing some of your savings in the company's stock. Before doing so, however, you want to perform a quick check of the company's financial performance. Use the Amazon.com Annual Report in Appendix A to gather your data (also found online at www.amazon.com, Investor Relations).

When you have completed your worksheet, answer the following question [Hint: See Amazon's Consolidated Balance Sheets, Consolidated Statements of Operations (income statement), and Consolidated Statements of Cash Flows]:

1. Net income (loss) affects both stock prices and dividends. What changes have occurred in Amazon's net income (loss) over the past two years? If you were in management at Amazon, would you include such a chart in your annual report? Why or why not?

Step-by-step:

1. Open a new Excel spreadsheet.
2. In column 1, create a bold-faced heading as follows:
   a. Chapter 1 Excel Application Exercise
   b. Amazon Financial Performance
   c. Today's Date
3. Two rows down, enter the following labels (one in each row):
   a. Income Statement Data (bold)
   b. Net Income (Loss) (in 000's)
   c. Percentage Change
4. Two rows below your heading, starting in the second column, set up three column headings, beginning with 2000 and ending with 2002 (or the last three fiscal years, if different from these).
5. Using the Amazon annual report, enter the net income (loss) data for the past three years, and use formulas to calculate the percentage change from year to year.
6. Enter the current assets and current liabilities data for at least two years.
7. Use the Chart Wizard to create a column chart showing how net income has changed (in percent). Title the chart "Net Income (Loss) Trend" and use the "percentage change" data for the chart data range. Position the chart appropriately on your worksheet.
8. Format all cells appropriately (width, dollars, percent, decimal places).
9. Save your worksheet and print a copy for your files.

END-OF-CHAPTER *Summary Problem*

A+ TIPS
CHECK YOUR RESOURCES

Jill Smith opens an apartment-locater business near a college campus. She is the sole owner of the proprietorship, which she names Campus Apartment Locators. During the first month of operations, July 20X6, she engages in the following transactions:

a. Smith invests $35,000 of personal funds to start the business.
b. She purchases on account office supplies costing $350.
c. Smith pays cash of $30,000 to acquire a lot next to the campus. She intends to use the land as a future building site for her business office.
d. Smith locates apartments for clients and receives cash of $1,900.
e. She pays $100 on the account payable she created in transaction (b).
f. She pays $2,000 of personal funds for a vacation.
g. She pays cash expenses for office rent, $400, and utilities, $100.
h. The business sells office supplies to another business for its cost of $150.
i. Smith withdraws cash of $1,200 for personal use.

Required

1. Analyze the preceding transactions in terms of their effects on the accounting equation of Campus Apartment Locators. Use Exhibit 1-7 as a guide, but show balances only after the last transaction.
2. Prepare the income statement, statement of owner's equity, and balance sheet of the business after recording the transactions. Use Exhibit 1-8 as a guide.

Solution

Requirement 1

PANEL A—Details of transactions

(a) Smith invested $35,000 cash to start the business.
(b) Purchased $350 of office supplies on account.
(c) Paid $30,000 to acquire land as a future building site.
(d) Earned service revenue and received cash of $1,900.
(e) Paid $100 on account.
(f) Paid for a personal vacation, which is not a transaction of the business.
(g) Paid cash expenses for rent, $400, and utilities, $100.
(h) Sold office supplies for cost of $150.
(i) Withdrew $1,200 cash for personal use.

PANEL B—Analysis of transactions:

	Assets: Cash	+	Assets: Office Supplies	+	Assets: Land	=	Liabilities: Accounts Payable	+	Owner's Equity: Jill Smith, Capital	Type of Owner's Equity Transaction
(a)	+35,000								+35,000	*Owner investment*
(b)			+350				+350			
(c)	−30,000				+30,000					
(d)	+ 1,900								+ 1,900	*Service revenue*
(e)	− 100						−100			
(f)	Not a transaction of the business									
(g)	− 400								− 400	*Rent expense*
	− 100								− 100	*Utilities expense*
(h)	+ 150		−150							
(i)	− 1,200								− 1,200	*Owner withdrawal*
Bal.	5,250		200		30,000		250		35,200	
	35,450						35,450			

Requirement 2: **Financial Statements of Campus Apartment Locators**

Campus Apartment Locators
Income Statement
Month Ended July 31, 20X6

Revenue:		
Service revenue		$1,900
Expenses:		
Rent expense	$400	
Utilities expense	100	
Total expenses		500
Net income		$1,400

Campus Apartment Locators
Statement of Owner's Equity
Month Ended July 31, 20X6

Jill Smith, capital, July 1, 20X6	$ 0
Add: Investment by owner	35,000
Net income for the month	1,400
	36,400
Less: Withdrawals by owner	(1,200)
Jill Smith, capital, July 31, 20X6	$35,200

Campus Apartment Locators
Balance Sheet
July 31, 20X6

Assets		Liabilities	
Cash	$ 5,250	Accounts payable	$ 250
Office supplies	200	**Owner's Equity**	
Land	30,000	Jill Smith, capital	35,200
Total assets	$35,450	Total liabilities and owner's equity	$35,450

REVIEW Accounting and the Business Environment

Quick Check

1. Generally accepted accounting principles (GAAP) are formulated by the
   a. Securities and Exchange Commission (SEC)
   b. Financial Accounting Standards Board (FASB)
   c. Institute of Management Accountants (IMA)
   d. American Institute of Certified Public Accountants (AICPA)

2. Which type of business organization is owned by its stockholders?
   a. Proprietorship
   b. Partnership
   c. Corporation
   d. All the above are owned by stockholders

3. Which accounting concept or principle specifically states that we should record transactions at amounts that can be verified?
   a. Entity concept
   b. Reliability principle
   c. Cost principle
   d. Going-concern concept

4. **Fossil** is famous for fashion wristwatches and leather goods. At the end of a recent year, Fossil's total assets added up to $381 million, and owners' equity was $264 million. How much did Fossil owe creditors?
   a. Cannot determine from the data given
   b. $381 million
   c. $264 million
   d. $117 million

5. Assume that Fossil sold watches for $50,000 to a department store on account. How would this transaction affect Fossil's accounting equation?
   a. Increase both assets and owners' equity by $50,000
   b. Increase both assets and liabilities by $50,000
   c. Increase both liabilities and owners' equity by $50,000
   d. No effect on the accounting equation because the effects cancel out

6. Refer to Fossil's sale of watches on account in the preceding question. Which parts of the accounting equation does a sale on account affect?
   a. Accounts Receivable and Accounts Payable
   b. Accounts Payable and Cash
   c. Accounts Payable and Owner, Capital
   d. Accounts Receivable and Owner, Capital

7. Assume that Fossil paid expenses totaling $35,000. How does this transaction affect Fossil's accounting equation?
   a. Increases assets and decreases liabilities
   b. Increases both assets and owners' equity
   c. Decreases both assets and owners' equity
   d. Decreases assets and increases liabilities

8. Consider the overall effects of transactions 5 and 7 on Fossil. What is Fossil's net income or net loss?
   a. Net income of $50,000
   b. Net loss of $35,000
   c. Net income of $15,000
   d. Cannot determine from the data given

9. The balance sheet reports
   a. Financial position on a specific date
   b. Results of operation on a specific date
   c. Financial position for a specific period
   d. Results of operations for a specific period

10. The income statement reports
    a. Financial position on a specific date
    b. Results of operations on a specific date
    c. Financial position for a specific period
    d. Results of operations for a specific period

Accounting Vocabulary

Accounting has a special vocabulary and it is important that you understand the following terms. They appear in the text and in the margins, and also in the glossary at the end of the book.

account payable (p. 11)
account receivable (p. 11)
accounting (p. 4)
accounting equation (p. 10)
asset (p. 10)
audit (p. 6)
balance sheet (p. 13)
capital (p. 11)
certified management accountant (CMA) (p. 6)
certified public accountant (CPA) (p. 6)
corporation (p. 8)
entity (p. 9)
expense (p. 12)
financial accounting (p. 5)
Financial Accounting Standards Board (FASB) (p. 6)
financial statements (p. 4)
generally accepted accounting principles (GAAP) (p. 9)
income statement (p. 18)
liability (p. 11)
management accounting (p. 5)
net earnings (p. 16)
net income (p. 16)
net loss (p. 16)
net profit (p. 16)
note payable (p. 11)
note receivable (p. 11)
owner's equity (p. 11)
owner withdrawals (p. 12)
partnership (p. 8)
proprietorship (p. 8)
revenue (p. 11)
shareholder (p. 8)
statement of cash flows (p. 18)
statement of earnings (p. 18)
statement of financial position (p. 13)
statement of operations (p. 18)
statement of owner's equity (p. 18)
stockholder (p. 8)
transaction (p. 12)

ASSESS *Your Progress*

A+ online homework

See *www.prenhall.com/horngren* for selected Starters, Exercises, and Problems.

Starters

Explaining assets, liabilities, owner's equity
(Obj. 1)

S1-1 Suppose you need a bank loan in order to purchase office equipment for **Jan's Perfect Presents,** which you own. In evaluating your loan request, the banker asks about the assets and liabilities of your business. In particular, the banker wants to know the amount of your owner's equity. In your own words, explain the meanings of *assets, liabilities,* and *owner's equity*. Also give the mathematical relationship among assets, liabilities, and owner's equity.

Explaining revenues, expenses
(Obj. 1)

S1-2 Gay Gillen eTravel has been open for one year, and Gillen wants to know the amount of the business's profit (net income) or net loss for the year. First, she must identify the revenues earned and the expenses incurred during the year. What are *revenues* and *expenses*? How do revenues and expenses enter into the determination of net income or net loss?

Applying accounting concepts and principles
(Obj. 2)

S1-3 Suppose you are starting a business, Web Master, to design Web sites for small businesses in your city. In organizing the business and setting up its accounting records, consider the following:

1. In keeping the books of the business, you must decide the amount to record for assets purchased and liabilities incurred. At what amount should you record assets and liabilities? Which accounting concept or principle provides guidance?
2. Should you account for your personal assets and personal liabilities along with the assets and the liabilities of the business, or should you keep the two sets of records separate? Why? Which accounting concept or principle provides guidance?

Applying accounting concepts and principles
(Obj. 2)

S1-4 Mac Mendelsohn owns and operates Mac's Floral Designs. He proposes to account for the shop's assets at current market value in order to have realistic amounts on the books if he must liquidate the business. Which accounting concept or principle does Mendelsohn's view violate? How should Mendelsohn account for the assets of the business? Which concept or principle governs this decision?

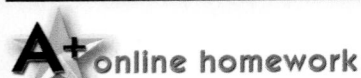

S1-5 You begin Job-Link Employment Service by investing $10,000 of your own money in a business bank account. Before starting operations, you borrow $8,000 cash by signing a note payable to Summit Bank. Write the business's accounting equation (Exhibit 1-5, page 11) after completing these transactions.

Using the accounting equation **(Obj. 3)**

S1-6 Alex Briggs owns 1-800-Fly-Europe, a travel agency near the campus of Tidewater Community College. The business has cash of $5,000 and furniture that cost $12,000. Debts include accounts payable of $8,000 and a $6,000 note payable. How much equity does Briggs have in the business? Using Briggs' figures, write the accounting equation (page 11) of the travel agency.

Using the accounting equation **(Obj. 3)**

S1-7 Review transaction 2 of Gay Gillen eTravel, on page 13. In that transaction, the business purchased land for $20,000. To buy the land, Gillen was obligated to pay for it. Why, then, did the business record no liability in this transaction?

Analyzing transactions **(Obj. 4)**

S1-8 Study Gay Gillen's transaction 4 on pages 14–15. Gillen recorded revenues earned by providing travel service for clients. Suppose the amount of revenue earned in transaction 4 was $4,000 instead of $5,500. How much are the business's cash and total assets after the transaction? How much is Gay Gillen, Capital?

Analyzing transactions **(Obj. 4)**

S1-9 Review transaction 9 of Gay Gillen eTravel, on page 17. Gillen collected cash from a client for whom she had provided travel services earlier. Why didn't the travel agency record any revenue in transaction 9?

Analyzing transactions **(Obj. 4)**

S1-10 Clements Auction Co. earns service revenue by selling antique furniture for customers. Clements' main expenses are the salaries paid to employees. Write the accounting equation to show the effects of

Analyzing transactions **(Obj. 4)**

a. Clements' earning $10,000 of service revenue on account and
b. Clements' $6,000 payment of salaries for October.

Show all appropriate headings, starting with the accounting equation. Also list the appropriate item under each heading. Assume Clements began with an adequate cash balance.

S1-11 Examine Exhibit 1-7 on page 19. The exhibit summarizes the transactions of Gay Gillen eTravel for the month of April 20X5. Suppose Gillen has completed only the first seven transactions and needs a bank loan on April 21. The vice president of the bank requires financial statements to support all loan requests.

Prepare the income statement, statement of owner's equity, and balance sheet that Gay Gillen would present to the banker after completing the first seven transactions on April 21, 20X5. Exhibit 1-8, page 21, shows the format of these statements.

Preparing the financial statements **(Obj. 5)**

S1-12 Gay Gillen wishes to know how well her business performed during April. The income statement in Exhibit 1-8, page 21, helps answer this question. Write the formula for measuring net income or net loss on the income statement.

Format of the income statement **(Obj. 5)**

S1-13 Bellmead Auto Repair has just completed operations for the year ended December 31, 20X8. This is the third year of operations for the company. As the proprietor, you want to know how well the business performed during the year. You also wonder where the business stands financially at the end of the year. To address these questions, you have assembled the following data:

Preparing the income statement **(Obj. 6)**

Insurance expense	$ 4,000	Salary expense	$42,000
Service revenue	101,000	Accounts payable	8,000
Accounts receivable	7,000	Owner, capital,	
Supplies expense	1,000	December 31, 20X7	13,000
Cash	16,000	Supplies	2,000
Fuel expense	6,000	Withdrawals by owner	36,000
Rent expense	8,000		

Prepare the income statement of Bellmead Auto Repair for the year ended December 31, 20X8. Follow the format shown in Exhibit 1-8, page 21.

Preparing the statement of owner's equity
(Obj. 6)

S1-14 Use the data in Starter 1-13 to prepare the statement of owner's equity of Bellmead Auto Repair for the year ended December 31, 20X8. Follow the format in Exhibit 1-8. Compute net income from the data in Starter 1-13.

Preparing the balance sheet
(Obj. 6)

S1-15 Use the data in Starter 1-13 to prepare the balance sheet of Bellmead Auto Repair at December 31, 20X8. The year-end balance sheet will show where the business stands financially at the end of the year. Follow the format in Exhibit 1-8. Owner's equity (Owner, capital) at December 31, 20X8, is $17,000.

A+ online homework

Exercises

Deciding on an investment
(Obj. 1)

E1-1 Suppose you have saved some money and you are considering an investment in **Amazon.com**. What accounting information will you use to decide whether or not to invest in Amazon? Which accounting principle do you hope Amazon's accountants follow closely? Explain your answer.

Explaining the income statement and the balance sheet
(Obj. 1)

E1-2 Shelly Herzog publishes a travel magazine. In need of cash, she asks Central Bank for a loan. The bank requires borrowers to submit financial statements to show results of operations and financial position. With little knowledge of accounting, Herzog doesn't know how to proceed. Explain to her the information provided by the balance sheet and the income statement. Indicate why a lender would require this information.

Business transactions
(Obj. 2)

E1-3 As manager of a **Kinko's Copies** store, you must deal with a variety of business transactions. Give an example of a transaction that has the described effect on the accounting equation:

a. Increase an asset and increase owner's equity.
b. Increase an asset and increase a liability.
c. Increase one asset and decrease another asset.
d. Decrease an asset and decrease owner's equity.
e. Decrease an asset and decrease a liability.

Transaction analysis
(Obj. 2)

E1-4 **Automatic Chef**, a proprietorship, supplies snack foods. The business experienced the following events. State whether each event (1) increased, (2) decreased, or (3) had no effect on the total assets of the business. Identify any specific asset affected.

a. Automatic Chef received a cash investment from the owner.
b. Cash purchase of land for a building site.
c. Paid cash on accounts payable.
d. Purchased machinery and equipment for a manufacturing plant; signed a promissory note in payment.
e. Performed service for a customer on account.
f. The owner withdrew cash from the business for personal use.
g. Received cash from a customer on account receivable.
h. The owner used personal funds to purchase a swimming pool for his home.
i. Sold land for a price equal to the cost of the land; received cash.
j. Borrowed money from the bank.

Accounting equation
(Obj. 3)

E1-5 Compute the missing amount in the accounting equation for each entity:

	Assets	Liabilities	Owner's Equity
Autozone	$?	$61,800	$21,000
Army-Navy Surplus	72,000	?	34,000
Amy's Hallmark	102,700	79,800	?

E1-6 Oracle Web Sites started 20X4 with total assets of $25,000 and total liabilities of $11,000. At the end of 20X4, Oracle's total assets stood at $31,000, and total liabilities were $14,000.

Accounting equation
(Obj. 3)

Required

1. Did the owner's equity of Oracle increase or decrease during 20X4? By how much?
2. Identify two possible reasons for the change in owner's equity during the year.

E1-7 Avis Rentals' balance sheet data at May 31, 20X6, and June 30, 20X6, follow:

Accounting equation
(Obj. 3)

	May 31, 20X6	June 30, 20X6
Total assets	$150,000	$195,000
Total liabilities	109,000	131,000

Required

Following are three assumptions about investments and withdrawals by the owner of the business during June. For each assumption, compute the amount of net income or net loss during June 20X6.

1. The owner invested $10,000 in the business and made no withdrawals.
2. The owner made no additional investments in the business but withdrew $5,000 for personal use.
3. The owner invested $30,000 in the business and withdrew $6,000 for personal use.

E1-8 Indicate the effects of the following business transactions on the accounting equation of an **Enterprise Rent-a-Car** location. Transaction (a) is answered as a guide.

Transaction analysis
(Obj. 4)

a. Received cash of $25,000 from the owner, who was investing in the business.
Answer: Increase asset (Cash)
Increase owner's equity (Capital)
b. Paid $700 cash to purchase supplies.
c. Earned rental revenue on account, $500.
d. Purchased on account office furniture at a cost of $600.
e. Received cash on account, $900.
f. Paid cash on account, $250.
g. Sold land for $12,000, which was the cost of the land.
h. Rented automobiles and received cash of $680.
i. Paid monthly office rent of $800.

E1-9 Ken Luikhart opens a medical practice. During the first month of operation, July, the business, titled Ken Luikhart, M.D., experienced the following events.

Transaction analysis; accounting equation
(Obj. 4)

Student Resource CD
spreadsheet

July 6	Luikhart invested $60,000 in the business by opening a bank account in the name of K. Luikhart, M.D.
9	Luikhart paid $55,000 cash for land. He plans to build an office building on the land.
12	He purchased medical supplies for $2,000 on account.
15	Luikhart officially opened for business.
15–31	During the rest of the month, he treated patients and earned service revenue of $7,000, receiving cash.
15–31	He paid cash expenses: employees' salaries, $1,400; office rent, $1,000; utilities, $300.
28	He sold supplies to another physician for the cost of those supplies, $500.
31	He paid $1,500 on account.

Required

Analyze the effects of these events on the accounting equation of the medical practice of K. Luikhart, M.D. Use a format similar to that of Exhibit 1-7, with headings for Cash; Medical Supplies; Land; Accounts Payable; and K. Luikhart, Capital.

Business transactions and net income
(Obj. 4)

E1-10 The analysis of Marstaller TV Service's first eight transactions follows. The owner of the business made only one investment to start the business and no withdrawals.

	Cash	+	Accounts Receivable	+	Equipment	=	Accounts Payable	+	Note Payable	+	Owner Capital
1.	+50,000										+50,000
2.	−750				+750						
3.					+100,000				+100,000		
4.			+800								+800
5.	−2,000										−2,000
6.	+2,200										+2,200
7.	−10,000						−10,000				
8.	+150		−150								

Required

1. Describe each transaction.
2. If these transactions fully describe the operations of Marstaller TV Service during the month, what was the amount of net income or net loss?

Business organization, balance sheet
(Obj. 5)

E1-11 The balances of the assets and liabilities of JD's Graphic Design at November 30, 20X9, follow. Also included are the revenue and expense figures of this service business for November.

Service revenue	$9,100	Office equipment	$15,500
Accounts receivable	6,900	Supplies	600
Accounts payable	2,500	Note payable	8,000
J.D. Power, capital	?	Rent expense	500
Salary expense	2,000	Cash	2,000

Required

1. What type of business organization is JD's Graphic Design? How can you tell?
2. Prepare the balance sheet of the business at November 30, 20X9.
3. What does the balance sheet report—financial position or operating results? Which financial statement reports the other information?

Income Statement
(Obj. 5)

Student Resource CD
spreadsheet

E1-12 The assets, liabilities, owner's equity, revenues, and expenses of Award Specialties, an engraving business, at December 31, 20X6, the end of its first year of operation, have the following balances. During the year, T. Kershaw, the owner, invested $15,000 in the business.

Office furniture	$ 45,000	Note payable	$41,000
Utilities expense........	6,800	Rent expense	24,000
Accounts payable	3,300	Cash	3,600
T. Kershaw, capital	27,100	Office supplies	4,800
Service revenue	161,200	Salary expense	60,000
Accounts receivable	9,000	Salaries payable	2,000
Supplies expense	4,000	Property tax expense	1,200

Required

1. Prepare the income statement of Award Specialties for the year ended December 31, 20X6. What is the result of operations for 20X6?
2. What was the amount of the proprietor's withdrawals during the year?

Evaluating the performance of a real company **(Obj. 6)**

E1-13 In this exercise you will practice using the data of a well-known company. The 20X1 annual report of **Fedex**, the overnight shipping company, reported revenue of $19.6 billion. Total expenses for the year were $19.0 billion. Fedex ended the year with total assets of $13.3 billion, and it owed debts totaling $7.4 billion. At year-end 20X0, Fedex reported total assets of $11.5 billion and total liabilities of $6.7 billion.

Required

1. Compute Fedex's net income for 20X1.
2. Did Fedex's owners' equity increase or decrease during 20X1? By how much?
3. How would you rate Fedex's performance for 20X1—good or bad? Give your reason.

Using the financial statements **(Obj. 6)**

E1-14 Compute the missing amount for Mars Company. You will need to prepare a statement of owner's equity.

Mars Co.	
Beginning:	
Assets	$ 50,000
Liabilities	20,000
Ending:	
Assets	$ 70,000
Liabilities	35,000
Owner's Equity:	
Investments by owner	$ 0
Withdrawals by owner	40,000
Income Statement:	
Revenues	$230,000
Expenses	?

Did Mars earn a net income or suffer a net loss for the year? Compute the amount.

Problems

(Group A)

A+ online homework

Entity concept, transaction analysis, accounting equation **(Obj. 2, 3, 4)**

P1-1A Lynn Greenspan practiced law with a partnership for 10 years. Recently she opened her own law office, which she operates as a proprietorship. The name of the new entity is Lynn Greenspan, Attorney. Greenspan experienced the following events during the organizing phase of the new business and its first month of operation. Some of the events were personal and did not affect the law practice. Others were business transactions and should be accounted for by the business.

July	1	Sold 1,000 shares of **Eastman Kodak** stock, which she had owned for several years, receiving $68,000 cash.
	2	Deposited the $68,000 cash from sale of the Eastman Kodak stock in her personal bank account.
	3	Received $170,000 cash from former law partners.
	5	Deposited $100,000 cash in a new business bank account titled Lynn Greenspan, Attorney.
	6	A representative of a large company telephoned Greenspan and told her of the company's intention to transfer its legal business to Lynn Greenspan, Attorney.

(*continued*)

7	Paid $500 cash for letterhead stationery for the new law office.
9	Purchased office furniture for the law office, agreeing to pay the account, $9,500, within 3 months.
23	Finished court hearings on behalf of a client and submitted her bill for legal services, $3,000.
30	Paid office rent, $1,900.
31	Withdrew $10,000 cash from the business for personal use.

Required

1. Analyze the effects of the preceding events on the accounting equation of the proprietorship of Lynn Greenspan, Attorney. Use a format similar to Exhibit 1-7.
2. At July 31, compute the business's
   a. Total assets
   b. Total liabilities
   c. Total owner's equity
   d. Net income or net loss for the month

Transaction analysis, accounting equation, financial statements
(Obj. 3, 4, 5)

P1-2A Daniel Peavy owns and operates an architectural firm called Peavy Design. The following amounts summarize the financial position of his business on April 30, 20X5:

Assets				= Liabilities +	Owner's Equity
Cash +	Accounts Receivable +	Supplies +	Land =	Accounts Payable +	Daniel Peavy, Capital
Bal. 1,720	3,240		24,100	5,400	23,660

During May 20X5, the following events occurred.

a. Peavy received $12,000 as a gift and deposited the cash in the business bank account.
b. Paid off the beginning balance of accounts payable.
c. Performed services for a client and received cash of $1,100.
d. Collected cash from a customer on account, $750.
e. Purchased supplies on account, $720.
f. Consulted on the interior design of a major office building and billed the client for services rendered, $5,000.
g. Invested personal cash of $1,700 in the business.
h. Recorded the following business expenses for the month:
   1. Paid office rent, $1,200.
   2. Paid advertising, $660.
i. Sold supplies to another interior designer for $80 cash, which was the cost of the supplies.
j. Withdrew cash of $4,000 for personal use.

Required

1. Analyze the effects of the preceding transactions on the accounting equation of Peavy Design. Adapt the format of Exhibit 1-7.
2. Prepare the income statement of Peavy Design for the month ended May 31, 20X5. List expenses in decreasing order by amount.
3. Prepare the statement of owner's equity of Peavy Design for the month ended May 31, 20X5.
4. Prepare the balance sheet of Peavy Design at May 31, 20X5.

Business transactions and analysis
(Obj. 3, 4)

P1-3A Jacobs-Cathey Heating & Cooling was recently formed. The balance of each item in the company's accounting equation follows for August 4 and for each of the nine following days:

	Cash	Accounts Receivable	Supplies	Land	Accounts Payable	Owner's Equity
Aug. 4	$2,000	$7,000	$ 800	$11,000	$3,800	$17,000
9	6,000	3,000	800	11,000	3,800	17,000
14	4,000	3,000	800	11,000	1,800	17,000
17	4,000	3,000	1,100	11,000	2,100	17,000
19	5,000	3,000	1,100	11,000	2,100	18,000
20	3,900	3,000	1,100	11,000	1,000	18,000
22	9,900	3,000	1,100	5,000	1,000	18,000
25	9,900	3,700	400	5,000	1,000	18,000
26	9,300	3,700	1,000	5,000	1,000	18,000
28	4,200	3,700	1,000	5,000	1,000	12,900

Required

A single transaction took place on each day. Describe briefly the transaction that most likely occurred on each day, beginning with August 9. Indicate which accounts were increased or decreased and by what amount. No revenue or expense transactions occurred on these dates.

P1-4A Collins Photographic Studio provides pictures for high-school yearbooks. The capital balance of L. Collins, owner of the company, was $50,000 at December 31, 20X8. During 20X9 he withdrew $16,000 for personal use. At December 31, 20X9, the business's accounting records show these balances:

Preparing the financial statements—simple situation **(Obj. 5)**

Accounts receivable	$ 8,000	Rent expense	$ 7,000
Note payable	12,000	Cash	16,000
L. Collins, capital	?	Accounts payable	6,000
Salary expense	22,000	Advertising expense	4,000
Equipment	65,000	Service revenue	70,000

Prepare the following financial statements for Collins Photographic Studio:

a. Income statement for the year ended December 31, 20X9
b. Statement of owner's equity for the year ended December 31, 20X9
c. Balance sheet at December 31, 20X9

P1-5A The amounts of (a) the assets and liabilities of Vail Financial Consultants at December 31, 20X4, and (b) the revenues and expenses of the company for the year ended on that date follow. The items are listed in alphabetical order.

Income statement, statement of owner's equity, balance sheet **(Obj. 5, 6)**

Accounts payable	$12,000	Note payable	$31,000
Accounts receivable	3,000	Property tax expense	2,000
Building	56,000	Rent expense	14,000
Cash	7,000	Salary expense	38,000
Equipment	21,000	Service revenue	108,000
Interest expense	4,000	Supplies	7,000
Interest payable	1,000	Utilities expense	3,000
Land	8,000		

The capital balance of Matthew Vail, the owner, was $43,000 at December 31, 20X3. During 20X4, Vail withdrew $32,000 for personal use.

Required

1. Prepare the income statement of Vail Financial Consultants for the year ended December 31, 20X4.
2. Prepare the company's statement of owner's equity for the year ended December 31, 20X4.
3. Prepare the company's balance sheet at December 31, 20X4.
4. Answer these questions about the company.
   a. Was the result of operations for the year a profit or a loss? How much?
   b. Did Vail drain off all the earnings for the year, or did he increase the company's capital during the period? How would his actions affect the company's ability to borrow?
   c. How much in total economic resources does the company have as it moves into the new year? How much does the company owe? What is the dollar amount of Vail's equity interest in the business at the end of the year?

Balance sheet, entity concept
(Obj. 2, 3, 5)

P1-6A Helen Chuy is a realtor. Chuy organized the business as a proprietorship on March 10, 20X6. Consider the following facts at March 31, 20X6:

a. Chuy had $15,000 in her personal bank account and $17,000 in her business bank account.
b. Office supplies on hand at the real estate office totaled $1,000.
c. Chuy's business spent $15,000 for an **Electronic Realty Associates** (ERA) franchise, which entitled Chuy to represent herself as an ERA agent. This franchise is an asset.
d. Chuy owed $34,000 on a note payable for some land that had been acquired by the business for a total price of $60,000.
e. Chuy owed $90,000 on a personal mortgage on her personal residence, which she acquired in 20X1 for a total price of $175,000.
f. Chuy owed $950 on her personal VISA credit card.
g. Chuy acquired business furniture for $12,000 on March 26. Of this amount, Chuy's business owed $6,000 on account at March 31.

Required

1. Prepare the balance sheet of the real estate business of Helen Chuy, Realtor, at March 31, 20X6.
2. Identify the personal items that would not be reported on the balance sheet of the business.

Correcting a balance sheet
(Obj. 5)

P1-7A The bookkeeper of Electronic Tax Service prepared the balance sheet of the company while the accountant was ill. The balance sheet contains numerous errors. In particular, the bookkeeper knew that the balance sheet should balance, so he plugged in the owner's equity amount to achieve this balance. The owner's equity amount, however, is not correct. All other amounts are accurate, but some are out of place.

Electronic Tax Service
Balance Sheet
Month Ended October 31, 20X7

Assets		Liabilities	
Cash	$ 5,400	Notes receivable	$ 3,000
Insurance expense	300	Interest expense	2,000
Land	31,500	Office supplies	800
Salary expense	3,300	Accounts receivable	2,600
Office furniture	6,700	Note payable	21,000
Accounts payable	3,000		
Utilities expense	2,100	**Owner's Equity**	
		Owner's equity	22,900
Total assets	$52,300	Total liabilities	$52,300

Required

1. Prepare the correct balance sheet, and date it correctly. Compute total assets, total liabilities, and owner's equity.
2. Identify the accounts that should *not* be presented on the balance sheet. State why you excluded them from the correct balance sheet you prepared. Where should these items be reported?

Problems

(Group B)

A+ online homework

Entity concept, transaction analysis, accounting equation
(Obj. 2, 3, 4)

P1-1B Jerry Ford practiced law with a partnership for five years. Recently he opened his own law office, which he operates as a proprietorship. The name of the new entity is Jerry Ford, Attorney. Ford experienced the following events during the organizing phase of his new business and its first month of operations. Some of the events were personal and did not affect his law practice. Others were business transactions and should be accounted for by the business.

Feb. 4	Received $100,000 cash from former law partners.
5	Deposited $80,000 cash in a new business bank account titled Jerry Ford, Attorney.
6	Paid $300 cash for letterhead stationery for the new law office.
7	Purchased office furniture for the law office. Ford agreed to pay the account payable, $7,000, within 3 months.
10	Sold 500 shares of **Intel** stock, which he had owned for several years, receiving $75,000 cash.
11	Deposited the $75,000 cash from sale of the Intel stock in his personal bank account.
12	A representative of a large company telephoned Ford and told him of the company's intention to transfer its legal business to Jerry Ford, Attorney.
18	Finished court hearings on behalf of a client and submitted a bill for legal services, $5,000. Ford expected to collect from this client within two weeks.
25	Paid office rent, $1,000.
28	Withdrew $10,000 cash from the business for personal use.

Required

1. Analyze the effects of the events on the accounting equation of the proprietorship of Jerry Ford, Attorney. Use a format similar to Exhibit 1-7 on page 19.
2. At February 28, compute:
   - **a.** Total assets
   - **b.** Total liabilities
   - **c.** Total owner's equity
   - **d.** Net income or net loss for February

Transaction analysis, accounting equation, financial statements
(Obj. 3, 4, 5)

P1-2B Monica Bass owns and operates an interior design studio called Enchanting Designs. The following amounts summarize the financial position of her business on August 31, 20X2:

	Assets				=	Liabilities	+	Owner's Equity
	Cash	+ Accounts Receivable	+ Supplies	+ Land	=	Accounts Payable	+	Monica Bass, Capital
Bal.	2,250	1,500		12,000		8,000		7,750

During September 20X2, the following events occurred.

a. Bass inherited $20,000 and deposited the cash in the business bank account.
b. Performed services for a client and received cash of $700.

c. Paid off the beginning balance of accounts payable.
d. Purchased supplies on account, $1,000.
e. Collected cash from a customer on account, $1,000.
f. Invested personal cash of $1,000 in the business.
g. Consulted on the interior design of a major office building and billed the client for services rendered, $2,400.
h. Recorded the following business expenses for the month:
   1. Paid office rent, $900.
   2. Paid advertising, $100.
i. Sold supplies to another business for $150 cash, which was the cost of the supplies.
j. Withdrew cash of $2,000 for personal use.

Required

1. Analyze the effects of the preceding transactions on the accounting equation of Enchanting Designs. Adapt the format of Exhibit 1-7, page 19.
2. Prepare the income statement of Enchanting Designs for the month ended September 30, 20X2. List expenses in decreasing order by amount.
3. Prepare the entity's statement of owner's equity for the month ended September 30, 20X2.
4. Prepare the balance sheet at September 30, 20X2.

Business transactions and analysis
(Obj. 3, 4)

P1-3B Little People Day Care Center was recently formed. The balance of each item in the company's accounting equation is shown for March 10 and for each of the nine following business days.

	Cash	Accounts Receivable	Supplies	Land	Accounts Payable	Owner's Equity
Mar. 10	$ 4,000	$4,000	$1,000	$ 8,000	$4,000	$13,000
11	13,000	4,000	1,000	8,000	4,000	22,000
12	6,000	4,000	1,000	15,000	4,000	22,000
15	6,000	4,000	3,000	15,000	6,000	22,000
16	5,000	4,000	3,000	15,000	5,000	22,000
17	7,000	2,000	3,000	15,000	5,000	22,000
18	15,000	2,000	3,000	15,000	5,000	30,000
19	12,000	2,000	3,000	15,000	2,000	30,000
22	11,000	2,000	4,000	15,000	2,000	30,000
23	3,000	2,000	4,000	15,000	2,000	22,000

Required

A single transaction took place on each day. Briefly describe the transaction that most likely occurred on each day, beginning with March 11. Indicate which accounts were increased or decreased and by what amounts. No revenue or expense transactions occurred on these dates.

Preparing the financial statements—simple situation
(Obj. 5)

P1-4B Robinson Chauffeur Service works weddings and prom-type parties. The capital balance of J. Robinson, the owner of the company, was $56,000 at December 31, 20X4. During 20X5 he withdrew $50,000 for personal use. At December 31, 20X5, the business's accounting records show these balances:

Accounts receivable	$ 3,000	Insurance expense	$ 4,000
Note payable	35,000	Cash	5,000
J. Robinson, capital	?	Accounts payable	1,000
Salary expense	14,000	Advertising expense	2,000
Automobiles	80,000	Service revenue	66,000

Prepare the following financial statements for Robinson Chauffeur Service:

a. Income statement for the year ended December 31, 20X5
b. Statement of owner's equity for the year ended December 31, 20X5
c. Balance sheet at December 31, 20X5

Income statement, statement of owner's equity, balance sheet
(Obj. 5, 6)

P1-5B Presented here are (a) the assets and liabilities of Ping Technology Consultants at December 31, 20X7, and (b) the revenues and expenses of the company for the year ended on that date. The items are listed in alphabetical order.

Accounts payable	$ 19,000	Land	$ 60,000
Accounts receivable	12,000	Note payable	85,000
Advertising expense	13,000	Property tax expense	4,000
Building	170,000	Rent expense	23,000
Cash	14,000	Salary expense	63,000
Equipment	20,000	Salary payable	1,000
Insurance expense	2,000	Service revenue	178,000
Interest expense	9,000	Supplies	3,000

The capital balance of Brian Sartor, the owner, was $150,000 at December 31, 20X6. During 20X7, Sartor withdrew $40,000 for personal use.

Required

1. Prepare Ping's income statement for the year ended December 31, 20X7.
2. Prepare the company's statement of owner's equity for the year ended December 31, 20X7.
3. Prepare the company's balance sheet at December 31, 20X7.
4. Answer these questions about the company:
   a. Was the result of operations for the year a profit or a loss? How much?
   b. Did Sartor drain off all the earnings for the year, or did he increase the company's capital during the period? How will his actions affect the company's ability to borrow?
   c. How much in total economic resources does the company have as it moves into the new year? How much does the company owe? What is the dollar amount of Sartor's equity interest in the business at the end of the year?

Balance sheet, entity concept
(Obj. 2, 3, 5)

P1-6B Lou Phillips is a realtor. She organized her business as a proprietorship on November 24, 20X4. Consider the following facts at November 30, 20X4.

a. Phillips owed $55,000 on a note payable for some undeveloped land that had been acquired by her business for a total price of $100,000.
b. Phillips' business had spent $20,000 for a **Century 21** real estate franchise, which entitled her to represent herself as a Century 21 agent. This franchise is a business asset.
c. Phillips owed $60,000 on a personal mortgage on her personal residence, which she acquired in 20X1 for a total price of $150,000.
d. Phillips had $8,000 in her personal bank account and $7,000 in her business bank account.
e. Phillips owed $1,800 on a personal charge account with the **Neiman-Marcus** store.
f. Phillips acquired business furniture for $17,000 on November 25. Of this amount, her business owed $6,000 on account at November 30.
g. Office supplies on hand at the real estate office totaled $1,000.
   1. Prepare the balance sheet of the real estate business of Lou Phillips, Realtor, at November 30, 20X4.
   2. Identify the personal items that would not be reported on the balance sheet of the business.

Correcting a balance sheet
(Obj. 5)

P1-7B The bookkeeper of Epson Printing Co. prepared the company's balance sheet while the accountant was ill. The balance sheet contains numerous errors. In particular, the bookkeeper knew that the balance sheet should balance, so he plugged in the owner's equity amount needed to achieve this balance. The owner's equity amount, however, is not correct. All other amounts are accurate, but some are out of place.

Epson Printing Co.
Balance Sheet
Month Ended July 31, 20X3

Assets		Liabilities	
Cash	$ 12,000	Accounts receivable	$ 23,000
Office supplies	1,000	Service revenue	68,000
Land	44,000	Property tax expense	800
Salary expense	2,500	Accounts payable	9,000
Office furniture	8,000		
Note payable	36,000	**Owner's Equity**	
Rent expense	4,000	Owner's equity	6,700
Total assets	$107,500	Total liabilities	$107,500

Required

1. Prepare the correct balance sheet, and date it correctly. Compute total assets, total liabilities, and owner's equity.
2. Identify the accounts that should *not* be presented on the balance sheet. State why you excluded them from the correct balance sheet you prepared. Where should these items be reported?

APPLY *Your Knowledge*

Decision Cases

Measuring net income
(Obj. 5, 6)

Case 1. Jimmy and Virginia Campbell saved all their married life with the dream of opening a bed and breakfast (B&B) in a quiet village in New England. They invested $300,000 of their own money and also got a $200,000 bank loan to round out the $500,000 they needed to get started. The Campbells bought a beautiful old Victorian home in Stowe, Vermont, for $200,000. It cost another $150,000 to renovate. They found most of the furniture at antique shops and flea markets—total cost was $50,000. Kitchen equipment cost $10,000, and a **Dell** computer set them back another $2,000.

Prior to the grand opening, the banker requests a report on their activities thus far. Jimmy and Virginia examine their bank statement and find it shows a cash balance of $88,000. They feel pretty good with that much net income in only six months. To better understand how well they are doing, they prepare the following income statement for presentation to the bank:

Old Victorian Bed and Breakfast
Income Statement
Six Months Ended June 30, 20X5

Revenues:	
Investments by owner	$300,000
Bank loan	200,000
Total revenues	500,000
Expenses:	
Cost of the house	$200,000
Repairs to house	150,000
Furniture expense	50,000
Kitchen equipment expense	10,000
Computer expense	2,000
Total expenses	412,000
Net income	$ 88,000

1. Suppose you are the Campbells' banker, and they have given you this income statement. Would you congratulate them on their net income? If so, explain why. If not, how would you advise them to measure the net income of the business? Does the amount of cash in the bank measure net income? Explain.
2. Show the Campbells how to prepare Old Victorian's balance sheet from their data.

Using financial statements to evaluate a loan request
(Obj. 1, 2, 6)

Case 2. The proprietors of two businesses, James Dobson Company and O'Reilly Public Relations, have sought business loans from you. To decide whether to make the loans, you have requested their balance sheets.

James Dobson Company
Balance Sheet
August 31, 20X4

Assets		Liabilities	
Cash	$ 9,000	Accounts payable	$ 12,000
Accounts receivable	14,000	Note payable	18,000
Merchandise inventory	85,000	Total liabilities	30,000
Store supplies	500		
Furniture and fixtures	9,000	**Owner's Equity**	
Building	80,000	James Dobson, capital	181,500
Land	14,000	Total liabilities	
Total assets	$211,500	and owner's equity	$211,500

O'Reilly Public Relations
Balance Sheet
August 31, 20X4

Assets		Liabilities	
Cash	$ 11,000	Accounts payable	$ 6,000
Accounts receivable	7,000	Note payable	168,000
Office supplies	1,000	Total liabilities	174,000
Office furniture	56,000	**Owner's Equity**	
Land	169,000	Bill O'Reilly, capital	70,000
		Total liabilities and	
Total assets	$244,000	owner's equity	$244,000

Required

1. Solely on the basis of these balance sheets, to which entity would you be more comfortable lending money? Explain fully, citing specific items and amounts from the balance sheets.
2. In addition to the balance sheet data, what other information would you require? Be specific.

Ethical Issues

Ethical Issue 1. The board of directors of McLane Wholesale Grocery is meeting to discuss the past year's results before releasing financial statements to the public. The discussion includes this exchange: Rebecca Stone, company president: "This has not been a good year! Revenue is down and expenses are way up. If we're not careful, we'll report a loss for the third year in a row. I can temporarily transfer some land that I own into the company's name, and that will beef up our balance sheet. Grant, can you save $500,000 from expenses? Then we can probably get the bank loan that we need."

Grant Tye, company chief accountant: "Rebecca, you are asking too much. Generally accepted accounting principles are designed to keep this sort of thing from happening."

Required

1. What is the fundamental ethical issue in this situation?
2. Discuss how Stone's proposals violate generally accepted accounting principles. Identify each specific concept or principle involved.

Ethical Issue 2. The tobacco companies have paid billions because of smoking-related illnesses. In particular, **Philip Morris**, a leading cigarette manufacturer, paid over $3 billion in one year.

Required

1. Suppose you are the chief financial officer (CFO) responsible for the financial statements of Philip Morris. What ethical issue would you face as you consider what to report in your company's annual report about the cash payments? What is the ethical course of action for you to take in this situation?
2. What are some of the negative consequences to Philip Morris for not telling the truth? What are some of the negative consequences to Philip Morris for telling the truth?

Financial Statement Case

Identifying items from a company's financial statements
(Obj. 3, 4)

This and similar cases in later chapters focus on the financial statement of a real company—**Amazon.com, Inc.,** the Internet shopping leader. As you work each case, you will gain confidence in your ability to use the financial statements of real companies.

Refer to Amazon.com's financial statements in Appendix A at the end of the book.

Required

1. How much in cash (including cash equivalents) did Amazon have on December 31, 2002?
2. What were the company's total assets at December 31, 2002? At December 31, 2001?
3. Write the company's accounting equation at December 31, 2002, by filling in the dollar amounts:

Assets = Liabilities + Stockholders' Equity

4. Identify Net sales (revenue) for the year ended December 31, 2002. How much did total revenue increase or decrease from 2001 to 2002?
5. How much net income or net loss did Amazon experience for 2002 and for 2001? Was 2002 better or worse than 2001? State your reasons.

Team Projects

Project 1. You are opening a pet kennel. Your purpose is to earn a profit, so you will need to establish the business. Assume you organize as a proprietorship.

1. Make a detailed list of 10 factors you must consider to establish the business.
2. Identify 10 or more transactions that your business will undertake to open and operate the kennel.
3. Prepare the kennel's income statement, statement of owner's equity, and balance sheet at the end of the first month of operations before you have had time to pay all the business's bills. Use made-up figures and include a complete heading for each financial statement. Date the balance sheet as of August 31, 20XX.
4. Discuss how you will evaluate the success of your business and how you will decide whether to continue its operation.

Project 2. You are promoting a rock concert in your area. Your purpose is to earn a profit, so you will need to establish the business. Assume you organize as a proprietorship.

Required

1. Make a detailed list of 10 factors you must consider to establish the business.
2. Describe 10 of the items your business must arrange in order to promote and stage the rock concert.
3. Prepare your business's income statement, statement of owner's equity, and balance sheet on August 31, 20XX, immediately after the rock concert and before you have had time to pay all the business's bills and to collect all receivables. Use made-up amounts, and include a complete heading for each financial statement. For the income statement and the statement of owner's equity, assume the period is the three months ended August 31, 20XX.
4. Assume that you will continue to promote rock concerts if the venture is successful. If it is unsuccessful, you will terminate the business within three months after the concert. Discuss how you will evaluate the success of your venture and how you will decide whether to continue in business.

For Internet Exercises, go to the Web site www.prenhall.com/horngren.

CHAPTER 2

Recording Business Transactions

A+ TIPS CHECK YOUR RESOURCES

- Visit the www.prenhall.com/horngren **Web site** for self-study quizzes, video clips, and other resources
- Try the **Quick Check** exercise at the end of the chapter to test your knowledge
- Learn the **key terms**
- Do the **Starter** exercises keyed in the margins
- Work the **mid-** and **end-of-chapter summary problems**
- Use the **Concept Links** to review material in other chapters
- Search the **CD** for review materials by chapter or by key word
- Watch the **tutorial videos** to review key concepts.
- Watch the **On Location Three Dog Bakery** video for the role of accounting in manufacturing and retail business.

LEARNING OBJECTIVES

1. Use accounting terms
2. Apply the rules of debit and credit
3. Record transactions in the journal
4. Post from the journal to the ledger
5. Prepare and use a trial balance
6. Analyze transactions without a journal

Frito-Lay

What is your favorite snack food? If you are like most people, it may be Doritos, Sun Chips, or plain potato chips. All of these are Frito-Lay products. Year in and year out, Frito-Lay leads the prepared-snack-food industry. How does this company deliver fresh quantities of chips to thousands of stores every day of the year?

One of Frito-Lay's great advantages is its accounting system. Route managers use handheld computers to record how many products are sold each day. The data are relayed to company headquarters, and managers can see instantly which products are moving and where. Suppose Doritos are selling well and potato chips are currently out of favor. Frito-Lay managers know to buy more corn for Doritos and less potatoes for chips. The company avoids waste by buying only what it needs to meet consumer demand.

The result? Frito-Lay is very profitable. This chapter shows how Frito-Lay and other companies record their business transactions. The procedures outlined here are followed by entities ranging from giants like Frito-Lay to a local travel agency such as Gay Gillen eTravel. ■

Sitemap

The following diagram summarizes the accounting process covered in this chapter.

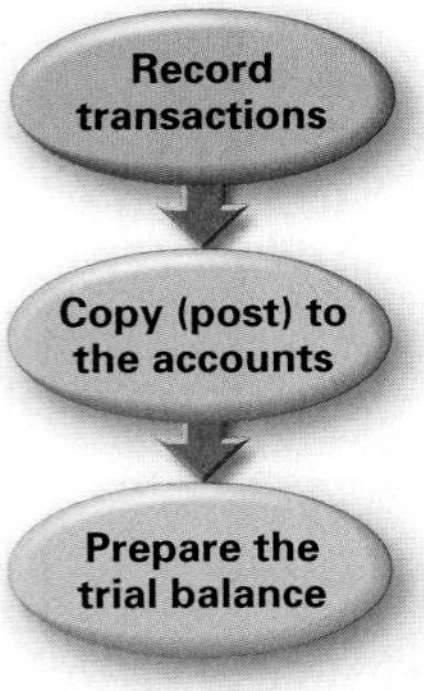

Accounting begins and ends with accounts.

1 *Use accounting terms*

Account
The detailed record of the changes in a particular asset, liability, or owner's equity during a period. The basic summary device of accounting.

The Account, the Ledger, and the Journal

The basic summary device of accounting is the **account**. This is the detailed record of all the changes that have occurred in a particular asset, liability, or owner's equity during a period. As we saw in Chapter 1, business transactions—such as buying and selling—cause the changes.

Accountants record transactions first in a **journal**. The journal is the chronological record of the transactions. Accountants then copy (post) the data to the accounts in a record called the **ledger**. A list of all the ledger accounts, along with their balances, is called a **trial balance**.

Take a moment to memorize these important terms. You will be using them over and over again.

- *Account* —the detailed record of the changes in a particular asset, liability, or owner's equity
- *Ledger* —the record holding all the accounts
- *Journal* —the chronological record of transactions
- *Trial balance* —the list of all the accounts with their balances

Accounts are grouped in three broad categories, according to the accounting equation ←:

In Chapter 1, p. 10, we learned that the accounting equation is the basic tool in all of accounting. It measures the assets of the business and the claims to those assets.

ASSETS = LIABILITIES + OWNER'S EQUITY

Stop & Think

Suppose you bought a $20,000 Pontiac Grand Am and had to borrow $12,000 to pay for it. Can you write your personal accounting equation for this transaction?

Answer

ASSETS	=	LIABILITIES	+	OWNER'S EQUITY
$20,000	=	$12,000	+	$8,000

Assets

Assets are economic resources that will benefit the business in the future. Most firms use the following asset accounts.

Cash The Cash account is a record of the cash effects of transactions. Cash includes money, such as a bank account balance, paper currency, coins, and checks. Successful companies such as Frito-Lay have plenty of cash.

Notes Receivable A business may sell goods or services and receive a *promissory note*. A note receivable is a written pledge that the customer will pay a fixed amount of money by a certain date. Notes Receivable is a record of the promissory notes the business expects to collect in cash. If you loan money to a friend and get him to sign a note, you have a note receivable from your friend.

Accounts Receivable A business may sell goods or services in exchange for an oral or implied promise of future cash receipt. Such sales are made on credit ("on account"). The Accounts Receivable account holds these amounts. Most sales in the United States and in other developed countries are made on account receivable. A receivable from your friend, if not supported by a formal note, could be an account receivable.

Prepaid Expenses A business often pays certain expenses, such as rent and insurance, in advance. A *prepaid expense* is an asset because the prepayment provides a future benefit for the business. The ledger has a separate asset account for each prepaid expense. Prepaid Rent, Prepaid Insurance, and Office Supplies are prepaid expense accounts. Your prepaid rent on your apartment or dorm room is an asset to you.

Land The Land account is a record of the cost of land a business owns and uses in its operations. Land held for sale is accounted for separately—in an investment account.

Building The cost of a business's buildings—office, warehouse, store, and the like—appear in the Buildings account. Frito-Lay owns buildings around the country, where it makes Doritos and other snack foods. But buildings held for sale are separate assets accounted for as investments.

Equipment, Furniture, and Fixtures A business has a separate asset account for each type of equipment—Computer Equipment, Office Equipment, and Store Equipment, for example. The Furniture and Fixtures account shows the cost of this asset. Frito-Lay has lots of manufacturing equipment.

Liabilities

Recall that a *liability* is a debt. A business generally has fewer liability accounts than asset accounts because a business's liabilities are summarized in a few accounts.

Notes Payable The Notes Payable account is the opposite of Notes Receivable. Notes Payable represents amounts the business must pay because it signed promissory notes to borrow money or to purchase goods or services.

Accounts Payable The Accounts Payable account is the opposite of Accounts Receivable. The oral or implied promise to pay a debt arising from a credit purchase appears in the Accounts Payable account. Such a purchase is said to be made on account. All companies, including Frito-Lay, Coca-Cola, and eBay, have accounts payable.

Journal
The chronological accounting record of an entity's transactions.

Ledger
The record holding all the accounts.

Trial Balance
A list of all the accounts with their balances.

Student ResourceCD
asset, expenses, liability, owner's equity, revenues

Accrued Liabilities An *accrued liability* is a liability for an expense that has not been paid. Taxes Payable, Interest Payable, and Salary Payable are liability accounts of Frito-Lay and most other companies.

Owner's Equity

The owner's claim to the assets of the business is called *owner's equity*. In a proprietorship or a partnership, owner's equity is split into separate accounts for the owner's capital balance and the owner's withdrawals.

Capital The Capital account shows the owner's claim to the assets of the business. Consider Gay Gillen eTravel. Subtracting total liabilities from total assets computes the travel agency's capital. The Capital balance equals the owner's investments in the business plus net income and minus any net losses and owner withdrawals.

See the statement of owner's equity in Chapter 1, Exhibit 1-8.

Withdrawals When Gay Gillen withdraws cash from the business for personal use, the travel agency's assets and owner's equity decrease. The amounts taken out of the business appear in a separate account titled Gay Gillen, Withdrawals, or Gay Gillen, Drawing. If withdrawals were recorded directly in the Capital account, the amount of owner withdrawals would not show up and the data might be lost. The Withdrawals account *decreases* owner's equity.

Revenues The increase in owner's equity created by delivering goods or services to customers is called *revenue*. The ledger contains as many revenue accounts as needed. Gay Gillen eTravel needs a Service Revenue account for amounts earned by providing travel services. If Gay Gillen eTravel lends money to an outsider, it needs an Interest Revenue account for the interest earned on the loan. If the business rents a building to a tenant, it needs a Rent Revenue account.

Expenses Expenses use up assets or create liabilities in the course of operating a business. Expenses have the opposite effect of revenues; expenses *decrease* owner's equity. A business needs a separate account for each type of expense, such as Salary Expense, Rent Expense, Advertising Expense, and Utilities Expense. Businesses strive to minimize their expenses in order to maximize net income—whether it's General Electric or Gay Gillen eTravel.

Exhibit 2-1 shows how asset, liability, and owner's equity accounts can be grouped in the ledger.

✔ Starter 2-1

✔ Starter 2-2

Exhibit 2-1

The Ledger (Asset, Liability, and Owner's Equity Accounts)

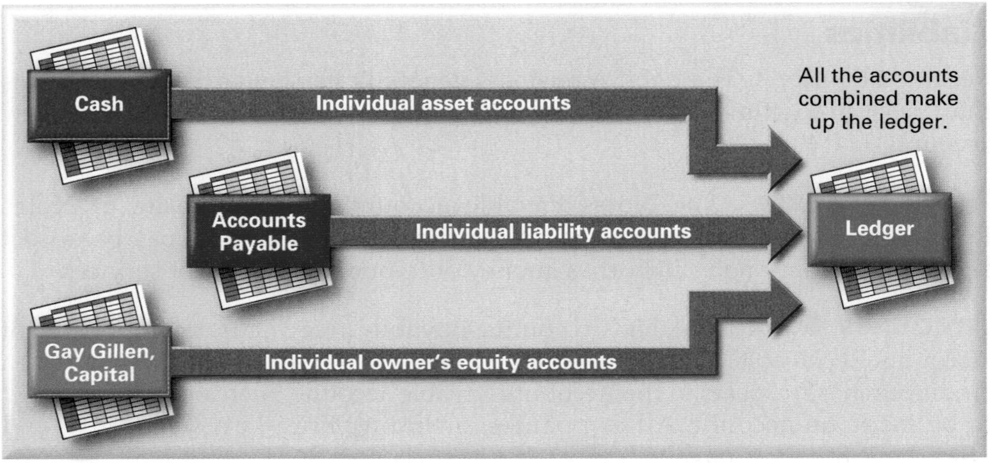

Double-Entry Accounting

Accounting is based on a *double-entry system,* which means that we record the *dual effects* of a business transaction. *Each transaction affects at least two accounts.* For example, Gay Gillen eTravel's $30,000 cash receipt from the owner increased both the Cash and the Capital of the business. It would be incomplete to record only the increase in cash without recording the increase in owner's equity.

Consider a cash purchase of supplies. What are the dual effects? The purchase (1) decreases cash and (2) increases supplies. A credit purchase of supplies (1) increases supplies and (2) increases accounts payable.

The T-Account

The most widely used account format is called the *T-account* because it takes the form of the capital letter "T." The vertical line in the T-account divides the account into its left and right sides, with the title at the top. For example, the Cash account of a business appears as follows.

Student Resource CD
asset, debits and credits, journal, ledger, liability, owner's equity, t-account

Cash	
(Left side) *Debit*	(Right side) *Credit*

The left side of the account is called the **debit** side, and the right side is called the **credit** side. The words *debit* and *credit* are new. To become comfortable using them, remember that

Debit
The left side of an account.

Credit
The right side of an account.

Debit = Left side   Credit = Right side

The terms *debit* and *credit* are deeply entrenched in business.[1] Debit and credit are abbreviated as follows:

Dr = Debit	Cr = Credit

Increases and Decreases in the Accounts

2 *Apply the rules of debit and credit*

The account category (asset, liability, equity) governs how we record increases and decreases. For any given account, increases are recorded on one side, and decreases are recorded on the other side. The following T-accounts provide a summary.

Assets	
Increases are recorded on the left (debit) side.	Decreases are recorded on the right (credit) side.

Liabilities and Owner's Equity	
Decreases are recorded on the left (debit) side.	Increases are recorded on the right (credit) side.

These are the *rules of debit and credit.*

In your study of accounting, forget the general usage of credit and debit. Remember that *debit means left side* and *credit means right side.* Whether an account is increased or decreased by a debit or a credit depends on the type of account.

In a computerized accounting system, the computer interprets debits and credits as increases or decreases by account category. For example, a computer reads a debit to Cash as an increase. The computer reads a debit to Accounts Payable as a decrease.

[1]The words *debit* and *credit* abbreviate the Latin terms *debitum* and *creditum.* Luca Pacioli, the Italian monk who wrote about accounting in the 15th century, popularized these terms.

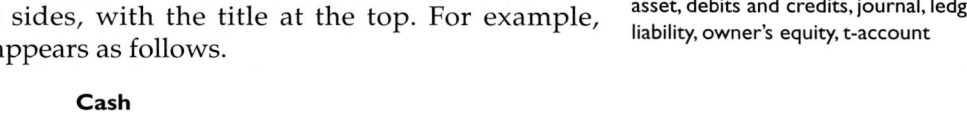

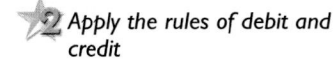

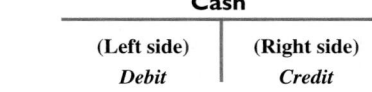

This pattern of recording debits and credits is based on the accounting equation:

Assets = Liabilities + Owner's Equity
Debits = Credits

Assets are on the opposite side of the equation from liabilities and owner's equity. Therefore, increases and decreases in assets are recorded in the opposite manner from increases and decreases in liabilities and owner's equity. Liabilities and owner's equity are on the same side, so they are treated in the same way. Exhibit 2-2 shows the relationship between the accounting equation and the rules of debit and credit.

Exhibit 2-2

The Accounting Equation and the Rules of Debit and Credit

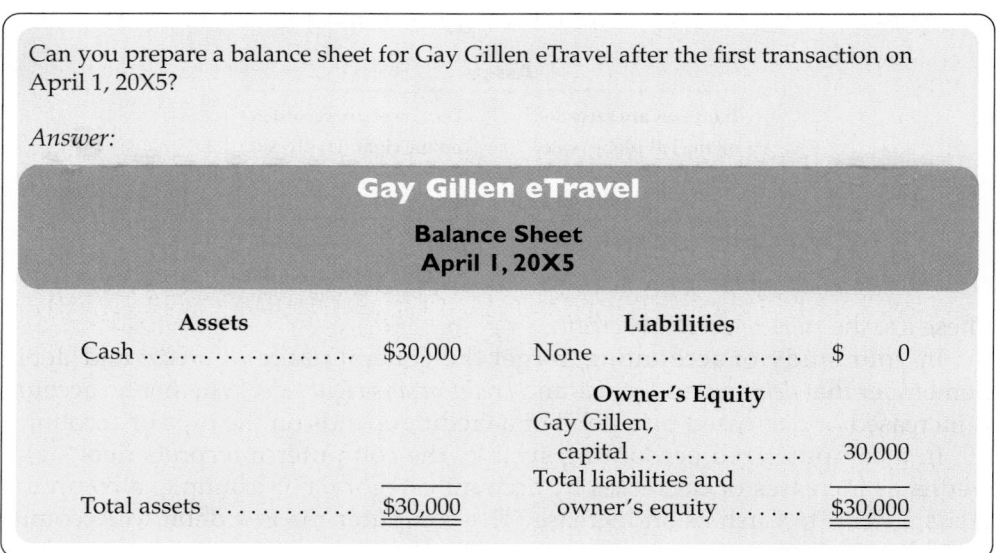

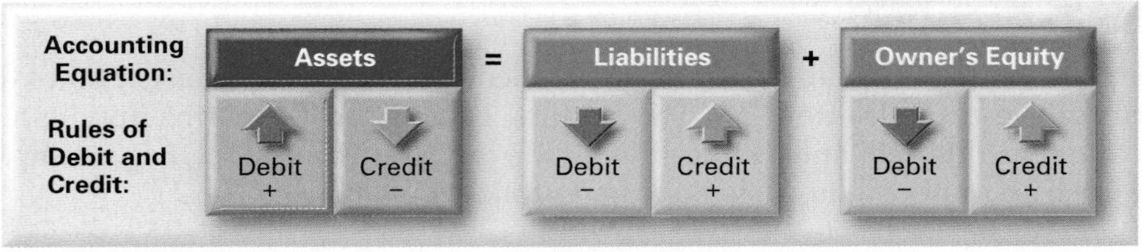

To illustrate the ideas diagrammed in Exhibit 2-2, reconsider the first transaction from Chapter 1. Gay Gillen eTravel received $30,000 cash from Gillen and gave her the owner's equity in the business. We are accounting for the business entity Gay Gillen eTravel. We are not accounting for Gay Gillen, the person. Which accounts of the business are affected? By what amounts? On what side (debit or credit)?

The answer: The business's Assets and Capital would increase by $30,000, as the T-accounts show.

Assets	=	Liabilities	+	Owner's Equity
Cash				**Gay Gillen, Capital**
Debit for increase, 30,000 (debit side)				Credit for increase, 30,000 (credit side)

The amount remaining in an account is called its *balance*. The first transaction gives Cash a $30,000 debit balance and Gay Gillen, Capital a $30,000 credit balance.

Stop & Think

Can you prepare a balance sheet for Gay Gillen eTravel after the first transaction on April 1, 20X5?

Answer:

Gay Gillen eTravel
Balance Sheet
April 1, 20X5

Assets		**Liabilities**	
Cash	$30,000	None	$ 0
		Owner's Equity	
		Gay Gillen, capital	30,000
Total assets	$30,000	Total liabilities and owner's equity	$30,000

Notice that Assets = Liabilities + Owner's Equity *and* that total debit amounts = total credit amounts. Exhibit 2-3 illustrates the accounting equation and Gay Gillen eTravel's first three transactions.

Exhibit 2-3 **The Accounting Equation and the First Three Transactions of Gay Gillen eTravel**

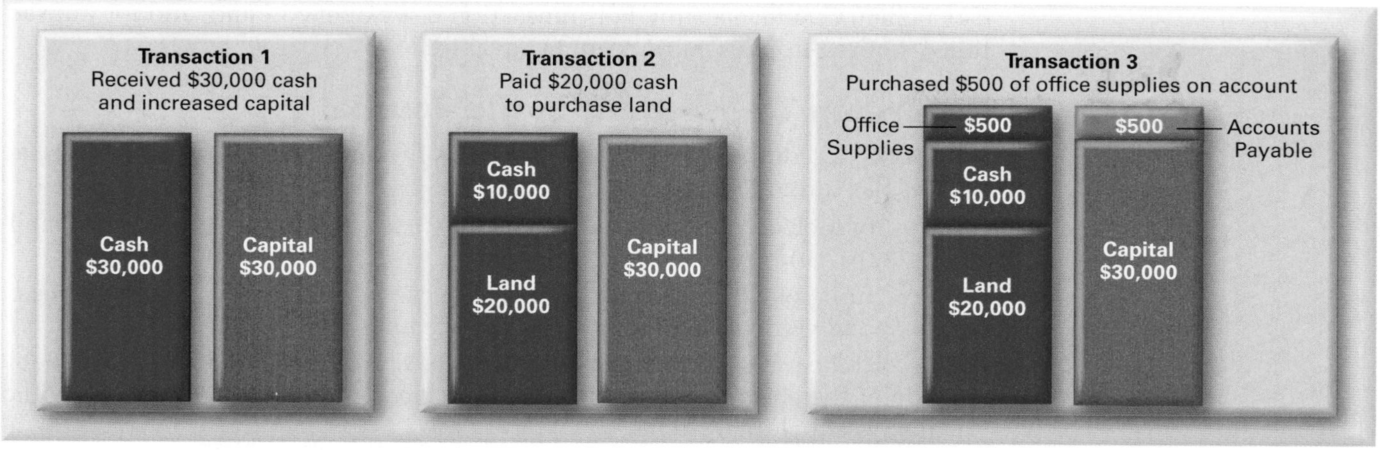

The second transaction is a $20,000 cash purchase of land. This transaction decreases (credits) Cash and increases (debits) Land, as shown in the T-accounts:

ASSETS = **LIABILITIES** + **OWNER'S EQUITY**

Cash

Debit	Credit
Balance 30,000	Credit for decrease, 20,000
Balance 10,000	

Land

Debit	Credit
Debit for increase, 20,000	
Balance 20,000	

Gay Gillen, Capital

Debit	Credit
	Balance 30,000

After this transaction, Cash has a $10,000 debit balance ($30,000 debit minus $20,000 credit), Land has a debit balance of $20,000, and Gay Gillen, Capital has a $30,000 credit balance.

Transaction 3 is a $500 purchase of office supplies on account. This transaction increases the asset Office Supplies and the liability Accounts Payable, as shown in the following accounts and in the right side of Exhibit 2-3 (labeled transaction 3):

ASSETS = **LIABILITIES** + **OWNER'S EQUITY**

Cash

Debit	Credit
Balance 10,000	

Office Supplies

Debit	Credit
Debit for increase, 500	
Balance 500	

Land

Debit	Credit
Balance 20,000	

Accounts Payable

Debit	Credit
	Credit for increase, 500
	Balance 500

Gay Gillen, Capital

Debit	Credit
	Balance 30,000

We create accounts as needed. The process of creating a new T-account is called *opening the account*. For transaction 1, we opened the Cash account and the Gay Gillen, Capital account. For transaction 2, we opened Land, and for transaction 3, Office Supplies and Accounts Payable.

3 *Record transactions in the journal*

Recording Transactions in the Journal

In practice, accountants record transactions first in a *journal*. The journalizing process has three steps:

1. Specify each account affected and classify each account by type (asset, liability, or owner's equity).
2. Determine whether each account is increased or decreased. Use the rules of debit and credit to debit or credit each account.
3. Record the transaction in the journal, including a brief explanation. The debit side of the entry is entered first and the credit side last. Total debits should always equal total credits.

Step 3, "Recording the transaction in the journal," is also called "making the journal entry" or "journalizing the transaction."

These steps are the same in a computerized system or a manual system. In step 3, the journal entry is generally entered into the computer by account number, and the account name pops up automatically.

Let's journalize the first transaction of Gay Gillen eTravel—the receipt of Gillen's $30,000 cash investment in the business.

STEP 1 The accounts affected by the receipt of cash from the owner (Exhibit 2-3) are *Cash* and *Gay Gillen, Capital*. Cash is an asset. Gay Gillen, Capital is an owner's equity account.

STEP 2 Both accounts increase by $30,000. Therefore, we debit Cash, the asset account, and we credit Gay Gillen, Capital, the owner's equity account.

STEP 3 The journal entry is

Journal			Page 1
Date	**Accounts and Explanation**	**Debit**	**Credit**
Apr. 1[a]	Cash[b] (↑ asset; debit)	30,000[d]	
	Gay Gillen, Capital[c] (↑ equity; credit) .		30,000[e]
	Received investment from owner.[f]		

Alongside Cash and Gay Gillen, Capital, we show an arrow to indicate an increase or a decrease in the account. We also give the type of account and the related debit or credit rule. These parenthetical notations are *not* part of the formal journal entry and are *not required*. But they will help you learn how to make journal entries.[2]

The journal entry includes (a) the date of the transaction, (b) the title of the account debited (printed flush left), (c) the title of the account credited (indented), the dollar amounts of the (d) debit and (e) credit, and (f) a short explanation of the transaction. Dollar signs are omitted in the money columns because it is understood that the amounts are in dollars. The journal presents the full story for each transaction. Exhibit 2-4 shows how Journal page 1 looks after Gillen has recorded the first transaction (without the extra notation).

Exhibit 2-4 **The Journal**

Journal			Page 1
Date	**Accounts and Explanation**	**Debit**	**Credit**
Apr. 1	Cash	30,000	
	Gay Gillen, Capital		30,000
	Received investment from owner.		

[2]We thank Michael Stemkoski for suggesting these aids to student learning.

Stop & Think

Make the journal entry to record a $1,600 payment on account.

1. What accounts are increased or decreased? Should they be debited or credited?
2. Make the journal entry with all notations and an explanation.

Answers:

1. Cash (an asset) decreases by $1,600. Accounts Payable (a liability) decreases by $1,600. To decrease an asset, we record a credit. To decrease a liability, we use a debit.
2. The journal entry is

Accounts Payable (↓ liability; debit)	1,600	
Cash (↓ asset; credit)		1,600
Made payment on account.		

Post from the journal to the ledger

Copying Information (Posting) from Journal to Ledger

Posting
Copying amounts from the journal to the ledger.

Posting in accounting means to copy the amounts from the journal to the ledger. Debits in the journal are posted as debits in the ledger, and credits in the journal are credits in the ledger. Debits never become credits, and credits never become debits. The investment transaction of Gay Gillen eTravel is posted to the ledger in Exhibit 2-5.

Exhibit 2-5
Making a Journal Entry and Posting to the Ledger

PANEL A—Journal Entry:

Accounts and Explanation	Debit	Credit
Cash	30,000	
Gay Gillen, Capital		30,000
Received investment from owner.		

PANEL B—Posting to the Ledger:

Cash		Gay Gillen, Capital	
30,000			30,000

- The Account, the Ledger, and the Journal
- Double-Entry Accounting
- **Flow of Accounting Data**
- Details of Journals and Ledgers
- Expanding the Accounting Equation
- Expanded Problem: Revenues and Expenses
- Quick Decision Making

The Flow of Accounting Data

Exhibit 2-6 summarizes the flow of data through the accounting system. In the pages that follow, we account for six of Gay Gillen eTravel's early transactions. In this first half of the chapter we do not account for any revenue or expense transactions. Those we save for the second half of the chapter. Keep in mind that we are accounting for the travel agency. We are *not* accounting for Gay Gillen's *personal* transactions.

Student Resource CD
account, debits and credits, journal, ledger, transaction analysis, trial balance

Exhibit 2-6 Flow of Accounting Data from the Journal to the Ledger

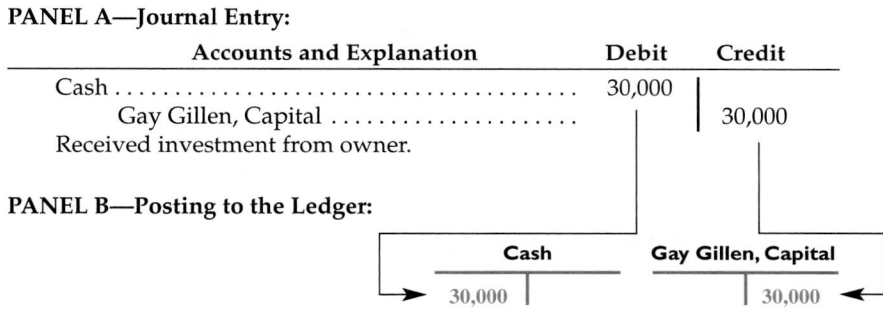

Transaction Analysis, Journalizing, and Posting to the Accounts

TRANSACTION 1 ANALYSIS The business received $30,000 cash that Gay Gillen invested to begin her travel agency. The business increased its asset cash, so we debit Cash. The business also increased owner's equity, so we credit Gay Gillen, Capital.

Accounting Equation

ASSETS	=	LIABILITIES	+	OWNER'S EQUITY
Cash				**Gay Gillen, Capital**
+30,000	=	0	+	+30,000

Journal Entry

Cash (↑ asset; debit)	30,000	
Gay Gillen, Capital (↑ equity; credit) ...		30,000
Received investment from owner.		

Ledger Accounts

Cash				Gay Gillen, Capital			
(1)	30,000					(1)	30,000

TRANSACTION 2 ANALYSIS Gillen paid $20,000 cash for land. The purchase decreased cash; therefore, credit Cash. The asset, land, increased, so we debit the Land account.

Accounting Equation

ASSETS		=	LIABILITIES	+	OWNER'S EQUITY
Cash	**Land**				
−20,000	+20,000	=	0	+	0

Journal Entry

Land (↑ asset; debit)	20,000	
Cash (↓ asset; credit)		20,000
Paid cash for land.		

Ledger Accounts

Cash				Land			
(1)	30,000	(2)	20,000	(2)	20,000		

TRANSACTION 3 ANALYSIS Gillen purchased $500 of office supplies on account. The asset office supplies increased, so we debit Office Supplies. The liability accounts payable also increased, so we credit Accounts Payable.

Accounting Equation

ASSETS	=	LIABILITIES	+	OWNER'S EQUITY
Office Supplies		**Accounts Payable**		
+500	=	+500	+	0

Journal Entry

Office Supplies (↑ asset; debit)	500	
Accounts Payable (↑ liability; credit) ...		500
Purchased supplies on account.		

Ledger Accounts

Office Supplies				Accounts Payable			
(3)	500					(3)	500

TRANSACTION 4 ANALYSIS Gillen paid $300 on the account payable created in transaction 3. The payment decreased cash; therefore, credit Cash. The payment decreased the liability accounts payable, so we debit Accounts Payable.

Accounting Equation

ASSETS	=	LIABILITIES	+	OWNER'S EQUITY
Cash		Accounts Payable		
–300	=	–300	+	0

Journal Entry

Accounts Payable (↓ liability; debit)	300	
Cash (↓ asset; credit)		300
Paid cash on account.		

Ledger Accounts

Cash

(1)	30,000	(2)	20,000
		(4)	300

Accounts Payable

(4)	300	(3)	500

TRANSACTION 5 ANALYSIS Gay Gillen remodeled her home with personal funds. This is not a transaction of the travel agency, so we make no entry on its books.

TRANSACTION 6 ANALYSIS Gillen withdrew $2,000 cash for personal living expenses. The withdrawal decreased the entity's cash; therefore, credit Cash. The transaction also decreased owner's equity. Decreases in equity that result from owner withdrawals are debited to a separate account, Withdrawals. Therefore, debit Gay Gillen, Withdrawals.

Accounting Equation

ASSETS	=	LIABILITIES	+	OWNERS' EQUITY
Cash				Gay Gillen, Withdrawals
–2,000	=	0		–2,000

Journal Entry

Gay Gillen, Withdrawals (↓ equity; debit)......	2,000	
Cash (↓ asset; credit)		2,000
Withdrawal by owner.		

Ledger Accounts

Cash

(1)	30,000	(2)	20,000
		(4)	300
		(6)	2,000

Gay Gillen, Withdrawals

(6)	2,000		

Each journal entry posted to the ledger is keyed by date or by transaction number. In this way, any transaction can be traced from the journal to the ledger and back to the journal. This linking allows you to locate any information you may need.

Accounts After Posting

We next show the accounts after posting the preceding transactions. The accounts are grouped under their headings.

Each account has a balance, denoted *Bal*. An account balance is the difference between the account's total debits and its total credits. For example, the $7,700 balance in the Cash account is the difference between

- Total debits, $30,000
- Total credits, $22,300 ($20,000 + $300 + $2,000)

The balance is the amount of cash left over after the journal entries have been posted to the account. We set an account balance apart from the transaction amounts by a horizontal line. The final figure in an account, below the horizontal line, is the balance.

ASSETS = LIABILITIES + OWNER'S EQUITY

Cash

(1)	30,000	(2)	20,000
		(4)	300
		(6)	2,000
Bal.	7,700		

Accounts Payable

(4)	300	(3)	500
		Bal.	200

Gay Gillen, Capital

		(1)	30,000
		Bal.	30,000

Office Supplies

(3)	500		
Bal.	500		

Gay Gillen, Withdrawals

(6)	2,000		
Bal.	2,000		

Land

(2)	20,000		
Bal.	20,000		

If the sum of an account's debits is greater than the sum of its credits, that account has a debit balance, as Cash does. If the sum of the credits is greater, the account has a credit balance, as for Accounts Payable.

The Normal Balance of an Account

Normal Balance
The balance that appears on the side of an account—debit or credit—where we record increases.

An account's **normal balance** appears on the side of the account—debit or credit—where we record *increases*. For example, Cash and other assets normally have a debit balance, so assets are called *debit-balance accounts*. Conversely, liabilities and owner's equity normally have a credit balance, so they are *credit-balance accounts*. Exhibit 2-7 illustrates the normal balances of assets, liabilities, and owner's equity.

Exhibit 2-7
Normal Balances of the Balance Sheet Accounts

Assets		=	Liabilities		+	Owner's Equity	
Normal Bal. Debit				Normal Bal. Credit			Normal Bal. Credit

An account that normally has a debit balance may occasionally have a credit balance. That indicates a negative amount of the item. For example, Cash will have a temporary credit balance if the business overdraws its bank account. Similarly, the liability Accounts Payable—normally a credit-balance account—will have a debit balance if the entity overpays its account. In other instances, an odd balance indicates an error. For example, a credit balance in Office Supplies, Office Furniture, or Buildings reveals an error because negative amounts of these assets make no sense.

✔ Starter 2-3

✔ Starter 2-4

✔ Starter 2-5

As we saw earlier, owner's equity contains the Capital account and the Withdrawals account. In total, these accounts show a normal credit balance. An individual owner's equity account with its normal credit balance is Gay Gillen, Capital. This account represents an *increase* in owner's equity. An owner's equity account that carries a normal debit balance is Gay Gillen, Withdrawals. Withdrawals represent a *decrease* in equity.

Revenues increase owner's equity, so the normal balance of a revenue is a credit. Expenses decrease equity, so the normal balance of an expense is a debit.

5 *Prepare and use a trial balance*

The Trial Balance

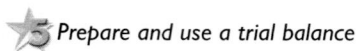

A trial balance lists all the accounts with their balances taken from the ledger—assets first, followed by liabilities and then owner's equity. In a manual accounting system, the trial balance provides a check on accuracy by showing whether total debits equal total credits. In all types of systems, the trial balance is a useful summary of the accounts and their balances. A trial balance may be taken at any time. The most common time is at the end of the accounting period. Exhibit 2-8 is the trial balance of Gay Gillen eTravel after the first six transactions.

Exhibit 2-8

Trial Balance

Gay Gillen eTravel

Trial Balance
April 30, 20X5

Account Title	Balance Debit	Balance Credit
Cash	$ 7,700	
Office supplies	500	
Land	20,000	
Accounts payable		$ 200
Gay Gillen, capital		30,000
Gay Gillen, withdrawals	2,000	
Total	$30,200	$30,200

MID-CHAPTER *Summary Problem*

A+ TIPS
CHECK YOUR RESOURCES

On August 1, 20X6, Liz Shea opens Shea's Research Service. She owns the proprietorship. During its first 10 days of operations, the business completes these transactions:

a. To begin operations, Shea deposits $40,000 of personal funds in a bank account titled Shea's Research Service. The business receives the cash and gives Shea capital (owner's equity).
b. Pays $30,000 cash for a small building to be used as an office.
c. Purchases office supplies for $500 on account.
d. Pays cash of $6,000 for office furniture.
e. Pays $150 on the account payable created in transaction (c).
f. Withdraws $1,000 cash for personal use.

Required

1. Give the accounting equation for each transaction. Then journalize these transactions and post to the accounts. Key the journal entries by letter.
2. Show all the T-accounts after posting.
3. Prepare the trial balance of Shea's Research Service at August 10, 20X6.

Solution

Requirement 1

a. Accounting Equation

ASSETS	=	LIABILITIES	+	OWNER'S EQUITY
Cash				**Liz Shea, Capital**
+40,000	=	0	+	$40,000

Journal Entry

Cash	40,000	
Liz Shea, Capital		40,000
Received investment from owner.		

Ledger Accounts

Cash			
(a)	40,000		

Liz Shea, Capital			
		(a)	40,000

b. Accounting Equation

ASSETS		=	LIABILITIES	+	OWNER'S EQUITY
Cash	Building				
−30,000	+30,000	=	0	+	0

Journal Entry

Building	30,000	
Cash		30,000
Purchased building.		

Ledger Accounts

Cash				Building			
(a)	40,000	(b)	30,000	(b)	30,000		

c. Accounting Equation

ASSETS	=	LIABILITIES	+	OWNER'S EQUITY
Office Supplies		Accounts Payable		
+500	=	+500	+	0

Journal Entry

Office Supplies	500	
Accounts Payable		500
Purchased office supplies on account.		

Ledger Accounts

Office Supplies				Accounts Payable			
(c)	500					(c)	500

d. Accounting Equation

ASSETS		=	LIABILITIES	+	OWNER'S EQUITY
Cash	Office Furniture				
−6,000	+6,000	=	0	+	0

Journal Entry

Office Furniture	6,000	
Cash		6,000
Purchased office furniture.		

Ledger Accounts

Cash				Office Furniture			
(a)	40,000	(b)	30,000	(d)	6,000		
		(d)	6,000				

e. Accounting Equation

ASSETS	=	LIABILITIES	+	OWNER'S EQUITY
Cash		Accounts Payable		
−150	=	−150	+	0

Journal Entry

Accounts Payable	150	
Cash		150
Paid cash on account.		

Ledger Accounts

Cash				Accounts Payable			
(a)	40,000	(b)	30,000	(e)	150	(c)	500
		(d)	6,000				
		(e)	150				

f. Accounting Equation

ASSETS	=	LIABILITIES	+	OWNER'S EQUITY
Cash				Liz Shea, Withdrawals
−1,000	=	0		−1,000

Journal Entry

Liz Shea, Withdrawals	1,000	
Cash		1,000
Withdrawal by owner.		

Ledger Accounts

Cash

(a)	40,000	(b)	30,000
		(d)	6,000
		(e)	150
		(f)	1,000

Liz Shea, Withdrawals

(f)	1,000		

Requirement 2

ASSETS = LIABILITIES + OWNER'S EQUITY

Cash

(a)	40,000	(b)	30,000
		(d)	6,000
		(e)	150
		(f)	1,000
Bal.	2,850		

Office Furniture

(d)	6,000		
Bal.	6,000		

Accounts Payable

(e)	150	(c)	500
		Bal.	350

Liz Shea, Capital

		(a)	40,000
		Bal.	40,000

Liz Shea, Withdrawals

(f)	1,000		
Bal.	1,000		

Office Supplies

(c)	500		
Bal.	500		

Building

(b)	30,000		
Bal.	30,000		

Requirement 3

Shea's Research Service
Trial Balance
August 10, 20X6

Account Title	Balance Debit	Balance Credit
Cash	$ 2,850	
Office supplies	500	
Office furniture	6,000	
Building	30,000	
Accounts payable		$ 350
Liz Shea, capital		40,000
Liz Shea, withdrawals	1,000	
Total	$40,350	$40,350

Details of Journals and Ledgers

To focus on the main points of journalizing and posting, we have omitted certain data. In practice, the journal and the ledger provide details to create a "trail" through the records. For example, a supplier may bill us twice for an item that we purchased. To prove we paid the first bill, we would search the records to find our payment. To see how this process works, let's take a closer look at the journal and the ledger.

Student Resource CD
chart of accounts, journal, ledger

DETAILS IN THE JOURNAL Exhibit 2-9, Panel A, describes a transaction, and Panel B shows the journal. The page number appears in the upper right corner, and the journal displays the following information:

- The *date* when the transaction occurred, April 1, 20X5.
- The *accounts* debited and credited and an explanation.

Exhibit 2-9

Journalizing and Posting

PANEL A —Illustrative Transactions

Date	Transaction
April 1, 20X5	Gay Gillen eTravel received cash of $30,000 from
	Gay Gillen, who was investing in the business.

PANEL B —Journal

Page 1

Date	Accounts and Explanation	Post Ref.	Debit	Credit
20X5				
Apr. 1	Cash	101	30,000	
	Gay Gillen, Capital	301		30,000
	Received investment from owner.			

PANEL C —Ledger 1 2 3 4

Account No. 101

Date	Item	Jrnl. Ref.	Debit	Date	Item	Jrnl. Ref.	Credit
20X5							
Apr. 1		J.1.	30,000				

Gay Gillen, Capital — Account No. 301

Date	Item	Jrnl. Ref.	Debit	Date	Item	Jrnl. Ref.	Credit
				20X5			
				Apr. 1		J.1.	30,000

- The *posting reference*, abbreviated Post. Ref. Use of this column will become clear when we discuss posting.
- The *debit* column, for the dollar amount debited.
- The *credit* column, for the dollar amount credited.

DETAILS IN THE LEDGER Exhibit 2-9, Panel C, shows the T-accounts affected by the first transaction: Cash and Gay Gillen, Capital. The account number appears at the upper right corner of each account. Each account has a separate column for

- The Date.
- The Item column, which can be used for any special notation.
- The Journal Reference column, abbreviated Jrnl. Ref. The use of this column will become clear when we discuss posting.
- The Debit column, with the amount debited.
- The Credit column, with the amount credited.

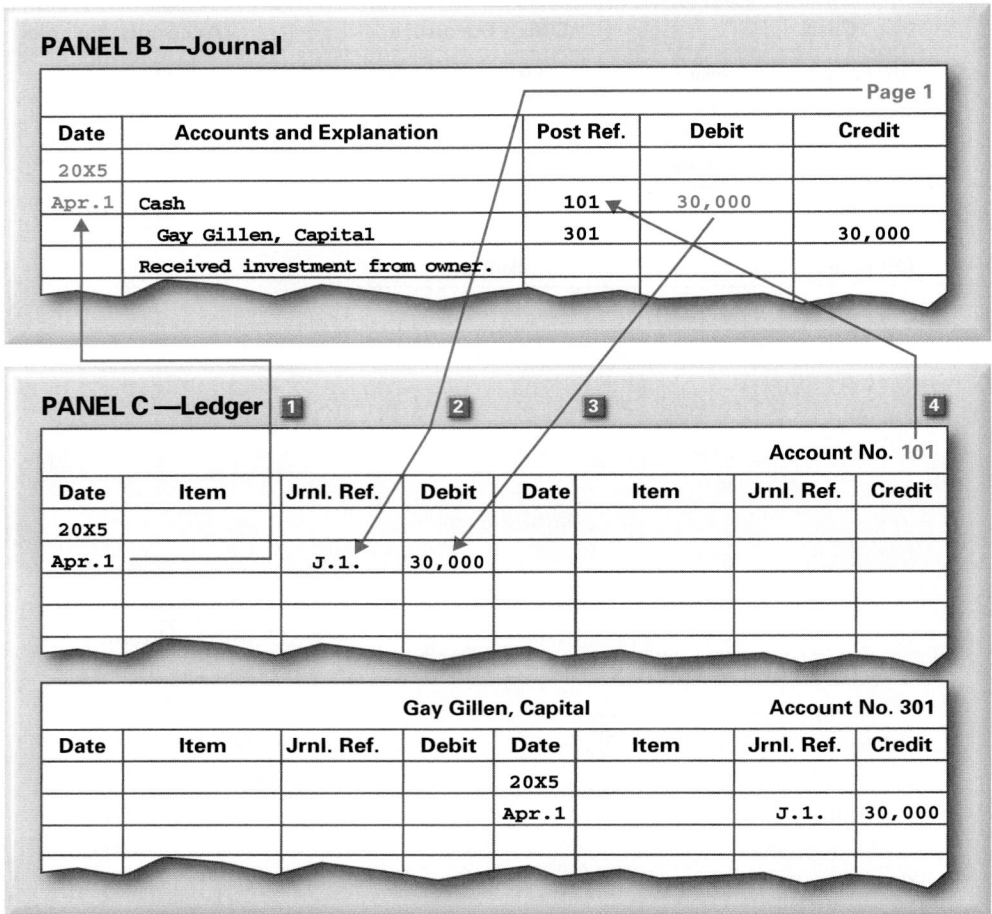

Posting from the Journal to the Ledger

Posting means copying information from the journal to the ledger. But how do we handle the details? Exhibit 2-9 illustrates the steps. Panel A describes the first transaction of the business entity, Gay Gillen eTravel; Panel B gives the journal; and Panel C shows the ledger.

The posting process includes four steps. After recording the transaction in the journal:

Arrow ①—Copy (post) the transaction **date** from the journal to the ledger.

Arrow ②—Copy (post) the journal page number from the journal to the ledger. **Jrnl. Ref.** means Journal Reference. **J.1** refers to Journal page 1. This step records where the data came from: Journal page 1.

Arrow ③—Copy (post) the dollar amount of the debit **($30,000)** from the journal as a debit to the Cash account in the ledger. Likewise, post the dollar amount of the credit (also **$30,000**) from the journal to the appropriate account in the ledger. Now the ledger accounts have their correct amounts.

Arrow ④—Copy (post) the account number **(101)** from the ledger back to the journal. This step records that the $30,000 debit to Cash has been posted to the Cash account in the ledger. Also, copy the account number **(301)** for Gay Gillen, Capital, back to the journal to show that the credit has been posted to the ledger. **Post. Ref.** is the abbreviation for Posting Reference.

After posting, you can prepare the trial balance.

The Four-Column Account: An Alternative to the T-Account

The ledger accounts illustrated in Exhibit 2-9 appear in T-account format, with the debit on the left and the credit on the right. The T-account clearly separates debits from credits and is used for teaching, where there isn't much detail. Another account format has four amount columns, as illustrated in Exhibit 2-10.

Exhibit 2-10

Account in Four-Column Format

Account Cash | Account No. 101

Date	Item	Jrnl. Ref.	Debit	Credit	Balance Debit	Balance Credit
20X5						
Apr. 1		J.1	30,000		30,000	
3		J.1		500	29,500	

The first pair of amount columns are for the amounts posted from individual entries, such as the $30,000 debit. The second pair of amount columns are for the account balance. The four-column format keeps a running balance in the account. For this reason, it is used more often in practice than the T-account format. In Exhibit 2-10, Cash has a debit balance of $30,000 after the first transaction and a debit balance of $29,500 after the second transaction.

Chart of Accounts

As you know, the ledger contains the accounts grouped under these headings:

- Balance sheet accounts: Assets, Liabilities, and Owner's Equity
- Income statement accounts: Revenues and Expenses

Organizations use a **chart of accounts** to list all their accounts along with the account numbers. Account numbers serve as posting references, illustrated by arrow 4 in Exhibit 2-9.

Chart of Accounts
List of all the accounts and their account numbers in the ledger.

Account numbers usually have two or more digits. Assets are often numbered beginning with 1, liabilities with 2, owner's equity with 3, revenues with 4, and expenses with 5. The second and third digits in an account number indicate where the account fits within the category. For example, Cash may be account number 101, the first asset account. Accounts Receivable may be account number 111, the second asset. Accounts Payable may be number 201, the first liability. All accounts are numbered by this system.

The chart of accounts for Gay Gillen eTravel appears in Exhibit 2-11. Notice the gap in account numbers between 111 and 141. Gillen may need to add another category of receivables—for example, Notes Receivable, which she might number 121. Or she may start selling some type of inventory, account number 131.

Exhibit 2-11

Chart of Accounts—Gay Gillen eTravel

Balance Sheet Accounts

Assets	Liabilities	Owner's Equity
101 Cash	201 Accounts Payable	301 Gay Gillen, Capital
111 Accounts Receivable	231 Notes Payable	311 Gay Gillen, Withdrawals
141 Office Supplies		
151 Office Furniture		
191 Land		

Income Statement Accounts (Part of Owner's Equity)

Revenues	Expenses
401 Service Revenue	501 Rent Expense
	502 Salary Expense
	503 Utilities Expense

Appendix B gives expanded charts of accounts that you will find helpful throughout this course. The first chart lists the typical accounts of a *service* proprietorship, such as Gay Gillen eTravel. The second chart is for a *merchandising* corporation, one that sells a product rather than a service. The third chart lists the accounts for a *manufacturing* company. You will use the manufacturing accounts in Chapters 19 through 26. Study the service proprietorship now, and refer to the other charts of accounts as needed later.

- ☐ The Account, the Ledger, and the Journal
- ☐ Double-Entry Accounting
- ☐ Flow of Accounting Data
- ☐ Details of Journals and Ledgers
- ■ Expanding the Accounting Equation
- ☐ Expanded Problem: Revenues and Expenses
- ☐ Quick Decision Making

Expanding the Accounting Equation: Revenues and Expenses

As we have noted, *revenues* are increases in owner's equity that result from delivering goods or services to customers. *Expenses* are decreases in equity that occur from using up assets or increasing liabilities in the course of operations. Therefore, we must expand the accounting equation. In Exhibit 2-12, revenues and expenses appear under equity because their net effect equals net income, which increases owner's equity. If expenses exceed the revenues, there is a net loss, which decreases owner's equity.

We can now express the rules of debit and credit in final form, as shown in Exhibit 2-13, Panel A. Panel B shows the *normal* balances of the five types of accounts: *Assets; Liabilities;* and *Owner's Equity* and its subparts, *Revenues and Expenses*. All of accounting is based on these five types of accounts.

Exhibit 2-12

The Accounting Equation Includes Revenues and Expenses

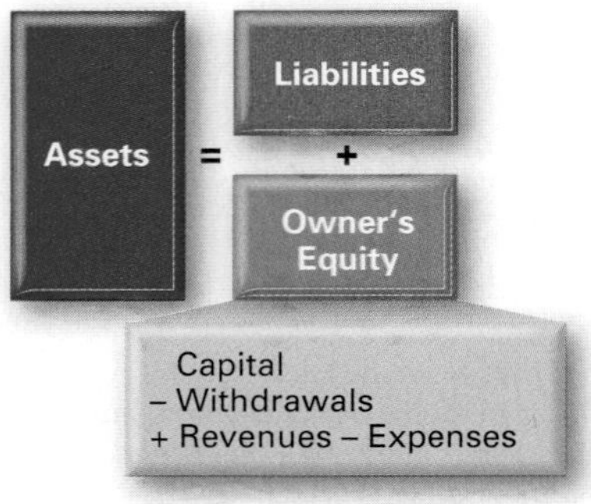

Before proceeding make sure you know the rules of debit and credit. Also make sure you know the normal balances of the five types of accounts.

Exhibit 2-13

Final Rules of Debit and Credit and the Normal Balance of Accounts

PANEL A—Rules of Debit and Credit

Assets		=	Liabilities		+	Capital	
Debit for increase	Credit for decrease		Debit for decrease	Credit for increase		Debit for decrease	Credit for increase

Withdrawals

Debit for increase	Credit for decrease

Revenues

Debit for decrease	Credit for increase

Expenses

Debit for increase	Credit for decrease

PANEL B—Normal Balances

Assets	Debit	
Liabilities		Credit
Owner's equity—overall		Credit
Capital		Credit
Withdrawals	Debit	
Revenues		Credit
Expenses	Debit	

Student Resource CD
debits and credits, expenses, revenues

Stop & Think

Compute the missing amount in each account.

1. **Cash**

Bal. 10,000	
20,000	13,000
Bal. X	

2. **Accounts Receivable**

Bal. 12,800	
45,600	X
Bal. 23,500	

3. **Annie Todd, Capital**

	Bal. X
22,000	56,000
	15,000
	Bal. 73,000

Answers:

1. The ending balance (*X*) for Cash is

$$X = \$10{,}000 + \$20{,}000 - \$13{,}000$$
$$X = \$17{,}000$$

2. We are given the beginning and ending balances. We can compute the credit entry (*X*) as follows for Accounts Receivable:

$$\$12{,}800 + \$45{,}600 - X = \$23{,}500$$
$$\$58{,}400 - \$23{,}500 = X$$
$$X = \$34{,}900$$

3. The Capital account has an ending credit balance of \$73,000. We can figure the beginning credit balance (*X*), as follows:

$$X + \$56{,}000 + \$15{,}000 - \$22{,}000 = \$73{,}000$$
$$X = \$73{,}000 - \$56{,}000 - \$15{,}000 + \$22{,}000$$
$$X = \$24{,}000$$

Expanded Problem Including Revenues and Expenses

Let's account for the revenues and expenses of the law practice of Brett Wilkinson, Attorney, for the month of July 20X7. We follow the same steps illustrated earlier in this chapter: Analyze the transaction, journalize, post to the ledger, and prepare the trial balance. To aid your learning of the journalizing process, we include the extra notation for each account debited or credited. Again, these notations are *not required*.

Student Resource CD
debits and credits, expenses, revenues, transaction analysis, trial balance

Transaction Analysis, Journalizing, and Posting

TRANSACTION 1 ANALYSIS Brett Wilkinson invested $10,000 cash in a business bank account to open his law practice. The business received the cash and gave Wilkinson owner's equity. The business's cash is increased; therefore, debit Cash. The owner's equity of the business increased, so credit Brett Wilkinson, Capital.

Journal Entry

	Debit	Credit
Cash (↑ asset; debit)	10,000	
Brett Wilkinson, Capital (↑ equity; credit)		10,000
Received investment from owner.		

Ledger Accounts

Cash			
(1)	10,000		

Brett Wilkinson, Capital			
		(1)	10,000

TRANSACTION 2 ANALYSIS Wilkinson performed service for a client and collected $3,000 cash. The asset cash is increased, so debit Cash. Revenue is increased; credit Service Revenue.

Journal Entry

	Debit	Credit
Cash (↑ asset; debit)	3,000	
Service Revenue (↑ revenue; credit)		3,000
Performed service and received cash.		

Ledger Accounts

Cash			
(1)	10,000		
(2)	3,000		

Service Revenue			
		(2)	3,000

TRANSACTION 3 ANALYSIS Wilkinson performed service for a client and billed the client for $500 on account receivable. Wilkinson expects to collect the $500 later. The asset accounts receivable is increased; therefore, debit Accounts Receivable. Service revenue is increased; credit Service Revenue. Remember that revenues are credit-balance accounts.

Journal Entry

	Debit	Credit
Accounts Receivable (↑ asset; debit)	500	
Service Revenue (↑ revenue; credit)		500
Performed service on account.		

Ledger Accounts

Accounts Receivable			
(3)	500		

Service Revenue			
		(2)	3,000
		(3)	500

TRANSACTION 4 ANALYSIS Wilkinson earned $700 service revenue by advising a client. Wilkinson received $300 cash immediately and billed the remaining $400 to the client. The assets cash and accounts receivable are increased; therefore, debit both asset accounts. Service revenue is increased; credit Service Revenue for the total amount earned.

Journal Entry

	Debit	Credit
Cash (↑ asset; debit)	300	
Accounts Receivable (↑ asset; debit)	400	
Service Revenue (↑ revenue; credit)		700
Performed service for cash and on account.		

Note: A transaction that debits or credits more than two accounts at the same time requires a *compound entry*. **As always, total debits must equal total credits.**

Ledger Accounts

Cash			
(1)	10,000		
(2)	3,000		
(4)	300		

Accounts Receivable			
(3)	500		
(4)	400		

Service Revenue			
		(2)	3,000
		(3)	500
		(4)	700

TRANSACTION 5 ANALYSIS Wilkinson paid the following cash expenses: office rent, $900; employee salary, $1,500; and utilities, $500. The asset cash is decreased; therefore, credit Cash for the sum of the three expense amounts. The expenses are increased, and each expense account is debited separately. Remember that expenses are debit-balance accounts, the opposite of revenues.

Journal Entry

Rent Expense (↑ expense; debit)	900	
Salary Expense (↑ expense; debit)	1,500	
Utilities Expense (↑ expense; debit)	500	
Cash (↓ asset; credit)		2,900
Paid cash expenses.		

Note: In practice, the business would record these three transactions separately. But we can record them together in a compound journal entry.

Ledger Accounts

Cash

(1)	10,000	(5)	2,900
(2)	3,000		
(4)	300		

Rent Expense

(5)	900		

Salary Expense

(5)	1,500		

Utilities Expense

(5)	500		

TRANSACTION 6 ANALYSIS Wilkinson received a telephone bill for $100 and will pay this expense next week. There is no cash payment now. Utilities expense is increased, so debit this expense. The liability accounts payable is increased, so credit Accounts Payable.

Journal Entry

Utilities Expense (↑ expense; debit)	100	
Accounts Payable (↑ liability; credit)		100
Received utility bill.		

Ledger Accounts

Accounts Payable

		(6)	100

Utilities Expense

(5)	500		
(6)	100		

TRANSACTION 7 ANALYSIS Wilkinson collected $200 cash from the client in transaction 3. Cash is increased, so debit Cash. Accounts receivable is decreased; credit Accounts Receivable.

Journal Entry

Cash (↑ asset; debit)	200	
Accounts Receivable (↓ asset; credit)		200
Received cash on account.		

Note: This transaction has no effect on revenue; the related revenue was recorded in transaction 3.

Ledger Accounts

Cash

(1)	10,000	(5)	2,900
(2)	3,000		
(4)	300		
(7)	200		

Accounts Receivable

(3)	500	(7)	200
(4)	400		

TRANSACTION 8 ANALYSIS Wilkinson paid the telephone bill from transaction 6. Cash is decreased, so credit Cash. Accounts payable is decreased; therefore, debit Accounts Payable.

Journal Entry

Accounts Payable (↓ liability; debit)	100	
Cash (↓ asset; credit)		100
Paid cash on account.		

Note: This transaction has no effect on expense because the related expense was recorded in transaction 6.

Ledger Accounts

Cash

(1)	10,000	(5)	2,900
(2)	3,000	(8)	100
(4)	300		
(7)	200		

Accounts Payable

(8)	100	(6)	100

✔ Starter 2-6

✔ Starter 2-7

✔ Starter 2-8

✔ Starter 2-9

Transaction 9 Analysis Wilkinson withdrew $1,000 cash for personal use. The asset cash decreased; credit Cash. The withdrawal decreased owner's equity; therefore, debit Brett Wilkinson, Withdrawals.

Journal Entry

Brett Wilkinson, Withdrawals (↓ equity; debit) . .	1,000	
Cash (↓ asset; credit)		1,000
Withdrew cash for personal use.		

Ledger Accounts

Cash

(1)	10,000	(5)	2,900
(2)	3,000	(8)	100
(4)	300	(9)	1,000
(7)	200		

Brett Wilkinson, Withdrawals

(9)	1,000		

Ledger Accounts After Posting

ASSETS

Cash

(1)	10,000	(5)	2,900
(2)	3,000	(8)	100
(4)	300	(9)	1,000
(7)	200		
Bal.	9,500		

Accounts Receivable

(3)	500	(7)	200
(4)	400		
Bal.	700		

LIABILITIES

Accounts Payable

(8)	100	(6)	100
		Bal.	0

OWNER'S EQUITY

Brett Wilkinson, Capital

		(1)	10,000
		Bal.	10,000

Brett Wilkinson, Withdrawals

(9)	1,000		
Bal.	1,000		

REVENUE

Service Revenue

		(2)	3,000
		(3)	500
		(4)	700
		Bal.	4,200

EXPENSES

Rent Expense

(5)	900		
Bal.	900		

Salary Expense

(5)	1,500		
Bal.	1,500		

Utilities Expense

(5)	500		
(6)	100		
Bal.	600		

Trial Balance

The trial balance lists the balance of each account.

✔ Starter 2-10

✔ Starter 2-11

Brett Wilkinson, Attorney
Trial Balance
July 31, 20X7

Account Title	Balance Debit	Balance Credit
Cash	$ 9,500	
Accounts receivable	700	
Accounts payable		$ 0
Brett Wilkinson, capital		10,000
Brett Wilkinson, withdrawals	1,000	
Service revenue		4,200
Rent expense	900	
Salary expense	1,500	
Utilities expense	600	
Total	$14,200	$14,200

Correcting Trial Balance Errors

In a trial balance, total debits and total credits should always be equal. If they are not, there is an error. Computerized accounting systems eliminate most errors because most software won't let you make a journal entry that doesn't balance. But computers cannot *eliminate* all errors because humans can input the wrong data.

Errors can be detected by computing the difference between total debits and total credits on the trial balance. Then perform one or more of the following actions:

1. Search the trial balance for a missing account. For example, suppose the accountant omitted Brett Wilkinson, Withdrawals, from Wilkinson's trial balance. The total amount of the debits would be $13,200 ($14,200 – $1,000). Trace each account from the ledger to the trial balance, and you will locate the missing account.
2. Divide the difference between total debits and total credits by 2. A debit treated as a credit, or vice versa, doubles the amount of error. Suppose Brett Wilkinson's accountant posted a $100 credit as a debit. Total debits contain the $100, and total credits omit the $100. The out-of-balance amount is $200. Dividing the difference by 2 identifies the $100 amount of the transaction. Then search the journal for a $100 transaction and trace to the account affected.

✔ Starter 2-12

✔ Starter 2-13

3. Divide the out-of-balance amount by 9. If the result is evenly divisible by 9, the error may be a *slide* (example: writing $300 as $30) or a *transposition* (example: treating $65 as $56). Suppose Wilkinson printed his $1,000 Withdrawal as $10,000 on the trial balance—a slide-type error. Total debits would differ from total credits by $9,000 ($10,000 – $1,000 = $9,000). Dividing $9,000 by 9 yields $1,000, the correct amount of withdrawals. Trace $1,000 through the ledger until you reach the Brett Wilkinson, Withdrawals account. You have then found the error.

A warning: Do not confuse the trial balance with the balance sheet. A trial balance is an internal document used only by company insiders. The public never sees a trial balance. Outsiders get only the company's financial statements.

The Seven Trillion Dollar Mistake

Accounting.com

"If we can send missiles to a bull's-eye at a . . . training camp in Afghanistan, we ought to be able to set up an accounting system at the Defense Department. . . . " This is what Senator Charles Grassley (R-Iowa) said in 1998 after embezzlements at U.S. military installations were allowed to occur because of weaknesses in the Pentagon's accounting system.

A year later, precision was still lacking at the Department of Defense. Pentagon money managers required almost $7 trillion of accounting adjustments to make their books balance. Each adjustment represents an accountant's correction of a discrepancy. The lesson of the $7 trillion mistake is this: Computers don't keep books; people do.

These bookkeeping errors affect all our pocketbooks. Without sound costing data, military managers simply can't make good decisions—like whether to close a base or keep it open. The public never knows the real cost of defense programs such as the missile defense shield or the cost of health care for military retirees. With more reliable accounting data, we would know how to vote on these issues.

Sources: Julia Malone, "Auditors cite failings in 11 of 24 agencies," *Atlanta Constitution*, March 31, 2000, p. A; 20. John M. Donnelly, "Pentagon's Finances Just Don't Add Up," *Los Angeles Times*, March 5, 2000, p. 8. Ralph Vartabedian, "Thefts Reveal Flawed Pentagon Contract System," *Los Angeles Times*, September 28, 1998, p. 1.

- ☐ The Account, the Ledger, and the Journal
- ☐ Double-Entry Accounting
- ☐ Flow of Accounting Data
- ☐ Details of Journals and Ledgers
- ☐ Expanding the Accounting Equation
- ☐ Expanded Problem: Revenues and Expenses
- ■ Quick Decision Making

Student Resource CD
transaction analysis

6 *Analyze transactions without a journal*

✔ **Starter 2-14**

Quick Decision Making

Often people must make quick decisions. Sometimes they can't take the time to follow all the steps in an accounting system. For example, suppose the **Frito-Lay** route manager needs more storage space to meet customer demand. He can purchase a small building for $70,000, or he can rent a building at an annual cost of $10,000. Whether to buy or rent depends on the financial effects of the two options.

The route manager doesn't need a full-blown accounting system to make this decision. If he knows a little accounting, he can figure out how the two options will affect his business. The following accounts summarize the effects of renting versus buying the building.

RENT THE BUILDING

Cash		Rent Expense	
	10,000	10,000	

BUY THE BUILDING

Cash		Building	
	70,000	70,000	

The accounts make it clear that buying will require more cash. But buying the building adds an asset to the business. This may motivate the route manager to borrow cash and buy the building. A low cash balance may force the manager to rent.

Companies do not actually keep their records in this short-cut fashion. But a decision maker who needs information immediately can quickly analyze the effects of a transaction on the financial statements. Simply record the transactions directly in the T-accounts.

Now you have seen how to account for transactions. Solidify your understanding of the accounting process by reviewing the Decision Guidelines.

Decision Guidelines

ANALYZING AND RECORDING TRANSACTIONS

Suppose the Frito-Lay route manager in the chapter-opening story stocks the shelves of 20 stores and earns service revenue. He opens a small office, hires a helper, and has a few other expenses. QuickBooks software is used for the accounting.

The route manager offers you a job as accountant for this small business. The pay is good. Can you answer the manager's questions, which are outlined in the Decision Guidelines? If so, you may get the job.

Decision	Guidelines
• Has a transaction occurred?	If the event affects the entity's financial position and can be reliably recorded—*Yes* If either condition is absent—*No*
• Where to record the transaction?	In the *journal,* the chronological record of transactions
• What to record for each transaction?	Increases and/or decreases in all the accounts affected by the transaction
• How to record an increase/decrease in a (an)	Rules of debit and credit:

	Increase	***Decrease***
Asset	Debit	Credit
Liability	Credit	Debit
Owner's Equity	Credit	Debit
Revenue	Credit	Debit
Expense	Debit	Credit

Decision Guidelines *(continued)*

Decision	Guidelines
• Where to store all the information for each account?	In the *ledger*, the record holding all the accounts
• Where to list all the accounts and their balances?	In the *trial balance*
• Where to report the results of operations?	In the income statement (Revenues – Expenses = Net income or Net loss)
• Where to report financial position?	In the balance sheet (Assets = Liabilities + Owner's equity)

Excel Application Exercise

Goal: Create an Excel spreadsheet to calculate total assets, total liabilities, total owner's equity, and net income (or loss) from the Brett Wilkinson, Attorney trial balance found in your text on page 64.

Scenario: In your interview with Wilkinson, he asks you to prepare a trial balance for his law practice. Your task is to create a simple spreadsheet to calculate total assets, total liabilities, total owner's equity, and net income (or loss) from a trial balance. When finished, answer these questions:

1. What are Brett Wilkinson's total assets?
2. What are Brett Wilkinson's total liabilities?
3. What is Brett Wilkinson's total owner's equity?
4. What is Brett Wilkinson's net income (or net loss) for the period?

Step-by-Step:

1. Open a new Excel spreadsheet.
2. Create a bold-faced heading for your spreadsheet that contains the following:
   - **a.** Chapter 2 Excel Application Exercise
   - **b.** Brett Wilkinson, Attorney
   - **c.** Trial Balance
   - **d.** July 31, 20X7
3. Two rows down from your worksheet heading, copy the heading format of the Brett Wilkinson trial balance. Make "Account Title" your first column (sized appropriately). Make two separate columns for the "Debit" and "Credit" balances.
4. Enter the account titles (without periods) and data from the trial balance under the correct headings. Create formulas for the column totals for the debit and credit balances. Format the data in each column.
5. Beginning two rows under the trial balance in the first column, enter the following descriptions:
   - **a.** Total Assets
   - **b.** Total Liabilities
   - **c.** Total Owner's Equity
   - **d.** Total Net Income (Loss)
6. In column two, across from each description, enter the formula to calculate the item.
7. Save your work to disk, and print a copy for your files.

END-OF-CHAPTER *Summary Problem*

The trial balance of Tomassini Computer Service Center on March 1, 20X2, lists the entity's assets, liabilities, and owner's equity on that date.

	Balance	
Account Title	**Debit**	**Credit**
Cash	$26,000	
Accounts receivable	4,500	
Accounts payable		$ 2,000
Larry Tomassini, capital		28,500
Total	$30,500	$30,500

A+ TIPS
CHECK YOUR RESOURCES

During March, the business engaged in the following transactions:

a. Borrowed $45,000 from the bank and signed a note payable in the name of the business.
b. Paid cash of $40,000 to a real estate company to acquire land.
c. Performed service for a customer and received cash of $5,000.
d. Purchased supplies on credit, $300.
e. Performed customer service and earned revenue on account, $2,600.
f. Paid $1,200 on account.
g. Paid the following cash expenses: salaries, $3,000; rent, $1,500; and interest, $400.
h. Received $3,100 on account.
i. Received a $200 utility bill that will be paid next week.
j. Withdrew $1,800 for personal use.

Required

1. Open the following accounts, with the balances indicated, in the ledger of Tomassini Computer Service Center. Use the T-account format.
   - Assets—Cash, $26,000; Accounts Receivable, $4,500; Supplies, no balance; Land, no balance
   - Liabilities—Accounts Payable, $2,000; Note Payable, no balance
   - Owner's Equity—Larry Tomassini, Capital, $28,500; Larry Tomassini, Withdrawals, no balance
   - Revenues—Service Revenue, no balance
   - Expenses—(none have balances) Salary Expense, Rent Expense, Utilities Expense, Interest Expense
2. Journalize each transaction. Key journal entries by transaction letter.
3. Post to the ledger.
4. Prepare the trial balance of Tomassini Computer Service Center at March 31, 20X2.

Solution

Requirement 1

ASSETS

Cash

Bal. 26,000	

Accounts Receivable

Bal. 4,500	

Supplies

Land

LIABILITIES

Accounts Payable

	Bal. 2,000

Note Payable

OWNER'S EQUITY

Larry Tomassini, Capital

	Bal. 28,500

Larry Tomassini, Withdrawals

REVENUE

Service Revenue

EXPENSES

Salary Expense

Rent Expense

Utilities Expense

Interest Expense

Requirement 2

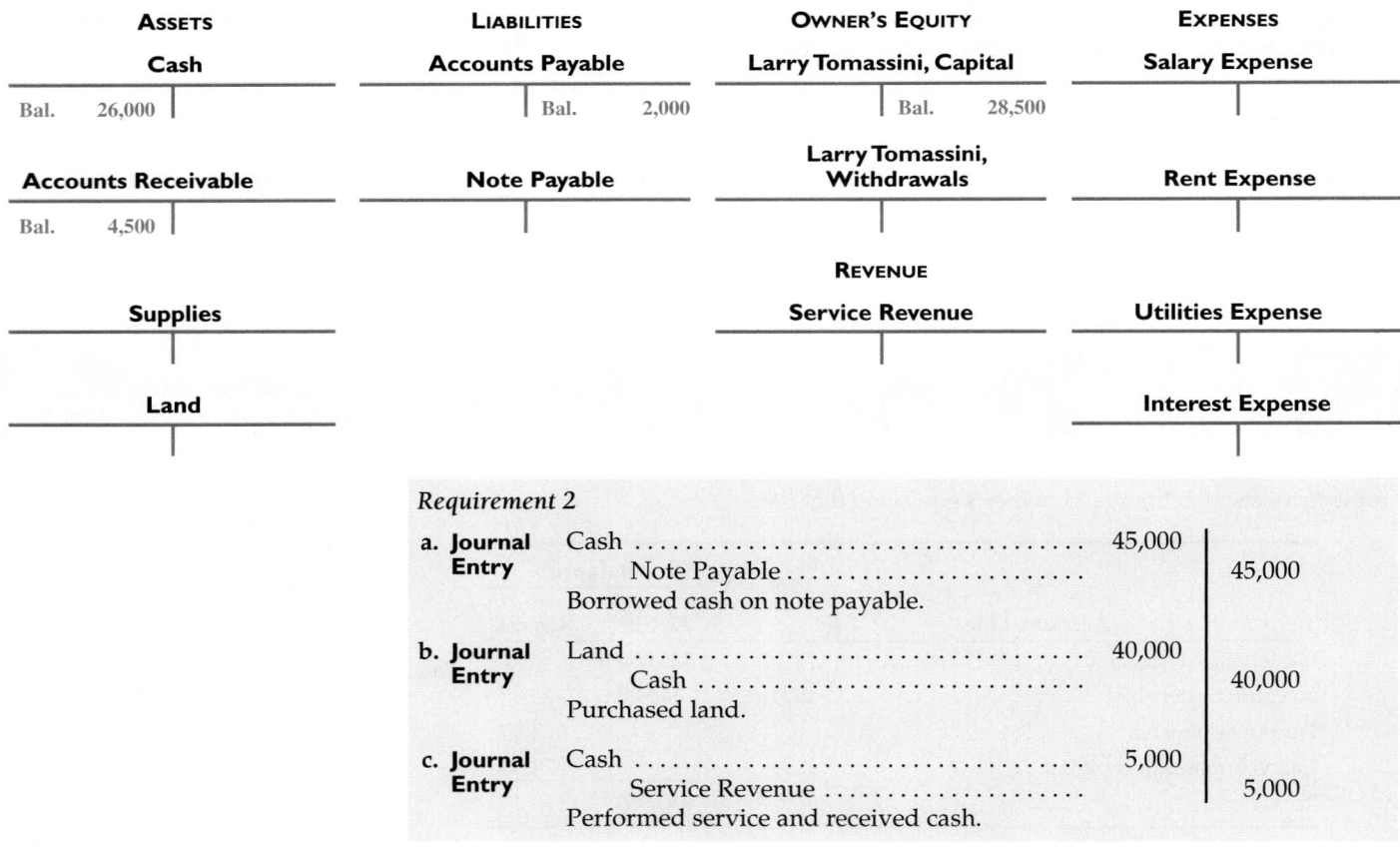

a. Journal Entry	Cash	45,000	
	Note Payable		45,000
	Borrowed cash on note payable.		
b. Journal Entry	Land	40,000	
	Cash		40,000
	Purchased land.		
c. Journal Entry	Cash	5,000	
	Service Revenue		5,000
	Performed service and received cash.		

d. Journal Entry	Supplies	300	
	Accounts Payable		300
	Purchased supplies on account.		
e. Journal Entry	Accounts Receivable	2,600	
	Service Revenue		2,600
	Performed service on account.		
f. Journal Entry	Accounts Payable	1,200	
	Cash		1,200
	Paid on account.		
g. Journal Entry	Salary Expense	3,000	
	Rent Expense	1,500	
	Interest Expense	400	
	Cash		4,900
	Paid expenses.		
h. Journal Entry	Cash	3,100	
	Accounts Receivable		3,100
	Received cash on account.		
i. Journal Entry	Utilities Expense	200	
	Accounts Payable		200
	Received utility bill.		
j. Journal Entry	Larry Tomassini, Withdrawals	1,800	
	Cash		1,800
	Owner withdrawal.		

Requirement 3

ASSETS

Cash

Bal.	26,000	(b)	40,000
(a)	45,000	(f)	1,200
(c)	5,000	(g)	4,900
(h)	3,100	(j)	1,800
Bal.	31,200		

Accounts Receivable

Bal.	4,500	(h)	3,100
(e)	2,600		
Bal.	4,000		

Supplies

(d)	300		
Bal.	300		

Land

(b)	40,000		
Bal.	40,000		

LIABILITIES

Accounts Payable

(f)	1,200	Bal.	2,000
		(d)	300
		(i)	200
		Bal.	1,300

Note Payable

		(a)	45,000
		Bal.	45,000

OWNER'S EQUITY

Larry Tomassini, Capital

		Bal.	28,500

Larry Tomassini, Withdrawals

(j)	1,800		
Bal.	1,800		

REVENUE

Service Revenue

		(c)	5,000
		(e)	2,600
		Bal.	7,600

EXPENSES

Salary Expense

(g)	3,000		
Bal.	3,000		

Rent Expense

(g)	1,500		
Bal.	1,500		

Interest Expense

(g)	400		
Bal.	400		

Utilities Expense

(i)	200		
Bal.	200		

Requirement 4

Tomassini Computer Service Center

Trial Balance
March 31, 20X2

Account Title	Balance Debit	Balance Credit
Cash	$31,200	
Accounts receivable	4,000	
Supplies	300	
Land	40,000	
Accounts payable		$ 1,300
Note payable		45,000
Larry Tomassini, capital		28,500
Larry Tomassini, withdrawals	1,800	
Service revenue		7,600
Salary expense	3,000	
Rent expense	1,500	
Interest expense	400	
Utilities expense	200	
Total	$82,400	$82,400

REVIEW *Recording Business Transactions*

Quick Check

1. Which sequence of actions correctly summarizes the accounting process?
   a. Prepare a trial balance, journalize transactions, post to the accounts
   b. Post to the accounts, journalize transactions, prepare a trial balance
   c. Journalize transactions, post to the accounts, prepare a trial balance
   d. Journalize transactions, prepare a trial balance, post to the accounts
2. The left side of an account is used to record
   a. Debits **c.** Debit or credit, depending on the type of account
   b. Credits **d.** Increases
3. Suppose a **Target** store has cash of $50,000, receivables of $60,000, and furniture and fixtures totaling $200,000. The store owes $80,000 on account and has a $100,000 note payable. How much is the store's owner equity?
   a. $20,000 **c.** $180,000
   b. $310,000 **d.** $130,000
4. A Target store purchased supplies of $1,000 on account. The journal entry to record this transaction is

a.	Inventory	1,000	
	Accounts Payable		1,000
b.	Accounts Payable	1,000	
	Supplies		1,000
c.	Supplies	1,000	
	Accounts Payable		1,000
d.	Supplies	1,000	
	Accounts Receivable		1,000

5. Posting a $1,000 purchase of supplies on account appears as follows:

a.

Supplies	
1,000	

Accounts Receivable	
	1,000

c.

Supplies	
	1,000

Accounts Payable	
1,000	

b.

Supplies	
1,000	

Accounts Payable	
	1,000

d.

Cash	
	1,000

Supplies	
1,000	

6. Which journal entry records Target's payment for the supplies purchased in transaction 4?

a.	Accounts Payable	1,000	
	Accounts Receivable		1,000
b.	Accounts Payable	1,000	
	Cash		1,000
c.	Cash	1,000	
	Accounts Payable		1,000
d.	Supplies	1,000	
	Cash		1,000

7. A Target store paid $500 for supplies and purchased additional supplies on account for $700. The store paid $300 of the accounts payable. What is the balance in the Supplies account?
   a. $500
   b. $900
   c. $1,200
   d. $1,500

8. **Kinko's Copies** recorded a cash collection on account by debiting Cash and crediting Accounts Payable. What will the trial balance show for this error?
   a. Too much for liabilities
   b. Too much for assets
   c. The trial balance will not balance
   d. Both a and b

9. Brett Wilkinson, Attorney, began the year with total assets of $120,000, liabilities of $70,000, and owner's equity of $50,000. During the year he earned revenue of $110,000 and paid expenses of $30,000. He also invested an additional $20,000 in the business and withdrew $60,000 for living expenses. How much is the law firm's equity at year-end?
   a. $90,000
   b. $120,000
   c. $130,000
   d. $160,000

10. How would Brett Wilkinson record his expenses for the year in the preceding question?

a.	Expenses	30,000	
	Cash		30,000
b.	Expenses	30,000	
	Accounts Payable		30,000
c.	Cash	30,000	
	Expenses		30,000
d.	Accounts Payable	30,000	
	Cash		30,000

Accounting Vocabulary

account (p. 44)
chart of accounts (p. 59)
credit (p. 47)
debit (p. 47)
journal (p. 45)
ledger (p. 45)
normal balance (p. 54)
posting (p. 51)
trial balance (p. 45)

ASSESS Your Progress

A+ online homework

See *www.prenhall.com/horngren* for selected Starters, Exercises, and Problems.

Starters

Using accounting terms
(Obj. 1)

S2-1 Review basic accounting definitions by completing the following crossword puzzle.

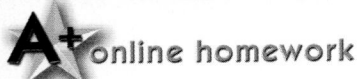

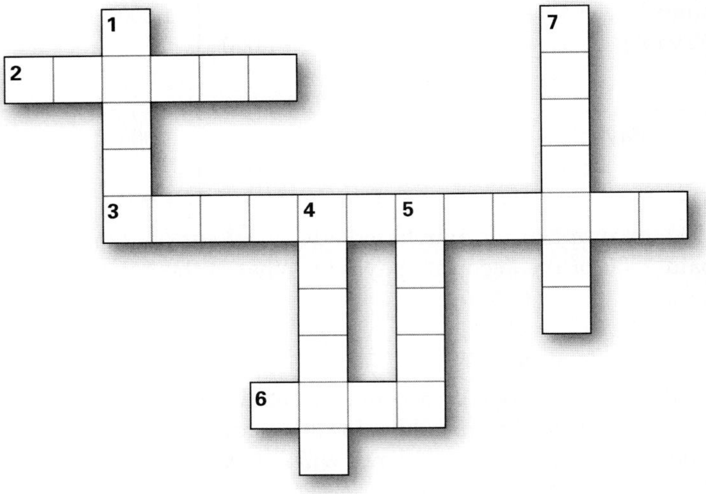

Down:
1. Left side of an account
4. Record holding the grouping of accounts
5. An economic resource
7. Record of transactions

Across:
2. Records an increase in a liability
3. List of accounts with their balances
6. Another word for liability

Using accounting terms
(Obj. 1)

S2-2 Tighten your grip on accounting by filling in the blanks to review some key definitions.

Lynn Bratton is describing the accounting process for a friend who is a philosophy major. Lynn states, "The basic summary device in accounting is the __________. The left side is called the __________ side, and the right side is called the __________ side. We record transactions first in a __________. Then we post (copy the data) to the __________. It is helpful to list all the accounts with their balances on a __________ __________."

Using accounting terms
(Obj. 1)

S2-3 Accounting has its own vocabulary and basic relationships. Match the accounting terms at left with the corresponding definitions at right.

______	1. Posting	A. Record of transactions
______	2. Normal balance	B. Always an asset
______	3. Payable	C. Left side of an account
______	4. Journal	D. Side of an account where increases are recorded
______	5. Receivable	E. Copying data from the journal to the ledger
______	6. Capital	F. Using up assets in the course of operating a business
______	7. Debit	G. Always a liability
______	8. Expense	H. Revenues – Expenses
______	9. Net income	I. Grouping of accounts
______	10. Ledger	J. Owner's equity in the business

Explaining the rules of debit and credit
(Obj. 2)

S2-4 Art Sudan is tutoring Nick Mull, who is taking introductory accounting. Art explains to Nick that *debits* are used to record increases in accounts and *credits* record decreases. Nick is confused and seeks your advice.

- When are credits increases? When are credits decreases?
- When are debits increases? When are debits decreases?

Exhibit 2-13, page 61, gives the rules of debit and credit.

S2-5 The accounting records of all businesses include three basic categories of accounts: assets, liabilities, and owner's equity. In turn, owner's equity holds the following categories: capital, withdrawals, revenues, and expenses. Identify which categories of all the accounts—including the subparts of owner's equity—have a normal debit balance and which categories of accounts have a normal credit balance. Exhibit 2-13, Panel B, on page 62, gives the normal balance in each category of account.

Normal account balances
(Obj. 2)

S2-6 Liana Garcia opened a medical practice in San Diego. Record the following transactions in the journal of Liana Garcia, M.D. Include an explanation with each journal entry.

Recording transactions
(Obj. 3)

September 1	Garcia invested $30,000 cash in a business bank account to start her medical practice. The business received the cash and gave Garcia owner's equity in the business.
2	Purchased medical supplies on account, $10,000.
2	Paid monthly office rent of $4,000.
3	Recorded $5,000 revenue for service rendered to patients. Received cash of $2,000 and sent bills to patients for the remainder.

S2-7 After operating for a month, Liana Garcia, M.D., completed the following transactions during the latter part of October:

Recording transactions
(Obj. 3)

October 15	Borrowed $50,000 from the bank, signing a note payable.
22	Performed service for patients on account, $3,600.
30	Received cash on account from patients, $2,000.
31	Received a utility bill, $200, which will be paid during November.
31	Paid monthly salary to nurse, $3,000.
31	Paid interest expense of $200 on the bank loan.

Journalize the transactions of Liana Garcia, M.D. Include an explanation with each journal entry.

S2-8 Stuart Deng purchased supplies on account for $5,000. Two weeks later, Deng paid half on account.

Journalizing transactions; posting
(Obj. 3, 4)

1. Journalize the two transactions for Stuart Deng. Include an explanation for each transaction.
2. Open the Accounts Payable T-account and post to Accounts Payable. Compute the balance, and denote it as *Bal.*

S2-9 Lance Alworth performed legal service for a client who could not pay immediately. Alworth expected to collect the $6,000 the following month. Later, he received $3,500 cash from the client.

Journalizing transactions; posting
(Obj. 3, 4)

1. Record the two transactions for Lance Alworth, Attorney. Include an explanation for each transaction.
2. Open these accounts: Cash; Accounts Receivable; Service Revenue. Post to all three accounts. Compute each account's balance, and denote as *Bal.*
3. Answer these questions based on your analysis:
   a. How much did Alworth earn? Which account shows this amount?
   b. How much in total assets did Alworth acquire as a result of the two transactions? Show the amount of each asset.

Note: Starter 2-10 should be used in connection with Starter 2-6.

Posting; preparing a trial balance
(Obj. 4, 5)

S2-10 Use the September transaction data for Liana Garcia, M.D., given in Starter 2-6.

1. Open the following T-accounts: Cash; Accounts Receivable; Medical Supplies; Accounts Payable; Liana Garcia, Capital; Service Revenue; Rent Expense.
2. After making the journal entries in Starter 2-6, post to the ledger. No dates or posting references are required. Compute the balance of each account, and denote it as *Bal.*
3. Prepare the trial balance, complete with a proper heading, at September 3, 20X8. Use the trial balance on page 64 as a guide.

Preparing a trial balance
(Obj. 5)

S2-11 Interfax Corporation reported the following summarized data at December 31, 20X3. Accounts appear in no particular order; dollar amounts are in millions.

Revenues	$29	Other liabilities	$19
Other assets	40	Cash	12
Accounts payable	1	Expenses	22
Capital	25		

Prepare the trial balance of Interfax Corporation at December 31, 20X3. List the accounts in proper order, as on page 64.

Correcting a trial balance
(Obj. 5)

S2-12 Brett Wilkinson, Attorney, prepared his trial balance on page 64. Suppose Wilkinson made an error: He erroneously listed his capital balance of $10,000 as a debit rather than a credit.

Compute the incorrect trial balance totals for debits and credits. Then refer to the discussion of correcting errors on page 65, and show how to correct this error.

Correcting a trial balance
(Obj. 5)

S2-13 Return to Brett Wilkinson's trial balance on page 64. Assume that Wilkinson accidentally listed his withdrawals as $100 instead of the correct amount of $1,000. Compute the incorrect trial balance totals for debits and credits. Then show how to correct this error, which is called a *slide*.

Analyzing transactions without a journal
(Obj. 6)

S2-14 Jane Avery established Bodyfit, a health club, with an initial cash investment of $100,000. The business immediately purchased equipment on a note payable for $80,000. Avery needs to know her account balances immediately and doesn't have time to journalize the transactions.

1. Open the following T-accounts on the books of Bodyfit. Cash; Equipment; Note Payable; Jane Avery, Capital.
2. Record the first two transactions directly in the T-accounts without using a journal.
3. Compute the balance in each account and show that total debits equal total credits.

A+ online homework

Exercises

Using accounting vocabulary
(Obj. 1)

E2-1 Sharpen your use of accounting terms by working this crossword puzzle.

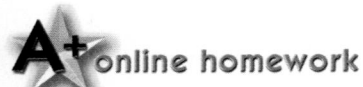

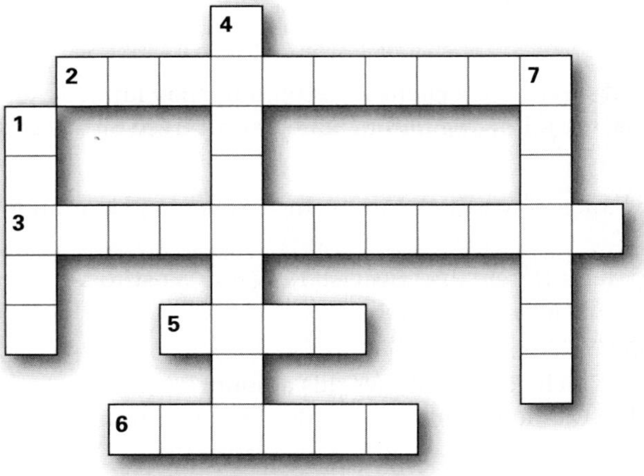

Down:

1. Records a decrease in a liability
4. Bottom line of an income statement
7. Revenue – net income = ________

Across:

2. Amount collectible from a customer
3. Statement of financial position
5. Copy data from the journal to the ledger
6. Records a decrease in an asset

Using debits and credits with the accounting equation
(Obj. 1, 2)

E2-2 → *Link Back to Chapter 1 (Accounting Equation).* **Coca-Cola** is famous worldwide for soft drinks. At the end of 20X1, Coca-Cola had total assets of $22 billion and liabilities totaling $11 billion.

Required

1. Write the company's accounting equation, and label each amount as a debit or a credit.
2. Coca-Cola's total revenues for 20X1 were $20 billion, and total expenses for the year were $16 billion. How much was Coca-Cola's net income (or net loss) for 20X1? Write the equation to compute Coca-Cola's net income, and indicate which element is a debit and which is a credit. Does net income represent a net debit or a net credit? Does net loss represent a net debit or a net credit? Review Exhibit 1-8, page 21, if needed.
3. During 20X1, the owners of Coca-Cola withdrew $2 billion in the form of dividends (same as owner Withdrawals). Did the dividends represent a debit or a credit?

Analyzing and journalizing transactions
(Obj. 2, 3)

E2-3 Record the following transactions in the journal of Elzinga Enterprises. Explanations are not required. Follow the pattern given for the December 1 transaction.

Dec. 1	Paid interest expense of $500.		
1	Interest Expense (↑ expense; debit)	500	
	Cash (↓ asset; credit)		500
5	Purchased office furniture on account, $800.		
10	Performed service on account for a customer, $1,600.		
12	Borrowed $7,000 cash, signing a note payable.		
19	Sold for $29,000 land that had cost this same amount.		
21	Purchased building for $140,000; signed a note payable.		
27	Paid the liability from December 5.		

Applying the rules of debit and credit; posting
(Obj. 2, 4)

Student ResourceCD
General Ledger, Peachtree, QuickBooks

E2-4 This exercise should be used only in connection with Exercise 2-3. Refer to the transactions of Elzinga Enterprises in Exercise 2-3.

Required

1. Open the following T-accounts with their December 1 balances: Cash, debit balance $3,000; Land, debit balance $29,000; Ken Elzinga, Capital, credit balance $32,000.
2. Post the transactions of Exercise 2-3 to the T-accounts affected. Use the dates as posting references. Start with December 1.
3. Compute the December 31 balance for each account, and prove that total debits equal total credits.

Journalizing transactions
(Obj. 3)

Student ResourceCD
GL, PT, QB

E2-5 Westview Landscaping completed the following transactions during March 20X8, its first month of operations:

Mar. 1	Ray Hawk invested $70,000 of cash to start the business.
2	Purchased supplies of $200 on account.
4	Paid $60,000 cash for a building to use for storage.
6	Performed service for customers and received cash, $3,000.
9	Paid $100 on accounts payable.
17	Performed service for customers on account, $1,600.
23	Received $1,200 cash from a customer on account.
31	Paid the following expenses: salary, $1,200; rent, $500.

Required

Record the preceding transactions in the journal of Westview Landscaping. Key transactions by date and include an explanation for each entry, as illustrated in the chapter. Use the following accounts: Cash; Accounts Receivable; Supplies; Building; Accounts Payable; Ray Hawk, Capital; Service Revenue; Salary Expense; Rent Expense.

Posting to the ledger and preparing a trial balance
(Obj. 4, 5)

E2-6 Refer to Exercise 2-5 for the transactions of Westview Landscaping.

Required

1. After journalizing the transactions of Exercise 2-5, post to the ledger, using T-account format. Key transactions by date. Date the ending balance of each account Mar. 31.
2. Prepare the trial balance of Westview Landscaping at March 31, 20X8.

Describing transactions and posting
(Obj. 2, 3)

E2-7 The journal of Vogue Career Services includes the following entries for May 20X6.

Required

1. Describe each transaction.
2. Set up the ledger using the following account numbers: Cash, 110; Accounts Receivable, 120; Supplies, 130; Accounts Payable, 210; Note Payable, 230; Laura Edwards, Capital, 310; Service Revenue, 410; Rent Expense, 510; Advertising Expense, 520; Utilities Expense, 530.
3. Post to the accounts. Write dates and journal references in the accounts, as illustrated in Exhibit 2-9, page 58. Compute the balance of each account after posting.
4. Prepare the trial balance of Vogue Career Services at May 31, 20X6.

Journal				Page 5
Date	**Accounts and Explanation**	**Post Ref.**	**Debit**	**Credit**
May 2	Cash		20,000	
	Laura Edwards, Capital			20,000
5	Cash		25,000	
	Note Payable			25,000
9	Supplies			200
	Accounts Payable			200
11	Accounts Receivable		2,600	
	Service Revenue			2,600
14	Rent Expense		3,200	
	Cash			3,200
22	Accounts Payable		300	
	Cash			300
25	Advertising Expense		400	
	Cash			400
27	Cash		1,400	
	Accounts Receivable			1,400
31	Utilities Expense		100	
	Accounts Payable			100

Journalizing transactions
(Obj. 3)

E2-8 The first five transactions of The Mane Event, a styling salon, have been posted to the accounts as follows:

Cash

(1)	22,000	(3)	40,000
(4)	37,000	(5)	6,000

Supplies

(2)	400		

Equipment

(5)	6,000		

Building

(3)	40,000		

Accounts Payable

		(2)	400

Note Payable

		(4)	37,000

Liz Adeva, Capital

		(1)	22,000

Required

Prepare the journal entries that served as the sources for the five transactions. Include an explanation for each entry as illustrated in the chapter.

Preparing a trial balance **(Obj. 5)**

E2-9 Prepare the trial balance of The Mane Event at October 31, 20X4, using the account data from Exercise 2-8.

Preparing a trial balance **(Obj. 5)**

Student ResourceCD spreadsheet

E2-10 The accounts of SW Bell Advertising follow with their normal balances at December 31, 20X4. The accounts are listed in no particular order.

Account	Balance
S. W. Bell, capital	$ 48,800
Insurance expense	700
Accounts payable	4,300
Service revenue	86,000
Land	29,000
Supplies expense	300
Cash	5,000
Salary expense	6,000
Building	125,000
Rent expense	2,000
S. W. Bell, withdrawals	6,000
Utilities expense	400
Accounts receivable	9,500
Note payable	45,000
Supplies	200

Required

Prepare the company's trial balance at December 31, 20X4, listing accounts in proper sequence, as illustrated in the chapter. For example, Supplies comes before Building and Land. List the largest expense first, the second-largest expense next, and so on.

Correcting errors in a trial balance **(Obj. 5)**

E2-11 The trial balance of Harvey Spark, M.D., at March 31, 20X9, does not balance:

Cash	$ 3,000	
Accounts receivable	2,000	
Supplies	600	
Land	66,000	
Accounts payable		$21,500
Harvey Spark, capital		41,600
Service revenue		9,700
Salary expense	1,700	
Rent expense	800	
Utilities expense	300	
Total	$74,400	$72,800

Investigation of the accounting records reveals that the bookkeeper

a. Recorded a $400 cash revenue transaction by debiting Accounts Receivable. The credit entry was correct.
b. Posted a $1,000 credit to Accounts Payable as $100.
c. Did not record utilities expense or the related account payable in the amount of $200.
d. Understated Harvey Spark, Capital, by $700.

Required

Prepare the correct trial balance at March 31, complete with a heading; journal entries are not required.

Recording transactions without a journal
(Obj. 6)

E2-12 Open the following T-accounts of Mike Reitmeier, CPA: Cash; Accounts Receivable; Office Supplies; Office Furniture; Accounts Payable; Mike Reitmeier, Capital; Mike Reitmeier, Withdrawals; Service Revenue; Salary Expense; Rent Expense.

Record the following transactions directly in the T-accounts without using a journal. Use the letters to identify the transactions. Compute the balance of each account.

a. Reitmeier opened an accounting firm by investing $15,000 cash and office furniture valued at $5,400.
b. Paid monthly rent of $1,500.
c. Purchased office supplies on account, $700.
d. Paid employee's salary, $1,800.
e. Paid $400 of the account payable created in transaction (c).
f. Performed accounting service on account, $1,600.
g. Withdrew $7,000 for personal use.

Preparing a trial balance
(Obj. 5)

E2-13 After recording the transactions in Exercise 2-12, prepare the trial balance of Mike Reitmeier, CPA, at May 31, 20X7.

Student Resource CD
GL, PT, QB
Analyzing transactions without a journal
(Obj. 6)

E2-14 Northern Starr Telecom began when Suzanne Starr invested $50,000 cash in a business bank account. During the first week, the business purchased supplies on credit for $8,000 and paid $12,000 cash for equipment. Starr later paid $5,000 on account.

Required

1. Open the following T-accounts: Cash; Supplies; Equipment; Accounts Payable; Suzanne Starr, Capital.
2. Record Starr's four transactions directly in the T-accounts without using a journal.
3. Compute the balance in each account, and show that total debits equal total credits. The T-accounts on page 54 provide a guide.

Analyzing accounting errors
(Obj. 2, 3, 4, 5)

E2-15 Kamran Saddiqi has trouble keeping his debits and credits equal. During a recent month, he made the following errors:

a. In journalizing a receipt of cash for service revenue, Saddiqi debited Cash for $80 instead of the correct amount of $800. Saddiqi credited Service Revenue for $80, the incorrect amount.
b. Saddiqi recorded a $120 purchase of supplies on account by debiting Supplies and crediting Accounts Payable for $210.
c. In preparing the trial balance, Saddiqi omitted a $50,000 note payable.
d. Saddiqi posted a $700 utility expense as $70. The credit posting to Cash was correct.
e. In recording a $400 payment on account, Saddiqi debited Supplies and credited Accounts Payable.

Required

1. For each of these errors, state whether total debits equal total credits on the trial balance.
2. Identify each account with an incorrect balance, and indicate the amount and direction of the error (such as "Accounts Receivable $500 too high").

Computing financial statement amounts without a journal
(Obj. 7)

E2-16 The owner of Specialty Medical Services needs to compute the following summary information from the accounting records:

a. Net income for the month of March
b. Total cash paid during March
c. Cash collections from customers during March
d. Cash paid on a note payable during March

The quickest way to compute these amounts is to analyze the following accounts:

Account	Balance Feb. 28	Balance Mar. 31	Additional Information for the Month of March
a. Owner, Capital	$ 9,000	$22,000	Withdrawals, $7,000
b. Cash................	7,000	2,000	Cash receipts, $70,000
c. Accounts Receivable ..	24,000	26,000	Revenues on account, $90,000
d. Note Payable	11,000	20,000	New borrowing on a note payable, $15,500

The net income for March can be computed as follows:

Owner, Capital

		Feb. 28 Bal.	**9,000**
March Withdrawals	**7,000**	March Net Income	X = $20,000
		March 31 Bal.	22,000

Use a similar approach to compute the other three items.

Continuing Exercise

Exercise 2-17 is the first exercise in a sequence that begins an accounting cycle. The cycle is completed in Chapter 5.

E2-17 Marsha Walker completed these transactions during the first half of December:

Recording transactions and preparing a trial balance
(Obj. 2, 3, 4, 5)

Student Resource CD
GL, PT, QB

Dec.	2	Invested $14,000 to start a consulting practice titled Marsha Walker, Consultant.
	2	Paid monthly office rent, $500.
	3	Paid cash for a Dell computer, $2,000. The computer is expected to remain in service for five years.
	4	Purchased office furniture on account, $3,600. The furniture should last for five years.
	5	Purchased supplies on account, $300.
	9	Performed consulting service for a client on account, $1,700.
	12	Paid utility expenses, $200.
	18	Performed service for a client and received cash for the full amount of $800.

Required

1. Open T-accounts in the ledger: Cash; Accounts Receivable; Supplies; Equipment; Furniture; Accounts Payable; Marsha Walker, Capital; Marsha Walker, Withdrawals; Service Revenue; Rent Expense; Utilities Expense; and Salary Expense.
2. Journalize the transactions. Explanations are not required.
3. Post to the T-accounts. Key all items by date, and denote an account balance as *Bal.* Formal posting references are not required.
4. Prepare a trial balance at December 18. In the Continuing Exercise of Chapter 3, we will add transactions for the remainder of December and prepare a trial balance at December 31.

Problems

(Group A)

A+ online homework

P2-1A → *Link Back to Chapter 1 (Balance Sheet, Income Statement).* Avery Patel, owner of Hillsboro Emergency Service, is selling the business. He offers the following trial balance to prospective buyers. Your best friend is considering buying the company. He seeks your advice in interpreting this information.

Using accounting terms and analyzing a trial balance
(Obj. 1)

Hillsboro Emergency Service

Trial Balance
December 31, 20X4

Cash	$ 7,000	
Accounts receivable	6,000	
Prepaid expenses	4,000	
Automobiles	251,000	
Accounts payable		$ 31,000
Note payable		180,000
Avery Patel, capital		33,000
Avery Patel, withdrawals	21,000	
Service revenue		112,000
Wage expense	38,000	
Fuel expense	14,000	
Rent expense	8,000	
Supplies expense	7,000	
Total	$356,000	$356,000

Required

Help your friend decide whether to buy Hillsboro Emergency Service by answering the following questions.

1. How much are the firm's total assets? total liabilities? net income or net loss?
2. Suppose Hillsboro earned all the service revenue on account. Make a single journal entry to record the revenue, set up the T-accounts affected, and post to the accounts. Then write a sentence to explain where the trial balance amount for Service Revenue comes from.
3. In your own words, describe the accounting process that results in Hillsboro's $7,000 balance for Cash. Use the following terms in your explanation: account, balance, journal, ledger, post, and trial balance.
4. If your friend were to join Avery Patel as a co-owner of Hillsboro Emergency Service, what form of business organization would the firm then take? If necessary, review Chapter 1.

Analyzing and journalizing transactions
(Obj. 2, 3)

Student Resource CD
GL, PT, QB

P2-2A Art Levitt practices medicine under the business title Art Levitt, M.D. During June, his medical practice engaged in the following transactions:

June 1	Levitt deposited $55,000 cash in the business bank account. The business gave Levitt owner's equity in the firm.
5	Paid monthly rent on medical equipment, $700.
9	Paid $22,000 cash to purchase land for an office site.
10	Purchased supplies on account, $1,200.
19	Borrowed $20,000 from the bank for business use. Levitt signed a note payable to the bank in the name of the business.
22	Paid $1,000 on account.
30	Revenues earned during the month included $6,000 cash and $5,000 on account.
30	Paid employees' salaries ($2,400), office rent ($1,500), and utilities ($400).
30	Withdrew $10,000 from the business for personal use.

Levitt's business uses the following accounts: Cash; Accounts Receivable; Supplies; Land; Accounts Payable; Notes Payable; Art Levitt, Capital; Art Levitt, Withdrawals; Service Revenue; Salary Expense; Rent Expense; Utilities Expense.

Required

Journalize each transaction, as shown for June 1. Show all notations as follows:

June 1	Cash (↑ asset; debit)	55,000	
	Art Levitt, Capital (↑ equity; credit) . .		55,000

Journalizing transactions, posting to T-accounts, and preparing a trial balance **(Obj. 2, 3, 4, 5)**

P2-3A Monica Kaska opened a law office on December 2 of the current year. During the first month of operations, the business completed the following transactions:

Dec. 2	Kaska deposited $30,000 cash in the business bank account Monica Kaska, Attorney.
3	Purchased supplies, $500, and furniture, $2,600, on account.
4	Performed legal service for a client and received cash, $1,500.
7	Paid cash to acquire land for a future office site, $22,000.
11	Prepared legal documents for a client on account, $900.
15	Paid secretary's salary, $570.
16	Paid for the furniture purchased December 3 on account.
18	Received $1,800 cash for helping a client sell real estate.
19	Defended a client in court and billed the client for $800.
29	Received partial collection from client on account, $400.
31	Paid secretary's salary, $570.
31	Paid rent expense, $700.
31	Withdrew $2,200 for personal use.

Required

Open the following T-accounts: Cash; Accounts Receivable; Supplies; Furniture; Land; Accounts Payable; Monica Kaska, Capital; Monica Kaska, Withdrawals; Service Revenue; Salary Expense; Rent Expense.

1. Record each transaction in the journal, using the account titles given. Key each transaction by date. Explanations are not required.
2. Post the transactions to the ledger, using transaction dates as posting references in the ledger. Label the balance of each account *Bal.*, as shown in the chapter.
3. Prepare the trial balance of Monica Kaska, Attorney, at December 31 of the current year.

Journalizing transactions, posting to accounts in four-column format, and preparing a trial balance **(Obj. 2, 3, 4, 5)**

P2-4A The trial balance of Robert Quiroga, Registered Dietician, at November 15, 20X3, follows.

Robert Quiroga, Registered Dietician

Trial Balance
November 15, 20X3

Account Number	Account	Debit	Credit
11	Cash	$ 3,000	
12	Accounts receivable	8,000	
13	Supplies	600	
14	Equipment	15,000	
21	Accounts payable		$ 4,600
31	Robert Quiroga, capital		20,000
32	Robert Quiroga, withdrawals	2,300	
41	Service revenue		7,100
51	Salary expense	1,800	
52	Rent expense	1,000	
	Total	$31,700	$31,700

During the remainder of November, Quiroga completed the following transactions:

Nov.	16	Collected $6,000 cash from a client on account.
	17	Performed a nutritional analysis for a hospital on account, $1,700.
	21	Used personal funds to pay for the renovation of private residence, $55,000.
	22	Purchased supplies on account, $800.
	23	Withdrew $2,100 for personal use.
	23	Paid on account, $2,600.
	24	Received $1,900 cash for consulting with **Kraft Foods**.
	30	Paid rent, $700.
	30	Paid employees' salaries, $2,100.

Required

1. Record the transactions that occurred November 16 to November 30 on page 6 of the journal. Include an explanation for each entry.
2. Post the transactions to the ledger, using dates, account numbers, journal references, and posting references. Open the ledger accounts listed in the trial balance together with their balances at November 15. Use the four-column account format illustrated in the chapter (Exhibit 2-10). Enter *Bal.* (for previous balance) in the Item column, and place a check mark (✓) in the journal reference column for the November 15 balance of each account.
3. Prepare the trial balance of Robert Quiroga, Registered Dietician, at November 30, 20X3.

Correcting errors in a trial balance
(Obj. 2, 5)

P2-5A ← *Link Back to Chapter 1 (Income Statement).* The trial balance for Online Cable Service does not balance. The following errors were detected:

a. The cash balance is understated by $400.
b. Rent expense of $350 was erroneously posted as a credit rather than a debit.
c. An $8,300 credit to Service Revenue was not posted.
d. A $600 debit to Accounts Receivable was posted as $60.
e. The balance of Utilities Expense is understated by $60.
f. A $100 purchase of supplies on account was neither journalized nor posted.
g. Office furniture should be listed in the amount of $21,300.

Online Cable Service
Trial Balance
March 31, 20X1

Cash	$ 6,200	
Accounts receivable	2,000	
Supplies	500	
Office furniture	22,300	
Computers	46,000	
Accounts payable		$ 2,700
Note payable		18,300
Meredith Ballard, capital		50,800
Meredith Ballard, withdrawals	5,000	
Service revenue		4,900
Salary expense	1,300	
Rent expense	500	
Advertising expense	300	
Utilities expense	200	
Total	$84,300	$76,700

Required

1. Prepare the correct trial balance at March 31. Journal entries are not required.
2. Prepare Online Cable Service's income statement for the month ended March 31, 20X1, to determine whether the business had a net income or a net loss for the month. Refer to Exhibit 1-8, page 21, if needed.

Recording transactions directly in T-accounts; preparing a trial balance **(Obj. 2, 5, 6)**

P2-6A Vince Serrano started Serrano Carpet Installers, and during the first month of operations (January 20X7), he completed the following selected transactions:

a. Serrano began the business with an investment of $18,000 cash and a van (automobile) valued at $13,000. The business gave Serrano owner's equity in the firm.
b. Borrowed $25,000 from the bank; signed a note payable.
c. Paid $32,000 for equipment.
d. Purchased supplies on account, $400.
e. Paid employee's salary, $1,300.
f. Received $800 for a carpet installation job performed for a bank.
g. Received an $800 bill for advertising expense that will be paid in the near future.
h. Paid $100 of the account payable created in transaction (d).
i. Installed carpet for a hotel on account, $3,300.
j. Received cash on account, $1,100.
k. Paid the following cash expenses:
(1) Rent, $1,000. **(2)** Insurance, $600.
l. Withdrew $2,600 for personal use.

Required

1. Open the following T-accounts: Cash; Accounts Receivable; Supplies; Equipment; Automobile; Accounts Payable; Note Payable; Vince Serrano, Capital; Vince Serrano, Withdrawals; Service Revenue; Salary Expense; Rent Expense; Advertising Expense; Insurance Expense.
2. Record the transactions directly in the T-accounts without using a journal. Use the letters to identify the transactions.
3. Prepare the trial balance of Serrano Carpet Installers at January 31, 20X7.

Note: Problem 2-7A should be used in conjunction with Problem 2-6A.

Preparing the financial statements **(Obj. 5)**

P2-7A → *Link Back to Chapter 1 (Income Statement, Statement of Owner's Equity, Balance Sheet).* Refer to Problem 2-6A. After completing the trial balance in Problem 2-6A, prepare the following financial statements for Serrano Carpet Installers:

1. Income statement for the month ended January 31, 20X7.
2. Statement of owner's equity for the month ended January 31, 20X7.
3. Balance sheet at January 31, 20X7.

Draw arrows to link the statements. If needed, use Exhibit 1-8, page 21, as a guide for preparing the financial statements.

Problems

(Group B)

A+ online homework

Using accounting terms and analyzing a trial balance **(Obj. 1)**

P2-1B → *Link Back to Chapter 1 (Balance Sheet, Income Statement).* Letrice Simkin, owner of the Simkin Law Firm, is considering adding another lawyer to the firm. Michelle McGuire is considering joining Simkin and asks to see Simkin's financial information. Simkin gives McGuire the firm's trial balance, which follows. Help McGuire decide whether to join the firm by answering these questions for her.

1. How much are the firm's total assets? total liabilities? net income or net loss?
2. Suppose Simkin earned all the service revenue on account. Make a single journal entry to record the revenue, set up the T-accounts affected, and post to the accounts. Then write a sentence to explain where the trial balance amount for Service Revenue comes from.

3. In your own words, describe the accounting process that results in Simkin's $12,000 balance for Cash. Use the following terms in your explanation: account, balance, journal, ledger, post, and trial balance.
4. If McGuire joins Simkin as a co-owner of the law firm, what form of business organization will the firm take? If necessary, review Chapter 1.

Simkin Law Firm
Trial Balance
December 31, 20X8

Cash	$ 12,000	
Accounts receivable	27,000	
Prepaid expenses	4,000	
Land	63,000	
Accounts payable		$ 35,000
Note payable		32,000
Letrice Simkin, capital		30,000
Letrice Simkin, withdrawals	48,000	
Service revenue		116,000
Rent expense	26,000	
Advertising expense	3,000	
Wage expense	23,000	
Supplies expense	7,000	
Total	$213,000	$213,000

Analyzing and journalizing transactions **(Obj. 2, 3)**

Student ResourceCD
GL, PT, QB

P2-2B Hollywood Theaters owns movie theaters in the shopping centers of a major metropolitan area. Its owner, James Stevens, engaged in the following business transactions:

April 1	Stevens invested $500,000 personal cash in the business by depositing that amount in a bank account titled Hollywood Theaters. The business gave Stevens owner's equity in the company.
2	Paid $400,000 cash to purchase a theater building.
5	Borrowed $220,000 from the bank. Stevens signed a note payable to the bank in the name of Hollywood Theaters.
10	Purchased theater supplies on account, $1,700.
15	Paid $800 on account.
15	Paid property tax expense on theater building, $1,200.
16	Paid employee salaries, $2,800, and rent on equipment, $1,800.
17	Withdrew $6,000 from the business for personal use.
30	Received $20,000 cash from revenue and deposited that amount in the bank. Label the revenue as Sales Revenue.

Hollywood Theaters uses the following accounts: Cash; Supplies; Building; Accounts Payable; Notes Payable; James Stevens, Capital; James Stevens, Withdrawals; Sales Revenue; Salary Expense; Rent Expense; Property Tax Expense.

Required

Journalize each transaction of Hollywood Theaters as shown for April 1. Show all notations as follows:

Apr. 1 Cash (↑ asset; debit)	500,000	
James Stevens, Capital (↑ equity; credit)		500,000

P2-3B Emily Smith started her practice as a registered dietician on September 3 of the current year. During the first month of operations, the business completed the following transactions:

Journalizing transactions, posting to T-accounts, and preparing a trial balance **(Obj. 2, 3, 4, 5)**

Sep. 3	Smith transferred $20,000 cash from her personal bank account to a business account titled Emily Smith, Registered Dietician. The business gave Smith owner's equity in the firm.
4	Purchased supplies, $200, and furniture, $1,800, on account.
6	Performed services for a hospital and received $4,000 cash.
7	Paid $15,000 cash to acquire land for a future office site.
10	Performed a nutritional analysis for a hotel and received its promise to pay the $800 within one week.
14	Paid for the furniture purchased September 4 on account.
15	Paid secretary's salary, $600.
17	Received partial collection from client on account, $500.
20	Prepared a nutrition plan for a school on account, $800.
28	Received $1,500 cash for consulting with **Procter & Gamble**.
30	Paid secretary's salary, $600.
30	Paid rent expense, $500.
30	Withdrew $2,900 for personal use.

Required

Open the following T-accounts: Cash; Accounts Receivable; Supplies; Furniture; Land; Accounts Payable; Emily Smith, Capital; Emily Smith, Withdrawals; Service Revenue; Salary Expense; Rent Expense.

1. Record each transaction in the journal, using the account titles given. Key each transaction by date. Explanations are not required.

2. Post the transactions to the ledger, using transaction dates as posting references in the ledger. Label the balance of each account *Bal.*, as shown in the chapter.

3. Prepare the trial balance of Emily Smith, Registered Dietician, at September 30 of the current year.

P2-4B The trial balance of Mark Power, CPA, is dated February 14, 20X3:

Journalizing transactions, posting to accounts in four-column format, and preparing a trial balance **(Obj. 2, 3, 4, 5)**

Mark Power, CPA
Trial Balance
February 14, 20X3

Account Number	Account	Debit	Credit
11	Cash	$ 2,000	
12	Accounts receivable	9,500	
13	Supplies	800	
14	Land	18,600	
21	Accounts payable		$ 3,000
31	Mark Power, capital		26,500
32	Mark Power, withdrawals	1,200	
41	Service revenue		7,200
51	Salary expense	3,600	
52	Rent expense	1,000	
	Total	$36,700	$36,700

During the remainder of February, Power completed the following transactions:

Feb. 15	Power collected $3,500 cash from a client on account.
16	Performed tax services for a client on account, $700.
20	Paid on account, $1,000.
21	Purchased supplies on account, $100.
21	Withdrew $1,200 for personal use.
21	Paid for a deck for private residence, using personal funds, $9,000.
22	Received cash of $5,500 for consulting work just completed.
28	Paid rent, $800.
28	Paid employees' salaries, $1,800.

Required

1. Record the transactions that occurred from February 15 to February 28 in page 3 of the journal. Include an explanation for each entry.
2. Open the ledger accounts listed in the trial balance, together with their balances at February 14. Use the four-column account format illustrated in the chapter (Exhibit 2-10). Enter *Bal.* (for previous balance) in the Item column, and place a check mark (✓) in the journal reference column for the February 14 balance in each account. Post the transactions to the ledger using dates, account numbers, journal references, and posting references.
3. Prepare the trial balance of Mark Power, CPA, at February 28, 20X3.

Correcting errors in a trial balance
(Obj. 2, 5)

P2-5B ← *Link Back to Chapter 1 (Income Statement).* The trial balance for Feelgood Fitness Center does not balance. The following errors were detected:

a. The cash balance is understated by $700.
b. The cost of the building was $93,000, not $96,000.
c. A $200 purchase of supplies on account was neither journalized nor posted.
d. The balance of Utilities Expense is overstated by $70.
e. Rent expense of $200 was erroneously posted as a credit rather than a debit.
f. A $300 debit to Accounts Receivable was posted as $30.
g. A $4,300 credit to Service Revenue was not posted.

Feelgood Fitness Center
Trial Balance
June 30, 20X2

Cash	$ 3,000	
Accounts receivable	10,000	
Supplies	900	
Equipment	85,100	
Building	96,000	
Accounts payable		$ 55,000
Note payable		72,000
Rob Rylander, capital		62,500
Rob Rylander, withdrawals	2,900	
Service revenue		6,500
Salary expense	2,100	
Rent expense	1,000	
Advertising expense	600	
Utilities expense	400	
Total	$202,000	$196,000

Required

1. Prepare the correct trial balance at June 30. Journal entries are not required.
2. Prepare the company's income statement for the month ended June 30, 20X2, in order to determine the business's net income or net loss for the month. Refer to Exhibit 1-8, page 21, if needed.

Recording transactions directly in T-accounts; preparing a trial balance **(Obj. 2, 5, 6)**

P2-6B Christie Clinton started a consulting service and during the first month of operations (June 20X3) completed the following selected transactions:

a. Clinton began the business with an investment of $5,000 cash and a building valued at $50,000. The business gave Clinton owner's equity in the business.
b. Borrowed $30,000 from the bank; signed a note payable.
c. Purchased office supplies on account, $2,100.
d. Paid $18,000 for office furniture.
e. Paid employee's salary, $2,200.
f. Performed consulting service on account for client, $5,100.
g. Paid $800 of the account payable created in transaction (c).
h. Received a $600 bill for advertising expense that will be paid in the near future.
i. Performed consulting service for customers and received cash, $1,600.
j. Received cash on account, $1,200.
k. Paid the following cash expenses:
(1) Rent on equipment, $700. **(2)** Utilities, $400.
l. Withdrew $7,500 for personal use.

Required

1. Open the following T-accounts: Cash; Accounts Receivable; Office Supplies; Office Furniture; Building; Accounts Payable; Note Payable; Christie Clinton, Capital; Christie Clinton, Withdrawals; Service Revenue; Salary Expense; Advertising Expense; Rent Expense; Utilities Expense.
2. Record each transaction directly in the T-accounts without using a journal. Use the letters to identify the transactions.
3. Prepare the trial balance of Clinton Consulting at June 30, 20X3.

Note: Problem 2-7B should be used in conjunction with Problem 2-6B.

Preparing the financial statements **(Obj. 5)**

P2-7B → *Link Back to Chapter 1 (Income Statement, Statement of Owner's Equity, Balance Sheet).* Refer to Problem 2-6B. After completing the trial balance in Problem 2-6B, prepare the following financial statements for Clinton Consulting Service:

1. Income statement for the month ended June 30, 20X3.
2. Statement of owner's equity for the month ended June 30, 20X3.
3. Balance sheet at June 30, 20X3.

Draw arrows to link the statements. If needed, use Exhibit 1-8, page 21, as a guide for preparing the financial statements.

APPLY *Your Knowledge*

Decision Cases

Recording transactions directly in T-accounts, preparing a trial balance, and measuring net income or loss **(Obj. 2, 5, 6)**

Case 1. You have been requested by a friend named Stephanie Bernina to advise her on the effects certain transactions will have on her business. Time is short, so you cannot journalize the transactions. Instead, you must analyze the transactions without a journal. Bernina will continue the business only if she can expect to earn monthly net income of $5,000. The following transactions occurred during March:

a. Bernina deposited $8,000 cash in a business bank account to start the company.
b. Paid $300 cash for supplies.
c. Incurred advertising expense on account, $700.
d. Paid the following cash expenses: secretary's salary, $1,400; office rent, $1,150.
e. Earned service revenue on account, $8,800.
f. Collected cash from customers on account, $1,200.

Required

1. Open the following T-accounts: Cash; Accounts Receivable; Supplies; Accounts Payable; Stephanie Bernina, Capital; Service Revenue; Salary Expense; Rent Expense; Advertising Expense; Utilities Expense; Interest Expense.
2. Record the transactions directly in the accounts without using a journal. Key each transaction by letter.
3. Prepare a trial balance at March 31, 20X9. List the largest expense first, the next largest second, and so on. The business name is Bernina Travel Planners.
4. Compute the amount of net income or net loss for this first month of operations. Would you recommend that Bernina continue in business?

Using the accounting equation
(Obj. 2)

Case 2. Answer the following questions. Consider each question separately.

1. When you deposit money in your bank account, the bank credits your account. Is the bank misusing the word *credit* in this context? Why does the bank use the term *credit* to refer to your deposit, and not *debit?*
2. Explain the advantages of double-entry bookkeeping over single-entry bookkeeping to a friend who is opening a used book store.
3. Your friend asks, "When revenues increase assets and expenses decrease assets, why are revenues credits and expenses debits and not the other way around?" Explain to your friend why revenues are credits and expenses are debits.

Ethical Issue

Brave Hearts, a charitable organization in Panama City, Florida, has a standing agreement with De Leon State Bank. The agreement allows Brave Hearts to overdraw its cash balance at the bank when donations are running low. In the past, Brave Hearts managed funds wisely and rarely used this privilege. Jacob Henson has recently become the president of Brave Hearts. To expand operations, Henson acquired office equipment and spent large amounts on fund-raising. During Henson's presidency, Brave Hearts has maintained a negative bank balance of approximately $6,000.

Required

What is the ethical issue in this situation? State why you approve or disapprove of Henson's management of Brave Hearts' funds.

Financial Statement Case

Journalizing transactions for a company
(Obj. 2, 3)

This problem helps you develop skill in recording transactions by using a company's actual account titles. Refer to the **Amazon.com** financial statements in Appendix A. Assume that Amazon completed the following selected transactions during December 2002:

Dec. 5	Earned sales revenue and collected cash, $110,000.
9	Borrowed $500,000 by signing a note payable.
12	Purchased equipment on account, $50,000.
17	Paid $100,000 of the note payable, plus interest expense of $8,000.
22	Paid half the account payable from December 12.
28	Paid a home-office electricity bill for $3,000 (this is an administrative expense).

Required

Journalize these transactions, using the following account titles taken from the Amazon.com financial statements: Cash; Equipment; Accounts Payable; Note Payable; Sales Revenue; Administrative Expense; and Interest Expense. Explanations are not required.

Team Project

Contact a local business and arrange with the owner to learn what accounts the business uses.

Required

1. Obtain a copy of the business's chart of accounts.
2. Prepare the company's financial statements for the most recent month, quarter, or year. You may use either made-up account balances or balances supplied by the owner.

If the business has a large number of accounts within a category, combine related accounts and report a single amount on the financial statements. For example, the company may have several cash accounts. Combine all cash amounts and report a single Cash amount on the balance sheet.

You will probably encounter numerous accounts that you have not yet learned. Deal with these as best you can. The chart of accounts given in Appendix B at the end of the book will be helpful.

Keep in mind that the financial statements report the balances of the accounts listed in the company's chart of accounts. Therefore, the financial statements must be consistent with the chart of accounts.

For Internet Exercises, go to the Web site www.prenhall.com/horngren.

CHAPTER 3

The Adjusting Process

A+ TIPS CHECK YOUR RESOURCES

- Visit the www.prenhall.com/horngren **Web site** for self-study quizzes, video clips, and other resources
- Try the **Quick Check** exercise at the end of the chapter to test your knowledge
- Learn the **key terms**
- Do the **Starter** exercises keyed in the margins
- Work the **end-of-chapter summary problems**
- Use the **Concept Links** to review material in other chapters
- Search the **CD** for review materials by chapter or by key word
- Watch the **tutorial videos** to review key concepts
- Watch the **On Location It's Just Lunch** video for an overview of accounting in business

IT'S just LUNCH!®

LEARNING OBJECTIVES

1. Distinguish accrual accounting from cash-basis accounting
2. Apply the revenue and matching principles
3. Make adjusting entries
4. Prepare an adjusted trial balance
5. Prepare the financial statements from the adjusted trial balance

What do dating and accounting have in common? Lots, if you are the owner of It's Just Lunch. Andrea McGinty founded It's Just Lunch as a service company and, in the process, turned dating into dollars. For a fee, It's Just Lunch will arrange lunch dates for busy professionals. After 10 years in business, McGinty's company is earning several million dollars a year in revenues and generating healthy profits.

According to It's Just Lunch,

- The average single professional has 8 first dates in a year.
- 78% of men will take 15 minutes on a first date to decide whether to see the person again.
- After 24 hours, the chance that a first date will call you again is 1 in 8.

For more information, you can visit the company's Web site at **www.itsjustlunch.com**. ■

It's Just Lunch

Sitemap

- Financial Statements and Adjusting Entries
- Adjusting the Accounts
- Prepaids and Accruals
- Adjusted Trial Balance
- The Financial Statements
- Ethical Issues
- Appendix: Alternative Treatment of Prepaid Expenses and Unearned Revenues

How does It's Just Lunch use accounting? How does McGinty know whether or not she is making money? It's Just Lunch measures assets, liabilities, revenues, and expenses like any other company. It records transactions and then prepares its financial statements at the end of the period.

In Chapter 2 we saw how to record transactions, post to the accounts, and prepare a trial balance. Here we take the accounting process a step further. It's Just Lunch comes to the end of the period, and the company's accounts must be updated. Its computers have depreciated, and It's Just Lunch owes some services to customers. This chapter shows how to adjust the books and ready the accounts for the financial statements.

- **Financial Statements and Adjusting Entries**
- Adjusting the Accounts
- Prepaids and Accruals
- Adjusted Trial Balance
- The Financial Statements
- Ethical Issues
- Appendix: Alternative Treatment of Prepaid Expenses and Unearned Revenues

Student Resource CD
accrual basis, cash basis, matching principle, revenue principle, time-period concept

1 *Distinguish accrual accounting from cash-basis accounting*

Accrual Accounting
Accounting that records the impact of a business event as it occurs, regardless of whether the transaction affected cash.

Cash-Basis Accounting
Accounting that records transactions only when cash is received or paid.

Financial Statements and Adjusting Entries

One step in financial statement preparation is the trial balance that we covered in Chapter 2. To measure income, a business must bring the records up to date at the end of the period. This process is called *adjusting the books*, and it requires special journal entries called *adjusting entries*. This chapter focuses on the adjustments that are needed to measure income.

Accountants have concepts and principles to guide the measurement of income. Chief among these are accrual accounting, the accounting period, the revenue principle, and the matching principle. In this chapter, we apply these principles to Gay Gillen eTravel for the month of April. It's Just Lunch and all other companies follow the same principles.

Accrual versus Cash-Basis Accounting

There are two ways to do accounting:

- **Accrual accounting** records the effect of each transaction as it occurs. Most businesses use the accrual basis as covered in this book.
- **Cash-basis accounting** records only cash receipts and cash payments. It ignores receivables, payables, and depreciation. Only very small businesses use the cash basis of accounting.

Suppose It's Just Lunch purchased $2,000 of office supplies on account. On the accrual basis, It's Just Lunch records Office Supplies and Accounts Payable as follows:

Office Supplies (↑ asset; debit)	2,000	
Accounts Payable (↑ liability; credit)		2,000
Purchased supplies on account.		

To help you learn to make journal entries, we repeat the special notations that we began in Chapter 2. As before, the arrows and the debit/credit notations are not required.

In contrast, cash-basis accounting ignores this transaction because It's Just Lunch paid no cash. The cash basis records only cash receipts and cash payments. In the cash basis,

- *Cash receipts are treated as revenues.*
- *Cash payments are treated as expenses.*

Under the cash basis, It's Just Lunch would record each cash payment as an expense and not as an asset. This is faulty accounting: It's Just Lunch acquired supplies, which are assets because they provide future benefit to the company.

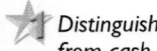

Now let's see how differently the accrual basis and the cash basis account for a revenue. Suppose It's Just Lunch performed service and earned the revenue but collected no cash. Under the accrual basis, It's Just Lunch records \$10,000 of revenue on account as follows:

Accounts Receivable (↑ asset; debit)..........	10,000	
Service Revenue (↑ revenue; credit).....		10,000
Earned revenue on account.		

Under the cash basis, It's Just Lunch would not even bother to record any revenue earned *on account* because there is no cash receipt. Instead, it would wait until the company receives the cash. Then it would record the cash receipt as revenue. As a result, cash-basis accounting never reports accounts receivable from customers. It shows the revenue in the wrong accounting period, when the cash is received. Revenue should be recorded when it is earned, and that is how the accrual basis operates.

Exhibit 3-1 illustrates the difference between the accrual basis and the cash basis. Keep in mind that the accrual basis is the correct way to do accounting. Panel A of the exhibit illustrates a revenue, and Panel B covers an expense.

Exhibit 3-1 **Accrual Accounting versus Cash-Basis Accounting**

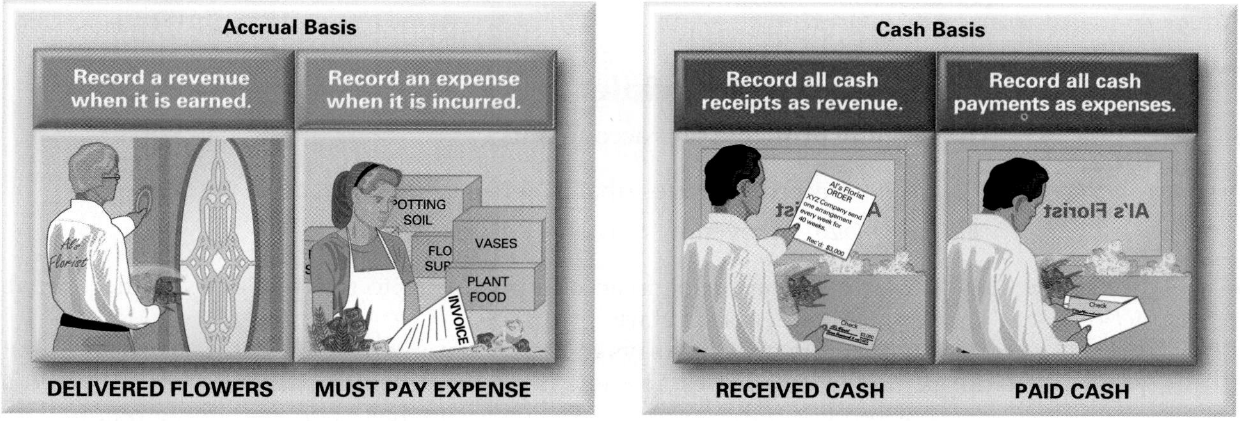

Now let's apply what you've learned. Work the Stop & Think.

Stop & Think

Suppose **It's Just Lunch** collects \$3,000 from customers on January 1. The company will earn the \$3,000 of revenue evenly during January, February, and March. How much service revenue will It's Just Lunch report each month under (a) accrual accounting and (b) cash-basis accounting?

Answer:

		Jan.	Feb.	Mar.
(a) *Accrual accounting:*	Service revenue	\$1,000	\$1,000	\$1,000
(b) *Cash-basis accounting:*	Service revenue	\$3,000		

Now suppose It's Just Lunch prepays \$6,000 for TV advertising. The ads will run during October, November, and December. How much advertising expense will It's Just Lunch report each month under the two methods of accounting?

Answer:

		Oct.	Nov.	Dec.
(a) *Accrual accounting:*	Advertising expense ...	\$2,000	\$2,000	\$2,000
(b) *Cash-basis accounting:*	Advertising expense ...	\$6,000		

Observe the vast differences between accrual accounting and the cash basis. The accrual basis is the correct way to do the accounting.

✔ **Starter 3-1**

✔ **Starter 3-2**

The Accounting Period

The only way to know for certain how successfully a business has operated is to close its doors, sell the assets, pay the liabilities, and give any leftover cash to the owners. This process of going out of business is called *liquidation*. It is not practical to measure income this way. Instead, businesses need periodic reports on their affairs. Accountants slice time into small segments and prepare financial statements for specific periods.

The basic accounting period is one year, and all businesses prepare annual financial statements. For about 60% of large companies in a recent survey, the annual accounting period runs the calendar year from January 1 through December 31. Other companies use a *fiscal year*, which ends on a date other than December 31. The year-end date is usually the low point in business activity for the year. Retailers are a notable example. For instance, **Wal-Mart**, **Target**, and most other retailers use a fiscal year that ends on January 31 because the low point in their activity falls after Christmas.

Companies also prepare financial statements for *interim* periods, so monthly statements are common. A series of monthly statements can be combined for quarterly and semiannual periods. Most of our discussions are based on an annual accounting period, but everything can be applied to interim periods as well.

2 Apply the revenue and matching principles

The Revenue Principle

Revenue Principle
The basis for recording revenues; tells accountants when to record revenue and the amount of revenue to record.

The **revenue principle** tells accountants

- *When* to record revenue—that is, when to make a journal entry
- The *amount* of revenue to record.

Revenue, defined in Chapter 1, p. 11, is the increase in owner's equity from delivering goods and services to customers in the course of operating a business.

"Recording" something in accounting means to make an entry in the journal. That is where the process starts.

The revenue principle says to record revenue when it has been earned—but not before. In most cases, revenue is earned when the business has delivered a good or service to the customer. The company has done everything required by the sale agreement, including transferring the item to the customer.

Exhibit 3-2 shows two situations that provide guidance on when to record revenue for Gay Gillen eTravel. The first situation illustrates when *not* to record revenue—because the client merely states his plan. Situation 2 illustrates when revenue should be recorded—after the travel agency has performed a service for the client.

Exhibit 3-2

Recording Revenue: The Revenue Principle

✔ **Starter 3-3**

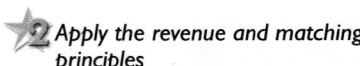

The revenue principle says to record revenue for the cash value of the item transferred to the customer. Suppose that to obtain a new client, Gillen performs travel service for the cut-rate price of $500. Ordinarily, Gillen would have charged $600 for this service. How much revenue should Gillen record? The answer is $500, because that was the value of the transaction. Gillen will not receive $600, so that is not the amount of revenue to record. She will receive only $500 cash, so she records that amount of revenue. The Accounting.com box entitled "Grossing Up the Revenue: Priceline.com" shows how Internet service companies, such as Priceline.com, have attempted to rewrite the accounting rules for recording their revenues.

The Matching Principle

The **matching principle** guides accounting for expenses. → Recall that expenses—such as rent, utilities, and advertising—are the costs of operating a business. Expenses are the costs of assets used up and liabilities incurred to earn revenue. The matching principle directs accountants to

An expense, defined in Chapter 1, p. 12, is a decrease in owner's equity that occurs from using assets or increasing liabilities in the course of operating a business.

1. Identify all expenses incurred during the period and measure the expenses.
2. Match the expenses against the revenues earned during the period.

Matching Principle
Guide to accounting for expenses. Identify all expenses incurred during the period, measure the expenses, and match them against the revenues earned during that same time period.

To match expenses against revenues means to subtract expenses from revenues. The goal is to compute net income or net loss. Exhibit 3-3 illustrates the matching principle.

There is a natural link between revenues and some expenses. For example, Gay Gillen may pay sales commissions to employees who sell the travel agency's services. *Cost of goods sold* is another example. If Ford Motor Company sells no automobiles, Ford has no cost of goods sold.

Grossing Up the Revenue: Priceline.com

Accounting.com

Suppose you're going to Australia. You want a cheap air ticket, and Priceline.com lets you "name your price" for airline tickets and hotel rooms. Your bid of $975 is accepted, and Priceline pockets the spread between your price and the amount Priceline pays the airline company. What should Priceline claim as revenue—the fee it earns, or the full price of your ticket?

Priceline.com and other Internet service companies record the entire value of the products sold through their sites. Priceline has defended this practice by saying it operates differently from a travel agency, which earns a fixed commission. Priceline purchases the airline ticket outright, assumes the full risk of ownership, and controls the profit on each sale. The Securities and Exchange Commission (SEC) and the Financial Accounting Standards Board (FASB) call this practice "grossing up" revenue.

Grossing up may be legal, but the SEC and the FASB are considering placing restrictions on it. The FASB now has added a project on revenue recognition to its agenda. "Revenue usually is the largest item in [a company's] financial statements, and revenue recognition issues top the list of reasons for financial restatements," say L. Todd Johnson, FASB senior project manager. "The FASB's proposed project would address such matters by developing one accounting standard that would apply to a broad range of industries."

Sources: Elizabeth McDonald, "Plump from Web Sales, Some Dot.Coms Face Crash Diet of Restriction on Booking Revenue," *The Wall Street Journal*, February 28, 2000, p. C4. Jeremy Kahn, "Presto Chango! Sales Are Huge!" *Fortune*, March 21, 2000, pp. 90–96. Also, http://www.fasb.org/news/nr052002.shtml.

Exhibit 3-3 Recording Expenses: The Matching Principle

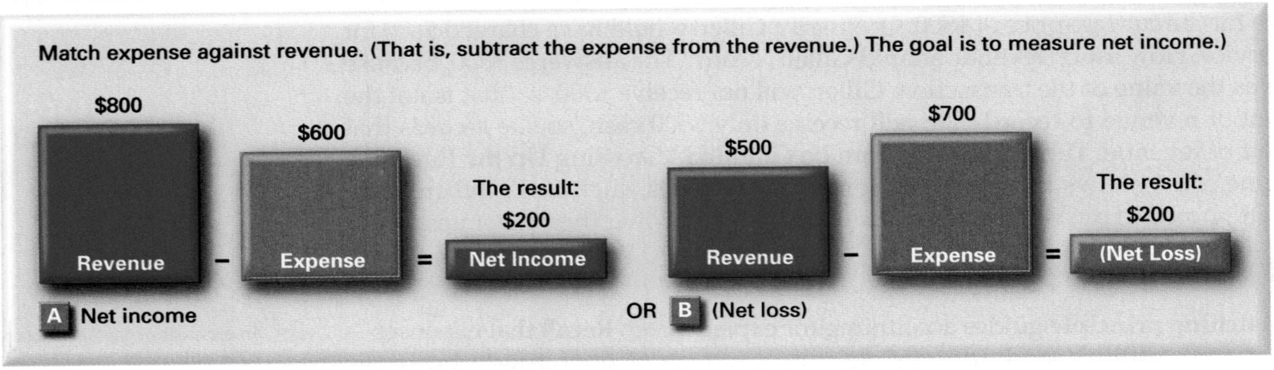

✔ Starter 3-4

Other expenses are not so easy to link to sales. For example, Gay Gillen eTravel's monthly rent expense occurs regardless of the revenues earned that month. The matching principle says to identify those expenses with a particular time period, such as a month or a year. Gay Gillen eTravel will record rent expense each month based on the lease agreement. Gillen also pays monthly salaries to some employees.

How does Gay Gillen account for a travel plan that begins in April and ends in May? How does she bring accounts up to date for the financial statements? To answer these questions, accountants use the time-period concept.

The Time-Period Concept

Time-Period Concept
Ensures that information is reported at regular intervals.

Managers need periodic readings on the business. The **time-period concept** ensures that information is reported often. To measure income accurately, companies update their accounts at the end of each period. Fossil, the fashion watch company, provides an example of an expense accrual. At December 31, 2002, Fossil recorded employee compensation of $11 million that the company owed its workers at year-end. The company's accrual entry, adapted and in millions of dollars, was

2002			
Dec. 31	Salary Expense (↑ expense; debit)	11	
	Salary Payable (↑ liability; credit)		11
	Accrued salary expense.		

This entry assigns the salary expense to 2002, the year when the employees worked for the company. Without this entry, 2002's expenses would be understated, and net income would be overstated. The accrual entry also records the liability for the balance sheet at December 31, 2002. Without this entry, total liabilities would be understated.

The remainder of the chapter shows how to adjust the accounts and bring the books up to date. What are the final products of the accounting process? The financial statements: the income statement, the balance sheet, and so on.

Adjusting the Accounts

Student ResourceCD
adjusting entries, adjustments, trial balance

3 Make adjusting entries

At the end of the period, the accountant prepares the statements. The end-of-period process begins with the trial balance. ← Exhibit 3-4 is the trial balance of Gay Gillen eTravel at April 30, 20X5. This *unadjusted trial balance* lists most of the revenues and expenses of the travel agency for April. But these trial balance amounts are incomplete because they omit certain revenue and expense transactions. That is why the trial balance is *unadjusted*. Usually, however, we refer to it simply as the trial balance, without the label "unadjusted."

Under cash-basis accounting, there is no need for adjustments to the accounts because all April cash transactions have already been recorded. However, accrual accounting requires adjusting entries at the end of the period. We must have correct balances for the financial statements. To see why, consider the Supplies account in Exhibit 3-4.

Exhibit 3-4
Unadjusted Trial Balance

Gay Gillen eTravel
Unadjusted Trial Balance
April 30, 20X5

Cash	$24,800	
Accounts receivable	2,250	
Supplies	700	
Prepaid rent	3,000	
Furniture	16,500	
Accounts payable		$13,100
Unearned service revenue		450
Gay Gillen, capital		31,250
Gay Gillen, withdrawals	3,200	
Service revenue		7,000
Salary expense	950	
Utilities expense	400	
Total	$51,800	$51,800

Gay Gillen eTravel uses supplies during the month. This reduces the quantity of supplies on hand and creates an expense, just like salary or rent. It is a waste of time to record supplies expense more than once a month. But by the end of the month, the $700 of Supplies on the unadjusted trial balance (Exhibit 3-4) is out of date. So how does Gillen account for supplies expense? Gillen must adjust the accounts at April 30 in order to show correct amounts for supplies and supplies expense. The adjusting process requires adjusting journal entries.

Adjusting entries assign revenues to the period when they are earned and expenses to the period when they are incurred. Adjusting entries also update the asset and liability accounts. Adjustments are needed to properly measure (1) the period's income on the income statement, and (2) the assets and the liabilities on the balance sheet. Adjusting entries are key to accrual accounting. This end-of-period process is called *adjusting the accounts, making the adjusting entries,* or *adjusting the books*. The two basic categories of adjustments are *prepaids* and *accruals.*

Adjusting Entry
Entry made at the end of the period to assign revenues to the period in which they are earned and expenses to the period in which they are incurred. Adjusting entries help measure the period's income and bring the related asset and liability accounts to correct balances for the financial statements.

☐ Financial Statements and Adjusting Entries
☐ Adjusting the Accounts
■ Prepaids and Accruals
☐ Adjusted Trial Balance
☐ The Financial Statements
☐ Ethical Issues
☐ Appendix: Alternative Treatment of Prepaid Expenses and Unearned Revenues

Prepaids and Accruals

In a *prepaid* adjustment, the cash transaction occurs before an expense or revenue is recorded. *Accrual*-type adjustments are the opposite of prepaids. Accruals record an expense or a revenue before the cash settlement.

Adjusting entries can be further divided into five categories:

1. Prepaid expenses
2. Depreciation
3. Accrued expenses
4. Accrued revenues
5. Unearned revenues

The core of this chapter shows how to account for these five types of adjusting entries. Study this material carefully, because it is the most challenging topic in all of introductory accounting.

Student ResourceCD
accruals, depreciation, prepaid expenses

Prepaid Expenses

Prepaid Expense
Advance payments of expenses. Examples include prepaid rent, prepaid insurance, and supplies.

Prepaid expenses are advance payments of expenses. Prepaid rent and prepaid insurance are examples of expenses that are paid in advance. All companies, large and small, must adjust their prepaid expenses. For example, McDonald's Corporation, the restaurant chain, makes prepayments for rent, insurance, and supplies. Keep in mind that prepaid expenses are assets, not expenses.

PREPAID RENT Landlords require tenants to pay rent in advance. This prepayment creates an asset for the renter. Suppose Gay Gillen eTravel prepays three months' office rent on April 1, 20X5. If the lease specifies a monthly rental of $1,000, the entry to record the payment is

Apr. 1	Prepaid Rent ($1,000 × 3)		
	(↑ asset; debit)	3,000	
	Cash (↓ asset; credit)		3,000
	Paid rent in advance.		

After posting, Prepaid Rent has a $3,000 debit balance.

ASSETS

Prepaid Rent

Apr. 1	3,000		

The trial balance at April 30, 20X5, lists Prepaid Rent with a debit balance of $3,000. Throughout April, Prepaid Rent maintains this beginning balance (Exhibit 3-4). But $3,000 is *not* the amount to report for Prepaid Rent on the balance sheet at April 30. Why?

At April 30, Prepaid Rent should be decreased for the amount of the asset that has been used up. The used-up portion is one-third of the prepayment. Recall that an asset that has expired is an *expense*. The adjusting entry transfers $1,000 ($3,000 × 1/3) of the Prepaid Rent to Rent Expense. The adjusting entry is

Apr. 30	Rent Expense ($3,000 × 1/3)		
	(↑ expense; debit)	1,000	
	Prepaid Rent (↓ asset; credit) ...		1,000
	To record rent expense.		

After posting, Prepaid Rent and Rent Expense show correct ending balances:

ASSETS — **Prepaid Rent**

Apr. 1	3,000	Apr. 30	1,000
Bal.	2,000		

→

EXPENSES — **Rent Expense**

Apr. 30	1,000		
Bal.	1,000		

Correct asset amount: $2,000 → **Total accounted for: $3,000** ← **Correct expense amount: $1,000**

The same analysis applies to the prepayment of three months of insurance. The only difference is in the account titles, which would be Prepaid Insurance instead of Prepaid Rent and Insurance Expense instead of Rent Expense. In a computerized system, the adjusting entry is programmed to recur automatically each accounting period.

The chapter appendix shows an alternative treatment of prepaid expenses. The end result on the financial statements is the same as illustrated here.

SUPPLIES Supplies are accounted for in the same way as prepaid expenses. On April 2, Gay Gillen paid $700 for office supplies:

Apr. 2	Supplies (↑ asset; debit)	700	
	Cash (↓ asset; credit).		700
	Paid cash for supplies.		

The April 30 trial balance, therefore, lists Supplies with a $700 debit balance, as shown in Exhibit 3-4. But Gillen's April 30 balance sheet should *not* report supplies of $700. Why?

During April, Gillen used supplies to conduct business. The cost of the supplies used becomes *supplies expense.* To measure supplies expense, Gillen counts the supplies on hand at the end of April. This is the amount of the asset still available to the business. Assume that supplies costing $400 remain at April 30. Subtracting the supplies on hand at the end of April ($400) from the supplies available ($700) measures supplies expense for the month ($300).

Cost of asset available	–	Cost of asset on hand at the end of the period	=	Cost of asset used (expense) during the period
$700	–	$400	=	$300

The April 30 adjusting entry to update the Supplies account and to record Supplies Expense for the month follows:

Apr. 30	Supplies Expense ($700 – $400)		
	(↑ expense; debit).	300	
	Supplies (↓ asset; credit)		300
	To record supplies expense.		

After posting, Supplies and Supplies Expense hold correct ending balances:

✔ Starter 3-5

ASSETS

Supplies

Apr. 2	**700**	**Apr. 30**	**300**
Bal.	400		

EXPENSES

Supplies Expense

Apr. 30	**300**		
Bal.	300		

Correct asset amount: $400	→	**Total accounted for: $700**	←	**Correct expense amount: $300**

The Supplies account then enters May with a $400 balance, and the adjustment process is repeated each month.

Stop & Think

At the beginning of the month, Supplies were $5,000. During the month, the company purchased $7,000 of supplies. At month's end, $3,000 of supplies were still on hand.

1. What was the cost of supplies used during the month? Where is this item reported?
2. What is the ending balance of Supplies? Where is this item reported?
3. Make the adjusting entry to update the Supplies account at the end of the month.

Answers:

1.	Beginning balance	$ 5,000
	+Purchases	7,000
	=Supplies available	12,000
	–Ending balance	(3,000)
	=Expense (supplies used)	$ 9,000

Report supplies expense among the expenses on the *income statement.*

2. The ending balance of Supplies is $3,000.
3. Adjusting entry: Report supplies among the assets on the *balance sheet.*

Supplies Expense	9,000	
Supplies		9,000

Depreciation

Plant Asset
Long-lived tangible assets—such as land, buildings, and equipment—used in the operation of a business.

Depreciation
The allocation of a plant asset's cost to expense over its useful life.

Accrual accounting is clearly illustrated by depreciation. **Plant assets** are long-lived tangible assets used in the operation of a business. Examples include land, buildings, equipment, and furniture and fixtures. As one accountant said, "All assets but land are on a march to the junkyard" because they decline in usefulness. This decline is an expense, and accountants systematically spread the cost of a plant asset over its useful life. This allocation of cost to expense is called **depreciation**. Land is the exception. We record no depreciation for land.

Similarity to Prepaid Expenses The concept underlying accounting for plant assets is the same as for a prepaid expense. The major difference between a prepaid expense and a plant asset is the length of time it takes for the asset to wear out. Prepaid expenses usually expire within a year, while most plant assets remain useful for several years. Consider Gay Gillen eTravel. Suppose that on April 3 Gillen purchased furniture on account for $16,500 and made this journal entry:

Apr. 3	Furniture (↑ asset; debit)	16,500	
	Accounts Payable (↑ liability; credit)		16,500
	Purchased furniture on account.		

After posting, the Furniture account has a $16,500 balance:

Assets

Furniture

Apr. 3	16,500	

Gillen believes the furniture will remain useful for 5 years and will be worthless at the end. One way to compute depreciation is to divide the cost of the asset ($16,500) by its expected useful life (5 years). This procedure—called the straight-line method—computes depreciation of $3,300 per year ($16,500/5 years). Depreciation for the month of April is $275 ($3,300/12 months = $275 per month).

The Accumulated Depreciation Account Depreciation expense for April is recorded by this entry:

Apr. 30	Depreciation Expense—Furniture (↑ expense; debit)	275	
	Accumulated Depreciation—Furniture (↓ asset; credit)		275
	To record depreciation on furniture.		

Accumulated Depreciation is credited instead of the Furniture account because it is helpful to keep the original cost in the Furniture account. Managers can then refer to the Furniture account to see how much the asset cost. This information may aid a decision about how much to pay for new furniture.

Depreciation is an estimate. The Accumulated Depreciation account holds the sum of all the depreciation recorded for the asset. The Accumulated Depreciation account increases over the life of the asset.

Accumulated Depreciation is a contra asset, which means an asset account with a normal credit balance. A **contra account** has two main characteristics:

Accumulated Depreciation
The cumulative sum of all depreciation expense recorded for an asset.

- A contra account follows a companion account.
- A contra account's normal balance (debit or credit) is opposite that of the companion.

Contra Account
An account that always has a companion account and whose normal balance is opposite that of the companion account.

Accumulated Depreciation is the contra account that follows Furniture. Furniture has a debit balance, so Accumulated Depreciation, a contra asset, has a credit balance. *All contra assets have credit balances.*

A business carries an accumulated depreciation account for each depreciable asset. If Gay Gillen eTravel has both building and furniture, it will carry two accounts: Accumulated Depreciation—Building and Accumulated Depreciation—Furniture.

After posting the depreciation entry, Gay Gillen's accounts appear as follows:

ASSETS				EXPENSES	
NORMAL ASSET		CONTRA ASSET			
Furniture		Accumulated Depreciation—Furniture		Depreciation Expense—Furniture	
Apr. 3 16,500			Apr. 30 275	Apr. 30 275	
Bal. 16,500			Bal. 275	Bal. 275	

BOOK VALUE The balance sheet reports both Furniture and Accumulated Depreciation. Because it's a contra account, the balance of Accumulated Depreciation is subtracted from Furniture. The resulting net amount of a plant asset (cost minus accumulated depreciation) is called its **book value**, as follows for Furniture:

Book value of plant assets:	
Furniture	$16,500
Less: Accumulated depreciation	(275)
Book value of the furniture	$16,225

Book Value (of a Plant Asset)
The asset's cost minus accumulated depreciation.

Suppose Gillen also owns a building that cost $48,000, with annual depreciation of $2,400 ($48,000/20 years). The amount of depreciation for one month would be $200 ($2,400/12), and the following entry records depreciation for April:

Apr. 30	Depreciation Expense—Building (↑ expense; debit)........................	200	
	Accumulated Depreciation—Building (↓ asset; credit).....................		200
	To record depreciation on building.		

✔ Starter 3-6

The April 30 balance sheet would report plant assets as shown in Exhibit 3-5.

Exhibit 3-5

Plant Assets on the Balance Sheet of Gay Gillen eTravel (April 30)

Plant Assets:		
Furniture	$16,500	
Less: Accumulated depreciation	(275)	$16,225
Building	$48,000	
Less: Accumulated depreciation	(200)	47,800
Plant assets, net		$64,025

Exhibit 3-6 shows how Fossil, the fashion watch company, reported Property, Plant, and Equipment as adapted from its annual report. The only new items are the last two. Leasehold improvements show Fossil's cost of changes made to assets that Fossil leases. An example would be the cost to paint the Fossil logo on delivery trucks that Fossil leases. The last item reports the cost of Fossil's plant assets that are under construction.

Exhibit 3-6

Fossil Reports Property, Plant, and Equipment

	Millions
Land	$ 8
Buildings	16
Furniture and fixtures	33
Computer equipment	19
Leasehold improvements	20
Construction in progress	27
	123
Less: Accumulated depreciation	(33)
	$ 90

Fossil's cost of plant assets was $123 million. Of this total cost, Fossil has depreciated $33 million. The book value of the company's plant assets is, therefore, $90 million.

Now let's return to Gay Gillen eTravel.

Accrued Expenses

Accrued Expense
An expense that the business has incurred but not yet paid.

Businesses often have expenses before they pay them. Consider an employee's salary. Gillen's salary expense grows as the employee works, so the expense is said to *accrue*. Another accrued expense is interest expense on a note payable. Interest accrues as the clock ticks. The term **accrued expense** refers to an expense the business has incurred but not yet paid. An accrued expense always creates a liability.

Companies don't make weekly journal entries to accrue expenses. That would be a waste of time. Instead they wait until the end of the period. They make an adjusting entry to bring each expense (and the related liability) up to date for the financial statements.

Remember the key differences between a prepaid expense and an accrued expense:

- A *prepaid expense* is paid first and expensed later.
- An *accrued expense* is expensed first and paid later.
- Prepaids and accruals are opposites.

Now let's see how to account for accrued expenses.

SALARY EXPENSE Suppose Gay Gillen pays her employee a monthly salary of $1,900, half on the 15th and half on the last day of the month. Here is a calendar for April with the two paydays circled:

April						
S	M	T	W	T	F	S
					1	2
3	4	5	6	7	8	9
10	11	12	13	14	(15)	16
17	18	19	20	21	22	23
24	25	26	27	28	29	(30)

To illustrate a salary accrual, assume that if either payday falls on a weekend, Gillen pays the following Monday. During April, Gillen paid the first half-month salary on Friday, April 15, and made the following entry:

Apr. 15	Salary Expense (↑ expense; debit).........	950	
	Cash (↓ asset; credit)...............		950
	To pay salary.		

After posting, Salary Expense shows its balance:

EXPENSES

Salary Expense

Apr. 15	950	

The trial balance at April 30 (Exhibit 3-4) includes Salary Expense, with a debit balance of $950. This is Gillen's salary expense for only the first half of April. The second half-month amount of $950 will be paid in May, so Gillen must accrue salary expense for the second half of April. At April 30, Gillen makes an adjusting entry as follows:

Apr. 30	Salary Expense (↑ expense; debit).........	950	
	Salary Payable (↑ liability; credit)....		950
	To accrue salary expense.		

This is accrual accounting in action. After posting, Salary Expense and Salary Payable hold their April 30 balances:

EXPENSES

Salary Expense

Apr. 15	950	
Apr. 30	950	
Bal.	1,900	

LIABILITIES

Salary Payable

	Apr. 30	950
	Bal.	950

Salary Expense holds a full month's salary, and Salary Payable shows the liability the company owes at April 30.

Stop & Think

Weekly salaries for a five-day workweek total $3,500, payable on a Friday. This month, November 30 falls on a Tuesday.

1. Which accounts require adjustment at November 30?
2. Make the adjusting entry.

Answers:

1. Salary Expense and Salary Payable require adjustment
2.

Salary Expense ($3,500 × 2/5)	1,400	
Salary Payable.		1,400
To accrue salary expense.		

✔ Starter 3-7

Accrued Revenues

Accrued Revenue
A revenue that has been earned but not yet collected in cash.

As we have just seen, some expenses occur before the cash payment, and that creates an accrued expense. Likewise, businesses also earn revenue before they receive the cash. This calls for an **accrued revenue**, which is a revenue that has been earned but not yet collected in cash.

Assume that Gay Gillen eTravel is hired on April 15 to perform travel services for It's Just Lunch. Under this agreement, Gillen will earn $500 monthly. During April, Gillen will earn half a month's fee, $250, for work April 15 through April 30. On April 30, Gillen makes the following adjusting entry to accrue the revenue earned during April 15 through 30:

Apr. 30	Accounts Receivable ($500 × 1/2)		
	(↑ asset; debit)	250	
	Service Revenue (↑ revenue; credit) . .		250
	To accrue service revenue.		

The unadjusted trial balance in Exhibit 3-4 shows that Accounts Receivable has an unadjusted balance of $2,250. Service Revenue's unadjusted balance is $7,000. Posting the adjustment increases both accounts to their correct balances at April 30.

ASSETS

Accounts Receivable		
	2,250	
Apr. 30	250	
Bal.	2,500	

REVENUES

Service Revenue		
		7,000
	Apr. 30	250
	Bal.	7,250

✔ Starter 3-8

Without the adjustment, Gillen's financial statements would be incomplete and misleading: They would understate both Accounts Receivable and Service Revenue. All accrued revenues are accounted for similarly: Debit a receivable and credit a revenue.

Now we turn to the final category of adjusting entries.

Unearned Revenues

Unearned Revenue
A liability created when a business collects cash from customers in advance of doing work. Also called **deferred revenue**.

Some businesses collect cash from customers in advance. Receiving cash before earning it creates a liability called **unearned revenue**, and the company owes a product or a service to the customer. Only when the job is completed will the business *earn* the revenue.

Suppose Intel Corporation engages Gillen to provide travel services, agreeing to pay her $450 monthly, beginning immediately. Gillen collects the first amount from Intel on April 20. Gillen records the cash receipt and a liability as follows:

Apr. 20	Cash (↑ asset; debit).	450	
	Unearned Service Revenue		
	(↑ liability; credit)		450
	Collected revenue in advance.		

Now the liability account Unearned Service Revenue shows that Gillen owes $450.

LIABILITIES

Unearned Service Revenue

		Apr. 20	450

Unearned Service Revenue is a liability because it represents Gillen's obligation to perform service for Intel.

The April 30 trial balance (Exhibit 3-4) lists Unearned Service Revenue with a $450 credit balance. During the last 10 days of the month—April 21 through April 30—Gillen will *earn* one-third (10 days divided by April's 30 days) of the $450, or $150. Therefore, Gillen makes the following adjustment to account for earning $150 of the revenue:

Apr. 30	Unearned Service Revenue ($450 × 1/3)		
	(↓ liability; debit)	150	
	Service Revenue (↑ revenue; credit) . .		150
	To record service revenue that was collected in advance.		

This adjusting entry shifts $150 of the total from liability to revenue. Service Revenue increases by $150, and Unearned Service Revenue decreases by $150. Now both accounts are up to date at April 30:

LIABILITIES

Unearned Service Revenue

Apr. 30	150	Apr. 20	450
		Bal.	300

REVENUES

Service Revenue

			7,000
		Apr. 30	250
		Apr. 30	150
		Bal.	7,400

Correct liability amount: $300 → **Total accounted for: $450** ← **Correct revenue amount: $150**

All revenues collected in advance are accounted for this way.

An unearned revenue to one company is a prepaid expense to the company that paid in advance. Consider Intel in the preceding example. Intel had prepaid travel expense—an asset. Gay Gillen eTravel had unearned service revenue—a liability.

✔ **Starter 3-9**

Remember this key point:

An unearned revenue is a liability, not a revenue.

Stop & Think

Consider the tuition you pay your college or university. Assume that one semester's tuition costs $1,500 and that you make a single payment up front. Can you make the journal entries to record the tuition transactions on your own books and on the books of your college or university?

Answer:

	Your Books			Your College's Books		
Start of Semester	Prepaid Tuition	1,500		Cash	1,500	
	Cash		1,500	Unearned Tuition		
	Paid semester tuition.			Revenue		1,500
				Collected revenue in advance.		
End of Semester	Tuition Expense	1,500		Unearned Tuition		
	Prepaid Tuition . . .		1,500	Revenue	1,500	
	To record tuition expense.			Tuition Revenue . .		1,500
				To record tuition revenue that was collected in advance.		

Exhibit 3-7 summarizes the timing of prepaid and accrual adjustments. The chapter appendix shows an alternative treatment for unearned revenues.

Exhibit 3-7 **Prepaid and Accrual Adjustments**

PREPAIDS—Cash transaction comes first.

	First			Later		
Prepaid Expenses	*Pay cash and record an asset:*			*Record an expense and decrease the asset:*		
	Prepaid Rent	XXX		Rent Expense	XXX	
	Cash		XXX	Prepaid Rent		XXX
Unearned Revenues	*Receive cash and record a liability:*			*Record a revenue and decrease the liability:*		
	Cash	XXX		Unearned Service Revenue	XXX	
	Unearned Service Revenue		XXX	Service Revenue		XXX

ACCRUALS—Cash transaction comes later.

	First			Later		
Accrued Expenses	*Accrue an expense and the related payable:*			*Pay cash and decrease the payable:*		
	Salary Expense	XXX		Salary Payable	XXX	
	Salary Payable		XXX	Cash		XXX
Accrued Revenues	*Accrue a revenue and the related receivable:*			*Receive cash and decrease the receivable:*		
	Interest Receivable	XXX		Cash	XXX	
	Interest Revenue		XXX	Interest Receivable		XXX

Source: The authors thank Darrel Davis and Alfonso Oddo for suggesting this exhibit.

Summary of the Adjusting Process

The adjusting process has two purposes:

1. Measure net income or net loss on the *income statement*. Every adjusting entry affects a *Revenue* or an *Expense*.
2. Update the *balance sheet*. Every adjusting entry affects an *Asset* or a *Liability*.

No adjusting entry debits or credits Cash because the cash transactions are recorded before the end of the period. Exhibit 3-8 summarizes the effects of the various adjusting entries.

Exhibit 3-8
Summary of Adjusting Entries

Category of Adjusting Entry	Debit	Credit
Prepaid expense	Expense	Asset
Depreciation	Expense	Contra asset
Accrued expense	Expense	Liability
Accrued revenue	Asset	Revenue
Unearned revenue	Liability	Revenue

Source: Adapted from material provided by Beverly Terry.

Exhibit 3-9 summarizes the adjusting entries of Gay Gillen eTravel at April 30. Panel A gives the data for each adjustment, Panel B shows the adjusting entries, and Panel C gives the accounts after posting. The adjustments are keyed by letter.

| Exhibit 3-9 | Journalizing and Posting the Adjusting Entries of Gay Gillen eTravel |

PANEL A—Information for Adjustments at April 30, 20X5

(a) Prepaid rent expired, $1,000. (e) Accrued service revenue, $250

(b) Supplies on hand, $400. (f) Service revenue that was collected in

(c) Depreciation on furniture, $275. advance and now has been earned, $150.

(d) Accrued salary expense, $950.

PANEL B—Adjusting Entries

(a) Rent Expense (↑ expense; debit) 1,000

 Prepaid Rent (↓ asset; credit)................................ 1,000

 To record rent expense.

(b) Supplies Expense (↑ expense; debit)............................. 300*

 Supplies (↓ asset; credit).................................... 300

 To record supplies used.

(c) Depreciation Expense—Furniture (↑ expense; debit)................ 275

 Accumulated Depreciation—Furniture (↓ asset; credit)......... 275

 To record depreciation on furniture.

(d) Salary Expense (↑ expense; debit)............................... 950

 Salary Payable (↑ liability; credit).......................... 950

 To accrue salary expense.

(e) Accounts Receivable (↑ asset; debit)............................ 250

 Service Revenue (↑ revenue; credit).......................... 250

 To accrue service revenue.

(f) Unearned Service Revenue (↓ liability; debit)....................... 150

 Service Revenue (↑ revenue; credit).......................... 150

 To record revenue that was collected in advance.

*Supplies available ($700) – supplies on hand ($400) = supplies expense ($300).

PANEL C—Ledger Accounts

ASSETS

Cash

| Bal. | 24,800 | |

Accounts Receivable

	2,250	
(e)	250	
Bal.	2,500	

Supplies

| | 700 | (b) | 300 |
| Bal. | 400 | |

Prepaid Rent

| | 3,000 | (a) | 1,000 |
| Bal. | 2,000 | |

Furniture

| Bal. | 16,500 | |

Accumulated Depreciation—Furniture

| | (c) | 275 |
| | Bal. | 275 |

LIABILITIES

Accounts Payable

| | Bal. 13,100 |

Salary Payable

| | (d) | 950 |
| | Bal. | 950 |

Unearned Service Revenue

| (f) | 150 | | 450 |
| | | Bal. | 300 |

OWNER'S EQUITY

Gay Gillen, Capital

| | Bal. | 31,250 |

Gay Gillen, Withdrawals

| Bal. | 3,200 | |

REVENUE

Service Revenue

			7,000
		(e)	250
		(f)	150
		Bal.	7,400

EXPENSES

Rent Expense

| (a) | 1,000 | |
| Bal. | 1,000 | |

Salary Expense

	950	
(d)	950	
Bal.	1,900	

Supplies Expense

| (b) | 300 | |
| Bal. | 300 | |

Depreciation Expense—Furniture

| (c) | 275 | |
| Bal. | 275 | |

Utilities Expense

| Bal. | 400 | |

- ☐ Financial Statements and Adjusting Entries
- ☐ Adjusting the Accounts
- ☐ Prepaids and Accruals
- ■ Adjusted Trial Balance
- ☐ The Financial Statements
- ☐ Ethical Issues
- ☐ Appendix: Alternative Treatment of Prepaid Expenses and Unearned Revenues

Student Resource CD
adjustments, trial balance

4 *Prepare an adjusted trial balance*

Adjusted Trial Balance
A list of all the accounts with their adjusted balances.

✔ Starter 3-10

✔ Starter 3-11

✔ Starter 3-12

✔ Starter 3-13

The Adjusted Trial Balance

This chapter began with the trial balance before any adjustments—the unadjusted trial balance (Exhibit 3-4). After the adjustments, the accounts appear as shown in Exhibit 3-9, Panel C. A useful step in preparing the financial statements is to list the accounts, along with their adjusted balances, on an **adjusted trial balance**. Exhibit 3-10 shows how to prepare the adjusted trial balance.

Exhibit 3-10 is a *work sheet*. We will continue this work sheet into Chapter 4. For now, simply note how clear this format is. The Account Titles and the Trial Balance are copied directly from the trial balance. The two Adjustments columns show the adjustment Debits and Credits. Each debit is identified by a letter keyed to Exhibit 3-9.

The Adjusted Trial Balance columns give the adjusted account balances. Each amount in these columns is computed by combining the trial balance amounts plus or minus the adjustments. For example, Accounts Receivable starts with a debit balance of $2,250. Adding the $250 debit from adjustment (e) gives Accounts Receivable an adjusted balance of $2,500. Supplies begins with a debit balance of $700. After the $300 credit adjustment, Supplies has a $400 balance. More than one entry may affect a single account, such as for Service Revenue. An account unaffected by the adjustments will show the same amount on both trial balances. For example, Cash, Furniture, Accounts Payable, Capital, and Withdrawals do not change.

Exhibit 3-10 **Preparation of Adjusted Trial Balance**

Gay Gillen eTravel
Preparation of Adjusted Trial Balance
April 30, 20X5

	Trial Balance		Adjustments		Adjusted Trial Balance		
Account Title	**Debit**	**Credit**	**Debit**	**Credit**	**Debit**	**Credit**	
Cash	24,800				24,800		Balance Sheet (Exhibit 3-13)
Accounts receivable	2,250		(e) 250		2,500		
Supplies	700			(b) 300	400		
Prepaid rent	3,000			(a) 1,000	2,000		
Furniture	16,500				16,500		
Accumulated depreciation				(c) 275		275	
Accounts payable		13,100				13,100	
Salary payable				(d) 950		950	
Unearned service revenue		450	(f) 150			300	
Gay Gillen, capital		31,250				31,250	Statement of Owner's Equity (Exhibit 3-12)
Gay Gillen, withdrawals	3,200				3,200		
Service revenue		7,000		(e) 250		7,400	Income Statement (Exhibit 3-11)
				(f) 150			
Rent expense			(a) 1,000		1,000		
Salary expense	950		(d) 950		1,900		
Supplies expense			(b) 300		300		
Depreciation expense			(c) 275		275		
Utilities expense	400				400		
	51,800	51,800	2,925	2,925	53,275	53,275	

The Financial Statements

The April financial statements of Gay Gillen eTravel can be prepared from the adjusted trial balance in Exhibit 3-10. In the right margin, we see how the accounts are distributed to the financial statements. As always, the income statement (Exhibit 3-11) reports the revenues and the expenses. The statement of owner's equity (Exhibit 3-12) shows why owner's capital changed during the period. Finally, the balance sheet (Exhibit 3-13) reports the assets, liabilities, and owner's equity.

- ☐ Financial Statements and Adjusting Entries
- ☐ Adjusting the Accounts
- ☐ Prepaids and Accruals
- ☐ Adjusted Trial Balance
- ■ The Financial Statements
- ☐ Ethical Issues
- ☐ Appendix: Alternative Treatment of Prepaid Expenses and Unearned Revenues

Student Resource CD
financial statements

5 *Prepare the financial statements from the adjusted trial balance*

Preparing the Statements

The financial statements should be prepared in this order:

1. Income statement—to determine net income
2. Statement of owner's equity—to compute ending capital
3. Balance sheet—which needs the ending capital amount to achieve its balancing feature

Exhibit 3-11
Income Statement

Gay Gillen eTravel
Income Statement
Month Ended April 30, 20X5

Revenue:		
Service revenue		$7,400
Expenses:		
Salary expense	$1,900	
Rent expense	1,000	
Utilities expense	400	
Supplies expense	300	
Depreciation expense	275	
Total expenses		3,875
Net income		$3,525

Exhibit 3-12
Statement of Owner's Equity

Gay Gillen eTravel
Statement of Owner's Equity
Month Ended April 30, 20X5

Gay Gillen, capital, April 1, 20X5	$31,250
Add: Net income	3,525
	34,775
Less: Withdrawals	(3,200)
Gay Gillen, capital, April 30, 20X5	$31,575

Exhibit 3-13
Balance Sheet

Gay Gillen eTravel
Balance Sheet
April 30, 20X5

Assets			Liabilities	
Cash		$24,800	Accounts payable	$13,100
Accounts receivable		2,500	Salary payable	950
Supplies		400	Unearned service revenue	300
Prepaid rent		2,000	Total liabilities	14,350
Furniture	$16,500			
Less: Accumulated depreciation	(275)	16,225	**Owner's Equity**	
			Gay Gillen, capital	31,575
Total assets		$45,925	Total liabilities and owner's equity	$45,925

All financial statements include these elements:

Heading

- Name of the entity—such as Gay Gillen eTravel
- Title of the statement—income statement, balance sheet, and so on
- Date, or period, covered by the statement—April 30, 20X5, or Month ended April 30, 20X5

Body of the statement

The income statement should list expenses in descending order by amount, as shown in Exhibit 3-11. However, Miscellaneous Expense, a catchall category, usually comes last.

Relationships Among the Financial Statements

The arrows in Exhibits 3-11, 3-12, and 3-13 show how the financial statements relate to each other. ←

The relationships among the financial statements were introduced in Chapter 1, p. 21. →

1. Net income from the income statement increases owner's equity in Exhibit 3-12. A net loss decreases owner's equity.
2. Ending capital from the statement of owner's equity is transferred to the balance sheet. The owner's ending capital is the final balancing amount for the balance sheet.

To solidify your understanding of these relationships, trace net income from the income statement to the statement of owner's equity. Then trace ending capital to the balance sheet.

Stop & Think

Examine Gay Gillen eTravel's adjusted trial balance in Exhibit 3-10. Suppose Gillen forgot to record the $1,000 of rent expense at April 30. What net income would the travel agency then report for April? What amounts of total assets, total liabilities, and owner's equity would Gay Gillen eTravel report at April 30?

Answer: Omitting the rent expense would produce these effects:

1. Net income would have been $4,525 ($3,525 + $1,000). See Exhibit 3-11.
2. Total assets would have been $46,925 ($45,925 + $1,000). See Exhibit 3-13.
3. Total liabilities (Exhibit 3-13) would have been unaffected by the error.
4. Owner's equity (Gay Gillen, Capital) would have been $32,575 ($31,575 + $1,000). See Exhibit 3-13.

- ☐ Financial Statements and Adjusting Entries
- ☐ Adjusting the Accounts
- ☐ Prepaids and Accruals
- ☐ Adjusted Trial Balance
- ☐ The Financial Statements
- ■ Ethical Issues
- ☐ Appendix: Alternative Treatment of Prepaid Expenses and Unearned Revenues

Student Resource CD
depreciation, ethics

Ethical Issues in Accrual Accounting

Like all areas of business, accounting poses ethical challenges. Accountants must be honest in their work. Only with complete and accurate information can people make wise decisions. An example will illustrate.

It's Just Lunch has done well as a business. The company has opened offices in most major cities in the United States. At this time, It's Just Lunch actually wishes to open an office in Nashville, Tennessee. Assume the company needs to borrow $100,000 to open the office. Suppose It's Just Lunch understated expenses in order to inflate net income on the income statement. A banker could be tricked into lending the company money. Then if It's Just Lunch could not pay the loan, the bank would lose—all because the banker relied on incorrect accounting information.

Accrual accounting provides opportunities for unethical accounting. It would be easy for a dishonest businessperson to overlook depreciation expense at the end of the year. Failing to record depreciation would overstate net income and paint a rosy picture of the company's financial situation. It is important for accountants to prepare accurate and complete financial statements because people rely on the data for their decisions.

Decision Guidelines

THE ACCOUNTING PROCESS

Take the role of Andrea McGinty, who founded **It's Just Lunch.** Assume it's now the end of the first year of operation, and McGinty wants to know where the business stands financially. The Decision Guidelines give a map of the accounting process to help McGinty manage the business.

Decision	Guidelines
Which basis of accounting better measures business income?	*Accrual basis*, because it provides more-complete reports of operating performance and financial position
How to measure revenues?	Revenue principle—Record revenues only after they're earned
How to measure expenses?	Matching principle—Subtract expenses from revenues in order to measure net income
Where to start with the measurement of income at the end of the period?	Unadjusted trial balance, usually referred to simply as the *trial balance*
How to update the accounts for the financial statements?	*Adjusting entries* at the end of the period
What are the categories of adjusting entries?	Prepaid expenses; Accrued revenues; Depreciation of plant assets; Unearned revenues; Accrued expenses
How do the adjusting entries differ from other journal entries?	**1.** Adjusting entries are made only at the end of the period. **2.** Adjusting entries never affect cash. **3.** All adjusting entries debit or credit • At least one *income statement* account (a revenue or an expense), and • At least one *balance sheet* account (an asset or a liability)
Where are the accounts with their adjusted balances summarized?	*Adjusted trial balance*, which aids preparation of the financial statements

Excel Application Exercise

Goal Create a spreadsheet that contains an income statement, a statement of owner's equity, and a balance sheet, complete with the formula relationships among all three statements.

Scenario The three financial statements are related. The relationships show up when net income changes. Using Exhibits 3-11, 3-12, and 3-13, replicate the income statement, statement of owner's equity, and balance sheet for Gay Gillen eTravel. When you are finished, you will change just two related variables, but you will see the effect ripple through all the statements you have created.

1. Change service revenue from $7,400 to $10,900 and cash from $24,800 to $28,300 (remember, every transaction requires at least one debit entry and one credit entry). What is the new net income figure?
2. What is the new balance for Gay Gillen, Capital on April 30, 20X5?
3. Did any other amounts change? If so, which ones?

Step-by-Step

1. Open a new Excel spreadsheet.
2. In column 1, create a bold-faced heading as follows:
   a. Chapter 3 Excel Application Exercise
   b. Gay Gillen eTravel
   c. Today's Date

Excel Application Exercise *(continued)*

3. Refer to Exhibit 3-11. Prepare the income statement as it appears in the text near the top of your spreadsheet, formatting and using formulas as appropriate. When finished, put a border around the income statement.
4. Refer to Exhibit 3-12. In your spreadsheet, prepare the statement of owner's equity as it appears in the text, to the right of the income statement. Be sure "Net Income" is a cell reference to your income statement's net income. Format and use formulas as appropriate. When finished, put a border around the statement of owner's equity.
5. Refer to Exhibit 3-13. Prepare the balance sheet as it appears in the text, below the income statement in your spreadsheet. Be sure "Gay Gillen, Capital" is a cell reference to the ending capital balance in your statement of owner's equity. When finished, put a border around the balance sheet.
6. Make the two changes in scenario question 1. Save your file to disk, and print a copy for comparison with Exhibits 3-11, 3-12, and 3-13.

END-OF-CHAPTER *Summary Problem*

A+ TIPS
CHECK YOUR RESOURCES

The trial balance of Clay Employment Services pertains to December 31, 20X9, which is the end of Clay's annual accounting period. Data needed for the adjusting entries include

a. Supplies on hand at year-end, $2,000.
b. Depreciation on furniture and fixtures, $20,000.
c. Depreciation on building, $10,000.
d. Salaries owed but not yet paid, $5,000.
e. Accrued service revenue, $12,000.
f. $32,000 of the unearned service revenue has been earned.

Required

1. Open the ledger accounts with their unadjusted balances. Show dollar amounts in thousands, as for Accounts Receivable:

Accounts Receivable	
370	

2. Journalize Clay's adjusting entries at December 31, 20X9. Key entries by letter, as in Exhibit 3-9.
3. Post the adjusting entries.
4. Write the trial balance on a work sheet, enter the adjusting entries, and prepare an adjusted trial balance, as shown in Exhibit 3-10.
5. Prepare the income statement, the statement of owner's equity, and the balance sheet. Draw arrows linking the three financial statements.

Clay Employment Services

Trial Balance
December 31, 20X9

Cash	$ 198,000	
Accounts receivable	370,000	
Supplies	6,000	
Furniture and fixtures	100,000	
Accumulated depreciation—furniture and fixtures		$ 40,000
Building	250,000	
Accumulated depreciation—building		130,000
Accounts payable		380,000
Salary payable		
Unearned service revenue		45,000
Jay Clay, capital		293,000
Jay Clay, withdrawals	65,000	
Service revenue		286,000

Salary expense	172,000	
Supplies expense		
Depreciation expense—furniture and fixtures		
Depreciation expense—building		
Miscellaneous expense	13,000	
Total	$1,174,000	$1,174,000

Solution

Requirements 1 and 3 (amounts in thousands)

Assets

Cash

Bal.	198		

Accounts Receivable

	370		
(e)	12		
Bal.	382		

Supplies

	6	(a)	4
Bal.	2		

Furniture and Fixtures

Bal.	100		

Accumulated Depreciation—Furniture and Fixtures

			40
		(b)	20
		Bal.	60

Building

Bal.	250		

Accumulated Depreciation—Building

			130
		(c)	10
		Bal.	140

Liabilities

Accounts Payable

		Bal.	380

Salary Payable

		(d)	5
		Bal.	5

Unearned Service Revenue

(f)	32		45
		Bal.	13

Owner's Equity

Jay Clay, Capital

		Bal.	293

Jay Clay, Withdrawals

Bal.	65		

Revenue

Service Revenue

			286
		(e)	12
		(f)	32
		Bal.	330

Expenses

Salary Expense

	172		
(d)	5		
Bal.	177		

Supplies Expense

(a)	4		
Bal.	4		

Depreciation Expense—Furniture and Fixtures

(b)	20		
Bal.	20		

Depreciation Expense—Building

(c)	10		
Bal.	10		

Miscellaneous Expense

Bal.	13		

Requirement 2

	20X9			
a.	Dec. 31	Supplies Expense ($6,000 – $2,000)	4,000	
		Supplies		4,000
		To record supplies used.		
b.	31	Depreciation Expense—Furniture and Fixtures	20,000	
		Accumulated Depreciation—Furniture and Fixtures		20,000
		To record depreciation expense on furniture and fixtures.		
c.	31	Depreciation Expense—Building	10,000	
		Accumulated Depreciation—Building		10,000
		To record depreciation expense on building.		
d.	31	Salary Expense	5,000	
		Salary Payable		5,000
		To accrue salary expense.		
e.	31	Accounts Receivable	12,000	
		Service Revenue		12,000
		To accrue service revenue.		
f.	31	Unearned Service Revenue	32,000	
		Service Revenue		32,000
		To record service revenue that was collected in advance.		

Requirement 4

Clay Employment Services

Preparation of Adjusted Trial Balance
December 31, 20X9 (amounts in thousands)

	Trial Balance		Adjustments		Adjusted Trial Balance	
Account Title	**Debit**	**Credit**	**Debit**	**Credit**	**Debit**	**Credit**
Cash	198				198	
Accounts receivable	370		(e) 12		382	
Supplies	6			(a) 4	2	
Furniture and fixtures	100				100	
Accumulated depreciation—furniture and fixtures		40		(b) 20		60
Building	250				250	
Accumulated depreciation—building		130		(c) 10		140
Accounts payable		380				380
Salary payable				(d) 5		5
Unearned service revenue		45	(f) 32			13
Jay Clay, capital		293				293
Jay Clay, withdrawals	65				65	
Service revenue		286		(e) 12 (f) 32		330
Salary expense	172		(d) 5		177	
Supplies expense			(a) 4		4	
Depreciation expense—furniture and fixtures			(b) 20		20	
Depreciation expense—building			(c) 10		10	
Miscellaneous expense	13				13	
	1,174	1,174	83	83	1,221	1,221

Requirement 5

Clay Employment Services

Income Statement
Year Ended December 31, 20X9 (amounts in thousands)

Revenue:		
Service revenue		$330
Expenses:		
Salary expense	$177	
Depreciation expense—furniture and fixtures	20	
Depreciation expense—building	10	
Supplies expense	4	
Miscellaneous expense	13	
Total expenses		224
Net income		$106

Clay Employment Services
Statement of Owner's Equity
Year Ended December 31, 20X9 (amounts in thousands)

Jay Clay, capital, January 1, 20X9	$293
Add: Net income	106
	399
Less: Withdrawals	(65)
Jay Clay, December 31, 20X9	$334

Clay Employment Services
Balance Sheet
December 31, 20X9 (amounts in thousands)

Assets			Liabilities	
Cash		$198	Accounts payable	$380
Accounts receivable		382	Salary payable	5
Supplies		2	Unearned service revenue	13
Furniture and fixtures	$100		Total liabilities	398
Less: Accumulated depreciation	(60)	40		
Building	$250		**Owner's Equity**	
Less: Accumulated depreciation	(140)	110	Jay Clay, capital	334
Total assets		$732	Total liabilities and owner's equity	$732

REVIEW *The Adjusting Process*

Quick Check

1. What are the features of accrual accounting and cash-basis accounting?
   a. Accrual accounting records all transactions.
   b. Cash-basis accounting records only cash receipts and cash payments.
   c. Accrual accounting is superior because it provides more information.
   d. All the above are true.
2. The revenue principle says
   a. Record revenue only after you have earned it.
   b. Record revenue only when you receive cash.
   c. Measure revenues and expenses in order to compute net income.
   d. Divide time into annual periods to measure revenue properly.
3. Adjusting the accounts is the process of
   a. Recording transactions as they occur during the period
   b. Updating the accounts at the end of the period
   c. Zeroing out account balances to prepare for the next period
   d. Subtracting expenses from revenues to measure net income
4. Which types of adjusting entries are natural opposites?
   a. Prepaids and depreciation
   b. Expenses and revenues
   c. Prepaids and accruals
   d. Net income and net loss

5. Assume that the weekly payroll of **It's Just Lunch** is $5,000. December 31, end of the year, falls on Monday, and the company will pay employees on Friday for the full week. What adjusting entry will It's Just Lunch make on Monday, December 31?

a. Salary Expense	1,000	
Salary Payable		1,000
b. Salary Expense	1,000	
Cash		1,000
c. Salary Payable	1,000	
Salary Expense		1,000

d. No adjustment is needed because the company will pay the payroll on Friday.

6. Assume It's Just Lunch gains a client who prepays $600 for a package of six dates. It's Just Lunch collects the $600 in advance and will provide the date arrangements later. After setting up two dates for the client, what should It's Just Lunch report on its income statement?
   a. Cash of $600
   b. Service revenue of $600
   c. Service revenue of $200
   d. Unearned service revenue of $400

7. Unearned revenue is always a (an)
   a. Liability
   b. Revenue
   c. Asset
   d. Owners' equity because you collected the cash in advance

8. Assume you prepay It's Just Lunch for a package of six dates. Which type of account should you have in your records?
   a. Accrued expense
   b. Prepaid expense
   c. Accrued revenue
   d. Unearned revenue

9. The adjusted trial balance shows
   a. Amounts that may be out of balance
   b. Revenues and expenses only
   c. Assets, liabilities, and owner's equity only
   d. Amounts ready for the financial statements

10. The accounting data flow from the
   a. Income statement to the statement of owner's equity
   b. Statement of owner's equity to the balance sheet
   c. Both a and b are correct
   d. None of the above is correct

Accounting Vocabulary

accrual accounting (p. 92)
accrued expense (p. 102)
accrued revenue (p. 104)
accumulated depreciation (p. 101)
adjusted trial balance (p. 108)
adjusting entry (p. 97)
book value (of a plant asset) (p. 101)
cash-basis accounting (p. 92)
contra account (p. 101)
deferred revenue (p. 104)
depreciation (p. 100)
matching principle (p. 95)
plant asset (p. 100)
prepaid expense (p. 98)
revenue principle (p. 94)
time-period concept (p. 96)
unearned revenue (p. 104)

ASSESS *Your Progress*

A+ online homework

See *www.prenhall.com/horngren* for selected Starters, Exercises, and Problems.

Starters

Comparing accrual accounting and cash-basis accounting
(Obj. 1)

S3-1 Suppose you work summers mowing lawns. Most of your customers pay you immediately after you cut their grass. A few ask you to send them a bill at the end of each month. It is now June 30 and you have collected $900 from cash-paying customers. Your remaining customers owe you $300. How much service revenue would you have under the (a) cash basis and (b) accrual basis? Which method of accounting provides more information about your lawn-service business? Explain your answer.

S3-2 **It's Just Lunch**, the business featured at the beginning of this chapter, uses client databases to help clients meet. Suppose It's Just Lunch paid $3,000 for a **Dell** computer. Review pages 92 and 93, and then describe how It's Just Lunch would account for the $3,000 expenditure under (a) the cash basis and (b) the accrual basis. State in your own words why the accrual basis is more realistic for this situation.

Accrual accounting versus cash-basis accounting for expenses
(Obj. 1)

S3-3 **Intel Corporation** produces Pentium© processors that drive many computers. Suppose Intel has completed production of 1,000 processor units that it expects to sell to **Gateway**. Assume that Intel's cost to manufacture each processor is $140 and that Intel sells each processor for $375.

Apply the revenue principle to determine (1) when Intel should record revenue for this situation and (2) the amount of revenue Intel should record for the sale of 1,000 processors.

Applying the revenue principle
(Obj. 2)

S3-4 Return to the **Intel Corporation** situation described in Starter 3-3. Suppose Intel has sold 1,000 Pentium© processors to **Gateway**. What will Intel record in order to apply the matching principle? Give the name of the expense that Intel will record, and specify its amount.

Applying the matching principle
(Obj. 2)

S3-5 Answer the following questions.

Adjusting prepaid expenses
(Obj. 3)

1. Prepaid expenses are discussed beginning on page 98. Focus on the accounting for prepaid rent. Assume that Gay Gillen's initial $3,000 prepayment of rent on April 1 (page 98) was for 6 months rather than 3. Give the adjusting entry to record rent expense at April 30. Include the date of the entry and an explanation. Then post to the two accounts involved, and show their balances at April 30.
2. Refer to the supplies example on pages 99–100. Assume that Gillen's travel agency has $500 of supplies on hand (rather than $400) at April 30. Give the adjusting entry, complete with date and explanation, at April 30. Post to the accounts and show their balances at April 30.

S3-6 **It's Just Lunch** uses computers for data searches. Suppose that on May 1 the company paid cash of $24,000 for **Dell** computers that are expected to remain useful for two years. At the end of two years, the value of the computers is expected to be zero.

Recording depreciation
(Obj. 3)

1. Make journal entries to record (a) purchase of the computers on May 1 and (b) depreciation on May 31. Include dates and explanations, and use the following accounts: Computer Equipment; Accumulated Depreciation—Computer Equipment; and Depreciation Expense—Computer Equipment.
2. Post to the accounts listed in requirement 1, and show their balances at May 31.
3. What is the equipment's book value at May 31?

S3-7 Suppose Gay Gillen borrowed $50,000 on October 1 by signing a note payable to Community One Bank. Gillen's interest expense for each month is $300.

Accruing and paying interest expense
(Obj. 3)

1. Make Gillen's adjusting entry to accrue interest expense at December 31. Date the entry and include its explanation.
2. Post to the two accounts affected by the adjustment.

S3-8 Return to the situation of Starter 3-7. Suppose you are accounting for the same transactions on the books of Community One Bank, which lent the money to Gay Gillen eTravel. Perform both requirements of Starter 3-7 for Community One Bank using its own accounts: Interest Receivable and Interest Revenue.

Accruing and receiving cash from interest revenue
(Obj. 3)

S3-9 **Yankee Clipper Magazine** collects cash from subscribers in advance and then mails the magazines to subscribers over a one-year period. Give the adjusting entry that Yankee Clipper makes to record the earning of $8,000 of Subscription Revenue that was collected in advance. Include an explanation for the entry, as illustrated in the chapter.

Accounting for unearned revenues
(Obj. 3)

S3-10 Study the T-accounts in Exhibit 3-9, Panel C, on page 107. Focus on the Supplies account. Which amount in the Supplies account appeared on the *unadjusted* trial balance

Contrasting the unadjusted and the adjusted trial balances
(Obj. 4)

(Exhibit 3-10, page 108)? Which amount will appear on the *adjusted* trial balance? Which amount will be reported on the balance sheet at April 30? Under what balance sheet category will Gillen report Supplies? Under what category, and on which financial statement, will Gillen report supplies used up?

Using the adjusted trial balance
(Obj. 4)

S3-11 In the Adjustments columns of Exhibit 3-10, page 108, two adjustments affected Service Revenue.

1. Make journal entries for the two adjustments. Date each entry and include an explanation.
2. The journal entries you just made affected three accounts: Accounts Receivable; Unearned Service Revenue; and Service Revenue. Show how Gay Gillen eTravel will report all three accounts in its financial statements at April 30. For each account, identify its (a) financial statement, (b) category on the financial statement, and (c) balance.

Preparing the balance sheet
(Obj. 5)

S3-12 Refer to the adjusted trial balance in Exhibit 3-10, page 108.

1. Focus on the *adjusted* figures. Compute Gillen's total assets and total liabilities at April 30. Compare your totals to the balance sheet amounts in Exhibit 3-13, page 109. Are they the same?
2. Why does a business need to make adjusting entries at the end of the period?

Preparing the income statement
(Obj. 5)

S3-13 Refer to the adjusted trial balance in Exhibit 3-10, page 108.

1. Focus on the *adjusted* figures. Compute Gillen's total revenues, total expenses, and net income for April. Compare your totals to the income statement amounts in Exhibit 3-11, page 109. Are they the same?
2. Why does a business need to make adjusting entries at the end of the period?

A+ online homework

Exercises

Cash basis versus accrual basis
(Obj. 1)

E3-1 Lexington Inn completed the following selected transactions during July:

July 1	Prepaid rent for three months, $3,000
5	Paid electricity expenses, $800.
9	Received cash for the day's room rentals, $2,600.
14	Paid cash for six television sets, $3,000.
23	Served a banquet, receiving a note receivable, $1,600.
31	Made the adjusting entry for rent (from July 1).
31	Accrued salary expense, $900.

Show how each transaction would be handled using the accrual basis. Give the amount of revenue or expense for July. Journal entries are not required. Use the following format for your answer, and show your computations:

Amount of Revenue (Expense) for July		
Date	**Revenue (Expense)**	**Accrual-Basis Amount**

Accrual accounting concepts and principles
(Obj. 1)

E3-2 Identify the accounting concept or principle (there may be more than one) that gives the most direction on how to account for each of the following situations:

a. Expenses of $1,200 must be accrued at the end of the period to measure income properly.
b. A customer states her intention to switch health clubs. Should the new health club record revenue based on this intention? Give the reason for your answer.

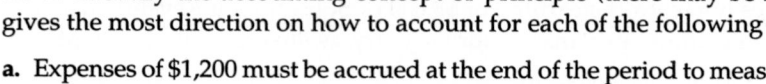

c. The owner of a business desires monthly financial statements to measure the progress of the entity on an ongoing basis.
d. Expenses of the period total $6,700. This amount should be subtracted from revenue to compute the period's net income.

E3-3 Suppose you start up your own photography business to shoot videos at college parties. The freshman class pays you $300 in advance just to guarantee your services for its party. The sophomore class promises you a minimum of $250 for filming its formal, and you end up collecting cash of $350 for this party. Answer the following questions about the correct way to account for your revenue under the accrual basis.

Cash versus accrual; applying the revenue principle
(Obj. 1, 2)

1. In addition to cash, what type of account was created when you received $300 from the freshman class? Name the new account.
2. When did you earn your revenue for both parties? What actually caused you to earn the revenue? Did you earn the revenue at the moment you received cash?

E3-4 Compute the amounts indicated by question marks for each of the following Prepaid Rent situations. For situation A, journalize the needed entry. Consider each situation separately.

Allocating prepaid expense to the asset and the expense
(Obj. 2, 3)

Student Resource CD
spreadsheet

	Situation			
	A	B	C	D
Beginning Prepaid Rent	$ 400	$500	$ 900	$ 600
Payments for Prepaid Rent during the year	1,400	?	1,100	?
Total amount to account for	?	?	2,000	1,500
Ending Prepaid Rent	300	400	?	700
Rent Expense	$?	$900	$1,200	$ 800

E3-5 Journalize the adjusting entries for the following adjustments at January 31, end of the accounting period.

Journalizing adjusting entries
(Obj. 3)

a. Employee salaries owed for Monday through Thursday of a five-day workweek; weekly payroll, $10,000.
b. Unearned service revenue earned, $500.
c. Depreciation, $3,000.
d. Prepaid rent expired, $300.
e. Interest revenue accrued, $3,800.

E3-6 Suppose the adjustments required in Exercise 3-5 were not made. Compute the overall overstatement or understatement of net income as a result of the omission of these adjustments.

Analyzing the effects of adjustments on net income
(Obj. 3)

E3-7 Journalize the adjusting entry needed at December 31 for each of the following independent situations.

Journalizing adjusting entries
(Obj. 3)

a. On October 1, we collected $6,000 rent in advance. We debited Cash and credited Unearned Rent Revenue. The tenant was paying one year's rent in advance.
b. Interest revenue of $800 has been earned but not yet received. The business holds a $20,000 note receivable.
c. Salary expense is $1,500 per day—Monday through Friday—and the business pays employees each Friday. This year December 31 falls on a Wednesday.
d. The unadjusted balance of the Supplies account is $3,100. Supplies on hand total $1,200.
e. Equipment was purchased last year at a cost of $10,000. The equipment's useful life is four years. Record the year's depreciation.
f. On September 1, when we prepaid $1,200 for a two-year insurance policy, we debited Prepaid Insurance and credited Cash.

Recording adjustments in T-accounts
(Obj. 3)

E3-8 The accounting records of Randall Roberts, Architect, include the following unadjusted balances at March 31: Accounts Receivable, $1,000; Supplies, $600; Salary Payable, $0; Unearned Service Revenue, $400; Service Revenue, $4,700; Salary Expense, $1,200; Supplies Expense, $0. Roberts' accountant develops the following data for the March 31 adjusting entries:

a. Service revenue accrued, $2,000.
b. Unearned service revenue that has been earned, $200.
c. Supplies on hand, $100.
d. Salary owed to employee, $400.

Open a T-account for each account and record the adjustments directly in the accounts, keying each adjustment by letter. Show each account's adjusted balance. Journal entries are not required.

Adjusting the accounts
(Obj. 3, 4)

E3-9 The adjusted trial balance of Stephen Perdue, Craftsman, is incomplete. Enter the adjustment amounts directly in the adjustment columns of the text.

Stephen Perdue, Craftsman

Preparation of Adjusted Trial Balance
May 31, 20X8

	Trial Balance		Adjustments		Adjusted Trial Balance	
Account Title	**Debit**	**Credit**	**Debit**	**Credit**	**Debit**	**Credit**
Cash	3,000				3,000	
Accounts receivable	4,500				7,600	
Supplies	1,000				800	
Equipment	32,300				32,300	
Accumulated depreciation		14,000				14,400
Salary payable						900
S. Perdue, capital		26,400				26,400
S. Perdue, withdrawals	5,100				5,100	
Service revenue		9,600				12,700
Salary expense	2,700				3,600	
Rent expense	1,400				1,400	
Depreciation expense					400	
Supplies expense					200	
	50,000	50,000			54,400	54,400

Journalizing adjustments
(Obj. 3, 4)

Student Resource CD
General Ledger, Peachtree, QuickBooks

E3-10 Make the journal entry for each adjustment needed to complete the adjusted trial balance in Exercise 3-9. Date the entries and include explanations.

Preparing the financial statements
(Obj. 5)

E3-11 Refer to the adjusted trial balance in Exercise 3-9. Prepare the Stephen Perdue, Craftsman, income statement and statement of owner's equity for the month ended May 31, 20X8, and its balance sheet on that date. Draw arrows linking the three statements.

Preparing the income statement
(Obj. 5)

E3-12 The accountant for Bill Glaze, Attorney, has posted adjusting entries (a) through (e) to the accounts at December 31, 20X6. Selected balance sheet accounts and all the revenues and expenses of the entity follow in T-account form.

Accounts Receivable

23,000	
(e) 1,000	

Supplies

4,000	(a) 1,000

Accumulated Depreciation—Equipment

	5,000
	(b) 2,000

Accumulated Depreciation—Building

	33,000
	(c) 5,000

Salary Payable

	(d) 1,500

Service Revenue

	105,000
	(e) 1,000

Salary Expense

28,000	
(d) 1,500	

Supplies Expense

(a) 1,000	

Depreciation Expense—Equipment

(b) 2,000	

Depreciation Expense—Building

(c) 5,000	

Required

1. Prepare the income statement of Bill Glaze, Attorney, for the year ended December 31, 20X6. List expenses in order from the largest to the smallest.
2. Were 20X6 operations successful? Give the reason for your answer.

Preparing the statement of owner's equity **(Obj. 5)**

E3-13 Blackhawk Data Processing began the year with capital of $90,000. On July 12, Kent Black (the owner) invested $12,000 cash in the business. On September 26, he transferred to the company land valued at $70,000. The income statement for the year ended December 31, 20X5, reported a net loss of $28,000. During this fiscal year, Black withdrew $1,500 each month for personal use.

Required

1. Prepare Blackhawk's statement of owner's equity for the year ended December 31, 20X5.
2. Did the owner's equity of the business increase or decrease during the year? What caused this change?

Computing financial statement amounts **(Obj. 5)**

E3-14 The adjusted trial balances of Quartz Control Corporation at December 31, 20X7, and December 31, 20X6, include these amounts:

	20X7	20X6
Supplies	$ 2,100	$ 1,500
Salary payable	3,100	3,700
Unearned service revenue	14,200	16,300

Analysis of the accounts at December 31, 20X7, reveals these transactions for 20X7:

Purchases of supplies	$ 8,400
Cash payments for salaries	84,600
Cash receipts in advance for service revenue	180,200

Compute the amount of supplies expense, salary expense, and service revenue to report on the Quartz Control income statement for 20X7.

Continuing Exercise

Exercise 3-15 continues the Marsha Walker, Consultant, situation begun in Exercise 2-17 of Chapter 2.

Adjusting the accounts, preparing an adjusted trial balance, and preparing the financial statements **(Obj. 3, 4, 5)**

Student Resource CD

GL, PT, QB

E3-15 Refer to Exercise 2-17 of Chapter 2. Start from the trial balance and the posted T-accounts that Marsha Walker, Consultant, prepared for her business at December 18, as follows:

Marsha Walker, Consultant

Trial Balance
December 18, 20XX

Account	Debit	Credit
Cash	$12,100	
Accounts receivable	1,700	
Supplies	300	
Equipment	2,000	
Furniture	3,600	
Accounts payable		$ 3,900
Marsha Walker, capital		14,000
Marsha Walker, withdrawals	—	
Service revenue		2,500
Rent expense	500	
Utilities expense	200	
Salary expense		
Total	$20,400	$20,400

Later in December, the business completed these transactions, as follows:

Dec. 21	Received $900 in advance for client service to be performed evenly over the next 30 days.
21	Hired a secretary to be paid $1,500 on the 20th day of each month. The secretary begins work immediately.
26	Paid $300 on account.
28	Collected $600 on account.
30	Withdrew $1,600 for personal use.

Required

1. Open these additional T-accounts: Accumulated Depreciation—Equipment; Accumulated Depreciation—Furniture; Salary Payable; Unearned Service Revenue; Depreciation Expense—Equipment; Depreciation Expense—Furniture; Supplies Expense.
2. Journalize the transactions of December 21 through 30.
3. Post to the T-accounts, keying all items by date.
4. Prepare a trial balance at December 31. Also set up columns for the adjustments and for the adjusted trial balance, as illustrated in Exhibit 3-10.
5. At December 31, Walker gathers the following information for the adjusting entries:
   a. Accrued service revenue, $400.
   b. Earned a portion of the service revenue collected in advance on December 21.
   c. Supplies on hand, $100.
   d. Depreciation expense—equipment, $50; furniture, $60.
   e. Accrued expense for secretary's salary—10 days worked.

   Make these adjustments directly in the adjustments columns, and complete the adjusted trial balance at December 31. Throughout the book, to avoid rounding errors, we base adjusting entries on 30-day months and 360-day years.
6. Journalize and post the adjusting entries. Denote each adjusting amount as *Adj.* and an account balance as *Bal.*
7. Prepare the income statement and the statement of owner's equity of Marsha Walker, Consultant, for the month ended December 31, and prepare the balance sheet at that date. Draw arrows linking the statements.

Problems

(Group A)

A+ online homework

Cash basis versus accrual basis
(Obj. 1, 2)

P3-1A The Española Medical Clinic completed these transactions during May:

May 2	Prepaid insurance for May through July, $900.
4	Paid water bill, $550.
5	Performed services on account, $3,000.
9	Purchased medical equipment for cash, $1,400.
12	Received cash for services performed, $7,400.
14	Purchased office equipment on account, $300.
28	Collected $500 on account from May 5.
29	Paid salary expense, $1,100.
30	Paid account payable from May 14.
31	Recorded adjusting entry for May insurance expense (see May 2).
31	Debited unearned revenue and credited revenue in an adjusting entry, $700.

Required

1. Show how each transaction would be handled using the accrual basis of accounting. Give the amount of revenue or expense for May. Journal entries are not required. Use the following format for your answer, and show your computations:

Amount of Revenue (Expense) for May		
Date	Revenue (Expense)	Accrual-Basis Amount

2. Compute May net income or net loss under the accrual basis of accounting.
3. Why is the accrual basis of accounting preferable to the cash basis?

Applying accounting principles
(Obj. 1, 2)

P3-2A Assume you own and operate Westview Nursery. Your greenhouse is quite large, and you employ 10 people. Write a business memo to your assistant manager to explain the difference between the cash basis of accounting and the accrual basis. Mention the roles of the revenue principle and the matching principle in accrual accounting. The format of a business memo follows.

Date: ______
To: Assistant Manager
From: (Student Name)
Subject: Difference between the cash basis and the accrual basis of accounting

Journalizing adjusting entries
(Obj. 3)
Student Resource CD
GL, PT, QB

P3-3A Journalize the adjusting entry needed on December 31, end of the current accounting period, for each of the following independent cases affecting Colorado River Rafting.

a. Details of Prepaid Insurance are shown in the account:

Prepaid Insurance	
Mar. 31 2,400	

Colorado pays liability insurance each year on March 31. Record insurance expense for the year ended December 31.

b. Colorado pays employees each Friday. The amount of the weekly payroll is $2,000 for a five-day workweek. The current accounting period ends on Monday.

c. Colorado has borrowed money, signing a note payable. For the current year, Colorado accrued interest expense of $600 that it will pay next year.

d. The beginning balance of Supplies was $2,600. During the year, Colorado purchased supplies for $6,100, and at December 31 the supplies on hand total $2,100.
e. Colorado is providing river-rafting trips for a large tour operator from Denver. The tour operator paid Colorado $12,000 as the annual service fee and Colorado recorded this amount as Unearned Service Revenue. The owner determines that Colorado has earned one-fourth the total fee during the current year.
f. Depreciation for the current year includes Canoe Equipment, $3,850; and Trucks, $1,300. Make a compound entry, as illustrated in Chapter 2.

Analyzing and journalizing adjustments
(Obj. 3)

Student Resource CD
GL, PT, QB

P3-4A Assume a U-Haul location's unadjusted and adjusted trial balances at April 30, 20X7, show the following data:

U-Haul
Adjusted Trial Balance
April 30, 20X7

	Trial Balance		Adjusted Trial Balance	
Account Title	**Debit**	**Credit**	**Debit**	**Credit**
Cash	6,200		6,200	
Accounts receivable	6,000		6,700	
Interest receivable			300	
Note receivable	4,100		4,100	
Supplies	1,000		300	
Prepaid rent	2,400		1,600	
Equipment	66,400		66,400	
Accumulated depreciation		16,000		17,200
Accounts payable		6,900		6,900
Wages payable				300
Paul Olen, capital		59,500		59,500
Paul Olen, withdrawals	3,600		3,600	
Rental revenue		9,500		10,200
Interest revenue				300
Wage expense	1,600		1,900	
Rent expense			800	
Depreciation expense			1,200	
Insurance expense	400		400	
Supplies expense			700	
Utilities expense	200		200	
	91,900	91,900	94,400	94,400

Required

Journalize the adjusting entries that account for the differences between the two trial balances.

Journalizing and posting adjustments to T-accounts; preparing the adjusted trial balance
(Obj. 3, 4)

Student Resource CD
GL, PT, QB

P3-5A The trial balance of Smoky Mountain Lodge at December 31, 20X5, and the data needed for the month-end adjustments follow.

Adjustment data:

a. Prepaid insurance still in force at December 31, $600.
b. Supplies used during the month, $600.
c. Depreciation for the month, $900.
d. Accrued advertising expense at December 31, $300. (Credit Accounts Payable.)
e. Accrued salary expense at December 31, $100.
f. Unearned service revenue still unearned at December 31, $1,100.

Smoky Mountain Lodge

Trial Balance
December 31, 20X5

Cash	$ 12,200	
Accounts receivable	14,100	
Prepaid insurance	3,100	
Supplies	800	
Building	412,700	
Accumulated depreciation		$311,600
Accounts payable		1,900
Salary payable		
Unearned service revenue		2,300
Rocky Rivers, capital		125,000
Rocky Rivers, withdrawals	2,900	
Service revenue		7,900
Salary expense	2,100	
Insurance expense		
Depreciation expense		
Advertising expense	800	
Supplies expense		
Total	$448,700	$448,700

Required

1. Open T-accounts for the accounts listed in the trial balance, inserting their December 31 unadjusted balances.
2. Journalize the adjusting entries and post them to the T-accounts. Key the journal entries and the posted amounts by letter.
3. Prepare the adjusted trial balance.
4. How will the company use the adjusted trial balance?

Preparing the financial statements from an adjusted trial balance
(Obj. 5)

P3-6A The adjusted trial balance of Air & Sea Travel at December 31, 20X6, follows.

Air & Sea Travel

Adjusted Trial Balance
December 31, 20X6

Cash	$ 1,300	
Accounts receivable	4,900	
Supplies	2,300	
Prepaid rent	1,600	
Office furniture	37,700	
Accumulated depreciation—office furniture		$ 4,800
Accounts payable		4,500
Unearned service revenue		600
Cindy Sorrel, capital		26,000
Cindy Sorrel, withdrawals	29,000	
Service revenue		106,000
Depreciation expense—office furniture	2,300	
Salary expense	39,900	
Rent expense	17,400	
Utilities expense	2,600	
Supplies expense	2,900	
Total	$141,900	$141,900

Required

1. Prepare Air & Sea Travel's 20X6 income statement, statement of owner's equity, and year-end balance sheet. List expenses in decreasing order on the income statement and show total liabilities on the balance sheet. Draw arrows linking the three financial statements.
2. a. Which financial statement reports Air & Sea Travel's results of operations? Were operations successful during 20X6? Cite specifics from the financial statements to support your evaluation.
   b. Which statement reports the company's financial position? Does Air & Sea Travel's financial position look strong or weak? Give the reason for your evaluation.

Preparing an adjusted trial balance and the financial statements
(Obj. 3, 4, 5)

Student Resource CD
GL, PT, QB

P3-7A The unadjusted trial balance of Pat Patillo, CPA, at July 31, 20X6, and the related month-end adjustment data follow.

Pat Patillo, CPA
Trial Balance
July 31, 20X6

Cash	$ 8,900	
Accounts receivable	11,600	
Prepaid rent	4,000	
Supplies	800	
Furniture	28,800	
Accumulated depreciation		$ 3,500
Accounts payable		3,400
Salary payable		
Pat Patillo, capital		39,100
Pat Patillo, withdrawals	4,000	
Accounting service revenue		15,000
Salary expense	2,400	
Rent expense		
Utilities expense	500	
Depreciation expense		
Supplies expense		
Total	$61,000	$61,000

Adjustment data:

a. Accrued accounting service revenue at July 31, $900.
b. Prepaid rent expired during the month. The unadjusted balance of prepaid rent relates to the period July through October.
c. Supplies on hand at July 31, $400.
d. Depreciation on furniture for the month. The estimated useful life of the furniture is 4 years.
e. Accrued salary expense at July 31 for 1 day only. The 5-day weekly payroll is $1,000.

Required

1. Using Exhibit 3-10 as an example, write the trial balance on a work sheet and prepare the adjusted trial balance of Pat Patillo, CPA, at July 31, 20X6. Key each adjusting entry by letter.
2. Prepare the income statement and the statement of owner's equity for the month ended July 31, 20X6, and the balance sheet at that date. Draw arrows linking the three statements.

Problems

(Group B)

A+ online homework

P3-1B Brazos Medical Clinic completed the following selected transactions during January:

Cash basis versus accrual basis
(Obj. 1, 2)

Jan. 1	Prepaid insurance for January through March, $600.
4	Performed medical service on account, $4,000.
5	Purchased office furniture on account, $150.
8	Paid property tax expense, $450.
11	Purchased office equipment for cash, $800.
19	Performed medical service and received cash, $700.
24	Collected $400 on account.
26	Paid account payable from January 5.
29	Paid salary expense, $900.
31	Recorded adjusting entry for January insurance expense (see Jan. 1).
31	Debited unearned revenue and credited revenue to adjust the accounts, $600.

Required

1. Show how each transaction would be handled using the accrual basis of accounting. Give the amount of revenue or expense for January. Journal entries are not required. Use the following format for your answer, and show your computations:

Amount of Revenue (Expense) for January		
Date	Revenue (Expense)	Accrual-Basis Amount

2. Compute January net income or net loss under the accrual basis of accounting.
3. State why the accrual basis of accounting is preferable to the cash basis.

P3-2B As the controller of Genie Car Wash, you have hired a new bookkeeper, whom you must train. He objects to making an adjusting entry for accrued salaries at the end of the period. He reasons, "We will pay the salaries within a week or two. Why not wait until payment to record the expense? In the end, the result will be the same." Write a business memo to explain to the bookkeeper why the adjusting entry for accrued salary expense is needed. The format of a business memo follows.

Applying accounting principles
(Obj. 1, 2)

Date: ______

To: New Bookkeeper

From: (Student Name)

Subject: Why the adjusting entry for salary expense is needed

P3-3B Journalize the adjusting entry needed on December 31, the end of the current accounting period, for each of the following independent cases affecting Metz Marketing Concepts.

Journalizing adjusting entries
(Obj. 3)
Student ResourceCD
GL, PT, QB

a. Each Friday, Metz pays employees for the current week's work. The amount of the payroll is $5,000 for a five-day workweek. The current accounting period ends on Thursday.

b. Details of Prepaid Insurance are shown in the account:

Prepaid Insurance	
April 30 3,000	

Metz pays insurance each year on April 30. Record insurance expense for the year ended December 31.

c. Metz has received notes receivable from some clients for professional services. During the current year, Metz has earned accrued interest revenue of $170, which will be collected next year.
d. The beginning balance of Supplies was $3,800. During the year, Metz purchased supplies costing $5,500, and at December 31, the supplies on hand total $2,900.
e. Metz designed a marketing campaign, and the client paid Metz $36,000 at the start of the project. Metz recorded this amount as Unearned Service Revenue. The campaign will run for several months. Metz estimates that the company has earned three-fourths of the total fee during the current year.
f. Depreciation for the current year includes: Office Furniture, $5,500; and Building, $3,700. Make a compound entry, as illustrated in Chapter 2.

Analyzing and journalizing adjustments **(Obj. 3)**

Student Resource CD
GL, PT, QB

P3-4B Howe Investment Brokers' unadjusted and adjusted trial balances at December 31, 20X7, follow.

Howe Investment Brokers
Adjusted Trial Balance
December 31, 20X7

	Trial Balance		Adjusted Trial Balance	
Account Title	**Debit**	**Credit**	**Debit**	**Credit**
Cash	4,100		4,100	
Accounts receivable	5,200		13,200	
Supplies	1,200		300	
Prepaid insurance	2,600		2,300	
Office furniture	21,600		21,600	
Accumulated depreciation		8,200		9,800
Accounts payable		6,400		6,400
Salary payable				1,000
Interest payable				400
Note payable		13,800		13,800
Sandy Howe, capital		13,500		13,500
Sandy Howe, withdrawals	29,400		29,400	
Commission revenue		66,900		74,900
Depreciation expense			1,600	
Supplies expense			900	
Utilities expense	5,000		5,000	
Salary expense	26,600		27,600	
Rent expense	12,200		12,200	
Interest expense	900		1,300	
Insurance expense			300	
	108,800	108,800	119,800	119,800

Required

Journalize the adjusting entries that account for the differences between the two trial balances.

Journalizing and posting adjustments to T-accounts; preparing the adjusted trial balance **(Obj. 3, 4)**

Student Resource CD
GL, PT, QB

P3-5B The trial balance of Unistar Alarm Systems at August 31, 20X6, and the data needed for the month-end adjustments follow.

Unistar Alarm Systems

Trial Balance
August 31, 20X6

Cash	$ 7,100	
Accounts receivable	19,800	
Prepaid rent	2,400	
Supplies	1,200	
Furniture	19,700	
Accumulated depreciation		$ 3,600
Accounts payable		3,300
Salary payable		
Unearned service revenue		2,800
John Wilhelm, capital		35,500
John Wilhelm, withdrawals	5,300	
Service revenue		15,600
Salary expense	3,800	
Rent expense		
Depreciation expense		
Advertising expense	1,500	
Supplies expense		
Total	$60,800	$60,800

Adjustment data:

a. Unearned service revenue still unearned at August 31, $1,600.
b. Prepaid rent still in force at August 31, $600.
c. Supplies used during the month, $700.
d. Depreciation for the month, $400.
e. Accrued advertising expense at August 31, $600. (Credit Accounts Payable.)
f. Accrued salary expense at August 31, $500.

Required

1. Open T-accounts for the accounts listed in the trial balance, inserting their August 31 unadjusted balances.
2. Journalize the adjusting entries and post them to the T-accounts. Key the journal entries and the posted amounts by letter.
3. Prepare the adjusted trial balance.
4. How will Unistar use the adjusted trial balance?

Preparing the financial statements from an adjusted trial balance
(Obj. 3, 4, 5)

P3-6B The adjusted trial balance of Doc's Recreation Center at December 31, 20X8, follows.

Doc's Recreation Center

Adjusted Trial Balance
December 31, 20X8

Cash	$ 2,340	
Accounts receivable	50,490	
Prepaid rent	1,350	
Supplies	970	
Equipment	75,690	
Accumulated depreciation—equipment		$ 22,240
Furniture	29,100	

(continued)

Accumulated depreciation—furniture		3,670
Accounts payable		13,600
Unearned service revenue		4,520
Interest payable		2,130
Salary payable		930
Note payable		45,000
D. Brooks, capital		32,380
D. Brooks, withdrawals	48,000	
Service revenue		209,790
Depreciation expense—equipment	11,300	
Depreciation expense—furniture	2,410	
Salary expense	87,800	
Rent expense	12,000	
Interest expense	4,200	
Utilities expense	3,770	
Insurance expense	3,150	
Supplies expense	1,690	
Total	$334,260	$334,260

Required

1. Prepare Doc's 20X8 income statement and statement of owner's equity and year-end balance sheet. List expenses in decreasing order on the income statement and show total liabilities on the balance sheet. Draw arrows linking the three financial statements.
2. **a.** Which financial statement reports Doc's results of operations? Were 20X8 operations successful? Cite specifics from the financial statements to support your evaluation.
   b. Which statement reports the company's financial position? Does Doc's financial position look strong or weak? Give the reason for your evaluation.

Preparing an adjusted trial balance and the financial statements
(Obj. 3, 4, 5)

Student Resource CD
GL, PT, QB

P3-7B Consider the unadjusted trial balance of Progressive Limo Service at October 31, 20X7, and the related month-end adjustment data.

Progressive Limo Service
Trial Balance
October 31, 20X7

Cash	$ 6,300	
Accounts receivable	8,000	
Prepaid rent	6,000	
Supplies	600	
Automobiles	120,000	
Accumulated depreciation		$ 3,000
Accounts payable		2,800
Salary payable		
Jack Dicorte, capital		131,000
Jack Dicorte, withdrawals	3,600	
Service revenue		9,400
Salary expense	1,400	
Rent expense		
Fuel expense	300	
Depreciation expense		
Supplies expense		
Total	$146,200	$146,200

Adjustment data:

a. Accrued service revenue at October 31, $2,000.
b. One-fourth of the prepaid rent expired during the month.
c. Supplies on hand October 31, $200.
d. Depreciation on automobiles for the month. The autos' expected useful lives are five years.
e. Accrued salary expense at October 31 for one day only. The five-day weekly payroll is $2,000.

Required

1. Write the trial balance on a work sheet, using Exhibit 3-10 as an example, and prepare the adjusted trial balance of Progressive Limo Service at October 31, 20X7. Key each adjusting entry by letter.
2. Prepare the income statement and the statement of owner's equity for the month ended October 31, 20X7, and the balance sheet at that date. Draw arrows linking the three financial statements.

APPLY *Your Knowledge*

Decision Cases

Valuing a business on the basis of its net income
(Obj. 3, 4)

Case 1. Chance Wayne has owned and operated Chance Wayne Advertising since its beginning 10 years ago. The company has prospered. Recently, Wayne mentioned that he has lost his zest for the business and would consider selling it for the right price.

Assume that you are interested in buying this business. You obtain its most recent monthly trial balance, which follows. Revenues and expenses vary little from month to month, and April is a typical month. Your investigation reveals that the trial balance does not include monthly revenues of $3,800 and expenses totaling $1,100. If you were to buy Chance Wayne Advertising, you would hire a manager so you could devote your time to other duties. Assume that this person would require a monthly salary of $4,000.

Chance Wayne Advertising
Trial Balance
April 30, 20XX

Cash	$ 9,700	
Accounts receivable	4,900	
Prepaid expenses	2,600	
Plant assets	221,300	
Accumulated depreciation		$189,600
Land	158,000	
Accounts payable		13,800
Salary payable		
Unearned advertising revenue		56,700
Chance Wayne, capital		137,400
Chance Wayne, withdrawals	9,000	
Advertising revenue		12,300
Rent expense		
Salary expense	3,400	
Utilities expense	900	
Depreciation expense		
Supplies expense		
Total	$409,800	$409,800

Required

1. Assume that the most you would pay for the business is 25 times the monthly net income *you could expect to earn* from it. Compute this possible price.
2. Wayne states that the least he will take for the business is his capital balance on April 30. Compute this amount.
3. Under these conditions, how much should you offer Wayne? Give your reason.

Completing the accounting cycle to compute net income
(Obj. 3, 5)

Case 2. One year ago, Bob Cervenka founded Total Restoration Service. Cervenka remembers that you took an accounting course while in college and comes to you for advice. He wishes to know how much net income the business earned during the past year in order to decide whether to keep the company going. His accounting records consist of the T-accounts from his ledger, which were prepared by an accountant who moved to another city. The ledger at December 31 follows. The accounts have *not* been adjusted.

Cash	Dec. 31 5,830	
Accounts Receivable	Dec. 31 12,360	
Prepaid Rent	Jan. 2 2,800	
Supplies	Jan. 2 2,600	
Equipment	Jan. 2 36,600	
Accumulated Depreciation		
Accounts Payable		Dec. 31 21,540
Unearned Service Revenue		Dec. 31 4,130
Salary Payable		
Bob Cervenka, Capital		Dec. 31 20,000
Bob Cervenka, Withdrawals	Dec. 31 28,420	
Service Revenue		Dec. 31 60,740
Salary Expense	Dec. 31 17,000	
Depreciation Expense		
Rent Expense		
Utilities Expense	Dec. 31 800	
Supplies Expense		

Cervenka indicates that at year-end, customers owe him $1,600 of accrued service revenue. These revenues have not been recorded. During the year, he collected $4,130 service revenue in advance from customers, but he earned only $600 of that amount. Rent expense for the year was $2,400, and he used up $2,100 of the supplies. Cervenka estimates that depreciation on his equipment was $5,900 for the year. At December 31, he owes his employee $1,200 accrued salary.

Required

Help Cervenka compute his net income for the year. Advise him whether to continue operating Total Restoration Service.

Ethical Issue

The net income of Bynum & Hobbs, a department store, decreased sharply during 2004. Ron Bynum, owner of the store, anticipates the need for a bank loan in 2005. Late in 2004, Bynum instructs the store's accountant to record a $6,000 sale of furniture to the Bynum family, even though the goods will not be shipped from the manufacturer until January 2005. Bynum also tells the accountant *not* to make the following December 31, 2004, adjusting entries:

Salaries owed to employees.	$900
Prepaid insurance that has expired	400

Required

1. Compute the overall effects of these transactions on the store's reported income for 2004.
2. Why is Bynum taking this action? Is his action ethical? Give your reason, identifying the parties helped and the parties harmed by Bynum's action.
3. As a personal friend, what advice would you give the accountant?

Financial Statement Case

Journalizing and posting transactions and tracing account balances to the financial statements
(Obj. 3, 5)

Amazon.com—like all other businesses—makes adjusting entries prior to year-end in order to measure assets, liabilities, revenues, and expenses properly. Examine Amazon's balance sheet and Note 3. Pay particular attention to Accumulated Depreciation, Interest Payable, and Unearned Revenue.

1. Open T-accounts for the following accounts with their balances at December 31, 2001 (amounts in thousands, as in the Amazon.com financial statements):

Accumulated Depreciation	$166,392
Interest Payable	68,632
Unearned Revenue	87,978

2. Assume that during 2002 Amazon.com completed the following transactions (amounts in thousands). Journalize each transaction (explanations are not required).
   a. Recorded depreciation expense, $76,946.
   b. Paid the beginning balance of interest payable.
   c. Accrued interest expense, $71,661.
   d. Earned sales revenue that had been collected in advance, $40,062.
3. Post to the three T-accounts. Then the balance of each account should agree with the corresponding amount reported in the December 31, 2002, balance sheet. Check to make sure they do agree with Amazon's actual balances. You can find Accumulated Depreciation in Note 3.

Team Project

Return to the chapter-opening story, which describes **It's Just Lunch**. Suppose your group is opening an It's Just Lunch office in your area. You must make some important decisions—where to locate, how to advertise, and so on—and you must also make some accounting decisions. For example, what will be the end of your business's accounting year? How often will you need financial statements to evaluate operating performance and financial position? Will you use the cash basis or the accrual basis? When will you account for the revenue that the business earns? How will you account for the expenses?

Required

Write a report (or prepare an oral presentation, as directed by your professor) to address the following considerations:

1. Will you use the cash basis or the accrual basis of accounting? Give a complete explanation of your reasoning.
2. How often do you want financial statements? Why? Discuss how you will use each financial statement.

3. What kind of revenue will you earn? When will you record it as revenue? How will you decide when to record the revenue?
4. Prepare a made-up income statement for It's Just Lunch for the year ended December 31, 20X5. List all the business's expenses, starting with the most important (largest dollar amount) and working through the least important (smallest dollar amount). Try to come as close as you can to the actual figures, as follows: Net revenues, $20,175,920; Net income, $2,018,516.
5. Using made-up dollar amounts, prepare all the adjusting entries your business will need at the end of the year. Identify the date of your adjustments.

For Internet Exercises, go to the Web site www.prenhall.com/horngren.

APPENDIX *to Chapter 3*

Alternative Treatment of Prepaid Expenses and Unearned Revenues

Chapters 1 through 3 illustrate the most popular way to account for prepaid expenses and unearned revenues. This appendix illustrates an alternative approach.

Prepaid Expenses

Prepaid expenses are advance payments of expenses such as Prepaid Insurance, Prepaid Rent, and Prepaid Advertising. Supplies are also accounted for as prepaid expenses.

When a business prepays an expense—rent, for example—it can debit an *asset* account (Prepaid Rent), as illustrated on page 98.

Aug. 1	Prepaid Rent (↑ asset; debit)............	xxx	
	Cash (↓ asset; credit)		xxx

Alternatively, it can debit an *expense* account to record this cash payment:

Aug. 1	Rent Expense (↑ expense; debit)	xxx	
	Cash (↓ asset; credit)		xxx

Either way, the business must adjust the accounts at the end of the period to report the correct amounts of the expense and the asset.

Prepaid Expense Recorded Initially as an Expense Prepaying an expense creates an asset. However, the asset may be so short-lived that it will expire in the current accounting period—within one year or less. Thus, the accountant may decide to debit the prepayment to an expense account at the time of payment. A $6,000 cash payment for rent (one year, in advance) on August 1 may be debited to Rent Expense:

20X6			
Aug. 1	Rent Expense (↑ expense; debit)......	6,000	
	Cash (↓ asset; credit)..........		6,000

At December 31, only five months' prepayment has expired (for August through December), leaving seven months' rent still prepaid. In this case, the accountant must transfer 7/12 of the original prepayment of $6,000, or $3,500, to the asset account Prepaid Rent. At December 31, 20X6, the business still has the benefit of the prepayment for January through July of 20X7. The adjusting entry at December 31 is

Adjusting Entries

20X6			
Dec. 31	Prepaid Rent ($6,000 × 7/12)		
	(↑ assets; debit)......................	3,500	
	Rent Expense (↓ expense; credit)..		3,500

After posting, the two accounts appear as follows (where CP = cash payment entry; Adj = adjusting entry):

Prepaid Rent

20X6		
Dec. 31 Adj.	**3,500**	
Dec. 31 Bal.	3,500	

Rent Expense

20X6		**20X6**	
Aug. 1 CP	**6,000**	**Dec. 31 Adj.**	**3,500**
Dec. 31 Bal.	2,500		

The balance sheet at the end of 20X6 reports Prepaid Rent of $3,500, and the income statement for 20X6 reports Rent Expense of $2,500, regardless of whether the business initially debits the prepayment to an asset account or to an expense account.

Unearned (Deferred) Revenues

Unearned (deferred) revenues arise when a business collects cash before earning the revenue. Unearned revenues are liabilities because the business that receives cash owes the other party goods or services to be delivered later.

Unearned (Deferred) Revenue Recorded Initially as a Revenue Receipt of cash in advance creates a liability, as recorded on page 104. Another way to account for the receipt of cash is to credit a *revenue account*. If the business has earned all the revenue within the same period, no adjusting entry is needed at the end of the period. However, if the business earns only part of the revenue at the end of the period, it must make an adjusting entry.

Suppose on October 1, 20X2, a law firm records as revenue the receipt of cash for a nine-month fee of $9,000 received in advance. The cash receipt entry is

20X2			
Oct. 1	Cash (↑ asset; debit)	9,000	
	Legal Revenue (↑ revenue, credit)		9,000

At December 31, the attorney has earned only 3/9 of the $9,000, or $3,000, for the months of October, November, and December. Accordingly, the firm makes an adjusting entry to transfer the unearned portion (6/9 of $9,000, or $6,000) from the revenue account to a liability account, as follows:

Adjusting Entries

20X2			
Dec. 31	Legal Revenue ($9,000 × 6/9)		
	(↓ revenue; debit)	6,000	
	Unearned Legal Revenue		
	(↑ liability; credit)...............		6,000

The adjusting entry transfers the unearned portion (6/9, or $6,000) of the original amount to the liability account because the law firm still owes legal service to the client during January through June of 20X3. After posting, the total amount ($9,000) is properly divided between the liability account ($6,000) and the revenue account ($3,000), as follows (where CR = cash receipt entry and Adj. = adjusting entry).

Unearned Legal Revenue				Legal Revenue			
		20X2		20X2		20X2	
		Dec. 31 Adj.	6,000	Dec. 31 Adj.	6,000	Oct. 1 CR	9,000
		Dec. 31 Bal.	6,000			Dec. 31 Bal.	3,000

The attorney's 20X2 income statement reports legal revenue of $3,000, and the balance sheet at December 31, 20X2, reports the unearned legal revenue of $6,000 as a liability. The result is the same whether the business initially credits a liability account or a revenue account.

Appendix Assignments

Exercises

Recording supplies transactions two ways

E3A-1 At the beginning of the year, supplies of $1,190 were on hand. During the year, Damon Air Conditioning Service paid $5,400 cash for supplies. At the end of the year, Damon has $860 of supplies on hand.

Required

1. Assume that Damon records supplies by initially debiting an *asset* account. Therefore, place the beginning balance in the Supplies T-account, and record the preceding entries directly in the accounts without using a journal.
2. Assume that Damon records supplies by initially debiting an *expense* account. Therefore, place the beginning balance in the Supplies Expense T-account, and record the preceding entries directly in the accounts without using a journal.
3. Compare the ending account balances under both approaches. Are they the same?

Recording unearned revenues two ways

E3A-2 At the beginning of the year, Avant Garde Advertising owed customers $2,750 for unearned service revenue collected in advance. During the year, Avant Garde received advance cash receipts of $7,000. At year-end, the liability for unearned revenue is $3,700.

Required

1. Assume that Avant Garde records unearned revenues by initially crediting a *liability* account. Open T-accounts for Unearned Service Revenue and Service Revenue, and place the beginning balance in Unearned Service Revenue. Journalize the cash collection and adjusting entries, and post their dollar amounts. As references in the T-accounts, denote a balance by *Bal.*, a cash receipt by *CR*, and an adjustment by *Adj*.
2. Assume that Avant Garde records unearned revenues by initially crediting a *revenue* account. Open T-accounts for Unearned Service Revenue and Service Revenue, and place the beginning balance in Service Revenue. Journalize the cash collection and adjusting entries, and post their dollar amounts. As references in the T-accounts, denote a balance by *Bal.*, a cash receipt by *CR*, and an adjustment by *Adj*.
3. Compare the ending balances in the two accounts.

Problem

Recording prepaid rent and rent revenue collected in advance two ways

P3A-1 Smart Pages Pack'n Mail completed the following transactions during 20X4:

Oct. 1	Paid $4,500 store rent covering the 6-month period ending March 31, 20X5.
Dec. 1	Collected $3,200 cash in advance from customers. The service revenue will be earned $800 monthly over the period ending March 31, 20X5.

Required

1. Journalize these entries by debiting an asset account for Prepaid Rent and by crediting a liability account for Unearned Service Revenue. Explanations are unnecessary.
2. Journalize the related adjustments at December 31, 20X4.
3. Post the entries to the ledger accounts, and show their balances at December 31, 20X4. Posting references are unnecessary.
4. Repeat requirements 1 through 3. This time, debit Rent Expense for the rent payment and credit Service Revenue for the collection of revenue in advance.
5. Compare the account balances in requirements 3 and 4. They should be equal.

CHAPTER 4

Completing the Accounting Cycle

A+ TIPS CHECK YOUR RESOURCES

- Visit the www.prenhall.com/horngren **Web site** for self-study quizzes, video clips, and other resources
- Try the **Quick Check** exercise at the end of the chapter to test your knowledge
- Learn the **key terms**
- Do the **Starter** exercises keyed in the margins
- Work the **mid-** and **end-of-chapter summary problems**
- Use the **Concept Links** to review material in other chapters
- Search the **CD** for review materials by chapter or by key word
- Watch the **On Location Merchandisers** video to review sale of inventory issues

LEARNING OBJECTIVES

1. Prepare an accounting work sheet
2. Use the work sheet to complete the accounting cycle
3. Close the revenue, expense, and withdrawal accounts
4. Classify assets and liabilities as current or long-term
5. Use the current ratio and the debt ratio to evaluate a company

Chicago Cubs

It's a beautiful day in Chicago. You are enjoying being at Wrigley Field, home of the **Chicago Cubs**. The **St. Louis Cardinals** are in town for a three-game series—one of the great sports rivalries in America. The bratwurst, pretzels, and drinks are refreshing, and the baseball should be even better.

St. Louis jumps to an early lead and stays up by two runs for most of the game. But then Chicago ties the score in the bottom of the ninth. Now the game goes into extra innings. How will it turn out?

In the top of the tenth inning, the Cardinals are shut out: three batters are up and down. Fortunately, the Cubs' Sammy Sosa is up next. And today, as at so many other Cubs games, Sammy hits a home run, a solo shot over the left-field wall, to win the game for Chicago. The final score is 6–5. Faithful Cubs fans go home happy.

What will the Wrigley Field scoreboard show at the start of tomorrow's game? Will it be 6–5 to carry over the score from the first game? Or will the scoreboard be set back to zero? The answer is obvious: After a game is finished, the scoreboard is always set back to zero.

In the same way, the accounting process sets the scoreboard back to zero at the end of each period. The process is called closing the books, and it is the main topic of this chapter. Here we show how companies close their books. The logic behind the closing process in accounting is the same as setting the scoreboard back to zero after a game. The final step in the process is to report the financial statements to the public.

Next period, we will repeat the accounting process outlined here. And the Cubs will travel to St. Louis, where the Busch Stadium scoreboard will start out with a score of 0–0.

Sitemap

Thus far, we have prepared financial statements from an adjusted trial balance. That approach works well for quick decision making, but companies take the process a step further. At the end of each period, after adjusting the accounts, they close their books. Whether the company is the Chicago Cubs baseball organization, Amazon.com, or Gay Gillen eTravel, the closing process follows the same pattern. Closing the books marks the end of the *accounting cycle* for a given period.

Accountants often use a document known as the *work sheet*. There are many different types of work sheets—in fact, as many as there are needs for data. Work sheets are useful because they summarize lots of data.

- ■ The Accounting Cycle
- □ The Work Sheet
- □ Completing the Cycle
- □ Classifying Assets and Liabilities
- □ Accounting Ratios
- □ Appendix: Reversing Entries

Student ResourceCD
accounting cycle

Accounting Cycle
Process by which companies produce their financial statements for a specific period.

The Accounting Cycle

The **accounting cycle** is the process by which companies produce their financial statements. For the Chicago Cubs, Amazon.com, or any other business, the first accounting step is to open the accounts. After a business has operated for one period, some of the account balances carry over to the next period. Therefore, the accounting cycle starts with the beginning asset, liability, and owner's equity account balances left over from the preceding period. Exhibit 4-1 outlines the complete accounting cycle of Gay Gillen eTravel and every other business. The boldface items in Panel A indicate the new concepts we introduce in this chapter. Accounting takes place at two different times:

- During the period—Journalizing transactions
  Posting to the accounts in the ledger
- End of the period —Adjusting the accounts, including journalizing and posting the adjusting entries
  Closing the accounts, including journalizing and posting the closing entries
  Preparing the financial statements (income statement, statement of owner's equity, and balance sheet)

The end-of-period work also readies the accounts for the next period. In Chapters 3 and 4, we cover the end-of-period accounting for a service business such as the Chicago Cubs and Gay Gillen eTravel. Chapter 5 shows how a merchandising entity such as Wal-Mart or Target adjusts and closes its books.

Exhibit 4-1 The Accounting Cycle

PANEL A

During the Period	End of the Period
1. Start with the account balances at the beginning of the period. **2.** Analyze and journalize transactions as they occur. **3.** Post journal entries to the accounts.	**4.** Compute the unadjusted balance in each account at the end of the period. **5.** Enter the trial balance on the work sheet, and complete the work sheet (optional). **6.** Using the adjusted trial balance or the full work sheet as a guide, **a.** Prepare the financial statements. **b.** Journalize and post the adjusting entries. **c. Journalize and post the closing entries.** **7.** Prepare the postclosing trial balance. This trial balance becomes step 1 for the next period.

PANEL B

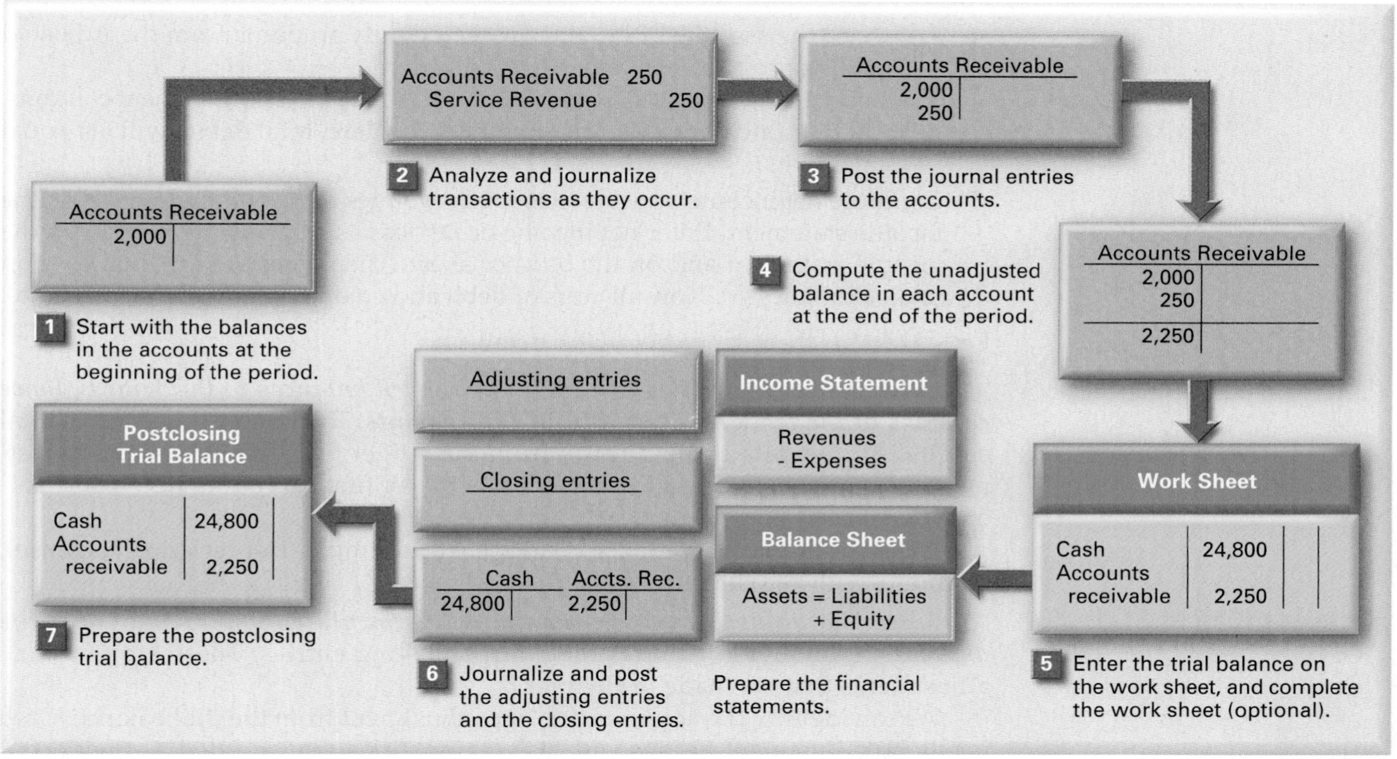

The Work Sheet

Accountants often use a **work sheet**—a document with several columns—to summarize data for the financial statements. The work sheet is not part of the ledger or the journal, and it is not a financial statement. It is merely a summary device. Listing all the accounts and their unadjusted balances helps identify the accounts that need adjustment. An Excel spreadsheet works well as an accounting work sheet.

Exhibits 4-2 through 4-6 illustrate the development of a typical work sheet for the business of Gay Gillen eTravel. The heading at the top covers essential data:

- Name of the business (Gay Gillen eTravel, in this case)
- Title of the document (Accounting Work Sheet)
- Period covered by the work sheet (Month ended April 30, 20X5, for Gay Gillen eTravel)

- The Accounting Cycle
- **The Work Sheet**
- Completing the Cycle
- Classifying Assets and Liabilities
- Accounting Ratios
- Appendix: Reversing Entries

Student ResourceCD
work sheet

Prepare an accounting work sheet

Work Sheet
A columnar document designed to help move data from the trial balance to the financial statements.

A step-by-step description of the work sheet follows.

Steps introduced in Chapter 3 for the adjusted trial balance:

1. Enter the account titles and their unadjusted ending balances in the Trial Balance columns of the work sheet, and total the amounts (Exhibit 4-2). Total debits equal total credits.
2. Enter the adjustments in the Adjustments columns, and total the amounts (Exhibit 4-3). Total debits equal total credits.
3. Compute each account's adjusted balance by combining the trial balance and the adjustment figures. Enter the adjusted amounts in the Adjusted Trial Balance columns (Exhibit 4-4). Then compute the total for each column. Total debits equal total credits.

Steps introduced in this chapter:

4. **a.** Extend the asset, liability, and owner's equity amounts from the Adjusted Trial Balance to the Balance Sheet columns.
   b. Extend the revenue and expense amounts to the Income Statement columns.
   c. Total the statement columns (Exhibit 4-5). Here, total debits will *not* equal total credits.
5. Compute net income or net loss as total revenues minus total expenses on the income statement. Enter net income or net loss as a balancing amount on the income statement and on the balance sheet. Then compute the final column totals (Exhibit 4-6). Now all pairs of debit and credit columns should be equal.

Let's examine these steps in greater detail.

1. ***Enter the account titles and their unadjusted balances in the Trial Balance columns of the work sheet, and total the amounts.*** Total debits must equal total credits. All the data come directly from the ledger accounts before the adjustments. Accounts are listed in proper order (Cash first, Accounts Receivable second, and so on).

An account may have a zero balance (for example, Depreciation Expense). Accounts with zero balances need to be adjusted.

✔ Starter 4-1

2. ***Enter the adjusting entries in the Adjustments columns, and total the amounts.*** Exhibit 4-3 includes the April adjusting entries. These are the same adjustments that we made in Chapter 3.

We can identify the accounts needing adjustment from the trial balance. Cash needs no adjustment because all cash transactions are recorded as they occur during the period. Consequently, Cash's balance is up-to-date.

Accounts Receivable is listed next. Has Gay Gillen earned any revenue she has not yet recorded? The answer is yes. At April 30, Gillen has earned $250 that she has not yet recorded because she will receive the cash later. For service revenue earned but not yet collected, Gillen debits Accounts Receivable and credits Service Revenue on the work sheet. A letter links the debit and the credit of each adjusting entry.

By moving down the trial balance, Gillen identifies the remaining accounts that need adjustment. Supplies is next. The business has used supplies during April, so Gillen debits Supplies Expense and credits Supplies. The other adjustments are analyzed and entered on the work sheet as we did in Chapter 3. After the adjustments are entered on the work sheet, the amount columns are totaled. Total debits equal total credits.

✔ Starter 4-2

3. ***Compute each account's adjusted balance by combining the trial balance and adjustment figures. Enter each account's adjusted amount in the Adjusted Trial Balance columns.*** Exhibit 4-4 shows the work sheet with the adjusted trial balance completed. For example, the Cash balance is up-to-date, so it receives no adjustment. Accounts Receivable's adjusted balance of $2,500 is computed by

adding the unadjusted amount of $2,250 to the $250 debit adjustment. We compute Supplies' adjusted balance by subtracting the $300 credit adjustment from the unadjusted debit balance of $700. An account may receive more than one adjustment, as Service Revenue does. On the adjusted trial balance, total debits equal total credits.

4. ***Extend (that is, copy) the asset, liability, and owner's equity amounts from the Adjusted Trial Balance to the Balance Sheet columns. Copy the revenue and expense amounts to the Income Statement columns. Total the statement columns.*** Every account is either a balance sheet account or an income statement account. Each account's balance should appear in only one column, as shown in Exhibit 4-5.

First, total the *income statement columns*, as follows:

Income Statement

■ Debits (Dr.) ⟶	Total expenses = $3,875	Difference = $3,525, a net income because revenues exceed expenses
■ Credits (Cr.) ⟶	Total revenues = $7,400	

Then total the *balance sheet* columns:

Balance Sheet

■ Debits (Dr.) ⟶	Total assets and withdrawals = $49,400	Difference = $3,525, a net income because total debits are greater
■ Credits (Cr.) ⟶	Total liabilities, owner's equity, and accumulated depreciation = $45,875	

5. ***Compute net income or net loss as total revenues minus total expenses on the income statement. Enter net income as the balancing amount on the income statement and as the balancing amount on the balance sheet. Then compute the adjusted column totals.*** Exhibit 4-6 presents the completed accounting work sheet, which shows net income of $3,525, computed as follows:

✔ Starter 4-3

Revenue (total credits on the income statement)	$7,400
Less: Expenses (total debits on the income statement)	(3,875)
Net income	$3,525

Net income of $3,525 is entered in the debit column of the income statement. This brings total debits on the income statement up to the total for credits on the income statement. The net income amount is then extended to the credit column of the balance sheet. Net income brings the balance sheet into balance.

If expenses exceed revenues, the result is a net loss. In that event, Net Loss is printed on the work sheet. The loss amount should be entered in the *credit* column of the income statement (to balance out) and in the *debit* column of the balance sheet (to balance out). After completion, total debits equal total credits in the Income Statement columns and in the Balance Sheet columns.

Discussion
Q: Why do the Income Statement columns appear before the Balance Sheet columns in the worksheet?
A: The amount of Net Income is transferred to the Capital account on the Balance Sheet.

Exhibit 4-2 Trial Balance

Gay Gillen eTravel

Accounting Work Sheet
Month Ended April 30, 20X5

Account Title	Trial Balance Dr.	Trial Balance Cr.	Adjustments Dr.	Adjustments Cr.	Adjusted Trial Balance Dr.	Adjusted Trial Balance Cr.	Income Statement Dr.	Income Statement Cr.	Balance Sheet Dr.	Balance Sheet Cr.
Cash	24,800									
Accounts receivable	2,250									
Supplies	700									
Prepaid rent	3,000									
Furniture	16,500									
Accumulated depreciation										
Accounts payable		13,100								
Salary payable										
Unearned service revenue		450								
Gay Gillen, capital		31,250								
Gay Gillen, withdrawals	3,200									
Service revenue		7,000								
Rent expense										
Salary expense	950									
Supplies expense										
Depreciation expense										
Utilities expense	400									
	51,800	51,800								
Net income										

Write the account titles and their unadjusted balances in the Trial Balance columns of the work sheet. Total the amounts.

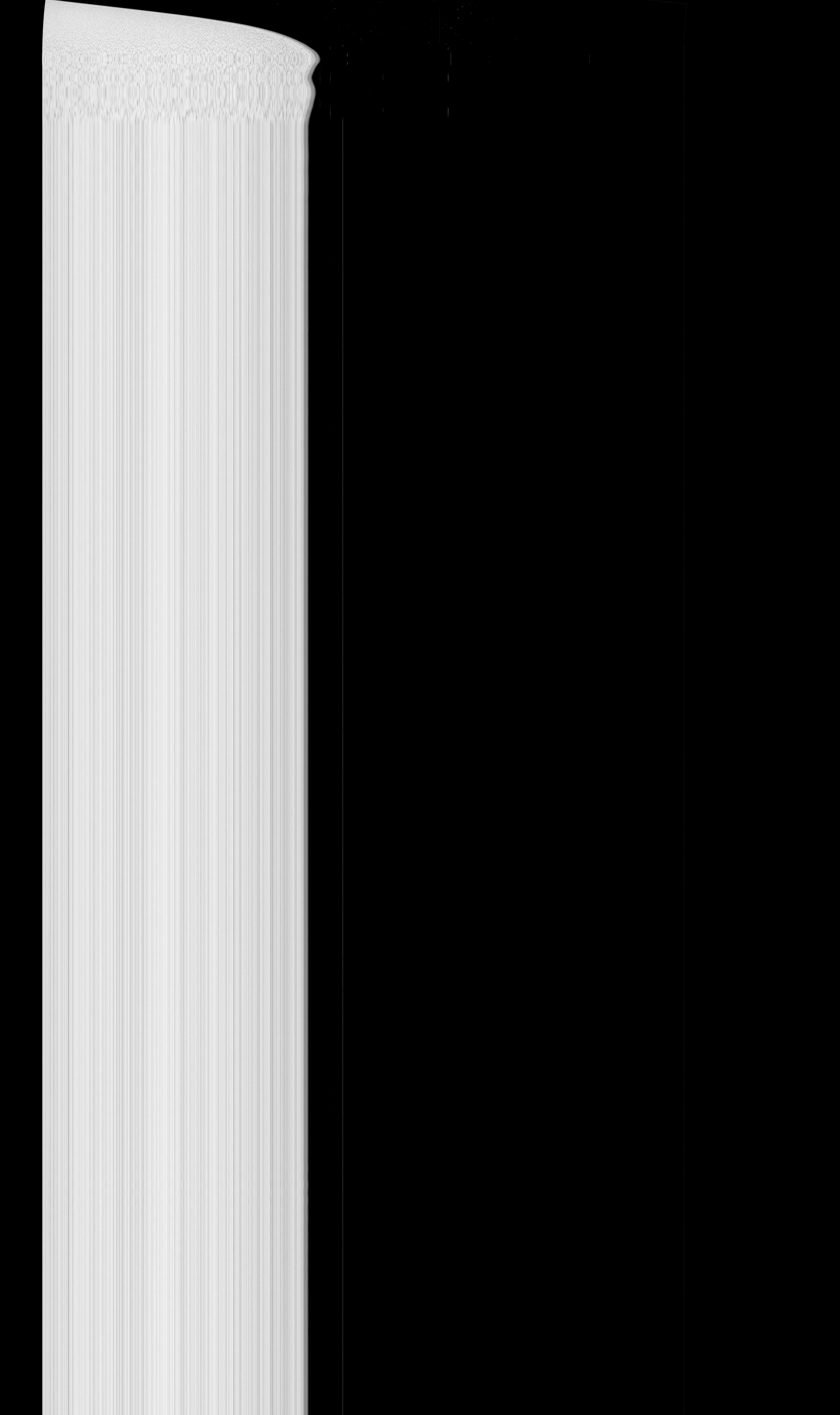

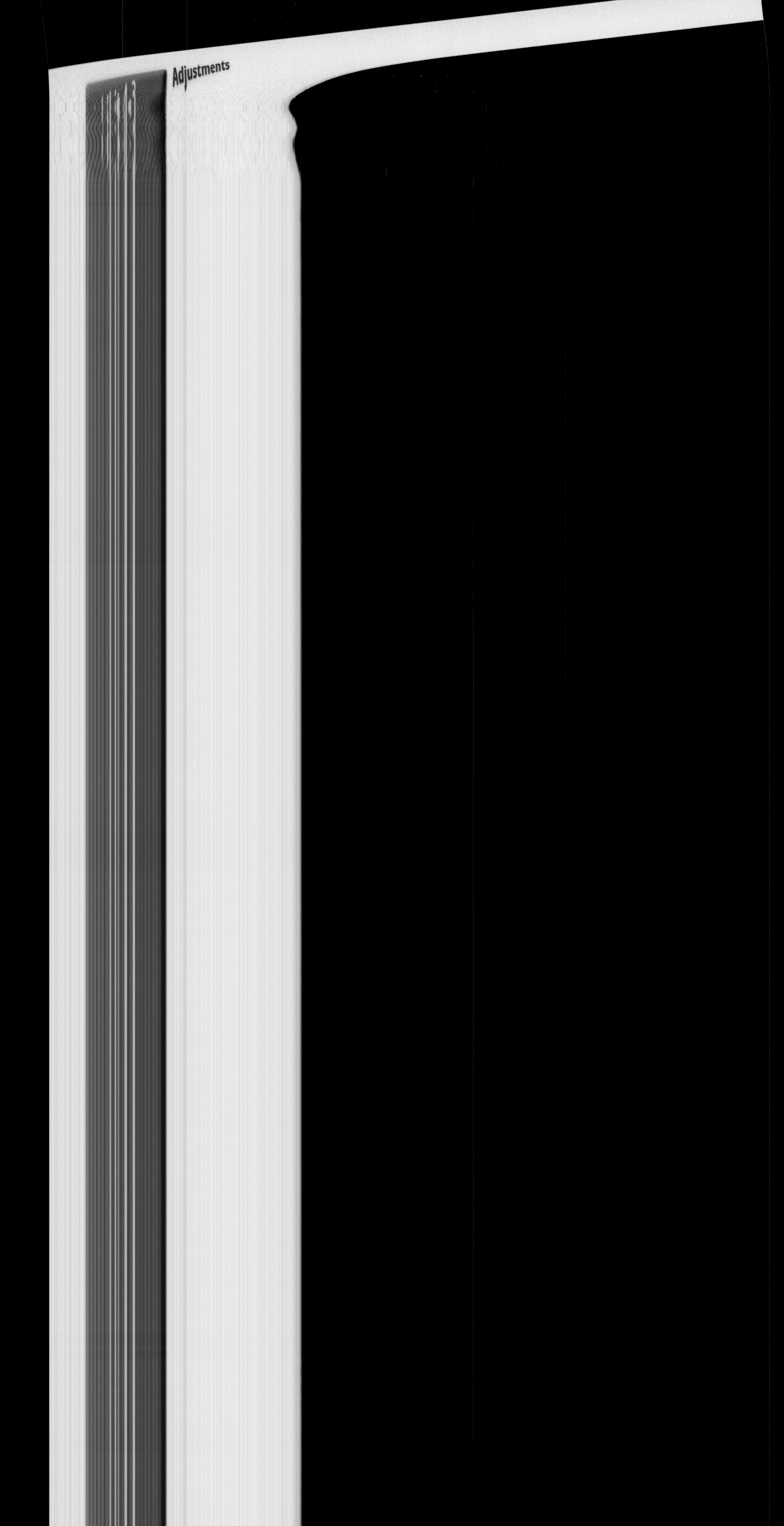

MID-CHAPTER *Summary Problem*

The trial balance of Clay Employment Services at December 31, 20X9, the end of its fiscal year, is as follows.

A+ TIPS
CHECK YOUR RESOURCES

Clay Employment Services

Trial Balance
December 31, 20X9

Cash	$ 198,000	
Accounts receivable	370,000	
Supplies	6,000	
Furniture and fixtures	100,000	
Accumulated depreciation—furniture and fixtures		$ 40,000
Building	250,000	
Accumulated depreciation—building		130,000
Accounts payable		380,000
Salary payable		
Unearned service revenue		45,000
Jay Clay, capital		293,000
Jay Clay, withdrawals	65,000	
Service revenue		286,000
Salary expense	172,000	
Supplies expense		
Depreciation expense—furniture and fixtures		
Depreciation expense—building		
Miscellaneous expense	13,000	
Total	$1,174,000	$1,174,000

Data needed for the adjusting entries include:

a. Supplies on hand at year-end, $2,000.
b. Depreciation on furniture and fixtures, $20,000.
c. Depreciation on building, $10,000.
d. Salaries owed but not yet paid, $5,000.
e. Accrued service revenue, $12,000.
f. Of the $45,000 balance of Unearned Service Revenue, $32,000 was earned during 20X9.

Required

Prepare the accounting work sheet of Clay Employment Services for the year ended December 31, 20X9. Key each adjusting entry by the letter corresponding to the data given.

Solution

Clay Employment Services
Work Sheet
Year Ended December 31, 20X9

Account Title	Trial Balance Dr.	Trial Balance Cr.	Adjustments Dr.	Adjustments Cr.	Adjusted Trial Balance Dr.	Adjusted Trial Balance Cr.	Income Statement Dr.	Income Statement Cr.	Balance Sheet Dr.	Balance Sheet Cr.
Cash	198,000				198,000				198,000	
Accounts receivable	370,000		(e) 12,000		382,000				382,000	
Supplies	6,000			(a) 4,000	2,000				2,000	
Furniture and fixtures	100,000				100,000				100,000	
Accumulated depreciation—furniture and fixtures		40,000		(b) 20,000		60,000				60,000
Building	250,000				250,000				250,000	
Accumulated depreciation—building		130,000		(c) 10,000		140,000				140,000
Accounts payable		380,000				380,000				380,000
Salary payable				(d) 5,000		5,000				5,000
Unearned service revenue		45,000	(f) 32,000			13,000				13,000
Jay Clay, capital		293,000				293,000				293,000
Jay Clay, withdrawals	65,000				65,000				65,000	
Service revenue		286,000		(e) 12,000 (f) 32,000		330,000		330,000		
Salary expense	172,000		(d) 5,000		177,000		177,000			
Supplies expense			(a) 4,000		4,000		4,000			
Depreciation expense—furniture and fixtures			(b) 20,000		20,000		20,000			
Depreciation expense—building			(c) 10,000		10,000		10,000			
Miscellaneous expense	13,000				13,000		13,000			
	1,174,000	1,174,000	83,000	83,000	1,221,000	1,221,000	224,000	330,000	997,000	891,000
Net income							106,000			106,000
							330,000	330,000	997,000	997,000

☐ The Accounting Cycle
☐ The Work Sheet
■ Completing the Cycle
☐ Classifying Assets and Liabilities
☐ Accounting Ratios
☐ Appendix: Reversing Entries

Completing the Accounting Cycle

The work sheet helps accountants prepare the financial statements, make the adjusting entries, and close the accounts. First, let's prepare the financial statements.

2 Use the work sheet to complete the accounting cycle

Preparing the Financial Statements

The financial statements can be prepared directly from the adjusted trial balance; see p. 108. This is why completion of the work sheet is optional.

The work sheet shows the amount of net income or net loss for the period, but we still must prepare the financial statements. Exhibit 4-7 shows the April financial statements for Gay Gillen eTravel (based on data from the work sheet in Exhibit 4-6). We can prepare Gillen's financial statements immediately after completing the work sheet.

Student Resource CD
adjusting entries, closing process, work sheet

Recording the Adjusting Entries

Adjusting the accounts requires journal entries and posting to the accounts. Panel A of Exhibit 4-8 repeats the April adjusting entries of Gay Gillen eTravel that we journalized in Chapter 3. Panel B shows the revenue and the expense

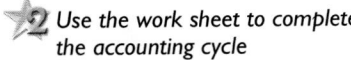

Exhibit 4-7

April Financial Statements of Gay Gillen eTravel

Gay Gillen eTravel

Income Statement
Month Ended April 30, 20X5

Revenue:		
Service revenue		$7,400
Expenses:		
Salary expense	$1,900	
Rent expense	1,000	
Utilities expense	400	
Supplies expense	300	
Depreciation expense	275	
Total expenses		3,875
Net income		$3,525

Gay Gillen eTravel

Statement of Owner's Equity
Month Ended April 30, 20X5

Gay Gillen, capital, April 1, 20X5	$31,250
Add: Net income	3,525
	34,775
Less: Withdrawals	(3,200)
Gay Gillen, capital, April 30, 20X5	$31,575

Gay Gillen eTravel

Balance Sheet
April 30, 20X5

Assets			Liabilities	
Cash		$24,800	Accounts payable	$13,100
Accounts receivable		2,500	Salary payable	950
Supplies		400	Unearned service revenue	300
Prepaid rent		2,000	Total liabilities	14,350
Furniture	$16,500			
Less: Accumulated depreciation	(275)	16,225	**Owner's Equity**	
			Gay Gillen, capital	31,575
Total assets		$45,925	Total liabilities and owner's equity	$45,925

accounts after all adjustments have been posted. *Adj.* denotes an amount posted from an adjusting entry. The adjusting entries should be journalized after they are entered on the work sheet. Only the revenue and expense accounts are presented in the exhibit in order to focus on the closing process.

Accountants can use the work sheet to prepare monthly or quarterly statements without journalizing and posting the adjusting entries. Many companies journalize and post the adjusting entries (as in Exhibit 4-8) only once annually—at the end of the year.

Exhibit 4-8 **Journalizing and Posting the Adjusting Entries**

PANEL A—Journalizing: **Page 4**

	Adjusting Entries		
Apr. 30	Accounts Receivable	250	
	Service Revenue		250
30	Supplies Expense	300	
	Supplies		300
30	Rent Expense	1,000	
	Prepaid Rent		1,000
30	Depreciation Expense	275	
	Accumulated Depreciation		275
30	Salary Expense	950	
	Salary Payable		950
30	Unearned Service Revenue	150	
	Service Revenue		150

PANEL B—Posting the Adjustments to the Revenue and Expense Accounts:

REVENUE

Service Revenue

			7,000
		Adj.	250
		Adj.	150
		Bal.	7,400

EXPENSES

Rent Expense

Adj.	1,000		
Bal.	1,000		

Salary Expense

	950		
Adj.	950		
Bal.	1,900		

Supplies Expense

Adj.	300		
Bal.	300		

Depreciation Expense

Adj.	275		
Bal.	275		

Utilities Expense

	400		
Bal.	400		

Adj. = Amount posted from an adjusting entry Bal. = Balance

3 *Close the revenue, expense, and withdrawal accounts*

Closing the Accounts
Step in the accounting cycle at the end of the period. Closing the accounts consists of journalizing and posting the closing entries to set the balances of the revenue, expense, and withdrawal accounts to zero for the next period.

Temporary Accounts
The revenue and expense accounts that relate to a particular accounting period and are closed at the end of the period. For a proprietorship, the owner withdrawal account is also temporary.

Permanent Accounts
Accounts that are *not* closed at the end of the period—the asset, liability, and capital accounts.

Closing the Accounts

Closing the accounts is the end-of-period process that gets the accounts ready for the next period. Closing consists of journalizing and posting the closing entries. The closing process zeroes out all the revenues and all the expenses in order to measure each period's net income separately from all other periods.

Recall that the income statement reports net income for only one period. For example, net income for the Chicago Cubs baseball organization for 2005 relates exclusively to 2005. At December 31, 2005, the Chicago Cubs' accountants close the company's revenue and expense accounts for that year. The revenue and expense account balances relate to only one accounting period and are therefore closed at the end of the period (December 31, 2005). For this reason, revenues and expenses are called **temporary accounts**. For example, Gay Gillen's balance of Service Revenue at April 30, 20X5, is $7,400. This balance relates exclusively to April and must be zeroed out before Gillen records revenue for May.

The owner's Withdrawal account is also a temporary account because it measures the owner's withdrawals for only one period. The Withdrawals account is also closed at the end of the period.

To better understand the closing process, contrast the temporary accounts with the **permanent accounts**—the asset, liability, and capital accounts. The asset, liability, and capital accounts are *not* closed at the end of the period because their balances are not used to measure income. Consider Cash, Accounts Receivable, Accounts Payable, and Gay Gillen, Capital. These accounts do not represent business *activity* for a single period, so they are not closed at the end of the period. Their balances carry over to the next period. For example, the Cash balance at December

31, 20X5, becomes the beginning balance for 20X6. The Accounts Receivable balance at December 31, 20X5, becomes the beginning balance for 20X6. The same is true for all the other assets, all the liabilities, and the owner's capital account.

Closing entries transfer the revenue, expense, and owner withdrawal balances to the capital account. As you know,

Closing Entries
Entries that transfer the revenue, expense, and owner withdrawal balances to the capital account.

REVENUES →	**increase Owner's Equity**
EXPENSES and OWNER WITHDRAWALS →	**decrease Owner's Equity**

Posting the closing entries transfers all the revenues, all the expenses, and the owner's withdrawals to the Capital account.

As an intermediate step, the revenues and the expenses are transferred first to an account titled **Income Summary**. This temporary account collects the sum of all the expenses (a debit) and the sum of all the revenues (a credit). The Income Summary account is like a "holding tank." The balance of Income Summary is then transferred to capital. Exhibit 4-9 gives a picture of the closing process. Observe that Owner's Capital is the final account in the closing process.

Income Summary
A temporary "holding tank" account into which revenues and expenses are transferred prior to their final transfer to the capital account.

Exhibit 4-9 **The Closing Process**

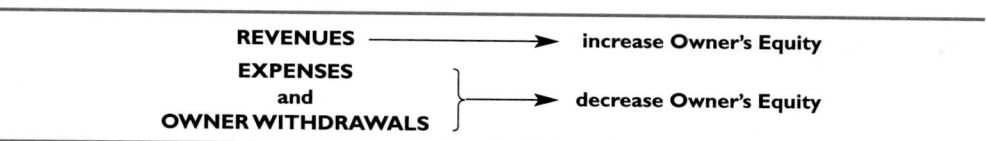

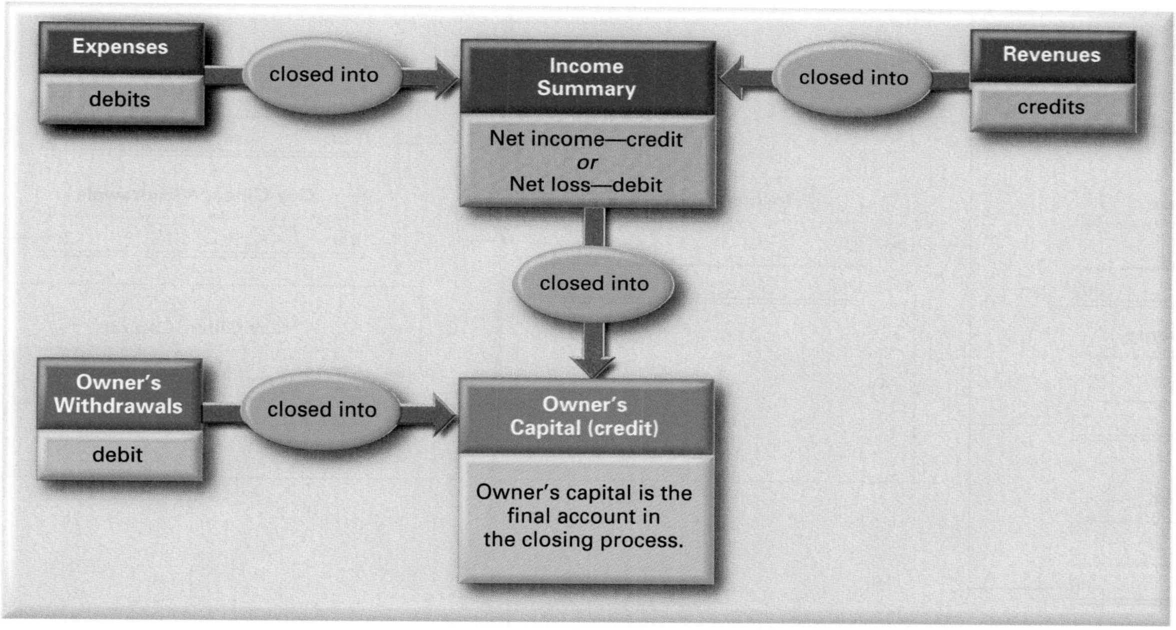

Closing Steps The steps in closing the books follow (the circled numbers are keyed to Exhibit 4-10).

① Debit each *revenue* account for the amount of its credit balance. Credit Income Summary for the total of the revenues. This closing entry transfers total revenues to the *credit* side of Income Summary.

② Credit each *expense* account for the amount of its debit balance. Debit Income Summary for the total of the expenses. This closing entry transfers total expenses to the *debit* side of Income Summary.

③ The Income Summary account now holds the net income (or net loss) of the period, but only for a moment. To close net income, we debit Income Summary for the amount of its *credit balance*, and credit the Capital account. This closing entry transfers net income to the owner's Capital account.

Exhibit 4-10 Journalizing and Posting the Closing Entries

PANEL A—Journalizing **Page 5**

Closing Entries

①	Apr. 30	Service Revenue	7,400	
		Income Summary		7,400
②	30	Income Summary	3,875	
		Rent Expense		1,000
		Salary Expense		1,900
		Supplies Expense		300
		Depreciation Expense		275
		Utilities Expense		400
③	30	Income Summary ($7,400 – $3,875)	3,525	
		Gay Gillen, Capital		3,525
④	30	Gay Gillen, Capital	3,200	
		Gay Gillen, Withdrawals		3,200

PANEL B—Posting

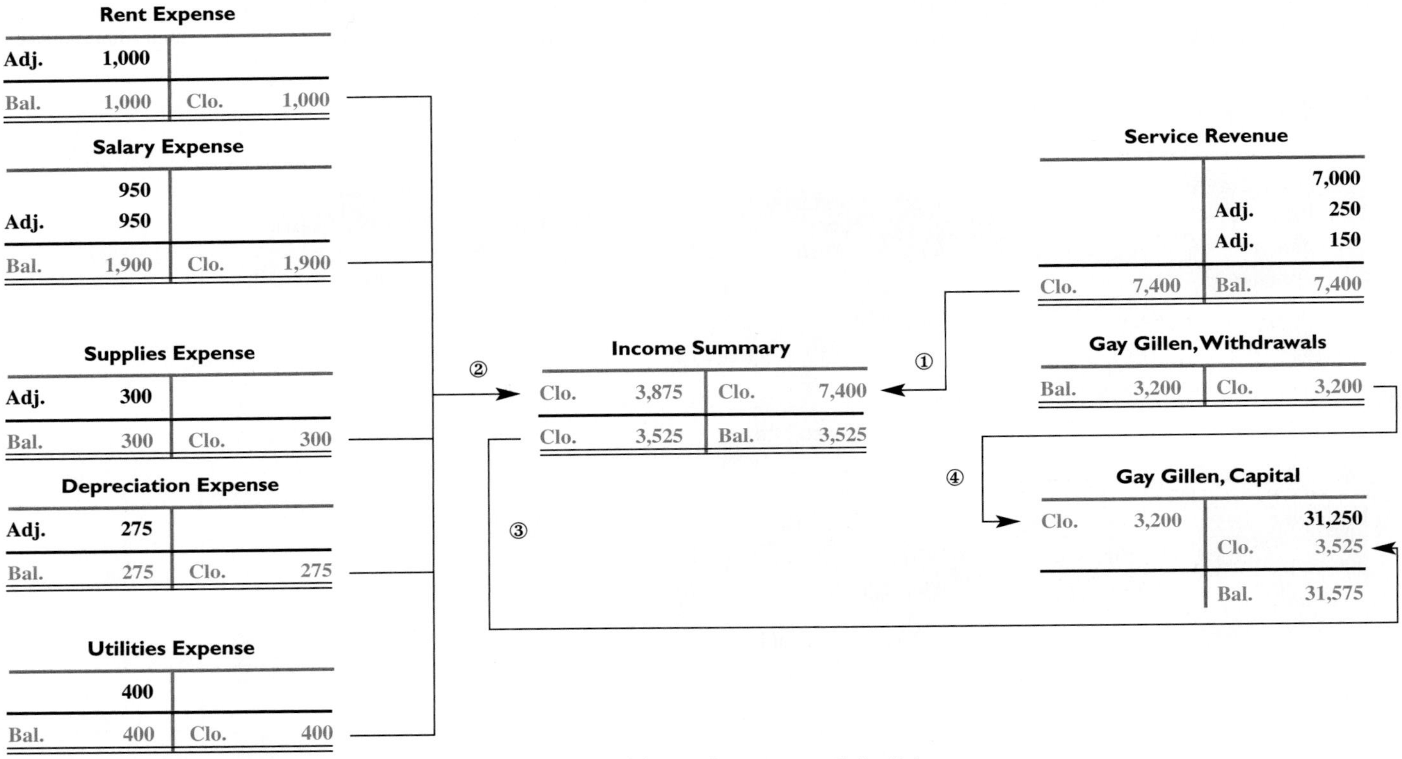
Rent Expense
Adj. 1,000
Bal. 1,000 Clo. 1,000
Salary Expense
950
Adj. 950
Bal. 1,900 Clo. 1,900
Supplies Expense
Adj. 300
Bal. 300 Clo. 300
Depreciation Expense
Adj. 275
Bal. 275 Clo. 275
Utilities Expense
400
Bal. 400 Clo. 400
②
Income Summary
Clo. 3,875 Clo. 7,400
Clo. 3,525 Bal. 3,525
③
①
④
Service Revenue
7,000
Adj. 250
Adj. 150
Clo. 7,400 Bal. 7,400
Gay Gillen, Withdrawals
Bal. 3,200 Clo. 3,200
Gay Gillen, Capital
Clo. 3,200 31,250
Clo. 3,525
Bal. 31,575

Adj. = Amount posted from an adjusting entry Clo. = Amount posted from a closing entry Bal. = Balance

✔ Starter 4-4
✔ Starter 4-5
✔ Starter 4-6
✔ Starter 4-7

④ Credit the *Withdrawals* account for the amount of its debit balance. Debit the owner's Capital account. This entry transfers the owner's withdrawals to the *debit* side of the Capital account.

These steps are best illustrated with an example. Suppose Gay Gillen closes the books at the end of April. Exhibit 4-10 shows the complete closing process for Gillen's travel agency. Panel A gives the closing journal entries, and Panel B shows the accounts after posting.

After the closing entries, Gay Gillen, Capital ends with a balance of $31,575. Trace this balance to the statement of owner's equity and also to the balance sheet in Exhibit 4-7.

CLOSING A NET LOSS What would the closing entries be if Gillen's travel agency had suffered a net *loss* during April? Suppose expenses totaled $7,700 and revenues remained $7,400. In that case, Gillen's business suffered a net loss of $300 for April. The loss shows up as a debit balance in Income Summary, as follows:

Income Summary

Clo.	7,700	Clo.	7,400
Bal.	300		

Closing entry ③ would then credit Income Summary and debit Gay Gillen, Capital, as follows:

③	Apr. 30	Gay Gillen, Capital	300	
		Income Summary		300

Then Income Summary would be closed out and Gay Gillen, Capital has its ending balance, as follows:

Income Summary

Clo.	7,700	Clo.	7,400
Bal.	300	Clo.	300

Gay Gillen, Capital

Clo.	300		31,250

Finally, the Withdrawals balance would be closed to Capital, as before. The double underline in an account means that the account has a zero balance; nothing more will be posted to the account in the current period.

Postclosing Trial Balance
List of the accounts and their balances at the end of the period after journalizing and posting the closing entries. This last step of the accounting cycle ensures that the ledger is in balance to start the next accounting period.

Postclosing Trial Balance

The accounting cycle can end with a **postclosing trial balance** (Exhibit 4-11). This optional step lists the accounts and their adjusted balances after closing.

Exhibit 4-11
Postclosing Trial Balance

✔ **Starter 4-8**

Gay Gillen eTravel
Postclosing Trial Balance
April 30, 20X5

Cash	$24,800	
Accounts receivable	2,500	
Supplies	400	
Prepaid Rent	2,000	
Furniture	16,500	
Accumulated depreciation		$ 275
Accounts payable		13,100
Salary payable		950
Unearned service revenue		300
Gay Gillen, capital		31,575
Total	$46,200	$46,200

Only assets, liabilities, and capital appear on the postclosing trial balance. No temporary accounts—revenues, expenses, or withdrawal accounts—are included because they have been closed. The ledger is up-to-date and ready for the next period's transactions.

Reversing entries are special journal entries that key off the adjustments at the end of the period. Reversing entries ease the accounting of the next period. They are optional, and we cover them in the appendix at the end of this chapter.

Reversing Entries
Special journal entries that ease the burden of accounting for transactions in the next period.

Student Resource CD
classified balance sheet, current assets, current liabilities, long-term liabilities

4 *Classify assets and liabilities as current or long-term*

Liquidity
Measure of how quickly an item can be converted to cash.

Current Asset
An asset that is expected to be converted to cash, sold, or consumed during the next 12 months, or within the business's normal operating cycle if the cycle is longer than a year.

Operating Cycle
Time span during which cash is paid for goods and services, which are then sold to customers from whom the business collects cash.

Long-Term Asset
An asset other than a current asset.

Plant or Fixed Asset
Another name for property, plant, and equipment.

Current Liability
A debt due to be paid with cash or with goods and services within one year or within the entity's operating cycle if the cycle is longer than a year.

Long-Term Liability
A liability other than a current liability.

✔ Starter 4-9

Classifying Assets and Liabilities

Assets and liabilities are classified as either *current* or *long-term* to indicate their relative liquidity. **Liquidity** measures closeness to cash, which is the most liquid asset. Accounts receivable is a relatively liquid asset because the receivables will be collected in the near future. Supplies are less liquid than receivables, and furniture and buildings are even less liquid because of their long lives.

Managers are interested in liquidity because business difficulties arise from a shortage of cash. How quickly can Amazon.com convert an asset to cash? How soon must Amazon pay a liability? These are questions of liquidity. A classified balance sheet helps to answer these questions.

Assets

CURRENT ASSETS **Current assets** will be converted to cash, sold, or used up during the next 12 months or within the business's normal operating cycle if the cycle is longer than a year. The **operating cycle** is the time span during which

1. Cash is used to acquire goods and services.
2. These goods and services are sold to customers.
3. The business collects cash.

For most businesses, the operating cycle is a few months. Cash, Accounts Receivable, Notes Receivable due within a year or less, and Prepaid Expenses are current assets. Merchandising entities such as Intel, Sears, and Dell Computer have another current asset: Inventory. Inventory holds the cost of the goods the business is holding for sale to customers.

LONG-TERM ASSETS **Long-term assets** are all assets other than current assets. One category of long-term assets is **plant assets** (also called **fixed assets**). Another name for plant assets is Property, Plant, and Equipment. Land, Buildings, Furniture and Fixtures, and Equipment are plant assets. Of these, Gay Gillen eTravel has only Furniture.

Other categories of long-term assets include Long-Term Investments and Other Assets (a catchall category). We discuss these categories in later chapters.

Liabilities

Business owners and managers need to know when they must pay their liabilities. Liabilities that must be paid immediately create a strain on cash. Therefore, the balance sheet lists liabilities in the order in which they must be paid. Balance sheets report two liability categories: *current liabilities* and *long-term liabilities*.

CURRENT LIABILITIES **Current liabilities** must be paid with cash or with goods and services within one year or within the entity's operating cycle if the cycle is longer than a year. Accounts Payable, Notes Payable due within one year, Salary Payable, Unearned Revenue, and Interest Payable are current liabilities.

LONG-TERM LIABILITIES All liabilities that are not current are classified as **long-term liabilities**. Many notes payable are payable after one year or the entity's operating cycle if the cycle is longer than a year. Some notes payable are paid in installments, with the first installment due within one year, the second installment due the second year, and so on. The first installment is a current liability, and the remaining installments are long-term liabilities. A $100,000 note payable to be paid $10,000 per year over 10 years would include:

- A current liability of $10,000 for next year's payment, and
- A long-term liability of $90,000.

A Detailed Balance Sheet

Thus far we have presented the *unclassified* balance sheet of Gay Gillen eTravel. Now we move up to the form of the balance sheet actually used in practice — called a classified balance sheet. Exhibit 4-12 presents Gillen's classified balance sheet.

Exhibit 4-12

Classified Balance Sheet of Gay Gillen eTravel

Gay Gillen eTravel
Balance Sheet
April 30, 20X5

Assets			Liabilities	
Current assets:			Current liabilities:	
Cash		$24,800	Accounts payable	$13,100
Accounts receivable		2,500	Salary payable	950
Supplies		400	Unearned service revenue	300
Prepaid rent		2,000	Total current liabilities	14,350
Total current assets		29,700	Long-term liabilities (None)	0
Fixed assets:			Total liabilities	14,350
Furniture	$16,500			
Less: Accumulated			**Owner's Equity**	
depreciation	(275)	16,225	Gay Gillen, capital	31,575
			Total liabilities and	
Total assets		$45,925	owner's equity	$45,925

Gillen classifies each asset and each liability as current or long-term. She could have labeled fixed assets as *long-term assets*, or as *plant assets*.

The classified balance sheet in Exhibit 4-12 reports more information—totals for current assets and current liabilities, which do not appear on an unclassified balance sheet. This is why actual balance sheets always classify the assets and the liabilities.

Stop & Think

Why is the classified balance sheet in Exhibit 4-12 more useful than an unclassified balance sheet (Exhibit 4-7) to (a) Gay Gillen and (b) a banker considering whether to lend $10,000 to Gillen?

Answer: A classified balance sheet indicates to Gillen and a banker

- Which of Gillen's liabilities, and the dollar amounts, that Gillen must pay within the next year
- Which of Gillen's assets are the most liquid and thus available to pay the liabilities
- Which assets and liabilities are long-term

Exhibit 4-13 presents a detailed balance sheet. To illustrate, we use the actual balance sheet of Dell Computer Corporation. You can understand all of Dell's account titles. Among the Current Assets are Short-term investments, which are investments that Dell expects to sell within one year. These assets are very liquid, which is why they come immediately after cash. Dell also reports inventory for the computers the company sells. And Dell has several different types of plant (fixed) assets. Everything else on Dell's balance sheet is similar to that of Gay Gillen eTravel.

Balance Sheet Forms

The balance sheet of Dell Computer in Exhibit 4-13 lists the assets at the top and the liabilities and owner equity below. This arrangement is known as the *report form*. The balance sheet of Gay Gillen eTravel in Exhibit 4-7 lists the assets at the left and the liabilities and the owner's equity at the right. That arrangement is known as the *account form*. Either form is acceptable; the report form used by Dell is more popular.

Exhibit 4-13

Dell Computer's Classified Balance Sheet

Dell Computer Corporation

Balance Sheet (Adapted)
January 31, 2002

Assets		*(millions)*
Current assets:		
Cash		$ 3,641
Short-term investments		273
Accounts receivable		2,269
Inventories		278
Prepaid expenses		1,416
Total current assets		7,877
Property, plant, and equipment:		
Land and buildings	$ 374	
Computer equipment	627	
Machinery and other equipment	437	
Total cost of property, plant, and equipment	1,438	
Less: Accumulated depreciation	(612)	
Property, plant, and equipment, net		826
Other assets		4,832
Total assets		$13,535
Liabilities		
Current liabilities:		
Accounts payable		$ 5,075
Salary payable		384
Taxes payable		264
Unearned revenue		322
Other current liabilities		1,474
Total current liabilities		7,519
Long-term notes payable		520
Other long-term liabilities		802
Total liabilities		8,841
Owner Equity		
Owner capital		4,694
Total liabilities and owner equity		$13,535

✔ Starter 4-10

Student Resource CD
current ratio, debt ratio

5 *Use the current ratio and the debt ratio to evaluate a company*

Accounting Ratios

Accounting is designed to provide information for decision making by business owners, managers, and lenders. A bank considering lending money to Gay Gillen must predict whether she can repay the loan. If Gillen already has a lot of debt, repayment is less certain than if she doesn't owe much money. To measure Gillen's (or Dell Computer's) financial position, decision makers use ratios that they compute from the company's financial statements. Two of the most widely used decision aids in business are the current ratio and the debt ratio.

Current Ratio

Current Ratio
Current assets divided by current liabilities. Measures the company's ability to pay current liabilities from current assets.

The **current ratio** measures a company's ability to pay its current liabilities. This ratio is computed as follows:

$$\text{Current ratio} = \frac{\text{Total current assets}}{\text{Total current liabilities}}$$

A company prefers to have a high current ratio because that means it has plenty of current assets to pay current liabilities. An increasing current ratio indicates improvement in ability to pay current debts.

A rule of thumb: A strong current ratio is 1.50, which indicates that the company has $1.50 in current assets for every $1.00 in current liabilities. A company with a current ratio of 1.50 would probably have little trouble paying its current liabilities. Most successful businesses operate with a current ratio of 1.50 or more. A current ratio of 1.00 is considered low.

Stop & Think

Compute **Dell Computer's** current ratio. Use the company's balance sheet in Exhibit 4-13 and show dollar amounts in millions.

Answer: $\text{Current} = \dfrac{\text{Total current assets}}{\text{Total current liabilities}} = \dfrac{\$7,877}{\$7,519} = 1.05$

How much in current assets does Dell have for every dollar the company owes in current liabilities?

Answer: $1.05

Is Dell's current ratio high or low? Is this ratio value risky?

Answer: Dell's current ratio is low, which makes it look risky. However, Dell operates successfully with a low current ratio because the company sells computers so fast.

Debt Ratio

Debt Ratio
Ratio of total liabilities to total assets. Tells the proportion of a company's assets that it has financed with debt.

A second decision aid is the **debt ratio**, which measures overall ability to pay debts. The debt ratio is computed as follows:

$$\text{Debt ratio} = \frac{\text{Total liabilities}}{\text{Total assets}}$$

The debt ratio indicates the proportion of a company's assets that are financed with debt. This ratio measures a business's overall ability to pay both current and long-term debts—total liabilities. The debt ratio measures debt-paying ability differently than the current ratio.

A *low* debt ratio is safer than a high debt ratio. Why? Because a company with low liabilities has low required payments. This company is unlikely to get into financial difficulty. By contrast, a business with a high debt ratio may have trouble paying its liabilities. When a company fails to pay its debts, the creditors can take the business away from its owner. The largest retail bankruptcy in history, Federated Department Stores, the parent company of Bloomingdale's, was due to high debt during an economic recession. People put off clothing purchases. Federated couldn't weather the downturn and had to declare bankruptcy.

A rule of thumb: A debt ratio below 0.60, or 60%, is considered safe for most businesses. A debt ratio above 0.80, or 80%, borders on high risk. Most companies have debt ratios in the range of 0.60 to 0.80.

✔ Starter 4-11

✔ Starter 4-12

Stop & Think

We saw that **Dell Computer** has a low current ratio, but Dell nevertheless operates successfully (profits are high, cash is plentiful, and the company grows steadily). Now compute Dell's debt ratio from the company's balance sheet in Exhibit 4-13. Show dollar amounts in millions.

Answer: $\text{Debt ratio} = \dfrac{\text{Total liabilities}}{\text{Total assets}} = \dfrac{\$8,841}{\$13,535} = 0.65, \text{ or } 65\%$

For each dollar of its total assets, how much does Dell owe in total liabilities?

Answer: $0.65

What percentage of Dell's total assets is financed with debt?

Answer: 0.65, or 65%

If you owed $0.65 for every dollar of your total assets, would you worry about your ability to pay your debts?

Answer: Probably not. A debt ratio of 65% is pretty safe.

Accounting.com

Dell Computer Corp.: Where Customer Focus Equals Solid Financials

Michael Dell dropped out of The University of Texas in 1984 to start **Dell Computer Corporation**. As he puts it, "My parents were upset, until I showed them my first financial statement." Dell began with $1,000 in seed money, and it was profitable from day one.

Today Dell is No. 1 in desktop PCs, No. 1 in the United States in low-end servers, and the country's No. 1 Internet retailer. Even with the PC industry in a slump, the company is on track to earn $2 billion net income in 2003. And while many technology stocks fell 80% from their 2000 peak, Dell's was down just 8% in 2002.

One of the main reasons Michael Dell was featured in *Business Week's* January 13, 2003, issue as one of "The Best Managers of the Year" is that he does not let the market valuation of his business cloud his vision. "There are two pieces of financials," says Dell. "One is the market's interpretation . . . stock price [and] credit ratings. Another is financial results. We don't have control of the market's reaction. We can focus on [keeping] our costs in line and [on having] the right mix of products." This focus fits with the company's mandate: ". . . The most important thing is to satisfy our customers. The second most important is to be profitable. If we don't do the first one well, the second one won't happen."

Dell has made a science of shaving costs from the PC-assembly process. Its process is so efficient that it rarely needs more than two hours' worth of parts inventory. Parts storage takes up a space no larger than your bedroom. Operating costs ate up only 10% of Dell's $35 billion revenue in 2002—compared with 21% at **Hewlett-Packard**, 25% at **Gateway**, and 46% at **Cisco**.

The direct-to-customer model has worked so well in PCs that Michael Dell wants to expand it into several other product lines, such as handhelds, servers, and storage systems. He knows that PCs alone will not keep his profit machine growing. Hewlett-Packard, Gateway, Cisco, and **IBM**: Watch out!

Based on: Kathryn Jones, "The Dell Way," *Business 2.0*, February 2003, www.business2.com/articles/mag/. Anonymous, "Michael Dell, Dell Computer," *Business Week*, January 13, 2003, p. 62. Del Jones, "Dell: Take Time to Build; Computer Chief Says Company Puts Its Focus on Customers," *USA Today*, October 10, 2002, p. B.06.

Managing Both the Current Ratio and the Debt Ratio

In general,

- A *high* current ratio is preferable to a low current ratio.
- A *low* debt ratio is preferable to a high debt ratio.

Which ratio gives the more reliable signal? Experienced lenders and investors examine a large number of ratios over several years to spot trends and turning points. They also consider other factors, such as the company's trend of net income.

As you progress through your study of accounting, we will introduce key ratios that people use for decision making. Chapter 18 summarizes all the ratios discussed in this book. It provides an overview of the more common ratios used to evaluate the success of a business.

Now study the Decision Guidelines feature, which summarizes what you have learned in this chapter, and do the Excel Application Exercise.

Decision Guidelines

COMPLETING THE ACCOUNTING CYCLE

Suppose you own the **Chicago Cubs** baseball organization, or suppose you are Michael Dell, working hard to get **Dell Computer** off the ground. How can you measure the success of your business? The Decision Guidelines describe the accounting process you will use to provide the information for your decisions.

Decision	Guidelines
How (where) to summarize the effects of all the entity's transactions and adjustments throughout the period?	Accountant's *work sheet* with columns for • Trial balance • Adjustments • Adjusted trial balance • Income statement • Balance sheet
What is the last *major* step in the accounting cycle?	*Closing entries* for the *temporary accounts:* • Revenues } Income statement accounts • Expenses } Income statement accounts • Owner's withdrawals
Why close out the revenues, expenses, and owner withdrawals?	Because these *temporary accounts* have balances that relate only to one accounting period and do *not* carry over to the next period.
Which accounts do *not* get closed out?	*Permanent (balance sheet) accounts:* • Assets • Liabilities • Owner's capital The balances of these accounts *do* carry over to the next period.
How do businesses classify their assets and liabilities for reporting on the balance sheet?	*Current* (within one year or the entity's operating cycle if longer than a year) *Long-term* (not current)
How do decision makers evaluate a company?	There are many ways, such as the company's net income (or net loss) on the income statement and the trend of net income from year to year. Another way to evaluate a company is based on the company's *financial ratios.* Two key ratios: $\text{Current ratio} = \frac{\text{Total current assets}}{\text{Total current liabilities}}$ The *current ratio* measures the ability to pay current liabilities with current assets. $\text{Debt ratio} = \frac{\text{Total liabilities}}{\text{Total assets}}$ The *debt ratio* measures the overall ability to pay liabilities. The debt ratio shows the proportion of the entity's assets that are financed with debt.

Excel Application Exercise

Goal: Create an Excel spreadsheet to calculate the current ratio and debt ratio for different companies, and use the results to answer questions about the companies. Requires Web research on **Amazon.com** and **Barnes & Noble.com**.

Scenario: You are deciding whether to buy the stock of two well-known online companies: Amazon.com and Barnes & Noble.com. You know that the current ratio and the debt ratio measure whether a company has the assets to cover its liabilities.

Your task is to create a simple spreadsheet to compare the current ratio and the debt ratio for each company. When done, answer these questions:

1. Do both companies have an acceptable current ratio? How can you tell?
2. Do both companies have an acceptable debt ratio? How can you tell?
3. What is the trend (up or down) for the ratios of both companies? Is the trend for each company positive or negative? Explain your answer.
4. Which company has the "better" current ratio? The "better" debt ratio?

Step-by-Step:

1. Locate the following current and prior-year information for Amazon.com and Barnes & Noble.com (found on the "Consolidated Balance Sheets"). For Amazon, use the annual report packaged with this text, or go to www.amazon.com, look under Services, click on "Investor Relations," then "Annual Reports." For Barnes & Noble.com, go to www.bn.com, click on "Investor Relations," then "Investor Information," and then "SEC Filings," and then "Annual Reports."
   a. Current Assets
   b. Total Assets
   c. Current Liabilities
   d. Long-Term Liabilities (You may have to compute this on the spreadsheet.)
   e. Total Liabilities (You may have to compute this on the spreadsheet.)
   f. Total Shareholders' Equity (Deficit)
   g. Total Liabilities and Shareholders' Equity
2. Open a new Excel spreadsheet.
3. Create a bold-faced heading for your spreadsheet that contains the following:
   a. Chapter 4 Excel Application Exercise
   b. The Current Ratio and Debt Ratio
   c. Amazon.com and Barnes & Noble.com Comparison
   d. Today's date
4. Two rows down from your worksheet heading, create a column heading titled "Amazon.com (in 000's)." Make it bold and underline the heading.
5. One row down from Amazon's column heading, create a row with the following bold, underlined column titles:
   a. Account
   b. FYxx (xx = the most recent fiscal year, for example, 02)
   c. FYyy (yy = the prior fiscal year, for example, 01)
6. Starting with the "Account" column heading, enter the data found in No. 1, above. You should have seven rows of data, with row descriptions (for example, "Current Assets"). Format the columns as necessary.
7. Skip a row at the end of your data, and then create a row titled "Current Ratio" and another row titled "Debt Ratio."
8. Enter the formula for each ratio in the "FYxx" and "FYyy" columns. You should have four formulas. Make both rows bold.
9. Repeat steps 4 through 8, substituting the Barnes & Noble.com title and data as appropriate.
10. Save your work to disk, and print a copy for your files.

END-OF-CHAPTER *Summary Problem*

A+ TIPS
CHECK YOUR RESOURCES

Refer to the data in the Mid-Chapter Summary Problem (Clay Employment Services, page 145–146).

Required

1. Journalize and post the adjusting entries. (Before posting to the accounts, enter into each account its balance as shown in the trial balance. For example, enter the $370,000 balance in the Accounts Receivable account before posting its adjusting entry.) Key adjusting entries by *letter*, as shown in the work sheet solution to the Mid-Chapter Summary Problem. You can take the adjusting entries straight from the work sheet on page 146.
2. Journalize and post the closing entries. (Each account should carry its balance as shown in the adjusted trial balance.) To distinguish closing entries from adjusting entries, key the closing entries by *number*. Draw arrows to illustrate the flow of data, as shown in Exhibit 4-10. Indicate the balance of the Capital account after the closing entries are posted.
3. Prepare the income statement for the year ended December 31, 20X9. List Miscellaneous Expense last among the expenses, a common practice.
4. Prepare the statement of owner's equity for the year ended December 31, 20X9. Draw an arrow linking the income statement to the statement of owner's equity.

5. Prepare the classified balance sheet at December 31, 20X9. Use the report form. All liabilities are current. Draw an arrow linking the statement of owner's equity to the balance sheet.

Solution

Requirement 1

Adjusting Entries

a.	Dec. 31	Supplies Expense.....................................	4,000		
		Supplies..		4,000	
b.	31	Depreciation Expense—Furniture and Fixtures	20,000		
		Accumulated Depreciation—Furniture and Fixtures. .		20,000	
c.	31	Depreciation Expense—Building....................	10,000		
		Accumulated Depreciation—Building.............		10,000	
d.	31	Salary Expense.....................................	5,000		
		Salary Payable		5,000	
e.	31	Accounts Receivable................................	12,000		
		Service Revenue................................		12,000	
f.	31	Unearned Service Revenue	32,000		
		Service Revenue................................		32,000	

Accounts Receivable		Supplies		Accumulated Depreciation—Furniture and Fixtures		Accumulated Depreciation—Building	
370,000		6,000	(a) 4,000		40,000		130,000
(e) 12,000					(b) 20,000		(c) 10,000

Salary Payable		Unearned Service Revenue		Service Revenue	
	(d) 5,000	(f) 32,000	45,000		286,000
					(e) 12,000
					(f) 32,000
					Bal. 330,000

Salary Expense		Supplies Expense		Depreciation Expense—Furniture and Fixtures		Depreciation Expense—Building	
172,000		(a) 4,000		(b) 20,000		(c) 10,000	
(d) 5,000		Bal. 4,000		Bal. 20,000		Bal. 10,000	
Bal. 177,000							

Requirement 2

Closing Entries

1.	Dec. 31	Service Revenue	330,000		
		Income Summary..........................		330,000	
2.	31	Income Summary...............................	224,000		
		Salary Expense		177,000	
		Supplies Expense		4,000	
		Depreciation Expense—Furniture and Fixtures .		20,000	
		Depreciation Expense—Building		10,000	
		Miscellaneous Expense		13,000	
3.	31	Income Summary ($330,000 − $224,000)	106,000		
		Capital		106,000	
4.	31	Capital	65,000		
		Withdrawals		65,000

Salary Expense

	172,000		
(d)	5,000		
Bal.	177,000	(2)	177,000

Supplies Expense

(a)	4,000		
Bal.	4,000	(2)	4,000

Depreciation Expense— Furniture & Fixtures

(b)	20,000		
Bal.	20,000	(2)	20,000

Depreciation Expense— Building

(c)	10,000		
Bal.	10,000	(2)	10,000

Miscellaneous Expense

	13,000		
Bal.	13,000	(2)	13,000

Income Summary

(2)	224,000	(1)	330,000
(3)	106,000	Bal.	106,000

Service Revenue

			286,000
		(e)	12,000
		(f)	32,000
(1)	330,000	Bal.	330,000

Jay Clay, Withdrawals

Bal.	65,000	(4)	65,000

Jay Clay, Capital

(4)	65,000		293,000
		(3)	106,000
		Bal.	334,000

Requirement 3

Clay Employment Services

Income Statement

Year Ended December 31, 20X9

Revenue:		
Service revenue		$330,000
Expenses:		
Salary expense	$177,000	
Depreciation expense—furniture and fixtures	20,000	
Depreciation expense—building	10,000	
Supplies expense	4,000	
Miscellaneous expense	13,000	
Total expenses		224,000
Net income		$106,000

Requirement 4

Clay Employment Services

Statement of Owner's Equity

Year Ended December 31, 20X9

Jay Clay, capital, January 1, 20X9	$293,000
Add: Net income	106,000
	399,000
Less: Withdrawals	(65,000)
Jay Clay, capital, December 31, 20X9	$334,000

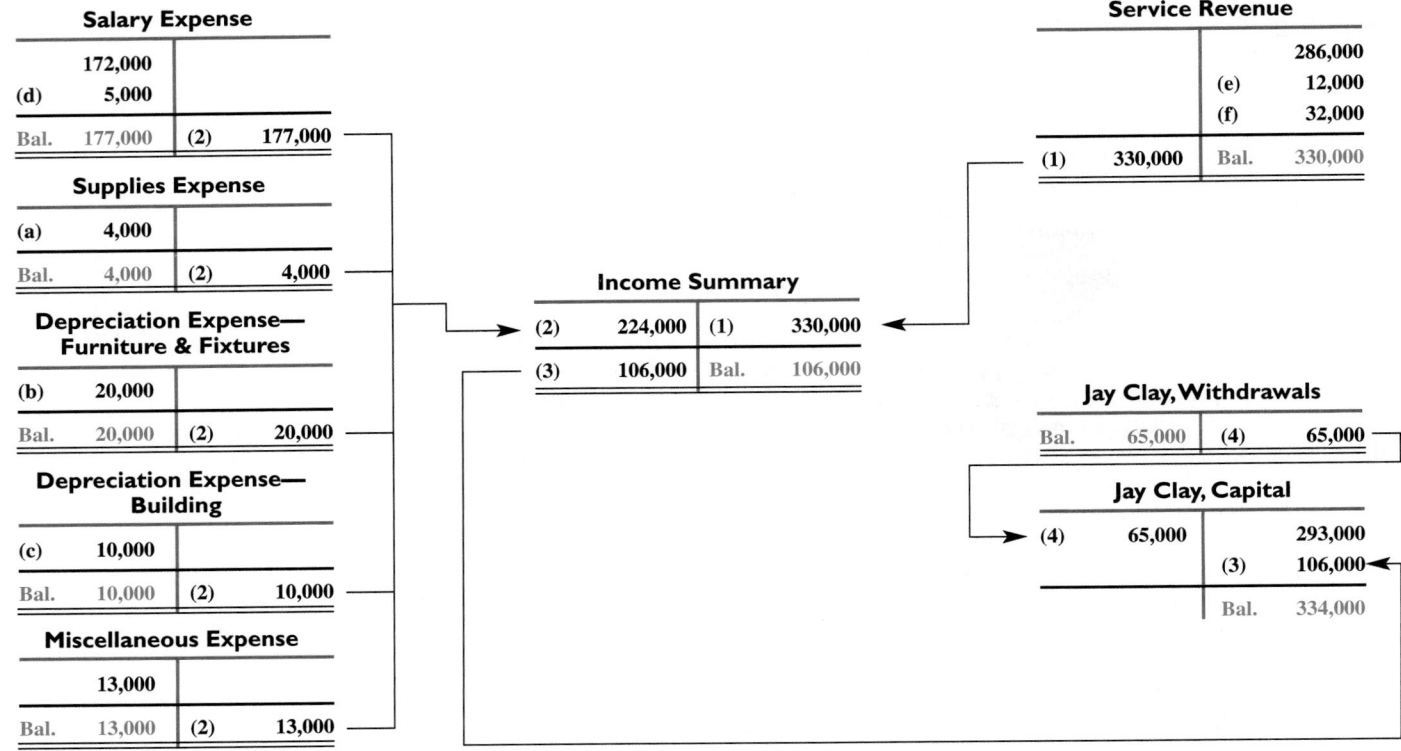

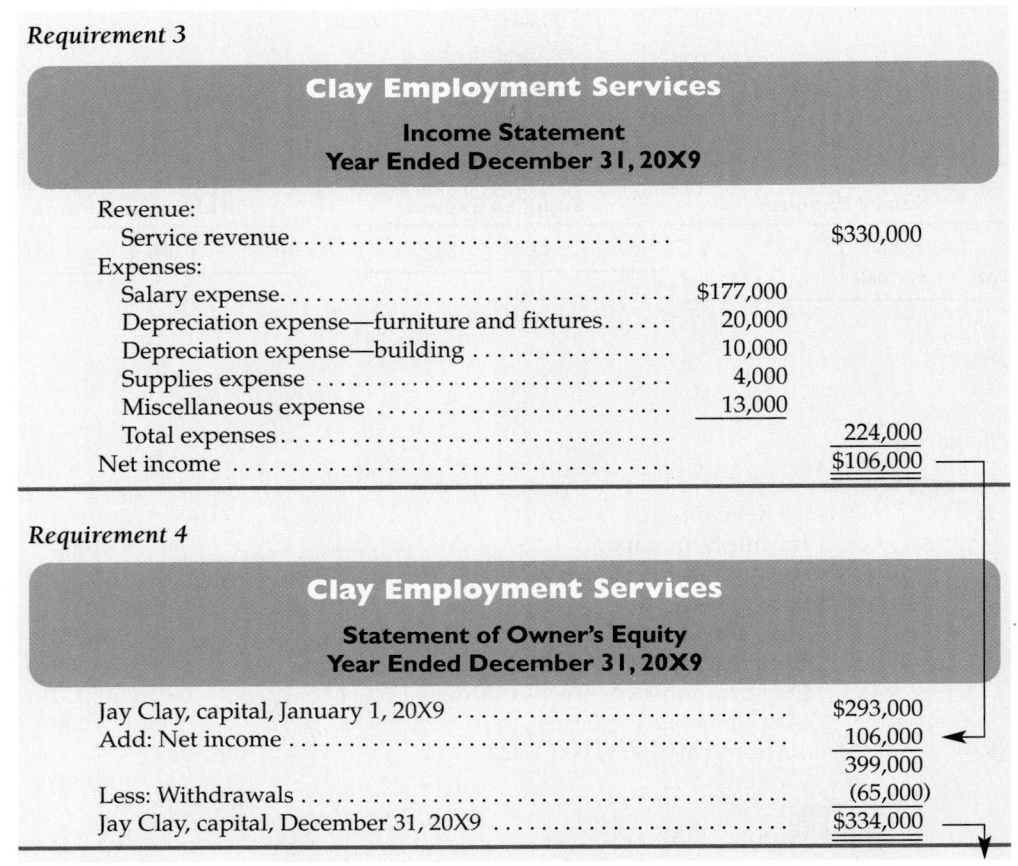

Requirement 5

Clay Employment Services
Balance Sheet
December 31, 20X9

Assets		
Current assets:		
Cash		$198,000
Accounts receivable		382,000
Supplies		2,000
Total current assets		582,000
Long-term assets:		
Furniture and fixtures	$100,000	
Less: Accumulated depreciation	(60,000)	40,000
Building	$250,000	
Less: Accumulated depreciation	(140,000)	110,000
Total assets		$732,000
Liabilities		
Current liabilities:		
Accounts payable		$380,000
Salary payable		5,000
Unearned service revenue		13,000
Total current liabilities		398,000
Owner's Equity		
Jay Clay, capital		334,000
Total liabilities and owner's equity		$732,000

REVIEW *Completing the Accounting Cycle*

Quick Check

1. Consider the steps in the accounting cycle in Exhibit 4-1, page 141. Which part of the accounting cycle provides information to help a bank decide whether to lend money to a company?
   a. Financial statements
   b. Adjusting entries
   c. Closing entries
   d. Postclosing trial balance
2. Which columns of the accounting work sheet show unadjusted amounts?
   a. Trial balance
   b. Adjustments
   c. Income Statement
   d. Balance Sheet
3. Which columns of the work sheet show net income?
   a. Adjusted Trial Balance
   b. Income Statement
   c. Balance Sheet
   d. Both b and c
4. Which situation indicates a net loss on the income statement?
   a. Total debits equal total credits
   b. Total debits exceed total credits
   c. Total credits exceed total debits
   d. None of the above
5. Assume that Supplies has a $6,000 unadjusted balance on the Trial Balance of **Dell Computer's** accounting work sheet. At year-end Dell counts supplies of $2,000. What adjustment will appear on Dell's work sheet?

a.	Supplies	4,000	
	Supplies Expense		4,000
b.	Supplies Expense	4,000	
	Supplies		4,000
c.	Supplies Expense	2,000	
	Supplies		2,000

   d. No adjustment is needed because the Supplies account already has a correct balance.

6. Which of the following accounts is not closed?
   - a. Salary Expense
   - b. Service Revenue
   - c. Accumulated Depreciation
   - d. Owner, Withdrawals

7. What do closing entries accomplish?
   - a. Transfer revenues, expenses, and owner withdrawals to the capital account
   - b. Zero out the revenues, expenses, and owner withdrawals to prepare these accounts for the next period
   - c. Bring the capital account to its correct ending balance
   - d. All of the above

8. Which of the following is not a closing entry?

a. Income Summary	XXX	
Rent Expense.		XXX
b. Salary Payable.	XXX	
Income Summary . .		XXX
c. Service Revenue	XXX	
Income Summary.		XXX
d. Owner, Capital	XXX	
Owner, Withdrawals . .		XXX

9. Assets and liabilities are listed on the balance sheet in order of their
   - a. Purchase date
   - b. Liquidity
   - c. Market value
   - d. Adjustments

10. Examine Gay Gillen eTravel's classified balance sheet in Exhibit 4-12, page 153. Gillen's current ratio at April 30, 20X5, is
    - a. 3.20
    - b. 0.31
    - c. 0.48
    - d. 2.07

Accounting Vocabulary

accounting cycle (p. 140)
closing the accounts (p. 148)
closing entries (p. 149)
current asset (p. 152)
current liability (p. 152)
current ratio (p. 154)
debt ratio (p. 155)
fixed asset (p. 152)
Income Summary (p. 149)
liquidity (p. 152)
long-term asset (p. 152)
long-term liability (p. 152)
operating cycle (p. 152)
permanent accounts (p. 148)
plant asset (p. 152)
postclosing trial balance (p. 151)
reversing entries (p. 151)
temporary accounts (p. 148)
work sheet (p. 142)

ASSESS *Your Progress*

A+ online homework

See *www.prenhall.com/horngren* for selected Starters, Exercises, and Problems.

Starters

Explaining items on the work sheet **(Obj. 1)**

S4-1 ← *Link Back to Chapter 3 (Adjusting Entries).* Return to the trial balance in Exhibit 4-2 on the acetate pages. In your own words, explain why the following accounts must be adjusted:

- a. Salary payable
- b. Unearned service revenue
- c. Supplies
- d. Prepaid rent
- e. Accumulated depreciation

Explaining items on the work sheet **(Obj. 1, 2)**

S4-2 ← *Link Back to Chapters 1, 2, and 3 (Definitions of Accounts).* Examine the Adjusted Trial Balance columns of Exhibit 4-4 on the acetate pages. Explain what the following items mean:

- a. Accounts receivable
- b. Supplies
- c. Prepaid rent
- d. Furniture
- e. Accumulated depreciation
- f. Accounts payable
- g. Unearned service revenue
- h. Service revenue
- i. Rent expense

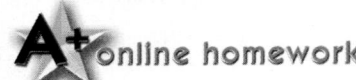

S4-3 Consider the Income Statement columns and the Balance Sheet columns of the work sheet in Exhibit 4-6 on the acetate pages. Answer the following questions:

Using the work sheet
(Obj. 1, 2)

1. What type of balance does the Owner's Capital account have—debit or credit?
2. Which Income Statement account has the same type of balance as the Capital account?
3. Which Income Statement accounts have the opposite type of balance?
4. What do we call the difference between total debits and total credits on the Income Statement? Into what account is the difference figure closed at the end of the period?

S4-4 Study Exhibit 4-5 on the acetate pages.

Making closing entries
(Obj. 3)

1. Journalize the closing entries for
   a. Owner's withdrawals
   b. Service revenue
   c. All the expenses (make a single closing entry for all the expenses)
   d. Income Summary
2. Set up all the T-accounts affected by requirement 1 and insert their adjusted balances (denote as *Bal.*) at April 30. Also set up a T-account for Income Summary. Post the closing entries to the accounts, denoting posted amounts as *Clo.*

S4-5 This exercise should be used in conjunction with Starter 4-4.

Analyzing the overall effect of the closing entries on the owner's capital account
(Obj. 3)

1. Return to Exhibit 4-5 on the acetate pages. Without making any closing entries or using any T-accounts, compute the ending balance of Gay Gillen, Capital.
2. Trace Gay Gillen's ending capital balance to its two appropriate places in Exhibit 4-7 (page 147). In which two financial statements do you find Gay Gillen, Capital? Where on each statement?

S4-6 **Oracle Corporation** reported the following items, adapted from its financial statements at May 31 (amounts in millions):

Making closing entries
(Obj. 3)

Sales and marketing expense	$2,622	Cash	$1,786
Other assets	477	Service revenue	5,139
Interest expense	21	Accounts payable	284
Long-term liabilities	382	Accounts receivable	2,238

Make Oracle's closing entries, as needed, for these accounts.

S4-7 This exercise should be used in conjunction with Starter 4-6. Use the data in Starter 4-6 to set up T-accounts for those accounts that **Oracle Corporation** closed out at May 31. Insert their account balances prior to closing, post the closing entries to these accounts, and show each account's ending balance after closing. Also show the Income Summary T-account. Denote a balance as *Bal.* and a closing entry amount as *Clo.*

Posting closing entries
(Obj. 3)

S4-8 After closing its accounts at May 31, 20XX, **Oracle Corporation** had the following account balances (adapted) with amounts given in millions:

Preparing a postclosing trial balance
(Obj. 3)

Long-term liabilities	$ 518	Property	$ 988
Other assets	825	Cash	1,786
Accounts receivable	2,479	Service revenue	0
Total expenses	0	Owners' equity	3,695
Accounts payable	284	Other current assets	1,182
Other current liabilities	2,759	Short-term notes payable	4

Prepare Oracle's postclosing trial balance at May 31, 20XX. List accounts in proper order, as shown in Exhibit 4-11.

Classifying assets and liabilities as current or long-term
(Obj. 4)

S4-9 **Lands' End** had sales of $1,320 million during the year ended January 31, 20X0, and total assets of $456 million at January 31, 20X0, the end of the company's fiscal year. The financial statements of Lands' End reported the following (all amounts in millions):

Sales revenue	$1,320	Land and buildings	$ 103
Inventory	162	Accounts payable	75
Receivables	18	Total expenses	1,073
Interest expense	2	Accumulated depreciation	117
Equipment	176	Accrued liabilities (such as	
Prepaid expenses	22	Salary payable)	44

1. Identify the assets (including contra assets) and liabilities.
2. Classify each asset and each liability as current or long-term.

Classifying assets and liabilities as current or long-term
(Obj. 4)

S4-10 ← *Link Back to Chapter 3 (Book Value).* Examine **Dell Computer's** balance sheet in Exhibit 4-13. Identify or compute the following amounts for Dell:

a. Total current assets
b. Total current liabilities
c. Book value of Property, plant, and equipment
d. Total long-term assets
e. Total long-term liabilities

Computing the current ratio and the debt ratio
(Obj. 5)

S4-11 Montez Printing Company has these account balances at December 31, 20X7:

Accounts payable	$ 5,000	Note payable, long-term	$ 9,000
Accounts receivable	6,000	Prepaid rent	1,000
Cash	3,000	Salary payable	2,000
Depreciation expense	4,000	Service revenue	31,000
Equipment	12,000	Supplies	2,000

Compute Montez's current ratio and debt ratio.

Computing and using the current ratio and the debt ratio
(Obj. 5)

S4-12 This exercise should be used in conjunction with Starter 4-8. Use the postclosing trial balance that you prepared for Starter 4-8 to compute **Oracle Corporation's** current ratio and debt ratio.

1. How much in *current* assets does Oracle have for every dollar of *current* liabilities that it owes? What ratio measures this relationship?
2. What percentage of Oracle's total assets are financed with debt? What is the name of this ratio?
3. What percentage of Oracle's total assets do the owners of the company actually own?

A+ online homework

Exercises

Preparing a work sheet
(Obj. 1)

Student Resource CD
spreadsheet
General Ledger, Peachtree, QuickBooks

E4-1 The trial balance of DaySpring Woodworking Service follows on page 165. Additional information at September 30, 20X6:

a. Accrued service revenue, $600
b. Depreciation, $100
c. Accrued salary expense, $500
d. Prepaid rent expired, $800
e. Supplies used, $1,600

Required

Complete DaySpring's work sheet for the month ended September 30, 20X6. How much was net income for September?

Journalizing adjusting and closing entries
(Obj. 2, 3)

E4-2 Journalize DaySpring's adjusting and closing entries in Exercise 4-1.

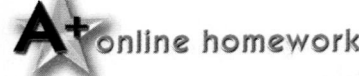

DaySpring Woodworking Service

Trial Balance
September 30, 20X6

Cash	$ 3,500	
Accounts receivable	3,400	
Prepaid rent	1,200	
Supplies	3,300	
Equipment	32,600	
Accumulated depreciation		$ 1,800
Accounts payable		3,600
Salary payable		
Gail Pfeiffer, capital		36,000
Gail Pfeiffer, withdrawals	2,000	
Service revenue		7,100
Depreciation expense		
Salary expense	1,800	
Rent expense		
Utilities expense	700	
Supplies expense		
Total	$48,500	$48,500

Posting adjusting and closing entries
(Obj. 2, 3)

Student ResourceCD

E4-3 Set up T-accounts for those accounts affected by the adjusting and closing entries in Exercise 4-2. Post the adjusting and closing entries to the accounts; denote adjustment amounts by *Adj.*, closing amounts by *Clo.*, and balances by *Bal.* Double underline the accounts with zero balances after you close them, and show the ending balance in each account.

Preparing a postclosing trial balance
(Obj. 2)

E4-4 After completing Exercises 4-1, 4-2, and 4-3, prepare the postclosing trial balance of DaySpring Woodworking Service at September 30, 20X6.

Adjusting the accounts
(Obj. 2)

E4-5 ← *Link Back to Chapter 2 (Adjusting Entries).* Pioneer Travel's accounting records include the following account balances:

	December 31, 20X1	20X2
Prepaid insurance	$1,400	$1,600
Unearned service revenue	4,100	3,100

During 20X2, Pioneer recorded the following:

a. Paid the annual insurance premium of $4,800.
b. Made the year-end adjustment to record insurance expense for the year. You must compute this amount.
c. Collected $17,000 cash in advance for service revenue to be earned later.
d. Made the year-end adjustment to record the earning of $18,000 service revenue that had been collected in advance.

Required

1. Set up T-accounts for Prepaid Insurance, Insurance Expense, Unearned Service Revenue, and Service Revenue. Insert beginning and ending balances for Prepaid Insurance and Unearned Service Revenue.
2. Journalize entries a through d above, and post to the T-accounts. Explanations are not required. Ensure that the ending balances for Prepaid Insurance and Unearned Service Revenue agree with the December 31, 20X2, balances given above.

Closing the books
(Obj. 3)

E4-6 Refer to the Pioneer Travel data in Exercise 4-5. After making the adjusting entries in Exercise 4-5, journalize Pioneer's closing entries at the end of 20X2. Also set up T-accounts for Insurance Expense and Service Revenue and post the closing entries to these accounts. What are their balances after closing?

Identifying and journalizing entries
(Obj. 3)

E4-7 From the following selected accounts of Daewoo Energy at June 30, 20X4, prepare the entity's closing entries:

Park Daewoo, capital	$ 21,600	Interest expense	$ 2,200
Service revenue	110,000	Accounts receivable	14,000
Unearned revenues	1,300	Salary payable	800
Salary expense	12,500	Depreciation expense	10,200
Accumulated depreciation	35,000	Rent expense	5,900
Supplies expense	1,700	Park Daewoo, withdrawals	40,000
Interest revenue	700	Supplies	1,400

What is Daewoo's ending capital balance at June 30, 20X4?

Identifying and journalizing closing entries
(Obj. 3)

E4-8 The accountant for MichiganTechnology.com has posted adjusting entries (a) through (e) to the following accounts at December 31, 20X8.

Accounts Receivable

	126,000		
(a)	9,500		

Supplies

	4,000	(b)	2,000

Accumulated Depreciation—Furniture

			5,000
		(c)	1,100

Accumulated Depreciation—Building

			33,000
		(d)	6,000

Salary Payable

		(e)	700

Felix Rohr, Capital

			52,400

Felix Rohr, Withdrawals

	61,400		

Service Revenue

			108,000
		(a)	9,500

Salary Expense

	26,000		
(e)	700		

Supplies Expense

(b)	2,000		

Depreciation Expense—Furniture

(c)	1,100		

Depreciation Expense—Building

(d)	6,000		

Required

1. Journalize MichiganTechnology.com's closing entries at December 31, 20X8.
2. Determine Felix Rohr's ending capital balance at December 31, 20X8.

Preparing a statement of owner's equity
(Obj. 3)

E4-9 From the following accounts of Chang Realty, prepare Chang's statement of owner's equity for the year ended December 31, 20X2.

Alvin Chang, Capital

Clo.	72,000	Jan. 1	164,000
		Clo.	143,000
		Bal.	235,000

Alvin Chang, Withdrawals

Mar. 31	19,000		
Jun. 30	17,000		
Sep. 30	19,000		
Dec. 31	17,000		
Bal.	72,000	Clo.	72,000

Income Summary

Clo.	85,000	Clo.	228,000
Clo.	143,000	Bal.	143,000

Identifying and recording adjusting and closing entries
(Obj. 2, 3)

E4-10 The trial balance and adjusted income statement amounts from the April work sheet of The Megan Price Decorator Guild follow:

Account Title	Unadjusted Trial Balance		Income Statement	
Cash	$14,200			
Supplies	2,400			
Prepaid rent	1,100			
Equipment	51,100			
Accumulated depreciation		$ 6,200		
Accounts payable		4,600		
Salary payable				
Unearned service revenue		4,400		

(continued)

Account Title	Unadjusted Trial Balance		Income Statement	
Long-term note payable		10,000		
Megan Price, capital.		34,800		
Megan Price, withdrawals	1,000			
Service revenue.		14,800		16,000
Salary expense	3,000		$ 3,800	
Rent expense.	1,200		1,400	
Depreciation expense.			300	
Supplies expense			400	
Utilities expense.	800		800	
	$74,800	$74,800	6,700	16,000
Net income or net loss.			?	
			$16,000	$16,000

Required

1. Journalize Price's adjusting and closing entries at April 30.
2. How much net income or net loss did Price earn for April? How can you tell?

Preparing a classified balance sheet **(Obj. 4, 5)**

E4-11 Refer to Exercise 4-10.

Required

1. After solving Exercise 4-10 use the data in that exercise to prepare the classified balance sheet of The Megan Price Decorator Guild at April 30 of the current year. Use the report format.
2. Compute Price's current ratio and debt ratio at April 30. One year ago, the current ratio was 1.50 and the debt ratio was 0.30. Indicate whether Price's ability to pay debts has improved, deteriorated, or remained the same during the current year.

Computing financial statement amounts **(Obj. 2, 4)**

E4-12 Data for the unadjusted trial balance of Joy's Dance Studio at December 31, 20X7, follow:

Cash.	$ 3,000	Service revenue	$ 93,600
Property, plant, and equipment	66,200	Salary expense	42,700
Accumulated depreciation .	21,800	Depreciation expense	
Accounts payable	6,100	Supplies expense	
		Insurance expense	

Adjusting data for 20X7 are

a. Accrued service revenue, $8,100.
b. Supplies used in operations, $600.
c. Accrued salary expense, $1,400.
d. Insurance expense, $1,800.
e. Depreciation expense, $2,900.

Joy Maddox, the owner, has received an offer to sell the company. She needs to know the net income for the year covered by these data.

Required

Without opening accounts, making journal entries, or using a work sheet, give Maddox the requested information. Prepare an income statement, and show all computations.

Continuing Exercise

This exercise continues the Marsha Walker, Consultant, situation begun in Exercise 2-17 of Chapter 2 and continued in Exercise 3-15 of Chapter 3.

Closing the books and preparing a classified balance sheet **(Obj. 3, 4, 5)**

E4-13 Refer to Exercise 3-15 of Chapter 3. Start from the posted T-accounts and the adjusted trial balance that Marsha Walker, Consultant, prepared for her business at December 31:

Marsha Walker, Consultant

Adjusted Trial Balance
December 31, 20XX

Account	Adjusted Trial Balance Debit	Adjusted Trial Balance Credit
Cash	$11,700	
Accounts receivable	1,500	
Supplies	100	
Equipment	2,000	
Accumulated depr.—equipment		$ 50
Furniture	3,600	
Accumulated depr.—furniture		60
Accounts payable		3,600
Salary payable		500
Unearned service revenue		600
Marsha Walker, capital		14,000
Marsha Walker, withdrawals	1,600	
Service revenue		3,200
Rent expense	500	
Utilities expense	200	
Salary expense	500	
Depreciation expense—equipment	50	
Depreciation expense—furniture	60	
Supplies expense	200	
Total	$22,010	$22,010

Required

1. Journalize and post the closing entries at December 31. Denote each closing amount as *Clo.* and an account balance as *Bal.*
2. Prepare a classified balance sheet at December 31.
3. If your instructor assigns it, complete the accounting work sheet at December 31.

Problems

A+ online homework

(Group A)

Preparing a work sheet
(Obj. 1)

P4-1A The trial balance of Lane's Interiors at May 31, 20X8, follows.

Lane's Interiors

Trial Balance
May 31, 20X8

Cash	$ 4,300	
Notes receivable	10,300	
Interest receivable		
Supplies	500	
Prepaid insurance	1,700	
Furniture	27,400	
Accumulated depreciation—furniture		$ 1,400
Building	53,900	
Accumulated depreciation—building		34,500
Land	18,700	
Accounts payable		14,700
Interest payable		
Salary payable		
Unearned service revenue		8,800

(continued)

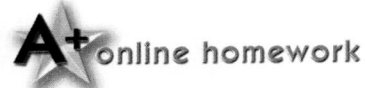

Note payable, long-term		18,700
K. Lane, capital		29,900
K. Lane, withdrawals	3,800	
Service revenue		16,800
Interest revenue		
Depreciation expense—furniture		
Depreciation expense—building		
Salary expense	2,100	
Insurance expense		
Interest expense		
Utilities expense	1,100	
Advertising expense	1,000	
Supplies expense		
Total	$124,800	$124,800

Additional data at May 31, 20X8:

a. Depreciation: furniture, $500; building, $400.
b. Accrued salary expense, $600.
c. Supplies on hand, $400.
d. Prepaid insurance expired, $300.
e. Accrued interest expense, $200.
f. Unearned service revenue earned during May, $4,400.
g. Accrued advertising expense, $100 (credit Accounts Payable).
h. Accrued interest revenue, $200.

Required

Complete Lane's work sheet for May. Key adjusting entries by letter.

Preparing a work sheet and the financial statements
(Obj. 1, 2)
Student ResourceCD
General Ledger, Peachtree, QuickBooks

P4-2A The unadjusted T-accounts of Ross Reagan, M.D., at December 31, 20X5, and the related year-end adjustment data follow.

Account	Debit	Credit
Cash	**Bal. 29,000**	
Accounts Receivable	**Bal. 44,000**	
Supplies	**Bal. 6,000**	
Equipment	**Bal. 102,000**	
Accumulated Depreciation		**Bal. 12,000**
Accounts Payable		**Bal. 16,000**
Salary Payable		
Unearned Service Revenue		**Bal. 2,000**
Note Payable, Long-Term		**Bal. 40,000**
Ross Reagan, Capital		**Bal. 41,000**
Ross Reagan, Withdrawals	**Bal. 54,000**	
Service Revenue		**Bal. 175,000**
Salary Expense	**Bal. 36,000**	
Supplies Expense		
Depreciation Expense		
Interest Expense	**Bal. 5,000**	
Insurance Expense	**Bal. 10,000**	

Adjustment data at December 31, 20X5:

a. Depreciation for the year, $5,000.
b. Supplies on hand, $2,000.
c. Accrued service revenue, $4,000.
d. Unearned service revenue earned during the year, $2,000.
e. Accrued salary expense, $4,000.

Required

1. Enter the trial balance on a work sheet, and complete the work sheet. Key each adjusting entry by the letter corresponding to the data given. List all the accounts, including those with zero balances. Leave a blank line under Service Revenue.

2. Prepare the income statement, the statement of owner's equity, and the classified balance sheet in account form.
3. Did Reagan have a good or a bad year during 20X5? Give the reason for your answer.

Journalizing adjusting and closing entries
(Obj. 2, 3)

Student Resource CD
GL, PT, QB

P4-3A The *unadjusted* trial balance of TexasOnline Service at April 30, 20X8, follows. Adjusting data at April 30, 20X8, consist of

a. Accrued service revenue, $2,200.
b. Depreciation for the year: equipment, $6,900; building, $3,700.
c. Accrued wage expense, $800.
d. Unearned service revenue earned during the year, $4,100.
e. Additional supplies used, $500.
f. Prepaid insurance expired, $700
g. Accrued interest expense, $1,200.

Required

1. Journalize the adjusting entries.
2. Journalize the closing entries.

TexasOnline Service
Adjusted Trial Balance
April 30, 20X8

Cash	$ 14,500	
Accounts receivable	43,700	
Supplies	3,600	
Prepaid insurance	2,200	
Equipment	63,900	
Accumulated depreciation—equipment		$ 28,400
Building	74,300	
Accumulated depreciation—building		18,200
Land	30,600	
Accounts payable		19,500
Interest payable		2,000
Wages payable		800
Unearned service revenue		3,600
Note payable, long-term		69,900
Jeff Trichel, capital		77,100
Jeff Trichel, withdrawals	27,500	
Service revenue		98,500
Depreciation expense—equipment		
Depreciation expense—building		
Wage expense	32,800	
Insurance expense	5,100	
Interest expense	8,100	
Utilities expense	4,900	
Supplies expense	6,800	
Total	$318,000	$318,000

Preparing an income statement
(Obj. 3)

P4-4A Refer to the data for TexasOnline Service in Problem 4-3A. After journalizing TexasOnline's adjusting and closing entries, prepare the company's income statement for the year ended April 30, 20X8. List expenses in descending order—that is, largest first, second-largest next, and so on.

Completing the accounting cycle
(Obj. 2, 3, 4)

Student Resource CD
GL, PT, QB

P4-5A The trial balance of Lange Party Productions at October 31, 20X6, follows, along with the data for the month-end adjustments.

Lange Party Productions
Trial Balance
October 31, 20X6

Account Number	Account Title	Debit	Credit
11	Cash	$ 4,900	
12	Accounts receivable	15,310	
13	Prepaid rent	2,200	
14	Supplies	840	
15	Equipment	26,830	
16	Accumulated depreciation—equipment		$ 3,400
21	Accounts payable		7,290
22	Salary payable		
23	Unearned service revenue		5,300
31	Melanie Lange, capital		28,290
32	Melanie Lange, withdrawals	3,900	
41	Service revenue		12,560
51	Salary expense	2,860	
52	Rent expense		
54	Depreciation expense—equipment		
56	Supplies expense		
	Total	$56,840	$56,840

Adjusting data at October 31:

a. Unearned service revenue still unearned, $800.
b. Prepaid rent still in force, $2,000.
c. Supplies used, $770.
d. Depreciation on equipment for the month, $250.
e. Accrued salary expense, $310.

Required

1. Open the accounts listed in the trial balance, inserting their October 31 unadjusted balances. Also open the Income Summary account, number 33. Use four-column accounts. Date the balances of the following accounts October 1: Prepaid Rent, Supplies, Equipment, Accumulated Depreciation—Equipment, Unearned Service Revenue, and Melanie Lange, Capital.
2. Enter the trial balance on a work sheet and complete the work sheet of Lange Party Productions for the month ended October 31, 20X6.
3. Prepare the income statement, statement of owner's equity, and classified balance sheet in report form.
4. Using the work sheet data that you prepare, journalize and post the adjusting and closing entries. Use dates and posting references. Use 12 as the journal page number.
5. Prepare a postclosing trial balance.

P4-6A Selected accounts of Mark Tynes, Architect, at December 31, 20X3, follow.

Preparing a classified balance sheet in report form
(Obj. 4, 5)

Required

1. Prepare Tynes's classified balance sheet in report form at December 31, 20X3. Show totals for total assets, total liabilities, and total liabilities and owner's equity.

Accounts payable	$34,700	Insurance expense	$ 600
Accounts receivable	41,500	Note payable, long-term	3,200
Accumulated depreciation—building	47,300	Other assets	2,300
		Other current liabilities	1,100
Accumulated depreciation—equipment	7,700	Prepaid insurance	600
		Prepaid rent	4,700
Building	55,900	Salary expense	17,800
Cash	3,400	Salary payable	2,400
Depreciation expense	1,900	Service revenue	71,100
Mark Tynes, capital	38,300	Supplies	3,800
Equipment	24,200	Unearned service revenue	1,700

2. Compute Tynes's current ratio and debt ratio at December 31, 20X3. At December 31, 20X2, the current ratio was 1.28 and debt ratio was 0.52. Did Tynes's ability to pay debts improve, deteriorate, or remain the same during 20X3?

Analyzing errors and journalizing adjusting entries
(Obj. 2)

P4-7A ← *Link Back to Chapter 2 (Accounting Errors).* The accountant of Vivid Image Photography encountered the following situations while adjusting and closing the books at February 28. Consider each situation independently.

a. The accountant failed to make the following adjusting entries at February 28:
   1. Depreciation of equipment, $700.
   2. Earned service revenue that had been collected in advance, $2,700.
   3. Accrued service revenue, $1,400.
   4. Insurance expense, $360.
   5. Accrued interest expense on a note payable, $520.

   Compute the overall net income effect of these omissions.

b. Record each of the adjusting entries identified in item a.

c. A $1,400 debit to Supplies was posted as $4,100.
   1. At what stage of the accounting cycle will this error be detected?
   2. What is the name of this type of error? Explain how to identify the error.

d. The $1,300 balance of Computer Software was entered as $13,000 on the trial balance.
   1. What is the name of this type of error?
   2. Assume that this is the only error in the trial balance. Which will be greater, the total debits or the total credits, and by how much?
   3. How can this type of error be identified?

A+ online homework

Problems

(Group B)

Preparing a work sheet
(Obj. 1)

P4-1B The trial balance of Roadster Tune Center at June 30, 20X3, follows.

Roadster Tune Center
Trial Balance
June 30, 20X3

Cash	$ 21,200	
Accounts receivable	37,800	
Supplies	17,600	
Prepaid insurance	2,300	
Equipment	32,600	
Accumulated depreciation—equipment		$ 26,200
Building	42,800	
Accumulated depreciation—building		10,500
Land	28,300	
Accounts payable		22,600
Interest payable		
Wages payable		
Unearned service revenue		10,500
Note payable, long-term		22,400
Dan Runyan, capital		79,100
Dan Runyan, withdrawals	4,200	
Service revenue		20,100
Depreciation expense—equipment		
Depreciation expense—building		
Wage expense	3,200	
Insurance expense		
Interest expense		
Utilities expense	1,100	
Advertising expense	300	
Supplies expense		
Total	$191,400	$191,400

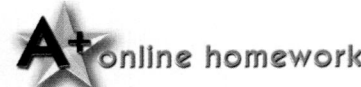

Additional data at June 30, 20X3:

a. Depreciation: equipment, $600; building, $300.
b. Accrued wage expense, $200.
c. Supplies on hand, $14,300.
d. Prepaid insurance expired during June, $500.
e. Accrued interest expense, $100.
f. Unearned service revenue earned during June, $4,900.
g. Accrued advertising expense, $100 (credit Accounts Payable).
h. Accrued service revenue, $1,100.

Required

Complete Roadster Tune Center's work sheet for June. Key adjusting entries by letter.

P4-2B The unadjusted T-accounts of Lake Air Studio, at December 31, 20X6, and the related year-end adjustment data follow.

Preparing a work sheet and the financial statements **(Obj. 1, 2)**

Student ResourceCD
GL, PT, QB

Adjustment data at December 31, 20X6:

a. Unearned service revenue earned during the year, $5,000.
b. Supplies on hand, $1,000.
c. Depreciation for the year, $9,000.
d. Accrued salary expense, $1,000.
e. Accrued service revenue, $2,000.

Required

1. Enter the trial balance on a work sheet, and complete the work sheet. Key each adjusting entry by the letter corresponding to the data given. List all the accounts, including those with zero balances. Leave a blank line under Service Revenue.
2. Prepare the income statement, the statement of owner's equity, and the classified balance sheet in account format.
3. Did Lake Air Studio have a good or a bad year during 20X6? Give the reason for your answer.

Account	Debit	Credit
Cash	Bal. 15,000	
Accounts Receivable	Bal. 36,000	
Supplies	Bal. 9,000	
Equipment	Bal. 99,000	
Accumulated Depreciation		Bal. 13,000
Accounts Payable		Bal. 6,000
Salary Payable		
Unearned Service Revenue		Bal. 5,000
Note Payable, Long-Term		Bal. 60,000
Betsy Willis, Capital		Bal. 36,000
Betsy Willis, Withdrawals	Bal. 62,000	
Service Revenue		Bal. 182,000
Salary Expense	Bal. 53,000	
Supplies Expense		
Depreciation Expense		
Interest Expense	Bal. 6,000	
Rent Expense	Bal. 15,000	
Insurance Expense	Bal. 7,000	

P4-3B The *unadjusted* trial balance of Oriental Rug Repair at June 30, 20X9 follows on the next page.

Journalizing adjusting and closing entries **(Obj. 2, 3)**

Student ResourceCD
GL, PT, QB

Adjusting data at June 30, 20X9:

a. Prepaid insurance expired, $2,200.
b. Accrued interest expense, $500.
c. Accrued service revenue, $900.
d. Accrued wage expense, $700.
e. Depreciation for the year: equipment, $7,300; building, $3,900.
f. Additional supplies used, $200.

Required

1. Journalize Oriental Rug Repair's adjusting entries.
2. Journalize the closing entries.

Oriental Rug Repair

Trial Balance
June 30, 20X9

Cash	$ 12,300	
Accounts receivable	26,400	
Supplies	31,200	
Prepaid insurance	3,200	
Equipment	135,800	
Accumulated depreciation—equipment		$ 16,400
Building	34,900	
Accumulated depreciation—building		16,800
Land	30,000	
Accounts payable		39,100
Interest payable		1,400
Wages payable		
Note payable, long-term		97,000
Linda Gallo, capital		49,400
Linda Gallo, withdrawals	45,300	
Service revenue		139,800
Depreciation expense—equipment		
Depreciation expense—building		
Wage expense	21,400	
Insurance expense	3,100	
Interest expense	8,500	
Utilities expense	4,300	
Supplies expense	3,500	
Total	$359,900	$359,900

Preparing an income statement
(Obj. 3)

P4-4B Refer to the data for Oriental Rug Repair in Problem 4-3B. After journalizing Oriental's adjusting and closing entries, prepare the company's income statement for the year ended June 30, 20X9. List expenses in descending order—that is, largest first, second-largest next, and so on.

Completing the accounting cycle
(Obj. 2, 3, 4)

Student Resource CD
GL, PT, QB

P4-5B The trial balance of Revere Silver Plating at August 31, 20X9, and the data for the month-end adjustments follow:

Revere Silver Plating

Trial Balance
August 31, 20X9

Account Number	Account Title	Debit	Credit
11	Cash	$ 3,800	
12	Accounts receivable	15,560	
13	Prepaid rent	1,290	
14	Supplies	20,900	
15	Equipment	15,350	
16	Accumulated depreciation—equipment		$ 12,800
17	Building	89,900	
18	Accumulated depreciation—building		28,600
21	Accounts payable		4,240
22	Salary payable		
23	Unearned service revenue		8,900
31	Paul Revere, capital		71,920
32	Paul Revere, withdrawals	4,800	
41	Service revenue		27,300
51	Salary expense	2,160	
52	Rent expense		
54	Depreciation expense—equipment		
55	Depreciation expense—building		
57	Supplies expense		
	Total	$153,760	$153,760

Adjustment data:

a. Unearned commission revenue still unearned at August 31, $6,500.
b. Prepaid rent still in force at August 31, $1,050.
c. Supplies used during the month, $5,340.
d. Depreciation on equipment for the month, $370.
e. Depreciation on building for the month, $130.
f. Accrued salary expense at August 31, $460.

Required

1. Open the accounts listed in the trial balance and insert their August 31 unadjusted balances. Also open the Income Summary account, number 33. Use four-column accounts. Date the balances of the following accounts as of August 1: Prepaid Rent, Supplies, Equipment, Accumulated Depreciation—Equipment, Building, Accumulated Depreciation—Building, Unearned Service Revenue, and Paul Revere, Capital.
2. Enter the trial balance on a work sheet and complete the work sheet of Revere Silver Plating for the month ended August 31, 20X9.
3. Prepare the income statement, the statement of owner's equity, and the classified balance sheet in report form.
4. Using the work sheet data that you prepare, journalize and post the adjusting and closing entries. Use dates and posting references. Use 7 as the journal page number.
5. Prepare a postclosing trial balance.

P4-6B Selected accounts of Noteworthy Communications at December 31, 20X6, follow:

Preparing a classified balance sheet in report form
(Obj. 4, 5)

Accounts payable	$ 15,100	Lori Stone, capital	$67,100
Accounts receivable	6,600	Note payable, long-term	27,800
Accumulated depreciation—		Other assets	3,600
equipment	37,800	Other current liabilities	4,700
Accumulated depreciation—		Prepaid insurance	1,100
computers	11,600	Prepaid rent	6,600
Equipment	114,400	Salary expense	24,600
Cash	16,500	Salary payable	3,900
Service revenue	93,500	Supplies	2,500
Computers	22,700	Unearned service revenue	5,400
Interest payable	600		

Required

1. Prepare Noteworthy's classified balance sheet in report form at December 31, 20X6. Show totals for total assets, total liabilities, and total liabilities and owner's equity.
2. Compute Noteworthy's current ratio and debt ratio at December 31, 20X6. At December 31, 20X5, the current ratio was 1.52 and the debt ratio was 0.39. Did the company's ability to pay debts improve or deteriorate during 20X6?

P4-7B ← *Link Back to Chapter 2 (Accounting Errors).* The accountant for River Square Retail Center encountered the following situations while adjusting and closing the books at December 31. Consider each situation independently.

Analyzing errors and journalizing adjusting entries
(Obj. 2)

a. The accountant failed to make the following adjusting entries at December 31:
   1. Accrued property tax expense, $200.
   2. Supplies expense, $1,090.
   3. Accrued interest revenue on a note receivable, $1,650.
   4. Depreciation of equipment, $400.
   5. Earned rent revenue that had been collected in advance, $1,100.

   Compute the overall net income effect of these omissions.
b. Record each adjusting entry identified in item a.
c. A $500 credit to Accounts Receivable was posted as a debit.
   1. At what stage of the accounting cycle will this error be detected?
   2. Describe the technique for identifying the amount of the error.

d. The $16,000 balance of Equipment was entered as $1,600 on the trial balance.
   1. What is the name of this type of error?
   2. Assume that this is the only error in the trial balance. Which will be greater, the total debits or the total credits, and by how much?
   3. How can this type of error be identified?

APPLY Your Knowledge

Decision Cases

Completing the accounting cycle to develop the information for a bank loan **(Obj. 3, 4)**

Case 1. One year ago, Donna Heinz founded United Rentals, and the business has prospered. Heinz comes to you for advice. She wishes to know how much net income the business earned during the past year. She also wants to know what her total capital is. The accounting records consist of the T-accounts in the ledger, which were prepared by an accountant who has moved. The accounts at December 31 are shown below.

Heinz indicates that, at year-end, customers owe her $1,600 accrued rent revenue, which she expects to collect early next year. These revenues have not been recorded. During the year, she collected $4,130 rent revenue in advance from customers, but the business has earned only $2,500 of that amount. Advertising expense for the year was $2,400, and she used up $2,100 of the supplies. Heinz estimates that depreciation on equipment was $5,900 for the year. At December 31, she owes her employee $1,200 accrued salary.

Heinz expresses concern that her withdrawals during the year might have exceeded the business's net income. To get a loan to expand the business, Heinz must show the bank that her capital account has grown from its original $40,000 balance. Has it? You and Heinz agree that you will meet again in one week.

Required

Prepare the financial statement that is needed to answer Heinz's question. Can Heinz expect to get the loan? Give your reason.

Account	Debit	Credit
Cash	Dec. 31 5,850	
Accounts Receivable	Dec. 31 12,360	
Prepaid Rent	Jan. 2 2,800	
Supplies	Jan. 2 2,600	
Equipment	Jan. 2 42,000	
Accumulated Depreciation		
Accounts Payable		Dec. 31 18,540
Salary Payable		
Unearned Rent Revenue		Dec. 31 4,130
Donna Heinz, Capital		Jan. 2 40,000
Donna Heinz, Withdrawals	Dec. 31 60,000	
Rent Revenue		Dec. 31 80,740
Salary Expense	Dec. 31 17,000	
Depreciation Expense		
Advertising Expense		
Utilities Expense	Dec. 31 800	
Supplies Expense		

Finding an error in the work sheet **(Obj. 1)**

Case 2. You are preparing the financial statements for the year ended October 31, 20X5, for Zadell Software Company.

- You began with the trial balance of the ledger, which balanced, and then made the required adjusting entries.
- To save time, you omitted preparing an adjusted trial balance.
- After making the adjustments on the work sheet, you extended the balances from the trial balance, adjusted for the adjusting entries, and computed amounts for the income statement and the balance sheet columns.

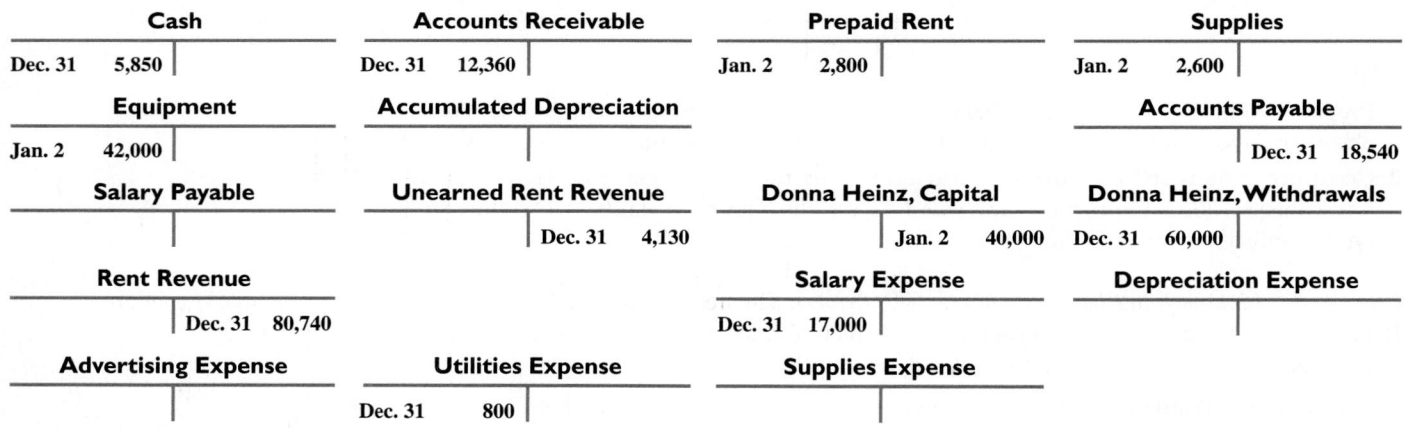

Required

a. When you added the total debits and the total credits on the income statement, you found that the credits exceeded the debits by $45,000. Did the business have a profit or a loss?

b. You took the balancing amount from the income statement columns to the debit column of the balance sheet and found that the total debits exceeded the total credits in the balance sheet. The difference between the total debits and the total credits on the balance sheet is $90,000. What is the cause of this difference? (Except for these errors, everything else is correct.)

Ethical Issue

← *Link Back to Chapter 3 (Revenue Principle).* Lords & Ladies Boutique wishes to expand and has borrowed $250,000. As a condition for making this loan, the bank requires that the store maintain a current ratio of at least 1.50.

Business has been good but not great. Expansion costs have brought the current ratio down to 1.40 at December 15. Josh Hemingway, owner of the boutique, is considering what might happen if the business reports a current ratio of 1.40 to the bank. One course of action for Hemingway is to record in December some revenue that the business will earn in January of next year. The contract for this job has been signed.

Required

1. Journalize the revenue transaction, and indicate how recording this revenue in December would affect the current ratio.

2. State whether it is ethical to record the revenue transaction in December. Identify the accounting principle relevant to this situation.

3. Propose a course of action that is ethical for Hemingway.

Financial Statement Case

Using a balance sheet **(Obj. 4, 5)**

This case, based on the balance sheet of **Amazon.com** in Appendix A, will familiarize you with some of the assets and liabilities of that company. Use the Amazon balance sheet to answer the following questions.

Required

1. Which balance sheet format does Amazon.com use?

2. Name the company's largest current asset and largest current liability at December 31, 2002.

3. Compute Amazon's current ratios at December 31, 2002 and 2001. Did the current ratio improve, worsen, or hold steady during 2002?

4. Under what category does Amazon report furniture, fixtures, and equipment?

5. What was the cost of the company's fixed assets at December 31, 2002? What was the amount of accumulated depreciation? What was the book value of the fixed assets? See Note 3 for the data.

Team Project

Aaron Grant formed a lawn service business as a summer job. To start the business on May 1, he deposited $1,000 in a new bank account in the name of the proprietorship. The $1,000 consisted of a $600 loan from his father and $400 of his own money. Aaron rented lawn equipment, purchased supplies, and hired other students to mow and trim customers' lawns.

At the end of each month, Aaron mailed bills to his customers. On August 31, he was ready to dissolve the business and return to Blue Mountain Community College. Because he was so busy, he kept few records other than his checkbook and a list of receivables from customers.

At August 31, Aaron's checkbook shows a balance of $2,000, and his customers still owe him $500. During the summer, he collected $5,500 from customers. His checkbook lists payments for supplies totaling $400, and he still has gasoline, weedeater cord, and other supplies that cost a total of $50. He paid his employees $1,800, and he still owes them $300 for the final week of the summer.

Aaron rented some equipment from Ludwig's Machine Shop. On May 1, he signed a six-month lease on mowers and paid $600 for the full lease period. Ludwig's will refund the unused portion of the prepayment if the equipment is in good shape. In order to get the refund, Aaron has kept the mowers in excellent condition. In fact, he had to pay $300 to repair a mower.

To transport employees and equipment to jobs, Aaron used a trailer that he bought for $300. He figures that the summer's work used up one-third of the trailer's service potential. The business checkbook lists a payment of $500 for cash withdrawals by Aaron during the summer. Aaron paid his father back during August.

Required

1. Prepare the income statement of Grant Lawn Service for the four months May through August.
2. Prepare the classified balance sheet of Grant Lawn Service at August 31.
3. Was Grant's summer work successful? Give the reason for your answer.

For Internet Exercises, go to the Web site www.prenhall.com/horngren.

APPENDIX *to Chapter 4*

Reversing Entries: An Optional Step

Reversing entries are special journal entries that ease the burden of accounting for transactions in a later period. Reversing entries are the exact opposites of certain adjusting entries at the end of the prior period. Reversing entries are used most often in conjunction with accrual-type adjustments, such as accrued salary expense and accrued service revenue. *Generally accepted accounting principles do not require reversing entries. They are used only for convenience and to save time.*

Accounting for Accrued Expenses

To see how reversing entries work, return to Gay Gillen's unadjusted trial balance at April 30 (Exhibit 4-2, page 144). Salary Expense has a debit balance of $950 for salaries paid during April. At April 30, the business still owes its employee an additional $950 for the last half of the month, so Gillen makes this adjusting entry:

	Adjusting Entries		
Apr. 30	Salary Expense	950	
	Salary Payable		950

After posting, the accounts are updated at April 30.[1]

Salary Payable

Debit		Credit	
		Apr. 30 Adj.	950
		Apr. 30 Bal.	950

Salary Expense

Debit		Credit	
Paid during April, CP	950		
Apr. 30 Adj.	950		
Apr. 30 Bal.	1,900		

After the adjusting entry,

- The April income statement reports salary expense of $1,900.
- The April 30 balance sheet reports salary payable of $950.

The $1,900 debit balance of Salary Expense is closed at April 30, 20X5, with this closing entry:

Closing Entries

Apr. 30	Income Summary	1,900	
	Salary Expense		1,900

After posting, Salary Expense has a zero balance as follows:

Salary Expense

Debit		Credit	
Paid during April, CP	950		
Apr. 30 Adj.	950		
Apr. 30 Bal.	1,900	Apr. 30 Clo.	1,900

Zero balance

Assume for this illustration that on May 5, the next payday, Gillen will pay the $950 of accrued salary left over from April 30 plus $100 of salary for the first few days of May. Gillen's next payroll payment will be $1,050 ($950 + $100).

Accounting Without a Reversing Entry

On May 5, the next payday, Gillen pays the payroll of $1,050 and makes this journal entry:

May 5	Salary Payable	950	
	Salary Expense	100	
	Cash		1,050

This method of recording the cash payment is correct. However, it wastes time because Gillen must refer back to the April 30 adjustments. Otherwise, she does not know the amount of the debit to Salary Payable (in this example, $950). Searching April's adjusting entries wastes time and money. To save time, accountants use reversing entries.

[1]Entry explanations used throughout this discussion are

Adj. = entry	CP = Cash payment entry—a credit to Cash
Bal. = Balance	CR = Cash receipt entry—a debit to Cash
Clo. = Closing entry	Rev. = Reversing entry

Making a Reversing Entry

Reversing Entry
An entry that switches the debit and the credit of a previous adjusting entry. The reversing entry is dated the first day of the new period.

A **reversing entry** switches the debit and the credit of a previous adjusting entry. *A reversing entry, then, is the exact opposite of a prior adjusting entry*. The reversing entry is dated the first day of the new period.

To illustrate reversing entries, recall that on April 30, Gillen made the following adjusting entry to accrue Salary Payable:

Adjusting Entries			
Apr. 30	Salary Expense	950	
	Salary Payable..............		950

The reversing entry simply reverses the debit and the credit of the adjustment:

Reversing Entries			
May 1	Salary Payable..................	950	
	Salary Expense		950

Observe that the reversing entry is dated the first day of the new period. It is the exact opposite of the April 30 adjusting entry. Ordinarily, the accountant who makes the adjusting entry also prepares the reversing entry at the same time. Gillen dates the reversing entry as of May 1 so that it affects only the new period. Note how the accounts appear after Gillen posts the reversing entry:

Salary Payable

May 1	Rev.	950	Apr. 30		Bal. 950
		Zero balance			

Salary Expense

Apr. 30		Bal. 1,900	Apr. 30		Clo. 1,900
		Zero balance			
			May 1	Rev.	950

The arrow shows the transfer of the $950 credit balance from Salary Payable to Salary Expense. This credit balance in Salary Expense does not mean that the entity has negative salary expense, as you might think. Instead, the odd credit balance in the Salary Expense account is merely a temporary result of the reversing entry. The credit balance is eliminated on May 5, when Gillen pays the payroll and debits Salary Expense in the customary manner:

May 5	Salary Expense	1,050	
	Cash		1,050

Then this cash payment entry is posted as follows:

Salary Expense

May 5	CP	1,050	May 1	Rev.	950
May 5	Bal.	100			

Now Salary Expense has its correct debit balance of $100, which is the amount of salary expense incurred thus far in May. The $1,050 cash disbursement also pays the liability for Salary Payable so that Salary Payable has a zero balance, which is correct.

Appendix Assignment

Problem

P4A-1 Refer to the data in Problem 4-5A, pages 170–171.

Using reversing entries

Required

1. Open accounts for Salary Payable and Salary Expense. Insert their unadjusted balances at October 31, 20X6.

2. Journalize adjusting entry (e) and the closing entry for Salary Expense at October 31. Post to the accounts.
3. On November 5, Lange Party Productions paid the next payroll amount of $500. This payment included the accrued amount at October 31, plus $190 for the first few days of November. Journalize this cash payment, and post to the accounts. Show the balance in each account.
4. Using a reversing entry, repeat requirements 1 through 3. Compare the balances of Salary Payable and Salary Expense computed using a reversing entry with those balances computed without the reversing entry (as they appear in your answer to requirement 3).

CHAPTER 5

Merchandising Operations

A+ TIPS CHECK YOUR RESOURCES

- Visit the www.prenhall.com/horngren **Web site** for self-study quizzes, video clips, and other resources
- Try the **Quick Check** exercise at end of chapter to test your knowledge
- Learn the **Key terms**
- Do the **Starter** exercises keyed in the margins
- Work the **Mid-** and **End-of-Chapter Summary Problems**
- Use the **Concept Links** in the text margins to review material in other chapters
- **Search the CD** for review materials by chapter or by key word

LEARNING OBJECTIVES

1. Account for the purchase of inventory
2. Account for the sale of inventory
3. Use sales and gross profit to evaluate a company
4. Adjust and close the accounts of a merchandising business
5. Prepare a merchandiser's financial statements
6. Use gross profit percentage and inventory turnover to evaluate a business

Amazon.com

What comes to mind when you hear Amazon.com? All around the world, millions of customers like you place orders using Amazon's online system. Thanks to global shippers like Fedex and UPS, customers in England, Japan, and Australia can expect the same fast delivery of DVDs and music that you enjoy.

Now you can go online with Amazon and buy clothing from Target, electronic games from Circuit City, and playthings from Toys "Я" Us. Amazon offers an incredible selection of products. For example, you can visit a big-box store such as Circuit City and find about 7,000 products; Amazon offers 45,000. How do Amazon and Circuit City manage all these goods? This chapter shows how companies keep track of their merchandise inventory. ■

Sitemap

- Merchandising Operations
- Accounting for Inventory: Perpetual System
- Adjusting and Closing Accounts
- Preparing Financial Statements
- Key Decision-Making Ratios

Inventory
All the goods that the company owns and expects to sell in the normal course of operations.

We shift gears in Chapter 5. The first four chapters focused on service companies such as Gay Gillen eTravel, the San Francisco Giants, and eBay. Here we begin working with merchandisers such as Amazon.com, Target, and Circuit City. A merchandiser differs from a service business in two important ways. A merchandiser sells *products*, whereas a service company provides a *service*. A merchandiser has an asset called *merchandise inventory*, such as DVDs, videos, and clothing. A service company carries no inventory.

Inventory includes all the goods a company owns and holds for sale in the normal course of operations. Throughout the remainder of the book we refer to merchandise inventory simply as inventory. It is a merchandiser's most important asset. This chapter demonstrates the central role of inventory in a business that sells merchandise. We illustrate accounting for the purchase and sale of inventory, and we also illustrate how to adjust and close the books of a merchandiser. The chapter also covers two ratios investors and creditors use to evaluate companies.

Before launching into merchandising, let's compare service entities, with which you are familiar, to merchandising companies. Exhibit 5-1 shows how the financial statements of a service entity (on the left) differs from a merchandiser (on the right).

Exhibit 5-1

Financial Statements of a Service Company and a Merchandiser

Service Co. * — Balance Sheet, June 30, 20XX		Merchandising Co. ** — Balance Sheet, June 30, 20XX	
Assets		**Assets**	
Current assets:		Current assets:	
Cash	$X	Cash	$X
Short-term investments	X	Short-term investments	X
Accounts receivable, net	X	Accounts receivable, net	X
Prepaid expenses	X	*Inventory*	*X*
		Prepaid expenses	X

*Such as Gay Gillen e-Travel

**Such as Amazon.com

Service Co. — Income Statement, Year Ended June 30, 20XX		Merchandising Co. — Income Statement, Year Ended June 30, 20XX	
Service revenue	$XXX →	*Sales revenue*	*$X,XXX*
Expenses: →		*Cost of goods sold*	*X*
Salary expense	X	*Gross profit*	*XXX*
Depreciation expense	X	Operating expenses:	
Income tax expense	X	Salary expense	X
Net income	$ X	Depreciation expense	X
		Income tax expense	X
		Net income	$ X

What Are Merchandising Operations?

Merchandising is the business activity of buying and selling products rather than services. Accounting for merchandising operations requires us to deal with these balance sheet and income statement items.

Balance Sheet:
- Inventory, an asset

Income Statement:
- Sales revenue (often abbreviated as Sales), a revenue
- Cost of goods sold, an expense

These items are italicized in Exhibit 5-1 for Merchandising Co. Let's begin with the operating cycle of a merchandising business.

Student Resource CD
periodic system, perpetual system

The Operating Cycle of a Merchandising Business

The operating cycle of a business is different from the accounting cycle. The operating cycle begins when a merchandiser buys inventory. The company then sells the goods to customers and collects cash. Exhibit 5-2 diagrams the operating cycle for *sales on account*.

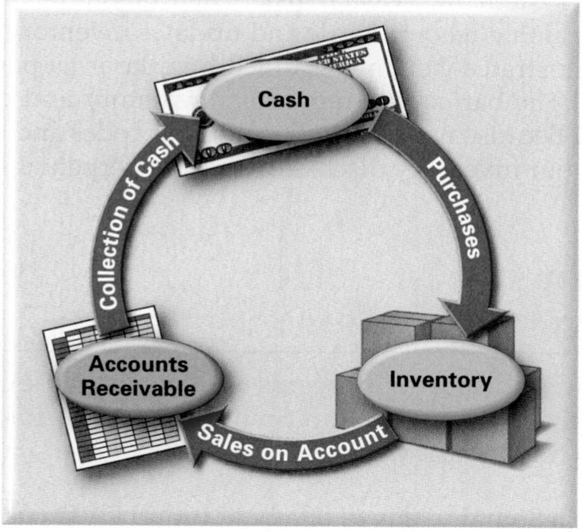

Exhibit 5-2
Operating Cycle of a Merchandiser

Now let's see how companies account for their inventory. The accounting cycle begins with journal entries, posts journal entries to the ledger accounts, and ends with the financial statements.

Inventory Systems: Perpetual and Periodic

There are two main types of inventory accounting systems:

- Periodic system
- Perpetual system

The **periodic inventory system** is used for relatively inexpensive goods. A convenience store without optical-scanning cash registers does not keep a daily running record of every loaf of bread and every key chain that it sells. Instead, the business counts its inventory at some regular interval to determine the quantities on hand. Restaurants and small retail stores also use the periodic system. Chapter 6 covers this system, which is becoming less and less popular as more businesses keep their inventory records by computer.

Periodic Inventory System
A system in which the business does not keep a continuous record of inventory on hand. At the end of the period, it makes a physical count of on-hand inventory and uses this information to prepare the financial statements.

Perpetual Inventory System
The accounting inventory system in which the business keeps a running record of inventory and cost of goods sold.

The **perpetual inventory system** keeps a running record of inventory and cost of goods sold. This system achieves control over the inventory. Even in a perpetual system, the business counts inventory at least once a year. The physical count establishes the correct amount of ending inventory for the financial statements and also serves as a check on the perpetual records.

The following chart compares the perpetual and periodic systems:

Perpetual Inventory System	Periodic Inventory System
■ Keeps a running record of all goods bought and sold.	■ Does *not* keep a running record of all goods bought and sold.
■ Inventory counted at least once a year.	■ Inventory counted at least once a year.

Integrated Inventory Systems

Bar code

An integrated inventory system records units purchased, units sold, and the quantities of goods on hand. Inventory systems are integrated with accounts receivable and sales. For example, Amazon.com's computers keep up-to-the-minute records, so managers can call up current inventory information at any time.

In a perpetual system, the "cash register" at a Target or a Circuit City store is a computer terminal that records a sale and updates inventory records. Bar codes such as the one illustrated here are scanned by a laser as part of the perpetual inventory system. The bar coding represents inventory and cost data that keep track of each item. Because most businesses use bar codes and computerized cash registers, we base our inventory discussions on the perpetual system.

Student Resource CD
cost of goods sold, gross profit, purchase of inventory, sale of inventory, sales revenue

Invoice
A seller's request for cash from the purchaser.

Accounting for Inventory in the Perpetual System

The cycle of a merchandising entity begins with the purchase of inventory. In this section, we trace the steps that Austin Sound Center, in Austin, Texas, takes to purchase and pay for inventory.

1. Suppose Austin Sound wants to offer JVC brand DVD players. Austin Sound orders DVD players from JVC.
2. JVC ships the goods and sends the invoice in Exhibit 5-3 to Austin Sound the same day. The **invoice** is the seller's request for a cash payment by the buyer. An invoice is also called a *bill*. To Austin Sound, the document is a purchase invoice.
3. After the inventory is received, Austin Sound pays JVC the invoice amount.

1 *Account for the purchase of inventory*

Purchase of Inventory

Here we use the actual invoice in Exhibit 5-3 — a $700 purchase of inventory—to illustrate the purchasing process. Suppose Austin Sound receives the goods on May 30. Austin Sound records this purchase on account as follows:

May 30	Inventory	700	
	Accounts Payable		700
	Purchased inventory on account.		

Exhibit 5-3 An Actual Invoice (Adapted)

1

JVC®

JVC SOUTHWEST BRANCH
P.O. BOX 100876
HOUSTON, TX 77212

Invoice	
Date	Number
5/27/05	410

3

Shipped To: AUSTIN SOUND CENTER
305 WEST MLK BLVD.
AUSTIN, TX 78701

2

Terms of Sale
3% 15, NET 30 DAYS

4

5

Quantity Ordered	Description	Model No.	Quantity Shipped	Unit Price	Total
7	DVD PLAYER	QLA200	7	$100.00	$700.00
				7 Pd.	06-10-05

Due Date & Due Amount	
06/11/05	06/26/05
$679 00	$700 00

8

Sub Total	$700.00
Ship. or Handl. Chg.	–
Tax (3%)	–
Total(s)	$700.00

6

Explanations:

1. The seller is JVC.
2. The purchaser is Austin Sound Center.
3. The invoice date, needed for determining whether the purchaser gets a discount for prompt payment (see 4).
4. Credit terms of the transaction: If it pays within 15 days of the invoice date, Austin Sound may deduct a 3% discount. Otherwise, the full amount—net—is due in 30 days. (The discussion of discounts starts on page 187.)
5. JVC shipped 7 DVD players to Austin Sound.
6. Total invoice amount is $700.
7. Austin Sound's payment date. How much did Austin pay? (See 8, which follows.)
8. Payment occurred 14 days after the invoice date—within the discount period—so Austin paid $679 ($700 – 3% discount).

The purchase of inventory on account increases Austin Sound's assets (Inventory) and liabilities (Accounts Payable), as shown by the accounting equation:

Assets	=	**Liabilities**	+	**Owner's Equity**
Inventory		**Accounts Payable**		
$700	=	$700	+	$0

The Inventory account is used only for goods purchased for resale. Supplies, equipment, and other assets are recorded in their own accounts. Inventory is an asset until sold.

Purchase Discounts Many businesses offer customers a purchase discount for early payment. JVC's credit terms of 3% 15, NET 30 DAYS mean that Austin Sound may deduct 3% of the total debt if Austin pays within 15 days of the invoice date. Otherwise, the full amount—NET—is due in 30 days. These credit terms can also be expressed as 3/15 n/30.

Terms of n/30 mean that no discount is offered and payment is due 30 days after the invoice date. Terms of *eom* mean that payment is due at the end of the current month.

Austin Sound paid within the discount period, so its cash payment entry is

June 10	Accounts Payable	700	
	Cash ($700 × 0.97)		679
	Inventory ($700 × 0.03)		21
	Paid within discount period.		

✔ Starter 5-1

Note that the discount is credited to the Inventory account. Why? Because the discount decreases Austin Sound's cost of goods, as shown in the Inventory account:

Inventory

May 30	700	June 10	21
Bal.	679		

But if Austin Sound pays this invoice after the discount period, Austin Sound must pay the full amount of $700. In that case, the payment entry is

June 24	Accounts Payable	700	
	Cash		700
	Paid after discount period.		

Inventory

May 30	700		

PURCHASE RETURNS AND ALLOWANCES Businesses allow customers to *return* merchandise that is defective, damaged, or otherwise unsuitable. Or the seller may deduct an *allowance* from the amount the buyer owes. Both purchase returns and purchase allowances decrease the buyer's cost of the inventory.

Suppose one DVD player purchased by Austin Sound (Exhibit 5-3) was damaged in shipment. Austin returns the merchandise to the seller and records the purchase return as follows:

June 3	Accounts Payable	100	
	Inventory		100
	Returned inventory to seller.		

A purchase return decreases Austin Sound's assets and its liabilities, as shown by the accounting equation:

✔ Starter 5-2
✔ Starter 5-3
✔ Starter 5-4

ASSETS	=	LIABILITIES	+	OWNER'S EQUITY
Inventory		Accounts Payable		
−$100	=	−$100	+	$0

Stop & Think

On September 15, Austin Sound purchases $1,000 of merchandise on account, with terms 2/10, n/30. Austin returns $100 of merchandise for credit on September 20, then makes payment in full on September 25. Journalize these transactions.

Answer: Three separate journal entries are needed. The purchase entry is

1. **Purchase:**	Sep. 15	Inventory	1,000	
		Accounts Payable		1,000

The second entry records the return of inventory, as follows:

2. **Return:**	Sep. 20	Accounts Payable	100	
		Inventory		100

Accounts Payable

Return	100	Purchase	1,000
		Bal.	900

The third entry records the payment of $882, as follows: Purchase amount, $1,000, minus the $100 return equals the net payable of $900. Now subtract the 2% discount ($900 × 0.02 = $18) to arrive at the final payment of $882.

3. **Payment:**	Sep. 25	Accounts Payable	900	
		Cash		882
		Inventory		18

TRANSPORTATION COSTS The transportation cost of moving inventory from seller to buyer can be significant. The purchase agreement specifies FOB terms to indicate who pays the shipping charges. *FOB* means *free on board*. FOB terms govern (1) when legal title to the goods passes from seller to buyer and (2) who pays the freight. Exhibit 5-4 summarizes FOB terms.

Exhibit 5-4 **FOB Terms Determine Who Pays Freight**

Freight costs are either *Freight in* or *Freight out*.

- Freight in is the transportation cost on *purchased goods*.
- Freight out is the transportation cost on *goods sold*.

Freight In FOB shipping point terms are most common, so the buyer pays the freight. Freight in becomes part of the cost of inventory. The buyer debits Inventory and credits Cash or Accounts Payable for the freight. Suppose Austin Sound pays a $60 shipping bill. Austin Sound's entry to record payment of the freight charge is

June 1	Inventory	60	
	Cash		60
	Paid a freight bill.		

The freight charge increases the cost of the inventory to $660, as follows:

Inventory

May 30	**Purchase**	**700**	**June 3**	**Return**	**100**
June 1	Freight in	60			
Bal.	Net cost	660			

Discounts are computed only on the account payable to the seller ($600), not on the transportation costs, because there is no discount on freight.

Under FOB shipping point terms, the seller sometimes prepays the transportation cost as a convenience and lists this cost on the invoice. A $5,000 purchase of goods, coupled with a related freight charge of $400, would be recorded as follows:

Mar. 12	Inventory ($5,000 + $400).	5,400	
	Accounts Payable		5,400
	Purchased inventory on account, including freight.		

If the buyer pays within the discount period, the discount will be computed on the $5,000 merchandise cost, not on the $5,400. For example, a 2% discount would be $100 ($5,000 × 0.02).

Freight Out Freight charges paid to ship goods sold to customers are called *freight out*. Freight out is delivery expense to the seller. Delivery expense is an operating expense. It is debited to the Delivery Expense account.

Stop & Think

This Stop & Think example is exactly like the preceding one, but with freight in. On September 15, Austin Sound purchased $1,000 of merchandise, with *$80 freight added*, for an invoice total of $1,080. Austin returns $100 of the goods for credit on September 20 and pays the account payable in full on September 25. Journalize these transactions.

Answer

Purchase:	Sept. 15	Inventory ($1,000 + $80)	1,080	
		Accounts Payable.		1,080
Return:	Sept. 20	Accounts Payable.	100	
		Inventory.		100
Payment:	Sept. 25	Accounts Payable ($1,080 − $100).	980	
		Inventory [($1,000 − $100) × 0.02].		18
		Cash ($1,000 + $80 − $100 − $18)		962

There is no discount on freight.

Accounting for Purchase Returns and Allowances, Discounts, and Transportation Costs Suppose Austin Sound buys $35,000 of audio/video inventory, takes a discount, and returns some of the goods. Austin Sound also pays some freight in. The following summary shows Austin Sound's total cost of this inventory. All amounts are assumed for this illustration.

Inventory

Debit		Credit	
Price paid for inventory	35,000	Purchase ret. & allow.	700
Freight in	2,100	Purchase discount	800
Balance	35,600		

DEBIT - BALANCE ACCOUNT		CREDITS TO INVENTORY				DEBIT TO INVENTORY		TOTAL COST OF THE INVENTORY
Inventory	−	Purchase Returns and Allowances	−	Purchase Discounts	+	Freight in	=	Inventory
$35,000	−	$700	−	$800	+	$2,100	=	$35,600

2 *Account for the sale of inventory*

Sales Revenue
The amount that a merchandiser earns from selling its inventory. Also called **sales.**

Cost of Goods Sold
The cost of the inventory that the business has sold to customers. Also called **cost of sales**.

Sale of Inventory

After a company buys inventory, the next step is to sell the goods. We shift now to the selling side and follow Austin Sound Center through a sequence of selling transactions. The amount a business earns from selling merchandise inventory is called **sales revenue** (often abbreviated as **sales**). A sale also creates an expense, Cost of Goods Sold, as the seller gives up the asset Inventory. **Cost of goods sold** is the entity's cost of its inventory that has been sold to customers. Cost of goods sold (often abbreviated as **cost of sales**) is the merchandiser's major expense.

After making a sale on account, Austin Sound may experience any of the following:

- ***A sales return:*** The customer may return goods to Austin Sound.
- ***A sales allowance:*** Austin Sound may grant a sales allowance to reduce the cash to be collected from the customer.
- ***A sales discount:*** If the customer pays within the discount period—under terms such as 2/10 n/30—Austin Sound collects the discounted amount.
- ***Freight out:*** Austin Sound may have to pay delivery expense to transport the goods to the buyer.

Let's begin with a cash sale.

CASH SALE Sales of retailers, such as Austin Sound, grocery stores, and restaurants, are often for cash. Cash sales of $3,000 are recorded by debiting Cash and crediting Sales Revenue as follows:

June 9	Cash	3,000	
	Sales Revenue		3,000
	Cash sale.		

Because Austin Sound sold goods, the business also must decrease the Inventory balance. Suppose these goods cost the seller $1,900. A second journal entry is needed to transfer the $1,900 cost of the goods from the Inventory account to Cost of Goods Sold, as follows: →

← *The recording of cost of goods sold along with sales revenue is an example of the matching principle (Chapter 3, p. 95)*

June 9	Cost of Goods Sold	1,900	
	Inventory		1,900
	Recorded the cost of goods sold.		

The Cost of Goods Sold account keeps a current balance throughout the period. In this example, cost of goods sold is not $3,000, because that's the selling price of the goods. Cost of goods sold is always based on the entity's cost, not the selling price.

After posting, the Cost of Goods Sold account holds the cost of the merchandise sold ($1,900 in this case):

Inventory			Cost of Goods Sold	
Purchases 50,000 (amount assumed)	Cost of sales 1,900	←→	June 9 1,900	

The computer automatically records the cost of goods sold entry. The cashier keys in the code number of the inventory that is sold, and optical scanners perform this task.

SALE ON ACCOUNT Most sales in the United States are made on account (on credit). A $5,000 sale on account is recorded as follows:

June 11	Accounts Receivable	5,000	
	Sales Revenue		5,000
	Sale on account.		

These goods cost the seller $2,900, so the related cost of goods sold entry is

June 11	Cost of Goods Sold	2,900	
	Inventory		2,900
	Recorded the cost of goods sold.		

When the cash comes in, the seller records the cash receipt on account as follows:

June 19	Cash	5,000	
	Accounts Receivable		5,000
	Collection on account.		

Stop & Think

How does the January 19 collection of cash affect revenue?

Answer: It doesn't affect revenue at all. The business recorded the revenue back when it made the sale.

Sales Returns and Allowances
Decreases in the seller's receivable from a customer's return of merchandise or from granting the customer an allowance from the amount owed to the seller. A contra account to Sales Revenue.

Sales Discount
Reduction in the amount receivable from a customer, offered by the seller as an incentive for the customer to pay promptly. A contra account to Sales Revenue.

Net Sales Revenue
Sales revenue less sales discounts and sales returns and allowances.

SALES DISCOUNTS AND SALES RETURNS AND ALLOWANCES We just saw that purchase returns and allowances and purchase discounts decrease the cost of inventory purchases. In the same way, **sales returns and allowances** and **sales discounts**, which are contra accounts to Sales Revenue, decrease the net amount of revenue earned on sales.

CREDIT-BALANCE ACCOUNT		DEBIT-BALANCE ACCOUNTS				CREDIT SUBTOTAL (*NOT* A SEPARATE ACCOUNT)
Sales Revenue	−	Sales Returns and Allowances	−	Sales Discounts	=	Net sales revenue[1]

Companies maintain separate accounts for Sales Discounts and Sales Returns and Allowances. Now let's examine a sequence of JVC sale transactions. Assume JVC is selling to Austin Sound Center.

On July 7, JVC sells stereo components for $7,200 on credit terms of 2/10 n/30. These goods cost JVC $4,700. JVC's entries to record this credit sale and the related cost of goods sold are

July 7	Accounts Receivable	7,200	
	Sales Revenue		7,200
	Sale on account.		
July 7	Cost of Goods Sold	4,700	
	Inventory		4,700
	Recorded cost of goods sold.		

Sales Returns Assume that the buyer returns $600 of the goods. JVC, the seller, records the sales return as follows:

July 12	Sales Returns and Allowances	600	
	Accounts Receivable		600
	Received returned goods.		

Accounts Receivable decreases because JVC will not collect cash for the returned goods. JVC receives the returned merchandise and updates inventory records. JVC must also decrease Cost of Goods Sold as follows (these goods cost JVC $400):

July 12	Inventory	400	
	Cost of Goods Sold		400
	Placed goods back in inventory.		

[1]Often abbreviated as Net sales.

Sales Allowances Suppose JVC grants a $100 sales allowance for damaged goods. A sales allowance is recorded as follows:

July 15	Sales Returns and Allowances	100	
	Accounts Receivable		100
	Granted a sales allowance for damaged goods.		

There is no inventory entry for a sales allowance because the seller receives no returned goods from the customer.

After these entries are posted, Accounts Receivable has a $6,500 debit balance, as follows:

Accounts Receivable

July 7	Sale	7,200	July 12	Return	600
			15	Allowance	100
Bal.		6,500			

Sales Discounts On July 17, the last day of the discount period, JVC collects $4,000 of this receivable. Assume JVC allows customers to take discounts on all amounts JVC receives within the discount period. JVC's cash receipt is $3,920 [$4,000 − ($4,000 × 0.02)], and the collection entry is

July 17	Cash	3,920	
	Sales Discounts ($4,000 × 0.02)	80	
	Accounts Receivable..............		4,000
	Cash collection within the discount period.		

✔ Starter 5-5

Suppose that JVC collects the remaining $2,500 on July 28. That date falls after the discount period, so there is no sales discount. JVC records this collection on account as follows:

July 28	Cash ($6,500 − $4,000)	2,500	
	Accounts Receivable.............		2,500
	Cash collection after the discount period.		

Now, JVC's Accounts Receivable balance is zero:

Accounts Receivable

July 7	Sale	7,200	July 12	Return	600
			15	Allowance	100
			17	Collection	4,000
			28	Collection	2,500
Bal.		–0–			

Evaluating Profitability: Sales Revenue, Cost of Goods Sold, and Gross Profit

3 Use sales and gross profit to evaluate a company

Managers and investors evaluate a business's profitability based on its net sales revenue, cost of goods sold, and gross profit. Net sales revenue minus cost of goods sold is called **gross profit**, or **gross margin**.

Gross Profit
Excess of net sales revenue over cost of goods sold. Also called **gross margin**.

Net sales revenue (abbreviated as Sales)	−	Cost of goods sold (same as Cost of sales)	=	Gross profit (same as Gross margin)

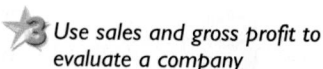

or, more simply,

$$\text{Sales} - \text{Cost of sales} = \text{Gross profit}$$

Gross profit, along with net income, is a measure of business success. A sufficiently high gross profit is vital to a merchandiser. Amazon.com's operations were quite successful during 2001. Amazon's gross profit was almost $800 million.

The following example will clarify the nature of gross profit. Suppose Amazon's cost to purchase a DVD is $15 and Amazon sells the DVD for $20. Amazon's gross profit per unit is $5, computed as follows:

✔ Starter 5-6
✔ Starter 5-7

Sales revenue earned by selling one DVD	$20
Less: Cost of goods sold for the DVD (what the DVD cost Amazon).........................	(15)
Gross profit on the sale of one DVD	$ 5

Accounting.com

Amazon.com: For E-Tailers Free Shipping Isn't Free, But It's Not a Cost, Either

Like most accounting students, Jennifer didn't have time to go Christmas shopping. She cruised the online mall and ended up buying all her presents from Amazon.com, the largest player in online retailing. Jennifer was lured by Amazon.com's huge selection and an offer of free shipping for all orders over $25.

Amazon.com views free shipping as a key factor in boosting its growth—revenue jumped 233% to $851 million in one year. Yet, the company doesn't send packages via eight trusty reindeer. Amazon has to pay freight companies to deliver DVD players, books, and blenders to customers around the world. How does an e-tailer—one that is just barely making a profit—account for these shipping and handling costs?

Fortunately for Amazon and other e-tailers, in the process of revolutionizing business, e-commerce has also bent certain accounting rules. One such rule is that the cost of products sold to customers is usually recorded as Cost of Goods Sold, a merchandiser's major expense. But online powerhouses like Amazon.com and Buy.com count some of this cost as "sales and marketing expenses." By listing these "fulfillment costs" as marketing expenses, both e-tailers and catalog houses such as L. L. Bean don't have to subtract the expense in arriving at gross profit.

Small wonder that this controversial approach came under investigation by the Financial Accounting Standards Board (FASB). The dot-com bubble had burst, and e-tailers were poised to reclassify shipping and handling costs as costs of goods sold. That would restate gross profit downward. However, the Emerging Issues Task Force of the FASB recommended that shipping and handling *revenue* should be included in sales, without giving any guidance about how to account for shipping and handling *costs*. So Amazon and other e-tailers are free to continue including shipping and handling costs under marketing expense. The result: Gross profits are still high.

Based on: Nick Winfield, "Survival Strategy: Amazon Takes Page from Wal-Mart to Prosper on Web—Internet Retailer Cuts Prices and Keeps Eye on Costs in Bid for High Volumes—Betting Big on Free Shipping," *The Wall Street Journal*, November 22, 2002, p. A1. Saul Hansell, "Amazon's Loss in Quarter Shows a Sharp Decrease," *The New York Times*, October 25, 2002, p. 8. Katherine Hobson, "Silver Lining: FASB Spares E-Tailers in Cost Ruling," *The Street.com*, August 8, 2000.

The gross profit reported on Amazon.com's 2001 income statement is the sum of the gross profits on all the DVDs and other products the company sold during the year.

Let's put into practice what you've learned in the first half of this chapter.

MID-CHAPTER *Summary Problem*

A+ TIPS
CHECK YOUR RESOURCES

Suppose Amazon.com engaged in the following transactions during June of the current year:

June 3	Purchased inventory on credit terms of 1/10 net eom (end of month), $1,600.
9	Returned 40% of the inventory purchased on June 3. It was defective.
12	Sold goods for cash, $920 (cost, $550).
15	Purchased goods for $5,000. Credit terms were 3/15 net 30.
16	Paid a $260 freight bill on goods purchased.
18	Sold inventory on credit terms of 2/10 n/30, $2,000 (cost, $1,180).
22	Received returned goods from the customer of the June 18 sale, $800 (cost, $480).
24	Borrowed money from the bank to take advantage of the discount offered on the June 15 purchase. Signed a note payable to the bank for the net amount.
24	Paid supplier for goods purchased on June 15, less the discount.
28	Received cash in full settlement of the account from the customer who purchased inventory on June 18, less the return on June 22.
29	Paid the amount owed on account from the purchase of June 3, less the June 9 return.

Required

1. Journalize the preceding transactions. Explanations are not required.
2. Set up T-accounts and post the journal entries to show the ending balances in the Inventory and the Cost of Goods Sold accounts.
3. Assume that the note payable signed on June 24 requires the payment of $95 interest expense. Was borrowing funds to take the cash discount a wise or unwise decision?

Solution

Requirement 1

June 3	Inventory	1,600	
	Accounts Payable		1,600
9	Accounts Payable ($1,600 × 0.40)	640	
	Inventory		640
12	Cash	920	
	Sales Revenue		920
12	Cost of Goods Sold	550	
	Inventory		550
15	Inventory	5,000	
	Accounts Payable		5,000
16	Inventory	260	
	Cash		260
18	Accounts Receivable	2,000	
	Sales Revenue		2,000
18	Cost of Goods Sold	1,180	
	Inventory		1,180

(*continued*)

June 22	Sales Returns and Allowances	800	
	Accounts Receivable		800
22	Inventory	480	
	Cost of Goods Sold		480
24	Cash [$5,000 – 0.03 ($5,000)]	4,850	
	Note Payable		4,850
24	Accounts Payable	5,000	
	Inventory ($5,000 × 0.03)		150
	Cash ($5,000 × 0.97)		4,850
28	Cash [($2,000 – $800) × 0.98]	1,176	
	Sales Discounts [($2,000 – $800) × 0.02]	24	
	Accounts Receivable ($2,000 – $800)		1,200
29	Accounts Payable ($1,600 – $640)	960	
	Cash		960

Requirement 2

Inventory

June 3	1,600	June 9	640
15	5,000	12	550
16	260	18	1,180
22	480	24	150
Bal.	4,820		

Cost of Goods Sold

June 12	550	June 22	480
18	1,180		
Bal.	1,250		

Requirement 3

Amazon's decision to borrow funds was wise because the discount ($150) exceeded the interest paid ($95). Thus Amazon was $55 better off.

- ☐ Merchandising Operations
- ☐ Accounting for Inventory: Perpetual System
- ■ Adjusting and Closing Accounts
- ☐ Preparing Financial Statements
- ☐ Key Decision-Making Ratios

Student Resource CD
adjusting, cost of goods sold, inventory, inventory turnover, work sheet

4 *Adjust and close the accounts of a merchandising business*

Adjusting and Closing the Accounts of a Merchandiser

A merchandiser adjusts and closes accounts the same way a service entity does. If a work sheet is used, the trial balance is entered, and the work sheet is completed to determine net income or net loss. The work sheet aids the adjusting and closing processes and preparation of the financial statements.

Adjusting Inventory Based on a Physical Count

The inventory account should stay current at all times. However, the actual amount of inventory on hand may differ from what the books show. Theft, damage, and errors occur. For this reason, businesses, like the bookstore chain Barnes & Noble, take a physical count of inventory at least once a year. The most common time to count inventory is at the end of the fiscal year. The business then adjusts the Inventory account based on the physical count.

Exhibit 5-5, Austin Sound's work sheet for the year ended December 31, 20X5, lists a $40,500 balance for inventory on the trial balance (first two columns). With no shrinkage—due to theft or error—the business should have inventory costing $40,500. But on December 31, when Austin Sound counts the inventory, the total cost of the goods on hand comes to only $40,200.

ACTUAL INVENTORY ON HAND	–	INVENTORY BALANCE BEFORE ADJUSTMENT	=	ADJUSTING ENTRY TO THE INVENTORY ACCOUNT
$40,200	–	$40,500	=	Credit of $300

Austin Sound then records this adjusting entry for inventory shrinkage:

Dec. 31	Cost of Goods Sold.	300	
	Inventory ($40,500 – $40,200)		300

This entry brings Inventory and Cost of Goods Sold to their correct balances.

Exhibit 5-5 Accounting Work Sheet

Austin Sound Center
Accounting Work Sheet
Year Ended December 31, 20X5

Account Title	Trial Balance Debit	Trial Balance Credit	Adjustments Debit	Adjustments Credit	Income Statement Debit	Income Statement Credit	Balance Sheet Debit	Balance Sheet Credit
Cash	2,850						2,850	
Accounts receivable	4,600						4,600	
Note receivable, current	8,000						8,000	
Interest receivable			(a) 400				400	
Inventory	**40,500**			**(b) 300**			**40,200**	
Supplies	650			(c) 550			100	
Prepaid insurance	1,200			(d) 1,000			200	
Furniture and fixtures	33,200						33,200	
Accumulated depreciation		2,400		(e) 600				3,000
Accounts payable		47,000						47,000
Unearned sales revenue		2,000	(f) 1,300					700
Wages payable				(g) 400				400
Interest payable				(h) 200				200
Note payable, long-term		12,600						12,600
C. Ernest, capital		25,900						25,900
C. Ernest, withdrawals	54,100						54,100	
Sales revenue		**168,000**		**(f) 1,300**		**169,300**		
Sales discounts	**1,400**				**1,400**			
Sales returns and allowances	**2,000**				**2,000**			
Interest revenue		600		(a) 400		1,000		
Cost of goods sold	**90,500**		**(b) 300**		**90,800**			
Wage expense	9,800		(g) 400		10,200			
Rent expense	8,400				8,400			
Depreciation expense			(e) 600		600			
Insurance expense			(d) 1,000		1,000			
Supplies expense			(c) 550		550			
Interest expense	1,300		(h) 200		1,500			
	258,500	258,500	4,750	4,750	116,450	170,300	143,650	89,800
Net income					53,850			53,850
					170,300	170,300	143,650	143,650

The physical count can also reveal that more inventory is present than the books show. In that case, the adjusting entry debits Inventory and credits Cost of Goods Sold.

To illustrate a merchandiser's adjusting and closing process, let's use Austin Sound's 20X5 work sheet in Exhibit 5-5. All the new accounts—Inventory, Cost of Goods Sold, and the contra accounts—are highlighted for emphasis.

Adjustment data at December 31, 20X5:

a. Interest revenue earned but not yet collected, $400.
b. Inventory on hand, $40,200.
c. Supplies on hand, $100.
d. Prepaid insurance expired during the year, $1,000.
e. Depreciation, $600.
f. Unearned sales revenue earned during the year, $1,300.
g. Accrued wage expense, $400.
h. Accrued interest expense, $200.

Preparing and Using the Work Sheet

The Exhibit 5-5 work sheet is similar to the work sheets we have seen so far, but there are a few differences. This work sheet does not include adjusted trial balance columns. In most accounting systems, a single operation combines trial balance amounts with the adjustments. The adjusted balances go directly to the income statement and balance sheet columns.

This work sheet is slightly different from the one introduced in the Chapter 4 acetates following p. 144—this work sheet contains four pairs of columns, not five.

Account Title Columns The trial balance lists the unadjusted amount for each account. There are a few accounts without balances. These accounts are affected by the adjusting process. Examples include Interest Receivable, Wages Payable, and Depreciation Expense. Accounts are listed in the order they appear in the ledger.

Trial Balance Columns Examine the Inventory account in the trial balance. Inventory has a balance of $40,500 before the physical count at the end of the year. Any difference between the Inventory amount on the trial balance ($40,500) and the correct amount based on the physical count ($40,200) is debited or credited to Cost of Goods Sold, as we just saw.

Adjustments Columns The adjustments are similar to those discussed in Chapters 3 and 4. The debit amount of each entry should equal the credit amount, and total debits should equal total credits.

Income Statement Columns The income statement columns in Exhibit 5-5 show adjusted amounts for the revenues and the expenses. Sales Revenue, for example, has an adjusted balance of $169,300.

The income statement totals indicate a net income or net loss.

- Net income: Total credits > Total debits
- Net loss: Total debits > Total credits

Austin Sound's total credits of $170,300 exceed the total debits of $116,450, so the company earned a net income.

Balance-Sheet Columns The only new item in the balance sheet columns is Inventory. The $40,200 balance is determined by the physical count at the end of the period.

Journalizing the Adjusting and Closing Entries

Exhibit 5-6 presents Austin Sound's adjusting entries, which are similar to those you have seen previously, except for the inventory adjustment [entry (b)]. → The closing entries in the exhibit also follow the pattern illustrated in Chapter 4.

← *Chapter 4, p. 148, explains closing entries in more detail.*

The *first closing entry* debits the revenue accounts for their ending balances. The offsetting credit of $170,300 transfers the sum of total revenues to Income Summary. This amount comes directly from the credit column of the income statement (Exhibit 5-5).

The *second closing entry* credits Cost of Goods Sold, the contra revenue accounts (Sales Discounts and Sales Returns and Allowances), and all the expense accounts. The offsetting $116,450 debit to Income Summary represents the amount of total expenses plus the contra revenues. These amounts come from the debit column of the income statement.

The *last two closing entries* close net income to the Capital account and also close Withdrawals into the Capital account.

Exhibit 5-6

Adjusting and Closing Entries for a Merchandiser

Journal

Adjusting Entries

a.	Dec. 31	Interest Receivable	400	
		Interest Revenue		400
b.	31	Cost of Goods Sold	300	
		Inventory		300
c.	31	Supplies Expense ($650 – $100)	550	
		Supplies		550
d.	31	Insurance Expense	1,000	
		Prepaid Insurance		1,000
e.	31	Depreciation Expense	600	
		Accumulated Depreciation		600
f.	31	Unearned Sales Revenue	1,300	
		Sales Revenue		1,300
g.	31	Wage Expense	400	
		Wages Payable		400
h.	31	Interest Expense	200	
		Interest Payable		200

Closing Entries

1.	Dec. 31	Sales Revenue	169,300	
		Interest Revenue	1,000	
		Income Summary		170,300
2.	31	Income Summary	116,450	
		Sales Discounts		1,400
		Sales Returns and Allowances		2,000
		Cost of Goods Sold		90,800
		Wage Expense		10,200
		Rent Expense		8,400
		Depreciation Expense		600
		Insurance Expense		1,000
		Supplies Expense		550
		Interest Expense		1,500
3.	31	Income Summary ($170,300 – $116,450)	53,850	
		C. Ernest, Capital		53,850
4.	31	C. Ernest, Capital	54,100	
		C. Ernest, Withdrawals		54,100

✔ **Starter 5-8**

✔ **Starter 5-9**

✔ **Starter 5-10**

Study Exhibits 5-5 and 5-6 carefully because they show the end-of-period process that leads to the financial statements.

Here is an easy way to remember the closing process. First, look at the work sheet. Then:

1. Debit all income statement accounts with a credit balance. Credit Income Summary for the total.
2. Credit all income statement accounts with a debit balance. Debit Income Summary for the total.
3. Compute the balance in the Income Summary account. A debit balance indicates a net loss; to close a net loss, credit Income Summary and debit Capital. If Income Summary has a credit balance, there is a net income; to close net income, debit Income Summary and credit Capital.
4. Withdrawals has a debit balance. Credit Withdrawals to close its balance, and debit Capital for the same amount. This is the final closing entry.

Preparing a Merchandiser's Financial Statements

Exhibit 5-7 shows Austin Sound's financial statements for 20X5.

Student Resource CD
income statement

5 Prepare a merchandiser's financial statements

Operating Expenses
Expenses, other than cost of goods sold, that are incurred in the entity's major line of business. Examples include rent, depreciation, salaries, wages, utilities, and supplies expense.

Income Statement The income statement begins with sales, cost of goods sold, and gross profit. Then come the **operating expenses,** which are those expenses other than cost of goods sold that occur in the entity's major line of business.

Many companies report operating expenses in two categories:

- *Selling expenses* are expenses related to marketing the company's products—sales salaries; sales commissions; advertising; depreciation, rent, and utilities on store buildings; and delivery expense.
- *General expenses* include office expenses, such as the salaries of the company president and office employees; depreciation; rent; utilities; and property taxes on the home office building.

Operating Income
Gross profit minus operating expenses plus any other operating revenues. Also called **income from operations**.

Other Revenue
Revenue that is outside the main operations of a business, such as a gain on the sale of plant assets.

Other Expense
Expense that is outside the main operations of a business, such as a loss on the sale of plant assets.

Gross profit minus operating expenses plus any other operating revenues equals **operating income**, or **income from operations**. Operating income measures the results of the entity's major ongoing activities.

The last section of Austin Sound's income statement is **other revenue and expense**. This category reports revenues and expenses that fall outside its main operations. Examples include gains and losses on the sale of plant assets (not inventory) and gains and losses on lawsuits.

The bottom line of the income statement is net income:

$$\text{Net income} = \text{Total revenues and gains} - \text{Total expenses and losses}$$

We often hear the term *bottom line*, that is, a final result. The *bottom line* is net income on the income statement.

Statement of Owner's Equity A merchandiser's statement of owner's equity looks exactly like that of a service business.

Balance Sheet If the business is a merchandiser, the balance sheet shows inventory as a major current asset. Service businesses usually have no inventory.

Exhibit 5-7

Financial Statements of Austin Sound Center

Austin Sound Center

Income Statement
Year Ended December 31, 20X5

Sales revenue		$169,300	
Less: Sales discounts	$ (1,400)		
Sales returns and allowances	(2,000)	(3,400)	
Net sales revenue			$165,900
Cost of goods sold			90,800
Gross profit			75,100
Operating expenses:			
Wage expense		$ 10,200	
Rent expense		8,400	
Insurance expense		1,000	
Depreciation expense		600	
Supplies expense		550	20,750
Operating income			54,350
Other revenue and (expense):			
Interest revenue		$ 1,000	
Interest expense		(1,500)	(500)
Net income			$ 53,850

✔ Starter 5-11

Austin Sound Center

Statement of Owner's Equity
Year Ended December 31, 20X5

C. Ernest, capital, December 31, 20X4	$25,900
Add: Net income	53,850
	79,750
Less: Withdrawals	(54,100)
C. Ernest, capital, December 31, 20X5	$25,650

Austin Sound Center

Balance Sheet
December 31, 20X5

Assets			Liabilities	
Current:			Current:	
Cash		$ 2,850	Accounts payable	$47,000
Accounts receivable		4,600	Unearned sales revenue	700
Note receivable		8,000		
Interest receivable		400	Wages payable	400
Inventory		40,200	Interest payable	200
Prepaid insurance		200		
Supplies		100	Total current liabilities	48,300
Total current assets		56,350	Long-term:	
Plant:			Note payable	12,600
Furniture and fixtures	$33,200		Total liabilities	60,900
Less: Accumulated depreciation	(3,000)	30,200	**Owner's Equity**	
			C. Ernest, capital	25,650
Total assets		$86,550	Total liabilities and owner's equity	$86,550

✔ Starter 5-12

Income Statement Formats: Multi-Step and Single-Step

For a review of balance sheet formats, see Chapter 4, p. 153.

The balance sheet appears in two formats:

- The report format (assets on top, . . . , owner's equity at bottom)
- The account format (assets at left, liabilities and owner's equity at right)

There are also two formats for the income statement:

- The multi-step format
- The single-step format

The multi-step format is by far the more popular.

Multi-Step Income Statement Format that contains subtotals to highlight significant relationships. In addition to net income, it reports gross profit and operating income.

MULTI-STEP INCOME STATEMENT The **multi-step format** lists important subtotals. In addition to net income, it also reports gross profit and income from operations. This format reports a merchandiser's results of operations especially well because gross profit and income from operations are important to investors. The income statements presented thus far in this chapter have been multi-step. Austin Sound's multi-step income statement for the year ended December 31, 20X5, appears in Exhibit 5-7.

Single-Step Income Statement Format that groups all revenues together and then lists and deducts all expenses together without drawing any subtotals.

SINGLE-STEP INCOME STATEMENT The **single-step format** groups all revenues together and all expenses together without drawing any subtotals. IBM and Wal-Mart use this format. The single-step format clearly distinguishes revenues from expenses, as Exhibit 5-8 shows. This format works well for service entities because they have no gross profit to report.

Exhibit 5-8
Single-Step Income Statement

Austin Sound Center
Income Statement
Year Ended December 31, 20X5

Revenues:	
Net sales (net of sales discounts, $1,400, and returns and allowances, $2,000)	$165,900
Interest revenue	1,000
Total revenues	166,900
Expenses:	
Cost of goods sold	90,800
Wage expense	10,200
Rent expense	8,400
Interest expense	1,500
Insurance expense	1,000
Depreciation expense	600
Supplies expenses	550
Total expenses	113,050
Net Income	$ 53,850

Two Key Ratios for Decision Making

Student Resource CD
gross profit, inventory turnover

Merchandise inventory is the most important asset for a merchandising business. Owners and managers use several ratios to evaluate operations, among them the gross profit percentage and the rate of inventory turnover.

The Gross Profit Percentage

Use gross profit percentage and inventory turnover to evaluate a business

A key decision tool highlights gross profit, which is net sales minus cost of goods sold. Merchandisers strive to increase the **gross profit percentage**, which is computed as follows:

Gross Profit Percentage
Gross profit divided by net sales revenue. A measure of profitability. Also called **gross margin percentage**.

For Austin Sound Center (Exhibit 5-7)

$$\text{Gross profit percentage} = \frac{\text{Gross profit}}{\text{Net sales revenue}} = \frac{\$75{,}100}{\$165{,}900} = 0.453 = 45.3\%$$

The gross profit percentage (also called the *gross margin percentage*) is one of the most carefully watched measures of profitability. A 45% gross margin means that each dollar of sales generates 45 cents of gross profit. On average, the goods cost the seller 55 cents. For most firms, the gross profit percentage changes little from year to year. A small increase may signal an important rise in income, and vice versa for a decrease.

Exhibit 5-9 compares Austin Sound's gross margin to that of Target and Amazon.com.

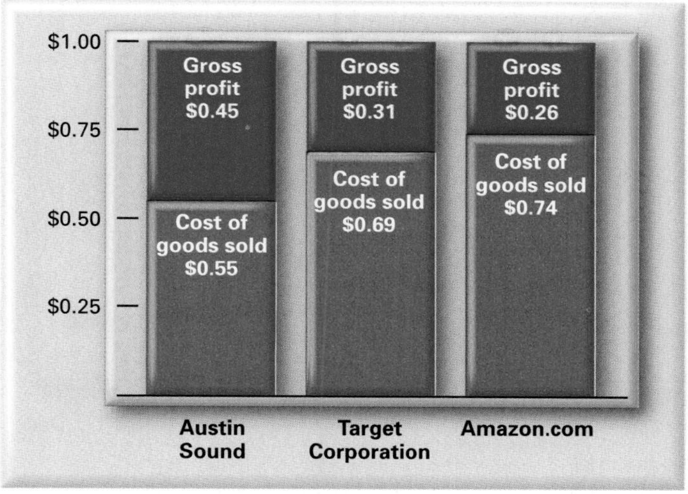

Exhibit 5-9
Gross Profit on $1 of Sales for Three Merchandisers

The Rate of Inventory Turnover

Owners and managers strive to sell inventory quickly because the inventory generates no profit until it is sold. The faster the sales, the higher the income. The slower the sales, the lower the income. Ideally, a business could operate with zero inventory. Most businesses, however, including Amazon.com and Target, must keeps goods on hand. **Inventory turnover**, the ratio of cost of goods sold to average inventory, indicates how rapidly inventory is sold. It is computed as follows:

Inventory Turnover
Ratio of cost of goods sold to average inventory. Measures the number of times a company sells its average level of inventory during a year.

For Austin Sound Center (Exhibit 5-7)

$$\text{Inventory turnover} = \frac{\text{Cost of goods sold}}{\text{Average inventory}} = \frac{\text{Cost of goods sold}}{(\text{Beginning inventory} + \text{Ending inventory})/2}$$

$$= \frac{\$90{,}800}{(\$38{,}600^{*} + \$40{,}200)/2} = 2.3 \text{ times per year}$$

*Taken from balance sheet at the end of the preceding period.

✔ Starter 5-13

✔ Starter 5-14

Inventory turnover is usually computed for an annual period, so the cost-of-goods sold figure is the amount for the entire year. Average inventory is computed from the beginning and ending balances. Austin Sound's beginning inventory would be taken from the balance sheet at the end of the preceding year.

A high turnover rate is desirable, and an increase in the turnover rate usually means higher profits. Inventory turnover varies from industry to industry. Grocery stores, for example, turn their goods over much faster than automobile dealers do. Retailers of electronic products, such as Austin Sound, have an average turnover of 3.6 times per year. A turnover rate of 2.3 times per year suggests that Austin Sound is not very efficient. Exhibit 5-10 compares the inventory turnover rate of Austin Sound and Amazon.com.

Exhibit 5-10 tells an interesting story. Amazon.com moves its merchandise six times as fast as Austin Sound.

In fact, the trick for merchandisers is in keeping enough goods to sell but not so much that inventory becomes a financial drain. According to analysts, disappointing sales from Home Depot show that the home improvement giant has not quite mastered the inventory balancing act. After Home Depot cut its inventory way back, customers started shopping at Home Depot's rival, Lowe's. Home Depot's sales dropped by 2%, and now the company is working hard to keep enough inventory on hand.[2]

Exhibit 5-10

Rate of Inventory Turnover for Two Merchandisers

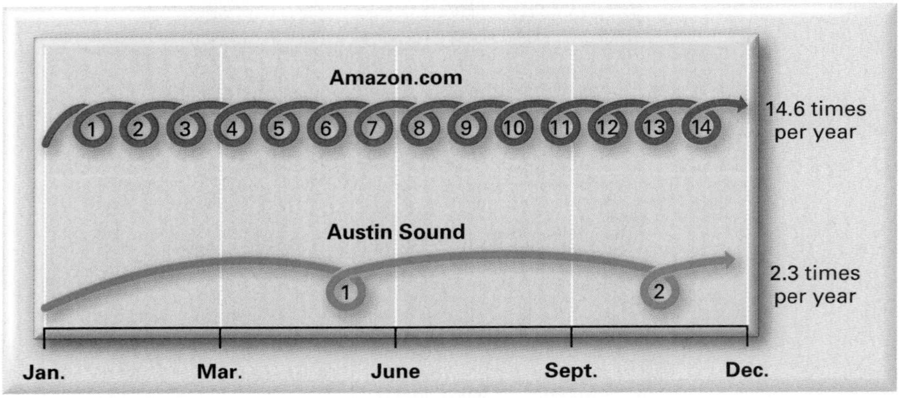

Stop & Think

Calculate the rate of inventory turnover for Safeway, Inc., the large grocery chain (amounts in millions).

Beginning inventory	$ 1,856
Ending inventory	2,445
Cost of goods sold	20,349

Answer

$$\text{Inventory turnover} = \frac{\text{Cost of goods sold}}{(\text{Beginning inventory} + \text{Ending inventory})/2}$$

$$= \frac{\$20,349}{(\$1,856 + \$2,445)/2} = 9.5 \text{ times per year}$$

[2]Chad Terhune, "Home Depot Earnings Fall 3.4% Amid First Quarterly Sales Drop, *The Wall Street Journal*, February 26, 2003, p. A.11.

Decision Guidelines

MERCHANDISING OPERATIONS AND THE ACCOUNTING CYCLE

Amazon.com and Kinko's Copy Centers are two very different companies. How do Amazon and Kinko's differ? How are they similar? The Decision Guidelines answer these questions.

Decision	Guidelines
How do merchandisers differ from service entities?	• Merchandisers, such as Amazon.com, buy and sell *merchandise inventory.* • Service entities, such as Kinko's, perform a *service.*
How do a merchandiser's financial statements differ from the statements of a service business?	
Income Statement:	**Balance sheet:** • Merchandiser has *inventory*, an asset. • Service business has no inventory.
Merchandiser Sales revenue .... $XXX −Cost of goods sold .... (X) = Gross profit .... XX −Operating expenses .... (X) = Net income .... $ X	***Service Business*** Service revenue .... $ XX −Operating expenses .... (X) = Net income .... $ X
Statements of Owner's Equity:	No difference
Which type of inventory system to use?	• *Perpetual system* shows the amount of *inventory* on hand (the asset) and the cost of goods sold (the expense) at all times. • *Periodic system* shows the correct balances of inventory and cost of goods sold only after a physical count of the inventory, which occurs at least once each year.
How do the adjusting and closing procedures of merchandisers and service entities differ?	Very little. The merchandiser may have to *adjust* the Inventory account for shrinkage. The merchandiser must *close* the Cost of Goods Sold account. Service entities have no inventory to adjust and no cost of goods sold to close.
How to format the merchandiser's income statement?	
Multi-Step Format Sales revenue .... $ XXX −Cost of goods sold .... (X) = Gross profit .... XX −Operating expenses .... (X) = Operating income .... X + Other revenues .... X −Other expenses .... (X) = Net income .... $ XX	**Single-Step Format** *Revenues:* Sales revenue .... $ XXX Other revenues .... X Total revenues .... XXXX *Expenses:* Cost of goods sold .... (X) Operating expenses .... (X) Other expenses .... (X) Total expenses .... XX Net income .... $ XX
How to evaluate inventory operations?	Two key ratios $\text{Gross profit percentage}^{*} = \dfrac{\text{Gross profit}}{\text{Net sales revenue}}$ $\text{Inventory turnover}^{*} = \dfrac{\text{Cost of goods sold}}{\text{Average inventory}}$

*In most cases—the higher, the better.

Excel Application Exercise

Goal: Create a spreadsheet to compute Amazon.com's gross profit percentage and inventory turnover for the past three years.

Scenario: You are intrigued by Amazon's ability to sell merchandise via the Internet and would like to invest in such a venture. Before doing so, however, you remember from your accounting course that ratio analysis is an important part of making an investment decision. You decide to calculate two key ratios: gross profit percentage and inventory turnover. (You may need to visit Amazon.com on the Web to find inventory data from past years. Look under Investor Relations at the bottom of the Home page.) When you have completed your worksheet, answer the following questions:

1. What has happened to Amazon's gross profit percentage over the past three years?
2. What can you tell about Amazon's inventory operations from its inventory turnover ratio for the past two years?

Step-by-Step:

1. Open a new Excel spreadsheet.
2. In column 1, create a bold-faced heading as follows:
   a. Chapter 5 Excel Application Exercise
   b. Evaluating Amazon Inventory Operations
   c. Today's Date
3. Two rows down and two columns over, create bold and underlined headings for the most recent three years (e.g., 2002, 2001, and 2000).
4. In column A, enter the following (one per row):
   a. Net Sales (in thousands)
   b. Cost of Goods Sold (Cost of Sales)
   c. Gross Profit
   d. Inventory
   e. Gross Profit Percentage
   f. Inventory Turnover
5. Locate the data for items **a-d** in the Amazon.com annual report (or on the Web) and enter it in the appropriate columns.
6. Calculate gross profit percentage and inventory turnover. To help visualize the data trends, use the Chart Wizard to create a bar graph of performance.
7. Format all columns, rows, and data as needed. Save your work and print a copy for your files.

END-OF-CHAPTER *Summary Problem*

A+ TIPS
CHECK YOUR RESOURCES

The adjustment data and trial balance of Jan King Distributing Company follow. (*The solution to Requirement 1 is on page 208.*)

Adjustment data at December 31, 20X6:

a. Supplies used during the year, $2,580.
b. Prepaid rent in force, $1,000.
c. Unearned sales revenue still not earned, $2,400.
d. Depreciation. The furniture and fixtures' estimated useful life is 10 years, and they are expected to be worthless when they are retired from service.
e. Accrued salaries, $1,300.
f. Accrued interest expense, $600.
g. Inventory on hand, $65,800.

Required

1. Enter the trial balance on a work sheet and complete the work sheet.
2. Journalize the adjusting and closing entries at December 31. Post to the Income Summary account as an accuracy check on the entries affecting that account. The credit balance closed out of Income Summary should equal net income computed on the work sheet.
3. Prepare the company's multi-step income statement, statement of owner's equity, and balance sheet in account format. Draw arrows linking the statements.
4. Compute the inventory turnover for 20X6. Inventory at December 31, 20X5, was $61,000. Turnover for 20X5 was 2.1 times. Would you expect Jan King Distributing Company to be more profitable or less profitable in 20X6 than in 20X5? Give your reason.

Jan King Distributing Company

Trial Balance
December 31, 20X6

Cash	$ 5,670	
Accounts receivable	37,100	
Inventory	60,500	
Supplies	3,930	
Prepaid rent	6,000	
Furniture and fixtures	26,500	
Accumulated depreciation		$ 21,200
Accounts payable		46,340
Salary payable		
Interest payable		
Unearned sales revenue		3,500
Note payable, long-term		35,000
Jan King, capital		23,680
Jan King, withdrawals	48,000	
Sales revenue		346,700
Sales discounts	10,300	
Sales returns and allowances	8,200	
Cost of goods sold	171,770	
Salary expense	82,750	
Rent expense	7,000	
Depreciation expense		
Utilities expense	5,800	
Supplies expense		
Interest expense	2,900	
Total	$476,420	$476,420

Solution

Requirement 2 (starts here; continues on p. 209)

Adjusting Entries

20X6			
Dec. 31	Supplies Expense	2,580	
	Supplies		2,580
31	Rent Expense	5,000	
	Prepaid Rent		5,000
31	Unearned Sales Revenue ($3,500 − $2,400)	1,100	
	Sales Revenue		1,100
31	Depreciation Expense ($26,500/10)	2,650	
	Accumulated Depreciation		2,650
31	Salary Expense	1,300	
	Salary Payable		1,300
31	Interest Expense	600	
	Interest Payable		600
31	Inventory ($65,800 − $60,500)	5,300*	
	Cost of Goods Sold		5,300

*Excess of inventory on hand over the balance in the Inventory account. This adjustment brings Inventory to its correct balance.

Requirement 1

Jan King Distributing Company

Accounting Work Sheet
Year Ended December 31, 20X6

	Trial Balance		Adjustments		Income Statement		Balance Sheet	
Account Title	Debit	Credit	Debit	Credit	Debit	Credit	Debit	Credit
Cash	5,670						5,670	
Accounts receivable	37,100						37,100	
Inventory	60,500		(g) 5,300				65,800	
Supplies	3,930			(a) 2,580			1,350	
Prepaid rent	6,000			(b) 5,000			1,000	
Furniture and fixtures	26,500						26,500	
Accumulated depreciation		21,200		(d) 2,650				23,850
Accounts payable		46,340						46,340
Salary payable				(e) 1,300				1,300
Interest payable				(f) 600				600
Unearned sales revenue		3,500	(c) 1,100					2,400
Note payable, long-term		35,000						35,000
Jan King, capital		23,680						23,680
Jan King, withdrawals	48,000						48,000	
Sales revenue		346,700		(c) 1,100		347,800		
Sales discounts	10,300				10,300			
Sales returns and allowances	8,200				8,200			
Cost of goods sold	171,770			(g) 5,300	166,470			
Salary expense	82,750		(e) 1,300		84,050			
Rent expense	7,000		(b) 5,000		12,000			
Depreciation expense			(d) 2,650		2,650			
Utilities expense	5,800				5,800			
Supplies expense			(a) 2,580		2,580			
Interest expense	2,900		(f) 600		3,500			
	476,420	476,420	18,530	18,530	295,550	347,800	185,420	133,170
Net income					52,250			52,250
					347,800	347,800	185,420	185,420

Closing Entries

20X6			
Dec. 31	Sales Revenue	347,800	
	Income Summary		347,800
31	Income Summary	295,550	
	Sales Discounts		10,300
	Sales Returns and Allowances		8,200
	Cost of Goods Sold		166,470
	Salary Expense		84,050
	Rent Expense		12,000
	Depreciation Expense		2,650
	Utilities Expense		5,800
	Supplies Expense		2,580
	Interest Expense		3,500
31	Income Summary ($347,800 – $295,550)	52,250	
	Jan King, Capital		52,250
31	Jan King, Capital	48,000	
	Jan King, Withdrawals		48,000

Income Summary

Clo.	295,550	Clo.	347,800
Clo.	52,250	Bal.	52,250

Requirement 3

Jan King Distributing Company

Income Statement
Year Ended December 31, 20X6

Sales revenue		$347,800	
Less: Sales discounts	$(10,300)		
Sales returns and allowances	(8,200)	(18,500)	
Net sales revenue			$329,300
Cost of goods sold			166,470
Gross profit			162,830
Operating expenses:			
Salary expense		$ 84,050	
Rent expense		12,000	
Utilities expense		5,800	
Depreciation expense		2,650	
Supplies expense		2,580	107,080
Income from operations			55,750
Other expense:			
Interest expense			3,500
Net income			$ 52,250

(continued)

Jan King Distributing Company

Statement of Owner's Equity
Year Ended December 31, 20X6

Jan King, capital, December 31, 20X5	$23,680
Add: Net income	52,250
	75,930
Less: Withdrawals	(48,000)
Jan King, capital, December 31, 20X6	$27,930

Jan King Distributing Company

Balance Sheet
December 31, 20X6

Assets			**Liabilities**	
Current:			Current:	
Cash		$ 5,670	Accounts payable	$46,340
Accounts receivable		37,100	Salary payable	1,300
Inventory		65,800	Interest payable	600
Supplies		1,350	Unearned sales revenue	2,400
Prepaid rent		1,000	Total current liabilities	50,640
Total current assets		110,920	Long-term:	
Plant:			Note payable	35,000
Furniture and fixtures	$26,500		Total liabilities	85,640
Less:				
Accumulated depreciation	(23,850)	2,650	**Owner's Equity**	
			Jan King, capital	27,930
Total assets		$113,570	Total liabilities and owner's equity	$113,570

Requirement 4

$$\text{Inventory turnover} = \frac{\text{Cost of goods sold}}{\text{Average inventory}} = \frac{\$166{,}470}{(\$61{,}000 + \$65{,}800)/2} = 2.6 \text{ times}$$

The increase in the rate of inventory turnover from 2.1 to 2.6 suggests higher profits in 20X6 than in 20X5.

REVIEW *Merchandising Operations*

Quick Check

1. Which account does a merchandiser, but not a service company, use?
   a. Inventory
   b. Sales revenue
   c. Cost of goods sold
   d. All of the above
2. The two main inventory accounting systems are the
   a. Purchase and sale
   b. Perpetual and periodic
   c. Cash and accrual
   d. Returns and allowances
3. The journal entry for the purchase of inventory on account is

a. Inventory	XXX	
Accounts Receivable		XXX
b. Accounts Payable	XXX	
Inventory		XXX
c. Inventory	XXX	
Accounts Payable		XXX
d. Inventory	XXX	
Cash		XXX

4. Amazon.com purchased inventory for $5,000 and also paid a $300 freight bill. Amazon returned half the goods to the seller and took a 2% purchase discount. What is Amazon's cost of the inventory that it kept?
   a. $2,750
   b. $2,800
   c. $2,700
   d. $2,500
5. Suppose Amazon.com had sales of $4.0 billion and sales returns of $0.9 billion. Cost of goods sold was $2.3 billion. How much gross profit did Amazon report?
   a. $0.8 billion
   b. $1.7 billion
   c. $2.6 billion
   d. Cannot be determined from the data given
6. Suppose Amazon.com's Inventory account showed a balance of $141 million before the year-end adjustments. The physical count of goods on hand totaled $144 million. To adjust the accounts, Amazon would make this journal entry (amounts in millions):

a. Inventory	3	
Accounts Receivable		3
b. Accounts Payable	3	
Inventory		3
c. Inventory	3	
Cost of Goods Sold		3
d. Cost of Goods Sold	3	
Inventory		3

7. Which account in question 6 would Amazon.com close at the end of the year?
   a. Inventory
   b. Accounts Receivable
   c. Accounts Payable
   d. Cost of Goods Sold
8. The final closing entry for a proprietorship is

a. Owner, Withdrawals	XXX	
Owner, Capital		XXX
b. Sales Revenue	XXX	
Income Summary		XXX
c. Owner, Capital	XXX	
Owner, Withdrawals		XXX
d. Income Summary	XXX	
Expenses		XXX

9. Which subtotals appear on a multi-step income statement, but not on a single-step income statement?
   a. Net sales and Cost of goods sold
   b. Gross Profit and Income from operations
   c. Cost of goods sold and net income
   d. Operating expenses and net income

10. Amazon.com made net sales of $3.12 billion, and cost of goods sold totaled $2.32 billion. Average inventory was $0.16 billion. What was Amazon.com's rate of inventory turnover for this period?
   a. 34% **c.** 19.5 times
   b. 14.5% **d.** 14.5 times

Accounting Vocabulary

cost of goods sold (p. 190)
cost of sales (p. 190)
gross margin (p. 193)
gross margin percentage (p. 203)
gross profit (p. 193)
gross profit percentage (p. 203)
income from operations (p. 200)
inventory (p. 184)
inventory turnover (p. 203)
invoice (p. 186)
multi-step income statement (p. 202)
net purchases (p. 233)
net sales revenue (p. 192)
operating expenses (p. 200)
operating income (p. 200)
other expense (p. 200)
other revenue (p. 200)
periodic inventory system (p. 185)
perpetual inventory system (p. 186)
sales (p. 190)
sales discount (p. 192)
sales returns and allowances (p. 192)
sales revenue (p. 190)
single-step income statement (p. 202)

ASSESS *Your Progress*

A+ online homework

See *www.prenhall.com/horngren* for selected Starters, Exercises, and Problems.

Starters

Recording purchase and cash payment transactions
(Obj. 1)

S5-1 You may have shopped at a **Gap** store. Suppose Gap purchases 2,000 pairs of slacks on account for $50,000. Credit terms are 2/10 n/30. Gap paid within the discount period. Journalize the following transactions for Gap:

a. Purchase of inventory. **b.** Payment on account.

Accounting for the purchase of inventory—purchase discount
(Obj. 1)

S5-2 **Toys "Я" Us** purchases inventory from a variety of suppliers, including **Mattel**, **Hasbro**, and **Tonka**. Suppose Toys "Я" Us buys $150,000 worth of **Lego** toys on credit terms of 3/15 n/45. Some of the goods are damaged in shipment, so Toys "Я" Us returns $50,000 (original amount, before any discounts) of the merchandise to Lego.

How much must Toys "Я" Us pay Lego

a. After the discount period? **b.** Within the discount period?

Recording purchase, purchase return, and cash payment transactions.
(Obj. 1)

S5-3 Refer to the **Toys "Я" Us** situation in Starter 5-2 and journalize the following transactions on the books of Toys "Я" Us. Explanations are not required.

a. Purchase of the goods on May 6, 20X5.
b. Return of the damaged goods on May 13.
c. Payment on May 15. Before journalizing this transaction, it is helpful to post the first two transactions to the Accounts Payable T-account.

S5-4 Suppose a **Lord & Taylor** store purchases $140,000 of women's sportswear on account from **Liz Claiborne, Inc.** Credit terms are 2/10 net 30. Lord & Taylor pays electronically, and Liz Claiborne receives the money on the tenth day.

Recording purchase transactions **(Obj. 1)**

Journalize Lord & Taylor's (a) purchase and (b) payment transactions. What was Lord & Taylor's net cost of this inventory?

Note: Starter 5-5 covers this same situation for the seller.

S5-5 **Liz Claiborne, Inc.**, sells $140,000 of women's sportswear to a **Lord & Taylor** store under credit terms of 2/10 net 30. Liz Claiborne's cost of the goods is $82,000, and Claiborne receives the appropriate amount of cash from Lord & Taylor on the tenth day.

Recording sales, cost of goods sold, and cash collections **(Obj. 2)**

Journalize Liz Claiborne's (a) sale, (b) cost of goods sold, and (c) cash receipt.

Note: Starter 5-4 covers the same situation for the buyer.

S5-6 Suppose **Prentice Hall,** the publisher, sells 1,000 books on account for $15 each (cost of these books is $8,000). One hundred of these books (cost, $800) were damaged in shipment, so Prentice Hall later received the damaged goods as sales returns. Then the customer paid the balance within the discount period. Credit terms were 2/15 net 30.

Recording sales, sales return, and collection entries **(Obj. 2, 3)**

Journalize Prentice Hall's (a) sale, (b) sale return, and (c) cash collection transactions. How much gross profit did Prentice Hall earn on this sale?

S5-7 **Intel Corporation**, famous for the Pentium© processor that powers personal computers, offers sales discounts to customers. Intel also allows its customers to return defective processors. Suppose that Intel made sales of $600,000 on credit terms of 3/10 net 30. Assume that Intel received sales returns of $12,000. Later, Intel collected cash within the discount period. Cost of goods sold for the period was $255,000 after all sales returns.

Computing net sales and gross profit **(Obj. 3)**

For this particular period, compute Intel's

a. Net sales revenue **b.** Gross profit

S5-8 Examine the work sheet of **Austin Sound Center** in Exhibit 5-5, page 197. Focus on adjusting entries (a) and (b). Which entry is exactly the same as for a service company? Which entry relates to a merchandiser only? Explain the reason for the merchandiser's adjusting entry.

Adjusting the accounts of a merchandiser **(Obj. 4)**

S5-9 Refer to the work sheet of **Austin Sound Center** in Exhibit 5-5, page 197. Based solely on the Income Statement columns of the work sheet, make two closing entries, as follows:

Making closing entries **(Obj. 4)**

- Journalize the closing entry for the *first account* listed that must be closed at the end of the period.
- Journalize the closing entry for the *last account* listed on the work sheet (not net income, which is not an account).

All closing entries for revenues and expenses follow the pattern of the closing entries you just made. Now make the final two closing entries of Austin Sound Center:

- Journalize the closing entry for net income.
- Journalize the closing entry for the Owner's Withdrawals account.

Set up a T-account for the Owner's Capital account, and insert the balance from the work sheet. Then post your closing entries to the Capital account. Its ending balance should be the same as the amount reported on Austin Sound's balance sheet in Exhibit 5-7 on page 201. Is it?

Closing the accounts
(Obj. 3)

S5-10 Refer to the income statement of Merchandising Co. in Exhibit 5-1, page 184.

1. Make two closing entries for Merchandising Co. at June 30, 20XX:
   - Close the revenue
   - Close the expenses
2. Which of Merchandising Co.'s balance sheet accounts will the company close at June 30, 20XX? Give your reason.

Preparing a merchandiser's income statement
(Obj. 5)

S5-11 **Dell Computer Corporation** reported these figures in its January 31, 20X1, financial statements (adapted, and in millions):

Cash	$ 3,809
Total operating expenses	3,552
Accounts payable	3,538
Owners' equity	5,308
Long-term liabilities	971
Inventory	391
Cost of goods sold	20,047
Other assets (long-term)	3,025
Other current liabilities	1,654
Property and equipment, net	765
Net sales revenue	25,265
Other current assets	873
Accounts receivable	2,608

Prepare Dell's multi-step income statement for the year ended January 31, 20X1.

Preparing a merchandiser's balance sheet
(Obj. 5)

S5-12 Use the data in Starter 5-11 to prepare **Dell Computer's** classified balance sheet at January 31, 20X1. Use the report format with all headings, and list accounts in proper order.

Computing the gross profit percentage and the rate of inventory turnover
(Obj. 6)

S5-13 Refer to the **Dell Computer** situation in Starter 5-12. Compute Dell's gross profit percentage and rate of inventory turnover for 20X1. One year earlier, at January 31, 20X0, Dell's inventory balance was $320 million.

Contrasting gross profit and cash flows
(Obj. 6)

S5-14 **Lands' End**, the catalog merchant, reported the following for the year ended January 31, 20X0 (adapted, with amounts in millions):

Cash collections from customers	$1,323
Selling, general, and administrative expenses	529
Cost of sales	727
Net sales revenue	1,320
Cash payments to suppliers	682

As an investor, you wonder which was greater, Lands' End's (a) gross profit, or (b) the company's excess of cash collections from customers over cash payments to suppliers? Compute both amounts to answer this question.

Exercises

A+ online homework

Journalizing transactions from a purchase invoice
(Obj. 1)

E5-1 As the proprietor of Davis Tire Co., you receive the following invoice from a supplier:

WHOLESALE DISTRIBUTORS, INC.
2600 Commonwealth Avenue
Boston, Massachusetts 02215

Invoice date: May 14, 20X6 **Payment terms:** 3/10 n/30

Sold to: Davis Tire Co.
4219 Crestwood Parkway
Lexington, Mass. 02173

Description	Quantity Shipped	Price	Amount
P135–X4 Radials....................................	4	$37.14	$ 148.56
L912 Belted-bias	8	41.32	330.56
R39 Truck tires......................................	10	60.02	600.20
Total...			$1,079.32

Due date:	Amount:
May 24, 20X6	$1,046.94
May 25 through June 13, 20X6	$1,079.32

Required

1. Davis received the invoice on May 15. Record the May 15 purchase on account. Carry amounts to the nearest cent throughout.
2. The R39 truck tires were ordered by mistake and were therefore returned to Wholesale Distributors. Journalize the return on May 19.
3. Record the May 22 payment of the amount owed.

Journalizing purchase transactions
(Obj. 1)

E5-2 On April 30, Stanley & Weaver Jewelers purchased inventory of $8,000 on account from Intergem Jewels, a jewelry importer. Terms were 3/15 net 45. On receiving the goods, Stanley & Weaver checked the order and found $1,000 of unsuitable merchandise. Stanley & Weaver returned the unsuitable merchandise to Intergem on May 4.

To pay the remaining amount owed, Stanley & Weaver borrowed the net amount of the invoice from the bank. On May 14, Stanley & Weaver signed a short-term note payable to the bank and immediately paid the borrowed funds to Intergem. On June 14, Stanley & Weaver paid the bank the net amount of the invoice, plus 1% monthly interest (rounded to the nearest dollar).

Required

Record the indicated transactions in the journal of Stanley & Weaver Jewelers. Explanations are not required.

Journalizing sales transactions
(Obj. 2)

E5-3 Refer to the business situation in Exercise 5-2. Journalize the transactions of Intergem Jewels. Intergem's gross profit is 40%, so cost of goods sold is 60% of sales. Explanations are not required.

Journalizing purchase and sales transactions
(Obj. 1, 2)

E5-4 Journalize, without explanations, the following transactions of Jan's Perfect Presents during the month of September:

Sept. 3	Purchased $1,900 of inventory on account under terms of 2/10 n/eom (end of month) and FOB shipping point.
7	Returned $300 of defective merchandise purchased on September 3.
9	Paid freight bill of $30 on September 3 purchase.
10	Sold inventory on account for $3,100. Payment terms were 3/15 n/30. These goods cost Jan's $1,700.
12	Paid amount owed on credit purchase of September 3, less the discount and the return.
16	Granted a sales allowance of $800 on the September 10 sale.
23	Received cash from September 10 customer in full settlement of her debt, less the allowance and the discount.

Computing gross profit and net income
(Obj. 3)

E5-5 General Electric (GE), the giant company known for home appliances and engines for jet aircraft, reported these figures for 2001 and 2000 (adapted and in billions):

	2001	2000
Net sales	$52.7	$54.8
Cost of sales	35.7	39.3
Total operating expenses and other expenses	3.3	2.8

Compute GE's (a) gross profit and (b) net income for each year. Which year was more successful?

Give your reason.

Evaluating a company's revenues, gross profit, and net income
(Obj. 3)

E5-6 Toys "Я" Us reported the following (adapted):

Toys "Я" Us, Inc.
Statements of Earnings (adapted)

	Fiscal Years Ended	
(In millions)	**January 31, 20X1**	**January 31, 20X0**
Net sales	$11,862	$11,170
Cost and expenses:		
Cost of sales	8,321	8,191
Other expenses	3,262	3,111
Net earnings (net loss)	$ 279	$ (132)

Toys "Я" Us, Inc.
Balance Sheets (partial, adapted)

Assets (In millions)	**January 31, 20X1**	**January 31, 20X0**
Current Assets:		
Cash and cash equivalents	$ 584	$ 410
Accounts and other receivables	182	204
Merchandise inventories	2,027	1,902
Prepaid expenses and other current assets	80	81
Total Current Assets	$2,873	$2,597

Required

1. Is Toys "Я" Us a merchandising entity, service business, or both? How can you tell? List the items in the Toys "Я" Us financial statements that influence your answer.
2. Compute Toys "Я" Us's gross profit for fiscal years 20X1 and 20X0. Did the gross profit increase or decrease in 20X1? Is this a good sign or a bad sign about the company?
3. Write a brief memo to investors advising them of Toys "Я" Us's trend of sales, gross profit, and net income. Indicate whether the outlook for Toys "Я" Us is favorable or unfavorable, based on this trend. Use the following memo format:

Date: ________

To: Investors

From: Student Name

Subject: Trend of sales, gross profit, and net income for Toys "Я" Us

E5-7 Supply the missing income statement amounts in each of the following situations:

Computing inventory and cost of goods sold amounts
(Obj. 3)

Sales	Sales Discounts	Net Sales	Cost of Goods Sold	Gross Profit
$98,300	(a)	$92,800	(b)	$33,000
62,400	$2,100	(c)	$44,100	(d)
91,500	1,800	89,700	59,400	(e)
(f)	3,000	(g)	72,500	39,600

E5-8 **Home Depot's** accounting records carried the following accounts (adapted, with amounts in millions) at January 31, 20X1:

Making closing entries
(Obj. 4)

Inventory	$ 5,489
Interest revenue	37
Accounts payable	1,993
Cost of goods sold	27,023
Other expense	1,597
Owner withdrawals	255
Selling expense	6,832
Sales revenue	38,434
Interest expense	28
Receivables	587
General and administrative expense	671

Required

1. Journalize all of Home Depot's closing entries at January 31, 20X1. Use an Owner Capital account.
2. Set up T-accounts for the Income Summary account and the Owner Capital account. Post to these accounts and take their ending balances. One year earlier, at January 31, 20X0, the Owner Capital balance was $8,740 million.

Journalizing closing entries
(Obj. 4)

E5-9 The trial balance and adjustments columns of the work sheet of Southside Development at March 31, 20X6 follow.

	Trial Balance		Adjustments	
Account Title	**Debit**	**Credit**	**Debit**	**Credit**
Cash	2,000			
Accounts receivable	8,500		(a) 12,000	
Inventory	36,100			(b) 4,290
Supplies	13,000			(c) 8,600
Equipment	42,470			
Accumulated depreciation		11,250		(d) 2,250
Accounts payable		9,300		
Salary payable				(e) 1,200
Note payable, long-term		7,500		
Jack Potter, capital		33,920		
Jack Potter, withdrawals	45,000			
Sales revenue		233,000		(a) 12,000
Sales discounts	2,000			
Cost of goods sold	111,600		(b) 4,290	
Selling expense	21,050		(c) 5,200	
			(e) 1,200	
General expense	10,500		(c) 3,400	
			(d) 2,250	
Interest expense	2,750			
Total	294,970	294,970	28,340	28,340

Compute the adjusted balance for each account that must be closed. Then journalize Southside's closing entries at March 31, 20X6. How much was Southside's net income or net loss?

Preparing a multi-step income statement
(Obj. 5)

Student Resource CD
spreadsheet

E5-10 Use the data in Exercise 5-9 to prepare the multi-step income statement of Southside Development for the year ended March 31, 20X6.

Preparing a merchandiser's multi-step income statement to evaluate the business
(Obj. 5, 6)

Student Resource CD
spreadsheet

E5-11 Selected amounts from the accounting records of Persnikity Tim's Coffee Shops are listed in alphabetical order.

Accounts payable	$ 16,200
Accumulated depreciation	18,700
Cost of goods sold	99,300
General expenses	23,500
Interest revenue	1,500
Inventory, December 31, 20X5	21,000
Inventory, December 31, 20X6	19,400
Owner's equity, December 31, 20X6	126,070
Sales discounts	9,000
Sales returns	4,600
Sales revenue	204,000
Selling expenses	37,800
Unearned sales revenue	6,500

Required

1. Prepare the business's multi-step income statement for the year ended December 31, 20X6.
2. Compute the rate of inventory turnover for the year. Last year the turnover rate was 3.8 times. Does this two-year trend suggest improvement or deterioration in inventory turnover?

Preparing a single-step income statement to evaluate the business
(Obj. 5, 6)
Student Resource CD
spreadsheet

E5-12 Prepare Persnikity Tim's Coffee Shops' single-step income statement for 20X6, using the data from Exercise 5-11. Compute the gross profit percentage, and compare it with last year's gross profit percentage of 50%. Does this two-year trend in the gross percentage suggest better or worse profitability during the current year?

Computing gross profit percentage and inventory turnover
(Obj. 6)

E5-13 **Motorola Systems** earned sales revenue of $55 million in 20X4. Cost of goods sold was $33 million, and net income reached $8 million, Motorola's highest ever. Total current assets included inventory of $6 million at December 31, 20X4. Last year's ending inventory was $4 million. The managers of Motorola need to know the company's gross profit percentage and rate of inventory turnover for 20X4. Compute these amounts.

Continuing Exercise. *This exercise completes the Marcia Walker, Consultant, situation from Exercise 2-17 of Chapter 2, Exercise 3-15 of Chapter 3, and Exercise 4-13 of Chapter 4.*

Accounting for both mechandising and service operations
(Obj. 1, 2, 4, 5)
Student Resource CD
General Ledger, Peachtree, QuickBooks

E5-14 Marcia Walker's consulting practice performs systems consulting. Walker has also begun selling accounting software. During January, the business completed these transactions:

Jan. 2	Completed a consulting engagement and received cash of $7,200.
2	Prepaid three months' office rent, $1,500.
7	Purchased accounting software inventory on account, $4,000.
16	Paid employee salary, $1,400.
18	Sold accounting software on account, $1,100 (cost $700).
19	Consulted with a client for a fee of $900 on account.
21	Paid on account, $2,000.
24	Paid utilities, $300.
28	Sold accounting software for cash, $600 (cost $400).
31	Recorded these adjusting entries:
	Accrued salary expense, $1,400.
	Accounted for expiration of prepaid rent.
	Depreciation of office furniture, $200.

Required

1. Open the following selected T-accounts in the ledger: Cash; Accounts Receivable; Accounting Software Inventory; Prepaid Rent; Accumulated Depreciation; Accounts Payable; Salary Payable; Marcia Walker, Capital; Income Summary; Service Revenue; Sales Revenue; Cost of Goods Sold; Salary Expense; Rent Expense; Utilities Expense; and Depreciation Expense.
2. Journalize and post the January transactions. Key all items by date. Compute each account balance, and denote the balance as *Bal.* Journalize and post the closing entries. Denote each closing amount as *Clo.* After posting all closing entries, prove the equality of debits and credits in the ledger.
3. Prepare the January income statement of Marcia Walker, Consultant. Use the single-step format.

A+ online homework

Problems

(Group A)

Explaining the perpetual inventory system
(Obj. 1, 2)

P5-1A Lens Masters is a regional chain of optical shops. The company offers a large selection of eyeglass frames, and Lens Masters stores provide while-you-wait service. The company has launched a vigorous advertising campaign to promote two-for-the-price-of-one frame sales.

Required

Lens Masters expects to grow rapidly and to increase its level of inventory. As the chief accountant of this company, you wish to install a perpetual inventory system. Write a one-paragraph business memo to the company president to explain how that system would work for the purchase and sale of eyeglasses. Use the following heading for your memo:

Date:	________
To:	Company president
From:	Chief Accountant
Subject:	How a perpetual inventory system works for purchases and sales

Accounting for the purchase and sale of inventory
(Obj. 1, 2)

P5-2A Assume the following transactions occurred between **Walgreen Co.**, the pharmacy chain, and Procter & Gamble (P&G), the consumer products company, during June of the current year:

June 8	P&G sold $6,000 worth of merchandise to Walgreen on terms of 2/10 n/30, FOB shipping point. P&G prepaid freight charges of $200 and included this amount in the invoice total. (P&G's entry to record the freight payment debits Accounts Receivable and credits Cash.) These goods cost P&G $2,100.
11	Walgreen returned $1,000 of the merchandise purchased on June 8. P&G accounted for the sales return and placed the goods back in inventory (P&G's cost, $400).
17	Walgreen paid $2,000 of the invoice amount owed to P&G for the June 8 purchase, less the discount. This payment included none of the freight charge.
26	Walgreen paid the remaining amount owed to P&G for the June 8 purchase.

Required

Journalize these transactions, first on the books of Walgreen Co. and, second, on the books of Procter & Gamble.

Journalizing purchase and sale transactions
(Obj. 1, 2)

P5-3A Hawkeye Electric company engaged in the following transactions during July:

July 2	Purchased inventory for cash, $800.
5	Purchased store supplies on credit terms of net eom, $600.
8	Purchased inventory of $3,000, plus freight charges of $230. Credit terms are 3/15 n/30.
9	Sold goods for cash,$1,200. Hawkeye's cost of these goods was $700.
11	Returned $200 of the inventory purchased on July 8. It was damaged.
12	Purchased inventory on credit terms of 3/10 n/30, $3,330.

(continued)

July 14	Sold inventory on credit terms of 2/10 n/30, $9,600 (cost $5,000).
16	Paid utilities expense, $275.
20	Received returned inventory from the July 14 sale, $400. Hawkeye shipped the wrong goods by mistake. Hawkeye's cost of the inventory received was $250.
21	Borrowed the amount owed on the July 8 purchase. Signed a note payable to the bank for $2,946, which takes into account the return of inventory on July 11.
21	Paid supplier for goods purchased on July 8 less the return and the discount.
23	Received $6,860 cash in partial settlement of his account from the customer who purchased inventory on July 14. Granted the customer a 2% discount and credited his account receivable for $7,000.
30	Paid for the store supplies purchased on July 5.

Required

1. Journalize the preceding transactions on the books of Hawkeye Electric Company.
2. Compute the amount of the receivable at July 31 from the customer to whom Hawkeye sold inventory on July 14. What amount of cash discount applies to this receivable at July 31?

Computing net sales, gross profit, and net income
(Obj. 3)

P5-4A The accounting records of Academy Security Systems at June 30, 20X8, list the following:

Cash	$ 13,600
Accounts receivable	8,100
Note payable	4,300
Sales revenue	199,100
Salary payable	1,800
Luke Stover, capital	36,000
Sales returns and allowances	12,100
Selling expenses	19,800
Luke Stover, withdrawals	30,400
Inventory: June 30, 20X7	23,800
June 30, 20X8	28,500
Equipment	44,700
Cost of goods sold	95,000
Accumulated depreciation—equipment	6,900
Sales discounts	3,400
General expenses	16,300
Accounts payable	23,800

Required

1. Prepare a multi-step income statement to show the computation of Academy Security Systems' net sales, gross profit, and net income for the year ended June 30, 20X8.
2. Luke Stover, owner of the business, strives to earn gross profit of $90,000 and net income of $50,000. Did he achieve these goals? Write a couple of sentences to explain.

Preparing a merchandiser's work sheet
(Obj. 4)

Student Resource CD
GL, PT, QB

P5-5A TravelMaster Supply Co.'s trial balance pertains to December 31, 20X7.

TravelMaster Supply Co.
Trial Balance
December 31, 20X7

Cash	$ 2,910	
Accounts receivable	10,190	
Inventory	101,760	
Store supplies	1,990	
Prepaid insurance	3,200	
Store fixtures	63,900	
Accumulated depreciation		$ 37,640
Accounts payable		29,770
Salary payable		
Interest payable		
Note payable, long-term		37,200
Elaine Lorens, capital		63,120
Elaine Lorens, withdrawals	36,300	
Sales revenue		290,000
Cost of goods sold	161,090	
Salary expense	46,580	
Rent expense	14,630	
Utilities expense	6,780	
Depreciation expense		
Insurance expense	5,300	
Store supplies expense		
Interest expense	3,100	
Total	$457,730	$457,730

Adjustment data at December 31, 20X7:

a. Insurance expense for the year, $6,090.
b. Store fixtures have an estimated useful life of 10 years and are expected to be worthless when they are retired from service.
c. Accrued salaries at December 31, $1,260.
d. Accrued interest expense at December 31, $870.
e. Store supplies on hand at December 31, $760.
f. Inventory on hand at December 31, $94,780.

Required

Complete TravelMaster's accounting work sheet for the year ended December 31, 20X7. Key adjusting entries by letter.

P5-6A Refer to the data in problem 5-5A.

Journalizing the adjusting and closing entries of a merchandising business **(Obj. 4)**

Required

1. Journalize the adjusting and closing entries of TravelMaster Supply Co.
2. Determine the December 31, 20X7, balance of Elaine Lorens, Capital.

P5-7A → *Link Back to Chapter 4 (Classified Balance Sheet).* Selected accounts of Omega Electronics are listed along with their balances before closing at July 31, 20X5.

Preparing a multi-step income statement and a classified balance sheet **(Obj. 3, 5)**

Accounts payable	$127,300
Accounts receivable	48,600
Accumulated depreciation—store equipment	16,400
A. L. Carson, capital, June 30	69,100
A. L. Carson, withdrawals	11,000
Cash	24,300
Cost of goods sold	360,900
General expense	75,800
Interest payable	3,000
Interest revenue	1,200
Inventory	187,300
Note payable, long-term	160,000
Salary payable	6,100
Sales discounts	8,300
Sales returns and allowances	17,900
Sales revenue	556,600
Selling expense	84,600
Store equipment	126,000
Supplies	4,300
Unearned sales revenue	9,300

Required

1. Prepare Omega Electronics' *multi-step* income statement for the month ended July 31, 20X5.
2. Prepare Omega's classified balance sheet in *report format* at July 31, 20X5. Show your computation of the July 31 balance of A. L. Carson, Capital.

P5-8A → *Link Back to Chapter 4 (Classified Balance Sheet).*

Preparing a single-step income statement and a classified balance sheet **(Obj. 3, 5)**

Required

1. Use the data of Problem 5-7A to prepare Omega Electronics' *single-step* income statement for the month ended July 31, 20X5.
2. Prepare Omega's classified balance sheet in *report format* at July 31, 20X5. Show your computation of the July 31 balance of A. L. Carson, Capital.

Using trial balance and adjustment data to prepare financial statements and evaluate the business; multi-step income statement
(Obj. 4, 5, 6)

P5-9A The trial balance and adjustment data of Bonds Baseball Cards at September 30, 20X9, follow:

	Trial Balance		Adjustments	
Account Title	**Debit**	**Credit**	**Debit**	**Credit**
Cash	7,300			
Accounts receivable	4,360		(a) 1,400	
Inventory	9,630		(b) 2,100	
Supplies	10,700			(c) 7,940
Equipment	99,450			
Accumulated depreciation		29,800		(d) 9,900
Accounts payable		13,800		
Salary payable				(f) 200
Unearned sales revenue		3,780	(e) 2,600	
Note payable, long-term		10,000		
B. Bonds, capital		58,360		
B. Bonds, drawing	39,000			
Sales revenue		216,000		(a) 1,400
				(e) 2,600
Sales returns	3,100			
Cost of goods sold	95,600			(b) 2,100
Selling expense	40,600		(c) 7,940	
			(f) 200	
General expense	21,000		(d) 9,900	
Interest expense	1,000			
Total	331,740	331,740	24,140	24,140

Required

1. Without completing a formal accounting work sheet, prepare the company's multi-step income statement for the year ended September 30, 20X9.
2. Compute the gross profit percentage and the inventory turnover for 20X9. Inventory on hand at September 30, 20X8, was $10,250. For 20X8 Bonds' gross profit percentage was 50% and the inventory turnover rate was 7.8 times. Does the two-year trend in these ratios suggest improvement or deterioration in profitability?

Problems

(Group B)

A+ online homework

Explaining the perpetual inventory system
(Obj. 1, 2)

P5-1B **Wal-Mart Stores, Inc.**, is the largest retailer in the world, with almost 4,000 stores. A key Wal-Mart advantage is its sophisticated perpetual inventory accounting system.

Required

You are the manager of a Wal-Mart store in Fort Lauderdale, Florida. Write a one-paragraph business memo to a new employee explaining how the company accounts for the purchase and sale of merchandise inventory. Use the following heading for your memo.

Date: ________

To: New Employee

From: Store Manager

Subject: Wal-Mart's perpetual inventory accounting system

P5-2B Assume the following transactions occurred between **Bristol-Myers Squibb (BMS)**, the health-care products company, and Walgreen Co., the pharmacy chain, during February of the current year:

Accounting for the purchase and sale of inventory
(Obj. 1, 2)

Feb. 6 BMS sold $8,000 worth of merchandise to Walgreen on terms of 3/10 n/30, FOB shipping point. BMS prepaid freight charges of $500 and included this amount in the invoice total. (BMS's entry to record the freight payment debits Accounts Receivable and credits Cash). These goods cost BMS $6,100.

10 Walgreen returned $900 of the merchandise purchased on February 6. BMS accounted for the $900 sales return and placed the goods back in inventory (BMS's cost, $590).

15 Walgreen paid $3,000 of the invoice amount owed to BMS for the February 6 purchase, less the discount. This payment included none of the freight charge.

27 Walgreen paid the remaining amount owed to BMS for the February 6 purchase.

Required

Journalize these transactions, first on the books of Walgreen and second on the books of Bristol-Myers Squibb.

P5-3B Belmont Software engaged in the following transactions during May:

Journalizing purchase and sale transactions
(Obj. 2)

May 3 Purchased office supplies for cash, $300.

7 Purchased inventory on credit terms of 3/10 net eom, $2,000.

8 Returned half the inventory purchased on May 7. It was not the inventory ordered.

10 Sold goods for cash, $450 (cost, $250).

13 Sold inventory on credit terms of 2/15 n/45, $3,900 (cost, $1,800).

16 Paid the amount owed on account from the purchase of May 7, less the return and the discount.

17 Received defective inventory as a sales return from May 13 sale, $900. Belmont's cost of the inventory received was $600.

18 Purchased inventory of $5,000 on account. Payment terms were 2/10 net 30.

26 Borrowed $4,900 from the bank to take advantage of the discount offered on the May 18 purchase. Signed a note payable to the bank for this amount.

28 Received cash in full settlement of the account from the customer who purchased inventory on May 13, less the return and the discount.

29 Purchased inventory for cash, $2,000, plus freight charges of $160.

Required

1. Journalize the preceding transactions on the books of Belmont Software.
2. The note payable signed on May 26 requires Belmont to pay $30 interest expense. Was the decision to borrow funds in order to take advantage of the cash discount wise or unwise? Support your answer by comparing the discount to the interest paid.

Computing net sales, gross profit, and net income
(Obj. 3)

P5-4B The accounting records of Copeland Appliance list the following at November 30, 20X7:

Accounts receivable	$ 18,000
Selling expenses	28,800
Furniture	37,200
Sales returns and allowances	3,200
Salary payable	300
Jim Copeland, capital	52,800
Sales revenue	199,600
Accounts payable	13,200
Inventory: November 30, 20X6	41,700
November 30, 20X7	41,500
Cash	29,000
Notes payable	21,600
Accumulated depreciation—furniture	13,600
Cost of goods sold	132,000
Sales discounts	2,100
General expenses	9,300

Required

1. Prepare a multi-step income statement to show the computation of Copeland's net sales, gross profit, and net income for the month ended November 30, 20X7.
2. Jim Copeland, owner of the company, strives to earn gross profit of $60,000 and net income of $20,000 each month. Did he achieve these goals? Write a sentence to explain.

Preparing a merchandiser's work sheet
(Obj. 4)

Student Resource CD
GL, PT, QB

P5-5B China Palace Restaurant's trial balance pertains to December 31, 20X9.

China Palace Restaurant
Trial Balance
December 31, 20X9

Cash	$ 1,270	
Accounts receivable	4,430	
Inventory	73,900	
Prepaid rent	4,400	
Fixtures	22,100	
Accumulated depreciation		$ 8,380
Accounts payable		6,290
Salary payable		
Interest payable		
Note payable, long-term		18,000
Jacob Xiang, capital		55,920
Jacob Xiang, withdrawals	39,550	
Sales revenue		170,150
Cost of goods sold	67,870	
Salary expense	24,700	
Rent expense	7,700	
Advertising expense	4,510	

(continued)

Utilities expense	3,880	
Depreciation expense		
Insurance expense	2,770	
Interest expense	1,660	
Total	$258,740	$258,740

Adjustment data at December 31, 20X9:

a. Total rent expense for the year, $10,200.
b. Store fixtures have an estimated useful life of 10 years and are expected to be worthless when they are retired from service.
c. Accrued salaries at December 31, $900.
d. Accrued interest expense at December 31, $360.
e. Inventory on hand at December 31, $71,000.

Required

Complete China Palace's accounting work sheet for the year ended December 31, 20X9. Key adjusting entries by letter.

Journalizing the adjusting and closing entries of a merchandising business **(Obj. 4)**

P5-6B Refer to the data in problem 5-5B.

1. Journalize the adjusting and closing entries.
2. Determine the December 31, 20X9, balance of Jacob Xiang, Capital.

Preparing a multi-step income statement and a classified balance sheet **(Obj. 3, 5)**

P5-7B →*Link Back to Chapter 4 (Classified Balance Sheet).* Selected accounts of Nature's Best Organic Products are listed along with their balances before closing at May 31, 20X9.

Accounts Payable	$ 16,900	Interest revenue	$ 400
Accounts receivable	33,700	Inventory	45,500
Accumulated depreciation—equipment	38,000	Note payable, long-term	45,000
		Salary payable	2,800
P. Debruge, capital, April 30, 20X9	73,900	Sales discounts	10,400
P. Debruge, withdrawals	9,000	Sales returns and allowances	18,000
Cash	7,800	Sales revenue	701,000
Cost of goods sold	362,000	Selling expenses	137,900
Equipment	146,000	Supplies	5,900
General expenses	116,700	Unearned sales revenue	13,800
Interest payable	1,100		

Required

1. Prepare the Nature's Best *multi-step* income statement for the month ended May 31, 20X9.
2. Prepare the Nature's Best classified balance sheet in *report format* at May 31, 20X9. Show your computation of the May 31 balance of P. Debruge, Capital.

Preparing a single-step income statement and a classified balance sheet **(Obj. 3, 5)**

P5-8B →*Link Back to Chapter 4 (Classified Balance Sheet).*

Required

1. Use the data of Problem 5-7B to prepare a *single-step* income statement for the month ended May 31, 20X9.
2. Prepare the Nature's Best classified balance sheet in *report format* at May 31, 20X9. Show your computation of the May 31 balance of P. Debruge, Capital.

Using trial balance and adjustment data to prepare financial statements and evaluate the business; multi-step income statement **(Obj. 4, 5, 6)**

P5-9B The trial balance and adjustments data of Mozart Music Company include the following accounts and balances at November 30, 20X4:

	Trial Balance		Adjustments	
Account Title	Debit	Credit	Debit	Credit
Cash	24,000			
Accounts receivable	14,500		(a) 4,000	
Inventory	36,330		(b) 1,010	
Supplies	2,800			(c) 2,400
Furniture	39,600			
Accumulated depreciation		6,300		(d) 2,450
Accounts payable		12,600		(f) 1,000
Salary payable				
Unearned sales revenue		13,570	(e) 6,700	
Note payable, long-term		15,000		
W. Mozart, capital		60,310		
W. Mozart, drawing	42,000			
Sales revenue		174,000		(a) 4,000 (e) 6,700
Sales returns	7,700			
Cost of goods sold	72,170			(b) 1,010
Selling expense	28,080		(f) 1,000	
General expense	13,100		(c) 2,400 (d) 2,450	
Interest expense	1,500			
Total	281,780	281,780	17,560	17,560

Required

1. Without entering the preceding data on a formal work sheet, prepare the company's multi-step income statement for the year ended November 30, 20X4.
2. Compute the gross profit percentage and the rate of inventory turnover for 20X4. Inventory on hand one year ago, at November 30, 20X3, was $32,650. For 20X3, Mozart's gross profit percentage was 55%, and inventory turnover was 1.91 times during the year. Does the two-year trend in these ratios suggest improvement or deterioration in profitability?

APPLY *Your Knowledge*

Decision Cases

Expanding a business **(Obj. 5)**

Case 1. Lauren Sever and Trey Hagins opened Party-Time T-Shirts to sell T-shirts for parties at their college. The company completed the first year of operations, and Sever and Hagins are generally pleased with operating results, as shown by the following income statement:

Party-Time T-Shirts
Income Statement
Year Ended December 31, 20X6

Net sales revenue	$350,000
Cost of goods sold	210,000
Gross margin	140,000
Operating expenses:	
Selling expense	40,000
General expense	25,000
Net income	$ 75,000

Sever and Hagins are considering how to expand the business. They each propose a way to increase profits to $100,000 during 20X7.

a. Sever believes they should advertise more heavily. She believes additional advertising costing $20,000 will increase net sales by 30% and leave general expense unchanged.

b. Hagins proposes selling higher-margin merchandise, such as party dresses. An importer can supply a minimum of 1,000 dresses for $40 each; Party-Time can mark these dresses up 100% and sell them for $80. Hagins realizes they will have to advertise the new merchandise, and this advertising will cost $5,000. Party-Time can expect to sell only 80% of these dresses during the coming year.

Required

Help Sever and Hagins determine which plan to pursue. Prepare a single-step income statement to show the expected net income under each plan.

Using the financial statements to decide on a business expansion
(Obj. 5, 6)

Case 2. → *Link Back to Chapter 4 (Classified Balance Sheet. Current Ratio; Debt Ratio).* Judy Brooks owns Heights Pharmacy, which has prospered during its second year of operation. In deciding whether to open another pharmacy in the area, Brooks has prepared the current financial statements of the business (below and on page 230). Brooks read in an industry trade journal that a successful pharmacy meets all of these criteria:

a. Gross profit percentage is at least 60%.
b. Current ratio is at least 2.0.
c. Debt ratio is no higher than 0.50.
d. Inventory turnover rate is at least 3.40. (Heights Pharmacy's inventory one year ago, at December 31, 20X7 was $16,390.)

Brooks believes the business meets all four criteria. She intends to go ahead with the expansion plan and asks your advice on preparing the pharmacy's financial statements in accordance with generally accepted accounting principles. When you point out that the statements include errors, Brooks assures you that all amounts are correct. But some items are listed in the wrong place.

Required

1. Compute the four ratios based on the Heights Pharmacy financial statements prepared by Brooks. Does the business appear to be ready for expansion?
2. Prepare a correct multi-step income statement and a correct classified balance sheet in report format.
3. On the basis of the corrected financial statements, compute correct measures of the four ratios listed in the trade journal.
4. Make a recommendation about whether Brooks should undertake the expansion.

Heights Pharmacy

Income Statement
Year Ended December 31, 20X8

Sales revenue	$195,000
Gain on sale of land	24,600
Total revenue	219,600
Cost of goods sold	85,200
Gross profit	134,400
Operating expenses:	
Salary expense	30,690
Interest expense	6,000
Depreciation expense	4,900
Utilities expense	3,730
Total operating expense	45,320
Income from operations	89,080

(continued)

Other expense:	
Sales returns	10,700
Net income	$ 78,380

Heights Pharmacy

Statement of Owner's Equity
Year Ended December 31, 20X8

J. Brooks, capital, December 31, 20X7	$ 30,000
Net income	78,380
J. Brooks, capital, December 31, 20X8	$108,380

Heights Pharmacy

Balance Sheet
December 31, 20X8

Assets	
Current:	
Cash	$15,030
Inventory	32,860
Store fixtures	63,000
Total current assets	110,890
Other:	
Withdrawals	65,000
Total assets	$175,890
Liabilities	
Current:	
Accumulated depreciation—store fixtures	$ 6,300
Accounts payable	10,310
Salary payable	900
Total current liabilities	17,510
Other:	
Note payable due in 90 days	50,000
Total liabilities	67,510
Owner's Equity	
J. Brooks, capital	108,380
Total liabilities and owner's equity	$175,890

Ethical Issue

Hunter Glass Company makes all sales under terms of FOB shipping point. The company usually receives orders for sales approximately one week before shipping inventory to customers. For orders received late in December, Donny Hunter, the owner, decides when to ship the goods. If profits are already at an acceptable level, Hunter delays shipment until January. If profits for the current year are lagging behind expectations, Hunter ships the goods during December.

Required

1. Under Hunter's FOB policy, when should the company record a sale?
2. Do you approve or disapprove of Hunter's manner of deciding when to ship goods to customers and record the sales revenue? If you approve, give your reason. If you disapprove, identify a better way to decide when to ship goods. (There is no accounting rule against Hunter's practice.)

Financial Statement Case

Closing entries and the gross profit percentage
(Obj. 4, 6)

This case uses both the income statement (statement of operations) and the balance sheet of Amazon.com in Appendix A. It will help you understand the closing process of a business.

Required

1. Journalize Amazon.com's closing entries for the revenues and expenses of 2002. Show all amounts in thousands as in the Amazon financial statements. You may be unfamiliar with certain revenues and expenses, but treat each item on the income statement as either a revenue or an expense. For example, Net Sales is the first revenue, and Interest Income is also a revenue. The last revenue is Cumulative Effect of Change in Accounting Principle. A loss is like an expense. In your closing entries ignore all subtotals such as Gross Profit, Total Operating Expenses, and Net Loss.
2. Create a T-account for Income Summary, post to that account, and then close Income Summary (debit Retained Earnings and credit Income Summary for $149,132). For this purpose, Retained Earnings is similar to the Owner's Capital account. How much was closed to Retained Earnings? How is this amount labeled on the income statement?

Team Project

With a small team of classmates, visit one or more merchandising businesses in your area. Interview a responsible official of the company to learn about its inventory policies and accounting system. Obtain answers to the following questions, write a report, and be prepared to make a presentation to the class if your instructor so directs:

Required

1. What merchandise inventory does the business sell?
2. From whom does the business buy its inventory? Is the relationship with the supplier new or longstanding?
3. What are the FOB terms on inventory purchases? Who pays the freight, the buyer or the seller? Is freight a significant amount? What percentage of total inventory cost is the freight?
4. What are the credit terms on inventory purchases—2/10 n/30, or other? Does the business pay early to get purchase discounts? If so, why? If not, why not?
5. How does the business actually pay its suppliers? Does it mail a check or pay electronically? What is the actual payment procedure?
6. Which type of inventory accounting system does the business use—perpetual or periodic? Is this system computerized?
7. How often does the business take a physical count of its inventory? When during the year is the count taken? Describe the count procedures followed by the company.
8. Does the owner or manager use the gross profit percentage and the rate of inventory turnover to evaluate the business? If not, show the manager how to use these ratios in decision making.
9. Ask any other questions your group considers appropriate.

APPENDIX to Chapter 5

Accounting for Merchandise in a Periodic Inventory System

After studying this appendix to Chapter 5, you should be able to:

A1. Account for purchase and sale of inventory
A2. Compute cost of goods sold
A3. Adjust and close the accounts of a merchandising business
A4. Prepare a merchandiser's financial statements

Purchasing Merchandise

Some businesses find it uneconomical to invest in a perpetual inventory system. These businesses use a periodic system.

A1 Account for the purchase and sale of inventory

Recording Purchases of Inventory All inventory systems use the Inventory account. But in a periodic system, purchases, purchase discounts, purchase returns and allowances, and transportation costs are recorded in separate accounts. Let's account for **Austin Sound Center's** purchase of the **JVC** goods in Exhibit 5A-1.

Exhibit 5A-1 **An Actual Invoice (Adapted)**

1 JVC®
JVC SOUTHWEST BRANCH
P.O. BOX 100876
HOUSTON, TX 77212

Invoice	
Date	Number
3 5/27/05	410

Shipped To: AUSTIN SOUND CENTER
2 305 WEST MLK BLVD.
AUSTIN, TX 78701

Terms of Sale 4
3% 15, NET 30 DAYS

5

Quantity Ordered	Description	Model No.	Quantity Shipped	Unit Price	Total
7	DVD PLAYER	QLA200	7	$100.00	$700.00
				7 Pd.	06-10-05
			Sub Total		$700.00
			Ship. or Handl. Chg.		–
			Tax (3%)		–
			Total(s)		$700.00 6

Due Date & Due Amount			
06/11/05		06/26/05	
$679 00		$700 00	

8

Explanations:

1 The seller is JVC.

2 The purchaser is Austin Sound Center.

3 The invoice date, needed for determining whether the purchaser gets a discount for prompt payment (see 4).

4 Credit terms of the transaction: If it pays within 15 days of the invoice date, Austin Sound may deduct a 3% discount. Otherwise, the full amount—net—is due in 30 days. (The discussion of discounts starts on page 187.)

5 JVC shipped 7 DVD players to Austin Sound.

6 Total invoice amount is $700.

7 Austin Sound's payment date. How much did Austin pay? (See 8, which follows.)

8 Payment occurred 14 days after the invoice date—within the discount period—so Austin paid $679 ($700 – 3% discount).

The following entries record the purchase and payment on account within the discount period. Assume that Austin Sound received the goods on May 30.

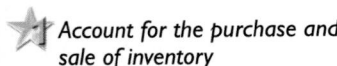

May 30	Purchases	700	
	Accounts Payable		700
	Purchased inventory on account		
June 10	Accounts Payable	700	
	Cash ($700 × 0.97)		679
	Purchase Discounts ($700 × 0.03)		21
	Paid on account.		

Recording Purchase Returns and Allowances Suppose that, prior to payment, Austin Sound returned to JVC goods costing $100 and also received from JVC a purchase allowance of $10. Austin Sound would record these transactions as follows:

June 3	Accounts Payable	100	
	Purchase Returns and Allowances		100
	Returned inventory to seller.		
June 4	Accounts Payable	10	
	Purchase Returns and Allowances		10
	Received a purchase allowance.		

During the period, the business records the cost of all inventory bought in the Purchases account. The balance of Purchases is a *gross* amount because it does not include subtractions for discounts, returns, or allowances. **Net purchases** is the remainder after subtracting the contra accounts from Purchases:

Net Purchases
Purchases less purchase discounts and purchase returns and allowances.

	Purchases (*debit*)
−	Purchase Discounts (*credit*)
−	Purchase Returns and Allowances (*credit*)
=	Net purchases (a *debit* subtotal, not a separate account)

Recording Transportation Costs Under the periodic system, costs to transport purchased inventory from seller to buyer are debited to the Freight In account, as shown for a $60 freight bill:

June 1	Freight In	60	
	Cash		60
	Paid a freight bill.		

Recording the Sale of Inventory

Recording sales is streamlined in the periodic system. With no running record of inventory to maintain, we can record a $3,000 sale as follows:

June 5	Accounts Receivable	3,000	
	Sales Revenue		3,000
	Sale on account.		

There is no accompanying entry to Inventory and Cost of Goods Sold in the periodic system.

Cost of goods sold (also called *cost of sales*) is the largest single expense of most businesses that sell merchandise, such as **Gap Inc.** and **Austin Sound**. It is the cost of the inventory the business has sold to customers. In a periodic system, cost of goods sold must be computed as in Exhibit 5A-2.

2 *Compute cost of goods sold*

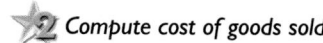

Exhibit 5A-2

Measuring Cost of Goods Sold in the Periodic Inventory System

PANEL A:

Beginning inventory	Purchases of inventory
+ Net purchases ←	− Purchase discounts
+ Freight in	− Purchase returns and allowances
= Cost of goods available for sale	= Net purchases
− Ending inventory	
= Cost of goods sold	

PANEL B:

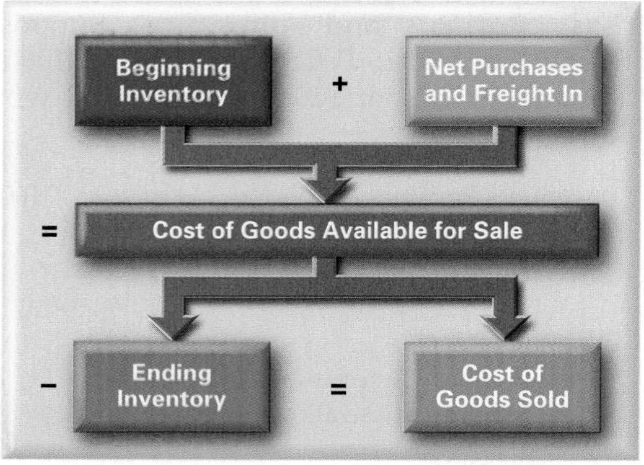

Exhibit 5A-3 summarizes the first half of this appendix by showing Austin Sound's net sales revenue, cost of goods sold, and gross profit on the income statement for the periodic system. (All amounts are assumed.)

Exhibit 5A-3

Partial Income Statement

Austin Sound Center

Income Statement

Year Ended December 31, 20X5

PANEL A—Detailed Gross Profit Section

Sales revenue				$169,300
Less: Sales discounts		$(1,400)		
Sales returns and allowances		(2,000)	(3,400)	
Net sales				$165,900
Cost of goods sold:				
Beginning inventory			$38,600	
Purchases			$91,400	
Less: Purchase discounts	$(3,000)			
Purch. returns & allow.	(1,200)	(4,200)		
Net purchases			87,200	
Freight in				5,200
Cost of goods available for sale			131,000	
Less: Ending inventory			(40,200)	
Cost of goods sold				90,800
Gross profit				$ 75,100

PANEL B—Gross Profit Section (Streamlined in Annual Reports to Outsiders)

Net sales	$165,900
Cost of goods sold	90,800
Gross profit	$ 75,100

Adjusting and Closing the Accounts

Adjust and close the accounts of a merchandising business

A merchandising business adjusts and closes the accounts much as a service entity does. The steps of this end-of-period process are the same: If a work sheet is used, the trial balance is entered and the work sheet is completed to determine net income or net loss. The work sheet provides the data for the adjusting and closing entries and the financial statements.

At the end of the period, before any adjusting or closing entries, the Inventory account still holds the cost of the last period's ending inventory, which becomes the beginning inventory of the current period. It is necessary to remove this beginning balance and replace it with the cost of the inventory on hand at the end of the current period. Various techniques may be used to update the inventory records.

To illustrate a merchandiser's adjusting and closing process under the periodic inventory system, let's use **Austin Sound's** December 31, 20X5, trial balance in Exhibit 5A-4. All the new accounts—Inventory, Freight In, and the contra accounts—are highlighted for emphasis. Additional data item (h) gives the ending inventory figure, $40,200.

Exhibit 5A-4
Trial Balance

Austin Sound Center
Trial Balance
December 31, 20X5

Cash	$ 2,850	
Accounts receivable	4,600	
Note receivable, current	8,000	
Interest receivable		
Inventory	38,600	
Supplies	650	
Prepaid insurance	1,200	
Furniture and fixtures	33,200	
Accumulated depreciation		$ 2,400
Accounts payable		47,000
Unearned sales revenue		2,000
Wages payable		
Interest payable		
Note payable, long-term		12,600
C. Ernest, capital		25,900
C. Ernest, withdrawals	54,100	
Sales revenue		168,000
Sales discounts	1,400	
Sales returns and allowances	2,000	
Interest revenue		600
Purchases	91,400	
Purchase discounts		3,000
Purchase returns and allowances		1,200
Freight in	5,200	
Wage expense	9,800	
Rent expense	8,400	
Depreciation expense		
Insurance expense		
Supplies expense		
Interest expense	1,300	
Total	$262,700	$262,700

Additional Data at December 31, 20X5:

a. Interest revenue earned but not yet collected, $400
b. Supplies on hand, $100
c. Prepaid insurance expired during the year, $1,000
d. Depreciation, $600
e. Unearned sales revenue earned during the year, $1,300
f. Accrued wage expense, $400
g. Accrued interest expense, $200
h. Inventory on hand, $40,200

This work sheet is slightly different from the one introduced in the Chapter 4 acetates. This work sheet contains four pairs of columns, not five.

Preparing and Using the Work Sheet in a Periodic System The Exhibit 5A-5 work sheet is similar to the work sheets we have seen so far, with a few differences. Most accounting systems combine trial balance amounts with the adjustments and extend the adjusted balances directly to the income statement and balance sheet columns. Therefore, the adjusted trial balance columns are omitted.

Account Title Columns. The Trial Balance lists the unadjusted amount for each account. A few accounts without balances are affected by the adjusting process. Examples include Interest Receivable, Wages Payable, and Depreciation Expense. Accounts are listed in the order they appear in the ledger.

Trial Balance Columns. Examine the Inventory account in the Trial Balance. The $38,600 amount is the cost of the beginning inventory. The work sheet is designed to replace this outdated amount with the new ending balance, which in our example is $40,200 [additional data item (h) for Exhibit 5A-4].

Adjustments Columns. The adjustments are similar to those discussed in Chapters 3 and 4. The debit amount of each entry should equal the credit amount, and total debits should equal total credits.

Income Statement Columns. The Income Statement columns in Exhibit 5A-5 show adjusted amounts for the revenues and the expenses. Sales Revenue, for example, has an adjusted balance of $169,300.

The income statement totals indicate whether the business had a net income or a net loss.

- Net income: Total credits > Total debits
- Net loss: Total debits > Total credits

Austin Sound's total credits of $214,700 exceed the total debits of $160,850, so the company earned a net income.

You may be wondering why the two inventory amounts appear in the Income Statement columns. The reason is that both beginning inventory and ending inventory enter the computation of cost of goods sold. *Placement of beginning inventory ($38,600) in the work sheet's Income Statement Debit column has the effect of adding beginning inventory to compute cost of goods sold. Placing ending inventory ($40,200) in the Credit column decreases cost of goods sold.*

Purchases and Freight In are in the Debit column because they are added to compute cost of goods sold. Purchase Discounts and Purchase Returns and Allowances are credits because they are subtracted in computing cost of goods sold—$90,800 on the income statement in Exhibit 5A-3.

Balance Sheet Columns. The only new item in the Balance Sheet columns is Inventory. The $40,200 balance is determined by the physical count at the end of the period.

Exhibit 5A-5 Accounting Work Sheet

Austin Sound Center

Accounting Work Sheet (Periodic Inventory System)
Year Ended December 31, 20X5

	Trial Balance		Adjustments		Income Statement		Balance Sheet	
Account Title	**Debit**	**Credit**	**Debit**	**Credit**	**Debit**	**Credit**	**Debit**	**Credit**
Cash	2,850						2,850	
Accounts receivable	4,600						4,600	
Note receivable, current	8,000						8,000	
Interest receivable			(a) 400				400	
Inventory	38,600				38,600	40,200	40,200	
Supplies	650			(b) 550			100	
Prepaid insurance	1,200			(c) 1,000			200	
Furniture and fixtures	33,200						33,200	
Accumulated depreciation		2,400		(d) 600				3,000
Accounts payable		47,000						47,000
Unearned sales revenue		2,000	(e) 1,300					700
Wages payable				(f) 400				400
Interest payable				(g) 200				200
Note payable, long-term		12,600						12,600
C. Ernest, capital		25,900						25,900
C. Ernest, withdrawals	54,100						54,100	
Sales revenue		168,000		(e) 1,300		169,300		
Sales discounts	1,400				1,400			
Sales returns and allowances	2,000				2,000			
Interest revenue		600		(a) 400		1,000		
Purchases	91,400				91,400			
Purchase discounts		3,000				3,000		
Purchase returns and allowances		1,200				1,200		
Freight in	5,200				5,200			
Wage expense	9,800		(f) 400		10,200			
Rent expense	8,400				8,400			
Depreciation expense			(d) 600		600			
Insurance expense			(c) 1,000		1,000			
Supplies expense			(b) 550		550			
Interest expense	1,300		(g) 200		1,500			
	262,700	262,700	4,450	4,450	160,850	214,700	143,650	89,800
Net income					53,850			53,850
					214,700	214,700	143,650	143,650

Journalizing Adjusting and Closing Entries Exhibit 5A-6 presents Austin Sound's adjusting entries. These entries follow the same pattern illustrated in Chapter 4 for a service entity and can be taken directly from the work sheet.

The exhibit also gives Austin Sound's closing entries. The first closing entry closes the revenue accounts. Closing entries 2 and 3 are new. Entry 2 closes the beginning Inventory balance ($38,600), along with Purchases and Freight In, into the Cost of Goods Sold account. Entry 3 sets up the ending balance of Inventory ($40,200) with a debit. Entry 3 also closes the Purchases contra accounts to Cost of Goods Sold.[1] Now Inventory and Cost of Goods Sold have their correct ending balances shown at the top of the next page.

Exhibit 5A-6

Adjusting and Closing Entries

Journal

Adjusting entries

a.	Dec. 31	Interest Receivable	400	
		Interest Revenue		400
b.	31	Supplies Expense ($650 – $100)	550	
		Supplies		550
c.	31	Insurance Expense	1,000	
		Prepaid Insurance		1,000
d.	31	Depreciation Expense	600	
		Accumulated Depreciation		600
e.	31	Unearned Sales Revenue	1,300	
		Sales Revenue		1,300
f.	31	Wage Expense	400	
		Wages Payable		400
g.	31	Interest Expense	200	
		Interest Payable		200

Closing Entries

1.	Dec. 31	Sales Revenue	169,300	
		Interest Revenue	1,000	
		Income Summary		170,300
2.	31	Cost of Goods Sold	135,200	
		Inventory (beginning balance)		38,600
		Purchases		91,400
		Freight In		5,200
3.	31	Inventory (ending balance)	40,200	
		Purchase Discounts	3,000	
		Purchase Returns and Allowances	1,200	
		Cost of Goods Sold		44,400
4.	31	Income Summary	116,450	
		Sales Discounts		1,400
		Sales Returns and Allowances		2,000
		Cost of Goods Sold ($135,200 – $44,400)		90,800
		Wage Expense		10,200
		Rent Expense		8,400
		Depreciation Expense		600
		Insurance Expense		1,000
		Supplies Expense		550
		Interest Expense		1,500
5.	31	Income Summary ($170,300 – $116,450)	53,850	
		C. Ernest, Capital		53,850
6.	31	C. Ernest, Capital	54,100	
		C. Ernest, Withdrawals		54,100

[1]Some accountants make the inventory entries as adjustments rather than as part of the closing process. The adjusting-entry approach adds these adjustments (shifted out of the closing entries):

Adjusting Entries

Dec. 31	Cost of Goods Sold	38,600	
	Inventory (beginning balance)		38,600
31	Inventory (ending balance)	40,200	
	Cost of Goods Sold		40,200

When these entries are posted, the Inventory account will look exactly as shown at the top of page 239, except that the journal references will be "Adj." instead of "Clo." The financial statements are unaffected by the approach used for these entries.

Inventory

Jan. 1	Bal.	38,600	Dec. 31	Clo.	38,600
Dec. 31	Clo.	40,200			

Cost of Goods Sold

Beg. Inventory	38,600	Pur. discounts	3,000
Purchases	91,400	Pur. returns and allowances	1,200
Freight in	5,200	End. inventory	40,200
Bal.	90,800		

Closing entry 4 then closes the Sales contra accounts and Cost of Goods Sold along with the other expense accounts into Income Summary. Closing entries 5 and 6 complete the closing process. All data for the closing entries are taken from the income statement columns of the work sheet.

Study Exhibits 5A-5 and 5A-6 carefully because they illustrate the entire end-of-period process that leads to the financial statements. As you progress through this book, you may want to refer to these exhibits to refresh your understanding of the adjusting and closing process for a merchandising business.

4 Prepare a merchandiser's financial statements

Preparing a Merchandiser's Financial Statements Exhibit 5A-7 presents Austin Sound's financial statements. The *income statement* through gross profit repeats Exhibit 5A-3. This information is followed by the *operating expenses,*

Exhibit 5A-7 Financial Statements of Austin Sound Center

Austin Sound Center

Income Statement
Year Ended December 31, 20X5

Sales revenue			$169,300	
Less: Sales discounts		$(1,400)		
Sales returns and allowances		(2,000)	(3,400)	
Net sales revenue				$165,900
Cost of goods sold:				
Beginning inventory			$ 38,600	
Purchases		$91,400		
Less: Purchase discounts	$(3,000)			
Purchase returns and allowances	(1,200)	(4,200)		
Net purchases			87,200	
Freight in			5,200	
Cost of goods available for sale			131,000	
Less: Ending inventory			(40,200)	
Cost of goods sold				90,800
Gross profit				75,100
Operating expenses:				
Wage expense			10,200	
Rent expense			8,400	
Insurance expense			1,000	
Depreciation expense			600	
Supplies expense			550	20,750
Income from operations				54,350
Other revenue and (expense):				
Interest revenue			1,000	
Interest expense			(1,500)	(500)
Net income				$ 53,850

(continued)

Austin Sound Center

Statement of Owner's Equity
Year Ended December 31, 20X5

C. Ernest, capital, December 31, 20X4	$25,900
Add: Net income	53,850
	79,750
Less: Withdrawals	(54,100)
C. Ernest, capital, December 31, 20X5	$25,650

Austin Sound Center

Balance Sheet
December 31, 20X5

Assets			Liabilities	
Current:			Current:	
Cash		$ 2,850	Accounts payable	$47,000
Accounts receivable		4,600	Unearned sales revenue	700
Note receivable		8,000	Wages payable	400
Interest receivable		400	Interest payable	200
Inventory		40,200	Total current liabilities	48,300
Prepaid insurance		200	Long-term:	
Supplies		100	Note payable	12,600
Total current assets		56,350	Total liabilities	60,900
Plant:				
Furniture and fixtures	$33,200		**Owner's Equity**	
Less: Accumulated depreciation	(3,000)	30,200	C. Ernest, capital	25,650
Total assets		$86,550	Total liabilities and owner's equity	$86,550

expenses other than cost of goods sold that occur in the entity's major line of business. Many companies report their operating expenses in two categories.

- ***Selling expenses*** relate to marketing the company's products—sales salaries, sales commissions, advertising, depreciation, rent, utilities, delivery expense, and so on.
- ***General expenses*** include office expenses, such as the salaries of office employees, and depreciation, rent, and other expenses on the home office building.

Gross profit minus operating expenses and plus any other operating revenues equals *operating income,* or *income from operations*. The last section of Austin Sound's income statement is *other revenue and expense*. This category reports revenues and expenses that are outside the company's main line of business.

Appendix Assignments

Exercises

Journalizing purchase and sale transactions
(Obj. A1)

E5A-1 Journalize, without explanations, the following transactions of Hunter Gift Shop during June. Use the periodic system.

June 3	Purchased $700 of inventory under terms of 2/10 n/eom (end of month) and FOB shipping point.
7	Returned $300 of defective merchandise purchased on June 3.
9	Paid freight bill of $30 on June 3 purchase.
10	Sold inventory for $3,200. Payment terms were 2/15 n/30.
12	Paid amount owed on credit purchase of June 3, less the discount and the return.
16	Granted a sales allowance of $800 on the June 10 sale.
23	Received cash from June 10 customer in full settlement of her debt, less the allowance and the discount.

Journalizing transactions from a purchase invoice
(Obj. A1)

E5A-2 As the proprietor of Davis Tire Company, you receive the following invoice from a supplier:

WHOLESALE DISTRIBUTORS, INC.
2600 Commonwealth Avenue
Boston, Massachusetts 02215

Invoice date: May 14, 20X6 **Payment terms:** 3/10 n/30

Sold to: Davis Tire Co.
4219 Crestwood Parkway
Lexington, Mass. 02173

Description	Quantity Shipped	Price	Amount
P135–X4 Radials....................................	4	$37.14	$ 148.56
L912 Belted-bias	8	41.32	330.56
R39 Truck tires..	10	60.02	600.20
Total..			$1,079.32

Due date:	**Amount:**
May 24, 20X6	$1,046.94
May 25 through June 13, 20X6	$1,079.32

Required

1. Davis received the invoice on May 15. Record the May 15 purchase on account. Carry amounts to the nearest cent throughout.
2. The R39 truck tires were ordered by mistake and were therefore returned to Wholesale Distributors. Journalize the return on May 19.
3. Record the May 22 payment of the amount owed.

Journalizing purchase transactions
(Obj. A1)

E5A-3 On April 30, Stanley & Weaver Jewelers purchased inventory of $8,000 on account from Intergem Jewels, a jewelry importer. Terms were 3/15 net 45. On receiving the goods, Stanley & Weaver checked the order and found $1,000 of unsuitable merchandise. Therefore, Stanley & Weaver returned $1,000 of merchandise to Intergem on May 4.

To pay the remaining amount owed, Stanley & Weaver borrowed the net amount of the invoice from the bank. On May 14, Stanley & Weaver signed a short-term note payable to the bank and immediately paid the borrowed funds to Intergem. On June 14, Stanley & Weaver paid the bank the net amount of the invoice, which Stanley & Weaver had borrowed, plus 1% monthly interest (round to the nearest dollar).

Required

Record the indicated transactions in the journal of Stanley & Weaver Jewelers. Use the periodic inventory system. Explanations are not required.

Journalizing sales transactions
(Obj. A1)

E5A-4 Refer to the business situation in Exercise 5A-3. Journalize the transactions of Intergem Jewels. Explanations are not required.

Problems

Accounting for the purchase and sale of inventory
(Obj. A1)

P5A-1 Assume that the following transactions occurred between Providence Medical Supply and a **Walgreen's** drug store during November of the current year:

Nov. 6	Providence Medical Supply sold $6,200 worth of merchandise to Walgreen's on terms of 2/10 n/30, FOB shipping point. Walgreen's also paid freight-in of $300.
10	Walgreen's returned $900 of the merchandise on November 6.
15	Walgreen's paid $3,000 of the invoice amount owed to Providence for the November 6 purchase, less the discount.
27	Walgreen's paid the remaining amount owed to Providence for the November 6 purchase.

Required

Journalize these transactions, first on the books of the Walgreen's drug store and second on the books of Providence Medical Supply. Use the periodic inventory system.

P5A-2 Preakness Wholesale Grocery engaged in the following transactions during May of the current year:

May 3	Purchased office supplies for cash, $300.
7	Purchased inventory on credit terms of 3/10 net 30, $2,000.
8	Returned half the inventory purchased on May 7. It was not the inventory ordered.
10	Sold goods for cash, $450.
13	Sold inventory on credit terms of 2/15 n/45, $3,900.
16	Paid the amount owed on account from the purchase of May 7, less the discount and the return.
17	Received defective inventory returned from the May 13 sale, $900.
18	Purchased inventory of $4,000 on account. Payment terms were 2/10 net 30.
26	Paid supplier for goods purchased on May 18, less the discount.
28	Received cash in full settlement of the account from the customer who purchased inventory on May 13, less the discount and the return.

Required

Journalize the preceding transactions. Use the periodic inventory system. Explanations are not required.

P5A-3 The year-end trial balance of Latham Sales Company pertains to March 31, 20X4.

Preparing a merchandiser's accounting work sheet, financial statements, and adjusting and closing entries **(Obj. A2, A3, A4)**

Latham Sales Company

Trial Balance
March 31, 20X4

Cash	$ 7,880	
Note receivable, current	12,400	
Interest receivable		
Inventory	130,050	
Prepaid insurance	3,600	
Notes receivable, long-term	62,000	
Furniture	6,000	
Accumulated depreciation		$ 4,000
Accounts payable		12,220
Sales commission payable		
Salary payable		
Unearned sales revenue		9,610
Ben Latham, capital		172,780
Ben Latham, withdrawals	66,040	
Sales revenue		440,000
Sales discounts	4,800	
Sales returns and allowances	11,300	
Interest revenue		8,600
Purchases	233,000	
Purchase discounts		3,100
Purchase returns and allowances		7,600
Freight in	10,000	
Sales commission expense	78,300	
Salary expense	24,700	
Rent expense	6,000	
Utilities expense	1,840	
Depreciation expense		
Insurance expense		
Total	$657,910	$657,910

Additional Data at March 31, 20X4:

a. Accrued interest revenue, $1,030.
b. Insurance expense for the year, $3,000.
c. Furniture has an estimated useful life of six years. Its value is expected to be zero when it is retired from service.
d. Unearned sales revenue still unearned, $7,400.
e. Accrued salary expense, $1,200.
f. Accrued sales commission expense, $1,700.
g. Inventory on hand, $133,200.

Required

1. Enter the trial balance on an accounting work sheet, and complete the work sheet for the year ended March 31, 20X4.
2. Journalize the adjusting and closing entries at March 31, 20X4.

3. Post to the Ben Latham, Capital account and to the Income Summary account as an accuracy check on the adjusting and closing process.
4. Prepare the company's multi-step income statement and statement of owner's equity for the year ended March 31, 20X4. Also prepare its classified balance sheet at that date. Long-term notes receivable should be reported on the balance sheet between current assets and plant assets in a separate section labeled Investments.

Comprehensive Problem for Chapters 1–5

Completing a Merchandiser's Accounting Cycle

The end-of-month trial balance of St. James Technology at January 31 of the current year follows. Additional data at January 31, 20XX:

a. Supplies consumed during the month, $1,500. Half is selling expense, and the other half is general expense.
b. Depreciation for the month: building, $4,000; fixtures, $4,800. One-fourth of depreciation is selling expense, and three-fourths is general expense.
c. Unearned sales revenue still unearned, $1,200.
d. Accrued salaries, a general expense, $1,150.
e. Accrued interest expense, $780.
f. Inventory on hand, $63,720. St. James uses the perpetual inventory system.

1. Using four-column accounts, open the accounts listed on the trial balance, inserting their unadjusted balances. Date the balances of the following accounts January 1: Supplies; Building; Accumulated Depreciation—Building; Fixtures; Accumulated Depreciation—Fixtures; Unearned Sales Revenue; and Dirk St. James, Capital. Date the balance of Dirk St. James, Withdrawals, January 31. Also open the Income Summary, account number 33.
2. Enter the trial balance on an accounting work sheet, and complete the work sheet for the month ended January 31 of the current year. St. James Technology groups all operating expenses under two accounts, Selling Expense and General Expense. Leave two blank lines under Selling Expense and three blank lines under General Expense.
3. Prepare the company's multi-step income statement and statement of owner's equity for the month ended January 31 of the current year. Also prepare the balance sheet at that date in report form.

Journalizing purchase and sales transactions
(Obj. A1)

St. James Technology
Trial Balance
January 31, 20XX

Account Number	Account	Balance Debit	Balance Credit
11	Cash	$ 16,430	
12	Accounts receivable	19,090	
13	Inventory	65,400	
14	Supplies	2,700	
15	Building	188,170	
16	Accumulated depreciation—building		$ 36,000
17	Fixtures	45,600	
18	Accumulated depreciation—fixtures		5,800
21	Accounts payable		28,300
22	Salary payable		
23	Interest payable		
24	Unearned sales revenue		6,560
25	Note payable, long-term		87,000
31	Dirk St. James, capital		144,980

(continued)

32	Dirk St. James, withdrawals	9,200	
41	Sales revenue		187,970
42	Sales discounts	7,300	
43	Sales returns and allowances	8,140	
51	Cost of goods sold	103,000	
54	Selling expense	21,520	
55	General expense	10,060	
56	Interest expense		
	Total	$496,610	$496,610

4. Journalize the adjusting and closing entries at January 31, using page 3 of the journal.
5. Post the adjusting and closing entries, using dates and posting references.

CHAPTER 6

Merchandise Inventory

A+ TIPS CHECK YOUR RESOURCES

- Visit the www.prenhall.com/horngren **Web site** for self-study quizzes, video clips, and other resources
- Try the **Quick Check** exercise at the end of the chapter to test your knowledge
- Learn the **key terms**
- Do the **Starter** exercises keyed in the margins
- Work the **mid-** and **end-of-chapter summary problems**
- Use the **Concept Links** to review material in other chapters
- Search the **CD** for review materials by chapter or by key word
- Watch the **tutorial videos** to review key concepts
- Watch the **On Location Teva Sports Sandals** video to review inventory and e-commerce issues

LEARNING OBJECTIVES

1. Compute perpetual inventory amounts under FIFO, LIFO, and average cost
2. Record perpetual inventory transactions
3. Compare the effects of FIFO, LIFO, and average cost
4. Compute periodic inventory amounts under FIFO, LIFO, and average cost
5. Apply the lower-of-cost-or-market rule to inventory
6. Measure the effects of inventory errors
7. Estimate ending inventory by the gross profit method

Columbia Sportswear Company

Columbia Sportswear Company® serves as the official outerwear supplier to the annual Kodak Albuquerque International Balloon Fiesta® in Albuquerque, New Mexico. Ballooning's largest and most spectacular event now hosts close to a thousand balloons and more than a million spectators. How do pilots and passengers stay warm at the higher altitudes?

For the eighth consecutive year, Columbia is outfitting pilots, sponsor guests, media personalities, and event staff with a special parka. "Columbia is very proud of its relationship with the . . .

celebration . . . ," said Chrisanthi Hatzantonis, Columbia Sportswear promotions manager. "This festival is . . . one of the most . . . visually stunning events I've attended."

Source: "Columbia Sportswear Takes Flight at World-Renowned Albuquerque Balloon Festival," press release, October 2, 2002. ■

Sitemap

- Inventory Costing Methods
- Inventory Costing: Perpetual System
- Inventory Costing: Periodic System
- Accounting Principles and Inventories
- Other Inventory Issues
- Appendix: Perpetual vs. Periodic

Columbia makes and markets over 50 different parkas and jackets for men, women, and children. Its line also includes specialized sports products like camouflaged hunting jackets, so how Columbia deals with inventory is vital to its success.

This chapter shows how Columbia Sportswear and other merchandisers apply various methods to account for their inventory. They can use the perpetual system, which we covered in Chapter 5, or the periodic system, which we introduce in this chapter.

But first let's review how merchandise inventory affects a company. Exhibit 6-1 gives the merchandising section of Columbia Sportswear's balance sheet and income statement. Inventories, cost of goods sold, and gross profit are highlighted. These amounts (X, Y, and Z) are left blank to indicate that throughout the chapter we will be computing them using various accounting methods.

Exhibit 6-1

Columbia Sportswear: Merchandising Sections of the Financial Statements

Columbia Sportswear Company
Balance Sheet (partial; adapted)
December 31, 20X1

	Millions
Assets	
Current assets:	
Cash	$ 79
Accounts receivable	155
Inventories	X
Prepaid expenses	18

Columbia Sportswear Company
Income Statement (partial; adapted)
Year Ended December 31, 20X1

	Millions
Net sales	$ 780
Cost of goods sold	Y
Gross profit	Z

The remainder of the chapter explores the various ways a company can determine the amounts of

- Ending inventory (X) in Exhibit 6-1
- Cost of goods sold (Y) and gross profit (Z) in Exhibit 6-1

Inventory Costing Methods

As we saw in Chapter 5,

Ending inventory	=	**Number of units on hand**	×	**Unit cost**
Cost of goods sold	=	**Number of units sold**	×	**Unit cost**

Companies determine the number of units from perpetual inventory records backed up by a physical count.

Unit cost = Purchase price – Purchase discounts

Exhibit 6-2 gives assumed inventory data for a line of Columbia Sportswear ski parkas.

Student Resource CD
average cost method, inventory costing, FIFO, LIFO

Exhibit 6-2
Perpetual Inventory Record—Quantities Only—Columbia Sportswear

Item: Sunrise Ski Parkas			
Date	**Quantity Purchased**	**Quantity Sold**	**Quantity on Hand**
Nov. 1			1
5	6		7
15		4	3
26	7		10
30		8	2
Totals	13	12	2

In this illustration, Columbia began November with 1 parka on hand. After buying and selling, Columbia had 2 parkas at the end of the month.

Assume that Columbia Sportswear's cost of each ski parka is $40. In this case,

Ending inventory	=	**Number of units on hand (Exhibit 6-2)**		**Unit Cost**		
		2	×	$40	=	$80
Cost of goods sold	=	**Number of units sold (Exhibit 6-2)**		**Unit cost**		
		12	×	$40	=	$480

What would Columbia's ending inventory and cost of goods sold be if the cost of ski parkas increased from $40 to $50 during the period? Companies face price increases during periods of inflation. To measure inventory amounts during such periods, the accounting profession has developed several costing methods.

Measuring the cost of inventory is easy when prices are constant. But the unit cost often changes. A ski parka that cost Columbia $40 in January may cost $45 or $50 later in the year. Suppose Columbia sells 10,000 ski parkas in November. How many of the parkas cost $40? How many cost $45 or $50? To compute ending inventory and cost of goods sold, Columbia must assign a cost to each item. The four costing methods GAAP allows are

1. Specific unit cost
2. Average cost
3. First-in, first-out (FIFO) cost
4. Last-in, first-out (LIFO) cost

A company can use any of these methods to account for its inventory.

Specific-Unit-Cost Method Inventory cost method based on the specific cost of particular units of inventory. Also called the **specific-identification method**.

The **specific-unit-cost** method is also called the **specific-identification method**. This method uses the specific cost of each unit of inventory. Some businesses deal in items that differ from unit to unit, such as automobiles, jewels, and real estate. For instance, a Chevrolet dealer may have two vehicles—a "stripped-down" model that cost $16,000 and a "loaded" model that cost $19,000. If the dealer sells the loaded model, cost of goods sold is $19,000, the cost of the specific unit. Suppose the stripped-down auto is the only unit left in inventory at the end of the period; ending inventory is $16,000, the dealer's cost of that particular car.

Amazon.com uses the specific-unit-cost method to account for its inventory. But very few other companies use this method, so we shift to the more popular inventory costing methods.

The other three methods are very different. First-in, first-out (FIFO) and last-in, first-out (LIFO) are exact opposites, and the average-cost method falls between the extremes of FIFO and LIFO. Exhibit 6-3 illustrates how each method works.

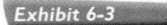

Exhibit 6-3

Cost Flows for the Three Most Popular Inventory Methods

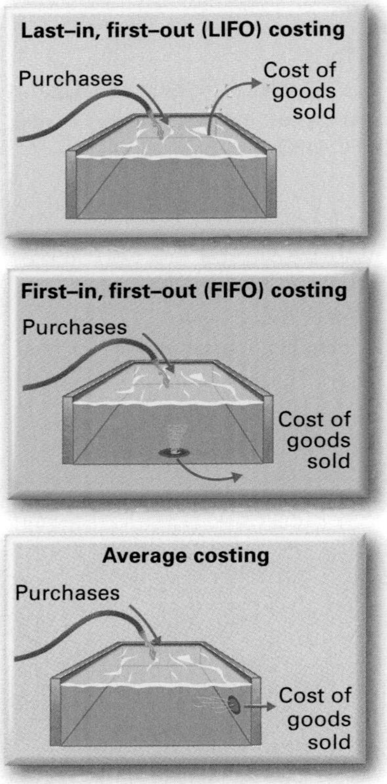

- Under the FIFO method, the cost of goods sold is based on the oldest purchases. This is illustrated by the Cost of goods sold coming from the *bottom* of the container.
- Under the LIFO method, the cost of goods sold is based on the most recent purchases. This is illustrated by the Cost of goods sold coming from the *top* of the container.
- Under the average method, the cost of goods sold is based on an average cost for the period. This is illustrated by the Cost of goods sold coming from the *middle* of the container.

Now let's see how to compute inventory amounts under the FIFO, LIFO, and average costing methods. The amounts we compute will complete Columbia's financial statements in Exhibit 6-1. We use the following transaction data for all the illustrations:

Columbia Sportswear Sunrise Ski Parka		**Number of Units**	**Unit Cost**
Nov. 1	Beginning inventory	1	$40
5	Purchase	6	45
15	Sale	4	
26	Purchase	7	50
30	Sale	8	

We begin with inventory costing in a perpetual system.

□ Inventory Costing Methods
■ **Inventory Costing: Perpetual System**
□ Inventory Costing: Periodic System
□ Accounting Principles and Inventories
□ Other Inventory Issues
□ Appendix: Perpetual vs. Periodic

Inventory Costing in a Perpetual System

As we shall see, the various inventory costing methods produce different amounts for ending inventory and cost of goods sold. Let's begin with the FIFO method.

Student Resource CD
average-cost method, cost of goods sold, FIFO, inventory turnover, LIFO, perpetual method, sales revenue

Compute perpetual inventory amounts under FIFO, LIFO, and average cost

First-In, First-Out (FIFO) Method

Columbia Sportswear actually uses the **FIFO method** to account for its inventory. FIFO costing is consistent with the physical movement of inventory for most companies. Under FIFO, the first costs incurred by Columbia each period are the first costs to be assigned to cost of goods sold. FIFO leaves in ending inventory the last—the most recent—costs incurred during the period. This is illustrated in the FIFO perpetual inventory record in Exhibit 6-4.

Exhibit 6-4

Perpetual Inventory Record: FIFO and Journal Entries for the Related Transactions

Sunrise Ski Parkas

	Purchases			Cost of Goods Sold			Inventory on Hand		
Date	Quantity	Unit Cost	Total Cost	Quantity	Unit Cost	Total Cost	Quantity	Unit Cost	Total Cost
Nov. 1							1	$40	$ 40
5	6	$45	$270				1	40	40
							6	45	270
15				1	$40	$ 40			
				3	45	135	3	45	135
26	7	50	350				3	45	135
							7	50	350
30				3	45	135			
				5	50	250	2	50	100
30	13		$620	12		$560	2		$100

Journal Entries: **(All purchases and sales on account. The sale price of a ski parka is $80 per unit.)**

Nov. 5	Inventory	270	
	Accounts Payable		270
15	Accounts Receivable (4 × $80)	320	
	Sales Revenue		320
15	Cost of Goods Sold ($40 + $135)	175	
	Inventory		175
26	Inventory	350	
	Accounts Payable		350
30	Accounts Receivable (8 × $80)	640	
	Sales Revenue		640
30	Cost of Goods Sold ($135 + $250)	385	
	Inventory		385

2 Record perpetual inventory transactions

Columbia began November with one ski parka that cost $40. After the November 5 purchase, the inventory on hand consists of 7 units (1 @ $40 plus 6 @ $45). On November 15, Columbia sold 4 units. Under FIFO, the first unit sold is costed at the oldest cost ($40 per unit). The next 3 units sold come from the group that cost $45 per unit. That leaves 3 units in inventory on hand, and those units cost $45 each. The remainder of the inventory record follows the same pattern.

First-In, First-Out (FIFO) Inventory Costing Method
Inventory costing method: the first costs into inventory are the first costs out to cost of goods sold. Ending inventory is based on the costs of the most recent purchases.

The FIFO monthly summary at November 30 is

- Cost of goods sold: 12 units that cost a total of $560
- Ending inventory: 2 units that cost a total of $100

Columbia measured cost of goods sold and inventory in this manner to prepare its financial statements in Exhibit 6-1.

✔ **Starter 6-1**

Stop & Think

How does the perpetual inventory record in Exhibit 6-4 help **Columbia Sportswear** manage its business? How will Columbia use the information in the perpetual inventory record? (To answer this question, consider how you would manage your inventory if you did *not* have any perpetual inventory records.) Explain your reasoning.

Answer: Columbia Sportswear uses perpetual inventory records to:

a. *Meet customer demand* for ski parkas. When a customer orders 10 parkas, Columbia can use the perpetual inventory records to determine whether the goods are available for sale.

b. *Prepare financial statements.* Each month Columbia gets inventory and cost of goods sold information from its inventory records, and uses this data to prepare monthly financial statements that managers use to operate the business.

c. *Keep track of merchandise* in order to keep from losing it to spoilage or theft.

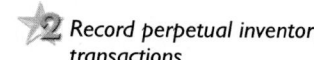

Last-In, First-Out (LIFO) Inventory Costing Method
Inventory costing method: the last costs into inventory are the first costs out to cost of goods sold. Leaves the oldest costs—those of beginning inventory and the earliest purchases of the period—in ending inventory.

Last-In, First-Out (LIFO) Method

LIFO is the opposite of FIFO. Under the **LIFO method**, cost of goods sold comes from the latest—the most recent—purchases. Ending inventory's cost comes from the oldest costs of the period. LIFO costing does not follow the flow of goods for most companies. LIFO often results in the highest cost of goods sold—and the lowest income tax. Low taxes are LIFO's main advantage. Exhibit 6-5 gives a perpetual inventory record for the LIFO method.

Exhibit 6-5

Perpetual Inventory Record: LIFO and Journal Entries for the Related Transactions

Sunrise Ski Parkas

	Purchases			Cost of Goods Sold			Inventory on Hand		
Date	Quantity	Unit Cost	Total Cost	Quantity	Unit Cost	Total Cost	Quantity	Unit Cost	Total Cost
Nov. 1							1	$40	$40
5	6	$45	$270				1	40	40
							6	45	270
15				4	$45	$ 180	1	40	40
							2	45	90
26	7	50	350				1	40	40
							2	45	90
							7	50	350
30				7	50	350			
				1	45	45	1	40	40
							1	45	45
30	13		$620	12		$575	2		$85

Journal Entries: **(All purchases and sales on account. The sale price of a ski parka is $80 per unit.)**

Nov. 5	Inventory	270	
	Accounts Payable		270
15	Accounts Receivable (4 × $80)	320	
	Sales Revenue		320
15	Cost of Goods Sold	180	
	Inventory		180
26	Inventory	350	
	Accounts Payable		350
30	Accounts Receivable (8 × $80)	640	
	Sales Revenue		640
30	Cost of Goods Sold ($350 + $45)	395	
	Inventory		395

Again, Columbia had 1 ski parka at the beginning of November. After the purchase on November 5, Columbia holds 7 units of inventory (1 @ $40 plus 6 @ $45). Columbia then sells 4 units on November 15. Under LIFO, the cost of goods sold always comes from the latest purchase. That leaves 3 ski parkas in inventory on November 15 (1 @ $40 plus 2 @ $45). The purchase of 7 units on November 26 adds a new $50 layer to inventory. Then the sale of 8 units on November 30 peels back units in LIFO order.

✔ **Starter 6-2**

The LIFO monthly summary at November 30 is

- Cost of goods sold: 12 units that cost a total of $575
- Ending inventory: 2 units that cost a total of $85

If Columbia used the LIFO method, it could measure cost of goods sold and inventory in this manner to prepare its financial statements in Exhibit 6-1.

Stop & Think

Examine Exhibit 6-4 (FIFO) and Exhibit 6-5 (LIFO). Focus on the sale of goods on November 15. Why is cost of goods sold different between FIFO costing and LIFO costing? Explain.

Answer: Cost of goods sold differs dramatically between FIFO costing and LIFO costing. The two methods make opposite assumptions about the timing of when costs leave inventory (an asset) and move into cost of goods sold (an expense).

- Under FIFO, the first costs into inventory are the first costs out to cost of goods sold. Under FIFO, the *oldest* costs are expensed first.
- Under LIFO, the last costs into inventory are the first costs out to cost of goods sold. The *newest* costs are expensed first.

FIFO and LIFO are opposites!

Average-Cost Method

Suppose Columbia Sportswear uses the **average-cost method** to account for its inventory of ski parkas. With this method, the business computes a new average cost per unit after each purchase. Ending inventory and cost of goods sold are then based on the average cost per unit. Exhibit 6-6 shows a perpetual inventory record for the average-cost method. We round average unit cost to the nearest cent and total cost to the nearest dollar.

Average-Cost Method
Inventory costing method based on the average cost of inventory during the period. Average cost is determined by dividing the cost of goods available for sale by the number of units available.

Exhibit 6-6

Perpetual Inventory Record: Average Cost and Journal Entries for the Related Transactions

Sunrise Ski Parkas

	Purchases			Cost of Goods Sold			Inventory on Hand		
Date	Quantity	Unit Cost	Total Cost	Quantity	Unit Cost	Total Cost	Quantity	Unit Cost	Total Cost
Nov. 1							1	$40.00	$ 40
5	6	$45	$270				7	44.29	310
15				4	$44.29	$177	3	44.29	133
26	7	50	350				10	48.30	483
30				8	48.30	386	2	48.30	97
30	13		$620	12		$563	2		$ 97

Journal Entries: **(All purchases and sales on account. The sale price of a ski parka is $80 per unit.)**

Nov. 5	Inventory	270	
	Accounts Payable		270
15	Accounts Receivable (4 × $80)	320	
	Sales Revenue		320
15	Cost of Goods Sold	177	
	Inventory		177
26	Inventory	350	
	Accounts Payable		350
30	Accounts Receivable (8 × $80)	640	
	Sales Revenue		640
30	Cost of Goods Sold	386	
	Inventory		386

After each purchase, Columbia computes a new average cost per unit. The new average unit cost on November 5 is:

	Total cost of inventory on hand		Number of units on hand		Average cost per unit
Nov. 5	$310	÷	7 units	=	$ 44.29

The goods sold on November 15 are then costed out at $44.29 per unit. Columbia then computes a new average cost after the November 26 purchase.

The average-cost summary at November 30 is

- Cost of goods sold: 12 units that cost a total of $563
- Ending inventory: 2 units that cost a total of $97

✔ Starter 6-3

If Columbia used the average-cost method, it would use these amounts to prepare its financial statements in Exhibit 6-1.

3 Compare the effects of FIFO, LIFO, and average cost

Comparing FIFO, LIFO, and Average Cost

Exhibit 6-7

Use of the Various Inventory Methods

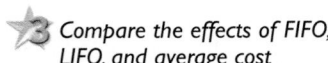

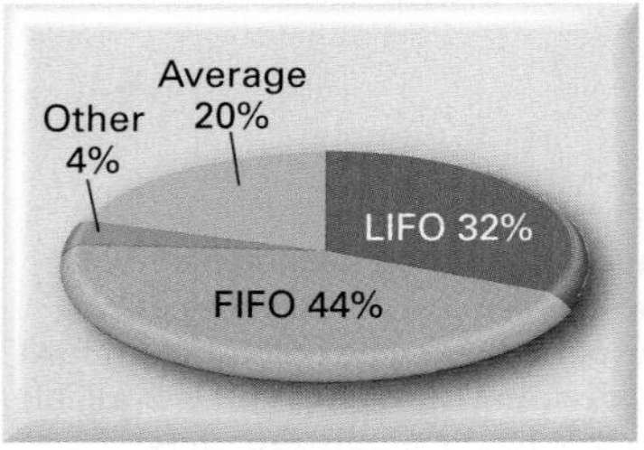

✔ Starter 6-4
✔ Starter 6-5
✔ Starter 6-6

Exhibit 6-7 shows that FIFO is the most popular inventory costing method. LIFO is next most popular and average cost ranks third.

What leads Columbia Sportswear to select the FIFO method, Lands' End to use LIFO, and Fossil (the watch company) to use average cost? The different methods have different benefits.

Exhibit 6-8 summarizes the results for the three inventory methods for Columbia Sportswear. It shows sales revenue, cost of goods sold, and gross profit for FIFO, LIFO, and average cost. All data come from Exhibits 6-4, 6-5, and 6-6.

Exhibit 6-8 shows that FIFO produces the lowest cost of goods sold and the highest gross profit. Net income is also the highest under FIFO when inventory costs are rising. Many companies wish to report high income in order to attract investors and borrow on good terms. FIFO offers this benefit.

LIFO results in the highest cost of goods sold and the lowest gross profit. That lets companies pay the lowest income taxes when inventory costs are rising. Low tax payments conserve a company's cash, but the downside of LIFO is that the company reports low net income.

The average-cost method generates gross profit, income tax, and net income amounts that fall between the extremes of FIFO and LIFO. Companies that seek a "middle-ground" solution, therefore, use the average-cost method for inventory.

Exhibit 6-8 **Comparative Results for FIFO, LIFO, and Average Cost**

	FIFO	LIFO	Average
Sales revenue	$ 960	$ 960	$ 960
Cost of goods sold	560	575	563
Gross profit	$ 400	$ 385	$ 397

MID-CHAPTER *Summary Problem*

A+ TIPS
CHECK YOUR RESOURCES

Fossil specializes in designer watches and leather goods. Assume Fossil began June holding 10 wristwatches that cost $50 each. Fossil sells these watches for $100 each. During June, Fossil bought and sold inventory as follows:

June 3	Sold 8 units for $100 each
16	Purchased 10 units @ $55 each
23	Sold 8 units for $100 each

Required

1. Prepare a perpetual inventory record for Fossil under
   - FIFO
   - LIFO
   - Average-Cost
2. Journalize all of Fossil's inventory transactions for June under all three costing methods.
3. Show the computation of gross profit for each method.
4. Which method maximizes net income? Which method minimizes income taxes?

Solution

1. Perpetual inventory records:

FIFO

Wristwatches

	Purchases			Cost of Goods Sold			Inventory on Hand		
Date	Quantity	Unit Cost	Total Cost	Quantity	Unit Cost	Total Cost	Quantity	Unit Cost	Total Cost
June 1							10	$50	$500
3				8	$50	$400	2	50	100
16	10	$55	$550				2	50	100
							10	55	550
23				2	50	100			
				6	55	330	4	55	220
30				16		$830	4		$220

LIFO

Wristwatches

	Purchases			Cost of Goods Sold			Inventory on Hand		
Date	Quantity	Unit Cost	Total Cost	Quantity	Unit Cost	Total Cost	Quantity	Unit Cost	Total Cost
June 1							10	$50	$500
3				8	$50	$400	2	50	100
16	10	$55	$550				2	50	100
							10	55	550
23				8	55	440	2	50	100
							2	55	110
30				16		$840	4		$210

Average Cost

Wristwatches

	Purchases			Cost of Goods Sold			Inventory on Hand		
Date	Quantity	Unit Cost	Total Cost	Quantity	Unit Cost	Total Cost	Quantity	Unit Cost	Total Cost
June 1							10	$50.00	$500
3				8	$50.00	$400	2	50.00	100
16	10	$55	$550				12	54.17	650
23				8	54.17	433	4	54.17	217
30				16		$833	4		217

2. Journal Entries:

		FIFO		LIFO		Average	
June 3	Accounts Receivable	800		800		800	
	Sales Revenue		800		800		800
3	Cost of Goods Sold.........	400		400		400	
	Inventory		400		400		400
16	Inventory	550		550		550	
	Accounts Payable....		550		550		550
23	Accounts Receivable	800		800		800	
	Sales Revenue		800		800		800
23	Cost of Goods Sold ($100 + $330)	430		440		433	
	Inventory		430		440		433

		FIFO	LIFO	Average
3.	Sales revenue ($800 + $800)	$1,600	$1,600	$1,600
	Cost of goods sold ($400 + $430)	830		
	($400 + $440)		840	
	($400 + $433)			833
	Gross profit	$ 770	$ 760	$ 767

4. FIFO maximizes net income.
LIFO minimizes income taxes.

Student Resource CD
average-cost method, cost of goods sold, FIFO, inventory costing, LIFO, periodic method, sales revenue

Inventory Costing in a Periodic System

We described the periodic inventory system briefly in Chapter 5. Accounting is simpler in a periodic system because the company keeps no daily running record of inventory on hand. The only way to determine the ending inventory and cost of goods sold in a periodic system is to count the goods—usually at the end of the year. The periodic system works well for a small business, in which the owner can control inventory by visual inspection.

The chapter appendix illustrates how the periodic system works. Journal entries in a periodic system are similar to journal entries in a perpetual system, except:

1. The periodic system uses four additional accounts. In the periodic system we record the purchase of inventory with a debit to the Purchases account, not to the Inventory account. Purchase discounts are credited to the Purchase Discount account, and purchase returns and allowances are credited to the Purchase Returns and Allowances account. Transportation charges on inventory purchases are debited to the Transportation-In account.
2. The end-of-period entries are more extensive in the periodic system because we must close out the beginning inventory balance and set up the cost of the ending inventory. The chapter appendix illustrates this process.

Cost of goods sold in a periodic inventory system is computed by the following formula (using assumed amounts for this illustration):

Beginning inventory	
(the inventory on hand at the end of the preceding period)......	$ 5,000
Net purchases (often abbreviated as Purchases)	20,000*
Cost of goods available for sale..............................	25,000
Less: Ending inventory	
(the inventory on hand at the end of the current period)......	(7,000)
Cost of goods sold..	$18,000

*Net purchases is determined as follows (all amounts assumed):

Purchases	$21,000
Less: Purchase discounts	(2,000)
Purchase returns and allowances	(5,000)
Add: Transportation-in..................................	6,000
Net purchases	$20,000

The application of the various costing methods (FIFO, LIFO, and average cost) in a periodic inventory system follows the pattern illustrated earlier for the perpetual system. To show how the periodic inventory system works, we use the same Columbia Sportswear data as we used for the perpetual system, as follows:

Columbia Sportswear Sunrise Ski Parka			
		Number of Units	Unit Cost
Nov. 1	Beginning inventory	1	$ 40
5	Purchase	6	45
15	Sale	4	
26	Purchase	7	50
30	Sale	8	
30	Ending inventory	2	?

Compute periodic inventory amounts under FIFO, LIFO, and average cost 4

First-In, First-Out (FIFO) Method

Columbia Sportswear could use the FIFO costing method with a periodic inventory system. The FIFO computations follow:

Beginning inventory (1 unit @ $40)	$ 40
Purchases (6 units @ $45 + 7 units @ $50)	620
Cost of goods available for sale (14 units)	660
Less: Ending inventory (2 units @ $50)	(100)
Cost of goods sold (12 units)	$560

Cost of goods available is always the sum of beginning inventory plus purchases. Under FIFO, the ending inventory comes from the latest—the most recent—purchases, which cost $50 per unit. Ending inventory is therefore $100, and cost of goods sold is $560. These amounts are exactly the same as we saw for FIFO in the perpetual system in Exhibit 6-4.

There are fewer journal entries in the periodic system because Columbia would record a sale with only a single entry. For example, Columbia's sale of 4 ski parkas for $80 each is recorded as follows:

Nov. 15	Accounts Receivable (4 × $80)	320	
	Sales Revenue		320

There is no cost of goods sold entry in the periodic system.

Last-In, First-Out (LIFO) Method

The LIFO method fits well with a periodic inventory system. Columbia's LIFO computations follow:

Beginning inventory (1 unit @ $40)	$ 40
Purchases (6 units @ $45 + 7 units @ $50)	620
Cost of goods available for sale (14 units)	660
Less: Ending inventory (1 unit @ $40 + 1 unit @ $45)	(85)
Cost of goods sold (12 units)	$575

Under LIFO, the ending inventory comes from the earliest units obtained—the single beginning unit that cost $40 plus 1 of the units purchased for $45. Ending inventory is therefore $85, and cost of goods sold is $575. These amounts are the same as we saw for the perpetual system in Exhibit 6-5. In some cases, the LIFO amounts can differ between the perpetual and the periodic systems.

✔ Starter 6-7

Average-Cost Method

In the average method, we compute a single average cost per unit for the entire period as follows:

Cost of goods available for sale		Number of units available for sale		Average cost per unit for the entire period
$660	÷	14 units	=	$47.14

This average cost per unit is then used to compute the ending inventory and cost of goods sold as follows:

Beginning inventory (1 unit @ $40) .	$ 40
Purchases (6 units @ $45 + 7 units @ $50)	620
Cost of goods available for sale	
(14 units @ average cost of $47.14)	660
Less: Ending inventory (2 units @ $47.14)	(94)
Cost of goods sold (12 units @ $47.14)	$566

Ending inventory and cost of goods sold under the periodic system differ from the amounts in a perpetual system. Why? Because under the perpetual system, a new average cost is computed after each purchase. But the periodic system uses a single average cost that is determined at the end of the period.

Accounting Principles and Inventories

Several accounting principles have special relevance to inventories. Among them are consistency, disclosure, materiality, and accounting conservatism.

CONSISTENCY PRINCIPLE The **consistency principle** states that businesses should use the same accounting methods and procedures from period to period. Consistency helps investors compare a company's financial statements from one period to the next.

Suppose you are analyzing a company's net income pattern over a two-year period. The company switched from LIFO to FIFO during that time. Its net income increased dramatically but only as a result of the change in inventory method. If you did not know of the change, you might believe that the company's income increased because of improved operations. Therefore, companies must report any changes in the accounting methods they use. Investors need this information to make wise decisions about the company.

DISCLOSURE PRINCIPLE The **disclosure principle** holds that a company's financial statements should report enough information for outsiders to make knowledgeable decisions about the company. In short, the company should report *relevant*, *reliable*, and *comparable* information about its economic affairs. With respect to inventories, the disclosure principle means disclosing the method being used to value inventories. Suppose a banker is comparing two companies—one using LIFO and the other FIFO. The FIFO company reports higher net income, but only because it uses the FIFO inventory method. Without knowledge of the accounting methods the companies are using, the banker could lend money to the wrong business.

MATERIALITY CONCEPT The **materiality concept** states that a company must perform strictly proper accounting *only* for items that are significant for the business's financial statements. Information is significant—or, in accounting terminology, *material*—when its presentation in the financial statements would cause someone to change a decision. The materiality concept frees accountants from having to report every last item in strict accordance with GAAP.

ACCOUNTING CONSERVATISM **Conservatism** in accounting means reporting items in the financial statements at amounts that lead to the most cautious immediate results. Conservatism appears in accounting guidelines such as

- "Anticipate no gains, but provide for all probable losses."
- "If in doubt, record an asset at the lowest reasonable amount and a liability at the highest reasonable amount."
- "When there's a question, record an expense rather than an asset."

✔ **Starter 6-8**

☐ Inventory Costing Methods
☐ Inventory Costing: Perpetual System
☐ Inventory Costing: Periodic System
■ **Accounting Principles and Inventories**
☐ Other Inventory Issues
☐ Appendix: Perpetual vs. Periodic

🖸 Student Resource CD
accounting principles

Consistency Principle
A business should use the same accounting methods and procedures from period to period.

Disclosure Principle
A business's financial statements must report enough information for outsiders to make knowledgeable decisions about the company.

Materiality Concept
A company must perform strictly proper accounting only for items that are significant to the business's financial statements.

Conservatism
Reporting the least favorable figures in the financial statements.

The goal is for financial statements to report realistic figures. The lower-of-cost-or-market rule is an example of accounting conservatism.

Other Inventory Issues

In addition to the basic inventory costing methods, accountants face other inventory issues. This section covers those topics, which include

- The lower-of-cost-or-market rule
- Effects of inventory errors
- Ethical issues
- Estimating inventory amounts

Student ResourceCD
ethics, gross profit method, inventory errors, lower of cost or market

5 *Apply the lower-of-cost-or-market rule to inventory*

Lower-of-Cost-or-Market Rule

The **lower-of-cost-or-market rule** (abbreviated as **LCM**) shows accounting conservatism in action. LCM requires that inventory be reported in the financial statements at whichever is lower—the inventory's historical cost or its market value. For inventories, *market value* generally means *current replacement cost* (that is, the cost to replace the inventory on hand). If the replacement cost of inventory falls below its historical cost, the business must write down the value of its goods. The business reports ending inventory at its LCM value on the balance sheet.

Lower-of-Cost-or-Market (LCM) Rule Rule that an asset should be reported in the financial statements at whichever is lower—its historical cost or its market value.

Suppose Columbia Sportswear paid $3,000 for inventory on September 26. By December 31, the inventory can now be replaced for $2,200, and the decline in value appears permanent. Market value is below FIFO cost, and the entry to write down the inventory to LCM follows:

Cost of Goods Sold (cost, $3,000 – market, $2,200)	800	
Inventory		800

In this case, Columbia's balance sheet would report this inventory as follows:

Balance Sheet	
Current assets:	
Inventory, at market (which is lower than FIFO cost)	$ 2,200

Companies often disclose LCM in notes to their financial statements, as shown here for Columbia Sportswear:

✔ Starter 6-9

✔ Starter 6-10

NOTE 2: STATEMENT OF SIGNIFICANT ACCOUNTING POLICIES
Inventories. Inventories are carried at the *lower of cost or market*. Cost is determined using the first-in, first-out method.

Effects of Inventory Errors

6 *Measure the effects of inventory errors*

Businesses count their inventories at the end of the period. As the period 1 segment of Exhibit 6-9 shows, an error in the ending inventory creates errors in cost of goods sold and gross profit. Compare period 1's ending inventory, which is overstated, with period 3, which is correct. Period 1 *should* look exactly like period 3.

Recall that one period's ending inventory becomes the next period's beginning inventory. Thus, the error in ending inventory carries over into the next period; note the amounts highlighted in Exhibit 6-9.

Exhibit 6-9 **Inventory Errors: An Example**

	Period 1		Period 2		Period 3	
	Ending Inventory Overstated by $5,000		*Beginning* Inventory Overstated by $5,000		Correct	
Sales revenue		$100,000		$100,000		$100,000
Cost of goods sold:						
Beginning inventory	$10,000		$ 15,000		$10,000	
Net purchases	50,000		50,000		50,000	
Cost of goods available for sale	60,000		65,000		60,000	
Ending inventory	(15,000)		(10,000)		(10,000)	
Cost of goods sold		45,000		55,000		50,000
Gross profit		$ 55,000		$ 45,000		$ 50,000
		$100,000 (Periods 1 and 2 combined)				

The correct gross profit is $50,000 for each period.

Source: The authors thank Carl High for this example.

Because ending inventory is *subtracted* to compute cost of goods sold in one period and the same amount is *added* as beginning inventory the next period, the error cancels out after two periods. The overstatement of cost of goods sold in period 2 counterbalances the understatement for period 1. Thus, total gross profit for the two periods combined is correct. These effects are summarized in Exhibit 6-10.

✔ Starter 6-11

Exhibit 6-10 **Effects of Inventory Errors**

✔ Starter 6-12

	Period 1		Period 2	
Inventory Error	Cost of Goods Sold	Gross Profit and Net Income	Cost of Goods Sold	Gross Profit and Net Income
Period 1 Ending inventory *overstated*	Understated	Overstated	Overstated	Understated
Period 1 Ending inventory *understated*	Overstated	Understated	Understated	Overstated

Online retailers try to avoid errors in accounting for their inventory. See the Accounting.com box titled, "Online Category Managers: The New B2B Force Behind Those Huge E-Tailer Inventories," on the next page.

Ethical Issues

No area of accounting has a deeper ethical dimension than inventory. Owners and managers of companies whose profits are lagging are sometimes tempted to "cook the books." The increase in reported income may lead investors and creditors to think the business is more successful than it really is.

There are two main schemes for cooking the books. The easiest way is simply to overstate ending inventory. In Exhibit 6-10, we saw how an error in ending inventory affects net income. A company can intentionally overstate its ending inventory. Such an error overstates assets and owner's equity, as shown in the accounting equation. The upward-pointing arrows indicate an overstatement—reporting more assets and equity than are actually present:

	ASSETS	=	LIABILITIES	+	OWNER'S EQUITY
Effect of overstating ending inventory:	↑	=	0	+	↑

Online Category Managers: The New B2B Force Behind Those Huge E-Tailer Inventories

A big advantage e-tailers have over brick-and-mortar concerns is a much wider selection of goods. Even big-box merchandisers like **Circuit City** have limited floor space. But for Circuitcity.com, cyberspace is the limit. And Circuitcity.com and other dot.com merchants don't have to pay for the goods! Their secret: the online "category manager."

Online category managers are third-party distributors that specialize in a specific product, like DVDs, sporting goods, jewelry, or electronic equipment. They ship directly to customers using e-tailing clients' labels. E-tailers pay a fee to integrate their e-commerce systems and then receive between 10% and 35% of the profit on each item sold—much less than if they owned the inventory themselves. But this is a small price to pay to avoid the risk of inventory ownership and headaches from accounting for the merchandise.

These behind-the-scenes inventory managers are growing faster than their clients. For example, 50% of online sales volume for struggling retailer **Kmart** comes through vendor partners. **GSI Commerce, Inc.**, a sporting goods manager, serves **Sports Authority** and **Athlete's Foot**. In 2001 GSI's sales more than doubled over 2000. Even e-commerce giant **Amazon.com** has tried to get a slice of the pie by becoming a vendor partner. "We created this business [inventory management] years ago, when people said it didn't make any sense," said Michael G. Rubin, chief executive of GSI. "[Now we've] proven what an opportunity this is."

Based on: Miguel Helft, "Still Alive and Growing Online, Without Fanfare," *The New York Times*, January 6, 2002, Sec. 3, p. 4. Bob Sechler, "E-Commerce (A Special Report): B2B—Inventories—Behind the Curtain: How Can Online Retailers Maintain Such Huge Inventories? Here's Their Secret," *The Wall Street Journal*, July 15, 2002, p. R12. Brian Garrity, "The State of E-Commerce," *Billboard*, March 17, 2001, pp. 60–62.

Accounting.com

HealthSouth Corp faces civil and criminal charges for overstating the company's inventory and other assets. However, the company's deft handling of its balance sheet made it practically impossible for investors to detect the scheme before it was too late.[1]

The second way of using inventory to cook the books involves sales. Sales schemes are more complex than simple inventory overstatements. **Datapoint Corporation** and **MiniScribe**, both computer-related concerns, were charged with creating fictitious sales to boost reported profits.

Datapoint is alleged to have hired drivers to transport its inventory around San Antonio so that the goods could *not* be physically counted. Datapoint's plan seemed to be that excluding goods from ending inventory would mean they had been sold. The scheme broke down when the trucks returned the goods to Datapoint. What would you think of a company with \$10 million in sales and \$4 million of sales returns?

MiniScribe is alleged to have cooked its books by shipping boxes of bricks labeled as computer parts to its distributors right before year-end. The scheme affected MiniScribe's reported assets and equity (assuming sales of \$10 million and cost of goods sold of \$6 million) as follows:

ASSETS	=	LIABILITIES	+	OWNER'S EQUITY
↑	=	0	+	↑

[1]Jonathan Weil, "Accounting Scheme Was Straightforward But Hard to Detect," *The Wall Street Journal*, March 20, 2003, p. C.1.

The bogus transactions increased MiniScribe's assets and equity by $4 million—but only temporarily. The scheme boomeranged when MiniScribe had to record the sales returns. In virtually every area, accounting imposes a discipline that brings out the facts sooner or later.

Estimating Inventory

7 *Estimate ending inventory by the gross profit method*

Often a business must *estimate* the value of its inventory. Suppose the company suffers a fire loss and must estimate the value of the inventory destroyed.

The **gross profit method** provides a way to estimate inventory as follows (amounts assumed for illustration):

Gross Profit Method
A way to estimate inventory on the basis of the cost-of-goods-sold model: Beginning inventory + Net purchases = Cost of goods available for sale. Cost of goods available for sale – Cost of goods sold = Ending inventory.

Beginning inventory
\+ Purchases
= Cost of goods available for sale
– Ending inventory
= Cost of goods sold

Rearranging *ending inventory* and *cost of goods sold* helps to estimate ending inventory (amounts assumed for illustration):

Beginning inventory
\+ Purchases
= Cost of goods available for sale
– Cost of goods sold (Sales – Gross Profit = COGS)
= Ending inventory

Suppose a fire destroys your inventory. To collect insurance, you must estimate the cost of the inventory destroyed—that is, the ending inventory. Using your normal *gross profit percent* (that is, gross profit divided by net sales revenue), you can estimate cost of goods sold. Then subtract cost of goods sold from goods available to estimate ending inventory. Exhibit 6-11 illustrates the gross profit method.

Exhibit 6-11
Gross Profit Method of Estimating Inventory (amounts assumed)

Beginning inventory		$14,000
Purchases		66,000
Cost of goods available for sale		80,000
Estimated cost of goods sold:		
Sales revenue	$100,000	
Less: Estimated gross profit of 40%	(40,000)	
Estimated cost of goods sold		(60,000)
Estimated cost of *ending inventory*		$20,000

Stop & Think

Beginning inventory is $70,000, net purchases total $298,000, and net sales are $500,000. With a normal gross profit rate of 40% of sales, how much is ending inventory?

Answer:

Beginning inventory		$ 70,000
Net purchases		298,000
Cost of goods available for sale		368,000
Estimated cost of goods sold:		
Net sales revenue	$500,000	
Less: Estimated gross profit of 40%	(200,000)	
Estimated cost of goods sold		(300,000)
Estimated cost of ending inventory		$ 68,000

Decision Guidelines

GUIDELINES FOR INVENTORY MANAGEMENT

Assume you are starting a business to sell school supplies to your college friends. You'll need to stock computer disks, notebooks, and other inventory items. To manage the business, you'll also need some accounting records. Here are some of the decisions you'll face.

Decision	Guidelines	System or Method
Which inventory system to use?	• Expensive merchandise • Cannot control inventory by visual inspection	Perpetual system
	• Can control inventory by visual inspection	Periodic system
Which costing method to use?	• Unique inventory items	Specific unit cost
	• The most current cost of ending inventory • Maximizes reported income when costs are rising	FIFO
	• The most current measure of cost of goods sold and net income • Minimizes income tax when costs are rising	LIFO
	• Middle-of-the-road approach for income tax and net income	Average-cost
How to estimate the cost of ending inventory?	• The cost-of-goods-sold model provides the framework	Gross profit method

Excel Application Exercise

Goal: Create an Excel spreadsheet that will compare gross profit, ending inventory, and cost of goods sold under the LIFO, FIFO, and average-cost methods of inventory valuation.

Scenario: Assume that during the first month of operating your school supplies business, you stock only 100 MB Zip disks. Your task is to create a spreadsheet and embedded graph that compare gross profit, ending inventory, and cost of goods sold under three methods: average cost, FIFO, and LIFO. For the first month of business, you have collected the following data for use in creating the spreadsheet:

August 1	Beginning inventory	50 units @ $4.00 cost per unit
10	Purchase	60 units @ $4.40 cost per unit
17	Purchase	100 units @ $4.75 cost per unit
31	Purchase	100 units @ $5.10 cost per unit
Sales for August:		*200 disks sold @ $10.00 each*

After you have prepared your spreadsheet, answer these questions:

1. Which method produces the lowest cost of goods sold? Why?
2. Which method produces the lowest ending inventory? Why?
3. If you want to maximize gross profit, which method should you choose? Does this method do a good job of matching inventory expense (cost of goods sold) to sales revenue?

Step-by-Step:

1. Open a new Excel spreadsheet.
2. Create a heading for your spreadsheet that contains the following:
   a. Chapter 6 Excel Application Exercise
   b. Inventory Management
   c. Today's date
3. At the top of your spreadsheet, create a "Data Section" for the August data. Set up columns for Date, Activity ("Beginning Inventory," "Purchases," "Goods Available for Sale," "Sales," and "Ending Inventory"), Units, Unit Cost, and Total Cost. Compute goods available for sale and ending inventory.
4. Include the calculation for "average unit cost" on a separate row in this section.
5. Next, create a section titled "Inventory Method Comparison" in bold print and underlined. Include one column for each method (average cost, FIFO, and LIFO). Include rows for Ending Inventory, Cost of Goods Sold, and Gross Profit. Format as necessary. Be sure your calculations are based on the "Data Section" figures. Do not "hard code" any amounts in this section.
6. When finished, create an embedded bar chart underneath the "Inventory Method Comparison" section that compares Gross Profit, Ending Inventory, and Cost of Goods Sold for all three methods. (*Hint*: Use the Chart Wizard button on the standard Excel toolbar.)
7. Save your spreadsheet, and print a copy for your files.

END-OF-CHAPTER *Summary Problem*

A+ TIPS
CHECK YOUR RESOURCES

Suppose a division of **IBM Corporation** that handles computer components has these inventory records for January 20X6:

Date	Item	Quantity	Unit Cost	Sale Price
Jan. 1	Beginning inventory	100 units	$ 8	
6	Purchase	60 units	9	
13	Sale	70 units		$20
21	Purchase	150 units	9	
24	Sale	210 units		22
27	Purchase	90 units	10	
30	Sale	30 units		25

Company accounting records reveal that operating expense for January was $1,900.

Required

Prepare the January income statement, showing amounts for FIFO, LIFO, and average cost. Label the bottom line "Operating income." (Round the average cost per unit to three decimal places and all other figures to whole-dollar amounts.) Show your computations, and use the periodic inventory model from pages 256–258 to compute cost of goods sold.

Solution

IBM Corporation

Income Statement for Computer Components
Month Ended January 31, 20X6

	FIFO		LIFO		Average Cost	
Sales revenue............................		$6,770		$6,770		$6,770
Cost of goods sold:						
Beginning inventory	$ 800		$ 800		$ 800	
Net purchases	2,790		2,790		2,790	
Cost of goods available for sale......................	3,590		3,590		3,590	
Ending inventory	(900)		(720)		(808)	
Cost of goods sold		2,690		2,870		2,782
Gross profit		4,080		3,900		3,988
Operating expenses		1,900		1,900		1,900
Operating income.........................		$2,180		$2,000		$2,088

Computations

Sales revenue:	(70 × $20) + (210 × $22) + (30 × $25)	= $6,770
Beginning inventory:	100 × $8	= $800
Purchases:	(60 × $9) + (150 × $9) + (90 × $10)	= $2,790
Ending inventory		
FIFO	90* × $10	= $900
LIFO	90 × $8	= $720
Average cost:	90 × $8.975**	= $808 (rounded from $807.75)

*Number of units in ending inventory = 100 + 60 − 70 + 150 − 210 + 90 − 30 = 90.
**$3,590/400 units† = $8.975 per unit.
†Number of units available = 100 + 60 + 150 + 90 = 400.

REVIEW Accounting for Merchandise Inventory

Quick Check

1. The chain store, **The Limited, Inc.**, made sales of $9,363 million and ended the year with inventories totaling $966 million. Cost of goods sold was $6,110 million. Total operating expenses were $2,734 million. How much net income did The Limited earn for the year?
   a. $519 million
   b. $3,253 million
   c. $5,663 million
   d. $6,629 million
2. Which inventory costing method assigns to ending inventory the latest—the most recent—costs incurred during the period?
   a. Specific unit cost
   b. First-in, first-out (FIFO)
   c. Last-in, first-out (LIFO)
   d. Average cost
3. Assume **Amazon.com** began June with 10 units of inventory that cost a total of $190. During June, Amazon purchased and sold goods as follows:

June 8	Purchase	30 units @ $20
14	Sale	25 units @ $40
22	Purchase	20 units @ $22
27	Sale	30 units @ $40

   Assume Amazon uses the FIFO inventory method and the perpetual inventory system. How much is Amazon's cost of goods sold for the transaction on June 14?
   a. $790
   b. $1,000
   c. $500
   d. $490
4. After the purchase on June 22, what is Amazon's cost of the inventory on hand?
   a. $300
   b. $440
   c. $740
   d. $720
5. Amazon's journal entry (entries) on June 14 is (are)

a. Accounts Receivable	490	
Inventory		490
b. Accounts Receivable	1,000	
Sales Revenue		1,000
c. Cost of Goods Sold	490	
Inventory		490
d. Both b and c		

6. Which inventory costing method results in the lowest net income during a period of rising inventory costs?
   a. Specific unit cost
   b. First-in, first-out (FIFO)
   c. Last-in, first-out (LIFO)
   d. Average cost
7. Suppose Amazon.com used the average-cost method and the periodic inventory system. Use the Amazon data in question 3 to compute the cost of the company's inventory on hand at June 30. Round unit cost to the nearest cent.
   a. $102.50
   b. $105.20
   c. $205.00
   d. $210.40
8. Which of the following is most closely tied to accounting conservatism?
   a. Consistency principle
   b. Disclosure principle
   c. Materiality concept
   d. Lower-of-cost-or-market rule
9. At December 31, 20X5, McAdam Company overstated ending inventory by $40,000. How does this error affect cost of goods sold and net income for 20X5?
   a. Overstates cost of goods sold; Understates net income
   b. Understates cost of goods sold; Overstates net income
   c. Overstates both cost of goods sold and net income
   d. Leaves both cost of goods sold and net income correct because the errors cancel each other

10. Suppose **Columbia Sportswear** suffered a fire loss and needs to estimate the cost of the goods destroyed. Beginning inventory was $100,000, purchases totaled $600,000, and sales came to $1,000,000. Columbia's normal gross profit percentage is 45%. Use the gross profit method to estimate the cost of the inventory lost in the fire.
    a. $150,000
    b. $250,000
    c. $300,000
    d. $350,000

Accounting Vocabulary

average-cost method (p. 253)
conservatism (p. 258)
consistency principle (p. 258)
disclosure principle (p. 258)
first-in, first-out (FIFO) inventory costing method (p. 251)
gross profit method (p. 262)
last-in, first-out (LIFO) inventory costing method (p. 252)
lower-of-cost-or-market (LCM) rule (p. 259)
materiality concept (p. 258)
specific identification method (p. 250)
specific-unit-cost method (p. 250)

ASSESS *Your Progress*

A+ online homework

See *www.prenhall.com/horngren* for selected Starters, Exercises, and Problems.

Starters

Measuring FIFO amounts in a perpetual system
(Obj. 1)

S6-1 Refer to **Columbia Sportswear's** perpetual inventory record, at FIFO cost, in Exhibit 6-4, page 251. Assume that Columbia began November with 5 ski parkas (instead of 1). Keep all other factors unchanged, and compute these FIFO amounts for Columbia:

a. Cost of goods sold for the November 15 transaction
b. Inventory on hand at November 15

Recording LIFO amounts in a perpetual system
(Obj. 1, 2)

S6-2 Use the LIFO perpetual inventory record of **Columbia Sportswear** in Exhibit 6-5, page 252. Assume that Columbia purchased 10 units (instead of 7) on November 26, and keep all other factors unchanged. Journalize Columbia's transactions under LIFO on November 30. The sale was half for cash and half on account. The sale price of the ski parkas was $70 each.

Measuring average-cost amounts in a perpetual system
(Obj. 1)

S6-3 The average-cost perpetual record of **Columbia Sportswear** appears in Exhibit 6-6, page 253. Suppose Columbia purchased 9 ski parkas (instead of 6) on November 5, and keep all other factors unchanged. Compute the cost of Columbia's inventory on hand at November 15.

Using a perpetual inventory system
(Obj. 1, 2)

S6-4 Use the FIFO inventory record in Exhibit 6-4, page 251, to prepare a T-account for the inventory. Show all dates and label each item in the T-account.

Comparing cost of goods sold under FIFO and LIFO
(Obj. 3)

S6-5 Study Exhibit 6-8, page 254, and answer these questions in your own words:

1. Why does FIFO produce the lowest cost of goods sold during a period of rising prices?
2. Why does LIFO produce the highest cost of goods sold during a period of rising prices?

Comparing ending inventory under FIFO and LIFO
(Obj. 3)

S6-6 Explain in your own words which inventory method results in the highest, and the lowest, cost of ending inventory. Prices are rising. The data in Exhibits 6-4, page 251, and 6-5, page 252, may help.

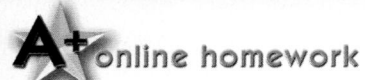

S6-7 St. Louis Dry Goods uses a periodic inventory system. St. Louis completed the following inventory transactions during April:

Computing FIFO and LIFO amounts in a periodic system **(Obj. 3, 4)**

April 1	Purchased 10 shirts @ $40
7	Sold 6 shirts for $70 each
13	Sold 2 shirts for $80 each
21	Purchased 3 shirts @ $50

Compute St. Louis's ending inventory and cost of goods sold under both LIFO and FIFO. Compute gross profit under both methods. Which method results in more gross profit?

S6-8 St. Louis Dry Goods uses a periodic inventory system. Use the St. Louis Dry Goods data in Starter 6-7 to compute ending inventory and cost of goods sold under the average-cost method. Round average unit cost to the nearest cent.

Computing average-cost amounts in a periodic system **(Obj. 4)**

S6-9 Assume **Columbia Sportswear** prepared the FIFO perpetual inventory record in Exhibit 6-4, page 251. It is now November 30 and Columbia is preparing monthly financial statements. Assume that Columbia's chief financial officer determines that the current replacement cost (market value) of the ending inventory is $90.

Make any adjusting entry that Columbia needs in order to apply the lower-of-cost-or-market rule at November 30. Then report the inventory on the balance sheet.

Applying the lower-of-cost-or-market rule; perpetual FIFO **(Obj. 5)**

S6-10 Suppose **Columbia Sportswear** uses the average-cost method and prepares the perpetual inventory record in Exhibit 6-6, page 253. It is now November 30, and Columbia is preparing monthly financial statements. Assume that Columbia's chief financial officer determines that the current market value of the ending inventory is $98.

What journal entry should Columbia make in order to apply the lower-of-cost-or-market rule at November 30? Explain. Then report the inventory on the balance sheet.

Applying the lower-of-cost-or-market rule; perpetual average cost **(Obj. 5)**

S6-11 **Target Corporation's** inventory data for the year ended January 31, 2002, as adapted, follow (in millions):

Effect of an inventory error—one year only **(Obj. 6)**

Beginning inventory	$ 4,248
Purchases	27,447
Cost of goods available	31,695
Less: Ending inventory	(4,449)
Cost of goods sold	$27,246

Assume that the ending inventory figure was accidentally overstated by $100 million. How would this error affect cost of goods sold and gross profit?

S6-12 Refer back to **Target Corporation's** inventory data in Starter 6-11. How would the inventory error affect Target's cost of goods sold and gross profit for the year ended January 31, 2003?

Next year's effect of an inventory error **(Obj. 6)**

S6-13 Asamax Insulation Company began the year with inventory of $350,000. Inventory purchases for the year totaled $1,600,000. Asamax managers estimate that cost of goods sold for the year will be $1,800,000. How much is Asamax's estimated cost of ending inventory? Use the gross profit method.

Estimating ending inventory by the gross profit method **(Obj. 7)**

S6-14 Cyrus Roofing began the year with inventory of $50,000 and purchased $160,000 of goods during the year. Sales for the year are $300,000, and Cyrus's gross profit percentage is 40% of sales. Compute Cyrus's estimated cost of ending inventory by the gross profit method.

Estimating ending inventory by the gross profit method **(Obj. 7)**

A+ online homework

Exercises

Measuring ending inventory and cost of goods sold in a perpetual system—FIFO
(Obj. 1)

E6-1 Picker Paradise carries a large inventory of guitars and other musical instruments. Picker uses the FIFO method and a perpetual inventory system. Company records indicate the following for a particular line of Honeydew guitars:

Date	Item	Quantity	Unit Cost
May 1	Balance	5	$70
6	Sale	3	
8	Purchase	10	80
17	Sale	4	
30	Sale	5	

Required

Prepare a perpetual inventory record for the guitars. Then determine the amounts Picker should report for ending inventory and cost of goods sold by the FIFO method.

Recording perpetual inventory transactions
(Obj. 2)

E6-2 After preparing the FIFO perpetual inventory record in Exercise 6-1, journalize Picker Paradise's May 8 purchase of inventory on account and cash sale on May 17 (sale price of each guitar was $140).

Measuring ending inventory and cost of goods sold in a perpetual system—LIFO
(Obj. 1)

E6-3 Refer to the Picker Paradise inventory data in Exercise 6-1. Assume that Picker Paradise uses the LIFO cost method. Prepare Picker's perpetual inventory record for the guitars on the LIFO basis. Then identify the cost of ending inventory and cost of goods sold for the month.

Applying the average-cost method in a perpetual inventory system
(Obj. 1)

E6-4 Refer to the Picker Paradise inventory data in Exercise 6-1. Assume that Picker uses the average-cost method. Prepare Picker's perpetual inventory record for the guitars on the average-cost basis. Round average cost per unit to the nearest cent and all other amounts to the nearest dollar.

Recording perpetual inventory transactions
(Obj. 2)

E6-5 Accounting records for Durall Luggage yield the following data for the year ended December 31, 20X5 (amounts in thousands):

Inventory, December 31, 20X4	$ 370
Purchases of inventory (on account)	3,105
Sales of inventory—80% on account; 20% for cash (cost $2,821)	4,395
Inventory, December 31, 20X5	?

Required

1. Journalize Durall's inventory transactions in the perpetual system. Show all amounts in thousands.
2. Report ending inventory on the balance sheet, and sales, cost of goods sold, and gross profit on the income statement (amounts in thousands).

Comparing FIFO and LIFO amounts for ending inventory
(Obj. 3)

E6-6 Assume that a **Toys "Я" Us** store bought and sold a video game (inventory) during December as follows:

Beginning inventory	10 units @ $20
Sale	6 units
Purchase	15 units @ $22
Sale	14 units

Toys "Я" Us uses the perpetual inventory system. Compute the cost of ending inventory under (a) FIFO and (b) LIFO. Which method results in higher cost of ending inventory? higher cost of goods sold?

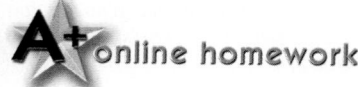

E6-7 Use the data in Exercise 6-6 to compute the cost of goods sold under (a) FIFO and (b) LIFO. You will need a complete perpetual inventory record for LIFO.

Comparing FIFO and LIFO amounts for cost of goods sold
(Obj. 3)

E6-8 Assume that a **Home Depot** store completed the following perpetual inventory transactions for a line of carpet.

Comparing FIFO, LIFO, and average-cost amounts
(Obj. 3)

Beginning inventory	20 rolls @ $200
Purchase	8 rolls @ $300
Sale	15 rolls @ $500

Compute cost of goods sold and gross profit under (a) FIFO, (b) LIFO, and (c) average cost (round average cost per unit to the nearest cent).

E6-9 The periodic inventory records of Flexon Prosthetics indicate the following at October 31:

Determining ending inventory and cost of goods sold by four methods: periodic system
(Obj. 4)

Student ResourceCD
spreadsheet

Oct. 1	Beginning inventory	9 units @ $160
8	Purchase	4 units @ 160
15	Purchase	12 units @ 170
26	Purchase	3 units @ 176

The physical inventory at October 31 counts 8 units on hand.

Required

Compute ending inventory and cost of goods sold, using each of the following methods.

1. Specific unit cost, assuming four $170 units and four $160 units are on hand
2. Average cost (round average unit cost to three decimal places)
3. First-in, first-out
4. Last-in, first-out

E6-10 Supply the missing amounts for each of the following companies:

Determining amounts for the income statement; periodic system
(Obj. 4)

Company	Net Sales	Beginning Inventory	Net Purchases	Ending Inventory	Cost of Goods Sold	Gross Profit
Maple	$101,800	$21,500	$62,700	$19,400	(a)	$37,000
Walnut	(b)	25,450	93,000	(c)	$94,100	43,200
Pine	94,700	(d)	54,900	22,600	62,500	(e)
Magnolia	84,300	10,700	(f)	8,200	(g)	47,100

Prepare the income statement for Magnolia Company, which uses the periodic inventory system. Include a complete heading and show the full computation of cost of goods sold. Magnolia's operating expenses for the year were $31,600.

E6-11 **Alcoa Enterprises,** which uses the FIFO method, has these account balances at December 31, 20X6, prior to releasing the financial statements for the year:

Applying the lower-of-cost-or-market rule to inventories
(Obj. 5)

Inventory		Cost of Goods Sold		Sales Revenue	
Beg. bal. 12,489					
End bal. 18,028		Bal. 113,245			Bal. 225,000

A year ago, when Alcoa prepared its 20X5 financial statements, the replacement cost of ending inventory was $13,051. Alcoa has determined that the replacement cost (current market value) of the December 31, 20X6, ending inventory is $16,840.

Required

Prepare Alcoa Enterprises' 20X6 income statement through gross profit to show how Alcoa would apply the lower-of-cost-or-market rule to its inventories. Include a complete heading for the statement.

Applying the lower-of-cost-or-market rule to inventories
(Obj. 5)

E6-12 Nash-Robin Foods reports inventory at the lower of FIFO cost or market. Prior to releasing its March 20X4 financial statements, Nash-Robin's preliminary income statement appears as follows:

Nash-Robin Foods
Income Statement (partial)

Sales revenue		$118,000
Cost of goods sold:		
Beginning inventory	$17,200	
Net purchases	51,700	
Cost of goods available for sale	68,900	
Ending inventory	(23,900)	
Cost of goods sold		45,000
Gross profit		$ 73,000

Nash-Robin has determined that the replacement cost of beginning inventory was $16,600, and the replacement cost of ending inventory is $18,300.

Required

Prepare the Nash-Robin income statement to apply the lower-of-cost-or-market rule to the company's beginning and ending inventory. Also show the relevant portion of Nash-Robin's balance sheet at March 31, 20X4.

Measuring the effect of an inventory error
(Obj. 6)

E6-13 Refer to the Nash-Robin income statement in Exercise 6-12, and ignore everything else. Assume that the ending inventory amount was miscounted and the cost ($23,900) is incorrect. Determine the correct amounts of cost of goods sold and gross profit if Nash-Robin's

a. Ending inventory is overstated by $3,000.
b. Ending inventory is understated by $3,000.

Start the computation of cost of goods sold with Cost of goods available for sale.

Correcting an inventory error—two years
(Obj. 6)

E6-14 Lazlo Power Tools reported the following comparative income statement for the years ended September 30, 20X2 and 20X1.

Lazlo Power Tools
Income Statements
Years Ended September 30, 20X2 and 20X1

	20X2		20X1	
Sales revenue		$137,300		$121,700
Cost of goods sold:				
Beginning inventory	$14,000		$12,800	
Net purchases	72,000		66,000	
Cost of goods available	86,000		78,800	
Ending inventory	(16,600)		(14,000)	
Cost of goods sold		69,400		64,800
Gross profit		67,900		56,900
Operating expenses		30,300		26,100
Net income		$ 37,600		$ 30,800

During 20X2, accountants for the company discovered that ending 20X1 inventory, as reported above, was overstated by $3,500. Prepare the corrected comparative income statement for the two-year period, complete with a heading for the statement. What was the effect of the error on net income for the two years combined? Explain your answer.

Estimating ending inventory by the gross profit method **(Obj. 7)**

E6-15 **General Electric Company (GE)** holds inventory all over the world. Assume that the records for a line of refrigerators show the following:

Beginning inventory	$ 150,000
Net purchases	800,000
Net sales	1,000,000
Gross profit rate	30%

Suppose this inventory, stored in Guatemala, was lost in a hurricane. Estimate the amount of the loss to GE. Use the gross profit method.

Estimating ending inventory by the gross profit method **(Obj. 7)**

Student ResourceCD spreadsheet

E6-16 Lake Huron Marineland uses a periodic inventory system. The company began January with inventory of $47,500. During January, the business made net purchases of $37,600 and had net sales of $60,000. For the past several years, Lake Huron's gross profit has been 40% of sales. Use the gross profit method to estimate the cost of the ending inventory for the monthly financial statements.

Problems

(Group A)

A+ online homework

Accounting for inventory in a perpetual system—FIFO **(Obj. 1, 2)**

P6-1A **Pier 1 Imports** operates almost 1,000 stores around the world. Assume you are dealing with a Pier 1 store in Dallas. Assume the store began with an inventory of 50 chairs that cost a total of $1,500. The store purchased and sold merchandise on account as follows:

Purchase 1	60 chairs @ $35
Sale 1	100 chairs @ $60
Purchase 2	80 chairs @ $40
Sale 2	70 chairs @ $70

Assume that Pier 1 uses the FIFO cost method. Cash payments on account totaled $5,100. Operating expenses were $2,400; the store paid two-thirds in cash and accrued the rest as Accounts Payable.

Required

1. Prepare a perpetual inventory record, at FIFO cost, for this merchandise.
2. Make journal entries to record the store's transactions.

Accounting for inventory in a perpetual system—average-cost **(Obj. 1, 3)**

P6-2A Refer to the **Pier 1 Imports** situation in Problem 6-1A. Keep all the data unchanged, except that Pier 1 actually uses the average-cost method.

Required

1. Prepare a perpetual inventory record at average cost. Round average unit cost to the nearest cent and all other amounts to the nearest dollar.
2. Prepare a multistep income statement for the Pier 1 Imports store for the month of February.

Using the perpetual inventory system—LIFO **(Obj. 1, 3)**

P6-3A Rambler Lawn Supply, which uses the LIFO method, began March with 50 units of inventory that cost $15 each. During March, Rambler completed these inventory transactions:

		Units	Unit Cost	Unit Sale Price
March 2	Purchase	12	$20	
8	Sale	40		$36
17	Purchase	24	25	
22	Sale	31		40

Required

1. Prepare a perpetual inventory record for the lawn supply merchandise.
2. Determine Rambler's cost of goods sold for March.
3. Compute gross profit for March.

Computing inventory by three methods—periodic system
(Obj. 3, 4)

P6-4A A Best Yet Electronic Center began December with 140 units of inventory that cost $75 each. During December, the store made the following purchases:

Dec. 3	217 @ $79
12	95 @ 82
18	210 @ 83
24	248 @ 87

The store uses the periodic inventory system, and the physical count at December 31 indicates that 229 units of inventory are on hand.

Required

1. Determine the ending inventory and cost-of-goods-sold amounts for the December financial statements under the average cost, FIFO, and LIFO methods. Round average cost per unit to the nearest cent and all other amounts to the nearest dollar.
2. Sales revenue for December totaled $90,000. Compute Best Yet's gross profit for December under each method.
3. Which method will result in the lowest income taxes for Best Yet? Why? Which method will result in the highest net income for Best Yet? Why?

Using the periodic inventory system—FIFO
(Obj. 4)

P6-5A Mesa Hardware Company, which uses a periodic inventory system, began 20X4 with 6,000 units of inventory that cost a total of $30,000. During 20X4, Mesa purchased merchandise on account as follows:

Purchase 1 (10,000 units costing)	$ 60,000
Purchase 2 (20,000 units costing)	140,000

At year-end, the physical count indicated 5,000 units of inventory on hand.

Required

1. How many units did Mesa sell during the year? The sale price per unit was $10. Determine Mesa's sales revenue for the year.
2. Compute cost of goods sold by the FIFO method. Then determine gross profit for the year.

Applying the lower-of-cost-or-market rule to inventories
(Obj. 5)

P6-6A **Revco Drug** has been plagued with lackluster sales, and some of the company's merchandise is gathering dust. It is now December 31, 20X7. Assume the current replacement cost of Revco's ending inventory is $700,000 below what Revco paid for the goods, which was $3,900,000. Before any adjustments at the end of the period, assume the Cost of Goods Sold account has a balance of $22,400,000.

What action should Revco take in this situation, if any? Give any journal entry required. At what amount should Revco report Inventory on the balance sheet? At what amount should the company report Cost of Goods Sold on the income statement? Discuss the accounting principle or concept that is most relevant to this situation.

Correcting inventory errors over a three-year period
(Obj. 6)

P6-7A The accounting records of Treviño's Mexican Restaurant show these data (in thousands):

	20X3		20X2		20X1	
Net sales revenue.		$210		$165		$170
Cost of goods sold:						
Beginning inventory	$ 15		$ 25		$ 40	
Net purchases.	135		100		90	
Cost of goods available.	150		125		130	
Less: Ending inventory.	(30)		(15)		(25)	
Cost of goods sold		120		110		105
Gross profit.		90		55		65
Operating expenses.		74		38		46
Net income		$ 16		$ 17		$ 19

In early 20X4, internal auditors discovered that the ending inventory for 20X1, as reported here, was understated by $8 thousand and that the ending inventory for 20X3 was overstated by $5 thousand. The ending inventory at December 31, 20X2, was correct.

Required

1. Show corrected income statements for the three years.
2. State whether each year's net income as reported here is understated or overstated. For each incorrect figure, indicate the amount of the understatement or overstatement.

Estimating ending inventory by the gross profit method; preparing the income statement
(Obj. 7)

Student ResourceCD
General Ledger, Peachtree, QuickBooks

P6-8A **Moss Motors** estimates its inventory by the gross profit method when preparing monthly financial statements. For the past two years, gross profit has averaged 30% of net sales. Assume further that the company's inventory records reveal the following data (amounts in thousands):

Inventory, March 1.	$ 292
Transactions during March:	
Purchases	6,585
Purchase discounts	149
Purchase returns	8
Sales.	8,657
Sales returns	17

Required

1. Estimate the March 31 inventory using the gross profit method.
2. Prepare the March income statement through gross profit for Moss Motors.

Problems

(Group B)

A+ online homework

Accounting for inventory using the perpetual system—LIFO
(Obj. 1, 2)

P6-1B **Toys "Я" Us** purchases inventory in crates of merchandise, so each unit of inventory is a crate of toys. Assume you are dealing with a single department in the Toys "Я" Us store in Santa Barbara, California.

Assume the department began January with an inventory of 20 units that cost a total of $1,200. During the month, the department purchased and sold merchandise on account as follows:

Purchase 1	30 units @ $ 65	Purchase 2	70 units @ $ 70
Sale 1	40 units @ $100	Sale 2	75 units @ $110

Toys "Я" Us uses the LIFO cost method.

Cash payments on account totaled $6,300. Department operating expenses for the month were $3,600. The department paid two-thirds in cash, with the rest accrued as Accounts Payable.

Required

1. Prepare a perpetual inventory record, at LIFO cost, for this merchandise.
2. Make journal entries to record the department's transactions.

Accounting for inventory in a perpetual system—average-cost
(Obj. 1, 3)

P6-2B Refer to the **Toys "Я" Us** situation in Problem 6-1B. Keep all the data unchanged, except assume that Toys "Я" Us uses the average-cost method.

Required

1. Prepare a perpetual inventory record at average cost. Round average unit cost to the nearest cent and all other amounts to the nearest dollar.
2. Prepare a multistep income statement for the Toys "Я" Us department for the month of January.

Using the perpetual inventory system—FIFO
(Obj. 1, 3)

P6-3B A **Samsonite** outlet store, which uses the FIFO method, began August with 50 units of inventory that cost $40 each. During August, the store completed these inventory transactions:

		Units	Unit Cost	Unit Sale Price
Aug. 3	Sale	40		$70
8	Purchase	80	44	
21	Sale	70		73
30	Purchase	20	48	

Required

1. Prepare a perpetual inventory record for the luggage inventory.
2. Determine the store's cost of goods sold for August.
3. Compute gross profit for August.

Computing inventory by three methods—periodic system
(Obj. 3, 4)

P6-4B Nelson Framing Co. began March with 73 units of inventory that cost $23 each. During the month, Nelson made the following purchases:

March 4	113 @ $26
12	81 @ 30
19	167 @ 32
25	44 @ 35

The company uses the periodic inventory system, and the physical count at March 31 includes 51 units of inventory on hand.

Required

1. Determine the ending inventory and cost-of-goods-sold amounts for the March financial statements under (a) average cost, (b) FIFO cost, and (c) LIFO cost. Round average cost per unit to the nearest cent and all other amounts to the nearest dollar.
2. Sales revenue for March totaled $20,000. Compute Nelson's gross profit for March under each method.
3. Which method will result in the lowest income taxes for Nelson? Why?
4. Which method will result in the highest net income for Nelson? Why?

Using the periodic inventory system—LIFO
(Obj. 4)

P6-5B Louisville Baseball Company, which uses a periodic inventory system, began 20X4 with 6,000 units of inventory that cost a total of $30,000. During 20X4, Louisville purchased merchandise on account as follows:

Purchase 1 (10,000 units costing)	$ 60,000
Purchase 2 (20,000 units costing)	140,000

At year-end, the physical count indicated 15,000 units of inventory on hand.

Required

1. How many units did Louisville sell during the year? The sale price per unit was $18. Determine Louisville's sales revenue for the year.
2. Compute cost of goods sold by the LIFO method. Then determine gross profit for the year.

Applying the lower-of-cost-or-market rule to inventories **(Obj. 5)**

P6-6B **The Army/Navy Surplus Store** has experienced lackluster sales, and some of the company's merchandise is gathering dust. It is now December 31, 20X5, and the current replacement cost of the ending inventory is $650,000 below what Army/Navy actually paid for the goods, which was $4,900,000. Before any adjustments at the end of the period, the company's Cost of Goods Sold account has a balance of $29,600,000.

What action should The Army/Navy Surplus Store take in this situation, if any? Give any journal entry required. At what amount should Army/Navy report Inventory on the balance sheet? At what amount should the company report Cost of Goods Sold on the income statement? Discuss the accounting principle or concept that is most relevant to this situation.

Correcting inventory errors over a three-year period **(Obj. 6)**

P6-7B The Victoria British Company books show the following data (in thousands). In early 20X4, internal auditors found that the ending inventory for 20X1 was overstated by $8 thousand and that the ending inventory for 20X3 was understated by $4 thousand. The ending inventory at December 31, 20X2, was correct.

(Thousands)	20X3		20X2		20X1	
Net sales revenue		$360		$285		$244
Cost of goods sold:						
Beginning inventory	$ 65		$ 55		$ 70	
Net purchases	195		135		130	
Cost of goods available	260		190		200	
Less: Ending inventory	(70)		(65)		(55)	
Cost of goods sold		190		125		145
Gross profit		170		160		99
Operating expenses		113		109		76
Net income		$ 57		$ 51		$ 23

Required

1. Show corrected income statements for the three years.
2. State whether each year's net income is understated or overstated. For each incorrect figure, indicate the amount of the understatement or overstatement.

Estimating ending inventory by the gross profit method; preparing the income statement **(Obj. 7)**

Student Resource CD
GL, PT, QB

P6-8B **The Roadster Factory** estimates its inventory by the gross profit method when preparing monthly financial statements. The gross profit has averaged 40% of net sales. Assume that the company's inventory records reveal the following data (amounts in thousands):

Inventory, July 1	$ 367
Transactions during July:	
Purchases	3,789
Purchase discounts	26
Purchase returns	12
Sales	6,430
Sales returns	25

Required

1. Estimate the July 31 inventory, using the gross profit method.
2. Prepare the July income statement through gross profit for The Roadster Factory.

APPLY *Your Knowledge*

Decision Cases

Increasing net income
(Obj. 3)

Case 1. Suppose you own a **Chevron** convenience store. Most of your sales come from gasoline, but you also sell fast food, snack items, and drinks. The store's summarized financial statements for 20X4, the most recent year, follow:

Chevron Convenience Store
Balance Sheet
December 31, 20X4

(Thousands)	Assets	Liabilities and Capital	
Cash	$ 30	Accounts payable	$ 35
Inventories	75	Note payable	280
Land and buildings, net	360	Total liabilities	315
		Owner, capital	150
Total assets	$465	Total liabilities and capital	$465

Chevron Convenience Store
Income Statement
Year Ended December 31, 20X4

	(Thousands)
Sales	$800
Cost of goods sold	660
Gross profit	140
Operating expenses	100
Net income	$ 40

Assume that you need to double net income. To accomplish your goal, it will be very difficult to raise the prices you charge because there is a **Texaco** store across the street. Also, you have little control over your cost of goods sold for gasoline because Chevron supplies all your gasoline and Chevron sets the price you must pay.

Identify several strategies for doubling net income.

Making inventory decisions
(Obj. 2, 3)

Case 2. Assume you are opening a clothing store that specializes in women's designer dresses. Each dress costs you anywhere from $200 to $500, and you plan to sell the dresses for $350 to $1,000 each.

To finance the business, you need a $50,000 loan, and your banker requires a set of forecasted financial statements. Assume you are preparing the statements and must make some decisions about how to do the accounting for the business. Answer the following questions (refer back to Chapter 5 if necessary):

1. Which type of inventory system will you use? Give your reason.
2. Show how to compute net purchases and net sales. How will you treat the cost of transportation-in?
3. How often do you plan to do a physical count of inventory on hand? What will the physical count accomplish?
4. Inventory costs are rising. Which inventory costing method will you use in order to:
   - **a.** Maximize net income?
   - **b.** Pay the least amount of income tax?

Ethical Issue

During 20X2, Darden Furniture Company changed to the LIFO method of accounting for inventory. Suppose that during 20X3, Darden changes back to the FIFO method and the following year switches back to LIFO again.

Required

1. What would you think of a company's ethics if it changed accounting methods every year?
2. What accounting principle would changing methods every year violate?
3. Who can be harmed when a company changes its accounting methods too often? How?

Financial Statement Case

Analyzing inventories
(Obj. 3, 4, 5)

The notes are an important part of a company's financial statements, giving valuable details that would clutter the tabular data presented in the statements. This case will help you learn to use a company's inventory notes. Refer to the **Amazon.com** financial statements and related notes in Appendix A and answer the following questions:

Required

1. How much was the Amazon.com merchandise inventory at December 31, 2002? At December 31, 2001?
2. How does Amazon value its inventories? Which cost method does the company use? See Note 1.
3. By rearranging the cost-of-goods-sold formula, you can compute purchases, which are not disclosed in the Amazon statements. How much were the company's inventory purchases during 2002?

Team Project

→ *Link Back to Chapter 5 (Gross Profit Percentage and Inventory Turnover).* Obtain the annual reports of as many companies as you have team members—one company per team member. Most companies post their financial statements on their Web sites.

Required

1. Identify the inventory method used by each company.
2. Compute each company's gross profit percentage and rate of inventory turnover for the most recent two years.
3. For the industries of the companies you are analyzing, obtain the industry averages for gross profit percentage and inventory turnover from Robert Morris Associates, *Annual Statement Studies*; Dun and Bradstreet, *Industry Norms and Key Business Ratios*; or Leo Troy, *Almanac of Business and Industrial Financial Ratios*.
4. How well does each of your companies compare to the average for its industry? What insight about your companies can you glean from these ratios?

For Internet Exercises, go to the Web site www.prenhall.com/horngren.

APPENDIX *to Chapter 6*

Comparing the Perpetual and Periodic Inventory Systems

Exhibit 6A-1 provides a side-by-side comparison of the two inventory accounting systems. It gives the journal entries, the T-accounts, and all financial-statement effects of both inventory systems.

In the periodic system, the purchase of inventory is *not* recorded in the Inventory account. Instead, purchases are recorded in the Purchases account,

Exhibit 6A-1 Comparing the Perpetual and Periodic Inventory Systems (amounts assumed)

Panel A—Recording in the Journal and Posting to the Accounts

Perpetual System

1. Credit purchases of $560,000:

Inventory	560,000	
Accounts Payable		560,000

2. Credit sales of $900,000 (cost $540,000):

Accounts Receivable	900,000	
Sales Revenue		900,000
Cost of Goods Sold	540,000	
Inventory		540,000

3. End-of-period entries:
No entries required. Both Inventory and Cost of Goods Sold are up-to-date.

Periodic System

1. Credit purchases of $560,000:

Purchases	560,000	
Accounts Payable		560,000

2. Credit sales of $900,000:

Accounts Receivable	900,000	
Sales Revenue		900,000

3. End-of-period entries to update Inventory and record Cost of Goods Sold:

a. Transfer the cost of beginning inventory ($100,000) to Cost of Goods Sold:

Cost of Goods Sold	100,000	
Inventory (beginning balance)		100,000

b. Record the cost of ending inventory ($120,000) based on a physical count:

Inventory (ending balance)	120,000	
Cost of Goods Sold		120,000

c. Transfer the cost of purchases to Cost of Goods Sold:

Cost of Goods Sold	560,000	
Purchases		560,000

Inventory and Cost of Goods Sold Accounts (Perpetual System)

Inventory (Dr.)	Inventory (Cr.)	Cost of Goods Sold (Dr.)	Cost of Goods Sold (Cr.)
100,000*	540,000	540,000	
560,000			
120,000			

*Beginning inventory was $100,000.

Inventory and Cost of Goods Sold Accounts (Periodic System)

Inventory (Dr.)	Inventory (Cr.)	Cost of Goods Sold (Dr.)	Cost of Goods Sold (Cr.)
100,000**	100,000	100,000	120,000
120,000		560,000	
		540,000	

**Beginning inventory was $100,000.

Panel B—Reporting in the Financial Statements

Perpetual System

Income Statement (partial)

Sales revenue	$900,000
Cost of goods sold	540,000
Gross profit	$360,000

Balance Sheet (partial)

Current assets:

Cash	$ XXX
Accounts receivable	XXX
Inventories	120,000

Periodic System

Sales revenue		$900,000
Cost of goods sold:		
Beginning inventory	$100,000	
Purchases	560,000	
Cost of goods available for sale	660,000	
Less: Ending inventory	(120,000)	
Cost of goods sold		540,000
Gross profit		$360,000

Current assets:

Cash	$ XXX
Accounts receivable	XXX
Inventories	120,000

which is an expense (see transaction 1 in the exhibit, right column). A sale transaction includes *no* cost of goods sold entry (transaction 2). How, then, does the business record inventory and cost of goods sold?

Transactions 3a and 3b give the end-of-period entries to update the Inventory account and record Cost of Goods Sold. Transaction 3c closes the Purchases account into Cost of Goods Sold to complete the periodic process.

Panel B of the exhibit shows the financial statements under both systems.

CHAPTER 7

Accounting Information Systems

A+ TIPS CHECK YOUR RESOURCES

- Visit the www.prenhall.com/horngren **Web site** for self-study quizzes, video clips, and other resources
- Try the **Quick Check** exercise at the end of the chapter to test your knowledge
- Learn the **key terms**
- Do the **Starter** exercises keyed in the margins
- Work the **mid-** and **end-of-chapter summary problems**
- Use the **Concept Links** to review material in other chapters
- Search the **CD** for review materials by chapter or by key word

LEARNING OBJECTIVES

1. Describe an effective accounting information system
2. Understand both computerized and manual accounting systems
3. Understand how spreadsheets are used in accounting
4. Use the sales journal, the cash receipts journal, and the accounts receivable ledger
5. Use the purchases journal, the cash payments journal, and the accounts payable ledger

With QuickBooks and Peachtree taking over, you'd think accountants would be worried. After all, why does a business need an accountant when these programs make the recordkeeping so user-friendly? But the reverse is true. The new software and Web applications are creating lots of opportunities for accountants. You may want to consider a career in accounting.

PriceKubecka

Many entrepreneurs are strapped for cash and can't pay an accountant to keep their books. Enter the Accounting Software Consultant. Brian Price of PriceKubecka has built a $400,000 business by consulting with small businesses. Clients range from mom-and-pop organizations that bring in $100,000 to $200,000 a year to a $2 million services firm. His typical client engagement generates $1,100 of service revenue for the firm. For a flat fee,

Price will install QuickBooks or other software and provide five hours of training. Of course, five hours is never enough, so clients end up buying more training time for $65 to $100 an hour.

The best part for Price is that clients then can do their own bookkeeping. That frees Price to do more fun things, such as analyzing financial information and helping clients make decisions. Price's clients also refer their friends to him, and that further grows the business.

Source: Adapted from Jeff Stimpson, "The New Consultant," *The Practical Accountant*, September 1999, pp. 325–42. ■

Sitemap

- Effective Accounting Systems
- Computerized and Manual Systems
- Special Journals
- The General Journal

Accounting Information System
The combination of personnel, records, and procedures that a business uses to provide financial data.

Every organization—from the smallest proprietorship to the largest corporation—needs accounting. An **accounting information system** is the combination of personnel, records, and procedures that provides financial data. You have already been using an accounting system in this text. It consists of two basic components: a journal and a ledger. Every accounting system has these components.

This simple system can handle only a few transactions each period. Businesses cope with heavy loads in two ways: computerization and specialization. We *computerize* to do the accounting faster and more reliably. *Specialization* combines similar transactions to speed the process. A key feature of specialization is the set of special journals that we cover in the second half of this chapter.

- ■ Effective Accounting Systems
- □ Computerized and Manual Systems
- □ Special Journals
- □ The General Journal

Effective Accounting Information Systems

Good personnel are critical to success. Employees must be both competent and honest. Design features also make the accounting system run efficiently. A good system—whether computerized or manual—must have

- Control
- Compatibility
- Flexibility
- Good cost/benefit relationship

1 Describe an effective accounting information system

Features of Effective Systems

Managers must *control* operations, or the company will lose focus. *Internal controls* safeguard assets and eliminate waste. For example, in companies such as Amazon.com, Coca-Cola, and Kinko's, managers control cash disbursements to avoid theft through unauthorized payments. VISA, MasterCard, and Discover keep accounts receivable records to ensure that they collect cash on time.

A *compatible* system is one that works smoothly with the company's personnel and organizational structure. An example is Bank of America, which is organized as a network of branch offices. Bank of America's top managers track revenues in each region where the bank does business. They must analyze loans in different geographic regions. If revenues in Texas are lagging, managers can focus on their Texas banks. They may move some top managers to their banks in Dallas or Houston.

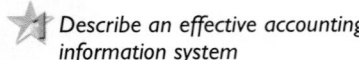

Organizations change over time. They develop new products, sell off unprofitable operations, and acquire new ones. Changes in the business may require a new accounting system. A well-designed system is *flexible* if it accommodates changes in the organization. Consider Monsanto Company's acquisition of the pharmaceuticals firm Searle, which features Nutrasweet. Monsanto's accounting system was flexible enough to fold Searle/Nutrasweet into Monsanto.

Control, compatibility, and flexibility cost money. Managers want a system that gives the most benefit at the least cost. This is a favorable *cost/benefit relationship*. Most small companies use off-the-shelf computerized accounting packages, and the very smallest businesses might not computerize at all. But large companies, such as the brokerage firm Edward Jones, have specialized information needs. Custom programming is a must. The benefits—in terms of good information—far outweigh the costs. The result? Better decisions.

✔ Starter 7-1

Components of a Computerized System

A computerized accounting system has three basic components:

- Hardware
- Software
- Company personnel

Hardware is the electronic equipment: computers, disk drives, monitors, printers, and the network that connects them. Most systems require a **network** to link different computers sharing the same information. In a networked system, the **server** stores the program and the data. With a network, a PriceWaterhouseCoopers auditor in London can work on the data of a client in Sydney, Australia. The result is a speedier audit for the client.

Hardware
Electronic equipment that includes computers, disk drives, monitors, printers, and the network that connects them.

Network
The system of electronic linkages that allows different computers to share the same information.

Server
The main computer in a network, where the program and data are stored.

✔ Starter 7-2

✔ Starter 7-3

Software is the set of programs that drives the computer. Accounting software reads, edits (alters), and stores transaction data. It also generates the reports managers use to run the business. Many software packages operate independently. For example, a company that owns a chain of gas stations may be only partly computerized. This small business may use software for employee payrolls. Other parts of the accounting system may not be automated.

For large enterprises, like Hershey Foods and Caterpillar Tractor, the accounting software is integrated into the company's **database**, or computerized storehouse of information.

Software
Set of programs or instructions that drive the computer to perform the work desired.

Database
A computerized storehouse of information.

- □ Effective Accounting Systems
- ■ Computerized and Manual Systems
- □ Special Journals
- □ The General Journal

How Computerized and Manual Systems Work

Student Resource CD
chart of accounts, ERP systems, spreadsheet program

2 *Understand both computerized and manual accounting systems*

Computerized accounting systems have replaced manual systems in many organizations—even in small businesses such as your neighborhood pharmacy. The three stages of data processing (inputs, processing, and outputs) are shown in Exhibit 7-1.

Exhibit 7-1

The Three Stages of Data Processing

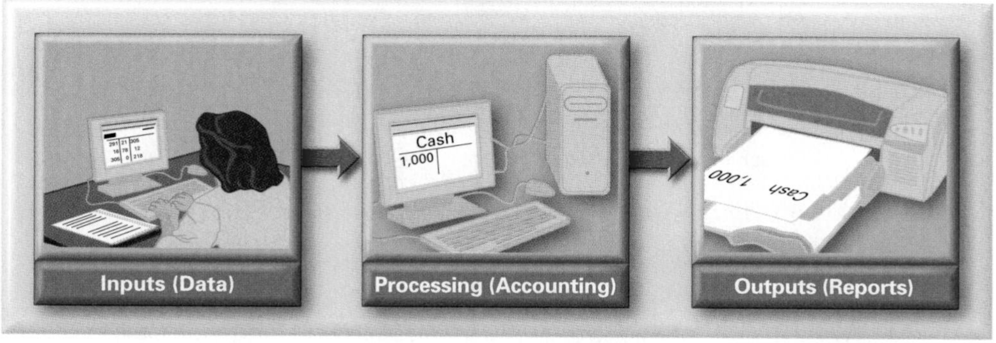

Inputs represent data from source documents, such as fax orders received from customers, sales receipts, and bank statements. Inputs are usually grouped by type. For example, a firm would enter cash-sale transactions separately from sales on account.

In a manual system, *processing* includes journalizing transactions, posting to the accounts, and preparing the financial statements. A computerized system also processes transactions, but without the intermediate steps (journal, ledger, and trial balance).

Outputs are the reports used for decision making, including the financial statements (income statement and balance sheet). Business owners can make better decisions with the reports produced by their accounting system. Exhibit 7-2 diagrams a computerized system. Start with data inputs in the lower left corner.

Exhibit 7-2

Overview of a Computerized Accounting System

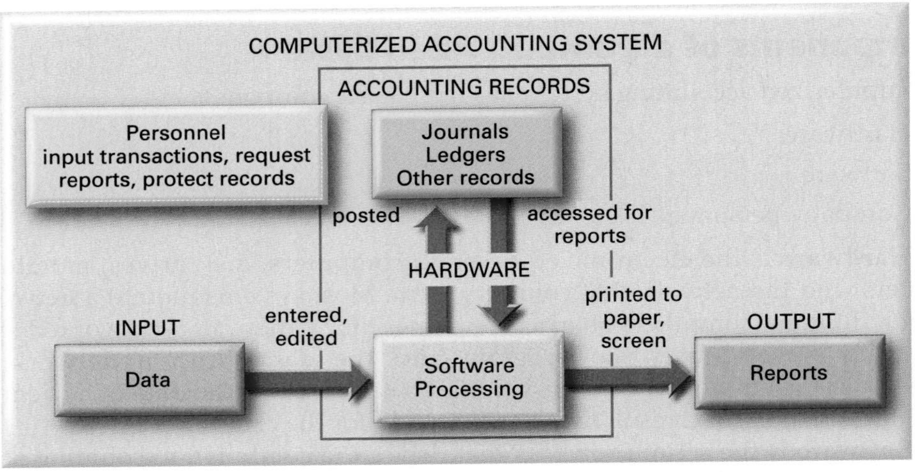

Designing a System: The Chart of Accounts

Recall from Chapter 2 that the chart of accounts lists all the accounts and their account numbers.

An accounting system begins with the chart of accounts. In the system of a large company such as Eastman Kodak, account numbers take on added importance. Recall that asset accounts generally begin with the digit 1, liabilities with the digit 2, owner's equity accounts with the digit 3, revenues with 4, and expenses with 5. Exhibit 7-3 diagrams one structure for computerized accounts. Assets are divided into current assets, fixed assets (property, plant, and equipment), and other assets. Among the current assets, we illustrate only three accounts: Cash in Bank (Account No. 111), Accounts Receivable (No. 112), and Prepaid Insurance (No. 115).

Exhibit 7-3

Account-Number Structure for Computerized Accounts

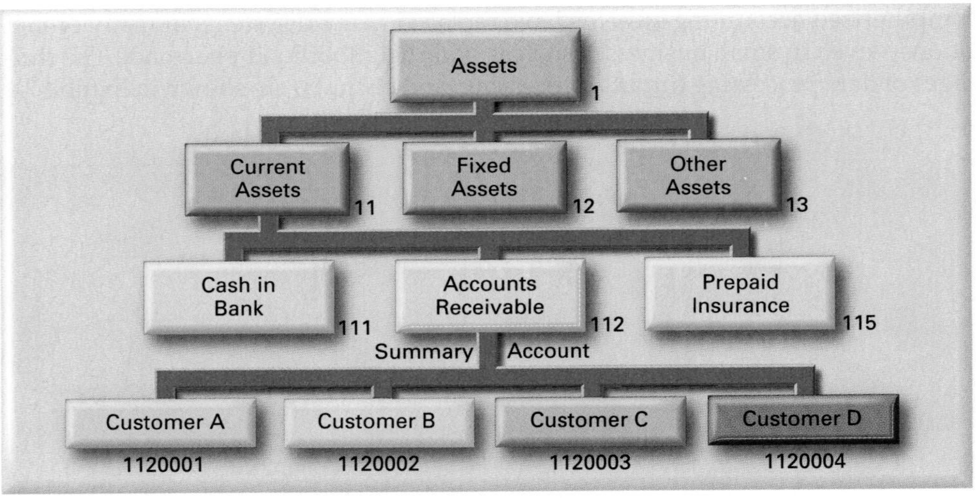

The account numbers in Exhibit 7-3 get longer and more detailed as you move from top to bottom. For example, Customer A's account number is 1120001: 112 represents Accounts Receivable, and 0001 refers to Customer A.

Computerized accounting systems rely on account *number ranges* to translate accounts and their balances into financial statements and other reports. For example, accounts numbered 101 through 399 (assets, liabilities, and owner's equity) are sorted to the balance sheet, while accounts numbered 401 through 599 (revenues and expenses) go to the income statement.

✔ Starter 7-4

Processing Transactions: Manual and Menu-Driven Systems

Recording transactions in an actual accounting system requires an additional step that we have skipped thus far. A business of any size classifies transactions by type for efficient handling. In a manual system, credit sales, cash receipts, purchases on account, and cash payments are treated as four separate categories. Each has its own special journal. For example:

- Credit sales are recorded in a *sales journal*.
- Cash receipts are entered in a *cash receipts journal*.
- Credit purchases of inventory and other assets are recorded in a *purchases journal*.
- Cash payments are entered in a *cash payments journal*.
- Transactions that do not fit any of the special journals, such as adjusting entries, are recorded in the *general journal*, which serves as the "journal of last resort."

Computerized systems are organized by function, or task. Access to functions is arranged in terms of menus. A **menu** is a list of options for choosing computer functions. In a *menu-driven* system, you first access the *main menu*. You then choose from one or more submenus until you finally reach the function you want.

Menu
A list of options for choosing computer functions.

Exhibit 7-4 illustrates one type of menu structure. The menu bar at the top gives the main menu. The accountant has chosen the General option (short for General Ledger), highlighted by the cursor. This action opened a submenu of four items: Transactions, Posting, Account Maintenance, and Closing. The Transactions option was then chosen (highlighted).

Exhibit 7-4

Main Menu of a Computerized Accounting System

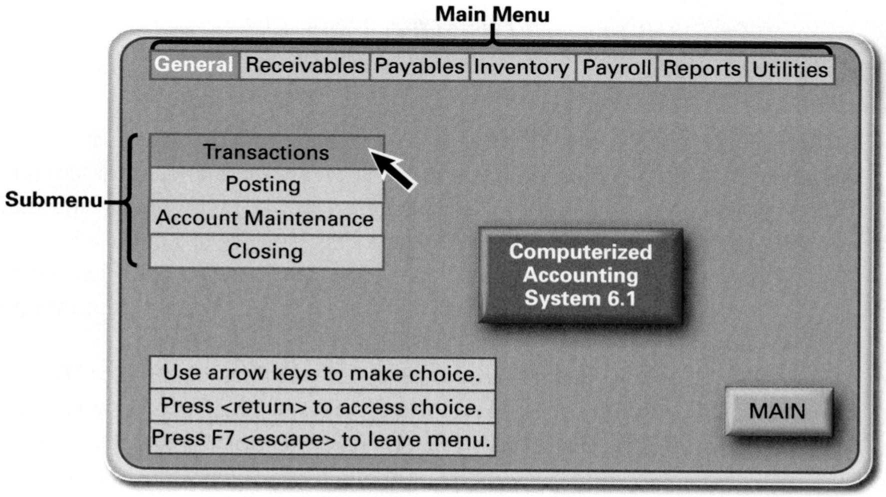

Online Processing
Computerized processing of related functions, such as the recording and posting of transactions, on a continuous basis.

Batch Processing
Computerized accounting for similar transactions in a group or batch.

Posting in a computerized system can be performed continuously (**online processing**) or later for a group of similar transactions (**batch processing**). In effect, data are "parked" in the computer to await posting. The posting then updates the account balances.

Enterprise Resource Planning (ERP) Systems

Enterprise Resource Planning (ERP) Software that can integrate all of a company's worldwide functions, departments, and data into a single system.

Data Warehouse A very large database holding data for a number of years and used for analysis rather than for transaction processing.

Many small businesses use QuickBooks or Peachtree. But larger companies like **Fujitsu** and **Allstate Insurance** are using **ERP** (enterprise resource planning) systems to manage their data. ERP systems such as SAP, Oracle, and PeopleSoft can integrate all company data into a single **data warehouse**. The ERP system feeds the data into software for all company activities—from purchasing to production and customer service.

Advantages of ERP systems include:

- A centralized ERP system can save lots of money.
- ERP helps companies adjust to changes. A change in sales ripples through the purchasing, shipping, and accounting systems.
- An ERP system can replace hundreds of separate software systems, such as different payroll and production software.

ERP is expensive. Major installations cost Fujitsu and Allstate over $40 million. Implementation also requires a large commitment of time and people. For example, **Hershey Foods** tried to shrink a four-year ERP project into two and a half years. The result? The software did not map into Hershey's operations, and disrupted deliveries hurt profits in the Halloween candy-buying season.

Accounting.com

Accounting Pioneers on the Virtual Frontier

As you saw in the chapter-opening story, computer and Internet technology are remaking the bookkeeping and tax aspects of accounting. There are "virtual" software consultants, and now there are "virtual" or "online" accountants. Slogans like "Real Accounting in a Virtual World" and "Outsourced Accounting Services for a Wired World" are advertising

- Basic bookkeeping
- Full-service outsourcing
- Real-time accounting
- 24-hour access to accounting data

TADOnline, founded by Lance and Deanna Gildea in San Diego, is one such service. TAD starts clients out scanning their invoices, bank statements, and other documents into the computer. Scanned documents are transmitted to TAD, and within minutes, TAD updates the client's accounts. Customers then use a Web browser to enter a home page prepared by TAD, where they can view, print, and download reports, checks, and other information. Soon clients will be able to get real-time access to their accounting data through a new Web-based service.

For clients—typically small- to mid-sized businesses—the key benefits of TADOnline are price and reliability. In some cases, TAD's monthly fees are half what it would cost to hire a bookkeeper—and TAD doesn't call in sick or take vacations. A big plus for the "virtual accountants" is being able to live wherever they please, regardless of where clients are located. For TAD's Lance and Deanna Gildea, that means San Diego half the year and scenic Vashon Island, Washington, for the other half.

Source: Adapted from Antoinette Alexander, "Pioneers on the Virtual Frontier," *Accounting Technology*, Jan./Feb. 2000, pp. 18–24.

Integrated Accounting Software: Spreadsheets

3 Understand how spreadsheets are used in accounting

Computerized accounting packages are organized by **modules**, which are integrated units that work together. Changes affecting one module will affect others. For example, a credit-sale transaction will update both Accounts Receivable/Sales and Inventory/Cost of Goods Sold. Accounting packages, such as QuickBooks and Peachtree, come as an integrated system.

Module
Separate compatible units of an accounting package that are integrated to function together.

Spreadsheets are computer programs that link data by means of formulas and functions. Spreadsheets are organized by *cells*, each defined by a row number and a column number. A cell can contain words (called labels), numbers, or formulas. The *cursor*, or electronic highlighter, indicates which cell is active. When the cursor is placed over any cell, information can be entered there for processing.

Spreadsheet
A computer program that links data by means of formulas and functions; an electronic work sheet.

Exhibit 7-5 shows an income statement on a spreadsheet screen. The labels were entered in cells A1 through A4. The dollar amount of revenues was entered in cell B2 and expenses in cell B3. A formula was placed in cell B4 as follows: =B2–B3. This formula computes net income in cell B4. If revenues increase to $170,000, net income automatically increases to $80,000. No other cells will change.

Exhibit 7-5
A Spreadsheet Screen

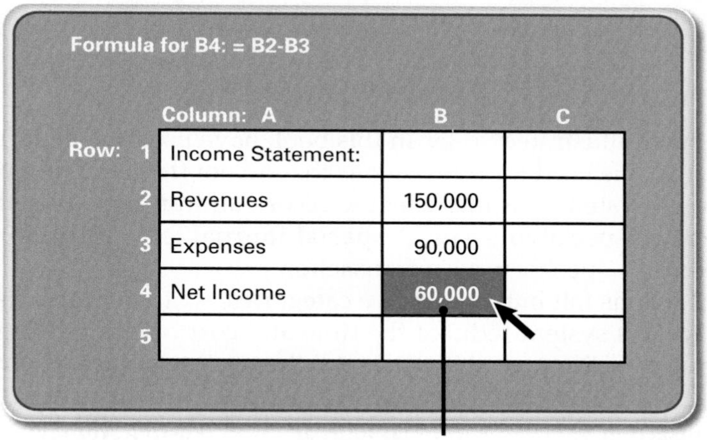

The power of a spreadsheet is apparent when large amounts of data are analyzed. Change only one number, and you save hours of manual calculations. Exhibit 7-6 shows the basic arithmetic operations in Excel.

Exhibit 7-6
Basic Arithmetic Operations in Excel Spreadsheets

✔ **Starter 7-5**

Operation	Symbol
Addition	+
Subtraction	–
Multiplication	*
Division	/
Addition of a range of cells	=SUM (beginning cell:ending cell)
Examples:	
Add cells A2 through A9	=SUM (A2:A9)
Divide cell C2 by cell D1	=C2/D1

A+ TIPS
CHECK YOUR RESOURCES

- ☐ Effective Accounting Systems
- ☐ Computerized and Manual Systems
- ■ Special Journals
- ☐ The General Journal

Special Journals

Exhibit 7-7 diagrams a typical accounting system for a merchandising business. The remainder of this chapter describes this system.

Exhibit 7-7 Overview of an Accounting System with Special Journals

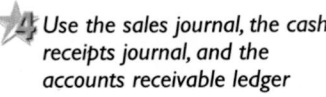

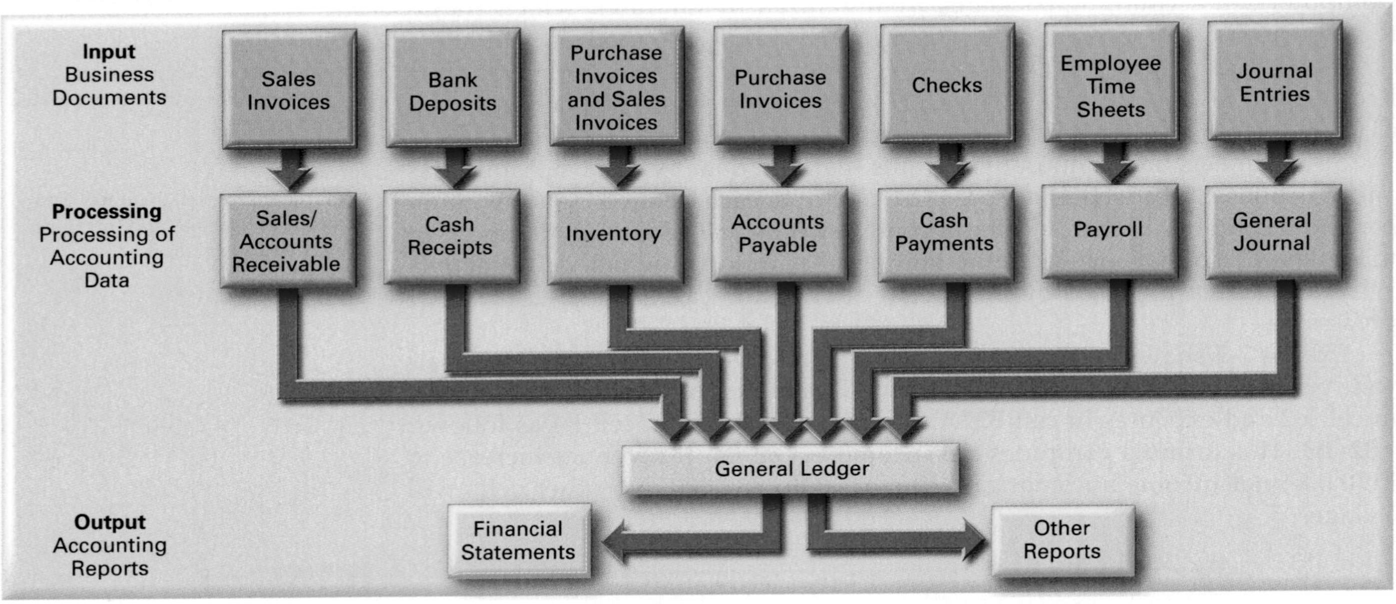

Special Journals in a Manual System

General Journal
Journal used to record all transactions that do not fit one of the special journals.

Special Journal
An accounting journal designed to record one specific type of transaction.

The journal entries illustrated so far in this book have used the **general journal**. The general journal is used for transactions that do not fit one of the special journals. In a manual system, it is inefficient to record all transactions in the general journal, so we use special journals. A **special journal** is an accounting journal designed to record a specific type of transaction.

Most transactions fall into one of five categories, so accountants use five different journals. This system reduces the time and cost of journalizing. The five types of transactions, the special journal, and the posting abbreviations follow.

✔ Starter 7-6

Transaction	Special Journal	Posting Abbreviation
1. Sale on account	Sales journal	S
2. Cash receipt	Cash receipts journal	CR
3. Purchase on account	Purchases journal	P
4. Cash payment	Cash payments journal	CP
5. All others	General journal	J

Student ResourceCD
special journals, transactions

4 *Use the sales journal, the cash receipts journal, and the accounts receivable ledger*

Adjusting and closing entries are entered in the general journal. Transactions are recorded in either the general journal or a special journal, but not in both.

You may be wondering why we cover manual accounting systems, since many businesses have computerized. There are three main reasons:

1. Learning a manual system will help you master accounting. One of the authors of this book has a friend who uses QuickBooks for his proprietorship. This man knows little beyond which keys to punch. If he knew the accounting, he could better manage his business and have more confidence that his records are accurate.
2. Learning a manual system will equip you to work with both manual and electronic systems. The accounting is the same regardless of the system.
3. Few small businesses have computerized all their accounting. Even companies that use QuickBooks or Peachtree keep some manual accounting records. Also, many small businesses use manual systems, and they follow the principles and procedures that we illustrate in this chapter.

Using the Sales Journal

Most merchandisers sell inventory on account. These credit sales are entered in the **sales journal**. Credit sales of assets other than inventory—for example, buildings—occur infrequently and are recorded in the general journal.

Sales Journal
Special journal used to record credit sales.

Exhibit 7-8 illustrates a sales journal (Panel A) and the related posting to the ledgers (Panel B) of Austin Sound Center, the company we introduced in Chapter 5. Each entry in the Accounts Receivable/Sales Revenue column of the sales journal in Exhibit 7-8 debits (Dr.) Accounts Receivable and credits (Cr.) Sales Revenue, as the heading indicates. For each transaction, the accountant

Exhibit 7-8 Sales Journal (Panel A) and Posting to the Ledgers (Panel B)

PANEL A—Sales Journal:

Sales Journal — Page 3

Date	Invoice No.	Account Debited	Post Ref.	Accounts Receivable Dr. Sales Revenue Cr.	Cost of Goods Sold Dr. Inventory Cr.
20X6					
Nov. 2	422	Maria Galvez	✔	935	505
13	423	Brent Harmon	✔	694	361
18	424	Susan Levy	✔	907	517
27	425	Clay Schmidt	✔	1,783	431
30		Total		4,319	1,814
				(112/410)	(511/131)

Individual accounts receivable are posted daily.

Totals can be posted at the end of the month.

Totals can be posted at the end of the month.

PANEL B—Posting to the Ledgers:

Accounts Receivable Subsidiary Ledger

Maria Galvez

Date	Jrnl. Ref.	Debit	Credit	Balance
Nov. 2	S.3	935		935

Brent Harmon

Date	Jrnl. Ref.	Debit	Credit	Balance
Nov. 13	S.3	694		694

Susan Levy

Date	Jrnl. Ref.	Debit	Credit	Balance
Nov. 18	S.3	907		907

Clay Schmidt

Date	Jrnl. Ref.	Debit	Credit	Balance
Nov. 27	S.3	1,783		1,783

General Ledger

Accounts Receivable — No. 112

Date	Jrnl. Ref.	Debit	Credit	Balance
Nov. 30	S.3	4,319		4,319

Inventory — No. 131

Date	Jrnl. Ref.	Debit	Credit	Balance
Nov. 30	Bal.			3,885
30	S.3		1,814	2,071

Sales Revenue — No. 410

Date	Jrnl. Ref.	Debit	Credit	Balance
Nov. 30	S.3		4,319	4,319

Cost of Goods Sold — No. 511

Date	Jrnl. Ref.	Debit	Credit	Balance
Nov. 30	S.3	1,814		1,814

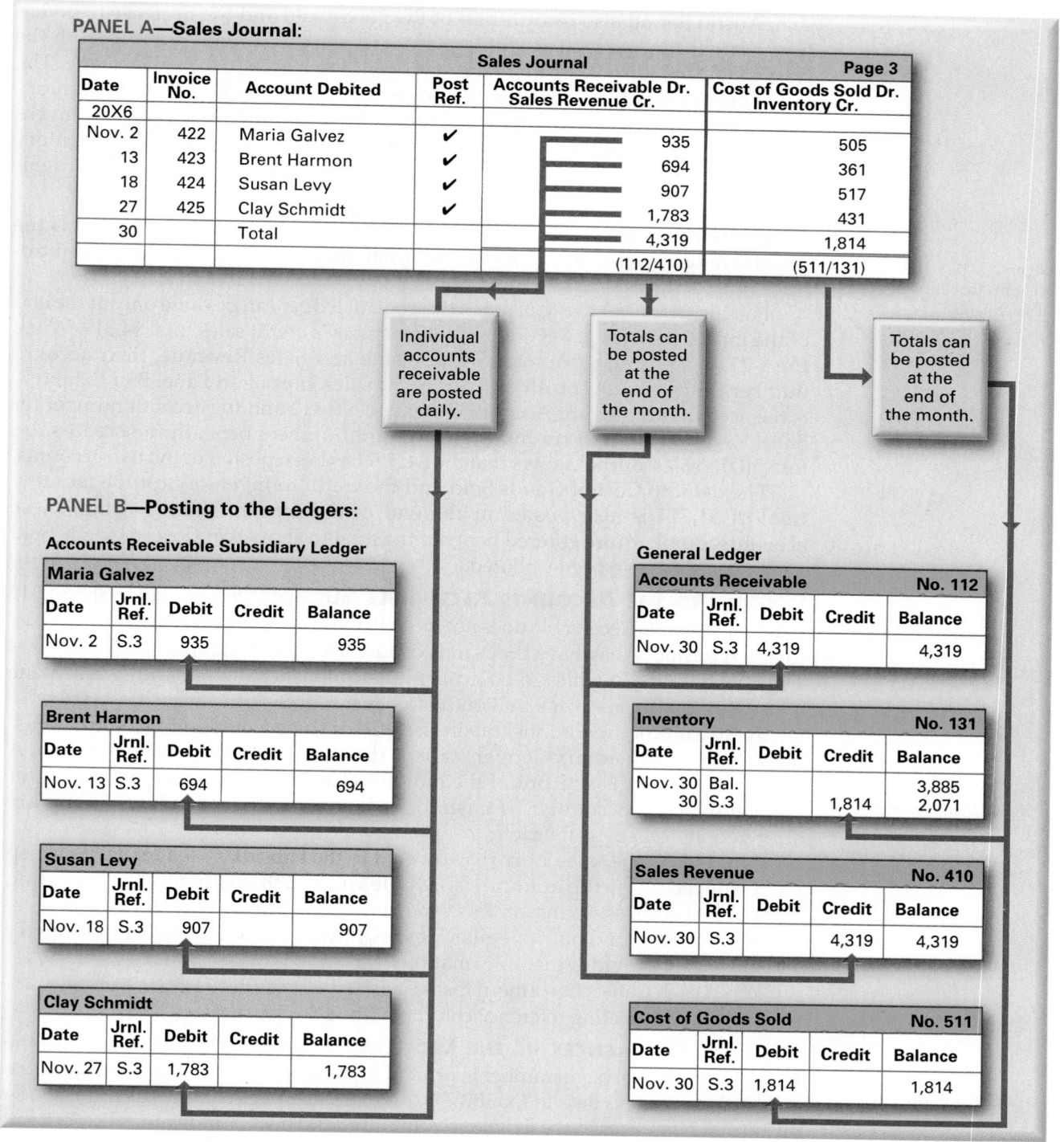

enters the date, invoice number, customer account, and transaction amount. This streamlined way of recording sales on account saves time.

In recording credit sales in previous chapters, we did not record the names of customers. In practice, the business must know the amount receivable from each customer. How else can the company ensure that it collects its receivables?

✔ Starter 7-7

✔ Starter 7-8

Consider the first transaction in Panel A. On November 2, Austin Sound sold goods on account to Maria Galvez for $935. The invoice number is 422. All this information appears on a single line in the sales journal. No explanation is necessary. The transaction's presence in the sales journal means it is a credit sale, debited to Accounts Receivable—Maria Galvez and credited to Sales Revenue.

Recall from Chapter 5 that Austin Sound uses a *perpetual* inventory system. Throughout this chapter we illustrate the perpetual system. When recording a sale, Austin Sound also records cost of the goods sold and the decrease in inventory. Many computerized accounting systems are programmed to read both the sales amount and the cost of goods sold from the bar code on the package. The far right column of the sales journal holds the cost of goods sold and inventory entry—$505 for the sale to Maria Galvez. If Austin Sound used a *periodic* inventory system, it would not record cost of goods sold or the decrease in inventory at the time of sale. The sales journal would need only one column to debit Accounts Receivable and credit Sales Revenue.

General Ledger
Ledger of accounts that are reported in the financial statements.

Posting to the General Ledger The ledger we have used so far is the **general ledger**, which holds the financial statement accounts. We will soon introduce other ledgers.

Posting from the sales journal to the general ledger can be done only at the end of the month. In Exhibit 7-8 (Panel A), November's credit sales total $4,319. When the $4,319 is posted to Accounts Receivable and Sales Revenue, their account numbers are written beneath the total in the sales journal. In Panel B of Exhibit 7-8, the account number for Accounts Receivable is 112 and the account number for Sales Revenue is 410. Printing these account numbers beneath the credit-sales total in the sales journal shows that the $4,319 has been posted to the two accounts.

The debit to Cost of Goods Sold and the credit to Inventory for the monthly total of $1,814 is also posted at the end of the month. After posting, these accounts' numbers are entered beneath the total to show that Cost of Goods Sold and Inventory have been updated.

Posting to the Accounts Receivable Subsidiary Ledger The $4,319 debit to Accounts Receivable does not identify the amount receivable from each customer. A business may have thousands of customers. For example, the Consumers Digest Company, a Chicago-based firm that publishes the bimonthly magazine *Consumers Digest*, has over a million customer accounts—one for each subscriber.

Subsidiary Ledger
Record of accounts that provides supporting details on individual balances, the total of which appears in a general ledger account.

To streamline operations, businesses place the accounts of individual customers in a subsidiary ledger called the Accounts Receivable ledger. A **subsidiary ledger** is a record of the individual accounts that make up a total for a general ledger account. The customer accounts in the subsidiary ledger are arranged in alphabetical order.

Amounts in the sales journal are posted to the subsidiary ledger *daily* to keep a current record of the amount receivable from each customer. Daily posting allows the business to answer customer inquiries. Suppose Maria Galvez telephones Austin Sound on November 3 to ask how much she owes. The subsidiary ledger readily provides that information, $935 in Exhibit 7-8, Panel B.

When each transaction amount is posted to the subsidiary ledger, a check mark is entered in the posting reference column of the sales journal (see Exh. 7-8, A).

Journal References in the Ledgers When amounts are posted to the ledgers, the journal page number is printed in the account to show the source of the data. All transaction data in Exhibit 7-8 originated on page 3 of the sales journal, so all journal references in the ledger accounts are S.3. The "S." indicates sales journal.

Trace all the postings in Exhibit 7-8. The most effective way to learn an accounting system is to study the flow of data. The arrows indicate the direction of the information. They also show the links between the individual customer accounts in the subsidiary ledger and the Accounts Receivable account. The Accounts Receivable balance in the general ledger should equal the sum of the individual customer balances in the subsidiary ledger, as follows:

General Ledger	
Accounts Receivable debit balance	$4,319
Subsidiary Ledger: Customer Accounts Receivable	
Customer	**Balance**
Maria Galvez	$ 935
Brent Harmon	694
Susan Levy	907
Clay Schmidt	1,783
Total accounts receivable	$4,319

Accounts Receivable in the general ledger is called a **control account**. A control account's balance equals the sum of the balances of a group of related accounts in a subsidiary ledger.

Control Account
An account whose balance equals the sum of the balances in a group of related accounts in a subsidiary ledger.

Stop & Think

Suppose Austin Sound had 400 credit sales for the month. How many postings to the general ledger would be made from the sales journal? (Ignore Cost of Goods Sold and Inventory.) How many postings would there be if all sales transactions were routed through the general journal?

Answer: There are only two postings from the sales journal to the general ledger: one to Accounts Receivable and one to Sales Revenue. There would be 800 postings from the general journal: 400 to Accounts Receivable and 400 to Sales Revenue. This difference clearly shows the benefit of a sales journal.

Using Documents as Journals

Many small businesses streamline their accounting by using business documents as journals. This avoids the need for special journals and saves money. For example, Austin Sound could keep sales invoices in a loose-leaf binder and let the invoices serve as the sales journal. At the end of the period, the accountant simply totals the sales on account and posts the total as a debit to Accounts Receivable and a credit to Sales Revenue. The accountant can also post directly from the invoices to customer accounts in the accounts receivable ledger.

Using the Cash Receipts Journal

Cash transactions are common in retail businesses. To record a high volume of cash receipts, accountants use the **cash receipts journal**.

Cash Receipts Journal
Special journal used to record cash receipts.

Exhibit 7-9, Panel A, illustrates the cash receipts journal. The related posting to the ledgers is shown in Panel B. The exhibit illustrates November transactions for Austin Sound Center.

Every transaction recorded in this journal is a cash receipt, so this special journal has a column for debits to Cash. The next column is for debits to Sales Discounts. In a typical merchandising business, the main sources of cash are cash sales and collections on account.

The cash receipts journal has credit columns for Accounts Receivable and Sales Revenue. The journal also has a credit column for Other Accounts, which lists other sources of cash. This Other Accounts column is also used to record the names of customers from whom cash is collected on account.

In Exhibit 7-9, the first cash sale occurred on November 6. Observe the debit to Cash and the credit to Sales Revenue ($517). Each sale entry is accompanied by

Exhibit 7-9 Cash Receipts Journal (Panel A) and Posting to the Ledgers (Panel B)

PANEL A—Cash Receipts Journal:

Cash Receipts Journal — Page 5

Date	Debits: Cash	Debits: Sales Discounts	Credits: Accounts Receivable	Credits: Sales Revenue	Other Accounts: Account Title	Other Accounts: Post Ref.	Other Accounts: Amount	Cost of Goods Sold Dr. Inventory Cr.
20X6								
Nov. 6	517			517				290
11	1,000				Note Payable to First Bank	221	1,000	
14	900	35	935		Maria Galvez	✔		
19	853			853				426
22	300		300		Brent Harmon	✔		
25	762				Interest Revenue	460	762	
28	1,802			1,802				991
30	6,134	35	1,235	3,172	Totals		1,762	1,707
	(101)	(420)	(112)	(410)			(X)	(511/131)

- Totals can be posted at the end of the month.
- Individual accounts receivable are posted daily.
- Individual amounts can be posted at the end of the month.
- Total is not posted.
- Totals can be posted at the end of the month.

PANEL B—Posting to the Ledgers:

Accounts Receivable Subsidiary Ledger

Maria Galvez

Date	Jrnl. Ref.	Debit	Credit	Balance
Nov. 2	S.3	935		935
14	CR. 5		935	-0-

Brent Harmon

Date	Jrnl. Ref.	Debit	Credit	Balance
Nov. 13	S.3	694		694
22	CR.5		300	394

Susan Levy

Date	Jrnl. Ref.	Debit	Credit	Balance
Nov. 18	S.3	907		907

Clay Schmidt

Date	Jrnl. Ref.	Debit	Credit	Balance
Nov. 27	S.3	1,783		1,783

General Ledger

Cash — No. 101

Date	Jrnl. Ref.	Debit	Credit	Debit Balance
Nov. 30	CR.5	6,134		

Accounts Receivable — No. 112

Date	Jrnl. Ref.	Debit	Credit	Debit Balance
Nov. 30	S.3	4,319		4,319
30	CR.5		1,235	3,084

Inventory — No. 131

Date	Jrnl. Ref.	Debit	Credit	Debit Balance
Nov. 30	Bal.			3,885
30	S.3		1,814	2,071
30	CR.5		1,707	364

Note Payable to First Bank — No. 221

Date	Jrnl. Ref.	Debit	Credit	Credit Balance
Nov. 11	CR.5		1,000	1,000

Sales Revenue — No. 410

Date	Jrnl. Ref.	Debit	Credit	Credit Balance
Nov. 30	S.3		4,319	4,319
30	CR.5		3,172	7,491

Sales Discounts — No. 420

Date	Jrnl. Ref.	Debit	Credit	Debit Balance
Nov. 30	CR.5	35		35

Interest Revenue — No. 460

Date	Jrnl. Ref.	Debit	Credit	Credit Balance
Nov. 25	CR.5		762	762

Cost of Goods Sold — No. 511

Date	Jrnl. Ref.	Debit	Credit	Debit Balance
Nov. 30	S.3	1,814		1,814
30	CR.5	1,707		3,521

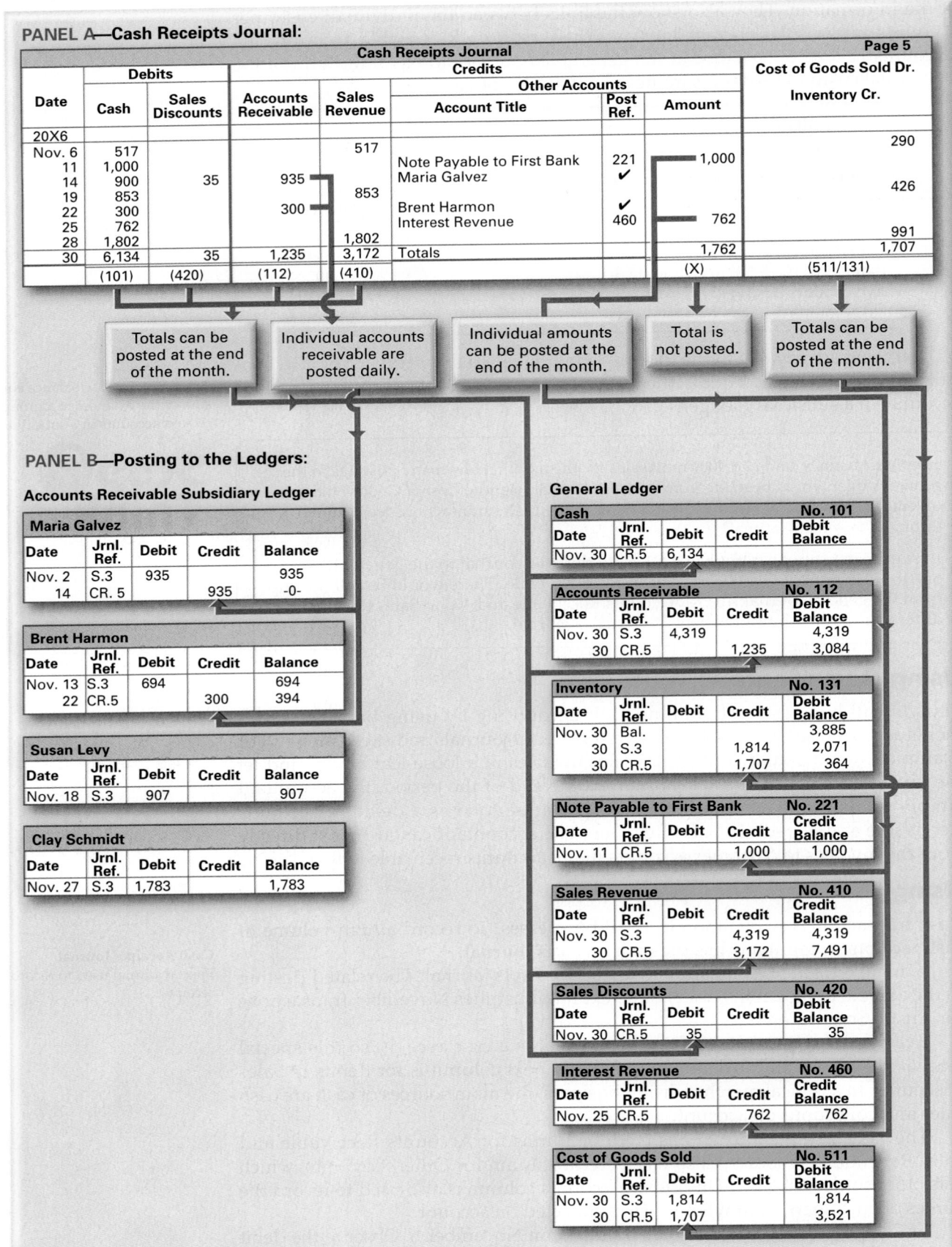

a separate entry that debits Cost of Goods Sold and credits Inventory for the cost of the merchandise sold. The column for this entry is at the far right of the journal.

On November 11, Austin Sound borrowed $1,000 from First Bank. Cash is debited, and Note Payable to First Bank is credited. We use the Other Accounts column because there is no specific credit column for borrowings. For this transaction, we print the account title, Note Payable to First Bank, in the Other Accounts/Account Title column.

The November 11 and 25 transactions illustrate a key fact. Different companies have different types of transactions, and they adapt special journals to their needs. In this case, the Other Accounts column is the catchall used to record all nonroutine cash receipts.

✔ Starter 7-9

On November 14, Austin Sound collected $900 from Maria Galvez. Back on November 2, Austin Sound sold $935 of merchandise to Galvez. The terms of sale allowed a $35 discount for prompt payment, and Galvez paid within the discount period. Austin records this cash receipt by debiting Cash and Sales Discounts and by crediting Accounts Receivable for $935. The customer's name appears in the Other Accounts/Account Title column.

In the cash receipts journal, as in all the journals, total debits should equal total credits. For the month, total debits ($6,169 = $6,134 + $35) equal total credits ($6,169 = $1,235 + $3,172 + $1,762). The debit to Cost of Goods Sold and the credit to Inventory are completely separate.

POSTING TO THE GENERAL LEDGER Column totals can be posted monthly. To indicate their posting, the account number is printed below the column total in the cash receipts journal. Note the account number for Cash (101) below the column total, and for the other column totals that are posted to the general ledger. Follow the arrows, which track the posted amounts.

The column total for *Other Accounts* is *not* posted. Instead, these credits are posted individually. In Exhibit 7-9, the November 11 transaction reads "Note Payable to First Bank." This account's number (221) in the Post. Ref. column shows that the transaction amount was posted individually. The letter x below the column indicates the column total was *not* posted.

POSTING TO THE SUBSIDIARY LEDGER Amounts from the cash receipts journal are posted to the accounts receivable ledger daily to keep the individual balances up to date. The postings to accounts receivable are credits. Trace the $935 posting to Maria Galvez's account. It reduces her balance to zero. The $300 receipt from Brent Harmon reduces his accounts receivable balance to $394.

After posting, the sum of the individual balances in the accounts receivable ledger equals the balance of Accounts Receivable in the general ledger, as follows:

General Ledger	
Accounts Receivable debit balance	$3,084
Subsidiary Ledger: Customer Accounts Receivable	
Customer	**Balance**
Brent Harmon	$ 394
Susan Levy	907
Clay Schmidt	1,783
Total accounts receivable	$3,084

Using the Purchases Journal

5 Use the purchases journal, the cash payments journal, and the accounts payable ledger

A merchandising business purchases inventory and supplies frequently. Such purchases are usually made on account. The **purchases journal** is designed to account for the purchases of inventory, supplies, and other assets *on account*. It can also be used to record expenses incurred *on account*. Cash purchases are recorded in the cash payments journal.

Purchases Journal
Special journal used to record all purchases of inventory, supplies, and other assets on account.

Exhibit 7-10 illustrates Austin Sound's purchases journal (Panel A) and posting to the ledgers (Panel B).[1] This purchases journal has special columns for credits to Accounts Payable and debits to Inventory, Supplies, and Other Accounts. A periodic inventory system would replace the Inventory column with a column titled "Purchases." The Other Accounts columns hold purchases of items other than inventory and supplies. Accounts Payable is credited for all transactions recorded in the purchases journal.

Exhibit 7-10 Purchases Journal (Panel A) and Posting to the Ledgers (Panel B)

PANEL A—Purchases Journal:

Purchases Journal — Page 8

				Credits	Debits				
							Other Accounts		
Date	Account Credited	Terms	Post Ref.	Accounts Payable	Inventory	Supplies	Account Title	Post Ref.	Amount
20X6									
Nov. 2	JVC Corp.	3/15 n/30	✔	700	700				
5	Pioneer Sound	n/30	✔	319	319				
9	City Office Supply Co.	2/10 n/30	✔	440			Fixtures	191	440
12	Audio Electronics, Inc.	n/30	✔	236	236				
13	JVC Corp.	3/15 n/30	✔	451	451				
19	City Office Supply Co.	2/10 n/30	✔	103		103			
23	O'Leary Furniture Co.	n/60	✔	627			Furniture	181	627
30	Totals			2,876	1,706	103			1,067
				(210)	(131)	(161)			(X)

Individual accounts payable are posted daily.

Totals can be posted at the end of the month.

Total is not posted.

Individual amounts can be posted at the end of the month.

PANEL B—Posting to the Ledgers:

Accounts Payable Subsidiary Ledger

Audio Electronics

Date	Jrnl. Ref.	Debit	Credit	Balance
Nov. 12	P.8		236	236

City Office Supply Co.

Date	Jrnl. Ref.	Debit	Credit	Balance
Nov. 9	P.8		440	440
19	P.8		103	543

JVC Corp.

Date	Jrnl. Ref.	Debit	Credit	Balance
Nov. 2	P.8		700	700
13	P.8		451	1,151

O'Leary Furniture Co.

Date	Jrnl. Ref.	Debit	Credit	Balance
Nov. 23	P.8		627	627

Pioneer Sound

Date	Jrnl. Ref.	Debit	Credit	Balance
Nov. 5	P.8		319	319

General Ledger

Inventory — No. 131

Date	Jrnl. Ref.	Debit	Credit	Debit Balance
Nov. 30	P.8	1,706		1,706

Supplies — No. 161

Date	Jrnl. Ref.	Debit	Credit	Debit Balance
Nov. 30	P.8	103		103

Furniture — No. 181

Date	Jrnl. Ref.	Debit	Credit	Debit Balance
Nov. 23	P.8	627		627

Fixtures — No. 191

Date	Jrnl. Ref.	Debit	Credit	Debit Balance
Nov. 9	P.8	440		440

Accounts Payable — No. 210

Date	Jrnl. Ref.	Debit	Credit	Credit Balance
Nov. 30	P.8		2,876	2,876

[1]This is the only special journal with the credit column placed to the left and the debit columns to the right. This arrangement of columns focuses on Accounts Payable (which is credited for each entry to this journal).

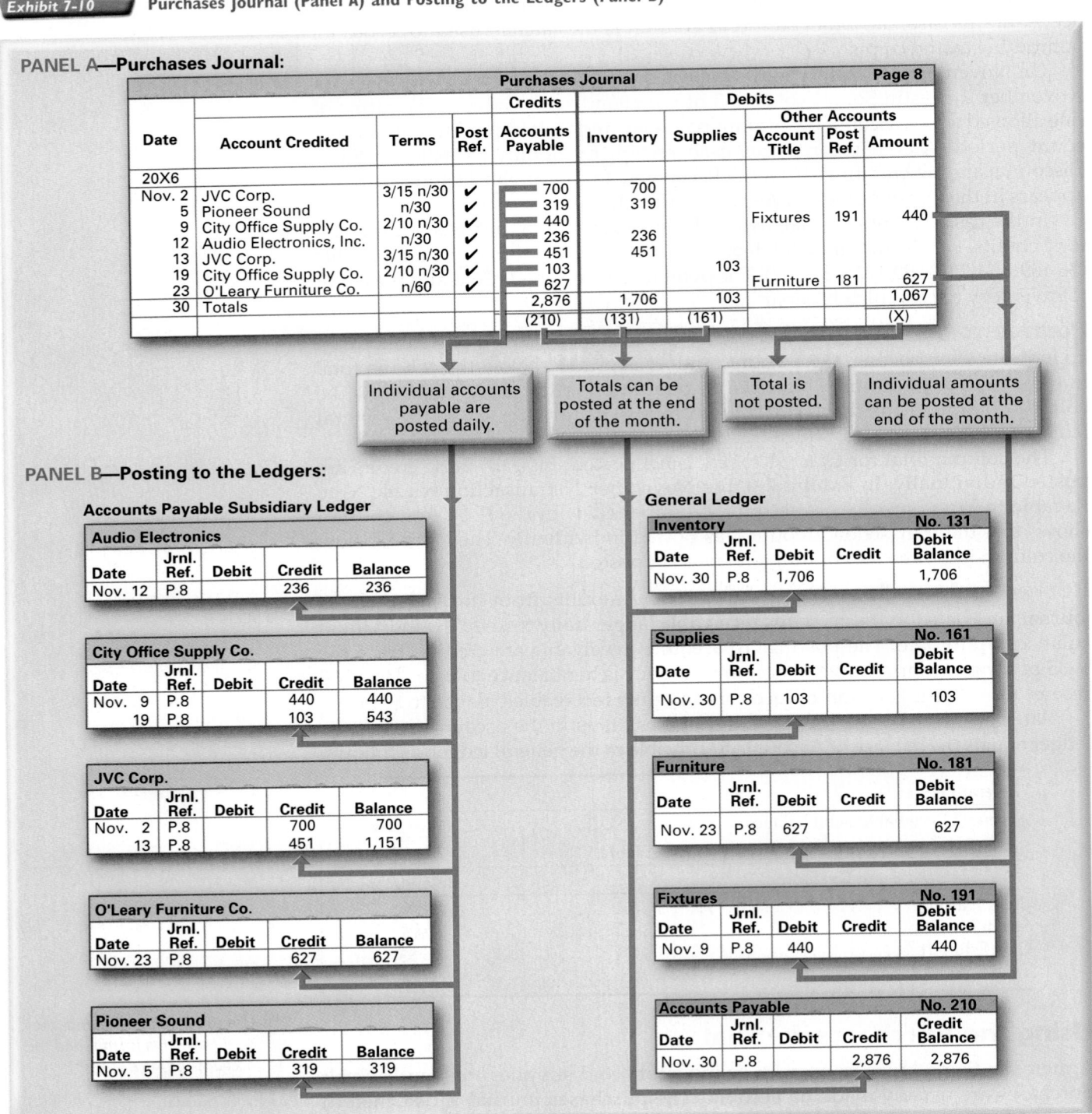

On November 2, Austin Sound purchased inventory costing $700 from JVC Corp. The creditor's name (JVC Corp.) is entered in the Account Credited column. The purchase terms of 3/15 n/30 are also entered to show the due date and the discount available. Accounts Payable is credited for the transaction amount, and Inventory is debited.

Note the November 9 purchase of fixtures from City Office Supply. The purchases journal holds no column for fixtures, so we use the Other Accounts debit column. Because this was a credit purchase, the accountant prints the creditor name (City Office Supply) in the Account Credited column and Fixtures in the Other Accounts/Account Title column. The total credits in the purchases journal ($2,876) must equal the total debits ($2,876 = $1,706 + $103 + $1,067).

ACCOUNTS PAYABLE SUBSIDIARY LEDGER To pay debts on time, a company must know how much it owes each creditor. Accounts Payable in the general ledger shows only a single total for the amount owed on account. It does not indicate the amount owed to each creditor. Companies keep an accounts payable ledger that is similar to the accounts receivable ledger.

The accounts payable ledger lists creditors in alphabetical order, along with amounts owed to them. Exhibit 7-10, Panel B, shows Austin Sound's accounts payable ledger, which includes accounts for Audio Electronics, City Office Supply, and others. After all the posting, the total of the individual balances in the subsidiary ledger equals the Accounts Payable balance in the general ledger.

POSTING FROM THE PURCHASES JOURNAL Posting from the purchases journal is similar to posting from the other special journals. Exhibit 7-10, Panel B, illustrates the posting process.

Individual accounts payable in the *accounts payable ledger* are posted daily, and column totals and other amounts to the *general ledger* at the end of the month. In the ledger accounts, P.8 means purchases journal page 8.

✔ Starter 7-10

Stop & Think

Contrast the number of *general ledger* postings from the purchases journal in Exhibit 7-10 with the number that would be required if the general journal were used to record the same seven transactions.

Answer: Use of the purchases journal requires only five *general ledger* postings—$2,876 to Accounts Payable, $1,706 to Inventory, $103 to Supplies, $440 to Fixtures, and $627 to Furniture. Without the purchases journal, there would have been 14 postings, two for each of the seven transactions.

Using the Cash Payments Journal

Businesses make most cash payments by check, and all checks are recorded in the **cash payments journal** (also called the *check register* and the *cash disbursements journal*). This special journal has columns for recording frequent cash payments.

Cash Payments Journal
Special journal used to record cash payments by check. Also called the **check register** or **cash disbursements journal**.

Exhibit 7-11, Panel A, shows the cash payments journal, and Panel B gives the postings to the ledgers. The cash payments journal has two debit columns—one for Other Accounts and one for Accounts Payable. It has two credit columns—one for credits to Inventory (for purchases discounts) and one for Cash. This special journal also has columns for the date and for the check number of each cash payment.

Suppose Austin Sound made numerous cash purchases of inventory. What additional column would its cash payments journal need? A Debit column for Inventory would be added.

All entries in the cash payments journal include a credit to Cash. Payments on account are debits to Accounts Payable. On November 15, Austin Sound paid JVC on account, with credit terms of 3/15 n/30 (for details, see the first transaction in Exhibit 7-10). Paying within the discount period, Austin took the 3% discount and paid $679 ($700 less the $21 discount). The discount is credited to Inventory.

Exhibit 7-11

Cash Payments Journal (Panel A) and Posting to the Ledgers (Panel B)

PANEL A—Cash Payments Journal:

Cash Payments Journal — Page 6

				Debits		Credits	
Date	Ck. No.	Account Debited	Post. Ref.	Other Accounts	Accounts Payable	Inventory	Cash
20X6							
Nov. 3	101	Rent Expense	541	1,200			1,200
8	102	Supplies	161	61			61
15	103	JVC Corp.	✔		700	21	679
20	104	Pioneer Sound	✔		119		119
26	105	Inventory	131	2,200			2,200
30		Totals		3,461	819	21	4,259
				(X)	(210)	(131)	(101)

Total is not posted.

Totals can be posted at the end of the month.

Individual accounts payable are posted daily.

Individual accounts can be posted at the end of the month.

PANEL B—Posting to the Ledgers:

Accounts Payable Subsidiary Ledger

Audio Electronics

Date	Jrnl. Ref.	Debit	Credit	Balance
Nov. 12	P.8		236	236

City Office Supply Co.

Date	Jrnl. Ref.	Debit	Credit	Balance
Nov. 9	P.8		440	440
19	P.8		103	543

JVC Corp.

Date	Jrnl. Ref.	Debit	Credit	Balance
Nov. 2	P.8		700	700
13	P.8		451	1,151
15	CP. 6	700		451

O'Leary Furniture Co.

Date	Jrnl. Ref.	Debit	Credit	Balance
Nov. 23	P.8		627	627

Pioneer Sound

Date	Jrnl. Ref.	Debit	Credit	Balance
Nov. 5	P.8		319	319
20	CP. 6	119		200

General Ledger

Cash — No. 101

Date	Jrnl. Ref.	Debit	Credit	Debit Balance
Nov. 30	CR. 5	6,134		6,134
30	CP. 6		4,259	1,875

Inventory — No. 131

Date	Jrnl. Ref.	Debit	Credit	Debit Balance
Nov. 30	P.8	1,706		1,706
26	CP. 6	2,200		3,906
30	CP. 6		21	3,885

Supplies — No. 161

Date	Jrnl. Ref.	Debit	Credit	Debit Balance
Nov. 30	P.8	103		103
8	CP. 6	61		164

Accounts Payable — No. 210

Date	Jrnl. Ref.	Debit	Credit	Credit Balance
Nov. 30	P.8		2,876	2,876
30	CP. 6	819		2,057

Rent Expense — No. 541

Date	Jrnl. Ref.	Debit	Credit	Debit Balance
Nov. 3	CP. 6	1,200		1,200

The Other Accounts column is used to record debits to accounts for which no special column exists. For example, on November 3, Austin Sound paid rent expense of $1,200. As with all other journals, the total debits ($4,280 = $3,461 + $819) should equal the total credits ($4,280 = $21 + $4,259).

✔ Starter 7-11

✔ Starter 7-12

Posting from the Cash Payments Journal Posting from the cash payments journal is similar to posting from the cash receipts journal. Individual creditor amounts are posted daily, and column totals and Other Accounts can be posted at the end of the month. (Exh. 7-11, Panel B, illustrates posting process).

Amounts in the Other Accounts column are posted individually (for example, Rent Expense—debit $1,200). When each amount in the Other Accounts column is posted to the general ledger, the account number is printed in the Post. Ref. column. The letter x below the column signifies that the total is *not* posted.

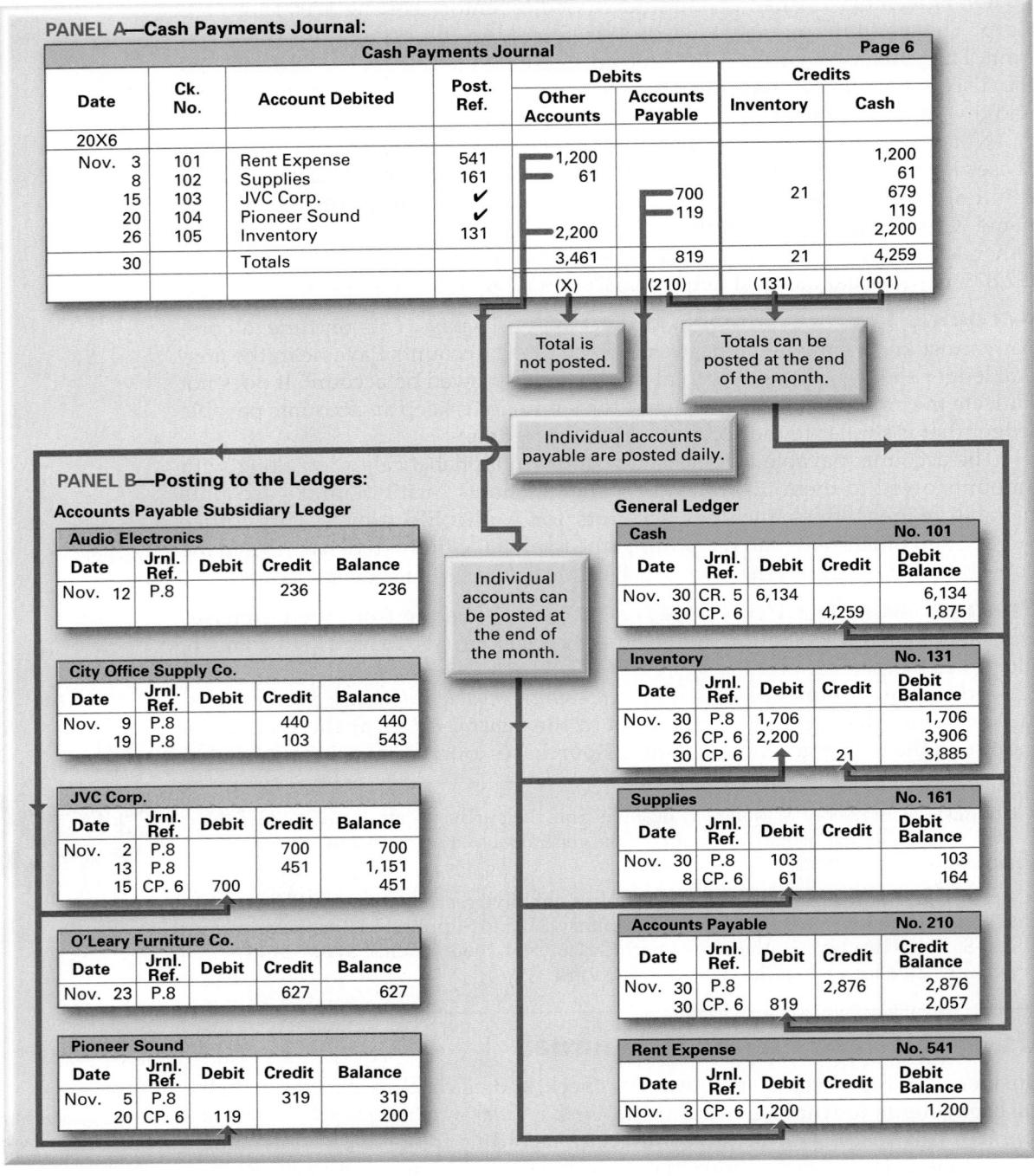

To review accounts payable, companies list individual creditor balances in the accounts payable ledger. The general ledger and subsidiary totals should agree.

General Ledger	
Accounts Payable credit balance	$2,057
Subsidiary Ledger: Accounts Payable	
Creditor	**Balance**
Audio Electronics	$ 236
City Office Supply	543
JVC Corp	451
O'Leary Furniture	627
Pioneer Sound	200
Total accounts payable	$2,057

□ Effective Accounting Systems
□ Computerized and Manual Systems
□ Special Journals
■ The General Journal

The Role of the General Journal

Special journals save time recording repetitive transactions. But some transactions do not fit a special journal. Examples include depreciation, the expiration of prepaid insurance, and the accrual of salary payable at the end of the period.

All accounting systems need a general journal. The adjusting entries and the closing entries are recorded in the general journal, along with other nonroutine transactions.

Student ResourceCD
credit memorandum, debit memorandum, general journal

Many companies record sales returns and allowances and purchase returns and allowances in the general journal. Let's turn now to sales returns and allowances and the related business document, the *credit memorandum*.

The Credit Memorandum—Recording Sales Returns and Allowances

Customers sometimes return merchandise to the seller. Sellers also grant sales allowances to customers because of product defects. The effect of sales returns and sales allowances is the same—both decrease net sales and accounts receivable. The document issued by the seller for a sales return or allowance is called a **credit memorandum**, or **credit memo**, because the company gives the customer credit for the returned merchandise. When a company issues a credit memo, it debits Sales Returns and Allowances and credits Accounts Receivable.

Credit Memorandum or Credit Memo A document issued by a seller to credit a customer account for returned merchandise.

On November 27, Austin Sound sold stereo speakers to Clay Schmidt for $1,783 on account. Later, Schmidt discovered a defect and returned the speakers. Austin Sound then issued to Schmidt a credit memo like the one in Exhibit 7-12.

Exhibit 7-12

Credit Memorandum Issued by Austin Sound Center

Credit Memorandum No. 27

Austin Sound Center
305 West Martin Luther King Blvd.
Austin, Texas 78701

Date December 1, 20X6

Customer Name Clay Schmidt
538 Rio Grande, Apt. 236
Austin, Texas 78703

Reason for Credit Defective merchandise returned

Description	Amount
4 Trailblazer JU5704 Speakers	$1,783

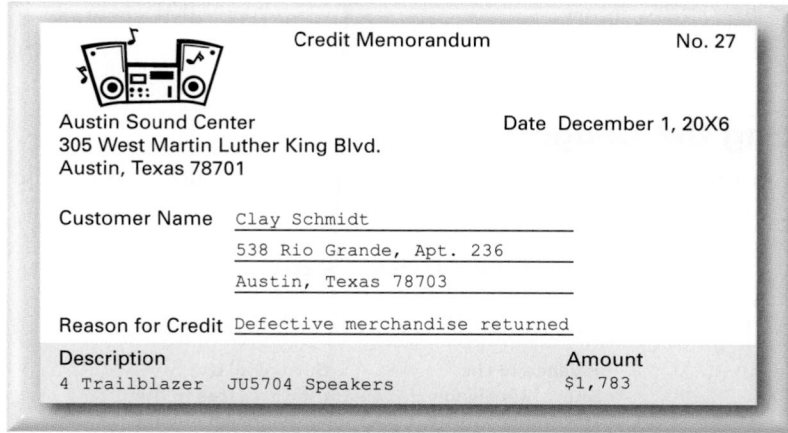

To record the *sale return* and the receipt of the defective speakers, Austin Sound would make these entries in the general journal:

General Journal — **Page 9**

Date	Accounts	Post Ref.	Debit	Credit
Dec. 1	Sales Returns and Allowances	430	1,783	
	Accounts Receivable—Clay Schmidt . .	112/✓		1,783
	Credit memo no. 27.			
Dec. 1	Inventory	131	431	
	Cost of Goods Sold	511		431
	Received defective goods from customer.			

Focus on the first entry. Sales Returns and Allowances is debited. Its account number (430) is written in the posting reference column. The credit entry requires two postings: one to Accounts Receivable in the general ledger (account number 112) and the other to Clay Schmidt in the accounts receivable ledger. These credits explain why the document is called a *credit memo*. The account number (112) denotes the posting to Accounts Receivable in the general ledger. The check mark (✓) denotes the posting to Schmidt's account in the subsidiary ledger.

The second entry records Austin Sound's receipt of the defective inventory from the customer. Now let's see how Austin Sound records the return of these defective speakers to JVC.

The Debit Memorandum—Recording Purchase Returns and Allowances

A purchase return occurs when a business returns goods to the seller. The purchaser receives a cash refund or replacement goods.

The purchaser may also send a document known as a **debit memorandum**, or **debit memo**. This document states that the buyer no longer owes for the goods. The buyer debits Accounts Payable and credits Inventory for the cost of the goods returned to the seller.

Debit Memorandum or Debit Memo A document issued by a buyer when returning merchandise. The memo informs the seller that the buyer no longer owes the seller for the amount of the returned purchases.

Many businesses record purchase returns in the general journal. Austin Sound would record its return of defective speakers to JVC as follows:

General Journal — **Page 9**

Date	Accounts	Post Ref.	Debit	Credit
Dec. 2	Accounts Payable—JVC Corp.	210/✓	431	
	Inventory	131		431
	Debit memo no. 16.			

Balancing the Ledgers

At the end of the period, after all postings, equality should exist as follows:

1. *General ledger:*

Total debits = Total credits

2. *General ledger and Accounts Receivable subsidiary ledger:*

Balance of the Accounts Receivable control account = Sum of all the customer balances in the Accounts Receivable ledger

3. *General ledger and Accounts Payable subsidiary ledger:*

Balance of the Accounts Payable control account = Sum of all the creditor balances in the Accounts Payable ledger

This process is called *balancing the ledgers,* or *proving the ledgers.* It helps ensure the accuracy of the accounting records.

Blending Computers and Special Journals in an Accounting Information System

Computerizing special journals requires no drastic change in system design. Systems designers can create a special screen for each accounting module—credit sales, cash receipts, credit purchases, and cash payments. The special screen for credit sales would ask the computer operator to enter the following information:

- Date
- Customer number
- Customer name
- Invoice number
- Dollar amount of the sale
- Cost of the goods sold

These data can generate debits to the accounts receivable ledger and the monthly statements for customers.

The Decision Guidelines feature focuses on major decisions accountants make as they use an information system.

Decision Guidelines

USING SPECIAL JOURNALS AND CONTROL ACCOUNTS

Suppose you start a business to do valet parking for large parties. It's not economical to computerize, so you set up a manual accounting system. How do you get started? The Decision Guidelines point you in the right direction.

Decision	Guidelines	
What are the main components of an accounting system?	Journals • General journal • Special journals	Ledgers • General ledger • Subsidiary ledgers: Accounts receivable Accounts payable
Where to record • Sales on account? • Cash receipts? • Purchases on account? • Cash payments? • All other transactions?	Journals • Sales journal • Cash receipts journal • Purchases journal • Cash payments journal • General journal	
How does the general ledger relate to the subsidiary ledgers?	See diagram below	

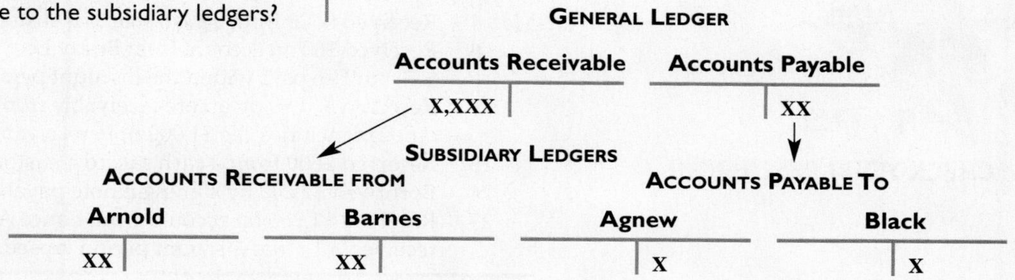

Decision Guidelines *(continued)*

Decision	Guidelines
When to post from the journals to the • General ledger? • Subsidiary ledgers?	—Monthly (or more often, if needed) —Daily
How to achieve control over • Accounts receivable? • Accounts payable?	Balance the ledgers, as follows: **General Ledger** = **Subsidiary Ledger** Accounts receivable = Sum of individual *customer* accounts receivable Accounts payable = Sum of individual *creditor* accounts payable

Excel Application Exercise

Goal: Create an Excel work sheet to prepare an income statement and balance sheet for a start-up business.

Scenario: You've started a valet parking business called First Class Valet. Although a computerized accounting system is beyond your current means, you have tracked your cash, supplies, revenues, expenses, and other items in a spreadsheet. The totals for each account at the end of your first month are as follows:

1.	Revenues:	$400
2.	Supplies On Hand:	$175
3.	Cash:	$300
4.	Supplies Expense:	$225
5.	(Your name), Capital, beginning of month:	$250
6.	Accounts Payable:	$50

In a new work sheet, prepare an income statement and balance sheet that show the results of your new business's activity at the end of its first month. When finished, answer these questions:

1. How well did your business do in its first month of operations? How did this affect your Capital account?

2. If you were to expand your business and hire an employee to assist with next month's parking engagements, what additional accounts might appear on next month's statements?

Step-by-Step:

1. Open a new Excel work sheet.

2. Create a bold-faced heading for your work sheet that contains the following:

a. Chapter 7 Excel Application Exercise

b. First Class Valet

c. Today's Date

3. Using the Chapter 3 Excel Application Exercise as a model, create an income statement and a balance sheet containing the accounts listed above, as well as any others you think are required.

4. Save your work, and print a copy for your files.

END-OF-CHAPTER *Summary Problem*

A+ TIPS
CHECK YOUR RESOURCES

Houlihan Company completed the following selected transactions during March:

Mar. 4	Received $500 from a cash sale to a customer (cost, $319).
6	Received $60 on account from Brady Lee. The full invoice amount was $65, but Lee paid within the discount period to gain the $5 discount.
9	Received $1,080 on a note receivable from Beverly Mann. This amount includes the $1,000 note receivable plus interest revenue.
15	Received $800 from a cash sale to a customer (cost, $522).
24	Borrowed $2,200 by signing a note payable to Interstate Bank.
27	Received $1,200 on account from Lance Albert. Collection was received after the discount period lapsed.

Required

The general ledger showed the following balances at February 28: Cash, $1,117; Accounts Receivable, $2,790; Note Receivable—Beverly Mann, $1,000; and Inventory, $1,819. The accounts receivable subsidiary ledger at February 28 contained debit balances as follows: Lance Albert, $1,840; Melinda Fultz, $885; Brady Lee, $65.

1. Record the transactions in the cash receipts journal, page 7.
2. Compute column totals at March 31. Show that total debits equal total credits in the cash receipts journal.
3. Post to the general ledger and the accounts receivable subsidiary ledger. Use complete posting references, including the following account numbers: Cash, 11; Accounts Receivable, 12; Note Receivable—Beverly Mann, 13; Inventory, 14; Note Payable—Interstate Bank, 22; Sales Revenue, 41; Sales Discounts, 42; Interest Revenue, 46; and Cost of Goods Sold, 51. Insert a check mark (✓) in the posting reference column for each February 28 account balance.
4. Show that the total of the customer balances in the subsidiary ledger equals the general ledger balance in Accounts Receivable.

Solution

Requirements 1 and 2

Cash Receipts Journal — **Page 7**

	Debits		Credits					
					Other Accounts			
Date	Cash	Sales Discounts	Accounts Receivable	Sales Revenue	Account Title	Post. Ref.	Amount	Cost of Goods Sold Debit Inventory Credit
Mar. 4	500			500				319
6	60	5	65		Brady Lee	✓		
9	1,080				Note Receivable—Beverly Mann	13	1,000	
					Interest Revenue	46	80	
15	800			800				522
24	2,200				Note Payable—Interstate Bank	22	2,200	
27	1,200		1,200		Lance Albert	✓		
31	5,840	5	1,265	1,300	Total		3,280	841
	(11)	(42)	(12)	(41)			(X)	(51/14)

Total Dr. = 5,845 Total Cr. = 5,845

Requirement 3

Accounts Receivable Ledger

Lance Albert

Date	Jrnl. Ref.	Debit	Credit	Balance
Feb. 28	✓			1,840
Mar. 27	CR.7		1,200	640

Melinda Fultz

Date	Jrnl. Ref.	Debit	Credit	Balance
Feb. 28	✓			885

Brady Lee

Date	Jrnl. Ref.	Debit	Credit	Balance
Feb. 28	✓			65
Mar. 6	CR.7		65	—

General Ledger

Cash — No. 11

Date	Jrnl. Ref.	Debit	Credit	Balance
Feb. 28	✓			1,117
Mar. 31	CR.7	5,840		6,957

Accounts Receivable — No. 12

Date	Jrnl. Ref.	Debit	Credit	Balance
Feb. 28	✓			2,790
Mar. 31	CR.7		1,265	1,525

Note Receivable—Beverly Mann — No. 13

Date	Jrnl. Ref.	Debit	Credit	Balance
Feb. 28	✓			1,000
Mar. 9	CR.7		1,000	—

Inventory — No. 14

Date	Jrnl. Ref.	Debit	Credit	Balance
Feb. 28	✓			1,819
Mar. 31	CR.7		841	978

Note Payable—Interstate Bank — No. 22

Date	Jrnl. Ref.	Debit	Credit	Balance
Mar. 24	CR.7		2,200	2,200

Sales Revenue — No. 41

Date	Jrnl. Ref.	Debit	Credit	Balance
Mar. 31	CR.7		1,300	1,300

Sales Discounts — No. 42

Date	Jrnl. Ref.	Debit	Credit	Balance
Mar. 31	CR.7	5		5

Interest Revenue — No. 46

Date	Jrnl. Ref.	Debit	Credit	Balance
Mar. 9	CR.7		80	80

Cost of Goods Sold — No. 51

Date	Jrnl. Ref.	Debit	Credit	Balance
Mar. 31	CR.7	841		841

Requirement 4

General Ledger

Accounts Receivable debit balance	$1,525

Accounts Receivable Subsidiary Ledger

Customer	Balance
Lance Albert	$ 640
Melinda Fultz	885
Total accounts receivable	$1,525

REVIEW *Accounting Information Systems*

Quick Check

1. The outputs of a computerized accounting system are called
   a. Software
   b. Processing steps
   c. Reports
   d. Trial balance
2. Account number 511 is most likely a (an)
   a. Asset
   b. Liability
   c. Owner equity
   d. Revenue
   e. Expense

3. The Excel formula to compute net income's percentage of sales in Exhibit 7-5, page 287, is
   a. =B4/B2
   b. =B4*B2
   c. =B2–B3
   d. =B4+B3
4. **Austin Sound** purchased inventory costing $8,000 from **Pioneer** on account. Where should Austin Sound record this transaction, and what account is credited?
   a. Cash payments journal; credit Cash
   b. Purchases journal; credit Accounts Payable
   c. Sales journal; credit Sales Revenue
   d. General journal; credit Inventory
5. Examine Austin Sound's sales journal in Exhibit 7-8, page 289. Based on these data, how much gross profit did Austin Sound earn during November?
   a. $4,319
   b. $1,814
   c. $2,505
   d. Cannot tell from the data given
6. Every transaction recorded in the cash receipts journal includes a
   a. Debit to Cash
   b. Debit to Accounts Receivable
   c. Debit to Sales Discounts
   d. Credit to Cash
7. The purchases journal is used to record all
   a. Purchases of inventory
   b. Purchases on account
   c. Purchases of assets
   d. Payments of purchases on account
8. The individual accounts in the accounts payable subsidiary ledger identify
   a. Customers
   b. Debtors
   c. Amounts to be collected
   d. Creditors
9. Which of the following is *not* a general ledger account?
   a. Sales Discounts
   b. Accounts Receivable
   c. Supplier Expense
   d. Jackson Wholesale Company
10. A debit memo is a (an)
    a. Report of all the debits to the Cash account
    b. Document for a purchase return
    c. Document for a sales return
    d. Entry to the Accounts Receivable account

Accounting Vocabulary

accounting information system (p. 282)
batch processing (p. 285)
cash disbursements journal (p. 295)
cash payments journal (p. 295)
cash receipts journal (p. 291)
check register (p. 295)
control account (p. 291)
credit memorandum or credit memo (p. 297)
data warehouse (p. 286)
database (p. 283)
debit memorandum or debit memo (p. 298)
Enterprise Resource Planning (p. 286)
general journal (p. 288)
general ledger (p. 290)
hardware (p. 283)
menu (p. 285)
module (p. 287)
network (p. 283)
online processing (p. 285)
purchases journal (p. 293)
sales journal (p. 289)
server (p. 283)
software (p. 283)
special journal (p. 288)
spreadsheet (p. 287)
subsidiary ledger (p. 290)

ASSESS *Your Progress*

Starters

Features of an effective information system
(Obj. 1)

A+ online homework

See *www.prenhall.com/horngren* for selected Starters, Exercises, and Problems.

S7-1 Suppose you have invested your life savings in a **McDonald's** franchise. The business is growing fast, and you need a better accounting information system. Consider the features of an effective system, as discussed on pages 282–283. Which do you regard as most important? Why? Which feature must you consider if your financial resources are limited?

Components of a computerized accounting system
(Obj. 1)

S7-2 Match each component of a computerized accounting system with its meaning.

Component		Meaning
A. Software	______	Electronic linkages that allow different computers to share the same information
B. Network	______	Electronic equipment
C. Server	______	Programs that drive a computer
D. Hardware	______	Main computer in a networked system

Accounting system vocabulary
(Obj. 1)

S7-3 Complete the crossword puzzle that follows.

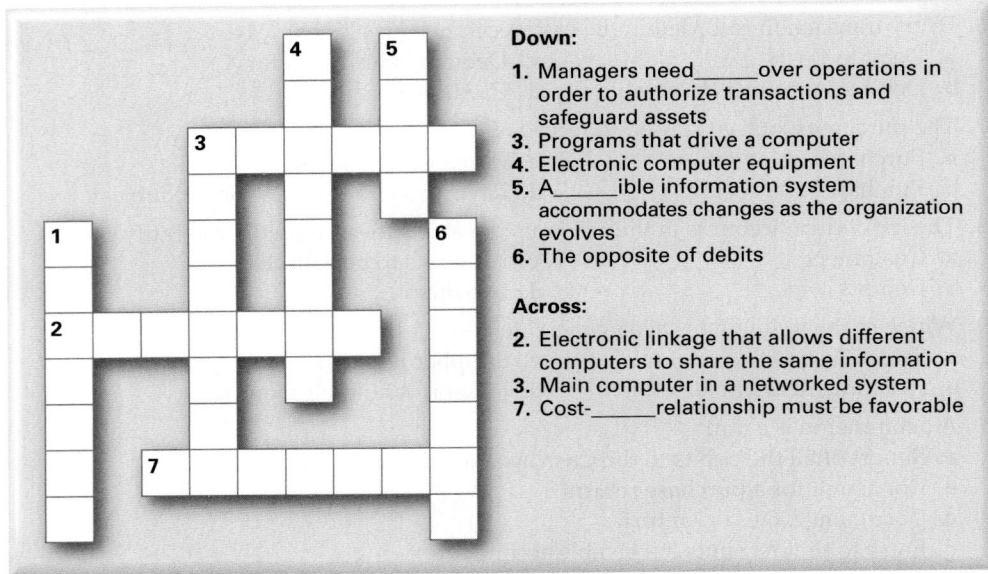

Down:

1. Managers need______over operations in order to authorize transactions and safeguard assets
3. Programs that drive a computer
4. Electronic computer equipment
5. A______ible information system accommodates changes as the organization evolves
6. The opposite of debits

Across:

2. Electronic linkage that allows different computers to share the same information
3. Main computer in a networked system
7. Cost-______relationship must be favorable

Setting up a chart of accounts
(Obj. 2)

S7-4 Use account numbers 11 through 16, 21, 22, 31, 32, 41, 51, and 52 to correspond to the following selected accounts from the general ledger of Casteel Map Company. List the accounts and their account numbers in proper order, starting with the most liquid current asset.

Randy Casteel, capital	Depreciation expense	Accounts receivable
Cost of goods sold	Cash	Note payable, long-term
Accounts payable	Randy Casteel, withdrawals	Computer equipment
Inventory	Supplies	
Sales revenue	Accumulated depreciation	

Using a spreadsheet
(Obj. 3)

S7-5 Refer to the spreadsheet screen in Exhibit 7-5, page 287. Suppose cells B1 through B4 are your business's actual income statement for the current year. You wish to develop your financial plan for the coming year. Revenues should increase by 10% and expenses by 17%. Write the formulas in cells C2 through C4 to compute expected revenues, expenses, and net income for the coming year.

Using the journals
(Obj. 4, 5)

S7-6 Use the following abbreviations to indicate the journal in which you would record transactions a through n.

J = General journal
S = Sales journal
CR = Cash receipts journal
P = Purchases journal
CP = Cash payments journal

Transactions:

_____ a. Cash sale of inventory
_____ b. Payment of rent
_____ c. Depreciation of computer equipment
_____ d. Purchases of inventory on account
_____ e. Collection of accounts receivable
_____ f. Expiration of prepaid insurance
_____ g. Sale on account
_____ h. Payment on account
_____ i. Cash purchase of inventory
_____ j. Collection of dividend revenue earned on an investment
_____ k. Prepayment of insurance
_____ l. Borrowing money on a long-term note payable
_____ m. Purchase of equipment on account
_____ n. Cost of goods sold along with a credit sale

S7-7 ← *Link Back to Chapter 5 (Gross Profit).* Use the sales journal and the related ledger accounts in Exhibit 7-8, page 289, to answer these questions about **Austin Sound Center**.

Using the sales journal and the related ledgers **(Obj. 4)**

1. After these transactions, how much does Susan Levy owe Austin Sound? Where do you obtain this information? Be specific.
2. If there were no discounts, how much would Austin Sound hope to collect from all its customers? Where is this amount stored in a single figure?
3. How much inventory did Austin Sound have on hand at the end of November? Where can you get this information?
4. What amount did Austin Sound post to the Sales Revenue account? When did Austin Sound post to the Sales Revenue account? Assume a manual accounting system.

S7-8

Using accounts receivable records **(Obj. 4)**

1. A business that sells on account must have good accounts receivable records to ensure collection from customers. What is the name of the detailed record of amounts collectible from individual customers?
2. Where does the total amount receivable from all the customers appear? Be specific.
3. A key control feature of **Austin Sound Center's** accounting system lies in the agreement between the detailed customer receivable records and the summary total in the general ledger. Use the data in Exhibit 7-8, page 289, to prove that Austin Sound's accounts receivable records are accurate.

S7-9 The cash receipts journal of **Austin Sound Center** appears in Exhibit 7-9, page 292, along with the company's various ledger accounts. Use the data in Exhibit 7-9 to answer the following questions raised by Charles Ernest, owner of the business.

Using cash receipts data **(Obj. 4)**

1. How much were total cash receipts during November?
2. How much cash did Austin Sound collect on account from customers? How much in total discounts did customers earn by paying quickly? How much did Austin Sound's accounts receivable decrease because of collections from customers during November?
3. How much were cash sales during November?
4. How much did Austin Sound borrow during November? Where else could you look to determine whether Austin Sound has paid off part of the loan?

S7-10 ← *Link Back to Chapters 1 and 2 (Recording transactions).* Use **Austin Sound's** purchases journal (Exhibit 7-10, page 294) to address these questions faced by Charles Ernest, owner of the business.

Using the purchases journal **(Obj. 5)**

1. How much were Austin Sound's total purchases of inventory during November?
2. Suppose it is December 1 and Ernest wishes to pay the full amount that Austin Sound owes on account. Examine only the purchases journal (page 294). Then make a general journal entry to record payment of the correct amount on December 1. Include an explanation.

Using the purchases journal and the cash payments journal
(Obj. 5)

S7-11 Refer to **Austin Sound Center's** purchases journal (Exhibit 7-10, page 294) and cash payments journal (Exhibit 7-11, page 296). Charles Ernest, the owner, has raised the following questions about the business.

1. How much did total credit purchases of inventory, supplies, fixtures, and furniture increase Austin Sound's accounts payable during November?
2. How much of the accounts payable did Austin Sound pay off during November?
3. At November 30, after all purchases and all cash payments, how much does Austin Sound owe **JVC Corp.**? How much in total does Austin Sound owe on account?

Using all the journals
(Obj. 4, 5)

S7-12 Answer the following questions about the November transactions of **Austin Sound Center**. You will need to refer to Exhibits 7-8 through 7-11, which begin on page 289.

1. How much cash does Austin Sound have on hand at November 30?
2. Determine Austin Sound's gross sales revenue and net sales revenue for November.
3. How did Austin Sound purchase furniture—for cash or on account? Indicate the basis for your answer.
4. From whom did Austin Sound purchase supplies on account? How much in total does Austin Sound owe this company on November 30?

A+ online homework

Exercises

Assigning account numbers
(Obj. 2)

E7-1 Assign account numbers (from the list that follows) to the accounts of Virtuoso Printers.

Inventory	Lisa Cohen, Withdrawals
Accounts Payable	Service Revenue
Lisa Cohen, Capital	Depreciation Expense

Numbers from which to choose:

101	211	321
131	281	411
191	311	531

Using a trial balance
(Obj. 2)

E7-2 The accounts of Madrid Jewelers show some of the company's adjusted balances before closing:

Total assets	$?	Long-term liabilities	$?
Current assets	43,600	Ronaldo Madrid, capital	8,600
Plant assets	63,400	Ronaldo Madrid, withdrawals	2,000
Total liabilities	?	Total revenues	40,000
Current liabilities	41,100	Total expenses	21,000

Compute the missing amounts. You must also compute ending owner's equity.

Using a spreadsheet to compute depreciation
(Obj. 3)

E7-3 Equipment listed on a spreadsheet has a cost of $500,000; this amount is located in cell B14. The years of the asset's useful life (20) are found in cell C6. Write the spreadsheet formula to express annual depreciation expense for the equipment. How much is annual depreciation?

Computing financial statement amounts with a spreadsheet
(Obj. 3)

E7-4 The following items are stored in the cells of a Mount Juliet Hotel spreadsheet:

Item	Cell
Total assets	B14
Current assets	B5
Fixed assets	B9
Total liabilities	C11
Current liabilities	C8
Long-term liabilities	C10

Write the spreadsheet formula to calculate Mount Juliet's

a. Current ratio **b.** Total owner's equity **c.** Debt ratio

E7-5 The sales and cash receipts journals of Cosmetics.com include the following entries:

Using the sales and cash receipts journals
(Obj. 4)

Sales Journal

Date	Account Debited	Post. Ref.	Accounts Receivable Dr. Sales Revenue Cr.	Cost of Goods Sold Dr. Inventory Cr.
May 7	L. Ewald	✓	80	36
10	T. Ross	✓	60	29
10	E. Lovell	✓	10	5
12	B. Goebel	✓	120	60
31	Total		270	130

Cash Receipts Journal

	Debits		Credits					
					Other Accounts			
Date	Cash	Sales Discounts	Accounts Receivable	Sales Revenue	Account Title	Post. Ref.	Amount	Cost of Goods Sold Dr. Inventory Cr.
May 16					L. Ewald	✓		
19					E. Lovell	✓		
24	300			300				190
30					T. Ross	✓		

Complete the cash receipts journal for those transactions indicated. There are no sales discounts. Also, total the journal and show that total debits equal total credits.

E7-6 The cash receipts journal of St. John Press follows.

Analyzing postings from the cash receipts journal
(Obj. 4)

Cash Receipts Journal **Page 7**

	Debits		Credits				
					Other Accounts		
Date	Cash	Sales Discounts	Accounts Receivable	Sales Revenue	Account Title	Post. Ref.	Amount
Jan. 2	794	16	810		Annan Corp.	(e)	
9	491		491		Kamm, Inc.	(f)	
19	4,480				Note Receivable	(g)	4,000
					Interest Revenue	(h)	480
30	314	7	321		J. T. Franz	(i)	
31	4,235			4,235			
31	10,314	23	1,622	4,235	Totals		4,480
	(a)	(b)	(c)	(d)			(j)

St. John's general ledger includes the following selected accounts, along with their account numbers:

Number	Account	Number	Account
101	Cash	511	Sales revenue
122	Accounts receivable	512	Sales discounts
123	Note receivable	513	Sales returns
139	Land	521	Interest revenue

Required

Indicate whether each posting reference (a) through (j) should be a

- Check mark (✓) for a posting to a customer account in the accounts receivable subsidiary ledger.
- Account number for a posting to an account in the general ledger. If so, give the account number.
- Letter (x) for an amount not posted.

Identifying transactions from postings to the accounts receivable ledger **(Obj. 4)**

E7-7 A customer account in the accounts receivable subsidiary ledger of Bernard Rapaport Company follows.

Lyndon Olsen

Date		Jrnl. Ref.	Dr.	Cr.	Balance Dr.	Balance Cr.
Nov. 3	....				403	
6	....	S.5	1,180		1,583	
14	....	J.8		191	1,392	
27	....	CR.9		703	689	

Required

Describe the three posted transactions.

Recording transactions in the general journal and in the purchases journal **(Obj. 5)**

E7-8 During April, St. Regis Sales Company completed these *credit purchase* transactions:

April 5 Purchased supplies, $555, from Sudan, Inc.
11 Purchased inventory, $1,200, from Greenbrier Corp. St. Regis uses a perpetual inventory system.
19 Purchased equipment, $14,300, from Saturn Co.
22 Purchased inventory, $2,210, from Milan, Inc.

Record these transactions first in the general journal—with explanations—and then in the purchases journal. Omit credit terms and posting references. Which procedure for recording transactions is quicker? Why?

Posting from the purchases journal; balancing the ledgers **(Obj. 5)**

E7-9 The purchases journal of Carlton Company follows.

Purchases Journal **Page 7**

Date	Account Credited	Terms	Post. Ref.	Account Payable Cr.	Inventory Dr.	Supplies Dr.	Other Accounts Dr. Acct. Title	Other Accounts Dr. Post. Ref.	Other Accounts Dr. Amt. Dr.
Sep. 2	Lancer Technologies	n/30		800	800				
5	Saturn Office Supply	n/30		175		175			
13	Lancer Technologies	2/10 n/30		1,409	1,409				
26	Faver Equipment Company	n/30		916			Equipment		916
30	Totals			3,300	2,209	175			916

Required

1. Open ledger accounts for Inventory, Supplies, Equipment, and Accounts Payable. Post to these accounts from the purchases journal. Use dates and posting references in the accounts.

2. Open accounts in the accounts payable subsidiary ledger for Faver Equipment Company, Lancer Technologies, and Saturn Office Supply. Post from the purchases journal. Use dates and journal references in the ledger accounts.
3. Balance the Accounts Payable control account in the general ledger with the total of the balances in the accounts payable subsidiary ledger.

Using the cash payments journal
(Obj. 5)

E7-10 During June, Sunset Greeting Cards had the following transactions:

June 1	Paid $490 on account to Rabin Associates, net of a $10 discount for an earlier purchase of inventory.
5	Purchased inventory for cash, $1,100.
9	Paid $375 for supplies.
16	Paid $4,062 on account to LaGrange Company; there was no discount.
21	Purchased furniture for cash, $960.
26	Paid $3,910 on account to Hallmark for an earlier purchase of inventory. The discount was $90.
30	Made a semiannual interest payment of $800 on a long-term note payable. The entire payment was for interest.

Required

1. Prepare a cash payments journal similar to the one illustrated in this chapter. Omit the check number (Ck. No.) and posting reference (Post. Ref.) columns.
2. Record the transactions in the cash payments journal.
3. Total the amount columns of the journal. Determine that total debits equal total credits.

Using business documents to record transactions
(Obj. 4)

E7-11 ←*Link Back to Chapter 5. (Recording Purchases, Sales, and Returns).* The following documents describe two business transactions.

Invoice

Date: May 14, 20X0
Sold to: Kendrick Tire Sales
Sold by: Goodyear Tire & Rubber Co.
Terms: 2/10 n/30

Items Purchased Tires

Quantity	Price	Total
8	$95	$ 760
4	70	280
5	60	300
Total		**$1,340**

Debit Memo

Date: May 20, 20X0
Sold to: Goodyear Tire & Rubber Co.
Sold by: Kendrick Tire Sales

Items Returned Tires

Quantity	Price	Total
1	$95	$95
1	70	70
Total		**$165**

Reason: Damaged in shipment

Required

Use the general journal to record these transactions and Kendrick's cash payment on May 21. Record the transactions first on the books of Kendrick Tire Sales and, second, on the books of Goodyear Tire & Rubber Company, which manufactures auto tires. Both Kendrick and Goodyear use a perpetual inventory system as illustrated in Chapter 5. Goodyear's cost of the tires sold to Kendrick was $690. Goodyear's cost of the returned merchandise was $80. Round to the nearest dollar. Explanations are not required. Set up your answer in the following format:

Date	Kendrick Journal Entries	Goodyear Journal Entries

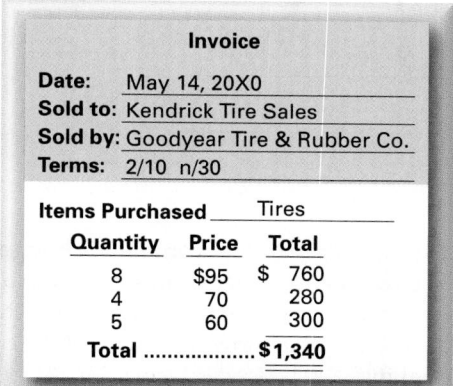

Using the special journals
(Obj. 4, 5)

E7-12 ← *Link Back to Chapter 5 (Gross Profit).*

Austin Sound Center's special journals in Exhibits 7-8 through 7-11 (pages 289–296) provide much of the data needed to prepare the financial statements. Austin Sound uses the *perpetual* inventory system. Charles Ernest, the owner, needs to know the business's gross profit for November. Compute the gross profit.

Problems

A+ online homework

(Group A)

Using a spreadsheet to prepare a partial balance sheet and evaluate financial position
(Obj. 3)

Student Resource CD
spreadsheet

P7-1A The following spreadsheet shows the assets of the Victoria British balance sheet:

Required

1. Write the word *number* in the cells (indicated by arrows) where numbers will be entered.
2. Write the appropriate formula in each cell that will need a formula. Choose from these symbols:
   + add   * multiply
   – subtract   / divide
   = SUM (beginning cell:ending cell)

	Column	
Row Number	**A**	**B**
5	Assets:	
6	Current assets:	
7	Cash ⟶	
8	Receivables ⟶	
9	Inventory ⟶	
10		______
11	Total current assets ⟶	
12		
13	Equipment ⟶	
14	Accumulated depreciation ⟶	
15		______
16	Equipment, net ⟶	
17		______
18	Total assets ⟶	
19		======

3. Last year Victoria British used this spreadsheet to prepare the company's budgeted balance sheet for the current year. The budgeted balance sheet shows the company's goal for total current assets at the end of the year. It is now one year later, and Victoria British has prepared its actual year-end balance sheet. State how the owner of the company can use this balance sheet in decision making.

Using the sales, cash receipts, and general journals
(Obj. 4)

Student Resource CD
General Ledger, Peachtree, QuickBooks

P7-2A The general ledger of Bisque Audio includes the following selected accounts, along with their account numbers:

Cash	111	Sales Revenue	411
Accounts Receivable	112	Sales Discounts	412
Notes Receivable	115	Sales Returns and Allowances	413
Inventory	131	Interest Revenue	417
Equipment	141	Gain on Sale of Land	418
Land	142	Cost of Goods Sold	511

All credit sales are on the company's standard terms of 2/10 n/30. Sales and cash receipts transactions in November were as follows:

Nov. 2	Sold inventory on credit to Grant Thornton $800. Bisque's cost of these goods was $314.
6	As an accommodation to another company, sold new equipment for its cost of $770, receiving cash in this amount.
6	Cash sales for the week totaled $2,107 (cost, $1,362).
8	Sold a sound system to McNair Co. on account, $2,830 (cost, $1,789).
9	Sold land that cost $22,000 for cash of $35,000. The difference is a gain on sale of land.
11	Sold goods on account to Nickerson Builders, $1,500 (cost, $800).
11	Received cash from Grant Thornton in full settlement of his account receivable from November 2.
13	Cash sales for the week were $1,995 (cost, $1,286).
15	Sold inventory on credit to Montez and Montez, a partnership, $900 (cost, $517).
18	Received inventory sold on November 8 to McNair Co. for $120. The goods we shipped were unsatisfactory. These goods cost Bisque $73.
19	Sold a sound system to Nickerson Builders on account, $3,900 (cost, $2,618).
20	Cash sales for the week were $2,330 (cost, $1,574).
21	Received $1,200 cash from McNair Co. in partial settlement of its account receivable. There was no discount.
22	Received cash from Montez and Montez for its account receivable from November 15.
22	Sold goods on account to Diamond Co., $2,022 (cost, $1,325).
25	Collected $4,200 on a note receivable, of which $200 was interest.
27	Cash sales for the week totaled $2,970 (cost, $1,936).
27	Sold inventory on account to Littleton Corporation, $2,290 (cost, $1,434).
28	Received goods sold on November 22 to Diamond Co. for $680. The goods were damaged in shipment. The salvage value of these goods was $96. Record the inventory at its salvage value.
30	Received $1,510 cash on account from McNair Co. There was no discount.

Required

1. Use the appropriate journal to record the preceding transactions in a sales journal (omit the Invoice No. column), a cash receipts journal, and a general journal. Bisque Audio records sales returns and allowances in the general journal.
2. Total each column of the cash receipts journal. Determine that total debits equal total credits.
3. Show how postings would be made from the journals by writing the account numbers and check marks in the appropriate places in the journals.

Correcting errors in the cash receipts journal
(Obj. 4)

P7-3A The following cash receipts journal shows 5 entries. All 5 entries are for legitimate cash receipt transactions, but the journal has some errors due to recording the transactions incorrectly. In fact, only 1 entry is correct, and each of the other 4 entries contains 1 error. Ignore posting references.

Cash Receipts Journal

	Debits		Credits					
					Other Accounts			
Date	Cash	3% Sales Discounts	Accounts Receivable	Sales Revenue	Account Title	Post. Ref.	Amount	Cost of Goods Sold Debit Inventory Credit
10/1	582	18	600		Alliance Chemicals			
9			650	650	Carl Ryther			
10	22,000			22,000	Land			
19	70							44
30	1,000			1,070				631
31	23,652	18	1,250	23,720	Totals			675

Total Dr. = $23,670 Total Cr. = $24,970

Required

1. Identify the correct entry.
2. Identify the error in each of the other four entries. Cost of Goods Sold and Inventory are correct.
3. Prepare a corrected cash receipts journal using the following format. All column totals are correct in the cash receipts journal that follows.

Cash Receipts Journal

	Debits		Credits					
					Other Accounts			
Date	**Cash**	**3% Sales Discounts**	**Accounts Receivable**	**Sales Revenue**	**Account Title**	**Post. Ref.**	**Amount**	**Cost of Goods Sold Debit Inventory Credit**
10/1	582	18	600		Alliance Chemicals			
9					Carl Ryther			
10					Land			
19								
30								
31	24,302	18	1,250	1,070	Totals		22,000	675

Total Dr. = $24,320 Total Cr. = $24,320

Using the purchases, cash payments, and general journals
(Obj. 5)

Student ResourceCD
GL, PT, QB

P7-4A The general ledger of Arlington Auto Sports includes the following accounts:

Cash	111	Equipment	189
Inventory	131	Accounts Payable	211
Prepaid Insurance	161	Rent Expense	562
Supplies	171	Utilities Expense	565

Transactions in January that affected purchases and cash payments were as follows:

Jan. 2	Paid monthly rent, debiting Rent Expense for $900.
5	Purchased inventory on credit from Sylvania Co., $5,000. Terms were 2/15 n/45.
6	Purchased supplies on credit terms of 2/10 n/30 from Harmon Sales, $800.
7	Paid gas and water utility bills, $400.
10	Purchased equipment on account from Lancer Co., $1,050. Payment terms were 2/10 n/30.
11	Returned the equipment to Lancer Co. It was defective.
12	Paid Sylvania Co. the amount owed on the purchase of January 5.
12	Purchased inventory on account from Lancer Co., $1,100. Terms were 2/10 n/30.
14	Purchased inventory for cash, $1,585.
15	Paid an insurance premium, debiting Prepaid Insurance, $2,410.
17	Paid electricity utility bill, $165.
19	Paid our account payable to Harmon Sales, from January 6.
20	Paid account payable to Lancer Co., from January 12.
21	Purchased supplies on account from Master Supply, $110. Terms were net 30.
22	Purchased inventory on credit terms of 1/10 n/30 from Linz Brothers, $3,400.
26	Returned inventory purchased for $500 on January 22, to Linz Brothers.
31	Paid Linz Brothers the net amount owed from January 22, less the return on January 26.

Required

1. Use the appropriate journal to record the preceding transactions in a purchases journal, a cash payments journal (omit the Check No. column), and a general journal. Arlington Auto Sports records purchase returns in the general journal.

2. Total each column of the special journals. Show that total debits equal total credits in each special journal.
3. Show how postings would be made from the journals by writing the account numbers and check marks in the appropriate places in the journals.

Using all the journals, posting, and balancing the ledgers **(Obj. 4, 5)**

P7-5A Prudhoe Bay Co. uses the perpetual inventory system and makes all credit sales on terms of 2/10 n/30. During March, Prudhoe Bay Co. completed these transactions:

Mar.	2	Issued invoice no. 191 for sale on account to L. E. Wooten, $2,350. Prudhoe Bay's cost of this inventory was $1,390.
	3	Purchased inventory on credit terms of 3/10 n/60 from Delwood Plaza, $5,900.
	4	Sold inventory for cash, $3,410 (cost, $1,820).
	5	Issued check no. 473 to purchase furniture for cash, $1,080.
	8	Collected interest revenue of $2,440.
	9	Issued invoice no. 192 for sale on account to Cortez Co., $6,250 (cost, $3,300).
	10	Purchased inventory for cash, $770, issuing check no. 474.
	12	Received $2,303 cash from L. E. Wooten in full settlement of her account receivable, net of the discount, from the sale of March 2.
	13	Issued check no. 475 to pay Delwood Plaza net amount owed from March 3.
	13	Purchased supplies on account from Havrilla Corp., $680. Terms were net end-of-month.
	15	Sold inventory on account to J. R. Wakeland, issuing invoice no. 193 for $740 (cost, $410).
	17	Issued credit memo to J. R. Wakeland for $740 for defective merchandise returned to us by Wakeland. Also accounted for receipt of the inventory at cost.
	18	Issued invoice no. 194 for credit sale to L. E. Wooten, $1,825 (cost, $970).
	19	Received $6,125 from Cortez Co. in full settlement of its account receivable from March 9.
	20	Purchased inventory on credit terms of net 30 from Jasper Sales, $2,150.
	22	Purchased furniture on credit terms of 3/10 n/60 from Delwood Plaza, $775.
	22	Issued check no. 476 to pay for insurance coverage, debiting Prepaid Insurance for $1,345.
	24	Sold supplies to an employee for cash of $80, which was Prudhoe Bay's cost.
	25	Issued check no. 477 to pay utilities, $380.
	28	Purchased inventory on credit terms of 2/10 n/30 from Havrilla Corp., $420.
	29	Returned damaged inventory to Havrilla Corp., issuing a debit memo for $420.
	29	Sold goods on account to Cortez Co., issuing invoice no. 195 for $560 (cost, $310).
	30	Issued check no. 478 to pay Havrilla Corp. on account from March 13.
	31	Received cash in full from L. E. Wooten on credit sale of March 18. There was no discount.
	31	Issued check no. 479 to pay monthly salaries of $5,100.

Required

1. Open the following general ledger accounts using Prudhoe Bay Co.'s account numbers:

Cash	111	Sales Revenue	411
Accounts Receivable	112	Sales Discounts	412
Supplies	116	Sales Returns and Allowances	413
Prepaid Insurance	117	Interest Revenue	419
Inventory	118	Cost of Goods Sold	511
Furniture	151	Salary Expense	531
Accounts Payable	211	Utilities Expense	541

2. Open these accounts in the subsidiary ledgers. Accounts receivable ledger: Cortez Co., J. R. Wakeland, and L. E. Wooten. Accounts payable ledger: Delwood Plaza, Havrilla Corp., and Jasper Sales.
3. Enter the transactions in a sales journal (page 8), a cash receipts journal (page 3), a purchases journal (page 6), a cash payments journal (page 9), and a general journal (page 4), as appropriate.

4. Post daily to the accounts receivable ledger and to the accounts payable ledger. On March 31, post to the general ledger.
5. Total each column of the special journals. Show that total debits equal total credits in each special journal.
6. Balance the total of the customer account balances in the accounts receivable ledger against Accounts Receivable in the general ledger. Do the same for the accounts payable ledger and Accounts Payable in the general ledger.

Problems

A+ online homework

(Group B)

Using a spreadsheet to prepare an income statement and evaluate operations
(Obj. 3)
Student Resource CD
spreadsheet

P7-1B The following spreadsheet shows the income statement of Boise Aeroquip:

	Column	
Row Number	**A**	**B**
5	Revenues:	
6	Service revenue →	
7	Rent revenue →	
8		______
9	Total revenue →	
10		
11	Expenses:	
12	Salary expense →	
13	Supplies expense →	
14	Rent expense →	
15	Depreciation expense →	
16		______
17	Total expenses →	
18		______
19	Net income →	
20		======

Required

1. Write the word *number* in the cells (indicated by arrows) where numbers will be entered.
2. Write the appropriate formula in each cell that will need a formula. Choose from these symbols:
   + add * multiply
   – subtract / divide
   = SUM (beginning cell:ending cell)
3. Last year, Boise used this spreadsheet to prepare the company's budgeted income statement to show the company's net income goal for the current year. It is now one year later, and Boise has prepared its actual income statement for this year. State how the owner of the company can use this income statement in decision making.

Using the sales, cash receipts, and general journals
(Obj. 4)
Student Resource CD
GL, PT, QB

P7-2B The general ledger of Grafton Appliances includes the following selected accounts, along with their account numbers:

Cash	11	Sales Revenue	41
Accounts Receivable	12	Sales Discounts	42
Inventory	13	Sales Returns and Allowances	43
Notes Receivable	15	Interest Revenue	47
Supplies	16	Cost of Goods Sold	51
Land	18		

All credit sales are on the company's standard terms of 2/10 n/30. Sales and cash receipts transactions in July were as follows:

July 2	Sold inventory on credit to Intelysis, Inc., $1,100. Grafton's cost of these goods was $600.
3	As an accommodation to a competitor, sold supplies at cost, $85, receiving cash.
7	Cash sales for the week totaled $1,890 (cost, $1,640).
9	Sold merchandise on account to A. L. Prince, $7,320 (cost, $5,110).
10	Sold land that cost $10,000 for cash of the same amount.
11	Sold goods on account to Sloan Electric, $5,104 (cost, $3,520).
12	Received cash from Intelysis in full settlement of its account receivable from July 2.
14	Cash sales for the week were $2,106 (cost, $1,530).
15	Sold inventory on credit to the partnership of Wilkie & Blinn, $3,650 (cost, $2,260).
18	Received inventory sold on July 9 to A. L. Prince for $600. The goods shipped were unsatisfactory. These goods cost Grafton $440.
20	Sold merchandise on account to Sloan Electric, $629 (cost, $450).
21	Cash sales for the week were $990 (cost, $690).
22	Received $4,000 cash from A. L. Prince in partial settlement of his account receivable.
25	Received cash from Wilkie & Blinn for its account receivable from July 15.
25	Sold goods on account to Olsen Co., $1,520 (cost, $1,050).
27	Collected $5,125 on a note receivable, of which $125 was interest.
28	Cash sales for the week totaled $3,774 (cost, $2,460).
29	Sold inventory on account to R. O. Bankston, $242 (cost, $170).
30	Received goods sold on July 25 to Olsen Co. for $40. The inventory was damaged in shipment. The salvage value of these goods was $10. Record the inventory at its salvage value.
31	Received $2,720 cash on account from A. L. Prince.

Required

1. Use the appropriate journal to record the preceding transactions in a sales journal (omit the Invoice No. column), a cash receipts journal, and a general journal. Grafton Appliances records sales returns and allowances in the general journal.
2. Total each column of the cash receipts journal. Show that total debits equal total credits.
3. Show how postings would be made by writing the account numbers and check marks in the appropriate places in the journals.

P7-3B The following cash receipts journal of Classic Car Parts contains 5 entries. All 5 entries are for legitimate cash receipt transactions, but the journal has some errors from recording the transactions incorrectly. In fact, only 1 entry is correct, and each of the other 4 entries contains 1 error. Ignore posting references.

Correcting errors in the cash receipts journal
(Obj. 4)

Cash Receipts Journal

	Debits		**Credits**					
					Other Accounts			
Date	**Cash**	**Sales Discounts**	**Accounts Receivable**	**Sales Revenue**	**Account Title**	**Post. Ref.**	**Amount**	**Cost of Goods Sold Debit Inventory Credit**
5/6		1,200		1,200				500
7	430	20			Paul Dalton		450	
10	8,200				Note Receivable		7,700	
					Interest Revenue		500	
18				300				150
24	1,000		700		Jaclyn Webb			
31	9,630	1,220	700	1,500	Totals		8,650	650
	Total Dr. = $10,850			Total Cr. = $10,850				

Required

1. Identify the correct entry.
2. Identify the error in each of the other 4 entries. Cost of Goods Sold and Inventory are correct.
3. Prepare a corrected cash receipts journal using the following format. All column totals are correct in the cash receipts journal that follows.

Cash Receipts Journal

	Debits		Credits					
					Other Accounts			
Date	Cash	Sales Discounts	Accounts Receivable	Sales Revenue	Account Title	Post. Ref.	Amount	Cost of Goods Sold Debit Inventory Credit
5/6								500
7					Paul Dalton			
10	8,200				Note Receivable		7,700	
					Interest Revenue		500	
18								150
24					Jaclyn Webb			
31	10,830	20	1,150	1,500	Totals		8,200	650

Total Dr. = $10,850 Total Cr. = $10,850

Using the purchases, cash payments, and general journals
(Obj. 5)

Student Resource CD
GL, PT, QB

P7-4B The general ledger of Tovar Technologies includes the following accounts:

Cash	111	Equipment	187
Inventory	131	Accounts Payable	211
Prepaid Insurance	161	Rent Expense	564
Supplies	171	Utilities Expense	583

Transactions in December that affected purchases and cash payments were as follows:

Dec. 2	Purchased inventory on credit from **Microsoft**, $4,000. Terms were 2/10 n/30.
3	Paid monthly rent, debiting Rent Expense for $2,000.
5	Purchased supplies on credit terms of 2/10 n/30 from Ross Supply, $450.
8	Paid electricity utility bill, $588.
9	Purchased equipment on account from A-1 Equipment, $6,100. Payment terms were net 30.
10	Returned the equipment to A-1 Equipment. It was damaged.
11	Paid Microsoft the amount owed on the purchase of December 2.
12	Purchased inventory on account from Wynne, Inc., $4,400. Terms were 3/10 n/30.
13	Purchased inventory for cash, $655.
14	Paid a semiannual insurance premium, debiting Prepaid Insurance, $1,200.
16	Paid our account payable to Ross Supply, from December 5.
18	Paid gas and water utility bills, $196.
21	Purchased inventory on credit terms of 1/10 n/45 from Software, Inc., $5,200.
21	Paid account payable to Wynne, Inc., from December 12.
22	Purchased supplies on account from Office Sales, Inc., $274. Terms were net 30.
26	Returned to Software, Inc., $1,200 of the inventory purchased on December 21.
31	Paid Software, Inc., the net amount owed from December 21 less the return on December 26.

Required

1. Tovar records purchase returns in the general journal. Use the appropriate journal to record Tovar's transactions in a purchases journal, a cash payments journal (omit the Check No. column), and a general journal.
2. Total each column of the special journals. Show that total debits equal total credits in each special journal.
3. Show how postings would be made from the journals by writing the account numbers and check marks in the appropriate places in the journals.

Using all the journals, posting, and balancing the ledgers
(Obj. 4, 5)

P7-5B Gifts & Toys uses the perpetual inventory system and makes all credit sales on terms of 2/10 n/30. Gifts & Toys completed the following transactions during May:

May 2	Issued invoice no. 913 for sale on account to K. D. Forbes, $2,000. Gifts & Toys' cost of this inventory was $900.
3	Purchased inventory on credit terms of 3/10 n/60 from Chicosky Co., $2,467.
5	Sold inventory for cash, $1,077 (cost, $480).
5	Issued check no. 532 to purchase furniture for cash, $2,185.
8	Collected interest revenue of $1,775.
9	Issued invoice no. 914 for sale on account to Bell Co., $5,550 (cost, $2,310).
10	Purchased inventory for cash, $1,143, issuing check no. 533.
12	Received cash from K. D. Forbes in full settlement of her account receivable from the sale on May 2.
13	Issued check no. 534 to pay Chicosky Co. the net amount owed from May 3. Round to the nearest dollar.
13	Purchased supplies on account from Manley, Inc., $441. Terms were net end-of-month.
15	Sold inventory on account to M. O. Brown, issuing invoice no. 915 for $665 (cost, $240).
17	Issued credit memo to M. O. Brown for $665 for defective merchandise returned to us by Brown. Also accounted for receipt of the inventory at cost.
18	Issued invoice no. 916 for credit sale to K. D. Forbes, $357 (cost, $127).
19	Received $5,439 from Bell Co. in full settlement of its account receivable from May 9. Bell earned a discount by paying early.
20	Purchased inventory on credit terms of net 30 from Sims Distributing, $2,047.
22	Purchased furniture on credit terms of 3/10 n/60 from Chicosky Co., $645.
22	Issued check no. 535 to pay for insurance coverage, debiting Prepaid Insurance for $1,000.
24	Sold supplies to an employee for cash of $54, which was Gifts & Toys' cost.
25	Issued check no. 536 to pay utilities, $453.
28	Purchased inventory on credit terms of 2/10 n/30 from Manley, Inc., $675.
29	Returned damaged inventory to Manley, Inc., issuing a debit memo for $675.
29	Sold goods on account to Bell Co., issuing invoice no. 917 for $496 (cost, $220).
30	Issued check no. 537 to pay Manley, Inc., in full on account from May 13.
31	Received cash in full from K. D. Forbes on credit sale of May 18. There was no discount.
31	Issued check no. 538 to pay monthly salaries of $1,950.

Required

1. Open the following general ledger accounts using the Gifts & Toys account numbers:

Cash	111	Sales Revenue	411
Accounts Receivable	112	Sales Discounts	412
Supplies	116	Sales Returns and Allowances	413
Prepaid Insurance	117	Interest Revenue	419
Inventory	118	Cost of Goods Sold	511
Furniture	151	Salary Expense	531
Accounts Payable	211	Utilities Expense	541

2. Open these accounts in the subsidiary ledgers: Accounts receivable ledger—Bell Co., M. O. Brown, and K. D. Forbes; accounts payable ledger—Chicosky Co., Manley, Inc., and Sims Distributing.

3. Enter the transactions in a sales journal (page 7), a cash receipts journal (page 5), a purchases journal (page 10), a cash payments journal (page 8), and a general journal (page 6), as appropriate.

4. Post daily to the accounts receivable ledger and to the accounts payable ledger. On May 31, post to the general ledger.

5. Total each column of the special journals. Show that total debits equal total credits in each special journal.

6. Balance the total of the customer balances in the accounts receivable ledger against Accounts Receivable in the general ledger. Do the same for the accounts payable ledger and Accounts Payable in the general ledger.

APPLY Your Knowledge

Decision Cases

Reconstructing transactions from amounts posted to the accounts receivable subsidiary ledger
(Obj. 4)

Case 1. A fire destroyed certain accounting records of Bullock Design Studio. The owner, Leigh Bullock, asks your help in reconstructing the records. *She needs to know (1) the beginning and ending balances of Accounts Receivable, (2) the credit sales, and (3) cash receipts on account from customers during April.* All of the sales are on account, with credit terms of 2/10 n/30. All cash receipts on account reached the store within the 10-day discount period, except as noted. The only accounting record preserved from the fire is the accounts receivable subsidiary ledger, which follows.

Garcia Sales

Date	Item	Jrnl. Ref.	Debit	Credit	Balance
Apr. 1	Balance				450
3		CR.8		450	-0-
25		S.6	3,600		3,600
29		S.6	1,100		4,700

Leewright, Inc.

Date	Item	Jrnl. Ref.	Debit	Credit	Balance
Apr. 1	Balance				2,800
15		S.6	2,600		5,400
29		CR.8		2,800*	2,600

*Cash receipt did not occur within the discount period.

Sally Jones

Date	Item	Jrnl. Ref.	Debit	Credit	Balance
Apr. 1	Balance				1,100
5		CR.8		1,100	-0-
11		S.6	400		400
21		CR.8		400	-0-
24		S.6	5,100		5,100

Jacques LeHavre

Date	Item	Jrnl. Ref.	Debit	Credit	Balance
Apr. 1	Balance				-0-
8		S.6	2,400		2,400
16		S.6	900		3,300
18		CR.8		2,400	900
19		J.5		200	700
27		CR.8		700	-0-

Designing a special journal
(Obj. 4, 5)

Case 2. AccuTrac Software creates and sells cutting-edge networking software. AccuTrac's quality control officer estimates that 20% of the company's sales and purchases of inventory are returned for additional debugging. AccuTrac needs special journals for

- Sales returns and allowances
- Purchase returns and allowances

Required

1. Design the two special journals. For each special journal, include a column for the appropriate business document (credit memo or debit memo).
2. Enter one transaction in each journal, using the **Austin Sound** transaction data illustrated on pages 289–298. Show all posting references, including those for column totals.

Ethical Issue

On a recent trip to Australia, Trevor Howard, sales manager of Elán, Inc., took his wife along at company expense. Meg Grayson, vice president of sales and Howard's boss, thought his travel and entertainment expenses seemed excessive. But Grayson approved the reimbursement because she owed Howard a favor. Grayson was aware that the company president reviews all expenses recorded in the cash payments journal, so Grayson recorded Howard's wife's expenses in the *general* journal as follows:

Sales Promotion Expense	9,100	
Cash.		9,100

Required

1. Does recording the transaction in the *general* journal rather than in the cash payments journal affect the amounts of cash and total expenses reported in the financial statements?
2. Why did Grayson record these expenses in the *general* journal?
3. What is the ethical issue in this situation? What role does accounting play in this issue?

Team Projects

Project 1. Preparing a Business Plan for a Merchandising Entity. As you work through Chapters 6 through 12, you will be examining in detail the current assets, current liabilities, and plant assets of a business. Most of the organizations that form the context for business activity in the remainder of the book are merchandising entities. Therefore, in a group or individually—as directed by your instructor—develop a plan for beginning and operating an audio/video store or other type of business. Develop your plan in as much detail as you can. Remember that the business manager who attends to the most details delivers the best product at the lowest price for customers!

Project 2. Preparing a Business Plan for a Service Entity. List what you have learned thus far in the course. On the basis of what you have learned, refine your plan for promoting a rock concert (from Team Project 2 in Chapter 1) to include everything you believe you must do to succeed in this business venture.

For Internet Exercises, go to the Web site www.prenhall.com/horngren.

Comprehensive Problem for Chapters 1–7

Completing the Accounting Cycle for a Merchandising Entity—Using Special Journals

Digital Meter Company closes its books and prepares financial statements at the end of each month. Digital uses the perpetual inventory system. The company completed the following transactions during August:

Aug.	1	Issued check no. 682 for August office rent of $1,000. (Debit Rent Expense.)
	2	Issued check no. 683 to pay the salary payable of $1,250 from July 31.
	2	Issued invoice no. 503 for sale on account to R. T. Loeb, $600. Digital's cost of this merchandise was $190.
	3	Purchased inventory on credit terms of 1/15 n/60 from Grant, Inc., $1,400.
	4	Received net amount of cash on account from Fullam Company, $2,156, within the discount period.
	4	Sold inventory for cash, $330 (cost, $104).
	5	Received from Park-Hee, Inc., merchandise that had been sold earlier for $550 (cost, $174). (Record this sales return in the general journal.)
	5	Issued check no. 684 to purchase supplies for cash, $780.
	7	Issued invoice no. 504 for sale on account to K. D. Skipper, $2,400 (cost, $759).
	8	Issued check no. 685 to pay Federal Company $2,600 of the amount owed at July 31. This payment occurred after the end of the discount period.

(continued)

Aug. 11	Issued check no. 686 to pay Grant, Inc., the net amount owed from August 3.
12	Received cash from R. T. Loeb in full settlement of her account receivable from August 2.
16	Issued check no. 687 to pay salary expense of $1,240.
19	Purchased inventory for cash, $850, issuing check no. 688.
22	Purchased furniture on credit terms of 3/15 n/60 from Beaver Corporation, $510.
23	Sold inventory on account to Fullam Company, issuing invoice no. 505 for $9,966 (cost, $3,152).
24	Received half the July 31 amount receivable from K. D. Skipper—after the end of the discount period.
26	Purchased supplies on credit terms of 2/10 n/30 from Federal Company, $180.
30	Returned damaged inventory to company from whom Digital made the cash purchase on August 19, receiving cash of $850.
31	Purchased inventory on credit terms of 1/10 n/30 from Suncrest Supply, $8,330.
31	Issued check no. 689 to Lester Mednick, owner of the business, for personal withdrawal, $1,700.

Required

1. Open these accounts with their account numbers and July 31 balances in the various ledgers.

General Ledger

101	Cash	$ 4,490	
102	Accounts Receivable	22,560	
105	Inventory	41,800	
109	Supplies	1,340	
117	Prepaid Insurance	2,200	
140	Note Receivable, Long-term	11,000	
160	Furniture	37,270	
161	Accumulated Depreciation		$10,550
201	Accounts Payable		12,600
204	Salary Payable		1,250
208	Unearned Sales Revenue		
220	Note Payable, Long-term		42,000
301	Lester Mednick, Capital		54,260
302	Lester Mednick, Withdrawals		
400	Income Summary		
401	Sales Revenue		
402	Sales Discounts		
403	Sales Returns and Allowances		
501	Cost of Goods Sold		
510	Salary Expense		
513	Rent Expense		
514	Depreciation Expense		
516	Insurance Expense		
519	Supplies Expense		

Accounts Receivable Subsidiary Ledger: Fullam Company, $2,200; R. T. Loeb, $0; Park-Hee, Inc., $11,590; K. D. Skipper, $8,770.

Accounts Payable Subsidiary Ledger: Beaver Corporation, $0; Federal Company, $12,600; Grant, Inc., $0; Suncrest Supply, $0.

2. Journalize the August transactions in a series of special journals: a sales journal (page 4), a cash receipts journal (page 11), a purchases journal (page 8), a cash payments journal (page 5), and a general journal (page 9). Digital makes all credit sales on terms of 2/10 n/30.

3. Post daily to the accounts receivable subsidiary ledger and the accounts payable subsidiary ledger. On August 31, post to the general ledger.

4. Prepare a trial balance in the Trial Balance columns of a work sheet, and use the following information to complete the work sheet for the month ended August 31:
   a. Supplies on hand, $990.
   b. Prepaid insurance expired, $550.
   c. Depreciation expense, $230.
   d. Accrued salary expense, $1,030.
   e. Unearned sales revenue, $450.*
   f. Inventory on hand, $46,700.

5. Journalize and post the adjusting and closing entries.

*At August 31, $450 of unearned sales revenue needs to be recorded as a credit to Unearned Sales Revenue. Debit Sales Revenue. Also, the cost of this merchandise ($142) needs to be removed from Cost of Goods Sold and returned to Inventory.

CHAPTER 8

Internal Control and Cash

A+ TIPS CHECK YOUR RESOURCES

- Visit the www.prenhall.com/horngren **Web site** self-study quizzes, video clips, and other resources
- Try the **Quick Check** exercise at the end of the chapter to test your knowledge
- Learn the **key terms**
- Do the **Starter** exercises keyed in the margins
- Work the **mid-** and **end-of-chapter summary problems**
- Use the **Concept Links** to review material in other chapters
- Search the **CD** for review materials by chapter or by key word
- Watch the **tutorial videos** to review key concepts

LEARNING OBJECTIVES

1. Define internal control
2. Tell how to achieve good internal control
3. Prepare a bank reconciliation and the related journal entries
4. Apply internal controls to cash receipts
5. Apply internal controls to cash payments
6. Make ethical business judgments

Darlyne Lopez worked as a cashier for the brokerage firm Merrill Lynch. Cashiers handle cash, so they are highly trusted employees. Lopez was so dedicated to the company that she never took a vacation and never missed a day of work. It took an auto accident to reveal that she was embezzling money.

Lopez stole $600,000 by using a well-known scheme. Here's how she did it: Merrill Lynch customers made deposits to their accounts through cashier Lopez, or so they thought. Lopez was quietly transferring customer deposits into her own account—and manipulating the Merrill Lynch customer records. She kept the scheme going for five years. When customers called to ask Lopez whether they got credit for a deposit, she would explain that the missing amount would show up on next month's statement. And it did as long as Lopez could apply Customer B's deposit to cover money stolen from Customer A.

Merrill Lynch

While Lopez was in the hospital, a co-worker took over as cashier. The new cashier couldn't explain the missing amounts. All the evidence pointed toward the missing employee. The Merrill Lynch office manager figured out why Lopez never missed a day of work: She had to be present to cover her tracks. After her stay in the hospital, she also did time in prison. All of this could have been avoided if Merrill Lynch had used some basic internal controls. ■

Sitemap

- Internal Control
- The Bank Account
- Managing Cash Receipts
- Managing Cash Payments
- Cash on the Balance Sheet
- Ethics and Accounting
- Appendix: Vouchers

To avoid situations like this, the Foreign Corrupt Practices Act requires companies under SEC jurisdiction to maintain a system of internal control. And the Sarbanes-Oxley Act of 2002 requires managers to give careful attention to internal control in their companies. This chapter discusses *internal control*—the organizational plan companies use to protect their assets. The chapter applies control techniques mainly to cash because cash is the most liquid asset. The chapter also provides a framework for making ethical judgments in business. The material covered is some of the most important in all of business. Unfortunately, it's often overlooked, as in the actual case of the cashier in the Merrill Lynch office.

- ■ Internal Control
- ☐ The Bank Account
- ☐ Managing Cash Receipts
- ☐ Managing Cash Payments
- ☐ Cash on the Balance Sheet
- ☐ Ethics and Accounting
- ☐ Appendix: Vouchers

Student Resource CD
e-commerce, internal control

1 *Define internal control*

Internal Control
Organizational plan and all the related measures adopted by an entity to safeguard assets, encourage employees to follow company policy, promote operational efficiency, and ensure accurate and reliable accounting records.

Internal Control

A key responsibility of managers is to control operations. Owners set goals, managers lead the way, and employees carry out the plan. **Internal control** is the organizational plan and all the related measures that an entity adopts to accomplish four objectives:

1. ***Safeguard assets.*** A company must safeguard its assets; otherwise it's throwing away resources. Merrill Lynch failed to safeguard customer cash, and Lopez blew the money on clothing, jewelry, and cars. In the end Merrill Lynch had to replace the missing $600,000—a total waste of company resources.

2. ***Encourage employees to follow company policy.*** Everyone in an organization needs to work toward the same goals. The international accounting firm of Arthur Andersen collapsed soon after a few members of the firm refused to follow its professional standards. They went against company policy and then certified financial statements that held large errors. Andersen fell apart.

3. ***Promote operational efficiency.*** Companies cannot afford to waste resources. WorldCom, a leading telephone-service provider, lent $366 million to its CEO. Is that an efficient use of WorldCom resources? Not to the company's enraged owners. WorldCom should have spent the money on new technology and better service for customers.

4. ***Ensure accurate, reliable accounting records.*** Good records are essential. Without reliable records, a manager cannot tell what investments to make or how much to charge for products. Banks cannot determine whether to make a loan. Enron Corporation collapsed when investors decided they couldn't rely on Enron's financial statements.

✔ Starter 8-1

Exhibit 8-1 diagrams the shield that internal controls provide for an organization. Protected by the wall, people do business safely and securely. How does a business achieve good internal control? The next section identifies the components of internal control.

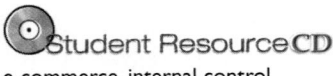

Exhibit 8-1

The Shield of Internal Control

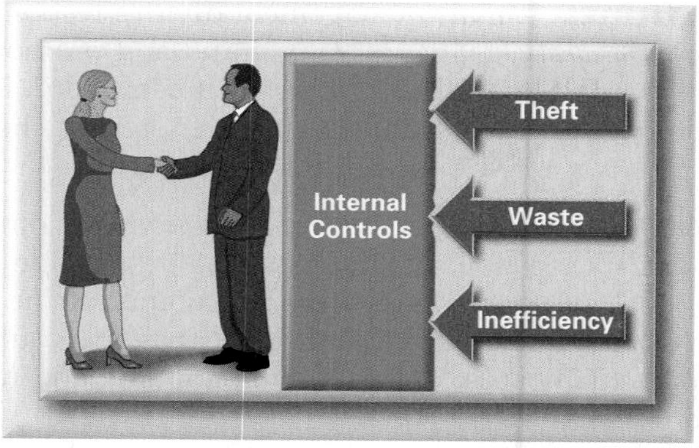

An Effective Internal Control System

Tell how to achieve good internal control

Whether the business is America Online, Merrill Lynch, or an Exxon gas station, an effective internal control system has the following characteristics.

Competent, Reliable, and Ethical Personnel Employees should be *competent, reliable*, and *ethical*. Paying good salaries to attract high-quality employees, training them to do the job, and supervising their work builds a competent staff.

Assigned Responsibilities In a business with good internal controls, no important duty is overlooked. Each employee has certain responsibilities. A model of *assignment of responsibilities* appears in Exhibit 8-2. This company has a vice president of accounting and finance. Two other officers, the treasurer and the controller, report to that vice president. The treasurer is responsible for cash management. The **controller** is the chief accounting officer.

Controller
The chief accounting officer of a company.

Within this organization, the controller approves invoices (bills) for payment, and the treasurer signs the checks. Notice that each officer has assigned duties so that all bases are covered.

Exhibit 8-2 An Organization Chart Showing Assignment of Responsibilities and Separation of Duties

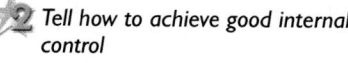

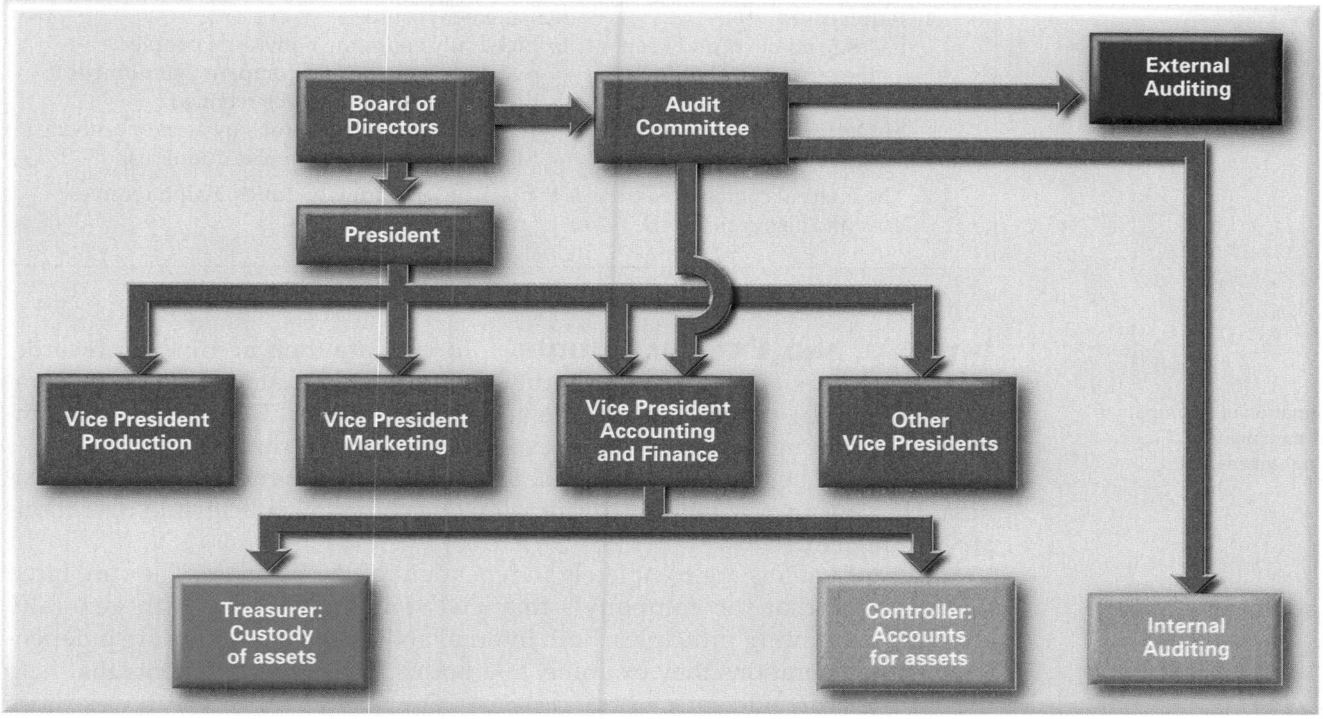

Separation of Duties Smart management divides responsibility between two or more people. *Separation of duties* limits fraud and promotes the accuracy of the accounting records. Separation of duties is illustrated in Exhibit 8-2, with the controller approving payments and the treasurer signing checks.

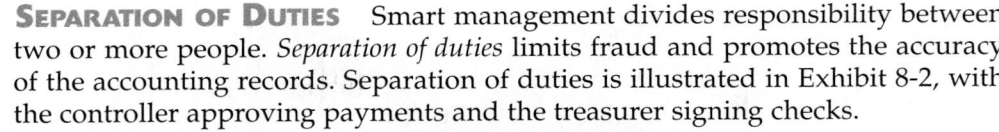

Separation of duties can be divided into two parts:

1. ***Separation of operations from accounting.*** Accounting should be completely separate from the operating departments, such as production and marketing. What would happen if sales personnel were to account for the company's revenue? Sales figures would be inflated, and top managers wouldn't know how much the company actually sold. This is why accounting and marketing (sales) are separate in Exhibit 8-2.

2. ***Separation of the custody of assets from accounting.*** Accountants must not handle cash and cashiers must not have access to the accounting records. If one employee has both cash-handling and accounting duties, that person can steal cash and conceal the theft by making a bogus entry on the books. We see this separation of duties in Exhibit 8-2. The treasurer handles cash, and the controller accounts for the cash. Neither person has both responsibilities. At Merrill Lynch, Darlyne Lopez had access to cash and to the company's accounting records. With both duties, she was able to apply one customer's cash deposit to another's account. The result was a $600,000 loss to the company.

✔ Starter 8-2

Stop & Think

Ralph works at Galaxy Theater. Occasionally, he must both sell tickets and take tickets as customers enter the theater. Standard procedure requires Ralph to tear each ticket, give half to the customer, and keep the other half. To control cash receipts, the manager compares each night's cash receipts with the number of ticket stubs on hand.

1. How could Ralph steal cash receipts and hide the theft? What additional steps should the manager take to strengthen internal control over cash receipts?
2. What is the internal control weakness in this situation? Explain the weakness.

Answers:

1. Ralph could
   a. Issue no ticket and keep the customer's cash.
   b. Destroy some tickets and keep the customers' cash.

   Management could
   a. Physically count the number of people watching a movie and compare that number to the number of ticket stubs retained.
   b. Account for all ticket stubs by serial number. Missing serial numbers raise questions.
2. The internal control weakness is the lack of separation of duties. Ralph receives cash and also controls the tickets.

Audit
An examination of a company's financial statements and the accounting system.

Internal and External Audits To validate their accounting records, most companies have a periodic audit. An **audit** is an examination of the company's financial statements and the accounting system. To evaluate the company's accounting system, auditors examine the internal controls.

Audits can be internal or external. *Internal auditors* are employees of the business. They ensure that employees are following company policies and operations are running efficiently.

External auditors are completely independent of the business. They are hired to determine that the company's financial statements agree with generally accepted accounting principles. Both internal and external auditors are independent of the operations they examine, and both suggest improvements that help the business run efficiently.

✔ Starter 8-3

Accounting.com

WorldCom, Inc.: Internal Auditor's Heroism Is Silver Lining in Cloud of Scandal

WorldCom, Inc.'s internal auditor, Cynthia Cooper, met with Controller David Myers on June 17, 2002. This was no ordinary coffee break. Cooper asked some questions that would later cost Myers his job and uncover a huge scandal.

Cooper wondered why WorldCom was counting everyday expenses as long-term assets. A company can boost reported profits by doing this, because expenses of one quarter are spread out over several years. When Cooper finished her audit, she revealed that WorldCom had inflated its income to the tune of $3.9 billion. When all the facts came out, this figure grew to a whopping $9 billion.

The internal audit forced WorldCom into the largest corporate bankruptcy in U.S. history, leaving creditors holding nearly $30 billion in bad receivables. It also turned Cooper into a national heroine. In December 2002, *Time* magazine named Cynthia Cooper, along with two other corporate whistleblowers, a "person of the year" for "doing right by just doing the job rightly."

Documents show how WorldCom's senior management overrode internal controls to hide the company's true financial condition. It turned out that Myers had promised to "do whatever necessary" to improve the company's profit margins. Fortunately, while Myers and other top WorldCom executives were doing what they deemed *necessary*, Internal Auditor Cynthia Cooper was doing what was *right*.

The Decision Guidelines at the end of this chapter outline the sad story of another auditor who did whatever was necessary to keep his client happy.

Based on: Yochi J. Dreazen and Deborah Solomon, "Leading the News: WorldCom Aide Conceded Flaws—Controller Said Company Was Forced to Disguise Expenses, Ignore Warnings," *The Wall Street Journal*, July 16, 2002, p. A3. Karen Kaplan and James S. Granelli, "*The Nation*; WorldCom Says It Inflated Books by $3.9 Billion," *Los Angeles Times*, June 26, 2002, p. A1. Associated Press, "The Nation; 3 Whistle-Blowers Get *Time* Magazine Honors," *Los Angeles Times*, December 23, 2002, p. A14. Peter Elstrom, "How to Hide $3.8 Billion in Expenses," *Business Week*, July 8, 2002, p. 41.

Documents and Records Business *documents and records* provide the details of business transactions. Documents include invoices and purchase orders, and records include the journals and ledgers. Documents should be prenumbered. A gap in the numbered sequence draws attention.

In a bowling alley a key document is the score sheet. The manager can compare the number of games scored with the amount of cash received. By multiplying the number of games by the price per game and comparing the revenue with cash receipts, the manager can see whether the business is collecting all the revenue.

Electronic Devices and Computer Controls Accounting systems are relying less on documents and more on digital storage devices. Computers shift the internal controls to the people who write the programs. Programmers then become the focus of internal controls because they can write programs that transfer company assets to themselves.

Businesses use electronic devices to protect assets. Retailers such as Target Stores, Macy's, and Dillard's control inventory by attaching an electronic sensor to merchandise. The cashier removes the sensor at checkout. If a customer tries to remove an item with the sensor attached, an alarm sounds. According to Checkpoint Systems, which manufactures the sensors, these devices reduce theft by as much as 50%.

OTHER CONTROLS Businesses keep cash and important documents in *fireproof vaults. Burglar alarms* protect buildings and other property.

Retailers receive most of their cash from customers on the spot. To safeguard cash, they use *point-of-sale terminals* that serve as a cash register and also record each transaction. Several times each day, a supervisor deposits the cash in the bank.

Employees who handle cash are in a tempting position. Many businesses purchase *fidelity bonds* on cashiers. The bond is an insurance policy that reimburses the company for any losses due to employee theft. Before issuing a fidelity bond, the insurance company investigates the employee's record.

✔ Starter 8-4

Mandatory vacations and *job rotation* require that employees be trained to do a variety of jobs. General Electric, Eastman Kodak, and other large companies move employees from job to job. This improves morale by giving employees a broad view of the business. Also, knowing someone else will be doing your job next month also keeps you honest. Had Merrill Lynch required Darlyne Lopez to take a vacation, her embezzlement would have been detected earlier.

Internal Controls for E-Commerce

E-Commerce creates its own risks. Hackers may gain access to confidential information that's unavailable in face-to-face transactions. To convince people to buy online, Amazon.com and EMusic.com must secure customer data.

PITFALLS E-Commerce pitfalls include:

- Stolen credit-card numbers
- Computer viruses and Trojan horses
- Impersonation of companies

Stolen Credit-Card Numbers Suppose you buy several CDs from EMusic.com. To make the purchase, your credit-card number must travel through cyberspace. Amateur hacker Carlos Salgado, Jr., used his home computer to steal 100,000 credit-card numbers with a combined limit exceeding $1 billion. Salgado was caught when he tried to sell the numbers to an undercover FBI agent.

Computer Virus
A malicious program that (a) reproduces itself, (b) enters program code without consent, and (c) performs destructive actions.

Trojan Horse
A malicious program that works like a virus but does not reproduce.

Computer Viruses and Trojan Horses A **computer virus** is a malicious program that (a) reproduces itself, (b) enters program code without consent, and (c) performs destructive actions. A **Trojan horse** works like a virus, but it does not reproduce. Viruses can destroy or alter data, make bogus calculations, and infect files. The International Computer Security Association reports that virtually all firms have found a virus in their system.

Suppose the U.S. Department of Defense takes bids for a missile defense system, and Raytheon and Lockheed-Martin bid on the contract. A hacker infects Raytheon's system and alters Raytheon's design. In evaluating the bids, Pentagon engineers label the Raytheon design as flawed even though Raytheon's is better and costs less. The American public winds up paying too much.

Impersonation Hackers sometimes create bogus Web sites, such as AOL4Free.com. The neat-sounding Web site attracts lots of visitors, and the hackers solicit confidential data from unsuspecting people. The hackers then use the data for illicit purposes.

Encryption
Rearranging plain-text messages by a mathematical process; the primary method of achieving confidentiality in e-commerce.

FIREWALLS AND ENCRYPTION Internet information can be secure, but the server holding the information may not be. Two standard techniques for securing e-commerce data are encryption and firewalls.

Encryption rearranges messages by a mathematical process. The encrypted message cannot be read by one who does not know the process. An accounting example uses check-sum digits for account numbers. Each account number has its last digit equal to the sum of the previous digits. For example, consider Customer Number 2237, where 2 + 2 + 3 = 7. Any account number that fails this test triggers an error message.

Firewalls limit access to a local network. They enable members of the local network to access the Internet but keep nonmembers out of the network. Usually several firewalls are built into the network. Think of a fortress with multiple walls protecting the king's chamber in the center. At the point of entry, passwords, PINs (personal identification numbers) and signatures are used. More-sophisticated firewalls are used deeper in the network.

Firewalls
Devices that enable members of a local network to access the Internet but keep nonmembers out of the network.

The Limitations of Internal Control

Unfortunately, most internal controls can be overcome. Collusion—two or more employees working as a team—can beat internal controls and defraud the firm. Consider Galaxy Theater. Ralph and another employee could design a scheme in which the ticket seller pockets the cash from 10 customers and the ticket taker admits 10 customers without tickets. To prevent this situation, the manager must take additional steps, such as matching the number of people in the theater against the number of ticket stubs retained. But that takes time away from other duties.

The stricter the internal control system, the more it costs. A system of internal control that is too complex can strangle the business with red tape. How tight should controls be? Internal controls must be judged in light of their costs and benefits.

The Bank Account as a Control Device

- ☐ Internal Control
- ■ The Bank Account
- ☐ Managing Cash Receipts
- ☐ Managing Cash Payments
- ☐ Cash on the Balance Sheet
- ☐ Ethics and Accounting
- ☐ Appendix: Vouchers

Cash is the most liquid asset because it is a medium of exchange. Increasingly, cash consists of electronic impulses with no paper checks or deposit slips. Cash is easy to conceal, easy to move, and relatively easy to steal. As a result, most businesses create specific controls for cash.

Keeping cash in a *bank account* helps control cash because banks have established practices for safeguarding customers' money. Banks also provide customers with detailed records of their transactions. To take full advantage, the business should deposit all cash receipts in the bank and make all cash payments through the bank. An exception is a petty cash transaction, which we will examine later.

Student Resource CD
bank reconciliation, ethics, internal control

The documents used to control a bank account include the

- Signature card
- Deposit ticket
- Check
- Bank statement
- Bank reconciliation

SIGNATURE CARD Banks require each person authorized to transact business through an account to sign a *signature card*. The bank uses the signature card to protect against forgery.

DEPOSIT TICKET Banks supply standard forms such as *deposit tickets*. The customer fills in the dollar amount of each deposit. As proof of the transaction, the customer keeps a deposit receipt.

CHECK To draw money from an account, the depositor writes a **check,** which is the document that tells the bank to pay the designated party a specified amount of money. There are three parties to a check: the *maker*, who signs the check, the *payee*, to whom the check is paid, and the *bank* on which the check is drawn.

Check
Document that instructs a bank to pay the designated person or business a specified amount of money.

Exhibit 8-3 shows a check drawn by Business Research, Inc., the maker. The check has two parts, the check itself and the *remittance advice* below. This is an optional attachment that tells the payee the reason for the payment. Business Research keeps a duplicate copy of the check for its cash payments journal.

Exhibit 8-3

Check with Remittance Advice

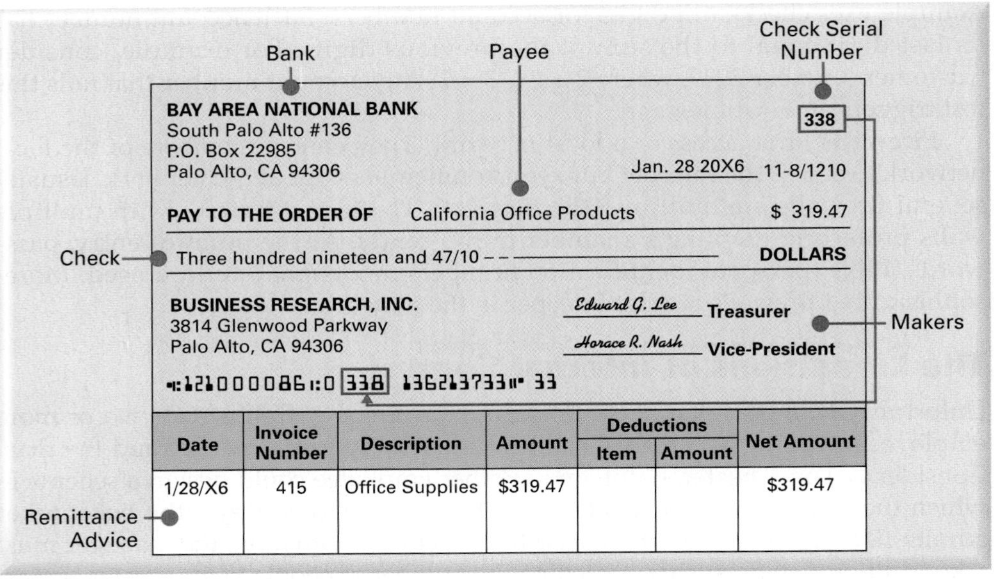

Bank Statement
Document the bank uses to report what it did with the depositor's cash. Shows the bank account's beginning and ending balances and lists the month's cash transactions conducted through the bank.

Electronic Funds Transfer (EFT)
System that transfers cash by electronic communication rather than by paper documents.

Bank Reconciliation
Document explaining the reasons for the difference between a depositor's cash records and the depositor's cash balance in its bank account.

BANK STATEMENT Banks send monthly statements to customers. A **bank statement** is the document on which the bank reports what it did with the customer's cash. The statement shows the account's beginning and ending balances and lists the cash receipts and payments transacted through the bank. Included with the statement are the maker's *canceled checks* (or photocopies of the paid checks). The statement also lists deposits and other changes in the account. Deposits appear in chronological order, and checks are listed by check number. Exhibit 8-4 is the bank statement of Business Research, Inc., for the month ended January 31, 20X6. The summary at the top shows the beginning balance, plus deposits minus withdrawals, and the ending balance. Details of the transactions follow.

Electronic funds transfer (EFT) is a system that moves cash by electronic communication. It is cheaper for a company to pay employees by EFT (direct deposit). Many people make mortgage, rent, and insurance payments by EFT and don't have to write checks for those payments. The monthly bank statement lists EFT deposits and payments.

The Bank Reconciliation

There are two records of a business's cash:

1. The Cash account in the company's general ledger (Exhibit 8-5).
2. The bank statement, which shows the cash receipts and payments transacted through the bank.

The books and the bank statement usually show different amounts. Differences arise because of a time lag in recording transactions. When you write a check, you immediately deduct the check in your checkbook. But the bank does not subtract the check from your account until it pays the check. That may take a few days, even weeks, if the payee waits to cash the check. Likewise, you immediately add the cash receipt for all deposits you make to your account. But it may take a day or two for the bank to add these amounts to your balance.

To ensure accurate cash records, you need to update your checkbook often—either online or after you receive your bank statement. All business entities do this. The result of this updating process is a document called the **bank reconciliation,** which is prepared by the company (not by the bank). Properly done, the bank reconciliation explains all differences between the company's cash records and the bank statement figures. It ensures that all cash transactions have been accounted for. It also establishes that bank and book (your own) records of cash are correct.

Exhibit 8-4 Bank Statement

BAY AREA NATIONAL BANK
SOUTH PALO ALTO #136 P.O. BOX 22985 PALO ALTO, CA 94306

ACCOUNT STATEMENT

Business Research, Inc.
3814 Glenwood Parkway
Palo Alto, CA 94306

CHECKING ACCOUNT 136–213733

CHECKING ACCOUNT SUMMARY AS OF 01/31/X6

BEGINNING BALANCE	TOTAL DEPOSITS	TOTAL WITHDRAWALS	SERVICE CHARGES	ENDING BALANCE
6,556.12	4,352.64	4,963.00	14.25	5,931.51

CHECKING ACCOUNT TRANSACTIONS

DEPOSITS	DATE	AMOUNT
Deposit	01/04	1,000.00
Deposit	01/04	112.00
Deposit	01/08	194.60
EFT—Collection of rent	01/17	904.03
Bank Collection	01/26	2,114.00
Interest	01/31	28.01

CHARGES	DATE	AMOUNT
Service Charge	01/31	14.25
Checks:		

CHECKS

Number	Amount
656	100.00
332	3,000.00
333	150.00
334	100.00
335	100.00
336	1,100.00

DAILY BALANCE

Date	Balance	Date	Balance
12/31	6,556.12	01/17	5,264.75
01/04	7,616.12	01/20	4,903.75
01/06	7,416.12	01/26	7,017.75
01/08	7,610.72	01/31	5,931.51
01/10	7,510.72		
01/12	4,360.72		

OTHER CHARGES	DATE	AMOUNT
NSF	01/04	52.00
EFT—Insurance	01/20	361.00

MONTHLY SUMMARY

Withdrawals: 8 Minimum Balance: 4,360.72 Average Balance: 6,085.19

Exhibit 8-5

Cash Records of Business Research, Inc.

General Ledger:

ACCOUNT Cash

Date	Item	Debit	Credit	Balance
20X6				
Jan. 1	Balance			6,556.12
2	Cash receipt	1,112.00		7,668.12
7	Cash receipt	194.60		7,862.72
31	Cash payments		6,160.11	1,702.61
31	Cash receipt	1,591.60		3,294.21

Cash Payments:

Check No.	Amount	Check No.	Amount
332	$3,000.00	338	$ 319.47
333	510.00	339	83.00
334	100.00	340	203.14
335	100.00	341	458.50
336	1,100.00		
337	286.00	Total	$6,160.11

3 *Prepare a bank reconciliation and the related journal entries*

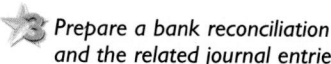

Preparing the Bank Reconciliation

Here are some common reconciling items. They all cause differences between the bank balance and the book balance. (We refer to your checkbook record of your cash as the "Book" records.)

Deposit in Transit
A deposit recorded by the company but not yet by its bank.

Outstanding Check
A check issued by the company and recorded on its books but not yet paid by its bank.

Bank Collection
Collection of money by the bank on behalf of a depositor.

1. Items to show on the *Bank* side of the bank reconciliation:
   a. **Deposits in transit** (outstanding deposits). The company has recorded these deposits, but the bank has not.
   b. **Outstanding checks.** The company has issued these checks and recorded them on its books, but the bank has not yet paid them.
   c. **Bank errors.** Correct all bank errors on the Bank side of the reconciliation.
2. Items to show on the *Book* side of the bank reconciliation:
   a. **Bank collections.** Banks sometimes collect money for their depositors. Many businesses have customers pay directly to the company bank account. This practice, called a *lock-box system,* reduces theft and circulates cash faster than if the cash is collected and deposited by company personnel. An example is a bank's collecting cash on a note receivable for the depositor. Bank collections are cash receipts.
   b. **Electronic funds transfers.** The bank may receive or pay cash on behalf of the depositor. An EFT may be a cash receipt or a cash payment.
   c. **Service charge.** This is the bank's fee for processing the depositor's transactions. It is a cash payment.
   d. **Interest revenue on checking account.** Depositors earn interest if they keep enough cash in their account. The bank notifies depositors of this interest on the bank statement. It is a cash receipt.
   e. **Nonsufficient funds (NSF) checks** are cash receipts that turn out to be worthless. NSF checks (sometimes called *hot checks*) should be subtracted on a bank reconciliation.
   f. **The cost of printed checks.** This cash payment is handled like a service charge.
   g. **Book errors.** Correct all book errors on the Book side of the reconciliation.

Nonsufficient Funds (NSF) Check
A "hot" check, one for which the maker's bank account has insufficient money to pay the check.

✔ Starter 8-5

BANK RECONCILIATION ILLUSTRATED The bank statement in Exhibit 8-4 shows that the January 31 bank balance of Business Research, Inc., is $5,931.51. However, the company's Cash account has a balance of $3,294.21, as shown in Exhibit 8-5. This situation calls for a bank reconciliation. Exhibit 8-6, panel A, lists the reconciling items, and panel B shows the completed reconciliation.

JOURNALIZING TRANSACTIONS FROM THE RECONCILIATION The bank reconciliation is an accountant's tool separate from the company books. It explains the effects of all cash receipts and all cash payments made through the bank. But it does *not* account for transactions in the journal. To get the transactions into the accounts, we must make journal entries and post to the general ledger. All items on the Book side of the bank reconciliation require journal entries.

Stop & Think

Why doesn't the company need to record the reconciling items on the Bank side of the reconciliation?

Answer: Those items have already been recorded on the company books.

Exhibit 8-6 **Bank Reconciliation**

PANEL A—Reconciling Items

1. Deposit in transit, $1,591.60
2. Bank error: The bank deducted $100 for a check written by another company. Add $100 to bank balance.
3. Outstanding checks:

Check No.	Amount
337	$286.00
338	319.47
339	83.00
340	203.14
341	458.50

4. EFT receipt of rent revenue, $904.03.
5. Bank collection of a note receivable, $2,114, including interest revenue of $114.
6. Interest revenue earned on bank balance, $28.01.
7. Book error: Check no. 333 for $150 paid to Brown Company on account, was recorded as $510. Add $360 to book balance.
8. Bank service charge, $14.25.
9. NSF check from L. Ross, $52.
10. EFT payment of insurance expense, $361.

PANEL B—Bank Reconciliation

Business Research, Inc.
Bank Reconciliation
January 31, 20X6

Bank		
Balance, January 31		$5,931.51
Add:		
1. Deposit of January 31 in transit		1,591.60
2. Correction of bank error		100.00
		7,623.11
Less:		
3. Outstanding checks		
No. 337	$286.00	
No. 338	319.47	
No. 339	83.00	
No. 340	203.14	
No. 341	458.50	(1,350.11)
Adjusted bank balance		$6,273.00

Books		
Balance, January 31		$3,294.21
Add:		
4. EFT receipt of rent revenue		904.03
5. Bank collection of note receivable ($2,000), plus interest revenue of $114		2,114.00
6. Interest revenue earned on bank balance		28.01
7. Correction of book error—overstated our check no. 333		360.00
		6,700.25
Less:		
8. Service charge	$ 14.25	
9. NSF check	52.00	
10. EFT payment of insurance expense	361.00	(427.25)
Adjusted book balance		$6,273.00

These amounts should agree.

Each reconciling item is treated in the same way in every situation. Here is a summary of how to treat the various reconciling items:

BANK BALANCE—ALWAYS

- *Add* deposits in transit.
- *Subtract* outstanding checks.
- *Add* or *subtract* corrections of bank errors.

BOOK BALANCE—ALWAYS

- *Add* bank collections, interest revenue, and EFT receipts.
- *Subtract* service charges, NSF checks, and EFT payments.
- *Add* or *subtract* corrections of book errors.

✔ Starter 8-6

The bank reconciliation in Exhibit 8-6 requires Business Research to make 10 journal entries. They are dated January 31 to bring the Cash account to the correct balance on that date. Numbers in parentheses correspond to the reconciling items listed in Exhibit 8-6, Panel A.

(4)	Jan. 31	Cash	904.03	
		Rent Revenue		904.03
		Receipt of monthly rent.		
(5)	31	Cash	2,114.00	
		Notes Receivable		2,000.00
		Interest Revenue		114.00
		Note receivable collected by bank.		
(6)	31	Cash	28.01	
		Interest Revenue		28.01
		Interest earned on bank balance.		
(7)	31	Cash	360.00	
		Accounts Payable —Brown Co.		360.00
		Correction of check no. 333.		
(8)	Jan. 31	Miscellaneous Expense[1]	14.25	
		Cash		14.25
		Bank service charge.		
(9)	31	Accounts Receivable —L. Ross	52.00	
		Cash		52.00
		NSF check returned by bank.		
(10)	31	Insurance Expense	361.00	
		Cash		361.00
		Payment of monthly insurance.		

These entries update the company's books.

The entry for the NSF check (entry 9) needs explanation. Upon learning that L. Ross's $52 check was not good, Business Research credits Cash to update the Cash account. Business Research still has a receivable from Ross, so the company debits Accounts Receivable—L. Ross.

✔ Starter 8-7

Stop & Think

The bank statement balance is $4,500 and shows a service charge of $15, interest earned of $5, and an NSF check for $300. Deposits in transit total $1,200 and outstanding checks are $575. The bookkeeper incorrectly recorded as $152 a check of $125 in payment of an account payable.

1. What is the adjusted balance?
2. Prepare the journal entries needed to update the company's books.

Answers:

1. $5,125 ($4,500 + $1,200 – $575)
2. Journal entries on the books:

Miscellaneous Expense	15	
Cash		15
Cash	5	
Interest Revenue		5
Accounts Receivable	300	
Cash		300
Cash ($152 – $125)	27	
Accounts Payable		27

How Owners and Managers Use the Bank Reconciliation

The bank reconciliation can be a powerful control device, as the following example illustrates.

Randy Vaughn is a CPA in Houston, Texas. Vaughn owns apartment complexes that his aunt manages. His accounting practice leaves little time to devote to the properties. Vaughn's aunt signs up tenants, collects the monthly rent, arranges custodial work, hires and fires employees, write the checks, and performs the bank reconciliation. This concentration of duties in one person is terri-

[1]Note: Miscellaneous Expense is debited for the bank service charge because the service charge pertains to no particular expense category.

ble from an internal control standpoint. Vaughn's aunt could be stealing from him. As a CPA, he is aware of this possibility.

Vaughn exercises some internal controls over his aunt's activities. Periodically, he drops by his properties to see whether the apartments are in good condition.

To control cash, Vaughn uses a bank reconciliation. On an irregular basis, he examines the bank reconciliations prepared by his aunt. He matches every paid check to the journal entry on the books. Vaughn would know immediately if his aunt were writing checks to herself. Vaughn sometimes prepares his own bank reconciliation to see whether he agrees with his aunt's work. To keep his aunt on her toes, Vaughn lets her know that he periodically audits her work.

Vaughn has a simple method for controlling cash receipts. He knows the occupancy level of his apartments. He also knows the monthly rent he charges. He multiplies the number of apartments—say 100—by the monthly rent (which averages $500 per unit) to arrive at expected monthly rent revenue of $50,000. By tracing the $50,000 revenue to the bank statement, Vaughn can tell that his rent money went into his bank account.

Control activities such as these are critical in small businesses. With only a few employees, a separation of duties may not be feasible. The owner must oversee the operations of the business, or the assets will slip away, as they did for Merrill Lynch in the chapter-opening story.

MID-CHAPTER *Summary Problem*

A+ TIPS

CHECK YOUR RESOURCES

The cash account of Baylor Associates at February 28, 20X6, is as follows:

Cash

Feb. 1	**Bal. 3,995**	**Feb. 3**	**400**
6	**800**	**12**	**3,100**
15	**1,800**	**19**	**1,100**
23	**1,100**	**25**	**500**
28	**2,400**	**27**	**900**
Feb. 28	**Bal. 4,095**		

Baylor Associates received the bank statement on February 28, 20X6 (as always, negative amounts are in parentheses):

Bank Statement for February 20X6

Beginning balance		$3,995
Deposits:		
Feb. 7	$ 800	
15	1,800	
24	1,100	3,700
Checks (total per day):		
Feb. 8	$ 400	
16	3,100	
23	1,100	(4,600)
Other items:		
Service charge		(10)
NSF check from M. E. Crown		(700)
Bank collection of note receivable for the company		1,000*
EFT—monthly rent expense		(330)
Interest on account balance		15
Ending balance		$3,070

*Includes principal of $881, plus interest of $119.

Additional data:

Baylor deposits all cash receipts in the bank and makes all payments by check.

Required

1. Prepare the bank reconciliation of Baylor Associates at February 28, 20X6.
2. Journalize the entries based on the bank reconciliation.

Solution

Requirement 1

Baylor Associates
Bank Reconciliation
February 28, 20X6

Bank:			
Balance, February 28, 20X6			$3,070
Add:	Deposit of February 28 in transit		2,400
			5,470
Less:	Outstanding checks issued on Feb. 25 ($500) and Feb. 27 ($900)		(1,400)
Adjusted bank balance, February 28, 20X6			$4,070
Books:			
Balance, February 28, 20X6			$4,095
Add:	Bank collection of note receivable, including interest of $119		1,000
	Interest earned on bank balance		15
			5,110
Less:	Service charge	$ 10	
	NSF check	700	
	EFT—Rent expense	330	(1,040)
Adjusted book balance, February 28, 20X6			$4,070

Requirement 2

Date	Accounts	Debit	Credit
Feb. 28	Cash	1,000	
	Note Receivable ($1,000 – $119)		881
	Interest Revenue		119
	Note receivable collected by bank.		
28	Cash	15	
	Interest Revenue		15
	Interest earned on bank balance.		
28	Miscellaneous Expense	10	
	Cash		10
	Bank service charge.		
Feb. 28	Accounts Receivable—M. E. Crown	700	
	Cash		700
	NSF check returned by bank.		
28	Rent Expense	330	
	Cash		330
	Monthly rent expense.		

Student Resource CD
cash receipts, internal control

Internal Control over Cash Receipts

Internal controls over cash receipts ensure that all cash receipts are deposited for safekeeping in the bank. Companies receive cash over the counter and through the mail. Each source of cash calls for its own security measures.

CASH RECEIPTS OVER THE COUNTER Exhibit 8-7 illustrates a cash receipt over the counter in a department store. The point-of-sale terminal (cash register) provides control over the cash receipts. Consider a Macy's store.

Company policy requires issuance of a receipt to ensure that each sale is recorded correctly. The cash drawer opens only when the clerk enters an amount on the keypad, and the machine records each transaction. At the end of the day, a manager proves the cash by comparing the total amount in the cash drawer against the machine's record of sales. This step helps prevent outright theft by the clerk.

At the end of the day, the cashier or other employee with cash-handling duties deposits the cash in the bank. The machine tape then goes to the accounting department as the basis for the journal entry to record sales revenue. These security measures, coupled with oversight by a manager, discourage theft.

Exhibit 8-7 **Cash Receipts Over the Counter**

CASH RECEIPTS BY MAIL Many companies receive cash by mail. Exhibit 8-8 shows how companies control cash received by mail. All incoming mail is opened by a mailroom employee. The mailroom then sends all customer checks to the treasurer, who deposits the money in the bank. The remittance advices go to the accounting department for the journal entries to Cash and customer accounts. As a final step, the controller compares the records of the day's cash receipts, as follows. Compare the

4 Apply internal controls to cash receipts

1. Bank deposit amount from the treasurer
2. Debit to Cash from the accounting department

This comparison ensures that the debit to Cash is for the amount actually deposited in the bank.

✔ Starter 8-8

Exhibit 8-8 **Cash Receipts by Mail**

Stop & Think

> What keeps the mailroom employee from pocketing a customer check and destroying the remittance advice?
>
> *Answer:* If a customer gets billed a second time, the customer can show the paid check to prove he/she has already paid. That will point to the dishonest mailroom employee.

✔ Starter 8-9

Many companies use a lock-box system to separate cash duties and establish control over cash receipts. Customers send their checks directly to the company's bank account. Internal control is tight because company personnel never touch incoming cash. The lock-box system improves efficiency because cash goes to work immediately.

Internal Control over Cash Payments

Cash payments are as important as cash receipts. It is therefore critical to control cash payments. Companies make most payments by check. They also pay small amounts from a petty cash fund. Let's begin with cash payments by check.

Student ResourceCD
cash payments, internal control

5 *Apply internal controls to cash payments*

Controls over Payment by Check

Payment by check is an important internal control. First, the check provides a record of the payment. Second, to be valid, the check must be signed by an authorized official. Before signing the check, the manager should study the evidence supporting the payment. To illustrate the internal control over cash payments, let's suppose the business is paying for merchandise inventory.

CONTROLS OVER PURCHASE AND PAYMENT The purchasing and payment process—outlined in Exhibit 8-9—starts when the company sends a *purchase order* to the supplier. When the supplier ships the merchandise, the supplier also mails the *invoice*, or bill. ← The goods arrive, and the receiving department checks the goods for damage and prepares a list of the goods received on a *receiving report*. The accounting department combines all the foregoing documents and forwards this *payment packet* to officers for approval. Exhibit 8-10 shows the documents that make up the payment packet.

We introduced the invoice in Chapter 5.

Exhibit 8-9
Cash Payments by Check

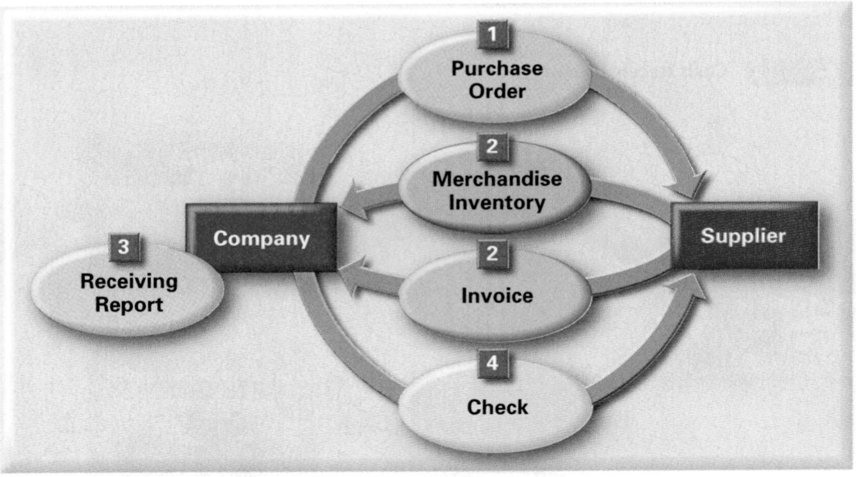

Exhibit 8-10
Payment Packet

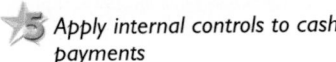

Before signing the check for payment, the controller or the treasurer should examine the packet to prove that all the documents agree. Only then does the company know that

1. It received the goods ordered.
2. It is paying only for the goods received.

These two proofs are needed for good internal control over cash payments by check.

After payment, the check signer punches a hole through the payment packet. Dishonest people have been known to run a bill through for cash payment two or more times. This hole alerts the company that it has paid the bill.

STREAMLINED PROCEDURES Technology is streamlining payment procedures. Evaluated Receipts Settlement (ERS) compresses the approval process into a single step: compare the receiving report to the purchase order. If those documents match, that proves **Kinko's** received the paper it ordered, and then Kinko's pays **Hammermill Paper**, the supplier.

An even more streamlined process bypasses people and documents altogether. In Electronic Data Interchange (EDI), Wal-Mart's computers communicate directly with the computers of suppliers like Hershey Foods and Procter & Gamble. When Wal-Mart's inventory of Hershey chocolate candy reaches a low level, the computer sends a purchase order to Hershey. Hershey ships the candy and invoices to Wal-Mart electronically. Then an electronic fund transfer (EFT) sends Wal-Mart's payment to Hershey.

✔ Starter 8-10

Controlling Petty Cash Payments

It is wasteful to get approval and write a check for an executive's taxi fare or the delivery of a package across town. To meet these needs, companies keep cash on hand to pay small amounts. This fund is called **petty cash**.

Petty Cash
Fund containing a small amount of cash that is used to pay for minor expenditures.

Even though petty cash payments are small, the business needs to set up controls such as the following:

1. Designate an employee to serve as custodian of the petty cash fund.
2. Keep a specific amount of cash on hand.
3. Support all fund payments with a petty cash ticket.

The petty cash fund is opened when a check for the designated amount is issued to Petty Cash. Assume that on February 28, the business creates a petty cash fund of $200. The custodian cashes a $200 check and places the money in the fund. Starting the fund is recorded as follows:

Feb. 28	Petty Cash	200	
	Cash in Bank		200
	To open the petty cash fund.		

For each petty cash payment, the custodian prepares a *petty cash ticket* like the one in Exhibit 8-11.

Exhibit 8-11
Petty Cash Ticket

PETTY CASH TICKET

Date Mar. 25, 20X6 **No.** 47

Amount $23.00

For Box of floppy diskettes

Debit Office Supplies, Acct. No. 145

Received by *Lewis Wright* **Fund Custodian** MAR

Signatures (or initials) identify the recipient of the cash (Lewis Wright) and the fund custodian (MAR). Requiring both signatures reduces fraudulent payments. The custodian keeps all the petty cash tickets in the fund. The sum of the cash plus the total of the ticket amounts should equal the opening balance ($200) at all times. Also, the Petty Cash account keeps its $200 balance at all times.

Maintaining the Petty Cash account at its designated balance is the nature of an **imprest system**. This clearly identifies the amount of cash for which the custodian is responsible, and that is the system's main internal control feature.

Imprest System
A way to account for petty cash by maintaining a constant balance in the petty cash account, supported by the fund (cash plus payment tickets) totaling the same amount.

Payments reduce the cash in the fund, so periodically the fund must be replenished. On March 31 this fund has $118 in cash and $82 in tickets. A check for $82 is issued to replenish the fund. The check is made payable to Petty Cash. The fund custodian cashes this check and puts $82 in the fund to return its actual cash to $200.

The petty cash tickets identify the accounts to be debited, as shown in the entry to replenish the fund:

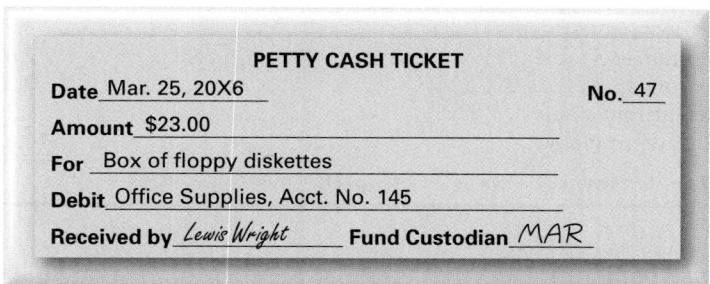

Mar. 31	Office Supplies	23	
	Delivery Expense	17	
	Miscellaneous Selling Expense	42	
	Cash in Bank		82
	To replenish the petty cash fund.		

✔ Starter 8-11

The Petty Cash account keeps its $200 balance at all times. Petty Cash is debited only when the fund is started (see the February 28 entry) or when its amount is changed. If the business raises the fund amount from $200 to $250, this would require a $50 debit to Petty Cash.

Student Resource CD
balance sheet

Reporting Cash on the Balance Sheet

Cash is the first asset listed on the balance sheet because it's the most liquid asset. Businesses often have many bank accounts and several petty cash funds, but they combine all cash amounts into a single total called "Cash and Cash Equivalents."

Cash equivalents include liquid assets such as time deposits. These are interest-bearing accounts that can be withdrawn with no penalty. These assets are sufficiently liquid to be reported along with cash. The balance sheet of Intel Corporation reported the following current assets:

Intel Corporation

Balance Sheet (Adapted)
December 31, 2001

	(In millions)
Assets	
Current assets:	
Cash and cash equivalents	$ 7,970
Short-term investments	3,580
Accounts receivable	2,607
Inventories	2,253
Other current assets	1,223
Total current assets	$17,633

Source: Intel Corporation. *Annual Report 2001*, p. 21.

Intel's cash balance means that Intel has $7,970 million available for immediate use. Cash that is restricted should not be reported as a current asset. For example, banks require customers to keep a *compensating balance* on deposit in order to borrow from the bank. The compensating balance is not included in the cash amount on the balance sheet.

Student Resource CD
ethics

Ethics and Accounting

A *Wall Street Journal* article described a Russian entrepreneur who was getting ahead in business by breaking laws. "Older people have an ethics problem," he said. "By that I mean they *have* ethics." Conversely, Roger Smith, the former chairman of General Motors, said, "Ethical practice is [. . .] good business." Smith has been around long enough to know that unethical behavior doesn't work. Sooner or later unethical conduct comes to light. Moreover, ethical behavior wins out in the long run because it is the right thing to do.

Corporate and Professional Codes of Ethics

Most large companies have a code of ethics to encourage employees to behave ethically. But codes of ethics are not enough by themselves. Senior management must set a high ethical tone. They must make it clear that the company will not tolerate unethical conduct.

As professionals, accountants are expected to maintain higher standards than society in general. Their ability to do business depends entirely on their reputation. Most independent accountants are members of the American Institute of Certified Public Accountants and must abide by the *AICPA Code of Professional Conduct*. Accountants who are members of the Institute of Management Accountants are bound by the *Standards of Ethical Conduct for Management Accountants*. →

← *See Chapter 19, p. 774.*

Ethical Issues in Accounting

6 *Make ethical business judgments*

In many situations, the ethical choice is easy. For example, stealing cash is both unethical and illegal. In our chapter-opening story, the cashier's actions landed her in prison. In other cases, the choices are more difficult. But in every instance, ethical judgments boil down to a personal decision: What should I do in a given situation? Let's consider three ethical issues in accounting.

SITUATION 1 Sonja Kleberg is preparing the income tax return of a client who has earned more income than expected. On January 2, the client pays for advertising and asks Sonja to backdate the expense to the preceding year. The tax deduction would help the client more in the year just ended than in the current year. Backdating would decrease taxable income of the earlier year and lower the client's tax payments. After all, there is a difference of only two days between January 2 and December 31. This client is important to Kleberg. What should she do?

She should refuse the request because the transaction took place in January of the new year.

What control device could prove that Kleberg behaved unethically if she backdated the transaction in the accounting records? An IRS audit could prove that the expense occurred in January rather than in December. Falsifying IRS documents is both unethical and illegal.

SITUATION 2 Jack Mellichamp's software company owes $40,000 to Bank of America. The loan agreement requires Mellichamp's company to maintain a current ratio (current assets divided by current liabilities) of 1.50 or higher. → At present, the company's current ratio is 1.40. At this level, Mellichamp is in violation of his loan agreement. He can increase the current ratio to 1.53 by paying off some current liabilities right before year-end. Is it ethical to do so?

← *For a review of the current ratio, see Chapter 4.*

Yes, because the action is a real business transaction.

Mellichamp should be aware that paying off the liabilities is only a delaying tactic. It will hold off the creditors for now, but the business still must improve in order to keep from violating the agreement.

SITUATION 3 David Duncan, the lead auditor of Enron Corporation, thinks Enron may be understating the liabilities on its balance sheet. Enron's transactions are very complex, and no one may ever figure this out. Duncan asks his firm's Standards Committee how he should handle the situation. They reply, "Require Enron to report all its liabilities." Enron is Duncan's most important

✔ Starter 8-12

client, and Enron is pressuring him to certify the liabilities. Duncan can rationalize that Enron's reported amounts are okay. What should Duncan do? To make his decision, Duncan could follow the framework outlined in the following Decision Guidelines feature.

Decision Guidelines

FRAMEWORK FOR MAKING ETHICAL JUDGMENTS

Weighing tough ethical judgments requires a decision framework. Answering these four questions will guide you through tough decisions. Let's apply them to David Duncan's situation.

Question	Decision Guideline
1. What is the ethical issue?	1. *Identify the ethical issue.* The root word of ethical is *ethics*, which Webster's dictionary defines as "the discipline dealing with what is good and bad and with moral duty and obligation." Duncan's ethical dilemma is to decide what he should do with the information he has uncovered.
2. What are Duncan's options?	2. *Specify the alternatives.* For David Duncan, the alternatives include (a) go along with Enron's liabilities as reported or (b) force Enron to report higher amounts of liabilities.
3. What are the possible consequences?	3. *Assess the possible outcomes.* a. If Duncan certifies Enron's present level of liabilities—and if no one ever objects—Duncan will keep this valuable client. But if Enron's actual liabilities turn out to be higher than reported, Enron investors may lose money and take Duncan to court. That would damage his reputation as an auditor and hurt his firm. b. If Duncan follows his company policy, he must force Enron to increase its reported liabilities. That will anger the company, and Enron may fire Duncan as its auditor. In this case, Duncan will save his reputation, but it will cost him some business in the short run.
4. What shall I do?	4. *Make the decision.* In the end Duncan went along with Enron and certified the company's liabilities. He went directly against his firm's policies. Enron later admitted understating its liabilities, Duncan had to retract his audit opinion, and Duncan's firm, **Arthur Andersen**, collapsed quickly. Duncan should have followed company policy, as we discuss on page 324. Rarely is one person smarter than a team of experts. Duncan got out from under his firm's umbrella of protection, and it cost him and many others dearly.

Excel Application Exercise

Goal: Create an Excel spreadsheet to help evaluate various options for an ethical dilemma.

Scenario: Consider the dilemma of Paul Van Allen, in textbook problem P8-7A. In addition to the facts in the problem, Van Allen's board is considering additional options. First, there is a comparable site in the same general area with an appraised value of $3.9 million. But this location is home to a woodland fungus that may aid in the treatment of diabetes. Second, the board is considering expanding the existing location's square footage by 25%. The board has received a bid of $3.2 million on the new construction from Van Allen's brother-in-law.

Assume the following: If the board makes an offer on Fletcher's property, it will propose a price of $3.5 million. If an offer is made on the comparable site, it will be $3.4 million. If the board chooses to remodel and expand the current location, the bid price will be accepted.

Your task is to create a spreadsheet that weights the issues associated with each scenario option and calculates the best choice.

After you have prepared your spreadsheet, answer these questions:

1. What additional issues did you include in your list?
2. Which option does your spreadsheet suggest the board choose?
3. For each option, which issue did you weigh the most (in other words, which issue was most important)?
4. If you were Van Allen, which option would you recommend to the board, and why?

Excel Application Exercise *(continued)*

Step-by-Step:

1. Open a new Excel worksheet.
2. Create a bold-faced heading for your spreadsheet that contains the following:
   a. Chapter 8 Excel Application Exercise
   b. Ethical Dilemma
   c. Today's Date
3. In row 5, create the following column headings:
   a. Issues
   b. Option 1 (Fletcher)
   c. Option 2 (Comp Site)
   d. Option 3 (Remodel)
   e. Option 4 (Do Nothing)
4. In the Issues column, list the issues that should be considered in making a decision. Add as many issues as you believe are relevant. Here's a starter list:
   a. Cost
   b. No potential environmental issues
   c. Absence of conflict of interest
   d. No exploitation of seller's circumstances
   e. Local community support
5. Next, using a range of 1 to 10, assign a score to each issue for each option. The higher the number, the more desirable it is for Van Allen and the board. For example, if the local community response for Option 1 is unimportant, the score should be close to 1 or 2. If the local community response to Option 2 is expected to be negative, it could be given a higher score to reflect the expected lack of support.
6. Underneath your last row of issues, create a "Total" row, and sum up the numbers for each column. This number represents the score for the option. Assuming all relevant issues have been appropriately ranked, the option with the highest score indicates the best choice.

END-OF-CHAPTER *Summary Problem*

Abbey Company established a $300 petty cash fund. James C. Brown (JCB) is the fund custodian. At the end of the week, the petty cash fund contains the following:

a. Cash: $171

b. Petty cash tickets, as follows:

No.	Amount	Issued to	Signed by	Account Debited
44	$14	B. Jarvis	B. Jarvis and JCB	Office Supplies
45	39	S. Bell	S. Bell	Delivery Expense
47	43	R. Tate	R. Tate and JCB	—
48	33	L. Blair	L. Blair and JCB	Travel Expense

A+ TIPS

CHECK YOUR RESOURCES

Required

1. Identify three internal control weaknesses revealed in the given data.
2. Prepare the general journal entries to record:
   a. Establishment of the petty cash fund.
   b. Replenishment of the fund. Assume that petty cash ticket no. 47 was issued for the purchase of office supplies.
3. What is the balance in the Petty Cash account immediately before replenishment? Immediately after replenishment?

Solution

Requirement 1

The three internal control weaknesses are

1. Petty cash ticket no. 46 is missing. There is no indication of what happened to this ticket. The company should investigate.
2. The petty cash custodian (JCB) did not sign petty cash ticket no. 45. This omission may have been an oversight on his part. However, it raises the question of whether he authorized the payment. Both the fund custodian and the recipient of cash should sign the ticket.
3. Petty cash ticket no. 47 does not indicate which account to debit. What did Tate do with the money, and what account should be debited? See 2b above.

Requirement 2

Petty cash journal entries:

a. Entry to establish the petty cash fund:

Petty Cash	300	
Cash in Bank		300

b. Entry to replenish the fund:

Office Supplies ($14 + $43)	57	
Delivery Expense	39	
Travel Expense	33	
Cash in Bank		129

Requirement 3

The balance in Petty Cash is *always* its specified balance, in this case $300.

REVIEW *Internal Control and Cash*

Quick Check

1. Which of the following is not part of the definition of internal control?
   a. Safeguard assets
   b. Encourage employees to follow company policy
   c. Promote operational efficiency
   d. Separation of duties
2. Internal auditors focus on __________; external auditors are more concerned with __________. Fill in the blanks.
   a. operations; financial statements
   b. e-commerce; fraud
   c. documents; records
   d. cash receipts; cash payments
3. Darice Goodrich receives cash from customers. Her other assigned job is to post the collections to customer accounts receivable. Her company has weak
   a. Ethics
   b. Separation of duties
   c. Assignment of responsibilities
   d. Computer controls
4. Encryption
   a. Creates firewalls to protect data
   b. Cannot be broken by hackers
   c. Avoids the need for separation of duties
   d. Rearranges messages by a special process
5. The document that explains all differences between the company's cash records and the bank's figures is called a
   a. Bank statement
   b. Bank reconciliation
   c. Bank collection
   d. Electronic fund transfer
6. Which items appear on the Book side of a bank reconciliation?
   a. Outstanding checks
   b. Deposits in transit
   c. Both a and b
   d. None of the above
7. Which items appear on the Bank side of a bank reconciliation?
   a. Outstanding checks
   b. Deposits in transit
   c. Both a and b
   d. None of the above
8. Navarro Company's Cash account shows an ending balance of $800. There are also a $20 service charge and an NSF check for $100. A $250 deposit is in transit, and outstanding checks total $400. What is Navarro's adjusted cash balance?
   a. $530
   b. $650
   c. $680
   d. $1,050
9. After performing a bank reconciliation, we need to journalize
   a. All items on the book side of the reconciliation
   b. All items on the bank side of the reconciliation
   c. All items on the reconciliation
   d. No items from the reconciliation because all cash transactions have already been recorded

10. Separation of duties is important for internal control of
   a. Cash receipts
   b. Cash payments
   c. Both of the above
   d. Neither of the above

Accounting Vocabulary

audit (p. 326)
bank collection (p. 332)
bank reconciliation (p. 330)
bank statement (p. 330)
check (p. 329)
computer virus (p. 328)
controller (p. 325)
deposit in transit (p. 332)
electronic funds transfer (EFT) (p. 330)
encryption (p. 328)
firewalls (p. 329)
imprest system (p. 339)
internal control (p. 324)
nonsufficient funds (NSF) check (p. 332)
outstanding check (p. 332)
petty cash (p. 339)
Trojan horse (p. 328)
voucher (p. 358)

ASSESS *Your Progress*

Starters

A+ online homework

See *www.prenhall.com/horngren* for selected Starters, Exercises, and Problems.

Definition of internal control
(Obj. 1)

S8-1 Internal controls are designed to safeguard assets, encourage employees to follow company policies, promote operational efficiency, and ensure accurate records. Which goal is most important? Which goal must the internal controls accomplish for the business to survive? Give your reason.

Applying the definition of internal control
(Obj. 1)

S8-2 Explain in your own words why separation of duties is often described as the cornerstone of internal control for safeguarding assets. Describe what can happen if the same person has custody of an asset and also accounts for the asset.

Characteristics of an effective system of internal control
(Obj. 2)

S8-3 How do external auditors differ from internal auditors? How does an external audit differ from an internal audit? How are the two types of audits similar?

Characteristics of an effective system of internal control
(Obj. 2)

S8-4 Review the characteristics of an effective system of internal control that begin on page 324. Then identify two things that **Merrill Lynch** in the chapter-opening story could have done to make it harder for cashier Darlyne Lopez to steal from the company and hide the theft. Explain how each new measure taken by Merrill Lynch would have accomplished its goal.

Aspects of a bank reconciliation
(Obj. 3)

S8-5 Answer the following questions about the bank reconciliation:

1. What is the difference between a bank statement and a bank reconciliation?
2. Is the bank reconciliation a journal, a ledger, an account, or a financial statement? If none of these, what is it?

Preparing a bank reconciliation
(Obj. 3)

S8-6 The Cash account of Good Times Video Productions reported a balance of $2,280 at May 31. Included were outstanding checks totaling $900 and a May 31 deposit in transit of $200. The bank statement, which came from Park Cities Bank, listed a May 31 balance of $3,600. Included in the bank balance was a May 30 collection of $630 on account from Kelly Brooks, a Good Times customer who pays the bank directly. The bank statement also shows a $20 service charge and $10 of interest revenue that Good times earned on its bank balance. *Prepare Good Times' bank reconciliation at May 31.*

Recording transactions from a bank reconciliation
(Obj. 3)

S8-7 After preparing Good Times Video's bank reconciliation in Starter 8-6, journalize the company's transactions that arise from the bank reconciliation. Include an explanation with each entry.

Control over cash receipts
(Obj. 4)

S8-8 Les Albrecht sells furniture for Lane's Interiors in Destin, Florida. Company procedure requires Albrecht to write a customer receipt for all sales. The receipt forms are prenumbered. Albrecht is having personal financial problems and takes $500 that he received from a customer. To hide his theft, Albrecht simply destroys the company copy of the sales receipt he gave the customer. What will alert Monica Lane, the owner, that something is wrong? What will this knowledge lead Lane to do?

Control over cash receipts by mail
(Obj. 4)

S8-9 Review the internal controls over cash receipts by mail, discussed on page 337. Exactly what is accomplished by the final step in the process, performed by the controller? What does a lock-box system accomplish?

S8-10 Answer the following questions about internal control over cash payments.

Internal control over payments by check
(Obj. 5)

1. A purchasing agent for Eastwood Company receives the goods that he purchases and also approves payment for the goods. How could this purchasing agent cheat his company? How could Eastwood avoid this internal control weakness?
2. Payment of cash payments by check carries two basic controls over cash. What are they?

Petty cash
(Obj. 5)

S8-11 Record the following selected transactions of Rosetree Florist in general journal format (explanations are not required):

April 1	Established a petty cash fund with a $200 balance.
30	The petty cash fund has $19 in cash and $181 in petty cash tickets that were issued to pay for Office Supplies ($111), Delivery Expense ($33), and Entertainment Expense ($37). Replenished the fund and recorded the expenses.

Making an ethical judgment
(Obj. 6)

S8-12 Nancy Allen, an accountant for Chinatown Express, discovers that her supervisor, Lee Kwan, made several errors last year. Overall, the errors overstated Chinatown's net income by 20%. It is not clear whether the errors were deliberate or accidental. What should Allen do?

A+ online homework

Exercises

Identifying internal control strengths and weaknesses
(Obj. 2)

E8-1 The following situations describe two equipment purchases and two cash receipts. In each pair, one situation's internal controls are much better than the other's. Evaluate the internal controls in each situation as strong or weak, and give the reason for your answers.

Equipment Purchases:

a. Centennial Homes policy calls for construction supervisors to request the equipment needed for construction jobs. The home office then purchases the equipment and has it shipped to the construction site.
b. Wayside Construction Company policy calls for project supervisors to purchase the equipment needed for construction jobs. The supervisors then submit the paid receipts to the home office for reimbursement. This policy enables supervisors to get the equipment they need quickly and keep construction jobs moving along.

Cash Receipts:

a. Cash received by mail goes straight to the accountant, who debits Cash and credits Accounts Receivable to record collections from customers. The accountant then deposits the cash in the bank.
b. Cash received by mail goes to the mail room, where a mail clerk opens envelopes and totals the cash receipts for the day. The mail clerk forwards customer checks to the treasurer for deposit in the bank and forwards the remittance slips to the accounting department for posting credits to customer accounts.

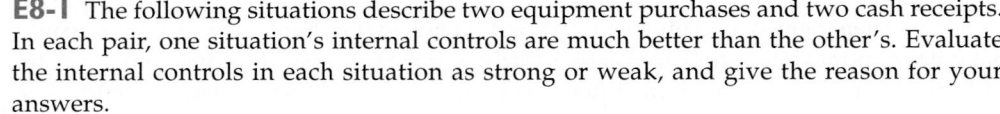

Identifying internal control strengths and weaknesses **(Obj. 2)**

E8-2 The following situations suggest a strength or a weakness in internal control. Identify each as *strength* or *weakness*, and give the reason for your answer.

a. Top managers delegate all internal control measures to the accounting department.
b. The accounting department orders merchandise and approves invoices for payment.
c. The operator of a computer has no other accounting or cash-handling duties.
d. Cash received over the counter is controlled by the sales clerk, who rings up the sale and places the cash in the register. The sales clerk matches the total recorded on the control tape stored in the register to each day's cash sales.
e. The officer who signs checks need not examine the payment packet because he is confident the amounts are correct.

Identifying internal controls **(Obj. 2)**

E8-3 Identify the missing internal control in the following situations. Select from these characteristics:

- Competent, reliable personnel
- Assignment of responsibilities
- Separation of duties
- Audits
- Electronic and computer controls
- Other controls (specify)

a. The same trusted employee has served as cashier for 10 years.
b. Grocery stores such as **Safeway** and **Meier's** purchase most merchandise from a few suppliers. At another grocery store, the manager decides to reduce paperwork. He eliminates the requirement that the receiving department prepare a receiving report, which lists the quantities of items actually received from the supplier.
c. When business is brisk, Stop-n-Go deposits cash in the bank several times during the day. The manager at one store wants to reduce the time employees spend delivering cash to the bank, so he starts a new policy. Cash will build up over Saturdays and Sundays, and the total two-day amount will be deposited on Sunday evening.
d. While reviewing the records of Discount Pharmacy, you find that the same employee orders merchandise and approves invoices for payment.
e. Business is slow at Fun City Amusement Park on Tuesday, Wednesday, and Thursday nights. To reduce expenses, the owner decides not to use a ticket taker on those nights. The ticket seller (cashier) is told to keep the tickets as a record of the number sold.

Classifying bank reconciliation items **(Obj. 3)**

E8-4 The following items could appear on a bank reconciliation:

a. Service charge
b. Deposits in transit
c. NSF check
d. Bank collection of a note receivable for us
e. Interest earned on bank balance
f. Book error: We credited Cash for $200. The correct amount was $2,000
g. Outstanding checks
h. Bank error: The bank decreased our account for a check written by another customer

Required

Classify each item as (1) an addition to the book balance, (2) a subtraction from the book balance, (3) an addition to the bank balance, or (4) a subtraction from the bank balance.

Preparing a bank reconciliation **(Obj. 3)**

E8-5 Jason Coe's checkbook lists the following:

Date	Check No.	Item	Check	Deposit	Balance
9/1					$ 525
4	622	JD's Art Café	$ 19		506
9		Dividends received		$ 116	622
13	623	General Tire Co.	43		579
14	624	ExxonMobil	58		521
18	625	Cash	50		471
26	626	Woodway Baptist Church	75		396
28	627	Bent Tree Apartments	275		121
30		Paycheck		1,500	1,621

Coe's September bank statement shows the following:

Balance				$525
Add: Deposits				116
Debit checks:	No.	Amount		
	622	$19		
	623	43		
	624	68*		
	625	50		(180)
Other charges:				
Printed checks			$18	
Service charge			12	(30)
Balance				$431

*This is the correct amount for check number 624.

Required

Prepare Coe's bank reconciliation at September 30. How much cash does Coe actually have on September 30?

Preparing a bank reconciliation
(Obj. 3)

E8-6 Zane Grey operates four Quik Pak convenience stores. He has just received the monthly bank statement at October 31 from City National Bank, and the statement shows an ending balance of $2,050. Listed on the statement are an EFT rent collection of $400, a service charge of $12, two NSF checks totaling $74, and a $9 charge for printed checks. In reviewing his cash records, Grey identifies outstanding checks totaling $467 and an October 31 deposit in transit of $1,788. During October, he recorded a $290 check by debiting Salary Expense and crediting Cash for $29. Grey's Cash account shows an October 31 balance of $3,327. *Prepare the bank reconciliation at October 31.*

Making journal entries from a bank reconciliation
(Obj. 3)

E8-7 Using the data from Exercise 8-6, make the journal entries Grey should record on October 31. Include an explanation for each entry.

Using a bank reconciliation as a control device
(Obj. 3)

E8-8 Barry Cruse owns Cruse Vacations. He fears that a trusted employee has been stealing from the company. This employee receives cash from customers and also prepares the monthly bank reconciliation. To check up on the employee, Cruse prepares his own bank reconciliation, as follows:

Cruse Vacations
Bank Reconciliation
August 31, 20X7

Bank		Books	
Balance, August 31	$3,000	Balance, August 31	$2,500
Add: Deposit in transit	400	Add: Bank collection	820
		Interest revenue	10
Less: Outstanding checks	(1,100)	Less: Service charge	(30)
Adjusted bank balance	$2,300	Adjusted book balance	$3,300

Which side of the reconciliation shows the true cash balance? What is Cruse's true cash balance? Does it appear that the employee has stolen from the company? If so, how much? Explain your answer.

Evaluating internal control over cash receipts
(Obj. 4)

E8-9 When you check out at a **Best Buy** store, the cash register displays the amount of the sale, the cash received from the customer, and any change returned to the customer. Suppose the register also produces a customer receipt but keeps no internal record of transactions. At the end of the day, the clerk counts the cash in the register and gives it to the cashier for deposit in the company bank account.

Write a memo to the store manager. Identify the internal control weakness over cash receipts, and explain how the weakness gives an employee the opportunity to steal cash. State how to prevent such a theft.

E8-10 Leather Goods Company created a $300 imprest petty cash fund. During the month, the fund custodian authorized and signed petty cash tickets as follows:

Accounting for petty cash
(Obj. 5)

Student Resource CD
General Ledger, Peachtree, QuickBooks

Petty Cash Ticket No.	Item	Account Debited	Amount
1	Delivery of goods to customers	Delivery Expense	$22
2	Mail package	Postage Expense	52
3	Newsletter	Supplies Expense	34
4	Key to closet	Miscellaneous Expense	3
5	Wastebasket	Miscellaneous Expense	13
6	Computer diskettes	Supplies Expense	85

Required

1. Make the general journal entries to (a) create the petty cash fund and (b) record its replenishment. Include explanations.
2. Describe the items in the fund both before and after replenishment.

E8-11

Control over petty cash
(Obj. 5)

1. Explain how an *imprest* petty cash system works. What is the main control feature of an imprest system?
2. Atlantic Press maintains an imprest petty cash fund of $400 which is under the control of Brenda Montague. At November 30, the fund holds $220 cash and petty cash tickets for travel expense, $80; office supplies, $60; and delivery expense, $40.

   Journalize **(a)** establishment of the petty cash fund on November 1 and **(b)** replenishment of the fund on November 30.
3. Prepare a T-account for the Petty Cash account of Atlantic Press, and post to the account. What is Petty Cash's balance at all times?

E8-12 Approximately 300 current and former members of the U.S. House of Representatives—on a regular basis—wrote a quarter million dollars of checks on the House bank without having the cash in their accounts. In effect, the delinquent check writers were borrowing money from each other on an interest-free, no-service-charge basis. The House closed its bank after the events became public.

Evaluating the ethics of conduct by government legislators
(Obj. 6)

Required

Suppose you are a new congressional representative from your state. Apply the ethical judgment framework outlined in the Decision Guidelines feature on page 342 to decide whether you would write NSF checks on a regular basis through the House bank.

Problems

(Group A)

A+ online homework

P8-1A San Marino Foreign Cars prospered during the recent economic expansion. Business was so good that the company used very few internal controls. A recent decline in automobile sales caused San Marino to experience a cash shortage. Mike Key, the company owner, is looking for ways to save money.

Identifying the characteristics of an effective internal control system
(Obj. 1, 2)

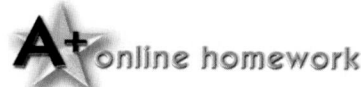

As a consultant for San Marino, write a memo to convince Key of the company's need for a system of internal control. Be specific in explaining how an internal control system could save the company money. Include the definition of internal control, and briefly discuss the characteristics of an effective internal control system, beginning with competent, reliable, and ethical personnel.

Correcting internal control weaknesses
(Obj. 2, 4, 5)

P8-2A Each of the following situations has an internal control weakness.

a. Computer programmers for Internet Solutions work under intense pressure. Facing tight deadlines, they sometimes bypass company policies and write programs without securing customer accounts receivable data.
b. Law firms use paraprofessional employees to perform routine tasks. For example, a legal paraprofessional might prepare first drafts of documents to assist a lawyer. In the law firm of Lee & Dunham, Joseph Lee, the senior partner, turns over most of his legal research to new members of his paraprofessional staff.
c. In evaluating internal control over cash payments, an auditor learns that the purchasing agent is responsible for purchasing diamonds for use in the company's manufacturing process. The purchasing agent also approves the invoices for payment and signs the checks.
d. Blake Lemmon owns an engineering firm. His staff consists of 12 engineers, and he manages the office. Often, his work requires him to travel. He notes that when he returns from business trips, the engineering jobs in the office have not progressed much. When he is away, his senior employees take over office management and neglect their engineering duties. One employee could manage the office.
e. Aimee Atkins has worked for Michael Riggs, MD, for many years. Atkins performs all accounting duties, including opening the mail, making the bank deposits, writing checks, and preparing the bank reconciliation. Riggs trusts Atkins completely.

Required

1. Identify the missing internal control characteristic in each situation.
2. Identify the possible problem caused by each control weakness.
3. Propose a solution to each internal control problem.

Preparing a bank reconciliation
(Obj. 3)

Student Resource CD
spreadsheet

P8-3A The cash records of Silver Maple Art Gallery for April 20X4 follows.

Cash Receipts (CR)		Cash Payments (CP)	
Date	**Cash Debit**	**Check No.**	**Cash Credit**
Apr. 2	$ 4,174	3113	$ 891
8	501	3114	147
10	559	3115	1,930
16	2,187	3116	664
22	1,854	3117	1,472
29	1,060	3118	1,000
30	337	3119	632
Total	$10,672	3120	1,675
		3121	100
		3122	2,413
		Total	$10,924

The Cash account of Silver Maple Art Gallery shows the following at April 30, 20X4:

Cash					
Date	**Item**	**Jrnl. Ref.**	**Debit**	**Credit**	**Balance**
Apr. 1	Balance				13,911
30		CR. 6	10,672		24,583
30		CP. 11		10,924	13,659

On April 30, 20X4, Silver Maple Art Gallery received the following bank statement:

Bank Statement for April 20X4

Beginning balance		$13,911
Deposits and other Credits:		
Apr. 1	$ 300 EFT	
4	4,174	
9	501	
12	559	
17	2,187	
22	1,300 BC	
23	1,854	10,875
Checks and other Debits:		
Apr. 7 (check no. 3113)	$ 891	
13 (check no. 3115)	1,390	
14	900 US	
15 (check no. 3114)	147	
18 (check no. 3116)	664	
21	200 EFT	
26 (check no. 3117)	1,472	
30 (check no. 3118)	1,000	
30	20 SC	(6,684)
Ending balance		$18,102

Explanations: EFT—electronic funds transfer; BC—bank collection; US—unauthorized signature; SC—service charge.

Additional data for the bank reconciliation:

a. The EFT deposit was a receipt of rent. The EFT debit was an insurance payment.
b. The unauthorized-signature check was received from a customer.
c. The $1,300 bank collection was for a note receivable.
d. The correct amount of check number 3115 is $1,390. (Silver Maple Art Gallery's accountant mistakenly recorded the check for $1,930.)

Required

Prepare the Silver Maple Art Gallery bank reconciliation at April 30, 20X4.

P8-4A The August 31 bank statement of Stop-n-Shop Food Mart has just arrived from United Bank. To prepare the Stop-n-Shop bank reconciliation, you gather the following data:

Preparing a bank reconciliation and the related journal entries
(Obj. 3)

Student Resource CD
spreadsheet

a. Stop-n-Shop's Cash account shows a balance of $6,409.31 on August 31.
b. The bank statement includes two charges for returned checks from customers. One is a $395.00 check received from Lakeland Express and returned due to "Unauthorized Signature." The other is an NSF check for $147.17 received from Veracruz, Inc.
c. Stop-n-Shop pays rent expense ($750) and insurance expense ($290) each month by EFT.
d. The Stop-n-Shop checks below are outstanding at August 31.

Check No.	Amount
237	$ 46.10
288	141.00
291	578.05
293	11.87
294	609.51
295	8.88
296	101.63

e. The bank statement includes a deposit of $1,191, collected by the bank on behalf of Stop-n-Shop Food Mart. Of the total, $1,000 is collection of a note receivable, and the remainder is interest revenue.
f. The bank statement shows that Stop-n-Shop earned $38.19 of interest on its bank balance during August. This amount was added to Stop-n-Shop's account by the bank.
g. The bank statement lists a $10 subtraction for the bank service charge.

h. On August 31, Stop-n-Shop deposited $316.15, but this deposit does not appear on the bank statement.

i. The bank statement includes a $300 deposit that Stop-n-Shop did not make. The bank erroneously credited the Stop-n-Shop account for another bank customer's deposit.

j. The August 31 bank balance is $7,527.22.

Required

1. Prepare the bank reconciliation for Stop-n-Shop Food Mart at August 31.
2. Record the journal entries necessary to bring the book balance of Cash into agreement with the adjusted book balance on the reconciliation. Include an explanation for each entry.

Identifying internal control weakness in cash receipts
(Obj. 4)

P8-5A Koala Bear Software makes all sales of its spreadsheet software on credit. Cash receipts arrive by mail. Nick Vaughn opens envelopes and separates the checks from the accompanying remittance advices. Vaughn forwards the checks to another employee, who makes the daily bank deposit but has no access to the accounting records. Vaughn sends the remittance advices, which show the cash received, to the accounting department for entry in the accounts. Vaughn's only other duty is to grant sales allowances to customers. (Recall that a *sales allowance* decreases the amount receivable.) When he receives a customer check for less than the full amount of the invoice, he records the sales allowance and forwards the document to the accounting department.

Required

You are a new employee of Koala Bear Software. Write a memo to the company president identifying the internal control weakness in this situation. State how to correct the weakness.

Accounting for petty cash transactions
(Obj. 5)

Student Resource CD
GL, PT, QB

P8-6A Suppose that on June 1, Reyna & Reyna, Consulting Engineers, opens a district office in Omaha and creates a petty cash fund with an imprest balance of $350. During June, Carol McColgin, fund custodian, signs the following petty cash tickets:

Petty Cash Ticket Number	Item	Amount
1	Postage for package received	$ 18
2	Decorations and refreshments for office party	13
3	Two boxes of floppy disks	20
4	Printer cartridges	27
5	Dinner money for sales manager entertaining a customer	50
6	Plane ticket for executive business trip to Chicago	169
7	Delivery of package across town	6

On June 30, prior to replenishment, the fund contains these tickets plus cash. The accounts affected by petty cash payments are Office Supplies Expense, Travel Expense, Delivery Expense, Entertainment Expense, and Postage Expense.

Required

1. Explain the characteristics and the internal control features of an imprest fund.
2. How much cash does this petty cash fund hold before it's replenished?
3. Make general journal entries to **(a)** create the fund and **(b)** replenish it. Include explanations. Also, briefly describe what the custodian does on these dates.
4. Make the entry on July 1 to increase the fund balance to $500. Include an explanation, and briefly describe what the custodian does.

Making an ethical judgment
(Obj. 7)

P8-7A Paul Van Allen is vice president of Tri-Cities Bank in Bristol, Virginia. Active in community affairs, Van Allen serves on the board of directors of Baker Publishing Company. Baker is expanding and relocating its plant. At a recent meeting, board members decided to buy 15 acres of land on the edge of town. The owner of the property, Jack Fletcher, is a customer of Tri-Cities Bank. Fletcher is completing a divorce, and Van Allen knows that Fletcher is eager to sell his property. In view of Fletcher's difficult situation, Van Allen believes he would accept almost any offer for the land. Realtors have appraised the property at $5 million.

Apply the ethical judgment framework from the Decision Guidelines (page 342) to help Van Allen decide what his role should be in Baker's attempt to buy the land from Fletcher.

Problems

(Group B)

online homework

Identifying the characteristics of an effective internal control system
(Obj. 1, 2)

P8-1B An employee of a Meyer's Department Store stole thousands of dollars from the company. Suppose Meyer's has installed a new system of internal controls. As a consultant for Meyer's Department Store, write a memo to the president explaining how internal controls safeguard assets.

Correcting internal control weaknesses
(Obj. 2, 4, 5)

P8-2B Each of the following situations has an internal control weakness.

a. MiniScribe Corporation, a private company, has never had an audit. MiniScribe's accountants falsified sales and inventory figures in order to get an important loan. The loan went through, but MiniScribe later went bankrupt and couldn't repay the bank.

b. Discount stores such as **Target** and **Sam's** receive a large portion of their sales revenue in cash, with the remainder in credit-card sales. To reduce expenses, one store manager ceases purchasing fidelity bonds on the cashiers.

c. The office supply company where Champs Sporting Goods purchases cash receipt forms recently notified Champs that their receipt forms were not prenumbered. Alex Champ, the owner, replied that he never uses the receipt numbers.

d. Centex Software specializes in programs with accounting applications. The company's most popular program prepares the journal, accounts receivable subsidiary ledger, and general ledger. In the company's early days, the owner and eight employees wrote the computer programs, sold the products to stores such as ComputerWorld, and performed the accounting. As the company has grown, the number of employees has increased dramatically. Recently, development of a new software program stopped while the programmers redesigned Centex's accounting system. Centex's accountants could have performed this task.

e. Lana Turner, a widow with no known sources of outside income, has been a trusted employee of Stone Products Company for 15 years. She performs all cash-handling and accounting duties, including opening the mail, preparing the bank deposit, accounting for all aspects of cash and accounts receivable, and preparing the bank reconciliation. She has just purchased a new Mercedes and a new home in an expensive suburb. Jeremy Stone, owner of the company, wonders how Turner can afford these luxuries.

Required

1. Identify the missing internal control characteristics in each situation.
2. Identify the possible problem caused by each control weakness.
3. Propose a solution to each internal control problem.

Preparing a bank reconciliation
(Obj. 3)

Student ResourceCD

P8-3B The cash records of **Mailboxes Etc.** for March 20X5 follow.

	Cash Receipts (CR)	Cash Payments (CP)	
Date	**Cash Debit**	**Check No.**	**Cash Credit**
Mar. 4	$2,716	1413	$ 465
9	544	1414	1,004
11	1,655	1415	450
14	896	1416	8
17	367	1417	775
25	890	1418	88
31	2,038	1419	126
Total	$9,106	1420	970
		1421	200
		1422	2,267
		Total	$6,353

The Cash account of Mailboxes shows the following on March 31, 20X5:

Cash					
Date	Item	Jrnl. Ref.	Debit	Credit	Balance
Mar. 1	Balance				12,188
31		CR. 10	9,106		21,294
31		CP. 16		6,353	14,941

On March 31, 20X5, Mailboxes received the bank statement that follows.

Bank Statement for March 20X5

Beginning balance		$12,188
Deposits and other Credits:		
Mar. 1	$ 625 EFT	
5	2,716	
10	544	
11	1,655	
15	896	
18	367	
25	890	
31	1,000 BC	8,693
Checks and other Debits:		
Mar. 8	$ 441 NSF	
9 (check no. 1413)	465	
13 (check no. 1414)	1,004	
14 (check no. 1415)	450	
15 (check no. 1416)	8	
19	340 EFT	
22 (check no. 1417)	775	
29 (check no. 1418)	88	
31 (check no. 1419)	216	
31	25 SC	(3,812)
Ending balance		$17,069

Explanations: BC—bank collection; EFT—electronic funds transfer; NSF—nonsufficient funds check; SC—service charge.

Additional data for the bank reconciliation:

a. The EFT deposit was a receipt of rent. The EFT debit was payment of insurance.
b. The NSF check was received from a customer.
c. The $1,000 bank collection was for a note receivable.
d. The correct amount of check 1419 is $216. Mailboxes Etc. mistakenly recorded the check for $126.

Required

Prepare the bank reconciliation of Mailboxes Etc. at March 31, 20X5.

Preparing a bank reconciliation and the related journal entries
(Obj. 3)

P8-4B The May 31 bank statement of Marlow Furniture Co. has just arrived from First State Bank. To prepare the bank reconciliation, you gather the following data.

a. The May 31 bank balance is $19,209.82.
b. The bank statement includes two charges for returned checks from customers. One is a $67.50 NSF check received from Sarah Batten and deposited on May 19. The other is a $195.03 check received from Lena Masters and deposited on May 21. It was returned due to "Unauthorized Signature."
c. The following Marlow checks are outstanding at May 31:

Check No.	Amount
616	$403.00
802	74.25
806	36.60
809	161.38
810	229.05
811	48.91

d. Marlow collects from a few customers by EFT. The May bank statement lists a $200 deposit for a collection on account from customer Jack Oates.

e. The bank statement includes two special deposits: $899.14, for dividend revenue, and $16.86, the interest revenue Marlow earned on its bank balance during May.

f. The bank statement lists a $6.25 subtraction for the bank service charge.

g. On May 31, the Marlow treasurer deposited $381.14, but this deposit does not appear on the bank statement.

h. The bank statement includes a $410.00 deduction for a check drawn by Marimont Freight Company. Marlow notified the bank of this bank error.

i. Marlow's Cash account shows a balance of $18,200.55 on May 31.

Required

1. Prepare the bank reconciliation for Marlow Furniture at May 31.

2. Record the entries called for by the reconciliation. Include an explanation for each entry.

Identifying internal control weakness in cash receipts **(Obj. 4)**

P8-5B Yamaha Marineland makes all sales on credit. Cash receipts arrive by mail. Kenneth Sartain in the mailroom opens envelopes and separates the checks from the accompanying remittance advices. Sartain forwards the checks to another employee, who makes the daily bank deposit but has no access to the accounting records. Sartain sends the remittance advices, which show cash received, to the accounting department for entry in the accounts. Sartain's only other duty is to grant sales allowances to customers. (Recall that a *sales allowance* decreases the amount receivable.) When Sartain receives a customer check for less than the full amount of the invoice, he records the sales allowance and forwards the document to the accounting department.

Required

You are a new employee of Yamaha Marineland. Write a memo to the company president identifying the internal control weakness in this situation. State how to correct the weakness.

Accounting for petty cash transactions **(Obj. 5)**

Student Resource CD
GL, PT, QB

P8-6B On April 1, City of Buena Vista, Arizona, creates a petty cash fund with an imprest balance of $400. During April, Elise Nelson, the fund custodian, signs the following petty cash tickets:

Petty Cash Ticket Number	Item	Amount
101	Office supplies	$86
102	Cab fare for executive	25
103	Delivery of package across town	37
104	Dinner money for city manager to entertain the governor	80
105	Inventory	85
106	Decorations for office party	19
107	Six boxes of floppy disks	44

On April 30, prior to replenishment, the fund contains these tickets plus cash. The accounts affected by petty cash payments are Office Supplies Expense, Travel Expense, Delivery Expense, Entertainment Expense, and Inventory.

Required

1. Explain the characteristics and the internal control features of an imprest fund.
2. How much cash does the petty cash fund hold before it's replenished?
3. Make general journal entries to **(a)** create the fund and **(b)** replenish it. Include explanations. Also, briefly describe what the custodian does on April 1 and April 30.
4. Make the May 1 entry to increase the fund balance to $500. Include an explanation, and briefly describe what the custodian does.

Making an ethical judgment
(Obj. 6)

P8-7B Tri State Bank in Cairo, Illinois, has a loan receivable from Cortez Manufacturing Company. Cortez is six months late in making payments to the bank, and Milton Reed, a Tri State vice president, is helping Cortez restructure its debt. Reed learns that Cortez is depending on landing a manufacturing contract from Peters & Sons, another Tri State client. Reed also serves as Peters' loan officer at the bank. In this capacity, he is aware that Peters is considering declaring bankruptcy. No one else outside Peters & Sons knows this. Reed has been a great help to Cortez Manufacturing, and Cortez's owner is counting on him to carry the company through this difficult restructuring. To help the bank collect on this large loan, Reed has a strong motivation to help Cortez survive.

Apply the ethical judgment framework from the chapter to help Reed plan his next action.

APPLY *Your Knowledge*

Decision Cases

Correcting an internal control weakness
(Obj. 1, 5)

Case 1. This case is based on an actual situation. A-1 Construction Company, headquartered in Terre Haute, Indiana, built a Rest Easy Motel 35 miles east of Terre Haute. The construction foreman, whose name was Monty, hired the 40 workers needed to complete the project. Monty had the construction workers fill out the necessary tax forms, and he sent the employment documents to the home office, which opened a payroll file for each employee.

Work on the motel began on April 1 and ended September 1. Each week, Monty filled out a time card of the hours worked by each employee during the week. Monty faxed the time sheets to the home office, which prepared the payroll checks on Friday morning. Monty drove to the home office after lunch on Friday, picked up the payroll checks, and returned to the construction site. At 5 P.M. on Friday, Monty distributed the payroll checks to the workers.

a. Describe in detail the main internal control weakness in this situation. Specify what negative result(s) could occur because of the internal control weakness.
b. Describe what you would do to correct the internal control weakness.

Using the bank reconciliation to detect a theft
(Obj. 3)

Case 2. Diamondback's Restaurant has poor internal control over its cash transactions. Genevieve Gilbreath, the owner, suspects Sam Knicks, the cashier, of stealing. Here are some details of the business's cash position at September 30.

a. The Cash account shows a balance of $6,502. This amount includes a September 30 deposit of $3,794 that does not appear on the September 30 bank statement.

b. The September 30 bank statement shows a balance of $3,124. The bank statement lists a $200 credit for a bank collection, an $8 debit for the service charge, and a $36 debit for an NSF check. The Diamondback's accountant has not recorded any of these items on the books.

c. At September 30, the following checks are outstanding:

Check No.	Amount
154	$116
256	150
278	353
291	190
292	206
293	245

d. The cashier handles all incoming cash and makes bank deposits. He also reconciles the monthly bank statement. Here is his September 30 reconciliation:

Balance per books, September 30		$17,502
Add: Outstanding checks		260
Bank collection		200
		17,962
Less: Deposits in transit	$3,794	
Service charge	8	
NSF check	36	3,838
Balance per bank, September 30		$14,124

Gilbreath asks you to determine whether the cashier has stolen cash from the business and, if so, how much. She also asks how the cashier concealed the theft. Perform your own bank reconciliation using the format illustrated in the chapter. There are no bank or book errors. Gilbreath also wants your input on changes that will improve Diamondback's internal controls.

Ethical Issue

Internal control over cash payments; ethical considerations
(Obj. 5, 6)

Pam Dilley owns rental properties in Michigan. Each property has a manager who collects rent, arranges for repairs, and runs advertisements in the local newspaper. The property managers transfer cash to Dilley monthly and prepare their own bank reconciliations. The manager in Lansing has been stealing from the company. To cover the theft, he understates the amount of the outstanding checks on the monthly bank reconciliation. As a result, each monthly bank reconciliation appears to balance. However, the balance sheet reports more cash than Dilley actually has in the bank. In negotiating the sale of the Lansing property, Dilley is showing the balance sheet to prospective investors.

Required

1. Identify two parties other than Dilley who can be harmed by this theft. In what ways can they be harmed?
2. Discuss the role accounting plays in this situation.

Financial Statement Case

Internal controls and cash
(Obj. 1, 3)

Study the audit opinion (labeled Report of Independent Auditors) of **Amazon.com** and the Amazon financial statements given at the end of Appendix A. Answer the following questions about the company.

Required

1. What is the name of Amazon.com's outside auditing firm (independent auditors)? What office of this firm signed the audit report? How long after the Amazon year-end did the auditors issue their opinion?
2. Who bears primary responsibility for the financial statements? How can you tell?
3. Does it appear that the Amazon internal controls are adequate? How can you tell?
4. What standard of auditing did the outside auditors use in examining the Amazon financial statements? By what accounting standards were the statements evaluated?
5. By how much did Amazon's cash balance (including cash equivalent) change during 2002? What were the beginning and ending cash balances?

Team Project

You are promoting a rock concert in your area. Each member of your team will invest $10,000 of their hard-earned money in this venture. It is April 1, and the concert is scheduled for June 30. Your promotional activities begin immediately, and ticket sales start on May 1. You expect to sell all the business's assets, pay all the liabilities, and distribute all remaining cash to the group members by July 31.

Required

Write an internal control manual that will help safeguard the assets of the business. The starting point of the manual is to assign responsibilities among the group members. Authorize individuals, including group members and any outsiders that you need to hire, to perform specific jobs. Separate duties among the group and any employees.

For Internet Exercises, go to the Web site www.prenhall.com/horngren.

APPENDIX *to Chapter 8*

- ☐ Internal Control
- ☐ The Bank Account
- ☐ Managing Cash Receipts
- ☐ Managing Cash Payments
- ☐ Cash on the Balance Sheet
- ☐ Ethics and Accounting
- ■ Appendix: Vouchers

Voucher
Instrument authorizing a cash payment.

The Voucher System

The voucher system for recording cash payments improves internal control over cash payments by formalizing the process of approving and recording invoices for payment.

A **voucher** is a document authorizing a cash payment. The accounting department prepares vouchers.

The voucher system uses (1) vouchers, (2) a voucher register (similar to a purchases journal), (3) an unpaid voucher file, (4) a check register (similar to a cash payments journal), and (5) a paid voucher file. The improvement in internal control comes from recording all payments through the voucher register. In a voucher system, all expenditures must be approved before payment can be made. This approval takes the form of a voucher. The larger the business, the more likely it is to need strict control over payments. The voucher system provides this control.

Exhibit 8A-1 Voucher

Front of Voucher

Voucher No. 326

BLISS WHOLESALE COMPANY

Payee Van Heusen, Inc.
Address 4619 Shotwell Avenue
Brooklyn, NY 10564

Due Date March 7
Terms 2/10, n/30

Date	Invoice No.	Description	Amount
Mar. 1	6380	144 men's shirts stock no. X14	$1,764

Approved *Jane Trent* **Controller** **Approved** *Bob Kraft* **Treasurer**

Back of Voucher

Voucher No. 326
Payee Van Heusen, Inc.
Invoice Amount $1,800
Discount 36
Net Amount $1,764

Due Date Mar. 7
Date Paid Mar. 6
Check No. 694

Account Distribution

Account Debited	Acct. No.	Amount
Inventory	105	$1,764
Store Supplies	145	
Salary Expense	538	
Advertising Expense	542	
Utilities Expense	548	
Delivery Expense	544	
Total		$1,764

Exhibit 8A-1 illustrates the voucher of Bliss Wholesale Company. In addition to the *payee, due date, terms, description*, and *invoice amount*, the voucher includes a section for designated officers to sign their approval for payment. The back of the voucher has places for recording the *account debited, date paid*, and *check number*. You should locate these eight items in Exhibit 8A-1.

CHAPTER 9

Receivables

A+ TIPS CHECK YOUR RESOURCES

- Visit the www.prenhall.com/horngren **Web site** for self-study quizzes, video clips, and other resources
- Try the **Quick Check** exercise at the end of the chapter to test your knowledge
- Learn the **key terms**
- Do the **Starter** exercises keyed in the margins
- Work the **mid-** and **end-of-chapter summary problems**
- Use the **Concept Links** to review material in other chapters
- Search the **CD** for review materials by chapter or by key word
- Watch the **tutorial videos** to review key concepts
- Watch the **On Location Oracle** video to review importance of receivables to a business

LEARNING OBJECTIVES

1. Design internal controls for receivables
2. Use the allowance method to account for uncollectibles by the percent-of-sales and aging-of-accounts methods
3. Use the direct write-off method to account for uncollectibles
4. Account for notes receivable
5. Report receivables on the balance sheet
6. Use the acid-test ratio and days' sales in receivables to evaluate a company

New York Jets and Oracle Corp.

What do a pro football team and a software company have in common? More than you might think. A New York Jets lineman must learn which opposing player to block, and that depends on the formation of the other team. In the information age, the Jets use software, not *X* and *O* diagrams, to map out plays. Oracle Corporation, the software company, has created an interactive multimedia show that turns football formations into live animation.

Carl Banks, director of player development for the Jets, uses the Oracle program as a teaching model. Says Banks, "By the time [players] hit the practice field, [they can't] visualize *X*'s and *O*'s as actual plays. Oracle has helped create [a] learning environment that increases [players'] retention by as much as 250%."

Oracle is one of the world's largest software companies, offering products and services to clients around the world. Accounts receivable are a significant asset for Oracle and most other businesses. Receivables present an accounting challenge: How much of a company's receivables can it collect? How much will be uncollectible? This chapter shows how to answer these and other questions about receivables. ■

Sitemap

- Receivables: An Introduction
- Uncollectibles (Bad Debts)
- Card (Credit, Bank, Debit) Sales
- Notes Receivable
- Accounting for Notes Receivable
- Decision Making Ratios
- Appendix: Discounting Notes Receivable

As Oracle grows, so do its revenues and receivables. Accounts receivable are Oracle's second-largest asset. This chapter shows how to predict how much of Oracle's receivables the company will collect in cash. The chapter also covers notes receivable, a more formal arrangement that includes a written promise and a stated interest rate.

A *receivable* arises when a company sells goods or services to another party on credit. The receivable is the seller's claim for the amount of the transaction. Each credit transaction involves two parties:

- The **creditor**, who sells something and obtains a receivable (an asset)
- The **debtor**, who makes the purchase and has a payable (a liability)

Creditor
The party to a credit transaction who sells goods or a service and obtains a receivable.

Debtor
The party to a credit transaction who makes a purchase and has a payable.

A receivable also arises when one person loans money to another. Here's an example: Suppose your best friend runs out of cash and needs $100 to make it to the end of the month. You lend $100 to your friend, and he promises to pay you back on May 31. You gave up your cash and got a $100 receivable from your friend. The receivable is an asset to you, just as the cash was. But the receivable is a slightly different asset: It's very close to cash, but it's not cash yet. In this situation, you are the creditor and your friend is the debtor.

This chapter focuses on accounting for receivables by the seller (the creditor).

- ■ Receivables: An Introduction
- □ Uncollectibles (Bad Debts)
- □ Card (Credit, Bank, Debit) Sales
- □ Notes Receivable
- □ Accounting for Notes Receivable
- □ Decision Making Ratios
- □ Appendix: Discounting Notes Receivable

Receivables: An Introduction

Types of Receivables

Receivables are monetary claims against businesses and individuals. The two major types of receivables are accounts receivable and notes receivable. A business's *accounts receivable* are the amounts to be collected from customers. Accounts receivable, which are *current assets*, are also called *trade receivables*.

Student Resource CD
accounts receivable, internal control, notes receivable, receivables

Receivables
Monetary claims against a business or an individual.

Accounts Receivable in the general ledger serves as a *control account* because it summarizes the total of the receivables from all customers. As we saw in Chapter 7, companies also keep a *subsidiary ledger* of the receivable from each customer ←. This is illustrated on the following page.

Chapter 7 introduced special journals and subsidiary ledgers, pp. 287–299. →

Notes receivable are more formal than accounts receivable. The debtor promises in writing to pay the creditor a definite sum at a future date—the *maturity* date. A written document known as a *promissory note* serves as the evidence. Notes receivable due within one year or less are *current assets*. Notes due beyond one year are *long-term*. Some notes receivable are collected in periodic installments. The portion due within one year is a current asset, and the remainder is a long-term asset. General Motors may hold a $6,000 note receivable from you, but only the $2,000 you owe this year is a current asset to GM. The remaining $4,000 is a long-term receivable.

GENERAL LEDGER			ACCOUNTS RECEIVABLE SUBSIDIARY LEDGER		
Accounts Receivable			**Acker**		
Bal.	15,000		Bal.	5,000	
			Dell		
			Bal.	4,000	
			Taft		
			Bal.	6,000	
			Total	15,000	

Other receivables is a miscellaneous category that may include loans to employees. Usually, these are long-term receivables, but they are current assets if due within one year or less. Long-term receivables are often reported as shown in Exhibit 9-1. Receivables are highlighted for emphasis.

Exhibit 9-1

Assets, with Receivables Highlighted

Example Company
Assets
Date

Assets		
Current:		
Cash		$X,XXX
Accounts receivable	$X,XXX	
Less: Allowance for uncollectible accounts	(XXX)	X,XXX
Notes receivable, short-term		X,XXX
Inventories		X,XXX
Prepaid expenses		X,XXX
Total		X,XXX
Investments and long-term receivables:		
Investments		X,XXX
Notes receivable, long-term		X,XXX
Other receivables		X,XXX
Total		X,XXX
Plant assets:		
Property, plant, and equipment		X,XXX
Total assets		$X,XXX

Establishing Internal Control over Collection of Receivables

1 Design internal controls for receivables

Businesses that sell on credit receive most cash receipts by mail. Internal control over collections is very important. → A critical element of internal control is the separation of cash-handling and cash-accounting duties. Consider the following case.

We introduced internal controls in Chapter 8.

Butler Supply Co. is family-owned and takes pride in the loyalty of its workers. Most company employees have been with the Butlers for years. The company makes 90% of its sales on account.

The office staff consists of a bookkeeper and a supervisor. The bookkeeper maintains the accounts receivable subsidiary ledger. He also makes the daily bank deposit. The supervisor prepares monthly financial statements and special reports.

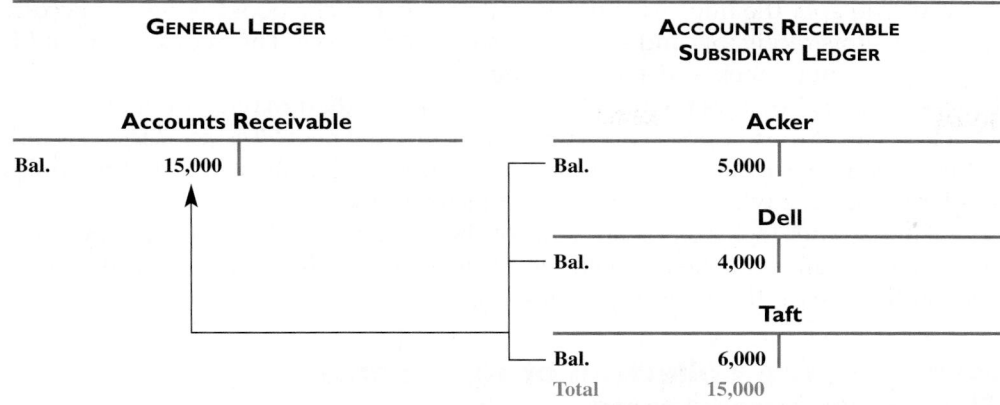

✔ Starter 9-1

Can you spot the internal control weakness here? The bookkeeper has access to the accounts receivable and also has custody of the cash. The bookkeeper could steal a customer check and write off the customer's account as uncollectible.[1] Unless someone reviews the bookkeeper's work, the theft may go undetected.

How can Butler Supply correct this control weakness? *The bookkeeper should not be allowed to handle cash.* Only the remittance advices should go to the bookkeeper to indicate which customer accounts to credit.

Using a bank lock box could achieve the same result. In a lock-box system, customers would send cash directly to Butler Supply's bank, which would then deposit the cash in the company's bank account. ←

We examined the lock-box system in detail in Chapter 8, p. 332. →

Managing the Collection of Receivables: The Credit Department

Most companies have a credit department to evaluate customers. The extension of credit requires a balancing act. The company doesn't want to lose sales to good customers, but it also wants to avoid uncollectible receivables.

✔ Starter 9-2

For good internal control over cash collections, the credit department should have no access to cash. For example, if a credit employee handles cash, he might pocket money received from a customer. He could then label the customer's account as uncollectible, and the company would write off the account receivable, as discussed in the next section. The company would stop billing that customer, and the employee would have covered his theft. For this reason, a sharp separation of duties is important.

The Decision Guidelines feature identifies the main issues in controlling and managing receivables. These guidelines serve as a framework for the remainder of the chapter.

Decision Guidelines

CONTROLLING, MANAGING, AND ACCOUNTING FOR RECEIVABLES

Butler Supply, Oracle Corporation, and all other companies that sell on credit face the same accounting challenges. The main issues in *controlling* and *managing* receivables, plus a plan of action, are as follows:

Issue	Action
Extend credit only to customers most likely to pay.	Run a credit check on prospective customers.
Separate cash-handing, credit, and accounting duties to keep employees from stealing cash collected from customers.	Design the internal control system to separate duties.
Pursue collection from customers to maximize cash flow.	Keep a close eye on collections from customers.

The main issues in *accounting* for receivables, and the related plan of action, are as follows:

Issue	Action
Report receivables at their *net realizable value*, the amount we expect to collect.	Estimate the amount of uncollectible receivables. The balance sheet reports receivables at net realizable value (accounts receivable minus the allowance for uncollectibles).
Report the expense associated with failure to collect receivables. This expense is called uncollectible-account expense.	The income statement reports the expense of failing to collect from customers.

[1]The bookkeeper would need to forge the endorsement on the check and deposit it in a bank account he controls.

Accounting for Uncollectibles (Bad Debts)

☐ Receivables: An Introduction
■ Uncollectibles (Bad Debts)
☐ Card (Credit, Bank, Debit) Sales
☐ Notes Receivable
☐ Accounting for Notes Receivable
☐ Decision Making Ratios
☐ Appendix: Discounting Notes Receivable

Selling on credit creates both a benefit and a cost.

- ***The benefit:*** The business increases revenues and profits by making sales to a wide range of customers.
- ***The cost:*** The company will be unable to collect from some customers, and that creates an expense. The expense is called **uncollectible-account expense**, **doubtful-account expense**, or **bad-debt expense**.

Uncollectible-account expense varies from company to company. The older the receivable, the less valuable it is because of the decreasing likelihood of collection. For Oracle Corporation, each $1 of accounts receivable is worth 86 cents. Uncollectible-account expense is an operating expense in the same way as salary expense and utilities expense. To account for uncollectible receivables, accountants use the allowance method or, in certain limited cases, the direct write-off method.

Student Resource CD
direct write-off, uncollectibles

Uncollectible-Account Expense
Cost to the seller of extending credit. Arises from the failure to collect from credit customers. Also called **doubtful-account expense**, or **bad-debt expense**.

The Allowance Method

Most companies use the **allowance method** to measure bad debts. They record uncollectible-account expense in the same period in which sales are made on account. The business doesn't wait to see which customers will not pay. Instead, it records an expense on the basis of estimates developed from past experience.

Allowance Method
A method of recording collection losses on the basis of estimates, instead of waiting to see which customers the company will not collect from.

The business records Uncollectible-Account Expense for the estimated amount and sets up **Allowance for Uncollectible Accounts** (or **Allowance for Doubtful Accounts**), a contra account to Accounts Receivable. This allowance account shows the amount of receivables the business expects *not* to collect.

Allowance for Uncollectible Accounts
A contra account, related to accounts receivable, that holds the estimated amount of collection losses. Also called **Allowance for Doubtful Accounts**.

Subtracting the allowance from Accounts Receivable yields the net amount that the company does expect to collect. Here are Oracle Corporation's figures, adapted and in millions:

Balance sheet (partial):	
Accounts receivable	$2,800
Less: Allowance for uncollectible accounts	(400)
Accounts receivable, net	$2,400

Customers owe Oracle $2,800 million, of which Oracle expects to collect $2,400 million. Oracle estimates it will not collect $400 million of these accounts receivable.

Another way to report receivables follows (in millions):

Accounts receivable, net of allowance for uncollectible accounts of $400	$2,400

The income statement can report Uncollectible-Account Expense (Doubtful-Account Expense) among the operating expenses, as follows (assumed figures in millions):

Income statement (partial):	
Expenses:	
Uncollectible-account expense	$5,000

Estimating Uncollectibles

2 *Use the allowance method to account for uncollectibles by the percent-of-sales and aging-of-accounts methods*

How are bad debts estimated? Companies use their past experience. There are two basic methods to estimate uncollectibles:

- Percent-of-sales
- Aging-of-accounts

Both approaches work with the allowance method.

Percent-of-Sales Method
A method of estimating uncollectible receivables that calculates uncollectible-account expense. Also called the **income-statement approach**.

PERCENT-OF-SALES METHOD The **percent-of-sales method** computes uncollectible-account expense as a percentage of net credit sales. This method is also called the **income-statement approach** because it focuses on the amount of expense. Uncollectible-account expense is recorded as an adjusting entry at the end of the period. Assume it is December 31, 20X6, and the accounts have these balances *before the year-end adjustments*:

Accounts Receivable		Allowance for Uncollectible Accounts	
120,000			500

Prior to any adjustments, net receivables total $119,500 ($120,000 – $500). This is more than the business expects to collect from customers. Based on prior experience, the credit department estimates that uncollectible-account expense is 2% of net credit sales, which were $500,000 for 20X6. The adjusting entry to record uncollectible-account expense for 20X6 and to update the allowance is

20X6			
Dec. 31	Uncollectible-Account Expense ($500,000 × 0.02)	10,000	
	Allowance for Uncollectible Accounts.		10,000
	Recorded expense for the year.		

The accounting equation shows that the transaction to record the expense decreases the business's assets by the amount of the expense:

ASSETS	=	LIABILITIES	+	OWNER'S EQUITY	–	EXPENSES
–10,000	=	0			–	10,000

Now the accounts are ready for reporting in the 20X6 financial statements.

✔ Starter 9-3

Accounts Receivable		Allowance for Uncollectible Accounts		
120,000				500
			Adj.	10,000
			End. Bal.	10,500

Customers owe the business $120,000, and now the allowance for uncollectible accounts is realistic. The balance sheet will report accounts receivable at the net amount of $109,500 ($120,000 – $10,500). The income statement will report 20X6's uncollectible-account expense of $10,000, along with the other operating expenses for the period.

Aging-of-Accounts Method
A way to estimate bad debts by analyzing individual accounts receivable according to the length of time they have been receivable from the customer. Also called the **balance-sheet approach**.

AGING-OF-ACCOUNTS The second popular approach for estimating uncollectibles is the **aging-of-accounts method**. This method is also called the **balance-sheet approach** because it focuses on accounts receivable. In the aging approach, individual accounts receivable are grouped according to how long they have been receivable from the customer. The computer sorts customer accounts by their age. For example, Schmidt Builders Supply groups its accounts receivable into 30-day periods, as Exhibit 9-2 shows.

Schmidt's accounts receivable total of $143,000 is shown at the far right of the exhibit. Of this amount, the aging schedule estimates that Schmidt will *not* collect $3,800. The following allowance for uncollectible accounts is not up-to-date *before the year-end adjustment*:

Accounts Receivable		Allowance for Uncollectible Accounts	
143,000			1,100

Exhibit 9-2 **Aging the Accounts Receivable of Schmidt Builders Supply**

	Age of Account				
Customer Name	**1–30 Days**	**31–60 Days**	**61–90 Days**	**Over 90 Days**	**Total Balance**
T-Bar-M Co.	$ 20,000				$ 20,000
Chicago Pneumatic Parts	10,000				10,000
Sarasota Pipe Corp.		$13,000	$10,000		23,000
Oneida, Inc.			3,000	$1,000	4,000
Other accounts	70,000	12,000	2,000	2,000	86,000
Totals	$100,000	$25,000	$15,000	$3,000	143,000
Estimated percentage uncollectible	× 0.1%	× 1%	× 5%	× 90%	
Allowance for Uncollectible Accounts balance	$ 100 +	$ 250 +	$ 750 +	$2,700 =	$ 3,800

The aging method brings the balance of the allowance account to the needed amount as determined by the aging schedule. In Exhibit 9-2, see the lower-right corner for the final result—a needed credit balance of $3,800.

To update the allowance, Schmidt makes this adjusting entry:

20X6			
Dec. 31	Uncollectible-Account Expense	2,700	
	Allowance for Uncollectible Accounts ($3,800 – $1,100)		2,700
	Recorded expense for the year.		

The expense decreases total assets and owner's equity. The accounting equation for the expense is

Assets	=	Liabilities	+	Owner's Equity	–	Expenses
–2,700	=	0			–	2,700

Now the balance sheet can report receivables at the amount that Schmidt expects to collect from customers, $139,200 ($143,000 – $3,800), as follows:

Accounts Receivable

143,000	

Allowance for Uncollectible Accounts

		1,100
	Adj.	2,700
	End. bal.	3,800

Net accounts receivable, 139,200

The *net* amount of accounts receivable—$139,200—is called *net realizable value* because it is the amount Schmidt expects to realize (collect in cash).

Using Percent-of-Sales and Aging Together In practice, companies use the percent-of-sales and the aging-of-accounts methods together.

- For *interim statements* (monthly or quarterly), companies use the percent-of-sales method because it is easier. This method focuses on the amount of uncollectible-account *expense*.
- At the end of the year, companies use the aging method to ensure that Accounts Receivable is reported at *net realizable value*. The aging method focuses on the amount of the receivables—the *asset*—that is uncollectible.
- Using the two methods together provides good measures of both the expense and the asset. Exhibit 9-3 summarizes and compares the two methods.

Exhibit 9-3

Comparing the Percent-of-Sales and Aging Methods

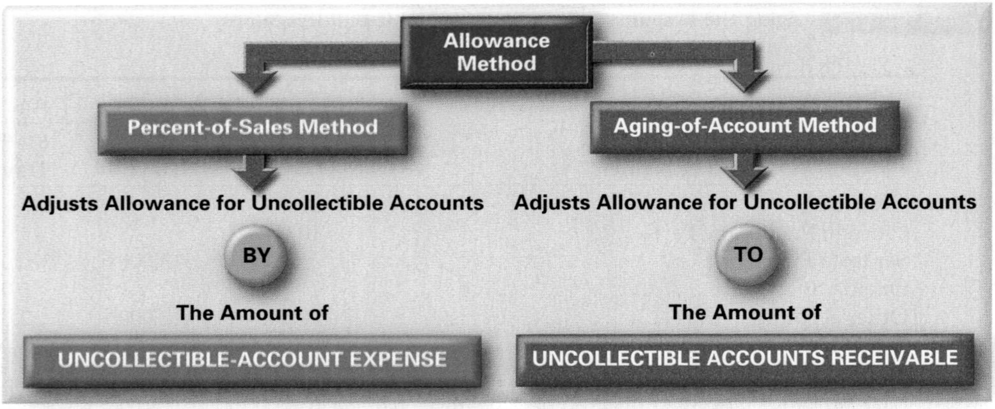

✔ Starter 9-4

Writing Off Uncollectible Accounts

Early in 20X7, Schmidt Builders Supply collects on most of its $143,000 accounts receivable and records the cash receipts as follows (amount assumed):

20X7			
Jan.–Mar.	Cash	123,000	
	Accounts Receivable		123,000
	Collected on account.		

Suppose that, after repeated attempts to collect, Schmidt's credit department determines that Schmidt cannot collect a total of $1,200 from customers Andrews ($900) and Jones ($300). Schmidt then writes off the receivables from these delinquent customers:

20X7			
Mar. 31	Allowance for Uncollectible Accounts	1,200	
	Accounts Receivable—Andrews		900
	Accounts Receivable—Jones........		300
	Wrote off uncollectible accounts.		

The write-off of uncollectible receivables has no impact on total assets, liabilities, or equity.

✔ Starter 9-5

✔ Starter 9-6

Assets	=	Liabilities	+	Owner's Equity
+1,200				
−1,200	=	0	+	0

Stop & Think

If the write-off of uncollectible accounts affects no expense or *net* receivables, then why write off the uncollectible account of customer Jones?

Answer: The business has decided that it will never collect from Jones. Therefore, eliminate Jones's account from the receivable records. That alerts the credit department not to waste time pursuing collection from Jones.

3 *Use the direct write-off method to account for uncollectibles*

Direct Write-Off Method
A method of accounting for uncollectible receivables, in which the company waits until the credit department decides that a customer's account receivable is uncollectible, and then debits Uncollectible-Account Expense and credits the customer's Account Receivable.

The Direct Write-Off Method

There is another way to account for uncollectible receivables that is not acceptable for most companies. Under the **direct write-off method**, Schmidt Builders would wait until it decides that it will never collect from the customer. Then Schmidt would write off the customer's account receivable by debiting

Uncollectible-Account Expense and crediting the customer's Account Receivable, as follows (using assumed data):

20X7			
Jan. 2	Uncollectible-Account Expense........	2,000	
	Accounts Receivable—Smith....		2,000
	Wrote off a bad account.		

The direct write-off method is defective for two reasons:

1. It does not set up an allowance for uncollectibles. As a result, the direct write-off method always reports the receivables at their full amount. Assets are overstated on the balance sheet because the business does not expect to collect the full amount.
2. It does not match uncollectible-account expense against revenue very well. In this example, Schmidt made the sale to Smith in 20X6 and should have recorded the uncollectible-account expense during 20X6. That's the only way to measure net income properly. By recording the uncollectible-account expense in 20X7, Schmidt overstates net income in 20X6 and understates net income in 20X7.

✔ Starter 9-7

Don't confuse the direct write-off method with the allowance method. The two methods of accounting for uncollectible receivables are opposites. A company uses one method or the other. The direct write-off method is acceptable only when the amount of uncollectible receivables is very low. It works well for retailers such as Wal-Mart, Lands' End, and Gap, because those companies carry almost no receivables.

Recovery of Accounts Previously Written Off

When an account receivable is written off as uncollectible, the receivable does not die: The customer still owes the money. However, the company stops pursuing collection and writes off the account as uncollectible.

Some companies turn delinquent receivables over to an attorney and recover some of the cash. This is called *recovery of a bad account*. Let's see how to record the recovery of an account that we wrote off earlier. Recall that on March 31, 20X7, Schmidt Builders Supply wrote off the $900 receivable from customer Andrews (see page 368). It is now January 4, 20X8, and Schmidt unexpectedly receives $900 from Andrews. To account for this recovery, Schmidt makes two journal entries to (1) reverse the earlier write-off and (2) record the cash collection, as follows:

(1) Accounts Receivable—Andrews	900	
Allowance for Uncollectible Accounts......		900
Reinstated Andrews' account receivable.		
(2) Cash	900	
Accounts Receivable—Andrews		900
Collected on account.		

☐ Receivables: An Introduction
☐ Uncollectibles (Bad Debts)
■ Card (Credit, Bank, Debit) Sales
☐ Notes Receivable
☐ Accounting for Notes Receivable
☐ Decision Making Ratios
☐ Appendix: Discounting Notes Receivable

Credit-Card, Bankcard, and Debit-Card Sales

Credit-Card Sales

Credit-card sales are common in both traditional and online retailing. Customers present credit cards like American Express and Discover to pay for purchases. The credit-card company then pays the seller and bills the customer, who pays the credit-card company.

Credit cards offer customers the convenience of buying without having to pay cash immediately. An American Express customer receives a monthly statement from American Express, detailing each transaction. The customer can write one check to cover the entire month's purchases.

Retailers also benefit from credit-card sales. They do not have to check a customer's credit rating. The credit-card company has already done so. Retailers do not have to keep accounts receivable records, and they do not have to collect cash from customers. These benefits do not come free. The seller receives less than 100% of the face value of the sale. The credit-card company takes a fee of 1 to 5% on the sale. Suppose you and your family have lunch at a **Red Lobster** restaurant. You pay the bill—$100—with a Discover card. Red Lobster's entry to record the $100 sale, subject to the credit-card company's 3% discount, is

Accounts Receivable—Discover	97	
Credit-Card Discount Expense	3	
Sales Revenue		100
Recorded credit-card sales.		

On collection of the cash, Red Lobster records the following:

Cash	97	
Accounts Receivable—Discover		97
Collected from Discover.		

Bankcard Sales

Most banks issue their own cards, known as *bankcards*, which operate much like credit cards. **VISA** and **MasterCard** are the two main bankcards. When an **Exxon** station makes a sale and takes a VISA card, the station receives cash at the point of sale. The cash received is less than the full amount of the sale because the bank deducts its fee. Suppose the Exxon station sells $150 of fuel to a family vacationing in its motor home. The station takes a VISA card, and the bank that issued the card charges a 2% fee. The Exxon station records the bankcard sale as follows:

Cash	147	
Bankcard Discount Expense ($150 × 0.02)	3	
Sales Revenue		150
Recorded a bankcard sale.		

✔ Starter 9-8

Debit-Card Sales

Debit cards are fundamentally different from credit cards and bankcards. Using a debit card to buy groceries is like paying with cash, except that you don't have to carry cash or write a check.

At **Target** (or **Kroger** or **Wal-Mart**), the buyer "swipes" the card through a special terminal, and the buyer's bank balance is automatically decreased. **Target's** Cash account is increased immediately—without having to deposit a check and wonder if it will clear the bank. With a debit card there is no third party, such as VISA or MasterCard, so there is no Credit-Card Discount Expense.

Merchant Beware: Credit Cards Boom with Online Sales . . . But So Does Fraud

Accounting.com

About 97% of all Web payments are made with credit cards. At the end of every month, e-tailers send up to 2.5% of their revenues to credit-card companies. **VISA**, **MasterCard**, **American Express**, and their cousins earn millions in transaction fees.

Who takes the hit when customers deny credit-card charges they actually made (*chargebacks*) or when criminals make purchases with stolen card numbers (*identity theft*)? The online merchants.

The anonymity of online transactions paves the way for both chargebacks and identity theft. It's harder to cheat in a face-to-face transaction. Industry analyst Gartner, Inc., reports that fraud costs online retailers more than $700 million in one year. Gartner's report also notes that credit-card fraud causes e-tailers to lose about 1% of their sales revenue. This is 19 times higher than the losses at traditional stores. Online theft puts a big dent in the bottom line and can even cause companies to go bankrupt. Case in point: **Flooz.com** sold online currency for electronic gift certificates. The company filed for bankruptcy after it was hit by $300,000 in credit-card fraud.

Source: Marcia Savage, "Online Fraud: New Twist on Old Issue," *Computer Reseller News*, March 27, 2000, p. 28. Leslie Beyer, "The Internet Revolution," *Credit Card Management*, November 1999, Mercedes M. Caroona, "VISA Teams Up with E-Tailers to Acquire Online Dominance," *Advertising Age*, December 6, 1999, p. 4. Patricia A. Murphy, "The Murky World of 'Net Chargebacks,'" *Credit Card Management*, February 2000, pp. 54–60. Amy Winn, "Business Online," *Atlanta Journal-Constitution*, March 5, 2002, p. D2. Sharon Gaudin, "Online Fraud Growing in Scale, Sophistication," *internetnews.com*, December 5, 2002.

MID-CHAPTER *Summary Problem*

A+ TIPS
CHECK YOUR RESOURCES

CPC International, Inc., produces Skippy peanut butter, Hellmann's mayonnaise, and Mazola corn oil. Suppose CPC's balance sheet at December 31, 20X5, reported the following:

	Millions
Notes and accounts receivable [total]	$549.9
Allowance for uncollectible accounts	(12.5)

Required

1. How much of the December 31, 20X5, balance of the receivable did CPC expect to collect? Stated differently, what was the net realizable value of these receivables?
2. Journalize, without explanations, 20X6 entries for CPC International, assuming:
   a. Total estimated Uncollectible-Account Expense was $19.2 million for the first three quarters of the year, based on the percent-of-sales method.
   b. Write-offs of accounts receivable totaled $23.6 million.
   c. December 31, 20X6, aging of receivables, which indicates that $15.3 million of the total receivables of $582.7 million is uncollectible. Post all three entries to Allowance for Uncollectible Accounts.
3. Show how CPC International's receivables and related allowance will appear on the December 31, 20X6, balance sheet.

   What is the net realizable value of receivables at December 31, 20X6? How much is uncollectible-account expense for 20X6?

Solution

Requirement 1

	(In millions)
Net realizable value of receivables ($549.9 – $12.5)	$537.4

Requirement 2

	(In millions)	
(a) Uncollectible-Account Expense........................	19.2	
Allowance for Uncollectible Accounts.............		19.2
(b) Allowance for Uncollectible Accounts	23.6	
Accounts Receivable............................		23.6
(c) Uncollectible-Account Expense ($15.3 – $8.1)............	7.2	
Allowance for Uncollectible Accounts.............		7.2

Allowance for Uncollectible Accounts

20X6 Write-offs	23.6	Dec. 31, 20X5 Bal.	12.5
		20X6 Expense	19.2
		Bal. before adj.	8.1
		Dec. 31, 20X6 Adj.	7.2
		Dec. 31, 20X6 Bal.	15.3

Requirement 3

	(In millions)
Notes and accounts receivable	$582.7
Less: Allowance for uncollectible accounts.................	(15.3)
Notes and accounts receivable, net........................	$567.4
Uncollectible-account expense for 20X6 ($19.2 + $7.2)	$26.4

Student Resource CD
notes receivable

Notes Receivable: An Overview

Notes receivable are more formal than accounts receivable. The debtor signs a promissory note as evidence of the debt. Before launching into the accounting, let's define the special terms used for notes receivable.

- **Promissory note:** A written promise to pay a specified amount of money at a particular future date.
- **Maker of the note (debtor):** The entity that signs the note and promises to pay the required amount; the maker of the note is the *debtor*.
- **Payee of the note (creditor):** The entity to whom the maker promises future payment; the payee of the note is the *creditor*.
- **Principal amount, or principal:** The amount loaned out by the payee and borrowed by the maker of the note.
- **Interest:** The revenue to the payee for loaning money; the expense to the debtor.
- **Interest period:** The period of time during which interest is computed. It extends from the original date of the note to the maturity date. Also called **note term**, or simply **time**.

- **Interest rate:** The percentage rate of interest specified by the note. Interest rates are almost always stated for a period of one year. A 9% note means that the amount of interest for *one year* is 9% of the note's principal amount.
- **Maturity date:** The date when final payment of the note is due. Also called the **due date**.
- **Maturity value:** The sum of the principal plus interest due at maturity.

Exhibit 9-4 illustrates a promissory note. Study it carefully.

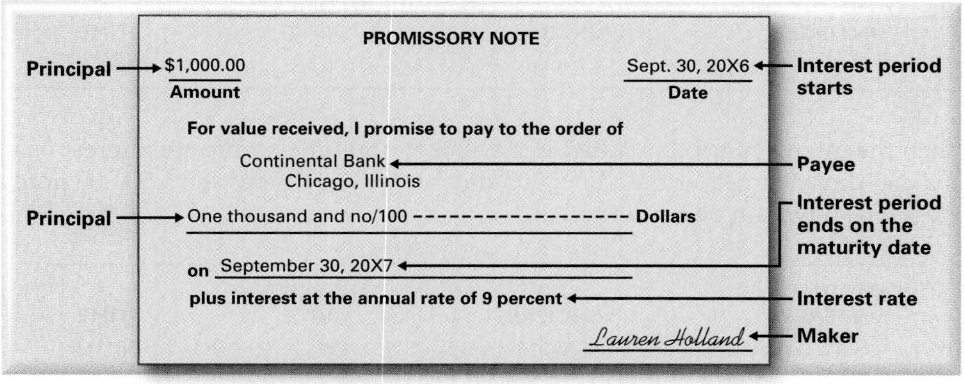

Exhibit 9-4
A Promissory Note

Identifying Maturity Date

Some notes specify the maturity date, as shown in Exhibit 9-4. Other notes state the period of the note in days or months. When the period is given in months, the note's maturity date falls on the same day of the month as the date the note was issued. A six-month note dated February 16 matures on August 16.

When the period is given in days, the maturity date is determined by counting the days from the date of issue. A 120-day note dated September 14, 20X6, matures on January 12, 20X7, as shown here:

Month	Number of Days	Cumulative Total
Sep. 20X6	30 – 14 = 16	16
Oct. 20X6	31	47
Nov. 20X6	30	77
Dec. 20X6	31	108
Jan. 20X7	12	120

In counting the days remaining for a note, remember to count the maturity date and to omit the date the note was issued.

Computing Interest on a Note

The formula for computing the interest on a note is

AMOUNT OF INTEREST	=	PRINCIPAL	×	INTEREST RATE	×	TIME

Using the data in Exhibit 9-4, Continental Bank computes interest revenue for one year as

AMOUNT OF INTEREST	=	PRINCIPAL	×	INTEREST RATE	×	TIME
$90		$1,000		0.09		1 yr

The maturity value of the note is $1,090 ($1,000 principal + $90 interest). The time element is 1 because the note's term is 1 year.

When the term of a note is stated in months, we compute the interest based on the 12-month year. Interest on a $2,000 note at 15% for three months is computed as

AMOUNT OF INTEREST	=	PRINCIPAL	×	INTEREST RATE	×	TIME
$75		$2,000		0.15		3/12

When the interest period is stated in days, we sometimes compute interest based on a 360-day year rather than on a 365-day year.[2] The interest on a $5,000 note at 12% for 60 days can be computed as

✔ Starter 9-9

AMOUNT OF INTEREST	=	PRINCIPAL	×	INTEREST RATE	×	TIME
$100		$5,000		0.12		60/360

Keep in mind that interest rates are stated as an annual rate. Therefore, the time in the interest formula should also be expressed in terms of a year.

Stop & Think

Practice calculating interest on
1. A $30,000, 12 1/2%, 180-day note
2. An $8,000, 9%, 6-month note

Answers:
1. ($30,000 × 0.125 × 180/360) = $1,875 2. ($8,000 × 0.09 × 6/12) = $360

- ☐ Receivables: An Introduction
- ☐ Uncollectibles (Bad Debts)
- ☐ Card (Credit, Bank, Debit) Sales
- ☐ Notes Receivable
- ■ Accounting for Notes Receivable
- ☐ Decision Making Ratios
- ☐ Appendix: Discounting Notes Receivable

Student Resource CD
accounts receivable, balance sheet, notes receivable

4 *Account for notes receivable*

Accounting for Notes Receivable

Recording Notes Receivable

Consider the loan agreement shown in Exhibit 9-4. After Lauren Holland signs the note, Continental Bank gives her $1,000 cash. At maturity, Holland pays the bank $1,090 ($1,000 principal plus $90 interest). The bank's entries are

Sep. 30, 20X6	Note Receivable—L. Holland	1,000	
	Cash		1,000
	Loaned out money.		
Sep. 30, 20X7	Cash..........................	1,090	
	Note Receivable—L. Holland ...		1,000
	Interest Revenue ($1,000 × 0.09 × 1)		90
	Collected note receivable.		

✔ Starter 9-10

Some companies sell merchandise in exchange for notes receivable. Suppose that on October 20, 20X8, General Electric sells household appliances for $15,000

[2] A 360-day year eliminates some rounding, which is consistent with our use of whole-dollar amounts throughout this book.

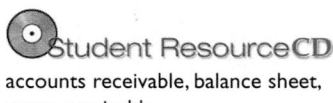

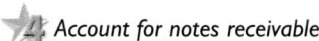

to Dorman Builders. Dorman signs a 90-day promissory note at 10% annual interest. General Electric's entries to record the sale and collection from Dorman are

Oct. 20, 20X8	Note Receivable— Dorman Builders	15,000	
	Sales Revenue		15,000
	Made a sale.		
Jan. 18, 20X9	Cash	15,375	
	Note Receivable— Dorman Builders		15,000
	Interest Revenue ($15,000 × 0.10 × 90/360)		375
	Collected note receivable.		

A company may accept a note receivable from a trade customer who fails to pay an account receivable. The customer signs a promissory note—that is, becomes the **maker of the note**—and gives it to the creditor, who becomes the **payee**. Suppose Sports Club cannot pay Hoffman Supply. Hoffman may accept a one-year, $2,400 note receivable, with 9% interest, from Sports Club on October 1, 20X8. Hoffman's entry is

Maker of a Note
The person or business that signs the note and promises to pay the amount required by the note agreement; the debtor.

Payee of a Note
The person or business to whom the maker of a note promises future payment; the creditor.

Oct. 1, 20X8	Note Receivable—Sports Club . . .	2,400	
	Accounts Receivable— Sports Club.		2,400
	Received a note on account.		

Accruing Interest Revenue

A note receivable may be outstanding at the end of an accounting period. The interest revenue earned on the note up to year-end is part of that year's earnings. Recall that interest revenue is earned over time, not just when cash is received. →

← *We saw in Chapter 3 on p. 104 that accrued revenue creates an asset because the revenue has been earned but not received.*

Let's continue with the Hoffman Supply note receivable from Sports Club. Hoffman Supply's accounting period ends December 31. How much of the total interest revenue does Hoffman earn in 20X8? How much does it earn in 20X9?

Hoffman will earn three months' interest in 20X8—for October, November, and December. In 20X9, Hoffman will earn nine months' interest—for January through September. At December 31, 20X8, Hoffman will make the following adjusting entry to accrue interest revenue:

Dec. 31, 20X8	Interest Receivable ($2,400 × 0.09 × 3/12)	54	
	Interest Revenue.		54
	Accrued interest revenue.		

Then, on the maturity date, Hoffman collects the principal and interest as follows:

Sep. 30, 20X9	Cash [$2,400 + ($2,400 × 0.09)] . . .	2,616	
	Note Receivable—Sports Club . .		2,400
	Interest Receivable ($2,400 × 0.09 × 3/12)		54
	Interest Revenue ($2,400 × 0.09 × 9/12)		162
	Collected note receivable plus interest.		

The entries for accrued interest at December 31, 20X8, and for collection in 20X9 assign the correct amount of interest to each year.

✔ **Starter 9-11**

A company holding a note may need cash before the note matures. A procedure for selling the note, called discounting a note receivable, appears in the chapter appendix.

Dishonored Notes Receivable

Dishonor of a Note
Failure of a note's maker to pay a note receivable at maturity. Also called **default on a note**.

If the maker of a note does not pay at maturity, the maker **dishonors**, or **defaults on**, the note. Because the term of the note has expired, the note agreement is no longer in force. But the payee still has a claim against the debtor. In this case, the payee will transfer the note receivable amount to Accounts Receivable. Suppose Rubinstein Jewelers has a 6-month, 10% note receivable for $1,200 from Mark Adair, and on the February 3 maturity date, Adair defaulted. Rubinstein Jewelers will record the default as follows:

Feb. 3	Accounts Receivable—M. Adair	1,260	
	Note Receivable—M. Adair............		1,200
	Interest Revenue ($1,200 × 0.10 × 6/12) ...		60
	Recorded a dishonored note receivable.		

Rubinstein will then pursue collection from Adair as an account receivable.

5 *Report receivables on the balance sheet*

Reporting Receivables on the Balance Sheet

Let's look at how some well-known companies report their receivables on the balance sheet. Terminology may vary. Intel Corporation, maker of the Pentium® processor, reports accounts receivable under Current Assets (in millions):

Accounts receivable, net of allowance for doubtful accounts of $67 ...	$3,700

The net realizable value of Intel's accounts receivable is $3,700 million. To compute Intel's total amount receivable, add the allowance to the net receivable: $67 + $3,700 = $3,767. Customers actually owe Intel $3,767 million, but Intel expects to collect only $3,700 million.

General Electric Company reports a single amount—net realizable value—for receivables in the balance sheet and uses an explanatory note to give the details (adapted, with amounts in millions):

✔ Starter 9-12

Current receivables (note 10)	$8,740
Note 10: Current Receivables......................	$9,060
Less: Allowance for losses.................	(320)
	$8,740

Stop & Think

1. How much did customers owe **General Electric (GE)**, as adapted?
2. How much did GE expect to collect?
3. How much did GE expect *not* to collect?

Answers:

1. $9,060 million
2. $8,740 million
3. $320 million

Computers and Accounts Receivable

Accounting for receivables by a large company like Oracle Corporation or M&M Mars requires thousands of postings for credit sales and cash collections. Manual accounting methods cannot keep up.

As we saw in Chapter 7, Accounts Receivable can be computerized. The order entry, shipping, and billing departments at M&M Mars work together to meet customer demand and ensure that Mars collects on its receivables, as shown in Exhibit 9-5.

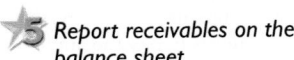

Exhibit 9-5

The Integration of Order Entry, Shipping, and Billing

Using Accounting Information for Decision Making

Student Resource CD
acid-test ratio, balance sheet, days' sales, quick ratio

6 *Use the acid-test ratio and days' sales in receivables to evaluate a company*

The balance sheet lists assets in order of liquidity (closeness to cash):

- Cash comes first because it is the liquid asset.
- Short-term investments come next because they are almost as liquid as cash.
- Current receivables are less liquid than short-term investments because the company must collect the receivables.
- Merchandise inventory is less liquid than receivables because the goods must first be sold.

The balance sheet of Oracle Corporation, as adapted, provides an example in Exhibit 9-6. Focus on the current assets at May 31, 2001. Oracle reports no inventory because the company earns revenue by providing services, not by selling products.

Exhibit 9-6

Oracle Corporation Balance Sheet

Oracle Corporation Balance Sheet (Partial, adapted) May 31, 2001 and May 31, 2000	(In millions) May 31, 2001	2000
Assets		
Current assets:		
Cash and cash equivalents	$4,400	$ 7,400
Short-term investments	1,400	300
Trade receivables net of allowance for doubtful accounts of $400 in 2001 and $300 in 2000	2,400	2,500
Prepaid expenses and other current assets	800	700
Total current assets	$9,000	$10,900
Liabilities		
Current liabilities:		
Total current liabilities	$3,900	$5,900

Oracle's balance-sheet data become more useful by showing the relationships among assets, liabilities, and revenues. Let's examine two important ratios.

Acid-Test (or Quick) Ratio

In Chapter 4, we discussed the current ratio, which measures ability to pay current liabilities with current assets. A more stringent measure of ability to pay current liabilities is the **acid-test** (or **quick) ratio**. The acid-test ratio reveals whether the entity can pay all its current liabilities if they come due immediately:

Acid-Test Ratio
Ratio of the sum of cash plus short-term investments plus net current receivables, to total current liabilities. Tells whether the entity could pay all its current liabilities if they came due immediately. Also called the **quick ratio**.

FOR ORACLE CORPORATION (EXHIBIT 9-6) (DOLLAR AMOUNTS IN MILLIONS)

$$\text{Acid-test ratio} = \frac{\text{Cash} + \text{Short-term investments} + \text{Net current receivables}}{\text{Total current liabilities}} \qquad \frac{\$4{,}400 + \$1{,}400 + \$2{,}400}{\$3{,}900} = 2.10$$

The higher the acid-test ratio, the more able the business is to pay its current liabilities. Oracle's acid-test ratio of 2.10 means that Oracle has $2.10 of quick assets to pay each $1 of current liabilities. This is an extremely strong position.

What is an acceptable acid-test ratio? That depends on the industry. Wal-Mart operates smoothly with an acid-test ratio of less than 0.20. Several things make this possible: Wal-Mart collects cash rapidly and has almost no receivables. The acid-test ratios for most department stores cluster about 0.80, while travel agencies average 1.10. In general, an acid-test ratio of 1.00 is considered safe.

Stop & Think

Use the data in Exhibit 9-6 to compute **Oracle Corporation's** current ratio at May 31, 2001. Then compare Oracle's current ratio and acid-test ratio. Why is the current ratio higher?

Answer:

$$\text{Current ratio} = \frac{\text{Total current assets}}{\text{Total current liabilities}} = \frac{\$9{,}000}{\$3{,}900} = 2.31$$

$$\text{Acid-test ratio} = 2.10$$

The current ratio is higher because it includes all current assets and not just cash, short-term investments, and receivables.

Days' Sales in Receivables

Days' Sales in Receivables Ratio of average net accounts receivable to one day's sales. Tells how many days' sales it takes to collect the average level of receivables. Also called the **collection period**.

After making a credit sale, the next step is to collect the receivable. **Days' sales in receivables**, also called the **collection period**, indicates how many days it takes to collect the average level of receivables. The shorter the collection period, the more quickly the organization can use its cash. The longer the collection period, the less cash is available for operations. Days' sales in receivables can be computed in two steps, as follows:[3]

FOR ORACLE CORPORATION (EXHIBIT 9-6) (DOLLAR AMOUNTS IN MILLIONS)

1. $$\text{One day's sales} = \frac{\text{Net sales (or Total revenues)}}{365 \text{ days}} = \frac{\$10{,}800^*}{365} = \$29.6 \text{ per day}$$

2. $$\text{Days' sales in average accounts receivable} = \frac{\text{Average net accounts receivable}}{\text{One day's sales}} = \frac{\left(\text{Beginning net receivables} + \text{Ending net receivables}\right) \div 2}{\text{One day's sales}}$$

$$= \frac{(\$2{,}500 + \$2{,}400)/2}{\$29.6} = 83 \text{ days}$$

* Adapted from Oracle Corporation's 2001 income statement, which is not reproduced here.

The length of the collection period depends on the credit terms of the sale. For example, sales on net 30 terms should be collected within approximately 30 days. When there is a discount, such as 2/10 net 30, the collection period may be shorter. Credit terms of net 45 result in a longer collection period.

We discussed sales discounts in Chapter 5, p. 187.

Investors and creditors do not evaluate a company on the basis of one or two ratios. Instead, they analyze all the information available. Then they stand back and ask, "What is our overall impression of this company?"

[3]Days' sales in average receivables can also be computed in this one step:

$$\text{Days' sales in average receivables} = \frac{\text{Average net receivables}}{\text{Net sales}} \times 365$$

Wal-Mart has a collection period of only 3 days. Why is it so short?

Answer: Wal-Mart sells for cash or credit cards and therefore has very low receivables. This makes the collection period very short.

Stop & Think

✔ Starter 9-13

✔ Starter 9-14

The Decision Guidelines feature summarizes some key decisions for receivables.

Decision Guidelines

ACCOUNTING FOR RECEIVABLES

Accounting for receivables is the same for your own start-up business as it is for a large company like **Oracle Coporation**. Suppose you open a business to maintain Web sites for local companies and you bill them monthly for your services. How should you account for your receivables? These guidelines show the way.

Decision	Guidelines
Accounts Receivable	
How much of our receivables will we collect?	Less than the full amount of the receivables because we cannot collect from some customers.
How to report receivables at their net realizable value?	**1.** Use the *allowance method* to account for uncollectible receivables. Set up the allowance for Uncollectible Accounts. **2.** Estimate uncollectibles by the **a.** *Percent-of-sales method* (income-statement approach) **b.** *Aging-of-accounts method* (balance-sheet approach) **3.** Write off uncollectible receivables as they prove uncollectible. **4.** $\text{Net accounts receivable} = \text{Accounts Receivable} - \text{Allowance for Uncollectible Accounts}$
Is there another way to account for uncollectible receivables?	The *direct write-off method* uses no Allowance for Uncollectibles. It simply debits Uncollectible-Account Expense and credits a customer's Account Receivable to write it off when it has proved uncollectible. This method is acceptable only when uncollectibles are insignficant.
Notes Receivable	
What two other accounts are related to notes receivable?	Notes receivable are related to: • *Interest Revenue.* • *Interest Receivable* (Interest revenue earned but not yet collected).
How to compute the interest on a note receivable?	$\text{Amount of interest} = \text{Principal} \times \text{Interest rate} \times \text{Time}$
Receivables in General	
What two decision aids use receivables to evaluate a company's financial position?	• $\text{Acid-test ratio} = \dfrac{\text{Cash} + \text{Short-term investments} + \text{Net current receivables}}{\text{Total current liabilities}}$ • $\text{Day's sales in average receivables} = \dfrac{\text{Average net accounts receivable}}{\text{One day's sales}}$
How to report receivables on the balance sheet?	Accounts (or Notes) Receivable . . . . $XXX Less: Allowance for uncollectible accounts . . . . (X) Accounts (or notes) receivable, net . . . . $ XX

Excel Application Exercise

Goal: Create a worksheet that shows accounts receivable activity for a company.

Scenario: You are the summer intern at **Amazon.com** headquarters in Seattle, Washington. Assume that shortly into your employment, your supervisor asks you to prepare an Excel spreadsheet that breaks down the month's accounts receivable by customer. She gives you the following partial data (all dollars are in thousands):

Customer ID	***Customer Name***	***May 31 Balance***	***Sales***	***Collections***
F01-235-00	Bookfair	$20,469	$22,500	$24,500
F07-988-45	Author Source	$18,752	$11,592	$12,980
W40-860-91	Instore Service Co.	$12,287	$14,765	$14,000

Assume Amazon's credit terms are net 30.

When you have completed your worksheet, answer the following questions:

1. How much cash did Amazon collect from these three customers during June?
2. How much do these three customers still owe Amazon at the end of June?
3. What are the days' sales in average accounts receivable from these three customers?

Step-by-Step:

1. Open a new Excel spreadsheet.
2. Create a bold-faced heading for your spreadsheet that contains the following:
   a. Chapter 9 Excel Application Exercise
   b. Amazon Accounts Receivable (in 000's)
   c. Today's Date
3. Two rows down from your heading, create a row containing the following column headings:
   a. Customer ID
   b. Customer Name
   c. Beginning Balance
   d. Sales
   e. Collections
   f. Ending Balance
4. Enter the data from the scenario into the spreadsheet. At the end of the entries, create a row for "Totals" and calculate totals for all financial columns.
5. Two rows beneath the scenario data, calculate the days' sales in average accounts receivable. Include a row for net sales underneath this calculation so that the net sales amount can be included as a variable in the days' sales in average accounts receivable.
6. Format your work. Experiment with the AutoFormat feature found by clicking "Format" on the menu bar (be sure to highlight the entire chart before doing so).
7. Save your worksheet and print a copy for your files.

END-OF-CHAPTER *Summary Problem*

A+ TIPS
CHECK YOUR RESOURCES

Suppose First Fidelity, Inc., engaged in the following transactions:

20X4	
Apr. 1	Loaned out $8,000 to Bland Co. Received a six-month, 10% note.
Oct. 1	Collected the Bland note at maturity.
Dec. 1	Loaned $6,000 to Flores, Inc., on a 180-day, 12% note.
Dec. 31	Accrued interest revenue on the Flores note.
20X5	
May 30	Collected the Flores note at maturity.

First Fidelity's accounting period ends on December 31.

Required

Explanations are not needed.

1. Record the 20X4 transactions on April 1 through December 1 on First Fidelity's books.
2. Make the adjusting entry needed on December 31, 20X4.
3. Record the May 30, 20X5, collection of the Flores note.

Solution

Requirement 1

20X4			
Apr. 1	Note Receivable—Bland Co.	8,000	
	Cash		8,000
Oct. 1	Cash ($8,000 + $400)	8,400	
	Note Receivable—Bland Co.		8,000
	Interest Revenue ($8,000 × 0.10 × 6/12)		400

Requirement 2

		Debit	Credit
20X4			
Dec. 1	Note Receivable—Flores, Inc.	6,000	
	Cash		6,000
31	Interest Receivable	60	
	Interest Revenue ($6,000 × 0.12 × 30/360).		60

Requirement 3

		Debit	Credit
20X5			
May 30	Cash ($6,000 + $360)	6,360	
	Note Receivable—Flores, Inc.		6,000
	Interest Receivable		60
	Interest Revenue ($6,000 × 0.12 × 150/360)		300

REVIEW Receivables

Quick Check

1. With good internal controls, the person who handles cash can also
   a. Account for cash receipts from customers
   b. Account for cash payments
   c. Issue credits to customers for merchandise returned to us
   d. None of the above
2. "Bad debts" are the same as
   a. Uncollectible accounts
   b. Doubtful accounts
   c. Both a and b
   d. None of the above
3. Which method of estimating uncollectible receivables focuses on Uncollectible Account Expense for the income statement?
   a. Aging-of-accounts approach
   b. Percent-of-sales approach
   c. Net-realizable-value approach
   d. All of the above.
4. Your company uses the allowance method to account for uncollectible receivables. At the beginning of the year, Allowance for Uncollectibles had a credit balance of $1,100. During the year you recorded Uncollectible-Account Expense of $2,000 and wrote off bad receivables of $2,100. What is your year-end balance in Allowance for Uncollectibles?
   a. $1,000
   b. $2,000
   c. $3,100
   d. $3,200
5. Your ending balance of Accounts Receivable is $20,000. Use the data in the preceding question to compute the net realizable value of Accounts Receivable at year-end. Or, stated differently, determine the net receivables to report on your year-end balance sheet.
   a. $18,000
   b. $19,000
   c. $20,000
   d. $21,000
6. What is wrong with the direct write-off method of accounting for uncollectibles?
   a. The direct write-off method does not set up an allowance for uncollectibles.
   b. The direct write-off method overstates assets on the balance sheet.
   c. The direct write-off method does not match expenses against revenue very well.
   d. All of the above.
7. At December 31, you have a $10,000 note receivable from a customer. Interest of 8% has also accrued for 6 months on the note. What will your financial statements report for this situation?
   a. Nothing, because you haven't received the cash yet.
   b. Balance sheet will report the note receivable of $10,000.
   c. Balance sheet will report the note receivable of $10,000 and interest receivable of $400.
   d. Income statement will report a note receivable of $10,000.

8. Return to the data in the preceding question. What will the income statement report for this situation?
   a. Nothing, because you haven't received the cash yet
   b. Interest revenue of $400
   c. Note receivable of $10,000
   d. Both b and c
9. At year-end, your company has cash of $10,000, receivables of $40,000, inventory of $50,000, and prepaid expenses totaling $5,000. Liabilities of $60,000 must be paid next year. What is your acid-test ratio?
   a. 0.83
   b. 1.67
   c. 1.75
   d. Cannot be determined from the data given
10. Return to the data in the preceding question. A year ago receivables stood at $60,000, and sales for the current year total $730,000. How many days did it take you to collect your average level of receivables?
   a. 45
   b. 35
   c. 25
   d. 20

Accounting Vocabulary

acid-test ratio (p. 377)
aging-of-accounts method (p. 366)
Allowance for Doubtful Accounts (p. 365)
Allowance for Uncollectible Accounts (p. 365)
allowance method (p. 365)
bad-debt expense (p. 365)
balance-sheet approach (p. 366)
collection period (p. 378)
creditor (p. 362)
days' sales in receivables (p. 378)
debtor (p. 362)
default on a note (p. 376)
direct write-off method (p. 368)
discounting a note receivable (p. 396)
dishonor of a note (p. 376)
doubtful-account expense (p. 365)
due date (p. 373)
income-statement approach (p. 366)
interest (p. 372)
interest period (p. 372)
interest rate (p. 373)
maker of a note (p. 375)
maturity date (p. 373)
maturity value (p. 373)
note term (p. 372)
payee of a note (p. 375)
percent-of-sales method (p. 366)
principal (p. 372)
principal amount (p. 372)
promissory note (p. 372)
quick ratio (p. 377)
receivables (p. 362)
time (p. 372)
uncollectible-account expense (p. 365)

ASSESS *Your Progress*

A+ online homework

See *www.prenhall.com/horngren* for selected Starters, Exercises, and Problems.

Starters

Internal control over the collection of receivables
(Obj. 1)

S9-1 Return to the Accounts Receivable T-accounts on page 363. Suppose Melanie Snyder is the accountant responsible for these records. What duty will a good internal control system withhold from Snyder? Why?

Internal control over the credit department
(Obj. 1)

S9-2 What duty must be withheld from a company's credit department in order to safeguard its cash? If the credit department does this job, what can a dishonest credit department employee do to hurt the company?

Applying the allowance method (percent-of-sales) to account for uncollectibles
(Obj. 2)

S9-3 During its first year of operations, Spring Break Travel earned revenue of $500,000 on account. Industry experience suggests that Spring Break's bad debts will amount to 2% of revenues. At December 31, 20X3, accounts receivable total $90,000. The company uses the allowance method to account for uncollectibles.

1. Journalize Spring Break Travel's uncollectible-account expense using the percent-of-sales method.
2. Show how Spring Break should report accounts receivable on its balance sheet at December 31, 20X3. Follow the reporting format illustrated in the middle of page 365.

Applying the allowance method (percent-of-sales) to account for uncollectibles **(Obj. 2)**

S9-4 ← *Link Back to Chapter 2 (Recording Service Revenue Transactions).* This exercise continues the situation of Starter 9-3, in which Spring Break Travel ended 20X3 with accounts receivable of $90,000 and an allowance for uncollectible accounts of $10,000.

During 20X4, Spring Break Travel completed these transactions:

1. Service revenue, $700,000 (ignore cost of goods sold).
2. Collections on account, $690,000.
3. Write-offs of uncollectibles, $15,000.
4. Uncollectible-account expense, 2% of service revenue.

Journalize Spring Break Travel's 20X4 transactions.

Applying the allowance method (aging-of-accounts) to account for uncollectibles **(Obj. 2)**

S9-5 ← *Link Back to Chapter 5 (Recording Sales Transactions).* Guardian Medical Group started 20X0 with accounts receivable of $120,000 and an allowance for uncollectible accounts with a $6,000 credit balance. Credit sales for 20X0 were $500,000, and cash collections on account totaled $420,000. During 20X0, Guardian wrote off uncollectible accounts receivable of $12,000. At December 31, 20X0, the aging of accounts receivable showed that Guardian will probably *not* collect $5,000 of its accounts receivable.

Journalize Guardian's (a) credit sales (ignore cost of goods sold), (b) cash collections on account, (c) write-offs of uncollectible receivables, and (d) uncollectible-account expense for the year. Prepare a T-account for Allowance for Uncollectible Accounts to show your computation of uncollectible-account expense for the year.

Applying the allowance method (aging-of-accounts) to account for uncollectibles **(Obj. 2)**

S9-6 Hot Button.com had the following balances at December 31, 20X1, before the year-end adjustments:

Accounts Receivable			Allowance for Uncollectible Accounts	
104,000				1,300

The aging of accounts receivable yields these data:

	Age of Accounts Receivable				
	0–30 Days	31–60 Days	61–90 Days	Over 90 Days	Total Receivables
Accounts receivable	$70,000	$20,000	$10,000	$4,000	$104,000
Percent uncollectible	× 1%	× 2%	× 5%	× 50%	

Journalize Hot Button's entry to adjust the allowance account to its correct balance at December 31, 20X1.

Applying the direct write-off method to account for uncollectibles **(Obj. 3)**

S9-7 Diane Feinstein is an attorney in San Francisco. Feinstein uses the direct write-off method to account for uncollectible receivables.

At May 31, Feinstein's accounts receivable were $8,000. During June, she earned service revenue of $20,000 on account and collected $22,000 from clients on account. She also wrote off uncollectible receivables of $1,000. What is Feinstein's balance of Accounts Receivable at June 30? Does she expect to collect all of this amount? Why or why not?

Recording credit-card sales **(Obj. 3)**

S9-8 Gas stations do a large volume of business by customer credit cards and bankcards. Suppose the **BP Amoco** station near Lenox Square in Atlanta, Georgia, had these transactions on a busy Saturday in July:

American Express credit-card sales	$10,000
VISA bankcard sales	8,000

Suppose **American Express** charges merchants 4% and **VISA** charges 3%. Record these sale transactions for the BP Amoco station.

Computing interest amounts on notes receivable
(Obj. 4)

S9-9 For each of the following notes receivable, compute the amount of interest revenue earned during 20X5. Use a 360-day year, and round to the nearest dollar.

	Principal	Interest Rate	Interest Period During 20X5
Note 1	$100,000	8%	6 months
Note 2	15,000	12%	75 days
Note 3	10,000	9%	60 days
Note 4	50,000	10%	3 months

Accounting for a note receivable
(Obj. 4)

S9-10 Deutsche Bank lent $100,000 to Johann Schroeder on a 90-day, 8% note. Record the following transactions for Deutsche Bank (explanations are not required):

a. Lending the money on June 12.
b. Collecting the principal and interest at maturity. Specify the date. For the computation of interest, use a 360-day year.

Accruing interest receivable and collecting a note receivable
(Obj. 4)

S9-11 Return to the promissory note in Exhibit 9-4, page 373. The accounting year of Continental Bank ends on December 31, 20X6. Journalize Continental Bank's (a) lending money on September 30, 20X6 and (b) accrual of interest revenue at December 31, 20X6. Carry amounts to the nearest cent.

Reporting receivables and other accounts in the financial statements
(Obj. 5)

S9-12 ←*Link Back to Chapters 1–3 (Debit/Credit Balances; Income Statement).* **Sprint Corporation**, the telecommunications company, included the following items in its financial statements (adapted, in millions):

Allowance for doubtful accounts	$ 117	Service revenue	$14,045
Cash	1,151	Other assets	355
Accounts receivable	2,581	Cost of services sold and other expenses	12,861
Accounts payable	1,027	Notes payable	3,281

1. How much net income did Sprint earn for the year?
2. Show how Sprint reported receivables on its classified balance sheet. Follow the reporting format shown in the middle of page 365.

Using the acid-test ratio and days' sales in receivables to evaluate a company
(Obj. 6)

S9-13 Vision Equipment, which makes VCRs, reported the following items at February 28, 20X6 (amounts in thousands, with last year's—20X5—amounts also given as needed):

Accounts payable	$ 449	Accounts receivable, net:	
Cash	215	February 28, 20X6	$ 220
Inventories:		February 28, 20X5	150
February 28, 20X6	190	Cost of goods sold	1,200
February 28, 20X5	160	Short-term investments	165
Net sales revenue	1,930	Other current assets	90
Long-term assets	410	Other current liabilities	145
Long-term liabilities	10		

Compute Vision Equipment's (a) acid-test ratio and (b) days' sales in average receivables for 20X6. Evaluate each ratio value as strong or weak. Assume Vision Equipment sells on terms of net 30.

Computing key ratios for a company
(Obj. 6)

S9-14 ← *Link Back to Chapter 4 (Current Ratio and Debt Ratio) and Chapter 5 (Gross Profit Percentage and Inventory Turnover).* Use the data in Starter 9-13 to compute the following 20X6 ratios for Vision Equipment:

a. Current ratio
b. Debt ratio
c. Gross profit percentage
d. Rate of inventory turnover

Exercises

A+ online homework

Identifying and correcting an internal control weakness
(Obj. 1)

E9-1 ← *Link Back to Chapter 8 (Internal Control Over Cash Receipts).* Suppose **Eastman Kodak** is opening an office in Little Rock, Arkansas. Anita Mills, the office manager, is designing the internal control system. Mills proposes the following procedures for credit checks on new customers, sales on account, cash collections, and write-offs of uncollectible receivables:

- The credit department runs a credit check on all customers who apply for credit. When an account proves uncollectible, the credit department authorizes the write-off of the account receivable.
- Cash receipts come into the credit department, which separates the cash received from the customer remittance slips. The credit department lists all cash receipts by customer name and amount of cash received.
- The cash goes to the treasurer for deposit in the bank. The remittance slips go to the accounting department for posting to customer accounts.
- The controller compares the daily deposit slip to the total amount posted to customer accounts. Both amounts must agree.

Identify the internal control weakness in this situation, and propose a way to correct it.

Using the allowance method for bad debts
(Obj. 2, 5)

E9-2 During October, German Imports had sales of $180,000, which included $120,000 in credit sales. October collections were $90,000. Other data include

- September 30 debit balance in Accounts Receivable, $28,000
- September 30 credit balance in Allowance for Uncollectible Accounts, $1,000
- Uncollectible-account expense, estimated as 2% of credit sales
- Write-offs of uncollectible receivables totaled $1,200

Required

1. Prepare journal entries to record sales, collections, uncollectible-account expense by the allowance method (percent-of-sales method), and write-offs of uncollectibles during October.
2. Show the ending balances in Accounts Receivable, Allowance for Uncollectible Accounts, and *net* accounts receivable at October 31. How much does German Imports expect to collect?

Using the direct write-off method for bad debts
(Obj. 3)

E9-3 Refer to Exercise 9-2.

Required

1. Record uncollectible-account expense for October using the direct write-off method.
2. What accounts receivable amount does German Imports report on its Oct. 31 balance sheet under the direct write-off method? Does it expect to collect the full amount?

Using the aging method to estimate bad debts
(Obj. 2, 5)

Student Resource CD
spreadsheet

E9-4 At December 31, 20X7, the Accounts Receivable balance of VISA Express is $300,000. The Allowance for Doubtful Accounts has a $3,900 credit balance. VISA prepares the following aging schedule for its accounts receivable:

	Age of Accounts			
Total Balance	**1–30 Days**	**31–60 Days**	**61–90 Days**	**Over 90 Days**
$300,000	$140,000	$80,000	$70,000	$10,000
Estimated percent uncollectible	0.5%	1.0%	6.0%	50%

Required

1. Journalize the year-end adjusting entry for doubtful accounts on the basis of the aging schedule. Show the T-account for the Allowance at December 31, 20X7.
2. Show how VISA Express will report Accounts Receivable on its December 31, 20X7 balance sheet.

Reporting bad debts by the allowance method
(Obj. 2, 5)

E9-5 Circuit Software made credit sales of $500,000 during 20X8. Experience indicates that uncollectible-account expense is 1/2 of 1% of credit sales.

At December 31, 20X8, Circuit Software's Accounts Receivable balance is $130,000, and Allowance for Uncollectibles stands at $1,600 before the year-end adjustment.

Record uncollectible-account expense for 20X8. Then report Circuit Software's receivables, net of the allowance, at December 31, 20X8.

Computing notes receivable amounts
(Obj. 4)

E9-6 On April 30, 20X7, First National Bank of Santa Fe, New Mexico, loaned $100,000 to Grant Thompson on a one-year, 9% note.

Required

1. Compute the interest for the years ended December 31, 20X7 and 20X8 for the Thompson note.
2. Which party has a
   - **a.** Note receivable?
   - **b.** Note payable?
   - **c.** Interest revenue?
   - **d.** Interest expense?
3. How much in total would Thompson pay the bank if he pays off the note early—say, on November 30, 20X7?

Recording notes receivable and accruing interest revenue
(Obj. 4)

Student Resource CD
General Ledger, Peachtree, QuickBooks

E9-7 Journalize the following transactions of Motor Sports Company, which ends its accounting year on June 30:

Apr. 1	Loaned $20,000 cash to Ahmed Fadal on a one-year, 8% note.
June 6	Sold goods to Lennox Corp., receiving a 90-day, 10% note for $3,000.
30	Made a single compound entry to accrue interest revenue on both notes. Use a 360-day year for interest computations.

Recording bankcard sales and a note receivable, and accruing interest revenue
(Obj. 4)

Student Resource CD
GL, PT, QB

E9-8 Record the following transactions in the journal of Spaceage Jewelry:

20X8	
Feb. 12	Recorded VISA bankcard sales of $60,000, less a 2% discount.
May 1	Loaned $20,000 to Peter Liu on a one-year, 12% note.
Dec. 31	Accrued interest revenue on the Liu note.
20X9	
May 1	Collected the maturity value of the Liu note.

Recording notes receivable transactions
(Obj. 4)

Student Resource CD
GL, PT, QB

E9-9 Acura Enterprises sells on account. When a customer account becomes four months old, Acura converts the account to a note receivable. During 20X6, Acura completed these transactions:

June 29	Sold goods on account to J. Lafferty, $10,000.
Nov. 1	Received a $10,000, 60-day, 9% note from J. Lafferty in satisfaction of his past-due account receivable.
Dec. 31	Collected the Lafferty note at maturity.

Required

Record the transactions in Acura's journal.

Evaluating ratio data
(Obj. 6)

E9-10 **Warnaco** reported the following amounts in its 20X9 financial statements. The 20X8 figures are given for comparison.

	20X9		20X8	
Current assets:				
Cash		$ 3,000		$ 10,000
Short-term investments		23,000		11,000
Accounts receivable	$80,000		$74,000	
Less: Allowance for uncollectibles	(7,000)	73,000	(6,000)	68,000
Inventory		192,000		189,000
Prepaid insurance		2,000		2,000
Total current assets		293,000		280,000
Total current liabilities		$104,000		$107,000
Net sales		$805,000		$732,000

Required

1. Determine whether Warnaco's acid-test ratio improved or deteriorated from 20X8 to 20X9. How does Warnaco's acid-test ratio compare with the industry average of 0.80?
2. Compare the days' sales in receivables for 20X9 with Warnaco's credit terms of net 30.

Analyzing an actual company's financial statements
(Obj. 6)

Student ResourceCD
spreadsheet

E9-11 **Dell Computer** sells on account. Recently, Dell reported these figures (in millions of dollars):

	2002	2001
Net sales	$31,168	$31,188
Receivables at end of year	2,269	2,424

Required

1. Compute Dell's average collection period on receivables during 2002.
2. Suppose Dell's normal credit terms for a sale on account are "net 30 days." How well does Dell's collection period compare to the company's credit terms? Is this good or bad for Dell? Explain.

Evaluating credit-card sales for profitability
(Obj. 2)

Student ResourceCD
spreadsheet

E9-12 Navigation Systems sells on store credit and manages its own receivables. Average experience for the past three years has been as follows:

	Total
Sales	$350,000
Cost of goods sold	210,000
Bad-debt expense	4,000
Other expenses	61,000

Bruce Slazenger, the owner, is considering whether to accept bankcards **(VISA, MasterCard)**. Typically, accepting bankcards increases total sales and cost of goods sold by 10%. But VISA and MasterCard charge approximately 2% of bankcard sales. If Slazenger switches to bankcards, he'll no longer have bad-debt expense. He can also save $5,000 on other expenses. After the switchover to bankcards, Slazenger expects cash sales of $200,000.

Required

Should Slazenger start accepting bankcards? Show the computations of net income under his present arrangement and under the bankcard plan.

Problems

(Group A)

A+ online homework

Controlling cash receipts from customers
(Obj. 1)

P9-1A Prism Imaging converts hard-copy documents to CD and DVD media. All work is performed on account, with regular monthly billing to customers. Eve Nations, the accountant for Prism, opens the mail. Company procedure requires her to separate customer checks from the remittance slips and then post collections to customer accounts. Nations deposits the checks in the bank. She computes each day's total amount posted to customer accounts and matches this total to the bank deposit slip. This procedure is intended to ensure that all receipts are deposited in the bank.

Required

As a consultant hired by Prism Imaging, write a memo to management evaluating the company's internal controls over cash receipts from customers. If the system is effective, identify its strong features. If the system has flaws, propose a way to strengthen the controls. Use the memorandum format that follows.

Date: ______

To:

From:

Subject:

Accounting for uncollectibles by the direct write-off and allowance methods
(Obj. 2, 3, 5)

P9-2A On May 31, Scuba Dive Equipment had a $210,000 debit balance in Accounts Receivable. During June, Scuba made sales of $560,000, all on credit. Other data for June include

- Collections on account, $567,400.
- Write-offs of uncollectible receivables, $8,900.

Required

1. Record sales and collections on account. Then record uncollectible-account expense and write-offs of customer accounts for June using the *allowance* method. Show all June activity in Accounts Receivable, Allowance for Uncollectible Accounts, and Uncollectible-Account Expense (post to these T-accounts). The May 31 unadjusted balance in Allowance for Uncollectible Accounts was $2,800 (credit). Uncollectible-account expense was estimated at 2% of credit sales.
2. Suppose Scuba Dive Equipment used a different method to account for uncollectible receivables. Record sales and collections on account. Then record uncollectible-account expense for June using the *direct write-off* method. Post to Accounts Receivable and Uncollectible-Account Expense and show their balances at June 30.
3. What amount of uncollectible-account expense would Scuba Dive Equipment report on its June income statement under each of the two methods? Which amount better matches expense with revenue? Give your reason.
4. What amount of *net* accounts receivable would Scuba Dive Equipment report on its June 30 balance sheet under each of the two methods? Which amount is more realistic? Give your reason.

Using the percent-of-sales and aging methods for uncollectibles
(Obj. 2, 5)

P9-3A The June 30, 20X7, balance sheet of Texas Golf Carts reports the following:

Accounts Receivable.	$143,000
Allowance for Uncollectible Accounts (credit balance)	3,200

At the end of each quarter, Texas Golf Carts estimates uncollectible-account expense to be 1 1/2% of credit sales. At the end of the year, the company ages its accounts receivable and adjusts the balance in Allowance for Uncollectible Accounts to correspond to the aging schedule. During July through December of 20X7, Texas Golf Carts completed the following transactions:

Aug. 9	Made a compound entry to write off uncollectible accounts: J. Aguilar, $200; Seaton Co., $100; and T. Taylor, $700.
Sep. 30	Recorded uncollectible-account expense equal to 1 1/2% of credit sales of $140,000.
Oct. 18	Wrote off as uncollectible the $500 account receivable from Lintz Co. and the $400 account receivable from Navisor Corp.
Dec. 31	Recorded uncollectible-account expense based on the aging of accounts receivable, which follows:

	Age of Accounts			
Total	**1–30 Days**	**31–60 Days**	**61–90 Days**	**Over 90 Days**
$163,000	$100,000	$40,000	$14,000	$9,000
Estimated percent uncollectible	0.1%	0.5%	5%	30%

Required

1. Record the transactions in the journal.
2. Open the Allowance for Uncollectible Accounts, and post entries affecting that account. Keep a running balance.
3. Show how Texas Golf Carts should report accounts receivable on its balance sheet at December 31, 20X7.

P9-4A ← *Link Back to Chapter 4 (Closing Entries).* Providence Medical Supply completed the following transactions during 20X4 and 20X5:

Using the percent-of-sales method for uncollectibles
(Obj. 2, 5)

Student Resource CD
GL, PT, QB

20X4	
Dec. 31	Estimated that uncollectible-account expense for the year was 3/4 of 1% on credit sales of $400,000, and recorded that amount as expense.
31	Made the closing entry for uncollectible-account expense.
20X5	
Jan. 17	Sold inventory to Mitch Vanez, $600, on account. Ignore cost of goods sold.
June 29	Wrote off the Mitch Vanez account as uncollectible after repeated efforts to collect from him.
Aug. 6	Received $200 from Mitch Vanez, along with a letter stating his intention to pay within 30 days. Reinstated his account in full.
Sept. 4	Received the balance due from Mitch Vanez.
Dec. 31	Made a compound entry to write off the following accounts as uncollectible: Bernard Klaus, $700; Marie Monet, $300; and Terry Fuhrman, $600.
31	Estimated that uncollectible-account expense for the year was 2/3 of 1% on credit sales of $480,000, and recorded that amount as expense.
31	Made the closing entry for uncollectible-account expense.

Required

1. Open general ledger accounts for Allowance for Uncollectible Accounts and Uncollectible-Account Expense. Keep running balances. All accounts begin with a zero balance.
2. Record the transactions in the general journal, and post to the two ledger accounts.
3. The December 31, 20X5, balance of Accounts Receivable is $139,000. Show how Accounts Receivable would be reported on the balance sheet at that date.

P9-5A The Bailey Insurance Agency received the following notes during 20X8.

Accounting for notes receivable, including accruing interest revenue
(Obj. 4)

Note	Date	Principal Amount	Interest Rate	Term
(1)	Dec. 23	$13,000	9%	1 year
(2)	Nov. 30	12,000	12%	6 months
(3)	Dec. 7	9,000	10%	30 days

Required

Identify each note by number, compute interest using a 360-day year for those notes with terms specified in days or years, and present entries in general journal form. Explanations are not required.

1. Determine the due date and maturity value of each note.
2. Journalize a single adjusting entry at December 31, 20X8, to record accrued interest revenue on all three notes.
3. For note (1), journalize the collection of principal and interest at maturity.

P9-6A ← *Link Back to Chapter 4 (Closing Entries).* Record the following transactions in the general journal of Triumph Auto Accessories. Explanations are not required.

Accounting for notes receivable, dishonored notes, and accrued interest revenue
(Obj. 4)

Student Resource CD
GL, PT, QB

20X4	
Dec. 19	Received a $3,000, 60-day, 12% note on account from Arnold Cohen.
31	Made an adjusting entry to accrue interest on the Cohen note.
31	Made a closing entry for interest revenue.
20X5	
Feb. 17	Collected the maturity value of the Cohen note.
June 1	Loaned $10,000 cash to Blues Brothers, receiving a 6-month, 11% note.
Oct. 31	Received a $1,500, 60-day, 12% note from Mark Phipps on his past-due account receivable.
Dec. 1	Collected the maturity value of the Blues Brothers note.
30	Mark Phipps dishonored his note at maturity; wrote off the note receivable as uncollectible, debiting Allowance for Uncollectible Accounts.

Journalizing uncollectibles, notes receivable, and accrued interest revenue
(Obj. 4)

Student Resource CD
GL, PT, QB

P9-7A Assume that **Pepperidge Farms**, famous for cookies, crackers, and other baked goods, completed the following selected transactions:

20X6	
Nov. 1	Sold goods to **Kroger**, receiving a $40,000, three-month, 9% note. Ignore cost of goods sold.
Dec. 31	Made an adjusting entry to accrue interest on the Kroger note.
31	Made an adjusting entry to record uncollectible-account expense based on an aging of accounts receivable. The aging analysis indicates that $57,400 of accounts receivable will not be collected. Prior to this adjustment, the credit balance in Allowance for Uncollectible Accounts is $42,600.
20X7	
Feb. 1	Collected the maturity value of the Kroger note.
June 23	Sold merchandise to Artesian Corp., receiving a 60-day, 10% note for $9,000. Ignore cost of goods sold.
Aug. 22	Artesian Corp. dishonored (failed to pay) its note at maturity; we converted the maturity value of the note to an account receivable.
Nov. 16	Loaned $6,000 cash to Crane, Inc., receiving a 90-day, 12% note.
Dec. 5	Collected in full on account from Artesian Corp.
31	Accrued the interest on the Crane, Inc., note.

Required

Record the transactions in the journal of Pepperidge Farms. Explanations are not required.

Using ratio data to evaluate a company's financial position
(Obj. 6)

Student Resource CD
spreadsheet

P9-8A ← *Link Back to Chapter 4 (Current Ratio)*. The comparative financial statements of Pizza Express Delis for 20X6, 20X5, and 20X4 include the following selected data:

	(In thousands)		
	20X6	**20X5**	**20X4**
Balance sheet			
Current assets:			
Cash	$ 82	$ 80	$ 60
Short-term investments	140	174	122
Receivables, net of allowance for doubtful accounts of $6, $6, and $5, respectively	257	265	218
Inventories	429	341	302
Prepaid expenses	21	27	46
Total current assets	929	887	748
Total current liabilities	$ 680	$ 700	$ 660
Income statement			
Sales revenue	$5,189	$4,995	$4,206
Cost of sales	2,734	2,636	2,418

Required

1. Compute these ratios for 20X6 and 20X5:
   a. Current ratio b. Acid-test ratio c. Days' sales in receivables
2. Write a memo explaining to the company owner which ratios improved from 20X5 to 20X6 and which ratios deteriorated. Which item in the financial statements increased and caused some ratios to improve and others to deteriorate? Discuss whether this factor conveys a favorable or an unfavorable impression about the company.

Problems

(Group B)

A+ online homework

Controlling cash receipts from customers
(Obj. 1)

P9-1B Downslope Ski Supply distributes ski gear to sporting goods stores. All sales are on credit, so virtually all cash receipts arrive in the mail. William Yang, the company owner, has just returned from a meeting with new ideas for the business. Among other things, Yang plans to institute stronger internal controls over cash receipts from customers.

Required

Assume you are William Yang. Write a memo to outline a set of procedures to ensure that (1) all cash receipts are deposited in the bank and (2) all cash receipts are posted as credits to customer accounts receivable. Use the memorandum format given in Problem 9-1A, page 388.

Accounting for uncollectibles by the direct write-off and allowance methods
(Obj. 2, 3, 5)

P9-2B On February 28, Hourglass Computers had a $75,000 debit balance in Accounts Receivable. During March, Hourglass made sales of $445,000, all on credit. Other data for March include

- Collections on account, $422,600.
- Write-offs of uncollectible receivables, $3,500.

Required

1. Record sales and collections on account. Then record uncollectible-account expense and write-offs of customer accounts using the *allowance* method. Show all March activity in Accounts Receivable, Allowance for Uncollectible Accounts, and Uncollectible-Account Expense (post to these T-accounts). The February 28 unadjusted balance in Allowance for Uncollectible Accounts was $800 (credit). Uncollectible-account expense was estimated at 2% of credit sales.
2. Suppose Hourglass Computers used a different method to account for uncollectible receivables. Record sales and collections on account. Then record uncollectible-account expense for March using the *direct write-off* method. Post to Accounts Receivable and Uncollectible-Account Expense and show their balances at March 31.
3. What amount of uncollectible-account expense would Hourglass Computers report on its March income statement under each of the two methods? Which amount better matches expense with revenue? Give your reason.
4. What amount of *net* accounts receivable would Hourglass Computers report on its March 31 balance sheet under each of the two methods? Which amount is more realistic? Give your reason.

Using the percent-of-sales and aging methods for uncollectibles
(Obj. 2, 5)

P9-3B The June 30, 20X9, balance sheet of RAM Technologies reports the following:

Accounts Receivable	$265,000
Allowance for Uncollectible Accounts (credit balance)	7,100

At the end of each quarter, RAM estimates uncollectible-account expense to be 2% of credit sales. At the end of the year, RAM ages its accounts receivable. RAM then adjusts the balance in Allowance for Uncollectible Accounts to correspond to the aging schedule. During the second half of 20X9, RAM completed the following transactions:

July	14	Made a compound entry to write off uncollectible accounts: T. J. Dooley, $700; Design Works, $2,400; and S. DeWitt, $100.
Sep.	30	Recorded uncollectible-account expense equal to 2% of credit sales of $140,000.
Nov.	22	Wrote off accounts receivable as uncollectible: Transnet, $1,300; **Webvan**, $2,100; and Alpha Group, $700.
Dec.	31	Recorded uncollectible-account expense based on the aging of receivables.

	Age of Accounts			
Total	**1–30 Days**	**31–60 Days**	**61–90 Days**	**Over 90 Days**
$255,000	$120,000	$80,000	$40,000	$15,000
Estimated percent uncollectible.....................	0.5%	1.0%	4%	50%

Required

1. Record the transactions in the journal.
2. Open the Allowance for Uncollectible Accounts, and post entries affecting that account. Keep a running balance.
3. Show how RAM Technologies should report accounts receivable on its December 31, 20X9, balance sheet.

Using the percent-of-sales method for uncollectibles
(Obj, 2, 5)

Student Resource CD
GL, PT, QB

P9-4B ← *Link Back to Chapter 4 (Closing Entries).* Mach-1 Sound Systems completed the following selected transactions during 20X1 and 20X2:

20X1		
Dec.	31	Estimated that uncollectible-account expense for the year was 2/3 of 1% on credit sales of $450,000 and recorded that amount as expense.
	31	Made the closing entry for uncollectible-account expense.
20X2		
Feb.	4	Sold inventory to Marian Holt, $1,500 on account. Ignore cost of goods sold.
July	1	Wrote off Marian Holt's account as uncollectible after repeated efforts to collect from her.
Oct.	19	Received $500 from Marian Holt, along with a letter stating her intention to pay within 30 days. Reinstated Holt's account in full.
Nov.	15	Received the balance due from Marian Holt.
Dec.	31	Made a compound entry to write off the following accounts as uncollectible: Kaycee Britt, $800; Tim Sands, $500; and Anna Chin, $1,200.
	31	Estimated that uncollectible-account expense for the year was 2/3 of 1% on credit sales of $585,000 and recorded the expense.
	31	Made the closing entry for uncollectible-account expense.

Required

1. Open general ledger accounts for Allowance for Uncollectible Accounts and Uncollectible-Account Expense. Keep running balances. All accounts begin with a zero balance.
2. Record the transactions in the general journal, and post to the two ledger accounts.
3. The December 31, 20X2, balance of Accounts Receivable is $164,500. Show how Accounts Receivable would be reported on the balance sheet at that date.

Accounting for notes receivable, including accruing interest revenue
(Obj. 4)

P9-5B Metro Bank loaned money and received the following notes during 20X8.

Note	Date	Principal Amount	Interest Rate	Term
(1)	Dec. 1	$12,000	9%	1 year
(2)	Oct. 31	11,000	12%	3 months
(3)	Nov. 19	15,000	10%	60 days

Required

Identify each note by number, compute interest using a 360-day year, and present entries in general journal form. Explanations are not required.

1. Determine the due date and maturity value of each note.
2. Journalize a single adjusting entry at December 31, 20X8, to record accrued interest revenue on all three notes.
3. For note (1), journalize the collection of principal and interest at maturity.

Accounting for notes receivable, dishonored notes, and accrued interest revenue
(Obj. 4)

Student ResourceCD
GL, PT, QB

P9-6B ← *Link Back to Chapter 4 (Closing Entries).* Record the following transactions in the general journal of Recognition Systems. Round all amounts to the nearest dollar. Explanations are not required.

20X6		
Dec.	21	Received a $2,800, 30-day, 10% note on account from Joe Fitzhugh.
	31	Made an adjusting entry to accrue interest on the Fitzhugh note.
	31	Made a closing entry for interest revenue.
20X7		
Jan.	20	Collected the maturity value of the Fitzhugh note.
Sept.	14	Loaned $6,000 cash to Bullseye Investors, receiving a three-month, 13% note.
	30	Received a $1,600, 60-day, 16% note from Chuck Powers on his past-due account receivable.
Nov.	29	Chuck Powers dishonored his note at maturity; wrote off the note as uncollectible, debiting Allowance for Uncollectible Accounts.
Dec.	14	Collected the maturity value of the Bullseye Investors note.

Journalizing uncollectibles, notes receivable, and accrued interest revenue
(Obj. 4)

Student ResourceCD
GL, PT, QB

P9-7B Assume that **Jones-Blair**, the paint manufacturer, completed the following selected transactions:

20X4		
Dec.	1	Sold goods to Kelly Paint Supply, receiving a $12,000, three-month, 10% note. Ignore cost of goods sold.
	31	Made an adjusting entry to accrue interest on the Kelly note.
	31	Made an adjusting entry to record uncollectible-account expense based on an aging of accounts receivable. The aging analysis indicates that $39,800 of accounts receivable will not be collected. Prior to this adjustment, the credit balance in Allowance for Uncollectible Accounts is $24,100.
20X5		
Mar.	1	Collected the maturity value of the Kelly Paint Supply note.
July	21	Sold merchandise to Mellon Co., receiving a 60-day, 9% note for $4,000. Ignore cost of goods sold.
Sep.	19	Mellon Co. dishonored its note (failed to pay) at maturity; we converted the maturity value of the note to an account receivable.
Nov.	21	Loaned $40,000 cash to Thermo Control, Inc., receiving a 90-day, 9% note.
Dec.	2	Collected in full on account from Mellon Co.
	31	Accrued the interest on the Thermo Control note.

Required

Record the transactions in the journal of Jones-Blair. Explanations are not required.

Using ratio data to evaluate a company's financial position
(Obj. 6)

Student ResourceCD
spreadsheet

P9-8B ← *Link Back to Chapter 4 (Current Ratio).* The comparative financial statements of Crispy Cream Pastries for 20X8, 20X7, and 20X6 include the data shown here:

	(In millions)		
	20X8	20X7	20X6
Balance sheet			
Current assets:			
Cash	$ 27	$ 26	$ 22
Short-term investments	93	101	69
Receivables, net of allowance for doubtful accounts of $7, $6, and $4, respectively	146	154	127
Inventories	454	383	341
Prepaid expenses	32	31	25
Total current assets	752	695	584
Total current liabilities	$ 400	$ 416	$ 388
Income statement			
Sales revenue	$2,671	$2,505	$1,944
Cost of sales	1,380	1,360	963

Required

1. Compute these ratios for 20X8 and 20X7:
   a. Current ratio b. Acid-test ratio c. Days' sales in receivables
2. Write a memo explaining to the company owner which ratios improved from 20X7 to 20X8 and which ratios deteriorated. Which item in the financial statements increased and caused some ratios to improve and others to deteriorate? Discuss whether this factor conveys a favorable or an unfavorable sign about the company.

APPLY *Your Knowledge*

Decision Cases

Comparing the allowance and direct write-off methods for uncollectibles
(Obj. 2, 3)

Case 1. Pappa Rollo Advertising has always used the direct write-off method to account for uncollectibles. The company's revenues, bad-debt write-offs, and year-end receivables for the most recent year follow.

Year	Revenues	Write-Offs	Receivables at Year-End
20X6	$170,000	$3,000	$20,0000

Pappa Rollo is applying for a bank loan, and the loan officer requires figures based on the allowance method of accounting for bad debts. Pappa Rollo estimates that bad debts run about 4% of revenues each year.

Required

Pappa Rollo must give the banker the following information:

1. How much more or less would net income be for 20X6 if Pappa Rollo were to use the allowance method for bad debts?
2. How much of the receivables balance at the end of 20X6 does Pappa Rollo expect to collect?

Compute these amounts, and then explain for Pappa Rollo why net income is more or less for 20X6 using the allowance method versus the direct write-off method for uncollectibles.

Uncollectible accounts and evaluating a business
(Obj. 2, 3)

Case 2. Heartland Cable Network performs service either for cash or on notes receivable. The business uses the direct write-off method to account for bad debts. Dan Pavlicek, the owner, has prepared the company's financial statements. Summary comparative income statements for 20X6 and 20X5 follow.

	20X6	20X5
Total revenue	$220,000	$195,000
Total expenses	107,000	103,000
Net income	$113,000	$ 92,000

On the basis of the increase in net income, Pavlicek wants to expand operations. He asks you to invest $50,000 in the business. You and Pavlicek have several meetings and you learn that notes receivable from customers were $200,000 at the end of 20X4 and $400,000 at the end of 20X5. Also, total revenues for 20X6 and 20X5 include interest at 13% on the year's beginning notes receivable balance. Total expenses include uncollectible-account expense of $2,000 each year, based on the direct write-off method. Pavlicek estimates that uncollectible-account expense would be 5% of sales revenue if the allowance method were used.

Required

1. Prepare for Heartland Cable a comparative single-step income statement for 20X6 and 20X5 that identifies service revenue, interest revenue, uncollectible-account expense, and other expenses, all computed in accordance with generally accepted accounting principles.
2. Is Heartland Cable's future as promising as Pavlicek's income statement makes it appear? Give the reason for your answer.

Ethical Issue

Show Biz Autos sells cars. Show Biz's bank requires Show Biz to submit quarterly financial statements in order to keep its line of credit. Show Biz's main asset is Notes Receivable. Therefore, Uncollectible-Account Expense and Allowance for Uncollectible Accounts are important accounts.

Lance Van Houten, the owner of Show Biz Autos, wants net income to increase in a smooth pattern, rather than increase in some periods and decrease in others. To report smoothly increasing net income, Van Houten underestimates Uncollectible-Account Expense in some periods. In other periods, Van Houten overestimates the expense. He reasons that over time the income overstatements roughly offset the income understatements.

Required

Is Van Houten's practice of smoothing income ethical? Why or why not?

Financial Statement Case

Analyzing accounts receivable and uncollectibles
(Obj. 2, 6)

Use the balance sheet and income statement (statement of operations) of **Amazon.com** in Appendix A.

1. Do accounts receivable appear to be an important asset for Amazon.com? What about Amazon's business affects the importance of accounts receivable?
2. Assume that all of "Accounts Receivable, Net and Other Current Assets" is accounts receivable. Further assume that gross receivables at December 31, 2002, were $118,000 thousand. Answer the following questions based on these data, plus what's reported on the balance sheet:
   a. How much did customers owe Amazon.com at December 31, 2002?
   b. How much did Amazon expect to collect from customers after December 31, 2002?
   c. Of the total receivable amount at December 31, 2002, how much did Amazon expect *not* to collect?
3. Compute Amazon.com's acid-test ratio at the end of 2002 and at the end of 2001. Marketable securities are short-term investments. Assume that other current assets are zero. If all the current liabilities came due immediately, could Amazon pay them?

Team Project

Notes Receivable of the Bank. Bob Opper and Denise Shapp worked for several years as sales representatives for **Xerox Corporation.** During this time, they became close friends as they acquired expertise with the company's full range of copier equipment. Now they see an opportunity to put their experience to work and fulfill lifelong desires to establish their own business. Lakeside College, located in their city, is expanding, and there is no copy center within five miles of the campus. Business in the area is booming, and the population in this section of the city is growing.

Opper and Shapp want to open a copy center, similar to a **Kinko's**, near the campus. A small shopping center across the street from the college has a vacancy that would fit their needs. Opper and Shapp each have $20,000 to invest in the business, and they forecast the need for $30,000 to renovate the store. Xerox Corporation will lease two large copiers to them at a total monthly rental of $4,000. With enough cash to see them through the first six months of operation, they are confident they can make the business succeed. The two work very well together, and both have excellent credit ratings. Opper and Shapp must borrow $80,000 to start the business, advertise its opening, and keep it running for its first six months.

Assume the role of Opper and Shapp, the partners who will own Lakeside Copy Center.

1. As a group, visit a copy center to familiarize yourselves with its operations. If possible, interview the manager or another employee. Then write a loan request that Opper and Shapp will submit to a bank with the intent of borrowing $80,000 to be paid back over three years. The loan will be a personal loan to the partnership of Opper and Shapp, not to Lakeside Copy Center. The request should specify all the details of Opper's and Shapp's plan that will motivate the bank to grant the loan. Include a budgeted income statement for the first six months of the copy center's operation.
2. As a group, interview a loan officer in a bank. Have the loan officer evaluate your loan request. Write a report, or make a presentation to your class—as directed by your instructor—to reveal the loan officer's decision.

For Internet exercises, go to the Web site www.prenhall.com/horngren.

APPENDIX *to Chapter 9*

Discounting a Note Receivable

A payee of a note receivable may need cash before the maturity date of the note. When this occurs, the payee may sell the note, a practice called **discounting a note receivable**. The price to be received for the note is determined by present-value concepts. ← But the transaction between the seller and the buyer of the note can take any form agreeable to the two parties. Here we illustrate one procedure used for discounting short-term notes receivable. To receive cash immediately, the seller accepts a lower price than the note's maturity value.

We discuss these concepts in Chapter 15. →

Discounting a Note Receivable Selling a note receivable before its maturity date.

To illustrate discounting a note receivable, suppose **General Electric** loaned $15,000 to Dorman Builders on October 20, 20X8. GE took a note receivable from Dorman. The maturity date of the 90-day 10% Dorman note is January 18, 20X9. Suppose GE discounts the Dorman note at First City Bank on December 9, 20X8, when the note is 50 days old. The bank applies a 12% annual interest rate to determine the discounted value of the note. The bank will use a discount rate that is higher than the note's interest rate in order to earn some interest on the transaction. The discounted value, called the *proceeds*, is the amount GE receives from the bank. The proceeds can be computed in five steps, as shown in Exhibit 9A-1. GE's entry to record discounting (selling) the note on December 9, 20X8, is

Dec. 9, 20X8	Cash	15,170	
	Note Receivable—Dorman Builders . .		15,000
	Interest Revenue ($15,170 – $15,000) . .		170
	Discounted a note receivable.		

When the proceeds from discounting a note receivable are less than the principal amount of the note, the payee records a debit to Interest Expense for the amount of the difference. For example, GE could discount the note receivable for cash proceeds of $14,980. The entry to record this discounting transaction is

Dec. 9, 20X8	Cash	14,980	
	Interest Expense	20	
	Note Receivable—Dorman Builders . .		15,000
	Discounted a note receivable.		

Step	Computation	
1. Compute the original amount of interest on the note receivable.	$15,000 × 0.10 × 90/360	= $375
2. Maturity value of the note = Principal + Interest	$15,000 + $375	= $15,375
3. Determine the period (number of days, months, or years) the *bank* will hold the note (the discount period).	Dec. 9, 20X8 to Jan. 18, 20X9	= 40 days
4. Compute the bank's discount on the note. This is the bank's interest revenue from holding the note.	$15,375 × 0.12 × 40/360	= $205
5. Seller's proceeds from discounting the note receivable = Maturity value of the note – Bank's discount on the note.	$15,375 – $205	= $15,170

The authors thank Doug Hamilton for suggesting this exhibit.

Exhibit 9A-1

Discounting (Selling) a Note Receivable: GE Discounts the Dorman Builders Note

Appendix Assignments

Exercise

Recording notes receivable and discounting a note
(Obj. 4)

E9A-1 Rider Systems, Inc., sells on account. When a customer account becomes three months old, Rider converts the account to a note receivable and immediately discounts the note to a bank. During 20X4, Rider completed these transactions:

Aug.	29	Sold goods on account to V. Moyer, $3,900.
Dec.	1	Received a $3,900, 60-day, 10% note from V. Moyer in satisfaction of his past-due account receivable.
	1	Sold the Moyer note by discounting it to a bank for $3,600.

Required

Record the transactions in Rider Systems' journal.

Problem

Discounting notes receivable
(Obj. 4)

P9A-1 A company received the following notes during 20X5. Notes (1), (2), and (3) were discounted on the dates and at the rates indicated.

Note	Date	Principal Amount	Interest Rate	Term	Date Discounted	Discount Rate
(1)	July 15	$6,000	6%	6 months	Oct. 15	8%
(2)	Aug. 19	9,000	8%	90 days	Aug. 30	10%
(3)	Sept. 1	8,000	9%	120 days	Nov. 2	12%

Required

Identify each note by number, compute interest using a 360-day year for those notes with terms specified in days, round all interest amounts to the nearest dollar, and present entries in general journal form. Explanations are not required.

1. Determine the due date and maturity value of each note.
2. Determine the discount and proceeds from the sale (discounting) of each note.
3. Journalize the discounting of notes (1) and (2).

CHAPTER 10

Plant Assets and Intangibles

A+ TIPS CHECK YOUR RESOURCES

- Visit the www.prenhall.com/horngren **Web site** for self-study quizzes, video clips, and other resources
- Try the **Quick Check** exercise at the end of the chapter to test your knowledge
- Learn the **key terms**
- Do the **Starter** exercises keyed in the margins
- Work the **mid-** and **end-of-chapter summary problems**
- Use the **Concept Links** to review material in other chapters
- Search the **CD** for review materials by chapter or by key word
- Watch the **tutorial videos** to review key concepts

LEARNING OBJECTIVES

1. Measure the cost of a plant asset
2. Account for depreciation
3. Select the best depreciation method for tax purposes
4. Account for the disposal of a plant asset
5. Account for natural resources
6. Account for intangible assets

American/Delta/United Airlines

Have you ever taken a flight on a commercial airline? Companies like American, Delta, or United have some of the most interesting assets in the world: Boeing and McDonnell-Douglas airplanes.

How long can a commercial airplane keep flying safely and efficiently? American and Delta use their planes for about 20 years. The airlines want to use a plane like a Boeing 737 for a long time because it keeps them from having to come up with the cash to buy new planes. Top managers walk a tightrope between getting the good out of a plane and using one that consumes less fuel.

How do the airlines account for the use of an airplane? They record depreciation over the plane's useful life. Managers also have to consider how much they can sell a plane for when it's taken out of service. The airlines don't depreciate this residual value because they get it back when they sell a plane. ■

Sitemap

This chapter covers these and other topics about plant assets. **Plant assets** are the long-term tangible assets a business uses to operate, such as airplanes for American, copy equipment for Kinko's, and automobiles for Hertz. The chapter also shows how to account for natural resources, such as oil and timber, and **intangibles**—those assets with no physical form, such as trademarks, copyrights, and goodwill.

Chapter 10 concludes our coverage of assets, except for investments. After completing this chapter, you should understand the various assets of a business and how to account for them. Let's begin with an example that is familiar to you.

You probably own an automobile—maybe a Chevy or a Honda. Your car is a plant asset if you use it for day-to-day operations. But if you bought the car to resell it, then it would not be a plant asset; it would be part of your inventory. As your car wears out, it depreciates in usefulness. You should record depreciation on all the plant assets used in a business, except for land.

Plant assets have their own terminology. Exhibit 10-1 shows which expense account applies to each category of plant asset.

Exhibit 10-1

Plant Assets and Their Related Expenses

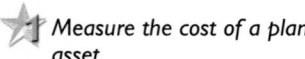

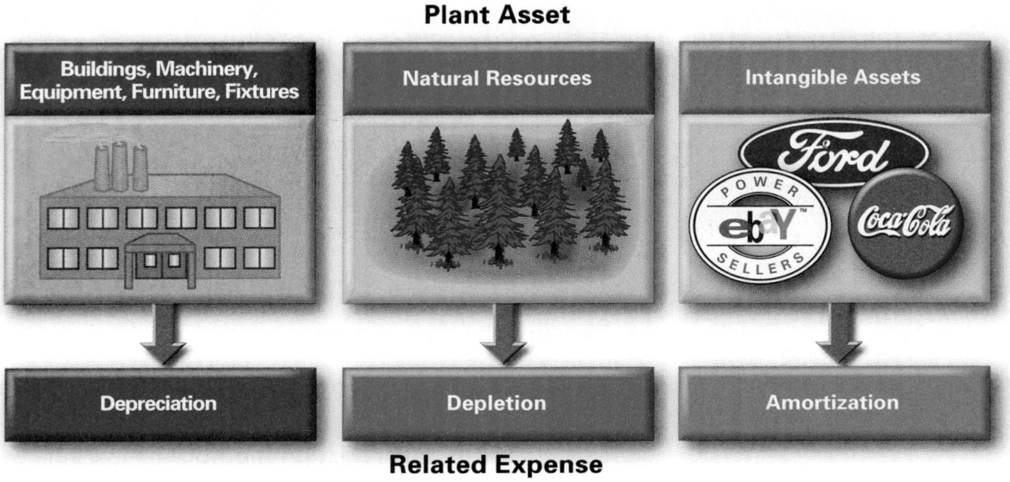

Plant Assets
Long-lived tangible assets, such as land, buildings, and equipment, used to operate a business.

Intangibles
Assets with no physical form. Valuable because of the special rights they carry. Examples are patents and copyrights.

Student Resource CD
capital expenditure, plant asset

1 *Measure the cost of a plant asset*

Measuring the Cost of Plant Assets

The *cost principle* says to carry an asset on the balance sheet at its cost—the amount paid for the asset. The general rule for measuring cost is

Cost of an asset = Sum of all the costs incurred to bring the asset to its intended purpose, net of all discounts

The *cost of a plant asset* is its purchase price plus applicable taxes, purchase commissions, and all other amounts paid to acquire the asset and make it ready for its intended use. In Chapter 6, we applied this principle to inventory. The types of costs differ for the various plant assets, so we discuss each asset individually.

Land and Land Improvements

The cost of land includes its purchase price, brokerage commission, survey and legal fees, and any back property taxes the purchaser pays. The cost also includes the cost of clearing the land and removing any unwanted buildings. The cost of land is not depreciated.

The cost does *not* include fencing, paving, sprinkler systems, and lighting. These separate plant assets—called *land improvements*—are subject to depreciation.

Suppose American Airlines signs a $500,000 note payable to purchase land. American also pays $40,000 in back property taxes, $8,000 in transfer taxes, $5,000 to remove an old building, and a $1,000 survey fee. What is the cost of this land? Exhibit 10-2 shows that all the costs incurred to bring the land to its intended use are part of the land's cost.

Exhibit 10-2

Measuring the Cost of a Plant Asset

Purchase price of land		$500,000
Add related costs:		
Back property taxes	$40,000	
Transfer taxes	8,000	
Removal of building	5,000	
Survey fee	1,000	
Total related costs		54,000
Total cost of land		$554,000

American Airlines' entry to record purchase of the land follows.

Land	554,000	
Note Payable		500,000
Cash		54,000

We would say that American Airlines *capitalized* the cost of the land at $554,000. This means that the company debited an asset account (Land) for $554,000.

Suppose American then pays $260,000 for fences, paving, lighting, and signs. The following entry records the cost of these land improvements.

Land Improvements	260,000	
Cash		260,000

Land and Land Improvements are two entirely separate asset accounts. The cost of land improvements is depreciated over the asset's useful life.

✔ Starter 10-1

Buildings

The cost of a building includes architectural fees, building permits, contractors' charges, and payments for material, labor, and overhead. The time to complete a building can be months, even years.

If the company constructs its own assets, the cost of the building may include the cost of interest on borrowed money. When an existing building is purchased, its cost includes all the usual items, plus all costs to repair and renovate the building for its intended use.

Machinery and Equipment

The cost of machinery and equipment includes its purchase price (less any discounts), plus transportation charges, insurance while in transit, sales and other taxes, purchase commission, installation costs, and the cost of testing the asset before it is used. After the asset is up and running, we no longer capitalize these costs to the Equipment account. Thereafter, insurance, taxes, and maintenance costs are recorded as expenses. American Airlines has an account for flight equipment, Kinko's has copy equipment, and Home Depot has delivery equipment for company trucks. All businesses have computer equipment.

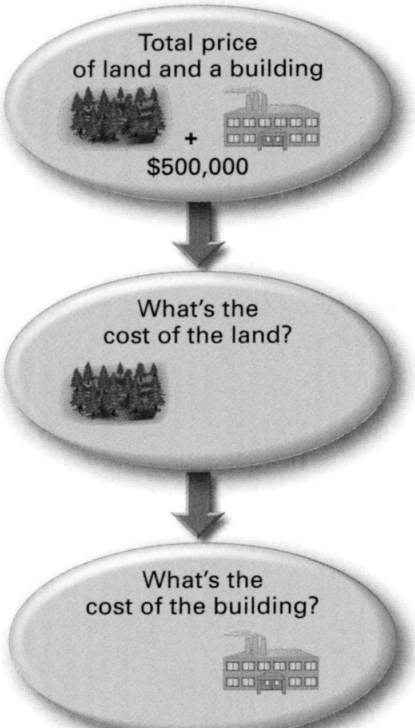
Total price
of land and a building
+
$500,000
What's the
cost of the land?
What's the
cost of the building?

Furniture and Fixtures

Furniture and fixtures include desks, chairs, file cabinets, and display racks. The cost of furniture and fixtures includes the basic cost of each asset (less any discounts), plus all other costs to get the assets ready for use. All companies have furniture and fixtures.

A Lump-Sum (Basket) Purchase of Assets

A company may purchase several assets as a group—in a "basket purchase"—for a single price. For example, **Delta Airlines** may pay one price for land and a building. For accounting purposes, Delta must identify the cost of each asset, as shown in the margin diagram. The total cost (100%) is divided among the assets according to their relative sales values. This allocation technique is called the *relative-sales-value method*.

Suppose Delta Airlines purchases land and a building in Kansas City for a communication center. The combined purchase price of land and building is $2,800,000. An appraisal indicates that the land's market (sales) value is $300,000 and that the building's market (sales) value is $2,700,000.

First, figure the ratio of each asset's market value to the total market value of both assets combined. Suppose the total appraised value is $2,700,000 + $300,000 = $3,000,000. Thus, the land, valued at $300,000, is 10% of the total market value. The building's appraised value is 90% of the total. The cost of each asset is determined as follows:

Asset	Market (Sales) Value	Percentage of Total Value				Total Purchase Price		Cost of Each Asset
Land	$ 300,000	$300,000/$3,000,000	=	10%	×	$2,800,000	=	$ 280,000
Building	2,700,000	$2,700,000/$3,000,000	=	90%	×	2,800,000	=	2,520,000
Total	$3,000,000			100%				$2,800,000

Suppose Delta pays cash. The entry to record the purchase of the land and building is

Land	280,000	
Building	2,520,000	
Cash		2,800,000

Stop & Think

How would **Kinko's** divide a $120,000 lump-sum purchase price for land, building, and equipment with estimated market values of $40,000, $95,000, and $15,000, respectively? Round decimals to three places.

Answer:

Asset	Market (Sales) Value	Percentage of Total Value				Total Purchase Price		Cost of Each Asset
Land	$ 40,000	$40,000/$150,000	=	26.7%	×	$120,000	=	$ 32,040
Building	95,000	$95,000/$150,000	=	63.3%	×	120,000	=	75,960
Equipment	15,000	$15,000/$150,000	=	10.0%	×	120,000	=	12,000
Total	$150,000			100.0%				$120,000

✔ Starter 10-2

Capital Expenditures

When a company spends money on a plant asset, it must decide whether to debit an asset account or an expense account. Examples of such expenditures range from General Motors buying robots for an assembly plant to you replacing the windshield on your automobile.

Expenditures that increase the asset's capacity or efficiency or that extend the asset's useful life are called **capital expenditures**. For example, GM's purchase of a robot and American Airlines' purchase of a Boeing 767 are capital expenditures. Also, the cost of a major overhaul that extends an asset's useful life is a capital expenditure. Repair work that generates a capital expenditure is called an **extraordinary repair**. Capital expenditures are debited to an asset account. For an extraordinary repair on a delivery truck, we would debit the Delivery Trucks account.

Capital Expenditure
Expenditure that increases the capacity or efficiency of an asset or extends its useful life. Capital expenditures are debited to an asset account.

Extraordinary Repair
Repair work that generates a capital expenditure.

Ordinary Repair
Repair work that is debited to an expense account.

Other expenditures do not extend an asset's capacity, but merely maintain the asset in working order. These costs are *expenses* and are immediately subtracted from revenue. Examples include the costs of repainting a truck, repairing a fender, and replacing tires. These costs for **ordinary repairs** are debited to Repair Expense.

The distinction between capital and maintenance expenditures requires judgment. Does the cost extend the life of the asset (a capital expenditure), or does it only maintain the asset in good order (an expense)? Exhibit 10-3 illustrates the distinction between (a) capital expenditures and (b) expenses for several delivery-truck expenditures.

Exhibit 10-3

Delivery-Truck Expenditures—Capital Expenditure or Expense?

CAPITAL EXPENDITURE: Debit an Asset Account	EXPENSE: Debit Repair and Maintenance Expense
Extraordinary repairs:	*Ordinary repairs:*
Major engine overhaul	Repair of transmission or engine
Modification for new use	Oil change, lubrication, and so on
Addition to storage capacity	Replacement of tires or windshield
	Paint job

Treating a capital expenditure as an expense, or vice versa, creates an accounting error. Suppose a company makes a capital expenditure and expenses this cost. This is an accounting error because the cost should have been debited to an asset account. This error overstates expenses and understates net income. On the balance sheet, the Equipment account is understated. Capitalizing an expense creates the opposite error. Expenses are understated, and net income is overstated. The balance sheet overstates assets.

✔ Starter 10-3

- ☐ Cost of Plant Assets
- ■ Plant Asset Depreciation
- ☐ Accounting for Plant Assets
- ☐ Natural Resources
- ☐ Intangibles
- ☐ Ethical Issues

Measuring Plant Asset Depreciation

As we've seen previously, *depreciation* is the allocation of a plant asset's cost to expense over its useful life. Depreciation matches the asset's cost (expense) against the revenue earned by the asset. → Exhibit 10-4 shows depreciation for the purchase of a Boeing 737 jet by United Airlines.

Student Resource CD
accelerated depreciation, depreciation, double-declining balance, plant asset, straight-line depreciation, units-of-production

See Chapter 3, page 95, for a discussion of the matching principle.

Exhibit 10-4

Depreciation and the Matching of Expense with Revenue

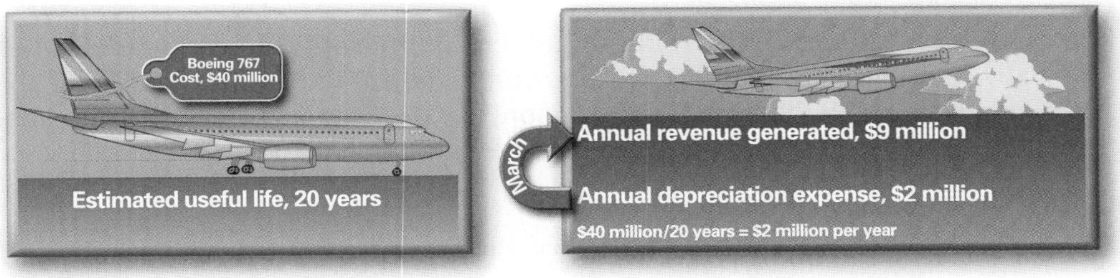

Suppose United Airlines buys a computer for use in its accounting system. United believes it will get four years of service from the computer, and it will then be worthless. Using the straight-line depreciation method, United expenses one-quarter of the asset's cost in each of its four years of use.

Let's contrast what depreciation is with what it is *not*.

1. *Depreciation is not a process of valuation*. Businesses do not record depreciation based on the market (sales) value of their plant assets.
2. *Depreciation does not mean that the business sets aside cash to replace an asset when it is used up*. Depreciation has nothing to do with establishing a cash fund.

Causes of Depreciation

All assets except land wear out. For some plant assets, *wear and tear* causes depreciation. For example, physical deterioration wears out the airplanes that American, Delta, and United fly. The store fixtures used to display merchandise in a Home Depot store are also subject to physical wear and tear.

Assets such as computers, software, and other electronic equipment may become *obsolete* before they wear out. An asset is obsolete when another asset can do the job more efficiently. Thus, an asset's useful life may be shorter than its physical life. Accountants usually depreciate computers over a short period—perhaps two to four years—even though the computers can continue working much longer. In all cases, the asset's cost is depreciated over its useful life.

Measuring Depreciation

Depreciation of a plant asset is based on three factors about an asset:

1. Cost 2. Estimated useful life 3. Estimated residual value

Cost is known. The other two factors are estimates.

Estimated Useful Life
Length of the service period expected from an asset. May be expressed in years, units of output, miles, or another measure.

Estimated Residual Value
Expected cash value of an asset at the end of its useful life. Also called **salvage value**.

Depreciable Cost
The cost of a plant asset minus its estimated residual value.

Estimated useful life is the length of the service period expected from the asset. Useful life may be expressed in years, units of output, miles, or another measure. For example, a building's life is stated in years, a bookbinding machine in the number of books it can bind, and a delivery truck in miles.

Estimated residual value—also called **salvage value**—is the expected cash value of an asset at the end of its useful life. A machine's useful life may be seven years. After seven years, the company expects to sell the machine as scrap metal. The expected cash receipt is the machine's estimated residual value. Estimated residual value is *not* depreciated because the business expects to receive this amount at the end. If there's no residual value, then the business depreciates the full cost of the asset. Cost minus residual value is called **depreciable cost**.

2 *Account for depreciation*

Depreciation Methods

Three major methods exist for computing depreciation:

- Straight-line
- Units-of-production
- Declining-balance

These methods allocate different amounts of depreciation to each period. But they all result in the same total depreciation for the asset. Exhibit 10-5 gives the data we will use to illustrate depreciation for an American Airlines baggage-handling truck. We cover the three most widely used methods.[1]

[1]We omit the sum-of-years'-digits method because only 7 of 600 companies in a recent poll used it.

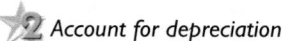

Exhibit 10-5

Data for Recording Depreciation on a Truck

Data Item	Amount
Cost of truck	$41,000
Less: Estimated residual value	(1,000)
Depreciable cost	$40,000
Estimated useful life:	
Years	5 years
Units of production	100,000 miles

STRAIGHT-LINE METHOD The **straight-line (SL) method** allocates an equal amount of depreciation to each year of asset use. Depreciable cost is divided by useful life in years to determine annual depreciation. The equation for SL depreciation, applied to the American Airlines truck from Exhibit 10-5, is

Straight-Line (SL) Depreciation Method
Depreciation method in which an equal amount of depreciation expense is assigned to each year of asset use.

$$\text{Straight-line depreciation} = \frac{\text{Cost} - \text{Residual value}}{\text{Useful life, in years}} = \frac{\$41{,}000 - \$1{,}000}{5}$$

$$= \$8{,}000 \text{ per year}$$

The entry to record each year's depreciation is

Depreciation Expense	8,000	
Accumulated Depreciation		8,000

This truck was purchased on January 1, 20X1, and a *straight-line depreciation schedule* is given in Exhibit 10-6. The final column in the exhibit shows the asset's *book value*, which is cost less accumulated depreciation. →

← We introduced book value in Chapter 3, page 101.

As an asset is used, accumulated depreciation increases and the asset's book value decreases. See the Accumulated Depreciation and Book Value columns in Exhibit 10-6. An asset's final book value is *residual value* ($1,000 in Exhibit 10-6). At the end, the asset is said to be *fully depreciated*.

Exhibit 10-6 **Straight-Line Depreciation for a Truck**

		Depreciation for the Year							
Date	Asset Cost	Depreciation Rate		Depreciable Cost		Depreciation Expense	Accumulated Depreciation	Book Value
1-1-20X1	$41,000							$41,000
12-31-20X1		0.20*	×	$40,000	=	$8,000	$ 8,000	33,000
12-31-20X2		0.20	×	40,000	=	8,000	16,000	25,000
12-31-20X3		0.20	×	40,000	=	8,000	24,000	17,000
12-31-20X4		0.20	×	40,000	=	8,000	32,000	9,000
12-31-20X5		0.20	×	40,000	=	8,000	40,000	1,000

* 1/5 year = 0.20 per year

Stop & Think

An asset with cost of $10,000, useful life of five years, and residual value of $2,000 was purchased on January 1. What is the SL depreciation for the first year? For the second year? For the fifth year?

Answer:

$$\text{SL depreciation} = \frac{\text{Cost} - \text{Residual value}}{\text{Useful life, in years}} = \frac{\$10{,}000 - \$2{,}000}{5}$$

$$= \$1{,}600 \text{ per year}$$ *every year*

Units-of-Production (UOP) Depreciation Method
Depreciation method by which a fixed amount of depreciation is assigned to each unit of output produced by an asset.

UNITS-OF-PRODUCTION (UOP) METHOD The **units-of-production (UOP) method** allocates a fixed amount of depreciation to each *unit of output* produced by the asset, as illustrated in Exhibit 10-7:

$$\text{Units-of-production depreciation per unit of output} = \frac{\text{Cost} - \text{Residual value}}{\text{Useful life, in units of production}} = \frac{\$41{,}000 - \$1{,}000}{100{,}000 \text{ miles}}$$

$$= \$0.40 \text{ per mile}$$

Assume that this truck is likely to be driven 20,000 miles the first year, 30,000 the second, 25,000 the third, 15,000 the fourth, and 10,000 during the fifth. The amount of UOP depreciation each period varies with the number of units the asset produces. Exhibit 10-7 shows the UOP schedule for this asset.

Exhibit 10-7 Units-of-Production Depreciation Schedule for a Truck

		Depreciation for the Year							
Date	Asset Cost	Depreciation Per Unit		Number of Units		Depreciation Expense	Accumulated Depreciation	Book Value
1-1-20X1	$41,000							$41,000
12-31-20X1		$0.40	×	20,000	=	$ 8,000	$ 8,000	33,000
12-31-20X2		0.40	×	30,000	=	12,000	20,000	21,000
12-31-20X3		0.40	×	25,000	=	10,000	30,000	11,000
12-31-20X4		0.40	×	15,000	=	6,000	36,000	5,000
12-31-20X5		0.40	×	10,000	=	4,000	40,000	1,000

Stop & Think

The asset in the preceding Stop & Think produced 3,000 units in the first year, 4,000 in the second, 4,500 in the third, 2,500 in the fourth, and 2,000 units in the last year. Its total estimated useful life is 16,000 miles. What is UOP depreciation for each year?

Answer:

$$\textbf{Depreciation per unit} = \frac{\textbf{Cost} - \textbf{Residual value}}{\textbf{Useful life, in units of production}} = \frac{\$10{,}000 - \$2{,}000}{16{,}000 \text{ miles}} = \$0.50 \text{ per mile}$$

Yr. 1: $1,500 (3,000 miles × $0.50)
Yr. 2: $2,000 (4,000 miles × $0.50)
Yr. 3: $2,250 (4,500 miles × $0.50)
Yr. 4: $1,250 (2,500 miles × $0.50)
Yr. 5: $1,000 (2,000 miles × $0.50)

Accelerated Depreciation Method
A depreciation method that writes off more of the asset's cost near the start of its useful life than the straight-line method does.

Double-Declining-Balance (DDB) Depreciation Method
An accelerated depreciation method that computes annual depreciation by multiplying the asset's decreasing book value by a constant percent that is two times the straight-line rate.

DOUBLE-DECLINING BALANCE METHOD Double-declining-balance depreciation is *accelerated*. An **accelerated depreciation method** writes off more depreciation near the start of an asset's life than the straight-line method does. The main accelerated depreciation method is **double-declining-balance (DDB)**. This method multiplies the asset's decreasing book value by a constant percentage that is 2 times the straight-line depreciation rate. DDB amounts can be computed in two steps:

1. Compute the straight-line depreciation rate per year. A 5-year asset has a straight-line rate of 1/5, or 20% per year. A 10-year asset has a straight-line rate of 1/10, or 10% per year, and so on.
   Multiply the straight-line rate by 2. The DDB rate for a 5-year asset is 40% per year (20% × 2 = 40%). For a 10-year asset, the DDB rate is 20% (10% × 2 = 20%).
2. Compute DDB depreciation for each year. Multiply the asset's book value (cost less accumulated depreciation) at the beginning of each year by the

DDB rate. Ignore residual value, except for the last year. The first-year depreciation for the truck in Exhibit 10-5 is

DDB depreciation for the first year	=	Asset book value at the beginning of the year	×	DDB rate
$16,400	=	$41,000	×	0.40

The same approach is used to compute DDB depreciation for all later years, except for the final year, as follows.

Final-year depreciation is the amount needed to bring the asset to its residual value. In the DDB schedule (Exhibit 10-8), final-year depreciation is $4,314—book value of $5,314 less the $1,000 residual value.

Exhibit 10-8 **Double-Declining-Balance Depreciation Schedule for a Truck**

		Depreciation for the Year						
Date	Asset Cost	DDB Rate		Book Value		Depreciation Expense	Accumulated Depreciation	Book Value
1-1-20X1	$41,000							$41,000
12-31-20X1		0.40	×	$41,000	=	$16,400	$16,400	24,600
12-31-20X2		0.40	×	24,600	=	9,840	26,240	14,760
12-31-20X3		0.40	×	14,760	=	5,904	32,144	8,856
12-31-20X4		0.40	×	8,856	=	3,542	35,686	5,314
12-31-20X5						4,314*	40,000	1,000

* Last-year depreciation is the amount needed to reduce book value to the residual amount ($5,314 – $1,000 = $4,314).

The DDB method differs from the other methods in two ways:

- Residual value is ignored at the start. In the first year, depreciation is computed on the asset's full cost.
- Final-year depreciation is the amount needed to bring the asset to residual value. Final-year depreciation is a "plug" figure.

Many companies change to the straight-line method during the next-to-last year of the asset's life. Let's use this plan to compute annual depreciation for 20X4 and 20X5. In Exhibit 10-8, book value at the end of 20X3 is $8,856, so depreciable cost is $7,856 after subtracting residual value of $1,000. Depreciable cost can be spread evenly over the last two years ($7,856 ÷ 2 remaining years = $3,928 per year).

Stop & Think

What is DDB depreciation for each year for the asset in the Stop & Think on page 405?

Answer: DDB rate = 1/5 × 2 = 40%

Yr. 1: $4,000 ($10,000 × 40%)
Yr. 2: $2,400 [($10,000 – $4,000 = $6,000) × 40%]
Yr. 3: $1,440 [($6,000 – $2,400 = $3,600) × 40%]
Yr. 4: $160 ($3,600 – $1,440 – $2,000*)

*Asset cost is not depreciated below residual value.

Comparing Depreciation Methods

Let's compare the depreciation methods we've just discussed. Annual amounts vary by method, but total depreciation is the same for all methods: $40,000.

✔ Starter 10-4

✔ Starter 10-5

Amount of Depreciation per Year			
			Accelerated Method
Year	Straight-Line	Units-of-Production	Double-Declining-Balance
1	$ 8,000	$ 8,000	$16,400
2	8,000	12,000	9,840
3	8,000	10,000	5,904
4	8,000	6,000	3,542
5	8,000	4,000	4,314
Total	$40,000	$40,000	$40,000

STRAIGHT-LINE Which method is best? That depends on the asset and the company's situation. A business should match an asset's expense against the revenue that the asset produces. For an asset that generates revenue evenly over time, the straight-line method follows the matching principle. Each period the asset is used, an equal amount of depreciation is recorded.

UNITS-OF-PRODUCTION The units-of-production method best fits an asset that depreciates due to wear and tear, rather than obsolescence. Depreciation is recorded only when the asset is used, and more use causes greater depreciation.

DOUBLE-DECLINING-BALANCE The accelerated method (DDB) works best for assets that produce more revenue in their early years. Higher depreciation in the early years is matched against those periods' greater revenue. This is the mark of an accelerated method.

COMPARISONS Exhibit 10-9 graphs annual depreciation for the three methods.

- The graph of straight-line depreciation is flat because annual depreciation is the same in all periods.
- Units-of-production depreciation follows no pattern because annual depreciation varies depending on the use of the asset.
- Accelerated depreciation is greater in the first year and less in the later years.

Exhibit 10-9

Depreciation Patterns for the Various Methods

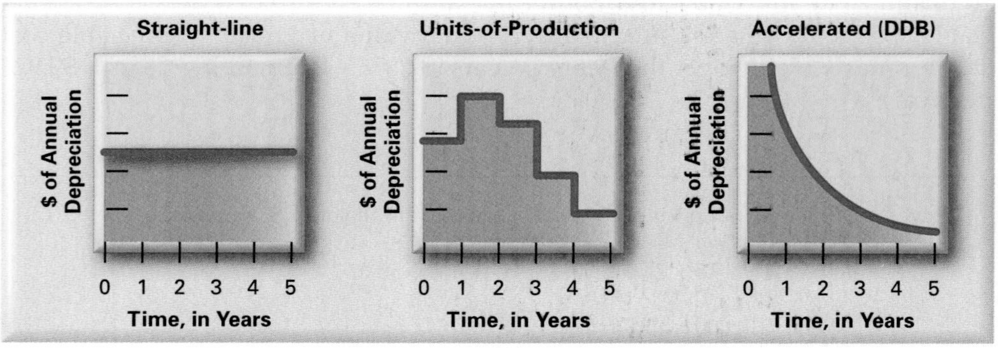

A recent survey of 600 companies, conducted by the American Institute of CPAs, indicated that the straight-line method is most popular. Exhibit 10-10 shows the percentages of companies that use each depreciation method.

Exhibit 10-10

Use of Depreciation Methods

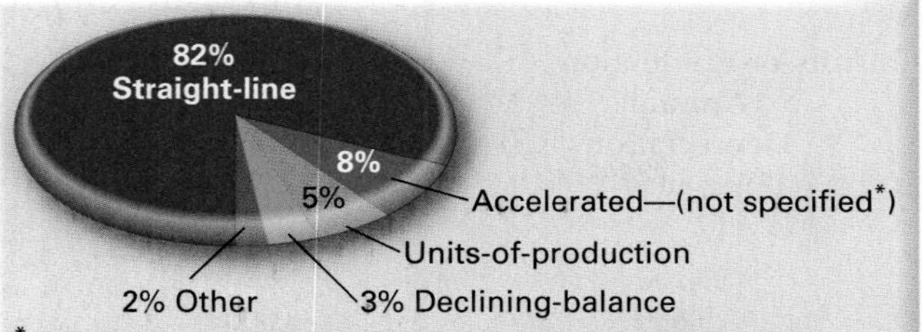

*Most of these are probably decling-balance methods because depreciation for income tax purposes is based on the declining-balance concept.

Source: Accounting Trends and Techniques

MID-CHAPTER *Summary Problem*

Quicker Copies purchased equipment on January 1, 20X5, for $44,000. Expected useful life is 10 years or 100,000 units of production, and residual value is $4,000. Under three depreciation methods, annual depreciation and total accumulated depreciation at the end of 20X5 and 20X6 are as follows:

A+ TIPS CHECK YOUR RESOURCES

	Method A		Method B		Method C	
Year	Annual Depreciation Expense	Accumulated Depreciation	Annual Depreciation Expense	Accumulated Depreciation	Annual Depreciation Expense	Accumulated Depreciation
20X5	$1,200	$1,200	$8,800	$ 8,800	$4,000	$4,000
20X6	5,600	6,800	7,040	15,840	4,000	8,000

Required

1. Identify the depreciation method used in each instance, and show the equation and computation for each. (Round amounts to the nearest dollar.)
2. Assume continued use of the same method through 20X7. Determine the annual depreciation expense, accumulated depreciation, and book value of the equipment for 20X5 through 20X7 under each method, assuming 12,000 units of production in 20X7.

Solution

Requirement 1

Method A: Units-of-Production

$$\text{Depreciation per unit} = \frac{\$44,000 - \$4,000}{100,000 \text{ units}} = \$0.40$$

20X5: $0.40 × 3,000 units = $1,200

20X6: $0.40 × 14,000 units = $5,600

Method B: Double-Declining-Balance

$$\text{Rate} = \frac{1}{10 \text{ years}} \times 2 = 10\% \times 2 = 20\%$$

20X5: 0.20 × $44,000 = $8,800

20X6: 0.20 × ($44,000 – $8,800) = $7,040

Method C: Straight-Line

Depreciable cost = $44,000 – $4,000 = $40,000

Each year: $40,000/10 years = $4,000

Requirement 2

Method A: Units-of-Production

Year	Annual Depreciation Expense	Accumulated Depreciation	Book Value
Start			$44,000
20X5	$1,200	$ 1,200	42,800
20X6	5,600	6,800	37,200
20X7	4,800	11,600	32,400

Method B: Double-Declining-Balance

Year	Annual Depreciation Expense	Accumulated Depreciation	Book Value
Start			$44,000
20X5	$8,800	$ 8,800	35,200
20X6	7,040	15,840	28,160
20X7	5,632	21,472	22,528

Method C: Straight-Line

Year	Annual Depreciation Expense	Accumulated Depreciation	Book Value
Start			$44,000
20X5	$4,000	$ 4,000	40,000
20X6	4,000	8,000	36,000
20X7	4,000	12,000	32,000

Computations for 20X7:

Units-of-production	$\$0.40 \times 12{,}000$ units = $4,800
Double-declining-balance	$0.20 \times \$28{,}160$ = $5,632
Straight-line	$40,000/10 years = $4,000

☐ Cost of Plant Assets
☐ Plant Asset Depreciation
■ Accounting for Plant Assets
☐ Natural Resources
☐ Intangibles
☐ Ethical Issues

Other Issues in Accounting for Plant Assets

Depreciation affects income taxes, and companies may have gains or losses when they sell plant assets.

Student ResourceCD
depreciation, plant asset, MACRS

3 *Select the best depreciation method for tax purposes*

Depreciation and Income Taxes

Most companies use straight-line depreciation for their financial statements. But they use a different depreciation method for income taxes. For tax purposes, most companies use an accelerated method.

Suppose you manage the United Airlines operation at Chicago's O'Hare airport. The IRS allows the DDB depreciation method, and you prefer accelerated to straight-line depreciation. Why? Because it provides the most depreciation expense as quickly as possible. The accelerated depreciation decreases your immediate tax payments and conserves your cash. You can then invest the cash and earn more income. This is a common strategy.

✔ **Starter 10-6**

To understand how depreciation affects cash flow, recall our earlier depreciation of the American Airlines truck: First-year depreciation is $8,000 under straight-line and $16,400 under double-declining-balance. Which tax deduction would you prefer? You would choose DDB depreciation because it gives you a greater tax deduction and saves cash.

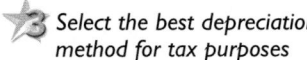

A special depreciation method called the *modified accelerated cost recovery system (MACRS)* is used for income tax purposes. Under MACRS, assets are divided into classes by asset life, as shown in Exhibit 10-11. MACRS depreciation is computed by the double-declining-balance method, the 150%-declining-balance method, or the straight-line method. Under 150% DB, the annual depreciation rate is computed by multiplying the straight-line rate by 1.50 (rather than by 2, as for DDB). For a 20-year asset, the straight-line rate is 0.05 (1/20 = 0.05), so the annual MACRS depreciation rate is 0.075 (0.05 × 1.50 = 0.075).

Exhibit 10-11

Selected Details of the Modified Accelerated Cost Recovery System (MACRS) Depreciation Method

Class Identified by Asset Life (Years)	Representative Assets	Depreciation Method
3	Racehorses	DDB
5	Automobiles, light trucks	DDB
10	Equipment	DDB
20	Certain real estate	150% DB
27 1/2	Residential rental property	SL
39	Nonresidential rental property	SL

Depreciation for Partial Years

Companies purchase plant assets whenever they need them. They don't wait until the beginning of a period. Therefore, companies develop policies to compute depreciation for partial years. Suppose Linens 'n Things purchases a building on *April 1* for $500,000. The building's estimated life is 20 years, with estimated residual value of $80,000. How does Linens 'n Things compute depreciation for the year ended December 31?

Many companies compute partial-year depreciation by first calculating a full year's depreciation. They then multiply full-year depreciation by the fraction of the year that they used the asset. Under the straight-line method, the year's depreciation for the Linens 'n Things building is $15,750, computed as follows:

Full-year depreciation: $\dfrac{\$500{,}000 - \$80{,}000}{20 \text{ years}} = \$21{,}000$

Partial-year depreciation: $\$21{,}000 \times 9/12 = \$15{,}750$

What if the company bought the asset on April 18? One policy is to record no depreciation on assets purchased after the 15th of the month. This policy also records a full month's depreciation on an asset bought on or before the 15th. In that case, the year's depreciation would be $14,000 for eight months ($21,000 × 8/12 = $14,000).

Partial-year depreciation is computed under the other depreciation methods in the same way—by applying the appropriate percentage of the year that the asset is used. Most companies use computerized systems to account for fixed assets. Such systems will automatically calculate the depreciation expense for each period.

✔ Starter 10-7

Changing the Useful Life of a Depreciable Asset

Estimating the useful life of a plant asset poses an accounting challenge. As the asset is used, the business may change its estimated useful life based on experience and new information. Walt Disney Company made such a change, called a *change in accounting estimate*. Disney refigured depreciation for theme-park assets. The following note in Disney's financial statements reports this change in accounting estimate:

Note 5

... [T]he Company extended the estimated useful lives of certain theme park ... assets based upon ... engineering studies. The effect of this change was to decrease depreciation by approximately $8 million. ...

Accounting changes like these are common because no one has perfect foresight. When a company makes an accounting change, generally accepted accounting principles require the business to report the nature, reason, and effect of the accounting change. The Disney example reports this information.

For a change in accounting estimate, the remaining book value of the asset is spread over the asset's remaining life. Assume that a Disney World hot dog stand cost $40,000. Suppose Disney originally believed the asset had an eight-year life with no residual value. Using the straight-line method, Disney would record depreciation of $5,000 each year ($40,000/8 years = $5,000).

Suppose Disney used the asset for two years. Accumulated depreciation reached $10,000. The asset's remaining depreciable book value (cost *less* accumulated depreciation *less* residual value) is $30,000 ($40,000 – $10,000). Suppose Disney management believes the hot dog stand will remain useful for 10 more years. The company would recompute depreciation as follows:

Asset's Remaining Depreciable Book Value	÷	(New) Estimated Useful Life Remaining	=	(New) Annual Depreciation
$30,000	÷	10 years	=	$3,000

✔ Starter 10-8

The yearly depreciation entry based on the new useful life is

Depreciation Expense—Hot Dog Stand.	3,000	
Accumulated Depreciation— Hot Dog Stand.		3,000

Revised straight-line depreciation is computed as follows:

$$\text{Revised SL depreciation} = \frac{\text{Cost} - \text{Accumulated depreciation} - \text{New residual value}}{\text{Estimated remaining useful life in years}}$$

Using Fully Depreciated Assets

A *fully depreciated asset* is one that has reached the end of its *estimated* useful life. No more depreciation is recorded for the asset. If the asset is no longer useful, it is disposed of. But the asset may still be useful, and the company may continue using this fully depreciated asset. The asset account and its accumulated depreciation remain on the books, but no additional depreciation is recorded.

Stop & Think

A fully depreciated asset has a cost of $80,000 and zero residual value. What is the asset's accumulated depreciation?

Answer: $80,000 (same as the asset's cost).

Now suppose the asset's residual value is $10,000. How much is accumulated depreciation?

Answer: $70,000 ($80,000 – $10,000).

4 *Account for the disposal of a plant asset*

Disposing of a Plant Asset

Eventually, an asset no longer serves its purpose. The asset may be worn out or obsolete. The owner may sell the asset or exchange it. If the asset cannot be sold or exchanged, then it is junked. Whatever the method of disposal, the business should bring depreciation up to date. That helps to measure the asset's final book value properly.

To record the disposal of a plant asset, credit the asset account and debit its accumulated depreciation. That removes the asset from the books. Suppose the final year's depreciation expense has just been recorded for a machine. Its cost was $6,000, and there is no residual value. The machine's accumulated depreciation thus totals $6,000. This asset cannot be sold or exchanged, so it is junked. The entry to record its disposal is

Accumulated Depreciation—Machinery . . .	6,000	
Machinery		6,000
To dispose of fully depreciated machine.		

Machinery

Debit	Credit
6,000	6,000

Accumulated Depreciation—Machinery

Debit	Credit
6,000	6,000

Now both accounts have a zero balance, as shown in the T-accounts at the right.

If assets are junked before being fully depreciated, the company records a loss equal to the asset's book value. Suppose Home Depot fixtures that cost $4,000 are junked at a loss. Accumulated depreciation is $3,000, and book value is therefore $1,000. Disposal of these store fixtures generates a loss, as follows:

Accumulated Depreciation—Store Fixtures	3,000	
Loss on Disposal of Store Fixtures	1,000	
Store Fixtures		4,000
To dispose of store fixtures.		

All losses, including this Loss on Disposal of Store Fixtures, decrease net income. Losses are reported along with expenses on the income statement.

SELLING A PLANT ASSET Suppose a Kinko's store sells furniture on September 30, 20X4, for $5,000 cash. The furniture cost $10,000 when purchased on January 1, 20X1, and has been depreciated on a straight-line basis. Kinko's estimated a 10-year life and no residual value. Prior to selling the furniture, Kinko's must update its depreciation. Partial-year depreciation must be recorded for nine months—from January 1, 20X4, to the sale date on September 30. The straight-line depreciation entry at September 30, 20X4, is

Sep. 30	Depreciation Expense ($10,000/10 years × 9/12). .	750	
	Accumulated Depreciation—Furniture . . .		750
	To update depreciation.		

Now the Furniture and the Accumulated Depreciation—Furniture accounts appear as follows.

Furniture

Debit		Credit
Jan. 1, 20X1	10,000	

Accumulated Depreciation—Furniture

Debit	Credit	
	Dec. 31, 20X1	1,000
	Dec. 31, 20X2	1,000
	Dec. 31, 20X3	1,000
	Sep. 30, 20X4	750
	Balance	3,750

Book Value = $6,250

Book value of the furniture is $6,250. Suppose Kinko's sells the furniture for $5,000 cash. The loss on the sale is $1,250, computed as follows:

Cash received from selling the asset		$5,000
Book value of asset sold:		
Cost	$10,000	
Less: Accumulated depreciation up to date of sale . . .	(3,750)	6,250
Gain (loss) on sale of the asset		($1,250)

Kinko's entry to sell the furniture is

Sep. 30 Cash	5,000	
Accumulated Depreciation—Furniture	3,750	
Loss on Sale of Furniture	1,250	
Furniture		10,000
To sell furniture.		

When recording the sale of a plant asset, the business must:

- Remove the balances in the asset account (Furniture, in this case) and its accumulated depreciation account
- Record a gain or loss if the cash received differs from the asset's book value.

In our example, cash of $5,000 is less than book value of $6,250. The result is a loss of $1,250.

If the sale price had been $7,000, Kinko's would have had a gain of $750 (Cash, $7,000 – asset book value, $6,250). The entry to record this gain would be

Sep. 30 Cash	7,000	
Accumulated Depreciation—Furniture	3,750	
Furniture		10,000
Gain on Sale of Furniture		750
To sell furniture.		

✔ Starter 10-9

A gain is recorded when an asset is sold for more than book value. A loss is recorded when the sale price is less than book value.

Gain (credit) = Sale proceeds > Book value

Loss (debit) = Sale proceeds < Book value

Gains increase net income, and losses decrease net income. All gains and losses are reported on the income statement.

Exchanging Plant Assets Businesses often exchange old plant assets for newer, more-efficient assets. The most common exchange transaction is a trade-in. For example, Domino's Pizza may trade in a five-year-old delivery car for a newer model. To record the exchange, Domino's must write off the old asset and its accumulated depreciation exactly as we just did for Kinko's disposal of furniture.

For most trade-ins, the business carries forward the book value of the old asset plus any cash payment as the cost of the new asset. For example, assume Domino's old delivery car cost $9,000 and has accumulated depreciation of $8,000. Book value is $1,000. Domino's trades in the old auto and pays cash of $10,000. Domino's records the trade-in with this journal entry:

Delivery Auto (new)	11,000	
Accumulated Depreciation (old)	8,000	
Delivery Auto (old)		9,000
Cash		10,000
Traded in old delivery car for new auto.		

Domino's cost of the new car is $11,000 (cash paid $10,000, plus the book value of the old auto, $1,000).

Accounting for Natural Resources

- ☐ Cost of Plant Assets
- ☐ Plant Asset Depreciation
- ☐ Accounting for Plant Assets
- ■ Natural Resources
- ☐ Intangibles
- ☐ Ethical Issues

Student Resource CD
depletion

5 *Account for natural resources*

Natural resources are plant assets. Examples include iron ore, oil, natural gas, and timber. Natural resources are like inventories in the ground (oil) or on top of the ground (timber). Natural resources are expensed through *depletion*. **Depletion expense** is that portion of the cost of natural resources that is used up in a particular period. Depletion expense is computed by the units-of-production formula:

$$\text{Depletion expense} = \frac{\text{Cost} - \text{Residual value}}{\text{Estimated total units of natural resource}} \times \text{Number of units removed}$$

Depletion Expense
Portion of a natural resource's cost used up in a particular period. Computed in the same way as units-of-production depreciation.

An oil well may cost $100,000 and hold 10,000 barrels of oil. Natural resources usually have no residual value. The depletion rate thus would be $10 per barrel ($100,000/10,000 barrels). If 3,000 barrels are extracted during the year, then depletion is $30,000 (3,000 barrels × $10 per barrel). The depletion entry for the year is

Depletion Expense (3,000 barrels × $10)	30,000	
Accumulated Depletion—Oil		30,000

If 4,500 barrels are removed next year, depletion is $45,000 (4,500 barrels × $10 per barrel).

Accumulated Depletion is a contra account similar to Accumulated Depreciation. Natural resources can be reported on the balance sheet as shown for oil in the following example:

Property, Plant, and Equipment:		
Land..........		$120,000
Buildings..........	$800,000	
Equipment	160,000	
	960,000	
Less: Accumulated depreciation..........	(410,000)	550,000
Oil..........	$380,000	
Less: Accumulated depletion..........	(80,000)	300,000
Property, plant, and equipment, net..........		$970,000

✔ Starter 10-10

Stop & Think

Ladue Paper Products pays $500,000 for land that holds 500,000 board feet of lumber. The land can be sold for $100,000 after the timber has been cut. If Ladue Paper harvests 200,000 board feet of lumber, how much depletion should be recorded?

Answer:

(Cost – Residual)	÷	Total output	=	Depletion rate	×	Production	=	Depletion
($500,000 – $100,000)	÷	500,000	=	$0.80 per foot	×	200,000	=	$160,000

Accounting for Intangible Assets

- ☐ Cost of Plant Assets
- ☐ Plant Asset Depreciation
- ☐ Accounting for Plant Assets
- ☐ Natural Resources
- ■ Intangibles
- ☐ Ethical Issues

Student Resource CD
amortization, goodwill, intangibles

6 *Account for intangible assets*

As we saw earlier in the chapter, *intangible assets* have no physical form. Instead, these assets convey special rights from patents, copyrights, trademarks, and so on.

In our technology-driven economy, intangibles rival tangible assets in value. Customer loyalty is all-important. Consider online pioneer eBay. The company has no physical products or equipment, but it helps people buy and sell everything from Batman toys to bathroom tiles. Each month eBay serves millions of customers. In a sense, eBay is a company of intangibles.

The intellectual capital of eBay or Intel is difficult to measure. But when one company buys another, we get a glimpse of the value of the acquired company. For example, America Online announced it would acquire Time Warner. AOL said it would give $146 billion of AOL stock for Time Warner's net tangible assets of only $9 billion. Why so much for so little? Because Time Warner's intangible assets were worth $190 billion. Intangibles can account for most of a company's market value, so companies are finding ways to value their intangibles, just as they do inventory and equipment.

A *patent* is an intangible asset that protects a secret process or formula. The acquisition cost of a patent is debited to the Patents account. The intangible is expensed through **amortization**, the systematic reduction of the asset's carrying value on the books. Amortization applies to intangibles exactly as depreciation applies to plant assets. Depreciation, depletion, and amortization are conceptually the same.

Amortization
Systematic reduction of the asset's carrying value on the books. Expense that applies to intangibles in the same way depreciation applies to plant assets and depletion to natural resources.

Amortization is computed over the asset's estimated useful life—usually by the straight-line method. Obsolescence often shortens an intangible's useful life. Amortization expense for an intangible asset can be written off directly against the asset account with no accumulated amortization account. The residual value of most intangibles is zero.

Some intangibles have indefinite lives. For them, the company records no systematic amortization each period. Instead, it accounts for any decrease in the value of the intangible, as we shall see for goodwill.

Specific Intangibles

Patent
A federal government grant giving the holder the exclusive right to produce and sell an invention for 20 years.

PATENTS A **patent** is a federal government grant conveying an exclusive 20-year right to produce and sell an invention. The invention may be a product or a process—for example, the Dolby noise-reduction process. Like any other asset, a patent may be purchased. Suppose General Electric Company (GE) pays $200,000 to acquire a patent on January 1. GE believes this patent's useful life is five years. Amortization expense is $40,000 per year ($200,000/5 years). Acquisition and amortization entries for this patent are

Jan. 1	Patents	200,000	
	Cash		200,000
	To acquire a patent.		
Dec. 31	Amortization Expense—Patents ($200,000/5)	40,000	
	Patents		40,000
	To amortize the cost of a patent.		

At the end of the first year, GE will report this patent at $160,000 ($200,000 minus the first year's amortization of $40,000), next year at $120,000, and so on.

Copyright
Exclusive right to reproduce and sell a book, musical composition, film, other work of art, or computer program. Issued by the federal government, copyrights extend 70 years beyond the author's life.

COPYRIGHTS A **copyright** is the exclusive right to reproduce and sell a book, musical composition, film, or other work of art or intellectual property. Copyrights also protect computer software programs, such as Microsoft Windows® and the Excel spreadsheet. Issued by the federal government, a copyright extends 70 years beyond the author's life.

A company may pay a large sum to purchase an existing copyright. For example, the publisher Simon & Schuster may pay $1 million for the copyright on a popular novel. Most copyrights have short useful lives.

Trademarks, Trade Names, or Brand Names
Assets that represent distinctive identifications of a product or service.

TRADEMARKS, BRAND NAMES **Trademarks** and **trade names** are assets that represent distinctive products or services, such as the CBS "eye" and

NBC's peacock. Legally protected slogans include Chevrolet's "Like a Rock" and Avis Rent A Car's "We try harder." The cost of a trademark or trade name is amortized over its useful life.

Franchises, Licenses Privileges granted by a private business or a government to sell a product or service under specified conditions.

FRANCHISES, LICENSES **Franchises** and **licenses** are privileges granted by a private business or a government to sell products or services under specified conditions. The Green Bay Packers football organization is a franchise granted by the National Football League. McDonald's restaurants and Holiday Inns are popular business franchises. The acquisition cost of a franchise or license is amortized over its useful life.

Goodwill Excess of the cost of an acquired company over the sum of the market values of its net assets (assets minus liabilities).

GOODWILL The term *goodwill* in accounting has a very different meaning from the everyday term, "goodwill among men." In accounting, **goodwill** is the excess of the cost to purchase another company over the market value of its net assets (assets minus liabilities).

Wal-Mart has expanded into Mexico. Suppose Wal-Mart acquired Mexana Company at a cost of $10 million. The sum of the market values of Mexana's assets was $9 million and its liabilities totaled $1 million, so Mexana's net assets totaled $8 million. In this case, Wal-Mart paid $2 million for goodwill, computed as follows:

Purchase price to acquire Mexana Company		$10 million
Market value of Mexana Company's assets	$ 9 million	
Less: Mexana Company's liabilities	(1 million)	
Market value of Mexana Company's net assets ...		8 million
Excess, called *goodwill*		$ 2 million

Wal-Mart's entry to record the purchase of Mexana Company, including the goodwill that Wal-Mart purchased, would be

Assets (Cash, Receivables, Inventories, Plant Assets, all at market value)......	9,000,000	
Goodwill	2,000,000	
Liabilities.......................		1,000,000
Cash		10,000,000
Purchased Mexana Company.		

Goodwill has some special features:

1. Goodwill is recorded only by a company that purchases another company. An outstanding reputation may create goodwill for a company, but that company never records goodwill for its own business. Instead, goodwill is recorded *only* by the acquiring entity when it buys another company.
2. According to generally accepted accounting principles (GAAP), goodwill is *not* amortized. Instead, the company measures the current value of its purchased goodwill each year. If the goodwill has increased in value, there is nothing to record. But if goodwill's value has decreased, then the company records a loss and writes the goodwill down. For example, suppose Wal-Mart's goodwill—purchased above—is worth only $1,500,000 at the end of the first year. In that case, Wal-Mart would make this entry:

✔ Starter 10-11

Loss on Goodwill	500,000	
Goodwill ($2,000,000 – $1,500,000) ..		500,000
Recorded loss on goodwill.		

Wal-Mart would then report this goodwill at its current value of $1,500,000.

Accounting.com

When Business Marriages Go Bust

Most partners enter a marriage with high expectations. It's the same with mergers and acquisitions (M&As). But in M&As, those expectations appear on a balance sheet in the form of *goodwill*, which is the excess of the cost to buy another company over the market value of its net assets. Accounting forces companies to measure their losses when M&As go sour.

The FASB used to require companies to write off goodwill evenly over a 40-year period (a process called *amortization*). Now the FASB requires companies to write goodwill down whenever it loses value. That means companies must revalue goodwill each year. Investors first saw the results of the new accounting rule at the start of 2002, when billions of dollars of goodwill evaporated. The huge write-offs reveal that many 1990s megamergers haven't lived up to expectations.

- **Qwest's** merger with **USWest** resulted in a $30 billion write-down.
- **America Online's** $54 billion write-down was an admission that its merger with **Time Warner** never lived up to the hype.

What effects do the huge write-offs have? Most analysts say goodwill write-offs hurt reported profits and depress stock prices. Others see them as one-time events that have little bearing on a company's future. For instance, the day after AOL's $54 billion write-off, the stock actually rose a little. Some companies will benefit from the rule change, for example, those who no longer have to record amortization. This new accounting rule might make companies think twice before getting hitched in the first place.

Based on: Joellen Perry, "The New Math of Mergers; Companies Are Writing Off the 'Goodwill' from Their Not-So-Good Deals," *U.S. News & World Report*, November 11, 2002, p. 40. Jeffrey Krasner, "Biotech Firms Wrestle with New Rules Accounting for Goodwill," *Boston Globe*, August 21, 2002, p. C1. Anne Tergesen, "How Much Is the Goodwill Worth? It Pays to Do the Math Before Your Stock Takes a Hit," *Business Week*, September 16, 2002, p. 83. Jonathan Weil, "Another Write-Off May Loom for AOL—Despite Stock's Recent Recovery, Investors Aren't Likely to Agree with Values Assigned to Assets," *The Wall Street Journal*, August 23, 2002, p. C1. Anonymous, "Qwest Sets Billions in Charges Related to Goodwill Value," *The Wall Street Journal*, October 29, 2002, p. A18.

Accounting for Research and Development Costs

✔ Starter 10-12

Accounting for research and development (R&D) costs is one of the toughest issues the accounting profession has faced. R&D is the lifeblood of companies such as **Procter & Gamble**, General Electric, Intel, and **Boeing** because it is vital to the development of new products and processes. But, in general, they do not report R&D assets on their balance sheets because GAAP requires companies to expense R&D costs as they incur those costs.

☐ Cost of Plant Assets
☐ Plant Asset Depreciation
☐ Accounting for Plant Assets
☐ Natural Resources
☐ Intangibles
■ Ethical Issues

Ethical Issues

The main ethical issue in accounting for plant assets is whether to capitalize or to expense a particular cost. In this area, companies have split personalities. On the one hand, they all want to save on taxes. This motivates them to expense all costs to decrease taxable income. But they also want to look as good as possible, with high net income and high amounts for assets.

In most cases, a cost that is capitalized or expensed for tax purposes must be treated the same way in the financial statements. What, then, is the ethical path? Accountants should follow the general guidelines for capitalizing a cost:

Capitalize all costs that provide a future benefit for the business, and expense all other costs, as outlined in the Decision Guidelines box that follows.

Many companies have gotten into trouble by capitalizing costs that were really expenses. They made their financial statements look better than the facts warranted. But there are very few cases of companies getting into trouble by following the general guidelines, or even by erring on the side of expensing questionable costs. This is another example of accounting conservatism. It works. →

← *We discussed accounting conservatism in Chapter 6, p. 258.*

Decision Guidelines

ACCOUNTING FOR PLANT ASSETS AND RELATED EXPENSES

Suppose you buy a **Curves International** franchise and invest in Nautilus and other fitness equipment. You have some decisions to make about how to account for the franchise and the equipment. The Decision Guidelines will help you maximize your cash flow and do the accounting properly.

Decision	Guidelines
Capitalize or expense a cost?	General rule: Capitalize all costs that provide *future benefit.* Expense all costs that provide *no future benefit.*
Capitalize or expense:	
• Cost associated with a new asset?	Capitalize all costs that bring the asset to its intended use.
• Cost associated with an existing asset?	Capitalize only those costs that add to the asset's usefulness or its useful life. Expense all other costs as maintenance or repairs.
Which depreciation method to use:	
• For financial reporting?	Use the method that best matches depreciation expense against the revenues produced by the asset.
• For income tax?	Use the method that produces the fastest tax deductions (MACRS). A company can use different depreciation methods for financial reporting and for income tax purposes. In the United States, this practice is considered both legal and ethical.

Excel Application Exercise

Goal: To create an Excel worksheet that calculates a proposed plant-asset investment's net income using different depreciation methods.

Scenario: Suppose the owner of the local **Curves International** franchise is considering investing in a new multistation weight machine. The following information is related to the acquisition and operation of the machine:

Initial investment	$100,000
Salvage value	$10,000
Useful life	6 years
Annual revenue attributable to the investment	$42,000
Annual operating expenses, excluding depreciation, associated with the investment	$14,000

The machine will be in use for 2,880 hours in year one; 2,550 hours each in years two and four; 2,190 hours in year five; and 1,460 hours each in years three and six.

When finished with your worksheet, answer these questions:

1. Which depreciation method produces the highest net income in year 1? In year 6? If it's not the same method for each year, why not?
2. Which method would Curves choose for tax purposes? Why?
3. Which method would Curves choose for reporting to bankers and creditors? Why? What if the company wanted to change methods after two years?

Step-by-Step:

1. Open a new Excel worksheet.
2. Prepare a bold-faced heading with the following information:
   a. Chapter 10 Excel Application Exercise
   b. Curves Depreciation Schedule
   c. Today's Date

Excel Application Exercise *(continued)*

3. Two rows under your heading, prepare four sections in your worksheet:

   Section 1 needs to contain the information listed in the table above, plus a line item for depreciation per unit.

   Section 2 will calculate net income from the investment using straight-line depreciation calculated using the SLN spreadsheet function. This section will have the following format:

   Section 2 Straight-Line Depreciation

	Year 0	1	2	3	4	5	6
Revenue							
Expenses							
Depreciation							
Net income							

   Section 3 will calculate net income from the investment using double-declining-balance depreciation (calculated using the DDB spreadsheet function). This section will have a format like that of Section 2.

   Section 4 will calculate net income from the investment using units-of-production depreciation (there is no Excel formula for this method). This section will have a format like that of Section 2, with the addition of a row for the annual units of production.

4. Format all cells appropriately, save your worksheet, and print a copy for your files.

END-OF-CHAPTER *Summary Problem*

A+ TIPS
CHECK YOUR RESOURCES

The following figures appear in the Answers to the Mid-Chapter Summary Problem, requirement 2, on page 410.

	Method B: Double-Declining-Balance			Method C: Straight-Line		
Year	Annual Depreciation Expense	Accumulated Depreciation	Book Value	Annual Depreciation Expense	Accumulated Depreciation	Book Value
Start			$44,000			$44,000
20X5	$8,800	$ 8,800	35,200	$4,000	$ 4,000	40,000
20X6	7,040	15,840	28,160	4,000	8,000	36,000
20X7	5,632	21,472	22,528	4,000	12,000	32,000

Quicker Copies purchased equipment on January 1, 20X5. Management has depreciated the equipment by using the double-declining-balance method. On July 1, 20X7, the company sold the equipment for $27,000 cash.

Required

1. Suppose the income tax authorities permit a choice between the two depreciation methods shown. Which method would you select for income tax purposes? Why?
2. Record Quicker Copies' depreciation for 20X7 and the sale of the equipment on July 1, 20X7.

Solution

Requirement 1

For tax purposes, most companies select the accelerated method because it results in the most depreciation in the earliest years of the equipment's life. Accelerated depreciation minimizes taxable income and income tax payments in the early years of the asset's life, thereby maximizing the business's cash at the earliest possible time.

Requirement 2

To record depreciation to date of sale and sale of Quicker Copies' equipment:

		Debit	Credit
20X7			
July 1	Depreciation Expense—Equipment ($5,632 × 1/2 year)	2,816	
	Accumulated Depreciation—Equipment		2,816
	To update depreciation.		
July 1	Cash	27,000	
	Accumulated Depreciation—Equipment ($15,840 + $2,816)	18,656	
	Equipment		44,000
	Gain on Sale of Equipment		1,656
	To record sale of equipment.		

REVIEW *Plant Assets and Intangibles*

Quick Check

1. Which cost is not recorded as part of the cost of a building?
   a. Construction materials and labor
   b. Annual building maintenance
   c. Real Estate commission paid to buy the building
   d. Earth-moving for the building's foundation
2. **FedEx** bought two used **Boeing** 707 airplanes. Each plane was worth $35 million, but the owner sold the combination for $60 million. How much is FedEx's cost of each plane?
   a. $30 million
   b. $35 million
   c. $60 million
   d. $70 million
3. How should you record a capital expenditure?
   a. Debit capital
   b. Debit an expense
   c. Debit a liability
   d. Debit an asset
4. Which depreciation method always produces the most depreciation in the first year?
   a. Straight-line
   b. Units-of-production
   c. Double-declining-balance
   d. All produce the same total depreciation
5. A FedEx airplane costs $50 million and is expected to fly 500 million miles during its 10-year life. Residual value is expected to be zero because the plane was used when acquired. If the plane travels 20 million miles the first year, how much depreciation should FedEx record under the units-of-production method?
   a. $2 million
   b. $5 million
   c. $10 million
   d. Cannot be determined from the data given
6. Which depreciation method would you prefer to use for income tax purposes? Why?
   a. Straight-line because it is simplest
   b. Units-of-production because it best tracks the asset's use
   c. Double-declining-balance because it gives the most total depreciation over the asset's life
   d. Double-declining-balance because it gives the fastest tax deductions for depreciation
7. A copy machine cost $40,000 when new and has accumulated depreciation of $37,000. Suppose **Kinko's** junks this machine, receiving nothing. What is the result of the disposal transaction?
   a. Gain of $3,000
   b. Loss of $3,000
   c. Gain of $37,000
   d. Loss of $40,000

8. Suppose Kinko's in the preceding question sold the machine for $5,000. What is the result of this disposal transaction?
   a. Gain of $2,000
   b. Loss of $2,000
   c. Gain of $3,000
   d. Gain of $5,000
9. Which method is used to compute depletion?
   a. Depletion method
   b. Straight-line method
   c. Units-of-production method
   d. Double-declining-balance method
10. Which intangible asset is recorded only as part of the acquisition of another company?
    a. Copyright
    b. Patent
    c. Franchise
    d. Goodwill

Accounting Vocabulary

accelerated depreciation method (p. 406)
amortization (p. 416)
brand names (p. 416)
capital expenditure (p. 403)
copyright (p. 416)
depletion expense (p. 415)
depreciable cost (p. 404)
double-declining-balance (DDB) depreciation method (p. 406)
estimated residual value (p. 404)
estimated useful life (p. 404)
extraordinary repair (p. 403)
franchises (p. 417)
goodwill (p. 417)
intangibles (p. 400)
licenses (p. 417)
ordinary repair (p. 403)
patent (p. 416)
plant assets (p. 400)
salvage value (p. 404)
straight-line (SL) depreciation method (p. 405)
trademark (p. 416)
trade name (p. 416)
units-of-production (UOP) depreciation method (p. 406)

ASSESS *Your Progress*

A+ online homework

See *www.prenhall.com/horngren* for selected Starters, Exercises, and Problems.

Starters

Measuring the cost of a plant asset
(Obj. 1)

S10-1 Page 401 of this chapter lists the costs included for the acquisition of land. First is the purchase price of the land, which is obviously included in the cost of the land. The reasons for including the other costs are not so obvious. For example, the removal of a building looks more like an expense. State why the costs listed are included as part of the cost of the land. After the land is ready for use, will these costs be capitalized or expensed?

Lump-sum purchase of assets
(Obj. 1)

S10-2 Return to the Stop & Think feature on page 402. Suppose at the time of your acquisition, the land has a current market value of $80,000, the building's market value is $60,000, and the equipment's market value is $20,000. Journalize the lump-sum purchase of the three assets for a total cost of $120,000. You sign a note payable for this amount.

Capitalizing versus expensing plant-asset costs
(Obj. 1)

S10-3 JetQuick Airways repaired one of its **Boeing** 767 aircraft at a cost of $800,000, which JetQuick paid in cash. JetQuick erroneously capitalized this cost as part of the cost of the plane.

1. Journalize both the incorrect entry the accountant made to record this transaction and the correct entry that the accountant should have made.
2. How will this accounting error affect JetQuick's net income? Ignore depreciation.

Computing depreciation by three methods—first year only
(Obj. 2)

S10-4 At the beginning of the year, JetQuick Airways purchased a used **Boeing** aircraft at a cost of $42,000,000. JetQuick expects the plane to remain useful for five years (6 million miles) and to have a residual value of $6,000,000. JetQuick expects the plane to be flown 750,000 miles the first year.

1. Compute JetQuick's first-year depreciation on the plane using the following methods:
   a. Straight-line
   b. Units-of-production
   c. Double-declining-balance
2. Show the airplane's book value at the end of the first year under the straight-line method.

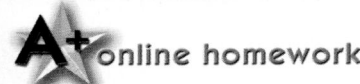

S10-5 At the beginning of 20X1, JetQuick Airways purchased a used **Boeing** aircraft at a cost of $42,000,000. JetQuick expects the plane to remain useful for five years (6 million miles) and to have a residual value of $6,000,000. JetQuick expects the plane to be flown 750,000 miles the first year and 1.5 million miles the second year. Compute second-year depreciation on the plane using the following methods:

Computing depreciation by three methods—second year **(Obj. 2)**

a. Straight-line **b.** Units-of-production **c.** Double-declining-balance

S10-6 This exercise uses the JetQuick Airways data from Starter 10-4. JetQuick is deciding which depreciation method to use for income tax purposes.

Selecting the best depreciation method for income tax purposes **(Obj. 3)**

1. Which depreciation method offers the tax advantage for the first year? Describe the nature of the tax advantage.
2. How much extra depreciation will JetQuick get to deduct for the first year as compared with using the straight-line method?

S10-7 On March 31, 20X2, JetQuick Airways purchased a used **Boeing** aircraft at a cost of $42,000,000. JetQuick expects to fly the plane for five years and to have a residual value of $6,000,000. Compute JetQuick's depreciation on the plane for the year ended December 31, 20X2, using the straight-line method.

Partial-year depreciation **(Obj. 2)**

S10-8 Return to the example of the **Disney World** hot dog stand on pages 411–412. Suppose that after using the hot dog stand for four years, the company determines that the asset will remain useful for only two more years. Record Disney's depreciation on the hot dog stand for year 5 by the straight-line method.

Computing and recording depreciation after a change in useful life **(Obj. 2)**

S10-9 Return to the **American Airlines** baggage-handling truck in Exhibits 10-6 and 10-8. Suppose American sold the truck on December 31, 20X2, for $28,000 cash, after using the truck for two full years. Depreciation for 20X2 has already been recorded. Make the journal entry to record American's sale of the truck under straight-line depreciation (Exhibit 10-6).

Recording a gain or loss on disposal under two depreciation methods **(Obj. 4)**

S10-10 **Chevron**, the giant oil company, holds huge reserves of oil and gas assets. Assume that at the end of 20X6, Chevron's cost of mineral assets totaled approximately $18 billion, representing 2.4 billion barrels of oil and gas reserves in the ground.

Accounting for the depletion of natural resources **(Obj. 5)**

1. Which depreciation method does Chevron use to compute its annual depletion expense for the minerals removed from the ground?
2. Suppose Chevron removed 0.8 billion barrels of oil during 20X7. Record Chevron's depletion expense for 20X7.

S10-11 Media-related companies have little in the way of tangible plant assets. Instead, their main asset is goodwill. When one media company buys another, goodwill is often the most costly asset acquired. Media Watch paid $700,000 to acquire *The Thrifty Nickel*, a weekly advertising paper. At the time of the acquisition, *The Thrifty Nickel's* balance sheet reported total assets of $1,200,000 and liabilities of $600,000. The fair market value of *The Thrifty Nickel's* assets was $800,000.

Accounting for goodwill **(Obj. 6)**

1. How much goodwill did Media Watch purchase as part of the acquisition of *The Thrifty Nickel?*
2. Journalize Media Watch's acquisition of *The Thrifty Nickel.*

S10-12 This exercise summarizes the accounting for patents and research and development costs.

Accounting for patents and research and development cost **(Obj. 6)**

Questor Applications paid $800,000 to research and develop a new software program. Questor also paid $500,000 to acquire a patent on other software. After readying the software for production, Questor's sales revenue for the first year totaled $1,700,000. Cost of goods sold was $200,000, and selling expenses were $400,000. All these transactions occurred during 20X5. Questor expects the patent to have a useful life of five years. Prepare Questor Applications' income statement for the year ended December 31, 20X5, complete with a heading.

Exercises

A+ online homework

Determining the cost of plant assets
(Obj. 1)

E10-1 Lone Star Lighting Systems purchased land, paying $80,000 cash as a down payment and signing a $120,000 note payable for the balance. In addition, Lone Star paid delinquent property tax of $2,100, title insurance costing $2,500, and a $5,400 charge for leveling the land and removing an unwanted building. The company constructed an office building on the land at a cost of $800,000. It also paid $51,000 for a fence around the property, $10,400 for the company sign near the entrance, and $6,000 for special lighting of the grounds. Determine the cost of the company's land, land improvements, and building. Which of the assets will Lone Star depreciate?

Measuring the cost of an asset
(Obj. 1)

E10-2 Dicorte Brothers manufactures conveyor belts. Early in January 20X7, Dicorte constructed its own building with borrowed money. The 6% loan was for $900,000. During the year, Dicorte spent the loan amount on construction of the building. At year-end, Dicorte paid the interest for one year.

Required

1. How much should Dicorte record as the cost of the building in 20X7?
2. Record all of Dicorte's transactions during 20X7.

Allocating cost to assets acquired in a lump-sum purchase
(Obj. 1)

E10-3 Perry's Tanning Salon bought three tanning beds in a $10,000 lump-sum purchase. An independent appraiser valued the tanning beds as follows:

Tanning Bed	Appraised Value
1	$3,000
2	5,000
3	4,000

Perry's paid $5,000 in cash and signed a note payable for $5,000. Record the purchase in the journal, identifying each tanning bed's cost in a separate Tanning Bed account. Round decimals to three places.

Distinguishing capital expenditures from expenses
(Obj. 1)

E10-4 Classify each of the following expenditures as a capital expenditure or an expense related to machinery: (a) purchase price; (b) ordinary recurring repairs to keep the machinery in good working order; (c) lubrication of the machinery before it is placed in service; (d) periodic lubrication after the machinery is placed in service; (e) major overhaul to extend useful life by three years; (f) sales tax paid on the purchase price; (g) transportation and insurance while machinery is in transit from seller to buyer; (h) installation; (i) training of personnel for initial operation of the machinery; and (j) income tax paid on income earned from the sale of products manufactured by the machinery.

Explaining the concept of depreciation
(Obj. 2)

E10-5 Jessica Brooks has just slept through the class in which Professor Dominguez explained the concept of depreciation. Because the next test is scheduled for Wednesday, Brooks telephones Hanna Svensen to get her notes from the lecture. Svensen's notes are concise: "Depreciation—Sounds like Greek to me." Brooks next tries Tim Lake, who says he thinks depreciation is what happens when an asset wears out. David Coe is confident that depreciation is the process of building up a cash fund to replace an asset at the end of its useful life. Explain the concept of depreciation for Brooks. Evaluate the explanations of Lake and Coe. Be specific.

Determining depreciation amounts by three methods
(Obj. 2, 3)

Student Resource CD
spreadsheet

E10-6 Providence Medical Center bought equipment on January 2, 20X6, for $15,000. The equipment was expected to remain in service four years and to perform 1,000 operations. At the end of the equipment's useful life, Providence estimates that its residual value will be $3,000. The equipment performed 100 operations the first year, 300 the second year, 400 the third year, and 200 the fourth year. Prepare a schedule of *depreciation expense* per year for the equipment under the three depreciation methods.

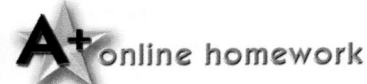

After two years under double-declining-balance depreciation, the company switched to the straight-line method. Show your computations.

Which method tracks the wear and tear on the equipment most closely? Which method would Providence prefer to use for income-tax purposes? Explain in detail why a taxpayer prefers this method.

E10-7 Jazzy Power Chair Co. paid $165,000 for equipment that is expected to have a seven-year life. The residual value of equipment is 10% of the asset's cost.

Selecting the best depreciation method for income tax purposes
(Obj. 3)

Select the appropriate MACRS depreciation method for income tax purposes. Then determine the extra amount of depreciation that Jazzy Power Chair Co. can deduct by using MACRS depreciation, versus straight-line, during the first two years of the equipment's life.

E10-8 Stagecoach Van Lines purchased a building for $700,000 and depreciated it on a straight-line basis over a 40-year period. The estimated residual value was $100,000. After using the building for 15 years, Stagecoach realized that wear and tear on the building would force the company to replace it before 40 years. Starting with the 16th year, Stagecoach began depreciating the building over a revised total life of 30 years and increased the estimated residual value to $175,000. Record depreciation expense on the building for years 15 and 16.

Changing a plant asset's useful life
(Obj. 2)

E10-9 On January 2, 20X6, Amy's Party Supplies purchased showroom fixtures for $10,000 cash, expecting the fixtures to remain in service five years. Amy's has depreciated the fixtures on a double-declining-balance basis, with zero residual value. On September 30, 20X7, Amy's sold the fixtures for $5,000 cash. Record both the depreciation expense on the fixtures for 20X7 and the sale of the fixtures on September 30, 20X7.

Analyzing the sale of a plant asset; DDB depreciation
(Obj. 4)

E10-10 J. B. Hunt is a large trucking company. Hunt uses the units-of-production (UOP) method to depreciate trucks because UOP depreciation best measures wear and tear. Hunt trades in used trucks often to keep driver morale high and to maximize fuel efficiency. Consider these facts about one Mack truck in the company's fleet.

Measuring a plant asset's cost, using UOP depreciation, and trading in an asset
(Obj. 1, 2, 4)

When acquired in 20X1, the tractor/trailer rig cost $350,000 and was expected to remain in service for 10 years or 1,000,000 miles. Estimated residual value was $100,000. The truck was driven 80,000 miles in 20X1, 120,000 miles in 20X2, and 160,000 miles in 20X3. After 40,000 miles in 20X4, the company traded in the Mack truck for a less-expensive Freightliner. Hunt paid cash of $50,000. Determine Hunt's cost of the new truck. Journal entries are not required.

E10-11 Tesoro Mining paid $398,500 for the right to extract mineral assets from a 200,000-ton mineral deposit. In addition to the purchase price, Tesoro also paid a $500 filing fee, a $1,000 license fee to the state of Colorado, and $60,000 for a geological survey of the property. Because the company purchased the rights to the minerals only, the company expected the asset to have zero residual value when fully depleted. During the first year, Tesoro removed 40,000 tons of the minerals. Make journal entries to record (a) purchase of the minerals (debit Mineral Asset), (b) payment of fees and other costs, and (c) depletion for the first year.

Recording natural resource assets and depletion
(Obj. 5)

E10-12 *Part 1.* Advantage Press manufactures high-speed printers. Advantage recently paid $1 million for a patent on a new laser printer. Although it gives legal protection for 20 years, the patent is expected to provide a competitive advantage for only 8 years. Assuming the straight-line method of amortization, make journal entries to record (a) the purchase of the patent and (b) amortization for year 1.

Recording a patent, amortization, and a change in the asset's useful life
(Obj. 6)

Part 2. After using the patent for 4 years, Advantage learns at an industry trade show that another company is designing a more-efficient printer. On the basis of this new information, Advantage decides, starting with year 5, to amortize the remaining cost of the patent over 2 remaining years, giving the patent a total useful life of 6 years. Record amortization for year 5.

Measuring and recording goodwill
(Obj. 6)

E10-13 **PepsiCo, Inc.**, has aggressively acquired other companies. Assume that PepsiCo purchased Kettle Chips Co. for $11 million cash. The market value of Kettle Chips' assets is $15 million, and it has liabilities of $10 million.

Required

1. Compute the cost of the goodwill purchased by PepsiCo.
2. Record the purchase of Kettle Chips by PepsiCo.

Capitalizing versus expensing costs; measuring the effect of an error
(Obj. 1)

E10-14 Papillon is a catalog merchant in France similar to **Lands' End** in the United States. Papillon uses automated shipping equipment. Assume that early in year 1, Papillon purchased equipment at a cost of 5 million euros (€5 million). Management expects the equipment to remain in service five years, with zero residual value. Papillon uses the straight-line depreciation method. Through an accounting error, Papillon accidentally expensed the entire cost of the equipment at the time of purchase.

Required

Prepare a schedule to show the overstatement or understatement in the following items at the end of each year over the five-year life of the equipment.

1. Equipment, net
2. Net income

Recording the sale of plant assets
(Obj. 2, 4)

E10-15 Assume that **General Motors Corporation's** comparative balance sheet reported these amounts:

	(In millions) December 31 20X2	20X1
Property:		
Land, plant, and equipment	$ 59,777	$ 59,565
Less accumulated depreciation	(34,363)	(34,641)
Net land, plant, and equipment	25,414	24,924

Required

Assume that on January 2, 20X3, GM sold 1/10 of its land, plant, and equipment for $3,000 million. Journalize this transaction for GM. Round to the nearest $1 million.

Problems

A+ online homework

(Group A)

Identifying the elements of a plant asset's cost
(Obj. 1, 2)

P10-1A Triumph Motorcycles incurred the following costs in acquiring land, making land improvements, and constructing and furnishing a new building.

a.	Purchase price of four acres of land	$200,000
b.	Landscaping (additional dirt and earthmoving)	8,100
c.	Fence around the boundary of the property	17,600
d.	Attorney fee for title search on the land	1,000
e.	Delinquent real estate taxes on the land to be paid by Triumph	5,900
f.	Company signs at front of the property	4,400
g.	Building permit for the building	500
h.	Architect's fee for the design of the building	22,500
i.	Labor to construct the building	709,000
j.	Materials used to construct the building	215,000
k.	Interest cost on construction loan for the building	9,000
l.	Landscaping (trees and shrubs)	6,400
m.	Parking lot and concrete walks	29,700
n.	Lights for the parking lot and walkways	10,300
o.	Salary of construction supervisor (85% to building; 15% to parking lot and concrete walks)	40,000
p.	Furniture for the building	107,100
q.	Transportation and installation of furniture	2,200

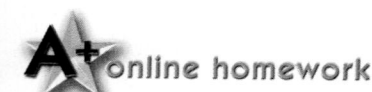

Triumph depreciates buildings over 40 years, land improvements over 20 years, and furniture over 8 years, all on a straight-line basis with zero residual value.

Required

1. Set up columns for Land, Land Improvements, Building, and Furniture. Show how to account for each cost by listing the cost under the correct account. Determine the total cost of each asset.
2. All construction was complete and the assets were placed in service on May 1. Record partial-year depreciation for the year ended December 31. Round to the nearest dollar.

Recording plant-asset transactions, exchange, and disposal
(Obj. 1, 2, 4)

Student Resource CD
General Ledger, Peachtree, QuickBooks

P10-2A Nelson Lewis provides freight service in Missouri, Kansas, and Illinois. The company's balance sheet includes Land, Buildings, and Motor-Carrier Equipment. Lewis has a separate accumulated depreciation account for each depreciable asset. During 20X7, Lewis completed the following transactions:

Jan.	1	Traded in motor-carrier equipment with accumulated depreciation of $90,000 (cost of $130,000) for similar new equipment with a cash cost of $176,000. Lewis received a trade-in allowance of $70,000 on the old equipment and paid the remainder in cash.
July	1	Sold a building that cost $550,000 and that had accumulated depreciation of $250,000 through December 31 of the preceding year. Depreciation is computed on a straight-line basis. The building has a 40-year useful life and a residual value of $50,000. Lewis received $100,000 cash and a $600,000 note receivable.
Oct.	31	Purchased land and a building for a cash payment of $300,000. An independent appraisal valued the land at $115,000 and the building at $230,000.
Dec.	31	Recorded depreciation as follows: Motor-carrier equipment has an expected useful life of 1,000,000 miles and an estimated residual value of $26,000. Depreciation is units-of-production. During the year, Lewis drove his truck 150,000 miles. Depreciation on buildings is straight-line. The new building has a 40-year useful life and a residual value equal to $20,000.

Required

Record the transactions in Nelson Lewis's journal.

Explaining the concept of depreciation
(Obj. 2)

P10-3A The board of directors of Ink Jet Products is reviewing the 20X6 annual report. A new board member—a professor—questions the company accountant about the depreciation amounts. The professor wonders why depreciation expense has decreased from $200,000 in 20X4 to $184,000 in 20X5 to $172,000 in 20X6. She states that she could understand the decreasing annual amounts if the company had been selling properties each year, but that has not occurred. Further, growth in the city is increasing the values of property. Why is the company recording depreciation when property values are increasing?

Required

Write a paragraph or two to explain the concept of depreciation and answer the professor's questions. Which depreciation method does Ink Jet Products appear to be using?

Computing depreciation by three methods and the advantage of accelerated depreciation for tax purposes
(Obj. 2, 3)

Student Resource CD
spreadsheet

P10-4A On January 3, 20X4, Tim Flanagan, Inc., paid $224,000 for equipment used in manufacturing automotive supplies. In addition to the basic purchase price, the company paid $700 transportation charges, $100 insurance for the equipment while in transit, $12,100 sales tax, and $3,100 for a special platform on which to place the equipment in the plant. Flanagan management estimates that the equipment will remain in service five years and have a residual value of $20,000. The equipment will produce 50,000 units the first year, with annual production decreasing by 5,000 units during each of the next four years (that is, 45,000 units in year 2; 40,000 units in year 3; and so on—a total of 200,000 units). In trying to decide which depreciation method to use, Flanagan has requested a depreciation schedule for each of three depreciation methods (straight-line, units-of-production, and double-declining-balance).

Required

1. For each depreciation method, prepare a depreciation schedule showing asset cost, depreciation expense, accumulated depreciation, and asset book value. For the units-of-production method, round depreciation per unit to three decimal places.
2. Flanagan prepares financial statements using the depreciation method that reports the highest income in the early years of asset use. For income tax purposes, the company uses the depreciation method that minimizes income taxes in the early years. Consider the first year Flanagan uses the equipment. Identify the depreciation methods that meet Flanagan's objectives, assuming the income tax authorities permit the use of any of the methods.

Accounting for intangibles, natural resources, and the related expenses
(Obj. 5, 6)

P10-5A *Part 1.* **Collins Foods International, Inc.**, is the majority owner of Sizzler Restaurants. Collins' balance sheet reports goodwill. Assume that Collins purchased this goodwill as part of the acquisition of another company, which carried these figures:

Book value of assets	$2.4 million
Market value of assets	2.7 million
Liabilities	2.2 million

Required

1. Make the journal entry to record Collins's purchase of the other company for $3.0 million cash.
2. How should Collins account for this goodwill after acquiring the other company? Explain in detail.

Part 2. **Georgia-Pacific's** balance sheet includes three assets: Natural Gas; Oil; and Coal. Suppose Georgia-Pacific paid $2.8 million cash for the right to work a mine with an estimated 100,000 tons of coal. Assume the company paid $60,000 to remove unwanted buildings from the land and $45,000 to prepare the surface for mining. Further, assume that Georgia-Pacific signed a $30,000 note payable to a company that will return the land surface to its original condition after the mining ends. During the first year, Georgia-Pacific removed 40,000 tons of coal, which it sold on account for $39 per ton. Operating expenses for the first year totaled $252,000, all paid in cash.

Required

1. Record all of Georgia-Pacific's transactions, including depletion, for the year.
2. Prepare the company's income statement for its coal operations for the year.

Reporting plant-asset transactions in the financial statements—a review
(Obj. 1, 2, 4)

P10-6A At the end of 2002, **The Coca-Cola Company** had total assets of $24.5 billion and total liabilities of $12.7 billion. Included among the assets were property, plant, and equipment with a cost of $9.0 billion and accumulated depreciation of $3.1 billion. During 2002, Coca-Cola earned total revenues of $20.2 billion and had total expenses of $17.1 billion.

Required

1. Show how Coca-Cola reported property, plant, and equipment on its balance sheet at December 31, 2002. What was the book value of property, plant, and equipment on that date?
2. How much was Coca-Cola's owners' equity at December 31, 2002?
3. Did Coca-Cola report net income or net loss on its 2002 income statement? Compute the amount.

Problems

(Group B)

A+ online homework

Identifying the elements of a plant asset's cost
(Obj. 1, 2)

P10-1B Carmel Apartments incurred the following costs to acquire land, make land improvements, and construct and furnish an apartment building:

a.	Purchase price of 3 acres of land	$150,000
b.	Delinquent real estate taxes on the land to be paid by Carmel	3,700
c.	Additional dirt and earthmoving	5,100
d.	Title insurance on the land acquisition	1,000
e.	Fence around the boundary of the property	44,200
f.	Building permit for the apartment building	200
g.	Architect's fee for the design of the building	32,000
h.	Signs near the approaches to the property	20,900
i.	Materials used to construct the building	814,000
j.	Labor to construct the building	734,000
k.	Interest cost on construction loan for the building	3,400
l.	Parking lots and concrete walks on the property	17,500
m.	Lights for the parking lot and walkways	8,900
n.	Salary of construction supervisor (90% to building; 10% to parking lot and concrete walks)	55,000
o.	Furniture	123,500
p.	Transportation of furniture from seller to the building	1,100
q.	Landscaping (trees and shrubs)	9,000

Carmel depreciates buildings over 40 years, land improvements over 20 years, and furniture over 8 years, all on a straight-line basis with zero residual value.

Required

1. Set up columns for Land, Land Improvements, Apartment Building, and Furniture. Show how to account for each cost by listing the cost under the correct account. Determine the total cost of each asset.
2. All construction was complete and the assets were placed in service on March 31. Record partial-year depreciation for the year ended December 31. Round to the nearest dollar.

Recording plant-asset transactions, exchange, and disposal
(Obj. 1, 2, 4)

Student Resource CD
GL, PT, QB

P10-2B Shepherd Smith Associates surveys American television-viewing trends. The company's balance sheet reports Land, Buildings, Office Equipment, Communication Equipment, and Televideo Equipment, with a separate accumulated depreciation account for each depreciable asset. During 20X6, Smith completed the following transactions:

May 1	Purchased communication and televideo equipment from the **Gallup** polling organization. Total cost was $80,000 paid in cash. An independent appraisal valued the communication equipment at $90,000 and the televideo equipment at $10,000.
July 30	Traded in old office equipment with book value of $11,000 (cost of $96,000 and accumulated depreciation of $85,000) for new equipment with a cash cost of $88,000. The seller gave Smith a trade-in allowance of $20,000 on the old equipment, and Smith paid the remainder in cash.
Sep. 1	Sold a building that had cost $475,000 (accumulated depreciation of $350,000 through December 31 of the preceding year). Depreciation is computed on a straight-line basis. The building has a 30-year useful life and a residual value of $47,500. Smith received $200,000 cash.
Dec. 31	Recorded depreciation as follows: Communication equipment and televideo equipment are depreciated by the straight-line method over a five-year life with zero residual value. Office equipment is depreciated straight-line over seven years with $9,000 residual value. Make separate depreciation entries for the equipment acquired on May 1 and on July 30.

Required

Record the transactions in the journal of Shepherd Smith Associates.

Explaining the concept of depreciation
(Obj. 2)

P10-3B The board of directors of Austin Healey Motor Company is having its regular quarterly meeting. Accounting policies are on the agenda, and depreciation is being discussed. A new board member, an attorney, has some strong opinions about two aspects of depreciation policy. Lance Lott argues that depreciation must be coupled with a fund to replace company assets. Otherwise, there is no substance to depreciation, he argues. Lott also challenges the three-year depreciable life of company computers. He states that the computers will last much longer and should be depreciated over at least five years.

Required

Write a memo to explain the concept of depreciation to Lott and to answer his arguments. Format your memo as follows:

MEMO

To: ______

From: ______

Subject: ______

Computing depreciation by three methods and the advantage of accelerated depreciation for tax purposes
(Obj. 2, 3)

Student Resource CD
spreadsheet

P10-4B On January 2, 20X4, McIntosh Speed Co. purchased a used trailer at a cost of \$63,000. Before placing the trailer in service, the company spent \$2,200 painting it, \$800 replacing tires, and \$4,000 overhauling the chassis. McIntosh management estimates that the trailer will remain in service for 6 years and have a residual value of \$14,200. The trailer's annual mileage is expected to be 18,000 miles in each of the first four years and 14,000 miles in each of the next two years—100,000 miles in total. In deciding which depreciation method to use, Larry McIntosh, the general manager, requests a depreciation schedule for each of the depreciation methods (straight-line, units-of-production, and double-declining-balance).

Required

1. Prepare a depreciation schedule for each depreciation method, showing asset cost, depreciation expense, accumulated depreciation, and asset book value. For the units-of-production method, round depreciation per mile to three decimal places.
2. McIntosh prepares financial statements using the depreciation method that reports the highest net income in the early years of asset use. For income-tax purposes, however, the company uses the depreciation method that minimizes income taxes in the early years. Consider the first year that McIntosh uses the trailer. Identify the depreciation methods that meet the general manager's objectives, assuming the income tax authorities permit the use of any of the methods.

Accounting for intangibles, natural resources, and the related expenses
(Obj. 5, 6)

P10-5B *Part 1.* **United Telecommunications, Inc.** (United Telecom), provides communication services in Florida, New Jersey, Texas, and other states. Assume that United Telecom purchased goodwill as part of the acquisition of Computer Printer Company, which had these figures:

Book value of assets	\$575,000
Market value of assets	906,000
Liabilities	406,000

Required

1. Make the journal entry to record United Telecom's purchase of Computer Printer Company for \$1,000,000 cash.
2. How should United Telecom account for goodwill after acquiring the other company? Explain in detail.

(continued)

Part 2. **Continental Pipeline Company** operates a pipeline that provides natural gas to the East Coast of the United States. The company's balance sheet includes the asset Oil and Gas Properties.

Suppose Continental paid $7,000,000 cash for oil and gas reserves with an estimated 500,000 barrels of oil. Assume the company paid $550,000 for additional geological tests of the property and $450,000 to prepare for drilling. During the first year of production, Continental removed 70,000 barrels of oil, which it sold on credit for $20 per barrel. Operating expenses related to this project totaled $185,000, all paid in cash.

Required

1. Record all of Continental's transactions, including depletion, for the year.
2. Prepare the company's income statement for this oil and gas project for the first year.

Reporting plant-asset transactions in the financial statements—a review
(Obj. 1, 2, 4)

P10-6B At the end of 2001, **Sprint Corporation**, the telecommunications company, had total assets of $45.8 billion and total liabilities of $33.2 billion. Included among the assets were property, plant, and equipment with a cost of $48.8 billion and accumulated depreciation of $19.8 billion. During 2001, Sprint earned total revenues of $26.1 billion and had total expenses of $27.5 billion.

Required

1. Show how Sprint Corporation would report property, plant, and equipment on its balance sheet at December 31, 2001.
2. How much was Sprint's owner's equity at December 31, 2001?
3. Did Sprint report net income or net loss on its 2001 income statement? Compute the amount.

APPLY *Your Knowledge*

Decision Cases

Measuring profitability based on different inventory and depreciation methods
(Obj. 2, 3)

Case 1. → *Link Back to Chapter 6 (Inventory Methods).* Suppose you are considering investing in two businesses, Payne Stewart and Michael Jordan. The two companies are virtually identical, and both began operations at the beginning of the current year. During the year, each company purchased inventory as follows:

Jan.	4	10,000 units at $4 =	$ 40,000
Apr.	6	5,000 units at 5 =	25,000
Aug.	9	7,000 units at 6 =	42,000
Nov.	27	10,000 units at 7 =	70,000
Totals		32,000	$177,000

During the first year, both companies sold 25,000 units of inventory.

In early January, both companies purchased equipment costing $143,000 (10-year estimated useful life and a $20,000 residual value). Stewart uses the inventory and depreciation methods that maximize reported income (FIFO and straight-line). By contrast, Jordan uses the inventory and depreciation methods that minimize income taxes (LIFO and double-declining-balance). Both companies' trial balances at December 31 included the following:

Sales revenue	$385,000
Operating expenses	80,700

Required

1. Prepare both companies' income statements.
2. Write an investment newsletter to address the following questions for your clients: Which company appears to be more profitable? Which company has more cash to invest in promising projects? If prices continue rising in both companies' industries over the long term, which company would you prefer to invest in? Why?

Plant assets and intangible assets
(Obj. 1, 6)

Case 2. The following questions are unrelated except that they all apply to fixed assets and intangible assets:

a. The manager of Ladue Company regularly buys plant assets and debits the cost to Repairs and Maintenance Expense. Why would he do that, since this action violates generally accepted accounting principles (GAAP)?
b. The manager of Clarkson Corporation regularly debits the cost of repairs and maintenance of plant assets to Plant and Equipment. Why would she do that, since she knows she is violating GAAP?
c. It has been suggested that, because many intangible assets have no value except to the company that owns them, they should be valued at $1.00 or zero on the balance sheet. Many accountants disagree with this view. Which view do you support? Why?

Ethical Issue

Ashton Village Apartments purchased land and a building for the lump sum of $4.1 million. To get the maximum tax deduction, Ashton Village's managers allocated 90% of the purchase price to the building and only 10% to the land. A more realistic allocation would have been 70% to the building and 30% to the land.

Required

1. Explain the tax advantage of allocating too much to the building and too little to the land.
2. Was Ashton Village's allocation ethical? If so, state why. If not, why not? Identify who was harmed.

Financial Statement Case

Plant assets
(Obj. 2, 3)

Refer to the **Amazon.com** financial statements, including Notes 1 and 3, in Appendix A, and answer the following questions.

Required

1. Which depreciation method does Amazon.com use for reporting in the financial statements? What type of depreciation method does the company probably use for income tax purposes? Why is this method preferable for tax purposes?
2. Depreciation expense is embedded in the operating expense amounts listed on the income statement. Note 3 gives the amount of depreciation expense. What was the amount of depreciation for 2002? Record Amazon's depreciation expense for 2002.
3. The statement of cash flows reports the purchases of fixed assets. How much were Amazon's fixed asset purchases during 2002? Journalize the company's purchase of fixed assets. Refer to Note 3 to determine the specific types of fixed assets purchased.

Team Project

Required

Visit a local business.

1. List all its plant assets.
2. If possible, interview the manager. Gain as much information as you can about the business's plant assets. For example, try to determine the assets' costs, the depreciation

method the company is using, and the estimated useful life of each asset category. If an interview is impossible, then develop your own estimates of the assets' costs, useful lives, and book values, assuming an appropriate depreciation method.

3. Determine whether the business has any intangible assets. If so, list them and learn as much as possible about their nature, cost, and estimated useful lives.
4. Write a detailed report of your findings and be prepared to present it to the class.

For Internet Exercises, go to the Web site www.prenhall.com/horngren.

CHAPTER 11

Current Liabilities and Payroll

A+ TIPS CHECK YOUR RESOURCES

- Visit the www.prenhall.com/horngren **Web site** for self-study quizzes, video clips, and other resources
- Try the **Quick Check** exercise at the end of the chapter to test your knowledge
- Learn the **key terms**
- Do the **Starter** exercises keyed in the margins
- Work the **mid**- and **end-of-chapter summary problems**
- Use the **Concept Links** to review material in other chapters
- Search the **CD** for review materials by chapter or by key word
- Watch the **tutorial videos** to review key concepts

LEARNING OBJECTIVES

1. Account for current liabilities of known amount
2. Account for current liabilities that must be estimated
3. Compute payroll amounts
4. Record basic payroll transactions
5. Use a payroll system
6. Report current liabilities on the balance sheet

General Motors

Most products are guaranteed against defects. Computers, video equipment, and automobiles are prime examples. When you buy a Sony camera or a new General Motors car, the manufacturer agrees to repair it if something goes wrong. Do you ever consider the guarantee when you buy a product? That may be what motivates you to select a Honda over a Chevrolet. If not, you should consider the product guarantee because it varies from company to company. Repairs can be expensive.

Product guarantees are called warranties, and warranties are a major liability of companies such as General Motors, Sony, and Goodyear Tire and Rubber Company. Warranties pose an accounting challenge because General Motors doesn't know which Chevrolets or Buicks will have to be recalled or repaired. But it's almost certain that some cars will have problems, so GM goes ahead and records a warranty liability based on estimates. ■

Sitemap

- Liabilities of Known Amount
- Estimated Liabilities
- Accounting for Payroll
- The Payroll System
- Reporting Liabilities
- Ethical Issues

- ■ Liabilities of Known Amount
- □ Estimated Liabilities
- □ Accounting for Payroll
- □ The Payroll System
- □ Reporting Liabilities
- □ Ethical Issues

1 *Account for current liabilities of known amount*

Student Resource CD
accrued expense/liability, current liabilities, payroll, short-term notes

In this chapter we will see how GM, Sony, and other companies account for their product warranties. We also will learn about other current liabilities, such as Accounts Payable and payroll. Recall that *current liabilities* are obligations due within one year or within the company's normal operating cycle if it is longer than one year. Obligations due beyond that period are classified as *long-term liabilities.*

Current Liabilities of Known Amount

The amounts of most current liabilities are known. A few must be estimated. Let's begin with current liabilities of known amount.

Accounts Payable

Amounts owed for products or services purchased on open account are *accounts payable*. We have seen many accounts payable illustrations in preceding chapters. For example, most businesses purchase inventory on account. **General Motors Corporation (GM)** reported accounts payable of $18.3 billion at December 31, 20X1 (see line 1 of Exhibit 11-1).

Let's see how GM's accounts payable get onto the company's balance sheet. One of GM's common transactions is the credit purchase of inventory. GM's accounts payable and inventory systems are integrated. When the inventory of a certain auto part dips below a certain level, the computer automatically places an order to buy the goods. GM records the purchase of inventory on account as follows (amount assumed):

Oct. 19	Inventory	600	
	Accounts Payable		600
	Purchase on account.		

The purchase increases both inventory and Accounts Payable. Then, to pay the liability, the computer debits Accounts Payable and credits Cash, as follows:

Nov. 12	Accounts Payable	600	
	Cash		600
	Paid on account.		

Exhibit 11-1
How General Motors Reports Its Current Liabilities

General Motors Corporation
Balance Sheet (partial; adapted)
December 31, 2001

	Liabilities	(In billions)
	Current Liabilities	
1	Accounts payable	$18.3
2	Loans payable	2.4
3	Accrued expenses payable	34.1
4	Other current liabilities	1.5
5	Total current liabilities	$56.3

Short-Term Notes Payable

Short-Term Note Payable
Promissory note payable due within one year, a common form of financing.

Short-term notes payable are a common form of financing. General Motors refers to this liability as Loans Payable (see Exhibit 11-1, line 2). Short-term notes payable are promissory notes that must be paid within one year. The following entries are typical for a short-term note used to purchase inventory:

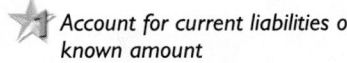

20X6			
Sep. 30	Inventory	8,000	
	Note Payable, Short-term		8,000
	Purchased inventory on a one-year, 10% note.		
Dec. 31	Interest Expense ($8,000 × 0.10 × 3/12)	200	
	Interest Payable		200
	Accrued interest expense at year-end.		

The balance sheet at December 31, 20X6, reports the Note Payable of $8,000 and Interest Payable of $200 as current liabilities. The income statement for 20X6 reports interest expense of $200. Both the balance sheet and the income statement are illustrated as follows:

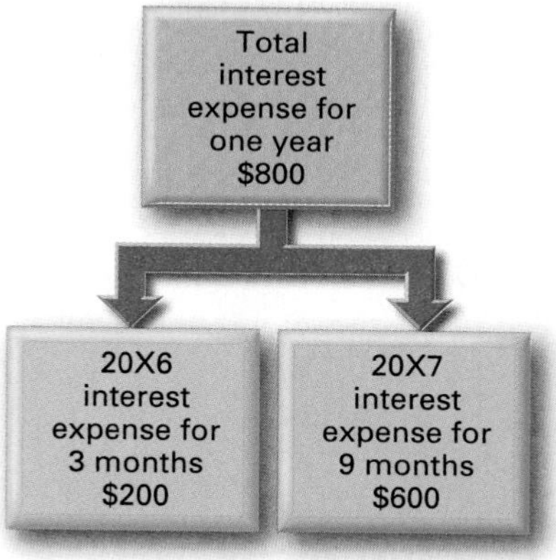

Balance Sheet December 31, 20X6		Income Statement Year Ended December 31, 20X6	
Liabilities		**Expenses**	
Current liabilities		Interest expense	$200
Note payable, short-term	$8,000		
Interest payable	200		

Interest expense of $200 was correctly allocated to 20X6. GM's interest expense will be $600 for 20X7. At maturity, GM will pay a full year's interest, allocated as shown in the margin diagram.

✔ Starter 11-1

✔ Starter 11-2

GM's entry for payment of the note in 20X7 is

20X7			
Sep. 30	Note Payable, Short-Term	8,000	
	Interest Payable	200	
	Interest Expense ($8,000 × 0.10 × 9/12)	600	
	Cash [$8,000 + ($8,000 × 0.10)]		8,800
	Paid note and interest at maturity.		

Sales Tax Payable

Most states levy sales tax on retail sales. Retailers collect the sales tax in addition to the price of the item sold. The retailers then owe the state the sales tax, so Sales Tax Payable is a current liability. For example, **ShowBiz Pizza Time, Inc.,** operator of Chuck E. Cheese pizza and entertainment centers, reports sales tax payable as a current liability.

Suppose one Saturday's sales at a ShowBiz Pizza Time totaled $10,000. The business collected an additional 5% in sales tax, which would equal $500 ($10,000 × 0.05). The business would record that day's sales as follows:

+

Cash ($10,000 × 1.05)	10,500	
Sales Revenue		10,000
Sales Tax Payable ($10,000 × 0.05)		500
To record cash sales and the related sales tax.		

Sales Tax Payable

	500

Companies forward the sales tax to the state at regular intervals. To pay the tax, they debit Sales Tax Payable and credit Cash.

Accounting.com

A Taxing Dilemma: Sales Tax Liability and the Internet

E-commerce offers two big pluses: shopping from home in your pajamas and no sales tax. Say you live in New York City and purchase a CD from a music store. You pay the retail price of $15.99, plus sales tax of 8.625%. A purchase of the same CD from **Amazon.com** will be $1.38 cheaper. Fortunately for online (and mail-order) customers, the U.S. Supreme Court ruled that only the U.S. Congress can require retailers to charge sales taxes if they don't have a physical location in a state.

But the e-commerce sales-tax loophole may not be so sweet after all. According to one study, states missed out on $13.3 billion in revenue from taxes in one year. Those billions could have been used to build schools, repair roads, and pay state and local employees.

With the 50 states projecting a total shortfall of $40 billion to $50 billion—growing to $75 billion in the following year—states are looking for ways to tax online sales. Over 30 states are considering online sales tax legislation as part of the Streamlined Sales Tax Project. Expect to hear more about sales taxes as online sales grow. And if you're starting your own dot.com, see EcommerceTax.com for up-to-the-minute news. How the sales tax is treated may influence how you set up your business.

Based on: Peter Schrag, "Loophole.com," *The Nation*, May 15, 2000, pp. 6–7. Anonymous, "United States: Offline," *The Economist*, March 25, 2000, p. 35. Patrick Thibodeau, "States Push to Require Online Sales Tax Collection," *Computerworld*, November 4, 2002, p. 21. Chris Gaither, "States Circle Net: Budget Woes Force Leaders to Revisit Levies on Online Sales," *Boston Globe*, January 2, 2003, p. C.11.

Current Portion of Long-Term Debt

Current Portion of Long-Term Debt Amount of the principal that is payable within one year. Also called **current maturity**.

Some long-term notes payable and bonds payable are paid in installments. The **current portion of long-term debt** is the amount of the principal payable within one year—a current liability. The remaining portion of the long-term debt is a long-term liability. At the end of the year, the company may make an adjusting entry to shift the current installment of the long-term debt to a current liability account, as follows (amount assumed):

Dec. 31	Long-Term Debt.	10,000	
	Current Portion of Long-Term Debt . . .		10,000

Stop & Think

Suppose **Dell Computer** owes $600,000 on long-term notes payable at December 31, 20X5. The borrowing agreement requires Dell to pay $200,000 of this debt on September 30, 20X6. Show how Dell will report both current and long-term liabilities on its balance sheet at December 31, 20X5.

Answer:

Current liabilities:	
Current maturities of long-term debt	$200,000
Long-term liabilities	
Long-term debt ($600,000 – $200,000)	400,000

Accrued Expenses (Accrued Liabilities)

Accrued Expense An expense that the business has not yet paid. Also called **accrued liability**.

We introduced accrued expenses in Chapter 3, p. 102.

An **accrued expense** is an expense that has not yet been paid. Therefore, an accrued expense creates a liability. This explains why accrued expenses are also called **accrued liabilities**. Accrued expenses typically occur with the passage of time, such as interest payable on long-term debt.

Like most other companies, General Motors has accrued liabilities for salaries payable, other payroll liabilities, interest payable, and income tax payable. We illustrated accounting for interest payable near the top of page 437. The second half of this chapter covers accounting for payroll liabilities.

Payroll, which is also called **employee compensation**, is a major expense. For service organizations—such as CPA firms and travel agencies—payroll is *the* major expense. Payroll expense for salaries or wages usually causes an accrued liability at year-end. We show how to account for payroll expenses later in the chapter.

Payroll
A major expense. Also called **employee compensation**.

Unearned Revenues

Unearned revenues are also called *deferred revenues*. → The business has received cash from customers before earning the revenue. The company therefore has an obligation to provide goods or services to the customer. Let's consider an example.

← *As we saw in Chapter 3, p. 104, an unearned revenue is a liability because it represents an obligation to provide a good or service.*

Dun & Bradstreet (D&B) Corporation provides credit reports for subscribers and collects cash in advance. By receiving cash before earning the revenue, D&B has a liability for future service. The liability account is called Unearned Subscription Revenue.

Assume that D&B charges $600 for a three-year subscription. D&B's entry to record the receipt of cash in advance would be

20X4			
Jan. 1	Cash	600	
	Unearned Subscription Revenue		600
	Received cash in advance.		

After receiving the cash on January 1, 20X4, D&B owes service to its customer over three years. D&B's liability is

Unearned Subscription Revenue	
	600

During 20X4, D&B performs one-third of the total service and earns $200 ($600 × 1/3) of the revenue. At December 31, 20X4, D&B makes the following adjusting entry to decrease Unearned Subscription Revenue, the liability, and increase Subscription Revenue:

20X4			
Dec. 31	Unearned Subscription Revenue	200	
	Subscription Revenue ($600 × 1/3)		200
	Earned revenue that was collected in advance.		

After posting, D&B still owes its subscribers $400 in services. D&B has earned $200 of the revenue, as follows:

Unearned Subscription Revenue

Dec. 31	200	Jan. 1	600
		Bal.	400

Subscription Revenue

		Dec. 31	200

Current Liabilities That Must Be Estimated

A business may know that a liability exists but not know the exact amount. It cannot simply ignore the liability. This liability must be reported on the balance sheet. A prime example is Estimated Warranty Payable, which is common for companies like General Motors and Sony. Another example is a contingent liability.

Student Resource CD
contingent liability, current liabilities

2 *Account for current liabilities that must be estimated*

Estimated Warranty Payable

Many companies guarantee their products against defects under *warranty* agreements. Ninety-day warranties and one-year warranties are common.

The matching principle says to record the *warranty expense* in the same period that we record the revenue. The expense occurs when you make a sale, not when you pay warranty claims. At the time of the sale, the company does not know the exact amount of warranty expense. But the business must estimate its warranty expense and the related liability.

For a review of the matching principle, see Chapter 3, p. 95.

Assume that **Whirlpool Corporation**, which manufactures appliances for **Sears**, made sales of $200,000, subject to product warranties. Whirlpool estimates that 3% of its products will require warranty payments. The company would record the sales and the warranty expense in the same period, as follows:

June 20	Accounts Receivable..............	200,000	
	Sales Revenue		200,000
	Sales on account.		
June 20	Warranty Expense ($200,000 × 0.03) . .	6,000	
	Estimated Warranty Payable. . .		6,000
	To accrue warranty expense.		

Assume that Whirlpool's warranty payments total $5,800. Whirlpool repairs the defective appliances and makes this journal entry:

Dec. 11	Estimated Warranty Payable	5,800	
	Cash		5,800
	To *repair* defective products sold under warranty.		

Whirlpool's expense on the income statement is the estimated amount of $6,000, not the $5,800 actually paid. After paying for these warranties, Whirlpool's liability account has a credit balance of $200.

Estimated Warranty Payable

5,800	**6,000**
	Bal. 200

Stop & Think

Maxim Company, a new company, made sales of $400,000 on account. The company estimated warranty repairs at 5% of the sales. Actual warranty payments were $19,000. Record sales, warranty expense, and warranty payments. How much is Maxim's estimated warranty payable at the end of the period?

Answer:

Accounts Receivable	400,000	
Sales Revenue..............................		400,000
Warranty Expense ($400,000 × 0.05)	20,000	
Estimated Warranty Payable		20,000
Estimated Warranty Payable	19,000	
Cash.....................................		19,000

Estimated Warranty Payable

19,000	**20,000**
	Bal. 1,000

✔ Starter 11-3

✔ Starter 11-4

Contingent Liabilities

A *contingent liability* is not an actual liability. Instead, it is a potential liability that depends on a *future* event. For example, suppose General Motors is sued because of auto accidents involving Chevy trucks. GM thus faces a contingent liability, which may or may not become an actual liability. If this lawsuit's outcome could hurt GM, it would be unethical for GM to withhold knowledge of the lawsuit. Another contingent liability arises when Company A *cosigns a note payable* for Company B. Company A has a contingent liability until the note comes due. If Company B pays off the note, the contingent liability ceases to exist. If not, Company A must pay Company B's debt, and Company A's liability becomes real.

The accounting profession divides contingent liabilities into three categories. Each category shows a likelihood that the contingency will cause a loss and a liability. The three categories of contingent liabilities, along with how to report them, are shown in Exhibit 11-2.

Exhibit 11-2

Contingent Liabilities: Three Categories

Likelihood of an Actual Loss	How to Report the Contingency
Remote	Ignore. Example: A frivolous lawsuit.
Reasonably possible	Describe the situation in a note to the financial statements. Example: The company is the defendant in a significant lawsuit and the outcome could go either way.
Probable, and the amount of the loss can be estimated	Record an expense (or loss) and an actual liability, based on estimated amounts. Example: Warranty expense and payable, as illustrated in the preceding section, beginning on page 439.

✔ Starter 11-5

At this halfway point in the chapter, review what you have learned by studying the Decision Guidelines.

Decision Guidelines

ACCOUNTING FOR CURRENT LIABILITIES

Suppose you're in charge of accounting for your student service club. The club decides to borrow $1,000 for a **Habitat for Humanity** project. The bank requires a balance sheet. These Decision Guidelines will help you report current liabilities accurately.

Decision	Guidelines
What are the two main issues in accounting for current liabilities?	• *Recording* the liability and the asset acquired or the expense incurred • *Reporting* the liability on the balance sheet
What are the two basic categories of current liabilities?	• Current liabilities of *known amount*: Accounts payable; Short-term notes payable; Sales tax payable; Current portion of long-term debt; Unearned revenues; Accrued expenses (accrued liabilities); Payroll liabilities; Salary, wages, commission, and bonus payable • Current liabilities that *must be estimated*: Estimated warranty payable

MID-CHAPTER *Summary Problem*

A+ TIPS
CHECK YOUR RESOURCES

Answer each question independently.

Required

1. A **Wendy's** hamburger restaurant made cash sales of $4,000 subject to a 5% sales tax. Record the sales and the related sales tax. Also record Wendy's payment of the tax to the state government.

2. Assume that at December 31, 20X6, **H. J. Heinz Company** reported its 6% long-term debt as follows:

Current Liabilities (In part)	Thousands
Portion of long-term debt payable within one year	$ 10,000
Interest payable ($200,000,000 × 0.06 × 6/12)	6,000
Long-Term Debt and Other Liabilities (In part)	
Long-term debt	$190,000

Assume that Heinz pays interest on June 30 each year.

Show how Heinz would report its liabilities on the year-end balance sheet one year later—December 31, 20X7. The current maturity of the long-term debt is $10 million each year until the liability is paid off.

3. How does a contingent liability differ from an actual liability?

Solution

1.

Cash ($4,000 × 1.05)	4,200	
Sales Revenue		4,000
Sales Tax Payable ($4,000 × 0.05)		200
To record cash sales and sales tax.		
Sales Tax Payable	200	
Cash		200
To pay sales tax.		

2. H. J. Heinz Company balance sheet at December 31, 20X7:

Current Liabilities (In part)	Thousands
Portion of long-term debt payable within one year	$ 10,000
Interest payable ($190,000,000 × 0.06 × 6/12)	5,700
Long-Term Debt and Other Liabilities (In part)	
Long-term debt	$180,000

3. A contingent liability is a *potential* liability; the contingency may or may not become an actual liability.

☐ Liabilities of Known Amount
☐ Estimated Liabilities
■ **Accounting for Payroll**
☐ The Payroll System
☐ Reporting Liabilities
☐ Ethical Issues

Student ResourceCD
payroll, payroll taxes, withholding taxes

3 *Compute payroll amounts*

Accounting for Payroll

Salaries and wages are so important that most businesses develop a special payroll system to account for labor costs.

Businesses pay employees at a base rate for a set number of hours—called *straight time*. For additional hours—called *overtime*—the employee may get a higher rate of pay.

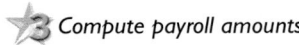

Lucy Childres is an accountant for Bobby Jones Golf Company. Lucy earns $600 per week for straight time (40 hours), so her hourly pay rate is $15 ($600/40). The company pays *time and a half* for overtime. That rate is 150% (1.5 times) the straight-time rate. Thus, Lucy earns $22.50 for each hour of overtime ($15.00 × 1.5 = $22.50). For working 42 hours during a week, she earns $645, computed as follows:

Straight-time pay for 40 hours	$600
Overtime pay for 2 overtime hours: 2 × $22.50	45
Total pay	$645

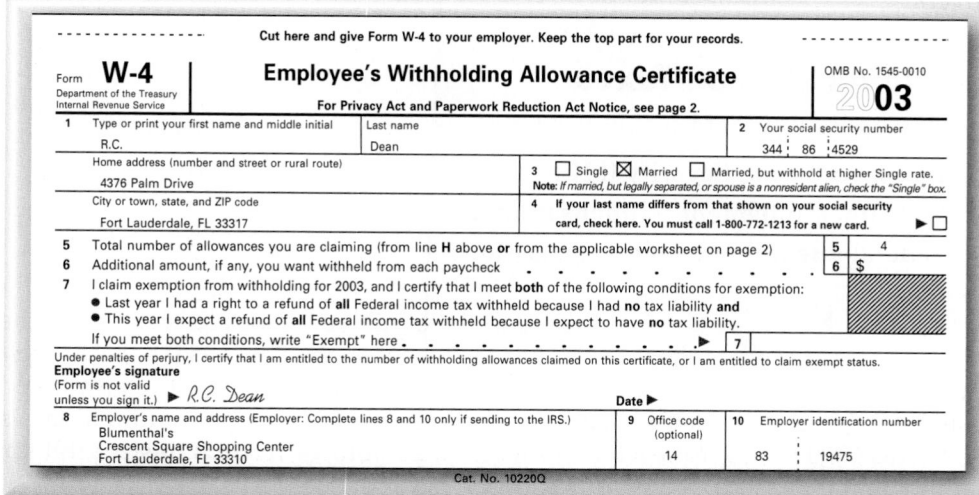

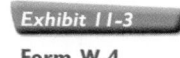

Gross Pay and Net Pay

The federal government requires employers to act as the collection agents for employee taxes. Employers deduct the taxes from employee checks. Insurance companies, labor unions, and other organizations may also receive pieces of employees' pay. Amounts withheld from an employee's check are called *deductions*.

Gross pay is the total amount of salary or wages, before taxes and other deductions. **Net pay**—or "take-home pay"—equals gross pay minus all deductions. Accounting for payroll is complex. Many companies also pay employee *benefits*, which are another form of compensation. Examples include health and life insurance.

Payroll Deductions

Payroll deductions fall into two categories:

- *Required deductions*, such as employee income tax and Social Security tax
- *Optional deductions*, including union dues, insurance premiums, charitable contributions, and other amounts withheld at the employee's request

After withholding, payroll deductions become the liability of the employer, who then pays the outside party—taxes to the government and charitable contributions to United Way or another charity.

Required Deductions: Employee Income Tax U.S. law requires companies to withhold income tax from employees' pay checks. The amount of income tax deducted from gross pay is called **withheld income tax**. The withholding depends on the amount of gross pay and on the number of *withholding allowances* the employee claims.

An employee files a Form W-4 with his employer to indicate the number of allowances claimed for withholding purposes. Each allowance lowers the amount of tax withheld. An unmarried taxpayer usually claims one allowance; a childless married couple, two allowances; a married couple with one child, three allowances; and so on. Exhibit 11-3 shows a W-4 for R. C. Dean, who claims four allowances (line 5).

Gross Pay
Total amount of salary, wages, commissions, or any other employee compensation before taxes and other deductions.

Net Pay
Gross pay minus all deductions. The amount of compensation that the employee actually takes home.

Withheld Income Tax
Income tax deducted from employees' gross pay.

Exhibit 11-3
Form W-4

Cut here and give Form W-4 to your employer. Keep the top part for your records.

Form **W-4** Department of the Treasury Internal Revenue Service — **Employee's Withholding Allowance Certificate** — For Privacy Act and Paperwork Reduction Act Notice, see page 2. — OMB No. 1545-0010 — **2003**

1 Type or print your first name and middle initial: R.C. — Last name: Dean — 2 Your social security number: 344 86 4529

Home address (number and street or rural route): 4376 Palm Drive — 3 ☐ Single ☒ Married ☐ Married, but withhold at higher Single rate.
Note: *If married, but legally separated, or spouse is a nonresident alien, check the "Single" box.*

City or town, state, and ZIP code: Fort Lauderdale, FL 33317 — 4 **If your last name differs from that shown on your social security card, check here. You must call 1-800-772-1213 for a new card.** ▶ ☐

5 Total number of allowances you are claiming (from line **H** above **or** from the applicable worksheet on page 2) — 5 — 4
6 Additional amount, if any, you want withheld from each paycheck — 6 — $
7 I claim exemption from withholding for 2003, and I certify that I meet **both** of the following conditions for exemption:
- Last year I had a right to a refund of **all** Federal income tax withheld because I had **no** tax liability **and**
- This year I expect a refund of **all** Federal income tax withheld because I expect to have **no** tax liability.

If you meet both conditions, write "Exempt" here ▶ 7

Under penalties of perjury, I certify that I am entitled to the number of withholding allowances claimed on this certificate, or I am entitled to claim exempt status.
Employee's signature (Form is not valid unless you sign it.) ▶ R.C. Dean — **Date** ▶

8 Employer's name and address (Employer: Complete lines 8 and 10 only if sending to the IRS.) Blumenthal's, Crescent Square Shopping Center, Fort Lauderdale, FL 33310 — 9 Office code (optional): 14 — 10 Employer identification number: 83 19475

Cat. No. 10220Q

REQUIRED DEDUCTIONS: EMPLOYEE SOCIAL SECURITY (FICA) TAX The *Federal Insurance Contributions Act (FICA)*, also known as the Social Security Act, created the Social Security Tax. The Social Security program provides retirement, disability, and medical benefits. The law requires employers to withhold **Social Security (FICA) tax** from employees' pay. The FICA tax has two components:

Social Security Tax
Federal Insurance Contributions Act (FICA) tax, which is withheld from employees' pay. Also called **FICA tax**.

1. Old age, survivors', and disability insurance (OASDI)
2. Health insurance (Medicare)

The amount of tax withheld varies from year to year. For 2003, the OASDI tax applies to the first $87,000 of employee earnings in a year. The taxable amount of earnings is adjusted annually. The OASDI tax rate is 6.2%. Therefore, the maximum OASDI tax that an employee paid in 2003 was $5,394 ($87,000 × 0.062).

The Medicare portion of the FICA tax applies to all employee earnings. This tax rate is 1.45%. An employee thus pays a combined FICA tax rate of 7.65% (6.2% + 1.45%) of the first $87,000 of annual earnings, plus 1.45% of earnings above $87,000.

To ease the computational burden and focus on the concepts, we assume that the FICA tax is 8% of the first $87,000 of employee earnings each year. (Use these numbers when you complete this chapter's assignment material, unless instructed otherwise.) For each employee who earns $87,000 or more, the employer withholds $6,960 ($87,000 × 0.08) and sends that amount to the federal government.

Assume that Rex Jennings, an employee, earned $80,000 prior to December. Jennings' salary for December is $7,000. How much FICA tax will be withheld from Jennings' December paycheck? The computation follows.

Employee earnings subject to the tax in one year	$87,000
Employee earnings prior to the current month	−80,000
Current pay subject to FICA tax......................	$ 7,000
FICA tax rate	×0.08
FICA tax to be withheld from current pay check........	$ 560

OPTIONAL DEDUCTIONS As a convenience to employees, many companies make payroll deductions and disburse cash according to employee instructions. Union dues, insurance payments, retirement savings plans, and gifts to charities such as United Way and Habitat for Humanity are examples.

✔ Starter 11-6

Many employers offer *cafeteria plans* that allow workers to select from a menu of insurance coverage. Suppose Ford Motor Company provides each employee with $500 of insurance coverage each month. One employee may use the monthly allowance to purchase life insurance. Another may select disability coverage. A third worker may choose a combination of life insurance and disability coverage.

Employer Payroll Taxes

Employers must pay at least three payroll taxes:

1. Employer **Social Security (FICA) tax**
2. State **unemployment compensation tax**
3. Federal **unemployment compensation tax**.

Unemployment Compensation Tax
Payroll tax paid by employers to the government, which uses the money to pay unemployment benefits to people who are out of work.

EMPLOYER FICA TAX In addition to the employee's Social Security tax, the employer must pay an equal amount into the program. The Social Security system is funded by equal contributions from the employee and the employer. Using our 8% Social Security tax rate, the employer's maximum annual tax is $6,960 ($87,000 × 0.08) for each employee. The employer records this payroll tax liability in the FICA Tax Payable account.

STATE AND FEDERAL UNEMPLOYMENT COMPENSATION TAXES State and federal unemployment taxes finance workmen's compensation for people laid off from work. *In recent years, employers have paid a combined tax of 6.2% on the first $7,000 of each employee's annual earnings.* The proportion paid to the state is 5.4%, plus 0.8% to the federal government. The employer uses the accounts Federal Unemployment Tax Payable and State Unemployment Tax Payable. Exhibit 11-4 shows a typical distribution of payroll costs for an employer company.

Exhibit 11-4

Typical Breakdown of Payroll Costs for One Employee

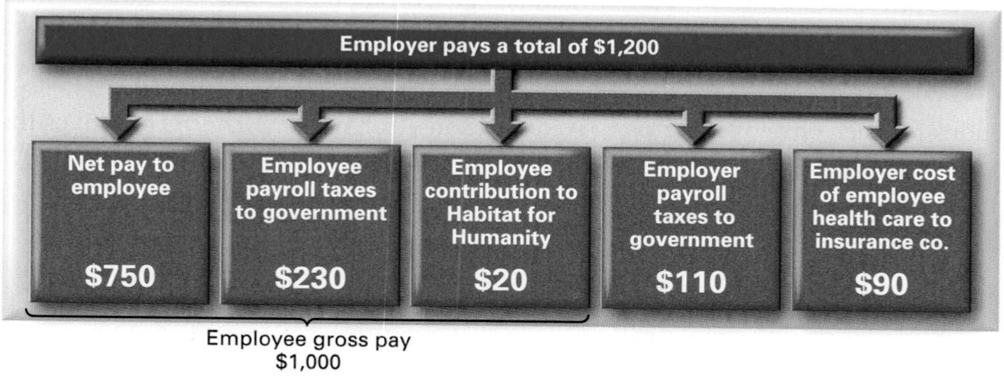

✔ Starter 11-7

Payroll Entries

4 *Record basic payroll transactions*

Exhibit 11-5 summarizes an employer's entries to record a monthly payroll of $10,000. All amounts are assumed for illustration only. Entry A records *salary expense*. *Gross salary* is $10,000, and net take-home pay is $7,860. There is a payable to Habitat for Humanity because several employees specify this charitable deduction. Entry B records *payroll tax expense,* which includes the $800 FICA tax plus state and federal unemployment taxes. Entry C records *benefits* paid by the employer. This company pays for health and life insurance on its employees, a common practice. The employer also pays cash into a pension plan for the benefit of employees after they retire.

Exhibit 11-5

Payroll Accounting by the Employer

A.	**Salary Expense**		
	Salary Expense (or Wage Expense or Commission Expense)	10,000	
	Employee Income Tax Payable		1,200
	FICA Tax Payable ($10,000 × 0.08)		800
	Payable to Habitat for Humanity		140
	Salary Payable to Employees (take-home pay)		7,860
	To record *salary expense.*		
B.	**Payroll Tax Expense**		
	Payroll Tax Expense	1,420	
	FICA Tax Payable ($10,000 × 0.08)		800
	State Unemployment Tax Payable ($10,000 × 0.054)		540
	Federal Unemployment Tax Payable ($10,000 × 0.008)		80
	To record employer's *payroll taxes.*		
C.	**Benefits Expense**		
	Health Insurance Expense	800	
	Life Insurance Expense	200	
	Pension Expense	500	
	Employee Benefits Payable		1,500
	To record employee benefits payable by employer.		

✔ Starter 11-8

✔ Starter 11-9

Stop & Think

What is the employer's total payroll expense in Exhibit 11-5?

Answer: $12,920 ($10,000 + $1,420 + $1,500)

Student Resource CD
payroll, payroll taxes, withholding taxes

5 *Use a payroll system*

We introduced the cash payments journal in Chapter 7, p. 295.

✔ **Starter 11-10**

The Payroll System

Good business means paying employees accurately and on time. A payroll system accomplishes these goals. The components of the payroll system are

- A payroll record
- Payroll checks
- Employee earnings record

Payroll Record

Each pay period the company organizes payroll data in a special journal called the *payroll record*. The payroll record resembles the cash payments journal and serves as a check register for recording payroll checks.

Exhibit 11-6 is a payroll record for **Blumenthal's**. The payroll record has sections for each employee's gross pay, deductions, and net pay. This record gives the employer the information needed to record salary expense for the week, as follows:

Dec. 31	Salary Expense	14,654.00	
	Employee Income Tax Payable....		3,367.76
	FICA Tax Payable..............		861.94
	Payable to Habitat for Humanity..		155.00
	Salary Payable.................		10,269.30

Exhibit 11-6 **Blumenthal's Payroll Record (Partial)**

Week Ended December 31, 2003

		Gross Pay			Deductions				Net Pay	
Employee Name	Hours	Straight-Time	Overtime	Total Salary Expense	Federal Income Tax	FICA Tax	Habitat for Humanity	Total	Amount	Check No.
Chen, W. L.*	40	500.00		500.00	71.05	40.00	2.50	113.55	386.45	1621
Dean, R. C.	46	400.00	90.00	490.00	59.94	39.20	2.00	101.14	388.86	1622
Ellis, M.	41	560.00	21.00	581.00	86.14	46.48		132.62	448.38	1623
Trimble, E. A.†	40	2,360.00		2,360.00	663.22		15.00	678.22	1,681.78	1641
Total		13,940.00	714.00	14,654.00	3,367.76	861.94	155.00	4,384.70	10,269.30	

*W. L. Chen earned gross pay of $500. His net pay was $386.45, paid with check number 1621.
† The business deducted no FICA tax from E. A. Trimble. She has already earned more than $87,000.
Note: For simplicity we ignore the additional tax for Medicare benefits.

Payroll Checks

Most companies pay employees by check or by electronic fund transfer (EFT). A *paycheck* has an attachment that details the payroll amounts. These figures come

Exhibit 11-7
Payroll Check

Blumenthal's 1622
Payroll Account
Fort Lauderdale, FL 12/31 2003

Pay to the Order of R.C. Dean $ 388.86

Three hundred eighty-eight & 86/100 .... **Dollars**

Republic Bank
Fort Lauderdale
Florida 33310

Anna Figaro
Treasurer

•A111900031A 0787C50000454C

Pay			Deductions				Net Pay	Check No.
Straight time	Overtime	Gross	Income tax	FICA	United Way	Total		
400.00	90.00	490.00	59.94	39.20	2.00	101.14	388.86	1622

from the payroll record in Exhibit 11-6. Exhibit 11-7 shows payroll check number 1622, issued to R. C. Dean for net pay of $388.86. To enhance your ability to use payroll data, trace all amounts on the check attachment to Dean's payroll record in Exhibit 11-6.

Many companies pay employees by electronic funds transfer. The employee can authorize the company to make deposits directly to his or her own bank account. This procedure saves time and money.

Earnings Record

The employer must file a payroll tax return with the federal and state governments. Exhibit 11-8 is the Form 941 that Blumenthal's filed with the Internal Revenue Service for the quarter ended December 31, 2003. These forms must be filed no later than one month after the end of a quarter.

The employer must also provide the employee with a wage and tax statement, Form W-2, at the end of the year. Exhibit 11-9 (on page 448) shows the earnings record of R. C. Dean for the last two weeks of 2003.

Exhibit 11-8

Payroll Tax Return

Form **941** (Rev. January 2003) Department of the Treasury Internal Revenue Service

Employer's Quarterly Federal Tax Return

▶ See separate instructions revised January 2002 for information on completing this return.

Please type or print.

Enter state code for state in which deposits were made only if different from state in address to the right (see page 2 of instructions). F L

Name (as distinguished from trade name) — Date quarter ended

Trade name, if any: Blumenthal's — Employer identification number

Address (number and street): Crescent Square Shopping Center, Fort Lauderdale, FL 33310-1234 — City, state, and ZIP code

OMB No. 1545-0029

T
FF
FD
FP
I
T

If address is different from prior return, check here ▶ ☐ — IRS Use

If you do not have to file returns in the future, check here ▶ ☐ and enter date final wages paid ▶

If you are a seasonal employer, see **Seasonal employers** on page 1 of the instructions and check here ▶ ☐

Line	Description	Box	Amount
1	Number of employees in the pay period that includes March 12th . . . ▶ 1		19
2	Total wages and tips, plus other compensation	2	113,654
3	Total income tax withheld from wages, tips, and sick pay	3	18,168
4	Adjustment of withheld income tax for preceding quarters of calendar year	4	—
5	Adjusted total of income tax withheld (line 3 as adjusted by line 4—see instructions)	5	18,168
6	Taxable social security wages . . . 6a 110,774 × 12.4% (.124) =	6b	13,736
	Taxable social security tips . . . 6c × 12.4% (.124) =	6d	
7	Taxable Medicare wages and tips . . . 7a 113,654 × 2.9% (.029) =	7b	3,296
8	Total social security and Medicare taxes (add lines 6b, 6d, and 7b). Check here if wages are not subject to social security and/or Medicare tax ▶ ☐	8	17,032
9	Adjustment of social security and Medicare taxes (see instructions for required explanation) Sick Pay $ ____ ± Fractions of Cents $ ____ ± Other $ ____ =	9	—
10	Adjusted total of social security and Medicare taxes (line 8 as adjusted by line 9—see instructions)	10	17,032
11	**Total taxes** (add lines 5 and 10)	11	35,200
12	Advance earned income credit (EIC) payments made to employees	12	—
13	Net taxes (subtract line 12 from line 11). **If $2,500 or more, this must equal line 17, column (d) below (or line D of Schedule B (Form 941))**	13	35,200
14	Total deposits for quarter, including overpayment applied from a prior quarter	14	35,200
15	**Balance due** (subtract line 14 from line 13). See instructions	15	–0–

16 **Overpayment.** If line 14 is more than line 13, enter excess here ▶ $ ____ and check if to be: ☐ Applied to next return or ☐ Refunded.

- **All filers:** If line 13 is less than $2,500, you need not complete line 17 or Schedule B (Form 941).
- **Semiweekly schedule depositors:** Complete Schedule B (Form 941) and check here ▶ ☐
- **Monthly schedule depositors:** Complete line 17, columns (a) through (d), and check here ▶ ☐

17 **Monthly Summary of Federal Tax Liability.** Do not complete if you were a semiweekly schedule depositor.

(a) First month liability	(b) Second month liability	(c) Third month liability	(d) Total liability for quarter
35,017	35,336	34,967	35,200

Sign Here Under penalties of perjury, I declare that I have examined this return, including accompanying schedules and statements, and to the best of my knowledge and belief, it is true, correct, and complete.

Signature ▶ *Anna Figaro* — Print Your Name and Title ▶ *Anna Figaro, Treasurer* — Date ▶ 1/30/03

For Privacy Act and Paperwork Reduction Act Notice, see back of Payment Voucher. Cat. No. 17001Z Form **941** (Rev. 1-2003)

Exhibit 11-9

Employee Earnings Record for 2003

EMPLOYEE NAME AND ADDRESS:	SOCIAL SECURITY NO.: 344-86-4529
DEAN, R. C.	MARITAL STATUS: MARRIED
4376 PALM DRIVE	WITHHOLDING EXEMPTIONS: 4
FORT LAUDERDALE, FL 33317	PAY RATE: $400 PER WEEK
	JOB TITLE: SALESPERSON

		Gross Pay				Deductions				Net Pay	
Week Ended	Hrs.	Straight-Time	Over-time	Total	To Date	Federal Income Tax	FICA Tax	United Way Charity	Total	Amount	Check No.
Dec. 24	48	400.00	120.00	520.00	22,720.00	66.75	41.60	2.00	110.35	409.65	1598
Dec. 31	46	400.00	90.00	490.00	23,210.00	59.94	39.20	2.00	101.14	388.86	1622
Total		20,800.00	2,410.00	23,210.00		1,946.72	1,856.80	104.00	3,907.52	19,302.48	

The employee earnings record is not a journal or a ledger, and it is not required by law. It is an accounting tool—like the work sheet—that the employer uses to prepare payroll tax reports to the Internal Revenue Service.

Exhibit 11-10 is the Wage and Tax Statement, Form W-2, for employee R. C. Dean. The employer prepares this statement and gives copies to the employee and to the Internal Revenue Service (IRS). Dean uses the W-2 to prepare his income tax return. To ensure that Dean is paying income tax on all his income from that job, the IRS matches Dean's income as reported on his tax return with his earnings as reported on the W-2.

Exhibit 11-10

Employee Wage and Tax Statement, Form W-2

a Control number 2222 Void ☐ For Official Use Only ▶ OMB No. 1545-0008

b Employer identification number: 83-19475

c Employer's name, address, and ZIP code:
Blumenthal's
Crescent Square Shopping Center
Fort Lauderdale, FL 33310-1234

d Employee's social security number: 344-86-4529

e Employee's name (first, middle initial, last): R.C. Dean
4376 Palm Drive
Fort Lauderdale, FL 33317

f Employee's address and ZIP code

1 Wages, tips, other compensation: 23,210.00	2 Federal income tax withheld: 1,946.72
3 Social security wages: 23,210.00	4 Social security tax withheld: 1,439.02
5 Medicare wages and tips: 23,210.00	6 Medicare tax withheld: 417.78
7 Social security tips	8 Allocated tips
9 Advance EIC payment	10 Dependent care benefits
11 Nonqualified plans	12 Benefits included in box 1
13 See instrs. for box 13	14 Other

15 Statutory employee ☐ Deceased ☐ Pension plan ☐ Legal rep. ☐ Deferred compensation ☐

16 State Employer's state ID no.	17 Sate wages, tips, etc	18 State income tax	19 Locality name	20 Local wages, tips, etc	21 Local income tax

Form **W-2** Wage and Tax Statement **2003**

Department of the Treasury—Internal Revenue Service

For Privacy Act and Paperwork Reduction Act Notice, see separate instructions.

Copy A For Social Security Administration—Send this entire page with Form W-3 to the Social Security Administration; photocopies are **not** acceptable.

Cat. No. 10134D

Paying the Payroll

Up to this point, we have talked only about *recording* payroll expenses and liabilities. We now turn to the *payment* of these liabilities. Most employers must record at least three cash payments for payrolls:

- Net pay to employees
- Payroll taxes and other payroll deductions
- Employee benefits

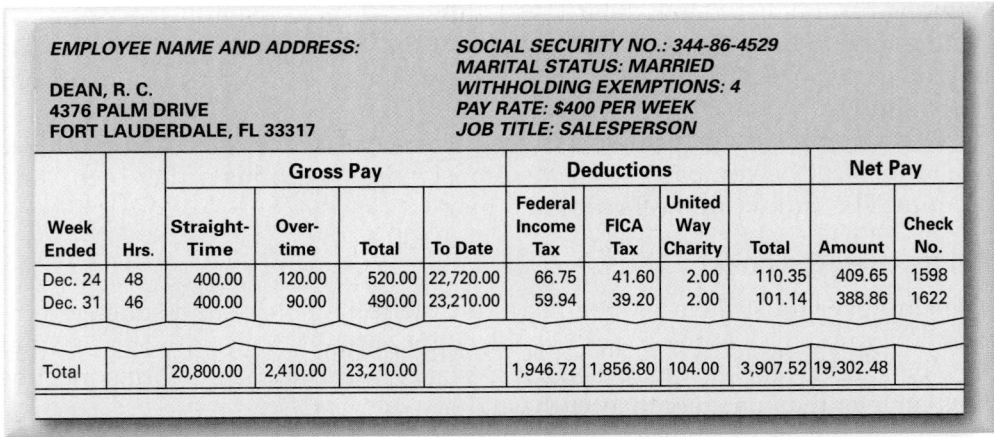

NET PAY TO EMPLOYEES When the company pays employees, it debits Salary Payable and credits Cash. Using the data in Exhibit 11-6, the company would make the following entry to record the cash payment (net pay) for the December 31 weekly payroll:

Dec. 31	Salary Payable	10,269.30	
	Cash		10,269.30

PAYROLL TAXES AND OTHER DEDUCTIONS The employer must send the government two sets of payroll taxes: those withheld from employees' pay and those paid by the employer. Based on the data in Exhibit 11-6, the business would record cash payments that can be summarized as follows (the unemployment tax amounts are assumed):

Dec. 31	Employee Income Tax Payable	3,367.76	
	FICA Tax Payable ($861.94 × 2)	1,723.88	
	Payable to Habitat for Humanity	155.00	
	State Unemployment Tax Payable	104.62	
	Federal Unemployment Tax Payable	15.50	
	Cash		5,366.76

BENEFITS The employer might pay for employees' insurance coverage and their pension plan. If the total cash payment for these benefits is $1,927.00, the entry is

Dec. 31	Employee Benefits Payable	1,927.00	
	Cash		1,927.00

Internal Control over Payroll

There are two main types of internal controls for payroll: controls for efficiency and controls to safeguard cash payments. →

← *Chapter 8 discusses internal controls over cash payments.*

EFFICIENCY Reconciling the bank account can be time-consuming because of the large number of paychecks. There may be many outstanding checks. To limit the number of outstanding checks, many companies use two payroll bank accounts. They pay the payroll from one bank account one month and from the other payroll account the next month. This way they can reconcile each account every other month, and that decreases accounting expense.

Payroll transactions are ideal for computer processing. Employee payroll data are stored in a file. The computer makes all calculations, prints the payroll record and the paychecks, and updates employee earnings records electronically.

SAFEGUARDING PAYROLL DISBURSEMENTS Owners and managers of small businesses can monitor their payrolls by personal contact with employees. Large corporations cannot. A particular risk is that a paycheck may be written to a fictitious person and cashed by a dishonest employee. To guard against this and other crimes, large businesses adopt strict internal control policies for payrolls.

The duties of hiring and firing employees should be separated from payroll accounting and from passing out paychecks. Issuing paychecks to employees with a photo ID ensures that only actual employees receive pay. A formal timekeeping system helps ensure that employees actually worked the number of hours claimed. Employees may punch time cards at the start and end of the workday to prove their attendance and number of hours worked.

✔ Starter 11-11

As we saw in Chapter 8, the foundation for good internal control is separation of duties. This is why companies have separate departments for the following payroll functions:

- Human Resources hires and fires employees
- Payroll maintains employee earnings records
- Accounting records all transactions
- Treasurer (or bursar) distributes paychecks to employees

Stop & Think

Centurion Homes of Omaha, Nebraska, builds houses with four construction crews. The foremen hire—and fire—workers and keep their hourly records. Each Friday morning, the foremen telephone their workers' hours to the home office, where accountants prepare the weekly paychecks. Around noon, the foremen pick up the paychecks. They return to the construction site and pay the workers at day's end. What is the internal control weakness in this situation? Propose a way to improve the internal controls.

Answer: The foremen control most of the payroll information, so they can forge the payroll records of fictitious employees and pocket their pay. To improve internal control, Centurion could hire and fire all workers through the home office. This would prove that all workers actually exist. Another way to improve the internal controls would be to have a home-office employee distribute paychecks on a surprise basis. Any unclaimed checks would arouse suspicion. This system would probably prevent foremen from cheating the company.

☐ Liabilities of Known Amount
☐ Estimated Liabilities
☐ Accounting for Payroll
☐ The Payroll System
■ Reporting Liabilities
☐ Ethical Issues

Student Resource CD
current liabilities

6 *Report current liabilities on the balance sheet*

✔ Starter 11-12

Reporting Payroll Expense and Liabilities

At the end of each period, the company reports all of its current liabilities on the balance sheet. At December 31, 20X6, Centurion Homes had the current liabilities shown in Exhibit 11-11. Centurion combines all payroll liabilities under a single heading: Compensation and Benefits Payable.

Exhibit 11-11

Current Liabilities on the Balance Sheet

Current Liabilities	
Accounts payable	$ 6,400
Compensation and benefits payable	3,800
Unearned revenue	4,500
Other accrued expenses and liabilities	5,700
Total current liabilities	$20,400

☐ Liabilities of Known Amount
☐ Estimated Liabilities
☐ Accounting for Payroll
☐ The Payroll System
☐ Reporting Liabilities
■ Ethical Issues

Ethical Issues in Reporting Liabilities

Accounting for liabilities poses an ethical challenge. Businesses want to look as successful as possible. They like to show high levels of net income because that makes the company look successful. High income also helps raise money from investors. And high asset values and low liabilities make the company look safe to lenders.

Owners and managers may be tempted to overlook some expenses and liabilities at the end of the accounting period. For example, a company can fail to accrue warranty expense. This will cause total expenses to be understated and net income to be overstated on the income statement.

Student Resource CD
contingent liabilities

Contingent liabilities also pose an ethical challenge. Because contingencies are not real liabilities, they are easy to overlook. But a contingent liability can be very important. Ethical business people do not play games with their accounting. Falsifying financial statements can ruin a reputation. It can also land a person in prison.

Decision Guidelines

ACCOUNTING FOR PAYROLL

CompUSA is a leading computer equipment chain. Suppose you manage a CompUSA store near your college and employ 10 people. What decisions must you make to account for payroll properly? The Decision Guidelines provide an outline for your actions.

Decision	Guidelines
What are the key elements of a payroll accounting system?	• Employee's Withholding Allowance Certificate, Form W-4 • Payroll record • Payroll checks • Employer's quarterly tax returns, such as Form 941 • Employee earnings record • Employee wage and tax statement, Form W-2
What are the key terms in the payroll area?	Gross pay (Total amount earned by the employee) – *Payroll deductions* **a.** Withheld income tax **b.** FICA (Social Security) tax—equal amount also payable by employer **c.** Optional deductions (insurance, savings, charitable contributions, union dues) = *Net (take-home) pay*
What is the employer's total payroll expense?	Gross pay + *Employer's payroll taxes* **a.** FICA (Social Security) tax—equal amount also payable by employee **b.** State and federal unemployment taxes + *Benefits for employees* **a.** Insurance (health, life, and disability) **b.** Pension (and other retirement) benefits **c.** Club memberships and other = *Employer's total payroll costs*
Where to report payroll costs?	• Payroll expenses on the income statement • Payroll liabilities on the balance sheet

Excel Application Exercise

Goal: Create a simple spreadsheet for computing payroll for a small company.

Scenario: Romano Service Co. has three employees for whom payroll must be calculated every two weeks. Hourly pay rates for each employee are as follows: J. Smith, $12.00; A. Jackson, $14.00; and B. Allen, $10.00. Overtime is paid at 1.5 times the hourly rate. Tax and withholding rates are as follows: Income tax, 11%; FICA, 8%; and pension plan, 10% of gross pay. Income tax, FICA, and pension are withheld from employee paychecks. During the current pay period, Smith worked 40 regular hours, Jackson worked 40 regular hours and 4 overtime hours, and Allen worked 38 hours.

Romano also must pay the employer portion for FICA (8%), plus state unemployment tax (5.4%) and federal unemployment tax (0.8%).

For each employee, calculate regular pay, overtime pay, gross pay, income tax withholding, FICA, pension plan amount, and net pay. Also calculate state and federal unemployment. When you have completed your work sheet, answer the following questions:

1. What is the net pay for each person?
2. What journal entries are required to record payroll expense for this period?
3. What is Romano's total payroll expense this period?

Excel Application Exercise *(continued)*

Step-by-Step:

1. Open a new Excel spreadsheet.
2. In column 1, create a bold-faced heading as follows:
   a. Chapter 11 Excel Application Exercise
   b. Romano Service Co.
   c. Pay Period Ending April 25, 20X5
3. Two rows down in column A, create a bold-faced heading titled, "Employee." In column B, create the same for "Pay Rate." In column C, enter the heading, "Regular Hours Worked," and in column D, enter "Overtime Hours Worked." Underline all four headings.
4. Enter the data for each employee under the appropriate headings.
5. Underneath the employee data in column A, enter titles for the overtime rate and all taxes/withholdings, one per row. In column B, enter the amount or percentage given in the exercise.
6. Below the employee and tax/withholding data, prepare the payroll calculations. Start with Employee Name in column A, and then enter titles for Regular Pay, Overtime Pay, Gross Pay, Income Tax Withholding, FICA, State Unemployment, Federal Unemployment, Pension Plan, and Net Pay. In the two columns after net pay, calculate state unemployment and federal unemployment taxes. These are not withheld from employee paychecks but are required to be paid by the employer.
7. Enter each employee name. Then create formulas for the calculation of all payroll items. At the end of each column, prepare a total.
8. Save your work sheet and print a copy for your files.

END-OF-CHAPTER *Summary Problem*

A+ TIPS
CHECK YOUR RESOURCES

Beth Denius, a clothing store, employs one salesperson, Alan Kingsley. His straight-time salary is $360 per week, with time-and-a-half pay for hours above 40 per week. Beth Denius withholds income tax (11.0%) and FICA tax (8.0%) from Kingsley's pay. She also pays payroll taxes for FICA (8.0%) and state and federal unemployment (5.4% and 0.8%, respectively). In addition, Denius contributes 10% of Kingsley's gross pay into his pension plan.

During the week ended December 26, 20X4, Kingsley worked 48 hours. Prior to this week, Kingsley had earned $5,470.

Required

1. Compute Kingsley's gross pay and net pay for the week.
2. Record the following payroll entries that Denius would make for:
   a. Kingsley's salary, including overtime
   b. Employer payroll taxes
   c. Expense for employee benefits
   d. Payment of cash to Kingsley
   e. Payment of all payroll taxes
   f. Payment for employee benefits
3. How much was Denius's total payroll expense for the week?

Solutions

Requirement 1

Gross pay:	Straight-time pay for 40 hours		$360.00
	Overtime pay:		
	Rate per hour ($360/40 × 1.5)	$13.50	
	Hours (48 – 40)	8	108.00
	Total gross pay		$468.00
Net pay:	Gross pay		$468.00
	Less: Withheld income tax ($468 × 0.11)	$51.48	
	Withheld FICA tax ($468 × 0.08)	37.44	88.92
	Net pay		$379.08

Requirement 2

a.	Sales Salary Expense	468.00	
	Employee Income Tax Payable		51.48
	FICA Tax Payable		37.44
	Salary Payable		379.08
b.	Payroll Tax Expense	66.45	
	FICA Tax Payable ($468 × 0.08)		37.44
	State Unemployment Tax Payable ($468 × 0.054)		25.27
	Federal Unemployment Tax Payable ($468 × 0.008)		3.74

c.	Pension Expense ($468 × 0.10)	46.80	
	Employee Benefits Payable		46.80
d.	Salary Payable	379.08	
	Cash		379.08
e.	Employee Income Tax Payable	51.48	
	FICA Tax Payable ($37.44 × 2)	74.88	
	State Unemployment Tax Payable	25.27	
	Federal Unemployment Tax Payable	3.74	
	Cash		155.37
f.	Employee Benefits Payable	46.80	
	Cash		46.80

Requirement 3

Denius incurred *total payroll expense* of $581.25 (gross salary of $468.00 + payroll taxes of $66.45 + benefits of $46.80). See entries **(a)** through **(c)**.

REVIEW *Current Liabilities and Payroll*

Quick Check

1. Known liabilities of uncertain amounts should be
   a. Estimated and accrued when they occur
   b. Ignored (Record them when paid.)
   c. Reported on the income statement
   d. Described in the notes to the financial statements
2. On January 1, 20X5, you borrowed $10,000 on a five-year, 8% note payable. At December 31, 20X6, you should record
   a. Note receivable of $10,000
   b. Nothing (The note is already on the books.)
   c. Interest payable of $800
   d. Cash receipt of $10,000
3. Your company sells $100,000 of goods and you collect sales tax of 3%. What current liability does the sale create?
   a. Accounts payable of $3,000
   b. Unearned revenue of $3,000
   c. Sales revenue of $103,000
   d. Sales tax payable of $3,000
4. At December 31, your company owes employees for three days of the five-day work-week. The total payroll for the week is $8,000. What journal entry should you make at December 31?
   a. Nothing, because you will pay the employees on Friday

b. Salary Expense	8,000	
Salary Payable		8,000
c. Salary Expense	4,800	
Salary Payable		4,800
d. Salary Expense	3,200	
Cash		3,200

5. What is unearned revenue?
   a. Receivable
   b. Current liability
   c. Revenue
   d. Current asset
6. **Sony** owed Estimated Warranty Payable of $1,000 at the end of 20X3. During 20X4, Sony made sales of $100,000 and expects product warranties to cost the company 3% of the sales. During 20X4, Sony paid $2,500 for warranties. What is Sony's Estimated Warranty Payable at the end of 20X4?
   a. $1,500
   b. $2,500
   c. $3,000
   d. $3,500

7. Payroll expenses include
   a. Salaries and wages
   b. Employee benefits
   c. Payroll taxes
   d. All of the above
8. What is the most that an employee paid the federal government for old age, survivors', and disability insurance (FICA tax) during 2003?
   a. $5,394.
   b. $87,000.
   c. Nothing. The employer paid it.
   d. There is no upper limit.
9. The document that an employer gives each employee at the end of the year to report annual earnings and taxes paid is the
   a. Payroll record
   b. Form 941
   c. Form W-2
   d. Form W-4
10. The foundation of internal control over payrolls is
    a. Paying the correct amount of payroll tax
    b. Accurately computing gross pay, deductions, and net pay
    c. Filing government tax forms on time
    d. Separating payroll duties

Accounting Vocabulary

accrued expense (p. 438)
accrued liability (p. 438)
current portion of long-term debt (p. 438)
current maturity (p. 438)
employee compensation (p. 439)
FICA tax (p. 444)
gross pay (p. 443)
net pay (p. 443)
payroll (p. 439)
short-term note payable (p. 436)
Social Security tax (p. 444)
unemployment compensation tax (p. 444)
withheld income tax (p. 443)

ASSESS *Your Progress*

A+ online homework

See *www.prenhall.com/horngren* for selected Starters, Exercises, and Problems.

Starters

Accounting for a note payable
(Obj. 1)

S11-1 Return to the $8,000 purchase of inventory on a short-term note payable that begins on page 436. Assume that the purchase of inventory occurred on June 30, 20X6, instead of September 30, 20X6. Journalize the company's (a) accrual of interest expense on December 31, 20X6 and (b) payment of the note plus interest on June 30, 20X7.

Reporting a short-term note payable and the related interest
(Obj. 1)

S11-2 Refer to the data in Starter 11-1. Show what the company would report for the note payable and related interest payable on its balance sheet at December 31, 20X6, and on its income statement for the year ended on that date.

Accounting for warranty expense and warranty payable
(Obj. 2)

S11-3 **Ford**, the automaker, guarantees its automobiles for three years or 36,000 miles, whichever comes first. Suppose Ford's experience indicates that the company can expect warranty costs to add up to 5% of sales.

Assume that Friendly Ford in Atlanta made sales totaling $600,000 during March 20X7, its first month of operations. The company received cash for 30% of the sales and notes receivable for the remainder. Payments to satisfy customer warranty claims totaled $25,000 during 20X7.

1. Record the sales, warranty expense, and warranty payments for Friendly Ford.
2. Post to the Estimated Warranty Payable T-account. At the end of 20X7, how much in estimated warranty payable does Friendly Ford owe its customers?

Applying GAAP; reporting warranties in the financial statements
(Obj. 2)

S11-4 Refer to the data given in Starter 11-3.

What amount of warranty expense will Friendly Ford report during 20X7? Does the warranty expense for the year equal the year's cash payments for warranties? Which accounting principle addresses this situation? Explain how the accounting principle works for measuring warranty expense.

S11-5 **Harley-Davidson, Inc.**, the motorcycle manufacturer, included the following note (adapted) in its annual report:

Interpreting an actual company's contingent liabilities **(Obj. 2)**

Notes to Consolidated Financial Statements
7 (in Part): Commitments and Contingencies (Adapted)
The Company self-insures its product liability losses in the United States up to $3 million.
Catastrophic coverage is maintained for individual claims in excess of $3 million up to $25 million.

1. Why are these *contingent* (versus real) liabilities?
2. How can a contingent liability become a real liability for Harley-Davidson? What are the limits to the company's product liabilities in the United States?

Starter 11-6 begins a sequence of exercises that ends with Starter 11-8.

S11-6 Examine the payroll situation of Lucy Childres on pages 442–443.

Computing an employee's total pay **(Obj. 3)**

1. Compute Childres's total pay for working 50 hours during the first week of February.
2. Childres is single, and her income tax withholding is 10% of total pay. Her only payroll deductions are payroll taxes. Compute Childres's net pay for the week. (Use an 8% FICA tax rate.)

S11-7 Return to the Lucy Childres payroll situation in Starter 11-6. Childres's employer, Bobby Jones Golf Company, pays all the standard payroll taxes plus benefits for employee pensions (5% of total pay), health insurance ($60 per employee per month), and disability insurance ($8 per employee per month).

Computing the payroll expense of an employer **(Obj. 3)**

Compute Bobby Jones's total expense of employing Lucy Childres for the 50 hours that she worked during the first week of February. Carry amounts to the nearest cent.

S11-8 After solving Starters 11-6 and 11-7, journalize for Bobby Jones Golf Company the following expenses related to the employment of Lucy Childres:

Making payroll entries **(Obj. 4)**

a. Salary expense **b.** Employer payroll taxes **c.** Benefits

Use Exhibit 11-5 (p. 445) to format your journal entries. Carry all amounts to the nearest cent.

S11-9 Suppose you work for an accounting firm all year and earn a monthly salary of $8,000. There is no overtime pay. Your withheld income taxes consume 15% of gross pay. In addition to payroll taxes, you elect to contribute 5% monthly to your pension plan. Your employer also deducts $200 monthly for your co-pay of the health insurance premium.

Computing payroll amounts late in the year **(Obj. 3)**

Compute your net pay for November. Use an 8% FICA tax rate on the first $87,000 of income.

S11-10 Refer to the payroll record in Exhibit 11-6, page 446.

Using a payroll system **(Obj. 5)**

1. How much was the company's total salary expense for the week?
2. How much cash did the employees take home for their work?
3. How much did *employees* pay this week for
   a. Federal income tax?
   b. FICA tax?
4. How much expense did the *employer* have this week for
   a. Employee federal income tax?
   b. FICA tax?

S11-11 ←*Link Back to Chapter 8 (Internal Controls).* What are some of the important elements of good internal control to safeguard payroll disbursements?

Internal controls over payroll disbursements **(Obj. 5)**

Reporting current liabilities
(Obj. 6)

S11-12 Study the payroll record of **Blumenthal's** in Exhibit 11-6, page 446. Assume Blumenthal's will pay this payroll on January 2, 2004. In addition to the payroll liabilities shown in the exhibit, Blumenthal's has the following current liabilities at December 31, 2003.

Accounts payable	$44,100
Employer FICA tax payable	862
Interest payable	1,110

Prepare the current liabilities section of Blumenthal's balance sheet at December 31, 2003. List current liabilities in descending order, starting with the largest first. Also list each of the payroll liabilities from Exhibit 11-6, rounded to the nearest dollar. Show total current liabilities.

A+ online homework

Exercises

Recording sales tax
(Obj. 1)

E11-1 Make general journal entries to record the following transactions of Club Havasu Vacations for a two-month period. Explanations are not required.

March 31	Recorded cash sales of $200,000 for the month, plus sales tax of 4% collected on behalf of the state of Arizona.
April 6	Sent March sales tax to the state.

Recording and reporting current liabilities
(Obj. 1)

E11-2 Assume the **Chicago Tribune** publishing company completed the following transactions during 20X8:

Nov. 1	Sold a six-month subscription, collecting cash of $180, plus sales tax of 5%.
Dec. 15	Remitted (paid) the sales tax to the state of Illinois.
31	Made the necessary adjustment at year-end to record the amount of subscription revenue earned during the year.

Journalize these transactions (explanations are not required). Then report the liability on the company's balance sheet at December 31, 20X8.

Accounting for warranty expense and warranty payable
(Obj. 2)

E11-3 The accounting records of Grafton Tire Company included the following at December 31, 20X5:

Estimated Warranty Payable

	Balance 3,000

In the past, Grafton's warranty expense has been 6% of sales. During 20X6, Grafton made sales of $200,000 and paid $10,000 to satisfy warranty claims.

Required

1. Journalize Grafton's warranty expense and cash payments to satisfy warranty claims during 20X6. Explanations are not required.
2. What balance of Estimated Warranty Payable will Grafton report on its balance sheet at December 31, 20X6?

Recording note payable transactions
(Obj. 1)

E11-4 Record the following note payable transactions of MG Publishing, Inc., in the company's general journal. Explanations are not required.

20X2	
May 1	Purchased equipment costing $15,000 by issuing a one-year, 6% note payable.
Dec. 31	Accrued interest on the note payable.
20X3	
May 1	Paid the note payable at maturity.

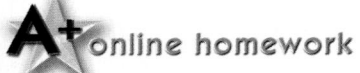

E11-5 Lana Gautier is manager of the women's sportswear department of Parisian Department Store in High Point, North Carolina. She earns a base monthly salary of $750 plus a 10% commission on her personal sales. Through payroll deductions, Gautier donates $25 per month to a charitable organization, and she authorizes Parisian to deduct $20 monthly for her health insurance. Tax rates on Gautier's earnings are 10% for income tax and 8% of the first $87,000 for FICA. During the first 11 months of the year, she earned $82,000.

Computing net pay
(Obj. 3)
Student ResourceCD
spreadsheet

Required

Compute Gautier's gross pay and net pay for December, assuming her sales for the month are $80,000.

E11-6 Mel O'Conner works as a cook for a **Steak 'n Shake** diner. His straight-time pay is $10 per hour, with time and a half for hours in excess of 40 per week. O'Conner's payroll deductions include withheld income tax of 7% of total earnings, FICA tax of 8% of total earnings, and a weekly deduction of $5 for a charitable contribution to United Fund.

Computing and recording gross pay and net pay
(Obj. 3, 4)
Student ResourceCD
spreadsheet

Required

Assuming O'Conner worked 50 hours during the week, (a) compute his gross pay and net pay for the week and (b) make a general journal entry to record the store's wage expense for O'Conner's work, including payroll deductions. Explanations are not required.

E11-7 **Mill Creek Golf Course** incurred salary expense of $92,000 for December. The pro shop's payroll expense includes employer FICA tax of 8% in addition to state unemployment tax of 5.4% and federal unemployment tax of 0.8%. Of the total salaries, $88,400 is subject to FICA tax, and $9,000 is subject to unemployment tax. Also, the store provides the following benefits for employees: health insurance (cost to the store, $2,060), life insurance (cost to the store, $350), and pension benefits (cost to the store, 6% of salary expense).

Recording a payroll
(Obj. 3, 4)

Required

Record Mill Creek's payroll taxes and its expenses for employee benefits. Explanations are not required.

E11-8 Jupiter Technologies has annual salary expense of $600,000. In addition, Jupiter incurs payroll tax expense equal to 9% of the total payroll. At December 31, Jupiter owes salaries of $4,000 and FICA and other payroll taxes of $1,000. Jupiter will pay these amounts early next year.

Reporting payroll expense and liabilities
(Obj. 6)

Required

Show what Jupiter will report for these facts on its income statement and year-end balance sheet.

E11-9 Unity Medical Group borrowed $3,000,000 on January 2, 20X1, by issuing a 9% long-term note payable that must be paid in three equal annual installments plus interest each January 2.

Reporting current and long-term liabilities
(Obj. 6)

Required

Insert the appropriate amounts to show how Unity would report its current and long-term liabilities.

	December 31		
	20X1	20X2	20X3
Current liabilities:			
Current portion of long-term note payable . .	$_____	$ _____	$ _____
Interest payable	_____	_____	_____
Long-term liabilities:			
Long-term note payable	_____	_____	_____

Reporting current and long-term liabilities
(Obj. 6)

E11-10 Assume that **Wilson Sporting Goods** completed these selected transactions during December 20X4.

a. Sales of $500,000 are subject to estimated warranty cost of 3%.
b. **Champs**, a chain of sporting goods stores, ordered $9,000 of tennis and golf equipment. With its order, Champs sent a check for $9,000 in advance. Wilson will ship the goods on January 3, 20X5.
c. The December payroll of $200,000 is subject to employee withheld income tax of 9%, FICA tax of 8% (employee and employer), state unemployment tax of 5.4%, and federal unemployment tax of 0.8%. On December 31, Wilson pays employees but accrues all tax amounts.

Required

Report each item at its correct amount on Wilson's balance sheet at December 31, 20X4. Show total current liabilities.

Analyzing current liabilities; using the current ratio
(Obj. 1, 6)

E11-11 ←*Link Back to Chapter 4 (Current Ratio)*. The balance sheets of **PepsiCo, Inc.**, for two years reported these figures:

	Billions	
	20X2	**20X1**
Total current assets	$ 4.6	$ 4.1
Noncurrent assets	14.2	13.0
	$18.8	$17.1
Total current liabilities	$ 3.7	$ 4.8
Noncurrent liabilities	9.5	7.4
Stockholders' equity	5.6	4.9
	$18.8	$17.1

Compute PepsiCo's current ratio and debt ratio for both years. Did the ratios improve or deteriorate in 20X2? Compute the debt ratio to 3 decimal places, and use Chapter 4 if necessary.

Recording current liabilities
(Obj. 1, 6)

E11-12 **PepsiCo, Inc.**, reported short-term notes payable and salary payable (adapted, in millions), as follows:

	December 31	
	20X2	**20X1**
Current liabilities (partial):		
Short-term notes payable	$707	$228
Salary payable	327	334

Assume that during 20X2, PepsiCo paid off both current liabilities that were left over from 20X1. Also assume that PepsiCo borrowed money on short-term notes payable and accrued salary expense during 20X2.

Required

Journalize all four of PepsiCo's transactions during 20X2.

A+ online homework

Problems

(Group A)

Journalizing liability transactions
(Obj. 1, 2)

Student Resource CD
General Ledger, Peachtree, QuickBooks

P11-1A The following transactions of SuperValue stores occurred during 20X5 and 20X6.

20X5		
Feb.	3	Purchased equipment for $10,000, signing a six-month, 9% note payable.
	28	Recorded the week's sales of $51,000, one-third for cash, and two-thirds on credit. All sales amounts are subject to a 5% sales tax.
Mar.	7	Sent last week's sales tax to the state.
Apr.	30	Borrowed $100,000 on a four-year, 9% note payable that calls for annual payment of interest each April 30.
Aug.	3	Paid the six-month, 9% note at maturity.
Nov.	30	Purchased inventory at a cost of $7,200, signing a three-month, 8% note payable for that amount.
Dec.	31	Accrued warranty expense, which is estimated at 3% of sales of $260,000.
	31	Accrued interest on all outstanding notes payable. Made a separate interest accrual entry for each note payable.
20X6		
Feb.	28	Paid off the 8% inventory note, plus interest, at maturity.
Apr.	30	Paid the interest for one year on the long-term note payable.

Required

Record the transactions in the company's general journal. Explanations are not required.

P11-2A The records of Excel Food Service show the following figures:

Computing and recording a payroll **(Obj. 3, 4)**

	Employee Earnings	
(a)	Straight-time earnings	$?
(b)	Overtime pay	5,109
(c)	Total employee earnings	?
	Deductions and Net Pay	
(d)	Withheld income tax	$ 9,293
(e)	FICA tax	6,052
(f)	Charitable contributions	?
(g)	Medical insurance	1,373
(h)	Total deductions	18,880
(i)	Net pay	64,813
	Account Debited	
(j)	Salary Expense	$?

Required

1. Determine the missing amounts on lines (a), (c), (f), and (j).
2. Journalize Excel's payroll for the month. No explanation is required.

P11-3A Jan Summers is a vice president at Harbor State Bank in Boston. During 20X5, she worked for the bank all year at a $6,500 monthly salary. She also earned a year-end bonus equal to 15% of her annual salary.

Computing and recording payroll amounts **(Obj. 3, 4)**

Student Resource CD
spreadsheet

Summers' federal income tax withheld during 20X5 was $820 per month, plus $2,480 on her bonus check. State income tax withheld came to $60 per month, plus $80 on the bonus. The FICA tax withheld was 8% of the first $87,000 of annual earnings. Summers authorized the following payroll deductions: United Fund contribution of 1% of total earnings and life insurance of $20 per month.

Harbor State Bank incurred payroll tax expense on Summers for FICA tax of 8% of the first $87,000 in total annual earnings. The bank also paid state unemployment tax of 5.4% and federal unemployment tax of 0.8% on the first $7,000 in annual earnings. The bank provided Summers with the following benefits: health insurance at a cost of $40 per month, and pension benefits to be paid to Summers during her retirement. During 20X5, the bank's cost of Summers' pension program was $4,000.

Required

1. Compute Summers' gross pay, payroll deductions, and net pay during 20X5. Round all amounts to the nearest dollar.
2. Compute the bank's total 20X5 payroll cost for Summers.
3. Prepare the bank's summary general journal entries to record its expense for:
   a. Summers' total earnings for the year, her payroll deductions, and her net pay. Debit Salary Expense and Executive Bonus Compensation as appropriate. Credit liability accounts for the payroll deductions and Cash for net pay.
   b. Employer payroll taxes for Summers. Credit liability accounts.
   c. Benefits provided to Summers. Credit a liability account.

Explanations are not required.

Journalizing, posting, and reporting liabilities
(Obj. 1, 2, 3, 4, 5, 6)

Student Resource CD
GL, PT, QB

P11-4A The Emerson Technology general ledger at September 30, 20X8, the end of the company's fiscal year, includes the following account balances before adjusting entries.

Accounts Payable	$ 88,200
Current Portion of Long-Term Debt	______
Interest Payable	______
Salary Payable	______
Employee Payroll Taxes Payable	______
Employer Payroll Taxes Payable	______
Unearned Rent Revenue	3,900
Long-Term Debt	100,000

The additional data needed to develop the adjusting entries at September 30 are as follows:

a. The long-term debt is payable in annual installments of $50,000, with the next installment due on January 31, 20X9. On that date, Emerson will also pay one year's interest at 6.6%. Interest was last paid on January 31. Make the adjusting entry to shift the current installment of the long-term debt to a current liability. Also accrue interest expense at year end.
b. Gross salaries for the last payroll of the fiscal year were $4,300. Of this amount, employee payroll taxes payable were $950.
c. Employer payroll taxes payable were $890.
d. On August 1, the company collected six months' rent of $3,900 in advance.

Required

1. Open the listed accounts, inserting their unadjusted September 30 balances.
2. Journalize and post the September 30 adjusting entries to the accounts opened. Key adjusting entries by letter.
3. Prepare the liabilities section of Emerson Technology's balance sheet at September 30, 20X8. Show total current liabilities and total liabilities.

Using a payroll record; recording a payroll
(Obj. 5)

P11-5A The payroll records of a Nissan Motor Systems' district office provided the following information for the weekly pay period ended December 29, 20X3:

Employee	Hours Worked	Weekly Earnings Rate	Federal Income Tax	Health Insurance	Earnings Through Previous Week
Clay Cooper	43	$ 400	$ 74	$ 16	$17,060
Tim LeMann	46	480	90	10	22,300
Lena Marx	48	1,400	319	46	86,200
Karen York	40	240	32	6	3,410

All employees are paid time and a half for hours worked in excess of 40 per week.

Required

For convenience, round all amounts to the nearest dollar. Show your computations. Explanations are not required for journal entries.

1. Enter the appropriate information in a payroll record similar to Exhibit 11-6, page 446. In addition to the deductions listed, the employer also withholds FICA tax: 8% of the first $87,000 of each employee's annual earnings.
2. Record the payroll information in the general journal.
3. Assume that the first payroll check is number 178, paid to Cooper. Record the check numbers in the payroll record. Also, prepare the general journal entry to record payment of net pay to the employees.
4. The employer's payroll taxes include FICA of 8% of the first $87,000 of each employee's annual earnings. The employer also pays unemployment taxes of 6.2% (5.4% for the state and 0.8% for the federal government) on the first $7,000 of each employee's annual earnings. Record the employer's payroll taxes in the general journal.

Reporting current liabilities
(Obj. 6)

P11-6A Following are pertinent facts about events during the current year at Marineland Boats.

a. December sales totaled $404,000, and Marineland collected sales tax of 5%. The sales tax will be sent to the state of Washington early in January.
b. Marineland owes $75,000 on a long-term note payable. At December 31, 6% interest for the year plus $25,000 of this principal are payable within one year.
c. On August 31, Marineland signed a six-month, 6% note payable to purchase a machine costing $80,000. The note requires payment of principal and interest at maturity.
d. Sales of $909,000 were covered by the Marineland product warranty. At January 1, estimated warranty payable was $11,300. During the year, Marineland recorded warranty expense of $27,900 and paid warranty claims of $30,100.
e. On October 31, Marineland received cash of $2,400 in advance for the rent on a building. This rent will be earned evenly over six months.

Required

For each item, indicate the account and the related amount to be reported as a current liability on Marineland's December 31 balance sheet.

Problems

(Group B)

A+ online homework

Journalizing liability transactions
(Obj. 1, 2)

Student Resource CD
GL, PT, QB

P11-1B The following transactions of Transocean Shipping occurred during 20X4 and 20X5:

20X4		
Jan.	9	Purchased equipment at a cost of $20,000, signing a six-month, 8% note payable for that amount.
	29	Recorded the week's sales of $40,000, three-fourths on credit, and one-fourth for cash. Sales amounts are subject to an additional 6% state sales tax.
Feb.	5	Sent the last week's sales tax to the state.
	28	Borrowed $200,000 on a four-year, 9% note payable that calls for annual installment payments of $50,000 principal plus interest. Record the short-term and the long-term portions of the note payable in two separate accounts.
July	9	Paid the six-month, 8% note at maturity.
Nov.	30	Purchased inventory for $3,000, signing a six-month, 10% note payable.
Dec.	31	Accrued warranty expense, which is estimated at 3% of sales of $650,000.
	31	Accrued interest on all outstanding notes payable. Made a separate interest accrual entry for each note payable.

(continued)

20X5	
Feb. 28	Paid the first installment and interest for one year on the long-term note payable.
May 31	Paid off the 10% note plus interest on maturity.

Required

Record the transactions in the company's general journal. Explanations are not required.

Computing and recording a payroll
(Obj. 3, 4)

P11-2B The records of Collegiate Specialties show the following figures:

	Employee Earnings	
(a)	Straight-time earnings	$16,431
(b)	Overtime pay	?
(c)	Total employee earnings	?
	Deductions and Net Pay	
(d)	Withheld income tax	$ 2,300
(e)	FICA tax	?
(f)	Charitable contributions	340
(g)	Medical insurance	668
(h)	Total deductions	5,409
(i)	Net pay	18,540
	Accounts Debited	
(j)	Salary Expense	$?

Required

1. Determine the missing amounts on lines (b), (c), (e), and (j).

2. Journalize this payroll for the month. No explanation is required.

Computing and recording payroll amounts
(Obj. 3, 4)

Student Resource CD
spreadsheet

P11-3B Brenda Gates is vice president of finance for Transco Leasing. During 20X5, she worked for the company all year at a $6,625 monthly salary. She also earned a year-end bonus equal to 10% of her salary.

Gates's federal income tax withheld during 20X5 was $737 per month, plus $1,007 on her bonus check. State income tax withheld came to $43 per month, plus $27 on the bonus. The FICA tax withheld was 8% of the first $87,000 in annual earnings. Gates authorized the following payroll deductions: United Fund contribution of 1% of total earnings and life insurance of $19 per month.

Transco incurred payroll tax expense on Gates for FICA tax of 8% of the first $87,000 in annual earnings. The company also paid state unemployment tax of 5.4% and federal unemployment tax of 0.8% on the first $7,000 in annual earnings. In addition, Transco provides Gates with health insurance at a cost of $35 per month and pension benefits. During 20X5, Transco paid $7,000 into Gates's pension program.

Required

1. Compute Gates's gross pay, payroll deductions, and net pay for the full year 20X5. Round all amounts to the nearest dollar.

2. Compute Transco's total 20X5 payroll cost for Brenda Gates.

3. Prepare Transco's summary general journal entries to record its expense for the following:

a. Gates's total earnings for the year, her payroll deductions, and her net pay. Debit Salary Expense and Executive Bonus Compensation as appropriate. Credit liability accounts for the payroll deductions and Cash for net pay.

b. Employer payroll taxes on Gates. Credit liability accounts.

c. Benefits provided to Gates. Credit a liability account. Explanations are not required.

Journalizing, posting, and reporting liabilities
(Obj. 1, 2, 3, 4, 5, 6)

Student Resource CD
GL, PT, QB

P11-4B The general ledger of Red Brick Investments at June 30, 20X8, the end of the company's fiscal year, includes the following account balances before adjusting entries.

Accounts Payable	$105,520
Current Portion of Long-Term Debt	_______
Interest Payable	_______
Salary Payable	_______
Employee Payroll Taxes Payable	_______
Employer Payroll Taxes Payable	_______
Unearned Rent Revenue	6,000
Long-Term Debt	200,000

The additional data needed to develop the adjusting entries at June 30 are as follows:

a. The long-term debt is payable in annual installments of $40,000 with the next installment due on July 31. On that date, Red Brick will also pay one year's interest at 9%. Interest was last paid on July 31 of the preceding year. Make the adjusting entry to shift the current installment of the long-term debt to a current liability. Also accrue interest expense at year end.

b. Gross salaries for the last payroll of the fiscal year were $5,044. Of this amount, employee payroll taxes payable were $1,088, and salary payable was $3,956.

c. Employer payroll taxes payable were $876.

d. On February 1, the company collected one year's rent of $6,000 in advance.

Required

1. Open the listed accounts, inserting the unadjusted June 30 balances.
2. Journalize and post the June 30 adjusting entries to the accounts opened. Key adjusting entries by letter.
3. Prepare the liabilities section of the balance sheet at June 30, 20X8. Show total current liabilities and total liabilities.

Using a payroll record; recording a payroll **(Obj. 5)**

P11-5B Assume that the payroll records of a district sales office of **Spalding Sporting Goods** provided the following information for the weekly pay period ended December 29, 20X6.

Employee	Hours Worked	Hourly Earnings Rate	Federal Income Tax	United Way Contributions	Earnings Through Previous Week
Larry Fisher	42	$40	$278	$35	$87,474
Felicia Jones	47	8	87	4	23,154
Joe Opper	40	11	64	4	4,880
Sara Tate	46	35	288	8	86,600

Employees are paid time and a half for hours over 40/week. Round all amounts to the nearest dollar. Show your computations. Explanations are not required for journal entries.

Required

1. Enter the appropriate information in a payroll record similar to Exhibit 11-6, page 446. In addition to the deductions listed, the employer also takes out FICA tax: 8% of the first $87,000 of each employee's annual earnings.
2. Record the payroll information in the general journal.
3. Assume that the first payroll check is number 319, paid to Larry Fisher. Record the check numbers in the payroll record. Also, prepare the general journal entry to record payment of net pay to the employees.
4. The employer's payroll taxes include FICA tax of 8% of the first $87,000 of each employee's earnings. The employer also pays unemployment taxes of 6.2% (5.4% for the state and 0.8% for the federal government) on the first $7,000 of each employee's annual earnings. Record the employer's payroll taxes in the general journal.

Reporting current liabilities
(Obj. 6)

P11-6B Following are pertinent facts about Falcon Jet's transactions during the current year.

a. On November 30, Falcon received cash of $6,000 in advance for the rent on a building. This rent will be earned evenly over three months.
b. December sales totaled $110,000, and Falcon collected an additional state sales tax of 7%. This amount will be sent to the state of Tennessee early in January.
c. Falcon owes $100,000 on a long-term note payable. At December 31, 6% interest on the full note and $20,000 of this principal are payable within one year.
d. Sales of $400,000 were covered by Falcon's product warranty. At January 1, estimated warranty payable was $8,000. During the year, Falcon recorded warranty expense of $22,000 and paid warranty claims of $24,000.
e. On September 30, Falcon signed a six-month, 9% note payable to purchase equipment costing $30,000. The note requires payment of principal and interest at maturity.

Required

For each item, indicate the account and the related amount to be reported as a current liability on Falcon's December 31 balance sheet.

APPLY *Your Knowledge*

Decision Cases

Identifying internal control weaknesses and their solution
(Obj. 5)

Case 1. Bluegrass Construction Co. operates throughout Kentucky. The owner, Art Waverly, oversees company operations and employs 15 work crews. Construction supervisors report directly to Waverly. Most supervisors are longtime employees, so Waverly trusts them. Waverly's office staff consists of an accountant and an office manager.

Because employee turnover is high in the construction industry, supervisors hire and fire their own crew members. Supervisors notify the office of all personnel changes. Also, supervisors forward to the office the employee W-4 forms. Each Thursday, the supervisors submit weekly time sheets for their crews, and the accountant prepares the payroll. At noon on Friday, the supervisors come to the office to get paychecks for distribution to the workers at 5 p.m.

The company accountant prepares the payroll, including the payroll checks. Waverly signs all payroll checks. To verify that each construction worker is a bona fide employee, the accountant matches the employee's endorsement signature on the back of the canceled payroll check with the signature on that employee's W-4 form.

Required

1. Identify one way that a supervisor can defraud Bluegrass Construction under the present system.
2. Discuss a control feature that Bluegrass can use to *safeguard* against the fraud you identified in requirement 1.

Contingent liabilities
(Obj. 1, 2)

Case 2. Microsoft Corporation is the defendant in numerous lawsuits claiming unfair trade practices. Microsoft has strong incentives not to disclose these contingent liabilities. However, GAAP requires that companies report their contingent liabilities.

Required

1. Why would a company prefer *not* to disclose its contingent liabilities?
2. Describe how a bank could be harmed if a company seeking a loan did not disclose its contingent liabilities.
3. What ethical tightrope must companies walk when they report contingent liabilities?

Ethical Issue

LTV, manufacturer of aircraft and aircraft-related electronic devices, has at times borrowed heavily to finance operations. Often LTV is able to earn operating income much higher than its interest expense and is therefore quite profitable. However, when the business cycle turns down, LTV's debt burden has pushed the company to the brink of bankruptcy. Operating income is sometimes less than interest expense.

Required

Is it unethical for managers to saddle a company with a high level of debt? Or is it just risky? Who can get hurt when a company takes on too much debt? Discuss.

Financial Statement Case

Current liabilities **(Obj. 1, 6)**

Details about a company's current liabilities appear in a number of places in the annual report. Use **Amazon.com's** financial statements to answer the following questions.

Required

1. Give the breakdown of Amazon.com's current liabilities at December 31, 2002. Give the January 2003 entry to record the payment of accounts payable that Amazon owed at December 31, 2002.
2. How much was Amazon's long-term debt at December 31, 2002? Of this amount, how much was due within one year? How much was payable beyond one year in the future?
3. The balance sheet lists no liability for Income Tax Payable. Why is this liability omitted?

Team Projects

Project 1. In recent years, the airline industry has dominated headlines. Consumers are shopping **Priceline.com** and other Internet sites for the lowest rates. The airlines have also lured customers with frequent-flyer programs, which award free flights to passengers who accumulate specified miles of travel. Unredeemed frequent-flyer mileage represents a liability that airlines must report on their balance sheets, usually as Air Traffic Liability.

Southwest Airlines, a profitable, no-frills carrier based in Dallas, has been rated near the top of the industry. Southwest controls costs by flying to smaller, less-expensive airports; using only one model of aircraft; serving no meals; increasing staff efficiency; and having a shorter turnaround time on the ground between flights. The fact that most of the cities served by Southwest have predictable weather maximizes its on-time arrival record.

Required

With a partner or group, lead your class in a discussion of the following questions, or write a report as directed by your instructor.

1. Frequent-flyer programs have grown into significant obligations for airlines. Why should a liability be recorded for those programs? Discuss how you might calculate the amount of this liability. Can you think of other industries that offer similar incentives that create a liability?
2. One of Southwest Airlines' strategies for success is shortening stops at airport gates between flights. The company's chairman has stated, "What [you] produce is lower fares for the customers because you generate more revenue from the same fixed cost in that airplane." Look up *fixed cost* in the index of this book. What are some of the "fixed costs" of an airline? How can better utilization of assets improve a company's profits?

Project 2. Consider three different businesses:

a. A bank b. A magazine publisher c. A department store

Required

For each business, list all of its liabilities—both current and long-term. If necessary, study Chapter 15 on long-term liabilities. Then compare your lists to identify what liabilities the three businesses have in common. Also identify the liabilities that are unique to each type of business.

For Internet Exercises, go to the Web site www.prenhall.com/horngren.

Comprehensive Problem for Chapters 8–11

COMPARING TWO BUSINESSES

Suppose you created a software package, sold the business, and now are ready to invest in a small resort property. Several locations look promising: Jekyll Island, Georgia; Bar Harbor, Maine; and Palm Springs, California. Each place has its appeal, but Jekyll Island wins out. Two small resorts are available. The property owners provide the following data:

	Island Resorts	Ocean Hideaway
Cash	$ 34,100	$ 63,800
Accounts receivable	20,500	18,300
Inventory	74,200	68,400
Land	270,600	669,200
Buildings	1,800,000	1,960,000
Accumulated depreciation—buildings	(105,000)	(822,600)
Furniture and fixtures	750,000	933,000
Accumulated depreciation—furniture and fixtures	(225,000)	(535,300)
Total assets	$2,619,400	$2,354,800
Total liabilities	$1,124,300	$1,008,500
Owners' equity	1,495,100	1,346,300
Total liabilities and owners' equity	$2,619,400	$2,354,800

Income statements for the last three years report total net income of $531,000 for Island Resorts and $283,000 for Ocean Hideaway.

INVENTORIES Island Resorts uses the FIFO inventory method, and Ocean Hideaway uses the LIFO method. If Island Resorts had used LIFO, its reported inventory would have been $7,000 lower. Three years ago, there was little difference between the LIFO and FIFO amounts for each company.

PLANT ASSETS Island Resorts uses the straight-line depreciation method and an estimated useful life of 40 years for buildings and 10 years for furniture and fixtures. Estimated residual values are $400,000 for buildings and $0 for furniture and fixtures. Island's buildings are 3 years old.

Ocean Hideaway uses the double-declining-balance method and depreciates buildings over 30 years. The furniture and fixtures, now 3 years old, are being depreciated over 10 years.

ACCOUNTS RECEIVABLE Island Resorts uses the direct write-off method for uncollectibles. Ocean Hideaway uses the allowance method. The Island Resorts owner estimates that $2,000 of the company's receivables are doubtful. Prior to the current year, uncollectibles were insignificant. Ocean Hideaway receivables are already reported at net realizable value.

Required

1. To compare the two resorts, convert Island Resorts' balance sheet to the accounting methods and the estimated useful lives used by Ocean Hideaway. Round all depreciation amounts to the nearest $100. The necessary revisions will not affect Island's total liabilities.
2. Convert Island Resorts' total net income for the last 3 years to reflect the accounting methods used by Ocean Hideaway. Round all depreciation amounts to the nearest $100.
3. Compare the two resorts' finances after you have revised Island Resorts' figures. Which resort looked better at the outset? Which looks better when they are placed on equal footing?

CHAPTER 12

Partnerships

A+ TIPS CHECK YOUR RESOURCES

- Visit the www.prenhall.com/horngren **Web site** for self-study quizzes, video clips, and other resources
- Try the **Quick Check** exercise at the end of the chapter to test your knowledge
- Learn the **key terms**
- Do the **Starter** exercises keyed in the margins
- Work the **mid-** and **end-of-chapter summary problems**
- Use the **Concept Links** to review material in other chapters
- Search the **CD** for review materials by chapter or by key word
- Watch the **tutorial videos** to review key concepts

LEARNING OBJECTIVES

1. Identify the characteristics of a partnership
2. Account for the partners' investments in a partnership
3. Allocate profits and losses to the partners
4. Account for the admission of a new partner
5. Account for a partner's withdrawal from the firm
6. Account for the liquidation of a partnership
7. Prepare partnership financial statements

Arthur Andersen LLP

Partnerships are very fragile indeed. Unlike corporations, which continue regardless of who owns the company, a partnership lives and dies with its owners: the partners. A case in point is **Arthur Andersen LLP**, the once-famous accounting firm. The previous edition of this book featured Arthur Andersen as a "profit-making machine," with "each partner's profit [averaging] well over half a million dollars a year." Now the firm is dead.

Arthur Andersen unraveled during 2002 and 2003. One of the world's largest—and most respected—accounting firms went from international star to has-been in a matter of months. What could cause such a rapid fall from grace?

The short answer is that the firm performed a few high-profile audits that proved to be flawed. Arthur Andersen's auditors okayed the financial statements of several companies that had been overstating their profits and their assets. The final blow came when the government indicted Andersen on the charge that a partner in the firm destroyed legal evidence. Immediately, hundreds of Andersen's clients began announcing that they were switching to other certified public accountants.

The partnership form of business organization contributed to the swiftness of Andersen's death. Why? Because a single partner can commit an entire firm to a legal liability. For this and other reasons, you should enter a business partnership very carefully.

Sitemap

- Partnership Characteristics
- Types of Partnerships
- Partnership Start-Up
- Profits and Losses, Drawings
- Admission of a Partner
- Withdrawal of a Partner
- Liquidation
- Financial Statements

The partnership form of business introduces some complexities that a proprietorship avoids. How much cash should a new partner contribute to the business? How should the partners divide profits and losses? How should a partner who leaves the firm be compensated for his or her share of the business? These issues were important to the partners of Arthur Andersen LLP (LLP is the abbreviation for limited liability partnership).

A **partnership** is an association of two or more persons who co-own a business for profit. This definition comes from the Uniform Partnership Act, which nearly every state in the United States has adopted to regulate partnership practice.

Forming a partnership is easy. It requires no permission from the government and no legal procedures. When two persons decide to go into business together, a partnership is automatically formed. A partnership brings together the assets and the experience of the partners. Business opportunities may open up to a partnership as two or more individuals pool their talents and resources. Their partnership may offer a fuller range of goods and services than any one person can offer alone.

Partnerships come in all sizes. Many have one or two partners, but some medical and law firms have 20 or more. The largest accounting firms have over 2,000 partners. Exhibit 12-1 lists the seven largest accounting firms in the United States and their revenues in 2002.

Exhibit 12-1 **The Seven Largest Accounting Partnerships in the United States**

Revenue Rank (2002)	Firm Name and Location	Accounting/Auditing Revenue (In millions)
1	PricewaterhouseCoopers, New York	$ 3,001
2	Ernst & Young, New York	2,664
3	Deloitte & Touche, Wilton, Connecticut	2,137
4	KPMG, New York	1,496
5	RSM McGladrey, Bloomington, Minnesota	205
6	Grant Thornton, Chicago	200
7	BDO Seidman, Chicago	145

Source: Adapted from *Accounting Today* (March 17–April 6, 2003).

Characteristics of a Partnership

■ Partnership Characteristics
□ Types of Partnerships
□ Partnership Start-Up
□ Profits and Losses, Drawings
□ Admission of a Partner
□ Withdrawal of a Partner
□ Liquidation
□ Financial Statements

A person cannot be forced to join a partnership, and partners cannot be forced to accept another person as a partner. The following characteristics distinguish partnerships from sole proprietorships and corporations.

1 Identify the characteristics of a partnership

The Written Agreement

A business partnership is like a marriage. To be successful, the partners must cooperate. But business partners don't vow to remain together for life. To lower the chances that any partner might misunderstand how the business is run, partners may draw up a **partnership agreement,** which is also called the **articles of partnership**. This agreement is a contract between the partners, so transactions involving the agreement are governed by contract law. The articles of partnership should make the following points clear:

1. Name, location, and nature of the business
2. Name, capital investment, and duties of each partner
3. Method of sharing profits and losses among the partners
4. Withdrawals of assets by the partners
5. Procedures for admitting new partners
6. Procedures for settling up with a partner who withdraws from the firm
7. Procedures for liquidating the partnership—selling the assets, paying the liabilities, and disbursing remaining cash to the partners

Partnership
An association of two or more persons who co-own a business for profit.

Partnership Agreement
The contract between partners that specifies such items as the name, location, and nature of the business; the name, capital investment, and duties of each partner; and the method of sharing profits and losses among the partners. Also called **articles of partnership**.

Limited Life

A partnership has a life limited by the length of time that all partners continue to own the business. If a partner withdraws, the old partnership ceases to exist. A new partnership may emerge to continue the same business, but the old partnership is dissolved. **Dissolution** is the ending of a partnership. The addition of a new partner dissolves the old partnership and creates a new partnership. Large partnerships such as PricewaterhouseCoopers retain the firm name even after partners resign from the firm.

Dissolution
Ending of a partnership.

Mutual Agency

Mutual agency in a partnership means that every partner can bind the business to a contract within the scope of the partnership's regular business operations. If Jana Jones, a partner in the firm of Willis & Jones, enters into a contract to provide legal service, then the firm of Willis & Jones—not just Jones—is bound to provide that service. If Jones signs a contract to construct her home, however, the partnership will not be bound to pay because that is a personal matter for Jones. It is not a transaction of the partnership.

Mutual Agency
Every partner can bind the business to a contract within the scope of the partnership's regular business operations.

Unlimited Liability

Each partner has an **unlimited personal liability** for the debts of the partnership. When a partnership cannot pay its debts, the partners must use their personal assets to meet the debt.

Suppose the Willis & Jones firm has had an unsuccessful year and the partnership's liabilities exceed its assets by $20,000. Willis and Jones must pay this amount with their personal assets. Because each partner has unlimited liability, if

Unlimited Personal Liability
When a partnership (or a proprietorship) cannot pay its debts with business assets, the partners (or the proprietor) must use personal assets to meet the debt.

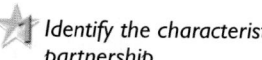

a partner is unable to pay his or her part of the debt, the other partner (or partners) must pay. If Jones can pay only $5,000 of the liability, Willis must pay $15,000.

Partners can avoid unlimited personal liability for partnership debts by forming a *limited partnership*. Ernst & Young LLP is a limited liability partnership, as are the other large accounting firms in Exhibit 12-1. In a limited partnership, the partners have limited liability similar to that of the stockholders in a corporation.

Co-Ownership of Property

Any asset—cash, inventory, computer software, and so on—that a partner invests in the partnership becomes the joint property of all the partners. The partner who invested the asset is no longer its sole owner.

No Partnership Income Taxes

✔ Starter 12-1

A partnership pays no income tax on its business income. Instead, the net income of the partnership becomes the taxable income of the partners. Suppose Willis & Jones, Attorneys, earned net income of $200,000, shared equally by the partners. The firm would pay no income tax *as a business entity*. But Willis and Jones would each pay personal income tax on $100,000 of partnership income.

Partners' Owner's Equity Accounts

Accounting for a partnership is much like accounting for a proprietorship. But a partnership has more than one owner, so it needs more than one owner's equity account.

Every partner in the business has an individual capital account. For example, the owner's equity account for Blake Willis would read "Willis, Capital." Similarly, each partner has a withdrawal account. If the number of partners is large, the general ledger may contain the single account Partners' Capital, or Owners' Equity. A subsidiary ledger can be used for individual partner accounts.

Exhibit 12-2 lists the advantages and disadvantages of partnerships (compared with proprietorships and corporations). A partnership is really a "multiple proprietorship." Most features of a proprietorship also apply to a partnership—in particular, limited life and unlimited liability.

Exhibit 12-2

Advantages and Disadvantages of Partnerships

Partnership Advantages	Partnership Disadvantages
Versus Proprietorships: **1.** Can raise more capital. **2.** Brings together the expertise of more than one person. **3.** 1 + 1 > 2 in a good partnership. If the partners work well together, they can add more value than by working alone. *Versus Corporations:* **1.** Less expensive to organize than a corporation, which requires a charter from the state. **2.** No taxation of partnership income, which is taxed to the partners as individuals.	**1.** Partnership agreement may be difficult to formulate. Each time a new partner is admitted or a partner withdraws, the business needs a new partnership agreement. **2.** Relationships among partners may be fragile. **3.** Mutual agency and unlimited personal liability create personal obligations for each partner.

Types of Partnerships

- □ Partnership Characteristics
- ■ Types of Partnerships
- □ Partnership Start-Up
- □ Profits and Losses, Drawings
- □ Admission of a Partner
- □ Withdrawal of a Partner
- □ Liquidation
- □ Financial Statements

Student Resource CD
general partnership, limited partnership, limited liability partnership, S corporation

There are two basic types of partnerships: general and limited.

General Partnerships

A **general partnership** is the basic form of partnership organization. Each partner is an owner of the business with all the privileges and risks of ownership. The profits and losses of the partnership pass through to the partners, who then pay personal income tax on their income.

General Partnership
A form of partnership in which each partner is an owner of the business, with all the privileges and risks of ownership.

Limited Partnerships

A **limited partnership** has at least two classes of partners. There must be at least one *general partner*, who takes primary responsibility for the business. The general partner also takes the bulk of the risk in the event the partnership goes bankrupt (liabilities exceed assets). Usually, the general partner is the last owner to receive a share of profits and losses. But the general partner may earn all excess profits after satisfying the limited partners' demands for income.

Limited Partnership
A partnership with at least two classes of partners: a general partner and limited partners.

The *limited partners* are so named because their liability for the partnership's debts is limited to their investment in the business. Limited partners usually have first claim to partnership profits and losses, but only up to a specified limit. In exchange for their limited liability, their potential for profits is also limited.

Most of the large accounting firms are organized as **limited liability partnerships**, or **LLPs**, which means that each partner's personal liability for the business's debts is limited to a certain amount. The LLP must carry a large insurance policy to protect the public in case the partnership is found guilty of malpractice. Medical, legal, and other firms of professionals can also be organized as LLPs.

Limited Liability Partnership
A form of partnership in which each partner's personal liability for the business's debts is limited to a certain amount. Also called **LLPs**.

S Corporations

An **S Corporation** is a corporation that is taxed the same as a partnership. This form of business organization derives its name from Subchapter S of the U.S. Internal Revenue Code.

S Corporation
A corporation taxed in the same way as a partnership.

An S corporation offers its owners the benefits of a corporation—no personal liability for business debts—and of a partnership—no double taxation. An ordinary (Subchapter C) corporation is subject to double taxation. First, the corporation pays corporate income tax on its income. Then, when the corporation pays dividends to the stockholders, they pay personal income tax on their dividend income.[1]

An S corporation pays no corporate income tax. Instead, the corporation's income flows directly to the stockholders (the owners), who pay personal income tax on their share of the S corporation's income. The one-time taxation of an S corporation's income is an important advantage over an ordinary corporation. From a tax standpoint, an S corporation operates like a partnership.

To qualify as an S corporation, a company can have no more than 75 stockholders, all of whom must be citizens or residents of the United States. Accounting for an S corporation resembles accounting for a partnership because the allocation of corporate income follows the same procedure used by partnerships.

[1]From time to time, U.S. presidents and congressmen propose eliminating the tax on dividends received by individuals.

Partnership Characteristics
Types of Partnerships
■ Partnership Start-Up
Profits and Losses, Drawings
Admission of a Partner
Withdrawal of a Partner
Liquidation
Financial Statements

2 Account for the partners' investments in a partnership

The Partnership Start-Up

Let's examine the start-up of a partnership. Partners in a new business may invest assets and liabilities. These contributions are entered in the books in the same way that a proprietor's assets and liabilities are recorded—debit the assets and credit the liabilities. Subtraction of liabilities from assets yields the amount of each partner's capital. Often, the partners hire an independent firm to appraise their assets and liabilities at current market value at the time a partnership is formed. This outside evaluation assures an objective accounting of assets, liabilities, and capital.

Assume that Dave Benz and Joan Hanna form a partnership to sell computer software. The partners agree on the following values:

Benz's Contributions

- Cash, $10,000; inventory, $70,000; and accounts payable, $85,000 (The appraiser believes that the current market values for these items equal Benz's values.)
- Accounts receivable, $30,000, less allowance for doubtful accounts of $5,000
- Computer equipment—cost, $800,000; accumulated depreciation, $200,000; current market value, $450,000

Hanna's Contributions

- Cash, $5,000
- Computer software: cost, $18,000; market value, $100,000

(continued on page 475)

Accounting.com

From Respected Partnership to Dead Duck: The Fall of Arthur Andersen

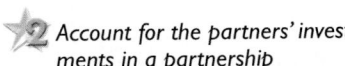

If you were considering an accounting career a few years ago, the respected firm of **Arthur Andersen** might have been your top choice. As of June 2001, **Andersen Worldwide** was a $9.3 billion global partnership with 85,000 employees in 84 countries. By late 2002, Andersen's payroll had dwindled to 3,000 and almost all 1,300 clients had switched to other accounting firms. Why? Because a few partners okayed the failed audits that Andersen performed for a handful of companies including **Enron**, **WorldCom**, **Adelphia**, and **Global Crossing**. The moral of the story is this: An accountant's good reputation attracts clients, and a bad reputation can kill you.

Cracks in the Arthur Andersen partnership began forming in the 1980s, when the firm shifted resources toward management consulting and away from auditing. Ill will between the auditing and consulting sides of the Andersen partnership resulted in a bitter divorce. **Andersen Consulting**, renamed **Accenture**, broke free from the accounting firm. "There is no question in my mind that Andersen took its eye off the ball," said Paul A. Volker, former Federal Reserve Board chairman. "Their compensation practices were based on how much revenue [they] could generate."

The death knell for the firm came with a criminal indictment. Andersen Worldwide could survive a few botched audits but not a criminal indictment. On October 16, 2002, the firm that once stood for "integrity" was sentenced for obstructing justice related to its work for Enron.

Based on: John A. Byrne, "Fall from Grace," *Business Week*, August 12, 2002, pp. 50–56. Carrie Johnson, "Arthur Andersen To Be Sentenced Today," *Washington Post*, October 16, 2002, p. E4. Robert Lea, "End of Andersen," *Management Today*, October 2002, pp. 46–53.

The partnership records the partners' investments at current market value because the partnership is buying the assets and assuming the liabilities at their current market values. The partnership entries are as follows:

Benz's Investment

June 1	Cash	10,000	
	Accounts Receivable	30,000	
	Inventory	70,000	
	Computer Equipment	450,000	
	Allowance for Doubtful Accounts		5,000
	Accounts Payable		85,000
	Benz, Capital ($560,000 – $90,000)		470,000
	To record Benz's investment in the partnership.		

Hanna's Investment

June 1	Cash	5,000	
	Computer Software	100,000	
	Hanna, Capital		105,000
	To record Hanna's investment in the partnership.		

The initial partnership balance sheet appears in Exhibit 12-3. The assets and liabilities are the same for a proprietorship and a partnership.

✔ Starter 12-2

✔ Starter 12-3

Exhibit 12-3

Partnership Balance Sheet

Benz and Hanna
Balance Sheet
June 1, 20X5

Assets			Liabilities	
Cash		$ 15,000	Accounts payable	$ 85,000
Accounts receivable	$30,000			
Less Allowance for doubtful accounts	(5,000)	25,000	**Capital**	
Inventory		70,000	Benz, capital	470,000
Computer equipment		450,000	Hanna, capital	105,000
Computer software		100,000	Total liabilities	
Total assets		$660,000	and capital	$660,000

Sharing Profits and Losses, and Partner Drawings

Allocating profits and losses among partners is one of the most challenging aspects of managing a partnership. If the partners have not drawn up an agreement or if the agreement does not state how the partners will divide profits and losses, then they share equally. If the agreement specifies a method for dividing profits but not losses, then losses are shared in the same proportion as profits. For example, a partner who gets 75% of the profits likewise absorbs 75% of any losses. Partners may agree to any profit-and-loss-sharing method they desire.

Student ResourceCD
allocation of profit and loss, partnership, partnership agreement, sharing profit and loss

3 *Allocate profits and losses to the partners*

Typical arrangements for dividing profits and losses among the partners include the following:

1. Sharing based on a stated fraction for each partner, such as 50/50 or 2/3 and 1/3 or 4:3:3 (which means 40% to Partner A, 30% to Partner B, and 30% to Partner C)
2. Sharing based on each partner's capital contribution

3. Sharing based on each partner's service to the partnership
4. Sharing based on a combination of each partner's stated fraction, capital contribution, and service

The sections that follow illustrate some of these profit-and-loss-sharing plans.

Sharing Based on a Stated Fraction

Partners may state a particular fraction of the total profits and losses each individual partner will share. Suppose the partnership agreement of Lou Cagle and Justin Dean allocates 2/3 of the business profits and losses to Cagle and 1/3 to Dean. This sharing rule can also be expressed as 2:1. If net income for the year is $90,000 and all revenue and expense accounts have been closed, the Income Summary account has a credit balance of $90,000:

Income Summary

	Bal.	90,000

The entry to close the profit to the partners' capital accounts is

Dec. 31	Income Summary	90,000	
	Cagle, Capital ($90,000 × 2/3)		60,000
	Dean, Capital ($90,000 × 1/3)		30,000
	To allocate net income to partners.		

Consider the effect of this entry. Does Cagle get $60,000 cash and Dean $30,000 cash? No. The increase in the partners' capital accounts cannot be linked to any particular asset, including cash. Instead, the entry indicates that Cagle's ownership in *all* the assets of the business increased by $60,000 and Dean's by $30,000.

If the year's operations resulted in a net loss of $66,000, the Income Summary account would have a debit balance of $66,000. In that case, the entry to close the loss to the partners' capital accounts would be

✔ Starter 12-4

Dec. 31	Cagle, Capital ($66,000 × 2/3)	44,000	
	Dean, Capital ($66,000 × 1/3)	22,000	
	Income Summary		66,000
	To allocate net loss to partners.		

Sharing Based on Capital Contributions and on Service

One partner may contribute more capital. Another partner may put more work into the business. Even among partners who log equal time, one person's experience may command a greater share of income. To reward the harder-working or the more-valuable person, the profits and losses may be divided based on a combination of contributed capital *and* service to the business. The Chicago-based law firm Baker & McKenzie, for example, has about 500 partners. Baker & McKenzie takes seniority into account in determining partner compensation.

Assume that Debbie Randolph and Nancy Scott formed a partnership in which Randolph invested $60,000 and Scott $40,000, for a total of $100,000. But Scott devotes more time to the partnership and earns the larger salary. Accordingly, the two partners have agreed to share profits as follows:

1. The first $50,000 of partnership profits is allocated on the basis of the partners' capital contributions.
2. The next $60,000 is allocated on the basis of service, with Randolph receiving $24,000 and Scott $36,000.
3. Any remaining amount will be allocated equally.

The partnership's net income for the first year is $125,000, and the partners share this profit as follows:

	Randolph	Scott	Total
Total net income			$125,000
Sharing of first $50,000 of net income, based on capital contributions:			
Randolph ($60,000/$100,000 × $50,000).....	$30,000		
Scott ($40,000/$100,000 × $50,000)		$20,000	
Total.............................			50,000
Net income remaining for allocation			75,000
Sharing of next $60,000, based on service:			
Randolph	24,000		
Scott...............................		36,000	
Total.............................			60,000
Net income remaining for allocation			15,000
Remainder shared equally:			
Randolph ($15,000 × 1/2).................	7,500		
Scott ($15,000 × 1/2)		7,500	
Total.............................			15,000
Net income remaining for allocation			$ 0
Net income allocated to the partners.........	$61,500	$63,500	$125,000

For this allocation, the closing entry is

Dec. 31	Income Summary...............	125,000	
	Randolph, Capital		61,500
	Scott, Capital..............		63,500
	To allocate net income to partners.		

✔ **Starter 12-5**

Partner Drawings of Cash and Other Assets

Like anyone else, partners need cash for personal expenses. Partnership agreements usually allow partners to withdraw assets from the business. Drawings from a partnership are recorded exactly as for a proprietorship. Assume that both Randy Lewis and Gerald Clark get monthly withdrawals of $3,500. The partnership records the March withdrawals with this entry:

Mar. 31	Lewis, Drawing..................	3,500	
	Clark, Drawing	3,500	
	Cash		7,000
	Monthly partner withdrawals of cash.		

During the year, each partner gets 12 monthly withdrawals, a total of $42,000 ($3,500 × 12). At the end of the period, the general ledger shows the following balances for the partners' drawing accounts:

Lewis, Drawing			Clark, Drawing	
Dec. 31 Bal. 42,000			Dec. 31 Bal. 42,000	

The drawing accounts are closed at the end of the period, exactly as for a proprietorship: Credit the partner's drawing account and debit his or her capital account.

Admission of a Partner

The addition of a new partner or the withdrawal of a partner dissolves the old partnership. We now discuss how partnerships dissolve—and how new partnerships arise.

☐ Partnership Characteristics
☐ Types of Partnerships
☐ Partnership Start-Up
☐ Profits and Losses, Drawings
■ Admission of a Partner
☐ Withdrawal of a Partner
☐ Liquidation
☐ Financial Statements

ⓞStudent ResourceCD

book value, partnership

★ *Account for the admission of a new partner*

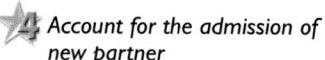

Often, a new partnership is formed to carry on the old partnership's business. In fact, the new firm may retain the dissolved partnership's name. PricewaterhouseCoopers LLP, for example, is an accounting firm that adds new partners and retires old ones each year. Thus, the old partnership may dissolve and a new partnership begin many times during a year. But the business retains its name and continues operating. Other partnerships may dissolve and then reform under a new name. Let's look at the ways a new member may be admitted into an existing partnership.

Admission by Purchasing a Partner's Interest

A person may become a member of a partnership by gaining the approval of the other partner (or partners) for entrance into the firm *and* by purchasing a present partner's interest in the business. Let's assume that Roberta Fisher and Benitez Garcia have a partnership that carries these figures:

Cash	$ 40,000	Total liabilities	$120,000
Other assets	360,000	Fisher, capital	110,000
		Garcia, capital	170,000
Total assets	$400,000	Total liabilities and capital	$400,000

Suppose Fisher receives an offer from Barry Holt, an outside party, to buy her $110,000 interest in the business for $150,000. Fisher agrees to sell out to Holt, and Garcia approves Holt as a new partner. The firm records the transfer of capital interest in the business with this entry:

Apr. 16	Fisher, Capital	110,000	
	Holt, Capital		110,000
	To transfer Fisher's equity in the business to Holt.		

The debit entry closes Fisher's capital account because she is no longer a partner in the firm. The credit side opens Holt's capital account. The entry amount is Fisher's capital balance ($110,000) and not the $150,000 that Holt paid Fisher to buy into the business. The full $150,000 goes to Fisher. In this example, the partnership receives no cash because the transaction was between Holt and Fisher, not between Holt and the partnership. Suppose Holt pays Fisher less than Fisher's capital balance. The entry on the partnership books is not affected. Fisher's equity is transferred to Holt at book value ($110,000).

✔ Starter 12-6

The old partnership has dissolved. Garcia and Holt draw up a new partnership agreement with a new profit-and-loss-sharing ratio and continue in business. If Garcia does not accept Holt as a partner, Holt gets no voice in management of the firm. However, under the Uniform Partnership Act, the purchaser shares in the profits and losses of the firm and in its assets at liquidation.

Admission by Investing in the Partnership

A person may be admitted as a partner by investing directly in the partnership rather than by buying an existing partner's interest. The new partner contributes assets—for example, cash or equipment—to the business. Assume that the partnership of Robin Ingel and Michael Jay has the following assets, liabilities, and capital:

Cash	$ 20,000	Total liabilities	$ 60,000
Other assets	200,000	Ingel, capital	70,000
		Jay, capital	90,000
Total assets	$220,000	Total liabilities and capital	$220,000

Laura Kahn offers to invest equipment and land (labeled Other Assets) with a market value of $80,000. Ingel and Jay agree to dissolve the existing partnership and to start up a new business, giving Kahn 1/3 interest [$80,000/($70,000 + $90,000 + $80,000) = 1/3] in exchange for the assets. Notice that Kahn is buying into the partnership at book value because her 1/3 investment ($80,000) equals 1/3 of the new partnership's total capital ($240,000). The entry to record Kahn's investment is

July 18	Other Assets........................	80,000	
	Kahn, Capital..................		80,000
	To admit L. Kahn as a partner with a one-third interest in the business.		

After this entry, the partnership books show

Cash...............	$ 20,000	Total liabilities..............	$ 60,000
Other assets.........		Ingel, capital	70,000
($200,000 + $80,000)	280,000	Jay, capital	90,000
		Kahn, capital	80,000
Total assets	$300,000	Total liabilities and capital....	$300,000

Kahn's 1/3 interest in the partnership does not necessarily entitle her to 1/3 of the profits. The sharing of profits and losses is a separate element in the partnership agreement.

✔ Starter 12-7

ADMISSION BY INVESTING IN THE PARTNERSHIP—BONUS TO THE OLD PARTNERS The more successful a partnership, the higher the payment demanded from a new partner. Partners in a business that is doing quite well might require an incoming person to pay them a bonus. The bonus increases the current partners' capital accounts.

Suppose that Hiro Nagasawa and Ralph Osburn's partnership has earned above-average profits for 10 years. The two partners share profits and losses equally. The partnership balance sheet carries these figures:

Cash...............	$ 40,000	Total liabilities..............	$100,000
Other assets.........	210,000	Nagasawa, capital...........	70,000
		Osburn, capital	80,000
Total assets	$250,000	Total liabilities and capital....	$250,000

The partners agree to admit Glen Parker to a 1/4 interest with his cash investment of $90,000. Parker's capital balance on the partnership books is only $60,000, computed as follows:

Partnership capital before Parker is admitted ($70,000 + $80,000)...	$150,000
Parker's investment in the partnership	90,000
Partnership capital after Parker is admitted	$240,000
Parker's capital in the partnership ($240,000 × 1/4)	$ 60,000
Bonus to the old partners ($90,000 – $60,000)	$ 30,000

In effect, Parker had to buy into the partnership at a price ($90,000) above the book value of his 1/4 interest ($60,000). Parker's investment of an extra $30,000 creates a *bonus* for the existing partners. The entry to record the receipt of Parker's investment is

Mar. 1	Cash..................................	90,000	
	Parker, Capital...................		60,000
	Nagasawa, Capital ($30,000 × 1/2)..		15,000
	Osburn, Capital ($30,000 × 1/2)		15,000
	To admit G. Parker as a partner with a one-fourth interest in the business.		

✔ Starter 12-8

Parker's capital account is credited for his 1/4 interest in the partnership. The *bonus* is allocated to the partners on the basis of their profit-and-loss ratio.

The new partnership's balance sheet reports these amounts:

Cash ($40,000 + $90,000)	$130,000	Total liabilities	$100,000
Other assets	210,000	Nagasawa, capital ($70,000 + $15,000)	85,000
		Osburn, capital ($80,000 + $15,000)	95,000
		Parker, capital	60,000
Total assets	$340,000	Total liabilities and capital	$340,000

Stop & Think

Mia and Susan are partners with capital balances of $25,000 and $75,000, respectively. They share profits and losses in a 30:70 ratio. Mia and Susan admit Tab to a 10% interest in a new partnership when Tab invests $20,000 in the business.

1. Journalize the partnership's receipt of cash from Tab.
2. What is each partner's capital in the new partnership?

Answers:

1. Cash	20,000	
Tab, Capital		12,000
Mia, Capital ($8,000 × 0.30)		2,400
Susan, Capital ($8,000 × 0.70)		5,600
To admit Tab with a 10% interest in the business.		

Partnership capital before Tab is admitted ($25,000 + $75,000)	$100,000
Tab's investment in the partnership	20,000
Partnership capital after Tab is admitted	$120,000
Tab's capital in the partnership ($120,000 × 1/10)	$ 12,000
Bonus to the old partners ($20,000 – $12,000)	$ 8,000

2. Partners' capital balances:

Mia, capital ($25,000 + 30% of $8,000)	$ 27,400
Susan, capital ($75,000 + 70% of $8,000)	80,600
Tab, capital	12,000
Total partnership capital	$120,000

ADMISSION BY INVESTING IN THE PARTNERSHIP—BONUS TO THE NEW PARTNER A new partner may be so important that the existing partners offer him or her a partnership share that includes a bonus. A law firm may want a former governor or other official as a partner because of the person's reputation and connections. A restaurant owner may want to go into partnership with a famous sports personality or a movie star. For example, **Planet Hollywood** opened its first restaurant in New York City with the help of celebrity partners Sylvester Stallone, Arnold Schwarzenegger, Bruce Willis, and Don Johnson.

Suppose Allan Page and Olivia Franco have a law partnership. The firm's balance sheet appears as follows:

Cash	$140,000	Total liabilities	$120,000
Other assets	360,000	Page, capital	230,000
		Franco, capital	150,000
Total assets	$500,000	Total liabilities and capital	$500,000

Page and Franco admit Martin Schiller, a former attorney general, as a partner with a 1/3 interest in exchange for his cash investment of \$100,000. Page and Franco share profits and losses in the ratio of 2/3 to Page and 1/3 to Franco. The computation of Schiller's equity in the partnership is

What they're thinking
We need Schiller: He's got lots of good connections.
What they say to Schiller
We'd like to offer you a deal.
Schiller
Franco
Page

Partnership capital before Schiller is admitted (\$230,000 + \$150,000) . .	\$380,000
Schiller's investment in the partnership	100,000
Partnership capital after Schiller is admitted	\$480,000
Schiller's capital in the partnership (\$480,000 × 1/3).	\$160,000
Bonus to the new partner (\$160,000 – \$100,000)	\$ 60,000

In this case, Schiller bought into the partnership at a price (\$100,000) below the book value of his interest (\$160,000). The bonus of \$60,000 went to Schiller from the other partners. The capital accounts of Page and Franco are debited for the \$60,000 difference between the new partner's equity (\$160,000) and his investment (\$100,000). The existing partners share this decrease in capital as though it were a loss, on the basis of their profit-and-loss ratio. The entry to record Schiller's investment is

Aug. 24	Cash	100,000	
	Page, Capital (\$60,000 × 2/3).	40,000	
	Franco, Capital (\$60,000 × 1/3)	20,000	
	Schiller, Capital		160,000
	To admit M. Schiller as a partner with a one-third interest in the business.		

The new partnership's balance sheet reports these amounts:

Cash		Total liabilities	\$120,000
(\$140,000 + \$100,000) . . .	\$240,000	Page, capital	
Other assets.	360,000	(\$230,000 – \$40,000)	190,000
		Franco, capital	
		(\$150,000 – \$20,000)	130,000
		Schiller, capital.	160,000
Total assets	\$600,000	Total liabilities and capital. . .	\$600,000

Stop & Think

John and Ron are partners with capital balances of \$30,000 and \$40,000, respectively. They share profits and losses in a 25:75 ratio. John and Ron admit Lou to a 20% interest in a new partnership when Lou invests \$10,000 in the business.

1. Journalize the partnership's receipt of cash from Lou.
2. What is each partner's capital in the new partnership?

Answers:

1. Cash	10,000	
John, Capital (\$6,000 × 0.25)	1,500	
Ron, Capital (\$6,000 × 0.75).	4,500	
Lou, Capital.		16,000
To admit Lou with a 20% interest in the business.		

Partnership capital before Lou is admitted (\$30,000 + \$40,000)	\$70,000
Lou's investment in the partnership.	10,000
Partnership capital after Lou is admitted.	\$80,000
Lou's capital in the partnership (\$80,000 × 0.20)	\$16,000
Bonus to the new partner (\$16,000 – \$10,000)	\$ 6,000

(continued)

Student Resource CD
allocation of profit and loss, book value, partnership

5 *Account for a partner's withdrawal from the firm*

2. Partners' capital balances:

John, capital ($30,000 – $1,500)	$28,500
Ron, capital ($40,000 – $4,500)	35,500
Lou, capital	16,000
Total partnership capital	$80,000

Withdrawal of a Partner

A partner may withdraw from the business for many reasons, including retirement, or a dispute. The resignation of a partner dissolves the old partnership. The partnership agreement should contain a provision to govern how to settle with a withdrawing partner. In the simplest case, a partner may resign and sell his or her interest to another partner in a personal transaction. The only entry needed to record this transfer of equity debits the withdrawing partner's capital account and credits the purchaser's capital account. The dollar amount of the entry is the capital balance of the withdrawing partner, regardless of the price paid by the purchaser. This situation is illustrated for Fisher and Holt on page 478.

The withdrawing partner may receive his or her share of the business in partnership assets other than cash. Then the question is what value to assign the partnership assets—book value or current market value? The settlement procedure may specify an independent appraisal to determine current market value. If market values have changed, the appraisal will result in revaluing the partnership assets. The partners share in any market-value changes their efforts caused.

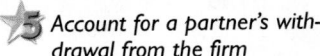

Suppose Keith Isaac is retiring from the partnership of Green, Henry, and Isaac. Before any asset appraisal, the partnership balance sheet reports the following:

Cash		$ 69,000	Total liabilities	$ 80,000
Inventory		44,000	Green, capital	54,000
Land		55,000	Henry, capital	43,000
Building	$95,000		Isaac, capital	21,000
Less Accum. depr.	(65,000)	30,000	Total liabilities and	
Total assets		$198,000	capital	$198,000

An independent appraiser revalues the inventory at $38,000 (down from $44,000) and the land at $101,000 (up from $55,000). The partners share the differences between these assets' market values and their prior book values on the basis of their profit-and-loss ratio.

The partnership agreement has allocated 1/4 of the profits to Susan Green, 1/2 to Charles Henry, and 1/4 to Keith Isaac. (This ratio may be written 1:2:1 for one part to Green, two parts to Henry, and one part to Isaac.) For each share that Green or Isaac has, Henry has two. The entries to record the revaluation of the inventory and land are

July 31	Green, Capital ($6,000 × 1/4)	1,500	
	Henry, Capital ($6,000 × 1/2)	3,000	
	Isaac, Capital ($6,000 × 1/4)	1,500	
	Inventory ($44,000 – $38,000)		6,000
	To revalue the inventory and allocate the loss to the partners.		
31	Land ($101,000 – $55,000)	46,000	
	Green, Capital ($46,000 × 1/4)		11,500
	Henry, Capital ($46,000 × 1/2)		23,000
	Isaac, Capital ($46,000 × 1/4)		11,500
	To revalue the land and allocate the gain to the partners.		

After the revaluations, the partnership balance sheet reports the following:

Cash		$ 69,000	Total liabilities	$80,000
Inventory		38,000	Green, capital ($54,000 – $1,500 + $11,500)	64,000
Land		101,000	Henry, capital ($43,000 – $3,000 + $23,000)	63,000
Building	$95,000		Isaac, capital ($21,000 – $1,500 + $11,500)	31,000
Less Accum. depr.	(65,000)	30,000		
Total assets		$238,000	Total liabilities and capital	$238,000

The books now carry the assets at current market value, which becomes the new book value, and the capital accounts are adjusted accordingly. As the balance sheet shows, Isaac has a claim to $31,000 in partnership assets. Now we can account for Keith Isaac's withdrawal from the business.

Withdrawal at Book Value

If Keith Isaac withdraws by receiving cash equal to the book value of his owner's equity, the entry will be

July 31	Isaac, Capital	31,000	
	Cash		31,000
	To record withdrawal of K. Isaac from the business.		

This entry records the payment of cash to Isaac and the closing of his capital account.

✔ Starter 12-9

Withdrawal at Less Than Book Value

The withdrawing partner may be so eager to leave the business that he or she is willing to take less than his or her equity. Assume that Keith Isaac withdraws from the business and agrees to receive partnership cash of $10,000 and the new partnership's note for $15,000. This $25,000 settlement is $6,000 less than Isaac's $31,000 equity in the business. The remaining partners share this $6,000 difference—which is a bonus to them—according to their profit-and-loss ratio.

Because Isaac has withdrawn from the partnership, a new agreement—and a new profit-and-loss ratio—must be drawn up. In forming a new partnership, Henry and Green may decide on any ratio that they see fit. Let's assume they agree that Henry will earn 2/3 of partnership profits and losses and Green 1/3. The entry to record Isaac's withdrawal at less than his book value is

July 31	Isaac, Capital	31,000	
	Cash		10,000
	Note Payable to K. Isaac		15,000
	Green, Capital ($6,000 × 1/3)		2,000
	Henry, Capital ($6,000 × 2/3)		4,000
	To record withdrawal of K. Isaac from the business.		

Isaac's account is closed, and Henry and Green may or may not continue the business as a new partnership.

Withdrawal at More Than Book Value

The settlement with a withdrawing partner may allow him or her to take assets of greater value than the book value of that partner's capital. Also, the remaining partners may be so eager for the withdrawing partner to leave that they pay him or her a bonus to withdraw from the business. In either case, the partner's withdrawal causes a decrease in the book equity of the remaining partners. This decrease is allocated to the partners on the basis of their profit-and-loss ratio.

The accounting for this situation follows the pattern illustrated for withdrawal at less than book value—with one exception. The remaining partners' capital accounts are debited because the withdrawing partner receives more than his or her book equity.

Stop & Think

Matt is withdrawing from the partnership of Matt, Lee, and Karla. The partners share profits and losses in a 1:2:3 ratio for Matt, Lee, and Karla, respectively. After the revaluation of assets, Matt's capital balance is $50,000, and the other partners agree to pay him $60,000. Journalize the payment to Matt and his withdrawal from the partnership.

Answer:

Matt, Capital	50,000	
Lee, Capital [($60,000 – $50,000) × 2/5]	4,000	
Karla, Capital [($60,000 – $50,000) × 3/5]	6,000	
Cash		60,000
To record withdrawal of Matt from the business.		

✔ Starter 12-10

Death of a Partner

6 *Account for the liquidation of a partnership*

The death of a partner dissolves a partnership. The partnership accounts are adjusted to measure net income or loss for the fraction of the year up to the date of death. Then they are closed to determine all partners' capital balances on that date. Settlement with the deceased partner's estate is based on the partnership agreement. The estate commonly receives partnership assets equal to the partner's capital balance. The partnership closes the deceased partner's capital account with a debit. This entry credits a payable to the estate.

Suppose Susan Green (of the partnership at the top of page 483) dies, and her capital balance is $64,000. Green's estate may request cash for her final share of the partnership's assets. At this time the business has only $39,000 of cash, so it must borrow. Let's assume the partnership borrows $50,000 and then pays Green's estate. The partnership's journal entries are

Aug. 1	Cash	50,000	
	Note Payable		50,000
	To borrow money.		
Aug. 1	Green, Capital	64,000	
	Cash		64,000
	To record withdrawal of Green from the business.		

Alternatively, a remaining partner may purchase the deceased partner's equity. The deceased partner's equity is debited, and the purchaser's equity is credited. The journal entry to record this transaction follows the pattern given on page 478 for the transfer of Fisher's equity to Holt. The amount of this entry is the ending credit balance in the deceased partner's capital account.

Student Resource CD
liquidation, partnership

Liquidation
The process of going out of business by selling the entity's assets and paying its liabilities. The final step in liquidation is the distribution of any remaining cash to the owner(s).

Liquidation of a Partnership

Admission of a new partner or withdrawal or death of an existing partner dissolves the partnership. However, the business may continue operating with no apparent change to outsiders, such as customers and creditors. In contrast, **liquidation** is the process of going out of business by selling an entity's assets and paying its liabilities. The final step in liquidation is the *distribution of the remaining cash to the owners.*

Before a business is liquidated, its books should be adjusted and closed. After closing, only asset, liability, and partners' capital accounts remain open.

Liquidation includes three steps:

1. Sell the assets. Allocate the gain or loss to the partners' capital accounts on the basis of the profit-and-loss ratio.
2. Pay the partnership liabilities.
3. Disburse the remaining cash to the partners on the basis of their capital balances.

In practice, the liquidation of a business can stretch over weeks or months. Selling every asset and paying every liability takes time. After the partners of Shea & Gould, one of New York's best-known law firms, voted to dissolve their partnership, the firm remained open for an extra year to collect bills and pay off liabilities.

To avoid excessive detail in our illustrations, we include only two asset categories—Cash and Noncash Assets—and a single liability category—Liabilities. Our examples assume that the business sells the noncash assets in a single transaction and then pays the liabilities in another single transaction.

Assume that Jane Akers, Elaine Bloch, and Mark Crane have shared profits and losses in the ratio of 3:1:1. (This ratio is equal to 3/5, 1/5, 1/5, or a 60%, 20%, 20% sharing ratio.) They decide to liquidate their partnership. After the books are adjusted and closed, the general ledger contains the following balances:

Cash	$ 10,000	Liabilities	$ 30,000
Noncash assets	90,000	Akers, capital	40,000
		Bloch, capital	20,000
		Crane, capital	10,000
Total assets	$100,000	Total liabilities and capital	$100,000

Sale of Noncash Assets at a Gain

Assume that the Akers, Bloch, and Crane partnership sells its noncash assets (shown on the balance sheet as $90,000) for cash of $150,000. The partnership realizes a gain of $60,000, which is allocated to the partners on the basis of their profit-and-loss-sharing ratio. The entry to record this sale and allocation of the gain is

Oct. 31	Cash	150,000	
	Noncash Assets		90,000
	Akers, Capital ($60,000 × 0.60)		36,000
	Bloch, Capital ($60,000 × 0.20)		12,000
	Crane, Capital ($60,000 × 0.20)		12,000
	To sell noncash assets at a gain.		

The partnership next must pay off its liabilities:

Oct. 31	Liabilities	30,000	
	Cash		30,000
	To pay liabilities.		

In the final liquidation transaction, the remaining cash is disbursed to the partners. *The partners share in the cash according to their capital balances.* (*Gains and losses* on the sale of assets are shared by the partners on the basis of their profit-and-loss-sharing ratio.) The amount of cash left in the partnership is $130,000—the $10,000 beginning balance plus the $150,000 cash sale of assets minus the

$30,000 cash payment of liabilities. The partners divide the remaining cash according to their capital balances:

Oct. 31	Akers, Capital ($40,000 + $36,000) . . .	76,000	
	Bloch, Capital ($20,000 + $12,000). . . .	32,000	
	Crane, Capital ($10,000 + $12,000) . . .	22,000	
	Cash.		130,000
	To pay cash in liquidation.		

A convenient way to summarize the transactions in a partnership liquidation is given in Exhibit 12-4. Remember: Upon liquidation, gains on the sale of assets are divided according to the *profit-and-loss ratio*. The final cash payment to the partners is based on *capital balances*.

Exhibit 12-4 **Partnership Liquidation—Sale of Assets at a Gain**

									Capital			
	Cash	+	Noncash Assets	=	Liabilities	+	Akers (60%)	+	Bloch (20%)	+	Crane (20%)
Balance before sale of assets	$ 10,000		$90,000		$30,000		$40,000		$20,000		$10,000
Sale of assets and sharing of gain	150,000		(90,000)				36,000		12,000		12,000
Balances	160,000		0		30,000		76,000		32,000		22,000
Payment of liabilities	(30,000)				(30,000)						
Balances	130,000		0		0		76,000		32,000		22,000
Payment of cash to partners	(130,000)						(76,000)		(32,000)		(22,000)
Balances	$ 0		$ 0		$ 0		$ 0		$ 0		$ 0

After the payment of cash to the partners, the business has no assets, liabilities, or owners' equity. All the balances are zero. By the accounting equation, partnership assets always *must* equal partnership liabilities plus partnership capital.

Sale of Noncash Assets at a Loss

✔ Starter 12-11

✔ Starter 12-12

Liquidation of a business often includes the sale of noncash assets at a loss. When this occurs, the partners' capital accounts are debited as they share the loss in their profit-and-loss-sharing ratio. Otherwise, the accounting follows the pattern illustrated for the sale of noncash assets at a gain.

Stop & Think

The liquidation of the Dirk & Cross partnership included the sale of assets at a $150,000 loss. Lorraine Dirk's capital balance of $45,000 was less than her $60,000 share of the loss. Allocation of losses to the partners created a $15,000 deficit (debit balance) in Dirk's capital account. Identify ways that the partnership could deal with the negative balance (a capital deficiency) in Dirk's capital account.

Answer: Two possibilities are

1. Dirk could contribute assets to the partnership in an amount equal to her capital deficiency.
2. Joseph Cross could absorb Dirk's capital deficiency by decreasing his own capital balance.

☐ Partnership Characteristics
☐ Types of Partnerships
☐ Partnership Start-Up
☐ Profits and Losses, Drawings
☐ Admission of a Partner
☐ Withdrawal of a Partner
☐ Liquidation
■ Financial Statements

Student Resource CD
allocation of profit and loss, financial statements, partnership

7 *Prepare partnership financial statements*

Partnership Financial Statements

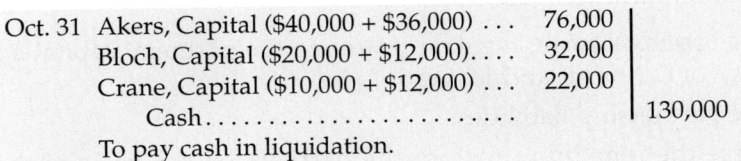

Partnership financial statements are much like those of a proprietorship. However, a partnership income statement includes a section showing the division of net income to the partners. For example, the partnership of Leslie Gray and Wayne Hayward might report its statements for the year ended December 31, 20X3, as shown in Exhibit 12-5. All amounts are assumed.

Exhibit 12-5

Financial Statements of a Partnership

Gray & Hayward Consulting

Income Statement
Year Ended December 31, 20X3

		Thousands
Revenues		$460
Expenses		(270)
Net income		$190
Allocation of net income:		
To Gray	$114	
To Hayward	76	$190

Gray & Hayward Consulting

Statement of Owners' Equity
Year Ended December 31, 20X3

	Thousands	
	Gray	Hayward
Capital, December 31, 20X2	$ 50	$ 40
Additional investments	10	—
Net income	114	76
Subtotal	174	116
Drawings	(72)	(48)
Capital, December 31, 20X3	$102	$ 68

Gray & Hayward Consulting

Balance Sheet
December 31, 20X3

Assets	Thousands
Cash and other assets	$170
Owners' Equity	
Gray, capital	$102
Hayward, capital	68
Total capital	$170

Large partnerships may not find it feasible to report the net income of every partner. Instead, the firm may report average earnings per partner, as shown in Exhibit 12-6 for a small firm.

Exhibit 12-6

Reporting Net Income for an Accounting Partnership

Price & Young

Income Statement
Year Ended August 31, 20X4

Fees for professional services	$1,500,000
Earnings for the year	$ 600,000
Average earnings per partner (2 partners)	$ 300,000

✔ Starter 12-13

✔ Starter 12-14

Decision Guidelines

ACCOUNTING FOR PARTNERSHIPS

Suppose you have a friend who's a biology major. Your friend has achieved amazing success growing plants hydroponically (in water). Your friend knows plants but has no sense for business, so the two of you form a partnership to take advantage of your respective skills. How do you organize? What decisions must you make? Consider these decision guidelines.

Decision	Guidelines
How to organize the business?	A partnership offers both advantages and disadvantages in comparison with proprietorships and corporations. (See Exhibit 12-2).
On what matters should the partners agree?	See "The Written Agreement" on page 471.
At what value does the partnership record assets and liabilities?	Current market value on the date of acquisition, because the partnership is buying its assets at their current market value.
How are partnership profits and losses shared among the partners?	• Equally if there is no profit-and-loss-sharing agreement. • As provided in the partnership agreement. Can be based on the partners' **a.** Stated fractions **b.** Capital contributions **c.** Service to the partnership **d.** Any combination of the above.
What happens when a partner withdraws from the firm?	The old partnership ceases to exist. The remaining partners may or may not form a new partnership.
How are new partners admitted to the partnership?	• *Purchase a partner's interest.* The old partnership is dissolved. The remaining partners may admit the new partner to the partnership. If not, the new partner gets no voice in management but shares in the profits and losses. Close the withdrawing partner's Capital account, and open a Capital account for the new partner. Carry over the old partner's Capital balance to the Capital account of the new partner. • *Invest in the partnership.* Buying in at book value creates no bonus to any partner. Buying in at a price above book value creates a bonus to the old partners. Buying in at a price below book value creates a bonus for the new partner.
How to account for the withdrawal of a partner from the business?	• First, adjust and close the books up to the date of the partner's withdrawal from the business. • Second, appraise the assets and the liabilities at their current market value. • Third, account for the partner's withdrawal. **a.** At book value (no change in remaining partners' Capital balances) **b.** At less than book value (increase the remaining partners' Capital balances) **c.** At more than book value (decrease the remaining partners' Capital balances)
What happens if the partnership goes out of business?	Liquidate the partnership, as follows: **a.** Adjust and close the partnership books up to the date of liquidation. **b.** Sell the partnership's assets. Allocate gain or loss to the partners' Capital accounts based on their profit-and-loss ratio. **c.** Pay the partnership liabilities. **d.** Pay any remaining cash to the partners based on their Capital balances.

Excel Application Exercise

Goal: Create a simple spreadsheet to prepare the financial statements of a partnership.

Scenario: Joey Ginsberg and Tommy Wong have decided to become partners and launch Hydro-Gro Partners, their hydroponic plant business. At the end of the year, Ginsberg prepares the new partnership's financial statements in Excel. The statements include an income statement, a statement of owners' equity, and a balance sheet. Revenues for the year were $8,000 and expenses were $4,500. Ginsberg had an initial investment of $700; Wong contributed $300. Ginsberg drew $630 from the business and Wong drew $440. Ginsberg and Wong agree to share profits and losses in proportion to their capital contributions.

When you have completed your work sheet, answer the following questions:

1. How much net income is allocated to Ginsberg? To Wong?
2. How much total capital does each partner have at year end?
3. What amount does the balance sheet report for the partnership's total capital at year-end?

Step-by-Step:

1. Open a new Excel spreadsheet.
2. In column 1, create a bold-faced heading as follows:
   - **a.** Chapter 12 Excel Application Exercise
   - **b.** Hydro-Gro Partners
   - **c.** Today's Date
3. Two rows down, enter the bold-faced title, "Partnership Financial Statements." Then, enter individual rows for revenues, expenses, investment by Ginsberg, investment by Wong, drawings by Ginsberg, and drawings by Wong. Enter the amounts in column B.
4. Using Exhibit 12-5 as your guide, create Hydro-Gro Partners' income statement and statement of owners' equity for the year ended December 31, 20X5, and the balance sheet on that date. Be sure all statements contain formulas based on the data supplied in the problem. (*Hint 1:* The allocation of net income is based on the relative proportion of the investment by each partner. Your formula needs to reflect this proportion. *Hint 2:* "Cash and other assets" must equal the total capital at year-end in the balance sheet.)
5. Save your work sheet and print a copy for your files.

END-OF-CHAPTER *Summary Problem*

The partnership of Taylor & Uvalde is considering admitting Steven Vaughn as a partner on January 1, 20X5. The partnership general ledger includes the following balances on that date:

Cash	$ 9,000	Total liabilities	$ 50,000
Other assets	110,000	Taylor, capital	45,000
		Uvalde, capital	24,000
Total assets	$119,000	Total liabilities and capital	$119,000

Ross Taylor's share of profits and losses is 60%, and Thomas Uvalde's share is 40%.

Required (Items 1 and 2 Are Independent)

1. Suppose that Vaughn pays Uvalde $31,000 to acquire Uvalde's interest in the business. Taylor approves Vaughn as a partner.
   - **a.** Record the transfer of owner's equity on the partnership books.
   - **b.** Prepare the partnership balance sheet immediately after Vaughn is admitted as a partner.
2. Suppose that Vaughn becomes a partner by investing $31,000 cash to acquire a one-fourth interest in the business.
   - **a.** Compute Vaughn's capital balance, and record his investment in the business.
   - **b.** Prepare the partnership balance sheet immediately after Vaughn is admitted as a partner. Include the heading.

A+ TIPS
CHECK YOUR RESOURCES

Solution

Requirement 1

a.

Jan. 1	Uvalde, Capital	24,000	
	Vaughn, Capital		24,000
	To transfer Uvalde's equity in the partnership to Vaughn.		

b. The balance sheet for the partnership of Taylor and Vaughn is identical to the balance sheet given for Taylor and Uvalde in the problem, except that Vaughn's name replaces Uvalde's name in the title and in the listing of Capital accounts.

Requirement 2

a. Computations of Vaughn's capital balance:

Partnership capital before Vaughn is admitted ($45,000 + $24,000)	$ 69,000
Vaughn's investment in the partnership	31,000
Partnership capital after Vaughn is admitted	$100,000
Vaughn's capital in the partnership ($100,000 × 1/4)	$ 25,000

Jan. 1	Cash	31,000	
	Vaughn, Capital		25,000
	Taylor, Capital [($31,000 – $25,000) × 0.60]		3,600
	Uvalde, Capital [($31,000 – $25,000) × 0.40]		2,400
	To admit Vaughn as a partner with a one-fourth interest in the business.		

b.

Taylor, Uvalde, & Vaughn
Balance Sheet
January 1, 20X5

Cash ($9,000 + $31,000)	$ 40,000	Total liabilities	$ 50,000
Other assets	110,000	Taylor, capital ($45,000 + $3,600)	48,600
		Uvalde, capital ($24,000 + $2,400)	26,400
		Vaughn, capital	25,000
Total assets	$150,000	Total liabilities and capital	$150,000

REVIEW *Partnerships*

Quick Check

1. How does a partnership get started?
   - **a.** The partners get a charter from the state.
   - **b.** The partners reach an agreement and simply begin operations.
   - **c.** The partners register with the Better Business Bureau.
   - **d.** All of the above.
2. Which characteristic identifies a partnership?
   - **a.** Limited life
   - **b.** No business income tax
   - **c.** Unlimited personal liability
   - **d.** All of the above

3. An S Corporation is taxed like a
   a. Corporation
   b. Partnership
   c. Either of the above, depending on the partners' decision
   d. None of the above
4. The partnership of Abbot and Brown splits profits in the ratio of 2/3 to Abbot and 1/3 to Brown. The partnership has a net loss of $450,000. What is Brown's share of the loss?
   a. $150,000
   b. $225,000
   c. $300,000
   d. Cannot be determined from the data given
5. Partner drawings
   a. Decrease partnership liabilities
   b. Increase partnership capital
   c. Decrease partnership capital
   d. Decrease partnership net income
6. Malcolm pays $100,000 to Lloyd to acquire Lloyd's $75,000 interest in a partnership. The journal entry to record this transaction is

a. Lloyd, Capital	100,000		
Malcolm, Capital . .		100,000	
b. Lloyd, Capital	75,000		
Malcolm, Capital . .		75,000	
c. Lloyd, Capital	25,000		
Malcolm, Capital . .		25,000	
d. Malcolm, Capital	75,000		
Lloyd, Capital		75,000	

7. Clark and Douglas admit Evans to their partnership, with Evans paying $50,000 more than the book value of her equity in the new partnership. Clark and Douglas have no formal profit-and-loss-sharing agreement. What effect does admission of Evans into the partnership have on the capital balances of Clark and Douglas?
   a. Cannot be determined from the data given
   b. Debit the Clark and Douglas capital accounts for $25,000 each
   c. Credit the Clark and Douglas capital accounts for $50,000 each
   d. Credit the Clark and Douglas capital accounts for $25,000 each
8. Tate retires from the partnership of Roberts, Smith, and Tate. The partners share profits and losses in the ratio of 3:3:4. Tate's capital balance is $40,000, and he receives $50,000 in final settlement. What is the effect on the capital accounts of Roberts and Smith?
   a. Roberts' capital decreases by $5,000.
   b. Smith's capital decreases by $5,000.
   c. Both *a* and *b*.
   d. None of the above.
9. The book value of the assets of the KLM partnership is $100,000. In liquidation, the partnership sells the assets for $130,000. How should the partnership account for the sale of the assets?
   a. Credit the assets for $100,000
   b. Debit cash for $130,000
   c. Increase the partners' capital accounts
   d. All of the above
10. Partnership financial statements report
    a. Revenues on the income statement
    b. Liabilities on the income statement
    c. Net income on the balance sheet
    d. Expenses on the balance sheet

Accounting Vocabulary

articles of partnership (p. 471)
dissolution (p. 471)
general partnership (p. 473)
limited liability partnership (p. 473)
limited partnership (p. 473)
liquidation (p. 484)
LLPs (p. 473)
mutual agency (p. 471)
partnership (p. 471)
partnership agreement (p. 471)
S Corporation (p. 473)
unlimited personal liability (p. 471)

ASSESS Your Progress

A+ online homework

See *www.prenhall.com/horngren* for selected Starters, Exercises, and Problems.

Starters

Partnership characteristics
(Obj. 1)

S12-1 After studying the characteristics of a partnership, write two short paragraphs, as follows:

1. Explain the *advantages* of a partnership over a proprietorship and a corporation.
2. Explain the *disadvantages* of a partnership over a proprietorship and a corporation.

A partner's investment in a partnership
(Obj. 2)

S12-2 Dean Hahn invests land in a partnership with Margo Klem. Hahn purchased the land in 20X1 for $300,000. A real estate appraiser now values the land at $400,000. Hahn wants $400,000 capital in the new partnership, but Klem objects. Klem believes that Hahn's capital contribution should be measured by the book value of his land.

Klem and Hahn seek your advice. Which value of the building is appropriate for measuring Hahn's capital—book value or current market value? State the reason for your answer. Give the partnership's journal entry to record Hahn's investment in the business.

Investments by partners
(Obj. 2)

S12-3 Seth Green and Nate Smith are forming the partnership Sun Development to develop a theme park near Panama City, Florida. Green contributes cash of $4 million and land valued at $10 million. When Green purchased the land in 20X1, its cost was $8 million. The partnership will assume Green's $3 million note payable on the land. Smith invests cash of $5 million and equipment worth $7 million.

1. Compute the partnership's total assets, total liabilities, and total owners' equity immediately after organizing.
2. Journalize the partnership's receipt of assets and liabilities from Green and from Smith. Record each asset at its current market value.

Partners' profits, losses, and capital balances
(Obj. 3)

S12-4 Examine the Benz and Hanna balance sheet in Exhibit 12-3, page 475. Note that Benz invested far more in the partnership than Hanna. Suppose the two partners fail to agree on a profit-and-loss-sharing ratio. For the first month (June 20X5), the partnership lost $20,000.

1. How much of this loss goes to Benz? How much goes to Hanna?
2. The partners withdrew no assets during June. What is each partner's capital balance at June 30? Prepare a T-account for each partner's capital to answer this question.

Dividing partnership profits based on capital contributions and service
(Obj. 3)

S12-5 Lawson, Martinez, and Norris have capital balances of $20,000, $30,000, and $50,000, respectively. The partners share profits and losses as follows:

a. The first $40,000 is divided based on the partners' capital balances.
b. The next $40,000 is based on service, shared equally by Lawson and Norris.
c. The remainder is divided equally.

Compute each partner's share of the business's $110,000 net income for the year.

Admitting a partner who purchases an existing partner's interest
(Obj. 4)

S12-6 Study the Ingel and Jay partnership balance sheet at the bottom of page 478. Claire Reynaldo pays $100,000 to purchase Michael Jay's interest in the partnership.

1. Journalize the partnership's transaction to admit Reynaldo to the partnership. What happens to the $10,000 difference between Reynaldo's payment and Jay's capital balance?
2. Must Robin Ingel accept Claire Reynaldo as a full partner? What right does Reynaldo have after purchasing Jay's interest in the partnership?

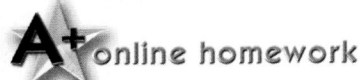

Admitting a partner who invests in the business
(Obj. 4)

S12-7 Return to the partnership balance sheet of Ingel and Jay near the bottom of page 478. Suppose Ann Teal invests cash of $80,000 to acquire a 1/3 interest in the partnership.

1. Does Teal's investment provide a bonus to the partners? Show calculations to support your answer.
2. Journalize the partnership's receipt of the $80,000 from Teal.

Admitting a new partner; bonus to the old partners
(Obj. 4)

S12-8 Refer to the partnership balance sheet of Page and Franco near the bottom of page 480. Page gets 2/3 of profits and losses, and Franco gets 1/3. Assume Neely invests $140,000 to acquire a 25% interest in the new partnership of Page, Franco, and Neely. Journalize the partnership's receipt of cash from Neely.

Withdrawal of a partner
(Obj. 5)

S12-9 Examine the Green, Henry, and Isaac balance sheet in the middle of page 482. The partners share profits and losses as follows: 25% to Green, 50% to Henry, and 25% to Isaac. Suppose Susan Green is withdrawing from the business, and the partners agree that no appraisal of assets is needed. How much in assets can Green take from the partnership? Give the reason for your answer, including an explanation of why the profit-and-loss-sharing ratio is not used for this determination.

Withdrawal of a partner; asset revaluation
(Obj. 5)

S12-10 Refer to the Green, Henry, and Isaac partnership balance sheet in the middle of page 482. Suppose Henry is retiring from the business and the partners agree to revalue the assets at current market value. A real-estate appraiser values the land at $95,000. The book values of all other assets approximate their current market value. The profit-and-loss ratio is 1:2:1.

Journalize (a) the revaluation of the land and (b) payment of $63,000 to Henry upon his retirement July 31.

Liquidation of a partnership at a loss
(Obj. 6)

S12-11 Use the data in Exhibit 12-4. Suppose the partnership of Akers, Bloch, and Crane liquidates by selling all noncash assets for $85,000. Complete the liquidation schedule as shown in Exhibit 12-4.

Liquidation of a partnership
(Obj. 6)

S12-12 This Starter builds on the solution to Starter 12-11. After completing the liquidation schedule in Starter 12-11, journalize the partnership's (a) sale of noncash assets for $85,000 (use a single account for Noncash Assets), (b) payment of liabilities, and (c) payment of cash to the partners. Include an explanation with each entry.

Partnership balance sheet
(Obj. 7)

S12-13 This Starter uses the Green, Henry, and Isaac balance sheet, after revaluation of inventory and land, given at the top of page 483. Assume Isaac has withdrawn from the partnership at his book value, receiving cash. Prepare the balance sheet of the new partnership of Green and Henry on July 31.

Partnership income statement
(Obj. 7)

S12-14 The partnership of Frost and Martin had these balances at September 30, 20X4:

Cash	$20,000	Service revenue	$140,000
Liabilities	40,000	Frost, capital	30,000
Martin, capital.	10,000	Total expenses	35,000
Other assets.	60,000		

Frost gets 60% of profits and losses, and Martin 40%. Prepare the partnership's income statement for the year ended September 30, 20X4.

Exercises

A+ online homework

Organizing a partnership
(Obj. 1)

E12-1 Ryan Amman, a friend from college, approaches you about forming a partnership to export software. Since graduating, Amman has worked for the International Trade Bank, developing important contacts among government officials and business leaders in South America. Amman believes he is in a unique position to capitalize on growing markets. With expertise in finance, you would have responsibility for the partnership's accounting and finance.

Required

Discuss the advantages and disadvantages of organizing the export business as a partnership rather than a proprietorship. Comment on how partnership income is taxed and how your taxes would change if you organized as an S corporation.

Recording a partner's investment
(Obj. 2)

E12-2 Vivien Monteros has been operating an apartment-locator service as a proprietorship. She and Barrett Schraeder have decided to reorganize the business as a partnership. Monteros's investment in the partnership consists of cash, $8,000; accounts receivable, $10,600; office furniture, $1,600; a small building, $55,000; accounts payable, $3,300; and a note payable to the bank, $10,000.

To determine Monteros's equity in the partnership, she and Schraeder hire an independent appraiser. The appraiser values all the assets and liabilities at their book value except the building, which has a current market value of $71,000. Also there are accrued expenses payable of $1,200.

Required

Make the entry on the partnership books to record Monteros's investment.

Computing partners' shares of net income and net loss
(Obj. 3)

Student Resource CD
spreadsheet

E12-3 David Coe and Jen Price form a partnership, investing $40,000 and $80,000, respectively. Determine their shares of net income or net loss for each of the following situations:

a. Net loss is $60,000 and the partners have no written partnership agreement.
b. Net income is $90,000, and the partnership agreement states that the partners share profits and losses on the basis of their capital contributions.
c. Net income is $98,000. The first $60,000 is shared on the basis of partner capital contributions. The next $30,000 is based on partner service, with Coe receiving 30% and Price receiving 70%. The remainder is shared equally.

Computing partners' capital balances
(Obj. 3)

E12-4 David Coe withdrew cash of $50,000 for personal use, and Jen Price withdrew cash of $40,000 during the year. Using the data from situation (c) in Exercise 12-3, journalize the entries to close (1) the income summary account and (2) the partners' drawing accounts. Explanations are not required. What was the overall effect on partnership capital?

Admitting a new partner
(Obj. 4)

E12-5 Adam Tse is admitted to a partnership. Prior to his admission, the partnership books show Sean Graham's capital balance at $100,000 and Kelly Ott's capital balance at $60,000. Compute each partner's equity on the books of the new partnership under the following plans:

a. Tse pays $90,000 for Ott's equity. Tse's payment goes directly to Ott.
b. Tse invests $40,000 to acquire a 1/5 interest in the partnership.
c. Tse invests $60,000 to acquire a 1/5 interest in the partnership.

Admitting a new partner
(Obj. 4)

E12-6 Make the partnership journal entry to record the admission of Tse under plans (a), (b), and (c) in Exercise 12-5. Explanations are not required.

Withdrawal of a partner
(Obj. 5)

E12-7 After the books are closed, Echols & Schaeffer's partnership balance sheet reports capital of $60,000 for Echols and $90,000 for Schaeffer. Echols is withdrawing from the firm. The partners agree to write down partnership assets by $40,000. They have shared profits and losses in the ratio of 1/4 to Echols and 3/4 to Schaeffer. The partnership agreement states that a withdrawing partner will receive assets equal to the book value of his owner's equity.

1. How much will Echols receive? Schaeffer will continue to operate the business as a proprietorship.
2. What is Schaeffer's beginning capital on the books of his new proprietorship?

E12-8 Lon Augustine is retiring from the partnership of Augustine, Rye, and Bermuda on May 31. The partner capital balances are Augustine, $36,000; Rye, $51,000; and Bermuda, $22,000. The partners agree to have the partnership assets revalued to current market values. The independent appraiser reports that the book value of the inventory should be decreased by $12,000, and the book value of the land should be increased by $32,000. The partners agree to these revaluations. The profit-and-loss ratio has been 5:3:2 for Augustine, Rye, and Bermuda, respectively. In retiring from the firm, Augustine receives $30,000 cash and a $30,000 note from the partnership.

Withdrawal of a partner
(Obj. 5)

Required

Journalize (a) the asset revaluations and (b) Augustine's withdrawal from the firm.

E12-9 Grant, Harris, and Isbell are liquidating their partnership. Before selling the noncash assets and paying the liabilities, the capital balances are Grant $23,000; Harris, $20,000; and Isbell, $11,000. The partnership agreement specifies no division of profits and losses.

Liquidation of a partnership
(Obj. 6)

Required

1. After selling the noncash assets and paying the liabilities, the partnership has cash of $54,000. How much cash will each partner receive in final liquidation?
2. After selling the noncash assets and paying the liabilities, the partnership has cash of $45,000. How much cash will each partner receive in final liquidation?

E12-10 Prior to liquidation, the accounting records of Park, Quade, and Ross included the following balances and profit-and-loss-sharing percentages:

Liquidation of a partnership
(Obj. 6)

							Capital				
	Cash	+	Noncash Assets	=	Liabilities	+	Park (40%)	+	Quade (30%)	+	Ross (30%)
Balances before sale of assets	$ 8,000		$57,000		$19,000		$20,000		$15,000		$11,000

The partnership sold the noncash assets for $72,000, paid the liabilities, and gave the remaining cash to the partners. Complete the summary of transactions in the liquidation of the partnership. Use the format illustrated in Exhibit 12-4.

E12-11 The partnership of West, Young, and Zeno is dissolving. Business assets, liabilities, and partners' capital balances prior to dissolution follow at the top of page 496. The partners share profits and losses as follows: West, 25%; Young, 45%; and Zeno, 30%.

Liquidation of a partnership
(Obj. 6)

Required

Create a spreadsheet or solve manually (see the top of page 496)—as directed by your instructor—to compute the ending balances in all accounts after the noncash assets are sold for $140,000 and for $90,000. Determine the unknown amounts. Identify two ways the partners can deal with the negative ending balance in Zeno's capital account.

E12-12 On December 31, 20X5, Cindy Dougherty and Marla Pehacek agree to combine their proprietorships as a partnership. Their balance sheets on December 31 are shown in the lower part of page 496.

Partnership balance sheet
(Obj. 7)

Required

Prepare the partnership balance sheet at December 31, 20X5.

Exercise 12-11 West, Young, and Zeno

	A	B	C	D	E	F
1			**West, Young & Zeno**			
2			**Sale of Noncash Assets**			
3			**(For $140,000)**			
4						
5		Noncash		West	Young	Zeno
6	Cash	Assets	Liabilities	Capital	Capital	Capital
7	$ 6,000	$126,000	$77,000	$12,000	$37,000	$6,000
8	140,000	(126,000)		?	?	?
9						
10	$146,000	$ 0	$77,000	$?	$?	$?
11						
12				=($A8–$B7) * .25		
13						
14						
15			**(For $90,000)**			
16		Noncash		West	Young	Zeno
17	Cash	Assets	Liabilities	Capital	Capital	Capital
18	$ 6,000	$126,000	$77,000	$12,000	$37,000	$6,000
19	90,000	(126,000)		?	?	?
20						
21	$96,000	$ 0	$77,000	$?	$?	$?
22						
23				=($A19–$B18) * .25		
24						

Exercise 12-12

Dougherty and Pehacek

	Dougherty's Business		Pehacek's Business	
	Book Value	Current Market Value	Book Value	Current Market Value
Assets				
Cash	$ 10,700	$ 10,700	$ 4,000	$ 4,000
Accounts receivable (net)	22,000	20,200	8,000	6,300
Inventory.............................	51,000	46,000	34,000	35,100
Plant assets (net).......................	121,800	103,500	53,500	57,400
Total assets	$205,500	$180,400	$99,500	$102,800
Liabilities and Capital				
Accounts payable.......................	$ 25,500	$ 25,500	$ 8,300	$ 8,300
Accrued expenses payable	9,200	9,200	1,400	1,400
Notes payable..........................	55,000	55,000		
Dougherty, capital	115,800	?		
Pehacek, capital			89,800	?
Total liabilities and capital	$205,500	$180,400	$99,500	$102,800

Problems

(Group A)

Writing a partnership agreement
(Obj. 1)

P12-1A Ron Jaworski and Lori Miller are forming a partnership, Compass Web Designs, to maintain Web sites for clients. Jaworski is skilled at systems design, and his designs can draw large sales volumes. Miller is a super salesperson and has already lined up several clients.

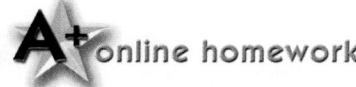

Required

Write a partnership agreement to cover all elements essential for Compass Web Designs to operate smoothly. Make up names, amounts, profit-and-loss percentages, and so on as needed.

Investments by partners
(Obj. 2, 7)

P12-2A On June 30, Alice Ogden and Dan Croyle formed a partnership. The partners agree to invest equal amounts of capital. Ogden invests her proprietorship's assets and liabilities (credit balances in parentheses), as follows:

	Ogden's Book Values	Current Market Values
Accounts receivable	$ 7,200	$ 7,200
Inventory	22,340	24,100
Prepaid expenses	1,700	1,700
Office equipment	45,900	27,600
Accumulated depreciation	(15,300)	0
Accounts payable	(19,100)	(19,100)

On June 30, Croyle invests cash in an amount equal to the current market value of Ogden's partnership capital. The partners decide that Ogden will earn two-thirds of partnership profits because she will manage the business. Croyle agrees to accept one-third of the profits. During the remainder of the year, the partnership earns net income of $90,000. Ogden's drawings are $39,000, and Croyle's drawings are $31,000.

Required

1. Journalize the partners' initial investments.
2. Prepare the partnership balance sheet immediately after its formation on June 30.
3. Journalize the December 31 entries to close the Income Summary account and the partners' drawing accounts.

Admitting a new partner
(Obj. 4)

P12-3A The owners of NBC partnership are considering admitting Sue Carter as a new partner. On March 31 of the current year, the capital accounts of the three existing partners and their shares of profits and losses are as follows:

	Capital	Profit-and-Loss Share
Nick Nelson	$ 40,000	15%
Luke Bright	100,000	30%
Lisa Clapton	160,000	55%

Required

Journalize the admission of Carter as a partner on March 31 for each of the following independent situations:

1. Carter pays Clapton $200,000 cash to purchase Clapton's interest in the partnership.
2. Carter invests $60,000 in the partnership, acquiring a one-sixth interest in the business.
3. Carter invests $80,000 in the partnership, acquiring a one-fourth interest in the business.

Computing partners' shares of net income and net loss; preparing the partnership income statement
(Obj. 3, 7)

Student Resource CD
General Ledger, Peachtree, QuickBooks

P12-4A Charles Lake, Liz Wood, and Hal Parks have formed a partnership. Lake invested $15,000, Wood $18,000, and Parks $27,000. Lake will manage the store; Wood will work in the store half-time; and Parks will not work in the business.

Required

1. Compute the partners' shares of profits and losses under each of the following plans:
   a. Net loss is $60,000, and the partnership agreement allocates 40% of profits to Lake, 25% to Wood, and 35% to Parks. The agreement does not specify the sharing of losses.

b. Net income for the year ended January 31, 20X4, is $210,000. The first $75,000 is allocated on the basis of partner capital contributions, and the next $36,000 is based on service, with Lake receiving $28,000 and Wood receiving $8,000. Any remainder is shared equally.

2. Revenues for the year ended January 31, 20X4, were $540,000, and expenses were $330,000. Under plan (b), prepare the partnership income statement for the year.

Withdrawal of a partner
(Obj. 4, 5)

P12-5A Priority Financial Planners is a partnership owned by three individuals. The partners share profits and losses in the ratio of 28% to Cary Black, 38% to Dick McNut, and 34% to Jen Tate. At December 31, 20X6, the firm has the following balance sheet:

Cash		$ 12,000	Total liabilities	$ 75,000
Accounts receivable	$ 22,000			
Less allowance for uncollectibles	(4,000)	18,000		
Building	$310,000		Black, capital	83,000
Less accumulated			McNut, capital	50,000
depreciation	(70,000)	240,000	Tate, capital	62,000
Total assets		$270,000	Total liabilities and capital	$270,000

McNut withdraws from the partnership on December 31, 20X6, to establish his own consulting practice.

Required

Record McNut's withdrawal from the partnership under the following plans:

1. In personal transactions, McNut sells his equity in the partnership to Ashley Napper and Jim Lucks, who each pay McNut $40,000 for half his interest. Black and Tate agree to accept Napper and Lucks as partners.
2. The partnership pays McNut cash of $20,000 and gives him a note payable for the remainder of his book equity in settlement of his partnership interest.
3. McNut receives cash of $10,000 and a note for $70,000 from the partnership.
4. The partners agree that the building is worth only $250,000 and that its accumulated depreciation should remain at $70,000. After the revaluation, the partnership settles with McNut by giving him cash of $10,000 and a note payable for the remainder of his book equity.

Liquidation of a partnership
(Obj. 6)

P12-6A The partnership of Parr, Johnston, & Rake has experienced operating losses for three consecutive years. The partners—who have shared profits and losses in the ratio of Parr, 10%; Johnston, 30%; and Rake, 60%—are liquidating the business. They ask you to analyze the effects of liquidation and present the following partnership balance sheet at December 31, end of the current year:

Cash	$ 27,000	Liabilities	$131,000
Noncash assets	202,000	Parr, capital	21,000
		Johnston, capital	39,000
		Rake, capital	38,000
Total assets	$229,000	Total liabilities and capital	$229,000

Required

1. Prepare a summary of liquidation transactions (as illustrated in Exhibit 12-4). The noncash assets are sold for $189,000.
2. Make the journal entries to record the liquidation transactions.

Capital amounts for the balance sheet of a partnership
(Obj. 7)

P12-7A ← *Link Back to Chapter 4 (Closing Entries).* VT&P is a partnership owned by Vela, Thomas, and Prago, who share profits and losses in the ratio of 5:3:2. The adjusted trial balance of the partnership at September 30, end of the current fiscal year, follows.

VT&P
Adjusted Trial Balance
September 30, 20XX

Cash	$ 10,000	
Noncash assets	177,000	
Liabilities		$135,000
Vela, capital		57,000
Thomas, capital		44,000
Prago, capital		21,000
Vela, drawing	45,000	
Thomas, drawing	37,000	
Prago, drawing	18,000	
Revenues		211,000
Expenses	181,000	
Totals	$468,000	$468,000

Required

1. Prepare the September 30 entries to close the revenue, expense, income summary, and drawing accounts.
2. Insert the opening capital balances in the partner capital accounts, post the closing entries to the capital accounts, and determine each partner's ending capital balance.

Problems

(Group B)

A+ online homework

Writing a partnership agreement
(Obj. 1)

P12-1B Anna Frank and Sara Gilbert are forming a partnership, Taxco Silver Co., to import silver jewelry from Mexico. Frank is especially artistic and will travel to Mexico to buy merchandise. Gilbert is a super salesperson and has already lined up several department stores to sell the jewelry.

Required

Write a partnership agreement to cover all elements essential for the business to operate smoothly. Make up names, amounts, profit-and-loss percentages, and so on as needed.

Investments by partners
(Obj. 2, 7)

P12-2B Beth Dalton and Kim Sperry formed a partnership on March 15. The partners agreed to invest equal amounts of capital. Sperry invested his proprietorship's assets and liabilities (credit balances in parentheses). See the table that follows.

	Sperry's Book Values	Current Market Values
Accounts receivable	$12,000	$12,000
Inventory	43,850	31,220
Prepaid expenses	3,700	3,700
Store equipment	36,700	26,600
Accumulated depreciation	(9,200)	(0)
Accounts payable	(22,300)	(22,300)

On March 15, Dalton invested cash in an amount equal to the current market value of Sperry's partnership capital. The partners decided that Sperry will earn 70% of partnership profits because he will manage the business. Dalton agreed to accept 30% of profits. During the period ended December 31, the partnership earned net income of $70,000. Dalton's drawings were $27,000, and Sperry's drawings totaled $41,000.

Required

1. Journalize the partners' initial investments.
2. Prepare the partnership balance sheet immediately after its formation on March 15.
3. Journalize the December 31 entries to close the Income Summary account and the partners' drawing accounts.

Admitting a new partner
(Obj. 4)

P12-3B Lost Pines Escape is a partnership, and its owners are considering admitting Duane Milano as a new partner. On July 31 of the current year, the capital accounts of the three existing partners and their shares of profits and losses are as follows:

	Capital	Profit-and-Loss Ratio
Eric Runyan	$48,000	1/6
Sara Braden	64,000	1/3
Ken Maness	88,000	1/2

Required

Journalize the admission of Milano as a partner on July 31 for each of the following independent situations:

1. Milano pays Maness $114,000 cash to purchase Maness's interest.
2. Milano invests $50,000 in the partnership, acquiring a one-fifth interest in the business.
3. Milano invests $50,000 in the partnership, acquiring a one-eighth interest in the business.

Computing partners' shares of net income and net loss; preparing the partnership income statement
(Obj. 3, 7)

Student ResourceCD
GL, PT, QB

P12-4B Rudy Trump, Monica Rivers, and Courtney Jetta have formed a partnership. Trump invested $20,000; Rivers, $40,000; and Jetta, $60,000. Trump will manage the store; Rivers will work in the store three-quarters of the time; and Jetta will not work.

Required

1. Compute the partners' shares of profits and losses under each of the following plans:
   a. Net loss is $47,000, and the partnership agreement allocates 45% of profits to Trump, 35% to Rivers, and 20% to Jetta. The agreement does not discuss the sharing of losses.
   b. Net income for the year ended September 30, 20X4, is $86,000. The first $30,000 is allocated on the basis of partner capital contributions. The next $30,000 is based on service, with $20,000 going to Trump and $10,000 going to Rivers. Any remainder is shared equally.
2. Revenues for the year ended September 30, 20X4, were $572,000, and expenses were $486,000. Under plan (b), prepare the partnership income statement for the year.

Withdrawal of a partner
(Obj. 4, 5)

P12-5B TMB Design is a partnership owned by three individuals. The partners share profits and losses in the ratio of 30% to Pam Tracy, 40% to Bill Mertz, and 30% to Cameron Brucks. At December 31, 20X3, the firm has the balance sheet that follows.

Cash		$ 25,000	Total liabilities	$103,000
Accounts receivable	$ 16,000			
Less allowance for uncollectibles	(1,000)	15,000		
Inventory		92,000	Tracy, capital	38,000
Equipment	130,000		Mertz, capital	49,000
Less accumulated depreciation	(30,000)	100,000	Brucks, capital	42,000
Total assets		$232,000	Total liabilities and capital	$232,000

Tracy withdraws from the partnership on this date.

Required

Record Tracy's withdrawal from the partnership under the following plans:

1. In personal transactions, Tracy sells her equity in the partnership to Walt Fair and Beverly Holtz, who each pay Tracy $35,000 for half her interest. Mertz and Brucks agree to accept Fair and Holtz as partners.
2. The partnership pays Tracy cash of $10,000 and gives her a note payable for the remainder of her book equity in settlement of her partnership interest.
3. Tracy receives cash of $6,000 and a note payable for $34,000 from the partnership.
4. The partners agree that the equipment is worth $160,000 and that accumulated depreciation should remain at $30,000. After the revaluation, the partnership settles with Tracy by giving her cash of $15,000 and inventory for the remainder of her book equity.

Liquidation of a partnership **(Obj. 6)**

P12-6B The partnership of Jackson, Pierce, & Fenner has experienced operating losses for three consecutive years. The partners—who have shared profits and losses in the ratio of Leigh Jackson, 15%; Trent Pierce, 60%; and Bruce Fenner, 25%—are liquidating the business. They ask you to analyze the effects of liquidation. They present the following condensed partnership balance sheet at December 31, end of the current year:

Cash	$ 7,000	Liabilities	$ 63,000
Noncash assets	163,000	Jackson, capital	24,000
		Pierce, capital	66,000
		Fenner, capital	17,000
		Total liabilities and	
Total assets	$170,000	capital	$170,000

Required

1. Prepare a summary of liquidation transactions (as illustrated in Exhibit 12-4). The noncash assets are sold for $141,000.
2. Make the journal entries to record the liquidation transactions.

Capital amounts for the balance sheet of a partnership **(Obj. 7)**

P12-7B ← *Link Back to Chapter 4 (Closing Entries).* ABS Company is a partnership owned by Alberts, Beech, and Sumner, who share profits and losses in the ratio of 1:3:4. The adjusted trial balance of the partnership at June 30, end of the current fiscal year, follows.

ABS Company

Adjusted Trial Balance
June 30, 20XX

Cash	$ 24,000	
Noncash assets	116,000	
Liabilities		$100,000
Alberts, capital		22,000
Beech, capital		41,000
Sumner, capital		62,000
Alberts, drawing	14,000	
Beech, drawing	35,000	
Sumner, drawing	54,000	
Revenues		108,000
Expenses	90,000	
Totals	$333,000	$333,000

Required

1. Prepare the June 30 entries to close the revenue, expense, income summary, and drawing accounts.
2. Insert the opening capital balances in the partners' capital accounts, post the closing entries to the capital accounts, and determine each partner's ending capital balance.

APPLY Your Knowledge

Decision Cases

Settling disagreements among partners
(Obj. 3)

Case 1. Kimberly Gardner invested $20,000 and Leah Johanssen invested $10,000 in a public relations firm that has operated for 10 years. Neither partner has made an additional investment. Gardner and Johanssen have shared profits and losses in the ratio of 2:1, which is the ratio of their investments in the business. Gardner manages the office, supervises the employees, and does the accounting. Johanssen, the moderator of a television talk show, is responsible for marketing. Her high profile generates important revenue for the business. During the year ended December 20X4, the partnership earned net income of $87,000, shared in the 2:1 ratio. On December 31, 20X4, Gardner's capital balance was $150,000, and Johanssen's capital balance was $100,000.

Required

Respond to each of the following situations.

1. During January 20X5, Gardner learned that revenues of $18,000 were omitted from the reported 20X4 income. She brings this omission to Johanssen's attention, pointing out that Gardner's share of this added income is two-thirds, or $12,000, and Johanssen's share is one-third, or $6,000. Johanssen believes that they should share this added income on the basis of their capital balances—60%, or $10,800, to Gardner and 40%, or $7,200, to herself. Which partner is correct? Why?
2. Assume that the 20X4 $18,000 omission was an account payable for an operating expense. On what basis would the partners share this amount?

Partnership issues
(Obj. 1, 5)

Case 2. The following questions relate to issues faced by partnerships.

1. The text states that a written partnership agreement should be drawn up between the partners in a partnership. One benefit of an agreement is that it provides a mechanism for resolving disputes between the partners. List five areas of dispute that might be resolved by a partnership agreement.
2. The statement has been made that "if you must take on a partner, make sure the partner is richer than you are." Why is this statement valid?
3. Corwin & Corwin is a law partnership. Natalie Corwin is planning to retire from the partnership and move to Israel. What options are available to Corwin to enable her to convert her share of the partnership assets to cash?

Ethical Issue

Tom Crenshaw and Lee Spitz operate Northern Engraving in Toledo, Ohio. The partners split profits and losses equally, and each takes an annual salary of $80,000. To even out the workload, Spitz does the buying and Crenshaw serves as the accountant. From time to time, they use small amounts of store merchandise for personal use. In preparing for a large party, Crenshaw took engraved invitations and other goods that cost $5,000. He recorded the transaction as follows:

Cost of Goods Sold	5,000	
Inventory		5,000

1. How should Crenshaw have recorded this transaction?
2. Discuss the ethical aspects of Crenshaw's action.

Team Project

Visit a business partnership in your area and interview one or more of the partners. Obtain answers to the following questions and ask your instructor for directions. As directed by your instructor, either (a) prepare a written report of your findings or (b) make a presentation to your class.

Required

1. Why did you organize the business as a partnership? What advantages does the partnership form of organization offer the business? What are the disadvantages of the partnership form of organization?
2. Is the business a general partnership or a limited partnership?
3. Do the partners have a written partnership agreement? What does the agreement cover? Obtain a copy if possible.
4. Who manages the business? Do all partners participate in day-to-day management, or is management the responsibility of only certain partners?
5. If there is no written agreement, what is the mechanism for making key decisions?
6. Has the business ever admitted a new partner? If so, when? What are the partnership's procedures for admitting a new partner?
7. Has a partner ever withdrawn from the business? If so, when? What are the partnership's procedures for settling up with a withdrawing partner?
8. If possible, learn how the partnership divides profits and losses among the partners.
9. Ask for any additional insights the partner you interview can provide about the business.

For Internet Exercises, go to the Web site www.prenhall.com/horngren.

CHAPTER 13

Corporations: Paid-in Capital and the Balance Sheet

TIPS CHECK YOUR RESOURCES

- Visit the www.prenhall.com/horngren **Web site** for self-study quizzes, video clips, and other resources
- Try the **Quick Check** exercise at the end of the chapter to test your knowledge
- Learn the **key terms**
- Do the **Starter** exercises keyed in the margins
- Work the **mid**- and **end-of-chapter summary problems**
- Use the **Concept Links** to review material in other chapters
- Search the **CD** for review materials by chapter or by key word
- Watch the **tutorial videos** to review key concepts
- Watch the **Amy's Ice Creams On Location** video for a review of forms of business ownership

LEARNING OBJECTIVES

1. Identify the characteristics of a corporation
2. Record the issuance of stock
3. Prepare the stockholders' equity section of a corporation balance sheet
4. Account for cash dividends
5. Use different stock values in decision making
6. Evaluate return on assets and return on stockholders' equity
7. Account for the income tax of a corporation

IHOP

Get on any interstate highway, and you'll see the distinctive shape of an IHOP (International House of Pancakes) building. We've all stopped at an IHOP for pancakes—or a sandwich. The restaurants are clean, the food is good, and the prices are right. Ever think about how IHOP swept across the country?

IHOP Corporation began as a small operation in Glendale, California. To grow the company, IHOP *went public*. This means IHOP offered its stock to anyone who would buy it. The initial public offering of IHOP stock was pretty successful: The company offered 6.2 million shares for $10 a share. As it turned out, investors bought 3.2 million shares. The $32 million (3.2 million × $10) IHOP received was used to open new restaurants and upgrade old ones.

Today, IHOP operates restaurants throughout the United States and in several foreign countries. The restaurants serve pancakes, sandwiches, and other casual food mainly to college students and families, which is the target market. Thanks to the sale of its stock, IHOP has become a large, well-known corporation. ■

Sitemap

This chapter covers the issuance of stock by corporations such as IHOP. Any company—large or small—can sell (issue) its stock to investors. All companies issue stock for the same reasons: to raise money, obtain assets, or pay off debt. Now let's explore how corporations differ from the proprietorships and partnerships we have been studying.

Corporations: An Overview

The corporation is the dominant form of business organization in the United States. IHOP is one example. Proprietorships and partnerships are more numerous, but corporations do much more business and are far larger. Most well-known companies, such as Amazon.com and Intel, are corporations. Their full names include *Corporation* or *Incorporated* (abbreviated *Corp.* and *Inc.*) to show that they are corporations—for example, Intel Corporation and Nike, Inc.

1 Identify the characteristics of a corporation

Student ResourceCD
corporation, limited liability, capital stock, stock

Characteristics of a Corporation

What makes the corporate form of organization so attractive? Several things. We now examine the features of corporations and their advantages and disadvantages.

Charter
Document that gives the state's permission to form a corporation.

Stockholder
A person who owns the stock of a corporation. Also called **shareholder**.

Stock
Shares into which the owners' equity of a corporation is divided.

SEPARATE LEGAL ENTITY A corporation is a business entity formed under the laws of a particular state. For example, the state of New York may grant a **charter**, a document that gives a business the state's permission to form a corporation. Neither a proprietorship nor a partnership requires a charter, because in the eyes of the law those businesses are the same as their owner(s).

A corporation is totally separate from its owners, who are called **stockholders** or **shareholders**. A corporation has many of the rights of a person. For example, a corporation may buy, own, and sell property. The assets and liabilities of IHOP belong to the corporation, not to its owners. The corporation may enter into contracts, sue, and be sued, just like an individual.

CONTINUOUS LIFE AND TRANSFERABILITY OF OWNERSHIP The owners' equity of a corporation is divided into shares of **stock**. Corporations have *continuous lives* regardless of who owns the stock. Stockholders may sell or trade stock to another person, give it away, or bequeath it in a will. Transfer of the stock does not affect the continuity of the corporation. By contrast, proprietorships and partnerships end when their ownership changes.

NO MUTUAL AGENCY *Mutual agency* means that all owners act as agents of the business. A contract signed by one owner is binding for the whole company. Mutual agency operates in partnerships but *not* in corporations. ← A stockholder of IHOP Corp. cannot commit IHOP to a contract (unless the person is also an officer in the business).

We introduced the idea of mutual agency for partnerships in Chapter 12, page 471. →

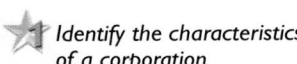

LIMITED STOCKHOLDER LIABILITY Stockholders have **limited liability** for corporation debts. That means they have no personal obligation for the corporation's liabilities. The most that a stockholder can lose on an investment in a corporation is the amount invested. In contrast, proprietors and partners are personally liable for all the debts of their businesses, unless the partnership is a limited liability partnership (LLP).

Limited Liability
No personal obligation of a stockholder for corporation debts. A stockholder can lose no more on an investment in a corporation's stock than the cost of the investment.

The combination of limited liability and no mutual agency means that persons can invest in a corporation without fear of losing all their personal wealth if the business fails. This feature enables a corporation to raise more money than proprietorships and partnerships.

SEPARATION OF OWNERSHIP AND MANAGEMENT Stockholders own a corporation, but a *board of directors*—elected by the stockholders—appoints the officers to manage the business. Stockholders may invest $1,000 or $1 million without having to manage the business.

Management's goal is to maximize the firm's value for the benefit of the stockholders. The separation of stockholders and management can create problems. Corporate officers may manage the business for their own benefit. The distance between the stockholders and management may make it difficult for stockholders to overturn bad management. How can stockholders protest? They can vote their shares on matters that come before them. In the extreme, they can sell their stock.

CORPORATE TAXATION Corporations are separate taxable entities. They pay several taxes not borne by proprietorships or partnerships, including an annual franchise tax levied by the state. The franchise tax keeps the corporate charter in force and enables the corporation to continue doing business. Corporations also pay federal and state income taxes just as individuals do.

Corporate earnings are subject to **double taxation**. First, corporations pay income taxes on corporate income. Then, stockholders pay personal income tax on the cash dividends they receive from corporations. Proprietorships and partnerships pay no business income tax. Instead, the tax falls solely on the owners.

Double Taxation
Corporations pay their own income taxes on corporate income. Then, the stockholders pay personal income tax on the cash dividends they receive from corporations.

GOVERNMENT REGULATION Because stockholders have only limited liability for corporation debts, outsiders can look no further than the corporation for payment of its debts. To protect persons who do business with corporations, government agencies monitor corporations. This *government regulation* creates some expenses not borne by proprietorships or partnerships.

Exhibit 13-1 summarizes the advantages and disadvantages of corporations.

Exhibit 13-1

Advantages and Disadvantages of a Corporation

Advantages	Disadvantages
1. Can raise more money than a proprietorship or partnership	1. Separation of ownership and management
2. Continuous life	2. Corporate taxation
3. Easy transfer of ownership	3. Government regulation
4. No mutual agency of the stockholders	
5. Limited liability of the stockholders	

Organizing a Corporation

The process of organizing a corporation begins when the *incorporators* obtain a charter from the state. The charter **authorizes** the corporation to issue a certain number of shares of stock. The incorporators pay fees, sign the charter, and file documents with the state. The corporation then becomes a legal entity. The stockholders agree to a set of **bylaws**, which act as their constitution.

Authorization of Stock
Provision in a corporate charter that gives the state's permission for the corporation to issue—that is, to sell—a certain number of shares of stock.

Bylaws
Constitution for governing a corporation.

Board of Directors
Group elected by the stockholders to set policy and to appoint the officers.

Chairperson
Elected by a corporation's board of directors, the most powerful person in the corporation.

Ultimate control of the corporation rests with the stockholders as they vote their shares of stock. For example, the stockholders elect the **board of directors**, which sets policy and appoints the officers. The board elects a **chairperson**, who is the most powerful person in the company. The board appoints the **president**, who is in charge of day-to-day operations. Most corporations also have a number of vice presidents. Exhibit 13-2 shows the authority structure in a corporation.

Exhibit 13-2 **Structure of a Corporation**

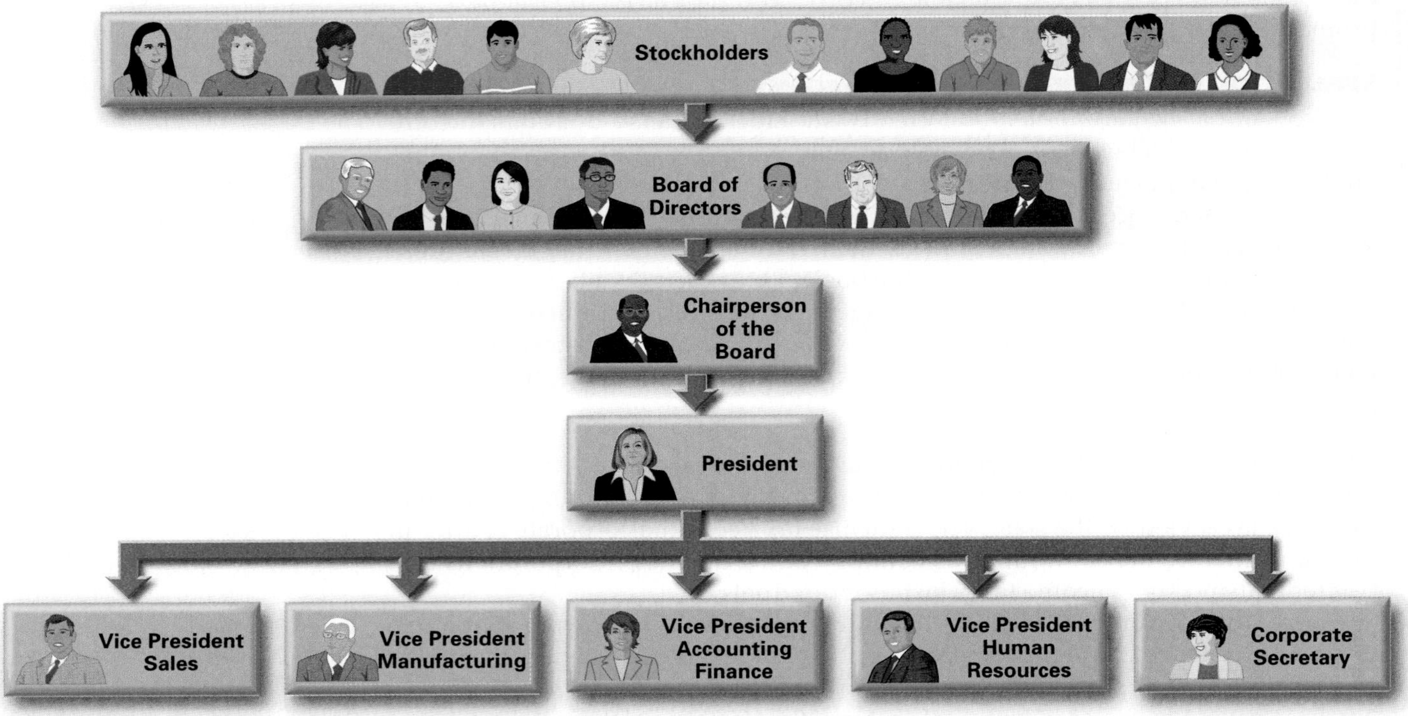

President
Chief operating officer in charge of managing the day-to-day operations of a corporation.

Capital Stock

A corporation issues *stock certificates* to the stockholders when they invest in the business. The stock represents the corporation's capital, so it is called *capital stock*. The basic unit of stock is a *share*. A corporation may issue a stock certificate for any number of shares. Exhibit 13-3 shows a stock certificate for 288 shares of

✔ Starter 13-1

Exhibit 13-3
Stock Certificate

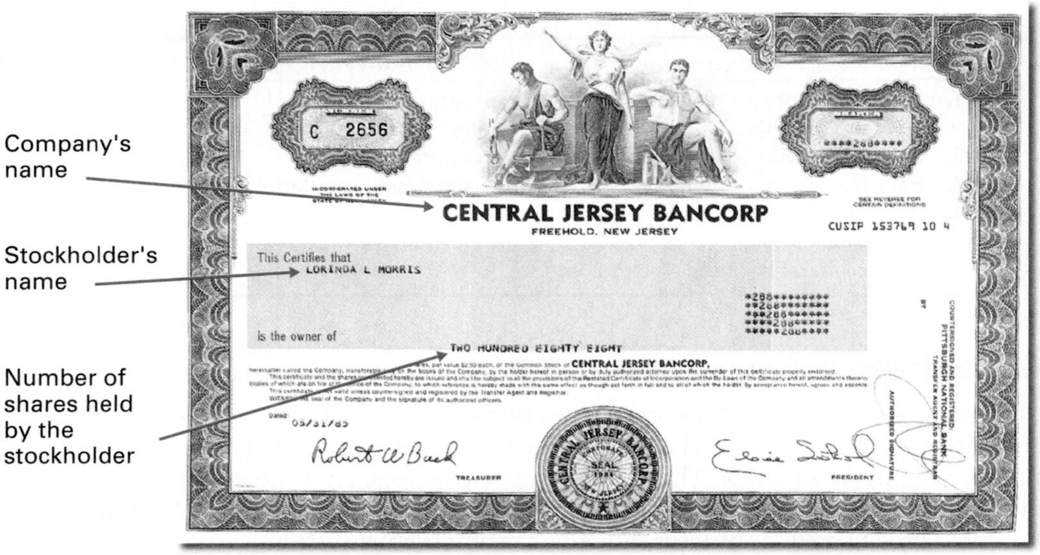

Central Jersey Bancorp common stock. The certificate shows the company's name, the stockholder's name, and the number of shares.

Stock that is held by the stockholders is said to be **outstanding**. The total shares of stock outstanding represent 100% ownership of the corporation.

Outstanding Stock
Stock in the hands of stockholders.

- ☐ Overview
- ■ Stockholders' Equity
- ☐ Issuing Stock
- ☐ Dividends
- ☐ Stock Values
- ☐ Evaluating Operations
- ☐ Income Taxes

Stockholders' Equity: The Basics

The balance sheet of a corporation reports assets and liabilities in the same way as for a proprietorship or a partnership. But the owners' equity of a corporation—called **stockholders' equity**—is reported differently. State laws require corporations to report the sources of their capital. There are two basic sources of capital:

- **Paid-in capital** (also called **contributed capital**) represents amounts received from the stockholders.
- **Retained earnings** is capital earned by profitable operations.

Exhibit 13-4 outlines a summarized version of the stockholders' equity of IHOP Corporation.

Stockholders' Equity
Owners' equity of a corporation.

Paid-in Capital
Capital from investments by the stockholders. Also called **contributed capital**.

Retained Earnings
Capital earned through profitable operation of the business.

Exhibit 13-4

Summarized Stockholders' Equity Sheet of IHOP Corporation (Amounts in Millions)

Stockholders' Equity	
Paid-in capital:	
Common stock	$ 89
Retained earnings	275
Total stockholders' equity	364

Student Resource CD
common stock, dividends, paid-in capital, preferred stock, retained earnings, share, stockholders' equity

✔ Starter 13-2

Paid-In Capital Comes from the Stockholders

Common stock is paid-in capital because it comes from the stockholders. Suppose IHOP is issuing common stock. IHOP's entry to record the receipt of $20,000 cash and the issuance of stock is

Oct. 20	Cash	20,000	
	Common Stock		20,000
	Issued stock.		

Common Stock
The basic form of capital stock. In a corporation, the common stockholders are the owners of the business.

This entry shows that issuing stock increases both the assets and the stockholders' equity of a corporation.

Retained Earnings Come from Profitable Operations

Profitable operations generate income, which increases stockholders' equity through a separate account called Retained Earnings. As we've just seen, a corporation needs more capital accounts than a proprietorship: A corporation uses a Common Stock account and a Retained Earnings account. Corporations close their revenues and expenses into Income Summary, and then they close net income to Retained Earnings. To illustrate, assume IHOP's revenues were $500,000 and expenses totaled $400,000 for December. The closing entries would be

Dec. 31	Sales Revenue	500,000	
	Income Summary		500,000
	To close sales revenue.		
31	Income Summary	400,000	
	Expenses (detailed)		400,000
	To close expenses.		

Now, the Income Summary account holds revenues, expenses, and net income.

Income Summary

Expenses	400,000	Revenues	500,000
		Balance (net income)	100,000

Finally, Income Summary's balance is closed to Retained Earnings.

Dec. 31	Income Summary...............	100,000	
	Retained Earnings.........		100,000
	To close net income to Retained Earnings.		

This closing entry completes the closing process. Income Summary is zeroed out, and Retained Earnings now holds net income, as follows:

Income Summary

Expenses	400,000	Revenues	500,000
Closing	100,000	Net income	100,000

Retained Earnings

		Closing (net income)	100,000

If IHOP has a net *loss*, Income Summary will have a debit balance. To close a $60,000 loss, the final closing entry credits Income Summary and debits Retained Earnings as follows:

Dec. 31	Retained Earnings..............	60,000	
	Income Summary		60,000
	To close *net loss* to Retained Earnings.		

Deficit
Debit balance in the Retained Earnings account.

A loss may cause a debit balance in the Retained Earnings account. This condition—called a Retained Earnings **deficit**—is reported on the balance sheet as a negative amount in stockholders' equity. HAL, Inc., which owns Hawaiian Airlines, Inc., reported this deficit:

Stockholders' Equity	(In millions)
Paid-in capital: Common stock	$ 50
Deficit	(193)
Total stockholders' equity	$ (143)

Corporations May Pay Dividends to the Stockholders

Dividends
Distributions by a corporation to its stockholders.

If the corporation has been profitable and has sufficient cash, it may distribute cash to the stockholders. Such distributions are called **dividends**. Dividends are similar to the withdrawals made by a proprietor. Dividends decrease both the assets and the retained earnings of the corporation. Most states prohibit using paid-in capital for dividends. Accountants use the term *legal capital* to refer to the portion of stockholders' equity that cannot be used for dividends.

Some people think of Retained Earnings as a fund of cash. It is not, because Retained Earnings is an element of stockholders' equity. Retained earnings has no particular relationship to cash or any other asset. *Remember that cash dividends are paid out of assets, not out of retained earnings.*

Stockholders' Rights

The ownership of stock entitles a stockholder to four basic rights, unless specific rights are withheld by contract:

1. ***Vote.*** Stockholders participate in management by voting on matters that come before them. This is a stockholder's sole right to manage the corporation. Each share of stock carries one vote.
2. ***Dividends.*** Stockholders receive a proportionate part of any dividend. Each share of stock receives an equal dividend with every other share of the same class.
3. ***Liquidation.*** Stockholders receive their proportionate share of any assets remaining after the corporation pays its liabilities in liquidation (goes out of business).
4. ***Preemption.*** Stockholders can maintain their proportionate ownership in the corporation. Suppose you own 5% of a corporation's stock. If the corporation issues 100,000 new shares of stock, it must offer you the opportunity to buy 5% (5,000) of the new shares. This right, called the *preemptive right*, is usually withheld from the stockholders.

Classes of Stock

Corporations issue different types of stock. The stock of a corporation may be either common or preferred and either par or no-par.

COMMON AND PREFERRED STOCK Every corporation issues *common stock*, the basic form of capital stock. The owners of a corporation are the common stockholders. Some companies issue Class A common stock, which carries the right to vote. They may also issue Class B common stock, which may be nonvoting. (Classes of stock may also be designated Series A, Series B, and so on.) There is a separate account for each class of stock.

Preferred stock gives its owners certain advantages over the common stockholders. Preferred stockholders receive dividends before the common stockholders, and they receive assets before the common stockholders if the corporation liquidates. Corporations pay a fixed amount of dividends on preferred stock. Investors usually buy preferred stock to earn those fixed dividends.

Preferred Stock
Stock that gives its owners certain advantages over common stockholders, such as the right to receive dividends before the common stockholders and the right to receive assets before the common stockholders if the corporation liquidates.

Owners of preferred stock also have the four basic stockholder rights, unless a right is specifically denied. The right to vote is sometimes withheld from preferred stockholders. Companies may issue different classes of preferred stock (Class A and Class B, or Series A and Series B, for example). Each class of stock is recorded in a separate account. Preferred stock is rarer than you might think. A recent survey of 600 corporations revealed that only 86 of them (14%) had some preferred stock outstanding (Exhibit 13-5).

Exhibit 13-5

Preferred Stock

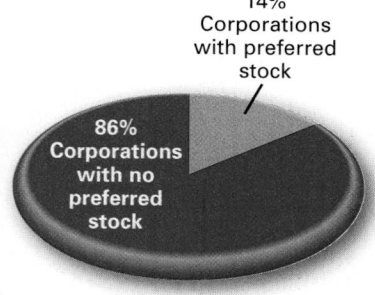

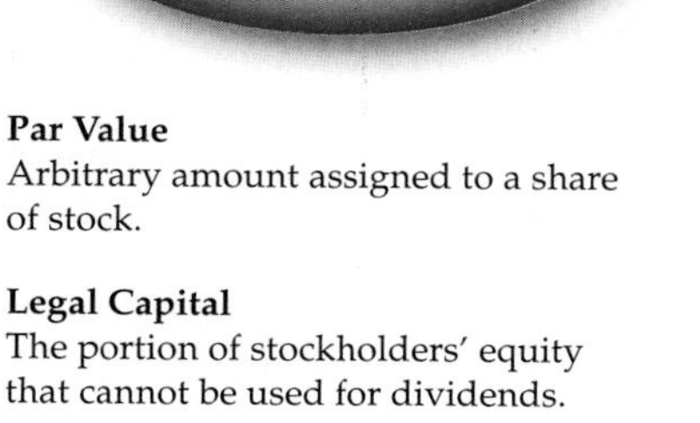

PAR VALUE, STATED VALUE, AND NO-PAR STOCK Stock may be par-value stock or no-par stock. **Par value** is an arbitrary amount assigned by a company to a share of its stock. Most companies set par value quite low to avoid legal difficulties from issuing their stock below par. Companies maintain a minimum amount of stockholders' equity for the protection of creditors, and this minimum represents the corporation's legal capital. For corporations with par-value stock, **legal capital** is usually the par value of the shares issued.

The common stock par value of Oracle Corporation, the software giant, is $0.01 (1 cent) per share. Pier 1 Imports' common carries a par value of $1 per share. Par value of preferred stock is often higher; some preferred stocks have par values of $25 or $100. Par value is used to compute dividends on preferred stock, as we shall see.

Par Value
Arbitrary amount assigned to a share of stock.

Legal Capital
The portion of stockholders' equity that cannot be used for dividends.

No-par stock does not have par value. Kimberly Clark, the paper company, has preferred stock with no par value. But some no-par stock has a **stated value**, which makes it similar to par-value stock. The stated value is an arbitrary amount that is similar to par value.

Stated Value
An arbitrary amount that accountants treat as though it were par value.

2 *Record the issuance of stock*

Student Resource CD
common stock, initial public offering, preferred stock

Issuing Stock

Large corporations such as Hewlett-Packard and Coca-Cola use huge quantities of money. They cannot finance all their operations through borrowing, so they raise capital by issuing stock. Corporations may sell the stock directly to stockholders or use the services of an *underwriter*, such as the brokerage firms Merrill Lynch and Morgan Stanley, Dean Witter. An underwriter agrees to buy all the stock it cannot sell to its clients.

The price that the corporation receives from issuing stock is called the *issue price*. Usually, the issue price exceeds the stock's par value because par value is quite low. In the following sections, we show how to account for the issuance of stock.

Issuing Common Stock

The Wall Street Journal is the most popular medium for advertising stock to attract investors. The ads are called *tombstones*. Exhibit 13-6 reproduces IHOP's tombstone, which appeared in *The Wall Street Journal*.

Exhibit 13-6

Announcement of Public Offering of IHOP Stock (Adapted)

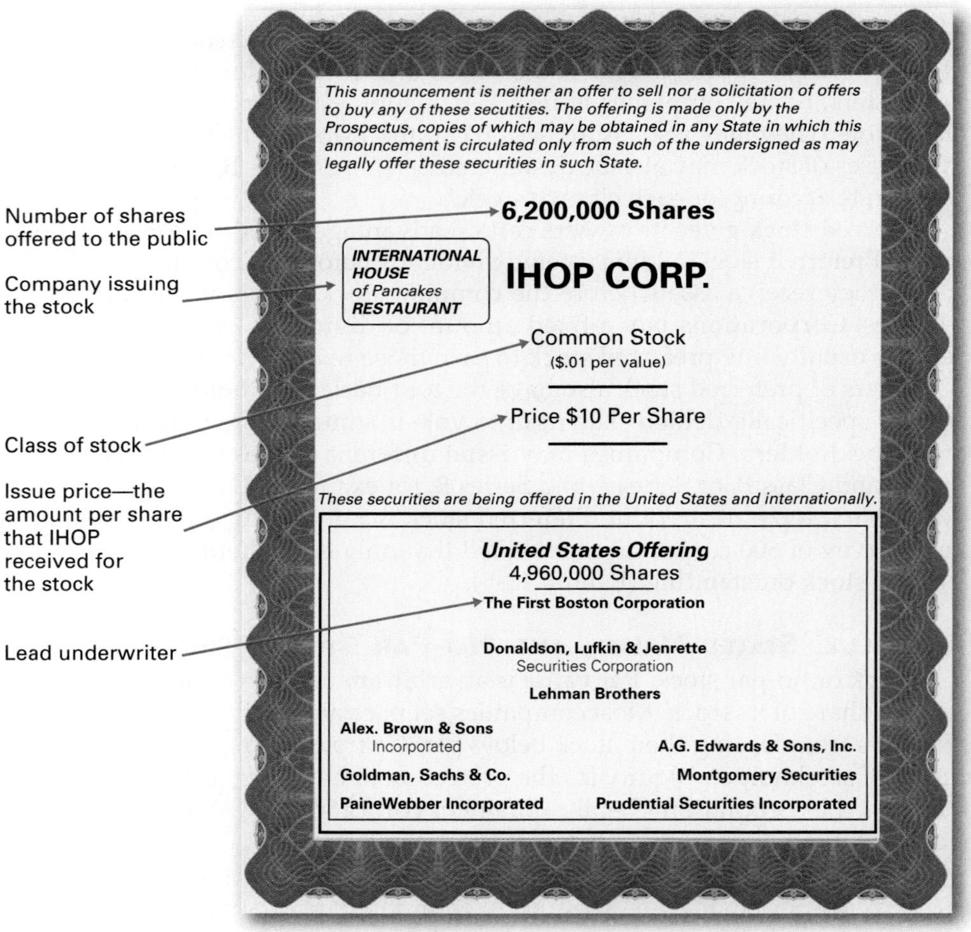

The lead underwriter of IHOP's public offering was The First Boston Corporation. Other brokerage firms and investment bankers also sold IHOP's stock to clients. IHOP's tombstone shows that IHOP hoped to raise approximately $62 million of capital. But in the final analysis, IHOP issued only 3.2 million of the shares and received cash of approximately $32 million.

COMMON STOCK AT PAR Suppose IHOP's common stock carried a par value of $10 per share. The stock issuance entry of 3.2 million shares would be

Jan. 31	Cash (3,200,000 × $10)	32,000,000	
	Common Stock.		32,000,000
	Issued common stock at par.		

Stop & Think

Prepare **IHOP's** classified balance sheet immediately after this issuance of stock. Assume zero balances prior to the transaction.

Answer:

IHOP Corporation
Balance Sheet
January 31, 20XX

Assets		**Liabilities**	
Current:			
Cash	$32,000,000	No liabilities	0
		Stockholders' Equity	
		Common stock	$32,000,000
		Total liabilities and	
Total assets	$32,000,000	stockholders' equity	$32,000,000

COMMON STOCK AT A PREMIUM Most corporations set par value low and issue common stock for a price above par. The amount above par is called a *premium*. IHOP's common stock has an actual par value of $0.01 (1 cent) per share. The $9.99 difference between issue price ($10) and par ($0.01) is a premium. This sale of stock increases the corporation's paid-in capital by the full $10, total issue price of the stock. Let's see how to account for the premium.

A premium on the sale of stock is not a gain, income, or profit because the entity is dealing with its own stockholders. This situation illustrates one of the fundamentals of accounting: *A company can have no profits or losses when buying or selling its own stock.*

With a par value of $0.01, IHOP's entry to record the issuance of the stock is

✔ Starter 13-3

July 31	Cash (3,200,000 × $10)	32,000,000	
	Common Stock (3,200,000 × $0.01) . .		32,000
	Paid-In Capital in Excess of Par—		
	Common (3,200,000 × $9.99).		31,968,000
	Issued common stock at a premium.		

Paid-In Capital in Excess of Par—Common is also called *Additional Paid-In Capital—Common*. Because both par value and premium amounts increase the corporation's capital, they appear in the stockholders' equity section of the balance sheet.

IHOP Corp. would report stockholders' equity on its balance sheet as follows, assuming that the corporate charter authorizes 40,000,000 shares of common stock and the balance of retained earnings is $26,000,000.

Stockholders' Equity	
Paid-in capital:	
Common stock, $0.01 par, 40 million shares	
authorized, 3.2 million shares issued	$ 32,000
Paid-in capital in excess of par	31,968,000
Total paid-in capital.	32,000,000
Retained earnings	26,000,000
Total stockholders' equity	$58,000,000

Common stock equals the total number of shares *issued* (3.2 million) multiplied by the par value per share ($0.01). The stock *authorization* reports the maximum number of shares the company may issue under its charter.

All transactions recorded in this section include the receipt of cash by the corporation for new stock issued to stockholders. These transactions are different from the vast majority of stock transactions reported each day in the financial press. In those transactions, stockholders are buying and selling stock to each other. The corporation doesn't journalize these transactions because its paid-in capital is unchanged.

NO-PAR COMMON STOCK When a company issues stock that has no par value, there can be no premium. A recent survey of 600 companies revealed 57 issues of no-par stock.

When a company issues no-par stock, it debits the asset received and credits the stock account. Rocky Mountain Corporation, which manufactures ski equipment, issues 4,000 shares of no-par common stock for $20 per share. The stock-issuance entry is

Aug. 14	Cash (4,000 × $20)	80,000	
	Common Stock		80,000
	Issued no-par common stock.		

Regardless of the stock's price, Cash is debited and Common Stock is credited for the cash received. There is no Paid-In Capital in Excess of Par for no-par stock.

Rocky Mountain's charter authorizes 10,000 shares of no-par stock, and the company has $151,000 in retained earnings. Rocky Mountain reports stockholders' equity on the balance sheet as follows:

Stockholders' Equity	
Paid-in capital:	
Common stock, no par, 10,000 shares authorized, 4,000 shares issued	$ 80,000
Retained earnings.	151,000
Total stockholders' equity	$231,000

Accounting.com

UPS Delivers the Dough at Record-Breaking IPO

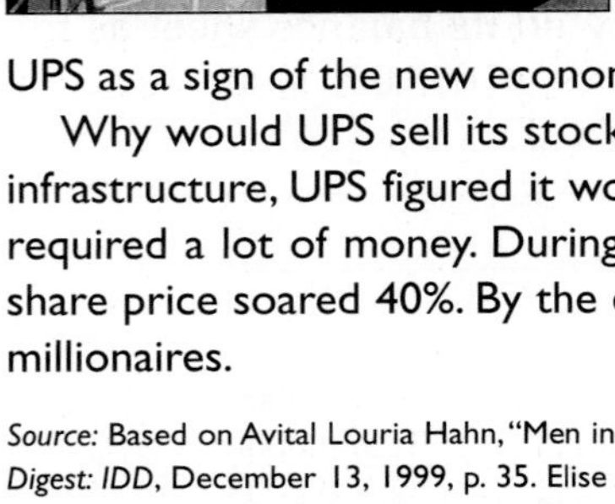

If you want stock in a company that operates in the global electronic marketplace, what comes to mind? Pioneering dot.coms like **Amazon.com** or **eBay?** Think again. There's a 97-year-old business whose workers drive old-fashioned brown trucks and run parcels up to your door. **UPS** is a business as traditional as apple pie. UPS raised a record-breaking $5.5 billion at its IPO (initial public offering) when it went public. All this money came from investors who saw UPS as a sign of the new economy.

Why would UPS sell its stock to the public? To build a cross-border, USA / European infrastructure, UPS figured it would need to acquire and merge with foreign firms. That required a lot of money. During the first hours of trading in UPS stock, the company's share price soared 40%. By the end of a week, the UPS workforce included 10,000 new millionaires.

Source: Based on Avital Louria Hahn, "Men in Brown: A Growth Story—UPS Recasts Itself for IPO," *The Investment Dealers' Digest: IDD*, December 13, 1999, p. 35. Elise Ackerman, "UPS Delivers as IPO Investors Give the World's No. 1 Package-Delivery Company Full Dot-Com Treatment," *U.S. News & World Report*, November 22, 1999, p. 53. Jenny Anderson, "Up, UPS and Away," *Institutional Investor*, January 2000, pp. 96–98.

No-Par Common Stock With a Stated Value Accounting for no-par stock with a stated value is identical to accounting for par-value stock. No-par common stock with a stated value uses an account titled Paid-In Capital in Excess of *Stated* Value—Common.

Common Stock for Assets Other Than Cash A corporation may issue stock and receive assets other than cash. It records the assets received at their current market value and credits the capital accounts accordingly. The assets' prior book value is irrelevant because the stockholder will demand stock equal to the market value of the asset given. Kahn Corporation issued 15,000 shares of its $1 par common stock for equipment worth $4,000 and a building worth $120,000. Kahn's entry is

Nov. 30	Equipment	4,000	
	Building	120,000	
	Common Stock (15,000 × $1)		15,000
	Paid-In Capital in Excess of Par—Common ($124,000 – $15,000)		109,000
	Issued common stock in exchange for equipment and a building.		

✔ Starter 13-4

Stop & Think

Prepare the stockholders' equity section of Kahn's balance sheet immediately after this transaction. Before this issuance of stock, Kahn already had outstanding 10,000 shares of common stock that the company had issued for $8 per share. Kahn's charter authorizes the issuance of 100,000 shares of common stock. Retained earnings is $500,000.

Answer:

Stockholders' Equity	
Paid-in capital:	
Common stock, $1 par, 100,000 shares authorized, 25,000 (10,000 + 15,000) shares issued	$ 25,000
Paid-in capital in excess of par ($70,000* + $109,000)	179,000
Total paid-in capital	204,000
Retained earnings	500,000
Total stockholders' equity	$704,000

*10,000 shares × ($8 – $1 par) = $70,000

✔ Starter 13-5

✔ Starter 13-6

Issuing Preferred Stock

Accounting for preferred stock follows the pattern illustrated for common stock. Chiquita Brands International, Inc., famous for its bananas, has some preferred stock outstanding. Assume Chiquita issued 100,000 shares of preferred stock at par value of $1 per share. The issuance entry is

July 31	Cash	100,000	
	Preferred Stock (100,000 shares × $1)		100,000
	Issued preferred stock at par.		

✔ Starter 13-7

Most preferred stock is issued at par value. Therefore, Paid-In Capital in Excess of Par is rare for preferred stock. For this reason, we do not cover it in this book.

Ethical Considerations

Issuance of stock for *cash* poses no ethical challenge. The company receives cash and issues stock, giving the stockholders certificates as evidence of their ownership.

Issuing stock for assets other than cash can pose an ethical challenge. The company issuing the stock often wishes to record a large amount for the asset received (such as land or a building) and for the stock being issued. Why? Because large asset and equity amounts make the business look successful. The desire to look good can motivate a company to record a high amount for the assets.

A company is supposed to record an asset received at its current market value. But one person's evaluation of a building can differ from another's. One person may appraise the building at a market value of $4 million. Another may honestly believe it is worth only $3 million. A company receiving the building in exchange for its stock must decide whether to record the building at $3 million, $4 million, or some other amount.

The ethical course of action is to record the asset at its current market value, as determined by independent appraisers. Public corporations are rarely found guilty of *understating* the asset values on their balance sheets but companies have been embarrassed by *overstating* asset values.

3 *Prepare the stockholders' equity section of a corporation balance sheet*

Review of Accounting for Paid-In Capital

Let's review the first half of this chapter by showing the stockholders' equity section of MedTech.com Corporation's balance sheet in Exhibit 13-7.

Exhibit 13-7

Part of MedTech.com Corporation's Balance Sheet

Stockholders' Equity	
Paid-in capital:	
Preferred stock, 5%, $100 par, 5,000 shares authorized, 400 shares issued	$ 40,000
Common stock, $10 par, 20,000 shares authorized, 5,000 shares issued	50,000
Paid-in capital in excess of par—common	70,000
Total paid-in capital	160,000
Retained earnings	90,000
Total stockholders' equity	$250,000

✔ Starter 13-8

✔ Starter 13-9

Note the two sections of stockholders' equity: paid-in capital and retained earnings. Also observe the order of the equity accounts:

- Preferred stock
- Common stock at par value
- Paid-in capital in excess of par—common
- Retained earnings (after the paid-in capital accounts)

Many companies label Paid-In Capital in Excess of Par—Common as **Additional Paid-In Capital** on the balance sheet. However, they are careful not to include preferred stock because that paid-in capital belongs to the preferred stockholders.

Additional Paid-In Capital
The paid-in capital in excess of par, common plus other accounts combined for reporting on the balance sheet.

Review the Decision Guidelines feature to solidify your understanding of stockholders' equity as it is reported on the balance sheet.

Decision Guidelines

STOCKHOLDERS' EQUITY OF A CORPORATION

Suppose you are interested in investing in stock. The following guidelines will help you sort out some of the relevant factors for your decision.

Decision	Guidelines
What are the two main segments of stockholders' equity?	• Paid-in capital • Retained earnings

Decision Guidelines *(continued)*

Decision	Guidelines
Which is more permanent, paid-in capital or retained earnings?	Paid-in capital is more permanent because corporations can use their retained earnings for dividends.
How are paid-in capital and retained earnings	
• Similar?	• Both represent the stockholders' equity (ownership) in the assets of the corporation.
• Different?	• Paid-in capital and retained earnings come from different sources: **a.** *Paid-in capital* comes from the corporation's stockholders, who invested in the company. **b.** *Retained earnings* comes from profitable operations.
What are the main categories of paid-in capital?	• Preferred stock • Common stock, plus paid-in capital in excess of par

MID-CHAPTER *Summary Problem*

A+ TIPS CHECK YOUR RESOURCES

1. Test your understanding of the first half of this chapter: Is each of the following statements true or false?
   a. Issuance of 1,000 shares of $5 par-value stock at $12 increases contributed capital by $7,000.
   b. The issuance of no-par stock with a stated value is fundamentally different from issuing par-value stock.
   c. A corporation issues its preferred stock in exchange for land and a building with a combined market value of $200,000. This transaction increases the corporation's owners' equity by $200,000 regardless of the assets' prior book value.
   d. A stockholder may bind the corporation to a contract.
   e. The policy-making body in a corporation is called the board of directors.
   f. The owner of 100 shares of preferred stock has greater voting rights than the owner of 100 shares of common stock.
   g. Par-value stock is worth more than no-par stock.
2. The brewery **Adolph Coors Company** has two classes of common stock. The company's balance sheet included the following (adapted):

Stockholders' Equity	
Capital stock	
Class A common stock, voting, $1 par value, authorized and issued 1,260,000 shares	$ 1,260,000
Additional paid-in capital—Class A common	2,011,000
Class B common stock, nonvoting, no par value, authorized and issued 46,200,000 shares	11,000,000
Retained earnings	872,403,000
	$886,674,000

Required

a. Record the issuance of the Class A common stock. The additional paid-in capital is related to the Class A common stock. Use the Coors account titles.
b. Record the issuance of the Class B common stock. Use the Coors account titles.
c. What is the total paid-in capital of the company?

Solutions

1. Answers to true/false statements:

a. False	**c.** True	**e.** True	**g.** False
b. False	**d.** False	**f.** False	

2. Adolph Coors Company:

a. Cash	3,271,000	
Class A Common Stock		1,260,000
Additional Paid-In Capital		2,011,000
To record issuance of Class A common stock.		
b. Cash	11,000,000	
Class B Common Stock		11,000,000
To record issuance of Class B common stock.		

c. Total paid-in capital is $14,271,000 ($1,260,000 + $2,011,000 + $11,000,000).

☐ Overview
☐ Stockholders' Equity
☐ Issuing Stock
■ Dividends
☐ Stock Values
☐ Evaluating Operations
☐ Income Taxes

Student Resource CD
dividends

Accounting for Cash Dividends

Corporations share their wealth with the stockholders through dividends. Corporations declare dividends from retained earnings and then pay with cash. The corporation must have enough *retained earnings* to declare the dividend and also have enough *cash* to pay the dividend.

Dividend Dates

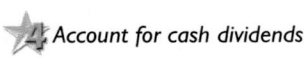

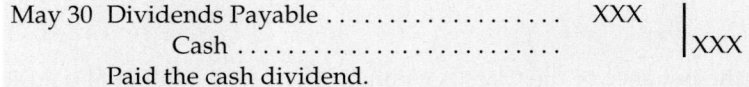

A corporation declares a dividend before paying it. The board of directors declares the dividend. The corporation has no obligation to pay a dividend until the board declares one. However, once the dividend is declared, it becomes a legal liability. Three relevant dates for dividends are

1. ***Declaration date.*** On the declaration date, the board of directors announces the intention to pay the dividend. The declaration creates a liability for the corporation.
2. ***Date of record.*** Those stockholders holding the stock on the date of record—a week or two after declaration—will receive the dividend when it's paid.
3. ***Payment date.*** Payment of the dividend usually follows the record date by a week or two.

Dividends on Preferred and Common Stock

Account for cash dividends

Declaration of a cash dividend is recorded by debiting Retained Earnings and crediting Dividends Payable, as follows:[1]

May 1	Retained Earnings	XXX	
	Dividends Payable		XXX
	Declared a cash dividend.		

Payment of the dividend usually follows declaration by a few weeks. Payment is recorded by debiting Dividends Payable and crediting Cash:

✔ Starter 13-10

May 30	Dividends Payable	XXX	
	Cash		XXX
	Paid the cash dividend.		

Dividends Payable is a current liability. When a company has issued both preferred stock and common stock, the preferred stockholders receive their dividends first. The common stockholders receive dividends only if the total dividend is large enough to satisfy the preferred requirement.

[1]Some accountants debit a Dividends account, which is closed to Retained Earnings. But most businesses debit Retained Earnings, as shown here.

Pine Industries, Inc., has 10,000 shares of preferred stock outstanding, plus common stock. Preferred dividends are paid at the annual rate of $1.50 per share. Exhibit 13-8 shows the division of dividends between preferred and common for two situations.

Exhibit 13-8

Dividing a Dividend Between Preferred Stock and Common Stock

Case A: Total dividend of $8,000:	
Preferred dividend (the full $8,000 goes to preferred because the annual preferred dividend is $15,000: 10,000 shares × $1.50)	$ 8,000
Common dividend (none because the total dividend did not cover the preferred dividend for the year)	0
Total dividend	$ 8,000
Case B: Total dividend of $50,000:	
Preferred dividend (10,000 shares × $1.50 per share)	$15,000
Common dividend ($50,000 – $15,000)	35,000
Total dividend	$50,000

✔ Starter 13-11

If Pine Industries' annual dividend is large enough to cover the preferred dividend for the year (Case B), the preferred stockholders receive their regular dividend, and the common stockholders receive the remainder. But if the year's dividend falls below the amount of the annual preferred dividend (Case A), the preferred stockholders receive the entire dividend, and the common stockholders get nothing that year.

The preferred-stock dividend preference can be stated as a percentage rate or a dollar amount. For example, preferred stock may be "6% preferred," which means that owners of the preferred stock receive an annual dividend of 6% of the par value of the stock. If par value is $100 per share, then the preferred stockholders get an annual dividend of $6 per share (6% of $100). The preferred stock may be "$3 preferred," which means that stockholders get an annual dividend of $3 per share regardless of the preferred stock's par value. The dividend rate on no-par preferred stock is stated in a dollar amount per share.

Dividends on Cumulative and Noncumulative Preferred

The allocation of dividends may be complex if the preferred stock is *cumulative*. Corporations sometimes fail to pay a dividend to their preferred stockholders. This is called *passing the dividend*, and the passed dividends are said to be *in arrears*. The owners of **cumulative preferred stock** must receive all dividends in arrears plus the current year's dividend before the common stockholders get a dividend.

Cumulative Preferred Stock Preferred stock whose owners must receive all dividends in arrears before the corporation pays dividends to the common stockholders.

The preferred stock of Pine Industries is cumulative. Suppose the company passed the 20X4 preferred dividend of $15,000. Before paying dividends to its common stockholders in 20X5, the company must first pay preferred dividends of $15,000 for both 20X4 and 20X5, a total of $30,000. *Preferred stock is cumulative in the eyes of the law unless it is labeled as noncumulative.* Most preferred stock is cumulative.

Assume that Pine Industries passes its 20X4 preferred dividend. In 20X5, the company declares a $50,000 dividend. The entry to record the declaration of this dividend is

Sep. 6	Retained Earnings	50,000	
	Dividends Payable, Preferred ($15,000 × 2)		30,000
	Dividends Payable, Common ($50,000 – $30,000)		20,000
	Declared a cash dividend.		

If the preferred stock is *noncumulative*, the corporation need not pay dividends in arrears. Suppose Pine Industries' preferred stock was noncumulative and the company passed the 20X4 preferred dividend. The preferred stockholders would lose the 20X4 dividend forever. Of course, the common stockholders would not receive a 20X4 dividend either. Before paying any common dividends in 20X5, the company would have to pay the 20X5 preferred dividend of $15,000.

Dividends in arrears are *not* a liability for the corporation. A liability for dividends arises only after the board of directors declares the dividend. Nevertheless, a corporation must report cumulative preferred dividends in arrears. This information alerts common stockholders about how much must be paid before the common stockholders will receive any dividends.

☐ Overview
☐ Stockholders' Equity
☐ Issuing Stock
☐ Dividends
■ Stock Values
☐ Evaluating Operations
☐ Income Taxes

5 *Use different stock values in decision making*

Different Values of Stock

There are several different *stock values* in addition to par value. Market value and book value are used for various investor decisions.

Market Value

Market Value
Price for which a person could buy or sell a share of stock.

A stock's **market value**, or *market price*, is the price for which a person could buy or sell a share of the stock. The corporation's net income, future prospects, and general economic conditions affect market value. The Internet and most newspapers report the market price of many stocks. Log on to any company's Web site to track its stock price. *In almost all cases, stockholders are more concerned about the market value of a stock than about any other value.*

Student ResourceCD
book value, market value

In the chapter-opening story, IHOP's stock had a market price of $10 when it was issued. Shortly thereafter, IHOP's stock shot up to $36, which means that the stock could be bought for $36 per share. The purchase of 100 shares of IHOP stock at $36 would cost $3,600 ($36 × 100), plus a commission. If you were selling 100 shares of IHOP stock, you would receive cash of $3,600 less a commission. The commission is the fee a stockbroker charges for buying or selling the stock. The price of a share of IHOP stock has fluctuated from $10 at issuance to a recent high of $26.

Book Value

Book Value
Amount of owners' equity on the company's books for each share of its stock.

The **book value** of a stock is the amount of owners' equity on the company's books for each share of its stock. If the company has only common stock outstanding, divide total stockholders' equity by the number of shares *outstanding*. A company with stockholders' equity of $180,000 and 5,000 shares of common stock has a book value of $36 per share ($180,000/5,000 shares).

If the company has both preferred stock and common stock outstanding, the preferred stockholders have the first claim to owners' equity. Therefore, we subtract preferred equity from total equity to compute book value per share of the common stock. To illustrate, Lille Corporation reports the following amounts:

Stockholders' Equity	
Paid-in capital:	
Preferred stock, 6%, $10 par, 5,000 shares issued	$ 50,000
Common stock, $1 par, 20,000 shares authorized, 10,000 shares issued	10,000
Paid-in capital in excess of par—common	170,000
Total paid-in capital	230,000
Retained earnings	420,000
Total stockholders' equity	$650,000

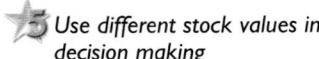

The book-value-per-share computation of common stock follows.

Common	
Total stockholders' equity	$650,000
Less stockholders' equity allocated to preferred	(50,000)
Stockholders' equity allocated to common	$600,000
Book value per share ($600,000/10,000 shares)	$ 60.00

✔ Starter 13-12

Book value is used in decision making. Book value may figure into the price to pay for a closely-held corporation, whose stock is not publicly traded. Also, a company may buy out a stockholder by agreeing to pay the book value of the person's stock.

Some investors compare the book value of a stock with its market value. The idea is that a stock selling below book value is underpriced and thus a good buy. But the relationship between book value and market value is far from clear. Other investors believe that if a stock sells below book value, the company must be experiencing difficulty. Exhibit 13-9 contrasts the book values and market prices for the stocks of three well-known companies. In all three cases, the stock price, which is the market value, exceeds book value—a sign of success. Dell Computer's stock price far exceeds its book value.

✔ Starter 13-13

Exhibit 13-9

Book Value and Market Value for Three Well-Known Companies

	Book Value Per Share	Recent Stock Price
IHOP Corp.	$17.12	$26.00
Fossil	7.34	18.13
Dell Computer	1.80	28.88

Evaluating Operations

Investors and creditors are constantly comparing companies' profits. IHOP's net income may not be comparable with the net income of a new company because IHOP is an established company and the other company is just getting started. IHOP's profits run into the millions, which far exceed a new company's net income. To compare companies, investors use standard profitability ratios. Two key measures are the rate of return on total assets and rate of return on common stockholders' equity.

6 *Evaluate return on assets and return on stockholders' equity*

Student Resource CD
rate of return, stockholders' equity

Rate of Return on Total Assets

The **rate of return on total assets**, or simply **return on assets**, measures a company's success in using assets to earn income for those who are financing the business.

- Stockholders hold the stock and therefore earn the *net income.*
- Creditors have loaned money to the corporation and thus earn *interest.*

Interest expense and net income are the returns to the two groups that have financed the corporation. The sum of net income plus interest expense is the numerator of the return-on-assets ratio. The denominator is average total assets. Return on assets is computed as follows, using data from the 2002 annual report of IHOP Corp. (dollar amounts in millions):

Rate of Return on Total Assets
The sum of net income plus interest expense divided by average total assets. Measures the success a company has in using its assets to earn income for those financing the business. Also called **return on assets.**

$$\text{RATE OF RETURN ON TOTAL ASSETS} = \frac{\text{NET INCOME} + \text{INTEREST EXPENSE}}{\text{AVERAGE TOTAL ASSETS}}$$

$$= \frac{\$41 + \$22}{(\$641 + \$820)/2} = \frac{\$63}{\$730.5} = 0.086$$

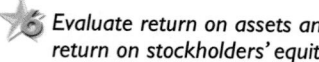

Net income and interest expense are taken from the income statement. Average total assets comes from the beginning and ending balance sheets.

What is a good rate of return on total assets? There is no single answer because rates of return vary widely by industry. For example, high-tech companies such as Intel and Microsoft earn higher returns than utility companies and manufacturers of consumer goods. In most industries, a return on assets of 10% is considered good.

Rate of Return on Common Stockholders' Equity

Rate of Return on Common Stockholders' Equity
Net income minus preferred dividends, divided by average common stockholders' equity. A measure of profitability. Also called **return on equity**.

Rate of return on common stockholders' equity, often called **return on equity**, shows the relationship between net income available to the common stockholders and average common equity. The numerator is net income minus preferred dividends. Preferred dividends are subtracted because the preferred stockholders have the first claim to dividends from net income. The denominator is average *common stockholders' equity*—total equity minus preferred equity. IHOP's rate of return on common stockholders' equity for 2002 is computed as follows (amounts in millions):

✔ Starter 13-14

✔ Starter 13-15

$$\text{RATE OF RETURN ON COMMON STOCKHOLDERS' EQUITY} = \frac{\text{NET INCOME} - \text{PREFERRED DIVIDENDS}}{\text{AVERAGE COMMON STOCKHOLDERS' EQUITY}}$$

$$= \frac{\$41 - \$0}{(\$312 + \$364)/2} = \frac{\$41}{\$338} = 0.121$$

IHOP has no preferred stock, so preferred dividends are zero.

IHOP's return on equity (12.1%) is higher than its return on assets (8.6%). This indicates a healthy company because IHOP is earning more for its stockholders than it is paying for interest expense. Companies borrow at one rate (say, 7%) and try to earn a higher rate (12%) on investments. This is what IHOP did. Borrowing at a lower rate than the return on equity is called *using leverage*.

If a company's return on assets exceeds its return on equity, the company is in trouble. Why?Because interest expense is greater than return on equity. Interest expense should always be lower than the return on equity. Investors and creditors use return on equity in much the same way they use return on total assets—to compare companies. The higher the rate of return, the more successful the company. IHOP's 12% return on common stockholders' equity would be considered fairly good in many industries.

☐ Overview
☐ Stockholders' Equity
☐ Issuing Stock
☐ Dividends
☐ Stock Values
☐ Evaluating Operations
■ Income Taxes

Accounting for Income Taxes by Corporations

7 *Account for the income tax of a corporation*

Corporations pay income tax just as individuals do, but not at the same rates. At this writing, the federal tax rate on most corporate income is 35%. Most states also levy a corporate income tax, so most corporations have a combined federal and state income tax rate of approximately 40%.

To account for income tax, the corporation measures

- Income tax expense, an expense on the income statement
- Income tax payable, a liability on the balance sheet

Let's illustrate accounting for income tax with a realistic example. In general, income tax expense and income tax payable can be computed as follows:[2]

$$\text{Income tax } \textit{expense} = \text{Income before tax—from the income statement} \times \text{Income tax rate}$$

$$\text{Income tax } \textit{payable} = \text{Taxable income—from the tax return filed with the IRS} \times \text{Income tax rate}$$

[2]The authors thank Jean Marie Hudson for suggesting this presentation.

The income statement and the income tax return are entirely separate documents. The income statement is the financial statement you've been studying throughout this course. The tax return is used only to report taxes to the IRS.

For most companies, income tax expense and income tax payable differ. The most important difference occurs when a corporation uses straight-line depreciation for the income statement and accelerated depreciation → for the tax return.

We learned in Chapter 10 that the MACRS depreciation method is used for tax purposes.

Continuing with the IHOP illustration, suppose for 20X6 that IHOP Corp. has

- Income before income tax of $70 million (This comes from the income statement.)
- Taxable income of $50 million (This comes from the tax return.)

IHOP will record income tax for 20X6 as follows (dollar amounts in millions and an income tax rate of 40%):

20X6			
Dec. 31	Income Tax Expense ($70 × 0.40)	28	
	Income Tax Payable ($50 × 0.40)		20
	Deferred Tax Liability		8
	Recorded income tax for the year.		

IHOP will pay the $20 million of Income Tax Payable within a few months. The Deferred Tax Liability account is long-term, so IHOP will pay this debt over a number of years. IHOP's 20X6 financial statements would report these figures (adapted, in millions):

Income Statement		Balance Sheet	
Income before income tax	$70	Current liabilities:	
Income tax expense	(28)	Income tax payable	$20
Net income	$42	Long-term liabilities:	
		Deferred tax liability	8*

*The beginning balance of Deferred tax liability was zero.

✔ Starter 13-16

Decision Guidelines

DIVIDENDS, STOCK VALUES, EVALUATING OPERATIONS, & CORPORATE INCOME TAX

Suppose you operate an **IHOP** restaurant near your college. You are naturally interested in how well the company as a whole is doing. Does IHOP pay dividends? What are IHOP's stock values? What are the rates of return on IHOP's assets and equity? The Decision Guidelines will help you evaluate the company.

Decision	Guidelines
Dividends	
Whether to declare a cash dividend?	• Must have enough retained earnings to declare the dividend. • Must have enough cash to pay the dividend.
What happens with a dividend?	• The corporation's board of directors declares the dividend. Then the dividend becomes a liability of the corporation. • The date of record fixes who will receive the dividend. • Payment of the dividend occurs later.
Who receives the dividend?	• Preferred stockholders receive their dividends first. Preferred dividends have a specified rate. • Common stockholders receive the remainder.

Decision Guidelines *(continued)*

Decision	Guidelines
Stock Values	
How much to pay for a stock?	Its market value.
How is book value used in decision making?	Sometimes used to help determine the market value of a stock that is not traded on a stock exchange.
Evaluating Operations	
How to evaluate the operations of a corporation?	Two measures that relate earnings to the amount stockholders have invested include: • Rate of return on assets • Rate of return on common stockholders' equity For a healthy company, return on stockholders' equity should exceed return on assets.
Accounting for Income Tax	
What are the three main tax accounts?	• Income tax expense • Income tax payable, a current liability • Deferred tax liability, usually a long-term liability
How to measure • Income tax expense?	Income before income tax (from the income statement) × Income tax rate
• Income tax payable?	Taxable income (from the income tax return filed with the Internal Revenue Service) × Income tax rate
• Deferred tax liability?	Difference between income tax expense and income tax payable for any one year

Excel Application Exercise

Goal: To create an Excel worksheet that compares the financial performances of two publicly traded stocks in the restaurant industry.

Scenario: Your task is to create an Excel worksheet that compares the historical performance of **IHOP** and **Cracker Barrel** on two key financial measures. Embedded graphs of each financial dimension also must be created. All data used in your spreadsheet will come from **Morningstar's** Web site.

When finished, answer these questions:

1. Which company has earned a consistently higher return on equity?
2. Which company has earned a consistently higher return on assets?

Step-by-Step:

1. Locate www.morningstar.com on the Web.
2. Under the "Morningstar Quicktake Reports" section, enter the ticker symbol for each company. IHOP's symbol is IHP, and Cracker Barrel's symbol is CBRL. To locate the required information, look under "Financial Statements." (Note: If the Web site differs from these headings, you may have to search other areas of the Web site.) Print out the pages used for each company.
3. Open a new Excel worksheet.
4. Create a bold-faced heading for your spreadsheet that contains the following:
   a. Chapter 13 Excel Application Exercise
   b. Investing in Stock
   c. Stock Performance Analysis
   d. Today's Date
5. Under the heading, create a bold-faced, underlined section titled "Return on Equity %." Move down one row. Create one column each for the past four years (for example, "2001," "2000," and so on). Create one row each for IHOP and Cracker Barrel.
6. Enter the "Return on Equity %" data for the past five years for each company.
7. Repeat steps 5 and 6 for "Return on Assets %."
8. Using the Excel Chart Wizard, create separate graphs for Return on Equity % and Return on Assets %. Resize and position each graph to the right of the data so that everything appears on one page when you print.
9. Save your work, and print your work sheet in landscape mode (with graphs) for your files.

END-OF-CHAPTER *Summary Problem*

Use the following accounts and related balances to prepare the classified balance sheet of Whitehall, Inc., at September 30, 20X4. Use the account format of the balance sheet.

Common stock, $1 par, 50,000 shares authorized, 25,000 shares issued	$25,000	Long-term note payable	$ 73,000
Dividends payable	4,000	Inventory	85,000
Cash	15,000	Property, plant, and equipment, net	225,000
Accounts payable	28,000	Accounts receivable, net	23,000
Retained earnings	80,000	Preferred stock, $3.50, no-par, 10,000 shares authorized, 2,000 shares issued	20,000
Paid-in capital in excess of par—common	115,000	Accrued liabilities	3,000

TIPS

CHECK YOUR RESOURCES

Compute the book value per share of Whitehall's common stock. No prior-year preferred dividends are in arrears, but Whitehall has not declared the current-year dividend.

Solution

Whitehall, Inc.

Balance Sheet
September 30, 20X4

Assets

Current:	
Cash	$ 15,000
Accounts receivable, net	23,000
Inventory	85,000
Total current assets	123,000
Property, plant, and equipment, net	225,000
Total assets	$348,000

Liabilities

Current:		
Accounts payable		$ 28,000
Dividends payable		4,000
Accrued liabilities		3,000
Total current liabilities		35,000
Long-term note payable		73,000
Total liabilities		108,000
Stockholders' Equity		
Paid-in capital:		
Preferred stock, $3.50, no-par, 10,000 shares authorized, 2,000 shares issued	$ 20,000	
Common stock, $1 par, 50,000 shares authorized, 25,000 shares issued	25,000	
Paid-in capital in excess of par—common	115,000	
Total paid-in capital	160,000	
Retained earnings	80,000	
Total stockholders' equity		240,000
Total liabilities and stockholders' equity		$348,000

Preferred equity:	
Carrying value	$ 20,000
Cumulative dividend for current year (2,000 shares × $3.50)	7,000
Stockholders' equity allocated to preferred	$ 27,000
Common:	
Total stockholders' equity	$240,000
Less stockholders' equity allocated to preferred	(27,000)
Stockholders' equity allocated to common	$213,000
Book value per share ($213,000/25,000 shares)	$8.52

REVIEW Corporations: Paid-In Capital and the Balance Sheet

Quick Check

1. Which characteristic of a corporation differs from a proprietorship and a partnership?
   a. Separate legal entity
   b. Double taxation
   c. Limited stockholder liability
   d. All of the above
2. Among the corporate characteristics listed in question 1, which is a disadvantage?
   a. Separate legal entity
   b. Double taxation
   c. Limited stockholder liability
   d. None of the above
3. The two basic sources of corporate capital are
   a. Paid-in capital and retained earnings
   b. Stock and bonds
   c. Common stock and preferred stock
   d. Retained earnings and dividends
4. Which class of stockholders takes the greater risk?
   a. Preferred
   b. Common
   c. Neither; bondholders take the most risk
   d. Both preferred and common take equal risk
5. Suppose **IHOP** issued 100,000 shares of its $0.05 par common stock at $1 per share. Which journal entry correctly records the issuance of this stock?

a.

Cash	100,000	
Common Stock		100,000

b.

Common Stock	100,000	
Cash		5,000
Paid-In Capital in Excess of Par		95,000

c.

Cash	100,000	
Common Stock		5,000
Paid-In Capital in Excess of Par		95,000

d.

Common Stock	100,000	
Cash		100,000

6. Suppose IHOP issues common stock to purchase a building. IHOP should record the building at
   a. Its market value
   b. Its book value
   c. The par value of the stock given
   d. A value assigned by the board of directors
7. Chewning Corporation has 10,000 shares of 5%, $10 par preferred stock and 50,000 shares of common stock outstanding. Chewning declared no dividends in 20X5. In 20X6, Chewning declares a total dividend of $25,000. How much of the dividends go to the common stockholders?
   a. $5,000
   b. $10,000
   c. $15,000
   d. None; it all goes to preferred
8. Techster Company has 10,000 shares of $1 par common stock outstanding, which Techster issued at $5 per share. Techster also has retained earnings of $80,000. How much is Techster's total stockholders' equity?
   a. $50,000
   b. $80,000
   c. $90,000
   d. $130,000
9. Dale Corporation has the following data:

Net income	$22,000	Average total assets	$300,000
Interest expense	8,000	Average common equity	100,000
Preferred dividends	10,000		

   Dale's return on common stockholders' equity is
   a. 4%
   b. 10%
   c. 12%
   d. 15%
10. A corporation's income tax expense is computed as follows:
   a. Income before tax × Income tax rate
   b. Taxable income × Income tax rate
   c. Net income × Income tax rate
   d. Return on equity × Income tax rate

Accounting Vocabulary

additional paid-in capital (p. 516)
authorization of stock (p. 507)
board of directors (p. 508)
book value (p. 520)
bylaws (p. 507)
chairperson (p. 508)
charter (p. 506)
common stock (p. 509)
contributed capital (p. 509)
cumulative preferred stock (p. 519)
deficit (p. 510)
dividends (p. 510)
double taxation (p. 507)
legal capital (p. 511)
limited liability (p. 507)
market value (p. 520)
outstanding stock (p. 509)
paid-in capital (p. 509)
par value (p. 511)
preferred stock (p. 511)
president (p. 508)
rate of return on common stockholders' equity (p. 522)
rate of return on total assets (p. 521)
retained earnings (p. 509)
return on assets (p. 521)
return on equity (p. 522)
shareholder (p. 506)
stated value (p. 511)
stock (p. 506)
stockholder (p. 506)
stockholders' equity (p. 509)

ASSESS *Your Progress*

Starters

A+ online homework

See *www.prenhall.com/horngren* for selected Starters, Exercises, and Problems.

Authority structure in a corporation
(Obj. 1)

S13-1 Consider the authority structure in a corporation, as diagrammed in Exhibit 13-2.

1. Who is in charge of day-to-day operations?
2. Who is in charge of accounting?
3. What group holds the ultimate power in a corporation?
4. Who is the most powerful person in the corporation?

The balance sheets of a corporation and a proprietorship
(Obj. 1)

S13-2 Examine the stockholders' equity of **IHOP Corporation** in Exhibit 13-4. Suppose IHOP were a proprietorship owned by Joe Hopper. How would the IHOP proprietorship balance sheet differ from the one given in Exhibit 13-4? How would the proprietorship balance sheet be similar to the one given in Exhibit 13-4?

Effect of a stock issuance on net income
(Obj. 2)

S13-3 Study **IHOP's** July 31 stock issuance entry at a premium on page 513, and answer these questions about the IHOP transaction.

1. IHOP received \$32,000,000 for the issuance of its stock. The par value of the IHOP stock was only \$32,000. Was the excess amount of \$31,968,000 a profit to IHOP? Did the excess affect net income? If not, what was it?
2. Suppose the par value of the IHOP stock had been \$1 per share, \$5 per share, or \$10 per share. Would a change in the par value of the company's stock affect IHOP's total paid-in capital? What does affect total paid-in capital?

Issuing stock to finance the purchase of assets
(Obj. 2)

S13-4 This exercise shows the similarity and the difference between two ways to acquire plant assets.

Case A—Issue stock and buy the assets in separate transactions:
Avisa, Inc., issued 10,000 shares of its \$10 par common stock for cash of \$700,000. In a separate transaction, Avisa purchased a building for \$500,000 and equipment for \$200,000. Journalize the two transactions.

Case B—Issue stock to acquire the assets:
Avisa issued 10,000 shares of its \$10 par common stock to acquire a building valued at \$500,000 and equipment worth \$200,000. Journalize this single transaction.

Compare the balances in all accounts after making both sets of entries. Are the account balances similar or different?

Issuing stock and interpreting stockholders' equity
(Obj. 2)

S13-5 The Coca-Cola Company reported the following on its balance sheet at December 31, 2002 (adapted, with amounts in millions, except for par value per share):

Common stock, $0.25 par value	
Authorized: 5,600 shares	
Issued: 3,500 shares	$ 875
Paid-in capital in excess of par	3,855
Retained earnings	24,506

1. Assume Coca-Cola issued all of its stock during 2002. Journalize the company's issuance of the stock for cash.
2. Was Coca-Cola's main source of stockholders' equity paid-in capital or profitable operations? How can you tell?

Issuing stock and analyzing retained earnings
(Obj. 2)

S13-6 At December 31, 2002, **The Coca-Cola Company** reported the following on its comparative balance sheet, which included 2001 amounts for comparison (adapted, with all amounts in millions except par value per share):

	December 31,	
	2002	2001
Common stock, $0.25 par value		
Authorized: 5,600 shares		
Issued: 3,500 shares in 2002	$ 875	
3,490 shares in 2001		$ 873
Paid-in capital in excess of par	3,855	3,520
Retained earnings	24,506	23,443

1. How much did Coca-Cola's total paid-in capital increase during 2002? What caused total paid-in capital to increase? How can you tell?
2. Did Coca-Cola have a profit or a loss for 2002? How can you tell?

Issuing stock
(Obj. 2)

S13-7 Bruner Corporation has two classes of stock: Common, $1 par: Preferred, $10 par. Journalize Bruner's issuance of

a. 1,000 shares of common stock for $50 per share
b. 1,000 shares of preferred stock for a total of $32,000

Explanations are not required.

Preparing the stockholders' equity section of a balance sheet
(Obj. 3)

S13-8 The financial statements of Manatee Corporation reported the following accounts (in thousands except for par value):

Paid-in capital in excess of par	$170	Net sales	$1,080
Cost of goods sold	588	Accounts payable	60
Common stock, $1 par,		Retained earnings	166
400 shares issued	400	Other current liabilities	52
Cash	240	Operating expenses	412
Long-term debt	76	Total assets	?

Prepare the stockholders' equity section of the Manatee balance sheet. Net income has already been closed to Retained Earnings.

Using stockholders' equity data
(Obj. 3)

S13-9 → *Link Back to Chapter 1 (Accounting Equation, Income Statement).* Use the Manatee Corporation data in Starter 13-8 to compute Manatee's

a. Net income **b.** Total liabilities **c.** Total assets

S13-10 Colombia Coffee Company earned net income of $85,000 during the year ended December 31, 20X8. On December 15, Colombia declared the annual cash dividend on its 6% preferred stock (par value, $100,000) and a $0.50 per share cash dividend on its common stock (50,000 shares). Colombia then paid the dividends on January 4, 20X9.

Accounting for cash dividends **(Obj. 4)**

Journalize for Colombia Company:

a. Declaring the cash dividends on December 15
b. Paying the cash dividends on January 4, 20X9

S13-11 Refer to the stockholders' equity of MedTech.com Corporation in Exhibit 13-7. Answer these questions about MedTech.com's dividends.

Dividing cash dividends between preferred and common stock **(Obj. 4)**

1. How much in dividends must MedTech.com declare each year before the common stockholders get any cash dividends for the year?
2. Suppose MedTech.com declares cash dividends of $20,000 for 20X5. How much of the dividends goes to preferred? How much goes to common?
3. Is MedTech.com's preferred stock cumulative or noncumulative? How can you tell?
4. Suppose MedTech.com passed the preferred dividend in 20X6 and 20X7. In 20X8, the company declares cash dividends of $9,000. How much of the dividends goes to preferred? How much goes to common?

S13-12 Refer to the stockholders' equity of MedTech.com Corporation in Exhibit 13-7. MedTech.com has not declared preferred dividends for three years (including the current year). Compute the book value per share of MedTech.com's common stock.

Book value per share of common stock **(Obj. 5)**

S13-13 Answer the following questions about various stock values.

Explaining the use of different stock values for decision making **(Obj. 5)**

1. Suppose you are an investor considering the purchase of **Intel** common stock as an investment. You have called your stockbroker to inquire about the stock. Which stock value are you most concerned about? Explain your reasoning.
2. How is the book value of a stock used in decision making?

S13-14 Answer these questions about two rates of return.

Computing and explaining return on assets and return on equity **(Obj. 6)**

1. Give the formula for computing (a) rate of return on common stockholders' equity and (b) rate of return on total assets.
2. Why are preferred dividends subtracted from net income to compute return on common stockholders' equity?
3. Why is interest expense added to net income to compute return on assets?

S13-15 **Coca-Cola's** 2002 financial statements reported the following items—with 2001 figures given for comparison (adapted, in millions):

Computing return on assets and return on equity for a leading company **(Obj. 6)**

	2002	2001
Balance sheet		
Total assets	$24,501	$22,417
Total liabilities	$12,701	$11,051
Total stockholders' equity (all common)	11,800	11,366
Total liabilities and equity	$24,501	$22,417
Income statement		
Net sales	$19,564	
Cost of goods sold	7,105	
Gross profit	12,459	
Selling, administrative, and general expenses	7,001	
Interest expense	199	
All other expenses, net	2,209	
Net income	$ 3,050	

Compute Coca-Cola's rate of return on total assets and rate of return on common stockholders' equity for 2002. Do these rates of return look high or low?

Accounting for a corporation's income tax
(Obj. 7)

S13-16 Harry's Hot Dogs had income before income tax of $100,000 and taxable income of $80,000 for 20X4, the company's first year of operations. The income tax rate is 40%.

1. Make the entry to record Harry's income taxes for 20X4.
2. Show what Harry's Hot Dogs will report on its 20X4 income statement, starting with income before income tax.

A+ online homework

Exercises

Organizing a corporation
(Obj. 1)

E13-1 Kyle Dietz and Joe Phipps are opening a limousine service to be named Good Times Limo. They need outside capital, so they plan to organize the business as a corporation. They come to you for advice. Write a memorandum informing them of the steps in forming a corporation. Identify specific documents used in this process, and name the different parties involved in the ownership and management of a corporation.

Issuing stock
(Obj. 2)
Student Resource CD
General Ledger (GL), QuickBooks (QB), Peachtree (PT)

E13-2 Carolina Systems completed the following stock issuance transactions:

April	19	Issued 1,000 shares of $1 par common stock for cash of $10.50 per share.
May	3	Sold 300 shares of $4.50, no-par preferred stock for $15,000 cash.
	11	Received inventory valued at $23,000 and equipment with market value of $11,000. Issued 3,000 shares of the $1 par common stock.

Required

1. Journalize the transactions. Explanations are not required.
2. How much paid-in capital did these transactions generate for Carolina Systems?

Issuing stock and preparing the stockholders' equity section of the balance sheet
(Obj. 2, 3)
Student Resource CD
GL, QB, PT

E13-3 The charter for Mohammed Rugs, Inc., authorizes the company to issue 100,000 shares of $3, no-par preferred stock and 500,000 shares of common stock with $1 par value. During its start-up phase, Mohammed completed the following transactions:

Aug.	6	Issued 500 shares of common stock to the promoters who organized the corporation, receiving cash of $15,000.
	12	Issued 300 shares of preferred stock for cash of $20,000.
	14	Issued 1,000 shares of common stock in exchange for land valued at $26,000.
	31	Closed net income of $25,000 into Retained Earnings.

Required

1. Record the transactions in the general journal.
2. Prepare the stockholders' equity section of the Mohammed Rugs balance sheet at August 31.

Recording issuance of no-par stock
(Obj. 2)

E13-4 Amalfi Furniture Co., located in Chicago, imports Mediterranean furniture. The corporation issued 5,000 shares of no-par common stock for $10 per share. Record issuance of the stock if the stock (a) is true no-par stock and (b) has stated value of $2 per share. Which type of stock results in more total paid-in capital?

Stockholders' equity section of a balance sheet
(Obj. 3)
Student Resource CD
GL, QB, PT

E13-5 The charter of Big Bear Corporation authorizes the issuance of 5,000 shares of Class A preferred stock, 1,000 shares of Class B preferred stock, and 10,000 shares of common stock. During a two-month period, Big Bear completed these stock-issuance transactions:

Nov. 23	Issued 2,000 shares of $1 par common stock for cash of $12.50 per share.
Dec. 2	Sold 300 shares of $4.50, no-par Class A preferred stock for $20,000 cash.
12	Received inventory valued at $25,000 and equipment with market value of $16,000 for 3,000 shares of the $1 par common stock.
17	Issued 1,000 shares of 5%, no-par Class B preferred stock with stated value of $50 per share. The issue price was stated value.

Required

Prepare the stockholders' equity section of the Big Bear Corporation balance sheet for the transactions given in this exercise. Retained Earnings has a balance of $70,000.

Paid-in capital for a corporation
(Obj. 2)

E13-6 ReadyTech Co. recently organized. The company issued common stock to an attorney in exchange for his patent with a market value of $40,000. In addition, ReadyTech received cash both for 2,000 shares of its $50 par preferred stock at par value and for 26,000 shares of its no-par common stock at $10 per share. Retained Earnings at the end of the first year was $70,000. Without making journal entries, determine the total paid-in capital created by these transactions.

Stockholders' equity section of a balance sheet
(Obj. 3)

Student Resource CD
spreadsheet

E13-7 Liston Fry Co. has the following selected account balances at June 30, 20X2. Prepare the stockholders' equity section of the company's balance sheet.

Common stock, no par with $1 stated value, 100,000 shares authorized and issued	$100,000	Inventory	$112,000
Accumulated depreciation—machinery and equipment	62,000	Machinery and equipment	109,000
Retained earnings	110,000	Preferred stock, 5%, $20 par, 20,000 shares authorized, 5,000 shares issued	100,000
		Paid-in capital in excess of stated value—common	90,000
		Cost of goods sold	81,000

Dividing dividends between preferred and common stock
(Obj. 4)

E13-8 Qualcomm Communications has the following stockholders' equity:

Preferred stock, 8%, $10 par, 100,000 shares authorized, 20,000 shares issued	$ 200,000
Common stock, $0.50 par, 500,000 shares authorized, 300,000 shares issued	150,000
Paid-in capital in excess of par—common	600,000
Total paid-in capital	950,000
Retained earnings	150,000
Total stockholders' equity	$1,100,000

First, determine whether preferred stock is cumulative or noncumulative. Then compute the amount of dividends to preferred and to common for 20X1 and 20X2 if total dividends are $15,000 in 20X1 and $50,000 in 20X2.

Computing dividends on preferred and common stock
(Obj. 4)

E13-9 The following elements of stockholders' equity are adapted from the balance sheet of Bullock Corporation.

Stockholders' Equity	$ Thousands
Preferred stock, cumulative, $2 par (Note 7), 50,000 shares issued	$100
Common stock, $0.10 par, 9,000,000 shares issued	900

Note 7. Preferred Stock:
Designated Annual Cash Dividend Per Share—$0.40.

Bullock paid no preferred dividends in 20X3.

Required

Compute the dividends to preferred and common for 20X4 if total dividends are $150,000 in 20X4.

Book value per share of common stock
(Obj. 5)

E13-10 The balance sheet of Westview Landscaping reported the following:

Preferred stock, $50 par value, 6%, 100 shares issued and outstanding	$ 5,000
Common stockholders' equity, 10,000 shares issued and outstanding	222,000
Total stockholders' equity	$227,000

Assume that Westview has paid preferred dividends for the current year and all prior years (no dividends in arrears). Compute the book value per share of the common stock.

Book value per share of common stock; preferred dividends in arrears
(Obj. 5)

E13-11 Refer to Exercise 13-10. Compute the book value per share of the common stock if three years' preferred dividends (including dividends for the current year) are in arrears. Round book value to the nearest cent.

Evaluating profitability
(Obj. 6)

E13-12 Columbus Furniture, Inc., reported these figures for 20X8 and 20X7:

	20X8	20X7
Income statement:		
Interest expense	$ 2,400,000	$ 7,100,000
Net income	18,000,000	18,700,000
Balance sheet:		
Total assets	326,000,000	317,000,000
Preferred stock, $1.30, no-par, 100,000 shares issued and outstanding	2,500,000	2,500,000
Common stockholders' equity	164,000,000	157,000,000
Total stockholders' equity	166,500,000	159,500,000

Compute rate of return on total assets and rate of return on common stockholders' equity for 20X8. Do these rates of return suggest strength or weakness? Give your reason.

Accounting for income tax by a corporation
(Obj. 7)

E13-13 The income statement of **Pier 1 Imports, Inc.**, reported income before income tax of $160 million during a recent year. Assume Pier 1's taxable income for the year was $100 million. The company's income tax rate was close to 40%.

1. Journalize Pier 1's entry to record income tax for the year.
2. Show how Pier 1 would report income tax on its income statement and on its balance sheet. Complete the income statement, starting with income before tax. For the balance sheet, assume all beginning balances were zero.

Accounting for an actual company's transactions
(Obj. 2, 4)

E13-14 **Wal-Mart Stores, Inc.**, completed many transactions during 20X2, including the following (adapted in billions):

a. Sales revenue—assume all for cash, $218.
b. Total expenses—90% paid in cash; 10% on account, $210.
c. Closing entries for sales revenue and total expenses.
d. Closing entry for net income to Retained Earnings.
e. Total cash dividends declared and then paid later, $1.

Required

Journalize these 20X2 transactions.

Problems

(Group A)

A+ online homework

P13-1A Del Chesser and Mark Bailes are opening a **Pier 1 Imports** store in a shopping center in Taos, New Mexico. The area is growing, and no competitors are located nearby. Their basic decision is how to organize the business. Chesser thinks the partnership form is best. Bailes favors the corporate form of organization. They seek your advice.

Organizing a corporation
(Obj. 1)

Required

Write a memo to Chesser and Bailes to make them aware of the advantages and disadvantages of organizing the business as a corporation. Use the following format for your memo:

Date:	__________
To:	Del Chesser and Mark Bailes
From:	Student Name
Subject:	Advantages and disadvantages of the corporate form of business organization

P13-2A Partners Craven and Thames wish to avoid the unlimited personal liability of the partnership form of business, so they are incorporating the company as C & T Services, Inc. The charter from the state of Arizona authorizes the corporation to issue 10,000 shares of 6%, $100 par preferred stock and 250,000 shares of no-par common stock. In its first month, C & T Services completed the following transactions:

Journalizing corporation transactions and preparing the stockholders' equity section of the balance sheet
(Obj. 2, 3)

Student Resource CD
GL, QB, PT

Jan. 3	Issued 6,300 shares of common stock to Craven and 3,800 shares to Thames, both for cash of $10 per share.
12	Issued 1,100 shares of preferred stock to acquire a patent with a market value of $110,000.
22	Issued 1,500 shares of common stock to other investors for $10 cash per share.

Required

1. Record the transactions in the general journal.
2. Prepare the stockholders' equity section of the C & T Services, Inc., balance sheet at January 31. The ending balance of Retained Earnings is $40,000.

P13-3A Delta Corporation was organized in 20X4. At December 31, 20X4, Delta's balance sheet reported the following stockholders' equity:

Issuing stock and preparing the stockholders' equity section of the balance sheet
(Obj. 2, 3)

Preferred stock, 5%, $10 par, 50,000 shares authorized, none issued	$ —
Common stock, $2 par, 100,000 shares authorized, 10,000 shares issued	20,000
Paid-in capital in excess of par—common	30,000
Retained earnings (Deficit)	(5,000)
Total stockholders' equity	$45,000

Required

Answer the following questions, making journal entries as needed.

1. What does the 5% mean for the preferred stock? After Delta issues preferred stock, how much in annual cash dividends will Delta expect to pay on 1,000 shares?
2. At what price per share did Delta issue the common stock during 20X4?
3. Were first-year operations profitable? Give your reason.
4. During 20X5, the company completed the following selected transactions. Journalize each transaction. Explanations are not required.
   a. Issued for cash 5,000 shares of preferred stock at par value.
   b. Issued for cash 1,000 shares of common stock at a price of $7 per share.
   c. Net income for the year was $50,000, and the company declared no dividends. Make the closing entry for net income.

(continued)

5. Prepare the stockholders' equity section of the Delta Corporation balance sheet at December 31, 20X5.

Stockholders' equity section of the balance sheet
(Obj. 3)

P13-4A Stockholders' equity information for two independent companies, Seville Enterprises, Inc., and Madrid Corp., is as follows:

- *Seville Enterprises, Inc.* Seville is authorized to issue 60,000 shares of $5 par common stock. All the stock was issued at $12 per share. The company incurred a net loss of $41,000 in 20X6. It earned net income of $30,000 in 20X7 and $90,000 in 20X8. The company declared no dividends during the three-year period.
- *Madrid Corp.* Madrid's charter authorizes the company to issue 10,000 shares of $2.50 preferred stock with par value of $50 and 120,000 shares of no-par common stock. Madrid issued 1,000 shares of the preferred stock at par. It issued 40,000 shares of the common stock for a total of $220,000. The company's Retained Earnings balance at the beginning of 20X8 was $64,000, and net income for the year was $90,000. During 20X8, the company declared the specified dividend on preferred and a $0.50 per share dividend on common. Preferred dividends for 20X7 were in arrears.

Required

For each company, prepare the stockholders' equity section of its balance sheet at December 31, 20X8. Show the computation of all amounts. Entries are not required.

Analyzing the stockholders' equity of an actual corporation
(Obj. 3, 4)

P13-5A Radioshack Corp. operates Radio Shack stores. Radioshack included the following stockholders' equity on its year-end balance sheet at December 31, 20X1, with all dollar amounts, except par value per share, adapted, and in millions:

Stockholders' Equity	($ Millions)
Preferred stock, 6% cumulative	$ 65
Common stock—par value $1 per share; 650,000,000 shares authorized, 236,000,000 shares issued	236
Paid-in capital in excess of par—common	70
Retained earnings	2,003
Other	(1,646)
Total	$ 728

Required

1. Identify the different issues of stock Radioshack has outstanding.
2. Give two summary entries to record issuance of all the Radioshack stock. Assume that all the stock was issued for cash. Explanations are not required.
3. Assume that preferred dividends are in arrears for 20X0 and 20X1. Record the declaration of a $50 million cash dividend on December 30, 20X2. Use separate Dividends Payable accounts for Preferred and Common. Round to the nearest $1 million. An explanation is not required.

Preparing a corporation balance sheet; measuring profitability
(Obj. 3, 6)

P13-6A → *Link Back to Chapter 1 (Accounting Equation).* The following accounts and June 30, 20X5, balances of Witt, Inc., are arranged in no particular order:

Property, plant, and equipment, net	$ 231,000	Accounts receivable, net	$ 46,000
Common stock, $1 par, 500,000 shares authorized, 236,000 shares issued	236,000	Paid-in capital in excess of par—common	19,000
Dividends payable	9,000	Accrued liabilities	26,000
Retained earnings	29,000	Long-term note payable	12,000
Preferred stock, $0.10, no-par, 10,000 shares authorized and issued	25,000	Inventory	81,000
		Prepaid expenses	10,000
		Cash	10,000
		Accounts payable	31,000
		Trademark, net	9,000

Required

1. Prepare the company's classified balance sheet in the account format at June 30, 20X5.
2. Compute Witt's rate of return on total assets and rate of return on common stockholders' equity for the year ended June 30, 20X5. For the rates of return, you will need these data:

Total assets, June 30, 20X4	$404,000
Common equity, June 30, 20X4	222,000
Net income, 20X5	51,000
Interest expense, 20X5	6,000

3. Do these rates of return suggest strength or weakness? Give your reason.

Computing dividends on preferred and common stock
(Obj. 4)

Student Resource CD
spreadsheet

P13-7A OnPoint Consulting, Inc., has 10,000 shares of $4.50, no-par preferred stock and 50,000 shares of no-par common stock outstanding. OnPoint declared and paid the following dividends during a three-year period: 20X1, $20,000; 20X2, $100,000; and 20X3, $200,000.

Required

1. Compute the total dividends to preferred stock and to common stock for each of the three years if
   a. Preferred is noncumulative. **b.** Preferred is cumulative.
2. For case (1b), journalize the declaration of the 20X3 dividends on December 28, 20X3, and the payment of the dividends on January 17, 20X4. Use separate Dividends Payable accounts for Preferred and Common.

Analyzing the stockholders' equity of a corporation
(Obj. 4, 5)

P13-8A The balance sheet of The Lopez Group reported the following:

Stockholders' Equity	
Nonvoting preferred stock, no-par	$320,000
Common stock, $1.50 par value, authorized 75,000 shares; issued 30,000 shares	45,000
Additional paid-in capital—common	240,000
Retained earnings	141,000
Total stockholders' equity	$746,000

Notes to the financial statements indicate that 8,000 shares of $3.00 preferred stock with a stated value of $40 per share are issued and outstanding. Preferred dividends are in arrears for three years, including the current year. On the balance sheet date, the market value of the Lopez common stock is $10 per share.

Required

1. Is the preferred stock cumulative or noncumulative? How can you tell?
2. What is the amount of the annual preferred dividend?
3. Which class of stockholders controls the company? Give your reason.
4. What is the total paid-in capital of the company?
5. What was the total market value of the common stock?
6. Compute the book value per share of the common stock.

Computing and recording a corporation's income tax
(Obj. 7)

P13-9A The accounting (not the income tax) records of Wolf Security Systems, Inc., provide the income statement for 20X8.

Total revenue		$680,000
Expenses:		
Cost of goods sold		$290,000
Operating expenses		180,000
Total expenses before tax		470,000
Income before income tax		$210,000

The operating expenses include depreciation of $50,000 computed under the straight-line method. In calculating taxable income on the tax return, Wolf uses MACRS. MACRS depreciation was $70,000 for 20X8. The corporate income tax rate is 40%.

Required

1. Compute Wolf's taxable income for the year.

2. Journalize the corporation's income tax for 20X8.

3. Prepare the corporation's single-step income statement for 20X8.

Problems

A+ online homework

(Group B)

Organizing a corporation
(Obj. 1)

P13-1B Megan Thomas and Ann Kraft are opening a **Cracker Barrel Restaurant** in Durango, Colorado. There are no competing family restaurants in the immediate vicinity. Their fundamental decision is how to organize the business. Thomas thinks the partnership form is best for their business. Kraft favors the corporate form of organization. They seek your advice.

Required

Write a memo to Thomas and Kraft to make them aware of the advantages and disadvantages of organizing the business as a corporation. Use the following format:

Date:	____________
To:	Megan Thomas and Ann Kraft
From:	Student Name
Subject:	Advantages and disadvantages of the corporate form of business organization

Journalizing corporation transactions and preparing the stockholders' equity section of the balance sheet
(Obj. 2, 3)

Student Resource CD
GL, QB, PT

P13-2B The partnership of Duran & Nueces needed additional capital to expand into new markets, so the business incorporated as Ventura, Inc. The charter from the state of Texas authorizes Ventura to issue 50,000 shares of 6%, $100-par preferred stock and 100,000 shares of no-par common stock. To start, Ventura completed the following transactions:

Dec. 2	Issued 9,000 shares of common stock to Duran and 12,000 shares to Nueces, both for cash of $5 per share.
10	Issued 500 shares of preferred stock to acquire a patent with a market value of $50,000.
27	Issued 12,000 shares of common stock to other investors for cash of $60,000.

Required

1. Record the transactions in the general journal.

2. Prepare the stockholders' equity section of the Ventura, Inc., balance sheet at December 31. The ending balance of Retained Earnings is $57,000.

Issuing stock and preparing the stockholders' equity section of the balance sheet
(Obj. 2, 3)

P13-3B Hudson Corporation was organized in 20X8. At December 31, 20X8, Hudson's balance sheet reported the following stockholders' equity:

Preferred stock, 6%, $50 par,	
100,000 shares authorized, none issued	$ —
Common stock, $1 par, 500,000 shares authorized,	
60,000 shares issued	60,000
Paid-in capital in excess of par—common	40,000
Retained earnings	25,000
Total stockholders' equity	$125,000

Required

Answer the following questions, making journal entries as needed.

1. What does the 6% mean for the preferred stock? After Hudson issues preferred stock, how much in annual cash dividends will Hudson expect to pay on 1,000 shares?
2. At what price per share did Hudson issue the common stock during 20X8?
3. Were first-year operations profitable? Give your reason.
4. During 20X9, the company completed the following selected transactions. Journalize each transaction. Explanations are not required.
   a. Issued for cash 1,000 shares of preferred stock at par value.
   b. Issued for cash 2,000 shares of common stock at a price of $3 per share.
   c. Net income for the year was $82,000, and the company declared no dividends. Make the closing entry for net income.
5. Prepare the stockholders' equity section of the Hudson Corporation balance sheet at December 31, 20X9.

P13-4B The following summaries for Yurman Jewelry, Inc., and Northern Insurance Company provide the information needed to prepare the stockholders' equity section of each company's balance sheet. The two companies are independent.

Stockholders' equity section of the balance sheet
(Obj. 3)

- *Yurman Jewelry, Inc.* Yurman Jewelry is authorized to issue 40,000 shares of $1 par common stock. All the stock was issued at $10 per share. The company incurred net losses of $50,000 in 20X1 and $14,000 in 20X2. It earned net income of $23,000 in 20X3 and $71,000 in 20X4. The company declared no dividends during the four-year period.
- *Northern Insurance Company.* Northern's charter authorizes the issuance of 50,000 shares of 7%, $15 par preferred stock and 500,000 shares of no-par common stock. Northern issued 1,000 shares of the preferred stock at $15 per share. It issued 100,000 shares of the common stock for $400,000. The company's retained earnings balance at the beginning of 20X4 was $120,000. Net income for 20X4 was $90,000, and the company declared the specified preferred dividend for 20X4. Preferred dividends for 20X3 were in arrears.

Required

For each company, prepare the stockholders' equity section of its balance sheet at December 31, 20X4. Show the computation of all amounts. Entries are not required.

P13-5B The **Procter & Gamble Company** reported the following stockholders' equity, as adapted, on its balance sheet at June 30, 20X3:

Analyzing the stockholders' equity of an actual corporation
(Obj. 3, 4)

Stockholders' Equity	$ Millions
Preferred stock, 6.125%—	
Authorized 600,000,000 shares; issued 1,634,000 shares	$ 1,634
Common stock—$1 stated value—	
Authorized 5,000,000,000 shares; issued 1,301,000,000	1,301
Additional paid-in capital, common	2,490
Retained earnings	11,980
Other	(3,699)
Total	$13,706

Required

1. Identify the different issues of stock Procter & Gamble has outstanding.
2. Make two summary journal entries to record issuance of all the Procter & Gamble stock. Assume all the stock was issued for cash. Explanations are not required.
3. Assume no preferred dividends are in arrears. Journalize the declaration of a $500 million dividend at June 30, 20X3. Use separate Dividends Payable accounts for Preferred and Common. Round to the nearest $1 million. An explanation is not required.

Preparing a corporation balance sheet; measuring profitability
(Obj. 3, 6)

P13-6B → *Link Back to Chapter 1 (Accounting Equation).* The following accounts and November 30, 20X6, balances of Omaha Mutual, Inc., are arranged in no particular order.

Common stock, $5 par, 100,000 shares authorized, 22,000 shares issued	$110,000	Retained earnings	$132,000
Dividends payable	3,000	Inventory	101,000
Additional paid-in capital—common	140,000	Property, plant, and equipment, net	278,000
Accounts payable	31,000	Prepaid expenses	13,000
Preferred stock, 4%, $10 par, 25,000 shares authorized, 3,700 shares issued	37,000	Goodwill	37,000
		Accrued liabilities	17,000
		Long-term note payable	104,000
		Accounts receivable, net	102,000
		Cash	43,000

Required

1. Prepare the company's classified balance sheet in the account format at November 30, 20X6.
2. Compute Omaha Mutual's rate of return on total assets and rate of return on common stockholders' equity for the year ended November 30, 20X6. For the rates of return, you will need these data:

Total assets, Nov. 30, 20X5	$581,000
Common equity, Nov. 30, 20X5	383,000
Net income, 20X5	47,200
Interest expense, 20X5	12,800

3. Do these rates of return suggest strength or weakness? Give your reason.

Computing dividends on preferred and common stock
(Obj. 4)

Student ResourceCD
spreadsheet

P13-7B Eastern Airlines has 5,000 shares of 5%, $10 par value preferred stock and 100,000 shares of $1.50 par common stock outstanding. During a three-year period, Eastern declared and paid cash dividends as follows: 20X1, $1,500; 20X2, $15,000; and 20X3, $23,000.

Required

1. Compute the total dividends to preferred stock and to common stock for each of the three years if
   a. Preferred is noncumulative.
   b. Preferred is cumulative.
2. For case (1b), journalize the declaration of the 20X3 dividends on December 22, 20X3, and the payment of the dividends on January 14, 20X4. Use separate Dividends Payable accounts for Preferred and Common.

Analyzing the stockholders' equity of a corporation
(Obj. 4, 5)

P13-8B The balance sheet of Maple Furniture, Inc., reported the following:

Stockholders' Equity	($ Thousands)
Cumulative preferred stock	$ 45
Common stock, $1 par, authorized 40,000,000 shares; issued 16,000,000 shares	16,000
Additional paid-in capital	217,000
Retained earnings (Deficit)	(77,165)
Total stockholders' equity	$155,880

Notes to the financial statements indicate that 9,000 shares of $1.50 preferred stock with a stated value of $5 per share are issued and outstanding. Preferred dividends are in arrears for two years, including the current year. On the balance sheet date, the market value of the Maple Furniture common stock was $9.50 per share.

Required

1. Is the preferred stock cumulative or noncumulative? How can you tell?
2. What is the amount of the annual preferred dividend?
3. What is the total paid-in capital of the company?
4. What was the total market value of the common stock?
5. Compute the book value per share of the common stock.

Computing and recording a corporation's income tax **(Obj. 7)**

P13-9B The accounting (not the income tax) records of Solarex Energy Corporation provide the income statement for 20X4.

Total revenue	$930,000
Expenses:	
Cost of goods sold	$430,000
Operating expenses	270,000
Total expenses before tax	700,000
Income before income tax	$230,000

The operating expenses include depreciation of $50,000 computed on the straight-line method. In calculating taxable income on the tax return, Solarex uses the modified accelerated cost recovery system (MACRS). MACRS depreciation was $80,000 for 20X4. The corporate income tax rate is 35%.

Required

1. Compute taxable income for the year.
2. Journalize the corporation's income tax for 20X4.
3. Prepare the corporation's single-step income statement for 20X4.

APPLY *Your Knowledge*

Decision Cases

Evaluating alternative ways to raise capital **(Obj. 2, 3)**

Case 1. Ray Link and Sam Chain have written a spreadsheet program (Link Chain) to rival Excel. They need additional capital to market the product, and they plan to incorporate the business. They are considering the capital structure for the corporation. Their primary goal is to raise as much capital as possible without giving up control of the business. Link and Chain plan to invest the software program in the company and receive 100,000 shares of the corporation's common stock. The partners have been offered $100,000 for the rights to the software program.

The corporation's plans for a charter include an authorization to issue 5,000 shares of preferred stock and 500,000 shares of $1 par common stock. Link and Chain are uncertain about the most desirable features for the preferred stock. Prior to incorporating, the partners are discussing their plans with two investment groups. The corporation can obtain capital from outside investors under either of the following plans:

- *Plan 1.* Group 1 will invest $100,000 to acquire 1,000 shares of $5, no-par preferred stock and $70,000 to acquire 70,000 shares of common stock. Each preferred share receives 50 votes on matters that come before the stockholders.
- *Plan 2.* Group 2 will invest $150,000 to acquire 1,500 shares of 6%, $100 par nonvoting, noncumulative preferred stock.

Required

Assume that the corporation is chartered.

1. Journalize the issuance of common stock to Link and Chain. Explanations are not required.
2. Journalize the issuance of stock to the outsiders under both plans. Explanations are not required.
3. Net income for the first year is $180,000 and total dividends are $30,000. Prepare the stockholders' equity section of the corporation's balance sheet under both plans.
4. Recommend one of the plans to Link and Chain. Give your reasons.

Characteristics of corporations' capital stock
(Obj. 2, 5)

Case 2. Answering the following questions will enhance your understanding of the capital stock of corporations. Consider each question independently of the others.

1. Preferred shares have advantages with respect to dividends and corporate liquidation. Why would investors buy common stock when preferred stock is available?
2. Why are capital stock and retained earnings shown separately in the shareholders' equity section of the balance sheet?
3. Chiu Wang, major shareholder of C-W, Inc., proposes to sell some land she owns to the company for common shares in C-W. What problem does C-W, Inc., face in recording the transaction?
4. If you owned 100 shares of stock in **Dell Computer Corporation** and someone offered to buy the stock for its book value, would you accept the offer? Why or why not?

Ethical Issue

Note: This case is based on an actual situation.

Jeremy Copeland paid $50,000 for a franchise that entitled him to market Success Associates software programs in the countries of the European Union. Copeland intended to sell individual franchises for the major language groups of western Europe—German, French, English, Spanish, and Italian. Naturally, investors considering buying a franchise from Copeland asked to see the financial statements of his business.

Believing the value of the franchise to be greater than $50,000, Copeland sought to capitalize his own franchise at $500,000. The law firm of St. Charles & LaDue helped Copeland form a corporation chartered to issue 500,000 shares of common stock with par value of $1 per share. Attorneys suggested the following chain of transactions:

a. A third party borrows $500,000 and purchases the franchise from Copeland.
b. Copeland pays the corporation $500,000 to acquire all its stock.
c. The corporation buys the franchise from the third party, who repays the loan.

In the final analysis, the third party is debt-free and out of the picture. Copeland owns all the corporation's stock, and the corporation owns the franchise. The corporation's balance sheet lists a franchise acquired at a cost of $500,000. This balance sheet is Copeland's most valuable marketing tool.

Required

1. What is unethical about this situation?
2. Who can be harmed? How can they be harmed? What role does accounting play?

Analyzing stockholders' equity
(Obj. 2, 6, 7)

Financial Statement Case

The **Amazon.com** financial statements appear in Appendix A. Answer the following questions about Amazon's stock.

Required

1. How much of Amazon's preferred stock was outstanding at December 31, 2002? How can you tell?
2. Examine Amazon.com's balance sheet. Which stockholders' equity account increased the most during 2002? What caused this increase? The statement of cash flows answers this question under Financing Activities.
3. Show how to compute the balances in Amazon.com's Common Stock account at the end of both 2002 and 2001.
4. Would it be meaningful to compute Amazon.com's return on equity? Explain your answer.

Team Project

Competitive pressures are the norm in business. **Lexus** automobiles (made in Japan) have cut into the sales of **Mercedes Benz** (a German company), Jaguar (now a division of Ford), **General Motors'** Cadillac Division, and **Ford's** Lincoln Division. **Dell, Gateway,** and **Compaq** computers have siphoned business away from **IBM**. Foreign steelmakers have reduced the once-massive U.S. steel industry to a fraction of its former size.

Indeed, corporate downsizing has occurred on a massive scale. During the past few years, each company or industry mentioned here has pared down plant and equipment, laid off employees, or restructured operations.

Required

1. Identify all the stakeholders of a corporation and the stake each group has in the company. A *stakeholder* is a person or a group who has an interest (that is, a stake) in the success of the organization.
2. Identify several measures by which a corporation may be considered deficient and which may indicate the need for downsizing. How can downsizing help to solve this problem? Discuss how each measure can indicate the need for downsizing.
3. Debate the downsizing issue. One group of students takes the perspective of the company and its stockholders, and another group of students takes the perspective of other stakeholders of the company.

For Internet exercises, go to the Web site www.prenhall.com/horngren.

CHAPTER 14

Retained Earnings, Treasury Stock, and the Income Statement

A+ TIPS CHECK YOUR RESOURCES

- Visit the www.prenhall.com/horngren **Web site** for self-study quizzes, video clips, and other resources
- Try the **Quick Check** exercise at the end of the chapter to test your knowledge
- Learn the **key terms**
- Do the **Starter** exercises keyed in the margins
- Work the **mid-** and **end-of-chapter summary problems**
- Use the **Concept Links** to review material in other chapters
- Search the **CD** for review materials by chapter or by key word
- Watch the **tutorial videos** to review key concepts

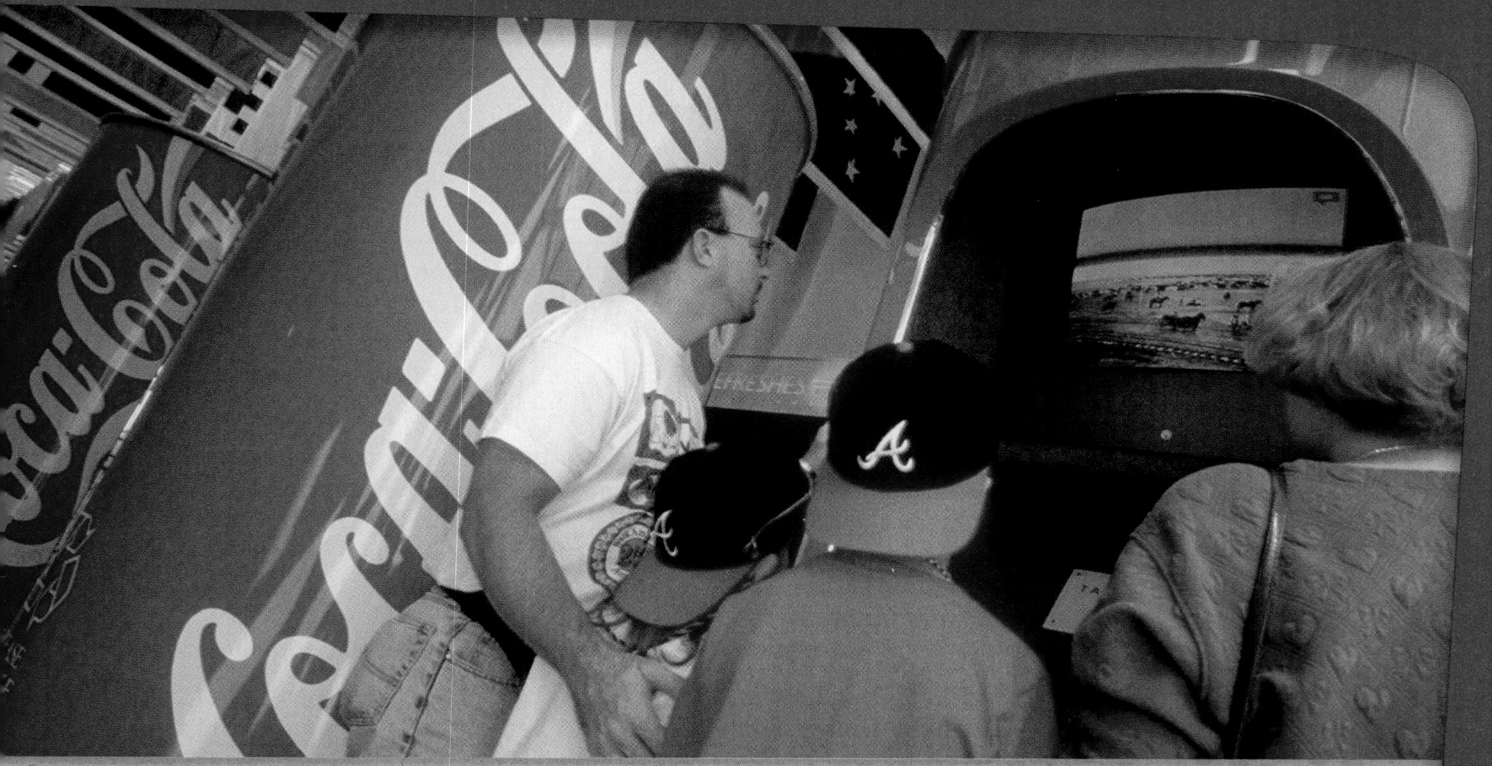

LEARNING OBJECTIVES

1. Account for stock dividends
2. Distinguish stock splits from stock dividends
3. Account for treasury stock
4. Report restrictions on retained earnings
5. Analyze a complex income statement
6. Prepare a statement of stockholders' equity

Coca-Cola/ Dell/ Pier 1

Coca-Cola, Dell Computer, and Pier 1 Imports are all leaders in their respective industries. What do these three companies have in common? A lot, including the fact that all three have bought back large amounts of their own stock. In Chapter 13 we saw how corporations raise capital by issuing their stock. Stock issuance increases stockholders' equity.

Companies also buy their own stock back from the stockholders. A stock repurchase decreases both corporate assets and equity. A company's own stock that it has repurchased is called treasury stock, because the company holds the stock in the corporate treasury. Coca-Cola, Dell, and Pier 1 have spent large sums to buy back their own stock. Coca-Cola's stock buybacks have totaled more than $14 billion—more than the company's total equity. Dell has spent over $2 billion—almost half of its total equity—to reacquire its own stock. ■

Why do companies repurchase their own stock? This chapter covers the topic of treasury stock, along with retained earnings, stock dividends, and the corporate income statement. Let's begin with retained earnings.

Sitemap

- Retained Earnings, Stock Dividends & Splits
- Treasury Stock
- Reporting Issues
- Corporate Income Statement

- ■ Retained Earnings, Stock Dividends & Splits
- □ Treasury Stock
- □ Reporting Issues
- □ Corporate Income Statement

Retained Earnings, Stock Dividends, and Stock Splits

We have seen that the owners' equity of a corporation is called *stockholders' equity* or *shareholders' equity*. The paid-in capital accounts and retained earnings make up stockholders' equity.

Retained Earnings

Retained Earnings carries the balance of the business's net income less all net losses and less all dividends accumulated over the corporation's lifetime. *Retained* means "held onto." Retained Earnings is the shareholders' stake in total assets that come from profits. A debit balance in Retained Earnings is called a *deficit*. Retained earnings deficits are rare because they can lead to corporate failure and bankruptcy.

When you see a balance sheet, remember these facts about Retained Earnings:

Student Resource CD
common stock, dividends, stock dividend, stock split

1. ***Credits to the Retained Earnings account arise only from net income.*** Retained Earnings shows how much net income a corporation has earned and retained in the business. Its balance is the cumulative, lifetime earnings of the company minus all net losses and all dividends.
2. ***The Retained Earnings account is not a reservoir of cash.*** Retained Earnings represents no asset in particular. In fact, the corporation may have a large balance in Retained Earnings but too little cash to pay a dividend.

Cash is an Asset. ≠ Retained Earnings is Stockholders' Equity.

Cash and Retained Earnings are two very different accounts, unrelated to each other.

Stop & Think

Assume that the beginning balance of Retained Earnings was $70,000. The net loss for the year was $80,000. What will the Retained Earnings balance be after this net loss?

Answer:

Retained Earnings

		Dec. 31, 20X0 Balance	70,000
Dec. 31, 20X1 Net loss	80,000		
Dec. 31, 20X1 Balance	10,000		

Stock Dividends

1 Account for stock dividends

Stock Dividend
A distribution by a corporation of its own stock to its stockholders.

A **stock dividend** is a distribution by a corporation of its own stock to its stockholders. Unlike cash dividends, stock dividends do not give any assets to the stockholders. Stock dividends

- Affect *only* stockholders' equity accounts (including Retained Earnings and Common Stock)
- Have *no* effect on total stockholders' equity

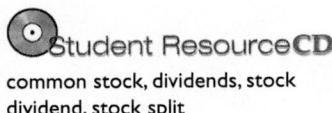

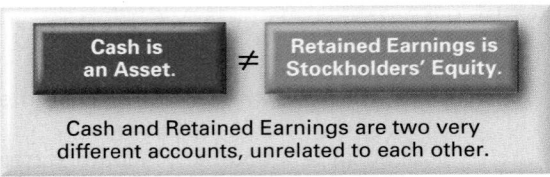

As Exhibit 14-1 shows, a stock dividend decreases Retained Earnings and increases Common Stock. Both accounts are stockholders' equity, so total equity is unchanged. This is a transfer from Retained Earnings to Common Stock. No asset or liability is affected by a stock dividend.

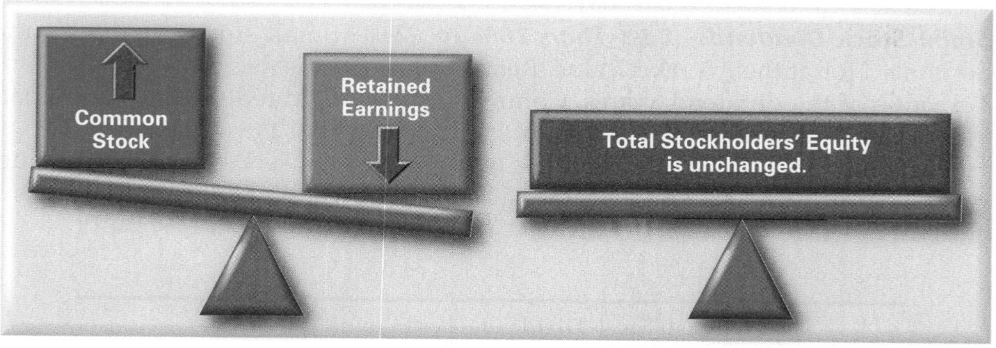

Exhibit 14-1

Effects of a Stock Dividend

The corporation distributes stock dividends to stockholders in proportion to the number of shares they already own. Suppose you own 300 shares of Pier 1 Imports' common stock. If Pier 1 distributes a 10% common stock dividend, you would receive 30 (300 × 0.10) additional shares. You would now own 330 shares of the stock. All other Pier 1 stockholders would also receive additional shares equal to 10% of their prior holdings. You and all the other Pier 1 stockholders would be in the same relative position after the dividend as before it.

WHY ISSUE STOCK DIVIDENDS? A company issues stock dividends for several reasons:

1. ***To continue dividends but conserve cash.*** A company may want to keep cash in the business. Yet it may also wish to continue dividends in some form.
2. ***To reduce the market price of its stock.*** A stock dividend may cause the market price of the company's stock to fall because of the increased supply of the stock. A share of Pier 1 Imports stock has traded at $20 recently. Doubling the shares outstanding by issuing a stock dividend would drop the stock's market price by approximately half, to $10 per share. The objective is to make the stock less expensive and thus more attractive to investors.

RECORDING STOCK DIVIDENDS The board of directors announces stock dividends on the declaration date. The date of record and the distribution date then follow. (These are the same dates used for a cash dividend.) The declaration of a stock dividend does *not* create a liability because the corporation is not obligated to pay assets. (Recall that a liability is a claim on *assets*.) Instead, the corporation has declared its intention to distribute its stock. Assume that Pier 1 Imports has the following stockholders' equity prior to a stock dividend:

Pier 1 Imports
Stockholders' Equity (Adapted)

Paid-in capital:	
Common stock, $1 par, 500,000 shares authorized, 100,000 shares issued	$100,000
Paid-in capital in excess of par	60,000
Total paid-in capital	160,000
Retained earnings	430,000
Total stockholders' equity	$590,000

The entry to record a stock dividend depends on its size. Generally accepted accounting principles distinguish between

- A *small* stock dividend (less than 20% to 25% of issued stock)
- A *large* stock dividend (25% or more of issued stock)

Stock dividends between 20% and 25% are rare.

Small Stock Dividends—Less Than 20% to 25% Small stock dividends are accounted for at their market value. Retained Earnings is decreased for the market value of the dividend shares, Common Stock is credited for the stock's par value, and Paid-In Capital in Excess of Par is credited for the remainder.

Assume Pier 1 Imports distributes a stock dividend when the market value of the company's common stock is $20 per share. Exhibit 14-2 illustrates the accounting for a 10% stock dividend.[1]

Exhibit 14-2
Accounting for Stock Dividends—Pier 1 Imports

Small Stock Dividend—For Example, 10%
(Accounted for at *market* value)

Retained Earnings		
(100,000 × 0.10 × $20 market value)	200,000	
Common Stock		
(100,000 × 0.10 × $1 par)		10,000
Paid-In Capital in Excess of Par		190,000

A stock dividend does not affect assets, liabilities, or total stockholders' equity. A stock dividend merely rearranges the stockholders' equity accounts, leaving total equity unchanged.

✔ Starter 14-1

✔ Starter 14-2

Large Stock Dividends—25% or More Large stock dividends are rare, so we do not illustrate them. Instead of large stock dividends, companies split their stock, as we illustrate in the next section.

Stock Splits

Stock Split
An increase in the number of outstanding shares of stock coupled with a proportionate reduction in the par value of the stock.

A **stock split** is fundamentally different from a stock dividend. A stock split increases the number of authorized, issued, and outstanding shares of stock. A stock split is also coupled with a proportionate reduction in the stock's par value. For example, if the company splits its stock 2 for 1, the number of outstanding shares is doubled and each share's par value is cut in half. A stock split decreases the market price of the stock—with the intention of making the stock more affordable. Most leading companies in the United States—General Electric, IBM, and many others—have split their stock.

The market price of a share of Pier 1 Imports common stock has been approximately $20. Assume that Pier 1 wishes to decrease the market price to approximately $10. Suppose Pier 1 decides to split the common stock 2 for 1, and the stock's market price drops from $20 to $10. A 2-for-1 stock split means that Pier 1 will have twice as many shares of stock outstanding after the split as before, and each share's par value is cut in half. Assume that Pier 1 had issued 100,000 shares of $1 par common stock before the split. The following table shows how a 2-for-1 split affects Pier 1 Imports' stockholders' equity.

[1]A stock dividend can be recorded with two journal entries—for (1) the declaration and (2) the stock distribution. But most companies record stock dividends with a single entry on the date of distribution, as we illustrate here.

Pier 1 Imports' Stockholders' Equity (Adapted)

Before 2-for-1 Stock Split		After 2-for-1 Stock Split	
Common stock, $1.00 par, 500,000 shares authorized, 100,000 shares issued	$100,000	Common stock, $0.50 par, 1,000,000 shares authorized, 200,000 shares issued	$100,000
Paid-in capital in excess of par	60,000	Paid-in capital in excess of par	60,000
Retained earnings	430,000	Retained earnings	430,000
Total stockholders' equity	$590,000	Total stockholders' equity	$590,000

After the 2-for-1 stock split, Pier 1 Imports would have 1 million shares authorized and 200,000 shares (100,000 shares × 2) of $0.50 (50 cents) par ($1.00/2) common stock outstanding. Total stockholders' equity would be exactly as before. Indeed, the balance in the Common Stock account does not even change. Only the par value of the stock and the number of shares change.

Because the stock split affects no account balances, no formal journal entry is needed. Instead, the split is recorded in a *memorandum entry* such as the following:

Aug. 19	Split the common stock 2 for 1. Called in the $1 par common stock and distributed two shares of $0.50 par common stock for each old share previously outstanding.

✔ Starter 14-3

Stock Dividends and Stock Splits Compared

2 *Distinguish stock splits from stock dividends*

Both stock dividends and stock splits increase the number of shares of stock owned by each stockholder. Neither stock dividends nor stock splits change investors' cost of the stock they own.

SIMILARITIES Consider Dell Computer Corporation, the leader in personal computers. Assume you own 100 shares of Dell stock.

- If Dell distributes a stock dividend or a stock split, your 100 shares increase, but your total cost is unchanged.
- Neither a stock dividend nor a stock split creates taxable income for the investor.

DIFFERENCES Stock dividends and stock splits differ in that

- A stock *dividend* shifts an amount from retained earnings to the stock account. Par value per share is unchanged.
- A stock *split* increases the number of shares of stock authorized, issued, and outstanding. Par value per share decreases.

Exhibit 14-3 summarizes the effects of dividends and stock splits on total stockholders' equity.

Exhibit 14-3

Effects of Dividends and Stock Splits on Total Stockholders' Equity

Event	Effect on Total Stockholders' Equity
Declaration of *cash* dividend	Decreases total equity
Payment of *cash* dividend	No effect on equity
Distribution of *stock* dividend	No effect on equity
Stock split	No effect on equity

Source: Adapted from material provided by Beverly Terry.

3 Account for treasury stock

Treasury Stock
A corporation's own stock that it has issued and later reacquired.

Student Resource CD
treasury stock

Treasury Stock

A company's own stock that it has issued and later reacquired is called **treasury stock.**[2] In effect, the corporation holds the stock in its treasury. Corporations such as Coca-Cola, Dell Computer, and Pier 1 Imports may purchase their own stock for several reasons:

1. The business is trying to increase net assets by buying its shares low and hoping to sell them for a higher price later.
2. The purchase supports the stock's market price by decreasing the supply of stock available.
3. Management wants to avoid a takeover by an outside party.

When a company buys its own stock back, the company gives up cash and becomes a smaller entity as a result. Now let's see how companies account for their treasury stock.

Purchase of Treasury Stock

We record the purchase of treasury stock by debiting Treasury Stock and crediting Cash. Suppose that Jupiter Cable Company had the following stockholders' equity before purchasing treasury stock:

Jupiter Cable Company
Stockholders' Equity [*Before* Purchase of Treasury Stock]

Common stock, $1 par, 10,000 shares authorized, 9,000 shares issued	$ 9,000
Paid-in capital in excess of par—common	12,000
Retained earnings	14,000
Total stockholders' equity	$35,000

On March 31, Jupiter purchases 1,000 shares of its common as treasury stock, paying cash of $5 per share. Jupiter records the purchase of treasury stock as follows:

Mar. 31	Treasury Stock—Common (1,000 × $5)	5,000	
	Cash		5,000
	Purchased treasury stock.		

Treasury Stock—Common

Debit	Credit
5,000	

The Treasury Stock account has a debit balance, which is the opposite of the other owners' equity accounts. Therefore, *Treasury Stock* is *a contra equity account.* Treasury stock is recorded at cost, without reference to par value. The Treasury Stock account is reported beneath Retained Earnings on the balance sheet. Treasury Stock's balance is subtracted from the sum of total paid-in capital and retained earnings, as follows:

Jupiter Cable Company
Stockholders' Equity [*After* Purchase of Treasury Stock]

Common stock, $1 par, 10,000 shares authorized, 9,000 shares issued	$ 9,000
Paid-in capital in excess of par—common	12,000
Retained earnings	14,000
Subtotal	35,000
Less: Treasury stock, 1,000 shares at cost	(5,000)
Total stockholders' equity	$30,000

[2]We illustrate the *cost* method of accounting for treasury stock because it is used most widely. Intermediate accounting courses also cover an alternative method.

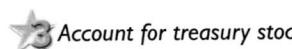

Total stockholders' equity decreases by $5,000, the cost of the treasury stock. Also, the stock *outstanding* decreases. *Outstanding* shares are computed as follows:

Shares of stock *issued*	9,000
Less: Shares of treasury stock	(1,000)
Shares of stock *outstanding*	8,000

Outstanding shares are important because only outstanding shares have voting rights, receive cash dividends, and receive assets if the corporation liquidates. Treasury stock doesn't carry a vote, receive dividends, or have a claim on assets in liquidation.

Stop & Think

Ethical Issue: Treasury stock transactions have a serious ethical and legal dimension. A company such as **Dell Computer** buying its own shares as treasury stock must be careful that its information releases are accurate. What will happen if Dell purchases treasury stock at $17 per share and one day later announces a technological breakthrough that will generate millions of dollars in new business?

Answer: Dell's stock price would likely rise in response to the new information. If it could be proved that Dell management withheld the information, a shareholder selling stock back to Dell could file a lawsuit against the company. The stockholder would claim that with the new information, he would have been able to sell the Dell stock at a higher price.

Sale of Treasury Stock

A company may sell its treasury stock at its cost, above cost, or below cost.

SALE AT COST If the stock is sold for cost—the same price the corporation paid to reacquire it—the entry debits Cash and credits Treasury Stock for the same amount.

SALE ABOVE COST If treasury stock is sold for more than its cost, the difference is credited to a new account, Paid-In Capital from Treasury Stock Transactions, because the excess came from the company's stockholders. Suppose Jupiter Cable Company resold its treasury shares for $9 per share (cost was $5). The entry is

Dec. 7	Cash (1,000 × $9)	9,000	
	Treasury Stock—Common (1,000 × $5 cost)		5,000
	Paid-In Capital from Treasury Stock Transactions		4,000
	Sold treasury stock.		

Treasury Stock—Common

5,000	5,000
0	

Paid-In Capital from Treasury Stock Transactions is reported with the other paid-in capital accounts on the balance sheet, beneath the Common Stock and Paid-In Capital in Excess of Par accounts, as shown here:

✔ Starter 14-4

Jupiter Cable Company

Stockholders' Equity [*After* Purchase and Sale of Treasury Stock]

Paid-in capital:	
Common stock, $1 par, 10,000 shares authorized, 9,000 shares issued	$ 9,000
Paid-in capital in excess of par—common	12,000
Paid-in capital from treasury stock transactions	4,000
Retained earnings	14,000
Total stockholders' equity	$39,000

Exhibit 14-4 tracks the stockholders' equity of Jupiter Cable Company to show how treasury stock transactions affect corporate equity.

Exhibit 14-4

Jupiter Cable Stockholders' Equity

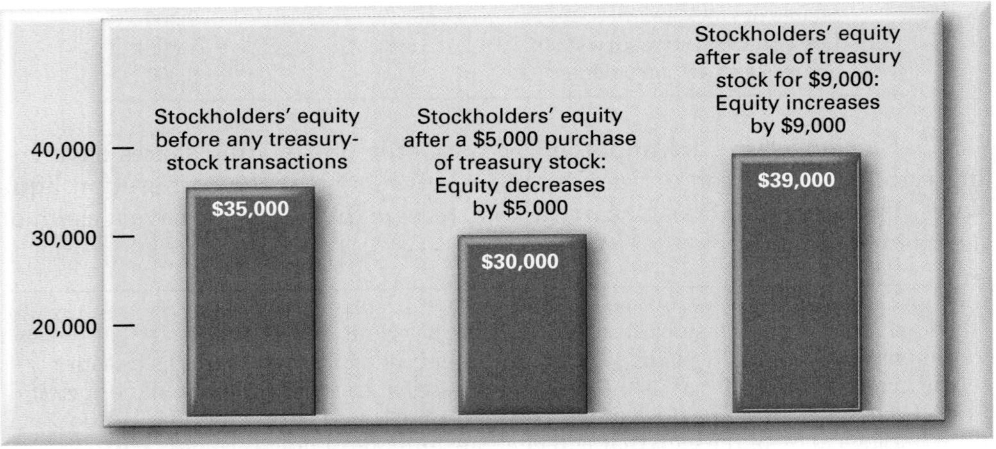

SALE BELOW COST The resale price of treasury stock can be less than cost. The shortfall is debited first to Paid-In Capital from Treasury Stock Transactions. If this account's balance is too small, then debit Retained Earnings for the remaining amount.

- □ Retained Earnings, Stock Dividends & Splits
- □ Treasury Stock
- ■ Reporting Issues
- □ Corporate Income Statement

Student Resource CD
retained earnings, stock buyback

Reporting Issues

Companies may retire their stock, restrict retained earnings, and vary the way they report stockholders' equity. This section covers these reporting issues.

Retirement of Stock

A corporation may purchase its own stock and *retire* it by canceling the stock certificates. Retirements of preferred stock are common because companies wish to avoid paying dividends on the preferred stock. The retired stock cannot be reissued.

Retiring stock decreases both the stock issued and the stock outstanding. In retiring stock, the corporation removes all the stock and the paid-in capital accounts related to the retired shares, such as Preferred Stock and Capital in Excess of Par.

4 *Report restrictions on retained earnings*

Restrictions on Retained Earnings

Dividends, purchases of treasury stock, and retirements of stock require a cash payment. These outlays decrease assets, so the corporation has fewer resources to pay liabilities. A bank may agree to loan $500,000 only if Jupiter Cable Company limits dividend payments and the purchase of treasury stock.

LIMITS ON DIVIDENDS AND TREASURY STOCK PURCHASES To ensure that corporations maintain a minimum level of stockholders' equity, state laws restrict the amount of treasury stock a corporation may purchase. The restriction often focuses on the balance of retained earnings. Companies usually report their retained earnings restrictions in notes to the financial statements. The following disclosure by RTE Corporation, a manufacturer of electronic transformers, is typical:

Notes to Consolidated Financial Statements

Note F—Long-Term Debt The . . . Company's loan agreements . . . restrict cash dividends and similar payments to shareholders. Under the most restrictive of these provisions, retained earnings of $4,000,000 were unrestricted as of December 31, 20X6.

With this restriction, the maximum dividend that RTE Corporation can pay its stockholders is $4,000,000.

Accounting.com

Are Stock Buybacks a Value Booster or a PR Gimmick?

What could signal more confidence than a company buying back lots of its own stock? Stock buybacks were a strategy for investing spare cash in the 1990s. Now the buyback has become a strategy for propping up a company's stock prices. For example, the stock of **Tenet Healthcare Corporation** plunged by 50% in a week, and the health-care giant paid $140 million to buy its own stock. The strategy worked because two weeks later, the stock had risen by 13%.

Purchases of a company's own shares reduce the number of outstanding shares, and earnings per share go up. A dramatic example of this occurred when **Deluxe**, the country's leading check printer, purchased 19 million of its own shares. Deluxe's stock price soared 116% after the buyback.

When the market falls, boosting stock prices becomes a priority, and there's a rush of buyback activity. In the second quarter of 2002, for instance, U.S. companies announced plans to repurchase $24 billion of their own stock. The key words here are "*announced plans*." Skeptical shareholders point out that buyback announcements aren't always followed by actual stock repurchases. Columnist John Ellis says, "Nothing so perfectly captures the fiber of today's whimpering CEOs than the stock buyback announcement." Ellis complains that CEOs don't always carry through on their buyback announcements: "While many have been announced, probably 6 out of 10 [buybacks] are nothing more than public relations gimmicks."

Dividend announcements are different. Unlike a buyback announcement, a cash dividend, once declared, becomes a real liability. The joke on Wall Street is this: Stock buybacks are like dating. A dividend is more like getting married.

Based on: Tom Petruno, "Stock Buybacks Face Increasing Scrutiny," *Los Angeles Times*, November 24, 2002, p. C.13. Shaheen Pasha, "Stock Buybacks Have Increased as Equities Fall," *The Wall Street Journal*, July 18, 2002, p. C9. John Ellis, "Strategy," *Fast Company*, October 2002, p. 74.

APPROPRIATIONS OF RETAINED EARNINGS **Appropriations** are restrictions on Retained Earnings that are recorded by formal journal entries. A corporation may *appropriate*—segregate in a separate account—a portion of Retained Earnings for a specific use. For example, the board of directors may appropriate part of Retained Earnings for expansion. Appropriated Retained Earnings can be reported as shown near the bottom of Exhibit 14-5.

Retained earnings appropriations are rare. Most companies report any retained earnings restrictions in the notes to the financial statements, as illustrated for RTE Corporation and in the real-world format of Exhibit 14-5.

Appropriation of Retained Earnings Restriction of retained earnings that is recorded by a formal journal entry.

✔ Starter 14-5

Variations in Reporting Stockholders' Equity

Accountants sometimes report stockholders' equity in ways that differ from our examples. We use a detailed format to help you learn the components of stockholders' equity. Companies assume that investors and creditors understand the details.

One of the most important skills you will learn in this course is how to read the financial statements of real companies. In Exhibit 14-5, we present a side-by-side comparison of our general teaching format and the format you are likely to encounter in actual balance sheets. Note the following points in the real-world format:

1. The heading Paid-In Capital does not appear. It is commonly understood that Preferred Stock, Common Stock, and Additional Paid-In Capital are elements of paid-in capital.
2. Preferred stock is often reported in a single amount that combines par value and premium.
3. For presentation in the financial statements, all additional paid-in capital appears as a single amount labeled Additional Paid-In Capital. Additional Paid-In Capital belongs to the common stockholders; therefore it follows Common Stock in the real-world format.
4. Often, total stockholders' equity ($4,000,000 in Exhibit 14-5) is not specifically labeled.

Exhibit 14-5 **Formats for Reporting Stockholders' Equity**

General Teaching Format

Stockholders' equity	
Paid-in capital:	
Preferred stock, 8%, $10 par, 30,000 shares authorized and issued	$ 300,000
Paid-in capital in excess of par—preferred	10,000
Common stock, $1 par, 100,000 shares authorized, 60,000 shares issued	60,000
Paid-in capital in excess of par—common	2,140,000
Paid-in capital from treasury stock transactions, common	9,000
Paid-in capital from retirement of preferred stock	11,000
Total paid-in capital	2,530,000
Retained earnings appropriated for contingencies	400,000
Retained earnings—unappropriated	1,100,000
Total retained earnings	1,500,000
Subtotal	4,030,000
Less: Treasury stock, common (1,000 shares at cost)	(30,000)
Total stockholders' equity	$4,000,000

Real-World Format

Stockholders' equity	
Preferred stock, 8%, $10 par, 30,000 shares authorized and issued	$ 310,000
Common stock, $1 par, 100,000 shares authorized, 60,000 shares issued	60,000
Additional paid-in capital	2,160,000
Retained earnings (Note 7)	1,500,000
Less: Treasury stock, common (1,000 shares at cost)	(30,000)
	$4,000,000

Note 7—Restriction on retained earnings.
At December 31, 20XX, $400,000 of retained earnings is restricted for contingencies by the company's board of directors. Accordingly, dividends are restricted to a maximum of $1,100,000.

Review the first half of the chapter by studying the following Decision Guidelines feature.

Decision Guidelines

ACCOUNTING FOR RETAINED EARNINGS, DIVIDENDS, AND TREASURY STOCK

Retained earnings, dividends, and treasury stock transactions are unique because they can affect a corporation's equity. The Decision Guidelines provide a foundation for you to understand their effects.

Decision	Guidelines		
How to record:			
• Distribution of a small stock dividend (20% to 25%)?	Retained Earnings.	Market value	
	Common Stock		Par value
	Paid-In Capital in Excess of Par . .		Excess
• Stock split?	Memorandum only: Split the common stock 2 for 1. Called in the outstanding $10 par common stock and distributed two shares of $5 par for each old share outstanding (amounts assumed).		

What are the effects of stock dividends and stock splits on:	*Effects of Stock* Dividend	Split
• Number of shares issued?	Increase	Increase
• Shares outstanding?	Increase	Increase
• Par value per share?	No effect	Decrease
• Total assets and total liabilities?	No effect	No effect
• Total stockholders' equity?	No effect	No effect
• Common Stock?	Increase	No effect
• Retained Earnings?	Decrease	No effect

How to record:			
• Purchase of treasury stock?	Treasury Stock	Cost	
• Sale of treasury stock?	Cash		Cost
At cost? (Amount received = Cost)	Cash	Amt received	
	Treasury Stock		Cost
Above cost?	Cash	Amt received	
	Treasury Stock		Cost
	Paid-In Capital from Treasury Stock Transactions		Excess
Below cost?	Cash	Amt received	
	Paid-In Capital from Treasury Stock Transactions	Amt up to prior bal	
	Retained Earnings	Excess	
	Treasury Stock		Cost

What are the effects of the purchase and sale of treasury stock on:	*Effects of* Purchase	Sale
• Total assets?	Decrease by full amount of payment	Increase by full amount of cash receipt
• Total stockholders' equity?	Decrease by full amount of payment	Increase by full amount of cash receipt

MID-CHAPTER *Summary Problem*

Simplicity Graphics, creator of magazine designs, reported shareholders' equity:

Shareholders' Equity	
Preferred stock, $1.00 par value	
Authorized—10,000 shares; Issued—None	$ —
Common Stock, $0.80 par value	
Authorized, 30,000 shares; Issued 14,000 shares	11,200
Capital in excess of par value	48,000
Earnings retained in business	89,000
	148,200
Less: Treasury stock, at cost (1,900 common shares)	(15,200)
	$133,000

A+ TIPS
CHECK YOUR RESOURCES

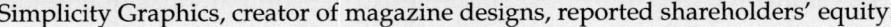

Required

1. What was the average issue price per share of the common stock?
2. Journalize the issuance of 1,000 shares of common stock at $4 per share. Use Simplicity's account titles.
3. How many shares of Simplicity's common stock are outstanding?
4. How many shares of common stock would be outstanding after Simplicity split its common stock 3 for 1?
5. Using Simplicity account titles, journalize the distribution of a 10% stock dividend when the market price of Simplicity common stock is $5 per share. Simplicity distributes the common stock dividend on the shares outstanding, which were computed in requirement 3.
6. Journalize the following treasury stock transactions, which occur in the order given:
   a. Simplicity purchases 500 shares of treasury stock at $8 per share.
   b. Simplicity sells 100 shares of treasury stock for $9 per share.

Solution

1. Average issue price of common stock was $4.23 per share [($11,200 + $48,000)/14,000 shares = $4.23]
2.

Cash (1,000 × $4)	4,000	
Common Stock (1,000 × $0.80)		800
Capital in Excess of Par Value		3,200
Issued common stock.		

3. Shares outstanding = 12,100 (14,000 shares issued minus 1,900 shares of treasury stock).
4. Shares outstanding after a 3-for-1 stock split = 36,300 (12,100 shares outstanding × 3).
5.

Earnings Retained in Business (12,100 × 0.10 × $5)	6,050	
Common Stock (12,100 × 0.10 × $0.80)		968
Capital in Excess of Par Value		5,082
Distributed a 10% common stock dividend.		

6.

a. Treasury Stock (500 × $8)	4,000	
Cash		4,000
Purchased treasury stock.		
b. Cash (100 × $9)	900	
Treasury Stock (100 × $8)		800
Paid-In Capital from Treasury Stock Transactions		100
Sold treasury stock.		

☐ Retained Earnings, Stock Dividends & Splits
☐ Treasury Stock
☐ Reporting Issues
■ **Corporate Income Statement**

5 *Analyze a complex income statement*

Student ResourceCD
comprehensive income, discontinued operations, earnings per share, extraordinary items, income statement, preferred stock, statement of shareholders' equity

The Corporate Income Statement: Analyzing Earnings

Now that we have covered stockholders' equity in detail, we turn to the corporate income statement. Net income (revenues plus gains minus expenses and losses) receives more attention than any other item in the financial statements. In fact, net income is probably the most important piece of information about a company. Net income measures how successfully the company has operated.

Suppose you are considering investing in the stock of Coca-Cola, Dell Computer, or Pier 1 Imports. You would examine these companies' income statements. Of particular interest is the amount of net income they can expect to earn year after year. To understand net income, let's examine Exhibit 14-6, which presents the income statement of Allied Electronics Corporation, a small manufacturer of precision instruments.

Continuing Operations

In Exhibit 14-6, the topmost section reports income from continuing operations. This part of the business should continue from period to period. Income from continuing operations, therefore, helps investors make predictions about future

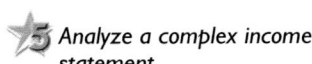

Exhibit 14-6 Income Statement of Allied Electronics Corporation

Allied Electronics Corporation

Income Statement
Year Ended December 31, 20X5

Continuing operations	Net sales revenue	$500,000
	Cost of goods sold	240,000
	Gross profit	260,000
	Operating expenses (detailed)	181,000
	Operating income	79,000
	Other gains (losses):	
	Gain on sale of machinery	11,000
	Income from continuing operations before income tax	90,000
	Income tax expense	36,000
	Income from continuing operations	54,000
Special items	Discontinued operations, income of $35,000, less income tax of $14,000	21,000
	Income before extraordinary item and cumulative effect of accounting change	75,000
	Extraordinary flood loss, $20,000, less income tax saving of $8,000	(12,000)
	Cumulative effect of accounting change, $10,000, less income tax of $4,000	6,000
	Net income	$ 69,000
Earnings per share	Earnings per share of common stock (20,000 shares outstanding):	
	Income from continuing operations	$2.70
	Income from discontinued operations	1.05
	Income before extraordinary item and cumulative effect of accounting change	3.75
	Extraordinary loss	(0.60)
	Cumulative effect of accounting change	0.30
	Net income	$3.45

earnings. We may use this information to predict that Allied Electronics Corporation will earn approximately $54,000 next year. The continuing operations of Allied Electronics include two items needing explanation.

First, Allied had a gain on the sale of machinery, which is outside the company's core business activity of selling electronics products. This explains why the gain is reported separately from Allied's sales revenue, cost of goods sold, and gross profit.

Second, income tax expense is subtracted to arrive at income from continuing operations. Allied Electronics' income tax rate is 40% ($90,000 × 0.40 = $36,000).

Special Items

After continuing operations, an income statement may include three types of special gains and losses:

✔ Starter 14-6

✔ Starter 14-7

- Discontinued operations
- Extraordinary gains and losses
- Cumulative effect of an accounting change

Discontinued Operations Most large corporations engage in several lines of business. For example, Sears, Roebuck & Co. is best known for its retail stores, but it also has a real-estate development company (Homart) and an insurance company (Allstate). Each identifiable division of a company is called a **segment of the business**. Allstate is the insurance segment of Sears.

Segment of the Business One of various separate divisions of a company.

A company may sell a segment of its business. For example, May Department Stores, the chain that operates Lord & Taylor and Foley's, sold Payless, its chain of shoe stores. Financial analysts typically do not include discontinued operations to predict a company's future income because the discontinued segments will generate no income in the future.

The income statement reports information on the discontinued segment under the heading Discontinued operations. Income from discontinued operations ($35,000) is taxed at 40% and reported by Allied Electronics Corporation, as shown in Exhibit 14-6. A loss on discontinued operations is reported similarly, with a subtraction for the income tax *savings* on the loss.

Companies dispose of old plant and equipment all the time. Gains and losses on these asset dispositions are *not* reported as discontinued operations. Gains and losses on normal asset dispositions are reported as "Other gains (losses)" up among continuing operations.

Extraordinary Gains and Losses (Extraordinary Items)

Extraordinary Gains and Losses
A gain or loss that is both unusual for the company and infrequent. Also called **extraordinary items**.

Extraordinary gains and losses, also called **extraordinary items**, are both unusual and infrequent. Losses from natural disasters (floods, earthquakes, and tornadoes) and the taking of company assets by a foreign government (expropriation) are extraordinary.

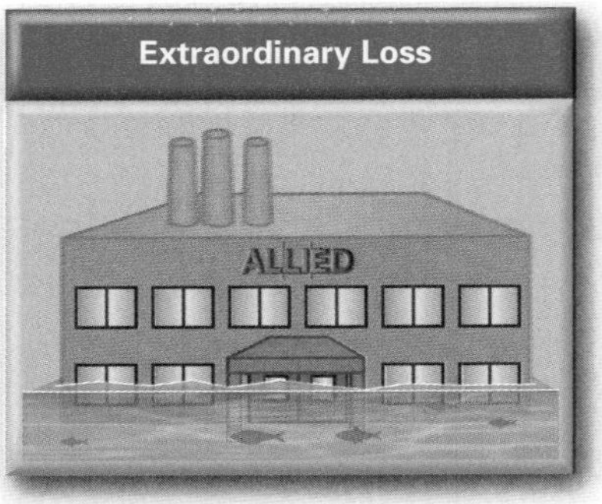

Extraordinary items are reported along with their income tax effect. During 20X5, Allied Electronics Corporation lost $20,000 of inventory in a flood. This flood loss reduced income and also reduced Allied's income tax. The tax effect decreases the net amount of the loss in the same way that the income tax reduces net income. An extraordinary loss can be reported along with its tax effect, as follows:

Extraordinary flood loss	$(20,000)
Less: Income tax saving	8,000
Extraordinary flood loss, net of tax	(12,000)

Trace this item to the income statement in Exhibit 14-6. An extraordinary gain is reported in the same way as a loss, net of the income tax.

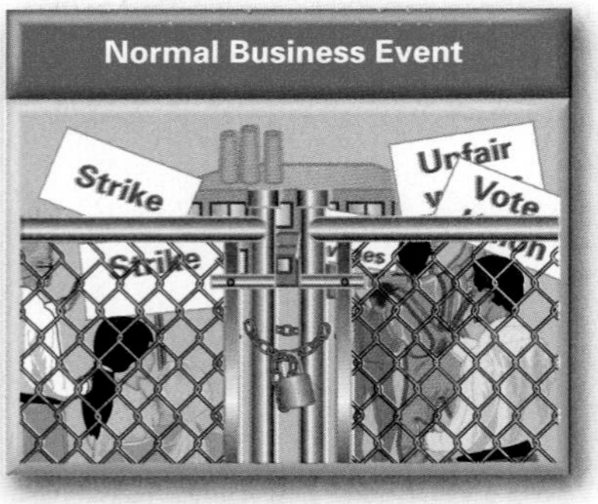

Gains and losses due to employee strikes, lawsuits, and the sale of plant assets are *not* extraordinary. These are normal business events. But they are outside the business's central operations, so they are reported on the income statement as other gains and losses. Examples include the gain on sale of machinery reported up in the Other gains (losses) section of Exhibit 14-6.

Cumulative Effect of a Change in Accounting Principle

For a review of depreciation methods, see Chapter 10. For a review of inventory methods, see Chapter 6. →

Companies sometimes change accounting methods, such as from double-declining-balance (DDB) to straight-line depreciation, or from first-in, first-out (FIFO) to average cost for inventory. ← An accounting change makes it difficult to compare one period's financial statements with the statements of earlier periods.

Investors and creditors can be misled into thinking that the current year is better when in fact the only difference is a change in accounting method. Investors must separate the effects of business operations from the effects created by accounting. Companies, therefore, report the effect of the accounting change in a special section of the income statement. This section appears after extraordinary items.

Allied Electronics Corporation has changed its method of accounting for depreciation from DDB to straight-line at the beginning of 20X5. If the company had been using straight-line depreciation every year, depreciation expense would have been less in prior years, and net income would have been higher. Exhibit 14-6 reports the $6,000 cumulative effect of this accounting change. A change from straight-line to double-declining-balance depreciation usually produces a negative cumulative effect.

✔ Starter 14-8

Stop & Think

Examine all the income tax amounts in Exhibit 14-6. How much was Allied Electronics' *total* income tax expense during 20X5?

Answer: \$46,000 = \$36,000 + \$14,000 − \$8,000 + \$4,000

Note that \$36,000 is the company's income tax expense from continuing operations: \$46,000 is *total* income tax expense.

Earnings per Share

The final segment of a corporate income statement presents the company's earnings per share, abbreviated as EPS. EPS is the most widely used of all accounting statistics. **Earnings per share (EPS)** reports the amount of net income for each share of the company's *outstanding common stock*. It is a key measure of success in business. EPS is computed as follows:

Earnings Per Share (EPS) Amount of a company's net income for each share of its outstanding common stock.

$$\textbf{Earnings per Share} = \frac{\textbf{Net income} - \textbf{Preferred dividends}}{\textbf{Average number of Common shares outstanding}}$$

Just as the corporation lists its different sources of income separately—from continuing operations, discontinued operations, and so on—it also shows a separate EPS figure for each element of income. Allied Electronics Corporation's EPS calculations are as follows:

Earnings per share of common stock (20,000 shares outstanding):	
Income from continuing operations (\$54,000/20,000)	\$2.70
Income from discontinued operations (\$21,000/20,000)	1.05
Income before extraordinary item and cumulative effect of accounting change (\$75,000/20,000)	3.75
Extraordinary loss (\$12,000/20,000)	(0.60)
Cumulative effect of accounting change (\$6,000/20,000)	0.30
Net income (\$69,000/20,000)	\$3.45

✔ Starter 14-9

The final section of Exhibit 14-6 reports the EPS figures for Allied Electronics.

Effect of Preferred Dividends on Earnings per Share Preferred dividends also affect EPS. Recall that EPS is earnings per share of *common* stock. Recall also that dividends on preferred stock are paid first. → Therefore, preferred dividends must be subtracted from income to compute EPS. Suppose Allied Electronics had 10,000 shares of preferred stock outstanding, each paying a \$1.00 dividend. The annual preferred dividend would be \$10,000 (10,000 × \$1.00). The \$10,000 would be subtracted from each of the income subtotals (lines 1, 3, and 6), resulting in the following EPS computations for the company:

← *Chapter 13, p. 511, provides detailed information on preferred stock.*

	Earnings per share of common stock (20,000 shares outstanding):	
1	Income from continuing operations (\$54,000 − \$10,000)/20,000	\$2.20
2	Income from discontinued operations (\$21,000/20,000)	1.05
3	Income before extraordinary item and cumulative effect of accounting change (\$75,000 − \$10,000)/20,000	3.25
4	Extraordinary loss (\$12,000/20,000)	(0.60)
5	Cumulative effect of accounting change (\$6,000/20,000)	0.30
6	Net income (\$69,000 − \$10,000)/20,000	\$2.95

✔ Starter 14-10

Basic and Diluted Earnings per Share Some corporations must report two sets of EPS figures, as follows:

- EPS based on outstanding common shares (*basic* EPS).
- EPS based on outstanding common shares plus the additional common shares that would arise from conversion of the preferred stock into common stock (*diluted* EPS). Diluted EPS is always lower than basic EPS.

Stop & Think

What makes earnings per share so useful as a business statistic?

Answer: Earnings per share is useful because it relates a company's income to one share of stock. Stock prices are quoted at an amount per share, and investors usually consider how much they must pay for a certain number of shares. Earnings per share is used to help determine the value of a share of stock.

Combined Statement of Income and Retained Earnings

Companies can report income and retained earnings on a single statement. Exhibit 14-7 illustrates how Allied Electronics would combine its income statement and its statement of retained earnings.

Exhibit 14-7

Combined Statement of Income and Retained Earnings

Allied Electronics Corporation

Summarized Statement of Income and Retained Earnings
Year Ended December 31, 20X5

Income statement	Sales revenue	$500,000
	Cost of goods sold	240,000
	Gross profit	260,000
	Expenses (listed individually)	191,000
Statement of retained earnings	Net income for 20X5	$ 69,000
	Retained earnings, December 31, 20X4	130,000
		199,000
	Dividends for 20X5	(54,000)
	Retained earnings, December 31, 20X5	$145,000

Reporting Comprehensive Income

Comprehensive Income
Company's change in total stockholders' equity from all sources other than from the owners.

As we have seen, all companies report net income or net loss on the income statement. There is another income figure. **Comprehensive income** is the company's change in total stockholders' equity from all sources other than from its owners. Comprehensive income includes net income plus some specific gains and losses, as follows:

- Unrealized gains or losses on certain investments
- Foreign-currency translation adjustments

These items do not enter into the determination of net income but instead are reported as other comprehensive income, as shown in Exhibit 14-8. Assumed figures are used for all items.

✔ Starter 14-11

Earnings per share applies only to net income and its components, as discussed earlier. Earnings per share is *not* reported for other comprehensive income.

Exhibit 14-8

Reporting Comprehensive Income

National Express Company

Income Statement
Year Ended December 31, 20X2

Revenues	$10,000
Expenses (summarized)	6,000
Net income	4,000
Other comprehensive income:	
Unrealized gain on investments	1,000
Comprehensive income	$ 5,000

Prior-Period Adjustments

A company may make an error in recording revenues or expenses. After the revenue and expense accounts are closed, Retained Earnings holds the error. The balance of Retained Earnings is wrong until corrected. Corrections to Retained Earnings for errors of an earlier period are called **prior-period adjustments**. The prior-period adjustment (correction) either increases or decreases the beginning balance of Retained Earnings and appears on that statement.

Prior-Period Adjustment
A correction to retained earnings for an error of an earlier period.

The year 2003 saw more prior-period adjustments than in the 20 previous years combined. Enron, Worldcom, Xerox, and many other companies restated their net income to correct accounting errors made in earlier years. To illustrate, assume De Graff Corporation recorded $30,000 of income tax expense for 20X7. The correct amount was $40,000. This error

- Understated expenses by $10,000
- Overstated net income by $10,000

In 20X8, the government required De Graff to pay the additional $10,000 in taxes for the prior year. De Graff's prior-period adjustment will decrease retained earnings as follows.

✔ Starter 14-12

De Graff Corporation

Statement of Retained Earnings
Year Ended December 31, 20X8

Retained earnings, December 31, 20X7, as originally reported	$390,000
Prior-period adjustment—To correct error in 20X7	(10,000)
Retained earnings, December 31, 20X7, as adjusted	380,000
Net income for 20X8	100,000
	480,000
Dividends for 20X8	(40,000)
Retained earnings, December 31, 20X8	$440,000

Statement of Stockholders' Equity

6 *Prepare a statement of stockholders' equity*

Most companies report a statement of stockholders' equity, which includes retained earnings. The statement of stockholders' equity is formatted exactly like a statement of retained earnings but with columns for each element of equity. The **statement of stockholders' equity** reports the changes in all categories of equity during the period:

Statement of Stockholders' Equity
Reports the changes in all categories of stockholders' equity during the period.

- Common stock
- Retained earnings
- Additional paid-in capital
- Treasury stock

Exhibit 14-9 uses assumed figures for Allied Electronics Corporation to illustrate the statement of stockholders' equity. Negative amounts—debits—appear in parentheses. If the company has preferred stock, the statement includes a column for Preferred Stock.

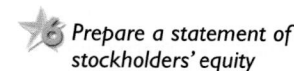

Exhibit 14-9 Statement of Stockholders' Equity

Allied Electronics Corporation

Statement of Stockholders' Equity
Year Ended December 31, 20X5

	Common Stock	Additional Paid-in Capital	Retained Earnings	Treasury Stock	Total
Balance, December 31, 20X4	$ 80,000	$160,000	$130,000	$(25,000)	$345,000
Issuance of stock	20,000	60,000			80,000
Net income			69,000		69,000
Cash dividends			(20,000)		(20,000)
Stock dividends—8%	8,000	26,000	(34,000)		0
Purchase of treasury stock				(10,000)	(10,000)
Sale of treasury stock		10,000		5,000	15,000
Balance, December 31, 20X5	$108,000	$256,000	$145,000	$(30,000)	$479,000

✔ Starter 14-13

Decision Guidelines

ANALYZING A CORPORATE INCOME STATEMENT

Three years out of college, you've saved $5,000 and are ready to start investing. Where do you start? You might begin by analyzing the income statements of **Coca-Cola, Dell Computer**, and **Pier I Imports**. These Decision Guidelines will help you understand a corporate income statement.

Decision	Guidelines	
What are the main sections of the income statement? See Exhibit 14-6 for an example.	Continuing operations	• Continuing operations, including other gains and losses and less income tax expense
	Special items	• Discontinued operations—gain or loss—less the income tax effect • Extraordinary gain or loss, less the income tax effect • Cumulative effect of an accounting change, less the income tax effect
		• Net income (or net loss) • Other comprehensive income (Exhibit 14-8)
What earnings-per-share (EPS) figures must a corporation report?	Earnings per share	• Earnings per share—applies only to net income (or net loss), not to other comprehensive income Separate EPS figures for • Income from continuing operations • Discontinued operations • Income before extraordinary item and cumulative effect of accounting change • Extraordinary gain or loss • Cumulative effect of accounting change • Net income (or net loss)
How to compute EPS for net income?		$\text{EPS} = \dfrac{\text{Net income} - \text{Preferred dividends}}{\text{Average number of common shares outstanding}}$

Excel Application Exercise

Goal: Create an Excel worksheet that charts the earnings-per-share (EPS) trend of a company with extraordinary items and/or changes in accounting principle.

Scenario: You are considering investing $5,000 in your favorite soft drink company, **Coca-Cola**. After taking a financial accounting class, you remember that smart investors investigate the financial performance of companies before investing. One measure of financial performance is earnings (net income) per share of common stock. When finished with your spreadsheet, answer these questions:

1. Why is EPS such a useful business statistic?
2. What is the trend in basic EPS (net income) for Coca-Cola?
3. List the EPS components given in the chapter. Fill in the amounts for Coca-Cola for the most recent year, and calculate EPS. Explain any difference between the amount you calculate and the one reported in the financial statements.
4. Besides EPS, what other financial measures should you examine prior to making an investment decision?

Step-by-Step:

1. Obtain a copy of the most recent annual report for Coca-Cola (online, try www.cocacola.com). Locate the Consolidated Statements of Income and Consolidated Balance Sheets.
2. Open a new Excel worksheet.
3. Create a bold-faced heading for your spreadsheet that contains the following:
   a. Chapter 14 Excel Application Exercise
   b. Coca-Cola Earnings-per-Share Analysis
   c. Today's Date
4. Move down two rows and enter the following title:
   Coca-Cola Company
   Income Statement
   Year Ended December 31, 2002 (or the most recent year)
   (In millions)
5. Copy the Consolidated Statements of Income, following the format used by Coca-Cola (leave out the description "Year Ended . . . "). Include all line items, using formulas where appropriate.
6. Starting with the row containing the three years' titles, highlight all rows of the income statement.
7. Click on the Chart Wizard. Select the line chart type with line markers displayed at each data value. Click next and select "Series in: rows." Then, click on the "Series" tab.
8. Remove from the series all line items except basic net income per share "before accounting change." You'll see lines disappear from your chart as you do this.
9. Then, click the "Add" button. Give the new series the name "EPS, net of changes." Click in the "Values" box, deleting any existing values. On the income statement, select the three amounts underneath the earnings-per-share line item "cumulative effect of accounting change" (these amounts do not have a name in the statement). The cell references should now be in the "Values" box. Click next.
10. Click on the "Titles" tab. For the chart title, enter "Earnings per Share." For the category X axis, enter "Year," and for the category Y axis, enter "EPS."
11. Click on the "Legend" tab, and click to move the legend to the bottom of the chart. Then, click on the "Data Labels" tab. Check "Value," then click "Finish." Position your chart to the right or bottom of your income statement.
12. Save your work, and print your work sheet in landscape mode (with graphs) for your files.

END-OF-CHAPTER *Summary Problem*

The following information was taken from the ledger of **Kraft Corporation** at December 31, 20X6.

A+ TIPS CHECK YOUR RESOURCES

Common stock, no-par, 45,000 shares issued	$180,000	Discontinued operations, income	$ 20,000
Sales revenue	620,000	Prior-period adjustment—credit to Retained Earnings	5,000
Extraordinary gain	26,000	Gain on sale of plant assets	21,000
Loss due to lawsuit	11,000	Cost of goods sold	380,000
General expenses	62,000	Income tax expense (saving):	
Preferred stock 8%	50,000	Continuing operations	32,000
Selling expenses	108,000	Discontinued operations	8,000
Retained earnings, beginning, as originally reported	103,000	Extraordinary gain	10,000
Cumulative effect of change in inventory method (debit)	(10,000)	Cumulative effect of change in inventory method	(4,000)
Dividends	16,000	Treasury stock, common (5,000 shares)	25,000

Required

Prepare a single-step income statement and a statement of retained earnings for Kraft Corporation for the year ended December 31, 20X6. Include the EPS presentation and show your computations. Kraft had no changes in its stock accounts during the year.

Solution

Kraft Corporation

Income Statement
Year Ended December 31, 20X6

Revenue and gains:		
Sales revenue		$620,000
Gain on sale of plant assets		21,000
Total revenues and gains		641,000
Expenses and losses:		
Cost of goods sold	$380,000	
Selling expenses	108,000	
General expenses	62,000	
Loss due to lawsuit	11,000	
Income tax expense	32,000	
Total expenses and losses		593,000
Income from continuing operations		48,000
Discontinued operations, income of $20,000, less income tax of $8,000		12,000
Income before extraordinary item and cumulative effect of change in inventory method		60,000
Extraordinary gain, $26,000, less income tax, $10,000		16,000
Cumulative effect of change in inventory method, $10,000, less income tax saving, $4,000		(6,000)
Net income		$ 70,000
Earnings per share:		
Income from continuing operations [($48,000 – $4,000)/40,000 shares]		$1.10
Income from discontinued operations ($12,000/40,000 shares)		0.30
Income before extraordinary item and cumulative effect of change in inventory method [($60,000 – $4,000)/40,000 shares]		1.40
Extraordinary gain ($16,000/40,000 shares)		0.40
Cumulative effect of change in inventory method ($6,000/40,000)		(0.15)
Net income [($70,000 – $4,000)/40,000 shares]		$1.65

Computations:

$$\text{EPS} = \frac{\text{Income} - \text{Preferred dividends}}{\text{Common shares outstanding}}$$

Preferred dividends: $50,000 × 0.08 = $4,000
Common shares outstanding:
45,000 shares issued – 5,000 treasury shares = 40,000 shares outstanding

Kraft Corporation

Statement of Retained Earnings
Year Ended December 31, 20X6

Retained earnings balance, beginning, as originally reported	$103,000
Prior-period adjustment—credit	5,000
Retained earnings balance, beginning, as adjusted	108,000
Net income for current year	70,000
	178,000
Dividends for current year	(16,000)
Retained earnings balance, ending	$162,000

REVIEW Retained Earnings, Treasury Stock, and the Income Statement

Quick Check

1. A company's own stock that it has issued and repurchased is called
   a. Issued stock
   b. Outstanding stock
   c. Stock dividend
   d. Treasury stock
2. A stock dividend
   a. Increases Common Stock
   b. Decreases Retained Earnings
   c. Has no effect on total equity
   d. All of the above
3. In a small stock dividend,
   a. Retained Earnings is debited for the market value of the shares issued.
   b. Common stock is debited for the par value of the shares issued.
   c. Paid-In Capital in Excess of Par is debited for the difference between the debits to Retained Earnings and to Common Stock.
   d. Net income is always decreased.
4. Stock splits
   a. Increase the number of shares of stock issued
   b. Decrease the par value of the stock
   c. Both a and b
   d. None of the above
5. Assume that **Pier 1 Imports** paid $10 per share to purchase 1,000 of its $1 par common as treasury stock. The purchase of treasury stock
   a. Decreased total equity by $1,000
   b. Increased total equity by $1,000
   c. Decreased total equity by $10,000
   d. Increased total equity by $10,000
6. Assume that Pier 1 Imports sold all 1,000 shares of its treasury stock for $15 per share. The sale of treasury stock
   a. Decreased total equity by $15,000
   b. Increased total equity by $15,000
   c. Decreased total equity by $5,000
   d. Increased total equity by $5,000
7. Analyze the income statement of Allied Electronics in Exhibit 14-6, page 555. Suppose you are predicting next year's net income. Allied is most likely to earn net income of $x next year. How much is $x?
   a. $54,000
   b. $75,000
   c. $79,000
   d. $90,000
8. Which of the following events would be an extraordinary loss?
   a. Loss on the sale of equipment
   b. Loss due to an earthquake
   c. Loss on discontinued operations
   d. All of the above are extraordinary items
9. What is the most widely followed statistic in accounting?
   a. Earnings per share
   b. Total assets
   c. Retained earnings
   d. Dividends
10. Earnings per share is *not* computed for
    a. Net income
    b. Discontinued operations
    c. Comprehensive income
    d. Extraordinary items

Accounting Vocabulary

appropriation of retained earnings (p. 551)
comprehensive income (p. 558)
earnings per share (EPS) (p. 557)
extraordinary gains and losses (p. 556)
extraordinary item (p. 556)
prior-period adjustment (p. 559)
segment of the business (p. 555)
statement of stockholders' equity (p. 559)
stock dividend (p. 544)
stock split (p. 546)
treasury stock (p. 548)

ASSESS *Your Progress*

A+ online homework

See *www.prenhall.com/horngren* for selected Starters, Exercises, and Problems.

Starters

Recording a small stock dividend
(Obj. 1)

S14-1 Benetech, Inc., has 200,000 shares of $2.50 par common stock outstanding. Benetech distributes a 5% stock dividend when the market value of its stock is $10 per share.

1. Journalize Benetech's distribution of the stock dividend on September 30. An explanation is not required.
2. What is the overall effect of the stock dividend on Benetech's total assets? On total stockholders' equity?

Comparing and contrasting cash dividends and stock dividends
(Obj. 1)

S14-2 → *Link Back to Chapter 13 (Cash Dividends)*. Compare and contrast the accounting for cash dividends and stock dividends. In the space provided, insert either "Cash dividends," "Stock dividends," or "Both cash dividends and stock dividends" to complete each of the following statements:

1. ____ increase paid-in capital by the same amount that they decrease Retained Earnings.
2. ____ decrease both total assets and total stockholders' equity, resulting in a decrease in the size of the company.
3. ____ decrease Retained Earnings.
4. ____ have no effect on a liability.

Accounting for a stock split
(Obj. 2)

S14-3 Examine **Pier 1 Imports'** stockholders' equity on page 545. Suppose Pier 1 split its common stock 2 for 1 in order to decrease the market price of its stock. The company's stock was trading at $20 immediately before the split.

1. Prepare the stockholders' equity section of Pier 1 Imports' balance sheet after the stock split.
2. Which account balances changed after the stock split? Which account balances were unchanged?

Accounting for the purchase and sale of treasury stock (above cost)
(Obj. 3)

S14-4 Celine Corporation began operations in 20X8. After issuing its common stock to the public, Celine completed the following treasury stock transactions:

a. Purchased 2,000 shares of the company's $1 par common stock as treasury stock, paying cash of $5 per share.
b. Sold 1,000 shares of the treasury stock for cash of $8 per share.

Journalize these transactions. Explanations are not required. Show how Celine will report treasury stock on its December 31, 20X8, balance sheet after completing the two transactions. In reporting the treasury stock, focus solely on the Treasury Stock account. You may ignore all other accounts.

Interpreting a restriction of retained earnings
(Obj. 4)

S14-5 Study Exhibit 14-5, page 552. The company's board of directors is preparing to declare a cash dividend.

1. The company has plenty of cash. What is the maximum amount of cash dividends the board of directors can declare? Explain how you arrived at your answer.
2. What is the nature of the retained earnings restriction in the exhibit? Why did the company restrict (appropriate) its retained earnings? Explain.

Preparing a corporate income statement
(Obj. 5)

S14-6 List the major parts of a complex corporate income statement for IMAX Corporation for the year ended December 31, 20X4. Include all the major parts of the income statement, starting with net sales revenue and ending with net income (net loss). You may ignore dollar amounts and earnings per share. Use Exhibit 14-6, page 555, as a guide.

Explaining the items on a complex corporate income statement **(Obj. 5)**

S14-7 Study the income statement of Allied Electronics Corporation in Exhibit 14-6, page 555. Answer these questions about the company's operations:

1. How much total gross profit did Allied earn on the sale of its products—before deducting any operating expenses? Name this item and give its amount.
2. Why is the gain on sale of machinery reported as Other gains (losses)?
3. What dollar amount of net income would most sophisticated investors predict for Allied Electronics to earn during 20X6 and beyond? Name this item, give its amount, and state your reason.

Preparing a corporate income statement **(Obj. 5)**

S14-8 H&R Young Corporation accounting records include the following items, listed in no particular order, at December 31, 20X3.

Extraordinary gain	$ 5,000	Other gains (losses)	$ (2,000)
Cost of goods sold	71,000	Net sales revenue	182,000
Operating expenses	64,000	Loss on discontinued	
Accounts receivable	19,000	operations	(15,000)

Income tax of 40% applies to all items.

Prepare H&R Young Corporation's income statement for the year ended December 31, 20X3. Use Exhibit 14-6, page 555, as a guide. Omit earnings per share.

Reporting earnings per share **(Obj. 5)**

S14-9 Return to the H&R Young Corporation data in Starter 14-8. H&R Young had 10,000 shares of common stock outstanding during 20X3. H&R Young declared and paid preferred dividends of $3,000 during 20X3.

Show how H&R Young reported EPS data on its 20X3 income statement.

Interpreting earnings-per-share data **(Obj. 5)**

S14-10 The **Procter & Gamble Company** has preferred stock outstanding, and the corporation issued additional common stock during the year.

1. Give the basic equation to compute earnings per share of common stock for net income.
2. List all the income items for which Procter & Gamble must report EPS data.

Reporting comprehensive income **(Obj. 5)**

S14-11 Use the H&R Young Corporation data in Starter 14-8. In addition, H&R Young had unrealized losses of $4,000 on investments during 20X3. Start with H&R Young's net income from Starter 14-8 and show how the company could report other comprehensive income on its 20X3 income statement.

Should H&R Young report EPS data for other comprehensive income?

Reporting a prior-period adjustment **(Obj. 6)**

S14-12 Examine De Graff Corporation's statement of retained earnings on page 559. Suppose instead that De Graff had overpaid 20X7 income tax expense by $10,000. Show how De Graff would report this prior-period adjustment on the statement of retained earnings for 20X8.

Using the statement of stockholders' equity **(Obj. 6)**

S14-13 ← *Link Back to Chapter 1 (Accounting Equation).* Use the statement of stockholders' equity in Exhibit 14-9, page 560, to answer the following questions about Allied Electronics Corporation.

1. Make a single journal entry to record Allied's declaration and payment of cash dividends during 20X5.
2. How much cash did the issuance of common stock bring in during 20X5?
3. What was the cost of the treasury stock that Allied purchased during 20X5? What was Allied's cost of the treasury stock that Allied sold during the year? For how much did Allied sell the treasury stock during 20X5?

Exercises

A+ online homework

Journalizing a stock dividend and reporting stockholders' equity
(Obj. 1)

E14-1 The stockholders' equity for Clifton, Inc., on December 31, 20X4, follows:

Stockholders' Equity	
Common stock, $1 par, 100,000 shares authorized, 50,000 shares issued	$ 50,000
Paid-in capital in excess of par	400,000
Retained earnings	120,000
Total stockholders' equity	$570,000

On April 30, 20X5, the market price of Clifton's common stock was $16 per share and the company distributed a 10% stock dividend.

Required

1. Journalize the distribution of the stock dividend.
2. Prepare the stockholders' equity section of the balance sheet after the stock dividend.

Journalizing cash and stock dividends
(Obj. 1)

E14-2 Hunter Racing Motors is authorized to issue 500,000 shares of $1 par common stock. The company issued 80,000 shares at $4 per share, and all 80,000 shares are outstanding. When the market price of common stock was $5 per share, Hunter distributed a 10% stock dividend. Later, Hunter declared and paid a $0.50 per share cash dividend.

Required

1. Journalize the distribution of the stock dividend.
2. Journalize both the declaration and the payment of the cash dividend.

Reporting stockholders' equity after a stock split
(Obj. 2)

E14-3 Harwood Travel, Inc., had the following stockholders' equity at May 31:

Common stock, $10 par, 200,000 shares authorized, 50,000 shares issued	$500,000
Paid-in capital in excess of par	100,000
Retained earnings	200,000
Total stockholders' equity	$800,000

On June 30, Harwood split its common stock 2 for 1. Make the necessary entry to record the stock split, and prepare the stockholders' equity section of the balance sheet immediately after the split.

Effects of stock issuance, dividends, and treasury stock transactions
(Obj. 1, 2, 3)

E14-4 Identify the effects of the following transactions on total stockholders' equity. Each transaction is independent.

a. Issuance of 50,000 shares of $10 par common at $15.
b. Purchase of 1,000 shares of treasury stock (par value $0.50) at $5 per share.
c. A 10% stock dividend. Before the dividend, 500,000 shares of $1 par common stock were outstanding; market value was $7 at the time of the dividend.
d. Sale of 600 shares of $1 par treasury stock for $5 per share. Cost of the treasury stock was $2 per share.
e. A 3-for-1 stock split. Prior to the split, 60,000 shares of $4 par common were outstanding.

Journalizing treasury stock transactions
(Obj. 3)

E14-5 Journalize the following transactions of **Foot Locker**, a chain of sports stores:

Feb. 4	Issued 20,000 shares of no-par common stock at $15 per share.
Apr. 22	Purchased 1,000 shares of treasury stock at $14 per share.
Aug. 22	Sold 600 shares of treasury stock at $20 per share.

Journalizing treasury stock transactions and reporting stockholders' equity **(Obj. 3)**

E14-6 Far Side, Inc., had the following stockholders' equity on November 30:

Stockholders' Equity	
Common stock, $5 par, 500,000 shares authorized, 50,000 shares issued	$250,000
Paid-in capital in excess of par	150,000
Retained earnings	520,000
Total stockholders' equity	$920,000

On December 30, Far Side purchased 5,000 shares of treasury stock at $10 per share. Journalize the purchase of the treasury stock, and prepare the stockholders' equity section of the balance sheet at December 31.

Reporting a retained earnings restriction **(Obj. 4)**

E14-7 The agreement under which Patterson, Inc., issued its long-term debt requires the restriction of $200,000 of the company's retained earnings balance. Total retained earnings is $250,000, and total paid-in capital is $500,000.

Required

Show how to report stockholders' equity on Patterson's balance sheet, assuming the following:

a. Patterson discloses the restriction in a note. Write the note.

b. Patterson appropriates retained earnings in the amount of the restriction and includes no note in its statements.

c. Patterson's cash balance is $100,000. What is the maximum amount of dividends Patterson can declare?

Preparing a multistep income statement **(Obj. 5)**

Student Resource CD

spreadsheet

E14-8 Schindler Corporation's accounting records include the following for 20X8:

Sales revenue	$410,000	Income tax expense—extraordinary gain	$ 6,000
Operating expenses (including income tax)	106,000	Income tax expense—change in depreciation method	3,000
Cumulative effect of change in depreciation method, a credit	7,000	Income tax saving—loss on discontinued operations	20,000
Cost of goods sold	245,000		
Loss on discontinued operations	50,000	Extraordinary gain	15,000

Required

Prepare a multistep income statement for 20X8. Omit earnings per share.

Computing earnings per share **(Obj. 5)**

E14-9 Tyler, Inc. earned net income of $74,000 for 20X6. The ledger reveals the following figures:

Preferred stock, $4.00 per year, no-par, 1,000 shares issued and outstanding	$ 50,000
Common stock, $10 par, 52,000 shares issued	520,000
Treasury stock, common, 2,000 shares at cost	36,000

Required

Compute Tyler's EPS for the year.

Computing earnings per share **(Obj. 5)**

E14-10 San Marcos, Inc., had 50,000 shares of common stock and 10,000 shares of 5%, $10 par preferred stock outstanding through December 31, 20X5. Income from continuing operations of 20X5 was $110,000, and loss on discontinued operations (net of income tax saving) was $8,000. The company had an extraordinary gain (net of tax) of $50,000.

Required

Compute San Marcos's EPS amounts for 20X5, starting with income from continuing operations.

Preparing a statement of retained earnings with a prior-period adjustment
(Obj. 6)

Student ResourceCD
spreadsheet

E14-11 The French Bakery reported a prior-period adjustment in 20X3. An accounting error caused net income of prior years to be understated by $5 million. Retained earnings at December 31, 20X2, as previously reported, stood at $395 million. Net income for 20X3 was $110 million, and dividends totaled $40 million.

Required

Prepare the company's statement of retained earnings for the year ended December 31, 20X3.

Preparing a combined statement of income and retained earnings
(Obj. 5, 6)

Student ResourceCD
spreadsheet

E14-12 The Ritz Hotel Company, a large hotel chain, had retained earnings of $410 million at December 31, 20X6. The company reported these figures for 20X7:

	($ Millions)
Net income	$140
Cash dividends—preferred	2
common	88

Required

Beginning with net income, prepare a combined statement of income and retained earnings for The Ritz Hotel Company for the year ended December 31, 20X7.

Computing comprehensive income
(Obj. 5)

E14-13 During 20X6, BMW Group earned income from continuing operations of $95,000. The company also sold its land-development segment (discontinued operations) at a gain of $30,000 and had an extraordinary loss of $8,000. At year-end, BMW had an unrealized loss on investments of $3,000.

1. Compute BMW's net income and comprehensive income for 20X6. All amounts are net of income taxes.
2. What would be the final EPS figure that BMW would report for 20X6? Show the amount. BMW had 20,000 shares of common stock (and no preferred stock) outstanding.

Preparing a statement of stockholders' equity
(Obj. 6)

E14-14 At December 31, 20X6, Labrador Corp. reported the following stockholders' equity.

Common stock, $5 par, 200,000 shares authorized, 120,000 shares issued	$ 600,000
Additional paid-in capital	100,000
Retained earnings	700,000
Treasury stock, 2,500 shares at cost	(80,000)
	$1,320,000

During 20X7, Labrador completed these transactions and events (listed in chronological order):

a. Sold 1,000 shares of treasury stock for $35 per share (cost of these shares was $30 per share).
b. Issued 500 shares of common stock at $20 per share.
c. Net income for the year was $200,000.
d. Declared and paid cash dividends of $100,000.

Required

Prepare Labrador Corp.'s statement of stockholders' equity for 20X7.

Recording a stock dividend and preparing a statement of stockholders' equity
(Obj. 1, 6)

E14-15 Omni Communications, Inc., began 20X5 with 2.9 million shares of $1 par common stock issued and outstanding. Beginning paid-in capital in excess of par was $6 million, and retained earnings was $7 million. In February 20X5, Omni issued 100,000 shares of stock at $11 per share. In September, when the stock's market price was $12 per share, the board of directors distributed a 10% stock dividend.

Required

1. Make the journal entries for the issuance of stock for cash and for the distribution of the 10% stock dividend.
2. Prepare the company's statement of stockholders' equity for the year ended December 31, 20X5.

Problems

(Group A)

A+ online homework

P14-1A **Titleist Sports Corporation** completed the following selected transactions during 20X6:

Journalizing stockholders' equity transactions
(Obj. 1, 3)

Student Resource CD
General Ledger (GL), QuickBooks (QB), Peachtree (PT)

Jan. 6	Declared a cash dividend on the 10,000 shares of $2.25, no-par preferred stock. Declared a $0.20 per share dividend on the 10,000 shares of common stock outstanding. The date of record is January 17, and the payment date is January 20.
Jan. 20	Paid the cash dividends.
Mar. 21	Split common stock 2 for 1 by calling in the 10,000 shares of $10 par common and issuing new stock in its place.
Apr. 18	Distributed a 10% stock dividend on the common stock. The market value of the common stock was $27 per share.
June 18	Purchased 2,000 shares of treasury common stock at $25 per share.
Dec. 22	Sold 1,000 shares of treasury common stock for $26 per share.

Required

Record the transactions in the general journal.

P14-2A The balance sheet of Quartz, Inc., at December 31, 20X5, reported 500,000 shares of $1 par common stock authorized with 100,000 shares issued. Paid-In Capital in Excess of Par had a balance of $300,000. Retained Earnings had a balance of $101,000. During 20X6, the company completed the following selected transactions:

Journalizing dividend and treasury stock transactions and reporting stockholders' equity
(Obj. 1, 2, 3)

Student Resource CD
GL, QB, PT

Feb. 15	Purchased 5,000 shares of the treasury stock at $4 per share.
Mar. 8	Sold 2,000 shares of treasury stock for $7 per share.
Sep. 28	Distributed a 10% stock dividend on the 97,000 shares of *outstanding* common stock. The market value of Quartz's common stock was $5 per share.
Dec. 31	Earned net income of $73,000 during the year. Closed net income to Retained Earnings.

Required

1. Record the transactions in the general journal. Explanations are not required.
2. Prepare the stockholders' equity section of the balance sheet at December 31, 20X6.

P14-3A Monahans Corporation is well positioned. Located in Tucson, Arizona, Monahans is the only company between Texas and California with reliable sources for its imported gifts. The company does a brisk business with specialty stores such as **Pier 1 Imports**. Monahans' recent success has made the company a prime target for a takeover. An investment group from Hong Kong is attempting to buy 51% of Monahans' outstanding stock against the wishes of Monahans' board of directors. Board members are convinced that the Hong Kong investors would sell the most desirable pieces of the business and leave little of value.

Purchasing treasury stock to fight off a takeover of the corporation
(Obj. 3)

At the most recent board meeting, several suggestions were advanced to fight off the hostile takeover bid. The suggestion with the most promise is to purchase a huge quantity of treasury stock. Monahans has the cash to carry out this plan.

Required

1. As a significant stockholder of Monahans Corporation, write a memorandum to explain to the board how the purchase of treasury stock would make it difficult for the Hong Kong group to take over Monahans. Include a discussion of the effect that purchasing treasury stock would have on stock outstanding and on the size of the corporation.
2. Suppose Monahans' management is successful in fighting off the takeover bid and later sells the treasury stock at prices greater than the purchase price. Explain what effect these sales will have on assets, stockholders' equity, and net income.

Journalizing dividend and treasury stock transactions; reporting retained earnings and stockholders' equity
(Obj. 1, 3)

Student Resource CD
GL, QB, PT

P14-4A The balance sheet of Swingline, Inc., at December 31, 20X8, presented the following stockholders' equity:

Paid-in capital:	
Common stock, $1 par, 250,000 shares authorized, 50,000 shares issued	$ 50,000
Paid-in capital in excess of par—common	350,000
Total paid-in capital	400,000
Retained earnings	99,000
Total stockholders' equity	$499,000

During 20X9, Swingline completed the following selected transactions:

Mar. 29	Distributed a 5% stock dividend on the common stock. The market value of Swingline common stock was $8 per share.
July 13	Purchased 2,000 shares of treasury stock at $8 per share.
Oct. 4	Sold 1,000 shares of treasury common stock for $9 per share.
Dec. 10	Declared a $0.20 per share cash dividend on the 51,500 shares of common stock outstanding. The date of record is December 17, and the payment date is January 2.
31	Closed the $71,000 net income to Retained Earnings.

Required

1. Record the transactions in the general journal.
2. Prepare the retained earnings statement at December 31, 20X9.
3. Prepare the stockholders' equity section of the balance sheet at December 31, 20X9.

Preparing a detailed income statement
(Obj. 5)

P14-5A The following information was taken from the records of Jeffries Corporation at June 30, 20X5:

Common stock, no-par, 22,000 shares authorized and issued	$350,000	Selling expenses	$ 120,000
Preferred stock, 6%, $25 par, 4,000 shares issued	100,000	General expenses	71,000
Retained earnings, beginning	63,000	Gain on discontinued operations	1,000
Income tax expense (tax saving):		Cost of goods sold	279,000
Continuing operations	28,000	Dividend revenue	19,000
Gain on discontinued operations	400	Treasury stock, common (2,000 shares)	28,000
Extraordinary loss (tax saving)	(15,400)	Extraordinary loss	42,000
		Net sales revenue	567,000

Required

Prepare a single-step income statement, including earnings per share, for Jeffries Corporation for the fiscal year ended June 30, 20X5.

P14-6A Eloy Santos, accountant for Airstream, Inc., was injured in an auto accident. Another employee prepared the following income statement for the fiscal year ended June 30, 20X4:

Preparing a corrected combined statement of income and retained earnings **(Obj. 5)**

Airstream, Inc.
Income Statement
June 30, 20X4

Revenues and gains:		
Sales		$733,000
Paid-in capital in excess of par—common		111,000
Total revenues and gains		844,000
Expenses and losses:		
Cost of goods sold	$383,000	
Selling expenses	103,000	
General expenses	91,000	
Sales returns	22,000	
Sales discounts	10,000	
Dividends	15,000	
Income tax expense—continuing operations	32,000	
Total expenses and losses		656,000
Income from operations		188,000
Other gains and losses:		
Loss on discontinued operations		(15,000)
Net income		$173,000
Earnings per share		$8.65

The individual *amounts* listed on the income statement are correct. However, some accounts are reported incorrectly, and one doesn't belong on the income statement at all. Also, income tax has not been applied to all appropriate figures. The income tax rate on discontinued operations is 40%. Airstream issued 24,000 shares of common stock in 20X1 and held 4,000 shares as treasury stock during fiscal year 20X4. Retained earnings at June 30, 20X3, was $209,000.

Required

Prepare a corrected combined statement of income and retained earnings for the fiscal year ended June 30, 20X4. Prepare the income statement in single-step format, and include earnings per share.

P14-7A The capital structure of Avian Company at December 31, 20X7, included 5,000 shares of $2 preferred stock and 120,000 shares of common stock. Common shares outstanding during 20X8 were 120,000. Income from continuing operations during 20X8 was $370,000. The company discontinued a segment of the business at a gain of $60,000 and also had an extraordinary loss of $48,000. Avian's board of directors has restricted $300,000 of retained earnings for expansion of the company's office facilities.

Computing earnings per share and reporting a retained earnings restriction **(Obj. 4, 5)**

Required

1. Compute Avian's earnings per share for 20X8. Start with income from continuing operations. Income and loss amounts are net of income tax.
2. Show two ways of reporting Avian's retained earnings restriction. Retained earnings at December 31, 20X7, was $120,000, and Avian declared cash dividends of $100,000 during 20X8.

Using a statement of stockholders' equity **(Obj. 6)**

P14-8A Business Analysts, Inc., reported the following statement of stockholders' equity for the year ended September 30, 20X9:

Business Analysts, Inc.

Statement of Stockholders' Equity
Year Ended September 30, 20X9

(Dollar amounts in thousands)	Common Stock	Additional Paid-in Capital	Retained Earnings	Treasury Stock	Total
Balance, September 30, 20X8	$173	$2,118	$1,706	$(18)	$3,979
Net income			520		520
Cash dividends			(117)		(117)
Issuance of stock (5,000 shares)	9	46			55
Stock dividend	18	92	(110)		—
Sale of treasury stock		5		11	16
Balance, September 30, 20X9	$200	$2,261	$1,999	$ (7)	$4,453

Required

1. What is the par value of the company's common stock?
2. At what price per share did the company issue its common stock during the year?
3. What was the cost of treasury stock sold during the year? What was the selling price of the treasury stock sold? What was the increase in total stockholders' equity from selling the treasury stock?
4. What overall effect did the stock dividend have on total stockholders' equity?

Problems

A+ online homework

(Group B)

Journalizing stockholders' equity transactions
(Obj. 1,3)

Student Resource CD
GL, QB, PT

P14-1B Alan Cook Corp. completed the following transactions during 20X9:

Feb. 2	Declared a cash dividend on the 5%, $100 par preferred stock (1,000 shares outstanding). Declared a $0.20 per share dividend on the 100,000 shares of common stock outstanding. The date of record is February 15 and the payment date is February 23.
Feb. 23	Paid the cash dividends.
June 10	Split common stock 2 for 1 by calling in the 100,000 shares of $10 par common and issuing new stock in its place.
July 30	Distributed a 10% stock dividend on the common stock. The market value of the common stock was $15 per share.
Oct. 26	Purchased 2,500 shares of treasury common stock at $14 per share.
Nov. 8	Sold 1,000 shares of treasury common stock for $17 per share.

Required

Record the transactions in Allen Cook's general journal.

Journalizing dividend and treasury stock transactions and reporting stockholders' equity
(Obj. 1, 2, 3)

Student Resource CD
GL, QB, PT

P14-2B The balance sheet of Recreation Concepts, Inc., at December 31, 20X6, reported 100,000 shares of no-par common stock authorized, with 30,000 shares issued and a Common Stock balance of $180,000. Retained Earnings had a balance of $140,000. During 20X7, the company completed the following selected transactions:

Mar. 15	Purchased 5,000 shares of treasury stock at $8 per share.
Apr. 30	Distributed a 20% stock dividend on the 25,000 shares of *outstanding* common stock. The market value of Recreation Concepts common stock was $10 per share.
Oct. 8	Sold 2,000 shares of treasury stock for $12 per share.
31	Earned net income of $110,000 during the year. Closed net income to Retained Earnings.

Required

1. Record the transactions in the general journal. Explanations are not required.
2. Prepare the stockholders' equity section of Recreation Concepts' balance sheet at December 31, 20X7.

Increasing dividends to fight off a takeover of the corporation
(Obj. 1)

P14-3B Cooper Fashions is ideally positioned in the clothing business. Located in Toledo, Ohio, Cooper is the only company with a distribution network for its imported goods. The company does a brisk business with specialty stores such as **Neiman Marcus, Saks Fifth Avenue**, and **Nordstrom**. Cooper's recent success has made the company a prime target for a takeover. Against the wishes of Cooper's board of directors, an investment group from Canada is attempting to buy 51% of Cooper's outstanding stock. Board members are convinced that the Canadian investors would sell off the most desirable pieces of the business and leave little of value.

At the most recent board meeting, several suggestions were advanced to fight off the hostile takeover bid. One suggestion is to increase the stock outstanding by distributing a 100% stock dividend. The intent is to spread the company's ownership in order to make it harder for the Canadian group to buy a controlling interest.

Required

As a significant stockholder of Cooper Fashions, write a short memo to explain to the board whether distributing the stock dividend would make it more difficult for the investor group to take over Cooper. Include in your memo a discussion of the effect that the stock dividend would have on assets, liabilities, and total stockholders' equity—that is, the dividend's effect on the size of the corporation.

Journalizing dividend and treasury stock transactions; reporting retained earnings and stockholders' equity
(Obj. 1, 3)

Student Resource CD
GL, QB, PT

P14-4B The balance sheet of Beta Concepts, Inc., at December 31, 20X6, reported the following stockholders' equity:

Paid-in capital:	
Common stock, $10 par, 100,000 shares authorized,	
20,000 shares issued	$200,000
Paid-in capital in excess of par—common	300,000
Total paid-in capital	500,000
Retained earnings	180,000
Total stockholders' equity	$680,000

During 20X7, Beta Concepts completed the following selected transactions:

Feb. 6	Distributed a 10% stock dividend on the common stock. The market value of Beta Concepts' stock was $24 per share.
July 29	Purchased 2,000 shares of treasury stock at $21 per share.
Nov. 13	Sold 400 shares of treasury stock for $22 per share.
27	Declared a $0.30 per share cash dividend on the 20,400 shares of common stock outstanding. The date of record is December 17, and the payment date is January 7, 20X8.
Dec. 31	Closed the $70,000 net income to Retained Earnings.

Required

1. Record the transactions in the general journal.
2. Prepare a retained earnings statement at December 31, 20X7.
3. Prepare the stockholders' equity section of the balance sheet at December 31, 20X7.

Preparing a detailed income statement
(Obj. 5)

P14-5B The following information was taken from the records of Courtyard Classics, Inc., at September 30, 20X8.

Cost of goods sold	$435,000	General expenses	$133,000
Retained earnings, beginning	88,000	Preferred stock, $2, no-par, 5,000 shares issued	200,000
Selling expenses	121,000	Common stock, $10 par, 25,000 shares authorized and issued	250,000
Income from discontinued operations	8,000	Net sales revenue	837,000
Income tax expense (tax saving):		Treasury stock, common (1,000 shares)	11,000
Continuing operations	72,000	Extraordinary loss	30,000
Income from discontinued operations	2,000		
Extraordinary loss (tax saving)	(12,000)		

Required

Prepare a single-step income statement, including earnings per share, for Courtyard Classics, Inc., for the fiscal year ended September 30, 20X8.

Preparing a corrected combined statement of income and retained earnings
(Obj. 5)

P14-6B Quincy Caldwell, accountant for Brooks Furniture Company, was injured in a boating accident. Another employee prepared the accompanying income statement for the year ended December 31, 20X3.

The individual *amounts* listed on the income statement are correct. However, some accounts are reported incorrectly, and one doesn't belong on the income statement at all. Also, income tax has not been applied to all appropriate figures. The income tax rate on discontinued operations was 40%. Brooks Furniture Company issued 52,000 shares of common stock in 20X1 and held 2,000 shares as treasury stock during 20X3. Retained earnings at December 31, 20X2, was $361,000.

Brooks Furniture Company
Income Statement
Year Ended December 31, 20X3

Revenue and gains:		
Sales		$362,000
Paid-in capital in excess of par—common		90,000
Total revenues and gains		452,000
Expenses and losses:		
Cost of goods sold	$105,000	
Selling expenses	67,000	
General expenses	61,000	
Sales returns	11,000	
Sales discounts	6,000	
Dividends	7,000	
Income tax expense	20,000	
Total expenses and losses		277,000
Income from operations		175,000
Other gains and losses:		
Loss on discontinued operations		(3,000)
Net income		$172,000
Earnings per share		$3.44

Required

Prepare a corrected combined statement of income and retained earnings for 20X3; include earnings per share. Prepare the income statement in single-step format.

Computing earnings per share and reporting a retained earnings restriction
(Obj. 4, 5)

P14-7B The capital structure of Smirnoff, Inc., at December 31, 20X6, included 20,000 shares of $1.25 preferred stock and 46,000 shares of common stock. Common stock outstanding during 20X7 totaled 46,000 shares. Income from continuing operations during 20X7 was $94,000. The company discontinued a segment of the business at a gain of $23,000, and also had an extraordinary gain of $11,500. Smirnoff's board of directors restricts $60,000 of retained earnings for contingencies.

Required

1. Compute Smirnoff's earnings per share for 20X7. Start with income from continuing operations. All income and loss amounts are net of income tax.
2. Show two ways of reporting Smirnoff's retained earnings restriction. Retained earnings at December 31, 20X6, was $100,000, and Smirnoff declared cash dividends of $20,000 during 20X7.

P14-8B Public Trust, Inc., reported the following statement of stockholders' equity for the year ended October 31, 20X4:

Using a statement of stockholders' equity **(Obj. 6)**

Public Trust, Inc.
Statement of Stockholders' Equity
Year Ended October 31, 20X4

(Dollar amounts in thousands)	Common Stock	Additional Paid-In Capital	Retained Earnings	Treasury Stock	Total
Balance, Oct. 31, 20X3	$427	$1,622	$904	$(117)	$2,836
Net income			336		336
Cash dividends			(194)		(194)
Issuance of stock (60,000 shares)	120	264			384
Stock dividend	22	48	(70)		—
Sale of treasury stock		9		19	28
Balance, Oct. 31, 20X4	$569	$1,943	$976	$ (98)	$3,390

Required

Answer these questions about Public Trust's stockholders' equity transactions.

1. What is the par value of the company's common stock?
2. At what price per share did Public Trust issue its common stock during the year?
3. What was the cost of treasury stock sold during the year? What was the selling price of the treasury stock sold? What was the increase in total stockholders' equity from selling the treasury stock?
4. What effect did the stock dividend have on total stockholders' equity?

APPLY *Your Knowledge*

Decision Cases

Case 1. Modem Transmission, Inc., had the following stockholders' equity amounts on June 30, 20X2:

Analyzing cash dividends and stock dividends **(Obj. 1)**

Common stock, no-par, 100,000 shares issued	$ 750,000
Retained earnings	790,000
Total stockholders' equity	$1,540,000

In the past, Modem has paid an annual cash dividend of $1 per share. Despite the large retained earnings balance, the board of directors wished to conserve cash for expansion. The board delayed the payment of cash dividends and in July distributed a 10% stock dividend. During August, the company's cash position improved. The board declared and paid a cash dividend of $0.9091 per share in September.

Suppose you owned 5,000 shares of Modem common stock, acquired three years ago, prior to the 10% stock dividend. The market price of the stock was $30 per share before any of these dividends.

Required

1. What amount of cash dividends did you receive last year—before the stock dividend? What amount of cash dividends will you receive after the stock dividend?
2. How does the stock dividend affect your proportionate ownership in Modem Transmission, Inc.? Explain.
3. Immediately after the stock dividend was distributed, the market value of Modem stock decreased from $30 per share to $27.273 per share. Does this decrease represent a loss to you? Explain.

Reporting special items
(Obj. 3, 5)

Case 2. The following accounting issues have arisen at T-Shirts Plus, Inc.:

1. T-Shirts Plus earned a significant profit in the year ended November 30, 20X6, because land that it held was purchased by the State of North Carolina for a new highway. The company proposes to treat the sale of land as operating revenue. Why do you think the company is proposing this plan? Is this disclosure appropriate?
2. Corporations sometimes purchase their own stock. When asked why they do so, T-Shirts Plus management responds that the stock is undervalued. What advantage would T-Shirts Plus gain by buying and selling its own undervalued stock?
3. The treasurer of T-Shirts Plus wants to report a large loss as an extraordinary item because the company produced too much product and cannot sell it. Why do you think the treasurer wants to report the loss as extraordinary? Would that be acceptable?

Ethical Issue

← *Link Back to Chapter 6 (Accounting Principles).* High Plains Production Company is an independent oil producer in Midland, Texas. In February, geologists discovered a pool of oil that tripled the company's proven reserves. Prior to disclosing the new oil to the public, top managers of the company quietly bought most of High Plains' stock for themselves. After the discovery was announced, the High Plains' stock price rose from $7 to $52.

Required

1. Did High Plains managers behave ethically? Explain your answer.
2. Identify the accounting principle relevant to this situation. Review Chapter 6 if necessary.
3. Who was helped and who was harmed by management's action?

Financial Statement Case

Complex income statement, earnings per share
(Obj. 5)

Use the **Amazon.com** financial statements in Appendix A to answer the following questions.

Required

1. Study Amazon.com's income statement, which the company labels "consolidated statement of operations." *Consolidated* means that Amazon owns other companies. Amazon reported one "special" item of income on its income statement. What was the special item, and what was its amount for 2002? Was this special item a gain or a loss? How can you tell?
2. Show how Amazon.com computed earnings per share of $(0.39) for 2002.
3. Prepare a T-account to show the beginning and ending balances and all activity in Retained Earnings (Accumulated Deficit) for 2002.

Team Project

Required

Obtain the annual reports (or annual report data) of five well-known companies. You can get the reports either from your college library or by mailing a request directly to the company (allow two weeks for delivery). Or you can visit the Web site for this book (http://www.prenhall.com/horngren) or the SEC EDGAR database, which includes the financial reports of most well-known companies.

1. After selecting five companies, examine their income statements to search for the following items:
   a. Income from continuing operations
   b. Discontinued operations
   c. Extraordinary gains and losses
   d. Cumulative effects of accounting changes
   e. Net income or net loss
   f. Earnings-per-share data
2. Study the companies' balance sheets to see
   a. What classes of stock each company has issued.
   b. Which item carries a larger balance—the Common Stock account, or Paid-In Capital in Excess of Par (also labeled Additional Paid-In Capital).
   c. What percentage of each company's total stockholders' equity is made up of retained earnings.
   d. Whether the company has treasury stock. If so, how many shares and how much is the cost?
3. Examine each company's statement of stockholders' equity for evidence of
   a. Cash dividends
   b. Stock dividends (Some companies use the term *stock split* to refer to a large stock dividend.)
   c. Treasury stock purchases and sales
4. As directed by your instructor, either write a report or present your findings to your class. You may be unable to understand *everything* you find, but neither can the Wall Street analysts! You will be amazed at how much you have learned.

For Internet exercises, go to the Web site www.prenhall.com/horngren.

CHAPTER 15

Long-Term Liabilities

A+ TIPS CHECK YOUR RESOURCES

- Visit the www.prenhall.com/horngren **Web site** for self-study quizzes, video clips, and other resources
- Try the **Quick Check** exercise at the end of the chapter to test your knowledge
- Learn the **key terms**
- Do the **Starter** exercises keyed in the margins
- Work the **mid-** and **end-of-chapter summary problems**
- Use the **Concept Links** to review material in other chapters
- Search the **CD** for review materials by chapter or by key word
- Watch the **tutorial videos** to review key concepts

LEARNING OBJECTIVES

1. Account for bonds payable transactions
2. Measure interest expense by the effective-interest method
3. Account for retirement and conversion of bonds payable
4. Report liabilities on the balance sheet
5. Show the advantages and disadvantages of borrowing

What's the best way to finance a company—issue stock or borrow the money? When the stock market declines, companies find it hard to sell their stock. They have to look to the bond market for cash to expand. For example, Amazon.com has borrowed by issuing convertible notes payable. Convertible bonds offer advantages for companies that need to borrow and for individuals with money to invest. By issuing convertible bonds, companies can borrow at lower interest rates than if they issued straight bonds. Then if a company's stock goes up, investors can swap the bonds for stock. Amazon gets a lower interest rate and investors can benefit if Amazon's stock price rises. They can convert the bonds into stock.

Amazon.com

Accessing bond information has never been easier. You can log on to www.investinginbonds.com for topics such as What Are Bonds? Also, www.convertbond.com provides data on convertible bonds plus chat rooms and search functions. These information sources make it easier for companies to borrow and for people to make informed investment decisions.

Sources: Forbes, May 22, 2000, "Best of the Web," p. 86; Jennifer Ablan, "Volume of Convertible Bond Offerings Continues to Rise with Big Deals by Technology Concerns," *The Wall Street Journal*, July 13, 2000, p. C25. ■

Sitemap

- Bonds: Introduction
- Issuing Bonds Payable
- Effective-Interest Method
- Additional Bond Topics
- Bonds versus Stock
- Lease Liabilities
- Appendix: Time Value of Money

Chapters 13 and 14 showed two ways to finance operations. Chapter 13 covered the stock accounts and additional paid-in capital, and Chapter 14 discussed profitable operations and retained earnings. This chapter shows the third way to finance a company: borrowing on long-term liabilities. The chapter appendix on the time value of money provides background on the valuation of long-term liabilities.

Before launching into accounting for bonds payable, let's compare stocks and bonds. The following chart shows how stocks and bonds differ.

Stocks	Bonds
1. Stock represents the *ownership* (equity) of the corporation.	1. Bonds represent a *liability* of the corporation.
2. Each shareholder is an *owner* of the corporation.	2. Each bondholder is a *creditor* of the corporation.
3. The corporation *may or may not* pay dividends.	3. The corporation *must* pay interest.
4. Dividends are *not* an expense of the corporation.	4. Interest is a *tax-deductible* expense of the corporation.
5. Corporation is *not* obligated to repay stock amounts to the shareholders.	5. Corporation *must* repay the bonds payable at maturity.

- ■ Bonds: Introduction
- □ Issuing Bonds Payable
- □ Effective-Interest Method
- □ Additional Bond Topics
- □ Bonds versus Stock
- □ Lease Liabilities
- □ Appendix: Time Value of Money

Bonds Payable
Groups of notes payable issued to multiple lenders called bondholders.

Student Resource CD
bonds payable, bond pricing, market interest rate, present value, stated interest rate

Bonds: An Introduction

Well-known companies such as Amazon.com, Inc., and eBay cannot borrow billions from a single lender because no bank will loan that much to a single company. Then how do corporations borrow the huge amounts they need to expand? They issue bonds payable to the public. **Bonds payable** are groups of notes issued to multiple lenders, called bondholders. Amazon can borrow millions of dollars from thousands of individual investors. Each investor buys a modest amount of Amazon bonds.

Purchasers of the bonds each receive a bond certificate, which shows the borrower's name, exactly like a note payable. The certificate states the *principal*, which is the amount the company has borrowed. This figure, typically stated in units of $1,000, is also called the bond's maturity value, or par value. The bond obligates the issuing company to pay the holder the principal amount at a specific future date, called the maturity date.

Bondholders lend their money to earn interest. The bond certificate states the interest rate that the issuer will pay and the dates the interest payments are due (generally twice a year). Exhibit 15-1 shows an actual bond certificate issued by Washington Public Power Supply System (WPPSS).

Exhibit 15-1 Bond Certificate (Adapted)

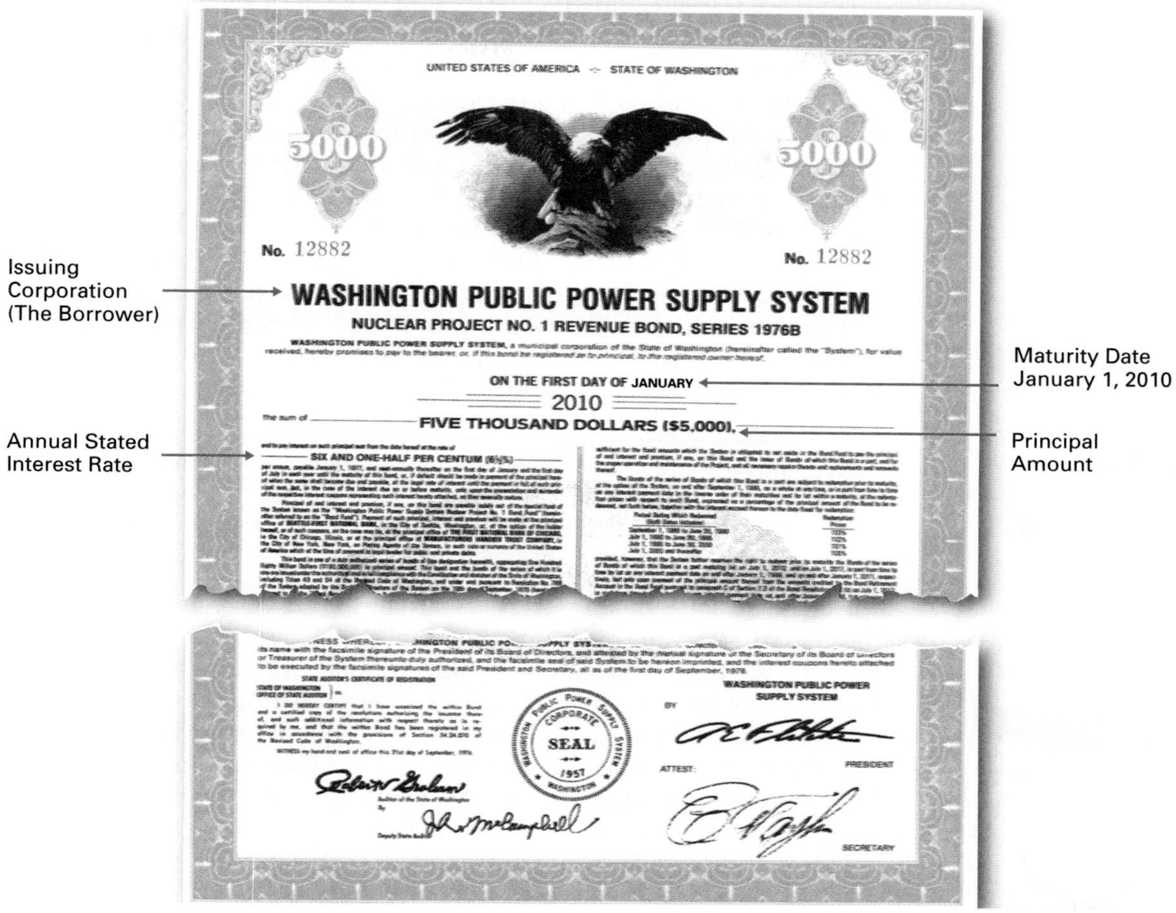

Review these bond fundamentals in Exhibit 15-1.

- ***Principal amount*** (also called maturity value, or par value). The amount the borrower must pay back to the lender.
- ***Maturity date*** The date on which the borrower must pay the principal amount to the lender.
- ***Stated interest rate*** The annual rate of interest that the borrower pays the lender.

Types of Bonds

All the bonds in a particular issue may mature at a specified time **(term bonds)**, or they may mature in installments **(serial bonds)**. Serial bonds are like installment notes payable.

Secured, or mortgage, bonds give the bondholder the right to take specified assets of the issuer (called *collateral*) if the company fails to pay interest or principal. A **mortgage** is an example of a secured note or bond. Unsecured bonds, called **debentures**, are backed only by the good faith of the borrower.

Term Bonds
Bonds that all mature at the same time for a particular issue.

Serial Bonds
Bonds that mature in installments over a period of time.

Mortgage
Borrower's promise to transfer the legal title to certain assets to the lender if the debt is not paid on schedule.

Debentures
Unsecured bonds backed only by the good faith of the borrower.

Bond Prices

A bond issued at a price above its maturity value is said to be issued at a **premium**, and a bond issued at a price below maturity value has a **discount**. As a bond nears maturity, its market price moves toward maturity value. On the

Premium
Excess of a bond's issue price over its maturity value. Also called **bond premium**.

Discount (on a Bond)
Excess of a bond's maturity value over its issue price. Also called a **bond discount**.

maturity date, the market value of a bond exactly equals its maturity value because the company pays that amount to retire the bond.

After a bond is issued, investors may buy and sell it through the bond market just as they buy and sell stocks through the stock market. The most famous bond market is the New York Exchange, which lists several thousand bonds. Bond prices are quoted at a percentage of their maturity value. For example, a $1,000 bond quoted at 100 is bought or sold for $1,000, which is 100% of its maturity value. The same bond quoted at 101.5 has a market price of $1,015 (101.5% of maturity value, or $1,000 × 1.015). A $1,000 bond quoted at 88.375 means 88.375% of $1,000, and it is priced at $883.75 ($1,000 × 0.88375).

✔ Starter 15-1

Exhibit 15-2 contains price information for the bonds of Ohio Edison Company, taken from *The Wall Street Journal*. On this particular day, 12 of Ohio Edison's 9 1/2% bonds maturing in 2006 (indicated by 06) were traded. The bonds' highest price on this day was $795 ($1,000 × 0.795). The lowest price of the day was $784.50 ($1,000 × 0.7845). The closing price (last sale of the day) was $795.

Exhibit 15-2

Bond Price Information for Ohio Edison Company (OhEd)

Bonds	Volume	High	Low	Close
OhEd 9 1/2 of 06	12	79.5	78.45	79.5

Present Value

The appendix to this chapter covers the time value of money in detail.

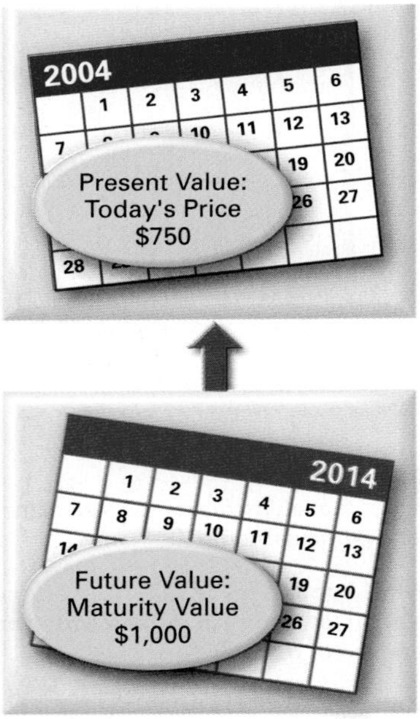

Present value is always less than future value.

Money earns income over time, a fact called the *time value of money*. Let's examine how the time value of money affects bond prices. Assume that a bond with a face value of $1,000 reaches maturity three years from today and carries no interest. As an investor, would you pay $1,000 to purchase the bond? No, because paying $1,000 today to receive the same amount later provides you with no income on the investment. How much would you pay today in order to receive $1,000 in three years? The answer is some amount *less* than $1,000. Suppose $750 is a fair price. By investing $750 now to receive $1,000 later, you will earn $250 over the three years. The company that issued the bonds sees the transaction this way: It pays you $250 interest for the use of your $750 for three years.

The amount that a person would invest *at the present time* to receive a greater amount in the future is called the **present value**. In our example, $750 is the present value, and the $1,000 to be received in three years is the future amount.

Present value is always less than future value. The difference between present value and future value is interest. We show how to compute present value in the chapter appendix. If your instructor so directs you, study the appendix now.

Bond Interest Rates

Bonds are sold at market price, which is the maximum amount an investor will pay for a bond. Market price is the bond's present value, which is the sum of the present value of the principal payment plus the present value of all the stated interest payments, which may be semiannual, annual, or quarterly.

Two interest rates work together to set the price of a bond:

- The **stated interest rate** is the interest rate that determines the amount of cash interest the borrower pays each year. The stated rate is printed on the bond and *does not change*. For example, Amazon.com's 10% notes payable have a stated interest rate of 10%. Thus, Amazon pays $1,000 of interest annually on each $10,000 bond. Each semiannual interest payment is $500 ($10,000 × 0.10 × 1/2).
- The **market interest rate** is the rate investors demand for loaning their money. The market interest rate *varies* daily. A company may issue bonds with a stated interest rate that differs from the market interest rate.

Present Value
Amount a person would invest now to receive a greater amount in the future.

Stated Interest Rate
Interest rate that determines the amount of cash interest the borrower pays and the investor receives each year.

Market Interest Rate
Interest rate that investors demand in order to loan their money. Also called the **effective interest rate**.

Amazon.com may issue its 10% notes when the market rate has risen to 11%. Will the Amazon notes attract investors in this market? No, because investors can earn 11% on other bonds and notes. Therefore, investors will purchase Amazon notes only at a price less than maturity value. The difference between the lower price and the notes' maturity value is a *discount*.

✔ Starter 15-2

Conversely, if the market interest rate is 8%, Amazon's 10% notes will be so attractive that investors will pay more than maturity value for them. The difference between the higher price and maturity value is a *premium*. Exhibit 15-3 shows how the stated interest rate and the market interest rate work together to determine the price of a bond.

Exhibit 15-3

Interaction of the Stated Interest Rate and the Market Interest Rate to Determine the Price of a Bond

Example: Bond with a Stated Interest Rate of 8%

Bond's Stated Interest Rate*		Market Interest Rate**		Issue Price of Bonds Payable
8%	=	8%	⇒	Maturity (par) value
8%	<	10%	⇒	Discount [price below maturity (par) value]
8%	>	6%	⇒	Premium [price above maturity (par) value]

*Determines the amount of each cash interest payment.
**Used to set the bond's market price.

✔ Starter 15-3

✔ Starter 15-4

☐ Bonds: Introduction
■ Issuing Bonds Payable
☐ Effective-Interest Method
☐ Additional Bond Topics
☐ Bonds versus Stock
☐ Lease Liabilities
☐ Appendix: Time Value of Money

Issuing Bonds Payable to Borrow Money

The basic entry to record issuing bonds payable debits Cash and credits Bonds Payable. The company may issue bonds for three different bond prices:

- At *maturity* (*par*) value
- At a *discount*
- At a *premium*

We begin with the simplest case: issuing bonds at maturity (par) value.

Issuing Bonds Payable at Maturity (Par) Value

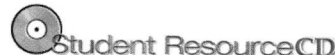

Account for bonds payable transactions

Student ResourceCD

amortizing bonds, bonds payable, bond discount, bond premium, stated interest rate

Suppose Amazon.com, Inc., has $50,000 of 8% bonds payable that mature in 5 years. Assume that Amazon issues these bonds at maturity (par) value on January 1, 2002. The issuance entry is

2002			
Jan. 1	Cash	50,000	
	Bonds Payable................		50,000
	Issued bonds payable.		

Amazon, the borrower, makes this one-time journal entry to record the receipt of cash and the issuance of bonds payable. Interest payments occur each January 1 and July 1. Amazon's entry to record the first semiannual interest payment is

2002			
July 1	Interest Expense ($50,000 × 0.08 × 6/12)	2,000	
	Cash		2,000
	Paid semiannual interest.		

At maturity, Amazon.com will record payment of the bonds as follows:

✔ Starter 15-5

2007			
Jan. 1	Bonds Payable.....................	50,000	
	Cash		50,000
	Paid off bonds payable at maturity.		

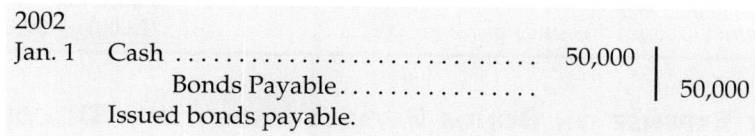

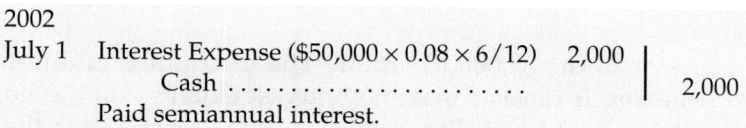

Stop & Think

How much interest expense will **Amazon.com** record for each year on these bonds?

Answer: $4,000 ($50,000 × 0.08)

Now we turn to the issuance of bonds payable at a discount.

Issuing Bonds Payable at a Discount

Bonds are often issued at a discount. We know that market conditions may force the issuing corporation to accept a discount price for its bonds. Suppose Amazon.com, Inc., issues $100,000 of its 9%, five-year bonds when the market interest rate is 9 1/2%. The market price of the bonds drops to 98, which means 98% of par value. Amazon receives $98,000 ($100,000 × 0.98) at issuance and makes the following journal entry:

2002			
Jan. 1	Cash ($100,000 × 0.98)	98,000	
	Discount on Bonds Payable	2,000	
	Bonds Payable		100,000
	Issued bonds payable at a discount.		

After posting, the bond accounts have these balances:

Bonds Payable		Discount on Bonds Payable	
	100,000	2,000	

Discount on Bonds Payable is a contra account to Bonds Payable. Bonds Payable minus the discount gives the carrying amount of the bonds. The relationship between Bonds Payable and the Discount account is similar to the relationship between Equipment and Accumulated Depreciation. Amazon would report these bonds payable as follows:

Long-term liabilities:		
Bonds payable	$100,000	
Less: Discount on bonds payable	(2,000)	$98,000

Interest Expense on Bonds Payable Issued at a Discount We saw that the stated interest rate and the market interest rate may differ. The market interest rate was 9 1/2% when Amazon.com issued its 9% bonds. The 1/2% interest-rate difference created the $2,000 discount on the bonds. Investors were willing to pay only $98,000 for a $100,000, 9% bond when they could purchase similar bonds and earn 9 1/2% on them. Amazon thus borrowed $98,000 cash but must pay $100,000 cash when the bonds mature five years later.

What happens to the $2,000 discount? The discount is additional interest expense to Amazon. It raises Amazon's interest expense on the bonds to the market interest rate of 9 1/2%. For each accounting period over the life of the bonds, the discount is accounted for as interest expense through a process called *amortization*. Amortization is the gradual reduction of an item over time.

Straight-Line Amortization of Bond Discount We can amortize a bond discount by dividing it into equal amounts for each interest period. This method is called *straight-line amortization*. In our example, the initial discount is $2,000, and there are 10 semiannual interest periods during the bonds' 5-year life.

Therefore, 1/10 of the $2,000 ($200) of bond discount is amortized each interest period. Amazon.com's first semiannual interest entry is[1]

2002			
July 1	Interest Expense	4,700	
	Cash ($100,000 × 0.09 × 6/12) ...		4,500
	Discount on Bonds Payable ($2,000/10)................		200
	Paid semiannual interest and amortized bond discount.		

Interest expense of $4,700 for the six-month period is the sum of

- The stated interest ($4,500, which is paid in cash)
- *Plus* the amortization of discount ($200)

✔ Starter 15-6

Discount on Bonds Payable is credited to amortize its balance. Ten amortization entries will decrease the discount to zero, and the carrying amount of the bonds payable will increase to the maturity value of $100,000.

Finally, the entry to pay off the bonds at maturity is

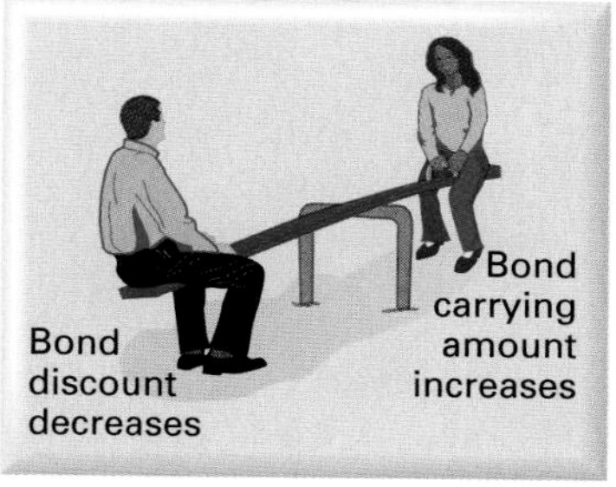

2007			
Jan. 1	Bonds Payable....................	100,000	
	Cash		100,000
	Paid off bonds payable at maturity.		

Stop & Think

How much interest expense will **Amazon** record each year on these bonds? How much cash interest will Amazon pay each year? What causes the difference?

Answer: Interest expense each year: $9,400 ($4,700 × 2)
Cash interest paid each year: $9,000 ($4,500 × 2)

The difference is caused by amortization of the bond discount.

Issuing Bonds Payable at a Premium

The issuance of bonds at a premium is rare because companies don't like to pay a stated interest rate higher than the market rate. To illustrate a bond premium, let's change the Amazon.com example. Assume that the market interest rate is 8% when Amazon issues its 9%, five-year bonds. Because 9% bonds are attractive in this market, investors will pay a premium to acquire them. Suppose the bonds are priced at 104 (104% of maturity value). In that case, Amazon receives $104,000 cash upon issuance. The entry to borrow money and issue bonds is

2002			
Jan. 1	Cash ($100,000 × 1.04)	104,000	
	Bonds Payable		100,000
	Premium on Bonds Payable ...		4,000
	Issued bonds payable at a premium.		

---

[1]Some accountants record the payment of interest and the amortization of bond discount in two separate entries, as follows:

2002			
July 1	Interest Expense.................................	4,500	
	Cash ($100,000 × 0.09 × 6/12)................		4,500
	Paid semiannual interest.		
July 1	Interest Expense.................................	200	
	Discount on Bonds Payable ($2,000/10).......		200
	Amortized discount on bonds payable.		

After posting, the bond accounts have the following balances:

Bonds Payable		Premium on Bonds Payable	
	100,000		4,000

Premium on Bonds Payable is added to Bonds Payable to determine the carrying amount of the bonds. Amazon.com would report these bonds payable as follows:

Long-term liabilities:		
Bonds payable	$100,000	
Plus: Premium on bonds payable	4,000	$104,000

INTEREST EXPENSE ON BONDS PAYABLE ISSUED AT A PREMIUM The 1% difference between the 9% stated interest rate on the bonds and the 8% market interest rate creates the $4,000 premium. Amazon borrows $104,000 cash but must pay only $100,000 at maturity. The premium is like a savings of interest expense to Amazon. The premium cuts Amazon's cost of borrowing and reduces interest expense to 8%, the market rate. We amortize the bond premium as a decrease in interest expense over the life of the bonds.

STRAIGHT-LINE AMORTIZATION OF BOND PREMIUM In our example, the beginning premium is $4,000, and there are 10 semiannual interest periods during the bonds' 5-year life. Therefore, 1/10 of the $4,000 ($400) of bond premium is amortized each interest period. Amazon.com's first semiannual interest entry is[2]

2002			
July 1	Interest Expense	4,100	
	Premium on Bonds Payable ($4,000/10)	400	
	Cash ($100,000 × 0.09 × 6/12)		4,500
	Paid semiannual interest and amortized bond premium.		

✔ Starter 15-7

Interest expense of $4,100 is

- The stated interest ($4,500, which is paid in cash)
- *Minus* the amortization of the premium

Stop & Think

Consider bonds issued at a discount. Which will be greater, the cash interest paid per period or the amount of interest expense? Answer the same question for bonds issued at a premium.

Answer: Discount: Interest expense > Stated interest paid
Premium: Stated interest paid > Interest expense

[2]The payment of interest and the amortization of bond premium can be recorded in separate entries as follows:

2002			
July 1	Interest Expense	4,500	
	Cash ($100,000 × 0.09 × 6/12)		4,500
	Paid semiannual interest.		
July 1	Premium on Bonds Payable ($4,000/10)	400	
	Interest Expense		400
	Amortized premium on bonds payable.		

Reporting Bonds Payable

Bonds payable are reported on the balance sheet at maturity value plus bond premium or minus bond discount. For example, in the preceding example of a bond premium, Amazon.com would report the following on its balance sheet at December 31, 2002:

Long-term liabilities:		
Bonds payable	$100,000	
Plus: Premium on bonds payable [$4,000 – (2 × $400)]	3,200	$103,200

Over the life of the bonds, 10 amortization entries will decrease the premium to zero. The payment at maturity will debit Bonds Payable and credit cash for $100,000.

Adjusting Entries for Interest Expense

Companies issue bonds when they need cash. The interest payments seldom occur on December 31 (or the end of the fiscal year). So interest expense must be accrued at the end of the period to measure income accurately. → The accrual entry should include the amortization of any bond discount or premium.

The adjusting entry for bond interest expense follows the pattern for the adjusting entries for other accrued liabilities, as in Chapters 3 (p. 105) and 11 (p. 450), except for the addition of the amortization of the premium or discount.

Xenon Corporation issued $100,000 of 8%, 10-year bonds at a $2,000 discount on October 1, 2006. The interest payments occur on March 31 and September 30 each year. On December 31, Xenon records interest for three months (October, November, and December) as follows:

2006			
Dec. 31	Interest Expense	2,050	
	Interest Payable ($100,000 × 0.08 × 3/12)		2,000
	Discount on Bonds Payable ($2,000/10 × 3/12)		50
	Accrued three months' interest and amortized bond discount.		

Interest Payable is credited for three months (October, November, and December). Discount on Bonds Payable must also be amortized for these three months.

Xenon's balance sheet at December 31, 2006, reports Interest Payable of $2,000 as a current liability. Bonds Payable are shown as follows:

Long-term liabilities:		
Bonds payable	$100,000	
Less: Discount on bonds payable ($2,000 – $50)	(1,950)	$98,050

Observe that the bonds' carrying amount increases by $50. The bonds' carrying amount continues to increase until it reaches $100,000 at maturity, when the discount will be fully amortized.

The next semiannual interest payment occurs on March 31, 2007:

✔ **Starter 15-8**

2007			
Mar. 31	Interest Expense	2,050	
	Interest Payable	2,000	
	Cash ($100,000 × 0.08 × 6/12)		4,000
	Discount on Bonds Payable ($2,000/10 × 3/12)		50
	Paid semiannual interest and amortized bond discount.		

✔ **Starter 15-9**

Amortization of a bond premium is similar except that Premium on Bonds Payable is debited.

Decision Guidelines

LONG-TERM LIABILITIES—PART A

Amazon.com has borrowed some money by issuing bonds payable. What type of bonds did Amazon issue? How much cash must Amazon pay each interest period? At maturity? The Decision Guidelines address these and other questions.

Decision	Guidelines
When will you pay off the bonds • At maturity? • In installments?	Type of bond to issue: • Term bonds • Serial bonds
Are the bonds secured? • Yes • No	Then they are • Mortgage or secured bonds • Debenture or unsecured bonds
How are bond prices • Quoted?	• As a percentage of maturity value (Example: A \$500,000 bond priced at \$510,000 would be quoted at 102 (\$510,000 ÷ \$500,000 = 1.02)
• Determined?	• Present value of the future principal amount to pay plus present value of the future interest payments (see chapter appendix)
What are the two interest rates used for bonds?	• The *stated interest rate* determines the amount of cash interest the borrower pays. This interest rate does not change. • The *market interest rate* is the rate investors demand for loaning their money. The market interest rate determines the borrower's true rate of interest expense. This rate varies daily.
What causes a bond to be priced at	When the bonds are issued,
• Maturity (par) value?	• The *stated* interest rate on the bond *equals* the *market* interest rate
• A premium?	• The *stated* interest rate on the bond is *greater than* the *market* interest rate
• A discount?	• The *stated* interest rate on the bond is *less than* the *market* interest rate
What is the relationship between interest expense and interest payments when bonds are issued at • Maturity (par) value? • A premium? • A discount?	• Interest expense *equals* Interest payment • Interest expense is *less than* Interest payment • Interest expense is *greater than* Interest payment
How to report bonds payable on the balance sheet?	Maturity (par) value { + Premium on bonds payable or – Discount on bonds payable }

MID-CHAPTER *Summary Problem*

A+ TIPS
CHECK YOUR RESOURCES

Assume that Alabama Power Company has an issue of 9% bonds payable that mature on May 1, 2028. The bonds are dated May 1, 2008, and Alabama Power pays interest each April 30 and October 31.

Required

1. Will the bonds be issued at par, at a premium, or at a discount if the market interest rate on the date of issuance is 8%? If the market interest rate is 10%?

2. Assume that Alabama Power issued $1,000,000 of the bonds at 104 on May 1, 2008.
   a. Record issuance of the bonds.
   b. Record the interest payment and amortization of the premium on October 31, 2008. Use the straight-line method of amortization.
   c. Accrue interest and amortize premium on December 31, 2008.
   d. Show how the company would report the bonds on the balance sheet at December 31, 2008.
   e. Record the interest payment and amortization of premium on April 30, 2009.

Solution

Requirement 1

Market Interest Rate	Bond Price
8%	Premium
10%	Discount

Requirement 2

2008			
a. May 1	Cash ($1,000,000 × 1.04)	$1,040,000	
	Bonds Payable		1,000,000
	Premium on Bonds Payable		40,000
	Issued bonds at a premium.		
b. Oct. 31	Interest Expense	44,000	
	Premium on Bonds Payable ($40,000/40)	1,000	
	Cash ($1,000,000 × 0.09 × 6/12)		45,000
	Paid semiannual interest and amortized bond premium.		
c. Dec. 31	Interest Expense	14,667	
	Premium on Bonds Payable ($40,000/40 × 2/6)	333	
	Interest Payable ($1,000,000 × 0.09 × 2/12)		15,000
	Accrued interest and amortized bond premium.		

d. Long-term liabilities:

Bonds payable, 9%	$1,000,000	
Premium on bonds payable ($40,000 – $1,000 – $333)	38,667	$1,038,667

2009			
e. Apr. 30	Interest Expense	29,333	
	Interest Payable	15,000	
	Premium on Bonds Payable ($40,000/40 × 4/6)	667	
	Cash ($1,000,000 × 0.09 × 6/12)		45,000
	Paid semiannual interest and amortized bond premium.		

Effective-Interest Method of Amortization

2 *Measure interest expense by the effective-interest method*

We began with the straight-line amortization method to introduce the concept of amortizing bonds. However, that method has a theoretical weakness. Under the straight-line method, each period's interest expense is the same dollar amount. But over their life, the bonds' carrying amount moves toward maturity. The amount of interest expense should also increase or decrease as the bonds move toward maturity.

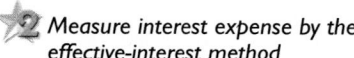

Student Resource CD
bond discount, bond premium, effective-interest method

Generally accepted accounting principles require that interest expense be measured using the *effective-interest method* unless the straight-line amounts are similar. In that case, either method is permitted. Total interest expense over the life of the bonds is the same under both methods. We now show how the effective-interest method works.

Effective-Interest Method for a Bond Discount

Assume that eBay Inc. issues $100,000 of 9% bonds at a time when the market rate of interest is 10%. These bonds mature in 5 years and pay interest semiannually, so there are 10 semiannual interest payments. The issue price of the bonds is $96,149,[3] and the discount on these bonds is $3,851 ($100,000 – $96,149). Exhibit 15-4 shows how to measure interest expense by the effective-interest method. (You will need an amortization table to account for bonds by the effective-interest method.)

Exhibit 15-4 Effective-Interest Method for a Bond Discount

PANEL A—Bond Data
Maturity value—$100,000
Stated interest rate—9%
Interest paid—4 1/2% semiannually, $4,500 ($100,000 × 0.045)
Market interest rate at time of issue—10% annually, 5% semiannually
Issue price—$96,149 on January 1, 2005

PANEL B—Amortization Table

	A	B	C	D	E
End of Semiannual Interest Period	Interest *Payment* (4 1/2% of maturity value)	Interest *Expense* (5% of preceding bond carrying amount)	Discount Amortization (B – A)	Discount Balance (D – C)	Bond Carrying Amount ($100,000 – D)
Jan. 1, 2005				$3,851	$ 96,149
July 1	$4,500	$4,807	$307	3,544	96,456
Jan. 1, 2006	4,500	4,823	323	3,221	96,779
July 1	4,500	4,839	339	2,882	97,118
Jan. 1, 2007	4,500	4,856	356	2,526	97,474
July 1	4,500	4,874	374	2,152	97,848
Jan. 1, 2008	4,500	4,892	392	1,760	98,240
July 1	4,500	4,912	412	1,348	98,652
Jan. 1, 2009	4,500	4,933	433	915	99,085
July 1	4,500	4,954	454	461	99,539
Jan. 1, 2010	4,500	4,961*	461	0	100,000

*Adjusted for effect of rounding.

Notes

- *Column A* The interest payments are constant—fixed by the stated interest rate and the bonds' maturity value.
- *Column B* The interest expense each period is the preceding bond carrying amount multiplied by the market interest rate. Interest expense increases as the bond carrying amount (E) increases.
- *Column C* The excess of interest expense (B) over interest payment (A) is the discount amortization.
- *Column D* The discount decreases by the amount of amortization for the period (C). Balance of discount + Bonds' carrying amount = Bonds' maturity value ($100,000) at all times.
- *Column E* The bonds' carrying amount increases from $96,149 at issuance to $100,000 at maturity.

[3]We compute this present value in the chapter appendix.

✔ Starter 15-10

The *accounts* debited and credited under the effective-interest method and the straight-line method are the same. Only the *amounts* differ.

Exhibit 15-4 gives the amounts for all the bond transactions of eBay. Let's begin with issuance of the bonds payable on January 1, 2005, and the first interest payment on July 1. Entries follow, using amounts from the respective lines of Exhibit 15-4.

2005			
Jan. 1	Cash (column E)	96,149	
	Discount on Bonds Payable (column D)	3,851	
	Bonds Payable (maturity value)		100,000
	Issued bonds at a discount.		

2005			
July 1	Interest Expense (column B)	4,807	
	Discount on Bonds Payable (column C)		307
	Cash (column A)		4,500
	Paid semiannual interest and amortized bond discount.		

✔ Starter 15-10

Stop & Think

How much interest expense will **eBay** record for 2005 on these bonds? How much cash interest will eBay pay each year? What causes the difference?

Answer: Interest expense for 2005: $9,630 ($4,807 + $4,823)

Cash interest paid each year: $9,000 ($4,500 × 2)

The difference is caused by amortization of the bond discount.

Exhibit 15-5 diagrams the carrying amount of bonds issued at a discount. Observe how it rises to maturity. All amounts are taken from Exhibit 15-4.

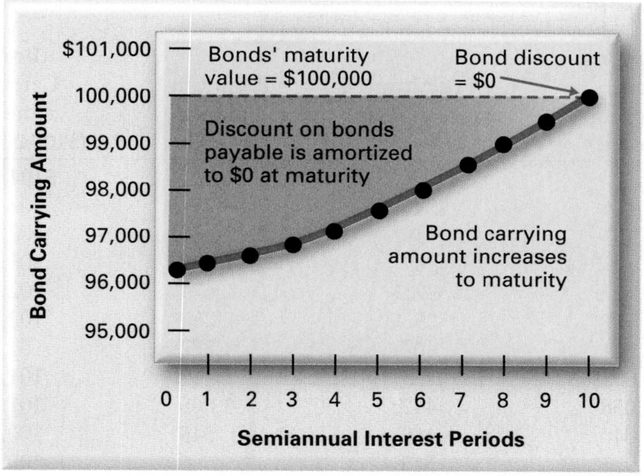

Exhibit 15-5

Carrying Amount for Bonds Payable Issued at a Discount

Effective-Interest Method for a Bond Premium

eBay may issue its bonds payable at a premium. Assume that eBay issues $100,000 of 5-year, 9% bonds when the market interest rate is 8%. The bonds' issue price is $104,100,[4] and the premium is $4,100.

[4]Again, we compute the present value of the bonds in the chapter appendix.

Exhibit 15-6 provides the data for all the bond transactions of eBay. Let's begin with issuance of the bonds on January 1, 2005, and the first interest payment on July 1. These entries follow.

2005			
Jan. 1	Cash (column E).	$104,100	
	Bonds Payable (maturity value). .		100,000
	Premium on Bonds Payable (column D).		4,100
	Issued bonds at a premium.		

2005			
July 1	Interest Expense (column B)	4,164	
	Premium on Bonds Payable (column C)	336	
	Cash (column A).		4,500
	Paid semiannual interest and amortized bond premium.		

Exhibit 15-6 Effective-Interest Method for a Bond Premium

PANEL A—Bond Data

Maturity value—$100,000
Stated interest rate—9%
Interest paid—4 1/2% semiannually, $4,500 ($100,000 × 0.045)
Market interest rate at time of issue—8% annually, 4% semiannually
Issue price—$104,100 on January 1, 2005

PANEL B—Amortization Table

	A	B	C	D	E
End of Semiannual Interest Period	**Interest *Payment* (4 1/2% of maturity value)**	**Interest *Expense* (4% of preceding bond carrying amount)**	**Premium Amortization (A – B)**	**Premium Balance (D – C)**	**Bond Carrying Amount ($100,000 + D)**
Jan. 1, 2005				$4,100	$104,100
July 1	$4,500	$4,164	$336	3,764	103,764
Jan. 1, 2006	4,500	4,151	349	3,415	103,415
July 1	4,500	4,137	363	3,052	103,052
Jan. 1, 2007	4,500	4,122	378	2,674	102,674
July 1	4,500	4,107	393	2,281	102,281
Jan. 1, 2008	4,500	4,091	409	1,872	101,872
July 1	4,500	4,075	425	1,447	101,447
Jan. 1, 2009	4,500	4,058	442	1,005	101,005
July 1	4,500	4,040	460	545	100,545
Jan. 1, 2010	4,500	3,955*	545	0	100,000

*Adjusted for effect of rounding.

Notes

- *Column A* The interest payments are constant—fixed by the stated interest rate and the bonds' maturity value.
- *Column B* The interest expense each period is the preceding bond carrying amount multiplied by the market interest rate. Interest expense decreases as the bond carrying amount decreases.
- *Column C* The excess of interest payment (A) over interest expense (B) is the premium amortization.
- *Column D* The premium balance decreases by the amount of amortization for the period. Bonds' carrying amount – Premium balance = Bonds' maturity value ($100,000) at all times.
- *Column E* The bonds' carrying amount decreases from $104,100 at issuance to $100,000 at maturity.

Stop & Think

How much interest expense will **eBay** record for 2005 on these bonds? How much cash interest will eBay pay each year? What causes the difference?

Answer:	Interest expense for 2005:	\$8,315 (\$4,164 + \$4,151)
	Cash interest paid each year:	\$9,000 (\$4,500 × 2)

The difference is caused by amortization of the bond premium.

✔ Starter 15-11

Exhibit 15-7 diagrams the carrying amount of the bonds issued at a premium. Observe how it falls to maturity. All amounts are taken from Exhibit 15-6.

Exhibit 15-7

Carrying Amount for Bonds Payable Issued at a Premium

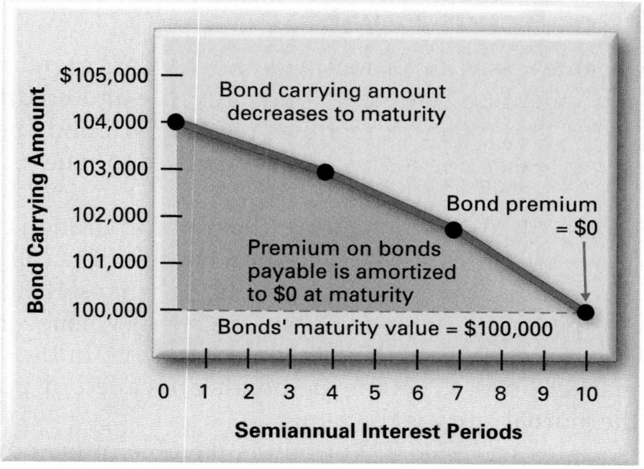

- ☐ Bonds: Introduction
- ☐ Issuing Bonds Payable
- ☐ Effective-Interest Method
- ■ Additional Bond Topics
- ☐ Bonds versus Stock
- ☐ Lease Liabilities
- ☐ Appendix: Time Value of Money

3 *Account for retirement and conversion of bonds payable*

Student Resource CD

callable bonds, convertible bonds, debenture

Additional Bond Topics

Companies that issue bonds payable face additional issues, such as

- Issuance of bonds payable between interest dates
- Retirement of bonds payable
- Convertible bonds payable
- Advantages and disadvantages of issuing bonds versus stock

Issuing Bonds Payable Between Interest Dates

In all the examples we've seen thus far, companies have issued bonds payable on an interest date, such as January 1. Corporations can also issue bonds between interest dates. That creates a complication.

Suppose Intel Corporation has \$100,000 of 8% bonds payable that are dated January 1. That means the interest starts accruing on January 1. Suppose Intel issues these bonds on April 1. How should we account for the interest for January, February, and March? At issuance on April 1, Intel collects three months' accrued interest from the bondholder and records the issuance of bonds payable as follows:

2005			
April 1	Cash	102,000	
	Bonds Payable		100,000
	Interest Payable		
	(\$100,000 × 0.08 × 3/12)		2,000
	Issued bonds two months after the date of the bonds.		

On the next interest date, Intel will pay six months' interest to whoever owns the bonds at that time. But Intel will record interest expense only for the three months the bonds have been outstanding (April, May, and June). To allocate interest expense to the correct months, Intel makes this entry on July 1 for the customary six-month interest payment:

2005			
July 1	Interest Payable (see entry on April 1) . . .	2,000	
	Interest Expense (for April, May, June). . .	2,000	
	Cash ($100,000 × 0.08 × 6/12)		4,000
	Paid six months' interest.		

✔ Starter 15-12

Retirement of Bonds Payable

Normally, companies wait until maturity to pay off, or *retire*, their bonds payable. The retirement entry debits Bonds Payable and credits Cash for the maturity value. But companies sometimes retire their bonds payable prior to maturity. The main reason for retiring bonds early is to relieve the pressure of paying interest.

Callable Bonds
Bonds that the issuer may call or pay off at a specified price whenever the issuer wants.

Some bonds are **callable**, which means that the corporation may *call*, or pay off, those bonds at a specified price whenever it chooses. The call price is usually 100 or a few percentage points above par value, perhaps 101 or 102. Callable bonds give the issuer the flexibility to pay off the bonds whenever it is beneficial. An alternative to calling the bonds is to purchase them in the open market at their current market price. Whether the bonds are called or purchased in the open market, the journal entry is the same.

ETrade Associates has $700,000 of bonds payable outstanding with a discount of $30,000. Lower interest rates have convinced management to pay off these bonds now. Assume that the bonds are callable at 103. If the market price of the bonds is 95, will ETrade call the bonds or purchase them in the open market? The market price is lower than the call price, so ETrade will pay off the bonds at their market price. Retiring the bonds at 95 results in a gain of $5,000, computed as follows:

Maturity value of bonds being retired	$700,000
Less: Discount	(30,000)
Carrying amount of bonds payable	670,000
Market price ($700,000 × 0.95)	665,000
Gain on retirement of bonds payable	$ 5,000

The following entry records retirement of the bonds, immediately after an interest date:

June 30	Bonds Payable	700,000	
	Discount on Bonds Payable . . .		30,000
	Cash ($700,000 × 0.95)		665,000
	Gain on Retirement of Bonds Payable		5,000
	Retired bonds payable.		

✔ Starter 15-13

The entry removes the bonds payable and the related discount from the accounts and records a gain on retirement. Any existing premium would be removed with a debit. If ETrade Associates retired only half of these bonds, the accountant would remove only half the discount or premium.

When retiring bonds before maturity, follow these steps: (1) Record partial-period amortization of discount or premium if the retirement date does not fall on an interest date. (2) Write off the portion of Discount or Premium that relates to the bonds being retired. (3) Compute gain or loss on retirement.

Convertible Bonds Payable

As the chapter-opening story indicates, convertible bonds and notes are popular. **Convertible bonds** and notes payable may be converted into the common stock of the issuing company at the option of the investor. These bonds, called convertible bonds, combine the benefits of interest and principal on the bonds with the opportunity for a gain on the stock. The conversion feature is so attractive that investors accept a lower interest rate than they would on non-convertible bonds. For example, Amazon.com's convertible bonds payable carry an interest rate of only 4 3/4%. The low cash interest payments benefit Amazon.com.

Convertible Bonds
Bonds that may be converted into the common stock of the issuing company at the option of the investor.

The issuance of convertible bonds payable is recorded like any other debt: Debit Cash and credit Convertible Bonds Payable. Then, if the market price of Amazon's stock gets above the market value of the bonds, the bondholders will convert the bonds into stock. The corporation records conversion by removing the bond accounts and crediting the stock accounts. The carrying amount of the bonds becomes the book value of the newly issued stock. There is no gain or loss.

Assume the Amazon bondholders convert $100,000 of the bonds into 2,000 shares of Amazon's common stock, which has a par value of $0.01 (1 cent) per share. Assume further that the carrying amount of the Amazon bonds is $90,000; thus, there is a discount of $10,000. To record the conversion, Amazon would make this journal entry:

May 14	Bonds Payable	100,000	
	Discount on Bonds Payable ($100,000 – $90,000)		10,000
	Common Stock (2,000 × $0.01)		20
	Paid-in Capital in Excess of Par—Common		89,980
	Recorded conversion of bonds payable.		

The entry closes the bonds payable account and its related discount. The carrying amount of the notes ($90,000) becomes the amount of new stockholders' equity ($89,980 + $20).

✔ Starter 15-14

Reporting Liabilities on the Balance Sheet

4 *Report liabilities on the balance sheet*

As we have seen, bonds come in all varieties. Companies report their bonds and notes payable among the liabilities on the balance sheet, divided between the current and long-term categories.

Serial bonds are payable in installments. The portion payable within one year is a current liability, and the remaining debt is long-term. For example, assume that Toys "Я" Us has $500,000 of notes payable maturing in various amounts in future years. Assume that the portion payable next year is $200,000. This amount is a current liability, and the remaining $300,000 is a long-term liability. Toys "Я" Us would report the following among its liabilities:

Current liabilities:	
Notes payable, current	$200,000
Long-term liabilities:	
Note payable, long-term..........	300,000

✔ Starter 15-15

Bonds payable are reported in a similar fashion.

Advantages and Disadvantages: Bonds versus Stock

5 *Show the advantages and disadvantages of borrowing*

Borrowing by issuing bonds payable carries a risk: The company may be unable to pay off the bonds. Why then do companies borrow so heavily? Because bonds are a cheaper source of money than stock. Borrowing can help a company increase its earnings per share of common stock. Companies thus face this decision: How shall we finance the expansion of the company?

Exhibit 15-8 shows the earnings-per-share (EPS) advantage of borrowing. ← Suppose that Vista.com, an Internet startup, has net income of $300,000 and 100,000 shares of common stock outstanding. Earnings per share of common stock is $3.00 ($300,000/100,000 shares). Vista needs $500,000 for expansion and the company is considering two finance plans:

Earnings per share (EPS) is a company's net income for each share of outstanding common stock (Chapter 14, p. 557). EPS may be the most important figure on the income statement. →

- Plan 1 is to borrow $500,000 at 10% (issue $500,000 of 10% bonds payable).
- Plan 2 is to issue 50,000 shares of common stock for $500,000.

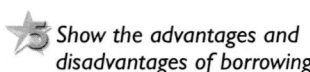

Borrow the money. Take a risk in hopes of increasing earnings per share.
Issue stock. It's safer, but earnings per share will drop.

Vista management believes the new cash can be used to earn income of $200,000 before interest and taxes.

EPS is higher if Vista.com borrows. If all goes well, Vista can earn more on the investment ($90,000) than the interest it pays on the bonds ($50,000). Earning more income on borrowed money than the related interest expense increases the earnings for common stockholders and is called using **leverage**. It is widely used to increase earnings per share of common stock.

Exhibit 15-8

Earnings-per-Share Advantage of Borrowing versus Issuing Stock

	Plan 1 Borrow $500,000 at 10%		**Plan 2 Issue $500,000 of Common Stock**	
Net income before expansion..........		$300,000		$300,000
Expected income on the new project before interest and income tax expenses	$200,000		$200,000	
Less: Interest expense ($500,000 × 0.10)	(50,000)		0	
Project income before income tax	150,000		200,000	
Less: Income tax expense (40%)..........	(60,000)		(80,000)	
Project net income		90,000		120,000
Total company net income		$390,000		$420,000
Earnings per share after expansion:				
Plan 1 ($390,000/100,000 shares)..........		$3.90		
Plan 2 ($420,000/150,000 shares)..........				$2.80

✔ Starter 15-16

Leverage
Earning more income on borrowed money than the related interest expense, thereby increasing the earnings for the owners of the business.

Borrowing can increase EPS, but borrowing has its disadvantages. Interest expense may be high enough to eliminate net income and lead to a cash shortage or even bankruptcy. This happens to lots of ambitious companies. Borrowing creates liabilities that must be paid during bad years as well as good years.

Lease Liabilities

☐ Bonds: Introduction
☐ Issuing Bonds Payable
☐ Effective-Interest Method
☐ Additional Bond Topics
☐ Bonds versus Stock
■ Lease Liabilities
☐ Appendix: Time Value of Money

A **lease** is a rental agreement in which the tenant (**lessee**) obtains the use of an asset by paying rent to the property owner (**lessor**). Leasing can avoid having to make a large initial cash down payment. Accountants divide leases into two types: operating leases and capital leases.

Operating Leases

Operating leases include many apartment leases and car-rental agreements. An operating lease gives the lessee use of an asset but no continuing right to the asset. The lessor keeps the usual rewards and risks of owning the leased asset. To account for an operating lease, the lessee debits Rent Expense and credits Cash for the amount of each lease payment. The lessee's books report no leased asset and no lease liability. This is why lessees prefer operating leases over capital leases. They report no liability.

Lease
Rental agreement in which the tenant (lessee) agrees to make rent payments to the property owner (lessor) to obtain the use of the asset.

Lessee
Tenant in a lease agreement.

Lessor
Property owner in a lease agreement.

Operating Lease
Usually a short-term or cancelable rental agreement.

Capital Leases

A capital lease requires the lessee to record both an asset and a lease liability. Capital leases are both long-term and noncancelable. A **capital lease** meets any *one* of the following criteria:

1. The lease transfers title of the leased asset to the lessee at the end of the lease term. Thus, the lessee becomes the legal owner of the leased asset.
2. The lease contains a *bargain purchase option*. The lessee can be expected to purchase the leased asset and become its legal owner.
3. The lease term is 75% or more of the estimated useful life of the leased asset. The lessee therefore uses up most of the leased asset's service potential.
4. The present value of the lease payments is 90% or more of the market value of the leased asset. In effect, the lease payments operate as installment payments for the leased asset.

Only those leases that meet *none* of these criteria are accounted for as operating leases.

Capital Lease
Lease agreement that meets any one of four criteria: (1) The lease transfers title of the leased asset to the lessee. (2) The lease contains a bargain purchase option. (3) The lease term is 75% or more of the estimated useful life of the leased asset. (4) The present value of the lease payments is 90% or more of the market value of the leased asset.

Accounting for a Capital Lease

Accounting for a capital lease is like accounting for a purchase of a long-term asset. The lessee records an asset and a lease liability even though the lessee may never actually own the property.

Safeway, the grocery chain, leases buildings for its stores. Suppose Safeway leases a store building for a 20-year period. This lease is similar to purchasing the building on an installment plan.

Suppose Safeway's liability under this capital lease totals $1,000,000. The lease liability measures Safeway's cost of the building. Safeway makes this entry at the beginning of the lease:

2006			
Jan. 1	Building	1,000,000	
	Lease Liability		1,000,000
	Acquired building under a capital lease.		

During the lease period, Safeway will report both the building and the lease liability on its balance sheet.

Accounting.com

Qwest: Swapping Bonds to Cut Debt Leaves Bondholders Wary

In the summer of 1998, Baby Bell phone company **USWest** made corporate history with the largest long-term bond issue: $1.5 billion in 30-year bonds. With the company's solid, investment-grade rating and a yield of 6.9 percent for 30 years, the bonds seemed the ideal investment vehicle. Yet individuals and large institutional investors alike are now unsure whether the bonds issued in 1998 will be paid in full at maturity.

USWest was bought by **Qwest Communications**, which sought to create the telecom company of the future. Old-economy USWest and new-economy Qwest never did mesh, and Qwest took on an enormous amount of debt to finance its fiber-optic dreams. Furthermore, the company's attempt to inflate revenue via illegal telecom-capacity swaps and other accounting shenanigans have landed former executives in jail, sunk the stock price, and sparked rumors of impending bankruptcy.

Qwest's capacity swaps were illegal, but a U.S. District judge decided that the company could go ahead with a bond swap to pare down its total debt of $24.5 billion. Qwest came up with a debt-for-debt swap for its institutional investors. It works like this: If a bondholder has a $100 face-value bond now trading at $80, Qwest will issue that holder an $80 face-value bond. In return for giving up the $20 difference, the bondholder gets a better rank among Qwest's creditors—in other words, it's more likely that they will get repaid. Qwest then gets to wipe that $20 off its balance sheet.

For those who bought Qwest's bonds at a discount as the company's troubles mounted, the deal is good. They can exchange bonds they bought at distressed values for little or no loss, get a better interest rate and higher standing among creditors. Those who bought the bonds at full face value are not so happy. In fact, bondholders owning about $4 billion of Qwest's bonds sued to stop the exchange, because those who abstain will be punished. They lost their case. Individual investors aren't even given the option to swap.

But who knows? Those who hold on to their Qwest bonds might benefit in the long run. If Qwest can cut its long-term debt, it becomes less likely that the company will go into bankruptcy, thus boosting the value of its bonds.

Based on: Stephanie N. Mehta, "Joe Nacchio's Dream Has Unraveled," *Fortune*, April 29, 2002, pp. 78–82. Kris Hudson, "Qwest Set to Shuffle Bond Debt," *Denver Post*, November 21, 2002, p. C1. Floyd Norris, "A Bond Swap Available Only to Big Players," *The New York Times*, December 18, 2002, p. C1. Kris Hudson, "Qwest Can Proceed on Bond Plan," *Denver Post*, December 19, 2002, p. C2.

Decision Guidelines

LONG-TERM LIABILITIES—PART B

Suppose **American Airlines** needs $500 million for new **Boeing** aircraft. American issues bonds payable to finance the purchase and now must account for the bonds payable. The Decision Guidelines outline some of the issues American must decide.

Decision	Guidelines
What happens to the bonds' carrying amount when bonds payable are issued at • Maturity (par) value? • A premium? • A discount?	 • Carrying amount *stays* at maturity (par) value. • Carrying amount *falls* gradually to maturity value. • Carrying amount *rises* gradually to maturity value.

How to account for the retirement of bonds payable?	At maturity date:
	Bonds Payable .... Maturity value
	    Cash .... Maturity value
	
	Before maturity date (assume a discount on the bonds and a gain on retirement):
	Bonds Payable .... Maturity value
	    Discount on Bonds Payable .. Balance
	    Cash .... Amount Paid
	    Gain on Retirement
	      of Bonds Payable .... Excess

How to account for the conversion of convertible bonds payable into common stock?	Remove the bonds payable (and related premium or discount) and credit Common Stock at par, plus any excess to Paid-In Capital in Excess of Par.
What are the advantages of financing operations with • Stock • Bonds (or notes) payable?	 • Creates no liability or interest expense. Less risky to the issuing corporation. • Results in higher earnings per share—under normal conditions.

Excel Application Exercise

Goal: Create an Excel worksheet to compare earnings per share under two financing scenarios: borrowing and issuing stock.

Scenario: Suppose **American Airlines** is building a new warehouse to serve its central hub operations. To finance construction of the warehouse, managers must decide whether to borrow the $5 million or issue stock. If borrowing is chosen, long-term bonds payable will be issued at 8%. If stock is chosen, 80,000 shares will be issued. Managers expect income before tax to increase by $700,000. Income tax expense is 40%. Net income before construction is $4 million, and shares outstanding before construction total 500,000.

Your task is to create a spreadsheet that compares earnings per share under the two scenarios described above. After completing the spreadsheet, answer these questions:

1. Which plan generates the higher earnings per share? Why?
2. Under what circumstances would American consider using debt to finance its new warehouse?
3. Under what circumstances would American consider the use of equity to finance its new warehouse?
4. Which option do you recommend? Why? Does your recommendation change if the bond interest rate is 10% rather than 8%?

Step-by-Step:

1. Open a new Excel worksheet.
2. Create a heading for your work sheet that contains the following:
   a. Chapter 15 Excel Application Exercise
   b. Financing with Debt or Stock
   c. American Airlines
   d. Today's date
3. Use Exhibit 15-8 in your textbook as a model for the layout of your spreadsheet. Label the long-term bonds as "Plan 1," and the issuance of common stock as "Plan 2." Be sure to set up the spreadsheet so that you can change variables, such as the interest rate on the bonds, without retyping any formulas in the body of the spreadsheet.
4. When finished, your spreadsheet should show earnings per share under both plans, and be capable of recomputing earnings per share simply by changing the interest rate on the bonds.
5. Save your work and print a copy of the work sheet (in landscape mode) for your files.

END-OF-CHAPTER *Summary Problem*

TIPS
CHECK YOUR RESOURCES

Trademark, Inc., has outstanding an issue of 8% convertible bonds payable that mature in 2020. Suppose the bonds were dated October 1, 2006, and pay interest each April 1 and October 1.

Required

1. With the bond data below, complete the following effective-interest amortization table through October 1, 2008:
- Maturity value—$100,000
- Stated interest rate—8%
- Interest paid—4% semiannually, $4,000 ($100,000 × 0.04)
- Market interest rate—9% annually, 4 1/2% semiannually
- Issue price—90.75 on October 1, 2006

	A	B	C	D	E
Semiannual Interest Date	Interest Payment (4% of maturity amount)	Interest Expense (4 1/2% of preceding bond carrying amount)	Discount Amortization (B – A)	Discount Balance (D – C)	Bond Carrying Amount ($100,000 – D)
10-1-06					
4-1-07					
10-1-07					
4-1-08					
10-1-08					

2. Using the amortization table, record the following transactions:

a. Issuance of the bonds on October 1, 2006.
b. Accrual of interest and amortization of discount on December 31, 2006.
c. Payment of interest and amortization of discount on April 1, 2007.
d. Conversion of one-third of the bonds payable into no-par common stock on October 2, 2008.
e. Retirement of two-thirds of the bonds payable on October 2, 2008. Purchase price of the bonds was 102.

Solution

Requirement 1

	A	B	C	D	E
Semiannual Interest Date	Interest Payment (4% of maturity amount)	Interest Expense (4 1/2% of preceding bond carrying amount)	Discount Amortization (B – A)	Discount Balance (D – C)	Bond Carrying Amount ($100,000 – D)
10-1-06				$9,250	$90,750
4-1-07	$4,000	$4,084	$84	9,166	90,834
10-1-07	4,000	4,088	88	9,078	90,922
4-1-08	4,000	4,091	91	8,987	91,013
10-1-08	4,000	4,096	96	8,891	91,109

Requirement 2

2006				
a.	Oct. 1	Cash ($100,000 × 0.9075)	90,750	
		Discount on Bonds Payable	9,250	
		Bonds Payable		100,000
		Issued bonds payable at a discount.		
b.	Dec. 31	Interest Expense ($4,084 × 3/6)	2,042	
		Discount on Bonds Payable ($84 × 3/6)		42
		Interest Payable ($4,000 × 3/6)		2,000
		Accrued interest and amortized bond discount.		
2007				
c.	Apr. 1	Interest Expense	2,042	
		Interest Payable	2,000	
		Discount on Bonds Payable ($84 × 3/6)		42
		Cash		4,000
		Paid semiannual interest and amortized bond discount.		
2008				
d.	Oct. 2	Bonds Payable ($100,000 × 1/3)	33,333	
		Discount on Bonds Payable ($8,891 × 1/3)		2,964
		Common Stock ($91,109 × 1/3)		30,369
		Recorded conversion of bonds payable.		
e.	Oct. 2	Bonds Payable ($100,000 × 2/3)	66,667	
		Loss on Retirement Bonds	7,260	
		Discount on Bonds Payable ($8,891 × 2/3)		5,927
		Cash ($100,000 × 2/3 × 1.02)		68,000
		Retired bonds payable before maturity.		

REVIEW *Long-Term Liabilities*

Quick Check

1. Which type of bond is unsecured?

a. Debenture bond
b. Mortgage bond
c. Serial bond
d. Common bond

2. A $100,000 bond priced at 103.5 can be bought or sold for

a. $100,000 + interest
b. $3,500
c. $103,500
d. $103,000 + $500 of interest

3. Which interest rate on a bond determines the amount of the semiannual interest payment?

a. Market rate
b. Effective rate
c. Semiannual rate
d. Stated rate

4. The final journal entry to record for bonds payable is

a.

Interest Expense	XXX	
Cash		XXX

b.

Cash	XXX	
Bonds Payable		XXX

c.

Bonds Payable	XXX	
Cash		XXX

d.

Discount on Bonds Payable	XXX	
Interest Expense		XXX

5. Lafferty Corporation's bonds payable carry a stated interest rate of 7%, and the market rate of interest is 8%. The price of the Lafferty bonds will be at
   a. Premium
   b. Discount
   c. Par value
   d. Maturity value
6. Bonds issued at a premium always have
   a. Interest expense less than the interest payments
   b. Interest expense greater than the interest payments
   c. Interest expense equal to the interest payments
   d. None of the above
7. Imported Cars of Sarasota has $500,000 of 10-year bonds payable outstanding. These bonds had a discount of $40,000 at issuance, which was 5 years ago. The company uses the straight-line amortization method. The carrying amount of Imported Cars' bonds payable is
   a. $460,000
   b. $480,000
   c. $500,000
   d. $520,000
8. Imported Cars issued its 8% bonds payable at a price of $440,000 (maturity value is $500,000). The market interest rate was 10% when Imported Cars issued its bonds. The company uses the effective-interest method for the bonds. Interest expense for the first year is
   a. $35,200
   b. $40,000
   c. $44,000
   d. $50,000
9. Milton Corporation issued bonds payable on August 1. Milton's bonds were dated July 1. Which statement is true of Milton's journal entry to record issuance of the bonds payable?
   a. Milton must pay one month's accrued interest.
   b. Milton will collect one month's accrued interest in advance.
   c. Milton will collect five months' accrued interest in advance.
   d. Milton will pay five months' interest on the next interest date.
10. Bull & Bear, Inc., retired $100,000 of its bonds payable, paying cash of $103,000. On the retirement date, the bonds payable had a discount of $2,000. The bond retirement created a
   a. Gain of $3,000
   b. Loss of $3,000
   c. Gain of $5,000
   d. Loss of $5,000

Accounting Vocabulary

bond discount (p. 581)
bond premium (p. 581)
bonds payable (p. 580)
callable bonds (p. 594)
capital lease (p. 597)
convertible bonds (p. 595)
debentures (p. 581)
discount (on a bond) (p. 581)
effective interest rate (p. 582)
lease (p. 597)
lessee (p. 597)
lessor (p. 597)
leverage (p. 596)
market interest rate (p. 582)
mortgage (p. 581)
operating lease (p. 597)
premium (p. 581)
present value (p. 582)
serial bonds (p. 581)
stated interest rate (p. 582)
term bonds (p. 581)

ASSESS *Your Progress*

A+ online homework

See *www.prenhall.com/horngren* for selected Starters, Exercises, and Problems.

Starters

Pricing bonds
(Obj. 1)

S15-1 Compute the price of the following 8% bonds:

a. $100,000 quoted at 92.6
b. $100,000 quoted at 102.5
c. $100,000 quoted at 77.75
d. $100,000 quoted at 110.375

Which bond will have the least interest expense over its life?
Which bond will have the most interest expense? Explain.

S15-2 **Washington Public Power Supply System (WPPSS)** borrowed money by issuing the bond payable in Exhibit 15-1. Assume the issue price was 96.5.

Determining bonds payable amounts **(Obj. 1)**

1. How much cash did WPPSS receive when it issued the bond payable?
2. How much must WPPSS pay back at maturity? When is the maturity date?
3. How much cash interest will WPPSS pay each six months? Carry the interest amount to the nearest cent.

S15-3 Assume the **WPPSS** bond in Exhibit 15-1 was issued at a price of 96.5. Was the market interest rate at the date of issuance 6 1/2%, above 6 1/2%, or below 6 1/2%? Explain.

Bond interest rates **(Obj. 1)**

S15-4 Determine whether the following bonds payable will be issued at maturity value, at a premium, or at a discount:

Determining bond prices at par, discount, or premium **(Obj. 1)**

a. The market interest rate is 7%. Chicago Corp. issues bonds payable with a stated rate of 8 1/2%.
b. Phoenix, Inc., issued 7% bonds payable when the market rate was 7 1/2%.
c. Tallahassee Corporation issued 8% bonds when the market interest rate was 8%.
d. Seattle Company issued bonds payable that pay cash interest at the stated rate of 7%. At the date of issuance, the market interest rate was 8 1/4%.

S15-5 Suppose **WPPSS** issued the 10-year bond in Exhibit 15-1 when the market interest rate was 6 1/2%. Assume that the fiscal year of WPPSS ends on December 31. Journalize the following transactions for WPPSS. Include an explanation for each entry.

Journalizing basic bond payable transactions **(Obj. 1)**

a. Issuance of the bond payable at par on January 1, 2000.
b. Payment of semiannual cash interest on July 1, 2000. (Round to the nearest dollar.)
c. Payment of the bonds payable at maturity. (Give the date.)

S15-6 Assume **WPPSS** issued the 10-year bond in Exhibit 15-1 at a price of 90 on January 1, 2000. Also assume that the WPPSS fiscal year ends on June 30. Journalize the following transactions for WPPSS. Include an explanation for each entry.

Issuing bonds payable at a discount; paying interest and amortizing discount by the straight-line method **(Obj. 1)**

a. Issuance of the bond payable on July 1, 2000.
b. Payment of semiannual interest and amortization of bond discount on July 1, 2000. (Use the straight-line method to amortize the discount. Round interest to the nearest dollar.)

S15-7 Assume **WPPSS** issued the 10-year bond payable in Exhibit 15-1 at a price of 110 on January 1, 2000. Also assume that the WPPSS fiscal year ends on December 31. Journalize the following transactions for WPPSS. Include an explanation for each entry.

Issuing bonds payable at a premium; paying interest and amortizing premium by the straight-line method **(Obj. 1)**

a. Issuance of the bond payable on January 1, 2000.
b. Payment of semiannual interest and amortization of bond premium on July 1, 2000. (Use the straight-line method to amortize the premium. Round interest to the nearest dollar.)

S15-8 Return to the **WPPSS** bond in Exhibit 15-1. Assume that WPPSS issued the 10-year bond payable on January 1, 2000, at a price of 90. Also assume that the WPPSS accounting year ends on December 31. Journalize the following transactions for WPPSS. Include an explanation for each entry.

Issuing bonds payable, accruing interest, and amortizing bond discount **(Obj. 1)**

a. Issuance of the bonds on July 1, 2000.
b. Accrual of semiannual interest expense and amortization of bond discount on December 31, 2000. Interest will be paid tomorrow, on January 1. (Use the straight-line amortization method, and round interest to the nearest dollar.)
c. Payment of the first semiannual interest amount on January 1, 2001.

S15-9 Use the situation in Starter 15-8, and show how **WPPSS** would report interest payable and the bond payable on its balance sheet at December 31, 2000.

Reporting interest payable and bonds payable on the balance sheet **(Obj. 5)**

Issuing bonds payable and amortizing discount by the effective-interest method **(Obj. 2)**

S15-10 Clever Path Information Systems issued $600,000 of 7%, 10-year bonds payable at a price of 90 on March 31, 20X3. The market interest rate at the date of issuance was 9%, and the bonds pay interest semiannually.

1. How much cash did Clever Path receive upon issuance of the bonds payable?
2. Prepare an effective-interest amortization table for the bond discount, through the first two interest payments. Use Exhibit 15-4 as a guide, and round amounts to the nearest dollar.
3. Record Clever Path's issuance of the bonds on March 31, 20X3, and on September 30, 20X3, payment of the first semiannual interest amount and amortization of the bond discount. Explanations are not required.

Issuing bonds payable and amortizing premium by the effective-interest method **(Obj. 2)**

S15-11 Sandals, Inc., issued $200,000 of 8%, 10-year bonds payable at a price of 110 on May 31, 20X5. The market interest rate at the date of issuance was 6%, and the Sandals bonds pay interest semiannually.

1. How much cash did Sandals receive upon issuance of the bonds payable?
2. Prepare an effective-interest amortization table for the bond premium, through the first two interest payments. Use Exhibit 15-6 as a guide, and round amounts to the nearest dollar.
3. Record Sandals' issuance of the bonds on May 31, 20X5, and, on November 30, 20X5, payment of the first semiannual interest amount and amortization of the bond premium. Explanations are not required.

Issuing bonds payable between interest dates and then paying the interest **(Obj. 1)**

S15-12 Assume **WPPSS** issued the 10-year bond in Exhibit 15-1 at par value on May 1, 2000, four months after the bond's original issue date of January 1, 2000. Assume that the fiscal year of WPPSS ends on December 31. Journalize the following transactions for WPPSS. Include an explanation for each entry.

a. Issuance of the bonds payable on May 1, 2000. (Carry amounts to the nearest cent.)
b. Payment of the first semiannual interest amount on July 1, 2000. (Carry amounts to the nearest cent.)

Accounting for the retirement of bonds payable **(Obj. 3)**

S15-13 Assume that Pacifica, Inc., issued the bonds payable in Exhibit 15-6. Pacifica has extra cash and wishes to retire the bonds payable on January 1, 2008, immediately after making the sixth semiannual interest payment. The bonds are quoted in the market at a price of 95.

1. What is Pacifica's carrying amount of the bonds payable on the retirement date?
2. How much cash must Pacifica pay to retire the bonds payable?
3. Compute Pacifica's gain or loss on the retirement of the bonds payable.
4. Journalize Pacifica's transaction to retire the bonds payable.

Accounting for the conversion of bonds payable **(Obj. 3)**

S15-14 ← *Link Back to Chapter 4 (Debt Ratio).* New Blue Corp. has $1,000,000 of convertible bonds payable outstanding, with a bond premium of $20,000 also on the books. The bondholders have notified New Blue that they wish to convert the bonds into stock. Specifically, the bonds may be converted into 200,000 shares of New Blue's $1 par common stock.

1. What is New Blue's carrying amount of its convertible bonds payable prior to the conversion?
2. Journalize New Blue's conversion of the bonds payable into common stock. No explanation is required.
3. How will the conversion affect New Blue's debt ratio?

Reporting liabilities **(Obj. 4)**

S15-15 Suburban Magazine, Inc., includes the following selected accounts in its general ledger at December 31, 20X8:

Notes payable, long-term.	$100,000	Accounts payable	$19,000
Bonds payable	350,000	Discount on bonds payable (all long-term)	6,000
Interest payable (due next year) . .	7,000		

Prepare the liabilities section of Suburban Magazine, Inc.'s balance sheet at December 31, 20X8, to show how the company would report these items. Report a total for current liabilities.

Earnings-per-share effects of financing with bonds versus stock
(Obj. 5)

S15-16 Leather Products, Inc. (LPI), needs to raise $1 million to expand company operations. LPI's president is considering two plans:

- Plan A: $1,000,000 of 8% bonds payable to borrow the money
- Plan B: 100,000 shares of common stock at $10 per share

Before any new financing, LPI expects to earn net income of $500,000, and the company already has 100,000 shares of common stock outstanding. LPI believes the expansion will increase income before interest and income tax by $200,000. LPI's income tax rate is 35%.

Prepare an analysis similar to Exhibit 15-8 to determine which plan is likely to result in the higher earnings per share. Which financing plan would you recommend for LPI?

Exercises

A+ online homework

Issuing bonds payable, paying and accruing interest
(Obj. 1)

E15-1 Neptune Corporation issued 8%, 20-year bonds payable with a maturity value of $500,000 on March 31. The bonds were issued at 100 and pay interest on March 31 and September 30. Record (a) issuance of the bonds on March 31, (b) payment of interest on September 30, and (c) accrual of interest on December 31.

Issuing bonds payable, paying interest, and amortizing discount by the straight-line method
(Obj. 1)

E15-2 On January 1, Quest Corp. issues 8%, 20-year bonds payable with a maturity value of $100,000. The bonds sell at 98 and pay interest on January 1 and July 1. Quest amortizes bond discount by the straight-line method. Record (a) issuance of the bonds on January 1, and (b) the semiannual interest payment on July 1.

Bond transactions at par, at a discount, and at a premium
(Obj. 1)

E15-3 Sandia, Inc., issued $100,000 of 10-year, 6% bonds payable on January 1, 20X6. Sandia pays interest each January 1 and July 1 and amortizes discount or premium by the straight-line method. The company can issue its bonds payable under various conditions:

a. Issuance at par (maturity) value
b. Issuance at a price of 95
c. Issuance at a price of 105

Required

1. Journalize Sandia's issuance of the bonds and first semiannual interest payment for each situation. Explanations are not required.
2. Which method results in the most interest expense for Sandia? Explain in detail.

Determining whether the bond price will be at par, at a discount, or at a premium
(Obj. 1)

E15-4 All Star Productions is planning to issue long-term bonds payable to borrow for a major expansion. The chief executive, Marty Boyd, asks your advice on some related matters, as follows:

a. The stated interest rate on the bonds is 7%, and the market interest rate is 8%. What type of price can All Star expect for the bonds?
b. All Star could raise the stated interest rate on the bonds to 9% (market rate is 8%). In that case, what type of price can All Star expect for the bonds?
c. At what type of bond price will All Star have total interest expense equal to the cash interest payments?
d. Under which type of price will All Star's total interest expense be less than the cash interest payments?
e. Under which type of price will All Star's total interest expense be greater than the cash interest payments?

Effective-interest method for bond discount; recording interest payments and interest expense
(Obj. 2)

Student ResourceCD

spreadsheet

E15-5 Autorama Corp. is authorized to issue 7%, 10-year bonds payable. On January 2, 20X4, when the market interest rate is 8%, the company issues $300,000 of the bonds and receives cash of $279,600. Autorama amortizes bond discount by the effective-interest method. Interest dates are January 2 and July 2.

Required

1. Prepare an amortization table for the first two semiannual interest periods. Follow the format of Exhibit 15-4.
2. Record issuance of the bonds payable and the first semiannual interest payment on July 2.

Effective-interest method for bond premium; recording interest accrual and payment and the related interest expense
(Obj. 2)

Student ResourceCD

spreadsheet

E15-6 On March 31, 20X2, the market interest rate is 7%. First Federal Bank issues $200,000 of 8%, 20-year bonds payable at 110. The bonds pay interest on March 31 and September 30. First Federal measures interest expense by the effective-interest method.

Required

1. Prepare an amortization table for the first two semiannual interest periods. Follow the format of Exhibit 15-6, Panel B.
2. Record issuance of the bonds on March 31, 20X2, and the semiannual interest payment on September 30.

Debt payment and discount amortization schedule
(Obj. 2)

Student ResourceCD

spreadsheet

E15-7 Einstein Productions issued $500,000 of 8 3/8% (0.08375), five-year bonds payable when the market interest rate was 9 1/2% (0.095). Einstein pays interest annually at year-end. The issue price of the bonds was $478,402.

Required

Create a spreadsheet model to prepare a schedule to measure interest expense on these bonds. Use the effective-interest method of amortization. Round to the nearest dollar, and format your answer as follows:

	A	B	C	D	E	F
1						
2						**Bond**
3		**Interest**	**Interest**	**Discount**	**Discount**	**Carrying**
4	**Date**	**Payment**	**Expense**	**Amortization**	**Balance**	**Amount**
5	1-1-X1				$ ☐	$478,402
6	12-31-X1	$ ☐	$ ☐	$ ☐		☐
7	12-31-X2					
8	12-31-X3					
9	12-31-X4					
10	12-31-X5					
		500000*.08375	+F5*.095	+C6−B6	500000−F5	+F5+D6

Issuing bonds between interest dates
(Obj. 1)

E15-8 Refer to the data for Neptune Corporation in Exercise 15-1. If Neptune issued the bonds payable on June 30, how much cash would Neptune receive upon issuance of the bonds?

Issuing bonds between interest dates and paying interest
(Obj. 1)

E15-9 Newton, Inc., issues $400,000 of 6%, 20-year bonds payable that are dated April 30. Record (a) issuance of bonds at par on May 31 and (b) the next semiannual interest payment on October 31.

Recording retirement of bonds payable
(Obj. 3)

E15-10 Microdot Printing issued $600,000 of 8% bonds payable at 97 on October 1, 20X0. These bonds mature on October 1, 20X8, and are callable at 102. Microdot pays interest each April 1 and October 1. On October 1, 20X5, when the bonds' market price is 101, Microdot retires the bonds in the most economical way available.

Required

Record the payment of the interest and amortization of bond discount at October 1, 20X5, and the retirement of the bonds on that date. Microdot uses the straight-line amortization method.

E15-11 Jacobs-Cathey Company issued $700,000 of 15-year, 8 1/2% bonds payable on July 31, 20X3, at a price of 98. The bonds may be converted into the company's common stock. Each $1,000 maturity amount of the bonds is convertible into 40 shares of $20 par stock. On July 31, 20X9, bondholders converted bonds into common stock.

Recording conversion of bonds payable **(Obj. 3)**

Required

1. What would cause the bondholders to convert their bonds into common stock?
2. Without making journal entries, compute the carrying amount of the bonds payable at July 31, 20X9. Jacobs-Cathey uses the straight-line method to amortize bond discount.
3. All amortization has been recorded properly. Journalize the conversion transaction at July 31, 20X9. No explanation is required.

E15-12 Shaker Village Food Industries reported the following at September 30:

Recording early retirement and conversion of bonds payable **(Obj. 3)**

Long-term liabilities:		
Convertible bonds payable	$400,000	
Less: Discount on bonds payable	(12,000)	$388,000

Required

1. Record retirement of half of the bonds on October 1 at the call price of 101.
2. Record conversion of the remainder of the bonds into 10,000 shares of Shaker Village's $5 par common stock on October 1. What would cause the bondholders to convert their bonds into stock?

E15-13 At December 31, Crestview Carpets owes $50,000 on accounts payable, plus salary payable of $14,000 and income tax payable of $8,000. Crestview also has $300,000 of bonds payable that require payment of a $30,000 installment next year and the remainder in later years. The bonds payable also require an interest payment of $7,000 at the end of each year.

Reporting liabilities **(Obj. 4)**

Report Crestview's liabilities on its year-end classified balance sheet. List liabilities in descending order (largest first, and so on).

E15-14 OK Copiers is considering two plans for raising $1,000,000 to expand operations. Plan A is to borrow at 9%, and plan B is to issue 100,000 shares of common stock. Before any new financing, OK has net income of $600,000 and 100,000 shares of common stock outstanding. Management believes the company can use the new funds to earn additional income of $420,000 before interest and taxes. The income tax rate is 40%.

Analyzing alternative plans for raising money **(Obj. 5)**

Required

Analyze OK Copiers' situation to determine which plan will result in higher earnings per share. Use Exhibit 15-8 as a guide.

Analyzing bond transactions
(Obj. 1, 2)

E15-15 This (partial and adapted) advertisement appeared in *The Wall Street Journal.*

BEAR STEARNS

New Issue

$300,000,000

MARK IV INDUSTRIES INC.

13 3/8% Subordinated Debentures due March 31, 2010
interest payable March 31 and September 30

Price 98.50% **March 31, 2000**

A *subordinated* debenture gives rights to the bondholder that are more restricted than the rights of other bondholders.

Required

Answer these questions about **Mark IV Industries'** debenture bonds payable:

1. Suppose Mark IV Industries issued these bonds payable at their offering price on March 31, 2000. Describe the transaction in detail, indicating who received cash, who paid cash, and how much.
2. Why is the stated interest rate on these bonds so high?
3. Compute Mark IV Industries' annual cash interest payment on the bonds.
4. Compute Mark IV Industries' annual interest expense under the straight-line amortization method.
5. Prepare an effective-interest amortization table for Mark IV Industries' first two interest payments on September 30, 2000, and March 31, 2001. Use Exhibit 15-4 as a guide and show all amounts in thousands. The market rate of interest on the bonds is 13.65% per year.
6. Compute Mark IV Industries interest expense for the first full year ended March 31, 2001, under the effective-interest method. Use the amortization table you prepared for requirement 5.

Analyzing bond transactions
(Obj. 1)

E15-16 Refer to the bond situation of **Mark IV Industries** in Exercise 15-15. Assume Mark IV Industries issued the bonds at the advertised price and that the company uses the straight-line amortization method and reports financial statements on a calendar-year basis.

Required

1. Journalize the following bond transactions of Mark IV Industries. Show all amounts in thousands of dollars. Explanations are not required.

2000	
Mar. 31	Issuance of the bonds.
Sep. 30	Payment of interest expense and amortization of discount on bonds payable.

2. What is Mark IV Industries' carrying amount of the bonds payable at
   a. September 30, 2000? **b.** March 31, 2001?

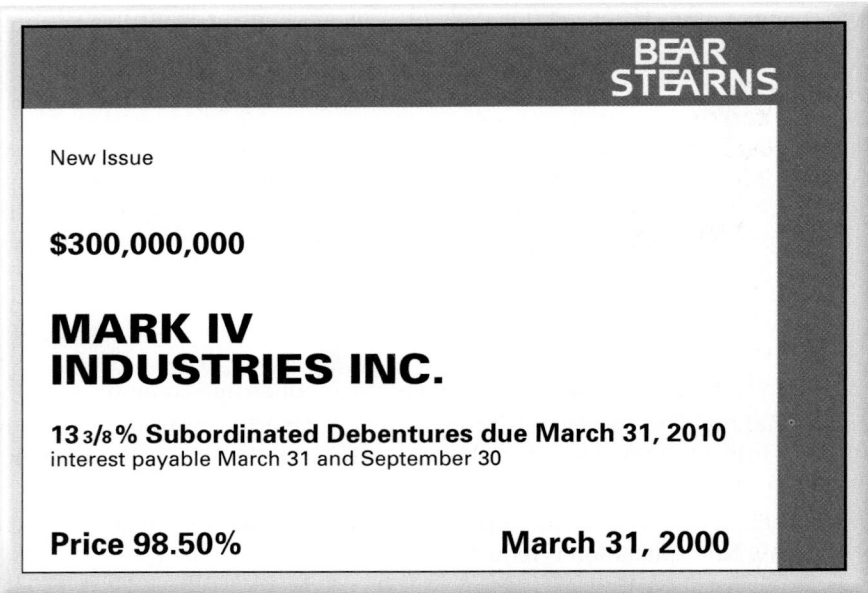

Problems

(Group A)

A+ online homework

Analyzing bonds, recording bond transactions at par, and reporting on the financial statements
(Obj. 1, 4)

Student ResourceCD
General Ledger, Peachtree, QuickBooks

P15-1A Mill Creek Golf Club issued $600,000 of 20-year, 9% bonds payable at maturity (par) value on February 1, 20X3. The bonds pay interest each January 31 and July 31, and the company ends its accounting year on December 31.

1. Fill in the blanks to complete these statements:
   a. Mill Creek's bonds are priced at (express the price as a percentage) ____.
   b. When Mill Creek issued its bonds, the market interest rate was ____%.
   c. The amount of bond discount or premium for Mill Creek to account for is $____ because the bonds were issued at ____.
2. Journalize for Mill Creek
   a. Issuance of the bonds payable on February 1, 20X3.
   b. Payment of interest on July 31, 20X3.
   c. Accrual of interest at December 31, 20X3.
   d. Payment of interest on January 31, 20X4.
   Explanations are not required.
3. Show what Mill Creek Golf Club will report on its income statement for the year ended December 31, 20X3, and on its balance sheet at December 31, 20X3.

Issuing notes payable and amortizing premium by the straight-line method
(Obj. 1)

P15-2A Assume that on April 1, 20X6, **Goretex Corp.** issues 8%, 10-year notes payable with maturity value of $400,000. The notes pay interest on March 31 and September 30, and Goretex amortizes premium and discount by the straight-line method.

Required

1. If the market interest rate is 7 1/2% when Goretex issues its notes, will the notes be priced at maturity (par) value, at a premium, or at a discount? Explain.
2. If the market interest rate is 9% when Goretex issues its notes, will the notes be priced at par, at a premium, or at a discount? Explain.
3. Assume that the issue price of the notes is 101. Journalize the following note payable transactions:
   a. Issuance of the notes on April 1, 20X6.
   b. Payment of interest and amortization of premium on September 30, 20X6.
   c. Accrual of interest and amortization of premium on December 31, 20X6.
   d. Payment of interest and amortization of premium on March 31, 20X7.

Determining bond price; recording bond transactions by the straight-line amortization method
(Obj. 1, 3)

P15-3A Global Positioning System (GPS) finances operations with both bonds and stock. Suppose GPS issued $200,000 of 10-year, 8% bonds payable under various market conditions. Match each market interest rate with the appropriate bond price, as follows:

Market Interest Rate	Bond Price
7%	?
8%	?
9%	?

The three possible bond prices are $187,000; $200,000; and $214,000. GPS pays annual interest each December 31.

After determining the respective bond prices, make the following journal entries for the bond premium situation (explanations are not required):

Dec. 31, 2008	Issuance of the bonds at a premium.
Dec. 31, 2009	Payment of interest and amortization of bond premium by the straight-line method.
Dec. 31, 2018	Payment of interest and amortization of bond premium by the straight-line method.
Dec. 31, 2018	Final payment of the bonds payable.

How much total interest expense will GPS have during the 10-year life of these bonds?

Analyzing a company's long-term debt and journalizing its transactions
(Obj. 2)

P15-4A The balance sheet of Cellular Tracking Company reported the following data on September 30, Year 1, end of the fiscal year:

Long-Term Debt	
5% bonds payable, net of	
discount of $55,200 (market interest rate of 8%)	$144,800

Cellular Tracking uses the effective-interest amortization method.

Required

1. Answer the following questions about Cellular Tracking's bonds payable:
   a. What is the maturity value of the 5% bonds?
   b. What is the carrying amount of the 5% bonds at September 30, Year 1?
   c. What is Cellular Tracking's annual cash interest payment on the 5% bonds?
2. Prepare an amortization table through September 30, Year 3, for the 5% bonds. Cellular Tracking pays interest annually on September 30.
3. Record the September 30, Year 3, interest payment and amortization of the discount on the 5% bonds.
4. What is the carrying amount of the 5% bonds at September 30, Year 3, immediately after the interest payment?

Recording bonds (at par) and reporting bonds payable on the balance sheet—bonds issued between interest dates
(Obj. 1)

Student Resource CD
GL, PT, QB

P15-5A The board of directors of Alpha Communications authorizes the issuance of $3 million of 9%, 20-year bonds payable. The semiannual interest dates are March 31 and September 30. The bonds are issued on April 30, 20X4, at par plus accrued interest.

Required

1. Journalize the following transactions:
   a. Issuance of the bonds on April 30, 20X4.
   b. Payment of interest on September 30, 20X4.
   c. Accrual of interest on December 31, 20X4.
   d. Payment of interest on March 31, 20X5.
2. Report interest payable and bonds payable as they would appear on the Alpha balance sheet at December 31, 20X4.

Issuing convertible bonds at a discount, using the effective-interest method, retiring bonds early, and reporting on the balance sheet
(Obj. 2, 3, 4)

Student Resource CD
GL, PT, QB

P15-6A On December 31, 20X7, Bible Distributing Company issues 8%, 10-year convertible bonds with a maturity value of $700,000. The semiannual interest dates are June 30 and December 31. The market interest rate is 9%, and the issue price of the bonds is 94. Bible Distributing Company amortizes bond premium and discount by the effective-interest method.

Required

1. Prepare an effective-interest-method amortization table for the first four semiannual interest periods.
2. Journalize the following transactions:
   a. Issuance of the bonds on December 31, 20X7. Credit Convertible Bonds Payable.
   b. Payment of interest on June 30, 20X8.
   c. Payment of interest on December 31, 20X8.
   d. Retirement of bonds with maturity value of $100,000 on December 31, 20X9. Bible Distributing Company purchases the bonds at 98 in the open market.
3. Prepare a balance sheet presentation of the bonds payable that are outstanding at December 31, 20X9.

Reporting liabilities on the balance sheet
(Obj. 4)

P15-7A The accounting records of Far Side Productions, Inc., include the following items:

Salary payable	$32,000	Accounts payable	$ 60,000
Bonds payable, current portion	25,000	Mortgage note payable—long-term	90,000
Discount on bonds payable (all long-term)	7,000	Interest payable	19,000
Income tax payable	16,000	Bonds payable, long-term ..	300,000

Required

Report these liabilities on Far Side Productions' balance sheet, including headings and totals for current liabilities and long-term liabilities.

Financing operations with debt or with stock
(Obj. 5)

P15-8A Market surveys show that consumers prefer upscale restaurants. To capitalize on this trend, Palomino, Inc., is embarking on a massive expansion. Plans call for opening 20 new restaurants within the next two years. Each restaurant is scheduled to be 30% larger than the company's existing locations and feature upgraded menus. Management estimates that company operations will provide $3 million of the cash needed for expansion. Palomino must raise the remaining $1.5 million from outsiders. The board of directors is considering obtaining the $1.5 million either through borrowing or by issuing common stock.

Required

1. Write a memo to company management. Discuss the advantages and disadvantages of borrowing and of issuing common stock to raise the needed cash. Use the following format for your memo:

Date:	______________
To:	Management of Palomino, Inc.
From:	Student Name
Subject:	Advantages and disadvantages of borrowing versus issuing stock to raise $1.5 million for expansion
Advantages and disadvantages of borrowing:	
Advantages and disadvantages of issuing stock:	

2. How will what you learned in this problem help you manage a business?

Problems

(Group B)

A+ online homework

Analyzing bonds, recording bonds at par, and reporting on the financial statements
(Obj. 1, 4)

Student ResourceCD
GL, PT, QB

P15-1B McLaren Ford Sales issued $500,000 of 10-year, 8% bonds payable at maturity (par) value on May 1, 20X5. The bonds pay interest each April 30 and October 31, and the company ends its accounting year on December 31.

Required

1. Fill in the blanks to complete these statements:
   a. McLaren's bonds are priced at (express the price as a percentage) ______.
   b. When McLaren issued its bonds, the market interest rate was ______%.
   c. The amount of bond discount or premium for McLaren to account for is $ ______ because the bonds were issued at ______.
2. Journalize for McLaren
   a. Issuance of the bonds payable on May 1, 20X5.
   b. Payment of interest on October 31, 20X5.
   c. Accrual of interest at December 31, 20X5.
   d. Payment of interest on April 30, 20X6.

   Explanations are not required.
3. Show what McLaren will report on its income statement for 20X5 and on its balance sheet at December 31, 20X5.

Issuing bonds and amortizing discount by the straight-line method
(Obj. 1)

P15-2B On March 1, 20X4, CD Warehouse issues 8 1/4%, 20-year bonds payable with maturity value of $400,000. The bonds pay interest on February 28 and August 31. CD Warehouse amortizes premium and discount by the straight-line method.

Required

1. If the market interest rate is 7 3/8% when CD Warehouse issues its bonds, will the bonds be priced at maturity (par) value, at a premium, or at a discount? Explain.
2. If the market interest rate is 8 7/8% when CD Warehouse issues its bonds, will the bonds be priced at par, at a premium, or at a discount? Explain.
3. The issue price of the bonds is 96. Journalize the following bond transactions:
   a. Issuance of the bonds on March 1, 20X4.
   b. Payment of interest and amortization of discount on August 31, 20X4.
   c. Accrual of interest and amortization of discount on December 31, 20X4.
   d. Payment of interest and amortization of discount on February 28, 20X5.

Determining bond price, recording bond transactions by the straight-line amortization method
(Obj. 1, 3)

P15-3B **UPS** finances operations with both bonds and stock. Suppose UPS issued $500,000 of 10-year, 7% bonds payable under various market conditions. Match each market interest rate with the appropriate bond price, as follows:

Market Interest Rate	Bond Price
6%	?
7%	?
8%	?

The three possible bond prices are $500,000; $537,000; and $466,000. Assume that UPS pays annual interest each December 31.

After determining the respective bond prices, make the following journal entries for the bond discount situation (explanations are not required):

Dec. 31, 2004	Issuance of the bonds at a discount.
Dec. 31, 2005	Payment of interest and amortization of bond discount by the straight-line method.
Dec. 31, 2014	Payment of interest and amortization of bond discount by the straight-line method.
Dec. 31, 2014	Final payment of the bonds payable.

How much total interest expense will UPS have during the 10-year life of these bonds?

Analyzing a company's long-term debt and journalizing its transactions
(Obj. 2)

P15-4B MUNY Digital's balance sheet reported the following data on September 30, Year 1, end of the fiscal year:

Long-Term Debt:	
6.00% bonds payable with a market interest rate of 8.00%, net of discount of $35,200	$164,800

MUNY Digital uses the effective-interest amortization method.

Required

1. Answer the following questions about MUNY Digital's bonds payable:
   a. What is the maturity value of the 6.00% bonds?
   b. What is the carrying amount of the 6.00% bonds at September 30, Year 1?
   c. What is MUNY's annual cash interest payment on the 6.00% bonds?
2. Prepare an amortization table through September 30, Year 3, for the 6.00% bonds. MUNY pays interest annually on September 30.
3. Record the September 30, Year 3 interest payment and amortization of the discount on the 6.00% bonds.
4. What is the carrying amount of the 6% bonds at September 30, Year 3, immediately after the interest payment?

P15-5B The board of directors of Galaxy Production Company authorizes the issuance of $8 million of 7%, 10-year bonds payable. The semiannual interest dates are May 31 and November 30. The bonds are issued on August 31, 20X5, at par plus accrued interest.

Recording bonds (at par) and reporting bonds payable on the balance sheet—bond issued between interest dates
(Obj. 1)

Student Resource CD
GL, PT, QB

Required

1. Journalize the following transactions:
   a. Issuance of the bonds on August 31, 20X5.
   b. Payment of interest on November 30, 20X5.
   c. Accrual of interest on December 31, 20X5.
   d. Payment of interest on May 31, 20X6.
2. Report interest payable and bonds payable as they would appear on the Galaxy balance sheet at December 31, 20X5.

P15-6B On December 31, 20X7, Early Bird Wireless, Inc., issues 9%, 10-year convertible bonds with a maturity value of $500,000. The semiannual interest dates are June 30 and December 31. The market interest rate is 8%, and the issue price of the bonds is 106.8. Early Bird measures interest expense by the effective-interest method.

Issuing convertible bonds at a premium, using the effective-interest method, retiring bonds early, and reporting on the balance sheet
(Obj. 2, 3, 4)

Student Resource CD
GL, PT, QB

Required

1. Prepare an effective-interest-method amortization table for the first four semiannual interest periods.
2. Journalize the following transactions:
   a. Issuance of the bonds on December 31, 20X7. Credit Convertible Bonds Payable.
   b. Payment of interest on June 30, 20X8.
   c. Payment of interest on December 31, 20X8.
   d. Retirement of bonds with maturity value of $100,000 on December 31, 20X9. Early Bird pays the call price of 102.
3. Prepare the balance sheet presentation of the bonds payable that are outstanding at December 31, 20X9.

P15-7B The accounting records of Modern Language Associates include the following items:

Reporting liabilities on the balance sheet
(Obj. 4)

Salary payable	$ 9,000	Mortgage note payable, long-term	$116,000
Bonds payable, long-term ..	160,000	Accounts payable	54,000
Premium on bonds payable (all long-term)	13,000	Bonds payable, current installment	20,000
Unearned sales revenue ...	3,000	Interest payable	14,000

Required

Report these liabilities on Modern Language Associates' balance sheet, including headings and totals for current liabilities and long-term liabilities.

P15-8B Two businesses are considering how to raise $10 million.

Financing operations with debt or with stock
(Obj. 5)

Jefferson Corporation is having its best year since it began operations in 1980. For each of the past 10 years, earnings per share have increased by at least 15%. The outlook for the future is equally bright, with new markets opening up and competitors unable to manufacture products of Jefferson's quality. Jefferson Corporation is planning a large-scale expansion.

Madison Company has fallen on hard times. Net income has been flat for the last six years, with this year falling by 10% from last year's level of profits. Top management has experienced turnover, and the company lacks leadership. To become competitive again, Madison Company desperately needs $10 million for expansion.

Required

1. Propose a plan for each company to raise the needed cash. Which company should borrow? Which company should issue stock? Consider the advantages and the disadvantages of raising money by borrowing and by issuing stock, and discuss them in your answer. Use the following memorandum headings to report your plans for the two companies:
   - Plan for Madison Company to raise $10 million
   - Plan for Jefferson Corporation to raise $10 million
2. How will what you learned in this problem help you manage a business?

APPLY *Your Knowledge*

Decision Cases

Analyzing alternative ways of raising $4 million
(Obj. 5)

Case 1. Business is going well for Email Designers. The board of directors of this family-owned company believes that Email Designers could earn an additional $1,000,000 income before interest and taxes by expanding into new markets. However, the $4,000,000 the business needs for growth cannot be raised within the family. The directors, who strongly wish to retain family control of the company, must issue securities to outsiders. They are considering three financing plans.

Plan A is to borrow at 6%. Plan B is to issue 100,000 shares of common stock. Plan C is to issue 100,000 shares of nonvoting, $2.50 preferred stock ($2.50 is the annual cash dividend for each share of preferred stock). Email Designers currently has net income of $2,000,000 and 400,000 shares of common stock outstanding. The company's income tax rate is 35%.

Required

1. Prepare an analysis similar to Exhibit 15-8 to determine which plan will result in the highest earnings per share of common stock.
2. Recommend one plan to the board of directors. Give your reasons.

Questions about long-term debt
(Obj. 1, 4 and Appendix to Chapter 15)

Case 2. → *Link Back to Chapter 4 (Debt Ratio).* The following questions are not related.

1. **IMAX Theater Corp.** needs to borrow $2 million to open new theaters. IMAX can borrow $2 million by issuing 8%, 20-year bonds at a price of 96. How much will IMAX actually be borrowing under this arrangement? How much must IMAX pay back at maturity? How will IMAX account for the difference between the amount borrowed and the amount paid back?
2. IMAX Corporation likes to borrow for longer periods when interest rates are low and for shorter periods when interest rates are high. Why is this a good business strategy?

Ethical Issue

Python.com owes $6 million on notes payable that will come due for payment in $1.5 million annual installments. The company has used its cash to advertise heavily in the competitive dotcom business environment. The result is that cash is scarce, and Python.com's management doesn't know where next year's note payment will come from. Python.com has prepared its balance sheet at December 31, 20X4, and it reports the following:

Liabilities	
Current:	
Accounts payable	$1,900,000
Salary payable and other accrued liabilities	300,000
Unearned revenue collected in advance	500,000
Income tax payable	200,000
Total current liabilities	2,900,000
Long-term:	
Notes payable	6,000,000

What is wrong with the way Python.com reported its liabilities? Why did Python.com report its liabilities this way? What is unethical about this way of reporting *these* liabilities? Who can be harmed as a result?

Financial Statement Case

Analyzing long-term debt **(Obj. 1, 2)**

The **Amazon.com** balance sheet, income statement (statement of operation's), and Note 6 in Appendix A provide details about the company's long-term debt. Use those data to answer the following questions.

Required

1. How much did Amazon.com owe on long-term debt at December 31, 2002? How much of this debt was payable in the coming year?
2. Journalize in a single entry Amazon's interest expense for 2002. Amazon paid cash of $139,896 thousand for interest.
3. Refer to Note 6 and compute the annual interest on Amazon's 4.75% convertible subordinated notes. Round to the nearest $1 thousand.

Team Project

Note: This project uses the chapter appendix.

Bermuda Corporation leases the equipment that it uses in operations. Bermuda prefers operating leases (versus capital leases) in order to keep the lease liability off its balance sheet and maintain a low debt ratio.

Bermuda is negotiating a 10-year lease on equipment with an expected useful life of 15 years. The lease requires Bermuda to make 10 annual lease payments of $20,000 each, due at the end of each year, plus a down payment that is due at the beginning of the lease term. The interest rate in the lease agreement is 10%. The leased asset has a market value of $160,000. The lease agreement specifies no transfer to title to the lessee and includes no bargain purchase option.

Write a report for Bermuda's management to explain how Bermuda should account for this lease—as an operating lease or as a capital lease. Use the following format for your report:

Date:	___________
To:	Bermuda Management
From:	Student Names
Subject:	Accounting for the company's equipment lease

For Internet exercises, go to the Web site www.prenhall.com/horngren.

APPENDIX *to Chapter 15*

Time Value of Money: Future Value and Present Value

This discussion of future value lays the foundation for present value but is not essential. For the valuation of long-term liabilities, some instructors may wish to begin in the middle of page 619.

The term *time value of money* refers to the fact that money earns interest over time. Interest is the cost of using money. To borrowers, interest is the expense of renting money. To lenders, interest is the revenue earned from lending. We must recognize the interest. Otherwise we overlook an important part of the transaction.

Suppose you invest $4,545 in corporate bonds that pay 10% interest each year. After one year, the value of your investment has grown to $5,000. The difference between your original investment ($4,545) and its future value ($5,000) is the amount of interest revenue you will earn ($455). Interest becomes more important as the time period lengthens because the amount of interest depends on how long the money is invested.

Let's consider a second example, but from the borrower's perspective. Suppose you purchase a machine for your business. The cash price of the machine is $8,000, but you cannot pay cash now. To finance the purchase, you sign an $8,000 note payable. The note requires you to pay the $8,000 plus 10% interest one year from the date of purchase. Is your cost of the machine $8,000, or is it $8,800 [$8,000 plus interest of $800 ($8,000 × 0.10)]? The cost is $8,000. The additional $800 is interest expense, which is not part of the cost of the machine.

Future Value

The main application of future value is the accumulated balance of an investment at a future date. In our first example, the investment earned 10% per year. After one year, $4,545 grew to $5,000, as shown in Exhibit 15A-1.

Exhibit 15A-1

Future Value

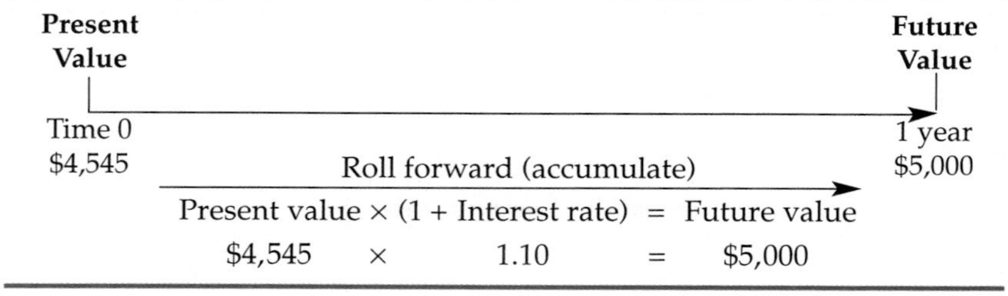

If the money were invested for five years, you would have to perform five such calculations. You would also have to consider the compound interest your investment is earning. *Compound interest* is the interest you earn not only on your principal amount, but also on the interest to date. Most business applications include compound interest. The following table shows the interest revenue earned each year at 10%:

End of Year	Interest	Future Value
0	—	$4,545
1	$4,545 × 0.10 = $455	5,000
2	5,000 × 0.10 = 500	5,500

Earning 10%, a $4,545 investment grows to $5,000 at the end of one year, to $5,500 at the end of two years, and so on. (Throughout this discussion, we round dollar amounts to the nearest dollar.)

Future-Value Tables The process of computing a future value is called *accumulating* because the future value is *more* than the present value. Mathematical tables ease the computational burden. Exhibit 15A-2, Future Value of $1, gives the future value for a single sum (a present value), $1, invested to earn a particular interest rate for a specific number of periods. Future value depends on three factors: (1) the amount of the investment, (2) the length of time between investment and future accumulation, and (3) the interest rate.

Exhibit 15A-2 **Future Value of $1**

Future Value of $1										
Period	4%	5%	6%	7%	8%	9%	10%	12%	14%	16%
1	1.040	1.050	1.060	1.070	1.080	1.090	1.100	1.120	1.140	1.160
2	1.082	1.103	1.124	1.145	1.166	1.188	1.210	1.254	1.300	1.346
3	1.125	1.158	1.191	1.225	1.260	1.295	1.331	1.405	1.482	1.561
4	1.170	1.216	1.262	1.311	1.360	1.412	1.464	1.574	1.689	1.811
5	1.217	1.276	1.338	1.403	1.469	1.539	1.611	1.762	1.925	2.100
6	1.265	1.340	1.419	1.501	1.587	1.677	1.772	1.974	2.195	2.436
7	1.316	1.407	1.504	1.606	1.714	1.828	1.949	2.211	2.502	2.826
8	1.369	1.477	1.594	1.718	1.851	1.993	2.144	2.476	2.853	3.278
9	1.423	1.551	1.689	1.838	1.999	2.172	2.358	2.773	3.252	3.803
10	1.480	1.629	1.791	1.967	2.159	2.367	2.594	3.106	3.707	4.411
11	1.539	1.710	1.898	2.105	2.332	2.580	2.853	3.479	4.226	5.117
12	1.601	1.796	2.012	2.252	2.518	2.813	3.138	3.896	4.818	5.936
13	1.665	1.886	2.133	2.410	2.720	3.066	3.452	4.363	5.492	6.886
14	1.732	1.980	2.261	2.579	2.937	3.342	3.797	4.887	6.261	7.988
15	1.801	2.079	2.397	2.759	3.172	3.642	4.177	5.474	7.138	9.266
16	1.873	2.183	2.540	2.952	3.426	3.970	4.595	6.130	8.137	10.748
17	1.948	2.292	2.693	3.159	3.700	4.328	5.054	6.866	9.276	12.468
18	2.026	2.407	2.854	3.380	3.996	4.717	5.560	7.690	10.575	14.463
19	2.107	2.527	3.026	3.617	4.316	5.142	6.116	8.613	12.056	16.777
20	2.191	2.653	3.207	3.870	4.661	5.604	6.727	9.646	13.743	19.461

The heading in Exhibit 15A-2 states $1. Future-value and present-value tables are based on $1 because unity (the value 1) is so easy to work with. Look at the Period column and the interest-rate columns 4–16%. In business applications, interest rates are always stated for the annual period of one year unless specified otherwise. In fact, an interest rate can be stated for any period, such as 3% per quarter or 5% for a six-month period. The length of the period is arbitrary.

An investment may promise a return (income) of 3% per quarter for six months (two quarters). In that case, you would be working with 3% interest for two periods. It would be incorrect to use 6% for one period because the interest is 3% compounded quarterly, and that amount differs from 6% compounded semiannually. Take care in studying future-value and present-value problems to align the interest rate with the appropriate number of periods.

Let's use Exhibit 15A-2. The future value of $1.00 invested at 8% for one year is $1.08 ($1.00 × 1.080, which appears at the junction under the 8% column and across from 1 in the Period column). The figure 1.080 includes both the principal (1.000) and the compound interest for one period (0.080).

Suppose you deposit $5,000 in a savings account that pays annual interest of 8%. The account balance at the end of one year will be $5,400. To compute the future value of $5,000 at 8% for one year, multiply $5,000 by 1.080 to get $5,400. Now suppose you invest in a 10-year, 8% certificate of deposit (CD). What will be the future value of the CD at maturity? To compute the future value of $5,000 at 8% for 10 periods, multiply $5,000 by 2.159 (from Exhibit 15A-2) to get $10,795.

This future value of $10,795 indicates that $5,000 earning 8% interest compounded annually grows to $10,795 at the end of 10 years. You can find any present amount's future value at a particular future date.

Future Value of an Annuity In the preceding example, we made an investment of a single amount. Other investments, called annuities, include multiple investments of an equal periodic amount at fixed intervals over the duration of the investment. Consider a family investing for a child's education. The Dietrichs can invest $4,000 annually to accumulate a college fund for 15-year-old Helen. The investment can earn 7% annually until Helen turns 18—a three-year investment. How much will be available for Helen on the date of the last investment? Exhibit 15A-3 shows the accumulation—a total future value of $12,860.

Exhibit 15A-3

Future Value of an Annuity

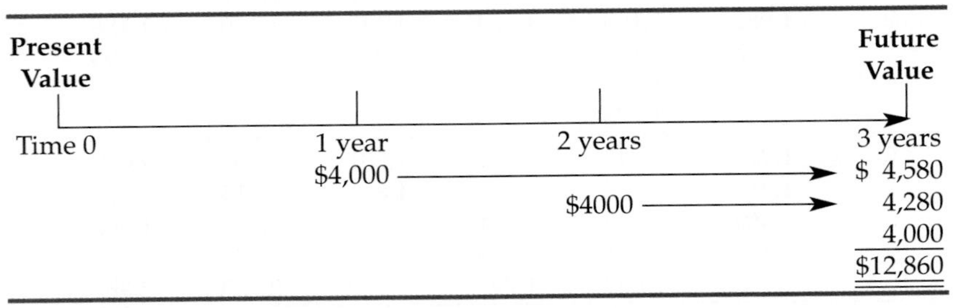

The first $4,000 invested by the Dietrichs grows to $4,580 over the investment period. The second amount grows to $4,280, and the third amount stays at $4,000 because it has no time to earn interest. The sum of the three future values ($4,580 + $4,280 + $4,000) is the future value of the annuity ($12,860), which can be computed as follows:

End of Year	Annual Investment	+	Interest	=	Increase for the Year	Future Value of Annuity
0	—		—		—	0
1	$4,000		—		$4,000	$ 4,000
2	4,000	+	($4,000 × 0.07 = $280)	=	4,280	8,280
3	4,000	+	($8,280 × 0.07 = $580)	=	4,580	12,860

As with the Future Value of $1 table (a lump sum), mathematical tables ease the strain of calculating annuities. Exhibit 15A-4, Future Value of Annuity of $1, gives the future value of a series of investments, each of equal amount, at regular intervals.

What is the future value of an annuity of three investments of $1 each that earn 7%? The answer 3.215 can be found in the 7% column and across from 3 in the Period column of Exhibit 15A-4. This amount can be used to compute the future value of the investment for Helen's education, as follows:

AMOUNT OF EACH PERIODIC INVESTMENT	×	FUTURE VALUE OF ANNUITY OF $1 (EXHIBIT 15A-4)	=	FUTURE VALUE OF INVESTMENT
$4,000	×	3.215	=	$12,860

This one-step calculation is much easier than computing the future value of each annual investment and then summing the individual future values. You can compute the future value of any investment consisting of equal periodic amounts at regular intervals. Businesses make periodic investments to accumulate funds for plant expansion and other uses—an application of the future value of an annuity.

Exhibit 15A-4 **Future Value of Annuity of $1**

Future Value of Annuity of $1										
Period	4%	5%	6%	7%	8%	9%	10%	12%	14%	16%
1	1.000	1.000	1.000	1.000	1.000	1.000	1.000	1.000	1.000	1.000
2	2.040	2.050	2.060	2.070	2.080	2.090	2.100	2.120	2.140	2.160
3	3.122	3.153	3.184	3.215	3.246	3.278	3.310	3.374	3.440	3.506
4	4.246	4.310	4.375	4.440	4.506	4.573	4.641	4.779	4.921	5.066
5	5.416	5.526	5.637	5.751	5.867	5.985	6.105	6.353	6.610	6.877
6	6.633	6.802	6.975	7.153	7.336	7.523	7.716	8.115	8.536	8.977
7	7.898	8.142	8.394	8.654	8.923	9.200	9.487	10.089	10.730	11.414
8	9.214	9.549	9.897	10.260	10.637	11.028	11.436	12.300	13.233	14.240
9	10.583	11.027	11.491	11.978	12.488	13.021	13.579	14.776	16.085	17.519
10	12.006	12.578	13.181	13.816	14.487	15.193	15.937	17.549	19.337	21.321
11	13.486	14.207	14.972	15.784	16.645	17.560	18.531	20.655	23.045	25.733
12	15.026	15.917	16.870	17.888	18.977	20.141	21.384	24.133	27.271	30.850
13	16.627	17.713	18.882	20.141	21.495	22.953	24.523	28.029	32.089	36.786
14	18.292	19.599	21.015	22.550	24.215	26.019	27.975	32.393	37.581	43.672
15	20.024	21.579	23.276	25.129	27.152	29.361	31.772	37.280	43.842	51.660
16	21.825	23.657	25.673	27.888	30.324	33.003	35.950	42.753	50.980	60.925
17	23.698	25.840	28.213	30.840	33.750	36.974	40.545	48.884	59.118	71.673
18	25.645	28.132	30.906	33.999	37.450	41.301	45.599	55.750	68.394	84.141
19	27.671	30.539	33.760	37.379	41.446	46.018	51.159	63.440	78.969	98.603
20	29.778	33.066	36.786	40.995	45.762	51.160	57.275	72.052	91.025	115.380

Present Value

Often a person knows a future amount and needs to know the related present value. Recall Exhibit 15A-1, in which present value and future value are on opposite ends of the same time line. Suppose an investment promises to pay you $5,000 at the *end* of one year. How much would you pay *now* to acquire this investment? You would be willing to pay the present value of the $5,000 future amount.

Present value also depends on three factors: (1) the amount of the future payment (or receipt), (2) the time span between investment and future receipt (or payment), and (3) the interest rate. Computing a present value is called *discounting* because the present value is *always less* than the future value.

In our example, the future receipt is $5,000. The investment period is one year. Assume that you demand an annual interest rate of 10% on your investment. With all three factors specified, you can compute the present value of $5,000 at 10% for one year.

$$\frac{\text{Future value}}{(1 + \text{Interest rate})} = \frac{\$5{,}000}{1.10} = \$4{,}545$$

By turning the data around into a future-value problem, we verify the present-value computation:

Amount invested (present value).	$4,545
Expected earnings ($4,545 × 0.10).	455
Amount to be received one year from now (future value). .	$5,000

This example illustrates that present value and future value are based on the same equation:

$$\text{Present value} \times (1 + \text{Interest rate}) = \text{Future value}$$

$$\frac{\text{Future value}}{(1 + \text{Interest rate})} = \text{Present value}$$

If the $5,000 is to be received two years from now, you will pay only $4,132 for the investment, as shown in Exhibit 15A-5.

Exhibit 15A-5

Two-Year Investment

$$\frac{\$4,545}{1.10} = \$4,132 \qquad \frac{\$5,000}{1.10} = \$4,545$$

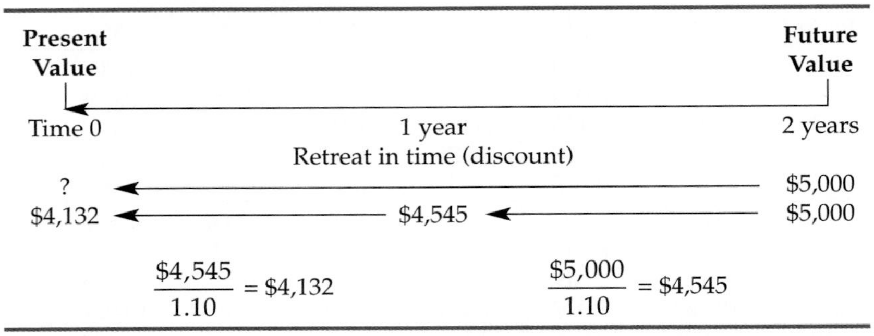

By turning the data around, we verify that $4,132 accumulates to $5,000 at 10% for two years:

Amount invested (present value) .	$4,132
Expected earnings for first year ($4,132 × 0.10)	413
Value of investment after one year .	4,545
Expected earnings for second year ($4,545 × 0.10)	455
Amount to be received two years from now (future value)	$5,000

You would pay $4,132—the present value of $5,000—to receive the $5,000 future amount at the end of two years at 10% per year. The $868 difference between the amount invested ($4,132) and the amount to be received ($5,000) is the return on the investment, the sum of the two interest receipts: $413 + $455 = $868.

Present-Value Tables We have shown the simple formula for computing present value. However, figuring present value "by hand" for investments spanning many years is burdensome. Present-value tables ease our work. Let's reexamine our examples of present value by using Exhibit 15A-6, Present Value of $1.

Exhibit 15A-6 Present Value of $1

					Present Value of $1				
Period	**4%**	**5%**	**6%**	**7%**	**8%**	**10%**	**12%**	**14%**	**16%**
1	0.962	0.952	0.943	0.935	0.926	0.909	0.893	0.877	0.862
2	0.925	0.907	0.890	0.873	0.857	0.826	0.797	0.769	0.743
3	0.889	0.864	0.840	0.816	0.794	0.751	0.712	0.675	0.641
4	0.855	0.823	0.792	0.763	0.735	0.683	0.636	0.592	0.552
5	0.822	0.784	0.747	0.713	0.681	0.621	0.567	0.519	0.476
6	0.790	0.746	0.705	0.666	0.630	0.564	0.507	0.456	0.410
7	0.760	0.711	0.665	0.623	0.583	0.513	0.452	0.400	0.354
8	0.731	0.677	0.627	0.582	0.540	0.467	0.404	0.351	0.305
9	0.703	0.645	0.592	0.544	0.500	0.424	0.361	0.308	0.263
10	0.676	0.614	0.558	0.508	0.463	0.386	0.322	0.270	0.227
11	0.650	0.585	0.527	0.475	0.429	0.350	0.287	0.237	0.195
12	0.625	0.557	0.497	0.444	0.397	0.319	0.257	0.208	0.168
13	0.601	0.530	0.469	0.415	0.368	0.290	0.229	0.182	0.145
14	0.577	0.505	0.442	0.388	0.340	0.263	0.205	0.160	0.125
15	0.555	0.481	0.417	0.362	0.315	0.239	0.183	0.140	0.108
16	0.534	0.458	0.394	0.339	0.292	0.218	0.163	0.123	0.093
17	0.513	0.436	0.371	0.317	0.270	0.198	0.146	0.108	0.080
18	0.494	0.416	0.350	0.296	0.250	0.180	0.130	0.095	0.069
19	0.475	0.396	0.331	0.277	0.232	0.164	0.116	0.083	0.060
20	0.456	0.377	0.312	0.258	0.215	0.149	0.104	0.073	0.051

For the 10% investment for one year, we find the junction in the 10% column and across from 1 in the Period column. The figure 0.909 is computed as follows: 1/1.10 = 0.909. This work has been done for us, and only the present values are given in the table. The heading in Exhibit 15A-6 states $1. To figure present value for $5,000, we multiply $5,000 by 0.909. The result is $4,545, which matches the result we obtained by hand.

For the two-year investment, we read down the 10% column and across the Period 2 row. We multiply 0.826 (computed as 0.909/1.10 = 0.826) by $5,000 and get $4,130, which confirms our earlier computation of $4,132 (the difference is due to rounding in the present-value table). Using the table, we can compute the present value of any single future amount.

Present Value of an Annuity Let's return to the investment example that provided the investor with only a single future receipt ($5,000 at the end of two years). Annuity investments provide multiple receipts of an equal amount at fixed intervals over the investment's duration.

Consider an investment that promises *annual* cash receipts of $10,000 to be received at the end of each of three years. Assume that you demand a 12% return on your investment. What is the investment's present value? What would you pay today to acquire the investment? The investment spans three periods, and you would pay the sum of three present values. The computation follows.

The present value of this annuity is $24,020. By paying this amount today, you will receive $10,000 at the end of each of the three years while earning 12% on your investment.

Year	Annual Cash Receipt	×	Present Value of $1 at 12% (Exhibit 15A-6)	=	Present Value of Annual Cash Receipt
1	$10,000	×	0.893	=	$ 8,930
2	10,000	×	0.797	=	7,970
3	10,000	×	0.712	=	7,120
	Total present value of investment			=	$24,020

The example illustrates repetitive computations of the three future amounts. One way to ease the computational burden is to add the three present values of $1 (0.893 + 0.797 + 0.712) and multiply their sum (2.402) by the annual cash receipt ($10,000) to obtain the present value of the annuity ($10,000 × 2.402 = $24,020).

An easier approach is to use a present value of an annuity table. Exhibit 15A-7 on the next page shows the present value of $1 to be received at the end of each period for a given number of periods. The present value of a three-period annuity at 12% is 2.402 (the junction of the Period 3 row and the 12% column). Thus, $10,000 received annually at the end of each of three years, discounted at 12%, is $24,020 ($10,000 × 2.402), which is the present value.

Present Value of Bonds Payable The present value of a bond—its market price—is the present value of the future principal amount at maturity plus the present value of the future stated interest payments. The principal is a single amount to be paid at maturity. The interest is an annuity because it occurs periodically.

Let's compute the present value of the 9%, five-year bonds of **eBay Inc.** The maturity value of the bonds is $100,000, and they pay 4 1/2% stated (cash) interest semiannually. At issuance, the market interest rate is expressed as 10%, but it is computed at 5% semiannually. Therefore, the market interest rate for each of the 10 semi-

Exhibit 15A-7 **Present Value of Annuity of $1**

	Present Value of Annuity of $1								
Period	**4%**	**5%**	**6%**	**7%**	**8%**	**10%**	**12%**	**14%**	**16%**
1	0.962	0.952	0.943	0.935	0.926	0.909	0.893	0.877	0.862
2	1.886	1.859	1.833	1.808	1.783	1.736	1.690	1.647	1.605
3	2.775	2.723	2.673	2.624	2.577	2.487	2.402	2.322	2.246
4	3.630	3.546	3.465	3.387	3.312	3.170	3.037	2.914	2.798
5	4.452	4.329	4.212	4.100	3.993	3.791	3.605	3.433	3.274
6	5.242	5.076	4.917	4.767	4.623	4.355	4.111	3.889	3.685
7	6.002	5.786	5.582	5.389	5.206	4.868	4.564	4.288	4.039
8	6.733	6.463	6.210	5.971	5.747	5.335	4.968	4.639	4.344
9	7.435	7.108	6.802	6.515	6.247	5.759	5.328	4.946	4.607
10	8.111	7.722	7.360	7.024	6.710	6.145	5.650	5.216	4.833
11	8.760	8.306	7.887	7.499	7.139	6.495	5.938	5.453	5.029
12	9.385	8.863	8.384	7.943	7.536	6.814	6.194	5.660	5.197
13	9.986	9.394	8.853	8.358	7.904	7.103	6.424	5.842	5.342
14	10.563	9.899	9.295	8.745	8.244	7.367	6.628	6.002	5.468
15	11.118	10.380	9.712	9.108	8.559	7.606	6.811	6.142	5.575
16	11.652	10.838	10.106	9.447	8.851	7.824	6.974	6.265	5.669
17	12.166	11.274	10.477	9.763	9.122	8.022	7.120	6.373	5.749
18	12.659	11.690	10.828	10.059	9.372	8.201	7.250	6.467	5.818
19	13.134	12.085	11.158	10.336	9.604	8.365	7.366	6.550	5.877
20	13.590	12.462	11.470	10.594	9.818	8.514	7.469	6.623	5.929

annual periods is 5%. We use 5% in computing the present value (PV) of the maturity and of the stated interest. The market price of these bonds is $96,149, as follows:

	Effective Annual Interest Rate ÷ 2	Number of Semiannual Interest Payments	
PV of principal:	↓	↓	
$100,000 × PV of single amount at 5%		for 10 periods	
($100,000 × 0.614—Exhibit 15A-6)			$61,400
PV of stated interest:			
($100,000 × 0.045) × PV of annuity at 5%		for 10 periods	
($4,500 × 7.722—Exhibit 15A-7)			34,749
PV (market price) of bonds			$96,149

The market price of the eBay bonds show a discount because the stated interest rate on the bonds (9%) is less than the market interest rate (10%). We discuss these bonds in more detail on pages 590–591.

Let's consider a premium price for the eBay bonds. Assume that the market interest rate is 8% at issuance. The market rate is 4% for each of the 10 semiannual periods:

	Effective Annual Interest Rate ÷ 2	Number of Semiannual Interest Periods	
PV of principal:	↓	↓	
$100,000 × PV of single amount at 4%		for 10 periods	
($100,000 × 0.676—Exhibit 15A-6)			$ 67,600
PV of stated interest:			
($100,000 × 0.045) × PV of annuity at 4%		for 10 periods	
($4,500 × 8.111—Exhibit 15A-7)			36,500
PV (market price) of bonds			$104,100

We discuss accounting for these bonds on page 591–592.

Appendix Assignments

Problems

Computing future values of investments

P15A-1 Gordon Riley is considering two plans for building an education fund for his children.

Plan A—Invest $2,000 each year to earn 10% annually for six years.

Plan B—Invest $10,000 now, to earn 8% annually for six years.

Which plan provides the larger amount at the end of six years? At the outset, which plan would you expect to provide the larger future amount?

Computing present-value amounts

P15A-2 Georgia-Atlantic Corp. needs new manufacturing equipment. Two companies can provide similar equipment but under different payment plans:

a. **General Electric (GE)** offers to let Georgia-Atlantic pay $60,000 each year for five years. The payments include interest at 12% per year. What is the present value of the payments?
b. **Westinghouse** will let Georgia-Atlantic make a single payment of $400,000 at the end of five years. This payment includes both principal and interest at 12%. What is the present value of this payment?
c. Georgia-Atlantic will purchase the equipment that costs the least, as measured by present value. Which equipment should Georgia-Atlantic select? Why?

Relating future-value and present-value amounts

P15A-3 This problem demonstrates the relationship between the future value of 1 and the present value of 1.

1. Rocky Tanner will need $10,000 at the end of 10 years to cover a business expense due at that time. To meet this future expense, Tanner can invest a sum today. His investment will earn 6% each year over the 10-year period. How much must Tanner invest today (present value)?
2. Now, let's turn this present-value situation around and view it in terms of a future value: Tanner has $5,580 to invest today. He can earn 6% each year over a 10-year period. How much will his investment be worth at the end of 10 years (future value)?

Computing the present values of various notes and bonds

P15A-4 Determine the present value of the following notes and bonds:

a. Ten-year bonds payable with maturity value of $88,000 and stated interest rate of 12%, paid semiannually. The market rate of interest is 12% at issuance.
b. Same bonds payable as in a, but the market interest rate is 14%.
c. Same bonds payable as in a, but the market interest rate is 10%.

Recording bond transactions

P15A-5 For each bond in Problem 15A-4, journalize issuance of the bond and the first semiannual interest payment. The company amortizes bond premium and discount by the straight-line method. Explanations are not required.

Computing a bond's present value, recording its issuance, interest payments, and amortization by the effective-interest method

P15A-6 On December 31, 20X1, when the market interest rate is 8%, Willis Realty Co. issues $400,000 of 7.25%, 10-year bonds payable. The bonds pay interest semiannually.

Required

1. Determine the present value of the bonds at issuance.
2. Assume that the bonds are issued at the price computed in requirement 1. Prepare an effective-interest method amortization table for the first two semiannual interest periods.
3. Using the amortization table prepared in requirement 2, journalize issuance of the bonds and the first two interest payments.

CHAPTER 16

Investments and International Operations

A+ TIPS CHECK YOUR RESOURCES

- Visit the www.prenhall.com/horngren **Web site** for self-study quizzes, video clips, and other resources
- Try the **Quick Check** exercise at the end of the chapter to test your knowledge
- Learn the **Key terms**
- Do the **Starter** exercises keyed in the margins
- Work the **mid-** and **end-of-chapter summary problems**
- Use the **Concept Links** to review material in other chapters
- Search the **CD** for review materials by chapter or by key word
- Watch the **tutorial videos** to review key concepts
- Watch the **On Location McDonald's International** video on consolidation accounting

LEARNING OBJECTIVES

1. Account for trading investments
2. Account for available-for-sale investments
3. Use the equity method for investments
4. Understand consolidated financial statements
5. Account for long-term investments in bonds
6. Account for transactions stated in a foreign currency

McDonald's

Have you ever invested in a stock? What type of company would interest you? **McDonald's? Panasonic? Nokia?** If you have some cash, you can invest in these companies' stocks. McDonald's is an American company, Panasonic is Japanese, and Nokia is headquartered in Finland. In a global economy, we do business with companies around the world as though they were next door.

Take McDonald's, for example. McDonald's recently invaded Disneyland-Paris and also entered Azerbaijan and Gibraltar. With restaurants in over 100 countries, McDonald's Corporation is one of the world's best-known companies.

McDonald's annual report featured a Chinese boy eating French fries. McDonald's bought those potatoes in China and must pay in Chinese currency, rather than dollars. In Russia, McDonald's pays for potatoes in rubles, and in France, in euros. Where does McDonald's get rubles and euros? That brings up accounting for international operations, the second topic of this chapter.

McDonald's has split its stock and has increased cash dividends over the years. Investors like rising stock prices and dividend increases. These topics bring up accounting for investments, the beginning topic of this chapter.

Sitemap

- Stock Investments
- Investments in Bonds and Notes
- International Operations

Investments can be a few shares of stock or the acquisition of an entire company. In earlier chapters, we discussed the stocks and bonds that IHOP and Amazon.com issued. Here we examine stocks and bonds for the investor who bought them. We begin with stock investments and then move to bonds. As you study investments, picture yourself as the investor. Your investment decisions would be similar to those of McDonald's or Amazon.com.

- Stock Investments
- Investments in Bonds and Notes
- International Operations

Student ResourceCD
available-for-sale investment, consolidation accounting, controlling interest, equity method, long-term investment, market-value method, minority interest, short-term investment, trading investment

✔ Starter 16-1

Stock Investments: An Overview

Some Basics

Stock Prices Stock prices are quoted as the market price per share—in dollars and cents. Newspapers and Internet news services such as nyse.com and nasdaq.com carry daily information on the stocks of thousands of corporations.

Exhibit 16-1 presents information for the common stock of McDonald's Corporation as it appeared in the media. During the previous 52 weeks, McDonald's stock reached a high price of $30.72 and a low of $12.12 per share. The annual cash dividend is $0.24 (24 cents) per share. On the previous day, McDonald's common stock closed at a price of $15.92 per share, which was $0.07 higher than the price of the preceding day.

Exhibit 16-1
Stock Price Information for McDonald's Corporation

52 weeks					
High	**Low**	**Stock Symbol**	**Dividend**	**Close**	**Net Change**
30.72	12.12	MCD	.24	15.92	.07

The owner of the stock in a corporation is the *investor*. The corporation that issued the stock is the *investee*. If you own shares of McDonald's stock, you are an investor and McDonald's is the investee.

Classifying Investments An investment is an asset to the investor. The investment may be short-term or long-term. **Short-term investments**—sometimes called **marketable securities**—are current assets. Short-term investments are liquid (readily convertible to cash), and the investor intends to convert them to cash within one year.

Short-Term Investment
A current asset; an investment that is readily convertible to cash and that the investor intends either to convert to cash within one year or use to pay a current liability. Also called a **marketable security**.

Long-Term Investment
A noncurrent asset; a separate asset category reported on the balance sheet between current assets and plant assets.

Investments that are not short-term are classified as **long-term investments** on the balance sheet. Long-term investments include stocks and bonds that the investor expects to hold longer than one year or that are not readily marketable—for instance, real estate held for sale. Exhibit 16-2 shows the positions of short-term and long-term investments on the balance sheet.

The balance sheet reports assets by order of liquidity, starting with cash. Short-term investments are the second-most-liquid asset. Long-term investments are less liquid than current assets but more liquid than property, plant, and equipment.

ASSETS		
Current Assets		
Cash	$X	
Short-term investments	X	
Accounts receivable	X	
Inventories	X	
Prepaid expenses	X	
Total current assets		$X
Long-term investments (or simply Investments)		X
Property, plant, and equipment		X
Intangible assets		X
Other assets		X

Exhibit 16-2

Reporting Investments on the Balance Sheet

TRADING AND AVAILABLE-FOR-SALE INVESTMENTS We begin stock investments with situations in which the investor owns less than 20% of the investee company. These investments in stock are classified as trading investments or as available-for-sale investments. **Trading investments** are to be sold in the very near future—days, weeks, or only a few months—with the intent of generating a profit on a quick sale. Trading investments are short-term.

Available-for-sale investments are all less-than-20% investments other than trading investments. Available-for-sale investments are current assets if the business expects to sell them within the next year or within the operating cycle if longer than a year. All other available-for-sale investments are long-term.

The investor accounts for trading investments and available-for-sale investments separately. We begin with trading investments.

Trading Investments
Investments that are to be sold in the very near future with the intent of generating profits on price changes.

Available-for-Sale Investments
All less-than-20% investments other than trading securities.

✔ Starter 16-2

Accounting for Trading Investments

1 *Account for trading investments*

The **market-value method** is used to account for trading investments because they will be sold in the near future at their current market value. Cost is the initial amount for a trading investment. Assume McDonald's Corporation has excess cash to invest. Suppose McDonald's buys 500 shares of Ford Motor Company stock for $50 per share on October 23, 20X5. Assume further that McDonald's management plans to sell this stock within three months. This is a trading investment, which McDonald's records as follows:

Market-Value Method
Used to account for all trading investments. These investments are reported at their current market value.

20X5			
Oct. 23	Short-Term Investment (500 × $50)	25,000	
	Cash		25,000
	Purchased investment.		

Short-Term Investment	
25,000	

Ford pays a cash dividend of $2 per share, so McDonald's would receive a dividend on the investment. McDonald's entry to record receipt of a cash dividend is

20X5			
Nov. 14	Cash (500 × $2.00)	1,000	
	Dividend Revenue		1,000
	Received cash dividend		

Trading investments are reported on the balance sheet at current market value, not at cost. This requires a year-end adjustment of the trading investment to current market value on the balance-sheet date. Assume that the Ford stock has decreased in value, and at December 31, 20X5, McDonald's investment in Ford stock is worth $20,000 ($5,000 less than the purchase price). At year-end, McDonald's would make the following adjustment:

Short-Term Investment

25,000	5,000
20,000	

20X5			
Dec. 31	Loss on Trading Investment ($25,000 – $20,000)	5,000	
	Short-Term Investment		5,000
	Adjusted trading investment to market value.		

The T-account shows the $20,000 ($25,000 – $5,000) balance of Short-Term Investment. McDonald's would report its trading investment on the balance sheet at December 31, 20X5, and the loss on trading investment on the 20X5 income statement, as follows:

Balance Sheet (Partial):		Income Statement (Partial):	
ASSETS		Other gains and losses:	
Current assets:		Gain (loss) on trading investment	$(5,000)
Short-term investments, at market value	$20,000		

If the investment's market value had risen above $25,000, McDonald's would have debited Short-Term Investment and credited Gain on Trading Investment.

When a company sells a trading investment, the gain or loss on the sale is the difference between the sale proceeds and the last carrying amount. Suppose McDonald's sells the Ford stock for $18,000 on January 19, 20X6. McDonald's would record the sale as follows:

Short-Term Investment

25,000	5,000
20,000	20,000

20X6			
Jan. 19	Cash	18,000	
	Loss on Sale of Investment	2,000	
	Short-Term Investment		20,000
	Sold investment.		

✔ Starter 16-3

✔ Starter 16-4

For reporting on the income statement, McDonald's could combine all gains and losses ($5,000 + $2,000) on short-term investments and report a single net amount under Other gains (losses). . . . $(7,000).

2 *Account for available-for-sale investments*

Accounting for Long-Term Available-for-Sale Investments

The **market-value method** is used to account for available-for-sale investments because the company expects to resell the stock at its market value. Available-for-sale investments therefore are reported on the balance sheet at their *current market value*, just like trading investments.

Suppose Dell Corporation purchases 1,000 shares of Hewlett-Packard Company (HP) common stock at the market price of $33. Dell plans to hold this stock for longer than a year and classifies it as a long-term available-for-sale investment. Dell's entry to record the investment is

20X1			
Feb. 23	Long-Term Available-for-Sale Investment (1,000 × $33)	33,000	
	Cash		33,000
	Purchased investment.		

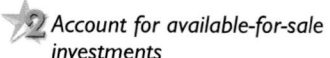

Dell receives a $0.60 per share cash dividend on the Hewlett-Packard stock. Dell's entry for receipt of the dividend is

20X1			
July 14	Cash (1,000 × $0.60)	600	
	Dividend Revenue................		600
	Received dividend.		

STOCK DIVIDEND VERSUS A CASH DIVIDEND A *stock* dividend is different from a cash dividend. → For a stock dividend, the investor records no dividend revenue. Instead, he makes a memorandum entry in the accounting records to show the new number of shares of stock held. The shares have increased, so the investor's cost per share decreases. For example, suppose Dell Corporation receives a 10% stock dividend from Hewlett-Packard. Dell would receive 100 shares (10% of 1,000 shares previously held) and make this memorandum entry:

For a review of stock dividends, see Chapter 14, page 544.

✔ **Starter 16-5**

MEMORANDUM—Receipt of stock dividend: Received 100 shares of Hewlett-Packard common stock in a 10% stock dividend. New cost per share is $30 (cost of $33,000 ÷ 1,100 shares).

For all future Hewlett-Packard investment transactions, Dell will use the new cost per share of $30.

REPORTING AVAILABLE-FOR-SALE INVESTMENTS Available-for-sale investments are reported on the balance sheet at market value. This requires an adjustment to current market value on the balance-sheet date. Assume that the market value of Dell's investment in Hewlett-Packard common stock is $36,000 on December 31, 20X1. In this case, Dell makes the following adjustment:

20X1			
Dec. 31	Allowance to Adjust Investment to		
	Market ($36,000 – $33,000)	3,000	
	Unrealized Gain on Investment.....		3,000
	Adjusted investment to market value.		

✔ **Starter 16-6**

Allowance to Adjust Investment to Market is a companion account to Long-Term Investment. The Allowance account brings the investment to current market value. Cost ($33,000) plus the Allowance ($3,000) equals the investment carrying amount ($36,000).

Long-Term Available-for-Sale Investment		Allowance to Adjust Investment to Market	
33,000		3,000	

Investment carrying amount = Market value of $36,000

Here the Allowance has a debit balance because the investment has increased in value. If the investment's value declines, the Allowance is credited. In that case, the investment carrying amount is cost *minus* the Allowance. The Allowance with a credit balance becomes a contra account. →

Other contra accounts are Accumulated Depreciation (Chapter 3) and Allowance for Uncollectible Accounts (Chapter 9).

The other side of the December 31 adjustment credits Unrealized Gain on Investment. If the investment declines, the company debits an Unrealized Loss. *Unrealized* means that the gain or loss resulted from a change in market value, not a sale. A gain or loss on the sale of an investment is said to be *realized* because the company receives cash. *Cash* turns a gain or loss into a realized gain or loss. For available-for-sale investments, the Unrealized Gain (or Loss) account is reported on the balance sheet as part of stockholders' equity, as shown here.

Balance Sheet (Partial)

ASSETS		STOCKHOLDERS' EQUITY	
Total current assets	$ XXX	Common stock	$ XXX
Long-term available-for-sale investments—at market value	36,000	Retained earnings	XXX
Property, plant, and equipment, net	XXX	Unrealized gain on investments	3,000

SELLING AN AVAILABLE-FOR-SALE INVESTMENT The sale of an available-for-sale investment can result in a *realized* gain or loss. Suppose Dell Corporation sells its investment in Hewlett-Packard stock for $32,000 during 20X2. Dell would record the sale as follows:

20X2			
May 19	Cash	32,000	
	Loss on Sale of Investment	1,000	
	Long-Term Available-for-Sale Investment (cost)		33,000
	Sold investment.		

✔ Starter 16-7

Dell would report the Loss on Sale of Investment as an "Other gain or loss" on the income statement.[1]

Stop & Think

Suppose Xenon Corporation holds the following long-term available-for-sale investments at December 31, 20X3:

Stock	Cost	Current Market Value
The Coca-Cola Company	$ 85,000	$ 71,000
Eastman Kodak Company	16,000	12,000
Scott Paper Company	122,000	136,000
	$223,000	$219,000

Show how Xenon will report long-term investments and the unrealized loss on its December 31, 20X3, balance sheet.

Answer:

Assets

Long-term available-for-sale investments, at market value $219,000

Stockholders' Equity

Unrealized gain (loss) on investments
($223,000 – $219,000) ....$ (4,000)

3 *Use the equity method for investments*

Accounting for Equity-Method Investments

An investor with a stock holding between 20% and 50% of the investee's voting stock owns a sizeable portion of the investee. With a 20% to 50% investment, the investor can *significantly influence* the investee's decisions on dividends and product lines. For this reason, investments in the range of 20% to 50% of another company are common. For example, General Motors owns nearly 40% of Isuzu Motors Overseas Distribution Corporation, and Dow Jones & Company, publisher of *The Wall Street Journal*, owns 50% of Smart Money, the magazine company.

[1]We omit the complex journal entry to adjust the Allowance account at year-end. That topic is covered in intermediate accounting courses.

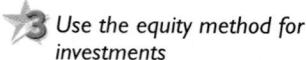

We use the **equity method** to account for 20% to 50% investments. A recent survey of 600 companies by *Accounting Trends & Techniques* showed that 43% of the companies held investments accounted for by the equity method. Investee companies are often called *affiliates* or *affiliated companies*.

Equity Method
Method used to account for investments in which the investor has 20% to 50% of the investee's voting stock and can significantly influence the decisions of the investee.

RECORDING THE INITIAL INVESTMENT Investments accounted for by the equity method are recorded initially at cost. Suppose Amazon.com pays $400,000 for 20% of the common stock of Drugstore.com. Amazon may refer to Drugstore.com as an *affiliated company*. Amazon's entry to record the purchase of this investment follows.

20X8			
Jan. 6	Long-Term Equity-Method Investment.......	400,000	
	Cash................................		400,000
	Purchased equity-method investment.		

ADJUSTING THE INVESTMENT ACCOUNT FOR INVESTEE NET INCOME Under the equity method, the investor applies its percentage of ownership to record its share of the investee's net income and dividends. Suppose Drugstore.com reported net income of $250,000 for the year. Amazon would record 20% of this amount as an increase in the investment account and as equity-method investment revenue, as follows:

Dec. 31	Long-Term Equity-Method Investment ($250,000 × 0.20)..........................	50,000	
	Equity-Method Investment Revenue		50,000
	Recorded investment revenue.		

The Investment Revenue account carries the Equity-Method label to identify its source. This labeling is similar to distinguishing Sales Revenue from Service Revenue.

The investor increases the Investment account and records Investment Revenue when the investee reports income. As the investee's equity increases, so does the Investment account on the investor's books.

RECEIVING DIVIDENDS ON AN EQUITY-METHOD INVESTMENT Amazon records its proportionate part of cash dividends received from Drugstore.com. Suppose Drugstore.com declares and pays a cash dividend of $100,000. Amazon receives 20% of this dividend and makes this journal entry:

20X9			
Jan. 17	Cash ($100,000 × 0.20)......................	20,000	
	Long-Term Equity-Method Investment..		20,000
	Received dividend on equity-method investment.		

The Investment account is credited for the receipt of a dividend on an equity-method investment. Why? Because the dividend decreases both the investee's equity and the investor's investment.

After the preceding entries are posted, Amazon.com's Investment account reflects its equity in the net assets of Drugstore.com:

✔ Starter 16-8

Long-Term Equity-Method Investment

20X8			**20X9**		
Jan. 6	**Purchase**	**400,000**	**Jan. 17**	**Dividends received**	**20,000**
Dec. 31	**Net income**	**50,000**			
20X9					
Jan. 17	**Balance**	**430,000**			

Amazon.com can report the long-term investment on the balance sheet and the revenue on the income statement as follows:

Balance Sheet (Partial):		Income Statement (Partial):	
ASSETS		Income from operations	$ XXX
Total current assets	$ XXX	Other revenue:	
Long-term equity-method investments	430,000	Equity-method investment revenue	50,000
Property, plant, and equipment, net	XXX	Net income	$ XXX

Selling an Equity-Method Investment There may be a gain or a loss on the sale of an equity-method investment. The gain or loss is the difference between the sale proceeds and the investment carrying amount. Suppose Amazon.com sells one-tenth of the Drugstore.com common stock for $40,000. The sale is recorded as follows:

Feb. 13	Cash	40,000	
	Loss on Sale of Investment	3,000	
	Long-Term Equity-Method Investment ($430,000 × 1/10)		43,000
	Sold investment.		

The following T-account summarizes the accounting for equity-method investments:

Long-Term Equity-Method Investment	
Cost	Share of losses
Share of income	Share of dividend received

Joint Ventures A *joint venture* is a separate entity owned by a group of companies. Joint ventures are used for risky endeavors such as oil exploration and the construction of nuclear power plants. Aramco, which stands for Arabian American Oil Company, is a joint venture half-owned by Saudi Arabia. Several multinational oil companies (ExxonMobil, ChevronTexaco, and others) own the remaining 50%.

A participant in a joint venture accounts for its investment by the equity method. Joint ventures are common in international business. Companies such as British Telecom, Total (of France) and Toyota partner with companies in other countries.

4 *Understand consolidated financial statements*

Controlling Interest
Ownership of more than 50% of an investee company's voting stock. Also called **majority interest**.

Parent Company
An investor company that owns more than 50% of the voting stock of a subsidiary company.

Subsidiary Company
A company in which a parent company owns more than 50% of the voting stock.

Exhibit 16-3

Ownership Structure of General Motors Corporation and Saturn Corporation

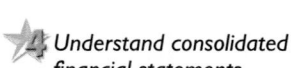

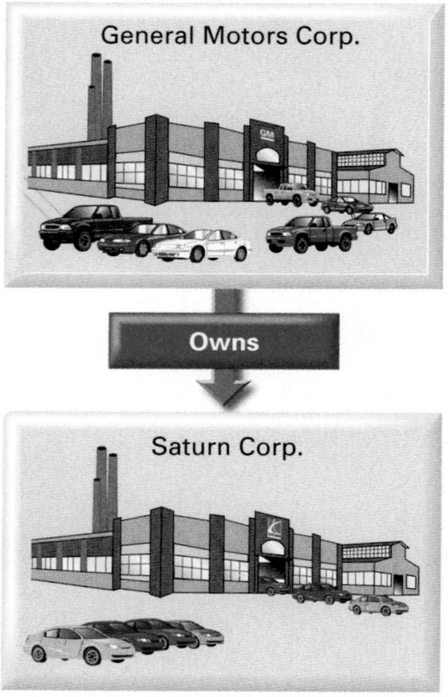

Accounting for Consolidated Subsidiaries

Most large corporations own controlling interests in other companies. A **controlling** (or **majority**) **interest** is the ownership of more than 50% of the investee's voting stock. A greater-than-50% investment enables the investor to elect a majority of the investee's board of directors and thereby control the investee. The corporation that controls the other company is called the **parent company**, and the company that is controlled by another corporation is called the **subsidiary**. A well-known example is Saturn Corporation, which is a subsidiary of General Motors, the parent company. Because GM owns Saturn Corporation, the stockholders of GM control Saturn, as diagrammed in Exhibit 16-3.

Why have subsidiaries? Why not have the corporation operate as a single legal entity? A subsidiary arrangement may save on income taxes, limit the parent's liabilities, and ease expansion into foreign countries. For example, McDonald's Corporation finds it easier to operate in France through a French subsidiary than through the U.S. parent company. Exhibit 16-4 shows some of the subsidiaries of three large automakers.

Exhibit 16-4

Selected Subsidiaries of Three Large Automobile Manufacturers

Parent Company	Selected Subsidiaries
General Motors Corporation	Saturn Corporation Hughes Aircraft Company
Ford Motor Company	Ford Aerospace Corporation Jaguar, Ltd.
DaimlerChrysler Corporation	Jeep/Eagle Corporation DaimlerChrysler Rail Systems

MAJORITY-OWNED SUBSIDIARIES *Consolidation accounting* is a way to combine the financial statements of two or more companies that have the same owners. Most published financial reports include consolidated statements. To understand real financial statements, you need to know the basics of consolidation accounting. **Consolidated statements** combine the balance sheets, income statements, and cash-flow statements of the parent company plus those of its majority-owned subsidiaries. The final outcome is a single set of statements as if the parent and its subsidiaries were the same entity.

Consolidated Statements
Financial statements of the parent company plus those of majority-owned subsidiaries as if the combination were a single legal entity.

In consolidation accounting, the assets, liabilities, revenues, and expenses of each subsidiary are added to the parent's accounts. The consolidated financial statements report the combined account balances. For example, Saturn's cash balance is added to the cash balance of General Motors, and the overall sum is reported on GM's balance sheet. The consolidated financial statements bear only the name of the parent company, in this case, General Motors Corporation.

Exhibit 16-5 shows which accounting method should be used for each type of stock investment.

GOODWILL AND MINORITY INTEREST Goodwill is an intangible asset that is recorded in the consolidation process and reported on the parent company's consolidated balance sheet. As we have seen, *goodwill* is the excess of the cost to acquire another company over the sum of the market value of its net assets. →

← *Chapter 10 discusses how to account for goodwill.*

A parent company may purchase less than 100% of a subsidiary company. For example, Nokia, the cellular telephone company, has a minority interest (owns less than 100% of) several other companies. **Minority interest** is the portion (less than 50%) of a subsidiary's stock that is owned by outside stockholders. Nokia Corporation, the parent company, therefore reports on its consolidated balance sheet an account titled Minority Interest. Most analysts treat Minority Interest as a liability.

✔ **Starter 16-9**

Exhibit 16-5

Accounting Methods for Investments by Percentage of Ownership

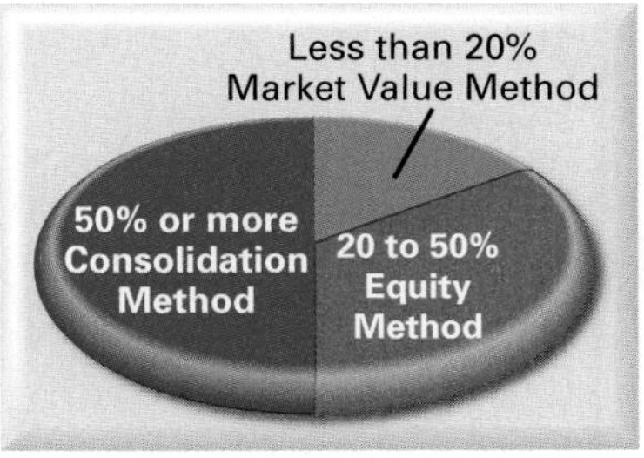

Minority Interest
A subsidiary company's equity that is held by stockholders other than the parent company.

INCOME OF A CONSOLIDATED ENTITY The income of a consolidated entity is the sum of

- Net income of the parent company, plus
- Parent's portion of the subsidiaries' net income

Suppose Parent Company owns all the stock of Subsidiary S-1 and 60% of the stock of Subsidiary S-2. During 20X8, Parent earned net income of $330,000, S-1 earned $150,000, and S-2 had a net loss of $100,000. Parent Company would report consolidated net income of $420,000, computed as follows:

	Net Income (Net Loss)	×	Parent Stockholders' Ownership	=	Parent's Consolidated Net Income (Net Loss)
Parent Company	$ 330,000	×	100%	=	$330,000
Subsidiary S-1	150,000	×	100%	=	150,000
Subsidiary S-2	(100,000)	×	60%	=	(60,000)
Consolidated net income					$420,000

Stop & Think

Answer these questions about consolidated financial statements:

1. Whose name appears on the consolidated statements—the parent company, the subsidiary company, or both?
2. Company A owns 90% of Company B. What is the remaining 10% of Company B's stock called, and where does it appear in Company A's financial statements?
3. Company C paid $1 million to acquire Company D, whose stockholders' equity (same as net assets) totaled $700,000. What is the $300,000 excess called? Which company reports the excess? Where in the financial statements is the excess reported?

Answers:

1. Parent company only
2. Minority interest—reported on (Parent) Company A's balance sheet among the liabilities
3. Goodwill—reported on (Parent) Company C's balance sheet as an intangible asset

☐ Stock Investments
■ Investments in Bonds and Notes
☐ International Operations

5 *Account for long-term investments in bonds*

Student Resource CD
bond investment, long-term investment, short-term investment

Accounting for Long-Term Investments in Bonds and Notes

Most companies invest far more in stocks than in bonds. The major holders of bonds are investment companies. The relationship between the issuing corporation and bondholders may be diagrammed as follows:

Issuing Corporation Has		Bondholder Has
Bonds payable	←——→	Investment in bonds
Interest expense	←——→	Interest revenue

The dollar amount of a bond transaction is the same for both the issuing corporation and the bondholder because money passes from one to the other. However, the accounts debited and credited differ. For example, the corporation has bonds payable; the bondholder has an investment. The corporation has interest expense, and the bondholder has interest revenue. Chapter 15 covered bonds payable. ←

See Chapter 15, pages 584–587 for discussion of bonds payable. →

An investment in bonds is classified as short-term (a current asset) or as long-term. *Short-term investments in bonds are rare.* Therefore, we focus on long-term investments in bonds. These are called **held-to-maturity investments**.

Held-to-Maturity Investments
Investment in bonds, notes, and other debt securities that the investor expects to hold until their maturity date.

Bond investments are recorded at cost. At maturity, the investor will receive the bonds' full face value. We must amortize any discount or premium, as we did for bonds payable in Chapter 15. Held-to-maturity investments are reported at their *amortized cost*.

Suppose an investor purchases $10,000 of 6% CBS bonds at a price of 94 (94% of maturity value) on July 1, 20X2. The investor intends to hold the bonds as a long-term investment until their maturity. Interest dates are June 30 and December 31. These bonds mature on July 1, 20X7, so they will be outstanding for 60 months. Let's amortize the discount by the straight-line method. ← The following are the bondholder's entries for this investment:

Straight-line amortization of premium or discount on a bond investment is calculated the same way as for bonds payable (see Chapter 15, page 584). →

20X2			
July 1	Long-Term Investment in Bonds ($10,000 × 0.94)	9,400	
	Cash		9,400
	Purchased bond investment.		

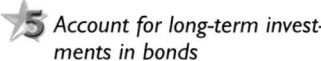

At December 31, the year-end entries are

Dec. 31	Cash ($10,000 × 0.06 × 6/12)	300	
	Interest Revenue		300
	Received interest.		
Dec. 31	Long-Term Investment in Bonds [($10,000 – $9,400)/5 × 6/12]..........	60	
	Interest Revenue		60
	Amortized discount on bond investment.		

✔ Starter 16-10

The financial statements at December 31, 20X2, report the following for this investment in bonds:

Balance sheet at December 31, 20X2:	
Long-term investments in bonds ($9,400 + $ 60)	$9,460
Income statement for 20X2:	
Other revenues:	
Interest revenue ($300 + $60)	$ 360

✔ Starter 16-11

Decision Guidelines

ACCOUNTING FOR LONG-TERM INVESTMENTS

Suppose you work for **Bank of America**. Your duties include accounting for the bank's investments. The following Decision Guidelines can serve as your checklist for using the appropriate method to account for each type of investment.

Decision	Guidelines
Investment Type	***Accounting Method***
Short-Term Investment	
Trading investment	Market value—report all gains (losses) on the income statement
Long-Term Investment	
Investor owns less than 20% of investee stock (available-for-sale investment)	Market value—report *unrealized* gains (losses) on the balance sheet —report *realized* gains (losses) from sale of the investment on the income statement
Investor owns between 20% and 50% of investee stock	Equity
Investment in a joint venture	Equity
Investor owns more than 50% of investee stock	Consolidation
Long-term investment in bonds (held-to-maturity investment)	Amortized cost

Excel Application Exercise

Goal: Create an Excel work sheet to chart foreign currency exchange rates.

Scenario: Your clothing boutique is expanding to offer merchandise made in other countries. In order to manage your company's foreign exchange rates, you are creating a spreadsheet to track currencies over the past 3 months for countries where you'll be doing business. The currencies you want to track against U.S. dollars are Canada dollars, euros, Australia dollars, and Swiss francs. When done, answer these questions:

1. Which currencies have strengthened, relative to the U.S. dollar, during the past 3 months? Which have weakened?
2. Which accounts are affected by foreign currency rate fluctuations?
3. What actions might a business take to manage its risk of a foreign exchange loss?

Step-by-Step:

1. Open a new Excel work sheet.
2. Create a heading for your work sheet that contains the following:
   a. Chapter 16 Excel Application Exercise
   b. Foreign Exchange Rates
   c. Today's Date
3. Launch your Web browser and go to www.xe.com/ict. This Web site specializes in reporting foreign-currency exchange rates. Under "Show me a currency table," choose "Based on USD (United States Currency)." Then, under "as of this date," click "the following date" and enter the current month, day 1 (the first day of the month), for the current year (e.g., 2003). Next, click on the button to generate a currency table.
4. On the table just created, locate the currencies listed in the exercise. You will be using the values listed under "USD per Unit." This is how much you'd need in US dollars to buy one unit of the foreign currency. For example, $1.60 USD equals 1 United Kingdom (British) pound.
5. Repeat the table creation process in steps 4 and 5 for the past 3 months. When done, you will have 3 data points for each currency.
6. Two rows down from your heading in your Excel spreadsheet in column A, enter the heading "Foreign Currency (USD per unit)." Starting in column B, set up 3 columns, one for each month of data with labels (Jan 1 2003, Feb 1 2003, etc.). Start with the oldest month first.
7. Return to column A. Under the "Foreign Currency" heading, list the names of the currencies, one per row (for example, Canada Dollars). Enter the monthly rate data collected for each currency in the appropriate columns.
8. Highlight all rows and columns, including titles. Click the Chart Wizard button. Select the "line" chart with markers displayed at each data value. Click next. Click next again.
9. Enter the chart title, "Foreign Currency Rates." Leave the **x** axis title blank. Enter the title, "USD per Unit" for the **y** axis. Click next.
10. Save your chart as an object in your spreadsheet and click finish. Size the chart to fit below your data.
11. When finished, save your work and print a copy for your files.

MID-CHAPTER *Summary Problem*

A+ TIPS
CHECK YOUR RESOURCES

Required

1. Identify the appropriate accounting method for each of the following situations:
   a. Investment in 25% of investee company's stock.
   b. Available-for-sale investment in stock.
   c. Investment in more than 50% of investee company's stock.
2. At what amount should the following available-for-sale investment portfolio be reported on the December 31 balance sheet? All the investments are less than 5% of the investee's stock.

Stock	Investment Cost	Current Market Value
Amazon.com	$ 5,000	$ 5,500
Intelysis	61,200	53,000
Procter & Gamble	3,680	6,230

   Journalize any adjusting entry required by these data.
3. Investor paid $67,900 to acquire a 40% equity-method investment in the common stock of Investee. At the end of the first year, Investee's net income was $80,000, and Investee declared and paid cash dividends of $55,000. Journalize Investor's (a) purchase of the investment, (b) share of Investee's net income, (c) receipt of dividends from Investee, and (d) sale of Investee stock for $80,100.

Solution

1. (a) Equity (b) Market value (c) Consolidation
2. Report the investments at market value, $64,730, as follows:

Stock	Investment Cost	Current Market Value
Amazon.com	$ 5,000	$ 5,500
Intelysis	61,200	53,000
Procter & Gamble	3,680	6,230
Totals	$69,880	$64,730

Adjusting entry:

Unrealized Loss on Investments ($69,880 – $64,730)	5,150	
Allowance to Adjust Investment to Market		5,150
To adjust investments to current market value.		

3. a. Long-Term Equity-Method Investment	67,900	
Cash		67,900
Purchased equity-method investment.		
b. Long-Term Equity-Method Investment ($80,000 × 0.40) ..	32,000	
Equity-Method Investment Revenue		32,000
Recorded investment revenue.		
c. Cash ($55,000 × 0.40)	22,000	
Long-Term Equity-Method Investment		22,000
Received dividend on equity-method investment.		
d. Cash	80,100	
Long-Term Equity-Method Investment ($67,900 + $32,000 – $22,000)		77,900
Gain on Sale of Investment		2,200
Sold investment.		

☐ Stock Investments
☐ Investments in Bonds and Notes
■ International Operations

Accounting for International Operations

Student Resource CD
exchange rate, exchange rate risk, foreign currency gains and losses, hedging

Accounting for business activities across national boundaries is called *international accounting*. Did you know that Coca-Cola, IBM, and Bank of America earn most of their revenue outside the United States? It is common for U.S. companies to do a large part of their business abroad. McDonald's and AMR (American Airlines) are also very active in other countries. Exhibit 16-6 shows the percentages of international sales for these companies.

Exhibit 16-6
Extent of International Business

Company	Percentage of International Sales
McDonald's	65%
IBM	60
AMR (American Airlines)	28

Foreign Currencies and Foreign-Currency Exchange Rates

If Boeing, a U.S. company, sells a 747 jet to Air France, will Boeing receive U.S. dollars or euros? If the transaction is stated in dollars, Air France must buy dollars to pay Boeing in U.S. currency. If the transaction is in euros, Boeing must sell euros. In either case, a step has been added to the transaction: One company must convert domestic currency into foreign currency, or vice versa.

Foreign-Currency Exchange Rate
The measure of one currency against another currency.

One nation's currency can be stated in terms of another country's monetary unit. The price of a foreign currency is called the **foreign-currency exchange rate**. In Exhibit 16-7, the U.S. dollar value of a European euro is $1.10. This means that one euro can be bought for $1.10. Other currencies are also listed in Exhibit 16-7.

Exhibit 16-7 Foreign-Currency Exchange Rates

Country	Monetary Unit	U.S. Dollar Value	Country	Monetary Unit	U.S. Dollar Value
Canada	Dollar	$0.69	Japan	Yen	$0.008
European Common Market	European currency unit	1.10	Mexico	Peso	0.096
Great Britain	Pound	1.59	Russia	Ruble	0.03

Source: The Wall Street Journal, April 29, 2003, p. C14.

Strong Currency
A currency that is rising relative to other nations' currencies.

Weak Currency
A currency that is falling relative to other nations' currencies.

We use the exchange rate to convert the price of an item stated in one currency to its price in a second currency. We call this conversion a *translation*. Suppose an item costs 200 Canadian dollars. To compute its cost in U.S. dollars, we multiply the amount in Canadian dollars by the conversion rate: 200 Canadian dollars × $0.69 = $138.

Currencies are described as "strong" or "weak." The exchange rate of a **strong currency** is rising relative to other nations' currencies. The exchange rate of a **weak currency** is falling relative to other currencies.

6 Account for transactions stated in a foreign currency

Foreign-Currency Transactions

More and more companies conduct transactions in foreign currencies. D. E. Shipp Belting of Waco, Texas, provides an example. Shipp makes conveyor belts for several industries, including M&M Mars, which makes Snickers candy bars in Waco. Farmers along the Texas–Mexico border use Shipp conveyor belts to process vegetables. Some of these customers are Mexican, so Shipp Belting conducts some of its business in pesos, the Mexican monetary unit.

COLLECTING CASH IN A FOREIGN CURRENCY Consider Shipp Belting's sale of conveyor belts to Artes de Mexico, a vegetable grower in Matamoros. The sale can be conducted in dollars or pesos. If Artes agrees to pay in dollars, the transaction is the same as selling to M&M Mars across town. But suppose Artes orders conveyor belts valued at 1,000 pesos (approximately $96). Further suppose that Artes demands to pay in pesos.

Shipp will need to convert the pesos to dollars. What if the peso strengthens (gains value) or weakens (loses value) before Shipp collects from Artes? Shipp will earn more or less than expected. Let's see how to account for this transaction.

Shipp Belting sells goods to Artes de Mexico for a price of 1,000 pesos on June 2. On that date, a peso was worth $0.096. One month later, on July 2, the peso has strengthened against the dollar and a peso is worth $0.100. Shipp still receives 1,000 pesos from Artes because that was the agreed price. Now the dollar value of Shipp's cash receipt is $4 more than the original amount, so Shipp ends up earning $4 more than expected. The following journal entries account for these transactions of Shipp Belting:

✔ Starter 16-12

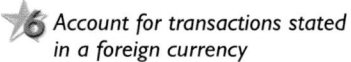

June 2	Accounts Receivable—Artes		
	(1,000 pesos × $0.096)	96	
	Sales Revenue		96
	Sale on account.		

July 2	Cash (1,000 pesos × $0.100)	100	
	Accounts Receivable—Artes		96
	Foreign-Currency Gain		4
	Collection on account.		

If Shipp had required Artes to pay at the time of the sale, Shipp would have received pesos worth $96. But during the 30-day credit period, Shipp was exposed to *foreign-currency exchange risk,* the risk of loss in an international transaction. In this case, Shipp experienced a $4 foreign-currency gain and received $4 more than expected, as shown in the collection entry on July 2.

PAYING CASH IN A FOREIGN CURRENCY Purchasing from a foreign company can create foreign-currency risk. Shipp Belting buys inventory from Gesellschaft Ltd., a Swiss company. The two companies decide on a price of 10,000 Swiss francs. On August 10, when Shipp receives the goods, the Swiss franc is priced at $0.72. When Shipp pays two weeks later, the Swiss franc has strengthened against the dollar and is now worth $0.78. This works to Shipp's disadvantage. Shipp would record the purchase of and payment for the inventory as follows:

Aug. 10	Inventory (10,000 Swiss francs × $0.72)	7,200	
	Accounts Payable—Gesellschaft Ltd.		7,200
	Purchase on account.		
Aug. 24	Accounts Payable—Gesellschaft Ltd.	7,200	
	Foreign-Currency Loss	600	
	Cash (10,000 Swiss francs × $0.78)		7,800
	Payment on account.		

In this case, the Swiss franc strengthened against the dollar (the dollar weakened), and that gave Shipp a foreign-currency loss. A company with a payable stated in a foreign currency hopes that the dollar gets stronger. The company can then use fewer dollars to pay the debt. But the dollar may weaken and force the company to pay more dollars for the foreign currency, as in the case of Shipp Belting.

REPORTING FOREIGN-CURRENCY GAINS AND LOSSES ON THE INCOME STATEMENT The Foreign-Currency Gain (Loss) account reports gains and losses on transactions in a currency other than the dollar. The company reports the *net amount* of these two accounts on the income statement as Other gains (losses). For example, Shipp Belting would combine a $600 foreign-currency loss and the $4 gain and report the net loss of $596 on the income statement, as follows:

Other gains (losses):	
Foreign-currency gain (loss), net ($600 – $4)	$(596)

These gains and losses fall into the "Other" category because they arise from outside activities. Buying and selling foreign currencies are not Shipp Belting's main business.

Managers examine these gains and losses to see how well the company is doing in foreign-currency transactions. The gains and losses may offset each other, with a small overall effect. But if losses grow large, managers will take action. One possible action is hedging.

HEDGING TO AVOID FOREIGN-CURRENCY LOSSES U.S. companies can avoid foreign-currency losses by requiring international transactions to be settled in dollars. But that strategy may alienate customers. Another protection is called hedging.

Hedging
Protecting oneself from losing money in one transaction by engaging in a counterbalancing transaction.

Hedging means to protect oneself from losing money by engaging in a counterbalancing transaction. Suppose Intel is selling goods to be collected in Japanese yen. Intel will receive a fixed number of yen in the future. If yen are losing value, they will be worth fewer dollars than the amount of Intel's receivable. Intel can expect a loss.

In other international transactions, Intel may have accumulated payables stated in another foreign currency, say euros. Losses on the yen may be offset by gains on the euros. This is a natural foreign-currency hedge. It is inexpensive because Intel has to take no special action to protect against foreign-currency loss.

Most companies do not have equal amounts of receivables and payables in foreign currency, so exactly offsetting receivables and payables is unlikely. To obtain a more-precise hedge, companies buy *futures contracts*, which are agreements for foreign currencies to be received in the future. Futures contracts can create a payable to exactly offset a receivable, and vice versa. Many companies use hedging to avoid losses.

Accounting.com

Avon Products Inc.: Staying Up When the Currency Goes Down

Cosmetics giant Avon Products often faces foreign-currency crises because a lot of the company's sales occur outside the United States. In fact, 39% of Avon's operating income comes from South America, so Avon is hit hard when the South American economy falters. CEO Andrea Jung once promised investors that Avon would earn $2.30 for each share of its stock. She then learned that the Argentine peso had devalued and the country's economy was reeling. In one moment, Argentina wiped out 5 cents of Avon's earnings. The company would face more bad news when Brazil went through a similar crisis.

Amazingly, Avon's profits and stock price keep climbing because the company is good at managing risk. To protect against volatile currencies, Avon buys raw materials and makes its products close to the markets where they are sold. Avon recently closed a British facility and moved it to Poland to be nearer Eastern and Central Europe because that part of the world is now the company's fastest-growing market.

Another key strategy is to sacrifice quick profits to grow market share. Avon is willing to take short-term losses to get long-term gains. In Mexico, for example, Avon sets prices low on brands aimed at the poor and the middle class. To keep profits high, the company raises prices on its premium brands.

Avon's main strength is keeping costs low. The company has cut 10 days off of inventory turnover. That saves on expenses. Avon also has reduced product-development cycles by more than 40%. That gets products to market and starts revenues flowing faster. Overall, Avon has trimmed total costs by $230 million. Lower costs mean higher profits.

Based on: Anonymous, "Susan Kropf & Andrea Jung: Avon Products," *Business Week*, January 13, 2003, p. 60. Allison Krampf, "Makeover Magic," *Barron's*, November 4, 2002, p. T6. Subrata N. Chakravarty, "Andrea Calling," *Institutional Investor*, August 2002, pp. 22–24. David Whitford, "A Currency Drowns—Can You Stay Afloat?" *Fortune*, March 1, 1999, pp. 229–235. Mel Mandell, "Asia: Converting Crisis to Opportunity," *World Trade*, April 1998, pp. 36–39. Fred R. Bleakley, "How U.S. Firm Copes with Asia Crisis—Avon Moves to Protect Against Volatile Currencies," *The Wall Street Journal*, December 26, 1997, p. A2.

International Accounting Standards

In this text, we focus on accounting principles that are generally accepted in the United States. Most accounting methods are consistent throughout the world. Double-entry, the accrual system, and the basic financial statements (balance sheet, income statement, and so on) are used worldwide. But some differences exist among countries, as shown in Exhibit 16-8.

Exhibit 16-8 Some International Accounting Differences

Country	Inventories	Goodwill	Research and Development Costs
United States	Specific unit cost, FIFO, LIFO, weighted-average.	Written down when current value decreases.	Expensed as incurred.
Germany	LIFO is unacceptable for tax purposes and is not widely used.	Amortized over 5 years.	Expensed as incurred.
Japan	Similar to U.S.	Amortized over 5 years.	May be capitalized and amortized over 5 years.
United Kingdom (Great Britain)	LIFO is unacceptable for tax purposes and is not widely used.	Amortized over useful life or not amortized if life is indefinite.*	Expense research costs. Some development costs may be capitalized.

* Proposal being considered.

Several organizations seek worldwide harmony of accounting standards. The International Accounting Standards Committee (IASC) is headquartered in London and operates much as the Financial Accounting Standards Board in the United States. It has the support of the accounting professions in the United States, most of the British Commonwealth countries, Japan, France, Germany, the Netherlands, and Mexico. However, the IASC has no authority to require compliance and must rely on cooperation by the various national accounting professions.

Decision Guidelines

FOREIGN-CURRENCY TRANSACTIONS

You've just opened a boutique to import clothing manufactured in China. Should you transact business in Chinese *renminbi* (the official currency unit), or in U.S. dollars? What foreign-currency gains or losses might occur? The Decision Guidelines will help you address these questions.

Decision	Guidelines
When to record a	
• Foreign-currency gain?	• When you receive foreign currency worth *more* U.S. dollars than the receivable on your books • When you pay foreign currency that costs *fewer* U.S. dollars than the payable on your books
• Foreign-currency loss?	• When you receive foreign currency worth *fewer* U.S. dollars than the receivable on your books • When you pay foreign currency that costs *more* U.S. dollars than the payable on your books

END-OF-CHAPTER *Summary Problem*

A+ TIPS
CHECK YOUR RESOURCES

Required

1. Journalize the following transactions of American Corp. Explanations are not required.

20X5	
Nov. 16	Purchased equipment on account for 40,000 Swiss francs when the exchange rate was $0.73 per Swiss franc.
27	Sold merchandise on account to a Belgian company for 7,000 euros. Each euro is worth $1.10.
Dec. 22	Paid the Swiss company when the franc's exchange rate was $0.725.
31	Adjusted for the change in the exchange rate of the euro. Its current exchange rate is $1.08.
20X6	
Jan. 4	Collected from the Belgian company. The exchange rate is $1.12.

2. In the 20X5 transactions, identify each of the following currencies as strong or weak:
   a. Swiss franc **b.** Euro **c.** U.S. dollar
   Which currency strengthened during 20X6? Which currency weakened during 20X6?

Solution

1. Entries for transactions stated in foreign currencies:

20X5			
Nov. 16	Equipment (40,000 × $0.73)	29,200	
	Accounts Payable		29,200
27	Accounts Receivable (7,000 × $1.10)	7,700	
	Sales Revenue		7,700
Dec. 22	Accounts Payable	29,200	
	Cash (40,000 × $0.725)		29,000
	Foreign-Currency Gain		200
31	Foreign-Currency Loss [7,000 × ($1.10 – $1.08)]	140	
	Accounts Receivable		140
20X6			
Jan. 4	Cash (7,000 × $1.12)	7,840	
	Accounts Receivable ($7,700 – $140)		7,560
	Foreign-Currency Gain		280

2. During 20X5,
   a. Swiss franc—weak **b.** Euro—weak **c.** U.S. dollar—strong
   During 20X6, the euro strengthened and the U.S. dollar weakened.

REVIEW *Investments and International Operations*

Quick Check

1. Suppose you are buying 100 shares of **McDonald's** stock. Use the data in Exhibit 16-1, page 626, to determine how much you must pay.
   a. $1,592
   b. $3,072
   c. $1,212
   d. $24

2. The two categories of stock investments in less than 20% of the investee's stock are
   a. Current and long-term
   b. Equity and consolidated
   c. Trading and available-for-sale
   d. Majority interest and minority interest

3. Suppose you hold 1,000 shares of **Intel** common stock as a trading investment. The stock cost you a total of $18,000, and you receive $80 in annual cash dividends. At December 31, your investment in Intel common stock is quoted at $19 per share. What will your *balance sheet* report for this investment?
   a. Short-term investment of $18,000
   b. Short-term investment of $19,000
   c. Unrealized gain of $1,000
   d. Dividend revenue of $80

4. Suppose you hold 1,000 shares of Intel common stock as a trading investment. The stock cost you a total of $18,000, and you receive $80 in annual cash dividends. At December 31, your investment in Intel common stock is quoted at $19 per share. What will your *income statement* report for this investment?
   a. Short-term investment of $18,000
   b. Short-term investment of $19,000
   c. Unrealized gain of $1,000
   d. Dividend revenue of $80 and Unrealized gain of $1,000

5. Suppose you hold 1,000 shares of Intel common stock as a long-term *available-for-sale* investment. The stock cost you a total of $18,000, and you receive $80 in annual cash dividends. At December 31, your investment in Intel common stock is quoted at $19 per share. What will your balance sheet report for this investment?
   a. Long-term investment of $18,000
   b. Long-term investment of $19,000
   c. Long-term investment of $19,000 and Unrealized gain of $1,000
   d. Dividend revenue of $80

6. Suppose you hold 20% of the common shares of Griffin Company as an equity-method investment. The stock cost you $18,000, and you receive no cash dividends. At December 31, Griffin reports net income of $15,000. What is the carrying amount of your investment for the December 31 balance sheet?
   a. $18,000
   b. $20,000
   c. $21,000
   d. $22,000

7. What is the minimum percentage ownership for a parent company to consolidate the financial statements of a subsidiary company?
   a. 50%
   b. > 50%
   c. 50.1%
   d. 100%

8. The journal entry to record the final transaction for a bond investment is

a. Cash	XXX	
Investment in Bonds		XXX
b. Cash	XXX	
Interest Revenue		XXX
c. Investment in Bonds	XXX	
Cash		XXX
d. Cash	XXX	
Bonds Payable		XXX

9. What causes a foreign-currency gain or loss?
   a. Buying a foreign currency
   b. Paying debts and collecting receivables in amounts that differ from the carrying amounts on your books
   c. Hedging activities
   d. Accounting differences in foreign countries

10. **IBM** purchased silicon chips on account from a Japanese supplier at a cost of 1,000,000 yen, with each yen valued at $0.008. One month later, when IBM paid the account, a yen was quoted at $0.009. Which journal entry records IBM's payment?

a. Accounts Payable	8,000	
Cash		8,000
b. Accounts Payable	9,000	
Foreign-Currency Loss		1,000
Cash		8,000
c. Cash	9,000	
Accounts Payable		9,000
d. Accounts Payable	8,000	
Foreign-Currency Loss	1,000	
Cash		9,000

Accounting Vocabulary

available-for-sale investments (p. 627)
consolidated statements (p. 633)
controlling interest (p. 632)
equity method (p. 631)
foreign-currency exchange rate (p. 638)
hedging (p. 640)
held-to-maturity investments (p. 634)
long-term investment (p. 626)
majority interest (p. 632)
marketable security (p. 626)
market-value method (p. 627)
minority interest (p. 633)
parent company (p. 632)
short-term investment (p. 626)
strong currency (p. 638)
subsidiary company (p. 632)
trading investments (p. 627)
weak currency (p. 638)

ASSESS *Your Progress*

A+ online homework

See *www.prenhall.com/horngren* for selected Starters, Exercises, and Problems.

Starters

Computing the cost of a stock investment
(Obj. 1, 2)

S16-1 Compute the cost of each investment. Round to the nearest dollar.

a. 200 shares of **Nokia** stock at 16.57.
b. 450 shares of **IBM** stock at 85.12. IBM pays a cash dividend of $0.60 per year.
c. 1,000 shares of **Nike** stock at 53.97.
d. 70 shares of **Target** stock at 33.12.

Classifying investments as trading or available-for-sale
(Obj. 1, 2)

S16-2 Milwaukee Corp. purchased 100 shares of stock in each of three companies:

a. Investment in **Intel Corporation** to be sold within the next 9 to 12 months
b. Investment in **AMR (American Airlines)** to be sold within the next 90 days
c. Investment in **Amazon.com** to be sold within the next two years

Classify each investment as (1) a current asset or a long-term asset and as (2) a trading investment or an available-for-sale investment.

Accounting for a trading investment loss
(Obj. 1)

S16-3 Frost Bank completed the following transactions during 20X4 and 20X5:

20X4	
Dec. 6	Purchased 1,000 shares of **Nissan** stock at a price of $52.25 per share, intending to sell the investment next week.
23	Received a cash dividend of $1.12 per share on the Nissan stock.
31	Adjusted the investment to its market value of $51 per share.
20X5	
Jan. 27	Sold the Nissan stock for $48 per share.

1. Classify Frost Bank's investment as trading or available-for-sale.
2. Journalize Frost Bank's investment transactions. Explanations are not required.

Accounting for a trading investment gain
(Obj. 1)

S16-4 Spitzer Electronics completed the following investment transactions during 20X6 and 20X7:

20X6	
Dec. 12	Purchased 500 shares of **Fedex** stock at a price of $59 per share, intending to sell the investment next week.
21	Received a cash dividend of $0.23 per share on the Fedex stock.
31	Adjusted the investment to its market value of $61 per share.
20X7	
Jan. 16	Sold the Fedex stock for $64.50 per share.

1. Classify Spitzer's investment as trading or available-for-sale.
2. Journalize Spitzer's investment transactions. Explanations are not required.

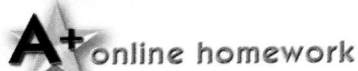

S16-5 **BankOne** buys 500 shares of **ChevronTexaco** stock, paying $64 per share. Suppose ChevronTexaco distributes a 10% stock dividend. Later, BankOne sells the ChevronTexaco stock for $60 per share.

Measuring gain or loss on the sale of an investment after receiving a stock dividend
(Obj. 2)

1. Compute BankOne's new cost per share after receiving the stock dividend.
2. Compute BankOne's gain or loss on the sale of this available-for-sale investment.

S16-6 Brookstone Financial, Inc., completed these long-term available-for-sale investment transactions during 20X7:

Accounting for an available-for-sale investment: unrealized loss
(Obj. 2)

20X7	
Jan. 14	Purchased 300 shares of **PepsiCo** stock, paying $43.45 per share. Brookstone intends to hold the investment for the indefinite future.
Aug. 22	Received a cash dividend of $0.60 per share on the PepsiCo stock.
Dec. 31	Adjusted the PepsiCo investment to its current market value of $12,600.

1. Journalize Brookstone's investment transactions. Explanations are not required.
2. Show how to report the investment and any unrealized gain or loss on Brookstone's balance sheet at December 31, 20X7.

S16-7 Use the data given in Starter 16-6. On August 4, 20X8, Brookstone Financial, Inc., sold its investment in **PepsiCo** stock for $45.15 per share.

Accounting for the sale of an available-for-sale investment
(Obj. 2)

1. Journalize the sale. No explanation is required.
2. How does the gain or loss that you recorded differ from the gain or loss that was recorded at December 31, 20X7 (in Starter 16-6)?

S16-8 Suppose on January 6, 20X5, **General Motors** paid $100 million for its 40% investment in **Isuzu**. Assume Isuzu earned net income of $20 million and paid cash dividends of $10 million during 20X5.

Accounting for a 40% investment in another company
(Obj. 3)

1. What method should General Motors use to account for the investment in Isuzu? Give your reason.
2. Journalize these three transactions on the books of General Motors. Show all amounts in millions of dollars and include an explanation for each entry.
3. Post to the Long-Term Equity-Method Investment T-account. What is its balance after all the transactions are posted?

S16-9 Answer these questions about consolidation accounting:

Understanding consolidated financial statements
(Obj. 4)

1. Define a parent company. Define a subsidiary company.
2. Which company's name appears on the consolidated financial statements? How much of the subsidiary's stock must the parent own before reporting consolidated statements?
3. How do consolidated financial statements differ from the financial statements of a single company?

S16-10 **Edward Jones Co.** owns vast amounts of corporate bonds. Suppose Edward Jones buys $1,000,000 of **Dow Jones & Co.** bonds at a price of 96. The Dow Jones bonds pay cash interest at the annual rate of 7% and mature within five years.

Working with a bond investment
(Obj. 5)

1. How much did Edward Jones pay to purchase the bond investment? How much will Edward Jones collect when the bond investment matures?
2. How much cash interest will Edward Jones receive each year from Dow Jones & Co.?
3. Will Edward Jones' annual *interest revenue* on the bond investment be more or less than the amount of *cash interest received* each year? Give your reason.
4. Compute Edward Jones' annual interest revenue on this bond investment. Use the straight-line method to amortize the discount on the investment.

Recording bond investment transactions
(Obj. 5)

S16-11 Return to Starter 16-10, the Edward Jones investment in Dow Jones & Co. bonds. Journalize on Edward Jones' books, along with an explanation for each entry:

a. Purchase of the bond investment on January 2, 20X4. Edward Jones expects to hold the investment to maturity.
b. Receipt of annual cash interest on December 31, 20X4.
c. Amortization of discount on December 31, 20X4.
d. Collection of the investment's face value at its maturity date on January 2, 20X9. (Assume the receipt of 20X8 interest and amortization of discount for 20X8 have already been recorded, so you may ignore these entries.)

Accounting for transactions stated in a foreign currency
(Obj. 6)

S16-12 Suppose **Nike Inc.** sells athletic shoes to a Russian company on March 14. Nike agrees to accept 2,000,000 Russian rubles. On the date of sale, the ruble is quoted at \$0.036. Nike collects half the receivable on April 19, when the ruble is worth \$0.034. Then, on May 10, when the price of the ruble is \$0.039, Nike collects the final amount.

Journalize these three transactions for Nike; include an explanation. Overall, how well did Nike come out in terms of a net foreign-currency gain or loss?

A+ online homework

Exercises

Accounting for a trading investment
(Obj. 1)

E16-1 **BankOne**, headquartered in Columbus, Ohio, holds huge portfolios of investments. Suppose BankOne completed the following investment transactions:

20X8	
Dec. 6	Purchased 1,000 shares of **Goodyear Tire & Rubber Co.** stock for \$70,000. BankOne plans to sell the stock within a week or two.
30	Received a quarterly cash dividend of \$0.85 per share on the Goodyear stock.
31	Adjusted the investment in Goodyear stock. Current market value is \$65,000, and BankOne plans to sell the stock early in 20X9.
20X9	
Jan. 14	Sold the Goodyear stock for \$71,000.

Required

1. Journalize the BankOne investment transactions. Explanations are not required.
2. Show how BankOne would report its investment in the Goodyear stock on the balance sheet at December 31, 20X8.

Journalizing transactions for an available-for-sale investment
(Obj. 2)

E16-2 Journalize the following long-term available-for-sale investment transactions of Cordant Communications. Explanations are not required.

a. Purchased 400 shares (8%) of Marcor Corporation common stock at \$38 per share, with the intent of holding the stock for the indefinite future.
b. Received cash dividend of \$1 per share on the Marcor investment.
c. At year-end, adjusted the investment account to current market value of \$45 per share.
d. Sold the Marcor stock for the market price of \$40 per share.

Journalizing transactions for an available-for-sale investment
(Obj. 2)

E16-3 Journalize the following investment transactions of **NEC Corporation**.

Aug. 1	Purchased 500 shares (2%) of Vardaman Corporation common stock as a long-term available-for-sale investment, paying \$44 per share.
Sep. 12	Received cash dividend of \$1 per share on the Vardaman investment.
Nov. 23	Received 50 shares of Vardaman common stock in a 10% stock dividend.
Dec. 4	Unexpectedly sold the Vardaman stock for \$39 per share.

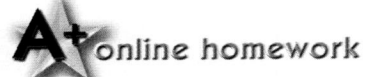

Accounting for long-term investment transactions
(Obj. 2)

E16-4 Late in the current year, Micron Instruments bought 1,000 shares of **National Geographic** common stock at $81.88, 600 shares of **AT&T Corp.** stock at $46.75, and 1,400 shares of **Hitachi** stock at $79—all as available-for-sale investments. At December 31, *The Wall Street Journal* reports National Geographic stock at $80.38, AT&T at $48.50, and Hitachi at $68.25.

Required

1. Determine the cost and the market value of the long-term investment portfolio at December 31.
2. Record any adjusting entry needed at December 31.
3. What two items would Micron Instruments report on its balance sheet for the information given? Make the necessary disclosures.

Accounting for transactions under the equity method
(Obj. 3)

E16-5 Newbold, Inc., owns equity-method investments in several other department-store companies. Newbold paid $2 million to acquire a 20% investment in Italian Imports Company. Italian Imports reported net income of $780,000 for the first year and declared and paid cash dividends of $500,000. Record the following in Newbold's journal: (a) purchase of the investment, (b) its proportion of Italian Imports' net income, and (c) receipt of the cash dividends.

Measuring gain or loss on the sale of an equity-method investment
(Obj. 3)

E16-6 Without making journal entries, record the transactions of Exercise 16-5 directly in the Newbold account, Long-Term Equity-Method Investment in Italian Imports. Assume that after all the noted transactions took place, Newbold sold its entire investment in Italian Imports for cash of $2,500,000. How much is Newbold's gain or loss on the sale of the investment?

Applying the appropriate accounting method for investments
(Obj. 3)

E16-7 Nasdaq, Inc., paid $145,000 for a 40% investment in the common stock of Auto Chief, Inc. For the first year, Auto Chief reported net income of $80,000 and at year-end declared and paid cash dividends of $20,000. On the balance sheet date, the market value of Nasdaq's investment in Auto Chief stock was $134,000.

Required

1. Which method is appropriate for Nasdaq to use in accounting for its investment in Auto Chief? Why?
2. Show everything that Nasdaq would report for the investment and any investment revenue in its year-end financial statements.
3. What role does the market value of the investment play in this situation?

Recording bond investment transactions
(Obj. 5)

E16-8 On June 30, 20X3, Greenbrier Corp. paid 92 for 6% bonds of **Dean Witter Financial Services** as a long-term held-to-maturity investment. The maturity value of the bonds will be $30,000 on June 30, 20X8. The bonds pay interest on June 30 and December 31.

Required

1. What method should Greenbrier Corporation use to account for its investment in the Dean Witter bonds?
2. Using the straight-line method of amortizing the discount, journalize all of Greenbrier's transactions on the bonds for 20X3.
3. Show how Greenbrier would report the bond investment on its balance sheet at December 31, 20X3.

Managing and accounting for foreign-currency transactions
(Obj. 6)

E16-9 Journalize the following foreign-currency transactions. Explanations are not required.

Nov. 17	Purchased inventory on account from a Japanese company. The price was 200,000 yen, and the exchange rate of the yen was $0.0083.
Dec. 16	Paid the Japanese supplier when the exchange rate was $0.0091.
19	Sold merchandise on account to a French company at a price of 60,000 euros. The exchange rate of the euro was $1.10.
30	Collected from the French company when the exchange rate was $1.14.

(*continued*)

On November 18, immediately after your purchase, which currency did you want to strengthen? Which currency did in fact strengthen? Explain your reasoning in detail.

Analyzing available-for-sale investments **(Obj. 2)**

E16-10 MAP Incorporated, which makes electronic connection devices, reported the stockholders' equity on its balance sheet, as adapted, at December 31, 20X8.

MAP Incorporated
Balance Sheet (Partial, adapted)
December 31, 20X8

Millions	**20X8**
Shareholders' Equity:	
Common stock	$ 226
Retained earnings	2,330
Treasury stock, at cost	(243)
Unrealized gains on available-for-sale investments	14
Total shareholders' equity	$2,327

Required

1. MAP's balance sheet also reports available-for-sale investments at $288 million. What was MAP's cost of the investments? What was the market value of the investments on December 31, 20X8?
2. Suppose MAP sold its available-for-sale investments in 20X9 for $259 million. Determine the gain or loss on the sale of the investments.

Problems

(Group A)

A+ online homework

Accounting for trading investments **(Obj. 1)**

Student Resource CD
General Ledger, Peachtree, QuickBooks

P16-1A During the second half of 20X2, the operations of Hercules Steel generated excess cash, which the company invested in securities, as follows:

July 3	Purchased 3,000 shares of common stock as a trading investment, paying $9.25 per share.
Aug. 14	Received cash dividend of $0.32 per share on the trading investment.
Sep. 15	Sold the trading investment for $10.50 per share.
Nov. 24	Purchased trading investments for $226,000.
Dec. 31	Adjusted the trading securities to their market value of $222,500.

Required

1. Record the transactions in the journal of Hercules Steel. Explanations are not required.
2. Post to the Short-Term Investment account. Then show how to report the short-term investment on the Hercules balance sheet at December 31, 20X2.

Accounting for available-for-sale and equity-method investments **(Obj. 2, 3)**

Student Resource CD
GL, PT, QB

P16-2A The beginning balance sheet of TalkNET, Inc., included the following:

Long-Term Equity-Method Investments $300,000

During the year, TalkNET completed the following investment transactions:

Mar. 2	Purchased 2,000 shares of DLV Inc., common stock as a long-term available-for-sale investment, paying $12.25 per share.
Apr. 21	Received cash dividend of $0.75 per share on the DLV investment.
Oct. 17	Received cash dividend of $50,000 from the equity-method investments.
Dec. 31	Received annual reports from the equity-method investee companies. Their total net income for the year was $550,000. Of this amount, TalkNET's proportion is 33%.
31	Adjusted the available-for-sale investment to market value. The market value of TalkNET's investment in DLV is $26,800.

Required

1. Record the transactions in the journal of TalkNET, Inc.
2. Post entries to the Long-Term Equity-Method Investments T-account, and determine its balance at December 31. Do likewise for the Long-Term Available-for-Sale Investment T-account and the Allowance to Adjust Investments to Market T-account.
3. Show how to report the Long-Term Available-for-Sale Investment and the Long-Term Equity-Method Investments accounts on TalkNET's balance sheet at December 31.

P16-3A Baldwin Company owns numerous investments in the stock of other companies. Assume that Baldwin completed the following long-term investment transactions:

Reporting investments on the balance sheet and the related revenue on the income statement
(Obj. 2, 3)

20X2	
Feb. 12	Purchased 20,000 shares, which exceeds 20% of the common stock of Growtech, Inc., at total cost of $700,000.
Aug. 9	Received cash dividend of $0.90 per share on the Growtech investment.
Oct. 16	Purchased 1,000 shares of Varnix Company common stock as an available-for-sale investment, paying $40 per share.
Dec. 31	Received annual report from Growtech, Inc. Net income for the year was $500,000. Of this amount, Baldwin's proportion is 30%.
31	Adjusted the available-for-sale investment in Varnix to current market value of $41,100.

Required

Show what Baldwin Company would report on its year-end balance sheet for these investments. It is helpful to use a T-account for the investment in Growtech stock.

P16-4A Financial institutions such as insurance companies hold large quantities of bond investments. Suppose Liberty Insurance Co. purchases $400,000 of 9% bonds of Inwood Corporation for 103 on January 1, 20X8. These bonds pay interest on June 30 and December 31 each year and mature in five years.

Accounting for a bond investment; straight-line amortization of premium
(Obj. 5)

Required

1. Journalize Liberty's purchase of the bonds as a long-term investment on January 1, 20X8 (to be held to maturity). Then record Liberty's receipt of cash interest and amortization of premium at June 30 and December 31, 20X8. The straight-line method is appropriate for amortizing premium.
2. Show how to report this long-term bond investment on Liberty Insurance Co.'s balance sheet at December 31, 20X8.

P16-5A ← *Link Back to Chapter 15 (Effective-Interest Amortization of Discount).* On December 31, 20X5, when the market interest is 8%, ChaseBank purchases $500,000 of **Michelin Corp.**, 7.4%, six-year bonds. The cost of this long-term bond investment is $486,123, and ChaseBank expects to hold the investment to maturity.

Accounting for a bond investment; effective-interest amortization of discount
(Obj. 5)

Required

Journalize the purchase on December 31, 20X5, the first semiannual interest receipt on June 30, 20X6, and the year-end interest receipt on December 31, 20X6. ChaseBank uses the effective-interest amortization method. Prepare a schedule for amortizing the discount on bond investment through December 31, 20X6. Use Exhibit 15-4 as a guide.

Recording foreign-currency transactions and reporting the transaction gain or loss
(Obj. 6)

Student Resource CD
GL, PT, QB

P16-6A DVD Burner Company completed the following transactions:

May	1	Sold inventory on account to Marconi Telegraph, an Italian public utility, for $20,000. The exchange rate of the euro is $1.06, and Marconi agrees to pay in dollars.
	10	Purchased supplies on account from a Canadian company at a price of Canadian $30,000. The exchange rate of the Canadian dollar is $0.70, and payment will be in Canadian dollars.
	17	Sold inventory on account to an English firm for 110,000 British pounds. Payment will be in pounds, and the exchange rate of the pound is $1.60.
	22	Collected from Marconi Telegraph.
June	18	Paid the Canadian company. The exchange rate of the Canadian dollar is $0.67.
	24	Collected from the English firm. The exchange rate of the British pound is $1.57.

Required

1. Record these transactions in DVD Burner's journal, and show how to report the net foreign-currency gain or loss on the income statement. Explanations are not required.
2. How will what you learned in this problem help you structure international transactions?

Problems

(Group B)

A+ online homework

Accounting for trading investments
(Obj. 1)

Student Resource CD
GL, PT, QB

P16-1B During the second half of 20X4, the operations of Pilot Corporation generated excess cash, which the company invested in securities, as follows:

July	2	Purchased 3,500 shares of common stock as a trading investment, paying $12.75 per share.
Aug.	21	Received cash dividend of $0.45 per share on the trading investment.
Sep.	16	Sold the trading investment for $13.50 per share.
Oct.	8	Purchased trading investments for $136,000.
Dec.	31	Adjusted the trading securities to their market value of $131,500.

Required

1. Record the transactions in the journal of Pilot Corporation. Explanations are not required.
2. Post to the Short-Term Investments account, and show how to report the short-term investments on Pilot's balance sheet at December 31, 20X4.

Accounting for available-for-sale and equity-method investments
(Obj. 2, 3)

Student Resource CD
GL, PT, QB

P16-2B The beginning balance sheet of Parr Investments Co. included the following:

Long-Term Equity-Method Investments $600,000

During the year Parr completed the following investment transactions:

Mar.	3	Purchased 5,000 shares of LBO Software common stock as a long-term available-for-sale investment, paying $9.25 per share.
May	14	Received cash dividend of $0.82 per share on the LBO investment.
Dec.	15	Received cash dividend of $31,000 from equity-method investments.
	31	Received annual reports from equity-method investee companies. Their total net income for the year was $620,000. Of this amount, Parr's proportion is 25%.
	31	Adjusted the available-for-sale investment to market value. The market value of Parr's investment in LBO is $44,100.

Required

1. Record the transactions in the journal of Parr Investments.
2. Post entries to the Long-Term Equity-Method Investments T-account, and determine its balance at December 31. Do likewise for the Long-Term Available-for-Sale Investment T-account and the Allowance to Adjust Investment to Market T-account.
3. Show how to report the Long-Term Available-for-Sale Investment and the Long-Term Equity-Method Investments on Parr's balance sheet at December 31.

P16-3B Ambassador Hotel Company owns stock in other companies. During 20X4, Ambassador completed the following long-term investment transactions:

Reporting investments on the balance sheet and the related revenue on the income statement
(Obj. 2, 3)

20X4	
May 1	Purchased 10,000 shares, which exceeds 20%, of the common stock of DeGaulle Company at total cost of $860,000.
Sep. 15	Received cash dividend of $6 per share on the DeGaulle investment.
Oct. 12	Purchased 1,000 shares of Cola Beverage Corporation common stock as an available-for-sale investment, paying $22.50 per share.
Dec. 31	Received annual report from DeGaulle Company. Net income for the year was $360,000. Of this amount, Ambassador's proportion is one third.
31	Adjusted the available-for-sale investment in Cola Beverage to current market value of $20,000.

Required

Show what Ambassador Hotel Company would report on its year-end balance sheet for these investments. (It is helpful to use a T-account for the investment in DeGaulle stock.)

P16-4B Financial institutions hold large quantities of bond investments. Suppose **Goldman Sachs** purchases $800,000 of 8% bonds of **Xerox Corporation** for 92 on January 1, 20X0. These bonds pay interest on June 30 and December 31 each year. They mature on January 1, 20X8.

Accounting for a bond investment; amortizing discount by the straight-line method
(Obj. 5)

Required

1. Journalize Goldman Sachs' purchase of the bonds as a long-term investment on January 1, 20X0 (to be held to maturity). Then record the receipt of cash interest and amortization of discount on June 30 and December 31, 20X0. The straight-line method is appropriate for amortizing discount.
2. Show how to report this long-term bond investment on Goldman Sachs' balance sheet at December 31, 20X0.

P16-5B ← *Link Back to Chapter 15 (Effective-Interest Amortization of Discount).* On December 31, 20X6, when the market interest rate is 10%, First Federal Bank purchases $400,000 of Yuma Inc., 9.5%, 10-year bonds. The cost of this bond investment was $387,578 and the investor expects to hold the investment to maturity.

Accounting for a bond investment; amortizing discount by the effective-interest method
(Obj. 5)

Required

Journalize First Federal's purchase on December 31, 20X6, the first semiannual interest receipt on June 30, 20X7, and the year-end interest receipt on December 31, 20X7. The investor uses the effective-interest amortization method. Prepare a schedule for amortizing the discount on the bond investment through December 31, 20X7. Use Exhibit 15-4 as a guide.

Recording foreign-currency transactions and reporting the transaction gain or loss **(Obj. 6)**

Student Resource CD
GL, PT, QB

P16-6B Suppose **Ralph Lauren** completed the following transactions:

May 4	Sold clothing on account to a Mexican department store for $71,000. The exchange rate of the Mexican peso is $0.10, and the customer agrees to pay in dollars.
13	Purchased inventory on account from a Canadian company at a price of Canadian $60,000. The exchange rate of the Canadian dollar is $0.75, and payment will be in Canadian dollars.
20	Sold goods on account to an English firm for 80,000 British pounds. Payment will be in pounds, and the exchange rate of the pound is $1.50.
27	Collected from the Mexican company.
June 21	Paid the Canadian company. The exchange rate of the Canadian dollar is $0.72.
July 17	Collected from the English firm. The exchange rate of the British pound is $1.47.

Required

1. Record these transactions in Ralph Lauren's journal, and show how to report the net foreign-currency gain or loss on the income statement. Explanations are not required.
2. How will what you learned in this problem help you structure international transactions?

APPLY *Your Knowledge*

Decision Cases

Explaining the market value and equity methods of accounting for investments **(Obj. 1, 2)**

Case 1. Carla Allman is the manager of Stagg Corp., whose year-end is December 31. The company made two investments during the first week of January 20X2. Both investments are to be held for the indefinite future. Information about the investments follows:

a. Stagg purchased 30% of the common stock of Frontenac Mfg. Co. for its book value of $250,000. During the year ended December 31, 20X2, Frontenac earned $146,000 and paid dividends totaling $53,000. At year-end, the market value of the Frontenac investment is $261,000.

b. One thousand shares of the common stock of St. John Medical Corporation were purchased as an available-for-sale investment for $95,000. During the year ended December 31, 20X2, St. John paid Stagg a dividend of $3,000. St. John earned a profit of $317,000 for that period, and at year-end, the market value of Stagg's investment in St. John stock was $92,000.

Allman has come to you to ask how to account for the investments. Stagg has never had such investments before. Explain the proper accounting to her by indicating that different accounting methods apply to different situations.

Required

Help Allman understand by writing a memo to

1. Describe the methods of accounting applicable to these investments.
2. Identify which method should be used to account for the investments in Frontenac Mfg. Co. and St. John Medical Corporation. Also indicate the dollar amount to report for each investment on the year-end balance sheet.

Understanding the consolidation method for investments
(Obj. 4)

Case 2. Caesar Saled inherited some investments, and he has received the annual reports of the companies. The financial statements of the companies are puzzling to Saled, and he asks you the following questions:

1. The companies label their financial statements as *consolidated* balance sheet, *consolidated* income statement, and so on. What are consolidated financial statements?
2. The consolidated balance sheet lists the asset Goodwill. What is goodwill? Does the presence of goodwill mean that the company's stock has increased in value?

Write a memo to answer each of Saled's questions.

Ethical Issue

Blaze Utilities owns 18% of the voting stock of Southwest Electric Power Company. The remainder of the Southwest stock is held by numerous investors with small holdings. Dee Falco, president of Blaze Utilities and a member of Southwest's board of directors, heavily influences Southwest Electric Power Company's policies.

Under the market-value method of accounting for investments, Blaze's net income increases as it receives dividend revenue from Southwest Power. Blaze Utilities pays President Falco a bonus computed as a percentage of Blaze's net income. Therefore, Falco can control her personal bonus to a certain extent by influencing Southwest's dividends.

A recession occurs in 20X0 and Blaze Utilities' income is low. Falco uses her power as a board member to have Southwest pay a large cash dividend. The action requires Southwest to borrow in order to pay the dividend.

Required

1. In getting Southwest to pay the large cash dividend, is Falco acting within her authority as a member of the Southwest board of directors? Are Falco's actions ethical? Whom can her actions harm?
2. Discuss how using the equity method of accounting for investments would decrease Falco's potential for manipulating her bonus.

Financial Statement Case

Accounting for investments
(Obj. 2, 3)

Refer to **Amazon.com's** financial statements in Appendix A. Answer the following questions about Amazon's investments.

1. Amazon.com reports Marketable Securities on the balance sheet. Amazon accounts for these investments as available-for-sale securities.
   - **a.** What amount is reported for Amazon's marketable securities at December 31, 2002? Does this amount represent cost or market value?
   - **b.** During 2002, Amazon's marketable securities increased in value by $20,294 thousand. Journalize this increase in value, dated December 31, 2002.
2. Amazon.com also reports Other Equity Investments among its long-term assets.
   - **a.** Which accounting method is used for these investments?
   - **b.** The income statement reports the results of operations by these investee companies. Were the investee companies' operations successful or unsuccessful during 2002? How can you tell? In your answer, give the dollar amount to prove your point.

Team Project

Pick a stock from *The Wall Street Journal* or other database or publication. Assume that your group purchases 1,000 shares of the stock as a short-term trading investment. Research the stock in *Value Line, Moody's Investor Record*, or other source to determine whether the company pays cash dividends and, if so, how much and at what intervals.

1. Track the stock for a period assigned by your professor. Over the specified period, keep a daily record of the price of the stock to see how well your investment has performed. Each day, search the Corporate Dividend News in *The Wall Street Journal* to keep a record of any dividends you've received. End the period of your analysis with a month end, such as September 30 or December 31.
2. Journalize all transactions that you have experienced, including the investment purchase, dividends received (both cash dividends and stock dividends), any year-end adjustment required by the accounting method that is appropriate for your investment, and the sale of your investment two ways: at a gain; and at a loss. Assume you will prepare financial statements on the ending date of your study.
3. Show what you will report on your company's balance sheet and income statement as a result of your investment transactions.

For Internet exercises, go to the Web site www.prenhall.com/horngren.

Comprehensive Problem for Chapters 13 to 16

Gateway International's Corporate Transactions

Gateway International's corporate charter authorizes the company to issue 1 million shares of $1 par-value common stock and 200,000 shares of 5%, $10 par-value preferred stock. During the first quarter of operations, Gateway completed the following selected transactions:

Oct.	1	Issued 75,000 shares of common stock for cash of $6 per share.
	5	Issued 2,000 shares of preferred stock, receiving cash of $22,000.
	30	Purchased 5,000 shares (20%) of the outstanding common stock of Newbold Corp. as a long-term equity-method investment, $85,000.
Nov.	1	Issued $200,000 of 9%, 10-year bonds payable at 94.
	14	Purchased long-term available-for-sale investments in the common stocks of **PepsiCo**, $22,000, and Data General, $31,000.
	19	Experienced a $13,000 extraordinary flood loss of inventory that cost $21,000. Cash received from the insurance company was $8,000. There is no income tax effect from this loss.
	30	Purchased 10,000 shares of Gateway common stock for the treasury at $5 per share.
Dec.	1	Received cash dividends of $1,100 on the PepsiCo investment.
	1	Sold 1,000 shares of the treasury stock for cash of $6.25 per share.
	29	Received a report from Newbold Corp. indicating that net income for November and December was $70,000.
	30	Sold merchandise on account, $716,000. Cost of the goods was $439,000. Operating expenses totaled $174,000, with $166,000 of this amount paid in cash. Gateway uses a perpetual inventory system.
	31	Accrued interest and amortized discount (straight-line method) on the bonds payable issued on November 1.
	31	Adjusted the available-for-sale investments to current market value. Market values of the available-for-sale investments: PepsiCo stock, $24,000, and the Data General stock, $30,000.
	31	Accrued income tax expense of $36,000.
	31	Closed all revenues, expenses, and losses to Retained Earnings in a single closing entry.
	31	Declared a quarterly cash dividend of $0.125 per share on the preferred stock. Record date is January 11, with payment scheduled for January 19.

Required

1. Record these transactions in the general journal. Explanations are not required.
2. Prepare a single-step income statement, including earnings per share, for the quarter ended December 31. Gateway had 72,000 shares of common stock outstanding. Remember to compute the preferred dividends for only 1/4 of the year.

CHAPTER 17

The Statement of Cash Flows

A+ TIPS CHECK YOUR RESOURCES

- Visit the www.prenhall.com/horngren **Web site** for self-study quizzes, video clips, and other resources
- Try the **Quick Check** exercise at the end of the chapter to test your knowledge
- Learn the **key terms**
- Do the **Starter** exercises keyed in the margins
- Work the **mid-** and **end-of-chapter summary problems**
- Use the **Concept Links** to review material in other chapters
- Search the **CD** for review materials by chapter or by key word
- Watch the **tutorial videos** to review key concepts

LEARNING OBJECTIVES

1. Identify the purposes of the statement of cash flows
2. Distinguish among operating, investing, and financing cash flows
3. Prepare a statement of cash flows by the indirect method
4. Prepare a statement of cash flows by the direct method

Why is cash flow so important? You can probably begin to answer that question from your own experience: It takes cash to pay the bills. You have a certain amount of income, and you have certain expenses: food, gas, entertainment, car insurance, and credit cards. The two have to match in quantity and in timing. You may borrow money for a large purchase, like a car, but if you have to borrow money for everyday living expenses, you are in trouble.

Businesses, including e-businesses, work the same way: They need enough cash flowing in to pay the bills and run their operations. Take eBay, a company that has revolutionized commerce. Lots of dot.coms have come and gone, but eBay is still going strong. One reason is that the company is both profitable and cash-rich. In 2001, eBay's operations provided more than $250 million of cash. In 2002, cash flow almost doubled—to $479 million—

eBay

quite an accomplishment for such a young company. Being cash-rich allows eBay to plan for expansion:

eBay Inc. Outlines Global Business Strategy

eBay Inc., . . . the world's online marketplace, [recently] outlined its strategy for growth. . . . eBay executives highlighted key areas of growth, both domestically and abroad. "The . . . potential of our business gives us great confidence in the future," said Meg Whitman, President and CEO of eBay. "The eBay marketplace is thriving. . . ." [eBay press release] ■

Sitemap

- Basic Concepts
- The Indirect Method
- The Direct Method
- Appendix: Work Sheet Approach

This chapter is devoted to analyzing cash flows because understanding cash flows is vital for making good business decisions. We will see how to prepare the statement of cash flows, which is the basis for the analysis, and how to interpret cash-flow information.

We begin by explaining the statement format, called the indirect approach, that is used by the vast majority of companies. We end the chapter with the alternate format of the statement of cash flows, the direct approach. This chapter will prepare you to analyze the cash flows of any company you encounter. It has three distinct sections:

- Introduction
- Preparing the Statement of Cash Flows by the Indirect Method, which begins on page 661
- Preparing the Statement of Cash Flows by the Direct Method, which begins on page 671

The introduction applies to all the cash-flow topics. To cover only the indirect method, instructors can assign the first two parts of the chapter. Those interested only in the direct method can cover the Introduction and proceed to the direct method on page 671.

- **Basic Concepts**
- The Indirect Method
- The Direct Method
- Appendix: Work Sheet Approach

Student ResourceCD

direct method, financing activities, indirect method, investing activities, operating activities, statement of cash flows

Basic Concepts: Statement of Cash Flows

A balance sheet reports financial position, and balance sheets for two periods show whether cash increased or decreased. For example, Anchor Corporation's comparative balance sheet reported the following:

	20X5	20X4	Increase (Decrease)
Cash	$22,000	$42,000	$(20,000)

You can see that Anchor's cash decreased by $20,000 during 20X5. But the balance sheet doesn't show *why* cash decreased. We need the cash-flow statement for that.

Statement of Cash Flows
Reports cash receipts and cash payments during the period.

Cash Flows
Cash receipts and cash payments.

The **statement of cash flows** reports **cash flows**—cash receipts and cash payments—during the period. It shows where cash came from and how it was spent. It explains the *causes* of the change in cash during any given time period. The statement of cash flows covers a span of time and therefore is dated "Year Ended December 31, 20X5" or "Month Ended June 30, 20X5." Exhibit 17-1 illustrates the time element of each financial statement.

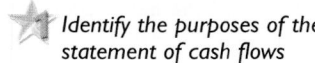

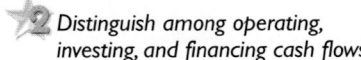

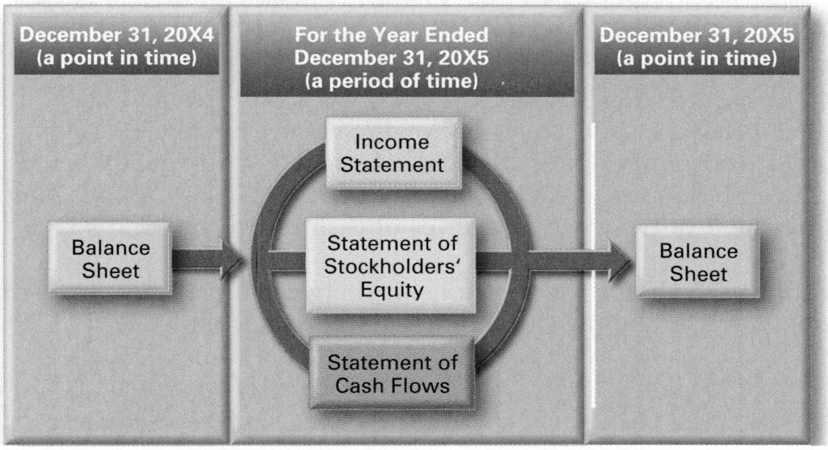

Exhibit 17-1

Timing of the Financial Statements

The statement of cash flows serves several purposes:

Identify the purposes of the statement of cash flows

1. ***Predicts future cash flows.*** Past cash receipts and payments are good predictors of future cash flows.
2. ***Evaluates management decisions.*** If managers make wise investment decisions, the business prospers. If they make unwise investments, the business suffers. The statement of cash flows reports cash flows from operations and also the investments the company is making. Investors and creditors use cash-flow information to evaluate managers' decisions.
3. ***Predicts ability to make debt payments to lenders and to pay dividends to stockholders.*** Lenders want to collect interest and principal on their loans. Stockholders want dividends on their investments. The statement of cash flows helps predict whether the business can make these payments.

✔ **Starter 17-1**

Cash Equivalents
Highly liquid short-term investments that can be readily converted into cash.

On a statement of cash flows, *Cash* means more than just cash on hand and cash in the bank. It includes **cash equivalents**, which are highly liquid short-term investments that can be readily converted into cash. Examples of cash equivalents are money-market investments and investments in U.S. government securities. Businesses invest cash in liquid assets rather than let the cash remain idle. Throughout this chapter, the term *cash* refers to cash and cash equivalents.

Distinguish among operating, investing, and financing cash flows

Operating, Investing, and Financing Activities

A business engages in three types of business activities:

- Operating activities
- Investing activities
- Financing activities

Operating Activities
Activities that create revenue or expense in the entity's major line of business; a section of the statement of cash flows. Operating activities affect the income statement.

Investing Activities
Activities that increase or decrease long-term assets; a section of the statement of cash flows.

Operating activities create revenues, expenses, gains, and losses. They affect *net income* on the income statement, which is a product of accrual accounting. The statement of cash flows reports the cash effects of operating activities. Operating activities also affect *current assets* and *current liabilities* on the balance sheet. Operating activities are the most important of the three categories. A successful business must generate most of its cash from day-to-day operations.

Investing activities increase and decrease *long-term assets*, such as computers and software, land, buildings, and equipment. The purchases and sales of these assets are investing activities. Loans to others and collections of loans are also investing activities. Investing activities are less critical than operating activities.

Financing Activities
Activities that obtain the cash needed to launch and sustain the business; a section of the statement of cash flows.

Financing activities obtain cash to launch a business and keep it running. Financing includes issuing stock, borrowing money, buying and selling treasury stock, and paying dividends. Paying off a loan is another financing activity. Financing cash flows relate to *long-term liabilities* and *owners' equity*. They are the least important of the three categories of cash flows, and that's why they are reported last.

Exhibit 17-2 shows the relationship between operating, investing, and financing activities and the various parts of the balance sheet.

Exhibit 17-2

Operating, Investing, and Financing Cash Flows and the Balance-Sheet Accounts

Accounting.com

Cash and Kisses Meet at Match.com

Who says "Money Can't Buy Me Love"? **Match.com**, the Internet dating service, is proving that money *can* buy at least the potential for love. Cash flow at the online dating service has surged as it has collected over $15 million a month from clients. For their fees, clients can post photos, contact other members, and receive alerts when potential matches show up.

Ticketmaster, Match.com's parent company, is delighted. Ticketmaster posted its first positive cash flow in 2001, thanks largely to Match.com. Analysts are not surprised: "Online dating [. . .] is one of the few [things] people will [pay] for online, [and. . .] companies are actually upping their prices."

Match.com's only big operating expense is advertising. The company has stayed on top by spending $50 million a year on TV ads. Yet, boasts the Ticketmaster chief executive, 30% to 70% of Match.com's advertising dollars are "instantly recouped."

Cash-rich Internet companies like Match.com can offer vital lessons about what works online. In general, these companies provide services that are information-intensive and require no physical transport of goods. There are no returned goods or other fulfillment costs to deal with.

For Match.com, fulfillment occurs off-screen: To date, the company boasts 1,300 marriages, hundreds of thousands of relationships, and more than 50 babies born of Match.com unions.

Based on: Robert Barker, "Is Ticketmaster Your Perfect Date?" *Business Week*, April 22, 2002, p. 108. Bob Tedeschi, "Online Matchmakers Are Helping to Bolster the Finances of Their Corporate Parents as They Raise the Romantic Hopes of Clients," *The New York Times*, February 4, 2002, p. C6. Julia Angwin, "Net Income: Latest Dot-Com Fad Is a Bit Old-Fashioned: It's Called 'Profitability,'" *The Wall Street Journal*, August 14, 2002, p. A1. Dennis McCafferty, "Hosting in the Name of Love," Hostingtech.com, October 2002.

Two Formats for Operating Activities

There are two ways to format operating activities on the statement of cash flows:

- **Indirect method**, which reconciles from net income to net cash provided by operating activities
- **Direct method**, which reports all cash receipts and cash payments from operating activities

Indirect Method
Format of the operating activities section of the statement of cash flows; starts with net income and reconciles to net cash provided by operating activities.

Direct Method
Format of the operating activities section of the statement of cash flows; lists the major categories of operating cash receipts and cash payments.

The two methods use different computations but produce the same amount of cash from operations. The indirect and direct methods have no effect on investing or financing activities. The following table summarizes the differences between these approaches for operating activities (all dollar amounts are assumed for the illustration).

Indirect Method		Direct Method	
Net income	$ 300	Collections from customers	$ 900
Adjustments:		*Deductions:*	
Depreciation, etc.	100	Payments to suppliers, etc.. . .	(500)
Net cash provided by operating activities. . . .	$ 400	Net cash provided by operating activities	$ 400

Let's begin with the indirect method because most companies use it.

✔ Starter 17-2

Preparing the Statement of Cash Flows by the Indirect Method

□ Basic Concepts
■ The Indirect Method
□ The Direct Method
□ Appendix: Work Sheet Approach

To prepare the statement of cash flows, you need data from the income statement and the balance sheet. Consider Anchor Corporation, a dealer in older British sports cars such as MG, Triumph, and Austin Healey. To prepare the statement of cash flows by the indirect method,

Student ResourceCD
indirect method, financing activities, investing activities, operating activities, financing cash flows, investing cash flows, operating cash flows

3 *Prepare a statement of cash flows by the indirect method*

Step 1 Lay out the template as shown in Exhibit 17-3. The exhibit is comprehensive. Steps 2 to 4 will complete the statement of cash flows.

Step 2 Use the comparative balance sheet to determine the increase or decrease in cash. The change in cash is the "check figure" for the statement of cash flows. Exhibit 17-4 gives the comparative balance sheet of Anchor Corporation at December 31, 20X5 and 20X4, with cash highlighted. Anchor's cash decreased by $20,000 during 20X5.

Step 3 From the income statement, take net income, depreciation, depletion, and amortization expense, and any gains or losses on the sale of assets. Exhibit 17-5 gives the income statement of Anchor Corporation for the year ended December 31, 20X5, with relevant items highlighted.

Step 4 Use data from the income statement and balance sheet to complete the statement of cash flows. The statement is complete only after you have explained year-to-year changes in all balance-sheet accounts.

Let's apply these steps to prepare the operating activities section of Anchor Corporation's statement of cash flows. Exhibit 17-6 gives the operating activities section of the statement of cash flows.

Exhibit 17-3

Template of the Statement of Cash Flows: Indirect Method

Anchor Corporation

Statement of Cash Flows
Year Ended December 31, 20X5

Cash flows from operating activities:
Net income
Adjustments to reconcile net income to net cash provided by operating activities:
+ Depreciation / amortization expense
+ Loss on sale of long-term assets
– Gain on sale of long-term assets
– Increases in current assets other than cash
+ Decreases in current assets other than cash
+ Increases in current liabilities
– Decreases in current liabilities
Net cash provided by operating activities

✔ Starter 17-3

Cash flows from investing activities:
Sales of long-term assets (investments, land, building, equipment, and so on)
– Purchases of long-term assets
Net cash provided by (used for) investing activities

Cash flows from financing activities:
Issuance of stock
+ Sale of treasury stock
– Purchase of treasury stock
+ Issuance of notes or bonds payable (borrowing)
– Payment of notes or bonds payable
– Payment of dividends
Net cash provided by (used for) financing activities

Net increase (decrease) in cash during the year
+ Cash at December 31, 20X4
= Cash at December 31, 20X5

Exhibit 17-4 **Comparative Balance Sheet**

Anchor Corporation

Comparative Balance Sheet
December 31, 20X5 and 20X4

(In thousands)	20X5	20X4	Increase (Decrease)	
Assets				
Current:				
Cash	$ 22	$ 42	$ (20)	
Accounts receivable	96	81	15	*Changes in current assets—Operating*
Inventory	143	145	(2)	
Plant assets, net of depreciation	464	219	245	*Changes in noncurrent assets—Investing*
Total	$725	$487	$238	
Liabilities				
Current:				
Accounts payable	$ 91	$ 57	$ 34	*Changes in current liabilities—Operating*
Accrued liabilities	5	9	(4)	
Long-term notes payable	160	77	83	
Stockholders' Equity				*Changes in long-term liabilities and common stock—Financing*
Common stock	359	258	101	
Retained earnings	110	86	24	*Change due to net income—Operating* *Change due to dividends—Financing*
Total	$725	$487	$238	

Exhibit 17-5

Income Statement

Anchor Corporation

Income Statement
Year Ended December 31, 20X5

	(In thousands)	
Revenues and gains:		
Sales revenue	$284	
Interest revenue	12	
Dividend revenue	9	
Gain on sale of plant assets	8	
Total revenues and gains		$313
Expenses:		
Cost of goods sold	$150	
Salary and wage expense	56	
Depreciation expense	18	
Other operating expense	17	
Interest expense	16	
Income tax expense	15	
Total expenses		272
Net income		$ 41

Exhibit 17-6

Statement of Cash Flows—Operating Activities by the Indirect Method

Anchor Corporation

Statement of Cash Flows
Operating Activities Only
For the Year Ended December 31, 20X5

		(In thousands)	
	Cash flows from operating activities:		
	Net income		$41
	Adjustments to reconcile net income to net cash provided by operating activities:		
Ⓐ	Depreciation	$ 18	
Ⓑ	Gain on sale of plant assets	(8)	
©	Increase in accounts receivable	(15)	
©	Decrease in inventory	2	
©	Increase in accounts payable	34	
©	Decrease in accrued liabilities	(4)	27
	Net cash provided by operating activities		$68

Cash Flows from Operating Activities

The operating section of the cash-flow statement begins with net income, taken from the income statement (Exhibit 17-5). Additions and subtractions, which follow, are labeled "Adjustments to reconcile net income to net cash provided by operating activities."

Operating Activities Are Related to the Transactions That Make Up Net Income (Revenues, Expenses, Gains, and Losses).[1]

[1]The authors thank Alfonso Oddo for suggesting this summary.

Ⓐ **DEPRECIATION, DEPLETION, AND AMORTIZATION EXPENSES** These expenses are added back to net income to reconcile from net income to cash flow. Let's see why. Depreciation is recorded as follows:

Depreciation Expense	18,000	
Accumulated Depreciation.............		18,000

You can see that depreciation does not affect cash. However, depreciation, like all other expenses, decreases net income. Therefore, in going from net income to cash flows, we add depreciation back to net income. The add-back cancels the earlier deduction.

Example: Suppose you had only two transactions during the period, a $1,000 cash sale and depreciation expense of $300. Net income is $700 ($1,000 – $300). But cash flow from operations is $1,000. To reconcile from net income ($700) to cash flow ($1,000), add back depreciation ($300). Also add back depletion and amortization.

Ⓑ **GAINS AND LOSSES ON THE SALE OF ASSETS** Sales of long-term assets are *investing* activities. A gain or loss on the sale is included in net income and therefore must be adjusted out of net income on the statement of cash flows. Exhibit 17-6 includes an adjustment for a gain. During 20X5, Anchor sold equipment for $62,000. The equipment's book value was $54,000, so there was a gain of $8,000.

The $62,000 sale is an investing cash flow, and the $8,000 gain on the sale must be removed from operating cash flow. We explain investing activities in the next section.

A loss on the sale of plant assets would be *added back* to net income. The cash received from selling the plant assets is then reported under investing activities.

Ⓒ **CHANGES IN THE CURRENT ASSET AND CURRENT LIABILITY ACCOUNTS** Most current assets and current liabilities result from operating activities. For example, accounts receivable result from sales, inventory relates to cost of goods sold, and so on. Changes in the current accounts are reported as adjustments to net income on the cash-flow statement. The reasoning follows:

↑ Current assets ⇒ ↓ Cash

1. ***An increase in a current asset other than cash means a decrease in cash.*** The reason is because it takes cash to acquire assets. If Accounts Receivable, Inventory, or Prepaid Expenses increase during the period, subtract the increase from net income to measure cash flow from operations.

↓ Current assets ⇒ ↑ Cash

2. ***A decrease in a current asset other than cash means an increase in cash.*** Suppose Anchor's Accounts Receivable decreased by $4,000. Anchor must have collected on the Accounts Receivable. Therefore, add decreases in Accounts Receivable and the other current assets to net income.

↓ Current liabilities ⇒ ↓ Cash

3. ***A decrease in a current liability means a decrease in cash.*** The payment of a current liability causes cash to decrease. Therefore, subtract decreases in current liabilities from net income.

↑ Current liabilities ⇒ ↑ Cash

The authors thank M. Suzanne Oliver for suggesting these displays.

4. ***An increase in a current liability means an increase in cash.*** Anchor's Accounts Payable increased. This means that cash was *not* spent to pay this liability, so Anchor has more cash on hand. Thus, increases in current liabilities are *added* to net income.

EVALUATING CASH FLOWS FROM OPERATING ACTIVITIES During 20X5, Anchor Corporation's operations provided net cash flow of $68,000. This amount exceeds net income, as it should because of the add-back of depreciation. However, to fully evaluate a company's cash flows, you must also examine its investing and financing activities. Let's see how to report those cash flows, as shown in Exhibit 17-7, which gives Anchor's full-blown statement of cash flows.

Anchor Corporation
Statement of Cash Flows
For the Year Ended December 31, 20X5

Exhibit 17-7
Statement of Cash Flows—Indirect Method

		(In thousands)	
Cash flows from operating activities:			
Net income			$ 41
Adjustments to reconcile net income to net cash provided by operating activities:			
Ⓐ	Depreciation	$ 18	
Ⓑ	Gain on sale of plant assets	(8)	
Ⓒ	Increase in accounts receivable	(15)	
Ⓒ	Decrease in inventory	2	
Ⓒ	Increase in accounts payable	34	
Ⓒ	Decrease in accrued liabilities	(4)	27
Net cash provided by operating activities			68
Cash flows from investing activities:			
Acquisition of plant assets		$ (317)	
Proceeds from sale of plant assets		62	
Net cash used for investing activities			(255)
Cash flows from financing activities:			
Proceeds from issuance of common stock		$ 101	
Proceeds from issuance of long-term notes payable		94	
Payment of long-term notes payable		(11)	
Payment of dividends		(17)	
Net cash provided by financing activities			167
Net decrease in cash			$ (20)
Cash balance, December 31, 20X4			42
Cash balance, December 31, 20X5			$ 22

✔ Starter 17-4

✔ Starter 17-5

✔ Starter 17-6

Cash Flows from Investing Activities

Investing activities affect long-term asset accounts, such as Plant Assets and Investments. Let's see how to compute the investing cash flows.

Computing Acquisitions and Sales of Plant Assets Companies keep separate accounts for Land, Buildings, Equipment, and other plant assets. But for computing investing cash flows, it is helpful to combine these accounts into a single Plant Assets account. Also, we subtract accumulated depreciation from the assets' cost and work with a single net figure for plant assets. This simplifies the computations.

To illustrate, observe that Anchor Corporation's

- Balance sheet reports beginning plant assets, net of depreciation, of $219,000 and an ending net amount of $464,000 (Exhibit 17-4).
- Income statement shows depreciation expense of $18,000 and an $8,000 gain on sale of plant assets (Exhibit 17-5).

Further, the acquisitions of plant assets total $317,000 (see Exhibit 17-7). How much, then, are the proceeds from the sale of plant assets? First, we must determine the book value of plant assets sold, as follows:

Plant Assets (Net)

Beginning balance	+	Acquisitions	−	Depreciation	−	Book value of assets sold	=	Ending balance
$219,000	+	$317,000	−	$18,000		− X	=	$464,000
						− X	=	$464,000 − $219,000 − $317,000 + $18,000
						X	=	$54,000

Now we can compute the sale proceeds:

Sale proceeds	=	Book value of assets sold	+	Gain	–	Loss
	=	$54,000	+	$8,000	–	$0
	=	$62,000				

Trace the sale proceeds of $62,000 to the statement of cash flows in Exhibit 17-7. If the sale resulted in a loss of $3,000, the sale proceeds would be $51,000 ($54,000 – $3,000), and the statement of cash flows would report $51,000 as a cash receipt from this investing activity.

The Plant Assets T-account provides another look at the computation of the book value of the assets sold.

Plant Assets (Net)

Beginning balance	**219,000**	**Depreciation**	**18,000**
Acquisitions	**317,000**	Book value of assets sold	54,000
Ending balance	**464,000**		

✔ Starter 17-7

Proceeds from the sale of an asset can be computed as follows:

Proceeds = Book value sold + Gain, or – Loss

The book-value information comes from the balance sheet; the gain or loss comes from the income statement. Exhibit 17-8 summarizes the computation of the investing cash flows.

Exhibit 17-8 **Computing Cash Flows from Investing Activities**

Receipts									
From sale of plant assets	Beginning plant assets (net)	+	Acquisition cost	–	Depreciation	–	Book value of assets sold	=	Ending plant assets (net)
	Cash received	=	Book value of assets sold	+ or –	Gain on sale / Loss on sale				
Payments									
For acquisition of plant assets	Beginning plant assets (net)	+	Acquisition cost	–	Depreciation	–	Book value of assets sold	=	Ending plant assets (net)

Cash Flows from Financing Activities

Financing activities affect the liability and stockholders' equity accounts, such as Long-Term Notes Payable, Bonds Payable, Common Stock, and Retained Earnings.

Computing Issuances and Payments of Long-Term Notes Payable

The beginning and ending balances of Long-Term Notes Payable or Bonds Payable are taken from the balance sheet. If either the amount of new issuances or the payments is known, the other amount can be computed. For Anchor Corporation, new issuances of notes payable total $94,000 (Exhibit 17-7). The computation of debt payments uses the Long-Term Notes Payable account, with amounts from Anchor Corporation's balance sheet in Exhibit 17-4:

Long-Term Notes Payable

Beginning balance	+	Issuance of new notes payable	–	Payment of notes payable	=	Ending balance
$77,000	+	$94,000		–X	=	$160,000
				–X	=	$160,000 – $77,000 – $94,000
				X	=	$11,000

Another view:

Long-Term Notes Payable

		Beginning balance	77,000
Payments	11,000	Issuance of new notes payable	94,000
		Ending balance	160,000

Computing Issuances of Stock and Purchases of Treasury Stock Cash flows for these financing activities can be determined by analyzing the stock accounts. For example, the amount of a new issuance of common stock is determined from Common Stock. Using data from Exhibits 17-4 and 17-7:

Common Stock

Beginning balance	+	Issuance of new stock	=	Ending balance
$ 258,000	+	$101,000	=	$359,000

Another view:

Common Stock

		Beginning balance	258,000
		Issuance of new stock	101,000
		Ending balance	359,000

Apart from the Anchor Corporation example, cash flows affecting Treasury Stock can be analyzed as follows:

Treasury Stock (Amounts assumed for illustration only)

Beginning balance	+	Purchase of treasury stock	=	Ending balance
$16,000	+	$3,000	=	$19,000

Another view:

Treasury Stock

Beginning balance	16,000		
Purchases of treasury stock	3,000		
Ending balance	19,000		

Computing Dividend Payments The amount of dividend payments can be computed by analyzing Retained Earnings. The T-accounts below provide another view.

Retained Earnings

Beginning balance	+	Net income	−	Dividends	=	Ending balance
$86,000	+	$41,000		−X	=	$110,000
				−X	=	$110,000 – $86,000 – $41,000
				X	=	$17,000

Retained Earnings

		Beginning balance	86,000
Dividends	17,000	Net income	41,000
		Ending balance	110,000

✔ Starter 17-8

A stock dividend has *no* effect on Cash and is *not* reported on the cash-flow statement. Exhibit 17-9 summarizes the computation of cash flows from financing activities, highlighted in color.

Exhibit 17-9 Computing Cash Flows from Financing Activities

Receipts							
From issuance of long-term notes payable	Beginning notes payable	+	Issuance of notes payable	−	Payment of notes payable	=	Ending long-term notes payable
From issuance of stock	Beginning stock	+	Issuance of new stock	=	Ending stock		
Payments							
Of long-term notes payable	Beginning notes payable	+	Issuance of notes payable	−	Payment of notes payable	=	Ending long-term notes payable
To purchase treasury stock	Beginning treasury stock	+	Cost of treasury stock	=	Ending treasury stock		
Of dividends	Beginning retained earnings	+	Net income	−	Dividends	=	Ending retained earnings

Stop & Think

Classify each of the following as an operating activity, an investing activity, or a financing activity:

a. Issuance of stock
b. Borrowing
c. Sales revenue
d. Payment of dividends
e. Purchase of land
f. Purchase of treasury stock
g. Paying bonds payable
h. Interest expense
i. Sale of equipment
j. Cost of goods sold
k. Purchase of another company
l. Making a loan

Answer:

a. Financing
b. Financing
c. Operating
d. Financing
e. Investing
f. Financing
g. Financing
h. Operating
i. Investing
j. Operating
k. Investing
l. Investing

Noncash Investing and Financing Activities

Companies make investments that do not require cash. They also obtain financing other than cash. Our examples thus far have included none of these transactions. Now suppose Anchor Corporation issued common stock of $320,000 to acquire a building. Anchor would journalize this transaction as follows:

Building	320,000	
Common Stock		320,000

This transaction would not be reported on the cash-flow statement because Anchor paid no cash. But the building and the common stock are important. *Noncash investing and financing activities* can be reported in a separate schedule that accompanies the statement of cash flows. Exhibit 17-10 illustrates noncash investing and financing activities (all amounts are assumed). This information follows the cash-flow statement or can be disclosed in a note.

Exhibit 17-10

Noncash Investing and Financing Activities (All amounts assumed)

	Thousands
Noncash Investing and Financing Activities:	
Acquisition of building by issuing common stock	$320
Acquisition of land by issuing note payable	70
Payment of note payable by issuing common stock	100
Total noncash investing and financing activities	$490

Now let's put into practice what you have learned about the statement of cash flows prepared by the indirect method.

MID-CHAPTER *Summary Problem*

Robins Corporation reported the following income statement and comparative balance sheet for 20X5, along with transaction data for 20X5:

CHECK YOUR RESOURCES

Robins Corporation
Income Statement
Year Ended December 31, 20X5

Sales revenue		$662,000
Cost of goods sold		560,000
Gross profit		102,000
Operating expenses:		
Salary expense	$46,000	
Depreciation expense	10,000	
Rent expense	2,000	
Total operating expenses		58,000
Income from operations		44,000
Other items:		
Loss on sale of equipment		(2,000)
Income before income tax		42,000
Income tax expense		16,000
Net income		$ 26,000

Robins Corporation
Balance Sheet
December 31, 20X5 and 20X4

Assets	20X5	20X4	Liabilities	20X5	20X4
Current:			Current:		
Cash and equivalents	$ 22,000	$ 3,000	Accounts payable	$ 35,000	$ 26,000
Accounts receivable	22,000	23,000	Accrued liabilities	7,000	9,000
Inventories	35,000	34,000	Income tax payable	10,000	10,000
Total current assets	79,000	60,000	Total current liabilities	52,000	45,000
Equipment, net	126,000	72,000	Bonds payable	84,000	53,000
			Owners' Equity		
			Common stock	52,000	20,000
			Retained earnings	27,000	19,000
			Less: Treasury stock	(10,000)	(5,000)
Total assets	$205,000	$132,000	Total liabilities and equity	$205,000	$132,000

Transaction Data for 20X5:	
Purchase of equipment	$140,000
Payment of dividends	18,000
Issuance of common stock to retire bonds payable	13,000
Issuance of bonds payable to borrow cash	44,000
Issuance of common stock	19,000
Sale of equipment (book value, $76,000)	74,000
Purchase of treasury stock	5,000

Required

Prepare Robins Corporation's statement of cash flows for the year ended December 31, 20X5. Format operating cash flows by the indirect method. Follow the four steps outlined below.

Requirement 1

Step 1 Lay out the template of the statement of cash flows.

Step 2 From the comparative balance sheet, determine the increase in cash during the year, $19,000.

Step 3 From the income statement, take net income, depreciation, and the loss on sale of equipment to the statement of cash flows.

Step 4 Complete the statement of cash flows. Account for the year-to-year change in each balance sheet account. Prepare a T-account to show the transaction activity in each long-term balance-sheet account.

Solution

Robins Corporation

Statement of Cash Flows
Year Ended December 31, 20X5

Cash flows from operating activities:		
Net income		$26,000
Adjustments to reconcile net income to net cash provided by operating activities:		
Depreciation	$ 10,000	
Loss on sale of equipment	2,000	
Decrease in accounts receivable	1,000	
Increase in inventories	(1,000)	
Increase in accounts payable	9,000	
Decrease in accrued liabilities	(2,000)	19,000
Net cash provided by operating activities		45,000
Cash flows from investing activities:		
Purchase of equipment	$(140,000)	
Sale of equipment	74,000	
Net cash used for investing activities		(66,000)
Cash flows from financing activities:		
Issuance of common stock	$ 19,000	
Payment of dividends	(18,000)	
Issuance of bonds payable	44,000	
Purchase of treasury stock	(5,000)	
Net cash provided by financing activities		40,000
Net increase in cash		$19,000
Cash balance, December 31, 20X4		3,000
Cash balance, December 31, 20X5		$22,000
Noncash investing and financing activities:		
Issuance of common stock to retire bonds payable		$13,000
Total noncash investing and financing activities		$13,000

Equipment, Net

Bal.	72,000		
	140,000		10,000
			76,000
Bal.	126,000		

Bonds Payable

Bal.	53,000		
	13,000		44,000
		Bal.	84,000

Common Stock

		Bal.	20,000
			13,000
			19,000
		Bal.	52,000

Retained Earnings

		Bal.	19,000
	18,000		26,000
		Bal.	27,000

Treasury Stock

Bal.	5,000		
	5,000		
Bal.	10,000		

Excel Application Exercise

Goal: To create an Excel work sheet that computes cash flows from operating activities using the indirect method.

Scenario: As an accountant at Ochoa, Inc., you have been asked to compute the net cash provided by operating activities using the indirect method for the month of March. Accounting records for the company reveal the following:

Cash sales	$ 9,000
Loss on sale of land	5,000
Net income	33,000
Depreciation	12,000
Increase in current assets other than cash	17,000
Acquisition of land	37,000
Decrease in current liabilities	9,000

Using the information provided in this exercise, determine the net cash flows from operating activities. When done, answer these questions:

1. Does Ochoa have net cash provided by (or used by) operating activities?
2. Evaluate Ochoa's operating cash flow as either strong or weak.
3. Based on the Application Exercise for this chapter, what decisions might investors make with this information?

Step-by-Step:

1. Open a new Excel work sheet.
2. Create a heading for your work sheet that contains:
   a. Chapter 17 Excel Application Exercise
   b. Ochoa, Inc.
   c. Statement of Cash Flows - Operating Activities
   d. For the Month Ended March 31, 20X5
3. Follow the statement of cash flows format in Exhibit 17-3 and use formulas for all computations.
4. Save your work and print a copy for your files.

- ☐ Basic Concepts
- ☐ The Indirect Method
- ■ The Direct Method
- ☐ Appendix: Work Sheet Approach

Preparing the Statement of Cash Flows by the Direct Method

Student Resource CD

direct method, financing activities, investing activities, operating activities, financing cash flows, investing cash flows, operating cash flows

4 *Prepare a statement of cash flows by the direct method*

The Financial Accounting Standards Board (FASB) has expressed a preference for the direct method of reporting cash flows from operating activities. Unfortunately, very few companies use this method because it takes more computations than the indirect method. But the direct method provides clearer information about the sources and uses of cash. Investing and financing cash flows are unaffected by operating cash flows.

To illustrate the statement of cash flows, we will be using Anchor Corporation, a dealer in older British sports cars such as MG, Triumph, and Austin Healey. To prepare the statement of cash flows by the direct method, proceed as follows:

STEP 1 Lay out the template of the statement of cash flows by the direct method, as shown in Exhibit 17-11.

Exhibit 17-11

Template of the Statement of Cash Flows: Direct Method

Anchor Corporation

Statement of Cash Flows
Year Ended December 31, 20X5

Cash flows from operating activities:
Receipts:
Collections from customers
Interest received
Dividends received on investments
Total cash receipts
Payments:
To suppliers
To employees
For interest and income tax
Total cash payments
Net cash provided by operating activities
Cash flows from investing activities:
Sales of long-term assets (investments, land, building, equipment, and so on)
– Purchases of long-term assets
Net cash provided by (used for) investing activities
Cash flows from financing activities:
Issuance of stock
+ Sale of treasury stock
– Purchase of treasury stock
+ Issuance of notes or bonds payable (borrowing)
– Payment of notes or bonds payable
– Payment of dividends
Net cash provided by (used for) financing activities
Net increase (decrease) in cash during the year
+ Cash at December 31, 20X4
= Cash at December 31, 20X5

STEP 2 Use the comparative balance sheet to determine the increase or decrease in cash during the period. The change in cash is the "check figure" for the statement of cash flows. The comparative balance sheet of Anchor Corporation at December 31, 20X5 and 20X4 shows that Anchor's cash decreased by $20,000 during 20X5. See Exhibit 17-4.

STEP 3 Use the available data to prepare the statement of cash flows. Suppose Anchor has assembled the summary of 20X5 transactions in Exhibit 17-12. These transactions give the data for both the income statement (Exhibit 17-5) and the statement of cash flows. Some transactions affect one statement and some, the other. For example, sales (item 1) are reported on the income statement, and cash collections (item 2) on the statement of cash flows. Other transactions, such as the cash receipt of dividend revenue (item 4) affect both statements. *The statement of cash flows reports only those transactions with cash effects* (those with an asterisk in Exhibit 17-12). Exhibit 17-13 gives Anchor Corporation's statement of cash flows for 20X5.

Cash Flows from Operating Activities

Operating cash flows are listed first because they are the most important source of cash. Exhibit 17-13 shows that Anchor is sound; its operating activities were the largest source of cash receipts, $290,000. Let's examine the operating cash flows (see page 674).

Exhibit 17-12

Summary of Anchor Corporation's 20X5 Transactions

Operating Activities

1. Sales on account, $284,000
*2. Collections from customers, $269,000
*3. Cash receipt of interest revenue, $12,000
*4. Cash receipt of dividend revenue, $9,000
5. Cost of goods sold, $150,000
*6. Payments to suppliers, $135,000
*7. Salary expense and payments, $56,000
8. Depreciation expense, $18,000
9. Other operating expense, $17,000
*10. Interest expense and payments, $16,000
*11. Income tax expense and payments, $15,000

Investing Activities

*12. Cash payments to acquire plant assets, $317,000
*13. Proceeds from sale of plant assets, $62,000, including $8,000 gain

Financing Activities

*14. Proceeds from issuance of common stock, $101,000
*15. Proceeds from issuance of long-term note payable, $94,000
*16. Payment of long-term note payable, $11,000
*17. Payment of cash dividends, $17,000

* Indicates a cash flow to be reported on the statement of cash flows
Note: Income statement data are used to prepare Exhibit 17-16, page 676.

Exhibit 17-13

Statement of Cash Flows—Direct Method

Anchor Corporation

Statement of Cash Flows
Year Ended December 31, 20X5

	(In thousands)	
Cash flows from operating activities:		
Receipts:		
Collections from customers	$ 269	
Interest received	12	
Dividends received	9	
Total cash receipts		$290
Payments:		
To suppliers	$(135)	
To employees	(56)	
For interest	(16)	
For income tax	(15)	
Total cash payments		(222)
Net cash provided by operating activities		68
Cash flows from investing activities:		
Acquisition of plant assets	$(317)	
Proceeds from sale of plant assets	62	
Net cash used for investing activities		(255)
Cash flows from financing activities:		
Proceeds from issuance of common stock	$ 101	
Proceeds from issuance of long-term notes payable	94	
Payment of long-term note payable	(11)	
Payment of dividends	(17)	
Net cash provided by financing activities		167
Net decrease in cash		**$ (20)**
Cash balance, December 31, 20X4		42
Cash balance, December 31, 20X5		$ 22

✔ Starter 17-9

Cash Collections from Customers Cash sales bring in cash immediately; collections of accounts receivable take longer. Both are reported on the statement of cash flows as "Collections from customers . . . $269,000" in Exhibit 17-13.

Cash Receipts of Interest The income statement reports interest revenue. Only the cash receipts of interest appear on the statement of cash flows—$12,000 in Exhibit 17-13.

Cash Receipts of Dividends Dividend revenue is reported on the income statement, and this cash receipt is reported on the statement of cash flows—$9,000 in Exhibit 17-13. (Dividends *received* are part of operating activities, but dividends *paid* are a financing activity.)

Payments to Suppliers Payments to suppliers include all payments for inventory and operating expenses except employee compensation, interest, and income taxes. *Suppliers* are those entities that provide the business with its inventory and essential services. In Exhibit 17-13, Anchor Corporation reports payments to suppliers of $135,000.

Payments to Employees This category includes payments for salaries and wages. Accrued amounts are not cash flows because they have not yet been paid. The statement of cash flows in Exhibit 17-13 reports only the cash payments ($56,000).

Payments for Interest Expense and Income Tax Expense These cash payments are reported separately from the other expenses. In the Anchor Corporation example, interest ($16,000) and income tax expenses ($15,000) equal their cash payments amounts. Therefore, the same amount appears on the income statement and the statement of cash flows.

Depreciation, Depletion, and Amortization Expense These expenses are *not* listed on the statement of cash flows because they do not affect cash.

Cash Flows from Investing Activities

Investing is critical because a company's investments determine its future course. Large purchases of plant assets signal expansion. Low levels of investing over a lengthy period indicate that the business is not replenishing assets.

Purchases of Plant Assets and Investments in Other Companies These cash payments acquire a long-term asset. The first investing activity reported by Anchor Corporation in Exhibit 17-13 is the purchase of plant assets ($317,000).

Proceeds from the Sale of Plant Assets and Investments These cash receipts are also investing activities. The sale of plant assets needs explanation. Exhibit 17-13 reports that Anchor Corporation received $62,000 cash from the sale of plant assets. The income statement shows an $8,000 gain on this transaction. What is the appropriate amount to show on the cash-flow statement? Report only the cash proceeds from the sale ($62,000), not the $8,000 gain. Investors and creditors are often critical of a company that sells large amounts of its plant assets. The sale may signal an emergency.

Cash Flows from Financing Activities

Cash flows from financing activities include the following:

PROCEEDS FROM ISSUANCE OF STOCK AND NOTES PAYABLE Readers of financial statements want to know how the entity obtains its financing. Issuing stock and borrowing money are two ways to finance a business. In Exhibit 17-13, Anchor Corporation issued common stock and received cash of $101,000. Anchor also issued long-term notes payable to borrow $94,000.

PAYMENT OF NOTES PAYABLE AND PURCHASES OF TREASURY STOCK The payment of notes payable decreases cash, which is the opposite of borrowing. Anchor Corporation reports long-term note payments of $11,000. Other transactions in this category include the purchase of treasury stock.

✔ Starter 17-10

PAYMENT OF CASH DIVIDENDS The payment of dividends decreases cash and is therefore a financing activity, as shown by Anchor's $17,000 payment in Exhibit 17-13. A stock dividend has *no* effect on cash and is *not* reported on the cash-flow statement.

✔ Starter 17-11

✔ Starter 17-12

Noncash Investing and Financing Activities

Companies make investments that do not require cash. They also obtain financing other than cash. Our examples thus far have included none of these transactions. Now suppose that Anchor Corporation issued common stock of $320,000 to acquire a building. Anchor would journalize this transaction as follows:

Building	320,000	
Common Stock.....................		320,000

This transaction would not be reported on the cash-flow statement because Anchor paid no cash. But the building and the common stock are important. Noncash investing and financing activities can be reported in a separate schedule that accompanies the statement of cash flows, as Exhibit 17-14 illustrates (all amounts are assumed). This information follows the cash-flow statement or can be disclosed in a note.

Exhibit 17-14

Noncash Investing and Financing Activities (All amounts assumed)

	Thousands
Noncash Investing and Financing Activities:	
Acquisition of building by issuing common stock.............	$320
Acquisition of land by issuing note payable..................	70
Payment of note payable by issuing common stock	100
Total noncash investing and financing activities	$490

Stop & Think

Classify each of the following as an operating activity, an investing activity, or a financing activity. Also identify those items that are not reported on the statement of cash flows prepared by the direct method.

a. Net income
b. Payment of dividends
c. Borrowing
d. Payment of cash to suppliers
e. Making a loan
f. Sale of treasury stock
g. Depreciation expense
h. Purchase of equipment
i. Issuance of stock
j. Purchase of another company
k. Payment of a note payable
l. Payment of income taxes
m. Collections from customers
n. Accrual of interest revenue
o. Expiration of prepaid expense
p. Receipt of cash dividends

Answer:

a. Not reported	e. Investing	i. Financing	m. Operating
b. Financing	f. Financing	j. Investing	n. Not reported
c. Financing	g. Not reported	k. Financing	o. Not reported
d. Operating	h. Investing	l. Operating	p. Operating

Now let's see how to compute the operating cash flows for the direct method.

Computing Operating Cash Flows by the Direct Method

How do we compute the operating cash flows for the direct method? We can use the income statement and the *changes* in the related balance sheet accounts, as diagrammed in Exhibit 17-15.

Exhibit 17-15 **Direct Method: Computing Cash Flows from Operating Activities**

Receipts/ Payments	From Income Statement Account	Change in Related Balance Sheet Account	
Receipts:			
From customers	Sales Revenue	+ Decrease in Accounts Receivable – Increase in Accounts Receivable	
Payments:			
To suppliers	Cost of Goods Sold	+ Increase in Inventory – Decrease in Inventory	+ Decrease in Accounts Payable – Increase in Accounts Payable
	Operating Expense	+ Increase in Prepaids – Decrease in Prepaids	+ Decrease in Accrued Liabilities – Increase in Accrued Liabilities

We thank Barbara Gerrity for suggesting this exhibit.

Data for computing Anchor Corporation's operating cash flows come from the income statement (Exhibit 17-16) and comparative balance sheet (Exhibit 17-17).

Exhibit 17-16
Income Statement

Anchor Corporation
Income Statement
Year Ended December 31, 20X5

		(In thousands)
Revenues and gains:		
Sales revenue	$284	
Interest revenue	12	
Dividend revenue	9	
Gain on sale of plant assets	8	
Total revenues and gains		$313
Expenses:		
Cost of goods sold	$150	
Salary and wage expense	56	
Depreciation expense	18	
Other operating expense	17	
Interest expense	16	
Income tax expense	15	
Total expenses		272
Net income		$ 41

Exhibit 17-17 Comparative Balance Sheet

Anchor Corporation
Comparative Balance Sheet
December 31, 20X5 and 20X4

(In thousands)	20X5	20X4	Increase (Decrease)	
Assets				
Current:				
Cash	$ 22	$ 42	$ (20)	
Accounts receivable	96	81	15	Changes in current assets—Operating
Inventory	143	145	(2)	
Plant assets, net of depreciation	464	219	245	Changes in noncurrent assets—Investing
Total	$725	$487	$238	
Liabilities				
Current:				
Accounts payable	$ 91	$ 57	$ 34	Changes in current liabilities—Operating
Accrued liabilities	5	9	(4)	
Long-term notes payable	160	77	83	Changes in long-term liabilities and common stock—Financing
Stockholders' Equity				
Common stock	359	258	101	
Retained earnings	110	86	24	Change due to net income—Operating Change due to dividends—Financing
Total	$725	$487	$238	

COMPUTING CASH COLLECTIONS FROM CUSTOMERS Collections can be computed by converting sales revenue (an accrual-basis amount) to the cash basis. Anchor Corporation's income statement (Exhibit 17-16) reports sales of $284,000. But cash collections are different. Exhibit 17-17 shows that Accounts Receivable increased from $81,000 at the beginning of the year to $96,000 at year-end, a $15,000 increase. Based on those amounts, Cash Collections equal $269,000.

Collections from Customers	=	Sales Revenue	−	Increase in Accounts Receivable
$269,000	=	$284,000	−	$15,000

COMPUTING PAYMENTS TO SUPPLIERS This computation includes two parts:

- Payments for inventory
- Payments for operating expenses (other than interest and income tax)

Payments for inventory are computed by converting cost of goods sold to the cash basis. We must analyze Cost of Goods Sold from the income statement and Inventory and Accounts Payable from the balance sheet. Payments for operating expenses (other than depreciation) use other operating expenses from the income statement and accrued liabilities from the balance sheet. Throughout, all amounts come from Exhibits 17-16 and 17-17.

Payments for Inventory	=	Cost of Goods Sold	−	Decrease in Inventory	−	Increase in Accounts Payable
$114,000	=	$150,000	−	$2,000	−	$34,000

Payments for Operating Expenses	=	Other Operating Expense	+	Decrease in Accrued Liabilities
$21,000	=	$17,000	+	$4,000

Payments to Suppliers	=	Payments for Inventory	+	Payments for Operating Expenses
$135,000	=	$114,000	+	$21,000

Computing Investing and Financing Cash Flows

The computations of investing and financing cash flows are given on pages 665–668.

Stop & Think

Viacom, Inc., the company that owns Paramount Pictures, Blockbuster Video, and MTV Music Television, reported the following for 2001 and 2000 (adapted, in millions):

At December 31,	**2001**	**2000**
Receivables, net	$ 3,582	$ 3,964
Inventory	5,224	5,035
Accounts payable	945	1,261
Year Ended December 31,	**2001**	**2000**
Revenues	$23,223	$20,044
Cost of goods sold	14,137	11,707

Based on these figures, how much cash did Viacom collect from customers during 2001? How much cash did Viacom pay for inventory during 2001?

Answer (In millions):

		Beginning Receivables	+	Revenues	−	Collections	=	Ending Receivables
Collections from customers	= $23,605	$3,964	+	$23,223	−	**$23,605**	=	$3,582
		Cost of Goods Sold	+	Increase in Inventory	+	Decrease in Accounts Payable	=	**Payments**
Payments for inventory and related services	= $14,642	$14,137	+	($5,224 − $5,035)	+	($1,261 − $945)	=	**$14,642**

Decision Guidelines

USING CASH-FLOW AND RELATED INFORMATION TO EVALUATE INVESTMENTS

Ann Browning is a private investor. Through the years, she has devised some guidelines for evaluating investments. Here are some of her guidelines.

Question	Financial Statement	What to Look For
Where is most of the company's cash coming from?	Statement of cash flows	Operating activities → Good sign Investing activities → Bad sign Financing activities → Okay sign
Do high sales and profits translate into more cash?	Statement of cash flows	Usually, but cash flows from *operating* activities must be the main source of cash for long-term success.
If sales and profits are low, how is the company generating cash?	Statement of cash flows	If *investing* activities are generating the cash, the business may be in trouble because it is selling off its long-term assets. If *financing* activities are generating the cash, that cannot go on forever. Sooner or later, investors will demand cash flow from operating activities.
Is the cash balance large enough to provide for expansion?	Balance sheet	The cash balance should be growing over time. If not, the company may be in trouble.
Can the business pay its debts?	Income statement	Increasing trend of net income.
	Statement of cash flows	Cash flows from operating activities should be the main source of cash.
	Balance sheet	Current ratio, debt ratio.

END-OF-CHAPTER *Summary Problem*

Granite Shoals Corporation reported the following comparative balance sheet and income statement for 20X6.

CHECK YOUR RESOURCES

Granite Shoals Corporation

Balance Sheet
December 31, 20X6 and 20X5

	20X6	20X5
Cash	$ 19,000	$ 3,000
Accounts receivable	22,000	23,000
Inventories	34,000	31,000
Prepaid expenses	1,000	3,000
Equipment (net)	90,000	79,000
Intangible assets	9,000	9,000
	$175,000	$148,000
Accounts payable	$ 14,000	$ 9,000
Accrued liabilities	16,000	19,000
Income tax payable	14,000	12,000
Long-term debt	45,000	50,000
Common stock	31,000	20,000
Retained earnings	64,000	40,000
Treasury stock	(9,000)	(2,000)
	$175,000	$148,000

Granite Shoals Corporation

Income Statement
Year Ended December 31, 20X6

Sales revenue	$190,000
Gain on sale of equipment	6,000
Total revenue and gains	196,000
Cost of goods sold	$ 85,000
Depreciation expense	19,000
Other operating expenses	36,000
Total expenses	140,000
Income before income tax	56,000
Income tax expense	18,000
Net income	$ 38,000

Required

Assume that **Berkshire Hathaway** is considering buying Granite Shoals Corporation. Berkshire Hathaway analysts need the following Granite Shoals cash-flow data for 20X6. There were no noncash investing and financing activities.

a. Collections from customers
b. Payments for inventory
c. Issuance of common stock
d. Payment of dividends

Solution

a.

Collections from customers	=	Sales revenue	+	Decrease in Accounts Receivables
$191,000	=	$190,000	+	$1,000

b.	Payments for inventory	=	Cost of goods sold	+	Increase in inventory	–	Increase in Accounts Payable
	$83,000	=	$85,000	+	$3,000	–	$5,000

c. Analyze Common Stock (let X = issuance)

Beginning	+	Issuance	=	Ending	
$20,000	+	X	=	$31,000	
		X	=		$11,000

d. Analyze Retained Earnings (let X = dividends)

Beginning	+	Net Income	–	Dividends	=	Ending	
$40,000	+	$38,000	–	X	=	$64,000	
				X	=		$14,000

REVIEW *the Statement of Cash Flows*

Quick Check

1. The three main categories of cash-flow activities are
   a. Direct and indirect
   b. Operating, investing, and financing
   c. Noncash investing and financing
   d. Current and long-term
2. The purposes of the cash-flow statement are to
   a. Predict future cash flows
   b. Evaluate management decisions
   c. Determine ability to pay liabilities and dividends
   d. All of the above
3. Financing activities are most closely related to
   a. Current assets and current liabilities
   b. Long-term assets
   c. Long-term liabilities and owners' equity
   d. Net income and dividends
4. Which item does *not* appear on a statement of cash flows prepared by the indirect method?
   a. Collections from customers
   b. Net income
   c. Depreciation
   d. Gain on sale of land
5. Euro Bistro earned net income of $60,000 after deducting depreciation of $4,000 and all other expenses. Current assets increased by $3,000, and current liabilities decreased by $5,000. How much was Euro Bistro's cash provided by operations (indirect method)?
   a. $48,000
   b. $50,000
   c. $52,000
   d. $56,000
6. The Plant Assets account of Canyon Corp. shows the following:

Plant Assets, Net

Beg.	100,000	Depr.	30,000
Purchase	400,000	Sale	?
End.	420,000		

   Canyon sold plant assets at a $10,000 gain. Where on the statement of cash flows should Canyon report the sale of plant assets? How much should Canyon report for the sale?
   a. Investing cash flows—sale of $40,000
   b. Investing cash flows—sale of $50,000
   c. Investing cash flows—sale of $60,000
   d. Financing cash flows—sale of $60,000

7. Columbia, Inc., borrowed $15,000, issued common stock of $10,000, and paid dividends of $25,000. What was Columbia's net cash provided (used) by financing activities?
   a. $0
   b. $25,000
   c. $(25,000)
   d. $50,000

8. Which item does *not* appear on a statement of cash flows prepared by the direct method?
   a. Net income
   b. Collections from customers
   c. Payments to suppliers
   d. Payments of income tax

9. Peppertree Copy Center had accounts receivable of $20,000 at the beginning of the year and $50,000 at year-end. Revenue for the year totaled $100,000. How much cash did Peppertree collect from customers?
   a. $170,000
   b. $150,000
   c. $120,000
   d. $70,000

10. Greenlawn Service had operating expense of $40,000. At the beginning of the year, Greenlawn owed $5,000 on accrued liabilities. At year-end, accrued liabilities were $8,000. How much cash did Greenlawn pay for operating expenses?
    a. $35,000
    b. $37,000
    c. $43,000
    d. $45,000

Accounting Vocabulary

cash equivalents (p. 659)
cash flows (p. 658)
direct method (p. 661)
financing activities (p. 660)
indirect method (p. 661)
investing activities (p. 659)
operating activities (p. 659)
statement of cash flows (p. 658)

ASSESS *Your Progress*

Starters

A+ online homework

See *www.prenhall.com/horngren* for selected Starters, Exercises, and Problems.

Purposes of the statement of cash flows
(Obj. 1)

S17-1 Describe how the statement of cash flows helps investors and creditors perform each of the following functions:

1. Predict future cash flows
2. Evaluate management decisions
3. Predict the ability to make debt payments to lenders and pay dividends to stockholders

Classifying cash-flow items
(Obj. 1)

S17-2 Answer these questions about the statement of cash flows:

a. What is the "check figure" for the statement of cash flows? Where do you get this check figure?
b. List the categories of cash flows in order of importance.
c. What is the first dollar amount to report for the indirect method?
d. What is the first dollar amount to report for the direct method?

Identifying items for reporting cash flows from operations—indirect method
(Obj. 2)

S17-3 Post Corporation is preparing its statement of cash flows by the *indirect* method. Post has the following items for you to consider in preparing the statement. Identify each item as

- Operating activity—addition to net income (O+), or subtraction from net income (O–)
- Investing activity (I)
- Financing activity (F)
- Activity that is not used to prepare the cash-flow statement (N)

Answer by placing the appropriate symbol in the blank space.

_______ a. Loss on sale of land	_______ f. Increase in accounts payable
_______ b. Depreciation expense	_______ g. Payment of dividends
_______ c. Increase in inventory	_______ h. Decrease in accrued liabilities
_______ d. Decrease in accounts receivable	_______ i. Issuance of common stock
_______ e. Purchase of equipment	_______ j. Gain on sale of building

Computing cash flows from operating activities—indirect method
(Obj. 3)

S17-4 Vis-à-Vis Printers reported these data for 20X7:

Income Statement	
Net income	$50,000
Depreciation	8,000
Balance sheet	
Increase in Accounts Receivable	6,000
Decrease in Accounts Payable	4,000

Compute Vis-à-Vis Printers' net cash provided by operations—indirect method.

Computing operating cash flows—indirect method
(Obj. 3)

S17-5 (Starter 17-6 is an alternate.) Mid-America Resources, Inc., accountants have assembled the following data for the year ended June 30, 20X5.

Payment of dividends	$ 6,000	Net income	$60,000
Proceeds from issuance of common stock	20,000	Purchase of equipment	40,000
Increase in current assets other than cash	30,000	Decrease in current liabilities	5,000
Purchase of treasury stock	5,000	Payment of note payable	30,000
		Proceeds from sale of land	60,000
		Depreciation expense	15,000

Prepare the *operating* activities section of Mid-America's statement of cash flows for the year ended June 30, 20X5. Mid-America uses the *indirect* method for operating cash flows.

Preparing a statement of cash flows—indirect method
(Obj. 3)

S17-6 Use the data in Starter 17-5 to prepare Mid-America's statement of cash flows for the year ended June 30, 20X5. Mid-America uses the *indirect* method for operating activities. Use Exhibit 17-7 as a guide, but you may stop after determining the net increase (or decrease) in cash.

Computing investing cash flows
(Obj. 3)

S17-7 Grace Chemical Company reported the following financial statements for 20X6:

Grace Chemical Company
Income Statement
Year Ended December 31, 20X6

	(In thousands)
Sales revenue	$710
Cost of goods sold	$340
Depreciation expense	60
Other expenses	200
Total expenses	600
Net income	$110

Grace Chemical Company

Comparative Balance Sheet
December 31, 20X6 and 20X5

(In thousands)

Assets	20X6	20X5	**Liabilities**	20X6	20X5
Current			Current		
Cash	$ 19	$ 16	Accounts payable	$ 47	$ 42
Accounts receivable	54	48	Salary payable	23	21
Inventory	80	84	Accrued liabilities	8	11
Prepaid expenses	3	2	Long-term notes payable	66	68
Long-term investments	75	90	**Stockholders' Equity**		
Plant assets, net	225	185	Common stock	40	37
			Retained earnings	272	246
Total	$456	$425	Total	$456	$425

Compute the amount of Grace Chemical's acquisition of plant assets, with Grace selling no plant assets.

S17-8 Use the Grace Chemical Company data in Starter 17-7 to compute

Computing financing cash flows **(Obj. 3)**

a. New borrowing or payment of long-term notes payable, with Grace having only one long-term note payable transaction during the year
b. Issuance of common stock, with Grace having only one common stock transaction during the year
c. Payment of cash dividends

S17-9 Wellness Health Laboratories began 20X4 with cash of $104,000. During the year, Wellness earned service revenue of $600,000 and collected $590,000 from customers. Expenses for the year totaled $420,000, of which Wellness paid $410,000 in cash to suppliers and employees. Wellness also paid $140,000 to purchase equipment and a cash dividend of $50,000 to its stockholders during 20X4.

Preparing a statement of cash flows—direct method **(Obj. 4)**

Prepare the company's statement of cash flows for the year ended December 31, 20X4. Format operating activities by the direct method.

S17-10 (Starter 17-11 is an alternate.) Mid-America Resources, Inc., has assembled the following data for the year ended June 30, 20X5.

Computing operating cash flows—direct method **(Obj. 4)**

Payment of dividends	$ 6,000
Proceeds from issuance of stock	20,000
Collections from customers	200,000
Proceeds from sale of land	60,000
Payments to suppliers	80,000
Purchase of equipment	40,000
Payments to employees	70,000
Payment of note payable	30,000

Prepare the *operating* activities section of Mid-America's statement of cash flows for the year ended June 30, 20X5. Mid-America uses the direct method for operating cash flows.

S17-11 Use the data in Starter 17-10 to prepare Mid-America's statement of cash flows for the year ended June 30, 20X5. Mid-America uses the *direct* method for operating activities. Use Exhibit 17-13, page 673, as a guide, but you may stop after determining the net increase (or decrease) in cash.

Preparing a statement of cash flows—direct method **(Obj. 4)**

S17-12 Use the Grace Chemical Company data in Starter 17-7 to compute the following:

Computing operating cash flows—direct method **(Obj. 4)**

a. Collections from customers
b. Payments for inventory

Exercises

A+ online homework

Identifying the purposes of the statement of cash flows
(Obj. 1)

E17-1 Biz Mart Stores, Inc., has experienced an unbroken string of 10 years of growth in net income. Nevertheless, the business is facing bankruptcy. Creditors are calling all of Biz Mart's outstanding loans for immediate payment, and the cash is simply not available. Attempts to explain where Biz Mart went wrong make it clear that managers placed undue emphasis on net income and gave too little attention to cash flows.

Required

Write a brief memo, in your own words, to explain to the managers of Biz Mart Stores the purposes of the statement of cash flows.

Identifying activities for the statement of cash flows—indirect method
(Obj. 2)

E17-2 Identify each of the following transactions as

- Operating activity (O)
- Investing activity (I)
- Financing activity (F)
- Noncash investing and financing activity (NIF)
- Transaction that is not reported on the statement of cash flows (N)

For each cash flow, indicate whether the item increases (+) or decreases (–) cash. The indirect method is used to report cash flows from operating activities.

______	**a.** Cash sale of land	______	**j.** Loss on sale of land
______	**b.** Issuance of long-term note payable to borrow cash	______	**k.** Acquisition of equipment by issuance of note payable
______	**c.** Depreciation of equipment	______	**l.** Payment of long-term debt
______	**d.** Purchase of treasury stock	______	**m.** Acquisition of building by issuance of common stock
______	**e.** Issuance of common stock	______	**n.** Accrual of salary expense
______	**f.** Increase in accounts payable	______	**o.** Decrease in inventory
______	**g.** Net income	______	**p.** Increase in prepaid expenses
______	**h.** Payment of cash dividend		
______	**i.** Decrease in accrued liabilities		

Classifying transactions for the statement of cash flows—indirect method
(Obj. 2, 3)

E17-3 Indicate whether each of the following transactions would result in an operating activity, an investing activity, or a financing activity for a statement of cash flows prepared by the *indirect* method and the accompanying schedule of noncash investing and financing activities.

a. Equipment	18,000	
Cash		18,000
b. Cash	7,200	
Long-Term Investment		7,200
c. Bonds Payable	45,000	
Cash		45,000
d. Building	164,000	
Note Payable, Long-Term		164,000
e. Loss on Disposal of Equipment	1,400	
Equipment Net		1,400
f. Dividends Payable	16,500	
Cash		16,500

g. Cash	81,000	
Common Stock		81,000
h. Treasury Stock	13,000	
Cash		13,000
i. Cash	60,000	
Sales Revenue		60,000
j. Land	87,700	
Cash		87,700
k. Depreciation Expense	9,000	
Accumulated Depreciation		9,000

Computing cash flows from operating activities—indirect method
(Obj. 3)

E17-4 The accounting records of Auto Chef Corporation reveal the following:

Net income	$22,000	Depreciation	$12,000
Sales revenue	9,000	Decrease in current liabilities	20,000
Loss on sale of land	5,000	Increase in current assets other than cash	27,000
Acquisition of land	37,000		

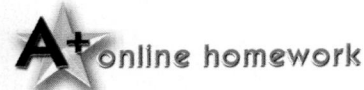

Required

Compute cash flows from operating activities by the indirect method. Use the format of the operating activities section of Exhibit 17-7. Also evaluate the operating cash flow of Auto Chef Corporation. Give the reason for your evaluation.

Computing cash flows from operating activities—indirect method
(Obj. 3)

E17-5 The accounting records of Ochoa, Inc.; include these accounts:

Cash

Mar. 1	5,000		
Receipts	447,000	Payments	448,000
Mar. 31	4,000		

Accounts Receivable

Mar. 1	18,000		
Sales	443,000	Collections	447,000
Mar. 31	14,000		

Inventory

Mar. 1	19,000		
Purchases	337,000	Cost of sales	335,000
Mar. 31	21,000		

Accounts Payable

		Mar. 1	14,000
Payments	332,000	Purchases	337,000
		Mar. 31	19,000

Accumulated Depreciation—Equipment

		Mar. 1	52,000
		Depreciation	3,000
		Mar. 31	55,000

Retained Earnings

		Mar. 1	64,000
Dividend	18,000	Net income	69,000
		Mar. 31	115,000

Compute Ochoa's net cash provided by (used for) operating activities during March. Use the indirect method.

Preparing the statement of cash flows—indirect method
(Obj. 3)

E17-6 The income statement and additional data of Crawford Properties, Inc., follow:

Crawford Properties, Inc.
Income Statement
Year Ended June 30, 20X6

Revenues:		
Sales revenue		$237,000
Expenses:		
Cost of goods sold	$103,000	
Salary expense	58,000	
Depreciation expense	29,000	
Income tax expense	9,000	199,000
Net income		$ 38,000

Additional data:

a. Acquisition of plant assets is $116,000. Of this amount, $101,000 is paid in cash and $15,000 by signing a note payable.
b. Proceeds from sale of land total $24,000.
c. Proceeds from issuance of common stock total $30,000.
d. Payment of long-term note payable is $15,000.
e. Payment of dividends is $11,000.
f. From the balance sheet:

	June 30, 20X6	June 30, 20X5
Current Assets:		
Cash	$27,000	$20,000
Accounts receivable	43,000	58,000
Inventory	92,000	85,000
Current Liabilities:		
Accounts payable	$35,000	$22,000
Accrued liabilities	13,000	21,000

Required

1. Prepare Crawford Properties, Inc.'s statement of cash flows for the year ended June 30, 20X6, using the indirect method. Include a separate section for noncash investing and financing activities.
2. Evaluate Crawford Properties' cash flows for the year. In your evaluation, mention all three categories of cash flows and give the reason for your evaluation.

Computing investing and financing amounts for the statement of cash flows
(Obj. 3)

E17-7 Compute the following items for the statement of cash flows:

a. Beginning and ending Retained Earnings are $45,000 and $73,000, respectively. Net income for the period is $62,000. How much are cash dividends?
b. Beginning and ending Plant Assets, net, are $103,000 and $107,000, respectively. Depreciation for the period is $16,000, and acquisitions of new plant assets total $27,000. Plant assets were sold at a $1,000 loss. What were the cash proceeds of the sale?

Identifying activities for the statement of cash flows—direct method
(Obj. 4)

E17-8 Identify each of the following transactions as

- Operating activity (O)
- Investing activity (I)
- Financing activity (F)
- Noncash investing and financing activity (NIF)
- Transaction that is not reported on the statement of cash flows (N)

For each cash flow, indicate whether the item increases (+) or decreases (–) cash. The direct method is used for cash flows from operating activities.

______	**a.** Collection of account receivable	______	**i.** Sale of land
______	**b.** Issuance of long-term note payable to borrow cash	______	**j.** Acquisition of equipment by issuance of note payable
______	**c.** Depreciation of equipment	______	**k.** Payment of long-term debt
______	**d.** Purchase of treasury stock	______	**l.** Acquisition of building by issuance of common stock
______	**e.** Issuance of common stock for cash	______	**m.** Purchase of equipment
______	**f.** Payment of account payable	______	**n.** Payment of wages to employees
______	**g.** Issuance of preferred stock for cash	______	**o.** Collection of cash interest
______	**h.** Payment of cash dividend	______	**p.** Sale of building

Classifying transactions for the statement of cash flows—direct method
(Obj. 4)

E17-9 Indicate where, if at all, each of the following transactions would be reported on a statement of cash flows prepared by the *direct* method and the accompanying schedule of noncash investing and financing activities.

a. Equipment	18,000		**g.** Salary Expense	4,300	
Cash		18,000	Cash		4,300
b. Cash	7,200		**h.** Cash	81,000	
Long-Term Investment		7,200	Common Stock		81,000
c. Bonds Payable	45,000		**i.** Treasury Stock	13,000	
Cash		45,000	Cash		13,000
d. Building	164,000		**j.** Cash	2,000	
Note Payable, Long-Term		164,000	Interest Revenue		2,000
e. Cash	1,400		**k.** Land	87,700	
Accounts Receivable		1,400	Cash		87,700
f. Dividends Payable	16,500		**l.** Accounts Payable	8,300	
Cash		16,500	Cash		8,300

Computing cash flows from operating activities—direct method
(Obj. 4)

E17-10 The accounting records of Auto Chef Corporation reveal the following:

Net income	$22,000	Payment of salaries and wages	$ 34,000
Payment of income tax	13,000	Depreciation	12,000
Collection of dividend revenue	7,000	Payment of interest	16,000
		Payment of dividends	7,000
Payment to suppliers	54,000	Collections from customers	102,000

Required

Compute cash flows from operating activities by the direct method. Use the format of the operating activities section of Exhibit 17-13. Also evaluate the operating cash flow of Auto Chef Corporation. Give the reason for your evaluation.

Identifying items for the statement of cash flows—direct method
(Obj. 4)

E17-11 Selected accounts of Crossroads Clinic, Inc., show the following:

Dividends Receivable

Beginning balance	**9,000**		
Dividend revenue	**40,000**	**Cash receipts of dividends**	**38,000**
Ending balance	**11,000**		

Land

Beginning balance	**90,000**		
Acquisition	**18,000**		
Ending balance	**108,000**		

Long-Term Notes Payable

		Beginning balance	**273,000**
Payments	**69,000**	**Issuance for cash**	**83,000**
		Ending balance	**287,000**

Required

For each account, identify the item or items that should appear on a statement of cash flows prepared by the direct method. State where to report the item.

Preparing the statement of cash flows—direct method
(Obj. 4)

E17-12 The income statement and additional data of Crawford Properties, Inc., follow:

Crawford Properties, Inc.
Income Statement
Year Ended June 30, 20X6

Revenues:		
Sales revenue	$229,000	
Dividend revenue	8,000	$237,000
Expenses:		
Cost of goods sold	$103,000	
Salary expense	45,000	
Depreciation expense	28,000	
Advertising expense	12,000	
Interest expense	2,000	
Income tax expense	9,000	199,000
Net income		$ 38,000

Additional data:

a. Collections from customers are $15,000 more than sales.
b. Payments to suppliers are the sum of cost of goods sold plus advertising expense.
c. Payments to employees are $1,000 more than salary expense.
d. Dividend revenue, interest expense, and income tax expense equal their cash amounts.
e. Acquisition of plant assets is $101,000.
f. Proceeds from sale of land total $24,000.
g. Proceeds from issuance of common stock total $30,000.
h. Payment of long-term note payable is $15,000.
i. Payment of dividends is $11,000.
j. Cash balance, June 30, 20X5, was $20,000.

Required

1. Prepare Crawford Properties' statement of cash flows for the year ended June 30, 20X6. Use the *direct* method.
2. Evaluate Crawford's cash flows for the year. In your evaluation, mention all three categories of cash flows and give the reason for your evaluation.

Computing amounts for the statement of cash flows—direct method
(Obj. 4)

E17-13 Compute the following items for the statement of cash flows:

a. Beginning and ending Accounts Receivable are $22,000 and $18,000, respectively. Credit sales for the period total $81,000. How much are cash collections?
b. Cost of goods sold is $90,000. Beginning Inventory balance is $25,000, and ending Inventory balance is $21,000. Beginning and ending Accounts Payable are $11,000 and $8,000, respectively. How much are cash payments for inventory?

Computing cash-flow amounts
(Obj. 3, 4)

E17-14 **Walgreen Company**, the nationwide pharmacy chain, reported the following in its financial statements for the year ended August 31, 20X1 (adapted, in millions):

	20X1	20X0
Income Statement		
Net sales	$24,623	$21,207
Cost of sales	18,048	15,466
Depreciation	269	230
Other operating expenses	4,883	4,248
Income tax expense	537	486
Net income	$ 886	$ 777
Balance Sheet		
Cash and equivalents	$ 17	$ 13
Accounts receivable	798	615
Inventories	3,482	2,831
Property and equipment, net	4,345	3,428
Accounts payable	1,547	1,364
Accrued liabilities	938	848
Long-term liabilities	478	464
Common stock	676	446
Retained earnings	4,531	3,788

Determine the following for Walgreen during 20X1:

a. Collections from customers
b. Payments for inventory
c. Payments of operating expenses
d. Acquisitions of property and equipment (no sales during 20X1)
e. Borrowing, with Walgreen paying no long-term liabilities
f. Proceeds from issuance of common stock
g. Payment of cash dividends

For operating cash flows, follow the approach outlined in Exhibit 17-15.

Problems

(Group A)

A+ online homework

Using cash-flow information to evaluate performance
(Obj. 1, 2)

P17-1A Top managers of Oasis Water, Inc., are reviewing company performance for 20X7. The income statement reports a 20% increase in net income over 20X6. However, most of the increase resulted from an extraordinary gain on insurance proceeds from storm damage to a building. The balance sheet shows a large increase in receivables. The cash-flow statement, in summarized form, reports the following:

Net cash used for operating activities	$(80,000)
Net cash provided by investing activities	40,000
Net cash provided by financing activities	50,000
Increase in cash during 20X7	$ 10,000

Required

Write a memo giving Oasis Water managers your assessment of 20X7 operations and your outlook for the future. Focus on the information content of the cash-flow data.

Preparing an income statement, balance sheet, and statement of cash flows—indirect method
(Obj. 2, 3)

P17-2A Scott Corporation, a furniture store, was formed on January 1, 20X8, when Scott issued common stock for $500,000. Early in January, Scott made the following cash payments:

a. $150,000 for equipment
b. $260,000 for inventory (2,000 pieces of furniture)
c. $20,000 for 20X8 rent on a store building

Later in the year, Scott purchased 1,000 units of furniture inventory on account. Cost of this inventory was $120,000. Before year-end, Scott paid $60,000 of this debt. Scott uses the FIFO method to account for inventory.

During 20X8, Scott sold 2,000 units of inventory for $200 each. Before year end, Scott collected 80% of this amount.

The store employs a salesperson whose annual pay is $45,000, of which Scott owes $4,000 at year-end. At the end of the year, Scott paid income tax of $10,000.

Late in 20X8, Scott paid cash dividends of $11,000.

For equipment, Scott uses the straight-line depreciation method, over 5 years, with zero residual value.

Required

1. Prepare Scott Corporation's income statement for the year ended December 31, 20X8. Use the single-step format, with all revenues listed together and all expenses together.
2. Prepare Scott's balance sheet at December 31, 20X8.
3. Prepare Scott's statement of cash flows for the year ended December 31, 20X8. Format cash flows from operating activities by the indirect method.

Preparing the statement of cash flows—indirect method
(Obj. 2, 3)

P17-3A Datex Corporation accountants have assembled the following data for the year ended December 31, 20X7.

Required

Prepare Datex Corporation's statement of cash flows using the *indirect* method to report operating activities. Include an accompanying schedule of noncash investing and financing activities.

Datex Corporation

	December 31, 20X7	20X6
Current Accounts:		
Current assets:		
Cash and cash equivalents	$85,000	$22,000
Accounts receivable	69,200	64,200
Inventories	80,000	83,000
Current liabilities:		
Accounts payable	$57,800	$55,800
Income tax payable	14,700	16,700

Transaction Data for 20X7:

Net income	$ 57,000	Purchase of treasury stock	$14,000
Issuance of common stock for cash	41,000	Loss on sale of equipment	11,000
Depreciation expense	21,000	Payment of cash dividends	18,000
Purchase of building	125,000	Issuance of long-term note payable to borrow cash	34,000
Retirement of bonds payable by issuing common stock	65,000	Sale of equipment	58,000

Preparing the statement of cash flows—indirect method
(Obj. 2, 3)

Student ResourceCD
spreadsheet

P17-4A The comparative balance sheet of Southern Bell Company at March 31, 20X9, reported the following:

	March 31, 20X9	20X8
Current Assets:		
Cash and cash equivalents	$ 6,200	$ 4,000
Accounts receivable	14,900	21,700
Inventories	63,200	60,600
Current Liabilities:		
Accounts payable	$30,100	$27,600
Accrued liabilities	10,700	11,100
Income tax payable	8,000	4,700

Southern Bell's transactions during the year ended March 31, 20X9, included the following:

Payment of cash dividend	$30,000	Depreciation expense	$ 17,300
Purchase of equipment	78,700	Purchase of building	47,000
Issuance of long-term note payable to borrow cash	50,000	Net income	70,000
		Issuance of common stock	11,000

Required

1. Prepare Southern Bell's statement of cash flows for the year ended March 31, 20X9, using the *indirect* method to report cash flows from operating activities.
2. Evaluate Southern Bell's cash flows for the year. Mention all three categories of cash flows and give the reason for your evaluation.

Preparing the statement of cash flows—indirect method
(Obj. 2, 3)

Student ResourceCD
spreadsheet

P17-5A The 20X5 comparative balance sheet and income statement of Town East Press follow.

Town East had no noncash investing and financing transactions during 20X5. During the year, there were no sales of land or equipment, no issuances of notes payable, no retirements of stock, and no treasury stock transactions.

Required

1. Prepare the 20X5 statement of cash flows, formatting operating activities by the indirect method.
2. How will what you learned in this problem help you evaluate an investment?

Town East Press

Comparative Balance Sheet

	December 31, 20X5	20X4	Increase (Decrease)
Current assets:			
Cash and cash equivalents	$ 6,700	$ 5,300	$ 1,400
Accounts receivable	25,300	26,900	(1,600)
Inventories	91,800	89,800	2,000
Plant assets:			
Land	89,000	60,000	29,000
Equipment, net	53,500	49,400	4,100
Total assets	$266,300	$231,400	$34,900
Current liabilities:			
Accounts payable	$ 30,900	$ 35,400	$(4,500)
Accrued liabilities	30,600	28,600	2,000
Long-term liabilities:			
Notes payable	75,000	100,000	(25,000)
Stockholders' equity:			
Common stock	88,300	64,700	23,600
Retained earnings	41,500	2,700	38,800
Total liabilities and stockholders' equity	$266,300	$231,400	$34,900

Town East Press

Income Statement
Year Ended December 31, 20X5

Revenues:		
Sales revenue		$213,000
Interest revenue		8,600
Total revenues		221,600
Expenses:		
Cost of goods sold	$70,600	
Salary expense	27,800	
Depreciation expense	4,000	
Other operating expense	10,500	
Interest expense	11,600	
Income tax expense	29,100	
Total expenses		153,600
Net income		$ 68,000

Preparing the statement of cash flows—direct method
(Obj. 2, 4)

P17-6A Accountants for Triad Associates, Inc., have developed the following data from the company's accounting records for the year ended April 30, 20X5:

a. Purchase of plant assets, $59,400
b. Proceeds from issuance of common stock, $8,000
c. Payment of dividends, $48,400
d. Collection of interest, $4,400
e. Payments of salaries, $93,600
f. Proceeds from sale of plant assets, $22,400
g. Collections from customers, $620,500
h. Cash receipt of dividend revenue, $4,100
i. Payments to suppliers, $368,500
j. Depreciation expense, $59,900
k. Proceeds from issuance of notes payable, $19,600
l. Payments of notes payable, $50,000
m. Interest expense and payments, $13,300
n. Income tax expense and payments, $37,900
o. Cash balance: April 30, 20X4, $39,300; April 30, 20X5, $47,200

Required

Prepare Triad Associates' statement of cash flows for the year ended April 30, 20X5. Use the direct method for cash flows from operating activities. Follow the format of Exhibit 17-13, but do *not* show amounts in thousands.

Preparing an income statement, balance sheet, and statement of cash flows—direct method
(Obj. 2, 4)

P17-7A Use the Scott Corporation data from Problem 17-2A.

Required

1. Prepare Scott Corporation's income statement for the year ended December 31, 20X8. Use the single-step format, with all revenues listed together and all expenses together.
2. Prepare Scott's balance sheet at December 31, 20X8.
3. Prepare Scott's statement of cash flows for the year ended December 31, 20X8. Format cash flows from operating activities by the direct method.

Preparing the statement of cash flows—direct method
(Obj. 2, 4)

Student Resource CD
spreadsheet

P17-8A Use the Town East Press data from Problem 17-5A.

Required

1. Prepare the 20X5 statement of cash flows by the direct method.
2. How will what you learned in this problem help you evaluate an investment?

Preparing the statement of cash flows—direct method
(Obj. 3, 4)

P17-9A To prepare the statement of cash flows, accountants for Internet Guide, Inc., have summarized 20X8 activity in the Cash account as follows:

Cash

Beginning balance	53,600	Payments on accounts payable	399,100
Receipts of interest	17,100	Payments of dividends	27,200
Collections from customers	673,700	Payments of salaries and wages	143,800
Issuance of common stock	47,300	Payments of interest	26,900
		Purchase of equipment	10,200
		Payments of operating expenses	34,300
		Payment of note payable	67,700
		Payment of income tax	18,900
Ending balance	63,600		

Required

Prepare the statement of cash flows of Internet Guide, Inc., for the year ended December 31, 20X8, using the *direct* method for operating activities.

A+ online homework

Problems

(Group B)

Using cash-flow information to evaluate performance
(Obj. 1, 2)

P17-1B Top managers of Internet Solutions, Inc., are reviewing company performance for 20X4. The income statement reports a 15% increase in net income, the fifth consecutive year with an income increase above 10%. The income statement includes a nonrecurring loss without which net income would have increased by 16%. The balance sheet shows modest increases in assets, liabilities, and stockholders' equity. The assets posting the largest increases are plant and equipment because the company is halfway through a 5-year expansion program. No other assets and no liabilities are increasing dramatically. A summarized version of the cash-flow statement reports the following:

Net cash provided by operating activities	$310,000
Net cash used for investing activities	(290,000)
Net cash provided by financing activities	70,000
Increase in cash during 20X4	$ 90,000

Required

Write a memo giving top managers of Internet Solutions your assessment of 20X4 operations and your outlook for the future. Focus on the information content of the cash-flow data.

Preparing an income statement, balance sheet, and statement of cash flows—indirect method
(Obj. 2, 3)

P17-2B Dohn Corporation, a discounter of men's suits, was formed on January 1, 20X6, when Dohn issued its common stock for $200,000. Early in January, Dohn made the following cash payments:

a. For store fixtures, $50,000
b. For inventory (1,000 men's suits), $100,000
c. For rent on a store building, $10,000

Later in the year, Dohn purchased 2,000 men's suits on account. Cost of each suit was $120, for a total of $240,000. Before year-end, Dohn paid $140,000 of this account payable. Dohn uses the FIFO method to account for inventory.

During 20X6, Dohn sold 2,500 units of inventory for $200 each. Before year end, Dohn collected 90% of this amount.

The store employs three people. The combined annual payroll is $90,000, of which Dohn owes $5,000 at year-end. At the end of the year, Dohn paid income tax of $30,000.

Late in 20X6, Dohn declared and paid cash dividends of $40,000.

For equipment, Dohn uses the straight-line depreciation method, over 5 years, with zero residual value.

Required

1. Prepare Dohn Corporation's income statement for the year ended December 31, 20X6. Use the single-step format, with all revenues listed together and all expenses together.
2. Prepare Dohn's balance sheet at December 31, 20X6.
3. Prepare Dohn's statement of cash flows for the year ended December 31, 20X6. Format cash flows from operating activities by the indirect method.

Preparing the statement of cash flows—indirect method
(Obj. 2, 3)

P17-3B Accountants for WWW.Smart, Inc., have assembled the following data for the year ended December 31, 20X4:

	December 31, 20X4	20X3
Current Accounts:		
Current assets:		
Cash and cash equivalents	$56,000	$34,000
Accounts receivable	70,100	73,700
Inventories	90,600	86,600
Current liabilities:		
Accounts payable	71,600	67,500
Income tax payable	5,900	6,800

Transaction Data for 20X4:

Depreciation expense	$30,200	Payment of cash dividends	$48,300
Purchase of equipment	69,000	Issuance of note payable to borrow cash	71,000
Acquisition of land by issuing long-term note payable	118,000	Net income	50,500
Payment of note payable	47,900	Issuance of preferred stock for cash	36,200
Gain on sale of equipment	3,500		

Required

Prepare WWW.Smart's statement of cash flows using the *indirect* method to report operating activities. Include an accompanying schedule of noncash investing and financing activities.

P17-4B The comparative balance sheet of CNA Leasing, Inc., at December 31, 20X5, reported the following:

Preparing the statement of cash flows—indirect method
(Obj. 2, 3)

	December 31, 20X5	December 31, 20X4
Current Assets:		
Cash and cash equivalents	$12,500	$22,500
Accounts receivable	26,600	29,300
Inventories	54,600	53,000
Current Liabilities:		
Accounts payable	$29,100	$28,000
Accrued liabilities	14,300	16,800

CNA's transactions during 20X5 included the following:

Payment of cash dividends	$17,000	Purchase of building	$124,000
Purchase of equipment	55,000	Net income	31,600
Issuance of long-term note payable to borrow cash	32,000	Issuance of common stock for cash	105,000
		Depreciation expense	17,700

Required

1. Prepare the statement of cash flows of CNA Leasing, Inc., for the year ended December 31, 20X5. Use the *indirect* method to report cash flows from operating activities.
2. Evaluate CNA's cash flows for the year. Mention all three categories of cash flows and give the reason for your evaluation.

Preparing the statement of cash flows—indirect method
(Obj. 2, 3)

P17-5B The 20X8 comparative balance sheet and income statement of Genie Marketing, Inc., follow.

Genie had no noncash investing and financing transactions during 20X8. During the year, there were no sales of land or equipment, no issuances of notes payable, no retirements of stock, and no treasury stock transactions.

Required

1. Prepare the 20X8 statement of cash flows, formatting operating activities by the indirect method.
2. How will what you learned in this problem help you evaluate an investment?

Genie Marketing, Inc.

Comparative Balance Sheet

	December 31, 20X8	December 31, 20X7	Increase (Decrease)
Current assets:			
Cash and cash equivalents	$ 21,000	$ 18,700	$ 2,300
Accounts receivable	46,500	43,100	3,400
Inventories	84,300	89,900	(5,600)
Plant assets:			
Land	35,100	10,000	25,100
Equipment, net	100,900	93,700	7,200
Total assets	$287,800	$255,400	$ 32,400
Current liabilities:			
Accounts payable	$ 31,100	$ 29,800	$ 1,300
Accrued liabilities	18,100	18,700	(600)
Long-term liabilities:			
Notes payable	55,000	65,000	(10,000)
Stockholders' equity:			
Common stock	131,100	122,300	8,800
Retained earnings	52,500	19,600	32,900
Total liabilities and stockholders' equity	$287,800	$255,400	$ 32,400

Genie Marketing, Inc.

Income Statement
Year Ended December 31, 20X8

Revenues:		
Sales revenue		$438,000
Interest revenue		11,700
Total revenues		449,700
Expenses:		
Cost of goods sold	$205,200	
Salary expense	76,400	
Depreciation expense	15,300	
Other operating expense	49,700	
Interest expense	24,600	
Income tax expense	16,900	
Total expenses		388,100
Net income		$ 61,600

Preparing the statement of cash flows—direct method
(Obj. 2, 4)

P17-6B Data Solutions, Inc., accountants have developed the following data from the company's accounting records for the year ended July 31, 20X5:

- **a.** Purchase of plant assets, $100,000
- **b.** Proceeds from issuance of notes payable, $44,100
- **c.** Payments of notes payable, $18,800
- **d.** Proceeds from sale of plant assets, $59,700
- **e.** Cash receipt of dividends, $2,700
- **f.** Payments to suppliers, $673,300
- **g.** Interest expense and payments, $37,800
- **h.** Collection of interest revenue, $11,700
- **i.** Payments of salaries, $104,000
- **j.** Income tax expense and payments, $56,400
- **k.** Depreciation expense, $27,700
- **l.** Collections from customers, $827,100
- **m.** Proceeds from issuance of common stock, $116,900
- **n.** Payment of cash dividends, $50,500
- **o.** Cash balance: July 31, 20X4—$53,800; July 31, 20X5—$75,200

Required

Prepare Data Solutions' statement of cash flows for the year ended July 31, 20X5. Use the direct method for cash flows from operating activities. Follow the format of Exhibit 17-13, but do *not* show amounts in thousands.

Preparing an income statement, balance sheet, and statement of cash flows—direct method
(Obj. 2, 4)

P17-7B Use the Dohn Corporation data from Problem 17-2B.

Required

1. Prepare Dohn Corporation's income statement for the year ended December 31, 20X6. Use the single-step format, with all revenues listed together and all expenses together.
2. Prepare Dohn's balance sheet at December 31, 20X6.
3. Prepare Dohn's statement of cash flows for the year ended December 31, 20X6. Format cash flows from operating activities by the direct method.

Preparing the statement of cash flows—direct method
(Obj. 2, 4)

P17-8B Use the Genie Marketing, Inc., data from Problem 17-5B.

Required

1. Prepare the 20X8 statement of cash flows by the direct method.
2. How will what you learned in this problem help you evaluate an investment?

Preparing the statement of cash flows—direct method
(Obj. 3, 4)

P17-9B To prepare the statement of cash flows, accountants for Rolex Paper Company have summarized 20X8 activity in the cash account as follows:

Cash

Beginning balance	**87,100**	**Payments of operating expenses**	**46,100**
Issuance of common stock	**60,800**	**Payment of note payable**	**89,300**
Receipts of interest revenue	**14,100**	**Payment of income tax**	**8,000**
Collections from customers	**308,100**	**Payments on accounts payable**	**101,600**
		Payment of dividends	**1,800**
		Payments of salaries and wages	**67,500**
		Payments of interest	**21,800**
		Purchase of equipment	**51,500**
Ending balance	**82,500**		

Required

Prepare Rolex's statement of cash flows for the year ended December 31, 20X8, using the *direct* method to report operating activities.

APPLY *Your Knowledge*

Decision Cases

Preparing and using the statement of cash flows to evaluate operations
(Obj. 3)

Case 1. The 20X6 comparative income statement and the 20X6 comparative balance sheet of Tennis, Tennis, Tennis! Inc., have just been distributed at a meeting of the company's board of directors. The members of the board of directors raise a fundamental question: Why is the cash balance so low? This question is especially troublesome to the board members because 20X6 showed record profits. As the controller of the company, you must answer the question.

Tennis, Tennis, Tennis! Inc.

Comparative Income Statement
Years Ended December 31, 20X6 and 20X5

(In thousands)	**20X6**	**20X5**
Revenues and gains:		
Sales revenue	$444	$310
Gain on sale of equipment (sale price, $33)	—	18
Total revenues and gains	$444	$328
Expenses and losses:		
Cost of goods sold	$221	$162
Salary expense	48	28
Depreciation expense	46	22
Interest expense	13	20
Amortization expense on patent	11	11
Loss on sale of land (sale price, $61)	—	35
Total expenses and losses	339	278
Net income	$105	$ 50

Tennis, Tennis, Tennis! Inc.

Comparative Balance Sheet
December 31, 20X6 and 20X5

(In thousands)	20X6	20X5
Assets		
Cash	$ 25	$ 63
Accounts receivable, net	72	61
Inventories	194	181
Long-term investments	31	0
Property, plant, and equipment	369	259
Accumulated depreciation	(244)	(198)
Patents	177	188
Totals	$624	$554
Liabilities and Owners' Equity		
Accounts payable	$ 63	$ 56
Accrued liabilities	12	17
Notes payable, long-term	179	264
Common stock	149	61
Retained earnings	221	156
Totals	$624	$554

Required

1. Prepare a statement of cash flows for 20X6 in the format that best shows the relationship between net income and operating cash flow. The company sold no plant assets or long-term investments and issued no notes payable during 20X6. There were *no* noncash investing and financing transactions during the year. Show all amounts in thousands.
2. Answer the board members' question: Why is the cash balance so low? In explaining the business's cash flows, identify two significant cash receipts that occurred during 20X5 but not in 20X6. Also point out the two largest cash payments during 20X6.
3. Considering net income and the company's cash flows during 20X6, was it a good year or a bad year? Give your reasons.

Using cash-flow data to evaluate an investment
(Obj. 1, 2)

Case 2. Carolina Technology, Inc., and Northwest Electric Power Corporation are asking you to recommend their stock to your clients. Because Carolina and Northwest earn about the same net income and have similar financial positions, your decision depends on their cash-flow statements, summarized as follows:

	Carolina		Northwest	
Net cash provided by operating activities:		$ 70,000		$ 30,000
Cash provided by (used for) investing activities:				
Purchase of plant assets	$(100,000)		$(20,000)	
Sale of plant assets	10,000	(90,000)	40,000	20,000
Cash provided by (used for) financing activities:				
Issuance of common stock		30,000		—
Paying off long-term debt		—		(40,000)
Net increase in cash		$10,000		$ 10,000

Based on their cash flows, which company looks better? Give your reasons.

Ethical Issue

Victoria British Auto Parts is having a bad year. Net income is only $37,000. Also, two important overseas customers are falling behind in their payments to Victoria, and Victoria's accounts receivable are ballooning. The company desperately needs a loan. The Victoria board of directors is considering ways to put the best face on the company's financial statements. Victoria's bank closely examines cash flow from operations. Daniel Peavey, Victoria's controller, suggests reclassifying as long-term the receivables from the slow-paying clients. He explains to the board that removing the $80,000 rise in accounts receivable from current assets will increase net cash provided by operations. This approach may help Victoria get the loan.

Required

1. Using only the amounts given, compute net cash provided by operations, both without and with the reclassification of the receivables. Which reporting makes Victoria look better?
2. Under what condition would the reclassification of the receivables be ethical? Unethical?

Financial Statement Case

Using the statement of cash flows **(Obj. 2, 3, 4)**

Use the **Amazon.com** statement of cash flows along with the company's other financial statements, all in Appendix A, to answer the following questions.

Required

1. Which method does Amazon use to report net cash flows from *operating* activities? How can you tell?
2. Amazon suffered a net loss during 2002. Did operations *provide* cash or *use* cash during 2002? Give the amount. How did operating cash during 2002 compare with 2001? Be specific, and state the reason for your answer.
3. Suppose Amazon reported net cash flows from operating activities by the direct method. Compute these amounts for the year ended December 31, 2002.
   a. Collections from customers (Assume that other current assets are zero)
   b. Payments for inventory
4. Evaluate 2002 in terms of net income, cash flows, balance sheet position, and overall results. Be specific.

Team Projects

Project 1. Each member of the team should obtain the annual report of a different company. Select companies in different industries. Evaluate each company's trend of cash flows for the most recent two years. In your evaluation of the companies' cash flows, you may use any other information that is publicly available—for example, the other financial statements (income statement, balance sheet, statement of stockholders' equity, and the related notes) and news stories from magazines and newspapers. Rank the companies' cash flows from best to worst and write a two-page report on your findings.

Project 2. Select a company and obtain its annual report, including all the financial statements. Focus on the statement of cash flows and, in particular, the cash flows from operating activities. Specify whether the company uses the direct method or the indirect method to report operating cash flows. As necessary, use the other financial statements (income statement, balance sheet, and statement of stockholders' equity) and the notes to prepare the company's cash flows from operating activities by the *other* method.

APPENDIX *to Chapter 17*

☐ Basic Concepts
☐ The Indirect Method
☐ The Direct Method
■ Appendix: Work Sheet Approach

The Work Sheet Approach to Preparing the Statement of Cash Flows

The body of this chapter discusses the uses of the statement of cash flows in decision making and shows how to prepare the statement using T-accounts. The T-account approach works well as a learning device. In practice, however, most companies face complex situations. In these cases, a work sheet can help in preparing the statement of cash flows. This appendix shows how to prepare the statement using a specially designed work sheet.

The work sheet starts with the beginning balance sheet and concludes with the ending balance sheet. Two middle columns—one for debit amounts and the other for credit amounts—complete the work sheet. These columns, labeled Transaction Analysis, hold the data for the statement of cash flows. Accountants can prepare the statement directly from the lower part of the work sheet. This appendix is based on the Anchor Corporation data used in the chapter. We begin with the indirect method for operating activities.

Preparing the Work Sheet—Indirect Method for Operating Activities

The indirect method reconciles net income to net cash provided by operating activities. Exhibit 17A-1 is the work sheet for preparing the statement of cash flows by the indirect method. Panel A shows the transaction analysis, and Panel B gives the statement of cash flows.

Transaction Analysis on the Work Sheet—Indirect Method Net income, transaction (a), is the first operating cash inflow. Net income is entered on the work sheet (Panel B) as a debit to Net Income under Cash flows from operating activities and as a credit to Retained Earnings. Next come the adjustments to net income, starting with depreciation—transaction (b)—which is debited to Depreciation and credited to Plant Assets, Net. Transaction (c) is the sale of plant assets. The $8,000 gain on the sale is entered as a credit to Gain on Sale of Plant Assets—a subtraction from net income—under operating cash flows. This credit removes the $8,000 gain from operations because the cash proceeds from the sale were $62,000, not $8,000. The $62,000 sale amount is then entered on the work sheet under investing activities. Entry (c) is completed by crediting the plant assets' book value of $54,000 to the Plant Assets, Net account.

Entries (d) through (g) reconcile net income to cash flows from operations for increases and decreases in the other current assets and for increases and decreases in the current liabilities. Entry (d) debits Accounts Receivable for its $15,000 increase during the year. This amount is credited to Increase in Accounts Receivable under operating cash flows. Entries (e), (f), and (g) adjust for the other current accounts.

Entries (h) through (l) account for the investing and financing transactions. Entry (h) debits Plant Assets, Net for their purchase and credits Purchase of plant assets under investing cash flows. Entry (i) debits Proceeds from issuance of common stock under financing cash flows. The offsetting debit is to Common Stock.

The final item in Exhibit 17A-1 is the Net decrease in cash—transaction (m) on the work sheet—a credit to Cash and a debit to Net decrease in cash. To prepare the statement of cash flows, the accountant can rewrite Panel B of the work sheet, adding subtotals for the three categories of activities.

Exhibit 17A-1 Work Sheet for Statement of Cash Flows—Indirect Method

Anchor Corporation

Work Sheet for Statement of Cash Flows (Indirect Method)
Year Ended December 31, 20X5

		In thousands		
	Balances	Transaction Analysis		Balances
	Dec. 31, 20X4	Debit	Credit	Dec. 31, 20X5
PANEL A—Balance-Sheet Accounts				
Cash	42		(m) 20	22
Accounts receivable	81	(d) 15		96
Inventory	145		(e) 2	143
Plant assets, net	219	(h) 317	(b) 18	
			(c) 54	464
Totals	487			725
Accounts payable	57		(f) 34	91
Accrued liabilities	9	(g) 4		5
Long-term notes payable	77	(k) 11	(j) 94	160
Common stock	258		(i) 101	359
Retained earnings	86	(l) 17	(a) 41	110
Totals	487	364	364	725
PANEL B—Statement of Cash Flows				
Cash flows from operating activities:				
Net income		(a) 41		
Add (subtract) items that affect net income and cash flow differently:				
Depreciation		(b) 18		
Gain on sale of plant assets			(c) 8	
Increase in accounts receivable			(d) 15	
Decrease in inventory		(e) 2		
Increase in accounts payable		(f) 34		
Decrease in accured liabilities			(g) 4	
Cash flows from investing activities:				
Purchase of plant assets			(h) 317	
Proceeds from sale of plant assets		(c) 62		
Cash flows from financing activities:				
Proceeds from issuance of common stock		(i) 101		
Proceeds from issuance of note payable		(j) 94		
Payment of note payable			(k) 11	
Payment of dividends			(l) 17	
		352	372	
Net decrease in cash		(m) 20		
Totals		372	372	

Noncash Investing and Financing Activities on the Work Sheet Noncash investing and financing activities can be analyzed on the work sheet. These transactions include both an investing activity and a financing activity, so they require two work-sheet entries. Suppose Anchor Corporation purchased a building by issuing common stock of $300,000. Exhibit 17A-2 illustrates the analysis of this transaction. Cash is unaffected. Work-sheet entry (a) records the purchase of the building, and entry (b) records the issuance of the stock.

Exhibit 17A-2 Noncash Investing and Financing Activities on the Work Sheet

Anchor Corporation

Work Sheet for Statement of Cash Flows
Year Ended December 31, 20X5

	Balances Dec. 31, 20X4	Transaction Analysis Debit	Transaction Analysis Credit	Balances Dec. 31, 20X5
PANEL A—Balance-Sheet Accounts				
Cash				
Building	600,000	(a) 300,000		900,000
Common stock	400,000		(b) 300,000	700,000
PANEL B—Statement of Cash Flows				
Noncash investing and financing transactions:				
Purchase of building by issuing common stock		(b) 300,000	(a) 300,000	

Preparing the Work Sheet—Direct Method for Operating Activities

The direct method separates operating activities into cash receipts and cash payments. Exhibit 17A-3 is the work sheet for the preparation of the statement of cash flows by the direct method.

Transaction Analysis on the Work Sheet—Direct Method For your convenience, we repeat the Anchor Corporation transaction data here.

Operating Activities:

a. Sales on account, $284,000
*b. Collections from customers, $269,000
*c. Cash receipt of interest revenue, $12,000
*d. Cash receipt of dividend revenue, $9,000
e. Purchase of inventory on account, $148,000
f. Cost of goods sold, $150,000
*g. Payments for inventory on account, $114,000
*h. Salary expense and payments, $56,000
i. Depreciation expense, $18,000
j. Accrual of other operating expense, $17,000
*k. Interest expense and payments, $16,000
*l. Income tax expense and payments, $15,000
*m. Payment of accrued liabilities, $21,000

Investing Activities:

*n. Cash payments to acquire plant assets, $317,000
*o. Proceeds from sale of plant assets, $62,000, including $8,000 gain

Financing Activities:

*p. Proceeds from issuance of common stock, $101,000
*q. Proceeds from issuance of long-term note payable, $94,000
*r. Payment of long-term note payable, $11,000
*s. Declaration and payment of cash dividends, $17,000

*Indicates a cash flow to be reported on the statement of cash flows.

The transaction analysis on the work sheet includes journal entries. Only balance-sheet accounts are used on the work sheet. Therefore, revenues are entered as credits to Retained Earnings, and expenses are entered as debits to Retained Earnings. For example, in transaction (a), sales on account are debited to Accounts Receivable and credited to Retained Earnings. Cash is neither debited nor credited because credit sales do not affect cash. But all transactions should be entered on the work sheet to identify all the cash effects of the period's transactions. In transaction (c), the collection of cash for interest revenue is entered by debiting Cash and crediting Retained Earnings.

Exhibit 17A-3 Work Sheet for Statement of Cash Flows—Direct Method

Anchor Corporation

Work Sheet for Statement of Cash Flows (Direct Method)
Year Ended December 31, 20X5

(in thousands)

	Balances	Transaction Analysis				Balances
	Dec. 31, 20X4	Debit		Credit		Dec. 31, 20X5
PANEL A—Balance-Sheet Accounts						
Cash	42			(t)	20	22
Accounts receivable	81	(a)	284	(b)	269	96
Inventory	145	(e)	148	(f)	150	143
Equipment, net	219	(n)	317	(i)	18	
				(o)	54	464
Totals	487					725
Accounts payable	57	(g)	114	(e)	148	91
Accrued liabilities	9	(m)	21	(j)	17	5
Long-term notes payable	77	(r)	11	(q)	94	160
Common stock	258			(p)	101	359
Retained earnings	86	(f)	150	(a)	284	110
		(h)	56	(c)	12	
		(i)	18	(d)	9	
		(j)	17	(o)	8	
		(k)	16			
		(l)	15			
		(s)	17			
Totals	487		1,184		1,184	725
PANEL B—Statement of Cash Flows						
Cash flows from operating activities:						
Receipts:						
Collections from customers		(b)	269			
Interest received		(c)	12			
Dividends received		(d)	9			
Payments:						
To suppliers				(g)	114	
				(m)	21	
To employees				(h)	56	
For interest				(k)	16	
For income tax				(l)	15	
Cash flows from investing activities:						
Purchase of plant assets				(n)	317	
Proceeds from sale of plant assets		(o)	62			
Cash flows from financing activities:						
Proceeds from issuance of common stock		(p)	101			
Proceeds from issuance of note payable		(q)	94			
Payment of note payable				(r)	11	
Payment of dividends				(s)	17	
			547		567	
Net decrease in cash		(t)	20			
Totals			567		567	

Entries (n) through (s) account for the investing and financing transactions. Entry (n) debits Equipment, Net for their purchase and credits Purchase of plant assets under investing cash flows. Entry (p) debits Proceeds from issuance of common stock under financing cash flows. The offsetting credit is to Common stock.

The final item in Exhibit 17A-3 is the Net decrease in cash—transaction (t) on the work sheet—a credit to cash and a debit to Net decrease in cash. To prepare the statement of cash flows, you can rewrite Panel B of the work sheet, adding subtotals for the three categories of activities.

Appendix Assignments

Problems

Preparing the work sheet for the statement of cash flows—indirect method

P17A-1 The 20X8 comparative balance sheet and income statement of Alden Group, Inc., follow. Alden had no noncash investing and financing transactions during 20X8.

Alden Group, Inc.

Comparative Balance Sheet

	December 31, 20X8	December 31, 20X7	Increase (Decrease)
Current assets:			
Cash and cash equivalents	$ 13,700	$ 15,600	$ (1,900)
Accounts receivable	41,500	43,100	(1,600)
Inventories	96,600	93,000	3,600
Plant assets:			
Land	35,100	10,000	25,100
Equipment, net	100,900	93,700	7,200
Total assets	$287,800	$255,400	$32,400
Current liabilities:			
Accounts payable	$ 24,800	$ 26,000	$ (1,200)
Accrued liabilities	24,400	22,500	1,900
Long-term liabilities:			
Notes payable	55,000	65,000	(10,000)
Stockholders' equity:			
Common stock	131,100	122,300	8,800
Retained earnings	52,500	19,600	32,900
Total liabilities and stockholders' equity	$287,800	$255,400	$32,400

Alden Group, Inc.

Income Statement for Year Ended December 31, 20X8

Revenues:		
Sales revenue		$438,000
Interest revenue		11,700
Total revenues		449,700
Expenses:		
Cost of goods sold	$205,200	
Salary expense	76,400	
Depreciation expense	15,300	
Other operating expense	49,700	
Interest expense	24,600	
Income tax expense	16,900	
Total expenses		388,100
Net income		$ 61,600

Required

Prepare the work sheet for the 20X8 statement of cash flows. Format cash flows from operating activities by the *indirect* method.

Preparing the work sheet for the statement of cash flows—direct method

P17A-2 Using the Alden Group, Inc., data from Problem 17A-1, prepare the work sheet for Alden's 20X8 statement of cash flows. Format cash flows from operating activities by the *direct* method.

CHAPTER 18

Financial Statement Analysis

A+ TIPS CHECK YOUR RESOURCES

- Visit the www.prenhall.com/horngren **Web site** for self-study quizzes, video clips, and other resources
- Try the **Quick Check** exercise at the end of the chapter to test your knowledge
- Learn the **key terms**
- Do the **Starter** exercises keyed in the margins
- Work the **mid-** and **end-of-chapter summary problems**
- Use the **Concept Links** to review material in other chapters
- Search the **CD** for review materials by chapter or by key word
- Watch the **tutorial videos** to review key concepts
- Watch the **On Location Financial Statement Analysis** video, in which people from three companies talk about how they use financial statements for decision making

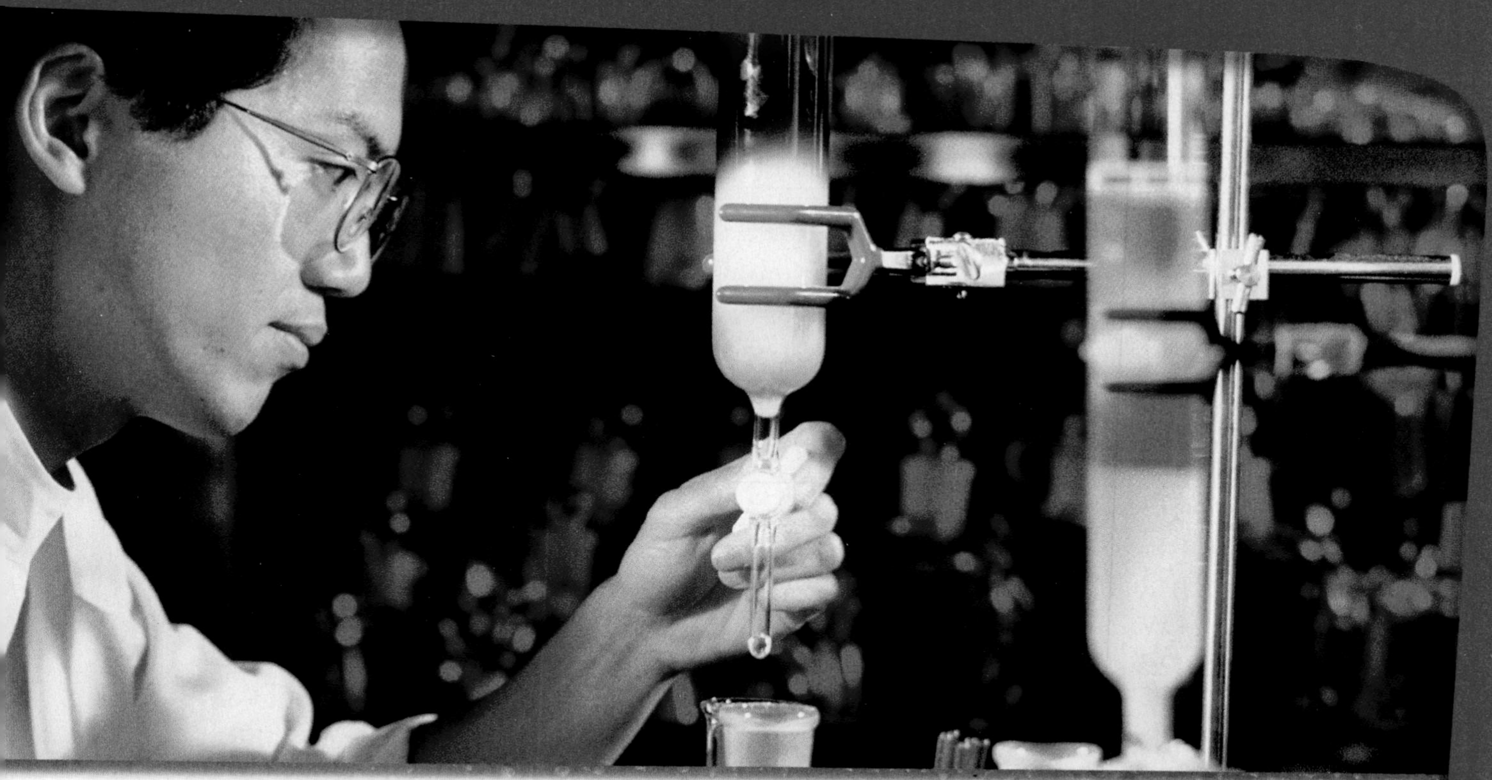

LEARNING OBJECTIVES

1. Perform a horizontal analysis of comparative financial statements
2. Perform a vertical analysis of financial statements
3. Prepare and use common-size financial statements
4. Compute the standard financial ratios
5. Measure economic value added

Bristol-Myers Squibb

You, or people you know, probably invest in stocks. How do you choose those investments? Do you pick large, established companies, or do you look for a new highflier? What kind of information do you use?

Some of the most important information about a company comes from its financial statements. To make an informed decision, you need to be able to analyze those statements, even if the company has been around a long time and is a household name. Take a look at what happened to health-care giant Bristol-Myers Squibb (BMS). Study BMS's 2002 income statement:

Bristol-Myers Squibb Company

Income Statement (Adapted)

(In millions)	Year Ended December 31, 2002	2001
Earnings		
1 **Net sales**	$18,119	$17,987
2 **Expenses**:		
3 Cost of goods sold	6,388	5,453
4 Marketing, selling, and administrative	3,923	3,894
5 Advertising and product promotion	1,295	1,299
6 Research and development	2,218	2,183
7 Other expense, net*	1,794	251
8 **Income before income tax**	2,501	4,907
9 Income taxes	435	73
10 **Net income**	$ 2,066	$ 4,834

*Includes discontinued operations.

You can see that 2002 was a tough year for the company. Net income (line 10) was down from 2001, and Wall Street wasn't happy.

Companies have to satisfy lots of people, from individual investors like you and me to Wall Street analysts. What analytical tools do people use to make decisions about a company like Bristol-Myers Squibb? They use many of the techniques we cover in this book. ■

Sitemap

- Horizontal Analysis
- Vertical Analysis
- Benchmarking
- Using Ratios
- Other Evaluation Tools

Investors and creditors can't evaluate a company by examining only one year's data. This is why most financial statements cover at least two periods, like the Bristol-Myers Squibb (BMS) income statement. In fact, most financial analysis covers trends of three to five years. This chapter illustrates some of the analytical tools for charting a company's progress through time.

The graphs in Exhibit 18-1 show some important data about BMS. They depict a three-year trend of net sales and research and development (R&D). Sales and R&D are important drivers of profits.

Exhibit 18-1 Financial Data of Bristol-Myers Squibb Company (Adapted)

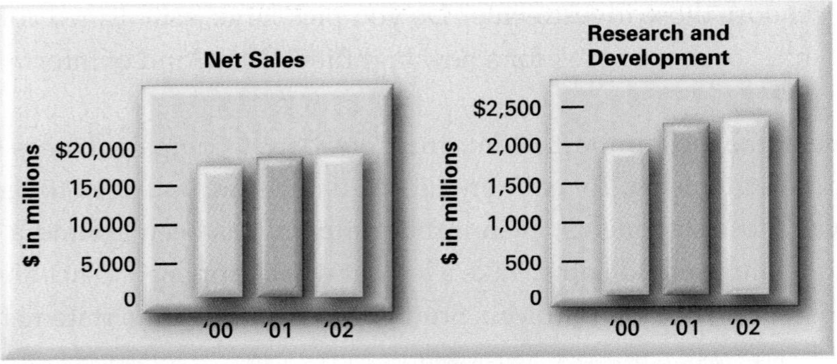

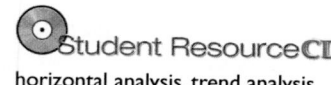

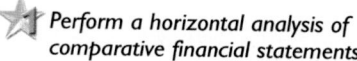

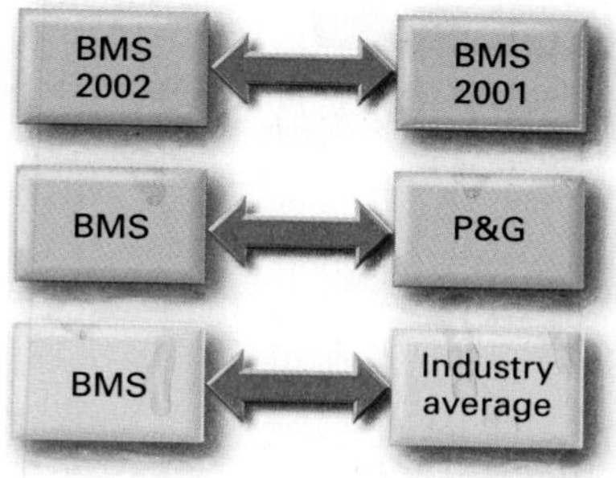

For BMS, both sales and research and development barely grew during 2002. These are not good signs for the future. How can we decide what we really think about BMS's performance in 2002? We need some way to compare that performance

- From one year to another
- With the performance of a competing company, like Procter & Gamble
- With the pharmaceuticals (health-care) industry

Then we will have a better idea of how to judge BMS's situation now and predict what might happen in the near future.

Horizontal analysis provides a direct year-to-year comparison of BMS's performance in 2002 and 2001. Another technique, vertical analysis, is the standard way to compare different companies. Let's begin with horizontal analysis.

Horizontal Analysis

■ **Horizontal Analysis**
□ Vertical Analysis
□ Benchmarking
□ Using Ratios
□ Other Evaluation Tools

Student ResourceCD
horizontal analysis, trend analysis

1 Perform a horizontal analysis of comparative financial statements

Horizontal Analysis
Study of percentage changes in comparative financial statements.

Many decisions hinge on whether the numbers—in sales, income, and expenses—are increasing or decreasing. Have sales risen from last year? By how much? We may find that sales have increased by $20,000. But considered alone, this fact is not very helpful. The *percentage change* in sales over time aids our understanding. It is more useful to know that sales have increased by 20% than to know that the increase is $20,000.

The study of percentage changes in comparative statements is called **horizontal analysis**. Computing a percentage change in comparative statements requires two steps:

1. Compute the dollar amount of the change from the earlier base period to the later period.
2. Divide the dollar amount of change by the base-period amount.

Illustration: Bristol-Myers Squibb

Horizontal analysis is illustrated for Bristol-Myers Squibb as follows (dollar amounts in millions):

			Increase (Decrease)	
	2002	2001	Amount	Percentage
Net sales	$18,119	$17,987	$132	0.7%

Sales increased by only 7/10 of 1% (0.007) during 2002, computed as follows:

STEP 1 Compute the dollar amount of change in sales from 2001 to 2002:

2002		2001		Increase
$18,119	–	$17,987	=	$132

STEP 2 Divide the dollar amount of change by the base-period amount. This computes the percentage change for the period:

$$\text{Percentage change} = \frac{\text{Dollar amount of change}}{\text{Base-year amount}}$$

$$= \frac{\$132}{\$17{,}987} = 0.007 = 0.7\%$$

Detailed horizontal analyses are shown in the two right-hand columns of Exhibits 18-2 and 18-3, the financial statements of BMS Company. The income statements reveal that net sales increased by 0.7% during 2002. But cost of goods sold grew by 17.1%, so gross profit fell by 6.4%. Net income was down by 57.3%. These results are not encouraging.

✔ Starter 18-1

Exhibit 18-2

Comparative Income Statement—Horizontal Analysis

Bristol-Myers Squibb Company

Income Statement (Adapted)
Years Ended December 31, 2002 and 2001

(Dollar amounts in millions)	2002	2001	Increase (Decrease) Amount	Increase (Decrease) Percentage
Net sales	$18,119	$17,987	$ 132	0.7%
Cost of goods sold	6,388	5,453	935	17.1
Gross profit	11,731	12,534	(803)	(6.4)
Operating expenses:				
Marketing, selling, and administrative	3,923	3,894	29	0.7
Advertising and product promotion	1,295	1,299	(4)	(0.3)
Research and development	2,218	2,183	35	1.6
Other expense, net	1,794	251	1,543	614.7
Income before income tax	2,501	4,907	(2,406)	(49.0)
Income tax expense	435	73	362	495.9
Net income	**$ 2,066**	**$ 4,834**	$(2,768)	(57.3)

The comparative balance sheet in Exhibit 18-3 shows that 2002 was not a growth year for BMS. Total assets fell by 10.6%. Fortunately, liabilities decreased by 15.1%, so the drop in stockholders' equity was only 1.2%.

Exhibit 18-3

Comparative Balance Sheet—Horizontal Analysis

Bristol-Myers Squibb Company

Balance Sheet (Adapted)
December 31, 2002 and 2001

(Dollar amounts in millions)	2002	2001	Increase (Decrease) Amount	Increase (Decrease) Percentage
Assets				
Current Assets:				
Cash and cash equivalents	$ 3,978	$ 5,500	$(1,522)	(27.7)%
Other current assets	5,997	7,749	(1,752)	(22.6)
Total current assets	9,975	13,249	(3,274)	(24.7)
Property, plant, and equipment, net	5,321	4,887	434	8.9
Intangible assets, net	6,768	7,203	(435)	(6.0)
Other assets	2,810	2,473	337	13.6
Total assets	**$24,874**	**$27,812**	$(2,938)	(10.6)
Liabilities				
Current Liabilities:				
Accounts payable	$ 1,553	$ 1,478	$ 75	5.1%
Other current liabilities	6,667	9,631	(2,964)	(30.8)
Total current liabilities	8,220	11,109	(2,889)	(26.0)
Long-term liabilities	7,687	7,628	59	0.8
Total liabilities	**15,907**	**18,737**	(2,830)	(15.1)
Stockholders' Equity				
Common stock	2,711	2,623	88	3.4
Retained earnings and other equity	6,256	6,452	(196)	(3.0)
Total stockholders' equity	**8,967**	**9,075**	(108)	(1.2)
Total liabilities and equity	**$24,874**	**$27,812**	$(2,938)	(10.6)

Trend Percentages

Trend percentages are a form of horizontal analysis. Trends indicate the direction a business is taking. How have sales changed over a five-year period? What trend does net income show? These questions can be answered by trend percentages over a representative period, such as the most recent three to five years.

Trend percentages are computed by selecting a base year whose amounts are set equal to 100%. The amounts for each following year are expressed as a percentage of the base amount. To compute trend percentages, divide each item for following years by the corresponding amount during the base year:

Trend Percentages
A form of horizontal analysis in which percentages are computed by selecting a base year as 100% and expressing amounts for following years as a percentage of the base amount.

$$\text{Trend \%} = \frac{\text{Any year \$}}{\text{Base year \$}}$$

BMS Company showed the following net sales for the past 6 years:

(In millions)	2002	2001	2000	1999	1998	1997
Net sales	$18,119	$17,987	$17,538	$16,502	$15,007	$13,698
Trend percentages	132%	131%	128%	120%	110%	100%

✔ Starter 18-2

We want trend percentages for the five-year period 1998 to 2002. The base year is 1997. Trend percentages are computed by dividing each year's amount by the 1997 amount. The trend percentages follow net sales (1997, the base year = 100%).

Net sales increased rapidly through 1999. The rate of growth slowed in 2000 and became a trickle in 2001 and 2002.

You can perform a trend analysis on any item you consider important. We selected net sales because sales drive profits. Trend analysis is widely used to predict the future.

Vertical Analysis

Horizontal analysis highlights changes in an item over time. However, no single technique gives a complete picture of a business.

Vertical analysis of a financial statement shows the relationship of each item to its base amount, which is the 100% figure. Every other item on the statement is then reported as a percentage of that base. For an income statement, net sales is the base. Suppose under normal conditions a company's gross profit is 70% of net sales. A drop to 60% may cause the company to suffer a loss. Investors view a large decline in gross profit with alarm.

Student ResourceCD
common-size statement, vertical analysis

2 *Perform a vertical analysis of financial statements*

Illustration: Bristol-Myers Squibb

Exhibit 18-4 shows the vertical analysis of BMS's income statement. In this case,

Vertical Analysis
Analysis of a financial statement that reveals the relationship of each statement item to a specified base, which is the 100% figure.

$$\text{Vertical analysis \%} = \frac{\text{Each income statement item}}{\text{Net sales}}$$

For example, the vertical-analysis percentage for Cost of goods sold for 2002 is 35.3% ($6,388/$18,119 = 0.353). Unfortunately for BMS, this percentage increased during 2002. Look further. Other expenses' percentages also increased. Consequently, the percentage for net income was down from 2001.

Exhibit 18-5 shows the vertical analysis of BMS's balance sheet. The base amount (100%) is total assets.

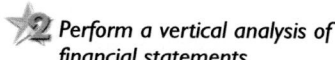

Exhibit 18-4

Comparative Income Statement—Vertical Analysis

Bristol-Myers Squibb Company

Income Statement (Adapted)
Years Ended December 31, 2002 and 2001

	2002		2001	
(Dollar amounts in millions)	Amount	Percent of Total	Amount	Percent of Total
Net sales	$18,119	100.0%	$17,987	100.0%
Cost of goods sold	6,388	35.3	5,453	30.3
Gross profit	11,731	64.7	12,534	69.7
Operating expenses:				
Marketing, selling, and administrative	3,923	21.7	3,894	21.7
Advertising and product promotion	1,295	7.1	1,299	7.2
Research and development	2,218	12.2	2,183	12.1
Other expense, net	1,794	9.9	251	1.4
Income before income tax	2,501	13.8	4,907	27.3
Income tax expense	435	2.4	73	0.4
Net income	**$ 2,066**	11.4%	**$ 4,834**	26.9%

Note: Percentage may contain slight rounding error.

Exhibit 18-5

Comparative Balance Sheet—Vertical Analysis

Bristol-Myers Squibb Company

Balance Sheet (Adapted)
December 31, 2002 and 2001

	2002		2001	
(Dollar amounts in millions)	Amount	Percent of Total	Amount	Percent of Total
Assets				
Current Assets:				
Cash and cash equivalents	$ 3,978	16.0%	$ 5,500	19.8%
Other current assets	5,997	24.1	7,749	27.8
Total current assets	9,975	40.1	13,249	47.6
Property, plant, and equipment, net	5,321	21.4	4,887	17.6
Intangible assets, net	6,768	27.2	7,203	25.9
Other assets	2,810	11.3	2,473	8.9
Total assets	**$24,874**	100.0%	**$27,812**	100.0%
Liabilities				
Current Liabilities:				
Accounts payable	$ 1,553	6.2%	$ 1,478	5.3%
Other current liabilities	6,667	26.8	9,631	34.7
Total current liabilities	8,220	33.0	11,109	40.0
Long-term liabilities	7,687	30.9	7,628	27.4
Total liabilities	**15,907**	63.9	**18,737**	67.4
Stockholders' Equity				
Common stock	2,711	10.9	2,623	9.4
Retained earnings and other equity	6,256	25.2	6,452	23.2
Total stockholders' equity	**8,967**	36.1	**9,075**	32.6
Total liabilities and equity	**$24,874**	100.0%	**$27,812**	100.0%

Note: Percentages may contain slight rounding error.

The vertical analysis of BMS's balance sheet reveals several things about the company's financial position:

✔ Starter 18-3

- Current assets make up 40.1% of total assets, compared to 47.6% in 2001. A high percentage of current assets can be bad because current assets earn a low rate of return.
- Intangibles make up 27.2% of total assets. This percentage is high because of the nature of the pharmaceutical business. Lenders dislike a high percentage of intangibles because, in a liquidation of the company, intangibles are often worthless. But in today's technology-driven economy, intangible assets are important.
- Total liabilities dropped to 63.9%, and stockholders' equity increased to 36.1% of total assets. Overall, BMS's creditworthiness improved a bit in 2002.

How Do We Compare One Company with Another?

3 *Prepare and use common-size financial statements*

The percentages in Exhibits 18-4 and 18-5 can be presented as a separate statement that reports only percentages (no dollar amounts). Such a statement is called a **common-size statement**.

Common-Size Statement
A financial statement that reports only percentages (no dollar amounts).

On a common-size income statement, each item is expressed as a percentage of net sales. Net sales is the *common size* to which we relate the other amounts. In the balance sheet, the common size is total assets. A common-size statement eases the comparison of different companies because amounts are stated in percentages.

Common-size statements may identify the need for corrective action. Exhibit 18-6 gives an example. In 2001, BMS had almost half of its resources tied up in current assets. As we have mentioned, cash, receivables, and inventories earn low rates of return, as compared with long-term assets. It appears that the top management of BMS made a serious shift during 2002. BMS invested in plant and equipment, and the company's long-term assets grew to 59.9% of total resources in 2002.

Exhibit 18-6

Common-Size Analysis of Current Assets

Bristol-Myers Squibb Company

Common-Size Analysis of Current and Long-Term Assets
December 31, 2002 and 2001

	Percent of Total Assets	
	2002	**2001**
Current assets	40.1%	47.6%
Long-term assets	59.9	52.4
Total assets	100.0%	100.0%

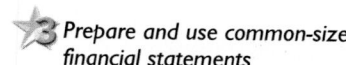

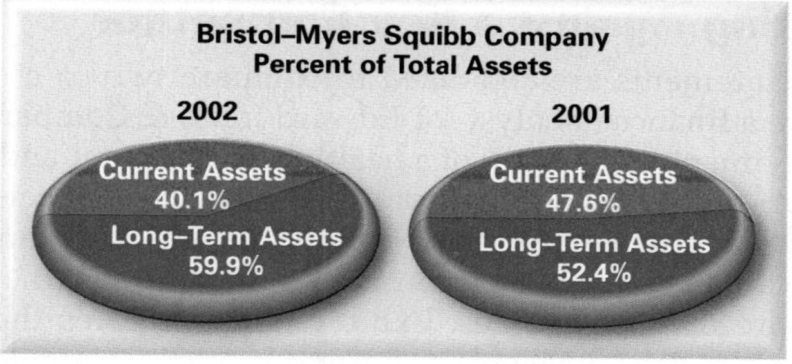

Benchmarking

Benchmarking is the practice of comparing a company with other companies that are leaders.

Stop & Think

Calculate the common-size percentages for the following income statement:

Net sales	$150,000
Cost of goods sold	60,000
Gross profit	90,000
Operating expense	40,000
Operating income	50,000
Income tax expense	15,000
Net income	$ 35,000

Answer:

Net sales	100%	(= $150,000 ÷ $150,000)
Cost of goods sold	40	(= $ 60,000 ÷ $150,000)
Gross profit	60	(= $ 90,000 ÷ $150,000)
Operating expense	27	(= $ 40,000 ÷ $150,000)
Operating income	33	(= $ 50,000 ÷ $150,000)
Income tax expense	10	(= $ 15,000 ÷ $150,000)
Net income	23%	(= $ 35,000 ÷ $150,000)

Student Resource CD
benchmarking

Benchmarking
The practice of comparing a company with other companies that are leaders.

Benchmarking Against the Industry Average

We study a company to gain insight into past results and future performance. Still, that knowledge is limited to the one company. We may learn that gross profit and net income have increased. This information is helpful, but it does not consider how other companies have fared over the same period. Have competitors profited even more? Investors need to know how a company compares with others in the same line of business. For example, during 2002, Johnson & Johnson and Procter & Gamble increased both sales and profits, while BMS's net income decreased.

Exhibit 18-7 gives the common-size income statement of BMS compared with the average for the pharmaceuticals (health-care) industry. The industry averages were adapted from Risk Management Association's *Annual Statement Studies*. Analysts at Merrill Lynch and Edward Jones & Co. specialize in a particular industry. For example, Merrill Lynch has health-care specialists, airline-industry specialists, and so on. They compare a company with others in the same industry. Exhibit 18-7 shows that BMS compares favorably with competing companies in its industry. BMS's gross profit percentage is much higher than the industry average. Even though 2002 was not a good year, BMS's percentage of net income is still higher than the industry average.

Benchmarking Against a Key Competitor

Common-size statements are also used to compare two or more companies. Suppose you are a financial analyst for Edward Jones & Company. You are considering an investment in the stock of a health-care company, and you are choosing between BMS and P&G. A direct comparison of their financial statements in dollar amounts is not meaningful because the amounts are so different. However, you can convert the two companies' income statements to common size and compare the percentages. Exhibit 18-8 compares the common-size income statements of Bristol-Myers Squibb and Procter & Gamble. The two companies earn similar percentages of net income to sales.

Exhibit 18-7

Common-Size Income Statement Compared with the Industry Average

Bristol-Myers Squibb Company

Common-Size Income Statement for Comparison with Industry Average
Year Ended December 31, 2002

	Bristol-Myers Squibb	Industry Average
Net sales	100.0%	100.0%
Cost of goods sold	35.3	51.6
Gross profit	64.7	48.4
Operating and other expenses	50.9	40.5
Income before income tax	13.8	7.9
Income tax expense	2.4	2.8
Net income	11.4%	5.1%

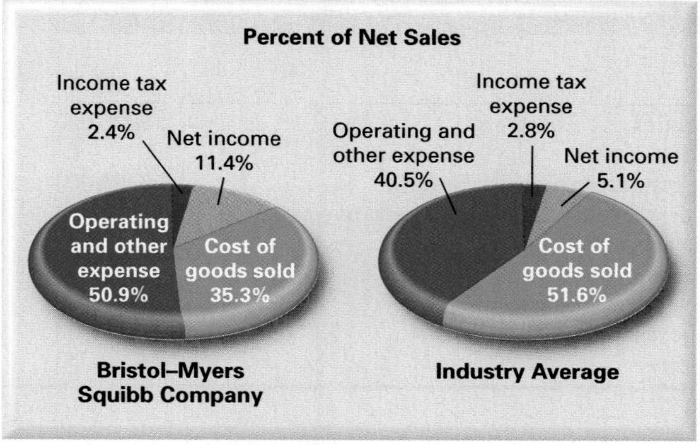

✔ Starter 18-4

Exhibit 18-8

Common-Size Income Statement Compared with a Key Competitor

Bristol-Myers Squibb Company

Common-Size Income Statement for Comparison with Key Competitor
Year Ended December 31, 2002

	Bristol-Myers Squibb	Procter & Gamble
Net sales	100.0%	100.0%
Cost of goods sold	35.3	52.2
Gross profit	64.7	47.8
Operating and other expenses	50.9	32.0
Income before income tax	13.8	15.8
Income tax expense	2.4	5.0
Net income	11.4%	10.8%

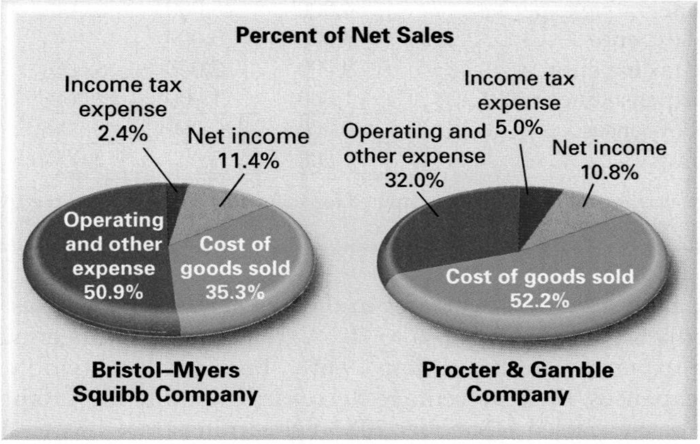

Now let's put your learning to practice. Work the mid-chapter summary problem, which reviews the concepts in the first half of this chapter.

MID-CHAPTER *Summary Problem*

A+ TIPS
CHECK YOUR RESOURCES

Perform a horizontal analysis and a vertical analysis of the comparative income statement of TRE Corporation, which makes metal detectors. State whether 20X3 was a good year or a bad year, and give your reasons.

TRE Corporation

Comparative Income Statement
Months Ended December 31, 20X3 and 20X2

	20X3	20X2
Total revenues	$275,000	$225,000
Expenses:		
Cost of products sold	$194,000	$165,000
Engineering, selling, and administrative expenses	54,000	48,000
Interest expense	5,000	5,000
Income tax expense	9,000	3,000
Other expense (income)	1,000	(1,000)
Total expenses	263,000	220,000
Net earnings	$ 12,000	$ 5,000

Solution

The horizontal analysis shows that total revenues increased 22.2%. This was greater than the 19.5% increase in total expenses, resulting in a 140% increase in net earnings.

TRE Corporation

Horizontal Analysis of Comparative Income Statement
Months Ended December 31, 20X3 and 20X2

			Increase (Decrease)	
	20X3	20X2	Amount	Percent
Total revenues	$275,000	$225,000	$50,000	22.2%
Expenses:				
Cost of products sold	$194,000	$165,000	$29,000	17.6
Engineering, selling, and administrative expenses	54,000	48,000	6,000	12.5
Interest expense	5,000	5,000	—	—
Income tax expense	9,000	3,000	6,000	200.0
Other expense (income)	1,000	(1,000)	2,000	—*
Total expenses	263,000	220,000	43,000	19.5
Net earnings	$ 12,000	$ 5,000	$ 7,000	140.0%

*Percentage changes are typically not computed for shifts from a negative to a positive amount, and vice versa.

The vertical analysis shows decreases in the percentages of net sales consumed by the cost of products sold (from 73.3% to 70.5%) and by the engineering, selling, and administrative expenses (from 21.3% to 19.6%). Because these two items are TRE's largest dollar expenses, their percentage decreases are quite important. The relative reduction in expenses raised December 20X3 net earnings to 4.4% of sales, compared with 2.2% the preceding December. The overall analysis indicates that December 20X3 was significantly better than December 20X2.

TRE Corporation

Vertical Analysis of Comparative Income Statement
Months Ended December 31, 20X3 and 20X2

	20X3		20X2	
	Amount	**Percent**	**Amount**	**Percent**
Total revenues	$275,000	100.0%	$225,000	100.0%
Expenses:				
Cost of products sold	$194,000	70.5	$165,000	73.3
Engineering, selling, and administrative expenses	54,000	19.6	48,000	21.3
Interest expense	5,000	1.8	5,000	2.2
Income tax expense	9,000	3.3	3,000	1.4**
Other expense (income)	1,000	0.4	(1,000)	(0.4)
Total expenses	263,000	95.6	220,000	97.8
Net earnings	$ 12,000	4.4%	$ 5,000	2.2%

**Number rounded up.

☐ Horizontal Analysis
☐ Vertical Analysis
☐ Benchmarking
■ Using Ratios
☐ Other Evaluation Tools

Using Ratios to Make Decisions

Online financial databases, such as Lexis/Nexis and the Dow Jones News Retrieval Service, provide financial data on thousands of corporations. Assume that you want to compare some companies' recent earnings histories. You might have the computer compare the companies on the basis of return on stockholders' equity. The computer could then give you the names of the 20 companies with the highest return on equity. A manager, lender, or financial analyst may use any ratio that is relevant to a particular decision.

Student Resource CD

accounts receivable turnover, acid-test ratio, current ratio, day's sales in receivables, debt ratio, dividend yield, earnings per share, inventory turnover ratio, P/E ratio, profitability ratio, return on net sales, return on stockholders' equity, return on total assets, times-interest-earned ratio

The ratios we discuss in this chapter may be classified as follows:

1. Measuring ability to pay current liabilities
2. Measuring ability to sell inventory and collect receivables
3. Measuring ability to pay long-term debt
4. Measuring profitability
5. Analyzing stock as an investment

Measuring Ability to Pay Current Liabilities

4 *Compute the standard financial ratios*

Working capital is defined as

Working capital = Current assets − Current liabilities

Working Capital
Current assets minus current liabilities; measures a business's ability to meet its short-term obligations with its current assets.

Working capital measures the ability to meet short-term obligations with current assets. To use working-capital data in decision making, analysts develop ratios. Two decision tools based on working-capital data are the *current ratio* and the *acid-test ratio.*

CURRENT RATIO The most widely used ratio is the **current ratio**, which is current assets divided by current liabilities. A company's current assets and current liabilities represent the core of day-to-day operations. The current ratio measures ability to pay current liabilities with current assets.

Current Ratio
Current assets divided by current liabilities. Measures ability to pay current liabilities with current assets.

Exhibit 18-9 gives the comparative income statement and balance sheet of Palisades Furniture, Inc. The current ratios of Palisades Furniture, Inc., at December 31, 20X5 and 20X4, follow, along with the average for the retail furniture industry:

Formula	Palisades' Current Ratio 20X5	Palisades' Current Ratio 20X4	Industry Average
Current ratio = $\frac{\text{Current assets}}{\text{Current liabilities}}$	$\frac{\$262,000}{\$142,000} = 1.85$	$\frac{\$236,000}{\$126,000} = 1.87$	1.50

Exhibit 18-9 Comparative Financial Statements

Palisades Furniture, Inc.
Comparative Income Statement
Years Ended December 31, 20X5 and 20X4

	20X5	20X4
Net sales	$858,000	$803,000
Cost of goods sold	513,000	509,000
Gross profit	345,000	294,000
Operating expenses:		
Selling expenses	126,000	114,000
General expenses	118,000	123,000
Total operating expenses	244,000	237,000
Income from operations	101,000	57,000
Interest revenue	4,000	—
Interest expense	24,000	14,000
Income before income taxes	81,000	43,000
Income tax expense	33,000	17,000
Net income	$ 48,000	$ 26,000

Palisades Furniture, Inc.
Comparative Balance Sheet
December 31, 20X5 and 20X4

	20X5	20X4
Assets		
Current Assets:		
Cash	$ 29,000	$ 32,000
Accounts receivable, net	114,000	85,000
Inventories	113,000	111,000
Prepaid expenses	6,000	8,000
Total current assets	262,000	236,000
Long-term investments	18,000	9,000
Property, plant, and equipment, net	507,000	399,000
Total assets	$787,000	$644,000
Liabilities		
Current Liabilities:		
Notes payable	$ 42,000	$ 27,000
Accounts payable	73,000	68,000
Accrued liabilities	27,000	31,000
Total current liabilities	142,000	126,000
Long-term debt	289,000	198,000
Total liabilities	431,000	324,000
Stockholders' Equity		
Common stock, no par	186,000	186,000
Retained earnings	170,000	134,000
Total stockholders' equity	356,000	320,000
Total liabilities and equity	$787,000	$644,000

✔ **Starter 18-5**

A high current ratio indicates a strong financial position and that the business has sufficient liquid assets to maintain normal business operations. Compare Palisades Furniture's current ratio of 1.85 with the industry average of 1.50 and with the current ratios of some well-known companies:

Company	Current Ratio
Chesebrough-Pond's Inc.	2.50
Wal-Mart Stores, Inc.	1.51
General Mills, Inc.	1.05

What is an acceptable current ratio? The answer depends on the industry. The norm for companies in most industries is around 1.50, as reported by the Risk Management Association. Palisades Furniture's current ratio of 1.85 is strong. In most industries, a current ratio of 2.0 is very strong.

Acid-Test Ratio The **acid-test** (or **quick) ratio** tells us whether the entity could pay all its current liabilities if they came due immediately. That is, could the company pass this *acid test*?

Acid-Test Ratio
Ratio of the sum of cash plus short-term investments plus net current receivables to total current liabilities. Tells whether the entity can pay all its current liabilities if they come due immediately. Also called the **quick ratio**.

To compute the acid-test ratio, we add cash, short-term investments, and net current receivables (accounts and notes receivable, net of allowances) and divide this sum by current liabilities. Inventory and prepaid expenses are the two current assets *not* included in the acid test because they are the least-liquid current assets. Palisades Furniture's acid-test ratios for 20X5 and 20X4 follow.

	Formula	Palisades' Acid-Test Ratio		Industry
		20X5	20X4	Average
Acid-test ratio =	(Cash + Short-term investments + Net current receivables) / Current liabilities	($29,000 + $0 + $114,000) / $142,000 = 1.01	($32,000 + $0 + $85,000) / $126,000 = 0.93	0.40

The company's acid-test ratio improved considerably during 20X5 and is significantly better than the industry average. Palisades' 1.01 acid-test ratio also compares favorably with the acid-test values of some well-known companies.

Company	Acid-Test Ratio
Chesebrough-Pond's Inc..	1.25
Wal-Mart Stores, Inc.	0.15
General Motors, Inc..	0.91

The norm for the acid-test ratio ranges from 0.20 for shoe retailers to 1.00 for manufacturers of equipment, as reported by the Risk Management Association. An acid-test ratio of 0.90 to 1.00 is acceptable in most industries.

Stop & Think

Schlotzky, Inc., has a current ratio of 2.00 and an acid-test ratio of only 0.70. Which account explains the big difference between these two measures of ability to pay current liabilities? Explain.

Answer: Inventory explains the difference. Inventory is included in the current ratio but not in the acid-test ratio. Prepaid expenses may also explain part of the difference, but inventory is more important.

Measuring Ability to Sell Inventory and Collect Receivables

The ability to sell inventory and collect receivables is fundamental to business success. Recall the operating cycle of a merchandiser: cash to inventory to receivables and back to cash. In this section, we discuss three ratios that measure the company's ability to sell inventory and collect receivables.

Inventory Turnover
Ratio of cost of goods sold to average inventory. Indicates how rapidly inventory is sold.

Inventory Turnover **Inventory turnover** measures the number of times a company sells its average level of inventory during a year. → A high rate of turnover indicates ease in selling inventory; a low rate indicates difficulty in selling. A value of 6 means that the company's average level of inventory has been sold six times during the year.

← *We introduced inventory turnover in Chapter 6, page 203.*

To compute inventory turnover, we divide cost of goods sold by the average inventory for the period. We use the cost of goods sold—not sales—because both cost of goods sold and inventory are stated *at cost*. Sales are stated at the sales value of inventory, which is not comparable with inventory cost.

Palisades Furniture's inventory turnover for 20X5 is

Formula	Palisades' Inventory Turnover	Industry Average
Inventory turnover = $\frac{\text{Cost of goods sold}}{\text{Average inventory}}$	$\frac{\$513,000}{\$112,000} = 4.6$	3.4

Cost of goods sold comes from the income statement (Exhibit 18-9). Average inventory is figured by averaging the beginning inventory ($111,000) and ending inventory ($113,000). (See the balance sheet, Exhibit 18-9.)

Inventory turnover varies widely with the nature of the business. For example, most manufacturers of farm machinery have an inventory turnover close to three times a year. In contrast, companies that remove natural gas from the ground hold their inventory for a very short period of time and have an average turnover of 30. Palisades Furniture's turnover of 4.6 times a year is high for its industry, which has an average turnover of 3.4.

Accounts Receivable Turnover
Measures a company's ability to collect cash from credit customers. To compute accounts receivable turnover, divide net credit sales by average net accounts receivable.

ACCOUNTS RECEIVABLE TURNOVER **Accounts receivable turnover** measures the ability to collect cash from credit customers. The higher the ratio, the more successfully the business collects cash. However, a receivable turnover that is too high may indicate that credit is too tight, causing the loss of sales to good customers.

To compute the accounts receivable turnover, we divide net credit sales by average net accounts receivable. Palisades Furniture's accounts receivable turnover ratio for 20X5 is computed as follows:

Formula	Palisades' Accounts Receivable Turnover	Industry Average
Accounts receivable turnover = $\frac{\text{Net credit sales}}{\text{Average net accounts receivable}}$	$\frac{\$858,000}{\$99,500} = 8.6$	51.0

Average net accounts receivable is figured by adding the beginning accounts receivable balance ($85,000) and the ending balance ($114,000), then dividing by 2.

Palisades' receivable turnover of 8.6 times per year is much slower than the industry average. Why the difference? Palisades is a hometown store that sells to local people who tend to pay their bills over time. Many larger furniture stores sell their receivables to other companies called *factors*, a practice that keeps receivables low and receivable turnover high. Palisades Furniture follows a different strategy.

Days' Sales in Receivables
Ratio of average net accounts receivable to one day's sale. Indicates how many days' sales remain in Accounts Receivable awaiting collection. Also called the **collection period**.

Recall from Chapter 9 (page 378) that days' sales in receivables indicates how many days it takes to collect the average level of receivables. ➡

DAYS' SALES IN RECEIVABLES The **days'-sales-in-receivables** ratio also measures the ability to collect receivables. This ratio tells us how many days' sales remain in Accounts Receivable. ⬅ To compute the ratio, we follow a two-step process:

First, divide net sales by 365 days to figure average sales for one day.

Second, divide this average day's sales amount into average net accounts receivable.

The data to compute this ratio for Palisades Furniture, Inc., for 20X5 are taken from the income statement and the balance sheet (Exhibit 18-9):

Formula	Palisades' Days' Sales in Accounts Receivable	Industry Average
Days' Sales in *average* Accounts Receivable:		
1. One day's sales $= \dfrac{\text{Net sales}}{\text{365 days}}$	$\dfrac{\$858,000}{\text{365 days}} = \$2,351$	
2. Days' sales in average accounts receivable $= \dfrac{\text{Average net accounts receivable}}{\text{One day's sales}}$	$\dfrac{\$99,500}{\$2,351} = \text{42 days}$	7 days

Average accounts receivable of $99,500 = ($85,000 + $114,000)/2.

✔ Starter 18-6

Palisades' ratio tells us that 42 average days' sales remain in accounts receivable and need to be collected. Palisades' days' sales in receivables is much higher (worse) than the industry average because Palisades collects its own receivables. Palisades Furniture remains competitive because of its personal relationship with customers. Without their good paying habits, the company's cash flow would suffer.

Measuring Ability to Pay Long-Term Debt

The ratios discussed so far yield insight into current assets and current liabilities. They help us measure ability to sell inventory, collect receivables, and pay current liabilities. Most businesses also have long-term debt. Two key indicators of a business's ability to pay long-term liabilities are the *debt ratio* and the *times-interest-earned ratio.*

DEBT RATIO Suppose you are a loan officer at a bank and you are evaluating loan applications from two companies with equal sales and total assets. Both companies have asked to borrow $500,000 and have agreed to repay the loan over a 10-year period. The first firm already owes $600,000 to another bank. The second owes only $250,000. Other things being equal, you are more likely to lend money to Company 2 because that company owes less than Company 1.

Debt Ratio
Ratio of total liabilities to total assets. Shows the proportion of a company's assets that is financed with debt.

This relationship between total liabilities and total assets—called the **debt ratio**—shows the proportion of assets financed with debt. → If the debt ratio is 1, then debt has been used to finance all the assets. A debt ratio of 0.50 means that the company has borrowed to finance half its assets; the owners of the business have financed the other half. The higher the debt ratio, the higher the strain of paying off loans.

← *We introduced the debt ratio in Chapter 4, page 155.*

The debt ratios for Palisades Furniture at the end of 20X5 and 20X4 follow:

Formula	Palisades' Debt Ratio 20X5	Palisades' Debt Ratio 20X4	Industry Average
Debt ratio $= \dfrac{\text{Total liabilities}}{\text{Total assets}}$	$\dfrac{\$431,000}{\$787,000} = 0.55$	$\dfrac{\$324,000}{\$644,000} = 0.50$	0.64

Palisades Furniture's debt ratio of 0.55 is not very high. Risk Management Association reports that the average debt ratio for most companies ranges from 0.57 to 0.67, with relatively little variation from company to company. Palisades' debt ratio indicates a fairly low-risk position compared with the industry average debt ratio of 0.64.

✔ Starter 18-7

Times-Interest-Earned Ratio
Ratio of income from operations to interest expense. Measures the number of times that operating income can cover interest expense. Also called the **interest-coverage ratio**.

TIMES-INTEREST-EARNED RATIO The debt ratio says nothing about ability to pay interest expense. Analysts use the **times-interest-earned ratio** to relate income to interest expense. This ratio is also called the **interest-coverage ratio.** It measures the number of times operating income can cover interest expense. A high interest-coverage ratio indicates ease in paying interest expense; a low ratio suggests difficulty.

To compute this ratio, we divide income from operations (operating income) by interest expense. Calculation of Palisades' times-interest-earned ratio follows.

Formula	Palisades' Times-Interest-Earned Ratio 20X5	20X4	Industry Average
$\text{Times-interest-earned ratio} = \dfrac{\text{Income from operations}}{\text{Interest expense}}$	$\dfrac{\$101{,}000}{\$24{,}000} = 4.21$	$\dfrac{\$57{,}000}{\$14{,}000} = 4.07$	2.80

The company's times-interest-earned ratio of around 4.00 is significantly better than the average for furniture retailers. The norm for U.S. business, as reported by Risk Management Association, falls in the range of 2.0 to 3.0. Based on its debt ratio and its times-interest-earned ratio, Palisades Furniture appears to have little difficulty *servicing its debt*, that is, paying liabilities.

Measuring Profitability

The fundamental goal of business is to earn a profit. Ratios that measure profitability are reported in the business press and discussed on Money Line. We examine four profitability measures.

Rate of Return on Net Sales
Ratio of net income to net sales. A measure of profitability. Also called **return on sales**.

RATE OF RETURN ON NET SALES In business, the term *return* is used broadly as a measure of profitability. Consider a ratio called the **rate of return on net sales**, or simply **return on sales**. (The word *net* is usually omitted for convenience, even though net sales is used to compute the ratio.) This ratio shows the percentage of each sales dollar earned as net income. Palisades Furniture's rate of return on sales follows.

Formula	Palisades' Rate of Return on Sales 20X5	20X4	Industry Average
$\text{Rate of return on sales} = \dfrac{\text{Net income}}{\text{Net sales}}$	$\dfrac{\$48{,}000}{\$858{,}000} = 0.056$	$\dfrac{\$26{,}000}{\$803{,}000} = 0.032$	0.008

Companies strive for a high rate of return on sales. The higher the rate of return, the more sales dollars are providing profit. The increase in Palisades Furniture's return on sales is significant and identifies the company as more successful than the average furniture store. Compare Palisades' rate of return on sales to the rates earned by some leading companies in other industries:

Company	Rate of Return on Sales
eBay	0.121
Bristol-Myers Squibb	0.114
Wal-Mart	0.031

RATE OF RETURN ON TOTAL ASSETS The **rate of return on total assets**, or simply **return on assets**, measures success in using assets to earn a profit. → Two groups finance a company's assets. Creditors have loaned money to the company, and they earn interest. Shareholders have invested in stock, and their return is the company's net income.

← *We first discussed the rate of return on total assets in Chapter 13, page 521.*

Rate of Return on Total Assets
Net income plus interest expense, divided by average total assets. This ratio measures a company's success in using its assets to earn income for the persons who finance the business. Also called **return on assets.**

The sum of interest expense and net income is thus the return to the two groups that have financed the company's assets. Computation of the return-on-assets ratio for Palisades Furniture follows.

Formula	Palisades' 20X5 Rate of Return on Total Assets	Industry Average
$\text{Rate of return on assets} = \dfrac{\text{Net income} + \text{Interest expense}}{\text{Average total assets}}$	$\dfrac{\$48{,}000 + \$24{,}000}{\$715{,}500} = 0.101$	0.078

Average total assets is the average of beginning and ending total assets from the comparative balance sheet: ($644,000 + $787,000)/2 = $715,500. Compare Palisades Furniture's rate of return on assets with the rates of some other companies:

Company	Rate of Return on Assets
General Electric	0.029
Procter & Gamble	0.116
Dell Computer	0.127

RATE OF RETURN ON COMMON STOCKHOLDERS' EQUITY A popular measure of profitability is **rate of return on common stockholders' equity**, often shortened to **return on equity**. → This ratio shows the relationship between net income and common stockholders' equity—how much income is earned for every $1 invested by the common shareholders.

← *We examined this ratio in detail in Chapter 13. For a review, see page 522.*

Rate of Return on Common Stockholders' Equity
Net income minus preferred dividends, divided by average common stockholders' equity. A measure of profitability. Also called **return on equity**.

To compute this ratio, we first subtract preferred dividends from net income to get net income available to the common stockholders. We then divide net income available to common stockholders by average common equity during the year. Common equity is total stockholders' equity minus preferred equity. The 20X5 rate of return on common stockholders' equity for Palisades Furniture follows.

Formula	Palisades' 20X5 Rate of Return on Common Stockholders' Equity	Industry Average
$\text{Rate of return on common stockholders' equity} = \dfrac{\text{Net income} - \text{Preferred dividends}}{\text{Average common stockholders' equity}}$	$\dfrac{\$48{,}000 - \$0}{\$338{,}000} = 0.142$	0.121

Average equity is the average of the beginning and ending balances [($356,000 + $320,000)/2 = $338,000]. Observe that Palisades' return on equity (0.142) is higher than its return on assets (0.101). This difference results from borrowing at one rate—say, 8%—and investing the funds to earn a higher rate, such as the firm's 14.2% return on equity. This practice is called **trading on the equity**, or using **leverage**. It is directly related to the debt ratio. The higher the debt ratio, the higher the leverage. Companies that finance operations with debt are said to *leverage* their positions.

Trading on the Equity
Earning more income on borrowed money than the related interest expense, thereby increasing the earnings for the owners of the business. Also called **leverage**.

Leverage usually increases profitability, but not always. Leverage can have a negative impact on profitability. Therefore, leverage is a double-edged sword, increasing profits during good times but compounding losses during bad times. Compare Palisades Furniture's rate of return on common stockholders' equity with the rates of some leading companies.

✔ Starter 18-8

Company	Rate of Return on Common Equity
General Electric (GE)	0.26
Procter & Gamble (P&G).	0.65
Dell Computer	0.35

Palisades Furniture is not as profitable as these leading companies. A return on equity of 15% to 20% year after year is considered good in most industries. GE, P&G, and Dell are exceptional performers. Palisades Furniture is okay.

Stop & Think

For an average company, rank the three rates of return from highest to lowest. Palisades Furniture is typical.

Answer:

1. Rate of return on common stockholders' equity
2. Rate of return on assets
3. Rate of return on net sales

Chapter 14 provides detailed treatment of EPS.

Earnings per Share (EPS) Amount of a company's net income for each share of its outstanding common stock.

Earnings per Share of Common Stock *Earnings per share of common stock*, or simply **earnings per share (EPS)**, is perhaps the most widely quoted of all financial statistics. EPS is the only ratio that must appear on the face of the income statement. EPS is the amount of net income earned for each share of the company's outstanding *common* stock.

Earnings per share is computed by dividing net income available to common stockholders by the number of common shares outstanding during the year. Preferred dividends are subtracted from net income because the preferred stockholders have a prior claim to dividends. Palisades Furniture, Inc., has no preferred stock outstanding and no preferred dividends. The firm's EPS for 20X5 and 20X4 follow (Palisades had 10,000 shares of common stock outstanding throughout 20X4 and 20X5).

	Palisades' Earnings per Share	
Formula	20X5	20X4
Earnings per share of common stock $= \dfrac{\text{Net income} - \text{Preferred dividends}}{\text{Number of shares of common stock outstanding}}$	$\dfrac{\$48{,}000 - \$0}{10{,}000} = \$4.80$	$\dfrac{\$26{,}000 - \$0}{10{,}000} = \$2.60$

Palisades Furniture's EPS increased 85%. Its stockholders should not expect this big a boost in EPS every year. Most companies strive to increase EPS by 10% to 15% annually, and leading companies do so. But even the most successful companies have an occasional bad year.

Analyzing Stock Investments

Investors purchase stock to earn a return on their investment. This return consists of two parts: (1) gains (or losses) from selling the stock at a price above or below purchase price and (2) dividends. The ratios we examine in this section help analysts evaluate stock in terms of market price or dividends.

PRICE/EARNINGS RATIO The **price/earnings ratio** is the ratio of the market price of a share of common stock to the company's earnings per share. It shows the market price of $1 of earnings. This ratio, abbreviated P/E, appears in *The Wall Street Journal* stock listings. P/E ratios play an important part in decisions to buy, hold, and sell stocks.

Price/Earnings Ratio
Ratio of the market price of a share of common stock to the company's earnings per share. Measures the value that the stock market places on $1 of a company's earnings.

Calculations for the P/E ratios of Palisades Furniture, Inc., follow. The market price of its common stock was $60 at the end of 20X5 and $35 at the end of 20X4. These prices can be obtained from a financial publication, a stockbroker, or the company's Web site.

	Palisades' Price/Earnings Ratio	
Formula	**20X5**	**20X4**
P/E ratio = $\dfrac{\text{Market price per share of common stock}}{\text{Earnings per share}}$	$\dfrac{\$60.00}{\$4.80} = 12.5$	$\dfrac{\$35.00}{\$2.60} = 13.5$

Palisades Furniture's P/E ratio of 12.5 means that the company's stock is selling at 12.5 times earnings. The decline from the 20X4 P/E ratio of 13.5 is no cause for alarm because the market price of the stock is not under Palisades Furniture's control. Net income is more controllable, and net income increased during 20X5.

✔ **Starter 18-9**

DIVIDEND YIELD **Dividend yield** is the ratio of dividends per share to the stock's market price per share. This ratio measures the percentage of a stock's market value that is returned annually as dividends. *Preferred* stockholders, who invest primarily to receive dividends, pay special attention to dividend yield.

Dividend Yield
Ratio of dividends per share of stock to the stock's market price per share. Tells the percentage of a stock's market value that the company returns to stockholders annually as dividends.

Palisades Furniture paid annual cash dividends of $1.20 per share of common stock in 20X5 and $1.00 in 20X4, and market prices of the company's common stock were $60 in 20X5 and $35 in 20X4. The firm's dividend yields on common stock follow.

	Dividend Yield on Palisades' Common Stock	
Formula	**20X5**	**20X4**
Dividend yield on common stock* = $\dfrac{\text{Dividend per share of common stock}}{\text{Market price per share of common stock}}$	$\dfrac{\$1.20}{\$60.00} = .020$	$\dfrac{\$1.00}{\$35.00} = .029$

*Dividend yields may also be calculated for preferred stock.

An investor who buys Palisades Furniture common stock for $60 can expect to receive 2% of the investment annually in the form of cash dividends.

Accounting.com

Expedia.com: Making Investors Happy and Rivals Scared

For an online travel stock, you might turn to the financial pages of a newspaper. The price/earnings (P/E) ratio of online travel giant **Expedia** was 67 in the first quarter of 2003. That means that one share of Expedia stock, valued at $63, was selling at 67 times its earnings per share. A P/E ratio of 67 is very high indeed. By contrast, the P/E ratio of competitor **Sabre Holdings**, Travelocity's owner, was only 10. Why the big difference between these similar companies?

Expedia is doing 55% more business than Travelocity. Why is Expedia so far ahead? Consider the story behind the company's financials: "Our big fat hairy dream is to be the largest seller of travel in the world. . . ," said Richard Barton, Expedia's former CEO.

Profit margins on airline tickets are razor-thin. So, unlike rivals, Expedia doesn't rely on airline bookings. It has expanded into hotel reservations and custom vacation packages, which earn higher profits. In the hotel market, Expedia was not content with the usual 10% commission on reservations. Barton bought hotel rooms at wholesale prices, marked them up as much as 26%, and then sold the rooms to consumers. A 26% markup beats a 10% markup any day.

Based on: Timothy J. Mullaney, "Expedia: Changing Pilots in Mid-Climb," *Business Week*, February 24, 2003, pp. 120–124. Kathy Bergen, "Air-Only Emphasis Trips Up Travel Sites: Online Firms Find Package Deals More Profitable," *Chicago Tribune*, December 1, 2002, p. 5-1. Andrew Chaikivsky, "The Best & Brightest: Business—Richard Barton, CEO, Expedia," *Esquire*, December 2002, p. 177.

Book Value per Share of Common Stock
Common stockholders' equity divided by the number of shares of common stock outstanding. The recorded amount for each share of common stock outstanding.

BOOK VALUE PER SHARE OF COMMON STOCK **Book value per share of common stock** is simply common equity divided by the number of common shares outstanding. Common equity equals total stockholders' equity less preferred equity. Palisades Furniture has no preferred stock outstanding. Its book-value-per-share-of-common-stock ratios follow (10,000 shares of common stock were outstanding).

Formula		Book Value per Share of Palisades' Common Stock	
		20X5	20X4
Book value per share of common stock	= (Total stockholders' equity – Preferred equity) / Number of shares of common stock outstanding	($356,000 – $0) / 10,000 = $35.60	($320,000 – $0) / 10,000 = $32.00

✔ Starter 18-10

✔ Starter 18-11

See Chapter 13, page 520, for a discussion of market value and book value.

Many experts argue that book value is not useful for investment analysis. It bears no relationship to market value and provides little information beyond stockholders' equity reported on the balance sheet. But some investors base their investment decisions on book value. For example, some investors rank stocks on the basis of the ratio of market price to book value. To these investors, the lower the ratio, the more attractive the stock.

Other Evaluation Tools

- ☐ Horizontal Analysis
- ☐ Vertical Analysis
- ☐ Benchmarking
- ☐ Using Ratios
- ■ Other Evaluation Tools

Economic Value Added

Student Resource CD
EVA

5 *Measure economic value added*

Coca-Cola, Quaker Oats, and other leading companies use **economic value added (EVA®)** to evaluate performance. EVA® measures whether operations have increased stockholder wealth. EVA® can be computed as follows:

$$\text{EVA}^{\circledR} = \text{Net income} + \text{Interest expense} - \text{Capital charge}$$

where

$$\text{Capital charge} = \left(\begin{matrix}\text{Notes}\\\text{payable}\end{matrix} + \begin{matrix}\text{Bonds}\\\text{payable}\end{matrix} + \begin{matrix}\text{Stockholders'}\\\text{equity}\end{matrix}\right) \times \begin{matrix}\text{Cost of}\\\text{capital}\end{matrix}$$

Economic Value Added (EVA®)
EVA = Net income + Interest expense − Capital charge. Used to evaluate a company's operating performance.

Cost of Capital
A weighted average of the returns demanded by the company's stockholders and lenders.

All amounts for the EVA® computation, except the cost of capital, are taken from the financial statements. The **cost of capital** is a weighted average of the returns demanded by the company's stockholders and lenders. The cost of capital varies with the company's level of risk. For example, stockholders and lenders would demand a higher return from a start-up company than from Coca-Cola because the new company is more risky. A new company would thus have a higher cost of capital than Coca-Cola. In the following discussions we assume a value for the cost of capital (such as 10%, 12%, or 15%).

The idea behind EVA® is that the returns to the company's stockholders (net income) and to its creditors (interest expense) should exceed the company's capital charge. The **capital charge** is the amount that investors *charge* for the use of their money. A positive EVA® amount suggests an increase in stockholder wealth, and the company's stock should remain attractive. If EVA® goes negative, stockholders probably will be unhappy and sell the stock, resulting in a decrease in the stock price.

Capital Charge
The amount that stockholders and lenders charge a company for the use of their money. Calculated as (Notes payable + Loans payable + Long-term debt + Stockholders' equity) × Cost of capital.

The Coca-Cola Company is a leading user of EVA.® Coca-Cola's EVA® for 2002 can be computed as follows, assuming a 10% cost of capital for the company (dollar amounts in millions):

$$\begin{aligned}
\text{Cola-Cola's EVA}^{\circledR} &= \begin{matrix}\text{Net}\\\text{income}\end{matrix} + \begin{matrix}\text{Interest}\\\text{expense}\end{matrix} - \left(\begin{matrix}\text{Loans and}\\\text{notes payable}\end{matrix} + \begin{matrix}\text{Long-term}\\\text{debt}\end{matrix} + \begin{matrix}\text{Stockholders'}\\\text{equity}\end{matrix}\right) \times \begin{matrix}\text{Cost of}\\\text{capital}\end{matrix}\\
&= \$3{,}050 + \$199 - [(\$2{,}475 + \$2{,}701 + \$11{,}800) \times 0.10]\\
&= \$3{,}249 - \$16{,}976 \times 0.10\\
&= \$3{,}249 - \$1{,}698\\
&= \$1{,}551
\end{aligned}$$

By this measure, Coca-Cola's operations during 2002 added $1.551 billion ($1,551 million) of value to its stockholders' wealth after meeting the company's capital charge. This performance is outstanding.

✔ Starter 18-12

Red Flags in Financial Statement Analysis

Another way to analyze a company's situation is to look for *red flags* that may signal financial trouble. Recent accounting scandals highlight the importance of these red flags. If the following conditions are present, the company may be too risky.

- ***Earnings Problems.*** Have income from continuing operations and net income decreased significantly for several years in a row? Has income turned into a loss? Most companies cannot survive consecutive loss years.
- ***Decreased Cash Flow.*** Cash flow validates earnings. Is cash flow from operations consistently lower than net income? Are the sales of plant assets a major source of cash? If so, the company may face a cash shortage.

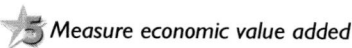

- ***Too Much Debt.*** How does the company's debt ratio compare to that of major competitors and to the industry average? If the debt ratio is much higher than average, the company may be unable to pay its debts.
- ***Inability to Collect Receivables.*** Are days' sales in receivables growing faster than for other companies in the industry? A cash shortage may be looming.
- ***Buildup of Inventories.*** Is inventory turnover slowing down? If so, the company may be unable to sell goods, or it may be overstating inventory. Recall from the cost-of-goods-sold model that one of the easiest ways to overstate net income is to overstate ending inventory.
- ***Movement of Sales, Inventory, and Receivables.*** Sales, receivables, and inventory generally move together. Increased sales lead to higher receivables and require more inventory to meet demand. Strange movements among these items may spell trouble.

Do these red flags reveal significant difficulties at Bristol-Myers Squibb (BMS)? Maybe so. Net income took a sharp downturn in 2002. Cash flow from operations was also down a lot. But receivables and inventories weren't up too much, and BMS's debt ratio isn't too high. Overall, we get mixed signals about BMS's financial health. Wall Street doesn't like mixed signals about a company. That's probably why the stock market didn't go for the company's performance in 2002.

Analyzing Nonfinancial Data

There is more to analyzing financial statements than performing horizontal and vertical analysis and computing the standard ratios. The nonquantitative parts of the annual report may hold more important information than the financial statements. For example, the president's letter may describe a turnover of top managers. The management discussion and analysis will reveal management's opinion of the year's results. And the auditor's report may indicate a major problem with the company. Let's consider each of these parts of a corporate annual report.

President's Letter to the Stockholders The president of the company gives his or her view of the year's results and outlines the direction top management is charting for the company. The most recent annual report of Procter & Gamble described the retirement of the company's chairman of the board and the election of a new chairman. A shift in top management or a major change in the company's direction is important to investors.

Management Discussion and Analysis (MD&A) The people who know the most about a company are its executives. For this reason, stockholders want to know what management thinks about the company's net income (or net loss), cash flows, and financial position. The MD&A section of the annual report discusses *why* net income was up or down, how the company invested the stockholders' money, and plans for future spending. Through the MD&A, investors may learn of the company's plan to discontinue a product line or to expand into new markets. These forward-looking data are not permitted in the historical financial statements, which are based on past transactions.

Auditor Report Both the president's letter and the MD&A express the views of corporate insiders. The financial statements are also produced by the management of the company. These people naturally want to describe the company in a favorable light. Therefore, all the information coming out of the company could be slanted to make the company look good.

Investors are aware of the possibility for management bias in the financial statements. For this reason, the Securities & Exchange Commission, a federal agency, requires that all financial statements of public corporations be audited by independent accountants. The auditors are not employees of the companies they audit. After auditing the Bristol-Myers Squibb (BMS) financial statements, PricewaterhouseCoopers (PwC), an international accounting firm, issued its professional opinion on the BMS statements. PwC stated that the BMS statements agreed with generally accepted accounting principles. This is how investors in the United States and in other developed countries gain assurance that they can rely on a company's financial statements. If the survival of BMS were in doubt, PwC's audit report would alert investors to the difficulty.

The Decision Guidelines summarize the most widely used ratios. The Excel Application Exercise provides an opportunity to apply your understanding of the ratios.

Decision Guidelines

USING RATIOS IN FINANCIAL STATEMENT ANALYSIS

Lane and Kay Collins operate a financial-services firm. They manage other people's money and do most of their own financial-statement analysis. How do they measure companies' ability to pay bills, sell inventory, collect receivables, and so on? They use the standard ratios we have covered throughout this book.

Ratio	Computation	Information Provided
Measuring ability to pay current liabilities:		
1. Current ratio	$\frac{\text{Current assets}}{\text{Current liabilities}}$	Measures ability to pay current liabilities with current assets
2. Acid-test (quick) ratio	$\frac{\text{Cash} + \text{Short-term investments} + \text{Net current receivables}}{\text{Current liabilities}}$	Shows ability to pay all current liabilities if they come due immediately
Measuring ability to sell inventory and collect receivables:		
3. Inventory turnover	$\frac{\text{Cost of goods sold}}{\text{Average inventory}}$	Indicates saleability of inventory—the number of times a company sells its average inventory during a year
4. Accounts receivable turnover	$\frac{\text{Net credit sales}}{\text{Average net accounts receivable}}$	Measures ability to collect cash from customers
5. Days' sales in receivables	$\frac{\text{Average net accounts receivable}}{\text{One day's sales}}$	Shows how many days' sales remain in Accounts Receivable—how many days it takes to collect the average level of receivables
Measuring ability to pay long-term debt:		
6. Debt ratio	$\frac{\text{Total liabilities}}{\text{Total assets}}$	Indicates percentage of assets financed with debt
7. Times-interest-earned ratio	$\frac{\text{Income from operations}}{\text{Interest expense}}$	Measures the number of times operating income can cover interest expense
Measuring profitability:		
8. Rate of return on net sales	$\frac{\text{Net income}}{\text{Net sales}}$	Shows the percentage of each sales dollar earned as net income
9. Rate of return on total assets	$\frac{\text{Net income} + \text{Interest expense}}{\text{Average total assets}}$	Measures how profitably a company uses its assets

Decision Guidelines *(continued)*

Ratio	Computation	Information Provided
10. Rate of return on common stockholders' equity	$\frac{\text{Net income} - \text{Preferred dividends}}{\text{Average common stockholders' equity}}$	Gauges how much income is earned for each dollar invested by common shareholders
11. Earnings per share of common stock	$\frac{\text{Net income} - \text{Preferred dividends}}{\text{Number of shares of common stock outstanding}}$	Gives the amount of net income earned for each share of the company's common stock
Analyzing stock as an investment:		
12. Price/earnings ratio	$\frac{\text{Market price per share of common stock}}{\text{Earnings per share}}$	Indicates the market price of $1 of earnings
13. Dividend yield	$\frac{\text{Annual dividend per share of common (or preferred) stock}}{\text{Market price per share of common (or preferred) stock}}$	Shows the percentage of a stock's market value returned as dividends to stockholders each year
14. Book value per share of common stock	$\frac{\text{Total stockholders' equity} - \text{Preferred equity}}{\text{Number of shares of common stock outstanding}}$	Indicates the recorded accounting amount for each share of common stock outstanding

Excel Application Exercise

Goal: Create an Excel work sheet that calculates financial ratios to compare PepsiCo and Coca-Cola. Then use the results to determine which company has the stronger financial performance.

Scenario: You've saved $5,000 from your summer internship at PepsiCo. You'd like to invest your savings in the stock of your employer, but your parents think the better investment would be stock in Coca-Cola, their favorite brand of soft drink. Before making your purchase, you decide to create an Excel work sheet that compares both companies on several key financial ratios.

Your task is to create an Excel spreadsheet to compare the following ratios for PepsiCo and Coca-Cola.

1. Acid-test (quick) ratio
2. Inventory turnover
3. Debt ratio
4. Return on net sales
5. Price/earnings ratio

When done with the work sheet, answer the following questions:

1. Which company is in a better position to pay all current liabilities if they come due immediately?
2. Which company's inventory is more "saleable"?
3. Which company is financing more of its assets with debt?
4. Which company earned more profit, as a percentage, on each sales dollar?
5. Which company's earnings have a higher market price per dollar of earnings?

Step-by-Step:

1. Locate the data required for each ratio in the annual reports of PepsiCo (www.pepsico.com) and Coca-Cola (www.cocacola.com). *Note:* For fiscal year-end stock prices, go to www.yahoo.com, and then select "Finance." Enter the ticker symbol (PEP for PepsiCo and KO for Coca-Cola), then select "Performance." You should be able to click on "historical prices" to enter the dates for each fiscal year-end.
2. Open a new Excel work sheet.
3. Create a bold-faced heading for your spreadsheet that contains the following:
   a. Chapter 18 Excel Application Exercise
   b. Using Ratios in Financial Statement Analysis
   c. PepsiCo and Coca-Cola Comparison
   d. Today's date
4. In the first column, enter the names of all five ratios. Skip a row between each ratio name.
5. Create bold-faced, underlined column headings for PepsiCo and Coca-Cola. Underneath, enter the "As of" date for the financial statements used in the analysis. (Fiscal year-ends may not match exactly.)
6. Enter the data located in step 1, using the correct ratio formulas found in the Decision Guidelines. For the P/E ratio, use basic EPS in the denominator. Format all cells as necessary.
7. Save your work, and print a copy for your files.

END-OF-CHAPTER *Summary Problem*

The following financial data are adapted from the annual reports of **Gap Inc.**, which operates Gap, Banana Republic, and Old Navy clothing stores:

A+ TIPS
CHECK YOUR RESOURCES

Gap Inc.

Five-Year Selected Financial Data (adapted)
Years Ended January 31,

Operating Results*	2002	2001	2000	1999
Net sales	$13,848	$13,673	$11,635	$9,054
Cost of goods sold	9,704	8,599	6,775	5,318
Interest expense	109	75	45	46
Income from operations	338	1,455	1,817	1,333
Net earnings (net loss)	(8)	877	1,127	824
Cash dividends	76	75	76	77
Financial Position				
Merchandise inventory	1,677	1,904	1,462	1,056
Total assets	7,591	7,012	5,189	3,963
Current ratio	1.48:1	0.95:1	1.25:1	1.20:1
Stockholders' equity	3,010	2,928	2,630	1,574
Average number of shares of common stock outstanding (in thousands)	860	879	895	576

*Dollar amounts are in thousands.

Required

Compute the following ratios for 2000 through 2002, and evaluate Gap's operating results. Are operating results strong or weak? Did they improve or deteriorate during the four-year period? Your analysis will reveal a clear trend.

1. Gross profit percentage
2. Net income as a percentage of sales
3. Earnings per share
4. Inventory turnover
5. Times-interest-earned ratio
6. Rate of return on stockholders' equity

Solution

	2002	2001	2000
1. Gross profit percentage	$\frac{\$13,848 - \$9,704}{\$13,848} = 29.9\%$	$\frac{\$13,673 - \$8,599}{\$13,673} = 37.1\%$	$\frac{\$11,635 - \$6,775}{\$11,635} = 41.8\%$
2. Net income as a percentage of sales	$\frac{\$(8)}{\$13,848} = (.06\%)$	$\frac{\$877}{\$13,673} = 6.4\%$	$\frac{\$1,127}{\$11,635} = 9.7\%$
3. Earnings per share	$\frac{\$(8)}{860} = \$(0.01)$	$\frac{\$877}{879} = \$1.00$	$\frac{\$1,127}{895} = \$1.26$
4. Inventory turnover	$\frac{\$9,704}{(\$1,677 + \$1,904)/2} = 5.4$ times	$\frac{\$8,599}{(\$1,904 + \$1,462)/2} = 5.1$ times	$\frac{\$6,775}{(\$1,462 + \$1,056)/2} = 5.4$ times
5. Times-interest-earned ratio	$\frac{\$338}{\$109} = 3.1$ times	$\frac{\$1,455}{\$75} = 19.4$ times	$\frac{\$1,817}{\$45} = 40.4$ times
6. Rate of return on stockholders' equity	$\frac{\$(8)}{(\$3,010 + \$2,928)/2} = (0.3\%)$	$\frac{\$877}{(\$2,928 + \$2,630)/2} = 31.6\%$	$\frac{\$1,127}{(\$2,630 + \$1,574)/2} = 53.6\%$

Evaluation: During this period, Gap's operating results deteriorated on all these measures except inventory turnover. The gross profit percentage is down sharply, as are the times-interest-earned ratio and all the return measures. From these data it is clear that Gap could sell its merchandise, but not at the markups the company enjoyed in the past. The final result, in 2002, was a net loss for the year.

REVIEW Financial Statement Analysis

Quick Check

The **Coca-Cola Company** reported these figures (adapted and in millions):

	2002	2001
Cash and equivalents	$ 2,345	$ 1,934
Receivables	2,097	1,882
Inventory	1,294	1,055
Prepaid expenses	1,616	2,300
Total current assets	7,352	7,171
Other assets	17,149	15,246
Total assets	$24,501	$22,417
Total current liabilities	$ 7,341	$ 8,429
Long-term liabilities	5,360	2,622
Common equity	11,800	11,366
Total liabilities and equity	$24,501	$22,417

	2002
Sales	$19,564
Cost of sales	7,105
Operating expenses	7,001
Operating income	5,458
Interest expense	199
Other expense	2,209
Net income	$ 3,050

1. Horizontal analysis of Coca-Cola's balance sheet for 2002 would report
   - a. 21% increase in Cash
   - b. Cash as 9.6% of total assets
   - c. Current ratio of 1.00
   - d. Inventory turnover of 6 times
2. Vertical analysis of Coca-Cola's balance sheet for 2002 would report
   - a. 21% increase in Cash
   - b. Cash as 9.6% of total assets
   - c. Current ratio of 1.00
   - d. Inventory turnover of 6 times
3. A common-size income statement for Coca-Cola would report (amounts rounded)
   - a. Sales of 100%
   - b. Cost of sales at 36%
   - c. Net income of 16%
   - d. All the above
4. Which statement best describes Coca-Cola's acid-test ratio?
   - a. Greater than 1
   - b. Equal to 1
   - c. Less than 1
   - d. None of the above
5. Coca-Cola's inventory turnover during 2002 was
   - a. 5 times
   - b. 6 times
   - c. 7 times
   - d. Not determinable from the data given
6. During 2002, Coca-Cola's days' sales in receivables ratio was
   - a. 30 days
   - b. 35 days
   - c. 37 days
   - d. 39 days
7. Which measure expresses Coca-Cola's times-interest-earned ratio?
   - a. 15 times
   - b. 20 times
   - c. 27 times
   - d. 51.8%
8. Coca-Cola's return on common stockholders' equity can be described as
   - a. Strong
   - b. Good
   - c. Average
   - d. Weak
9. The company has 2,500 million shares of common stock outstanding. What is Coca-Cola's earnings per share?
   - a. 2.04
   - b. 3.6 times
   - c. $3.05
   - d. $1.22
10. Coca-Cola's stock has traded recently around $44 per share. Use your answer to question 9 to measure the company's price/earnings ratio.
    - a. 69
    - b. 44
    - c. 1.00
    - d. 36

Accounting Vocabulary

accounts receivable turnover (p. 718)
acid-test ratio (p. 717)
benchmarking (p. 712)
book value per share of common stock (p. 724)
capital charge (p. 725)
collection period (p. 718)
common-size statement (p. 711)
cost of capital (p. 725)
current ratio (p. 715)
days' sales in receivables (p. 718)
debt ratio (p. 719)
dividend yield (p. 723)
earnings per share (EPS) (p. 722)
economic value added (EVA)® (p. 725)
horizontal analysis (p. 707)
interest-coverage ratio (p. 720)
inventory turnover (p. 717)
leverage (p. 721)
price/earnings ratio (p. 723)
quick ratio (p. 717)
rate of return on common stockholders' equity (p. 721)
rate of return on net sales (p. 720)
return on assets (p. 721)
return on equity (p. 721)
return on sales (p. 720)
rate of return on total assets (p. 721)
return on stockholders' equity (p. 721)
times-interest-earned ratio (p. 720)
trading on the equity (p. 721)
trend percentages (p. 709)
vertical analysis (p. 709)
working capital (p. 715)

ASSESS *Your Progress*

Starters

A+ online homework

See *www.prenhall.com/horngren* for selected Starters, Exercises, and Problems.

Horizontal analysis of revenues and gross profit
(Obj. 1)

S18-1 **Nike, Inc.**, reported the following on its 2002 comparative income statement:

(in millions)	2002	2001	2000
Revenues	$9,893	$9,489	$8,995
Cost of sales	6,005	5,785	5,404

Perform a horizontal analysis of revenues and gross profit—both in dollar amounts and in percentages—for 2002 and 2001.

Trend analysis of revenues and net income
(Obj. 1)

S18-2 **Nike, Inc.**, reported the following revenues and net income amounts:

(in millions)	2002	2001	2000	1999
Revenues	$9,893	$9,489	$8,995	$8,777
Net income	664	590	579	451

1. Show Nike's trend percentages for revenues and net income. Use 1999 as the base year.
2. Which measure increased faster during 2000–2002?

Vertical analysis to correct a cash shortage
(Obj. 2)

S18-3 Perfect 10 Sporting Goods reported the following amounts on its balance sheets at December 31, 20X6, 20X5, and 20X4:

	20X6	20X5	20X4
Cash and receivables	$ 38,000	$ 30,000	$ 25,000
Inventory	48,000	36,000	24,000
Property, plant, and equipment, net	96,000	88,000	87,000
Total assets	$182,000	$154,000	$136,000

Sales and profits are high. Nevertheless, the company is experiencing a cash shortage. Perform a vertical analysis of Perfect 10 assets at the end of years 20X6, 20X5, and 20X4. Use the analysis to explain the reason for the cash shortage.

Common-size income statements of two leading companies
(Obj. 3)

S18-4 **Nike, Inc.,** and **Home Depot** are leaders in their respective industries. Compare the two companies by converting their income statements (adapted) to common size.

(in millions)	Nike	Home Depot
Net sales	$9,489	$19,536
Cost of goods sold	5,785	14,101
Other expense	3,114	4,497
Net income	$ 590	$ 938

Which company earns more net income? Which company's net income is a higher percentage of its net sales? Which company is more profitable? Explain your answer.

Evaluating a company's current ratio
(Obj. 4)

S18-5 Use the **Bristol-Myers Squibb** balance sheet data in Exhibit 18-3, page 708.

1. Compute the company's current ratio at December 31, 2002 and 2001.
2. Did Bristol-Myers Squibb's current ratio value improve, deteriorate, or hold steady during 2002?

Computing inventory turnover and days' sales in receivables
(Obj. 4)

S18-6 Use the **Bristol-Myers Squibb** 2002 income statement (page 708) and balance sheet (page 708) to compute the following (amounts in millions):

a. The rate of inventory turnover for 2002. Inventory was $1,573 at the end of 2002 and $1,699 at the end of 2001.
b. Days' sales in average receivables during 2002. All sales are made on account. Receivables were $2,968 at the end of 2002 and $3,992 at the end of 2001. (Round dollar amounts to one decimal place.)

Measuring ability to pay liabilities
(Obj. 4)

S18-7 Use the financial statements of **Bristol-Myers Squibb Company** (page 708).

1. Compute the debt ratio at December 31, 2002.
2. Is Bristol-Myers Squibb's ability to pay its liabilities strong or weak? Explain your reasoning.

Measuring profitability
(Obj. 4)

S18-8 Use the financial statements of **Bristol-Myers Squibb Company** (page 710) to determine or, if necessary, to compute these profitability measures for 2002.

a. Rate of return on net sales.
b. Rate of return on total assets. Interest expense for 2002 was $410 million.
c. Rate of return on common stockholders' equity.

Are these rates of return strong or weak? Explain.

Computing EPS and the price/earnings ratio
(Obj. 4)

S18-9 The annual report of **Dell Computer Corporation** for fiscal year 2002 included the following items (in millions):

Preferred stock outstanding	$0
Net income	$1,246
Number of shares of common stock outstanding	2,602

1. Compute earnings per share (EPS) for Dell. Round to the nearest cent.
2. Compute Dell's price/earnings ratio. The price of a share of Dell stock is $26.85.

S18-10 A skeleton of **Campbell Soup Company's** income statement (as adapted) appears as follows (amounts in millions):

Using ratio data to reconstruct an income statement
(Obj. 4)

Income Statement

Net sales	$7,278
Cost of goods sold	(a)
Selling and administrative expenses	1,716
Interest expense	(b)
Other expenses	151
Income before taxes	1,042
Income tax expense	(c)
Net income	$ (d)

Use the following ratio data to complete Campbell Soup's income statement:

a. Inventory turnover was 5.53 (beginning inventory was $787; ending inventory was $755).
b. Rate of return on sales is 0.0959.

S18-11 A skeleton of **Campbell Soup Company's** balance sheet (as adapted) appears as follows (amounts in millions):

Using ratio data to reconstruct a balance sheet
(Obj. 4)

Balance Sheet

Cash	$ 53	Total current liabilities	$2,164
Receivables	(a)	Long-term debt	(e)
Inventories	755	Other long-term liabilities	826
Prepaid expenses	(b)		
Total current assets	(c)		
Plant assets, net	(d)		
Other assets	2,150	Stockholders' equity	2,468
Total assets	$6,315	Total liabilities and equity	$ (f)

Use the following ratio data to complete Campbell Soup's balance sheet:

a. Current ratio is 0.7306.
b. Acid-test ratio is 0.3161.

S18-12 Use the financial statements of **Bristol-Myers Squibb** (page 710).

Measuring economic value added
(Obj. 5)

1. Compute economic value added (EVA®) by the company's operations during 2002. Use beginning-of-year amounts to compute the capital charge. Interest expense was $410 million, and interest-bearing debt totaled $6,411 million. Assume that the company's cost of capital is 12%. Round all amounts to the nearest million dollars.
2. Should the company's stockholders be happy with the EVA® for 2002?

Exercises

A+ online homework

E18-1 What were the dollar amount of change and the percentage of change in Micron Electronics' working capital during 2005 and 2006? Is this trend favorable or unfavorable?

Computing year-to-year changes in working capital
(Obj. 1)

	2006	2005	2004
Total current assets	$302,000	$290,000	$280,000
Total current liabilities	150,000	157,000	140,000

Horizontal analysis of an income statement
(Obj. 1)

Student Resource CD
spreadsheet

E18-2 Prepare a horizontal analysis of the following comparative income statement of Newsletter E-Mail, Inc. Round percentage changes to the nearest one-tenth percent (three decimal places):

Newsletter E-Mail, Inc.
Comparative Income Statement
Years Ended December 31, 2005 and 2004

	2005	2004
Total revenue	$430,000	$373,000
Expenses:		
Cost of goods sold	$202,000	$188,000
Selling and general expenses	98,000	93,000
Interest expense	7,000	4,000
Income tax expense	42,000	37,000
Total expenses	349,000	322,000
Net income	$ 81,000	$ 51,000

Why did net income increase by a higher percentage than total revenues during 2005?

Computing trend percentages
(Obj. 1)

E18-3 Compute trend percentages for Metro Graphics' net revenues and net income for the following 5-year period, using year 1 as the base year. Round to the nearest full percent.

(in thousands)	Year 5	Year 4	Year 3	Year 2	Year 1
Total revenue	$1,418	$1,187	$1,106	$1,009	$1,043
Net income	132	114	83	71	85

Which grew faster during the period, total revenue or net income?

Vertical analysis of a balance sheet
(Obj. 2)

E18-4 Consolidated Water System of Sierra, Nevada, has requested that you perform a vertical analysis of its balance sheet to determine the component percentages of its assets, liabilities, and stockholders' equity.

Consolidated Water System of Sierra, Nevada
Balance Sheet
December 31, 20X5

Assets	
Total current assets	$ 42,000
Property, plant, and equipment, net	247,000
Other assets	35,000
Total assets	$324,000
Liabilities	
Total current liabilities	$ 48,000
Long-term debt	108,000
Total liabilities	156,000
Stockholders' Equity	
Total stockholders' equity	168,000
Total liabilities and stockholders' equity	$324,000

Preparing a common-size income statement
(Obj. 3)

Student Resource CD
spreadsheet

E18-5 Prepare a comparative common-size income statement for Newsletter E-Mail, Inc., using the 2005 and 2004 data of Exercise 18-2 and rounding percentages to one-tenth percent (three decimal places). To an investor, how does 2005 compare with 2004? Explain your reasoning.

E18-6 The financial statements of Cunningham Financial Group include the following items:

Computing five ratios
(Obj. 4)

Student ResourceCD
spreadsheet

	Current Year	Preceding Year
Balance sheet:		
Cash	$ 17,000	$ 22,000
Short-term investments	11,000	26,000
Net receivables	64,000	73,000
Inventory	77,000	71,000
Prepaid expenses	16,000	8,000
Total current assets	$185,000	$200,000
Total current liabilities	$131,000	$ 91,000
Income statement:		
Net credit sales	$454,000	
Cost of goods sold	297,000	

Required

Compute the following ratios for the current year:

a. Current ratio
b. Acid-test ratio
c. Inventory turnover
d. Days' sales in average receivables

E18-7 Pinnacle Market Research Corporation has asked you to determine whether the company's ability to pay current liabilities and long-term debts improved or deteriorated during 20X4. To answer this question, compute ratios for 20X4 and 20X3:

Analyzing the ability to pay current liabilities
(Obj. 4)

Student ResourceCD
spreadsheet

a. Current ratio
b. Acid-test ratio
c. Debt ratio
d. Times-interest-earned ratio

Summarize the results of your analysis in a written report.

	20X4	20X3
Cash	$ 61,000	$ 47,000
Short-term investments	28,000	—
Net receivables	102,000	116,000
Inventory	237,000	272,000
Total assets	543,000	489,000
Total current liabilities	275,000	221,000
Long-term debt	46,000	52,000
Income from operations	165,000	158,000
Interest expense	48,000	39,000

E18-8 Compute four ratios that measure ability to earn profits for Save the Planet's Air, Inc., whose comparative income statement follows:

Analyzing profitability
(Obj. 4)

Save the Planet's Air, Inc.
Comparative Income Statement
Years Ended December 31, 20X6 and 20X5

Dollars in Thousands	20X6	20X5
Net sales	$174,000	$158,000
Cost of goods sold	93,000	86,000
Gross profit	81,000	72,000
Selling and general expenses	46,000	41,000
Income from operations	35,000	31,000
Interest expense	9,000	10,000
Income before income tax	26,000	21,000
Income tax expense	8,000	8,000
Net income	$ 18,000	$ 13,000

(continued)

Additional data:

	20X6	20X5	20X4
Total assets	$204,000	$191,000	$171,000
Common stockholders' equity	$ 96,000	$ 89,000	$ 79,000
Preferred dividends	$ 3,000	$ 3,000	$ 0
Common shares outstanding during the year	20,000	20,000	18,000

Did the company's operating performance improve or deteriorate during 20X6?

Evaluating a stock as an investment
(Obj. 4)

E18-9 Evaluate the common stock of Friedman Energy Company as an investment. Specifically, use the three stock ratios to determine whether the common stock has increased or decreased in attractiveness during the past year.

	20X4	20X3
Net income	$ 58,000	$ 55,000
Dividends—common	20,000	20,000
Dividends—preferred	12,000	12,000
Total stockholders' equity at year-end (includes 80,000 shares of common stock)	580,000	500,000
Preferred stock, 6%	200,000	200,000
Market price per share of common stock	$ 11.50	$ 7.75

Using economic value added to measure corporate performance
(Obj. 5)

E18-10 Two companies with very different economic-value-added (EVA®) profiles are **Oracle Corporation**, the world's second-largest software company, and **Wells Fargo & Company**, the nationwide banking conglomerate. Adapted versions of the two companies' financial statements are presented here (in millions):

	Oracle	Wells Fargo
Balance sheet data:		
Total assets	$11,030	$307,569
Interest-bearing debt	$ 304	$195,781
All other liabilities	4,448	84,574
Stockholders' equity	6,278	27,214
Total liabilities and equity	$11,030	$307,569
Income statement data:		
Total revenue	$10,860	$ 26,891
Interest expense	24	6,741
All other expenses	8,275	16,727
Net income	$ 2,561	$ 3,423

Required

Compute the EVA® for each company and then decide which company's stock you would rather hold as an investment. Assume Oracle's cost of capital is 15%, and Wells Fargo's is 5%. Round to the nearest $1 million.

Using ratio data to reconstruct a company's balance sheet
(Obj. 4)

E18-11 The following data (dollar amounts in millions) are adapted from the financial statements of **Wal-Mart Stores, Inc.**

Total current assets	$ 10,196
Accumulated depreciation	$ 1,448
Total liabilities	$ 11,806
Preferred stock	$ 0
Debt ratio	60.342%
Current ratio	1.51

Required

Complete the following condensed balance sheet. Report amounts to the nearest $ 1 million.

Current assets		$?
Property, plant, and equipment	$?	
Less Accumulated depreciation	(?)	?
Total assets		$?
Current liabilities		$?
Long-term liabilities		?
Stockholders' equity		?
Total liabilities and stockholders' equity		$?

Problems

(Group A)

online homework

P18-1A Net sales, net income, and total assets for XT Communications, Inc., for a four-year period follow:

Trend percentages, return on sales, and comparison with the industry
(Obj. 1, 4)

(in thousands)	20X8	20X7	20X6	20X5
Net sales	$357	$313	$266	$281
Net income	29	21	11	18
Total assets	286	254	209	197

Required

1. Compute trend percentages for each item for 20X6 through 20X8. Use 20X5 as the base year and round to the nearest percentage.
2. Compute the rate of return on net sales for 20X6 through 20X8, rounding to three decimal places. In the telecommunications industry, rates above 5% are considered good, and rates above 7% are outstanding.
3. How does XT Communications' return on net sales compare with that of the industry?

P18-2A Top managers of Escalade Technology Corporation have asked your help in comparing the company's profit performance and financial position with the average for the cell phone industry. The accountant has given you the company's income statement and balance sheet and also the following data for the industry:

Common-size statements, analysis of profitability, and comparison with the industry
(Obj. 2, 3, 4)

Escalade Technology Corporation
Income Statement Compared with Industry Average
Year Ended December 31, 20X5

	Escalade	Industry Average
Net sales	$957,000	100.0%
Cost of goods sold	652,000	65.9
Gross profit	305,000	34.1
Operating expenses	204,000	28.1
Operating income	101,000	6.0
Other expenses	13,000	0.4
Net income	$ 88,000	5.6%

Escalade Technology Corporation
Balance Sheet Compared with Industry Average
December 31, 20X5

	Escalade	Industry Average
Current assets	$486,000	74.4%
Fixed assets, net	117,000	20.0
Intangible assets, net	24,000	0.6
Other assets	3,000	5.0
Total	$630,000	100.0%
Current liabilities	$246,000	45.6%
Long-term liabilities	136,000	19.0
Stockholders' equity	248,000	35.4
Total	$630,000	100.0%

Required

1. Prepare a common-size income statement and balance sheet for Escalade. The first column of each statement should present Escalade's common-size statement, and the second column should show the industry averages.

2. For the profitability analysis, compute Escalade's (a) ratio of gross profit to net sales, (b) ratio of operating income to net sales, and (c) ratio of net income to net sales. Compare these figures with the industry averages. Is Escalade's profit performance better or worse than the average for the industry?
3. For the analysis of financial position, compute Escalade's (a) ratios of current assets and current liabilities to total assets and (b) ratio of stockholders' equity to total assets. Compare these ratios with the industry averages. Is Escalade's financial position better or worse than average for the industry?

Effects of business transactions on selected ratios
(Obj. 4)

P18-3A Financial statement data on Thunderbird Medical Supply include the following:

Cash	$ 47,000	Accounts payable	$ 96,000
Accounts receivable, net	123,000	Accrued liabilities	50,000
Inventories	289,000	Long-term liabilities	224,000
Total assets	933,000	Net income	119,000
Short-term notes payable	72,000	Common shares outstanding	22,000

Required

1. Compute Thunderbird's current ratio, debt ratio, and earnings per share. Use the following format for your answer:

Requirement 1

Current Ratio	Debt Ratio	Earnings per Share

2. Compute the three ratios after evaluating the effect of each transaction that follows. Consider each transaction *separately*.
   a. Borrowed $27,000 on a long-term note payable.
   b. Issued 10,000 shares of common stock, receiving cash of $108,000.
   c. Purchased merchandise of $48,000 on account, debiting Inventory.
   d. Received cash on account, $6,000.

   Format your answer as follows:

Requirement 2

Transaction Letter	Current Ratio	Debt Ratio	Earnings per Share

Using ratios to evaluate a stock investment
(Obj. 4)

P18-4A Comparative financial statement data of Advanced Automotive Company follow:

Advanced Automotive Company

Comparative Income Statement
Years Ended December 31, 20X6 and 20X5

	20X6	20X5
Net sales	$667,000	$599,000
Cost of goods sold	378,000	283,000
Gross profit	289,000	316,000
Operating expenses	129,000	147,000
Income from operations	160,000	169,000
Interest expense	57,000	41,000
Income before income tax	103,000	128,000
Income tax expense	34,000	53,000
Net income	$ 69,000	$ 75,000

Advanced Automotive Company

Comparative Balance Sheet
December 31, 20X6 and 20X5

	20X6	20X5	20X4*
Current assets:			
Cash	$ 37,000	$ 40,000	
Current receivables, net	208,000	151,000	$138,000
Inventories	352,000	286,000	184,000
Prepaid expenses	5,000	20,000	
Total current assets	602,000	497,000	
Property, plant, and equipment, net	287,000	276,000	
Total assets	$889,000	$773,000	707,000
Total current liabilities	$286,000	$267,000	
Long-term liabilities	245,000	235,000	
Total liabilities	531,000	502,000	
Preferred stockholders' equity, 4%, $20 par	50,000	50,000	
Common stockholders' equity, no par	308,000	221,000	148,000
Total liabilities and stockholders' equity	$889,000	$773,000	

*Selected 20X4 amounts.

Other Information:

1. Market price of Advanced Automotive's common stock: $36.75 at December 31, 20X6, and $50.50 at December 31, 20X5.
2. Common shares outstanding: 15,000 during 20X6 and 14,000 during 20X5.
3. All sales on credit.

Required

1. Compute the following ratios for 20X6 and 20X5:
   a. Current ratio
   b. Inventory turnover
   c. Times-interest-earned ratio
   d. Return on common stockholders' equity
   e. Earnings per share of common stock
   f. Price/earnings ratio
2. Decide whether (a) Advanced's financial position improved or deteriorated during 20X6 and (b) the investment attractiveness of its common stock appears to have increased or decreased.
3. How will what you learned in this problem help you evaluate an investment?

Using ratios to decide between two stock investments; measuring economic value added
(Obj. 4, 5)

P18-5A Assume that you are considering purchasing stock in a company in the music industry. You have narrowed the choice to Blues, Inc., and Sonic Sound Corporation and have assembled the following data:

Selected income-statement data for the current year:

	Blues	Sonic
Net sales (all on credit)	$603,000	$519,000
Cost of goods sold	484,000	387,000
Interest expense	—	8,000
Net income	56,000	38,000

Selected balance-sheet and market-price data at the *end* of the current year:

	Blues	Sonic
Current assets:		
Cash	$ 45,000	$ 39,000
Short-term investments	6,000	13,000
Current receivables, net	169,000	164,000
Inventories	211,000	183,000
Prepaid expenses	19,000	15,000
Total current assets	450,000	414,000
Total assets	974,000	938,000
Total current liabilities	366,000	338,000
Total liabilities	667,000*	691,000*
Common stock, $1 par (150,000 shares)	150,000	
$5 par (20,000 shares)		100,000
Total stockholders' equity	307,000	247,000
Market price per share of common stock	$ 8	$ 47.50

*Includes bonds payable: Blues, $3,000, and Sonic, $303,000.

Selected balance-sheet data at the *beginning* of the current year:

	Blues	Sonic
Current receivables, net	$142,000	$193,000
Inventories	209,000	197,000
Total assets	842,000	909,000
Common stock, $1 par (150,000 shares)	150,000	
$5 par (20,000 shares)		100,000

Your strategy is to invest in companies that have low price/earnings ratios but appear to be in good shape financially. Assume that you have analyzed all other factors and that your decision depends on the results of ratio analysis.

Required

1. Compute the following ratios for both companies for the current year and decide which company's stock better fits your investment strategy.
   - **a.** Acid-test ratio
   - **b.** Inventory turnover
   - **c.** Days' sales in average receivables
   - **d.** Debt ratio
   - **e.** Earnings per share of common stock
   - **f.** Price/earnings ratio
2. Compute each company's economic-value-added (EVA®) measure and determine whether their EVA®s confirm or alter your investment decision. Each company's cost of capital is 10%. Round all amounts to the nearest $1,000.

Analyzing a company based on its ratios
(Obj. 4)

P18-6A Take the role of an investment analyst at **Edward Jones Company**. It is your job to recommend investments for your client. The only information you have are the ratio values for two companies in the graphics software industry.

Ratio	GraphTech, Inc.	Core Software Company
Days' sales in receivables	51	43
Inventory turnover	9	7
Gross profit percentage	62%	71%
Net income as a percent of sales	16%	14%
Times-interest earned	12	18
Return on equity	29%	36%
Return on assets	19%	14%

Write a report to the Edward Jones investment committee. Recommend one company's stock over the other. State the reasons for your recommendation.

Problems

(Group B)

A+ online homework

P18-1B Net revenues, net income, and common stockholders' equity for xCel Corporation, a manufacturer of contact lenses, for a four-year period follow.

Trend percentages, return on common equity, and comparison with the industry **(Obj. 1, 4)**

(in thousands)	2008	2007	2006	2005
Net revenues	$781	$714	$641	$662
Net income	51	45	32	48
Ending common stockholders' equity	366	354	330	296

Required

1. Compute trend percentages for each item for 2006 through 2008. Use 2005 as the base year. Round to the nearest percent.
2. Compute the rate of return on common stockholders' equity for 2006 through 2008, rounding to three decimal places. In the contact lens industry, rates of 13% are average, rates above 16% are good, and rates above 20% are outstanding. xCel has no preferred stock outstanding.
3. How does xCel's return on common stockholders' equity compare with the industry?

P18-2B Bose Stereo Shops has asked you to compare the company's profit performance and financial position with the average for the stereo industry. The proprietor has given you the company's income statement and balance sheet, as well as the industry average data for retailers.

Common-size statements, analysis of profitability, and comparison with the industry **(Obj. 2, 3, 4)**

Bose Stereo Shops
Income Statement Compared with Industry Average
Year Ended December 31, 20X6

	Bose	Industry Average
Net sales	$781,000	100.0%
Cost of goods sold	497,000	65.8
Gross profit	284,000	34.2
Operating expenses	163,000	19.7
Operating income	121,000	14.5
Other expenses	6,000	0.4
Net income	$115,000	14.1%

Bose Stereo Shops
Balance Sheet Compared with Industry Average
December 31, 20X6

	Bose	Industry Average
Current assets	$350,000	70.9%
Fixed assets, net	74,000	23.6
Intangible assets, net	4,000	0.8
Other assets	22,000	4.7
Total	$450,000	100.0%
Current liabilities	$207,000	48.1%
Long-term liabilities	62,000	16.6
Stockholders' equity	181,000	35.3
Total	$450,000	100.0%

Required

1. Prepare a common-size income statement and balance sheet for Bose. The first column of each statement should present Bose's common-size statement, and the second column, the industry averages.
2. For the profitability analysis, compute Bose's (a) ratio of gross profit to net sales, (b) ratio of operating income to net sales, and (c) ratio of net income to net sales. Compare these figures with the industry averages. Is Bose's profit performance better or worse than the industry average?

3. For the analysis of financial position, compute Bose's (a) ratio of current assets to total assets and (b) ratio of stockholders' equity to total assets. Compare these ratios with the industry averages. Is Bose's financial position better or worse than the industry averages?

Effects of business transactions on selected ratios
(Obj. 4)

P18-3B Financial statement data of Biz Mart Discount Center include the following items (dollars in thousands):

Cash	$ 22,000
Accounts receivable, net	102,000
Inventories	149,000
Total assets	657,000
Short-term notes payable	49,000
Accounts payable	103,000
Accrued liabilities	38,000
Long-term liabilities	191,000
Net income	71,000
Common shares outstanding	40,000

Required

1. Compute Biz Mart's current ratio, debt ratio, and earnings per share. Use the following format for your answer:

Requirement 1

Current Ratio	Debt Ratio	Earnings per Share

2. Compute the three ratios after evaluating the effect of each transaction that follows. Consider each transaction *separately*.
   a. Purchased store supplies of $46,000 on account.
   b. Borrowed $125,000 on a long-term note payable.
   c. Issued 5,000 shares of common stock, receiving cash of $120,000.
   d. Received cash on account, $19,000.
   Format your answer as follows:

Requirement 2

Transaction (Letter)	Current Ratio	Debt Ratio	Earnings per Share

Using ratios to evaluate a stock investment
(Obj. 4)

P18-4B Comparative financial-statement data of i2 Networks, Inc., follow.

i2 Networks, Inc.
Comparative Income Statement
Years Ended December 31, 20X9 and 20X8

	20X9	20X8
Net sales	$462,000	$427,000
Cost of goods sold	229,000	218,000
Gross profit	233,000	209,000
Operating expenses	136,000	134,000
Income from operations	97,000	75,000
Interest expense	11,000	12,000
Income before income tax	86,000	63,000
Income tax expense	30,000	27,000
Net income	$ 56,000	$ 36,000

i2 Networks, Inc.

Comparative Balance Sheet
December 31, 20X9 and 20X8

	20X9	20X8	20X7*
Current assets:			
Cash	$ 96,000	$ 97,000	
Current receivables, net	112,000	116,000	$103,000
Inventories	147,000	162,000	207,000
Prepaid expenses	16,000	7,000	
Total current assets	371,000	382,000	
Property, plant, and equipment, net	214,000	178,000	
Total assets	$585,000	$560,000	598,000
Total current liabilities	$206,000	$223,000	
Long-term liabilities	119,000	117,000	
Total liabilities	325,000	340,000	
Preferred stockholders' equity, 6%, $100 par	100,000	100,000	
Common stockholders' equity, no par	160,000	120,000	90,000
Total liabilities and stockholders' equity	$585,000	$560,000	

*Selected 20X7 amounts.

Other information:

1. Market price of i2 Networks' common stock: $53 at December 31, 20X9, and $32.50 at December 31, 20X8.
2. Common shares outstanding: 10,000 during 20X9 and 9,000 during 20X8.
3. All sales on credit.

Required

1. Compute the following ratios for 20X9 and 20X8:
   a. Current ratio
   b. Inventory turnover
   c. Times-interest-earned ratio
   d. Return on common stockholders' equity
   e. Earnings per share of common stock
   f. Price/earnings ratio
2. Decide (a) whether i2 Networks' financial position improved or deteriorated during 20X9 and (b) whether the investment attractiveness of its common stock appears to have increased or decreased.
3. How will what you learned in this problem help you evaluate an investment?

Using ratios to decide between two stock investments; measuring economic value added
(Obj. 4, 5)

P18-5B Assume that you are purchasing an investment and have decided to invest in a company in the air-conditioning/heating business. You have narrowed the choice to Caremark Laboratories and AmeriCorp, Inc., and have assembled the following data:

Selected income-statement data for the current year:

	Caremark	AmeriCorp
Net sales (all on credit)	$371,000	$497,000
Cost of goods sold	209,000	258,000
Interest expense	—	19,000
Net income	48,000	72,000

Selected balance-sheet data at the *beginning* of the current year:

	Caremark	AmeriCorp
Current receivables, net	$ 40,000	$ 48,000
Inventories	93,000	88,000
Total assets	259,000	270,000
Common stock, $1 par (10,000 shares)	10,000	
$2.50 par (5,000 shares)		12,500

Selected balance-sheet and market-price data at the *end* of the current year:

	Caremark	AmeriCorp
Current assets:		
Cash	$ 22,000	$ 19,000
Short-term investments	20,000	18,000
Current receivables, net	42,000	46,000
Inventories	87,000	100,000
Prepaid expenses	2,000	3,000
Total current assets	173,000	186,000
Total assets	265,000	328,000
Total current liabilities	108,000	98,000
Total liabilities	108,000*	131,000*
Common stock, $1 par (10,000 shares)	10,000	
$2.50 par (5,000 shares)		12,500
Total stockholders' equity	157,000	197,000
Market price per share of common stock	$ 51	$ 112

*Includes notes payable: Caremark, $1,000, and AmeriCorp, $86,000.

Your strategy is to invest in companies that have low price/earnings ratios but appear to be in good shape financially. Assume that you have analyzed all other factors and that your decision depends on the results of ratio analysis.

Required

1. Compute the following ratios for both companies for the current year, and decide which company's stock better fits your investment strategy.

a. Acid-test ratio
b. Inventory turnover
c. Days' sales in average receivables
d. Debt ratio
e. Earnings per share of common stock
f. Price/earnings ratio

2. Compute each company's economic-value-added (EVA®) measure and determine whether their EVA®s confirm or alter your investment decision. Each company's cost of capital is 12%. Round all amounts to the nearest $1,000.

Analyzing a company based on its ratios
(Obj. 4)

P18-6B Take the role of an investment analyst at **Goldman Sachs**. It is your job to recommend investments for your clients. The only information you have are ratio values for two companies in the pharmaceuticals industry.

Ratio	Pratt Corp.	Jacobs, Inc.
Days' sales in receivables	36	42
Inventory turnover	6	8
Gross profit percentage	49%	51%
Net income as a percentage of sales	7.2%	8.3%
Times-interest-earned	16	9
Return on equity	32.3%	21.5%
Return on assets	12.1%	16.4%

Write a report to Goldman Sachs' investment committee. Recommend one company's stock over the other. State the reasons for your recommendation.

APPLY *Your Knowledge*

Decision Cases

Assessing the effects of transactions on a company
(Obj. 4)

Case 1. **AOL Time Warner, Inc.**, had a bad year in 2001; the company suffered a net loss. The loss pushed most of the return measures into the negative column, and the current ratio dropped below 1.0. The company's debt ratio is still only 0.27. Assume top management of AOL Time Warner is pondering ways to improve the company's ratios. In particular, management is considering the following transactions:

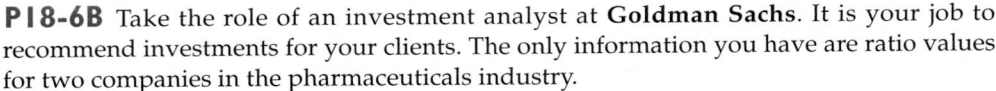

1. Borrow $100 million of long-term debt.
2. Purchase treasury stock for $500 million cash.
3. Expense one-fourth of goodwill carried on the books at $128 million.
4. Sell advertising, and the advertisements will run immediately.
5. Purchase trademarks from **NBC**, paying $20 million cash.

Required

Top management wants to know the effects of these transactions (increase, decrease, or no effect) on the following ratios of AOL Time Warner:

a. Current ratio **b.** Debt ratio **c.** Return on equity

Understanding the components of accounting ratios **(Obj. 4)**

Case 2. Consider the following business situations:

a. Pinehurst Corporation's owners are concerned because the number of days' sales in receivables has increased over the previous two years. Explain why the ratio might have increased.

b. Sara Fulton has asked you about the stock of a particular company. She finds it attractive because it has a high dividend yield relative to another stock she is also considering. Explain to her the meaning of the ratio and the danger of making a decision based on dividend yield alone. Suggest other information (ratios) Sara should consider as she makes her investment decision.

c. Nathanael Smith is the controller of Saturn Ltd., a dance club whose year-end is December 31. Smith prepares checks for suppliers in December and posts them to the appropriate accounts in that month. However, he holds on to the checks and mails them to the suppliers in January. What financial ratio(s) are most affected by the action? What is Smith's purpose in undertaking this activity?

Ethical Issue

Balmoral Golf Corporation's long-term debt agreements make certain demands on the business. For example, Balmoral may not purchase treasury stock in excess of the balance of retained earnings. Also, long-term debt may not exceed stockholders' equity, and the current ratio may not fall below 1.50. If Balmoral fails to meet any of these requirements, the company's lenders have the authority to take over management of the company.

Changes in consumer demand have made it hard for Balmoral to attract customers. Current liabilities have mounted faster than current assets, causing the current ratio to fall to 1.47. Before releasing financial statements, Balmoral management is scrambling to improve the current ratio. The controller points out that an investment can be classified as either long-term or short-term, depending on management's intention. By deciding to convert an investment to cash within one year, Balmoral can classify the investment as short-term—a current asset. On the controller's recommendation, Balmoral's board of directors votes to reclassify long-term investments as short-term.

Required

1. What effect will reclassifying the investments have on the current ratio? Is Balmoral's true financial position stronger as a result of reclassifying the investments?
2. Shortly after the financial statements are released, sales improve; so, too, does the current ratio. As a result, Balmoral management decides not to sell the investments it had reclassified as short-term. Accordingly, the company reclassifies the investments as long-term. Has management behaved unethically? Give the reasoning underlying your answer.

Financial Statement Case

Measuring profitability and analyzing stock as an investment **(Obj. 4)**

Amazon.com's financial statements in Appendix A reveal some unusual relationships for a company with a bright future. Answer these questions about Amazon.com.

1. What is most unusual about the balance sheet?
2. What is most unusual about the income statement (statement of operations)?

3. Consider Amazon's profitability ratios, ratios that measure the ability to pay long-term debt, and ratios for analyzing stock as an investment. What about Amazon makes these ratios meaningless? How can Amazon.com continue as a going business? The statement of cash flows helps to answer this critical question.

Team Projects

Project 1. Select an industry you are interested in, and use the leading company in that industry as the benchmark. Then select two other companies in the same industry. For each category of ratios in the Decision Guidelines on pages 727 and 728, compute at least two ratios for all three companies. Write a two-page report that compares the two companies with the benchmark company.

Project 2. Select a company and obtain its financial statements. Convert the income statement and the balance sheet to common size, and compare the company you selected to the industry average. Risk Management Association's *Annual Statement Studies*, **Dun & Bradstreet's** *Industry Norms & Key Business Ratios*, and Prentice Hall's *Almanac of Business and Industrial Financial Ratios*, by Leo Troy, publish common-size statements for most industries.

For Internet exercises, go to the Web site www.prenhall.com/horngren.

Comprehensive Problem for Chapters 17 and 18

Analyzing a Company for Its Investment Potential

In its 2003 annual report, **Wal-Mart Stores, Inc.**, includes an 11-year financial summary (see pp. 748–749). Analyze the company's financial summary for the fiscal years 1999 to 2003 to decide whether to invest in the common stock of Wal-Mart. Include the following sections in your analysis, and fully explain your final decision.

1. Trend analysis for net sales and net income (use 1999 as the base year)
2. Profitability analysis
3. Measuring ability to sell inventory (Wal-Mart uses the LIFO method)
4. Measuring ability to pay debts
5. Measuring dividends

Wal-Mart Stores, Inc.

11-Year Financial Summary (Partial; adapted)

(Dollar Amounts in Millions Except per Share Data)	2003	2002	2001
Net sales	**$244,524**	$217,799	$191,329
Net sales increase	**12%**	14%	16%
Domestic comparative store sales increase	**5%**	6%	5%
Other income—net	**2,001**	1,873	1,787
Cost of sales	**191,838**	171,562	150,255
Operating, selling, and general and administrative expenses	**41,043**	36,173	31,550
Interest costs:			
Debt	**803**	1,083	1,104
Capital leases	**260**	274	279
Interest income	**(138)**	(171)	(188)
Provision for income taxes	**4,487**	3,897	3,692
Minority interest and equity in unconsolidated subsidiaries	**(193)**	(183)	(129)
Cumulative effect of accounting change, net of tax	—	—	—
Net income	**8,039**	6,671	6,295
Per share of common stock:			
Basic net income	**1.81**	1.49	1.41
Diluted net income	**1.81**	1.49	1.40
Dividends	**0.30**	0.28	0.24
Financial Position			
Current assets	**$ 30,483**	$ 27,878	$ 26,555
Inventories at LIFO cost	**24,891**	22,614	21,442
Net property, plant, and equipment and capital leases	**51,904**	45,750	40,934
Total assets	**94,685**	83,527	78,130
Current liabilities	**32,617**	27,282	28,949
Long-term debt	**16,607**	15,687	12,501
Long-term obligations under capital leases	**3,001**	3,045	3,154
Shareholders' equity	**39,337**	35,102	31,343
Financial Ratios			
Current ratio	**0.9**	1.0	0.9
Inventories/working capital	**(11.7)**	38.2	(9.0)
Return on assets	**9.2%**	8.5%	8.7%
Return on shareholders' equity	**21.6%**	20.1%	22.0%

2000	1999	1998	1997	1996	1995	1994	1993
$165,013	$137,634	$117,958	$104,859	$93,627	$82,494	$67,344	$55,484
20%	17%	12%	12%	13%	22%	21%	26%
8%	9%	6%	5%	4%	7%	6%	11%
1,615	1,391	1,290	1,293	1,138	904	633	490
129,664	108,725	93,438	83,510	74,505	65,586	53,444	44,175
27,040	22,363	19,358	16,946	15,021	12,858	10,333	8,321
779	535	558	629	693	520	331	143
266	268	229	216	196	186	186	180
(204)	(189)	(54)	(26)	(9)	(10)	(12)	(7)
3,338	2,740	2,115	1,794	1,606	1,581	1,358	1,171
(170)	(153)	(78)	(27)	(13)	4	(4)	4
(198)	—	—	—	—	—	—	—
5,377	4,430	3,526	3,056	2,740	2,681	2,333	1,995
1.21	0.99	0.78	0.67	0.60	0.59	0.51	0.44
1.20	0.99	0.78	0.67	0.60	0.59	0.51	0.44
0.20	0.16	0.14	0.11	0.10	0.09	0.07	0.05
$ 24,356	$ 21,132	$ 19,352	$ 17,993	$17,331	$15,338	$12,114	$10,198
19,793	17,076	16,497	15,897	15,989	14,064	11,014	9,268
35,969	25,973	23,606	20,324	18,894	15,874	13,176	9,793
70,349	49,996	45,384	39,604	37,541	32,819	26,441	20,565
25,803	16,762	14,460	10,957	11,454	9,973	7,406	6,754
13,672	6,908	7,191	7,709	8,508	7,871	6,156	3,073
3,002	2,699	2,483	2,307	2,092	1,838	1,804	1,772
25,834	21,112	18,503	17,143	14,756	12,726	10,753	8,759
0.9	1.3	1.3	1.6	1.5	1.5	1.6	1.5
(13.7)	3.9	3.4	2.3	2.7	2.6	2.3	2.7
9.5%	9.6%	8.5%	7.9%	7.8%	9.0%	9.9%	11.1%
22.9%	22.4%	19.8%	19.2%	19.9%	22.8%	23.9%	25.3%

Appendix A

2 0 0 2

amazon.com®

ANNUAL REPORT (EXCERPTED)

amazon.com

To our shareholders:

In many ways, Amazon.com is not a normal store. We have deep selection that is unconstrained by shelf space. We turn our inventory 19 times in a year. We personalize the store for each and every customer. We trade real estate for technology (which gets cheaper and more capable every year). We display customer reviews critical of our products. You can make a purchase with a few seconds and one click. We put used products next to new ones so you can choose. We share our prime real estate—our product detail pages—with third parties, and, if they can offer better value, we let them.

One of our most exciting peculiarities is poorly understood. People see that we're determined to offer both world-leading customer experience *and* the lowest possible prices, but to some this dual goal seems paradoxical if not downright quixotic. Traditional stores face a time-tested tradeoff between offering high-touch customer experience on the one hand and the lowest possible prices on the other. How can Amazon.com be trying to do both?

The answer is that we transform much of customer experience—such as unmatched selection, extensive product information, personalized recommendations, and other new software features—into largely a fixed expense. With customer experience costs largely fixed (more like a publishing model than a retailing model), our costs as a percentage of sales can shrink rapidly as we grow our business. Moreover, customer experience costs that remain variable—such as the variable portion of fulfillment costs—improve in our model as we reduce defects. Eliminating defects improves costs and leads to better customer experience.

We believe our ability to lower prices and simultaneously drive customer experience is a big deal, and this past year offers evidence that the strategy is working.

First, we do continue to drive customer experience. The holiday season this year is one example. While delivering a record number of units to customers, we also delivered our best-ever experience. Cycle time, the amount of time taken by our fulfillment centers to process an order, improved 17% compared with last year. And our most sensitive measure of customer satisfaction, contacts per order, saw a 13% improvement.

Inside existing product categories, we've worked hard to increase selection. Electronics selection is up over 40% in the U.S. alone over the prior year, and we now offer 10 times the selection of a typical big box electronics store. Even in U.S. books, where we've been working for 8 years, we increased selection by 15%, mostly in harder-to-find and out-of-print titles. And, of course, we've added new categories. Our Apparel and Accessories store has more than 500 top clothing brands, and in its first 60 days, customers bought 153,000 shirts, 106,000 pairs of pants, and 31,000 pairs of underwear.

In this year's American Customer Satisfaction Index, the most authoritative study of customer satisfaction, Amazon.com scored an 88, the highest score ever recorded—not just online, not just in retailing—but the highest score ever recorded in any service industry. In ACSI's words:

> "Amazon.com continues to show remarkably high levels of customer satisfaction. With a score of 88 (up 5%), it is generating satisfaction at a level unheard of in the service industry.... Can customer satisfaction for Amazon climb more? The latest ACSI data suggest that it is indeed possible. Both service and the value proposition offered by Amazon have increased at a steep rate."

Second, while focused on customer experience, we've also been lowering price substantially. We've been doing so broadly across product categories, from books to electronics, and we've eliminated shipping fees with our 365 day-per-year Free Super Saver Shipping on orders over $25. We've been taking similar actions in every country in which we do business.

Our pricing objective is not to discount a small number of products for a limited period of time, but to offer low prices everyday and apply them broadly across our entire product range. To illustrate this point, we recently did a price comparison versus a major well-known chain of book superstores. We did not hand pick a choice group of books against which we wanted to compare. Instead, we used their published list of their 100 bestsellers for 2002. It was a good representation of the kinds of books people buy most, consisting of 45 hardcover titles and 55 paperbacks across many different categories, including Literature, Romance, Mystery and Thrillers, Nonfiction, Children's, Self-Help, and so on.

We priced all 100 titles by visiting their superstores in both Seattle and New York City. It took us six hours in four of their different superstores to find all 100 books on their list. When we added up everything we spent, we discovered that:

- At their stores, these 100 bestselling books cost $1,561. At Amazon.com, the same books cost $1,195 for a total savings of $366, or 23%.
- For 72 of the 100 books, our price was cheaper. On 25 of the books, our price was the same. On 3 of the 100, their prices were better (we subsequently reduced our prices on these three books).
- In these physical-world superstores, only 15 of their 100 titles were discounted—they were selling the other 85 at full list price. At Amazon.com, 76 of the 100 were discounted and 24 were sold at list price.

To be sure, you may find reasons to shop in the physical world—for instance, if you need something immediately—but, if you do so, you'll be paying a premium. If you want to save money and time, you'll do better by shopping at Amazon.com.

Third, our determination to deliver low price *and* customer experience is generating financial results. Net sales this year increased 26% to a record $3.9 billion, and unit sales grew at an even faster 34%. Free cash flow—our most important financial measure—reached $135 million, a $305 million improvement over the prior year.[1]

In short, what's good for customers is good for shareholders.

Once again this year, I attach a copy of our original 1997 letter and encourage current and prospective shareowners to take a look at it. Given how much we've grown and how much the Internet has evolved, it's notable that the fundamentals of how we do business remain the same.

As always, we at Amazon.com are grateful to our customers for their business and trust, to each other for our hard work, and to our shareholders for their support and encouragement.

Jeffrey P. Bezos
Founder and Chief Executive Officer
Amazon.com, Inc.

---

[1] Free cash flow for 2002 of $135 million is net cash provided by operating activities of $174 million less purchases of fixed assets of $39 million. Free cash flow for 2001 of negative $170 million is net cash used in operating activities of $120 million less purchases of fixed assets of $50 million.

REPORT OF ERNST & YOUNG LLP, INDEPENDENT AUDITORS

The Board of Directors and Stockholders
Amazon.com, Inc.

We have audited the accompanying consolidated balance sheets of Amazon.com, Inc. as of December 31, 2002 and 2001, and the related consolidated statements of operations, stockholders' equity (deficit) and cash flows for each of the three years in the period ended December 31, 2002. Our audits also included the financial statement schedule listed at Item 15(a)(2). These financial statements and schedule are the responsibility of the Company's management. Our responsibility is to express an opinion on these financial statements and schedule based on our audits.

We conducted our audits in accordance with auditing standards generally accepted in the United States. Those standards require that we plan and perform the audit to obtain reasonable assurance about whether the financial statements are free of material misstatement. An audit includes examining, on a test basis, evidence supporting the amounts and disclosures in the financial statements. An audit also includes assessing the accounting principles used and significant estimates made by management, as well as evaluating the overall financial statement presentation. We believe that our audits provide a reasonable basis for our opinion.

In our opinion, the financial statements referred to above present fairly, in all material respects, the consolidated financial position of Amazon.com, Inc. at December 31, 2002 and 2001, and the consolidated results of its operations and its cash flows for each of the three years in the period ended December 31, 2002, in conformity with accounting principles generally accepted in the United States. Also, in our opinion, the related financial statement schedule, when considered in relation to the basic financial statements taken as a whole, presents fairly in all material respects the information set forth therein.

As discussed in Note 1 to the consolidated financial statements, the Company adopted the full provisions of Statement of Financial Accounting Standards No. 141, Business Combinations, and No. 142, Goodwill and Other Intangible Assets, effective January 1, 2002. The Company also adopted Statement of Financial Accounting Standards No. 133, Accounting for Derivative Instruments and Hedging Activities, effective January 1, 2001. In addition, as discussed in Note 1 to the consolidated financial statements, effective January 1, 2002, the Company prospectively changed its inventory costing method to the first-in first-out method of accounting.

/s/ Ernst & Young LLP

Seattle, Washington
January 17, 2003

amazon.com

1997 LETTER TO SHAREHOLDERS
(Reprinted from the 1997 Annual Report)

To our shareholders:

Amazon.com passed many milestones in 1997: by year-end, we had served more than 1.5 million customers, yielding 838% revenue growth to $147.8 million, and extended our market leadership despite aggressive competitive entry.

But this is Day 1 for the Internet and, if we execute well, for Amazon.com. Today, online commerce saves customers money and precious time. Tomorrow, through personalization, online commerce will accelerate the very process of discovery. Amazon.com uses the Internet to create real value for its customers and, by doing so, hopes to create an enduring franchise, even in established and large markets.

We have a window of opportunity as larger players marshal the resources to pursue the online opportunity and as customers, new to purchasing online, are receptive to forming new relationships. The competitive landscape has continued to evolve at a fast pace. Many large players have moved online with credible offerings and have devoted substantial energy and resources to building awareness, traffic, and sales. Our goal is to move quickly to solidify and extend our current position while we begin to pursue the online commerce opportunities in other areas. We see substantial opportunity in the large markets we are targeting. This strategy is not without risk: it requires serious investment and crisp execution against established franchise leaders.

It's All About the Long Term

We believe that a fundamental measure of our success will be the shareholder value we create over the *long term*. This value will be a direct result of our ability to extend and solidify our current market leadership position. The stronger our market leadership, the more powerful our economic model. Market leadership can translate directly to higher revenue, higher profitability, greater capital velocity, and correspondingly stronger returns on invested capital.

Our decisions have consistently reflected this focus. We first measure ourselves in terms of the metrics most indicative of our market leadership: customer and revenue growth, the degree to which our customers continue to purchase from us on a repeat basis, and the strength of our brand. We have invested and will continue to invest aggressively to expand and leverage our customer base, brand, and infrastructure as we move to establish an enduring franchise.

Because of our emphasis on the long term, we may make decisions and weigh tradeoffs differently than some companies. Accordingly, we want to share with you our fundamental management and decision-making approach so that you, our shareholders, may confirm that it is consistent with your investment philosophy:

- We will continue to focus relentlessly on our customers.

- We will continue to make investment decisions in light of long-term market leadership considerations rather than short-term profitability considerations or short-term Wall Street reactions.

- We will continue to measure our programs and the effectiveness of our investments analytically, to jettison those that do not provide acceptable returns, and to step up our investment in those that work best. We will continue to learn from both our successes and our failures.

- We will make bold rather than timid investment decisions where we see a sufficient probability of gaining market leadership advantages. Some of these investments will pay off, others will not, and we will have learned another valuable lesson in either case.

- When forced to choose between optimizing the appearance of our GAAP accounting and maximizing the present value of future cash flows, we'll take the cash flows.

- We will share our strategic thought processes with you when we make bold choices (to the extent competitive pressures allow), so that you may evaluate for yourselves whether we are making rational long-term leadership investments.

- We will work hard to spend wisely and maintain our lean culture. We understand the importance of continually reinforcing a cost-conscious culture, particularly in a business incurring net losses.

- We will balance our focus on growth with emphasis on long-term profitability and capital management. At this stage, we choose to prioritize growth because we believe that scale is central to achieving the potential of our business model.

- We will continue to focus on hiring and retaining versatile and talented employees, and continue to weight their compensation to stock options rather than cash. We know our success will be largely affected by our ability to attract and retain a motivated employee base, each of whom must think like, and therefore must actually be, an owner.

We aren't so bold as to claim that the above is the "right" investment philosophy, but it's ours, and we would be remiss if we weren't clear in the approach we have taken and will continue to take.

With this foundation, we would like to turn to a review of our business focus, our progress in 1997, and our outlook for the future.

Obsess Over Customers

From the beginning, our focus has been on offering our customers compelling value. We realized that the Web was, and still is, the World Wide Wait. Therefore, we set out to offer customers something they simply could not get any other way, and began serving them with books. We brought them much more selection than was possible in a physical store (our store would now occupy 6 football fields), and presented it in a useful, easy-to-search, and easy-to-browse format in a store open 365 days a year, 24 hours a day. We maintained a dogged focus on improving the shopping experience, and in 1997 substantially enhanced our store. We now offer customers gift certificates, 1-Click^{SM} shopping, and vastly more reviews, content, browsing options, and recommendation features. We dramatically lowered prices, further increasing customer value. Word of mouth remains the most powerful customer acquisition tool we have, and we are grateful for the trust our customers have placed in us. Repeat purchases and word of mouth have combined to make Amazon.com the market leader in online bookselling.

By many measures, Amazon.com came a long way in 1997:

- Sales grew from $15.7 million in 1996 to $147.8 million—an 838% increase.

- Cumulative customer accounts grew from 180,000 to 1,510,000—a 738% increase.

- The percentage of orders from repeat customers grew from over 46% in the fourth quarter of 1996 to over 58% in the same period in 1997.

- In terms of audience reach, per Media Metrix, our Web site went from a rank of 90th to within the top 20.

- We established long-term relationships with many important strategic partners, including America Online, Yahoo!, Excite, Netscape, GeoCities, AltaVista, @Home, and Prodigy.

Infrastructure

During 1997, we worked hard to expand our business infrastructure to support these greatly increased traffic, sales, and service levels:

- Amazon.com's employee base grew from 158 to 614, and we significantly strengthened our management team.
- Distribution center capacity grew from 50,000 to 285,000 square feet, including a 70% expansion of our Seattle facilities and the launch of our second distribution center in Delaware in November.
- Inventories rose to over 200,000 titles at year-end, enabling us to improve availability for our customers.
- Our cash and investment balances at year-end were $125 million, thanks to our initial public offering in May 1997 and our $75 million loan, affording us substantial strategic flexibility.

Our Employees

The past year's success is the product of a talented, smart, hard-working group, and I take great pride in being a part of this team. Setting the bar high in our approach to hiring has been, and will continue to be, the single most important element of Amazon.com's success.

It's not easy to work here (when I interview people I tell them, "You can work long, hard, or smart, but at Amazon.com you can't choose two out of three"), but we are working to build something important, something that matters to our customers, something that we can all tell our grandchildren about. Such things aren't meant to be easy. We are incredibly fortunate to have this group of dedicated employees whose sacrifices and passion build Amazon.com.

Goals for 1998

We are still in the early stages of learning how to bring new value to our customers through Internet commerce and merchandising. Our goal remains to continue to solidify and extend our brand and customer base. This requires sustained investment in systems and infrastructure to support outstanding customer convenience, selection, and service while we grow. We are planning to add music to our product offering, and over time we believe that other products may be prudent investments. We also believe there are significant opportunities to better serve our customers overseas, such as reducing delivery times and better tailoring the customer experience. To be certain, a big part of the challenge for us will lie not in finding new ways to expand our business, but in prioritizing our investments.

We now know vastly more about online commerce than when Amazon.com was founded, but we still have so much to learn. Though we are optimistic, we must remain vigilant and maintain a sense of urgency. The challenges and hurdles we will face to make our long-term vision for Amazon.com a reality are several: aggressive, capable, well-funded competition; considerable growth challenges and execution risk; the risks of product and geographic expansion; and the need for large continuing investments to meet an expanding market opportunity. However, as we've long said, online bookselling, and online commerce in general, should prove to be a very large market, and it's likely that a number of companies will see significant benefit. We feel good about what we've done, and even more excited about what we want to do.

1997 was indeed an incredible year. We at Amazon.com are grateful to our customers for their business and trust, to each other for our hard work, and to our shareholders for their support and encouragement.

Jeffrey P. Bezos
Founder and Chief Executive Officer
Amazon.com, Inc.

AMAZON.COM, INC.

CONSOLIDATED BALANCE SHEETS

	December 31, 2002	December 31, 2001
	(In thousands, except per share data)	
ASSETS		
Current assets:		
Cash and cash equivalents	$ 738,254	$ 540,282
Marketable securities	562,715	456,303
Inventories	202,425	143,722
Accounts receivable, net and other current assets	112,282	67,613
Total current assets	1,615,676	1,207,920
Fixed assets, net	239,398	271,751
Goodwill, net	70,811	45,367
Other intangibles, net	3,460	34,382
Other equity investments	15,442	28,359
Other assets	45,662	49,768
Total assets	$ 1,990,449	$ 1,637,547
LIABILITIES AND STOCKHOLDERS' DEFICIT		
Current liabilities:		
Accounts payable	$ 618,128	$ 444,748
Accrued expenses and other current liabilities	314,935	305,064
Unearned revenue	47,916	87,978
Interest payable	71,661	68,632
Current portion of long-term debt and other	13,318	14,992
Total current liabilities	1,065,958	921,414
Long-term debt and other	2,277,305	2,156,133
Commitments and contingencies		
Stockholders' deficit:		
Preferred stock, $0.01 par value:		
Authorized shares — 500,000		
Issued and outstanding shares — none	—	—
Common stock, $0.01 par value:		
Authorized shares — 5,000,000		
Issued and outstanding shares — 387,906 and 373,218 shares, respectively	3,879	3,732
Additional paid-in capital	1,649,946	1,462,769
Deferred stock-based compensation	(6,591)	(9,853)
Accumulated other comprehensive income (loss)	9,662	(36,070)
Accumulated deficit	(3,009,710)	(2,860,578)
Total stockholders' deficit	(1,352,814)	(1,440,000)
Total liabilities and stockholders' deficit	$ 1,990,449	$ 1,637,547

See accompanying notes to consolidated financial statements.

AMAZON.COM, INC.

CONSOLIDATED STATEMENTS OF OPERATIONS (Adapted)

	Years Ended December 31,		
	2002	2001	2000
	(In thousands, except per share data)		
Net sales	$3,932,936	$3,122,433	$ 2,761,983
Cost of sales	2,940,318	2,323,875	2,106,206
Gross profit	992,618	798,558	655,777
Operating expenses:			
Fulfillment	392,467	374,250	414,509
Marketing	125,383	138,283	179,980
Technology and content	215,617	241,165	269,326
General and administrative	79,049	89,862	108,962
Stock-based compensation	68,927	4,637	24,797
Amortization of goodwill and other intangibles	5,478	181,033	321,772
Restructuring-related and other	41,573	181,585	200,311
Total operating expenses	928,494	1,210,815	1,519,657
Income (loss) from operations	64,124	(412,257)	(863,880)
Interest income	23,687	29,103	40,821
Interest expense	(142,925)	(139,232)	(130,921)
Other income (expense), net	5,623	(1,900)	(10,058)
Other gains (losses), net	(96,273)	(2,141)	(142,639)
Total non-operating expenses, net	(209,888)	(114,170)	(242,797)
Loss before equity in losses of equity-method investees	(145,764)	(526,427)	(1,106,677)
Equity in losses of equity-method investees, net	(4,169)	(30,327)	(304,596)
Loss before change in accounting principle	(149,933)	(556,754)	(1,411,273)
Cumulative effect of change in accounting principle	801	(10,523)	—
Net loss	$ (149,132)	$ (567,277)	$(1,411,273)
Basic and diluted loss per share:			
Prior to cumulative effect of change in accounting principle	$ (0.40)	$ (1.53)	$ (4.02)
Cumulative effect of change in accounting principle	0.01	(0.03)	—
	$ (0.39)	$ (1.56)	$ (4.02)
Shares used in computation of loss per share:			
Basic and diluted	378,363	364,211	350,873

• • •

See accompanying notes to consolidated financial statements.

AMAZON.COM, INC.

CONSOLIDATED STATEMENTS OF CASH FLOWS

	Years Ended December 31,		
	2002	2001	2000
		(In thousands)	
CASH AND CASH EQUIVALENTS, BEGINNING OF PERIOD	$ 540,282	$ 822,435	$ 133,309
OPERATING ACTIVITIES:			
Net loss	(149,132)	(567,277)	(1,411,273)
Adjustments to reconcile net loss to net cash provided by (used in) operating activities:			
Depreciation of fixed assets and other amortization	82,274	84,709	84,460
Stock-based compensation	68,927	4,637	24,797
Equity in losses of equity-method investees, net	4,169	30,327	304,596
Amortization of goodwill and other intangibles	5,478	181,033	321,772
Non-cash restructuring-related and other	3,470	73,293	200,311
Gain on sale of marketable securities, net	(5,700)	(1,335)	(280)
Other losses (gains), net	96,273	2,141	142,639
Non-cash interest expense and other	29,586	26,629	24,766
Cumulative effect of change in accounting principle	(801)	10,523	—
Changes in operating assets and liabilities:			
Inventories	(51,303)	30,628	46,083
Accounts receivable, net and other current assets	(32,948)	20,732	(8,585)
Accounts payable	156,542	(44,438)	22,357
Accrued expenses and other current liabilities	4,491	50,031	93,967
Unearned revenue	95,404	114,738	97,818
Amortization of previously unearned revenue	(135,466)	(135,808)	(108,211)
Interest payable	3,027	(345)	34,341
Net cash provided by (used in) operating activities	174,291	(119,782)	(130,442)
INVESTING ACTIVITIES:			
Sales and maturities of marketable securities and other investments	553,289	370,377	545,724
Purchases of marketable securities	(635,810)	(567,152)	(184,455)
Purchases of fixed assets, including internal-use software and Web site development	(39,163)	(50,321)	(134,758)
Investments in equity-method investees and other investments	—	(6,198)	(62,533)
Net cash provided by (used in) investing activities	(121,684)	(253,294)	163,978
FINANCING ACTIVITIES:			
Proceeds from exercise of stock options and other	121,689	16,625	44,697
Proceeds from issuance of common stock, net of issuance costs	—	99,831	—
Proceeds from long-term debt and other	—	10,000	681,499
Repayment of capital lease obligations and other	(14,795)	(19,575)	(16,927)
Financing costs	—	—	(16,122)
Net cash provided by financing activities	106,894	106,881	693,147
Effect of exchange-rate changes on cash and cash equivalents	38,471	(15,958)	(37,557)
Net increase (decrease) in cash and cash equivalents	197,972	(282,153)	689,126
CASH AND CASH EQUIVALENTS, END OF PERIOD	$ 738,254	$ 540,282	$ 822,435
SUPPLEMENTAL CASH FLOW INFORMATION:			
Fixed assets acquired under capital leases and other financing arrangements	$ 3,023	$ 5,597	$ 9,303
Equity securities received for commercial agreements	—	331	106,848
Stock issued in connection with business acquisitions and minority investments	—	5,000	32,130
Cash paid for interest	111,589	112,184	67,252

See accompanying notes to consolidated financial statements.

AMAZON.COM, INC.

CONSOLIDATED STATEMENTS OF STOCKHOLDERS' EQUITY (DEFICIT)

	Common Stock		Additional Paid-In Capital	Deferred Stock-Based Compensation	Accumulated Other Comprehensive Income (Loss)	Accumulated Deficit	Total Stockholders' Equity (Deficit)
	Shares	Amount					
	(In thousands)						
Balance at December 31, 1999	345,155	$3,452	$1,194,369	$(47,806)	$ (1,709)	$ (882,028)	$ 266,278
Net loss	—	—	—	—	—	(1,411,273)	(1,411,273)
Foreign currency translation losses, net	—	—	—	—	(364)	—	(364)
Change in unrealized gain (loss) on available-for-sale securities, net	—	—	—	—	(303)	—	(303)
Comprehensive loss	—	—	—	—	—	—	(1,411,940)
Issuance of capital stock, net of issuance costs	866	8	30,977	—	—	—	30,985
Exercise of common stock options, net	11,119	111	41,995	—	—	—	42,106
Public offering of equity-method investee	—	—	76,898	—	—	—	76,898
Note receivable for common stock	—	—	27	—	—	—	27
Deferred stock-based compensation, net of adjustments	—	—	(5,963)	2,528	—	—	(3,435)
Amortization of deferred stock-based compensation	—	—	—	31,830	—	—	31,830
Balance at December 31, 2000	357,140	3,571	1,338,303	(13,448)	(2,376)	(2,293,301)	(967,251)
Net loss	—	—	—	—	—	(567,277)	(567,277)
Foreign currency translation losses, net	—	—	—	—	(1,257)	—	(1,257)
Change in unrealized gain (loss) on available-for-sale securities, net	—	—	—	—	7,005	—	7,005
Net unrealized losses on Euro-based currency swap	—	—	—	—	(17,337)	—	(17,337)
Reclassification of currency gains on 6.875% PEACS	—	—	—	—	(9,811)	—	(9,811)
Cumulative effect of change in accounting principle	—	—	—	—	(12,294)	—	(12,294)
Comprehensive loss	—	—	—	—	—	—	(600,971)
Issuance of capital stock, net of issuance costs	8,989	90	98,716	—	—	—	98,806
Exercise of common stock options, net	6,089	61	14,989	—	—	—	15,050
Repayments of note receivable for common stock	—	—	1,130	—	—	—	1,130
Deferred stock-based compensation, net of adjustments	1,000	10	9,631	(4,797)	—	—	4,844
Amortization of deferred stock-based compensation	—	—	—	8,392	—	—	8,392
Balance at December 31, 2001	373,218	3,732	1,462,769	(9,853)	(36,070)	(2,860,578)	(1,440,000)
Net loss	—	—	—	—	—	(149,132)	(149,132)
Foreign currency translation gains, net	—	—	—	—	16,910	—	16,910
Change in unrealized gain (loss) on available-for-sale securities, net	—	—	—	—	20,294	—	20,294
Net unrealized gains on Euro-based currency swap	—	—	—	—	8,528	—	8,528
Comprehensive loss	—	—	—	—	—	—	(103,400)
Exercise of common stock options, net	14,728	147	121,542	—	—	—	121,689
Deferred stock-based compensation, net of adjustments	(40)	—	1,592	(2,828)	—	—	(1,236)
Amortization of deferred stock-based compensation	—	—	—	6,090	—	—	6,090
Variable accounting and other stock compensation amortization	—	—	64,043	—	—	—	64,043
Balance at December 31, 2002	387,906	$3,879	$1,649,946	$ (6,591)	$ 9,662	$(3,009,710)	$(1,352,814)

See accompanying notes to consolidated financial statements.

AMAZON.COM, INC.

NOTES TO CONSOLIDATED FINANCIAL STATEMENTS (Excerpts; Adapted)

Note 1 — Description of Business and Accounting Policies (Partial)

Description of Business

Amazon.com, Inc., a Fortune 500 company, commenced operations on the World Wide Web in July 1995. The Company seeks to offer Earth's Biggest Selection and to be Earth's most customer-centric company, where customers can find and discover anything they may want to buy online. The Company and its sellers list new, used and collectible items in categories such as apparel and accessories, electronics, computers, kitchen and housewares, books, music, DVDs, videos, cameras and photo items, office products, toys, baby items and baby registry, software, computer and video games, cell phones and service, tools and hardware, travel services, magazine subscriptions and outdoor living items. Through Amazon Marketplace, the Merchants@ program, zShops and Auctions, participating businesses or individuals can sell their products to Amazon.com's customers.

The Company operates six global Web sites: *www.amazon.com, www.amazon.co.uk, www.amazon.de, www.amazon.fr, www.amazon.co.jp* and *www.amazon.ca.* The Company also owns and operates the Internet Movie Database at *www.imdb.com* ("IMDb"), which is a source of information on movie and entertainment titles and cast and crew members. IMDb offers IMDb Pro, a subscription service designed for the entertainment industry.

Principles of Consolidation

The consolidated financial statements include the accounts of the Company and its wholly owned subsidiaries. All intercompany balances and transactions have been eliminated.

Use of Estimates

The preparation of financial statements in conformity with accounting principles generally accepted in the United States requires estimates and assumptions that affect the reported amounts of assets and liabilities, revenues and expenses, and related disclosures of contingent assets and liabilities in the consolidated financial statements and accompanying notes. Estimates are used for, but not limited to, inventory valuation, depreciable lives, sales returns, receivables valuation, restructuring-related liabilities, incentive discount offers, valuation of investments, taxes and contingencies. Actual results could differ materially from those estimates.

Business Combinations

For business combinations that have been accounted for under the purchase method of accounting, the Company includes the results of operations of the acquired business from the date of acquisition. Net assets of the companies acquired are recorded at their fair value at the date of acquisition. The excess of the purchase price over the fair value of tangible and identifiable intangible net assets acquired is included in goodwill on the accompanying consolidated balance sheets.

Cash and Cash Equivalents

The Company classifies all highly liquid instruments with an original maturity of three months or less at the time of purchase as cash equivalents.

Inventories

Inventories, consisting of products available for sale, are valued at the lower of cost or market value. The Company makes judgments, based on currently-available information, about the likely method of disposition (whether through sales to individual customers, returns to product vendors or liquidations), and expected recoverable values of each disposition category. Based on this evaluation, which is applied consistently from period to period, the Company records a valuation allowance to adjust the carrying amount of its inventories to lower of cost or market value.

Accounting Changes

Inventories

Effective January 1, 2002, the Company prospectively changed its inventory costing method to the first-in first-out ("FIFO") method of accounting. This change resulted in a cumulative increase in inventory of $0.8 million, with a corresponding amount recorded to "Cumulative effect of change in accounting principle" on the consolidated statements of operations. The Company evaluated the effect of the change on each quarter of 2001 and determined such effect to be less than $1.2 million individually and in the aggregate. The Company determined this change to be preferable under accounting principles generally accepted in the United States since, among other reasons, it facilitates the Company's record keeping process, significantly improves its ability to provide cost-efficient fulfillment services to third-party companies as part of its services offering and results in increased consistency with others in the industry. The Company received a letter of preferability for this change in inventory costing from its independent auditors.

• • •

Fixed Assets

Fixed assets are stated at cost less accumulated depreciation, which includes the amortization of assets recorded under capital leases. Fixed assets, including assets purchased under capital leases, are depreciated on a straight-line basis over the estimated useful lives of the assets (generally two to ten years).

Included in fixed assets is the cost of internal-use software, including software used to upgrade and enhance the Company's Web sites. The Company expenses all costs related to the development of internal-use software other than those incurred during the application development stage. Costs incurred during the application development stage are capitalized and amortized over the estimated useful life of the software (generally two years).

• • •

Cost of Sales

Cost of sales consists of the purchase price of consumer products sold by the Company, inbound and outbound shipping charges, packaging supplies and certain costs associated with service revenues. Costs associated with service revenues classified as cost of services generally include direct and allocated indirect fulfillment-related costs to ship products on behalf of third-party sellers, costs to provide customer service, credit card fees and other related costs.

Outbound shipping charges and the cost of tangible supplies used to package products for shipment to customers totaled $404 million, $376 million, and $340 million in 2002, 2001 and 2000, respectively.

Fulfillment

Fulfillment costs represent those costs incurred in operating and staffing the Company's fulfillment and customer service centers, including costs attributable to: receiving, inspecting and warehousing inventories; picking, packaging and preparing customers' orders for shipment; credit card fees and bad debt costs; and responding to inquiries from customers. Fulfillment costs also include amounts paid to third-party co-sourcers that assist the Company in fulfillment and customer service operations. Certain Services segment fulfillment-related costs incurred on behalf of other businesses are classified as cost of sales rather than fulfillment.

Marketing

Marketing expenses consist of advertising, promotional, and public relations expenditures, and payroll and related expenses for personnel engaged in marketing and selling activities. The Company expenses general media advertising costs as incurred. The Company enters into certain online promotional agreements with third parties to increase traffic to its Web sites. Costs associated with these promotional agreements consist of fixed payments, variable activity-based payments, or a combination of the two. Fixed payments are amortized ratably over the corresponding agreement term and variable payments are expensed in the period incurred. The Company receives reimbursements from vendors for certain general media and other advertising costs. Such reimbursements are recorded as a reduction of expense. Advertising expense and other promotional costs were $114 million, $125 million and $172 million in 2002, 2001 and 2000, respectively. Prepaid advertising costs were $1 million and $2 million at December 31, 2002 and 2001, respectively.

Technology and Content

Technology and content expenses consist principally of payroll and related expenses for development, editorial, systems, and telecommunications operations personnel; and systems and telecommunications infrastructure.

Technology and content costs are expensed as incurred, except for certain costs relating to the development of internal-use software, including upgrades and enhancements to the Company's Web sites, that are capitalized and depreciated over two years. Fixed assets associated with capitalized internal-use software, net of accumulated depreciation, was $23 million and $24 million at December 31, 2002 and 2001, respectively. Costs capitalized during the application development stage for internal-use software, offset by corresponding amortization, was a net expense of $1 million in 2002, and net deferrals of $3 million and $14 million in 2001 and 2000, respectively.

• • •

Note 2 — Cash, Cash Equivalents and Marketable Securities

The following tables summarize, by major security type, the Company's cash and marketable securities (in thousands):

	December 31, 2002			
	Cost or Amortized Cost	Gross Unrealized Gains	Gross Unrealized Losses	Estimated Fair Value
Cash	$ 302,964	$ —	$ —	$ 302,964
Commercial paper and short-term obligations	429,943	5,347	—	435,290
Cash and cash equivalents	732,907	5,347	—	738,254
Certificates of deposit	19,494	2,832	—	22,326
Commercial paper and short-term obligations	2,073	—	—	2,073
Corporate notes and bonds	42,586	355	—	42,941
Asset-backed and agency securities	309,549	7,166	—	316,715
U.S. Treasury notes and bonds	172,145	2,616	(35)	174,726
Equity securities	3,934	—	—	3,934
Marketable securities	549,781	12,969	(35)	562,715
Total	$1,282,688	$18,316	$(35)	$1,300,969

• • •

Note 3 — Fixed Assets

Fixed assets, at cost, consist of the following (in thousands):

	December 31,	
	2002	2001
Furniture, fixtures and leasehold improvements	$ 112,943	$ 109,227
Technology infrastructure and other computer equipment	57,086	58,140
Software purchased or developed for internal use	94,561	70,944
Equipment and other fixed assets acquired under capital leases	218,146	199,832
	482,736	438,143
Less accumulated depreciation	(243,338)	(166,392)
Fixed assets, net	$ 239,398	$ 271,751

Depreciation expense on fixed assets was $77 million, $83 million and $83 million, which includes amortization of fixed assets acquired under capital lease obligations of $7 million, $9 million and $11 million for 2002, 2001 and 2000, respectively.

• • •

Note 6 — Long-Term Debt and Other

The Company's long-term debt and other long-term liabilities are summarized as follows (in thousands):

	December 31,	
	2002	2001
4.75% Convertible Subordinated Notes	$1,249,807	$1,249,807
6.875% PEACS	724,500	608,787
Senior Discount Notes	255,597	231,830
Long-term restructuring liabilities	31,614	20,640
Euro currency swap	12,159	33,265
Capital lease obligations	8,491	16,415
Other long-term debt	8,456	10,381
	2,290,624	2,171,125
Less current portion of capital lease obligations	(7,506)	(9,922)
Less current portion of other long-term debt	(5,813)	(5,070)
	$2,277,305	$2,156,133

• • •

Note 15 — Segment Information

The Company presents information to its chief operating decision maker in four segments: North America Books, Music, and DVD/Video ("BMVD"); North America Electronics, Tools, and Kitchen ("ETK"); International; and Services. Accordingly, the Company discloses its segment financial information along these lines.

• • •

BMVD Segment

The BMVD segment includes retail sales from *www.amazon.com* and *www.amazon.ca* of books, music and DVD/video products and magazine subscription commissions. This segment also includes commissions from sales of these products, new, used or collectible, through Amazon Marketplace, amounts earned from sales of these products by other businesses through the Merchants@ program and product revenues from stores offering these products through the Syndicated Stores program.

ETK Segment

The ETK segment includes *www.amazon.com* retail sales of electronics, home improvement and home and garden products, as well as our mail-order catalog sales. This segment also includes commissions from sales of these products, new, used or collectible, through Amazon Marketplace and amounts earned from sales of these products by other businesses through the Merchants@ program, such as with Office Depot, and will include revenues from stores offering these products, if any, through the Syndicated Stores program.

International Segment

The International segment includes all retail sales of the following internationally-focused Web sites: *www.amazon.co.uk, www.amazon.de, www.amazon.fr* and *www.amazon.co.jp.* These international sites share a common Amazon.com experience, but are localized in terms of language, products, customer service and fulfillment. To the extent available on these sites, this segment includes commissions and other amounts earned from sales of products through Amazon Marketplace and revenues from stores offering products through the Syndicated Stores program, such as *www.waterstones.co.uk* and *www.virginmega.co.jp,* and amounts earned from sales of products by other businesses through the Merchants@ program. The International segment includes export sales from *www.amazon.co.uk, www.amazon.de, www.amazon.fr* and *www.amazon.co.jp* (including export sales from these sites to customers in the U.S. and Canada), but excludes export sales from *www.amazon.com* and *www.amazon.ca.* Operating results for the International segment are affected by movements in foreign exchange rates. During 2002, International segment revenues improved $47 million, and operating results improved $4 million in comparison to the prior year due to changes in foreign exchange rates.

Services Segment

The Services segment consists of commissions, fees and other amounts earned from the services business, including the Merchant.com program (such as *www.target.com*), and to the extent full product categories are not also offered by the Company through its online retail stores, the Merchants@ program, such as the apparel store, Toysrus.com and Babiesrus.com stores, and portions of the Target store at *www.amazon.com,* as well as the commercial agreement with America Online, Inc. This segment also includes Auctions, zShops, Amazon Payments and miscellaneous marketing and promotional agreements.

Included in Services segment revenues are equity-based service revenues of $13 million, $27 million and $79 million for 2002, 2001 and 2000, respectively.

The Company measures the results of operations of its reportable segments using a pro forma measure. Pro forma results from operations, which exclude stock-based compensation, amortization of goodwill and other intangibles, and restructuring-related and other charges, are not in conformity with accounting principles generally accepted in the United States. Stock-based compensation, amortization of goodwill and other intangibles, and restructuring-related and other costs are not allocated to segment results. All other centrally-incurred operating costs are fully allocated to segment results. There are no internal transactions between the Company's reporting segments.

Information on reportable segments and reconciliation to consolidated net loss is as follows (in thousands):

Year Ended 2002:

	North America					
	Books, Music and DVD/Video	Electronics, Tools and Kitchen	Total	International	Services	Consolidated
Net sales	$1,873,291	$645,031	$2,518,322	$1,168,935	$245,679	$3,932,936
Gross profit	527,542	89,863	617,405	249,089	126,124	992,618
Pro forma income (loss) from operations	211,363	(73,220)	138,143	(640)	42,599	180,102
Stock-based compensation						(68,927)
Amortization of other intangibles						(5,478)
Restructuring-related and other						(41,573)
Total non-operating expenses, net						(209,888)
Equity in losses of equity-method investees, net						(4,169)
Cumulative effect of change in accounting principle						801
Net loss						$ (149,132)

Year Ended 2001:

	North America					
	Books. Music and DVD/Video	Electronics, Tools and Kitchen	Total	International	Services	Consolidated
Net sales	$1,688,752	$ 547,190	$2,235,942	$ 661,374	$225,117	$3,122,433
Gross profit	453,129	78,384	531,513	140,606	126,439	798,558
Pro forma income (loss) from operations	156,753	(140,685)	16,068	(103,112)	42,042	(45,002)
Stock-based compensation						(4,637)
Amortization of goodwill and other intangibles						(181,033)
Restructuring-related and other						(181,585)
Total non-operating expenses, net						(114,170)
Equity in losses of equity-method investees, net						(30,327)
Cumulative effect of change in accounting principle						(10,523)
Net loss						$ (567,277)

Year Ended 2000:

	North America					
	Books, Music and DVD/Video	Electronics, Tools and Kitchen	Total	International	Services	Consolidated
Net sales	$1,698,266	$ 484,151	$2,182,417	$ 381,075	$198,491	$ 2,761,983
Gross profit	417,452	44,655	462,107	77,436	116,234	655,777
Pro forma income (loss) from operations	71,441	(269,890)	(198,449)	(145,070)	26,519	(317,000)
Stock-based compensation						(24,797)
Amortization of goodwill and other intangibles						(321,772)
Restructuring-related and other						(200,311)
Total non-operating expenses, net						(242,797)
Equity in losses of equity-method investees, net						(304,596)
Net loss						$(1,411,273)

Net sales to customers outside of the U.S. represented approximately 35%, 29% and 22% of net sales for 2002, 2001 and 2000, respectively. Other than sales into the United Kingdom, which represents approximately 11% of total net sales in 2002, no individual foreign country, geographical area or customer accounted for more than 10% of net sales in any of the periods presented.

Depreciation expense, by segment, was as follows (in thousands):

	North America					
Year Ended December 31,	Books, Music and DVD/Video	Electronics, Tools and Kitchen	Total	Services	International	Consolidated
2002	$25,774	$19,051	$44,825	$7,339	$21,194	$73,358
2001	29,317	21,670	50,987	8,349	24,108	83,444
2000	29,501	26,818	56,319	7,649	18,970	82,938

At December 31, 2002 and 2001, fixed assets, net totaled $196 million and $228 million in the United States, respectively, and $43 million and $44 million in other countries, respectively.

Note 16 — Quarterly Results (Unaudited)

The following tables contain selected unaudited statement of operations information for each quarter of 2002, 2001 and 2000. The Company believes that the following information reflects all normal recurring adjustments necessary for a fair presentation of the information for the periods presented. The operating results for any quarter are not necessarily indicative of results for any future period. Unaudited quarterly results were as follows (in thousands, except per share data):

	Year Ended December 31, 2002			
	Fourth Quarter	Third Quarter	Second Quarter	First Quarter
Net sales	$1,428,610	$851,299	$805,605	$847,422
Gross profit	335,159	216,167	218,167	223,125
Income (loss) before change in accounting principle	2,651	(35,080)	(93,553)	(23,951)
Cumulative effect of change in accounting principle	—	—	—	801
Net income (loss)	2,651	(35,080)	(93,553)	(23,150)
Basic income (loss) per share(1):				
Prior to cumulative effect of change in accounting principle	$ 0.01	$ (0.09)	$ (0.25)	$ (0.06)
Cumulative effect of change in accounting principle	—	—	—	—
	$ 0.01	$ (0.09)	$ (0.25)	$ (0.06)
Diluted income (loss) per share(1):				
Prior to cumulative effect of change in accounting principle	$ 0.01	$ (0.09)	$ (0.25)	$ (0.06)
Cumulative effect of change in accounting principle	—	—	—	—
	$ 0.01	$ (0.09)	$ (0.25)	$ (0.06)
Shares used in computation of income (loss) per share:				
Basic	383,702	379,650	376,937	373,031
Diluted	407,056	379,650	376,937	373,031

	Year Ended December 31, 2001			
	Fourth Quarter	Third Quarter	Second Quarter	First Quarter
Net sales	$1,115,171	$ 639,281	$ 667,625	$ 700,356
Gross profit	274,049	162,192	179,720	182,597
Income (loss) before change in accounting principle	5,087	(169,874)	(168,359)	(223,608)
Cumulative effect of change in accounting principle	—	—	—	(10,523)
Net income (loss)	5,087	(169,874)	(168,359)	(234,131)

	Year Ended December 31, 2001			
	Fourth Quarter	Third Quarter	Second Quarter	First Quarter
Basic and diluted income (loss) per share(1):				
Prior to cumulative effect of change in accounting principle	$ 0.01	$ (0.46)	$ (0.47)	$ (0.63)
Cumulative effect of change in accounting principle	—	—	—	(0.03)
	$ 0.01	$ (0.46)	$ (0.47)	$ (0.66)
Shares used in computation of basic income (loss) per share	371,420	368,052	359,752	357,424
Shares used in computation of diluted income (loss) per share	384,045	368,052	359,752	357,424

	Year Ended December 31, 2000			
	Fourth Quarter	Third Quarter	Second Quarter	First Quarter
Net sales	$ 972,360	$ 637,858	$ 577,876	$ 573,889
Gross profit	224,300	167,279	136,064	128,134
Net loss	(545,140)	(240,524)	(317,184)	(308,425)
Basic and diluted loss per share(1)	$ (1.53)	$ (0.68)	$ (0.91)	$ (0.90)
Shares used in computation of basic and diluted loss per share	355,681	353,954	349,886	343,884

(1) The sum of quarterly per share amounts may not equal per share amounts reported for year-to-date periods. This is due to changes in the number of weighted-average shares outstanding and the effects of rounding for each period.

Appendix B

Typical Charts of Accounts for Different Types of Businesses

(For Businesses Discussed in Chapters 1–12)

Service Proprietorship

Assets

Cash
Accounts Receivable
Allowance for Uncollectible Accounts
Notes Receivable, Short-Term
Interest Receivable
Supplies
Prepaid Rent
Prepaid Insurance
Notes Receivable, Long-Term
Land
Furniture
Accumulated Depreciation—Furniture
Equipment
Accumulated Depreciation—Equipment
Building
Accumulated Depreciation—Building

Liabilities

Accounts Payable
Notes Payable, Short-Term
Salary Payable
Wage Payable
Employee Income Tax Payable
FICA Tax Payable
State Unemployment Tax Payable
Federal Unemployment Tax Payable
Employee Benefits Payable
Interest Payable
Unearned Service Revenue
Notes Payable, Long-Term

Owner's Equity

Owner, Capital
Owner, Withdrawals

Revenues and Gains

Service Revenue
Interest Revenue
Gain on Sale of Land (or Furniture, Equipment, or Building)

Expenses and Losses

Salary Expense
Payroll Tax Expense
Rent Expense
Insurance Expense
Supplies Expense
Uncollectible-Account Expense
Depreciation Expense—Furniture
Depreciation Expense—Equipment
Depreciation Expense—Building
Property Tax Expense
Interest Expense
Miscellaneous Expense
Loss on Sale of Land (Furniture, Equipment, or Building)

Service Partnership

Same as Service Proprietorship, except for Owners' Equity:

Owners' Equity

Partner 1, Capital
Partner 2, Capital
Partner *N*, Capital

Partner 1, Drawing
Partner 2, Drawing
Partner *N*, Drawing

(For Businesses Discussed in Chapters 13–26)

Merchandising Corporation

Assets

Cash
Short-Term Investments (Trading Securities)
Accounts Receivable
Allowance for Uncollectible Accounts
Notes Receivable, Short-Term
Interest Receivable
Inventory
Supplies
Prepaid Rent
Prepaid Insurance
Notes Receivable, Long-Term
Investments in Stock (Available-for-Sale Securities)
Investments in Bonds (Held-to-Maturity Securities)
Other Receivables, Long-Term
Land
Land Improvements
Furniture and Fixtures
Accumulated Depreciation—Furniture and Fixtures
Equipment
Accumulated Depreciation—Equipment
Buildings
Accumulated Depreciation—Buildings
Franchises
Patents
Leaseholds
Goodwill

Liabilities

Accounts Payable
Notes Payable, Short-Term
Current Portion of Bonds Payable
Salary Payable
Wage Payable
Employee Income Tax Payable
FICA Tax Payable
State Unemployment Tax Payable
Federal Unemployment Tax Payable
Employee Benefits Payable
Interest Payable
Income Tax Payable
Unearned Sales Revenue
Notes Payable, Long-Term
Bonds Payable

Stockholder's Equity

Preferred Stock
Paid-in Capital in Excess of Par—Preferred
Common Stock
Paid-in Capital in Excess of Par—Common
Paid-in Capital from Treasury Stock Transactions
Paid-in Capital from Retirement of Stock
Retained Earnings
Foreign Currency Translation Adjustment
Treasury Stock

Revenues and Gains

Sales Revenue
Interest Revenue
Dividend Revenue
Equity-Method Investment Revenue
Unrealized Gain on Investments
Gain on Sale of Investments
Gain on Sale of Land (Furniture and Fixtures, Equipment, or Buildings)
Discontinued Operations—Gain
Extraordinary Gains

Expenses and Losses

Cost of Goods Sold
Salary Expense
Wage Expense
Commission Expense
Payroll Tax Expense
Rent Expense
Insurance Expense
Supplies Expense
Uncollectible-Account Expense
Depreciation Expense—Land Improvements
Depreciation Expense—Furniture and Fixtures
Depreciation Expense—Equipment
Depreciation Expense—Buildings
Amortization Expense—Franchises
Amortization Expense—Leaseholds
Loss on Goodwill
Income Tax Expense
Unrealized Loss on Investments
Loss on Sale of Investments
Loss on Sale of Land (Furniture and Fixtures, Equipment, or Buildings)
Discontinued Operations—Loss
Extraordinary Losses

Manufacturing Corporation

Same as Merchandising Corporation, except for Assets and Expenses:

Assets

Inventories:
- Materials Inventory
- Work in Process Inventory
- Finished Goods Inventory

Expenses (Contra Expenses If Credit Balance)

Direct Materials Price Variance
Direct Materials Efficiency Variance
Direct Labor Price Variance
Direct Labor Efficiency Variance
Manufacturing Overhead Flexible Budget Variance
Manufacturing Overhead Production Volume Variance

Appendix C

Present Value Tables and Future Value Tables

This appendix provides present value tables and future value tables (more complete than those in the Chapter 15 appendix and in Chapter 26).

Exhibit C-1

Present Value of $1

	Present Value										
Periods	**1%**	**2%**	**3%**	**4%**	**5%**	**6%**	**7%**	**8%**	**9%**	**10%**	**12%**
1	0.990	0.980	0.971	0.962	0.952	0.943	0.935	0.926	0.917	0.909	0.893
2	0.980	0.961	0.943	0.925	0.907	0.890	0.873	0.857	0.842	0.826	0.797
3	0.971	0.942	0.915	0.889	0.864	0.840	0.816	0.794	0.772	0.751	0.712
4	0.961	0.924	0.888	0.855	0.823	0.792	0.763	0.735	0.708	0.683	0.636
5	0.951	0.906	0.883	0.822	0.784	0.747	0.713	0.681	0.650	0.621	0.567
6	0.942	0.888	0.837	0.790	0.746	0.705	0.666	0.630	0.596	0.564	0.507
7	0.933	0.871	0.813	0.760	0.711	0.665	0.623	0.583	0.547	0.513	0.452
8	0.923	0.853	0.789	0.731	0.677	0.627	0.582	0.540	0.502	0.467	0.404
9	0.914	0.837	0.766	0.703	0.645	0.592	0.544	0.500	0.460	0.424	0.361
10	0.905	0.820	0.744	0.676	0.614	0.558	0.508	0.463	0.422	0.386	0.322
11	0.896	0.804	0.722	0.650	0.585	0.527	0.475	0.429	0.388	0.350	0.287
12	0.887	0.788	0.701	0.625	0.557	0.497	0.444	0.397	0.356	0.319	0.257
13	0.879	0.773	0.681	0.601	0.530	0.469	0.415	0.368	0.326	0.290	0.229
14	0.870	0.758	0.661	0.577	0.505	0.442	0.388	0.340	0.299	0.263	0.205
15	0.861	0.743	0.642	0.555	0.481	0.417	0.362	0.315	0.275	0.239	0.183
16	0.853	0.728	0.623	0.534	0.458	0.394	0.339	0.292	0.252	0.218	0.163
17	0.844	0.714	0.605	0.513	0.436	0.371	0.317	0.270	0.231	0.198	0.146
18	0.836	0.700	0.587	0.494	0.416	0.350	0.296	0.250	0.212	0.180	0.130
19	0.828	0.686	0.570	0.475	0.396	0.331	0.277	0.232	0.194	0.164	0.116
20	0.820	0.673	0.554	0.456	0.377	0.312	0.258	0.215	0.178	0.149	0.104
21	0.811	0.660	0.538	0.439	0.359	0.294	0.242	0.199	0.164	0.135	0.093
22	0.803	0.647	0.522	0.422	0.342	0.278	0.226	0.184	0.150	0.123	0.083
23	0.795	0.634	0.507	0.406	0.326	0.262	0.211	0.170	0.138	0.112	0.074
24	0.788	0.622	0.492	0.390	0.310	0.247	0.197	0.158	0.126	0.102	0.066
25	0.780	0.610	0.478	0.375	0.295	0.233	0.184	0.146	0.116	0.092	0.059
26	0.772	0.598	0.464	0.361	0.281	0.220	0.172	0.135	0.106	0.084	0.053
27	0.764	0.586	0.450	0.347	0.268	0.207	0.161	0.125	0.098	0.076	0.047
28	0.757	0.574	0.437	0.333	0.255	0.196	0.150	0.116	0.090	0.069	0.042
29	0.749	0.563	0.424	0.321	0.243	0.185	0.141	0.107	0.082	0.063	0.037
30	0.742	0.552	0.412	0.308	0.231	0.174	0.131	0.099	0.075	0.057	0.033
40	0.672	0.453	0.307	0.208	0.142	0.097	0.067	0.046	0.032	0.022	0.011
50	0.608	0.372	0.228	0.141	0.087	0.054	0.034	0.021	0.013	0.009	0.003

Exhibit C-1
(cont'd)

Present Value											
14%	15%	16%	18%	20%	25%	30%	35%	40%	45%	50%	Periods
0.877	0.870	0.862	0.847	0.833	0.800	0.769	0.741	0.714	0.690	0.667	1
0.769	0.756	0.743	0.718	0.694	0.640	0.592	0.549	0.510	0.476	0.444	2
0.675	0.658	0.641	0.609	0.579	0.512	0.455	0.406	0.364	0.328	0.296	3
0.592	0.572	0.552	0.516	0.482	0.410	0.350	0.301	0.260	0.226	0.198	4
0.519	0.497	0.476	0.437	0.402	0.328	0.269	0.223	0.186	0.156	0.132	5
0.456	0.432	0.410	0.370	0.335	0.262	0.207	0.165	0.133	0.108	0.088	6
0.400	0.376	0.354	0.314	0.279	0.210	0.159	0.122	0.095	0.074	0.059	7
0.351	0.327	0.305	0.266	0.233	0.168	0.123	0.091	0.068	0.051	0.039	8
0.308	0.284	0.263	0.225	0.194	0.134	0.094	0.067	0.048	0.035	0.026	9
0.270	0.247	0.227	0.191	0.162	0.107	0.073	0.050	0.035	0.024	0.017	10
0.237	0.215	0.195	0.162	0.135	0.086	0.056	0.037	0.025	0.017	0.012	11
0.208	0.187	0.168	0.137	0.112	0.069	0.043	0.027	0.018	0.012	0.008	12
0.182	0.163	0.145	0.116	0.093	0.055	0.033	0.020	0.013	0.008	0.005	13
0.160	0.141	0.125	0.099	0.078	0.044	0.025	0.015	0.009	0.006	0.003	14
0.140	0.123	0.108	0.084	0.065	0.035	0.020	0.011	0.006	0.004	0.002	15
0.123	0.107	0.093	0.071	0.054	0.028	0.015	0.008	0.005	0.003	0.002	16
0.108	0.093	0.080	0.060	0.045	0.023	0.012	0.006	0.003	0.002	0.001	17
0.095	0.081	0.069	0.051	0.038	0.018	0.009	0.005	0.002	0.001	0.001	18
0.083	0.070	0.060	0.043	0.031	0.014	0.007	0.003	0.002	0.001		19
0.073	0.061	0.051	0.037	0.026	0.012	0.005	0.002	0.001	0.001		20
0.064	0.053	0.044	0.031	0.022	0.009	0.004	0.002	0.001			21
0.056	0.046	0.038	0.026	0.018	0.007	0.003	0.001	0.001			22
0.049	0.040	0.033	0.022	0.015	0.006	0.002	0.001				23
0.043	0.035	0.028	0.019	0.013	0.005	0.002	0.001				24
0.038	0.030	0.024	0.016	0.010	0.004	0.001	0.001				25
0.033	0.026	0.021	0.014	0.009	0.003	0.001					26
0.029	0.023	0.018	0.011	0.007	0.002	0.001					27
0.026	0.020	0.016	0.010	0.006	0.002	0.001					28
0.022	0.017	0.014	0.008	0.005	0.002						29
0.020	0.015	0.012	0.007	0.004	0.001						30
0.005	0.004	0.003	0.001	0.001							40
0.001	0.001	0.001									50

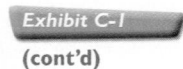

Exhibit C-2

Present Value of Annuity of $1

	Present Value										
Periods	1%	2%	3%	4%	5%	6%	7%	8%	9%	10%	12%
1	0.990	0.980	0.971	0.962	0.952	0.943	0.935	0.926	0.917	0.909	0.893
2	1.970	1.942	1.913	1.886	1.859	1.833	1.808	1.783	1.759	1.736	1.690
3	2.941	2.884	2.829	2.775	2.723	2.673	2.624	2.577	2.531	2.487	2.402
4	3.902	3.808	3.717	3.630	3.546	3.465	3.387	3.312	3.240	3.170	3.037
5	4.853	4.713	4.580	4.452	4.329	4.212	4.100	3.993	3.890	3.791	3.605
6	5.795	5.601	5.417	5.242	5.076	4.917	4.767	4.623	4.486	4.355	4.111
7	6.728	6.472	6.230	6.002	5.786	5.582	5.389	5.206	5.033	4.868	4.564
8	7.652	7.325	7.020	6.733	6.463	6.210	5.971	5.747	5.535	5.335	4.968
9	8.566	8.162	7.786	7.435	7.108	6.802	6.515	6.247	5.995	5.759	5.328
10	9.471	8.983	8.530	8.111	7.722	7.360	7.024	6.710	6.418	6.145	5.650
11	10.368	9.787	9.253	8.760	8.306	7.887	7.499	7.139	6.805	6.495	5.938
12	11.255	10.575	9.954	9.385	8.863	8.384	7.943	7.536	7.161	6.814	6.194
13	12.134	11.348	10.635	9.986	9.394	8.853	8.358	7.904	7.487	7.103	6.424
14	13.004	12.106	11.296	10.563	9.899	9.295	8.745	8.244	7.786	7.367	6.628
15	13.865	12.849	11.938	11.118	10.380	9.712	9.108	8.559	8.061	7.606	6.811
16	14.718	13.578	12.561	11.652	10.838	10.106	9.447	8.851	8.313	7.824	6.974
17	15.562	14.292	13.166	12.166	11.274	10.477	9.763	9.122	8.544	8.022	7.120
18	16.398	14.992	13.754	12.659	11.690	10.828	10.059	9.372	8.756	8.201	7.250
19	17.226	15.678	14.324	13.134	12.085	11.158	10.336	9.604	8.950	8.365	7.366
20	18.046	16.351	14.878	13.590	12.462	11.470	10.594	9.818	9.129	8.514	7.469
21	18.857	17.011	15.415	14.029	12.821	11.764	10.836	10.017	9.292	8.649	7.562
22	19.660	17.658	15.937	14.451	13.163	12.042	11.061	10.201	9.442	8.772	7.645
23	20.456	18.292	16.444	14.857	13.489	12.303	11.272	10.371	9.580	8.883	7.718
24	21.243	18.914	16.936	15.247	13.799	12.550	11.469	10.529	9.707	8.985	7.784
25	22.023	19.523	17.413	15.622	14.094	12.783	11.654	10.675	9.823	9.077	7.843
26	22.795	20.121	17.877	15.983	14.375	13.003	11.826	10.810	9.929	9.161	7.896
27	23.560	20.707	18.327	16.330	14.643	13.211	11.987	10.935	10.027	9.237	7.943
28	24.316	21.281	18.764	16.663	14.898	13.406	12.137	11.051	10.116	9.307	7.984
29	25.066	21.844	19.189	16.984	15.141	13.591	12.278	11.158	10.198	9.370	8.022
30	25.808	22.396	19.600	17.292	15.373	13.765	12.409	11.258	10.274	9.427	8.055
40	32.835	27.355	23.115	19.793	17.159	15.046	13.332	11.925	10.757	9.779	8.244
50	39.196	31.424	25.730	21.482	18.256	15.762	13.801	12.234	10.962	9.915	8.305

Exhibit C-2

(cont'd)

Present Value

14%	15%	16%	18%	20%	25%	30%	35%	40%	45%	50%	Periods
0.877	0.870	0.862	0.847	0.833	0.800	0.769	0.741	0.714	0.690	0.667	1
1.647	1.626	1.605	1.566	1.528	1.440	1.361	1.289	1.224	1.165	1.111	2
2.322	2.283	2.246	2.174	2.106	1.952	1.816	1.696	1.589	1.493	1.407	3
2.914	2.855	2.798	2.690	2.589	2.362	2.166	1.997	1.849	1.720	1.605	4
3.433	3.352	3.274	3.127	2.991	2.689	2.436	2.220	2.035	1.876	1.737	5
3.889	3.784	3.685	3.498	3.326	2.951	2.643	2.385	2.168	1.983	1.824	6
4.288	4.160	4.039	3.812	3.605	3.161	2.802	2.508	2.263	2.057	1.883	7
4.639	4.487	4.344	4.078	3.837	3.329	2.925	2.598	2.331	2.109	1.922	8
4.946	4.772	4.607	4.303	4.031	3.463	3.019	2.665	2.379	2.144	1.948	9
5.216	5.019	4.833	4.494	4.192	3.571	3.092	2.715	2.414	2.168	1.965	10
5.553	5.234	5.029	4.656	4.327	3.656	3.147	2.752	2.438	2.185	1.977	11
5.660	5.421	5.197	4.793	4.439	3.725	3.190	2.779	2.456	2.197	1.985	12
5.842	5.583	5.342	4.910	4.533	3.780	3.223	2.799	2.469	2.204	1.990	13
6.002	5.724	5.468	5.008	4.611	3.824	3.249	2.814	2.478	2.210	1.993	14
6.142	5.847	5.575	5.092	4.675	3.859	3.268	2.825	2.484	2.214	1.995	15
6.265	5.954	5.669	5.162	4.730	3.887	3.283	2.834	2.489	2.216	1.997	16
6.373	6.047	5.749	5.222	4.775	3.910	3.295	2.840	2.492	2.218	1.998	17
6.467	6.128	5.818	5.273	4.812	3.928	3.304	2.844	2.494	2.219	1.999	18
6.550	6.198	5.877	5.316	4.844	3.942	3.311	2.848	2.496	2.220	1.999	19
6.623	6.259	5.929	5.353	4.870	3.954	3.316	2.850	2.497	2.221	1.999	20
6.687	6.312	5.973	5.384	4.891	3.963	3.320	2.852	2.498	2.221	2.000	21
6.743	6.359	6.011	5.410	4.909	3.970	3.323	2.853	2.498	2.222	2.000	22
6.792	6.399	6.044	5.432	4.925	3.976	3.325	2.854	2.499	2.222	2.000	23
6.835	6.434	6.073	5.451	4.937	3.981	3.327	2.855	2.499	2.222	2.000	24
6.873	6.464	6.097	5.467	4.948	3.985	3.329	2.856	2.499	2.222	2.000	25
6.906	6.491	6.118	5.480	4.956	3.988	3.330	2.856	2.500	2.222	2.000	26
6.935	6.514	6.136	5.492	4.964	3.990	3.331	2.856	2.500	2.222	2.000	27
6.961	6.534	6.152	5.502	4.970	3.992	3.331	2.857	2.500	2.222	2.000	28
6.983	6.551	6.166	5.510	4.975	3.994	3.332	2.857	2.500	2.222	2.000	29
7.003	6.566	6.177	5.517	4.979	3.995	3.332	2.857	2.500	2.222	2.000	30
7.105	6.642	6.234	5.548	4.997	3.999	3.333	2.857	2.500	2.222	2.000	40
7.133	6.661	6.246	5.554	4.999	4.000	3.333	2.857	2.500	2.222	2.000	50

Exhibit C-3

Future Value of $1

	Future Value												
Periods	1%	2%	3%	4%	5%	6%	7%	8%	9%	10%	12%	14%	15%
1	1.010	1.020	1.030	1.040	1.050	1.060	1.070	1.080	1.090	1.100	1.120	1.140	1.150
2	1.020	1.040	1.061	1.082	1.103	1.124	1.145	1.166	1.188	1.210	1.254	1.300	1.323
3	1.030	1.061	1.093	1.125	1.158	1.191	1.225	1.260	1.295	1.331	1.405	1.482	1.521
4	1.041	1.082	1.126	1.170	1.216	1.262	1.311	1.360	1.412	1.464	1.574	1.689	1.749
5	1.051	1.104	1.159	1.217	1.276	1.338	1.403	1.469	1.539	1.611	1.762	1.925	2.011
6	1.062	1.126	1.194	1.265	1.340	1.419	1.501	1.587	1.677	1.772	1.974	2.195	2.313
7	1.072	1.149	1.230	1.316	1.407	1.504	1.606	1.714	1.828	1.949	2.211	2.502	2.660
8	1.083	1.172	1.267	1.369	1.477	1.594	1.718	1.851	1.993	2.144	2.476	2.853	3.059
9	1.094	1.195	1.305	1.423	1.551	1.689	1.838	1.999	2.172	2.358	2.773	3.252	3.518
10	1.105	1.219	1.344	1.480	1.629	1.791	1.967	2.159	2.367	2.594	3.106	3.707	4.046
11	1.116	1.243	1.384	1.539	1.710	1.898	2.105	2.332	2.580	2.853	3.479	4.226	4.652
12	1.127	1.268	1.426	1.601	1.796	2.012	2.252	2.518	2.813	3.138	3.896	4.818	5.350
13	1.138	1.294	1.469	1.665	1.886	2.133	2.410	2.720	3.066	3.452	4.363	5.492	6.153
14	1.149	1.319	1.513	1.732	1.980	2.261	2.579	2.937	3.342	3.798	4.887	6.261	7.076
15	1.161	1.346	1.558	1.801	2.079	2.397	2.759	3.172	3.642	4.177	5.474	7.138	8.137
16	1.173	1.373	1.605	1.873	2.183	2.540	2.952	3.426	3.970	4.595	6.130	8.137	9.358
17	1.184	1.400	1.653	1.948	2.292	2.693	3.159	3.700	4.328	5.054	6.866	9.276	10.76
18	1.196	1.428	1.702	2.026	2.407	2.854	3.380	3.996	4.717	5.560	7.690	10.58	12.38
19	1.208	1.457	1.754	2.107	2.527	3.026	3.617	4.316	5.142	6.116	8.613	12.06	14.23
20	1.220	1.486	1.806	2.191	2.653	3.207	3.870	4.661	5.604	6.728	9.646	13.74	16.37
21	1.232	1.516	1.860	2.279	2.786	3.400	4.141	5.034	6.109	7.400	10.80	15.67	18.82
22	1.245	1.546	1.916	2.370	2.925	3.604	4.430	5.437	6.659	8.140	12.10	17.86	21.64
23	1.257	1.577	1.974	2.465	3.072	3.820	4.741	5.871	7.258	8.954	13.55	20.36	24.89
24	1.270	1.608	2.033	2.563	3.225	4.049	5.072	6.341	7.911	9.850	15.18	23.21	28.63
25	1.282	1.641	2.094	2.666	3.386	4.292	5.427	6.848	8.623	10.83	17.00	26.46	32.92
26	1.295	1.673	2.157	2.772	3.556	4.549	5.807	7.396	9.399	11.92	19.04	30.17	37.86
27	1.308	1.707	2.221	2.883	3.733	4.822	6.214	7.988	10.25	13.11	21.32	34.39	43.54
28	1.321	1.741	2.288	2.999	3.920	5.112	6.649	8.627	11.17	14.42	23.88	39.20	50.07
29	1.335	1.776	2.357	3.119	4.116	5.418	7.114	9.317	12.17	15.86	26.75	44.69	57.58
30	1.348	1.811	2.427	3.243	4.322	5.743	7.612	10.06	13.27	17.45	29.96	50.95	66.21
40	1.489	2.208	3.262	4.801	7.040	10.29	14.97	21.72	31.41	45.26	93.05	188.9	267.9
50	1.645	2.692	4.384	7.107	11.47	18.42	29.46	46.90	74.36	117.4	289.0	700.2	1,084

Exhibit C-4

Future Value of Annuity $1

	Future Value												
Periods	1%	2%	3%	4%	5%	6%	7%	8%	9%	10%	12%	14%	15%
1	1.000	1.000	1.000	1.000	1.000	1.000	1.000	1.000	1.000	1.000	1.000	1.000	1.000
2	2.010	2.020	2.030	2.040	2.050	2.060	2.070	2.080	2.090	2.100	2.120	2.140	2.150
3	3.030	3.060	3.091	3.122	3.153	3.184	3.215	3.246	3.278	3.310	3.374	3.440	3.473
4	4.060	4.122	4.184	4.246	4.310	4.375	4.440	4.506	4.573	4.641	4.779	4.921	4.993
5	5.101	5.204	5.309	5.416	5.526	5.637	5.751	5.867	5.985	6.105	6.353	6.610	6.742
6	6.152	6.308	6.468	6.633	6.802	6.975	7.153	7.336	7.523	7.716	8.115	8.536	8.754
7	7.214	7.434	7.662	7.898	8.142	8.394	8.654	8.923	9.200	9.487	10.09	10.73	11.07
8	8.286	8.583	8.892	9.214	9.549	9.897	10.26	10.64	11.03	11.44	12.30	13.23	13.73
9	9.369	9.755	10.16	10.58	11.03	11.49	11.98	12.49	13.02	13.58	14.78	16.09	16.79
10	10.46	10.95	11.46	12.01	12.58	13.18	13.82	14.49	15.19	15.94	17.55	19.34	20.30
11	11.57	12.17	12.81	13.49	14.21	14.97	15.78	16.65	17.56	18.53	20.65	23.04	24.35
12	12.68	13.41	14.19	15.03	15.92	16.87	17.89	18.98	20.14	21.38	24.13	27.27	29.00
13	13.81	14.68	15.62	16.63	17.71	18.88	20.14	21.50	22.95	24.52	28.03	32.09	34.35
14	14.95	15.97	17.09	18.29	19.60	21.02	22.55	24.21	26.02	27.98	32.39	37.58	40.50
15	16.10	17.29	18.60	20.02	21.58	23.28	25.13	27.15	29.36	31.77	37.28	43.84	47.58
16	17.26	18.64	20.16	21.82	23.66	25.67	27.89	30.32	33.00	35.95	42.75	50.98	55.72
17	18.43	20.01	21.76	23.70	25.84	28.21	30.84	33.75	36.97	40.54	48.88	59.12	65.08
18	19.61	21.41	23.41	25.65	28.13	30.91	34.00	37.45	41.30	45.60	55.75	68.39	75.84
19	20.81	22.84	25.12	27.67	30.54	33.76	37.38	41.45	46.02	51.16	63.44	78.97	88.21
20	22.02	24.30	26.87	29.78	33.07	36.79	41.00	45.76	51.16	57.28	72.05	91.02	102.4
21	23.24	25.78	28.68	31.97	35.72	39.99	44.87	50.42	56.76	64.00	81.70	104.8	118.8
22	24.47	27.30	30.54	34.25	38.51	43.39	49.01	55.46	62.87	71.40	92.50	120.4	137.6
23	25.72	28.85	32.45	36.62	41.43	47.00	53.44	60.89	69.53	79.54	104.6	138.3	159.3
24	26.97	30.42	34.43	39.08	44.50	50.82	58.18	66.76	76.79	88.50	118.2	158.7	184.2
25	28.24	32.03	36.46	41.65	47.73	54.86	63.25	73.11	84.70	98.35	133.3	181.9	212.8
26	29.53	33.67	38.55	44.31	51.11	59.16	68.68	79.95	93.32	109.2	150.3	208.3	245.7
27	30.82	35.34	40.71	47.08	54.67	63.71	74.48	87.35	102.7	121.1	169.4	238.5	283.6
28	32.13	37.05	42.93	49.97	58.40	68.53	80.70	95.34	113.0	134.2	190.7	272.9	327.1
29	33.45	38.79	45.22	52.97	62.32	73.64	87.35	104.0	124.1	148.6	214.6	312.1	377.2
30	34.78	40.57	47.58	56.08	66.44	79.06	94.46	113.3	136.3	164.5	241.3	356.8	434.7
40	48.89	60.40	75.40	95.03	120.8	154.8	199.6	259.1	337.9	442.6	767.1	1,342	1,779
50	64.46	84.58	112.8	152.7	209.3	290.3	406.5	573.8	815.1	1,164	2,400	4,995	7,218

Appendix D

Check Figures*

Chapter 1

Quick Check 1 b; 2 c; 3 b; 4 d; 5 a; 6 d; 7 c; 8 c; 9 a; 10 d

S1-1 NCF
S1-2 NCF
S1-3 NCF
S1-4 NCF
S1-5 Owner, Capital $10,000
S1-6 Briggs, Capital $3,000
S1-7 NCF
S1-8 Gillen, Capital $34,000
S1-9 NCF
S1-10 Owner, Capital: (a) $10,000 (b) −$6,000
S1-11 Net income $5,200
Total assets $35,400
S1-12 NCF
S1-13 Net income $40,000
S1-14 Owner, capital, Dec. 31, 20X8 $17,000
S1-15 Total assets $25,000
E1-1 NCF
E1-2 NCF
E1-3 NCF
E1-4 NCF
E1-5 Amy's Hallmark Owner's Equity $22,900
E1-6 1. Increase in equity $3,000
E1-7 1. Net income $13,000
3. Net loss $1,000
E1-8 NCF
E1-9 Total assets $64,800
E1-10 2. Net income $1,000
E1-11 2. Total assets $25,000
E1-12 1. Net income $65,200
2. Capital, ending $27,100
E1-13 1. Net income $0.6 billion
2. Owner equity, ending $5.9 billion
E1-14 Net income $45,000
P1-1A 2. a. Total assets $100,600
d. Net income $1,100
P1-2A 1. Total assets $38,320
2. Net income $4,240
P1-3A NCF
P1-4A a. Net income $37,000
b. L. Collins, capital $71,000
c. Total assets $89,000
P1-5A 1. Net income $47,000
2. Matthew Vail, capital $58,000
3. Total assets $102,000
P1-6A 1. Total assets $105,000
P1-7A 1. Total assets $50,000
P1-1B 2. a. Total assets $81,000
d. Net income $4,000
P1-2B 1. Total assets $29,850
2. Net income $2,100
P1-3B NCF
P1-4B a. Net income $46,000
b. J. Robinson, capital $52,000
c. Total assets $88,000
P1-5B 1. Net income $64,000
2. Brian Sartor, capital $174,000
3. Total assets $279,000
P1-6B 1. Total assets $145,000
P1-7B 1. Total assets $88,000
Case 1 2. Total assets $500,000
Case 2 NCF
Financial Statement Case 2. Total assets Dec. 31, 2002 $1,990,449,000
4. Net sales increased $810,503,000

Chapter 2

Quick Check 1 c; 2 a; 3 d; 4 c; 5 b; 6 b; 7 c; 8 d; 9 a; 10 a

S2-1 NCF
S2-2 NCF
S2-3 NCF
S2-4 NCF
S2-5 NCF
S2-6 NCF
S2-7 NCF
S2-8 NCF
S2-9 3. a. Earned $6,000
b. Total assets $6,000
S2-10 3. Trial bal. total $45,000
S2-11 Trial bal. total $74 mil.
S2-12 Incorrect Trial bal. total debits $24,200
S2-13 Incorrect Trial bal. total debits $13,300
S2-14 Total debits $180,000
E2-1 NCF
E2-2 1. Owners' equity $11 bil.
2. Net income $4 bil.
E2-3 NCF
E2-4 Total debits $180,600
E2-5 NCF
E2-6 2. Trial bal. total $74,700
E2-7 4. Trial bal. total $47,600
E2-8 NCF
E2-9 Trial bal. total $59,400
E2-10 Trial bal. total $184,100
E2-11 Trial bal. total $74,600
E2-12 Cash bal. $4,300
E2-13 Trial bal. total $22,300
E2-14 3. Total debits $53,000
E2-15 NCF
E2-16 b. Cash paid $75,000
c. Cash collected $88,000
E2-17 4. Trial bal. total $20,400
P2-1A 1. Total assets $268,000
Net income $45,000
P2-2A NCF
P2-3A 3. Trial bal. total $35,500
P2-4A 3. Trial bal. total $33,500
P2-5A 1. Trial bal. total $85,100
2. Net income $10,140
P2-6A 3. Trial bal. total $61,200
P2-7A 1. Net income $400
2. Vince Serrano, capital Jan. 31, 20X7 $28,800
3. Total assets $54,900
P2-1B 1. Total assets $106,000
Net income $57,000
P2-2B NCF
P2-3B 3. Trial bal. total $27,300
P2-4B 3. Trial bal. total $42,000
P2-5B 1. Trial bal. total $200,500
2. Net income $6,370
P2-6B 3. Trial bal. total $93,600
P2-7B 1. Net income $2,800
2. Christie Clinton, capital Dec. 31, 20X3 $50,300
3. Total assets $82,200
Case 1 3. Trial bal. total $17,500
4. Net income $5,550
Case 2 NCF
Financial Statement Case Dec. 5 Debit Cash $110,000; Credit Sales Revenue $110,000

Chapter 3

Quick Check 1 d; 2 a; 3 b; 4 c; 5 a; 6 c; 7 a; 8 b; 9 d; 10 c

S3-1 Service revenue:
Cash basis $900;
Accrual basis $1,200
S3-2 NCF
S3-3 2. Revenue $375,000
S3-4 Expense $140,000
S3-5 1. Prepaid Rent bal. $2,500
Rent Expense bal. $500
S3-6 3. Book value $23,000
S3-7 2. Interest Payable at Dec. 31 $900
S3-8 2. Interest Receivable at Dec. 31 $900
S3-9 NCF
S3-10 Supplies to report on balance sheet $400
S3-11 Income statement reports service revenue $7,400
S3-12 1. Total assets $45,925
Total liabilities $14,350
S3-13 1. Net income $3,525
E3-1 NCF

*(NCF = No check figure)

E3-2 NCF
E3-3 NCF
E3-4 A. Rent Expense $1,500
B. Total to account for $1,300
E3-5 NCF
E3-6 Overall, net income is overstated by $7,000
E3-7 NCF
E3-8 Service Revenue bal. $6,900
E3-9 Adjusted trial bal. total $54,400
E3-10 NCF
E3-11 Net income $7,100; S. Perdue, capital $28,400; Total assets $29,300
E3-12 1. Net income $68,500
E3-13 1. Kent Black, capital Dec. 31, 20X5 $126,000
E3-14 Supplies expense $7,800
Salary expense $84,000
Service revenue $182,300
E3-15 7. Net income $1,690; Marsha Walker, capital $14,090; Total assets $18,790
P3-1A 2. Net income $9,150
P3-2A NCF
P3-3A a. Insurance Expense $1,800
d. Supplies Expense $6,600
P3-4A Rental Revenue $700; Interest Revenue $300; Wage Expense $300
P3-5A 3. Adjusted trial bal. total $450,000
P3-6A 1. Net income $40,900; Cindy Sorrel, capital Dec. 31, 20X6 $37,900; Total assets $43,000
P3-7A 2. Net income $10,800; Pat Patillo, capital, July 31, 20X6 $45,900; Total assets $49,500
P3-1B 2. Net income $3,750
P3-2B NCF
P3-3B a. Salary Expense $4,000
d. Supplies Expense $6,400
P3-4B Commission Revenue $8,000; Supplies Expense $900; Salary Expense $1,000
P3-5B 3. Adjusted trial bal. total $62,300
P3-6B 1. Net income $83,470; D. Brooks, capital Dec. 31, 20X8 $67,850; Total assets $134,030
P3-7B 2. Net income $5,400; Jack Dicorte, capital, Oct. 31, 20X7 $132,800; Total assets $136,000
Case 1 1. Your highest price $167,500
2. Wayne's lowest price $139,100
Case 2 Net income $33,540
Financial Statement Case 3. Account balances—all credits: Accum. Depr. $243,338,000; Interest Payable $71,661,000; Unearned Revenue $47,916,000
E3A-1 Supplies bal. $860
E3A-2 Unearned Service Revenue bal. $3,700
E3A-1 Prepaid Rent bal. $2,250; Unearned Service Revenue bal. $2,400

Chapter 4

Quick Check 1 a; 2 a; 3 d; 4 b; 5 b; 6 c; 7 d; 8 b; 9 b; 10 d
S4-1 NCF
S4-2 NCF
S4-3 NCF
S4-4 1. d. Close $3,525
2. Gay Gillen, Capital $31,575
S4-5 1. Gay Gillen, Capital $31,575
S4-6 NCF
S4-7 Income Summary Credit bal. $2,496 mil.
S4-8 Trial bal. total $7,260 mil.
S4-9 NCF
S4-10 c. $826 mil.
d. $5,658 mil.
e. $1,322 mil.
S4-11 Current ratio 1.71
Debt ratio 0.67
S4-12 1. $1.79
2. 49%
E4-1 Net income $2,200
E4-2 Sep. 30 Close net income of $2,200 to Gail Pfeiffer, Capital
E4-3 Gail Pfeiffer, Capital bal. $36,200
E4-4 Trial bal. total $42,200
E4-5 2. b. Insurance Expense $4,600
E4-6 Ending balances of Insurance Expense and Service Revenue are zero
E4-7 Park Daewoo, Capital bal. $59,800
E4-8 Felix Rohr, Capital bal. $72,700
E4-9 Alvin Chang, Capital, Dec. 31, 20X2 $235,000
E4-10 2. Net income $9,300
E4-11 1. Total assets $61,700
2. Current ratio of current year 1.99
E4-12 Net income $52,300
E4-13 1. Marsha Walker, Capital bal. $14,090;
2. Total assets $18,790
3. Net income $1,690
P4-1A Net income $15,000
P4-2A 1. Net income $117,000
2. Ross Reagan, capital $104,000; Total assets $164,000
P4-3A 2. Close net income of $33,300
P4-4A Net income $33,300
P4-5A 2. Net income $12,670
3. Total assets $45,460
5. Postclosing trial bal. total $49,110
P4-6A 1. Total assets $81,400
2. Debt ratio 20X3 0.53
P4-7A a. Overall, net income is understated by $2,520
P4-1B Net income $16,400
P4-2B 1. Net income $90,000
2. Betsy Willis, Capital $64,000; Total assets $131,000
P4-3B 2. Close net income of $85,100
P4-4B Net income $85,100
P4-5B 2. Net income $21,000
3. Total assets $99,320
5. Postclosing trial bal. total $141,220
P4-6B 1. Total assets $124,600
2. Debt ratio 20X6 0.46
P4-7B a. Overall, net income is understated by $1,060
Case 1 Net income $55,440
Case 2 NCF
Financial Statement Case 3. Current ratio at Dec. 31, 2002 1.52
5. Book value $239,398,000
Team Project 1. Net income $2,750
2. Total assets $2,950
P4A-1 All balances are the same both without and with reversing entries.

Chapter 5

Quick Check 1 d; 2 b; 3 c; 4 a; 5 a; 6 c; 7 d; 8 c; 9 b; 10 d
S5-1 NCF
S5-2 a. $100,000
b. $97,000
S5-3 c. Credit Cash for $97,000
S5-4 Cost of inventory $137,200
S5-5 c. Debit Cash for $137,200
S5-6 Gross profit $6,030
S5-7 b. Gross profit $315,360
S5-8 NCF
S5-9 C. Earnest, Capital bal. $25,650
S5-10 NCF
S5-11 Net income $1,666 mil.
S5-12 Total assets $11,471 mil.
S5-13 Gross profit % 20.7%
Invy. turnover 56.4 times
S5-14 b. Excess of collections over payments $641 mil.
E5-1 May 22 Credit Cash for $464.75
E5-2 June 14 Credit Cash for $6,858
E5-3 May 14 Debit Cash for $6,790
E5-4 Sept. 23 Debit Cash for $2,231
E5-5 b. Net income for 2001 $13.7 bil.
E5-6 2. Gross profit for 20X1 $3,541 mil.
E5-7 f. $115,100
g. $112,100
E5-8 2. Owner Capital bal. $10,805 mil.
E5-9 Net income $80,760
E5-10 Net income $80,760
E5-11 1. Net income $31,300
2. Invy. turnover—current year 4.9 times
E5-12 Net income $31,300
Gross profit %—current year 48%

E5-13 Gross profit % 40%
Invy. turnover 6.6 times
E5-14 3. Net income $4,900
P5-1A NCF
P5-2A NCF
P5-3A 2. Receivable $2,200
P5-4A 1. Net income $52,500
P5-5A Net income $35,000
P5-6A 2. Elaine Lorens, Capital bal. $61,820
P5-7A 1. Net income $10,300
2. Total assets $374,100
P5-8A 1. Net income $10,300
2. Total assets $374,100
P5-9A 1. Net income $42,760
2. Invy. turnover for 20X9 8.5 times
P5-1B NCF
P5-2B NCF
P5-3B 2. Belmont was $70 better off as a result of borrowing.
P5-4B 1. Net income $24,200
P5-5B Net income $48,190
P5-6B 2. Jacob Xiang, Capital bal. $64,560
P5-7B 1. Net income $56,400
2. Total assets $200,900
P5-8B 1. Net income $56,400
2. Total assets $200,900
P5-9B 1. Net income $57,310
2. Invy. turnover for 20X4 2.03 times
Case 1 Net income: Sever's plan $97,000
Hagins' plan $102,000
Case 2 2. Net income $78,380
Total assets $104,590
Financial Statement Case Dec. 31 Credit Income Summary for total revenues of $3,963,047,000. Then debit Income Summary for total expenses of $4,112,179,000. Finally, credit Income Summary for net loss of $149,132,000.

Chapter 5 Appendix

E5A-1 June 23 Debit Cash for $2,352
E5A-2 May 22 Credit Cash for $469.54
E5A-3 May 14 Credit Cash for $6,790
June 14 Credit Cash for $6,858
E5A-4 May 14 Debit Cash for $6,790
P5A-1 Nov. 27 Walgreen credits Cash for $2,300. Providence debits Cash for $2,300.
P5A-2 May 26 Credit Cash for $3,920.
May 28 Debit Cash for $2,940.
P5A-3 1. Net income $88,850
3. Ben Latham, Capital bal. $195,590
4. Total assets $218,110

Chapter 6

Quick Check 1 a; 2 b; 3 d; 4 c; 5 d; 6 c; 7 a; 8 d; 9 b; 10 a
S6-1 a. COGS $160
b. Inventory $310
S6-2 COGS $400
S6-3 Inventory $267
S6-4 Inventory bal. $100
S6-5 NCF
S6-6 NCF
S6-7 Gross profit: FIFO $260; LIFO $230
S6-8 COGS $338
S6-9 Report Inventory at $90
S6-10 NCF
S6-11 COGS understated by $100 mil.
S6-12 COGS overstated by $100 mil.
S6-13 Ending invy. $150,000
S6-14 Estimated cost of ending invy. $30,000
E6-1 End. invy. $240; COGS $910
E6-2 May 17 COGS $300
E6-3 End. invy. $220; COGS $930
E6-4 COGS $915; May 31 Invy. $235
E6-5 2. Gross profit $1,574 thou.
E6-6 End. invy.: FIFO $110; LIFO $102
E6-7 COGS: FIFO $420; LIFO $428
E6-8 Gross profit: FIFO $4,500; LIFO $3,700; Avg. $4,071
E6-9 COGS: Avg. $3,320; FIFO $3,270; LIFO $3,368
E6-10 a. $64,800; c. $24,350; d. $30,200; f. $34,700
E6-11 Gross profit $110,567
E6-12 Gross profit $68,000; End. invy. $18,300
E6-13 Gross profit is $70,000 with invy. overstated; $76,000 with invy. understated
E6-14 Net income: 20X2 $41,100; 20X1 $27,300
E6-15 Estimated cost of invy. destroyed $250,000
E6-16 Estimated cost of end. invy. $49,100
P6-1A 1. COGS $6,000; End. invy. $800
P6-2A 1. COGS $6,016; End. invy. $784
2. Net income $2,484
P6-3A 1. COGS $1,365; End. invy. $225
3. Gross profit $1,315
P6-4A 2. Gross profit: Avg. $34,293; FIFO $35,484; LIFO $33,092
P6-5A 1. Sales revenue $310,000
2. COGS $195,000
P6-6A NCF
P6-7A 1. Net income: 20X3 $11,000; 20X2 $9,000; 20X1 $27,000
P6-8A 1. Estimated cost of end. invy. $672,000
2. Gross profit $2,592,000
P6-1B 1. COGS $7,750; End. invy. $300
P6-2B 1. COGS $7,705; End. invy. $345
2. Net income $945
P6-3B 1. COGS $4,640; End. invy. $1,840
3. Gross profit $3,270
P6-4B 2. Gross profit: Avg. $7,555; FIFO $7,833: LIFO $7,242
P6-5B 1. Sales revenue $378,000
2. COGS $155,000
P6-6B NCF
P6-7B 1. Net income: 20X3 $61,000; 20X2 $59,000; 20X1 $15,000
P6-8B 1. Estimated cost of end. invy. $275,000
2. Gross profit $2,562,000
Case 1 NCF
Case 2 NCF
Financial Statement Case 3. Purchases $2,999,021,000

Chapter 7

Quick Check 1 c; 2 e; 3 a; 4 b; 5 c; 6 a; 7 b; 8 d; 9 d; 10 b
S7-1 NCF
S7-2 NCF
S7-3 NCF
S7-4 NCF
S7-5 NCF
S7-6 NCF
S7-7 NCF
S7-8 NCF
S7-9 2. Decrease in Accounts Receivable $1,235
S7-10 2. Credit Cash $2,876
S7-11 1. Increase in Accounts Payable $2,876
S7-12 2. Net sales revenue $7,456
E7-1 NCF
E7-2 Total assets $107,000
E7-3 NCF
E7-4 NCF
E7-5 Total debit to Cash $450
E7-6 NCF
E7-7 NCF
E7-8 Purchases journal: Total credit to Accounts Payable $18,265
E7-9 3. Total Accounts Payable $3,300
E7-10 Total credit to Cash $11,697
E7-11 Kendrick: Credit Cash for $1,151
E7-12 Gross profit $3,935
P7-1A NCF
P7-2A 1. Cash receipts journal: Total debit to Cash $53,748
P7-3A 3. Corrected cash receipts journal: Total debit to Cash $24,302
P7-4A 1. Cash payments journal: Total credit to Cash $15,109
P7-5A 6. Total Accounts Receivable $560
Total Accounts Payable $2,925
P7-1B NCF
P7-2B 1. Cash receipts journal: Total debit to Cash $35,345

P7-3B 3. Corrected cash receipts journal: Total debit to Cash $10,830
P7-4B 1. Cash payments journal: Total credit to Cash $17,237
P7-5B 6. Total Accounts Receivable $496
Total Accounts Payable $2,692
Case 1 Cash receipts journal: Total debit to Cash $7,749
Case 2 NCF

Chapter 8

Quick Check 1 d; 2 a; 3 b; 4 d; 5 b; 6 d; 7 c; 8 c; 9 a; 10 c
S8-1 NCF
S8-2 NCF
S8-3 NCF
S8-4 NCF
S8-5 NCF
S8-6 Adjusted balance $2,900
S8-7 NCF
S8-8 NCF
S8-9 NCF
S8-10 NCF
S8-11 April 30 Credit Cash for $181
S8-12 NCF
E8-1 NCF
E8-2 NCF
E8-3 NCF
E8-4 NCF
E8-5 Adjusted balance $1,581
E8-6 Adjusted balance $3,371
E8-7 NCF
E8-8 NCF
E8-9 NCF
E8-10 1. Credit Cash in Bank for $209
E8-11 3. Petty Cash balance $400
E8-12 NCF
P8-1A NCF
P8-2A NCF
P8-3A Adjusted balance $14,679
P8-4A 1. Adjusted balance $6,046.33
P8-5A NCF
P8-6A 3. June 30 Credit Cash in Bank for $303
P8-7A NCF
P8-1B NCF
P8-2B NCF
P8-3B Adjusted balance $15,670
P8-4B 1. Adjusted balance $19,047.77
P8-5B NCF
P8-6B 3. April 30 Credit Cash in Bank for $376
P8-7B NCF
Case 1 NCF
Case 2 Cashier stole $1,000
Financial Statement Case 5. Cash increased by $197,972,000

Chapter 9

Quick Check 1 d; 2 c; 3 b; 4 a; 5 b; 6 d; 7 c; 8 b; 9 a; 10 c
S9-1 NCF
S9-2 NCF
S9-3 Accts. Rec., net $80,000
S9-4 Uncollectible-Account Expenses $14,000
S9-5 Allowance for Uncollectible Accts. bal. $5,000
S9-6 Uncollectible-Account Expense $2,300
S9-7 June 30 Accts. Rec. bal. $5,000
S9-8 Debit Cash for $7,760
S9-9 Note 1 $4,000
Note 2 $375
S9-10 a. Credit Cash for $100,000
b. Debit Cash for $102,000
S9-11 b. Debit Interest Receivable for $22.50
S9-12 1. Net income $1,184 mil.
2. Accts. Rec., net $2,464 mil.
S9-13 a. 1.01 b. 35 days
S9-14 a. 1.48 c. 0.38
b. 0.47 d. 6.9 times
E9-1 NCF
E9-2 2. Accts. Rec., net $54,600
E9-3 2. Accts. Rec. bal. $56,800
E9-4 2. Accts. Rec., net $289,300
E9-5 Accts. Rec., net $125,900
E9-6 1. Interest for:
20X7 $6,000
20X8 $3,000
E9-7 June 30 Debit Interest Receivable for $420
E9-8 May 1, 20X9 Debit Cash for $22,400
E9-9 Dec. 31 Debit Cash for $10,150
E9-10 1. 20X9 0.95
2. 32 days
E9-11 1. 27 days
E9-12 Net income:
Without bankcards $75,000;
With bankcards $94,300
P9-1A NCF
P9-2A Uncollectible-Acct. Expense:
1. $11,200
2. $8,900
P9-3A 3. Accts. Rec., net $159,300
P9-4A 3. Accts. Rec., net $134,400
P9-5A 1. Note 1 $14,170; Note 2 $12,720; Note 3 $9,075
3. Debit Cash for $14,170
P9-6A Feb. 17, 20X5 Debit Cash for $3,060
Dec. 1, 20X5 Debit Cash for $10,550
P9-7A Dec. 31, 20X6 Debit Uncollectible-Acct. Expense for $14,800
P9-8A 1. Ratios for 20X6:
a. 1.37 c. 18 days
b. 0.70
P9-1B NCF
P9-2B Uncollectible-Acct. Expense:
1. $8,900; 2. $3,500
P9-3B 3. Accts. rec., net $244,500
P9-4B 3. Accts. rec., net $160,100
P9-5B 1. Note 1 $13,080; Note 2 $11,330; Note 3 $15,250
3. Debit Cash for $13,080
P9-6B Jan. 20, 20X7 Debit Cash for $2,823
Dec. 14, 20X7 Debit Cash for $6,195
P9-7B Dec. 31, 20X4 Debit Uncollectible-Acct. Expense for $15,700
P9-8B 1. Ratios for 20X8:
a. 1.88 c. 20 days
b. 0.67
Case 1 2. Expected amount to collect $16,200
Case 2 1. Net income: 20X6 $106,600; 20X5 $85,550
Financial Statement Case 2. b. Expect to collect $112,282,000
c. Expect not to collect $5,718,000
3. Acid-test ratio for 2002 1.33

Chapter 10

Quick Check 1 b; 2 a; 3 d; 4 c; 5 a; 6 d; 7 b; 8 a; 9 c; 10 d
S10-1 NCF
S10-2 Land $60,000; Building $45,000; Equipment $15,000
S10-3 2. Net income overstated by $800,000
S10-4 2. Book value $34,800,000
S10-5 2nd-year depreciation:
b. UOP $9,000,000; DDB $10,080,000
S10-6 2. Extra tax deduction with DDB $9,600,000
S10-7 $5,400,000
S10-8 Depreciation Expense $10,000
S10-9 Gain on Sale $3,000
S10-10 2. Depletion Expense $6.0 bil.
S10-11 Goodwill $500,000
S10-12 Net income $200,000
E10-1 Land $210,000; Land improvements $67,400; Building $800,000
E10-2 1. Cost of building $954,000
E10-3 Bed 1 $2,500; Bed 2 $4,170; Bed 3 $3,330
E10-4 NCF
E10-5 NCF
E10-6 20X9 Depreciation: SL $3,000; UOP $2,400; DDB $375
E10-7 Extra depreciation with DDB $38,388
E10-8 Depreciation for Year 16 $20,000
E10-9 Gain on sale $800
E10-10 Cost of new truck $300,000
E10-11 c. Depletion Expense $92,000
E10-12 Part 2. Amortization Expense for year 5 $250,000
E10-13 Goodwill $6,000,000
E10-14 Year 5: Equipment is correct; Net income is overstated by 1 million euros
E10-15 Gain on sale $458 mil.

P10-1A 2. Depreciation: Land Improvements $2,480; Building $16,500; Furniture $9,108
P10-2A Dec. 31 Depreciation Expense: Motor-Carrier Equip. $18,000; Buildings $750
P10-3A NCF
P10-4A 1. Book value at Dec. 31, 20X7: SL $64,000; UOP $53,000; DDB $31,104
P10-5A Part 1. Goodwill $2,500,000
Part 2. Net income $134,000
P10-6A 1. Book value $5.9 bil.;
2. Owners' equity $11.8 bil.;
3. Net income $3.1 bil.
P10-1B 2. Depreciation: Land Improvements $3,975; Building $30,621; Furniture $11,681
P10-2B Dec. 31 Depreciation Expense: Comm. Equip. $9,600; Televideo Equip. $1,067; Office Equip. $4,167
P10-3B NCF
P10-4B 1. Book value at Dec. 31, 20X8: SL $23,500; UOP $22,012; DDB $14,200
P10-5B Part 1. Goodwill $500,000
Part 2. Net income $95,000
P10-6B 1. Book value $29.0 bil.;
2. Owners' equity $12.6 bil.;
3. Net loss $1.4 bil.
Case 1 1. Net income: Stewart $164,000; Jordan $126,700
Case 2 NCF
Financial Statement Case
2. Depreciation expense $77 mil.
3. Purchases of fixed assets $39,613,000

Chapter 11

Quick Check 1 a; 2 c; 3 d; 4 c; 5 b; 6 a; 7 d; 8 a; 9 c; 10 d
S11-1 b. Credit Cash for $8,800
S11-2 Interest Expense $400
S11-3 2. Estimated Warranty Payable bal. $5,000
S11-4 NCF
S11-5 NCF
S11-6 2. Net pay $676.50
S11-7 Total expense $1,000.40
S11-8 a. Salary Payable $676.50
S11-9 Net pay $5,640
S11-10 1. Total salary expense $14,654;
2. Net pay $10,269.30
S11-11 NCF
S11-12 Total current liabilities $60,726
E11-1 Mar. 31 Debit Cash for $208,000
E11-2 Unearned subscription revenue bal. $120
E11-3 2. Estimated Warranty Payable bal. $5,000
E11-4 May 1, 20X3 Credit Cash for $15,900
E11-5 Net pay $7,430
E11-6 a. Net pay $462.50
E11-7 Payroll Tax Expense $7,630
E11-8 Salary expense $600,000; Salary payable $4,000
E11-9 20X1: Current portion of long-term note payable $1,000,000; Interest payable $270,000
E11-10 Total current liabilities $86,400
E11-11 Ratios for 20X2:
Current 1.24; Debt 0.702
E11-12 NCF
P11-1A NCF
P11-2A 1. c. $83,693
P11-3A 1. Net pay $68,483
2. Total cost $101,574
P11-4A 3. Total liabilities $200,390
P11-5A 1. Total net pay $2,334
3. Credit Cash for $2,334
4. Debit Payroll Tax Expense for $181
P11-6A NCF
P11-1B NCF
P11-2B 1. c. $23,949
P11-3B 1. Net pay $68,993
P11-4B 2. Total cost $102,264
3. Total liabilities $331,440
P11-5B 1. Total net pay $3,412
3. Credit Cash for $3,412
4. Debit Payroll Tax Expense for $127
P11-6B NCF
Case 1 NCF
Case 2 NCF
Financial Statement Case
1. Debit Accounts Payable for $618,128,000; Credit Cash for $618,128,000
2. Total long-term debt $2,290,623,000

Chapter 12

Quick Check 1 b; 2 d; 3 b; 4 a; 5 c; 6 b; 7 d; 8 c; 9 d; 10 a
S12-1 NCF
S12-2 Debit Land for $400,000
S12-3 1. Total equity $23 mil.
S12-4 2. Benz, Capital $460,000
Hanna, Capital $95,000
S12-5 Lawson $38,000; Martinez $22,000; Norris $50,000
S12-6 NCF
S12-7 Teal, Capital $80,000
S12-8 Credit Page, Capital $6,667; Franco, Capital $3,333; Neely, Capital $130,000
S12-9 NCF
S12-10 a. Credit Green, Capital $10,000; Henry, Capital $20,000; Isaac, Capital $10,000
S12-11 Pay Akers $37,000; Bloch $19,000; Crane $9,000
S12-12 Final entry: Debit Akers, Capital $37,000; Bloch, Capital $19,000; Crane, Capital $9,000
S12-13 Green, capital $64,000; Henry, capital $63,000
S12-14 Net income: Frost $63,000; Martin $42,000
E12-1 NCF
E12-2 Credit Monteros, Capital for $76,700
E12-3 c. Coe $33,000; Price $65,000
E12-4 Partnership capital increased by $8,000
E12-5 c. Tse, capital $44,000; Graham, capital $108,000; Ott, capital $68,000
E12-6 c. Credit Tse, Capital for $44,000; Graham, Capital for $8,000; Ott, Capital for $8,000
E12-7 1. Echols receives $50,000;
2. Scheffer's equity $60,000
E12-8 b. Debit Augustine, Capital for $46,000; Rye, Capital for $8,400; Bermuda, Capital for $5,600
E12-9 2. Grant gets $20,000, Harris $17,000, and Isbell $8,000
E12-10 Pay Park $26,000, Quade $19,500, Ross $15,500
E12-11 Selling for $140,000: West, Capital $15,500; Young, Capital $43,300; Zeno, Capital $10,200
E12-12 Total assets $283,200; Klatt, capital $90,700; Stover, capital $93,100
P12-1A NCF
P12-2A 2. Total assets $102,100;
Ogden, capital $41,500;
Croyle, capital $41,500
P12-3A Carter's capital:
2. $60,000
3. $95,000
P12-4A 1. b. Net income to:
Lake $79,750
Wood $63,500
Parks $66,750
P12-5A 3. Debit McNut, Capital for $50,000; Black, Capital for $13,548; Tate, Capital for $16,452
P12-6A 1. Pay Parr $19,700, Johnston $35,100, Rake $30,200
P12-7A 2. Capital balances:
Vela $27,000
Thomas $16,000
Prago $9,000
P12-1B NCF
P12-2B 2. Total assets $124,740;
Dalton, capital $51,220;
Sperry, capital $51,220
P12-3B Milano's capital:
2. $50,000
3. $31,250
P12-4B 1. b. Net income to:
Trump $33,667
Rivers $28,667
Jetta $23,666
P12-5B 3. Debit Tracy, Capital for $38,000; Mertz, Capital for $1,143; Brucks, Capital for $857
P12-6B 1. Pay Jackson $20,700; Pierce $52,800; Fenner $11,500

P12-7B 2. Capital balances:
Alberts $10,250
Beech $12,750
Sumner $17,000
Case 1 NCF
Case 2 NCF

Chapter 13

Quick Check 1 d; 2 b; 3 a; 4 b; 5 c; 6 a; 7 c; 8 d; 9 c; 10 a
S13-1 NCF
S13-2 NCF
S13-3 NCF
S13-4 Balances: Building $500,000; Equip. $200,000
S13-5 1. Paid-in Capital in Excess of Par $3,855
S13-6 1. Total increase in paid-in capital $337 mil.
S13-7 a. Paid-in Capital in Excess—Common $49,000
S13-8 Total stockholders' equity $736,000
S13-9 a. Net income $80,000; c. Total assets $924,000
S13-10 NCF
S13-11 4. Preferred gets $6,000; common gets $3,000
S13-12 Book value per share of common $40.80
S13-13 NCF
S13-14 NCF
S13-15 ROA 13.8%
ROE 26.3%
S13-16 2. Net income $60,000
E13-1 NCF
E13-2 2. Total paid-in capital $59,500
E13-3 2. Total stockholders' equity $86,000
E13-4 Both plans result in total paid-in capital of $50,000
E13-5 Total stockholders' equity $206,000
E13-6 Total paid-in capital $400,000
E13-7 Total stockholders' equity $400,000
E13-8 20X2: Preferred gets $17,000; common gets $33,000
E13-9 Preferred gets $40,000; Common gets $110,000
E13-10 Book value per share of common $22.20
E13-11 Book value per share of common $22.11
E13-12 ROA 0.063
ROE 0.111
E13-13 2. Net income $96 mil.
Deferred tax liability $24 mil.
E13-14 d. Close net income of $8 mil. to Retained Earnings
P13-1A NCF
P13-2A 2. Total stockholders' equity $266,000
P13-3A 5. Total stockholders' equity $152,000
P13-4A Total stockholders' equity: Seville $799,000; Madrid $399,000
P13-5A 3. Dividends Payable: Preferred $12 mil.; Common $38 mil.
P13-6A 1. Total assets $387,000; Total S/E $309,000
2. ROA 0.144; ROE 0.198
P13-7A 1. b. 20X2: Preferred gets $70,000; Common gets $30,000
P13-8A 6. Book value per share of common $11.80
P13-9A 3. Net income $126,000
P13-1B NCF
P13-2B 2. Total stockholders' equity $272,000
P13-3B 5. Total stockholders' equity $263,000
P13-4B Total stockholders' equity: Yurman $430,000; Northern $622,900
P13-5B 3. Dividends Payable: Preferred $100 mil.; Common $400 mil.
P13-6B 1. Total assets $574,000; Total S/E $419,000
2. ROA 0.104; ROE 0.120
P13-7B 1. b. 20X2: Preferred gets $3,500; common gets $11,500
P13-8B 5. Book value per share of common $9.74
P13-9B 3. Net income $149,500
Case 1 3. Total stockholders' equity: Plan 1 $420,000; Plan 2 $400,000
Case 2 NCF
Financial Statement Case 3. At Dec. 31, 2002, Common shares issued 387,906,000; Common Stock balance $3,879,000

Chapter 14

Quick Check 1 d; 2 d; 3 a; 4 c; 5 c; 6 b; 7 a; 8 b; 9 a; 10 c
S14-1 Paid-in Capital in Excess of Par $75,000
S14-2 NCF
S14-3 1. Total stockholders' equity $590,000
S14-4 Balance sheet reports Treasury stock $(5,000)
S14-5 NCF
S14-6 NCF
S14-7 NCF
S14-8 Net income $21,000
S14-9 EPS for net income $1.80
S14-10 NCF
S14-11 Comprehensive income $17,000
S14-12 Retained earnings Dec. 31, 20X8 $460,000
S14-13 2. $80,000
3. Sold treasury stock for $15,000
E14-1 2. Total stockholders' equity $570,000
E14-2 NCF
E14-3 Total stockholders' equity $800,000
E14-4 d. Increase stockholders' equity by $3,000
E14-5 Aug. 22 Credit Paid-in Capital from Treasury Stock Transactions for $3,600
E14-6 Total stockholders' equity $870,000
E14-7 b. Total stockholders' equity $750,000
E14-8 Net income $42,000
E14-9 EPS $1.40
E14-10 EPS for net income $2.94
E14-11 Retained earnings Dec. 31, 20X3 $470 mil.
E14-12 Retained earnings Dec. 31, 20X7 $460 mil.
E14-13 1. Comprehensive income $114,000
2. EPS $5.85
E14-14 Total stockholders' equity Dec. 31, 20X7 $1,465,000
E14-15 2. Total stockholders' equity Dec. 31, 20X5 $17,000,000
P14-1A Dec. 22 Credit Paid-in Capital from Treasury Stock Transactions for $1,000
P14-2A 2. Total stockholders' equity $568,000
P14-3A NCF
P14-4A 3. Total stockholders' equity $552,700
P14-5A Net income $62,000; EPS for net income $2.80
P14-6A Retained earnings June 30, 20X4 $277,000; EPS for net income $4.15
P14-7A EPS for net income $3.10
P14-8A 1. Par value $1.80
2. Price per share $11.00
3. Increase in equity $16,000
P14-1B Nov. 8 Credit Paid-in Capital from Treasury Stock Transactions for $3,000
P14-2B 2. Total stockholders' equity $414,000
P14-3B NCF
P14-4B 3. Total stockholders' equity $710,680
P14-5B Net income $64,000; EPS for net income $2.25
P14-6B Retained earnings Dec. 31, 20X3 $444,200; EPS for net income $1.80
P14-7B 1. EPS for net income $2.25
P14-8B 1. Par value $2
2. Price per share $6.40
3. Increase in equity $28,000
Case 1 NCF
Case 2 NCF
Financial Statement Case 2. Basic EPS (loss per share) $(0.39)
3. Accumulated Deficit balance—debit of $3,009,710,000

Chapter 15

Quick Check 1 a; 2 c; 3 d; 4 c; 5 b; 6 a; 7 b; 8 c; 9 b; 10 d

S15-1 c. $77,750
d. $110,375
S15-2 a. $4,825
c. $162.50
S15-3 NCF
S15-4 NCF
S15-5 NCF
S15-6 July 1, 2000 Interest Expense $188
S15-7 July 1, 2000 Interest Expense $138
S15-8 Dec. 31, 2000 Interest Expense $188
S15-9 LT liabilities: Bonds payable, net $4,550
S15-10 2. Bond carrying amount. Mar. 31, 20X4 $546,749
S15-11 2. Bond carrying amount May 31, 20X6 $217,158
S15-12 Interest Expense July 1, 2000 $54.17
S15-13 Gain on retirement of bonds $6,872
S15-14 2. Paid-in Capital in Excess of Par $820,000
S15-15 Total current liabilities $26,000; LT bonds payable, net $344,000
S15-16 EPS: Plan A $5.78; Plan B $3.15
E15-1 c. Dec. 31 Interest Expense $10,000
E15-2 July 1 Interest Expense $4,050
E15-3 At July 1:
b. Credit Discount for $250
c. Debit Premium for $250
E15-4 NCF
E15-5 1. Bond carrying amount 1-2-X5 $280,995
E15-6 1. Bond carrying amount 3-31-X3 $219,390
E15-7 Bond carrying amount 12-31-X5 $500,000
E15-8 Total cash received $510,000
E15-9 b. Oct. 31 Interest Expense $10,000
E15-10 Oct. 1 Loss on Retirement of Bonds $12,750
E15-11 2. Bond carrying amount July 31, 20X9 $691,600
E15-12 2. Oct. 1 Credit Paid-in Capital in Excess of Par for $144,000
E15-13 NCF
E15-14 EPS: Plan A $7.98; Plan B $4.26
E15-15 4. Interest expense $40,575,000
5. Bond carrying amount Mar. 31, 2001 $295,717
6. Interest expense $40,343,000
E15-16 2. a. $295,725
b. $295,950
P15-1A 2. Interest Expense Jan. 31, 20X4 $4,500; 3. Interest expense for 20X3 $49,500; Interest payable $22,500
P15-2A 3. d. Interest Expense Mar. 31, 20X7 $7,900
P15-3A Interest Expense:
Dec. 31, 2009 $14,600
Dec. 31, 2018 $14,600
P15-4A 2. Bond carrying amount Sep. 30, Year 3 $148,095
P15-5A 1. d. Interest Expense Mar. 31, 20X5 $67,500
2. Interest payable at Dec. 31, 20X4 $67,500
P15-6A 3. Convertible bonds payable, net $569,903
P15-7A Total current liabilities $152,000
Total LT liabilities $383,000
P15-8A NCF
P15-1B 2. Interest Expense, Apr. 30, 20X6 $13,333
3. Interest expense $26,667; Interest payable $6,667
P15-2B 3. d. Interest Expense Feb. 28, 20X5 $5,633
P15-3B Interest Expense:
Dec. 31, 2005 $38,400
Dec. 31, 2014 $38,400
P15-4B 2. Bond carrying amount Sep. 30, Year 3 $167,263
P15-5B 1. d. Interest Expense May 31, 20X6 $233,333
2. Interest payable at Dec. 31, 20X5 $46,667
P15-6B 3. Convertible bonds payable, net $423,327
P15-7B Total current liabilities $100,000
Total LT liabilities $289,000
P15-8B NCF
Case 1 EPS: Plan A $6.24; Plan B $5.30; Plan C $6.00
Case 2 NCF
Financial Statement Case
3. Annual interest $59,366,000

Chapter 15 Appendix

P15A-1 Future value:
Plan A $15,432
Plan B $15,870
P15A-2 Present value:
GE $216,300
Westinghouse $226,800
P15A-3 1. Invest $5,580 today
P15A-4 Present value of bonds:
a. $88,018
b. $78,640
c. $98,975
P15A-5 Interest expense for bonds issued at:
12% $5,280
14% $5,748
10% $4,731
P15A-6 2. Bond carrying amount 12-31-X2 $380,838
3. Interest expense Dec. 31, 20X2 $15,205

Chapter 16

Quick Check 1 a; 2 c; 3 b; 4 d; 5 c; 6 c; 7 b; 8 a; 9 b; 10 d

S16-1 a. $3,314
b. $38,304
S16-2 NCF
S16-3 2. Jan. 27, 20X5 Loss on Sale $3,000
S16-4 2. Jan. 16, 20X7 Gain on Sale $1,750
S16-5 2. Gain on sale $1,000
S16-6 2. Unrealized loss $435
S16-7 1. Gain on Sale $510
S16-8 3. LT Equity-Method Investment bal. $104 mil.
S16-9 NCF
S16-10 4. Annual interest revenue $78,000
S16-11 b. Interest Revenue $70,000
c. Interest Revenue $8,000
S16-12 Overall foreign-currency gain $1,000
E16-1 1. Jan. 14, 20X9 Gain on Sale $6,000
E16-2 d. Gain on Sale $800
E16-3 Dec. 4 Loss on Sale $550
E16-4 3. LT available-for-sale investments $205,030; Unrealized loss $15,500
E16-5 b. Equity-Method Investment Revenue $156,000
E16-6 Gain on sale $444,000
E16-7 2. LT Equity-Method Investment bal. $169,000
E16-8 3. LT investment in bonds $27,840
E16-9 Dec. 16 Foreign-Currency Loss $160
Dec. 30 Foreign-Currency Gain $2,400
E16-10 1. Cost $274 mil.
2. Loss on sale $15 mil.
P16-1A 1. Dec. 31 Loss on Trading Investment $3,500
P16-2A 3. LT available-for-sale investments $26,800; LT equity-method investments $431,500
P16-3A LT Equity-Method Investment bal. $832,000; Unrealized gain $1,100
P16-4A 2. LT investment in bonds $409,600
P16-5A Investment carrying amount 12-31-X6 $488,051
P16-6A Income statement reports Foreign-currency loss, net $2,400
P16-1B 1. Dec. 31 Loss on Trading Investment $4,500
P16-2B 3. LT available-for-sale investment $44,100; LT equity-method investments $724,000
P16-3B LT Equity-Method Investment bal. $920,000; Unrealized loss $2,500
P16-4B 2. LT investment in bonds $744,000

P16-5B Investment carrying amount 12-31-X7 $388,355
P16-6B Income statement reports Foreign-currency loss, net $600
Case 1 NCF
Case 2 NCF
Financial Statement Case 1.a. Market value $562,715,000

Chapter 17

Quick Check 1 b; 2 d; 3 c; 4 a; 5 d; 6 c; 7 a; 8 a; 9 d; 10 b
S17-1 NCF
S17-2 NCF
S17-3 NCF
S17-4 Net cash from operating $48,000
S17-5 Net cash from operating $40,000
S17-6 Net cash from operating $40,000; Net increase in cash $39,000
S17-7 Acquisitions of plant assets $100,000
S17-8 a. $2,000 c. $84,000
b. $3,000
S17-9 Net cash from operating $180,000; Cash balance ending $94,000
S17-10 Net cash from operating $50,000
S17-11 Net cash from operating $50,000; Net increase in cash $54,000
S17-12 a. $704,000
b. $331,000
E17-1 NCF
E17-2 NCF
E17-3 NCF
E17-4 Net cash used for operating $(8,000)
E17-5 Net cash from operating $79,000
E17-6 1. Net cash from operating $80,000; investing ($77,000); financing $4,000
E17-7 a. $34,000
b. $6,000
E17-8 NCF
E17-9 NCF
E17-10 Net cash used for operating $(8,000)
E17-11 NCF
E17-12 Net cash from operating $80,000; investing ($77,000); financing $4,000
E17-13 a. $85,000
b. $89,000
E17-14 a. $24,440 mil.
b. $18,516 mil.
c. $4,793 mil.
d. $1,186 mil.
e. $14 mil.
f. $230 mil.
g. $143 mil.
P17-1A NCF
P17-2A 1. Net income $35,000
2. Total assets $588,000
3. Net cash used for operating $(71,000); Cash bal., Dec. 31, 20X8 $268,000
P17-3A Net cash from operating $87,000; investing $(67,000); financing $43,000; Total non-cash investing and financing $65,000
P17-4A 1. Net cash from operating $96,900; investing $(125,700); financing $31,000
P17-5A 1. Net cash from operating $69,100; investing $(37,000); financing $(30,600)
P17-6A Net cash from operating $115,700; investing $(37,000); financing $(70,800)
P17-7A 1. Net income $35,000; 2. Total assets $588,000; 3. Net cash used for operating $(71,000); Cash balance Dec. 31, 20X8 $268,000
P17-8A 1. Net cash from operating $69,100; investing $(37,100); financing $(30,600)
P17-9A Net cash from operating $67,800; investing $(10,200); financing $(47,600)
P17-1B NCF
P17-2B 1. Net income $80,000 2. Total assets $345,000 3. Net cash from operating $85,000; Cash bal., Dec. 31, 20X6 $195,000
P17-3B Net cash from operating $80,000; investing $(69,000); financing $11,000; Total non-cash investing and financing $118,000
P17-4B 1. Net cash from operating $49,000; investing $(179,000); financing $120,000
P17-5B 1. Net cash from operating $79,800; investing $(47,600); financing $(29,900)
P17-6B Net cash from operating $(30,000); investing $(40,300); financing $91,700
P17-7B 1. Net income $80,000 2. Total assets $345,000 3. Net cash from operating $85,000; Cash bal., Dec. 31, 20X6 $195,000
P17-8B 1. Net cash from operating $79,800; investing $(47,600); financing $(29,900)
P17-9B Net cash from operating $77,200; investing $(51,500); financing $(30,300)
Case 1 1. Net cash from operating $140,000; investing $(141,000); financing $(37,000)
Case 2 NCF
Financial Statement Case 3. a. Collections $3,888,267,000
b. Payments $2,825,641,000

Chapter 17 Appendix

P17A-1 Column totals:
Dec. 31, 20X7 $255,400
Dec. 31, 20X8 $287,800
17A-2 Column totals:
Dec. 31, 20X7 $255,400
Dec. 31, 20X8 $287,800

Chapter 18

Quick Check 1 a; 2 b; 3 d; 4 c; 5 b; 6 c; 7 c; 8 a; 9 d; 10 d
S18-1 2002 Gross profit increase 5.0%
S18-2 1. Trend % for 2002 revenue 113%
S18-3 20X6 Cash 20.9% of total assets
S18-4 Net income % of sales: Nike 6.2%; Home Depot 4.8%
S18-5 1. Current ratio for 2002 1.21
S18-6 a. 3.9 times
b. 70 days
S18-7 1. Debt ratio 0.64
S18-8 a. 11.4% c. 22.9%
b. 9.4%
S18-9 1. $0.48
2. 56 times
S18-10 d. $698 mil.
S18-11 a. $631 mil.
c. $1,581 mil.
f. $6,315 mil.
S18-12 1. EVA® $1,858 mil.
E18-1 2006 Increase in working capital 14.3%
E18-2 Total revenue increased 15.3%; Net income increased 58.8%
E18-3 Trend % for Year 5:
Total revenue 136%
Net income 155%
E18-4 Total current assets 13.0%; Long-term debt 33.3%
E18-5 % for 2005: COGS 47.0%; Net income 18.8%
E18-6 a. 1.41 c. 4.01 times
b. 0.70 d. 55 days
E18-7 Ratios for 20X4:
a. 1.56 c. 0.59
b. 0.69 d. 3.44 times
E18-8 Ratios for 20X6:
a. 0.103 c. 0.162
b. 0.137 d. $0.75
E18-9 Ratios for 20X4:
a. 20 c. $4.75
b. 0.022
E18-10 EVA®: Oracle $1,598 mil.; Wells Fargo −$986 mil.
E18-11 Total assets $19,565 mil.; Current liabilities $6,752 mil.

P18-1A 1. Trend % for 20X8: Net sales 127%; Net income 161%; Total assets 145%
2. Return on sales for 20X8 0.081
P18-2A 1. Gross profit 31.9%; Net income 9.2%; Current assets 77.1%; Stockholders' equity 39.4%
P18-3A 2. a. Current ratio 2.23; Debt ratio 0.49; EPS no effect
P18-4A 1. Ratios for 20X6:
a. 2.10 d. 0.253
b. 1.18 e. $4.47
c. 2.81 f. 8.2
P18-5A 1. Blues ratios:
a. 0.66 d. 0.68
b. 2.30 e. $0.37
c. 94 days f. 21.6
2. Blues EVA® $25,000
P18-6A NCF
P18-1B 1. Trend % for 2008: Net revenues 118%; Net income 106%; Common stockholders' equity 124%
2. ROE for 2008 0.142
P18-2B 1. Gross profit 36.4%; Net income 14.7%; Current assets 77.8%; Stockholders' equity 40.2%
P18-3B 2. a. Current ratio 1.35; Debt ratio 0.61; EPS No effect
P18-4B 1. Ratios for 20X9:
a. 1.80 d. 0.357
b. 1.48 e. $5.00
c. 8.82 f. 10.6
P18-5B 1. Caremark ratios:
a. 0.78 d. 0.41
b. 2.32 e. $4.80
c. 40 days f. 10.6
2. Caremark EVA® $29,000
P18-6B NCF
Case 1 NCF
Case 2 NCF
Financial Statement Case NCF

Chapter 19

Quick Check 1 d; 2 a; 3 b; 4 b; 5 d; 6 c; 7 d; 8 a; 9 a; 10 c
S19-1 NCF
S19-2 NCF
S19-3 NCF
S19-4 NCF
S19-5 NCF
S19-6 CGS $41,000
S19-7 CGM $35,000
S19-8 Total MOH $15,275
S19-9 DM used $19,700
S19-10 NCF
S19-11 NCF
S19-12 Total expected benefits $199 million
S19-13 NCF
S19-14 NCF
E19-1 NCF
E19-2 Total inventoriable product costs $142
E19-3 Total inventoriable product costs $33,000
E19-4 NCF
E19-5 Total current assets $214,000
E19-6 CGM $213,000
E19-7 NI $49,000
E19-8 a. CGS $15,000
b. Beg. Materials inv. $2,000
c. End. FG inv. $5,100
E19-9 NCF
E19-10 Expected benefits exceed costs by $84,500
E19-11 NCF
P19-1A Total MOH $4,775
Total inventoriable product costs $34,575
P19-2A Part One: Hannah's Pets Op. Inc. $13,500
Part Two: Best Friends Manufacturing CGM $67,655; Op. Inc. $35,545
Part Three: Best Friends' Manufacturing total inventories $15,695
P19-3A Direct labor $71,000; CGM $162,000; Op. Inc. $100,000
P19-4A *Req 1:* Total benefits if project succeeds $830,000
Req 2: Expected value of the benefits exceed cost by $109,000
P19-5A *Req 2:* Expected value of the benefits falls short of costs by $57,000
P19-6A Present value of benefits exceeds costs by $227,000
P19-7A *Req 1:* Present value of expected benefits $1,102,600
Req 2: Expected value of benefits falls short of costs by $27,400
P19-8A NCF
P19-1B Total MOH $415
Total inventoriable product costs $12,145
P19-2B Part One: Precious Memories Op. Inc. $33,750
Part Two: Forever Manufacturing CGM $72,750; Op. Inc. $44,000
Part Three: Forever Manufacturing total inventories $11,500
P19-3B Manufacturing overhead $40,000; Beg. FG inv. $124,000
P19-4B *Req 1:* Total benefits if project succeeds $470,500
Req 2: Expected value of the benefits exceeds cost by $78,850
P19-5B NCF
P19-6B Present value of benefits exceeds costs by $3,200
P19-7B *Req 1:* Expected value of benefits from additional business $49,560
Req 2: Present value of expected benefits exceeds cost by $9,560
P19-8B NCF
Case 1 End. Materials inv $143,000; End. WIP inv. $239,000; End FG inv. $150,000
Case 2 NCF
Ethical Issue NCF
Financial Statement Case NCF
Team Project NCF

Chapter 20

Quick Check 1 b; 2 d; 3 c; 4 d; 5 a; 6 a; 7 c; 8 b; 9 d; 10 a
S20-1 NCF
S20-2 NCF
S20-3 Ending Materials Inv., $43,500
S20-4 DM, $200
S20-5 NCF
S20-6 Total MOH, $65,000
S20-7 Total cost, $1,180
S20-8 Indirect materials used, $2,000
S20-9 MOH is $1,000 underallocated
S20-10 MOH is $25,000 underallocated
S20-11 NCF
S20-12 DL for Client 367, $770
S20-13 Indirect cost for Client 367, $350
E20-1 NCF
E20-2 WIP Inv., $8,400
E20-3 MOH allocated, $21,000
E20-4 Item f is closing underallocated MOH
E20-5 1. End. WIP Inv., $11,000
4. GP on G-65, $8,000
E20-6 2. MOH allocated, $102,240
3. Underallocated MOH, $2,360
E20-7 2. MOH allocated, $440,000
3. Underallocated MOH, $70,000
E20-8 1. Overallocated MOH, $10,000
3. Adjusted CGS, $590,000
E20-9 1. b. Indirect cost allocation rate, 70%
2. Total predicted cost, $58,718
E20-10 1. MH used, 20,250
2. Underallocated overhead, $243,000
P20-1A 1. c. March CGS, $3,000
April CGS, $2,900
4. GP for Job 5, $900
P20-2A 2. End. WIP Inv., $102,400
FG Inv., $92,820
5. GP for Chalet 13, $34,220
P20-3A 1. MOH allocated, $1,134
Total job cost, $4,504
P20-4A 1. PMOHR, $25/MH
3. Underallocated MOH, $22,000

P20-5A 2. End. WIP Inv., $99,090
FG Inv., $60,550
4. CGM, $63,200
P20-6A 2. GoVacation.com, $74,890
3. Port Armour, $5,950
P20-1B 1. c. Nov. CGS, $1,400
Dec. CGS, $3,650
2. Transferred to FG in Nov., $3,300
Transferred to FG in Dec., $3,850
P20-2B 2. End. WIP Inv., $272,900
FG Inv., $117,620
5. GP for House 304, $51,340
P20-3B 1. MOH allocated, $648
Total job cost, $2,373
P20-4B 1. PMOHR, $7/MH
3. Underallocated MOH, $49,750
P20-5B 2. End. WIP Inv., $38,080
FG Inv., $21,280
4. CGM, $49,160
P20-6B 2. Organic Foods, $128,500
3. SunNow.com, $9,575
Case 1 NCF
Case 2 NCF
Ethical Issue NCF
Team Project 1. Delta's profit per flight 1247, $1,004.79
2. JetBlue's profit per flight 53, $2,659.55

Chapter 21

Quick Check 1 b; 2 c; 3 d; 4 a; 5 c; 6 a; 7 d; 8 d; 9 b; 10 d
S21-1 NCF
S21-2 2. Cost per liter, $0.84
S21-3 2. EU of DM, 200,000
EU of CC, 192,000
S21-4 EU of DM, 50,000
EU of CC, 43,000
S21-5 CC/EU, $1.90
S21-6 DM/EU, $0.60; CC/EU, $0.25
S21-7 2. End. WIP Inv., $32,000
S21-8 End. WIP Inv., $32,000
S21-9 2. EU of TI costs, 168,000
EU of DM, 154,000
EU of CC, 163,800
S21-10 TI cost/EU, $0.82; DM/EU, $0.20; CC/EU, $0.35
S21-11 End. WIP Inv., $14,910
S21-12 End. WIP Inv., $14,910
E21-1 NCF
E21-2 NCF
E21-3 2. EU of DM, 8,000
3. End. WIP Inv., $1,440
E21-4 2. End. WIP Inv., $1,440
3. Avg. Cost/gal. CTO, $1.00
E21-5 1. EU of DM 18,000
2. CC/EU, $1.40
3. End. WIP Inv., $10,610
E21-6 2. EU of CC, 7,710
3. End. WIP Inv., $3,146.50
E21-7 3. Avg. Cost/gal. CTO, $2.35
E21-8 Costs transferred out, $392,400
E21-9 2. Mixing Dep't. EU of TI costs, 90,000
Heating Dep't. EU of TI costs, 86,000
E21-10 2. EU of TI, 35,000
3. End. WIP Inv., $75,996
P21-1A 2. EU of DM, 20,400
CC/EU, $0.25
3b. End. WIP Inv., $1,560
P21-2A 2. EU of CC, 11,700
CC/EU, $25
3b. End. WIP Inv., $172,500
P21-3A 2. EU of CC, 14,160
3. CC/EU, $1
3b. End. WIP Inv., $3,570
P21-4A 2. EU of CC, 2,900
TI cost/EU, $15; CC/EU, $24
3. Costs transferred out, $110,000
P21-5A 2. EU of CC, 19,800
3. TI cost/EU, $0.14
3b. End. WIP Inv., $3,078
P21-1B 2. EU of CC, 90,560
CC/EU, $3.05
3b. End. WIP Inv., $131,688
P21-2B 2. EU of CC, 4,600
CC/EU, $0.90
3b. End. WIP Inv., $210
P21-3B 2. EU of CC, 2,370
3. CC/EU, $0.80
3b. End. WIP Inv., $1,281
P21-4B 2. EU of CC, 608
TI cost/EU, $40; CC/EU, $93
3. Costs transferred out, $77,000
P21-5B 2. EU of CC, 6,000
3. TI cost/EU, $85
3. b. End. WIP Inv., $447,000
Case 3. Op. Inc., $1,800
5. Selling price per box, $12.93
Ethical Issue NCF
Team Project 1. Max. TI cost/lb., $0.23
2. Cutting Dep't. cost/lb., $0.17

Chapter 21 Appendix

S21A-1 2. EU of TI, 160,000
EU of CC, 160,600
S21A-2 DM/EU, $0.20
S21A-3 End. WIP Inv., $15,330
E21A-1 1a. 40%, 25%
2. Mixing Dep't. EU of DM 75,000
Cooking Dep't. EU of CC 76,700
E21A-2 2. EU of CC, 25,900
3. b. End. WIP Inv., $79,200
P21A-1 2. EU of DM, 3,100
DM/EU, $8; CC/EU, $16
3. Costs transferred out, $123,140
P21A-2 2. EU of CC, 17,700
CC/EU, $0.11
3b. End. WIP Inv., $3,648
P21A-3 2. EU of DM, 2,200
TI cost/EU, $12; DM/EU, $11
3. Costs transferred out, $116,300

Chapter 22

Quick Check 1 b; 2 d; 3 a; 4 b; 5 b; 6 a; 7 b; 8 a; 9 a; 10 c
S22-1 NCF
S22-2 1c. Total cost, $33
S22-3 a. BEP, 6,875 tickets
S22-4 1. CM ratio, 0.66667
S22-5 7,875 tickets
S22-6 NCF
S22-7 B is the total expense line
S22-8 1. 9,167 tickets
2. 6,111 tickets
S22-9 1. BEP, 5,000 tickets
S22-10 a. Margin of safety, 125 tickets
c. Margin of safety, 1.79%
S22-11 b. Margin of safety, $10,500
S22-12 VC Op. Inc., $106,500
S22-13 1. AC Op. Inc., $101,500
S22-14 NCF
E22-1 NCF
E22-2 Op. Loss when sales are $250,000 = $20,000
BEP, $283,333
E22-3 1. CM ratio, 50%
2. BEP, 100,000 packages
E22-4 1. BEP, $12,000
2. Sales required to earn target income, $24,500
E22-5 2. Op. Loss when sales are $500,000 = $240,000
E22-6 3. BEP, 500 students, $50,000
E22-7 2. BEP, 1,200,000 tickets
E22-8 1. Margin of safety, $40,000
E22-9 1. AC Op. Inc., $675,000
VC Op. Inc., $525,000
3. Increase in Op. Inc., $75,000
P22-1A NCF
P22-2A CM ratio:
Q 0.70
S 0.60
T 0.711
P22-3A 1. VE per show, $15,200
2. BEP, 38 shows
3. Target shows, 96 shows
P22-4A 1. BEP, 150,000 cartons
2. Target sales, $2,000,000
3. Op. Inc., $2,070,000
4. BEP, $2,535,750
P22-5A 1. BEP, 24 trades
2. Target sales, $14,400
4. BEP, 32 trades
P22-6A 1. AC product cost/meal
Jan., $4.50
Feb., $4.70
2. a. AC Op. Inc
Jan., $900
Feb., $1,040
P22-1B NCF
P22-2B A CM ratio, 0.550
B CM per unit, $3.75
C CM ratio, 0.491
P22-3B 1. VE per show, $27,200
2. BEP, 9 shows
3. Target shows, 139 shows

P22-4B 1. BEP, 87,000 flags
2. Target sales, $1,094,000
3. Op. Loss, $132,600
4. BEP, 108,576 flags
P22-5B 1. BEP, 40 trades
2. Target sales, $42,000
4. BEP, 50 trades
P22-6B 1. AC product cost/game
Oct., $19
Nov., $20
2. a. AC Op. Inc.
Oct., $17,000
Nov., $17,900
Case 1 BEP, 4,800 meals
To earn target Op. Inc., 7,500 meals
Case 2 NCF
Ethical Issue NCF
Financial Statement Case
3. 2002 CM, $899,769
4. 2002 CM ratio, 0.22878
5. 2002 BEP, $3,652,614
Team Project 1. Op. Loss in 20X6, $1.5 million
2. Adopting ad campaign will increase Op. Inc. by $1.5 million

Chapter 22 Appendix

S22A-1 WA CM/unit, $66.91
S22A-2 a. 3,737 total tickets
E22A-1 BEP, 264 standard and 176 chrome
E22A-2 WA CM/unit, $125;
CM per Classic, $300
P22A-1 1. BEP, 12,000 small and 4,000 large
3. Op. Inc., $31,750

Chapter 23

Quick Check 1 d; 2 a; 3 a; 4 d; 5 b; 6 c; 7 a; 8 c; 9 d; 10 b
S23-1 NCF
S23-2 NCF
S23-3 Feb. sales, $770,000
S23-4 Jan. purchases, $490,750
Feb. purchases, $585,650
S23-5 June cash sales, $24,000
S23-6 May purchases, $48,000
S23-7 May cash collections, $71,000
S23-8 May cash payments for purchases, $47,600
S23-9 January cash collections, $548,330
S23-10 Grippers must borrow $34,070
S23-11 NCF
S23-12 NCF
S23-13 NCF
S23-14 NCF
E23-1 NI this year, $220,000
E23-2 Purchases, qtr. ended June 30, $88,500
Purchases, qtr. ended Sept. 30, $80,700
E23-3 Qtr. 2 NI, $856,960
Qtr. 3 NI, $950,546
E23-4 b. Sept. cash receipts from customers, $106,830
E23-5 1. Nov. borrowing, $1,000
E23-6 Feb. borrowing, $11,100
March interest paid, $74
E23-7 Total assets, $30,280
Owners' Equity, $25,980
E23-8 NCF
E23-9 Total cell phone Op. Inc. Var., $45,000 F
P23-1A May CGS, $15,500
May NI, $14,300
June NI, $9,500
P23-2A 1a. May cash collections, $42,660
b. May cash payments for purchases, $18,125
c. May cash payments for op. expenses, $8,708
2. May ending cash balance, $26,827
June ending cash balance, $39,991
P23-3A 1. Ending cash balance, $55,000
Total Assets, $143,900
Owners' Equity, $115,600
2. Net increase in cash, $14,400
3. Cash available, $76,800
P23-4A 1. Ending cash balance, $29,500
Total Assets, $131,900
Owners' Equity, $103,600
P23-5A NCF
P23-6A 1. Dayton Op. Inc. Var., $6,100U
Other Ohio stores Op. Inc. Var., $4,400 F
Companywide Op. Inc. Var., $86,000 U
P23-1B Aug. CGS, $120,000
Aug. NI, $26,000
Sept. NI, $28,000
P23-2B 1a. Aug. cash collections, $199,000
b. Aug. cash payments for purchases, $124,720
c. Aug. cash payments for op. expenses, $40,090
2. Aug. ending cash balance, $56,190
Sept. ending cash balance, $97,250
P23-3B 1. Ending cash balance, $45,200
Total Assets, $172,700
Owners' Equity, $145,600
2. Net decrease in cash, $5,000
P23-4B 1. Ending cash balance, $31,200
Total Assets, $162,700
Owners' Equity, $135,600
P23-5B NCF
P23-6B 1. Store No. 23 Op. Inc. Var., $2,000 F
Other Dallas stores Op. Inc. Var., $9,000 F
Texas Op. Inc. Var., $44,400 F
Case 1 NCF
Case 2 1. NI cotton mats, $235
NI linen mats, $225
Ethical Issue NCF
Financial Statement Case
3. Company-wide total Op. Inc. Var., $225,104 F
North American Books, Music, DVD/Video Op. Inc. Var., $54,610 F
Team Project NCF

Chapter 23 Appendix

S23A-1 NCF
S23A-2 Software Dep't., $200,000
E23A-1 Marketing cost allocated to Welding, $4,200
Total indirect costs allocated to Priming, $25,400
E23A-2 1. Chrome Op. Inc., $75,800
P23-A1 1. Housekeeping cost, $24/room
Total Club expense, $99,480
2. Club cost $184.22/room
Regular cost $92.57/room

Chapter 24

Quick Check 1 a; 2 a; 3 d; 4 e; 5 b; 6 b; 7 d; 8 c; 9 d; 10 c
S24-1 1. 4-Pool Op. Loss, $4,000
S24-2 2. Actual expenses, $80,000
4. FB Var., $12,000F
S24-3 Total FB Var., $12,000F; Total SVV, $4,000F
S24-4 1. Relevant range, 0–11 pools
S24-5 NCF
S24-6 NCF
S24-7 DM Eff. Var., $2,800U
S24-8 DM Eff. Var. for onion, $0.70U
S24-9 DL Price Var., $17,500F
S24-10 NCF
S24-11 VMOHR = $7/DLH
S24-12 FB Var., $4,000U; PVV, $12,000F
S24-13 NCF
S24-14 NCF
S24-15 CGS, $364,000
S24-16 Op. Inc., $85,500
E24-1 Op. Inc. at 70,000 units, $170,000
E24-2 NCF
E24-3 Total FB Var., $9,000U;
Static Budget Op. Inc., $20,000
E24-4 Sales Revenue FB Var., $210,000F; Static Budget Op. Inc., $441,000
E24-5 Actual price, $10.50/lb.
E24-6 DM Price Var., $72,500F;
DL Eff. Var., $6,500F
E24-7 NCF
E24-8 NCF

E24-9 MOH FB Var., $2,200U; PVV, $3,000F
E24-10 GP, $228,500
P24-1A 1. 60,000 units: SR, $180,000; CGS, $69,000; Op. Inc., $20,700
P24-2A 1. Total Exp. FB Var., $4,000U; Total Exp. SVV, $7,550U
P24-3A 1. FB Gross Profit, $4,204,000 2. DM Price Var., $42,840F; DM Eff. Var., $58,000F; MOH FB Var., $28,220U 3. Total FB Var., $68,120F
P24-4A 1. DL hrs. worked, 5,860 hrs. 2. DL Price Var., $2,930F
P24-5A 1. DL Price Var., $4,896U; DL Eff. Var., $25,568F 3. PVV, $1,760U
P24-6A 1. DL Price Var., $920F 2. MOH FB Var., $6,400F 3. Total Man. Cost Variances, $16,890F
P24-1B 1. 11,000 units: SR, $253,000; CGS, $110,000; Op. Inc., $47,625
P24-2B 1. Total Exp. FB Var., $4,225U; Total Exp. SVV, $40,675U
P24-3B 1. FB Gross Profit, $260,068 2. DM Price Var., $1,230F; DM Eff. Var., $2,403U; MOH FB Var., $15,960U 3. Total FB Var., $16,773U
P24-4B 1. DL hrs. worked, 3,900 hrs. 2. DL Price Var., $1,950U
P24-5B 1. DL Price Var., $4,200U; DL Eff. Var., $2,628U 3. PVV, $1,134F
P24-6B 1. DL Price Var., $330U 2. MOH FB Var., $11,540U 3. Total Man. Cost Variances, $15,870U
Case 1 Total FB Var., $23,025 F Total SVV, $133,600U
Case 2 DL Eff. Var., $96U
Ethical Issue NCF
Team Project NCF

Chapter 25

Quick Check 1 c; 2 a; 3 a; 4 b; 5 d; 6 c; 7 d; 8 c; 9 a; 10 c
S25-1 2. Aldehyde, $3,360
S25-2 1. Setup cost/lb. of PH, $44.80
S25-3 1. MOH/lb. of PH, $138.80 2. GP/lb. of aldehyde, $1.57
S25-4 2. TC of Webb, $49,120 3. Op. Inc. of Greg, $3,380
S25-5 NCF
S25-6 NCF
S25-7 Doc. Prep., $32/page
S25-8 1. TC of Webb, $45,800 2. Op. Loss of Greg, $16,700
S25-9 NCF
S25-10 NCF
S25-11 NCF
S25-12 NCF
S25-13 CC are $660 underallocated
S25-14 NCF
S25-15 2. Net advantage to implementing quality program, $100,000
E25-1 1. Mat. Handling, $4/part 2. Ind. mfg. cost/wheel, $143.40
E25-2 1. Total budgeted indirect mfg. costs, $461,500 2. ABC indirect cost/Deluxe wheel, $296 3. Original system indirect cost/Deluxe wheel, $276.90
E25-3 1. ABC GP for Standard, $59.50 2. Original system GP for Standard, $40.40
E25-4 Total cost of Deluxe, $347
E25-5 NCF
E25-6 2. EB RIP, $480,000 3. CC, $720,000 overallocated
E25-7 1. CC, $1,020,000 underallocated 2. EB FG, $324,000
E25-8 NCF
E25-9 NCF
E25-10 2. Net advantage to undertaking TQM, $10,000
E25-11 2. Job 409 Lathe turns, 20,000
P25-1A Mfg. product cost, $92.70
P25-2A 1. Total mfg. cost of Standard, $288,000 2. Full product cost of Standard, $78/unit 4. Sale price, $120
P25-3A 2. X-Secure indirect cost, $199,600/unit 3. X-Page indirect cost, $33.33/unit
P25-4A 1. Total cost, $25.20/unit 3. Indirect cost, $13.41/unit
P25-5A 2. CC, $64,000 overallocated 3. EB RIP, $2,000
P25-6A 2. Net benefit, $51,000
P25-1B Mfg. product cost, $147.80
P25-2B 1. Total mfg. cost of Standard, $146,700 2. Full product cost of Standard, $72.90/unit 4. Sale price, $68.50
P25-3B 2. Commercial indirect cost, $132.80/unit 3. Travel pack indirect cost, $2.40/unit
P25-4B 1. Total cost, $6.21/unit 3. Indirect cost, $2.82/unit
P25-5B 2. CC, $79,000 overallocated 3. EB RIP, $1,000
P25-6B 2. Net benefit, $5,000
Case 1 1. Original system cost/unit of Job A, $5,460 2. ABC cost/unit of Job A, $5,072.50
Case 2 Savings required, $620
Ethical Issue NCF
Financial Statement Case NCF
Team Project 2. Ind. cost allocation rate, $16.125/DLH; Total cost/lb. of Headless shrimp, $3.96125 3. Scheduling, $100/batch; Chilling, $0.02/lb.; Total indirect cost/lb. of Headless shrimp, $0.995; Total cost/lb. of Headless shrimp, $4.795

Chapter 26

Quick Check 1 b; 2 c; 3 d; 4 d; 5 a; 6 d; 7 a; 8 c; 9 b; 10 a
S26-1 NCF
S26-2 Expected decrease in Op. Inc., $1,000
S26-3 NCF
S26-4 NCF
S26-5 Regular CM/unit, $125
S26-6 Advantage to outsourcing, $13,500
S26-7 NCF
S26-8 Advantage to processing further, $2,000
S26-9 Average annual net cash inflow, $2,880,000
S26-10 Payback period, 4.51 years
S26-11 ARR, 24%
S26-12 NPV, $3,272,000
S26-13 IRR, over 16%
S26-14 NCF
E26-1 1. Increase in Op. Inc., $2,500 2. Decrease in Op. Inc., $2,500
E26-2 1. Increase in Op. Inc., $320,000
E26-3 Decrease in Op. Inc., $40,000
E26-4 Decrease in Op. Inc., $10,000
E26-5 Total CM of moderately priced line, $39,000
E26-6 Advantage to making switch, $1.50/unit
E26-7 Advantage to buying and using facilities for other product, $100,000
E26-8 Advantage to processing further, $100
E26-9 Payback period, 4 years
E26-10 ARR Veras, 37%
E26-11 NPV Project B, $(7,040)
E26-12 IRR Project A, between 14% and 16%
E26-13 1. 12 oz. cans of Coca-Cola, CM/linear foot, $7.50 2. 360 12 oz. cans of Coca-Cola
P26-1A 1. Increase in Op. Inc., $35,000
P26-2A 1. Decrease in Op. Inc., $104,000 2b. Operating loss, $52,000
P26-3A 2. Deluxe: CM, $1,440 / MH; Total CM at capacity, $6,480,000
P26-4A 1. Advantage to making, $2,460 2. Net cost to buy and make another product, $31,060

P26-5A 1. Cost of further processing, $56,400
3. Advantage to selling as is, $19,920

P26-6A 1. ARR, 31.2%;
NPV, $733,360

P26-7A 1. Plan B's ARR, 7.8%
Plan B's NPV, $(959,000)
3. IRR, 12%–14%

P26-1B 1. Increase in Op. Inc., $2,500

P26-2B 1. Decrease in Op. Inc., $22,500
2b. Op. Inc. $193,000

P26-3B 2. Spas:
CM, $1.95/sq. ft.;
Total CM at capacity, $15,600

P26-4B 1. Advantage to making, $26,600
2. Net cost to buy and make snack bars, $846,600

P26-5B 1. Cost of further processing, $120,000
3. Advantage to process further, $30,000

P26-6B 1. ARR, 6%;
NPV, $(1,052,125)

P26-7B 1. Plan A's ARR, 12%
Plan A's NPV, $(835,360)
3. IRR, 14%–16%

Case 1 1. Total cost/mailbox per month, $64
2. Total advantage to outsourcing, $21,850
3. Advantage to insourcing extra services, $1,150

Case 2 1. Total earnings if he chooses the meat packing plant, $9,450

Ethical Issue Advantage to outsourcing, $18,000/year

Financial Statement Case 2. Annual net cash inflow, $13,439,602
3.b. ARR, 18.6%

Team Project 2. Annual cash inflow advantage to insourcing, $7,972,000
3.b. ARR, 22.1%
c. NPV, $3,964,024

Glossary

Absorption Costing. The costing method that assigns both variable and fixed manufacturing costs to products.

Accelerated Depreciation Method. A depreciation method that writes off more of the asset's cost near the start of its useful life than the straight-line method does.

Account. The detailed record of the changes in a particular asset, liability, or owner's equity during a period. The basic summary device of accounting.

Account Payable. A liability backed by the general reputation and credit standing of the debtor.

Account Receivable. A promise to receive cash from customers to whom the business has sold goods or for whom the business has performed services.

Accounting. The information system that measures business activities, processes that information into reports, and communicates the results to decision makers.

Accounting Cycle. Process by which companies produce their financial statements for a specific period.

Accounting Equation. The basic tool of accounting, measuring the resources of the business and the claims to those resources: Assets = Liabilities + Owner's Equity.

Accounting Information System. The combination of personnel, records, and procedures that a business uses to provide financial data.

Accounting Rate of Return. A measure of profitability computed by dividing the average annual operating income from an asset by the average amount invested in the asset.

Accounts Receivable Turnover. Measures a company's ability to collect cash from credit customers. To compute accounts receivable turnover, divide net credit sales by average net accounts receivable.

Accrual Accounting. Accounting that records the impact of a business event as it occurs, regardless of whether the transaction affected cash.

Accrued Expense. An expense that the business has not yet paid. Also called **accrued liability**.

Accrued Revenue. A revenue that has been earned but not yet collected in cash.

Accumulated Depreciation. The cumulative sum of all depreciation expense recorded for an asset.

Acid-Test Ratio. Ratio of the sum of cash plus short-term investments plus net current receivables, to total current liabilities. Tells whether the entity could pay all its current liabilities if they came due immediately. Also called the **quick ratio**.

Activity-Based Costing (ABC). Focuses on *activities* as the fundamental cost objects. The costs of those activities become building blocks for compiling the indirect costs of products, services, and customers.

Activity-Based Management. Using activity-based cost information to make decisions that increase profits while satisfying customers' needs.

Additional Paid-In Capital. The paid-in capital in excess of par, common plus other accounts combined for reporting on the balance sheet.

Adjusted Trial Balance. A list of all the accounts with their adjusted balances.

Adjusting Entry. Entry made at the end of the period to assign revenues to the period in which they are earned and expenses to the period in which they are incurred. Adjusting entries help measure the period's income and bring the related asset and liability accounts to correct balances for the financial statements.

Aging-of-Accounts Method. A way to estimate bad debts by analyzing individual accounts receivable according to the length of time they have been receivable from the customer. Also called the **balance-sheet approach**.

Allocation base. A common denominator that links indirect costs to cost objects. Ideally, the allocation base is the primary cost driver of the indirect cost.

Allowance for Uncollectible Accounts. A contra account, related to accounts receivable, that holds the estimated amount of collection losses. Also called **Allowance for Doubtful Accounts**.

Allowance Method. A method of recording collection losses on the basis of estimates, instead of waiting to see which customers the company will not collect from.

Amortization. Systematic reduction of the asset's carrying value on the books. Expense that applies to intangibles in the same way depreciation applies to plant assets and depletion to natural resources.

Annuity. A stream of equal periodic cash flows.

Appraisal Costs. Costs incurred to *detect* poor-quality goods or services.

Appropriation of Retained Earnings. Restriction of retained earnings that is recorded by a formal journal entry.

Asset. An economic resource that is expected to be of benefit in the future.

Audit. An examination of a company's financial statements and the accounting system.

Authorization of Stock. Provision in a corporate charter that gives the state's permission for the corporation to issue—that is, to sell—a certain number of shares of stock.

Available-for-Sale Investments. All less-than-20% investments other than trading securities.

Average-Cost Method. Inventory costing method based on the average cost of inventory during the period. Average cost is determined by dividing the cost of goods available for sale by the number of units available.

Balance Sheet. An entity's assets, liabilities, and owner's equity as of a specific date. Also called the **statement of financial position**.

Bank Collection. Collection of money by the bank on behalf of a depositor.

Bank Reconciliation. Document explaining the reasons for the difference between a depositor's cash records and the depositor's cash balance in its bank account.

Bank Statement. Document the bank uses to report what it did with the depositor's cash. Shows the bank account's beginning and ending balances and lists the month's cash transactions conducted through the bank.

Batch Processing. Computerized accounting for similar transactions in a group or batch.

Benchmarking. The practice of comparing a company with other companies that are leaders.

Board of Directors. Group elected by the stockholders to set policy and to appoint the officers.

Bonds Payable. Groups of notes payable issued to multiple lenders called bondholders.

Book Value. Amount of owners' equity on the company's books for each share of its stock.

Book Value (of a Plant Asset). The asset's cost minus accumulated depreciation.

Book Value per Share of Common Stock. Common stockholders' equity divided by the number of shares of common stock outstanding. The recorded amount for each share of common stock outstanding.

Breakeven Point. The sales level at which operating income is zero: Total revenues equal total expenses.

Budget. Quantitative expression of a plan that helps managers coordinate and implement the plan.

Bylaws. Constitution for governing a corporation.

Callable Bonds. Bonds that the issuer may call or pay off at a specified price whenever the issuer wants.

Capital Budgeting. Budgeting for the acquisition of capital assets—assets used for a long period of time.

Capital Charge. The amount that stockholders and lenders charge a company for the use of their money. Calculated as (Notes payable + Loans payable + Long-term debt + Stockholders' equity)

Capital Expenditure. Expenditure that increases the capacity or efficiency of an asset or extends its useful life. Capital expenditures are debited to an asset account.

Capital Expenditures Budget. A company's plan for purchases of property, plant, equipment, and other long-term assets.

Capital Lease. Lease agreement that meets any one of four criteria: (1) The lease transfers title of the leased asset to the lessee. (2) The lease contains a bargain purchase option. (3) The lease term is 75% or more of the estimated useful life of the leased asset. (4) The present value of the lease payments is 90% or more of the market value of the leased asset.

Cash Budget. Details how the business expects to go from the beginning cash balance to the desired ending balance. Also called the **statement of budgeted cash receipts and payments**.

Cash Equivalents. Highly liquid short-term investments that can be readily converted into cash.

Cash Flows. Cash receipts and cash payments.

Cash Payments Journal. Special journal used to record cash payments by check. Also called the **check register** or **cash disbursements journal**.

Cash Receipts Journal. Special journal used to record cash receipts.

Cash-Basis Accounting. Accounting that records transactions only when cash is received or paid.

Certified Management Accountant (CMA). A licensed accountant who works for a single company.

Certified Public Accountant (CPA). A licensed accountant who serves the general public rather than one particular company.

Chairperson. Elected by a corporation's board of directors, the most powerful person in the corporation.

Chart of Accounts. List of all the accounts and their account numbers in the ledger.

Charter. Document that gives the state's permission to form a corporation.

Check. Document that instructs a bank to pay the designated person or business a specified amount of money.

Closing Entries. Entries that transfer the revenue, expense, and owner withdrawal balances to the capital account.

Closing the Accounts. Step in the accounting cycle at the end of the period. Closing the accounts consists of journalizing and posting the closing entries to set the balances of the revenue, expense, and withdrawal accounts to zero for the next period.

Common Stock. The basic form of capital stock. In a corporation, the common stockholders are the owners of the business.

Common-Size Statement. A financial statement that reports only percentages (no dollar amounts).

Comprehensive Income. Company's change in total stockholders' equity from all sources other than from the owners.

Computer Virus. A malicious program that (a) reproduces itself, (b) enters program code without consent, and (c) performs destructive actions.

Conservatism. Reporting the least favorable figures in the financial statements.

Consistency Principle. A business should use the same accounting methods and procedures from period to period.

Consolidated Statements. Financial statements of the parent company plus those of majority-owned subsidiaries as if the combination were a single legal entity.

Constraint. A factor that restricts production or sale of a product.

Continuous Improvement. A philosophy requiring employees to continually look for ways to improve performance.

Contra Account. An account that always has a companion account and whose normal balance is opposite that of the companion account.

Contribution Margin. Sales revenue minus variable expenses.

Contribution Margin Income Statement. Income statement that groups costs by behavior —variable costs or fixed costs— and highlights the contribution margin.

Contribution Margin Ratio. Ratio of contribution margin to sales revenue.

Control Account. An account whose balance equals the sum of the balances in a group of related accounts in a subsidiary ledger.

Controller. The chief accounting officer of a company.

Controlling. Evaluating the results of business operations by comparing the actual results to the plan.

Controlling Interest. Ownership of more than 50% of an investee company's voting stock. Also called **majority interest**.

Conversion Costs. Direct labor plus manufacturing overhead.

Convertible Bonds. Bonds that may be converted into the common stock of the issuing company at the option of the investor.

Copyright. Exclusive right to reproduce and sell a book, musical composition, film, other work of art, or computer program. Issued by the federal government, copyrights extend 70 years beyond the author's life.

Corporation. A business owned by stockholders; it begins when the state approves its articles of incorporation. A corporation is a legal entity, an "artificial person," in the eyes of the law.

Cost Allocation. Assigning indirect costs (such as manufacturing overhead) to cost objects (such as jobs or production processes).

Cost Assignment. A general term that refers to both tracing direct costs and allocating indirect costs to cost objects.

Cost Behavior. Describes how costs change as volume changes.

Cost Driver. The primary factor that causes a cost.

Cost Object. Anything for which managers want a separate measurement of costs.

Cost of Capital. A weighted average of the returns demanded by the company's stockholders and lenders.

Cost of Goods Manufactured. The manufacturing (or plant-related) cost of the goods that finished the production process this period.

Cost of Goods Sold. The cost of the inventory that the business has sold to customers. Also called **cost of sales**.

Cost Tracing. Assigning direct costs (such as direct materials and direct labor) to cost objects (such as jobs or production processes) that used those costs.

Cost-Benefit Analysis. Weighing costs against benefits to help make decisions.

Cost-Volume-Profit (CVP) Analysis. Expresses the relationships among costs, volume, and profit or loss.

Credit. The right side of an account.

Credit Memorandum or Credit Memo. A document issued by a seller to credit a customer account for returned merchandise.

Creditor. The party to a credit transaction who sells goods or a service and obtains a receivable.

Cumulative Preferred Stock. Preferred stock whose owners must receive all dividends in arrears before the corporation pays dividends to the common stockholders.

Current Asset. An asset that is expected to be converted to cash, sold, or consumed during the next 12 months, or within the business's normal operating cycle if the cycle is longer than a year.

Current Liability. A debt due to be paid with cash or with goods and services within one year or within the entity's operating cycle if the cycle is longer than a year.

Current Portion of Long-Term Debt. Amount of the principal that is payable within one year. Also called **current maturity**.

Current Ratio. Current assets divided by current liabilities. Measures the company's ability to pay current liabilities from current assets.

Customer Service. Support provided for customers after the sale.

Data Warehouse. A very large database holding data for a number of years and used for analysis rather than for transaction processing.

Database. A computerized storehouse of information.

Days' Sales in Receivables. Ratio of average net accounts receivable to one day's sales. Indicates how many days' sales it takes to collect the average level of receivables. Also called the **collection period**.

Debentures. Unsecured bonds backed only by the good faith of the borrower.

Debit. The left side of an account.

Debit Memorandum or Debit Memo. A document issued by a buyer when returning merchandise. The memo informs the seller that the buyer no longer owes the seller for the amount of the returned purchases.

Debt Ratio. Ratio of total liabilities to total assets. Shows the proportion of a company's assets that it has financed with debt.

Debtor. The party to a credit transaction who makes a purchase and has a payable.

Deficit. Debit balance in the Retained Earnings account.

Depletion Expense. Portion of a natural resource's cost used up in a particular period. Computed in the same way as units-of-production depreciation.

Deposit in Transit. A deposit recorded by the company but not yet by its bank.

Depreciable Cost. The cost of a plant asset minus its estimated residual value.

Depreciation. The allocation of a plant asset's cost to expense over its useful life.

Design. Detailed engineering of products and services, or processes for producing them.

Direct Cost. A cost that can be specifically traced to a cost object.

Direct Labor. The compensation of employees who physically convert materials into the company's products; labor costs that are directly traceable to finished products.

Direct Materials. Materials that become a physical part of a finished product and whose costs are traceable to the finished product.

Direct Method. Format of the operating activities section of the statement of cash flows; lists the major categories of operating cash receipts and cash payments.

Direct Write-Off Method. A method of accounting for uncollectible receivables, in which the company waits until the credit department decides that a customer's account receivable is uncollectible, and then debits Uncollectible-Account Expense and credits the customer's Account Receivable.

Disclosure Principle. A business's financial statements must report enough information for outsiders to make knowledgeable decisions about the company.

Discount (on a Bond). Excess of a bond's maturity value over its issue price. Also called a **bond discount**.

Discount Rate. Management's minimum desired rate of return on an investment. Also called the **hurdle rate, required rate of return**, and **cost of capital**.

Discounting a Note Receivable. Selling a note receivable before its maturity date.

Dishonor of a Note. Failure of a note's maker to pay a note receivable at maturity. Also called **default on a note**.

Dissolution. Ending of a partnership.

Distribution. Delivery of products or services to customers.

Dividend Yield. Ratio of dividends per share of stock to the stock's market price per share. Tells the percentage of a stock's market value that the company returns to stockholders annually as dividends.

Dividends. Distributions by a corporation to its stockholders.

Double Taxation. Corporations pay their own income taxes on corporate income. Then, the stockholders pay personal income tax on the cash dividends they receive from corporations.

Double-Declining-Balance (DDB) Depreciation Method. An accelerated depreciation method that computes annual depreciation by multiplying the asset's decreasing book value by a constant percent that is two times the straight-line rate.

Earnings Per Share (EPS). Amount of a company's net income for each share of its outstanding common stock.

Economic Value Added (EVA). EVA = Net income + Interest expense − Capital charge. Used to evaluate a company's operating performance.

Efficiency Variance. Measures whether the quantity of materials or labor used to make the actual number of outputs is within the standard allowed for that number of outputs. This is computed as the difference in quantities (actual quantity of input used minus standard quantity of input allowed for the actual number of outputs) multiplied by the standard price per unit of the input.

Electronic Funds Transfer (EFT). System that transfers cash by electronic communication rather than by paper documents.

Encryption. Rearranging plain-text messages by a mathematical process; the primary method of achieving confidentiality in e-commerce.

Entity. An organization or a section of an organization that, for accounting purposes, stands apart from other organizations and individuals as a separate economic unit.

Equity Method. Method used to account for investments in which the investor has 20% to 50% of the investee's voting stock and can significantly influence the decisions of the investee.

Equivalent Units. Express the amount of work done during a period in terms of fully complete units of output.

Enterprise Resource Planning (ERP). Software systems that can integrate all of a company's worldwide functions, departments, and data into a single system.

Estimated Residual Value. Expected cash value of an asset at the end of its useful life. Also called **salvage value**.

Estimated Useful Life. Length of the service period expected from an asset. May be expressed in years, units of output, miles, or another measure.

Expense. Decrease in owner's equity that occurs from using assets or increasing liabilities in the course of delivering goods or services to customers.

External Failure Costs. Costs incurred when the company does not detect poor-quality goods or services until *after* delivery to customers.

Extraordinary Gains and Losses. A gain or loss that is both unusual for the company and infrequent. Also called **extraordinary items**.

Extraordinary Repair. Repair work that generates a capital expenditure.

Financial Accounting. The branch of accounting that focuses on information for people outside the firm.

Financial Accounting Standards Board (FASB). The private organization that determines how accounting is practiced in the United States.

Financial Budget. The case budget (cash inflows and outflows), the budgeted period-end balance sheet, and the budgeted statement of cash flows.

Financial Statements. Documents that report on a business in monetary amounts, providing information to help people make informed business decisions.

Financing Activities. Activities that obtain the cash needed to launch and sustain the business; a section of the statement of cash flows.

Finished Goods Inventory. Completed goods that have not yet been sold.

Firewalls. Devices that enable members of a local network to access the Internet but keep nonmembers out of the network.

First-In, First-Out (FIFO) Inventory Costing Method. Inventory costing method: the first costs into inventory are the first costs out to cost of goods sold. Ending inventory is based on the costs of the most recent purchases.

First-In, First-Out (FIFO) Process Costing Method. A process costing method that values each equivalent unit of work at the cost per equivalent unit in effect during the period the work is done.

Flexible Budget. A summarized budget that managers can easily compute for several different volume levels. Flexible budgets separate variable costs from fixed costs; it is the variable costs that put the "flex" in the flexible budget.

Flexible Budget Variance. The difference arising because the company actually earned more or less revenue, or incurred more or less cost, than expected for the actual level of output. This equals the difference between the actual amount and a flexible budget amount.

Foreign-Currency Exchange Rate. The measure of one currency against another currency.

Franchises, Licenses. Privileges granted by a private business or a government to sell a product or service under specified conditions.

Full Product Costs. The costs of all resources used throughout the value chain for a product.

General Ledger. Ledger of accounts that are reported in the financial statements.

General Partnership. A form of partnership in which each partner is an owner of the business, with all the privileges and risks of ownership.

Generally Accepted Accounting Principles (GAAP). Accounting guidelines, formulated by the Financial Accounting Standards Board, that govern how accountants measure, process, and communicate financial information.

Goodwill. Excess of the cost of an acquired company over the sum of the market values of its net assets (assets minus liabilities).

Gross Pay. Total amount of salary, wages, commissions, or any other employee compensation before taxes and other deductions.

Gross Profit. Excess of net sales revenue over cost of goods sold. Also called **gross margin**.

Gross Profit Method. A way to estimate inventory on the basis of the cost-of-goods-sold model: Beginning inventory + Net purchases = Cost of goods available for sale. Cost of goods available for sale − Cost of goods sold = Ending inventory.

Gross Profit Percentage. Gross profit divided by net sales revenue. A measure of profitability. Also called **gross margin percentage**.

Hardware. Electronic equipment that includes computers, disk drives, monitors, printers, and the network that connects them.

Hedging. Protecting oneself from losing money in one transaction by engaging in a counterbalancing transaction.

Held-to-Maturity Investments. Investment in bonds, notes, and other debt securities that the investor expects to hold until their maturity date.

Horizontal Analysis. Study of percentage changes in comparative financial statements.

Imprest System. A way to account for petty cash by maintaining a constant balance in the petty cash account, supported by the fund (cash plus payment tickets) totaling the same amount.

Income Statement. Summary of an entity's revenues, expenses, and net income or net loss for a specific period. Also called the **statement of earnings** or the **statement of operations**.

Income Summary. A temporary "holding tank" account into which revenues and expenses are transferred prior to their final transfer to the capital account.

Indirect Cost. A cost that cannot be specifically traced to a cost object.

Indirect Labor. Labor costs that are difficult to trace to specific products.

Indirect Materials. Materials whose costs cannot conveniently be directly traced to particular finished products.

Indirect Method. Format of the operating activities section of the statement of cash flows; starts with net income and reconciles to net cash provided by operating activities.

Intangibles. Assets with no physical form. Valuable because of the special rights they carry. Examples are patents and copyrights.

Interest. The revenue to the payee for loaning money; the expense to the debtor.

Interest period. The period of time during which interest is computed. It extends from the original date of the note to the maturity date. Also called **note term**, or simply **time**.

Interest rate. The percentage rate of interest specified by the note. Interest rates are almost always stated for a period of one year. A 9% note means that the amount of interest for one year is 9% of the note's principal amount.

Internal Control. Organizational plan and all the related measures adopted by an entity to safeguard assets, encourage employees to follow company policies, promote operational efficiency, and ensure accurate and reliable accounting records.

Internal Failure Costs. Costs incurred when the company detects and corrects poor-quality goods or services *before* delivery to customers.

Internal Rate of Return (IRR). The rate of return (based on discounted cash flows) that a company can expect to earn by investing in the project. The discount rate that makes the net present value of the project's cash flows equal to zero.

Inventoriable Product Costs. All costs of a product that GAAP requires companies to treat as an asset for external financial reporting. These costs are not expensed until the product is sold.

Inventory. All the goods that the company owns and expects to sell in the normal course of operations.

Inventory Turnover. Ratio of cost of goods sold to average inventory. Measures the number of times a company sells its average level of inventory during a year.

Investing Activities. Activities that increase or decrease long-term assets; a section of the statement of cash flows.

Invoice. A seller's request for cash from the purchaser.

Job Cost Record. Document that accumulates the direct materials, direct labor, and manufacturing overhead costs assigned to each individual job.

Job Costing. System for assigning costs to a specific unit or to a small batch of products or services that (1) pass through production steps as a distinct identifiable job and (2) can vary considerably in materials, labor, and overhead costs.

Journal. The chronological accounting record of an entity's transactions.

Just-in-Time (JIT). A system in which a company produces just in time to satisfy needs. Suppliers deliver materials just in time to begin production, and finished units are completed just in time for delivery to customers.

Just-in-Time (JIT) Costing. A standard costing system that starts with output completed and then assigns manufacturing costs to units sold and to inventories. Also called **backflush costing**.

Labor Time Record. Identifies the employee, the amount of time spent on a particular job, and the labor cost charged to the job; a record used to assign direct labor cost to specific jobs.

Last-In, Last-Out (LIFO) Inventory Costing Method. Inventory costing method: the last costs into inventory are the first costs out to cost of goods sold. Leaves the oldest costs—those of beginning inventory and the earliest purchases of the period—in ending inventory.

Lease. Rental agreement in which the tenant (lessee) agrees to make rent payments to the property owner (lessor) to obtain the use of the asset.

Ledger. The record holding all the accounts.

Legal Capital. The portion of stockholders' equity that cannot be used for dividends.

Lessee. Tenant in a lease agreement.

Lessor. Property owner in a lease agreement.

Leverage. Earning more income on borrowed money than the related interest expense, thereby increasing the earnings for the owners of the business.

Liability. An economic obligation (a debt) payable to an individual or an organization outside the business.

Limited Liability. No personal obligation of a stockholder for corporation debts. A stockholder can lose no more on an investment in a corporation's stock than the cost of the investment.

Limited Liability Partnership. A form of partnership in which each partner's personal liability for the business's debts is limited to a certain amount. Also called **LLPs**.

Limited Partnership. A partnership with at least two classes of partners: a general partner and limited partners.

Liquidation. The process of going out of business by selling the entity's assets and paying its liabilities. The final step in liquidation is the distribution of any remaining cash to the owner(s).

Liquidity. Measure of how quickly an item can be converted to cash.

Long-Term Asset. An asset other than a current asset.

Long-Term Investment. A noncurrent asset; a separate asset category reported on the balance sheet between current assets and plant assets.

Long-Term Liability. A liability other than a current liability.

Lower-of-Cost-or-Market (LCM) Rule. Rule that an asset should be reported in the financial statements at whichever is lower—its historical cost or its market value.

Maker of a Note. The person or business that signs the note and promises to pay the amount required by the note agreement; the debtor.

Management Accounting. The branch of accounting that focuses on information for internal decision makers of a business.

Management by Exception. Directs management's attention to important differences between actual and budgeted amounts.

Manufacturing Company. A company that uses labor, plant, and equipment to convert raw materials into new finished products.

Manufacturing Overhead. All manufacturing costs other than direct materials and direct labor. Also called **factory overhead** or **indirect manufacturing cost**.

Margin of Safety. Excess of expected sales over breakeven sales. Drop in sales a company can absorb without incurring an operating loss.

Market Interest Rate. Interest rate that investors demand in order to loan their money. Also called the **effective interest rate**.

Market Value. Price for which a person could buy or sell a share of stock.

Marketing. Promotion of products or services.

Market-Value Method. Used to account for all trading investments. These investments are reported at their current market value.

Master Budget. The set of budgeted financial statements and supporting schedules for the entire organization. Includes the operating budget, the capital expenditures budget, and the financial budget.

Matching Principle. Guide to accounting for expenses. Identify all expenses incurred during the period, measure the expenses, and match them against the revenues earned during that same time period.

Materiality Concept. A company must perform strictly proper accounting only for items that are significant to the business's financial statements.

Materials Inventory. Raw materials for use in manufacturing.

Materials Requisition. Request for the transfer of materials to the production floor, prepared by the production team.

Maturity Date. The date when final payment of the note is due. Also called the **due date**.

Maturity Value. The sum of the principal plus interest due at maturity.

Menu. A list of options for choosing computer functions.

Merchandising Company. A company that resells products previously bought from suppliers.

Minority Interest. A subsidiary company's equity that is held by stockholders other than the parent company.

Mixed Costs. Costs that have both variable and fixed components.

Module. Separate compatible units of an accounting package that are integrated to function together.

Mortgage. Borrower's promise to transfer the legal title to certain assets to the lender if the debt is not paid on schedule.

Multi-Step Income Statement. Format that contains subtotals to highlight significant relationships. In addition to net income, it reports gross profit and operating income.

Mutual Agency. Every partner can bind the business to a contract within the scope of the partnership's regular business operations.

Net Income. Excess of total revenues over total expenses. Also called **net earnings** or **net profit**.

Net Loss. Excess of total expenses over total revenues.

Net Pay. Gross pay minus all deductions. The amount of compensation that the employee actually takes home.

Net Present Value (NPV). The decision model that brings cash inflows and outflows back to a common time period by discounting these expected future cash flows to their present value, using a minimum desired rate of return.

Net Purchases. Purchases less purchase discounts and purchase returns and allowances.

Net Sales Revenue. Sales revenue less sales discounts and sales returns and allowances.

Network. The system of electronic linkages that allows different computers to share the same information.

Nonsufficient Funds (NSF) Check. A "hot" check, one for which the maker's bank account has insufficient money to pay the check.

Normal Balance. The balance that appears on the side of an account—debit or credit—where we record increases.

Note Payable. A written promise of future payment.

Note Receivable. A written promise for future collection of cash.

Online Processing. Computerized processing of related functions, such as the recording and posting of transactions, on a continuous basis.

Operating Activities. Activities that create revenue or expense in the entity's major line of business; a section of the statement of cash flows. Operating activities affect the income statement.

Operating Budget. Projects sales revenue, cost of goods sold, and operating expenses, leading to the budgeted income statement that projects operating income for the period.

Operating Cycle. Time span during which cash is paid for goods and services, which are then sold to customers from whom the business collects cash.

Operating Expenses. Expenses, other than cost of goods sold, that are incurred in the entity's major line of business. Examples include rent, depreciation, salaries, wages, utilities, and supplies expense.

Operating Income. Gross profit minus operating expenses plus any other operating revenues. Also called **income from operations**.

Operating Lease. Usually a short-term or cancelable rental agreement.

Opportunity Cost. The benefit forgone by not choosing an alternative course of action.

Ordinary Repair. Repair work that is debited to an expense account.

Other Expense. Expense that is outside the main operations of a business, such as a loss on the sale of plant assets.

Other Revenue. Revenue that is outside the main operations of a business, such as a gain on the sale of plant assets.

Outsourcing. A make-or-buy decision: managers decide whether to buy a component product or service or produce it in-house.

Outstanding Check. A check issued by the company and recorded on its books but not yet paid by its bank.

Outstanding Stock. Stock in the hands of stockholders.

Overallocated (Manufacturing) Overhead. The manufacturing overhead allocated to Work in Process Inventory is more than the amount of manufacturing overhead costs actually incurred.

Overhead Flexible Budget Variance. Shows how well management has controlled overhead costs. It is the difference between the actual overhead cost and the flexible budget overhead for the actual number of outputs.

Owner Withdrawals. Amounts removed from the business by an owner.

Owner's Equity. The claim of a business owner to the assets of the business. Also called **capital**.

Paid-in Capital. Capital from investments by the stockholders. Also called **contributed capital**.

Par Value. Arbitrary amount assigned to a share of stock.

Parent Company. An investor company that owns more than 50% of the voting stock of a subsidiary company.

Partnership. An association of two or more persons who co-own a business for profit.

Partnership Agreement. The contract between partners that specifies such items as the name, location, and nature of the business; the name, capital investment, and duties of each partner; and the method of sharing profits and losses among the partners. Also called **articles of partnership**.

Patent. A federal government grant giving the holder the exclusive right to produce and sell an invention for 20 years.

Payback. The length of time it takes to recover, in net cash inflows, the dollars of a capital outlay.

Payee of a Note. The person or business to whom the maker of a note promises future payment; the creditor.

Payroll. A major expense. Also called **employee compensation**.

Percent-of-Sales Method. A method of estimating uncollectible receivables that calculates uncollectible-account expense. Also called the **income-statement approach**.

Period Costs. Operating costs that are expensed in the period in which they are incurred.

Periodic Inventory System. A system in which the business does not keep a continuous record of inventory on hand. At the end of the period, it makes a physical count of on-hand inventory and uses this information to prepare the financial statements.

Permanent Accounts. Accounts that are *not* closed at the end of the period—the asset, liability, and capital accounts.

Perpetual Inventory System. The accounting inventory system in which the business keeps a running record of inventory and cost of goods sold.

Petty Cash. Fund containing a small amount of cash that is used to pay for minor expenditures.

Planning. Choosing goals and deciding how to achieve them.

Plant Assets. Long-lived tangible assets, such as land, buildings, and equipment, used to operate a business.

Plant or Fixed Asset. Another name for property, plant, and equipment.

Postclosing Trial Balance. List of the accounts and their balances at the end of the period after journalizing and posting the closing entries. This last step of the accounting cycle ensures that the ledger is in balance to start the next accounting period.

Posting. Copying amounts from the journal to the ledger.

Predetermined Manufacturing Overhead Rate. Estimated manufacturing overhead allocation rate computed at the beginning of the year, calculated as the total estimated manufacturing overhead costs divided by the total estimated quantity of the manufacturing overhead allocation base. Also called the **budgeted manufacturing overhead rate**.

Preferred Stock. Stock that gives its owners certain advantages over common stockholders, such as the right to receive dividends before the common stockholders and the right to receive assets before the common stockholders if the corporation liquidates.

Premium. Excess of a bond's issue price over its maturity value. Also called **bond premium**.

Prepaid Expense. Advance payments of expenses. Examples include prepaid rent, prepaid insurance, and supplies.

Present Value. Amount a person would invest now to receive a greater amount in the future.

President. Chief operating officer in charge of managing the day-to-day operations of a corporation.

Prevention Costs. Costs incurred to *avoid* poor-quality goods or services.

Price Variance. Measures how well the business keeps unit prices of material and labor inputs within standards. This is computed as the difference in prices (actual price per unit minus standard price per unit) of an input multiplied by the actual quantity of the input.

Price/Earnings Ratio. Ratio of the market price of a share of common stock to the company's earnings per share. Measures the value that the stock market places on $1 of a company's earnings.

Principal Amount, or Principal. The amount loaned out by the payee and borrowed by the maker of the note.

Prior-Period Adjustment. A correction to retained earnings for an error of an earlier period.

Process Costing. System for assigning costs to large numbers of identical units that usually proceed in a continuous fashion through a series of uniform production steps or processes.

Production Cost Report. Summarizes a processing department's operations for a period.

Production or Purchases. Resources used to produce a product or service, or to purchase finished merchandise.

Production Volume Variance. Arises when actual production differs from expected production. It is the difference between (1) the manufacturing overhead cost in the flexible budget for actual outputs and (2) the standard overhead allocated to production.

Promissory note. A written promise to pay a specified amount of money at a particular future date.

Proprietorship. A business with a single owner.

Purchases Journal. Special journal used to record all purchases of inventory, supplies, and other assets on account.

Rate of Return on Common Stockholders' Equity. Net income minus preferred dividends, divided by average common stockholders' equity. A measure of profitability. Also called **return on equity**.

Rate of Return on Net Sales. Ratio of net income to net sales. A measure of profitability. Also called **return on sales**.

Rate of Return on Total Assets. Net income plus interest expense, divided by average total assets. Measures the success a company has in using its assets to earn income for those financing the business. Also called **return on assets**.

Receivables. Monetary claims against a business or an individual.

Relevant Information. Expected future data that differs among alternatives.

Relevant Range. The band of volume where total fixed costs remain constant and where the variable cost per unit remains constant.

Research and Development (R&D). Researching and developing new or improved products or services, or the processes for producing them.

Responsibility Accounting. A system for evaluating the performance of each responsibility center and its manager.

Responsibility Center. A part or subunit of an organization whose manager is accountable for specific activities.

Retained Earnings. Capital earned through profitable operation of the business.

Revenue. Amounts earned by delivering goods or services to customers. Revenues increase owner's equity.

Revenue Principle. The basis for recording revenues; tells accountants when to record revenue and the amount of revenue to record.

Reversing Entries. Special journal entries that ease the burden of accounting for transactions in the next period.

S Corporation. A corporation taxed in the same way as a partnership.

Sales Discount. Reduction in the amount receivable from a customer, offered by the seller as an incentive for the customer to pay promptly. A contra account to Sales Revenue.

Sales Journal. Special journal used to record credit sales.

Sales Mix. Combination of products that make up total sales.

Sales Returns and Allowances. Decreases in the seller's receivable from a customer's return of merchandise or from granting the customer an allowance from the amount owed to the seller. A contra account to Sales Revenue.

Sales Revenue. The amount that a merchandiser earns from selling its inventory. Also called **sales**.

Sales Volume Variance. The difference arising only because the number of units actually sold differs from the static budget units. This equals the difference between a static budget amount and a flexible budget amount.

Segment of the Business. One of various separate divisions of a company.

Sensitivity Analysis. A "what if" technique that asks what results will be if actual prices or costs change, or if an underlying assumption changes.

Serial Bonds. Bonds that mature in installments over a period of time.

Server. The main computer in a network, where the program and data are stored.

Service Company. A company that sells intangible services, rather than tangible products.

Short-Term Investment. A current asset; an investment that is readily convertible to cash and that the investor intends either to convert to cash within one year or use to pay a current liability. Also called a **marketable security**.

Short-Term Note Payable. Promissory note payable due within one year, a common form of financing.

Single-Step Income Statement. Format that groups all revenues together and then lists and deducts all expenses together without drawing any subtotals.

Social Security Tax. Federal Insurance Contributions Act (FICA) tax, which is withheld from employees' pay. Also called **FICA tax**.

Software. Set of programs or instructions that drive the computer to perform the work desired.

Specific-Unit-Cost Method. Inventory cost method based on the specific cost of particular units of inventory. Also called the **specific-identification method**.

Spreadsheet. A computer program that links data by means of formulas and functions; an electronic work sheet.

Standard Cost. A budget for a single unit.

Stated Interest Rate. Interest rate that determines the amount of cash interest the borrower pays and the investor receives each year.

Stated Value. An arbitrary amount that accountants treat as though it were par value.

Statement of Cash Flows. Reports cash receipts and cash payments during a period.

Statement of Owner's Equity. Summary of the changes in an entity's owner's equity during a specific period.

Statement of Stockholders' Equity. Reports the changes in all categories of stockholders' equity during the period.

Static Budget. The budget prepared for only one level of sales volume. Also called the **master budget**.

Stock. Shares into which the owners' equity of a corporation is divided.

Stock Dividend. A distribution by a corporation of its own stock to its stockholders.

Stock Split. An increase in the number of outstanding shares of stock coupled with a proportionate reduction in the par value of the stock.

Stockholder. A person who owns the stock of a corporation. Also called **shareholder**.

Stockholders' Equity. Owners' equity of a corporation.

Straight-Line (SL) Depreciation Method. Depreciation method in which an equal amount of depreciation expense is assigned to each year of asset use.

Strong Currency. A currency that is rising relative to other nations' currencies.

Subsidiary Company. A company in which a parent company owns more than 50% of the voting stock.

Subsidiary Ledger. Record of accounts that provides supporting details on individual balances, the total of which appears in a general ledger account.

Sunk Cost. A past cost that cannot be changed regardless of which future action is taken.

Supply-Chain Management. Exchange of information with suppliers and customers to reduce costs, improve quality, and speed delivery of goods and services from suppliers, through the company itself, and on to customers.

Target Cost. Allowable cost to develop, produce, and deliver the product or service. Equals target price minus desired profit.

Target Price. What customers are willing to pay for the product or service.

Temporary Accounts. The revenue and expense accounts that relate to a particular accounting period and are closed at the end of the period. For a proprietorship, the owner withdrawal account is also temporary.

Term Bonds. Bonds that all mature at the same time for a particular issue.

Throughput Time. The time between buying raw materials and selling finished products.

Time Record. Source document used to trace direct labor to specific jobs.

Time Value of Money. The fact that money can be invested to earn income over time.

Time-Period Concept. Ensures that information is reported at regular intervals.

Times-Interest-Earned Ratio. Ratio of income from operations to interest expense. Measures the number of times that operating income can cover interest expense. Also called the **interest-coverage ratio**.

Total Fixed Costs. Costs that do not change in total despite wide changes in volume.

Total Quality Management (TQM). A philosophy of delighting customers by providing them with superior products and services. Requires improving quality and eliminating defects and waste throughout the value chain.

Total Variable Costs. Costs that change in total in direct proportion to changes in volume.

Trademarks, Trade Names, or Brand Names. Assets that represent distinctive identifications of a product or service.

Trading Investments. Investments that are to be sold in the very near future with the intent of generating profits on price changes.

Trading on the Equity. Earning more income on borrowed money than the related interest expense, thereby increasing the earnings for the owners of the business. Also called **leverage**.

Transaction. An event that affects the financial position of a particular entity and can be recorded reliably.

Transferred-in Costs. Costs incurred in a previous process that are carried forward as part of the product's cost when it moves to the next process.

Treasury Stock. A corporation's own stock that it has issued and later reacquired.

Trend Percentages. A form of horizontal analysis in which percentages are computed by selecting a base year as 100% and expressing amounts for following years as a percentage of the base amount.

Trial Balance. A list of all the accounts with their balances.

Trojan Horse. A malicious program that works like a virus but does not reproduce.

Uncollectible-Account Expense. Cost to the seller of extending credit. Arises from the failure to collect from credit customers. Also called **doubtful-account expense**, or **bad-debt expense**.

Underallocated (Manufacturing) Overhead. The manufacturing overhead allocated to Work in Process Inventory is less than the amount of manufacturing overhead costs actually incurred.

Unearned Revenue. A liability created when a business collects cash from customers in advance of doing work. Also called **deferred revenue**.

Unemployment Compensation Tax. Payroll tax paid by employers to the government, which uses the money to pay unemployment benefits to people who are out of work.

Units-of-Production (UOP) Depreciation Method. Depreciation method by which a fixed amount of depreciation is assigned to each unit of output produced by an asset.

Unlimited Personal Liability. When a partnership (or a proprietorship) cannot pay its debts with business assets, the partners (or the proprietor) must use personal assets to meet the debt.

Value Chain. The activities that add value to a firm's products and services. Includes R&D, design, production or purchases, marketing, distribution, and customer service.

Value Engineering. Reevaluating activities to reduce costs while satisfying customer needs.

Variable Costing. The costing method that assigns only variable manufacturing costs to products.

Variance. The difference between an actual amount and the budget. A variance is labeled as favorable if it increases operating income and unfavorable if it decreases operating income.

Vertical Analysis. Analysis of a financial statement that reveals the relationship of each statement item to a specified base, which is the 100% figure.

Voucher. Instrument authorizing a cash payment.

Weak Currency. A currency that is falling relative to other nations' currencies.

Weighted-Average Process Costing Method. A process costing method that costs all equivalent units of work with a weighted average of the previous period's and the current period's cost per equivalent unit.

Withheld Income Tax. Income tax deducted from employees' gross pay.

Work in Process Inventory. Goods that are partway through the manufacturing process but not yet complete.

Work Sheet. A columnar document designed to help move data from the trial balance to the financial statements.

Working Capital. Current assets minus current liabilities; measures a business's ability to meet its short-term obligations with its current assets.

Company Index

*Real companies are in **bold** type.*

Subject Index